THE OXFORD HANDBOOK OF

PRICING

MANAGEMENT

OXFORD HANDBOOKS IN FINANCE

SERIES EDITOR: MICHAEL DEMPSTER
University of Cambridge and Cambridge Systems Associates Limited

THE OXFORD HANDBOOK OF BANKING
Edited by Allen N. Berger, Philip Molyneux, and John O. S. Wilson

THE OXFORD HANDBOOK OF CREDIT DERIVATIVES
Edited by Alexander Lipton and Andrew Rennie

**THE OXFORD HANDBOOK OF QUANTITATIVE
ASSET MANAGEMENT**
Edited by Bernhard Scherer and Kenneth Winston

THE OXFORD HANDBOOK OF PRICING MANAGEMENT
Edited by Özalp Özer and Robert Phillips

THE OXFORD HANDBOOK OF

PRICING

MANAGEMENT

Edited by

ÖZALP ÖZER

and

ROBERT PHILLIPS

OXFORD

UNIVERSITY PRESS

Great Clarendon Street, Oxford, OX2 6DP,
United Kingdom

Oxford University Press is a department of the University of Oxford.
It furthers the University's objective of excellence in research, scholarship,
and education by publishing worldwide. Oxford is a registered trade mark of
Oxford University Press in the UK and in certain other countries

First Edition published in 2012
First published in paperback 2014

Impression: 1

Published in the United States of America by Oxford University Press
198 Madison Avenue, New York, NY 10016, United States of America

British Library Cataloguing in Publication Data

Data available

ISBN 978-0-19-954317-5 (hbk)
ISBN 978-0-19-871481-1 (pbk)

Printed in Great Britain on acid free paper by
CPI Group (UK) Ltd, Croydon, CR0 4YY

Links to third party websites are provided by Oxford in good faith and
for information only. Oxford disclaims any responsibility for the materials
contained in any third party website referenced in this work.

CONTENTS

PART III PRICING FUNDAMENTALS

PART IV PRICING TACTICS

PART V ORGANIZATION AND PROCESSES

PART VI CURRENT CHALLENGES AND FUTURE PROSPECTS

LIST OF FIGURES

List of Tables

LIST OF BOXES

List of Contributors

Andy Atherton is COO of Brand.net. Andy has extensive experience in pricing, as Yahoo!'s VP of Global Pricing & Yield Management for display advertising; as a co-founder of Optivo, a price-optimization start-up; and as a consultant at RB Webber, developing their pricing practice.

Yossi Aviv develops and applies operations research models to study problems in supply chain management and revenue management. His current research focuses on dynamic pricing under strategic consumer behavior. Aviv holds several editorial positions, and teaches courses on quantitative decision modeling, operations management, and supply chain management.

Brenda A. Barnes has held positions as Vice President of global pricing and revenue management for Delta Air Lines and Starwood Hotels & Resorts, management positions at American Airlines, and as an advisor to leading hospitality companies and airlines. She holds an MBA from the University of Texas and a BS in Accounting and Computer Science from Minnesota State University.

Warren Bidmead is Division Marketing Director for Brown Forman Beverages, a diversified producer of Wines and Spirits. Prior to Brown Forman, Mr. Bidmead was with Del Monte Foods where he was Director of Customer Marketing for the company's vegetable business. He also served in various business development and corporate strategy positions for Del Monte. He started his career with Gallo Sales Company. Mr. Bidmead earned a BSc in Business Administration from California State University Sacramento, and an MBA from Pepperdine University.

Robert C. Blattberg is the Timothy W. McGuire Distinguished Service Professor of Marketing and Director of the Center for Marketing Technology and Information at the Tepper School, Carnegie-Mellon University. Previously he was the Polk Bros. Distinguished Professor of Retailing at the Kellogg School of Management, Northwestern University and the Charles H. Kellstadt Professor of Marketing and Director of the Center for Marketing Information Technology in the Graduate School of Business at the University of Chicago. Professor Blattberg received a BA degree in mathematics from Northwestern University, and MSc and PhD degrees in Industrial Administration from Carnegie-Mellon University. While at Northwestern and Chicago, Professor Blattberg has taught marketing strategy, marketing management, retailing behavior, and statistics. Professor Blattberg's primary research is in the areas of marketing information technology, database marketing, sales promotions, and retailing. His articles have appeared in the *Journal of Marketing Research, Management Science, Marketing Science, Econometrica, Journal of Marketing, Journal of Direct Marketing*, and other leading academic journals. His monograph, *Assessing and Capturing the Soft Benefits of Scanning*, has served as a guidepost for numerous retailers. He has co-authored the books *Sales Promotions* (Prentice Hall, 1990), which is widely recognized as the most authoritative publication on promotions, and *The Marketing Information Revolution* (Harvard Business Press, January 1994). He has completed a five-part set of guides on Category Management, published in 1995–96 by the Food Marketing Institute and translated into Spanish and Japanese. In 2001 he co-authored the book *Customer Equity* (Harvard Business Press, 2001) and his most recent book is *Database Marketing: Theory and Practice* (Springer, 2008). In addition to his teaching, writing, and research responsibilities, Professor Blattberg consults to leading retailers, consumer goods manufacturers, and database marketers.

E. Andrew Boyd served as Chief Scientist and Senior Vice President of Science and Research at a pricing firm for over a decade. Prior to that, he was a tenured faculty member at Texas A&M University. He is an INFORMS Fellow. Dr. Boyd received his AB with Honors at Oberlin College with majors in Mathematics and Economics in 1981, and his PhD in Operations Research from the Massachusetts Institute of Technology in 1987.

Richard A. Briesch is the Marilyn and Leo Corrigan Endowed Professor of Marketing, Cox School of Business, Southern Methodist University. His primary areas of research are the modeling of consumer decision making, pricing, sales promotions, and non-parametric methods. His articles have appeared in *Journal of the American Statistical Association, Journal of Consumer Research, Journal of Consumer Psychology, Journal of Business and Economic Statistics, Journal of Marketing Research, Marketing Science, Journal of Retailing,* and other leading academic journals. He won the William R. Davidson Award for the best paper in the *Journal of Retailing,* and was a finalist for the Paul Green award in 2010 in the *Journal of Marketing Research.* Over the past ten years, Professor Briesch has also consulted for many regional, national, and multinational firms.

Simon Caufield is a management consultant serving clients in the banking, finance, and insurance sectors. His interests lie in applying models of customer behavior and product profitability to risk, pricing, and marketing as well as strategy and valuation. In 2002, Simon and Robert Phillips co-founded Nomis Solutions, a software company providing price optimization software for the consumer lending industry. Simon's fifteen years' experience in consumer credit pricing covers mortgages, auto loans, credit cards, unsecured consumer loans, and home equity loans for clients such as American Express, Barclays, Citigroup, and Lloyds Banking Group. He is the founder and managing director of Sensible Investors. Simon also writes a twice monthly investment newsletter called "True Value" for the Moneyweek Group of companies. He holds an MA in Engineering Mathematics from Cambridge University and an MBA from London Business School.

Xin Chen is an Associate Professor at the Department of Industrial and Enterprise Systems Engineering at the University of Illinois at Urbana-Champaign. His research interests include supply chain management, inventory management, and optimization. He is co-author of the book *The Logic of Logistics* (Springer, 2005).

Greg Cudahy is the North American managing partner of Accenture's Operations practice. With more than twenty-five years of experience in management consulting and technology, Mr. Cudahy focuses on strategy development and capability building in support of cost reduction, price management, and sales and marketing strategy. He additionally focuses on total supply chain transformations by balancing demand-related factors with organizations' supply-side capabilities. Based in Atlanta, Mr. Cudahy has worked across a variety of industries with special emphasis on consumer goods and media/high technology. In 2005, he was named by *World Trade Magazine* as one of the Top 50 Supply Chain Pioneers.

Yosun Denizeri is the Vice President of Merchandise Planning at Caché, a women's apparel brand based in the US. She specializes in developing assortment planning and pricing strategies and in-season price management methods that maximize profitability and return on investment in the retail environment. Previously, she worked at the GAP Inc. leading merchandising, planning, and distribution initiatives for Banana Republic, GAP, Old Navy, and Outlet brands and at Decision Focus Incorporated and Manugistics specializing in price optimization and revenue management. She holds a BS and an MS in Operations Research from Cornell University.

Michael Freimer is the Chief Scientist at SignalDemand Inc., a software company providing predictive analytics and optimization for commodity-based value chains. He has held academic positions at Penn State's Smeal College of Business and Cornell's School of Operations Research & Industrial Engineering and School of Hotel Administration.

Guillermo Gallego is a Professor at the Industrial Engineering and Operations Research Department at Columbia University and a world-renowned expert in pricing optimization, revenue management, inventory theory, and supply chain optimization. He has published over 60 papers in operations research, management science, and pricing journals including seminal papers in *Supply Chain*, *Inventory Theory*, and *Dynamic Pricing*. His graduate students are associated with prestigious universities.

Tiffany Gilbert is a senior manager in Accenture's Global Pricing & Profit Optimization practice. She helps clients improve their pricing confidence and make effective use of price negotiation tactics. Prior to joining Accenture, Ms. Gilbert was corporate counsel for companies in the financial services, manufacturing, and software industry and specialized in creating and negotiating optimal deal structures. Ms. Gilbert is based in Atlanta.

Thomas G. Jacobson is the global managing director of Accenture's Pricing & Profit Optimization. Mr. Jacobson has led a number of engagements across a variety of industries for clients around the world, helping them transform business strategy, processes, organization, and technology to maximize profitable growth. He contributed to the 2011 book *Contextual Pricing* and received the "Distinguished Pricing Award for Contributions to the Field of Pricing Practice" from Fordham/Babson University in 2010. Before joining Accenture, he served in an executive role at a price- and- profit- optimization software company. Mr. Jacobson is based in Boston.

Junko Kaji is a writer and editor at Deloitte Services LP.

Murat Kaya joined Sabancı University in 2007, after receiving his PhD degree from Stanford University. During his PhD study, Dr. Kaya worked for several projects at HP Labs in Palo Alto. His current research focuses primarily on behavioral operations management and supply chain contracting.

Sheryl E. Kimes is a Professor at the Cornell Hotel School and holds the Distinguished Singapore Tourism Board Chair in Asian Hospitality Management. From 2005 to 2006, she served as Interim Dean of the Hotel School. Her area of specialization is revenue management. Professor Kimes earned her doctorate in Operations Management in 1987 from the University of Texas at Austin.

Edward Kintz is a Master Business Consultant within the Manufacturing & Distribution Industry vertical for Hewlett-Packard's Business Intelligence Solutions (BIS). His primary responsibilities are to provide subject matter expertise in the transportation industry, project management, strategy development, and thought leadership focused on identifying tangible business value realized through delivering information management solutions. Prior to joining HP Kintz worked at DHL as Senior Director of Finance and prior to DHL as the Senior Director of Pricing Services at Consolidated Freightways.

Praveen K. Kopalle is Professor of Marketing at the Tuck School of Business at Dartmouth, Dartmouth College. Praveen received his PhD from Columbia University, New York, his MBA from the Indian Institute of Management, Bangalore, and his BE from Osmania University, Hyderabad. His research interests include pricing and promotions, new product development, and game theory.

Warren H. Lieberman is President of Veritec Solutions, a pricing and revenue management consulting firm based in Belmont, California. Dr. Lieberman pioneered the application of advanced pricing and revenue management techniques in the cruise industry in 1988, providing design and technical leadership. Since that time, he has worked for ten cruise lines; his pricing work spans twenty industries. Dr. Lieberman serves on the editorial board for the *Journal of Revenue and Pricing Management* and on the Board of Directors of INFORMS, the world's largest Society for Operations Research Professionals. He has published numerous articles and holds a PhD in Operations Research from Yale University.

Michelle Mahoney is a senior manager in Accenture's Sales and Pricing organization and the global pricing capability lead. She helps clients achieve their company's pricing strategies by working with them to improve their pricing confidence, make effective use of price negotiation tactics, and understand how to optimize deal profitability. Prior to working at Accenture, Ms. Mahoney worked in sales and marketing. Ms. Mahoney is based in Denver.

Julie Meehan is a principal in Deloitte Consulting LLP's Pricing and Profitability Management Practice. She helps companies with both strategic and operational pricing improvements, including developing pricing and sales channel strategies, improving price execution capabilities, building organizational alignment and pricing capabilities, and performing in-depth analytics to diagnose and remedy issues related to poor profitability. She frequently writes and speaks on the topic of pricing and guest lectures at several leading undergraduate and graduate programs in the US.

Larry Montan is a Director in Deloitte Consulting LLP's Sales Effectiveness practice. He helps companies address the sales force implications of pricing transformations, including issues related to performance metrics and pay, selling roles, training, sales processes, organization, leadership alignment, and salesforce adoption of new pricing processes, technology, and initiatives.

Michael Neal is founder, CEO, and Chairman of SignalDemand. He was previously co-founder of DemandTec (Nasdaq: DMAN), the largest provider of consumer demand management software. Previously he consulted at Deloitte and Accenture, applying mathematics to key problems in the Food and Consumer Goods industries, and he holds several patents in related fields. Neal earned his MBA from the J. B. Fuqua School of Business at Duke University and a BA in Economics and Statistics from the University of Florida. He serves as director on several corporate and industry association boards.

Shmuel S. Oren is Professor of Industrial Engineering and Operations Research at the University of California at Berkeley. He holds a PhD in Engineering Economic Systems from Stanford University and is a Fellow of INFORMS and of the IEEE. His academic research and consulting have focused on optimization, pricing policies, and on the design of electricity markets.

Özalp Özer is Professor of Management at the University of Texas at Dallas. He was also a faculty member at Columbia University and Stanford University. His areas of specialization include pricing management, supply chain management, global production and distribution system design, contract and incentive design, capacity and inventory planning. His articles on these topics have appeared in leading academic journals such as *Management Science* and *Operations Research*. He has also received several teaching awards by vote of students at Columbia and Stanford. National Science Foundation and Fortune 500 companies have supported his research and teaching activities. He is an active consultant to industries such as high technology and retail. He has been invited to present his work in national and international conferences and in lectures at universities, such as MIT Sloan Business School of Management, INSEAD, and London Business School. He received his PhD and MS degrees from Columbia University.

Robert Phillips is Professor of Professional Practice at Columbia University and Founder and Chief Science Officer at Nomis Solutions. He is also Director of the Center for Pricing and Revenue Management at Columbia University. Dr. Phillips has years of experience in pricing and revenue management in a wide variety of industries including airlines, hotels, rental cars, automotive, air freight, cruise lines, retail, and financial services. He is the former CEO of Talus Solutions and of Decision Focus Incorporated and author of the widely used textbook *Pricing and Revenue Optimization*. Dr. Phillips has served as a lecturer at the Stanford University Graduate School of Business and has published in many journals. He received his PhD from Stanford University in Engineering Economic Systems.

Robert D. Pierce is founder and CEO of PriceSimplicity, Inc. Formerly Chief Scientist at SignalDemand, Inc., he has held research and executive positions in academia and the software industry. He holds a PhD in Theoretical Physics from U.C. Berkeley and undergraduate degrees in Math and Physics from Brown University.

Rama Ramakrishnan was formerly the Chief Scientist at Oracle Retail and a consultant at McKinsey & Company. An expert in data-driven decision-making, he helps organizations use data and analytics to drive business performance. He also teaches the graduate course in decision methodologies for managers at MIT Sloan School of Management. He has a PhD from MIT and a BS from IIT.

Diogo Rau is a former Partner with McKinsey's Business Technology Office in San Francisco where he led McKinsey's IT organization and governance practice in North America, and served technology and financial services firms on a range of strategy, organization, and technology issues.

Garrett J. van Ryzin is the Paul M. Montrone Professor of Decision, Risk and Operations at the Columbia University Graduate School of Business. His research interests include analytical pricing, stochastic optimization, and operations management. He is co-author (with Kalyan Talluri) of the book *The Theory and Practice of Revenue Management.*

Tiago Salvador is a senior principal in Accenture's Pricing & Profit Optimization practice. Mr. Salvador focuses on global pricing transformation initiatives, from pricing strategy through execution and organization design and alignment in a variety of industries. In addition, Mr. Salvador has led engagements in growth strategy, new product development, sales and market strategy, and customer strategy and segmentation. Mr. Salvador is based in Chicago.

Julian Short is the managing director of Accenture's Pricing and Profit Optimization practice in Europe, Africa, and Latin America. He has led multiple engagements across a variety of industries encompassing the complete range of pricing capabilities, including pricing strategy, process, organization, and technology development and implementation. Mr. Short is based in London.

Robert A. Shumsky is Professor of Business Administration at the Tuck School of Business at Dartmouth. His research interests include the application of game theory to the coordination of service supply chains in which pricing and service design decisions are distributed among multiple firms.

David Simchi-Levi is Professor of Engineering Systems at MIT. His research focuses on developing and implementing robust and efficient techniques for logistics and manufacturing systems. He has published widely in professional journals on both practical and theoretical aspects of logistics and supply chain management. Professor Simchi-Levi co-authored the books *Managing the Supply Chain* (McGraw-Hill, 2004), *The Logic of Logistics* (Springer, 2005), as well as the award-winning *Designing and Managing the Supply Chain* (McGraw-Hill, 2007). His new book *Operations Rules: Delivering Customer Value through Flexible Operations* was published by MIT Press in September 2010. Professor Simchi-Levi has consulted and collaborated extensively with private and public organizations. He is the founder of LogicTools (now part of IBM), which provides software solutions and professional services for supply chain planning.

Michael Simonetto is the Global Leader of Deloitte's Pricing and Profitability Management Practice. He has thirty years of work experience, across a number of industries and topics. Mike guest lectures extensively at some of the top MBA programs in the USA, and has published a significant number of pricing related articles.

ManMohan S. Sodhi is Professor of Operations and Supply Chain Management at Cass Business School, City University London and Executive Director, Munjal Global Manufacturing Institute, Indian School of Business. His research is broadly in the area of supply chain management and more specifically in supply chain risk. Prior to his academic career, he worked at Accenture and at other consulting firms with clients in consumer electronics, commodity and specialty chemicals, petroleum products distribution, hospitality industry procurement, and airlines. He has taught at the University of Michigan Business School (Ross) and has a PhD in management science from the UCLA Anderson School.

Navdeep S. Sodhi is Managing Director at Six Sigma Pricing. His global pricing experience, as practitioner and consultant, spans chemicals, airlines, medical device, electronics, outsourced business services, and business-to-business manufacturing. He is a past recipient of the Award of Excellence from the Professional Pricing Society. He has published in the *Harvard Business Review* and has co-authored a book on *Six Sigma Pricing* (FT Press, 2008). Mr. Sodhi has an MBA from Georgetown University.

Catalina Stefanescu is an Associate Professor and the Director of Research at the European School of Management and Technology (ESMT) in Berlin. Prior to joining ESMT, she was Assistant Professor of Decision Sciences at the London Business School. She received her PhD and MS in Operations Research from Cornell University, and her BS in Mathematics from the University of Bucharest.

Richard Steinberg is Chair in Operations Research and Head of the Management Science Group at the London School of Economics. His primary area of research is auctions. He has advised both the US Federal Communications Commission and the UK Department of Energy and Climate Change on auction design.

Lisabet Summa is a founder and Culinary Director of Big Time Restaurant Group, a multi-venue, multi-concept enterprise, headquartered in West Palm Beach, Florida. She has worked in fine dining at Maxim's and Charlie Trotter's and as a culinary instructor.

Kalyan Talluri is an ICREA Research Professor in the Department of Economics and Business at the Universitat Pompeu Fabra in Barcelona. He received an MS degree from Purdue University and a PhD in Operations Research from MIT. His research interests are in the pricing of consumer goods and services and the operational implementation of pricing tactics.

Sushil Verma has over twenty years of experience in building and marketing mathematical applications in the areas of pricing, demand, and supply-chain management. Dr. Verma is the founder of and currently president at Enumerica. Prior to that, he worked at SignalDemand, i2, and AMD. He graduated from UC Berkeley with a PhD in Operations Research.

Madhu Vudali is Vice-President, Product at Brand.net. Before Brand.net, Mr. Vudali held a variety of roles relating to pricing and yield management: Senior Director of Pricing and Yield Management for Yahoo!'s US display advertising, product manager for pricing at Rapt, and a consultant at DFI/Talus.

Gustavo Vulcano is an Associate Professor at the Leonard N. Stern School of Business, New York University. He obtained his BS and MS in Computer Science at the University of Buenos Aires, Argentina; and his PhD in Decision, Risk and Operations from the Graduate School of Business, Columbia University. His research interests are primarily in revenue management, including modeling and the development of computational algorithms to solve problems within that area.

Thomas A. Weber is Director of the Management of Technology and Entrepreneurship Institute and Chair of Operations, Economics and Strategy at Ecole Polytechnique Fédérale de Lausanne. His research is concerned with decision-making, optimization, and information economics. A graduate of École Centrale Paris, Technical University Aachen, and

MIT, Weber worked as senior consultant for the Boston Consulting Group, and received his doctorate from the Wharton School.

Paul Willmott is a Director with McKinsey's Business Technology Office in London and a leader in McKinsey's IT Organisation and Governance Practice. Since joining McKinsey in 1996, he has served firms across various sectors on strategy, organization, and technology issues.

Robert Wilson has taught courses on pricing and related topics at the Stanford Graduate School of Business for forty-six years. His consulting includes topics involving pricing, and in recent years focuses on the electricity industry. His book on *Nonlinear Pricing* is the standard reference on the subject.

Graham Young is Vice President, Revenue Management with JDA Software International. In his twenty-five-year career in revenue management and pricing, Mr. Young has led innovative visioning studies and successful pioneering implementations for more than thirty clients across the airline, hospitality, cruise, and media sectors worldwide.

Yanchong Zheng is Assistant Professor of Operations Management at the MIT Sloan School of Management. Her research focuses on studying behavioral issues in an operations context. She uses both analytical modeling and empirical methods to investigate how nonpecuniary factors impact strategic interactions between forms as well as between firms and consumers. She received her PhD at Stanford University.

Jon Zimmerman has applied quantitative methods in a variety of industries including wireless communications, travel, and e-commerce. His experience includes leading strategic pricing for T-Mobile USA, creating the customer analytics group at Expedia, and working as consultant for Decision Focus, Inc. where he developed revenue management capabilities for major airlines and hotel chains. Jon earned an ME in Systems Engineering from the University of Virginia, and a BS in Industrial Engineering from Stanford University.

PART I

INTRODUCTION

CHAPTER 1

INTRODUCTION

ÖZALP ÖZER AND
ROBERT PHILLIPS

"Pricing is the moment of truth—all of marketing comes to focus in the pricing decision." Harvard Business School Professor E. Raymond Corey wrote these words more than thirty years ago and they remain as true today as they were then. As noted in Chapter 34 in this volume by Thomas Jacobson and his co-authors from Accenture, pricing remains one of the most powerful levers to increase profitability available to most companies—a 1 percent increase in pricing will lead to a 7–15 percent improvement in operating profit. Yet, despite its importance, pricing is a scattered and under-managed process in many organizations. The pricing process within a company often incorporates input from the sales, marketing, and finance divisions. Many different individuals from many different groups typically influence the final price in a transaction. This fragmentation is mirrored in academia— there is no one home for "pricing studies" in the university. Rather, pricing is a topic of interest in a number of different fields including economics, operations research, management science, operations management, marketing, and, increasingly, computer science. One of the purposes of this book is to bring together insights and results from each of these fields regarding pricing into one volume.

The theory and practice of pricing have greatly advanced over the last twenty-five years. There is strong interest in and need for better pricing methods in industry and a growing number of conferences, consultants, and software vendors seeking to help fill that need. Pricing is a growing field of research and teaching within a number of different university departments. Because pricing is both a critical corporate function and a field of academic study, we have commissioned articles for this volume from both pricing practitioners and from leading researchers in pricing. We hope that including authors from these broad communities will serve two purposes. First, we wish to emphasize that what may seem theoretically optimal in pricing may not be practical. Secondly, we hope to stimulate future research inspired by the specific pricing challenges faced in different industries.

The scope of this handbook is primarily the prices set (or negotiated) between a profit-maximizing company and its customers. Except for the article entitled "For what IT's Worth: Pricing Internal IT Services," by Diogo Rau and Paul Willmott, we do not consider internal transfer pricing. In addition, we have not addressed the pricing of social goods or services nor have we addressed some topics that could conceivably be included in the broad definition of pricing such as wages.

ORGANIZATION AND CONTENTS OF THIS VOLUME

This book is divided into six parts. After the introductory section, Part II, Pricing in Selected Industries, introduces the wide variety of pricing approaches that are taken in different industries. The first chapter in this part discusses three approaches to understanding why a particular mechanism is used in a particular setting. The remaining chapters are written primarily by practitioners and consultants describing the pricing challenges in fourteen different industries. Part III, Pricing Fundamentals, contains chapters describing some of the fundamental concepts from economics and management science useful for analyzing pricing across many settings. Part IV, Pricing Tactics, describes specific pricing tactics such as nonlinear pricing and markdown management and how prices are analyzed and set using each tactic. Part V, Organization and Processes, discusses the issues involved in creating an effective pricing organization and an effective pricing process. Finally, Part VI, Current Challenges and Future Prospects, describes some promising areas for current and future research. We next describe the contents of each part in more detail.

Part II: Pricing in Selected Industries

The processes by which prices are set, updated, evaluated, and managed can vary widely from industry to industry and even from company to company within an industry. Understanding how prices are set, communicated, and updated in a particular industry is a fundamental pre-condition for modeling the pricing process within that industry or prescribing approaches (analytical or otherwise) for improving pricing. A pricing optimization or analytic approach built for a passenger airline is unlikely to work for pricing wine, health care, or telecommunication services. The purpose of this section is to give a sample of how pricing is performed in a number of different industries.

In his chapter, Robert Phillips discusses a "pricing modality" as the mechanism by which buyers, sellers, and intermediaries determine the price for a transaction in a market and compares three approaches to understanding why a particular modality will predominate within a particular market at a given time. He stresses the variety of ways in which prices can be determined and claims that arguments from optimality cannot predict which modality will predominate in a given industry at a particular time. He provides examples from three different markets—television advertising, movie tickets, and retail pricing—to support his thesis.

The authors of the remaining chapters in this part are primarily practitioners and consultants. They describe how pricing is performed in fourteen different industries ranging from airlines and cruise lines to health care and consumer credit as well as pricing in the Grand Bazaar in Istanbul. Each author has provided a summary of the key processes and issues involved in setting prices in the industry of interest, a discussion of why prices are set the way they are in that industry, and a discussion of current and future trends. These chapter are not only useful for those looking to understand pricing in those industries; taken together, they provide vivid evidence of the wide variety of pricing approaches in use today.

Part III: Pricing Fundamentals

While pricing practices vary from industry to industry and even from company to company within an industry, there are analytical approaches that can be applied to pricing situations independent of the setting. The chapters in this part describe some of the fundamental tools and concepts that can be used to analyze pricing.

In "Price Theory in Economics", Thomas Weber describes how prices are treated in economic theory. He introduces the basic concepts of consumer choice including rational preferences and utility functions. He then shows how consumer choice combined with the elements of an exchange economy can give rise to equilibrium prices that are efficient. He then discusses the important issue of market externalities and nonmarket goods. He also describes the relationship between information and pricing which leads quite naturally to the question of how pricing mechanisms can be designed to be informative and efficient.

One of the key elements in pricing analysis is representing how demand will change as prices change. Garrett van Ryzin's chapter "Models of Demand" provides a primer on such models. He shows how the forms of demand models can be derived from the underlying principles of consumer choice. He describes the desirable properties of such models and discusses a number of such models in common use. Finally he describes how the parameters of these models can be estimated from sales and pricing data.

In most markets, pricing satisfies the conditions of a game as originally defined by von Neumann and Morgenstern: the results of a pricing action by firm A will depend upon how its competitors react and vice versa. There is a long tradition of game theory being applied to pricing: in 1883, Joseph Bertrand used game theoretic reasoning to argue that prices in a perfect market would equilibrate to marginal cost. In their chapter entitled "Game Theory Models of Pricing", Praveen Kopalle and Rob Shumsky introduce the basic concepts of game theory as applied to pricing. They describe the classic models of Bertrand and Cournot competition and introduce Stackleberg pricing games. They show how game theory can be used to derive insights about pricing behavior in a variety of settings from dynamic pricing, to promotions, to airline revenue management.

Neoclassical economics was based on the assumption that consumer behavior followed certain axioms of rationality. Since the pioneering work of Kahnemann and Tversky in the 1970s, it has been increasingly demonstrated that actual consumer behavior can deviate significantly from rationality. *Behavioral economics* is the term that has been given to the study of these deviations from rationality and their implications. In their chapter, Özalp Özer and Yanchong Zheng discuss the implications of the findings of behavioral economics for pricing. They describe the principal regularities that have been found in deviation from "economically rational" behavior such as loss aversion, framing, and concern for fairness. They then show how these can influence price response for both consumers and businesses.

Part IV: Pricing Tactics

The chapters in this part describe and provide an overview of specific pricing management problems, their settings, and approaches to determining prices within these settings. This part also illustrates the wide variety of methodologies that are needed to support pricing decisions and processes faced in different industries. One key dimension that is particularly important in determining the appropriate pricing tactic is the amount of "customization" that the seller can apply to his pricing and how it is applied. At one extreme—typically found in business-to-business settings—the seller has considerable information about each buyer and their needs and the ability to quote a different price for each transaction based on that information. A "customized pricing" approach is often used to set the price in this case. At the other extreme, the seller may have limited information about each customer and/or little ability to set different prices for different customers. In this case, some sort of "list pricing" is used, often with various promotions, markdowns, or "nonlinear pricing" approaches to segment potential customers. If capacity or inventory is scarce and perishable, then pricing a unit needs to incorporate the possibility of selling the item later at a higher price—this is the classic "revenue management" problem. Finally, when there are many potential buyers contending to purchase a scarce item, sellers often use auctions as a mechanism to maximize their revenue and ensure that the item is purchased by the seller with the highest valuation. This section covers tactical pricing in all of these settings.

Customized pricing describes a pricing modality in which the seller has the ability to set the price to a customer based on some knowledge of that customer's identity and expressed needs. It is an approach widely used in business-to-business settings as well as in consumer lending and insurance. Robert Phillips' chapter describes how customized pricing works in a number of different market settings. It further describes how to determine the customized prices that best meet corporate goals given a bid–response function as well as how to estimate a bid–response function given historical sales data.

Nonlinear pricing is the phrase used to describe pricing schemes in which the price is not strictly proportional to the amount purchased (hence nonlinear). It is a tactic that is widely used in many industries. Shmuel Oren's chapter on nonlinear pricing describes direct and indirect price discrimination methods such as bundling, quantity discounts, Ramsey pricing, priority pricing, efficient rationing, and pricing through quality (product attribute) differentiation and self-selection. The chapter also covers nonlinear pricing applications in different industries such as electric power and telecommunication.

List pricing refers to the situation in which a seller sets a price and each potential customer decides whether or not to purchase at that price. It is one of the most common pricing modalities and is the standard for most retail trade (on-line and off-line) in Western economies. The chapter by Yossi Aviv and Gustavo Vulcano entitled "Dynamic List Pricing" describes methods for setting and adjusting list prices over time in order to maximize profitability. They discuss response estimation for list pricing, how to incorporate multiple products that are complements or substitutes, the forecasting process, dynamic list pricing when customers are strategic (for example, when they wait for sales and time their purchase decision), and the effect of product assortment on optimal dynamic list pricing methods.

In their chapter entitled "Sales Promotions", Robert Blattberg and Richard Briesch describe how temporary discounts of various sorts can be used to drive sales and improve profitability. There are a vast number of sales promotions types ranging from coupons, to temporary sales, to "buy one get one free". Blattberg and Briesch describe the different sales promotions mechanisms in use and how they work. They discuss what is known about the effects of the different promotions and their effectiveness. Finally, they describe how the effects of promotions can be analyzed and how managers can select the right promotional approach in a particular situation.

The *markdown management* problem is faced by retailers who sell inventory that either deteriorates (such as fresh food) or becomes less valuable over time (such as fashion goods). In such situations, the retailer needs to determine how much discount to apply and how to update that discount over time in order to maximize revenue from his inventory. In the chapter entitled "Markdown Management", Rama Ramakrishnan reviews the reasons for markdowns and the characteristics of industries in which they occur. He formulates the markdown management problem and describes the business rules and operating practices that constrain markdown decisions. He discusses the different approaches that are used to solve the markdown management problem and some of the challenges faced in implementing automated markdown management systems.

Following deregulation in the United States, airlines faced the problem of how many seats to allocate to different fares on different flights. This was the origin of *revenue management*, which has become an important tool for increasing profitability in many industries including hotels, rental cars, cruise lines, and freight carriers. The chapter by Kalyan Talluri entitled "Revenue Management" notes that the key characteristics of revenue management industries include limited supply and immediate perishability. In this situation, it can be optimal to reject low-fare customers even when supply is available in order to preserve capacity for later booking higher-fare customers. The chapter describes the field of application of revenue management, describes approaches to revenue management applicable to a single resource (such as a flight leg) as well as how revenue management can be applied to a network of resources (such as an airline schedule).

Auctions are among the most durable market mechanisms: the ancient Romans used them to sell property and Google uses them to sell keywords. Richard Steinberg's chapter "Auction Pricing" gives some historical background on auctions and describes the different varieties of auction, such as English, Dutch, Japanese, candle, silent, sealed-bid, Vickery, and simultaneous ascending auctions. The chapter summarizes the most important results from auction theory including the optimality of the Vickery auction and the revelation principle. It also describes some of the current topics in auction research including approaches to combinatorial auctions.

One of the newest trends in service operations is offering virtual modifications of an underlying service in order to segment customers and increase profitability. One example is the use of "opaque" channels such as Priceline and Hotwire to sell airline seats. Opaque channels are inferior to traditional booking channels because the identity of the airline and the exact time of departure are unknown at the time of booking. Another example of a virtual modification is an "option" by which a seller offers a discount conditional on their right to recall the service at some point before delivery. In their chapter, "Services Engineering: Design and Pricing of Service Features", Guillermo Gallego and Catalina Stefanescu discuss a number of such virtual modifications including fulfillment and repayment options, flexible services, opaque selling, and bundling/unbundling. In each case, they discuss how pricing is intimately linked to the design of the product.

The chapter by Murat Kaya and Özalp Özer entitled "Pricing in Business-to-Business Contracts" discusses how pricing terms in supply chain contracts are used to share profits, align incentives, share risks, and signal or screen information across firms. For example, pricing can be used to signal quality and screen private information such as demand forecasts. Their chapter also highlights some of the issues that a firm should consider when designing a pricing contract, such as channel coordination, efficiency, and risk. The chapter reviews a variety of pricing contract structures including wholesale price, revenue sharing agreements, consumer and manufacture rebates, buy-back agreements, advance purchase contracts, capacity reservations, and service-level agreements.

The chapter by Xin Chen and David Simchi-Levi entitled "Pricing and Inventory Management" surveys academic research on price optimization models in which inventory replenishment plays a critical role. The chapter summarizes some of the optimal policies that can be used to jointly optimize prices and inventory replenishment decisions for systems with finite planning horizons and multiple decision periods. The chapter covers topics such as base-stock list price policy and (s,S,p) policy.

Part V: Organization and Processes

The chapters in this part address the practical issues involved in managing the pricing process. These include establishing the right pricing organization; hiring the right mix of people into the organization; establishing processes for setting, updating, and evaluating prices; determining ways to measure the success of pricing; and providing the right incentives to the people involved in pricing decisions.

A precondition for pricing success is an effective pricing organization. The chapter entitled "Structuring and Managing an Effective Pricing Organization" by Michael Simonetto and his co-authors from Deloitte Consulting discusses the challenges that companies face in developing and managing their pricing organizations. In many companies, pricing decisions and processes are dispersed across finance, sales, marketing, and operations. The authors argue that the pricing process should be closely managed and coordinated with other corporate decisions. They present an approach for structuring and managing a pricing organization to accomplish this.

Selling globally adds complexity to pricing. In their chapter, "Global Pricing Strategy", Greg Cudahy and his co-authors from Accenture discuss the issues faced by companies selling into many different countries. They focus on the specific challenge of transforming an underperforming global pricing organization into a more effective one and illustrate with the example of a chemical manufacturing company.

Lean and *Six Sigma* are methodologies originally developed to improve the efficiency and quality of manufacturing operations. Six Sigma was designed to reduce the quality variation of manufacturing outputs while Lean manufacturing was designed to reduce waste at every step of a process. In their chapter, "Using Lean Six Sigma to Improve Pricing Execution", ManMohan Sodhi and Navdeep Sodhi describe how the two methodologies can be applied to the pricing process to increase efficiency and reduce "bad" pricing quotes. They illustrate the concept with a case study application to a US-based global manufacturer of industrial equipment.

In business-to-business selling, prices are often set through a complex process of negotiation. In the chapter "Mastering your Profit Destiny in Business-to-Business Settings", Thomas Jacobson and his co-authors from Accenture discuss the challenges that sellers face in this environment. They stress that procurement departments are becoming far more sophisticated and use a variety of tactics to negotiate better deals. They describe these tactics and also make recommendations that can help sellers maintain reasonable prices in the face of aggressive procurement departments.

Part VI: Current Challenges and Future Prospects

The concluding chapter by Özalp Özer and Robert Phillips describes two specific areas of current research that they believe will be significant for the future of pricing management. One area they discuss is the need for more empirical studies of pricing—categorizing and understanding how pricing is performed in different companies and different industries, what pricing processes and organizations are most effective, and what benefits have been delivered by automated systems. A second area is pricing with unknown response—the need for companies to learn about customer response at the same time that they are trying to make money. Some studies have shown that seemingly rational processes by which companies might update their customer response models based on new information could lead to suboptimal pricing. More research is needed to understand how pervasive this issue might be in practice and how such processes could be improved.

A reader intrepid enough to read all of the chapters in this book should gain a strong appreciation of the challenges posed by pricing in the real world. She would have an excellent overview of the "state-of-the art" in analytical approaches used to improve pricing and of current thought in how pricing should be organized and performed within an organization. While many readers will not read all the chapters, we hope that any reader with an interest in pricing will find something valuable and interesting in every chapter.

References

Corey, E. R. (1976) *Industrial Marketing: Cases and Concepts.* Englewood Cliffs, NJ: Prentice-Hall.

PART II

PRICING IN SELECTED INDUSTRIES

CHAPTER 2

WHY ARE PRICES SET THE WAY THEY ARE?

ROBERT PHILLIPS

2.1 INTRODUCTION

One of the themes of this book is the wide variety of pricing approaches that are used in different industries and, correspondingly, the wide variety of methodologies that are needed to support pricing. Different approaches to pricing used in different industries include:

- On-line advertisements are typically sold in a sort of auction based on the number of impressions that they garner (Vudali and Atherton, Chapter 7).
- In Western economies, most retail transactions typically use a fixed price modality. That is, the seller posts a price and prospective buyers either pay that price or do not purchase.
- Less-than-truckload trucking services are typically sold to large purchasers as annual contracts based on a discount from a standard tariff (see Kintz, Chapter 13).
- Airline tickets are sold individually using highly dynamic and differentiated prices (see Barnes, Chapter 3).

This chapter explores the question of why this disparity in pricing mechanisms exists and persists—even among markets that often appear superficially very similar.

To address this question, we define the concept of a *pricing modality*. The pricing modality is the way that buyers, sellers, and intermediaries interact in a market to determine the price for a particular transaction. In the terms of Mark Granovetter (1992), prices themselves are an "outcome" while a pricing modality is an "institution". Depending upon the situation, a pricing modality can either be a particular instance of an economic

I would like to gratefully acknowledge the useful comments of Mike Harrison of the Stanford Business School, Danielle Logue of Oxford University, Özalp Özer of the University of Texas at Dallas, Richard Steinberg of the London School of Economics, Kalinda Ukanwa Zeiger, and an anonymous referee.

institution or part of a larger economic institution (e.g., a "market structure"). Some examples of pricing modalities include:

- *Fixed pricing.* A seller chooses a price. That price is posted in a market. The item for sale (product or service) is available at that price to all buyers in the market.
- *Bargaining.* A price is negotiated between an individual buyer and a seller. The "price" is the final point of agreement—assuming that agreement is reached.
- *Dictatorship.* A government or state agency chooses and enforces prices.
- *Seller auction.* A seller accepts bids from two or more potential buyers. Buyers may or may not be allowed to update their offers. The ultimate price is determined by the seller's choice of buyer but may also depend on the other bids as well.
- *Customized pricing.* A potential buyer solicits offers or bids from potential suppliers, often through a "request for proposal" or "request for quote" process. The price results from the buyer's choice of which bid to accept.
- *Contingent pricing.* The buyer and seller agree on a table of prices or pricing formula that determines the final price based on uncertain future outcomes.

A pricing modality describes the "rules of the game" in a given market. These rules are understood by all buyers, sellers, and intermediaries as well as by outside observers such as reporters, regulators, and stock analysts. In some cases, the predominant modality may be mandated by regulation, but more often it is simply a matter of common understanding among all parties.

We note that pricing in most industries is a messy business, with great variation among industries and even among different companies within the same industry. In many cases, only insiders fully appreciate the subtleties of how prices are set, communicated, evaluated, and updated within their industry. In many cases, industries that seem superficially very similar operate under very different pricing modalities. This raises the questions: Why do certain pricing modalities prevail in certain markets and industries? Why are prices set using different modalities in markets that appear to be very similar? How do prevailing market modalities influence how people think about prices? How do they influence what people consider "fair" or "unfair" in economic transactions?

Definitively answering these questions is beyond the scope of this chapter. However, this chapter does seek to establish some specific points. The first is that the pricing modality in use in a particular market generally cannot be predicted purely by reference to principles of economic optimality. Pricing modalities are neither ahistoric nor asocial—understanding history and the broader social setting is often necessary to understand why a particular pricing modality is in place in a particular market at a particular time. Second, over time, pricing modalities tend to become normative for all participants—buyers, sellers, and intermediaries. An attempt by any player to unilaterally deviate from the norm may not succeed even if it would lead to an improved situation for all participants. Finally, the fact that pricing modalities have a past means that they can also have a future. That is, the pricing modality in use in a particular market can shift due to changes in technology, regulatory environment, or social and demographic characteristics. When this happens, incumbents who are heavily invested in the previous modality may find themselves at a relative disadvantage.

The next section discusses three different approaches to explaining and understanding the reasons why particular modalities hold in particular markets. The subsequent two sections discuss two markets—pricing for television advertising and pricing of movie tickets in the United States—in which arguments from economic equilibrium are seemingly unable to explain the predominant pricing modalities. The next section discusses the rise of fixed pricing as the dominant modality for retail transactions. This history is interesting because of the extent to which fixed pricing has become the standard for "fairness" in retail pricing. The final section summarizes the main points.

2.2 APPROACHES TO PRICING MODALITIES

Broadly speaking, there are three pure approaches used to explain the use of a particular pricing modality within a particular market:

- The *market equilibrium* approach analyzes economic institutions strictly in terms of the incentives and information of the players (buyers, sellers, and intermediaries); the nature of the goods and services being sold; and the regulatory and technological environment in place. Given this, it seeks to show that a particular pricing modality is the (ideally unique) Nash equilibrium of the underlying game.

- *Institutional history* views economic institutions as the outcome of historical development involving the interplay among changing technologies, regulations, players, and industry structures. The institutional history viewpoint emphasizes the role of the past in determining the pricing modality currently used in a particular market.

- *Economic sociology* emphasizes the roles of social structures, norms, expectations, and the extent and nature of social ties in determining the form of economic institutions.

We will briefly discuss each of these three pure approaches as they apply to pricing.

2.2.1 Market equilibrium

The market equilibrium approach assumes that the pricing modality currently in place in a market can be determined entirely from consideration of the players (buyers, sellers, and intermediaries) in that market and their preferences, the information available to each player and how it is revealed over time, the distribution technology, the characteristics of the product or service for sale, and the regulatory environment. Four examples of this approach as applied to pricing include:

- In a pioneering example of game-theoretic reasoning, Bertrand (1883) argued that competitive pressures would force sellers of identical goods to set their margins to zero. Prices would then equal marginal costs.

- Riley and Zeckhauser (1983) used a mathematical model to show that a seller encountering risk-neutral buyers should quote a fixed price rather than bargain or use a randomized pricing strategy. They showed that this holds whether or not the seller knows the distribution of willingness-to-pay within the buyer population.

- Lazear (1986) considered the case of a seller holding a fixed stock of a good whose value to customers is highly uncertain—for example, a dress at the start of the spring season. He shows that the optimal policy for such a seller is to start initially with a high price which he should then sequentially lower until the entire stock is sold. This corresponds to the "markdown policy" commonly used by sellers of fashion goods (Ramakrishnan, Chapter 25).

- Dana (1998) showed how the advance purchase discount policy adopted by airlines, rental cars, and other related industries can be derived from a model in which customers have uncertain demand for the service. This result holds even in the absence of market power on the part of the seller.

These are just four examples among many—the argument from equilibrium is, to a large extent, the defining characteristic of modern economic theory. Economists employ a range of analytic tools to establish market equilibria—and, thereby, pricing modalities. As one example, the "no arbitrage" principle provides a limit to the extent to which a market can support price discrimination. As another, the assumption of profit-maximizing sellers interacting with utility-maximizing buyers often enables a set of possible equilibria to be determined as the set of joint solutions to mathematical optimization problems.

It is unquestionable that the argument from equilibrium has been extremely successful in providing insights into the structure of markets. To name just one example, it was long believed—by many retailers among others—that the need to mark down unsold inventory was solely the result of mistakes in buying, merchandising, or pricing. For example, a pamphlet issued to managers at a leading San Francisco department store entitled "How to Avoid Wasteful Markdowns" warned:

> High markdowns benefit no one. Not the store. Not the manufacturer. Not the customer. The store loses in value of assets or inventory. The manufacturer loses in future sales and by loss of prestige of his product. The customer is getting merchandise that is not up to standard, at a low price it is true, but, remember—she would rather have fresh, new merchandise that she can be proud of and with real value at regular price than pay less for questionable merchandise. (Emporium 1952)

Economic analysis such as that by Lazear (1986) has helped retailers understand that, far from being evidence of mismanagement, markdowns can be an effective and profitable way to manage sales of seasonal merchandise.

Game theory has proven to be a particularly important tool for analyzing markets. The demonstration that a pricing modality is a unique pure-strategy Nash equilibrium is a powerful result. It means that, under the current modality, no player (buyer, seller, or intermediary) could unilaterally do better by changing his actions. This can be a strong explanation for the persistence of a particular modality over time. Furthermore, in many cases, it can be shown that a sequence of "best response" moves will lead to an equilibrium—see, for example, Gallego et al. (2006). While this type of result cannot be used to explain the origin of a modality (why buyers and sellers interact on the basis of fixed prices) it can provide some justification for the persistence of the modality over time.

However, game theory explanations for market structure have a number of well-known drawbacks. First of all, a one-shot game may have multiple pure Nash equilibria. In this case, some refinement or restriction of the Nash criterion needs to be used to predict which equilibrium would prevail. Worse still is the case of games that admit only mixed-strategy Nash equilibria. For large games (those with many players and/or many possible actions), the computation of all Nash equilibria is a computationally difficult problem (Papadimitrou 2007). It is not clear how sellers would have access to the computational power needed to calculate the mixed-strategy solution that can arise, for example, in the case of a finite number of capacity-constrained Bertrand–Edgeworth oligopolists (Allen and Hellwig 1986). And, even if players had access to sufficient computational power, there is no accepted way to predict what would happen in a one-shot game that admits only mixed-strategy equilibria.

A further challenge to the use of game theory has come from the field of experimental economics—in particular, the finding that, in many experimental situations, the strategies adopted by the players do not correspond to a Nash equilibrium. The classic example is the "ultimatum game" in which one player (the "Proposer") is given a sum of money and proposes a split of the money to a second player (the "Responder") who decides whether or not to accept the proposed split. If the Responder accepts, than each player receives the proposed split. If the Responder rejects the proposed split than both players receive nothing. The unique Nash equilibrium for this game is for the Proposer to propose the smallest possible amount to the Responder and for the Responder to accept. However, Fehr and Schmidt (1999) found that in more than 70 percent of games, the Proposer offered between 40 and 50 percent to the Responder. Furthermore, Responders routinely rejected offers of 10–20 percent of the money. In almost all ultimatum game experiments, either the Proposer or the Responder (and sometimes both) play a strategy that is strongly dominated in the game theoretic sense—the Proposer by proposing to give away more than the minimum, the Responder by rejecting positive offers. These results have been replicated in a wide variety of settings (Henrich et al. 2001; Camerer 2003: 48–59; Henrich et al. 2004). While there are substantial variations between cultures, deviation from Nash equilibrium is the rule rather than the exception. Experimental economists have found deviations from "optimal play" in many other types of game (Camerer 2003). The implications and interpretations of these deviations from optimality can be controversial[1] but it is increasingly apparent that arguments from game theory need to be used with great care. Experimental economics has shown that a Nash equilibrium may be neither descriptive nor reliably normative for a particular market (Özer and Zheng, Chapter 20).

2.2.2 Institutional history

In his book, *Institutions, Institutional Change and Economic Performance* (1990), Douglass North asserts that neoclassical economics cannot explain the origin and persistence of many economic institutions.

> [neoclassical economics] does not provide much insight into such organizations as the medieval manor, the Champagne fairs, or the suq (the bazaar market that characterizes

---

[1] See, for example, the commentaries and responses in Henrich et al. (2005).

much of the Middle East and North Africa). Not only does it not characterize these organizations' exchange processes very well, it does not explain the persistence for millenia of what appear to be very inefficient forms of exchange. (North 1990: 11)

North, and other institutional historians, seek to explain the origin, development, and persistence of economic institutions over time in terms of social change. They view arguments from pure economic equilibrium as having insufficient explanatory power because they take for granted much of what needs to be explained. "Asserting that a particular game is an equilibrium outcome in a larger meta-game whose rules reflect only the attributes of the available technology and the physical world is useful yet unsatisfactory, because it simply pushes the question of institutional origin back one step. What is the origin of the meta-game?" (Greif 2006: 11). Institutional historians seek to supplement (rather than replace) economic analysis with the understanding of an economic institution as the outcome of an evolutionary process.

If understanding history is necessary, then the rationale for an existing pricing modality cannot be entirely explained from current conditions. The implication is that if history were different, then the present would be different. This is the definition of *historical contingency*—an existing economic institution has the form it does, at least in part, because of past events and cannot be fully explained without reference to history. If history needs to be evoked to explain the present, then the final form of the institution cannot be "optimal" with respect to current conditions. This idea is very similar to the concept of *path-dependence* introduced by Paul David. Specifically, David was interested in how an apparently sub-optimal standard could become dominant over a very large market even in the presence of a superior alternative. The particular example that he evoked was the *QWERTY* keyboard layout.

QWERTY—named for the sequence of the first six keys on the upper left side of the keyboard—is the name given to the most common keyboard layout. It was by far the prevalent layout for typewriters and is still the dominant layout for computer keyboards, PDAs, cell-phones, Blackberries, and so on. The QWERTY layout was originally designed by the American Christopher Sholes and adopted in its current form by the Remington Corporation in 1874. QWERTY is evidently inefficient since three of the four most common English letters (E, T, and A) are allocated to the weaker left hand. According to David (1985), this was a conscious decision on the part of early typewriter designers to slow typists down in order to keep the keys from jamming.

The Remington was the first commercial typewriter available in America and the fact that it had a QWERTY layout set the course for the future:

> QWERTY's early dominance meant that typewriter users became committed to the layout. From 1874 to 1881, the only typewriters commercially available were Remington machines with QWERTY keyboards, and typists learned to use them. Some of those typists set up typing schools, where they taught the QWERTY keyboard familiar to them. Their pupils took jobs at offices with the keyboards they knew. Many businesses newly equipping themselves with typewriters ordered QWERTY machines, because it was easy to find typists trained to operate them. (Diamond 1997: 5)

Over time, the design of typewriters evolved so that key jamming was no longer a limiting factor on typing speed—yet QWERTY remained dominant. In 1932, William Dealey and August Dvorak introduced a new layout—the so-called *Dvorak keyboard*—which had been designed to make typing both faster and less fatiguing. Navy tests showed that retraining QWERTY typists to Dvorak increased their accuracy by 68 percent and their speed by 74 percent (Diamond 1997).

Nonetheless, despite its superiority, the Dvorak typewriter did not displace QWERTY. Interested parties including manufacturers, typists, and typing schools simply had too much invested in the status quo to change. Put another way, the "switching costs" in terms of both variable and fixed costs for participants to convert from QWERTY to Dvorak were too high to justify the change. As a result, David argued that a "sub-optimal" technology continued to dominate the market, even though a superior technology had been available for many years.[2]

While the specific details of the QWERTY example are somewhat controversial, there is no question that there are many examples of customs and standards in which path-dependence clearly plays a role. Examples include left-hand driving in the UK versus right-hand driving in the USA; the varying width or "gauge" of railroad tracks in different countries; 110 volt electric power in the USA versus 220 volt power most other places; etc. Institutional history is both necessary and sufficient to explain, for example, the use of different power plug configurations in different countries. There is no "argument from optimality" that explains the use of a different power plug in the UK than in Italy. Thus, at some level, any controversy is not about the existence of "path-dependent" institutions, but rather the extent to which a sub-optimal institution can long persist in the face of superior alternatives.[3]

2.2.3 Economic sociology

The market equilibrium approach is asocial in the sense that it makes no reference to any sphere of social interaction or normative behavior among the parties except as manifest in their preferences and externally imposed regulations. Economic sociologists claim that the core models of economics are overly simplistic and reductive in that they are built around the assumption of economic individualism. This ignores the fact that the set of activities defined and labeled as "economic" is, in fact, part of a larger social structure. The sociologist Mark Granovetter noted that economic actions are "embedded in concrete, ongoing systems of social relations" (Granovetter 1985: 487). Economic sociology emphasizes the "social embeddedness" of the economy. Granovetter and other economic sociologists emphasize that economic transactions are merely a particular type of social interaction

[2] Both the specifics of the triumph of the QWERTY keyboard over the Dvorak and the concept of path-dependence have been strongly contested. In Lewin (2003), Liebowitz and Margolis argue that the Navy tests were biased in favor of Dvorak and that there is no firm evidence that the Dvorak keyboard is actually superior to the QWERTY keyboard. They go on to argue that path-dependence—at least in the sense that David defined it—does not play an important role in the evolution of economic institutions. See David (2000) for his response.

[3] We note that the fact that players will agree on *some* standard in most situations *is* often explainable using game theory—even when the nature of the standard that is chosen is not. Traffic lights provide an excellent example—the value of a "coordinated equilibrium" over all possible non-coordinated equilibria is sufficiently high for all players (drivers) that the rise of some coordination mechanism seems inevitable (Tardos and Vazirani 2007: 14–15.) However, the widespread adoption of stop lights with "green means go", "amber means caution", and "red means stop" rather than, say "blue means stop" while "white means go", is only explainable by reference to details of technological and institutional history.

and the modes of economic interaction within a society, the institutions that are built around economic activities, and the allowable sets of outcomes are strongly mediated by broader social factors. To the extent that this is true, an economic institution cannot fully be understood without reference to the surrounding social context.

An example of the economic sociology approach is the study by Yakubovich et al. (2005) of electric power pricing. During the formative years of the electric power industry in the United States, there was a spirited debate about how electricity should be priced. Electricity was unique in the sense that the cost of providing electric service was driven not only by the demand for electric power at any particular moment, but also by the need to build capacity to accommodate the highest anticipated demand during the year—the so-called "peak demand".[4] Two different approaches to pricing were proposed; the Wright system and the Barstow system. Ultimately, the Wright system prevailed. The authors argue that economic theory "does not lead to any strong prediction as to which pricing system we should expect to have been adopted" (Yakubovich et al. 2005: 580). The Wright system prevailed not due to its intrinsic superiority nor from persuasive argument, "but from complex manipulations and exercises of power by leading industry actors, who mobilized support through their personal networks and domination of industry trade associations" (ibid.: 581–2). This emphasis on the importance of personal networks in determining economic outcomes is a particular hallmark of the work of economic sociologists.

Another example of the sociological approach to pricing is Stephen Gelber's (2005) study of bargaining for new cars. The fact that bargaining is accepted (and even expected) in new car sales is a clear exception to the fixed pricing modality that otherwise dominates retail sales in the United States. Gelber argues that bargaining has survived in automobile sales because it is one of the last remaining markets in which men make the majority of the purchasing decisions and that men are more comfortable in the conflict-fraught (and hence masculine) process of bargaining while women strongly prefer the more passive role implied by fixed pricing. "If department stores turned male customers into women by offering them a single price in a feminine environment, then car dealers turned women into men by not posting one true price for their new cars..." (Gelber 2005: 138). He sees the current mode of bargaining for automobiles as a direct descendent from the male-dominated horse-trading market of the late eighteenth and early nineteenth centuries.

Gelber's analysis is purist in the sense that it focuses almost entirely on the historical and sociological dimensions of the automobile market. He mentions but does not explore the fact that bargaining is likely to be more prevalent for "big-ticket" items such as automobiles and houses than it is for "small-ticket" items such as groceries or clothing. He presents no evidence that other retail items with predominately male buyers such as shop tools or hunting equipment are more prone to bargaining than retail items with predominantly female buyers. While his analysis is incomplete, it is not necessarily wrong. Both auto manufacturers and dealers have long been aware that women seem more averse to bargaining than men (*Business Week* 2007). If a particular manufacturer or dealer thought that abandoning bargaining in order to attract more female customers was to its advantage, there is no reason why it could not do so. And, in fact, there have been sporadic attempts to introduce fixed pricing for automobiles over time, ranging from Sears in 1912 (Emmet and Jeuck 1950: 220–1) to more recent attempts by Saturn and others (*Business Week* 2007). The

---

[4] For more information on electric power pricing, see the chapter by Wilson, Chapter 4.

fact that bargaining has survived as the dominant modality in the face of these and other attempts to institute fixed pricing still requires explanation.

We note that both "path-dependence" economists and economic sociologists view the structure of economic institutions as not fully explainable from a "closed" examination of the market itself without reference to history or context. The difference between them is one of emphasis. Sociologists tend to explain differences in terms of different societal norms or social structures while the "path-dependence approach" emphasizes the importance of history—particularly the way that market structures can become "locked in" early in the development of a market and then persist through time.

2.2.4 Application to pricing modalities

None of the three approaches described above can, by itself, fully explain the variety of pricing modalities used in various markets around the world. In particular, arguments from market equilibrium usually need to be supplemented by references to history and social factors if a particular market is to be understood. We discuss three specific examples in which the argument from pure equilibrium would appear to fail: the television advertising market in the United States, movie ticket pricing, and fixed pricing in retailing.

2.3 WHY IS TELEVISION ADVERTISING SOLD IN AN UPFRONT MARKET IN THE UNITED STATES?

In the United States, advertising inventory is sold by television networks such as CBS and NBC and purchased primarily by advertising agencies on behalf of their clients, the advertisers themselves. The market for this inventory has a curious structure. The bulk of television advertising is bought and sold in a short period in May known as the *upfront market*. The upfront market for prime-time advertising typically commences shortly after the networks have announced their fall (autumn) schedules. During a very intense period lasting from a few days to a few weeks, the television networks such as ABC, CBS, Fox, and NBC, sell the majority of their inventory for the next television season, where the "season" lasts from September to the following August. While the details of the upfront market are quite complicated, the typical transaction consists of an agreement to air an advertiser's commercials in certain shows for the next year along with a guarantee to provide a minimum number of impressions (viewers) in certain demographics such as "Adult Males, 18–42". If the network does not deliver the promised impressions it is obliged to compensate by providing additional slots to the advertiser or other consideration. If the network over-delivers it is simply a benefit to the advertiser. Typically the networks sell 70–80 percent of their anticipated capacity during the upfront market with the remaining capacity sold during the season on a spot basis in the so-called *scatter market*.

This is a simplified description of a market of great complexity. More details on how the US television advertising market works can be found in Lotz (2007) and in Phillips and

Young (Chapter 11). For our purposes, it is sufficient to note that the market has several features that do not have an obvious benefit to any of the participants:

1. During the upfront period, billions of dollars in complex commitments are negotiated among multiple parties in a short hectic period of a few days or weeks. Mistakes are not uncommon and, given the number of deals being negotiated and the short time period, none of the parties has the ability to "optimize" its responses to proposals made by other parties (Phillips and Young, Chapter 11).

2. The timing of the market—sales commitments in May for delivery from September through the following August—does not correspond to either the calendar year nor to the fiscal year of any participant. Nor does it correspond to the typical "media planning" calendar used by advertisers and agencies (Lotz 2007).

3. Both buyers and sellers are making commitments with substantial financial implications in the face of considerable uncertainty—neither the networks nor the advertisers know how shows are likely to perform in the coming season. If a network overestimates the impressions that will be generated by a new show, it runs the risk of needing to compensate advertisers with additional inventory. The opportunity cost of these "make-ups" can be substantial.

Given that it does not appear to be a particularly efficient market mechanism, how did the upfront market come to be and why does it persist? There are many other more obvious and convenient ways in which television advertising could be bought and sold. In other industries with fixed, perishable capacity, buyers can purchase future units in bulk at almost any time during the year. Thus, even very large groups such as conferences can enter negotiations at any time with airlines and hotels to purchase future capacity: there is no "upfront market" for airline seats or hotel rooms. Furthermore, other countries lack the upfront/scatter market structure. In addition, at various times over the years, advertisers and agencies have suggested that the industry should eliminate the upfront market in favor of a "continuous market" in which impressions and/or advertising slots could be purchased as needed (Ephron 2003). More recently, a group of advertisers led by Chevrolet pushed for an "e-Bay style" market for television advertising (McClellan 2010). But these efforts have come to naught and the upfront market has remained largely unchanged for almost fifty years. This suggests that we must look to the history of the upfront market to provide an explanation.

2.3.1 The history of the upfront market

Commercial television appeared in a serious form in the United States in the years following World War II. The "big three" television networks—ABC, CBS, and NBC— were originally radio networks and the structure of the new industry closely followed the established structure of radio. Despite some initial moves at government subsidy, the new medium of television, like its predecessor, radio, soon became 100 percent advertiser funded. Early television, like radio, was dominated by a small number of networks, each with a national organization of affiliated stations.

During the so-called "golden age" of live television (from the end of World War II into the late 1950s), advertisers typically sponsored an entire season of shows. In many cases, the sponsors' name would be in the title—*The Ford Theatre Hour, The Chrysler Shower of Stars, The Kraft Playhouse*. This approach had been adopted directly from radio. During the golden age, "it was standard for all networks to pay a program's production costs and additional fees for the network's airtime, based on the time of the day that the show aired and the number of affiliates that carried a program" (Weinstein 2004: 42). Most programs of the period were variety shows or staged plays that lent themselves well to live broadcast. Commercials consisted of celebrity endorsements or live product demonstrations. Since advertisers financed an entire series, all of the advertisements during a show would be from a single sponsor. Negotiations between sponsors and the networks apparently took place during February with final commitments in place by the first of March (Ephron 2003). Negotiations were for the opportunity to sponsor an entire series—there was little or no market for individual slots.[5]

During the period from the mid-1950s through the early 1960s, the industry moved from a *sponsor-centric* model to a *network-centric model*. Under the sponsor-centric model, shows were sponsored by one or two advertisers and produced by advertising agencies such as J. Walter Thompson and McCann-Erickson. By the 1957 fall season, only three shows were still produced by an agency—the remainder were network-produced or purchased by the network from independent producers (Mashon 2007: 149). The responsibility for developing, financing, and producing shows was moving from the sponsors and the agencies to the networks. In this new world:

> a program series was contracted to the network, not to the sponsor, as was previously the case. The network would schedule the program and either sell sponsorships or participation to interested advertisers. Since this new responsibility brought with it greater financial risks, the networks began to share the cost of pilots with the show's producers. If a pilot show was accepted for network scheduling, the network retained its financial interest in the series. (Heighton and Cunningham 1976: 34)

The shift from single-sponsor shows to multiple-sponsor shows was gradual but inexorable: during the 1956–57 season, 75 percent of prime-time programs were single-sponsor, by the 1964–65 season the fraction had dropped to only 13 percent (Boddy 1990).

By mid-1960s, single sponsorship was almost extinct. Instead, the networks developed their own programs or purchased them from independent producers or Hollywood studios and scheduled them as they saw fit. Instead of sponsoring shows, advertisers—through their intermediaries, the agencies—now purchased slots across many different shows often spread among two or more networks.

The modern upfront market seems to have emerged during the transition of commercial television from a sponsor-centric model to a network-centric model. However, the roots of the upfront market may go back to the days before television, when radio was the dominant

---

[5] A fascinating exception to this pattern was the so called "fourth network"; the DuMont Television Network. Founded by DuMont Laboratories, a television set manufacturer, in 1946, DuMont did not have a radio heritage. Because of this, and because it was under severe financial stress for almost the entirety of its existence, DuMont was far more flexible than the "big three" networks in how it sold advertising. It would air unsponsored programs and allow advertisers to buy individual or multiple slots (Weinstein 2004: 411–13.). However, DuMont ceased effective operations in 1955 and did not play any meaningful role in the development of the future television advertising market.

entertainment medium. Since at least the 1930s radio programming typically followed a September to May season. A commonly cited rationale was that audiences were lighter during the summer months and performers liked to take a summer vacation (Hettinger and Neff 1938: 159). As a result, network advertising contracts for radio, like their later television counterparts, usually started in October and lasted until the following April or May (Hettinger 1933: 186). Television seems to have inherited the idea of a fall season from radio—probably a direct result of the fact that the big three networks came from radio. Although early television shows could premier any time of the year, a season starting in September and lasting until April or May became standard for all four networks (ABC, CBS, DuMont, and NBC) by the 1951–52 season (Castleman and Podrazik 1982). Completing negotiations by the end of February gave advertisers and their agencies the time necessary to script and prepare the (live) shows for the new season. As the networks moved from selling shows and show times to selling slots, it is easy to see how the annual negotiation cycle moved from (a) selling single-show sponsorships to (b) selling both sponsorships and slots to (c) selling only slots. The upfront system was evidently well in place by 1962, when an advertising executive could complain, "the advertiser must make his decisions in March, knowing that he will have to live with them for the entire year that begins the following October!" (Foreman 1962: 44).

2.3.2 Is the upfront market an example of path-dependence?

A pure economic equilibrium explanation for the upfront market would be that it is the only "logical" market structure given the basic institutional and technological characteristics of the market for television advertising. Allaz and Vila (1993) present a two-period model of oligopolistic suppliers with constrained capacity in which a forward market forms despite the fact that it makes the sellers as a whole worse-off than selling on the spot market alone. They do not apply their approach to television advertising, but their analysis could plausibly serve as a starting point for a model of the upfront market. Such a model would need to reflect the fact that the television network ad market is not only oligopsonistic—with only six major sellers—but also highly concentrated on the buyers' side with four large advertising agencies accounting for almost 40 percent of total upfront ad spend (Ephron 2003).

Any explanation of the upfront market needs to account for the fact that advertising markets in countries other than the United States are structured quite differently. In Canada, the upfront market is quite small (about 20 percent of the total) and most advertising is sold on the scatter market. In Australia and New Zealand there is no upfront market per se—advertisers contract periodically throughout the year with the networks (Graham Young, personal communication). It seems unlikely that these differences represent unique technological or current regulatory environments within these countries. Rather, it seems likely that, to a large extent, they reflect the different historical pathways of commercial television in the different countries. For example most European television industries have a much longer tradition of both government support and control than the American industry. It is also significant that advertising markets in other media such as newspapers and magazines do not have upfront markets. Neither do group sales for airlines, hotels, or cruise lines.

A key element in the persistence of the upfront market appears to be the institutional and human capital infrastructure that has developed around it. The upfront market is avidly anticipated and followed by media journalists and stock analysts. The volume of upfront sales made by a network is considered an indicator of corporate performance and the total volume of upfront sales is seen as an indicator of the financial health of the television industry. Prior to the upfront market, equity analysts prepare detailed forecasts of network performance. As a typical example, one analyst predicted of the 2007 upfront market: "The market will grow 4.7% to just under $9.5 billion with CBS moving up 5.3% to $2.5 billion, ABC climbing 4.3% to $2.04 billion, NBC rising 3.9% to $1.98 billion and Fox going 5% to $1.98 billion" (Friedman 2007). Similar analysis of upfront "winners" and "losers" takes place once the market is complete and the networks have announced the results. In the face of such scrutiny, network executives are understandably reluctant to "opt out" of the upfront market.

The upfront/scatter market structure is woven deeply into the fabric of the television industry. Both the networks and the advertising agencies have invested many years and dollars in developing the capabilities needed to operate in this environment. The large advertising agencies employ specialists in developing and negotiating upfront deals. The networks have both people and systems focused exclusively on extracting as much revenue as possible in the upfront market. Equity analysts and journalists use upfront market performance as important financial indicators. Deviating from the current modality would require abandoning this familiar world, writing off millions of dollars in investment and sailing into unknown waters. The sociological view of the upfront market might be as an industrial norm that persists due to its ritual importance as described by Lotz (2007).

This does not mean that the upfront/scatter market structure is not a Nash equilibrium of some game. If a large agency, a large advertiser, or a major network saw that it was to their advantage to withdraw unilaterally from the upfront market, they would surely do so. If enough players withdrew, the upfront market would collapse. Thus, it is unquestionably true that all the major players believe it is in their interest to participate—at least as long as others participate. This, by definition, implies that the upfront market is a Nash equilibrium of some game. The question is, what game? How big does the "television advertising market game" need to be defined before the upfront market falls out as a unique subgame-perfect Nash equilibrium—if it ever does? It could be argued that equity analysts and network shareholders might need to be included as players since their expectations are cited as a reason for continued network. On the other hand, equity analysts only follow the upfront market because it has been important historically. In other words, the motivations and even the identities of the "players" cannot be specified without reference to history.

2.4 WHY DO MOVIE TICKETS COST THE SAME ON TUESDAY NIGHTS AS SATURDAY NIGHTS?

When the movie *Dreamgirls* opened in December, 2006, theaters in Los Angeles, New York, and San Francisco charged $25.00 per ticket—almost twice the usual price—during the first ten days of its run. Despite the high price, enough people flocked to the musical to fill almost all of the available seats. Ticket prices were lowered to their usual levels after the initial two weeks and the movie went on to a successful nationwide run (Hessel 2007).

The unusual thing about the differential pricing of *Dreamgirls* tickets is precisely how unusual it is. While movie theaters do employ many standard promotional approaches such as student/senior discounts or matinee discounts, they do not vary their pricing according to the popularity or genre of a movie, nor do they change it over time as demand begins to dwindle. In other words, they do not practice *revenue management* as do many industries such as the passenger airlines with which they share similar characteristics. As with passenger airlines, the seating capacity of movie theaters is fixed and immediately perishable—an empty seat is an irrecoverable source of lost revenue. As in airlines and other revenue management industries, demand for movie seats is uncertain but follows predictable patterns. For example, demand is reliably stronger during the summer and holidays than during other times of the year and is stronger on weekend nights than on week nights or during matinees. Demand tends to decline or "decay" after release in a fairly consistent fashion (Einav 2007). Furthermore, demand predictably varies among genres: during the period from 1985 through 1999, the average revenue per movie for science fiction movies was more than seven times the average for documentaries (Orbach 2004). R-rated movies tend to have lower box-office returns than G or PG rated movies (Sawhney and Eliashberg 1996). Both the cost of a motion picture and the amount of marketing and advertising expenditure have strong positive correlations with total revenue (Eliashberg et al. 2006). On the surface, this would seem to indicate that movies would be a strong candidate for dynamic pricing or revenue management.

Of course, forecasting demand for movie seats is far from an exact science. There will always be high-profile, high-budget flops such as *Waterworld* and surprise, low-budget hits such as *Little Miss Sunshine*. Nonetheless, there is no readily apparent reason why the industry could not benefit from more differentiated pricing. It would not be difficult to use some of the factors described above to develop a model of demand by theater that had sufficient predictive power to support profitable revenue management. Broadway theaters, whose demand is arguably less predictable than movies, routinely use various forms of price differentiation ranging from different prices for different seating qualities to half-price tickets sold through the TKTS outlet on the day of the show (Leslie 2004). Even professional sporting events—long known for pricing conservatism—have begun to vary prices according to the anticipated demand for individual games.[6] Why are movie theaters reluctant to follow suit?

Orbach (2004) and Orbach and Einav (2007) have examined the "riddle of motion picture pricing" in some detail. The current near-uniformity of prices within a theater is particularly puzzling because prior to 1970 there was significant pricing differentiation. According to Orbach, "throughout the 1950s and 1960s there was a clear distinction between pricing of regular and event movies. Exhibitors also maintained price variation between weekdays and weekends and among different types of seat" (Orbach 2004: 348). Furthermore, theaters and theater chains still differentiate prices according to geography: "Admission fees in certain cities are as much as three times higher than in other cities" (Orbach 2004: 322). Given that

---

[6] See, for example, the pricing scheme for the Colorado Rockies in Phillips (2005: 106).

theaters and theater chains are not allergic to price-differentiation among cities and price differentiation worked in the past, why do they universally maintain uniform pricing within the same theater? Orbach and Einav discuss six possible reasons:

1. Perceived unfairness of differentiated prices on the part of consumers.

2. Price may be a quality signal. A discount price might lead consumers to believe that a particular movie is inferior, thus leading to a sharp decrease in demand.

3. Demand uncertainty.

4. Menu and monitoring costs. These are particularly relevant at large multiplexes in which a single ticket taker provides entry to many different movies.

5. Agency problems. A distributor does not care about concession revenue, which can be a large component of profitability for an exhibitor.

6. Double marginalization. An industry structure in which a monopolistic supplier (such as the studio) sells to customers through a monopolistic distributor (such as a theater) has been shown to result in higher-than-optimal pricing to customers as well as lower-than-optimal profits for both the supplier and the distributor.

Orbach and Einav dismiss all of these reasons as either not applicable or as insufficient to explain uniform pricing. Their arguments seem persuasive. It is very difficult to argue that uniform movie pricing is now optimal when differential pricing was successful in the past and is used successfully in similar settings such as Broadway theaters and sporting events. In the absence of a more persuasive explanation, Orbach and Einav hypothesize that tacit pressure from movie distributors is the reason for uniform pricing. According to Orbach (2004), the shift from differentiated to uniform pricing can be dated to the release of *The Godfather* in 1970. *The Godfather* was released with uniform pricing nationwide and became the highest grossing movie to date. As Orbach (2004: 350) notes, "It is implausible that all exhibitors across the country decided individually to charge a regular price for *The Godfather*." This suggests (but does not prove) that some central coordination—presumably from the distributors—was involved.

It is important to note that, in theory, distributors are prohibited from influencing pricing by the terms of the Supreme Court judgment in *United States vs. Paramount* (1948) and a series of related consent decrees. Prior to *Paramount*, a cartel of eight distributors controlled the production, distribution, and exhibition of movies in the United States. The outcome of the Paramount case included prohibitions against direct and indirect distributor intervention in box-office pricing. Thus, if distributors are influencing prices, it must be through a tacit channel.

The hypothesis that tacit pressure by distributors influences theater prices is supported by statements from the exhibitors. For example, the executive director of a small Tucson theater commented, with respect to variable pricing, "The whole subject is very intriguing, but we're not going to do anything to disrupt our relationships with our distributors because they're our life blood. It might have to be something done by one chain that had 5,000 screens and the sufficient power over distributors to do it."[7] But there is no "smoking

---

[7] Quoted in Stauffer (2007).

gun"—no documented evidence of explicit pressure applied by distributors on exhibitors to adopt uniform pricing. This is not entirely unexpected, since such pressure would almost surely be judged to be in violation of the Paramount agreement.

Orbach (2004) invokes "conservatism" as an explanation for the persistence of uniform pricing: "Conservatism in this context is the adherence of the industry to an established practice without examining its justifications. In the exhibition market, conservatism seems to be fed by unexamined concerns that the transition to variable pricing would be financially disadvantageous" (Orbach 2004: 363–4). Ultimately, appeals to "conservatism" or inertia as rationales are somewhat unsatisfactory. Unlike the upfront market for television advertising, there does not appear to be significant monetary or human capital investment in uniform pricing by theater operators—it would be quite easy for a particular operator to institute differentiated pricing. This strongly implies that theater managers have significant doubts whether differentiated pricing would be successful in generating additional revenue and/or they fear some sort of adverse reaction either from consumers, competitors, or distributors. The upshot is that the question of why movie tickets cost the same on Tuesday night as they do on Saturday night remains open. The lack of pricing differentiation certainly appears to be suboptimal from a market equilibrium point of view, but the factors preventing theater owners from moving to more differentiated pricing have yet to be definitively identified.

2.5 Why do retailers sell at fixed prices?

The most important trend in pricing in modern times has been the rise of retail fixed pricing. The *fixed pricing modality* incorporates four elements:

1. The seller unilaterally chooses a price.
2. The seller posts the price in a market for potential buyers to see.
3. Potential customers observe the price and choose whether or not to purchase.
4. Transactions take place exclusively at posted or advertised prices.

It should be made clear that fixed-pricing is in no way inconsistent with price-differentiation, customer segmentation, volume discounts, dynamic pricing, or other common pricing tactics. A movie theater selling tickets at $12.50 to the general public but offering senior citizens a $2.00 discount is still practicing fixed pricing. So is a retailer running a "buy one get one free" promotion in its stores, as is a grocery store offering a "25 cents off a gallon of milk" coupon to some of its customers. In all of these cases, the seller has unilaterally set prices and communicated them to customers (albeit with potentially different prices to different customers)—the only decision that a customer faces is whether or not to buy at the price available to her.

About 50 percent of consumer expenditure in the United States is spent on goods and services that are sold in markets that (almost) exclusively use fixed prices. These include food, beverages, household supplies, gasoline, public transportation, and entertainment. Categories of expenditure that are typically transacted using modalities other than fixed pricing include housing, vehicle purchases, and insurance.[8] While about 50 percent of household *expenditure dollars* are spent on a fixed price basis, the percentage of household *transactions* that take place on a fixed price basis is unquestionably much higher. The non-fixed price transactions are "big ticket" items such as housing and vehicle purchases which are typically purchased less than once a year. Almost all common purchases such as buying a meal at a restaurant, groceries at a grocery store, books at a bookstore, personal items at a drugstore, or clothing from a department store, are fixed price transactions. Given its ubiquity, many might find it surprising that retail fixed pricing is less than 150 years old.

2.5.1 The prehistory of fixed pricing

Bargaining or haggling was the dominant pricing modality for buying and selling almost everything in the West from Classical times well into the nineteenth century. Buyers and sellers haggled over the price of produce in a market, over the price of shoes, of tailored clothing, of skilled handiwork, of land, of horses, of almost anything. In the classical world, auctions were also common—many unique and expensive items such as slaves, land, or furniture were commonly sold at auction.[9] Fixed pricing was, at best, a distant third—indeed, with the possible exception of inns and taverns (Casson 1974), it is difficult to find evidence of anything at all being sold at a fixed price during Classical times.

The situation continued past the fall of Rome, through the Medieval world, through the Renaissance and into the modern age. Individual purchases were typically based on bargaining or negotiation. Transactions among merchants, traders, and their agents (the "B-to-B" economy of the time) were based on various types of contracts and agreements that were undoubtedly intensely negotiated.

Fixed and posted pricing began to appear in various urban institutions starting in the eighteenth century. The first coffee houses in London opened in the mid-seventeenth century and apparently charged fixed and relatively stable prices (Ackroyd 2000: 319–24). Restaurants appeared in Paris sometime before the French Revolution. They differed from inns and taverns in that they catered to locals, not travelers. According to a 1773 description of a restaurant, "the price of each item is specific and fixed", while the 1835 edition of the *Dictionnaire de L'Académie Française* noted that the prices at a restaurant are "indicated on a sort of placard". Later, the placards would be replaced (or supplemented) with printed menus with prices—a practice adapted from the *menus de hote* provided to guests at dinner parties (Spang 2000). Computations for large parties needed to be kept simple in the days before the cash register so a common practice was to charge a fixed price for the meal with prices for beverages listed separately. Hotels, which arose in the United States in the years following the American Revolution, also advertised and posted prices as early as the 1820s (Sandoval-Strausz 2007).

---

[8] Calculations were based on 2006 expenditure figures by category available on-line at http://www.bls.gov/news.release/cpi.t01.htm. Details of underlying calculations are available from the author.

[9] The Romans in particular made widespread use of auctions—Trimalchio in *The Satyricon* is going to sell his "surplus furniture" at auction [Petronius 1997: 29]. In 193 AD, the Praetorian Guard, after killing the emperor Pertinax, sold the entire Roman Empire at an auction. Didius Julianus won with a bid of 250,000 sesterces per man.

Carriage lines in England and America in the late eighteenth century advertised fixed prices. For example, the *New York Times* of March 13, 1789 carried an advertisement for "New York & Baltimore Stages" that offered "Fare for each passenger 4 dollars, way passengers 4d per mile."[10] One of the most important early fixed pricers were the railroads. Railroad travel was an easily standardized product that lent itself naturally to fixed pricing. Indeed, railroads were not only early fixed pricers, they were also pioneers in price discrimination as recognized by the French economist Dupuit in 1849:

> It is not because of the few thousand francs which would have to be spent to put a roof over the third-class carriages or to upholster the third-class seats that some company or other has open carriages with wooden benches.... What the company is trying to do is to prevent the passengers who can pay the second class fare from traveling third class; it hits the poor, not because it wants to hurt them, but to frighten the rich. And it is again for the same reason that the companies, having proved almost cruel to the third-class passengers and mean to the second-class ones, become lavish in dealing with first-class passengers. Having refused the poor what is necessary, they give the rich what is superfluous.[11]

Thus, "fixed pricing" was hardly unknown by the mid-nineteenth century. Yet bargaining was unquestionably the dominant modality for the vast majority of purchases. After all, restaurants were primarily for the urban middle and upper classes at a time when the vast majority of the population was rural. A railroad trip would be a rarity for most people and only about 20 percent of the population in 1840 could afford to stay in a hotel (Sandoval-Strausz 2007). Most people, most of the time, did their buying in stores—and in stores, before the 1860s, bargaining was almost universal.[12] In smaller stores, the proprietor knew the cost of every good and negotiated every deal personally. Larger stores with numbers of clerks often utilized the "price code" system in which information on price-tags was listed in a code that the customer could not read:

> Every merchant selected a Price Symbol as soon as he went into business, and it was made a password to his sales methods. It had to contain ten letters, preferably not two were alike and it could not be too easy to decipher. Some of these were "Baltimore," "Comb basket," "Black Snake," "Prudential," "Cumberland," the first ten letters of the Greek alphabet, and special symbols such as those used by the J. D. McGraw house in Louisville, Mississippi...
>
> $$\wedge \vee 7 Z \mathcal{S} \vee \vee \theta \phi \times$$
>
> Thus markings on goods became "$\wedge$ Z $\times \times$" or $14.00. Always it was the practice to mark goods with both the purchase and selling prices.... One of the favorite pastimes for the few customers who understood the use of code words was that of trying to guess what they meant. (Clark 1944: 317–18)

This system favored buyers who were most willing and able to haggle. As John Wanamaker described retail trade prior to 1865, "There was no selling price for goods—there was an asking price, and the most persistent haggler bought the goods far below the unwary" (Wanamaker 1911: 27). It was not just customers who haggled with merchants—haggling was standard throughout the retail supply chain. "Manufacturers and importers bargained for the highest amounts they could get from wholesalers and jobbers. Wholesalers and

---

[10] Reprinted in Crow (1946: following p. 18).   [11] Quoted in Ekelund and Hébert (1999: 225).
[12] In some stores, basic commodities such as tea, sugar, salt, meal, and flour were sold at fixed prices prior to the Civil War (Norris 1962: 456).

jobbers put the squeeze on retailers for the last possible dime, and retailers in turn charged their customers as much as they feel the traffic would bear" (Scull 1967: 79). Haggling (or "higgling" as it was also called) had the benefit of enabling the savvy retailer to practice price discrimination. "A prosperous customer was quoted one price—subject, of course, to considerable negotiation—while a less affluent customer was quoted a lower price, also subject to adjustment if the customer had the time and stamina to negotiate" (Scull 1967: 79).

A glimpse of this world can be seen in Emile Zola's novel *The Belly of Paris*, which is set in the Les Halles market in Paris in the 1850s. Haggling is the basis of every transaction and *caveat emptor* is the rule. A naive servant who overpays for a fish is jeered and hectored by the other stall owners when she tries to return it (Zola 1873/2007). Other glimpses can be seen from contemporary marketplaces in traditional economies. In rural Mexico, "[for maize] one dealer observed asked $4.50 a pesada, sold fairly readily at $4.40 and would go to $4.20. If the client were very persistent, he might even sell at $4.00. If so, however, he managed to short weight the client of about half a kilogram of grain by clever manipulation.... Yet for regular customers who have agreed on a 'good' price, most dealers add a little maize after the weighing is complete" (Beals 1975: 167).

The system of bargaining for goods was the standard in Western society for millennia. However, as the 1860s dawned, this was about to change.

2.5.2 The fixed pricing revolution

It is impossible to determine which retailer was the first to use fixed pricing. Quaker merchants, who had a reputation for probity[13] are often credited with being the first to set fixed—although not necessarily posted—prices. In a 1658 tract entitled *A Warning to the Merchants of London*, the most influential early Quaker, George Fox, enjoined merchants to desist from the "cozening and cheating and defrauding" practice of haggling and adopt a fixed price policy (Kent 1990: 142). According to Daniel Defoe in *The Complete English Tradesman* (1726), Quakers "resolved to ask no more than they would take upon any occasion whatsoever and chose rather to lose the sale of their goods, ..., rather than abate a farthing from the price they had asked."[14] A dry-goods store founded by A. T. Stewart in 1826 is often credited with being the first to employ fixed prices in the United States (Scull 1967: 81). Some Parisian stores, such as the Petit Dunkerque, were advertising fixed and marked prices in the late 1830s and the Ville de Paris, the largest *magasin de nouveautés* in Paris, also featured fixed and marked prices by 1845 (Miller 1981).

The idea of fixed retail pricing was clearly in the air by the 1860s. But it was the arrival of those "grand emporiums of commerce", the first large department stores, that established the fixed price policy as the standard. Retail stores selling many different lines of goods with an emphasis on customer service and variety began to appear in the 1850s and 1860s

---

[13] So much so that many merchants falsely identified themselves as "Quaker", leading to an appeal by representatives of the Religious Society of Friends to the New York Legislature to prohibit the fraudulent use of the word "Quaker" in trade. See "Fight for Name 'Quaker'", *The New York Times*, p. 32, March 26, 1913.

[14] Defoe (1726: 245). Allen (2008: 37) describes the tension in a small store between an assistant who bargains with a customer and the Quaker owner who expects the goods to be sold "at the prices marked".

more-or-less simultaneously in the United States and France and a little later in England. Which of these establishments qualifies as the first "department store" is a matter of lively (if inconclusive) debate among business historians.[15] What is certain is that four of the most important early department stores were A. T. Stewart's Cast Iron Palace in New York (1862), Rowland Hussey Macy's eponymous New York store (1865), Aristide Boucicaut's Bon Marché in Paris (1850s), and John Wanamaker's Grand Depot (later known as "Wanamaker's") in Philadelphia (1876). Each of these pioneering entrepreneurs brought great energy and marketing savvy to their respective enterprises. All were experienced retailers and all—with the exception of Boucicaut—had experimented with a fixed price policy at previous establishments.[16]

Stewart, Macy, Boucicaut, and Wanamaker all became known for their fixed price policies and money-back guarantees at their stores. Stewart put price tags on all of his goods and advertised his "one-price" policy in the newspapers (Scull 1967: 81). Wanamaker boasted of his Grand Depot that "The prices of goods were put down at the beginning to the lowest point that they could be sold for and there was no underground way to get them. All were on the ground floor from the first" (Wanamaker 1911: 47). In New York, in Paris, and in Philadelphia, the new retail emporiums and their fixed price policies proved enormously popular. Smaller retailers were forced to adopt the new policies whether they liked it or not—the introduction of fixed prices by one of the new giants into a new line of business often resulted in general conversion to the new prices. When Wanamaker started selling pianos in 1899, "such thing as a fixed price for a piano, marked in plain figures, was rarely known" (Wanamaker 1911: 87). Once Wanamaker entered the business, other piano makers adopted the fixed price system in order to compete.

The fixed price policy coupled with money-back guarantees spread from the great stores of the East Coast to the rest of the country. Wayland Tonning (1956) studied the spread of fixed pricing in Champaign-Urbana, Illinois. He found that there was very sporadic advertising of a "one-price policy" in various stores between 1866 and 1872. In 1872, the Scott & Willis store opened, advertising "All Goods Marked in Plain Figures and ONE PRICE Strictly Adhered To". Competing stores gradually adopted the one-price policy combined with money-back guarantees. By the turn of the century, the one-price policy was the standard in Champaign-Urbana. This was simply one example of the process that occurred between 1870 and 1890, during which fixed pricing moved from being a rare exception to the norm for American retailers. By 1890, "One Price for Every Man" was being advertised proudly by grocers even in remote rural Georgia (Wetherington 1994: 172).

By the turn of the century, the fixed price policy was well on its way to being standard operating procedure for major retail establishments throughout North America and Western Europe. In 1905, prices in London stores were "almost invariably fixed, so that bargaining is unnecessary" (Baedeker 1905: 25). George Gissing's novel *Will Warburton*

---

[15] See, for example, Resseguie (1965).

[16] Macy had maintained a fixed price policy (along with a cash-back guarantee) at four different stores before coming to New York City. All four failed, but Macy maintained a firm belief in fixed prices and money-back guarantees. A. T. Stewart opened his first store in 1826, on a "one-price policy" in order both to make his clerks more efficient and to increase customer loyalty (Scull 1967). "Not two prices,—one price and only one," was John Wanamaker's motto when he founded his first store—a men's and boys' clothing store—in 1861 (Wanamaker 1911: 28).

(written in 1902–03, but published in 1905) has one merchant chide another who deviated from fixed pricing, "That'll never do behind the counter, sir, never!"

As the twentieth century progressed, fixed pricing became more and more firmly established among American retailers. Nonetheless, a 1947 handbook advised returning American servicemen who opened small retail stores to: "Maintain a strictly one-price policy. All your merchandise should be ticketed with the exact price; under no circumstance deviate from the price shown. Sometimes people are inclined to haggle and bargain with the owner of a small shop, whereas they wouldn't think of questioning prices in a large store. Correct that impression; never bargain or compromise."[17] What is interesting is not the advice itself, but the fact that it was still thought necessary. Even in post-World War II America, the norm of fixed pricing needed to be enforced.

2.5.3 Why fixed pricing?

Fixed pricing was a critical component of the business model of the new department stores. For one thing, without fixed prices there could be no money-back guarantees. The two went hand-in-hand—mass-volume merchants could not keep the records needed to enable "money-back" guarantees. Under the new regime, the customer lost her right (if that's what it was) to argue for a lower price. In return, the merchant relieved the customer of some of the risk of purchasing through the money-back guarantee.

Fixed prices were critical to the new stores in other ways. Many observers of contemporary markets within so-called "traditional" economies have noted the sophisticated skills required for sellers to thrive in these markets: not only must a seller be able to estimate the willingness-to-pay of each prospective buyer, they must also know the cost of each item and the magnitude of overheads in order to run a long-term business that not only sustains itself but provides a sufficient profit margin (Geertz 1978; Robertson 1983). In the small shops that preceded the advent of the department stores, sales clerks performed long apprenticeships before they could be trusted with full responsibility. List-pricing massively simplified the job. It enabled Wanamaker, Macy, and Boucicaut to recruit thousands of workers for their new stores who could become productive sales clerks after only minimal training.

Furthermore, fixed pricing enabled centralization of the pricing function and generated economies of scale in pricing. In a bargaining modality, selling 10,000 identical items requires 10,000 negotiations and 10,000 pricing decisions. In a fixed price modality, selling 10,000 identical items requires no negotiation and only a single pricing decision. The superior efficiency of fixed pricing was recognized by A. T. Stewart as early as 1826. Given that fixed pricing reduces the average time consumed for a new car sale by 82 percent (*Business Week* 2007) it is likely that the time savings from a fixed price policy were substantial, particularly as retail stores grew in size and scope. Some retail historians have claimed that, prior to the advent of fixed pricing, retailing required a much greater number of clerks relative to total sales than afterwards.[18] The increased efficiency of fixed pricing led

---

[17] Greenberg and Schindall (1946: 64, italics in original).

[18] For example, Crow (1946: 142–3) claims that "Old account books show that before the days of fixed prices and retail advertising the storekeeper had to employ two or three times as many clerks as needed today to sell the same quantity of goods". Note also Walter Benjamin's speculation that "The gain in time

to savings that could be passed along to customers in the form of lower prices—thus further increasing the advantage of the larger stores.

The combination of low and fixed prices with unprecedented size and scope meant that the new stores were really something new under the sun. They were acknowledged as such not only by shoppers but also by writers, academics, and journalists. In Paris, Emile Zola was fascinated by Aristide Boucicaut and his creation, The Bon Marché, which he saw as a new, hygienic, and efficient mode of commerce, replacing the old world of small specialized shops and customer haggling. Zola's novel, *La Bonheur des Femmes*—literally "The Ladies' Paradise"—is based closely on The Bon Marché; and its entrepreneurial owner, Octave Mouret, is based on Aristide Boucicaut. In Zola's novel,[19] the new store attracts customers in droves with its bright lights, its modern design, and its seemingly endless displays of merchandise of all sorts, as well as with its fixed prices, listed on tags, and its return policy. The fixed and posted prices are an integral part of the machinery of commercial seduction: even outside the front door, "on the pavement itself, was a mountain of cheap goods, placed at the entrance as a bait, bargains which stopped the women as they passed by.... Denise saw a piece of tartan at forty-five centimes, strips of American mink at one franc, and mittens at twenty-five centimes. It was a giant fairground display, as if the shop were bursting and throwing its surplus stock into the street" (Zola 1883/1995: 4–5).

Fixed prices were even part of the marketing displays at *La Bonheur des Femmes*:

> There was something for every whim, from evening wraps at twenty-nine francs to the velvet coat prices at eighteen hundred francs. The dummies' round bosoms swelled out the material, their wide hips exaggerated the narrow waists and their missing heads were replaced by large price tags with pins stuck through them into the red bunting round the collars, while mirrors on either side of the windows had been skillfully arranged to reflect the dummies, multiplying them endlessly, seeming to fill the street with these beautiful women for sale with huge price tags where their heads should have been (Zola 1883/1995: 6).

As Zola recognized, fixed and posted prices made possible entirely new retail and marketing strategies. When a small silk retailer, Robineau, tries to undercut the price of silk at the Ladies' Paradise by 10 centimes, he inadvertently starts the first price war. "And, in fact, the following week Mouret boldly reduced the price of the Paris-Paradise (silk) by twenty centimes... those twenty centimes meant a dead loss, for the silk was already being sold at cost. It was a severe blow for Robineau; he had not thought that his rival would lower his prices, for such suicidal competitions, such loss-leading sales were then unknown" (Zola 1883/1995: 197). Mouret triumphs by his ability to go ever lower than his competitor and Robineau is ultimately forced out of business.

Fixed prices combined with the power of advertising also enabled the "loss leader":

> "We'll lose a few centimes on these goods, I'll grant you. But so what? It won't be such a disaster if it enables us to attract all the women here and hold them at our mercy, their heads turned at the sight of our piles of goods, emptying their purses without counting!... After that you can sell the other goods at prices as high as anywhere else, and they'll still think yours are cheapest. For example, our Cuir-d'Or, that taffeta at seven francs fifty, which is on

realized by the abolition of bargaining may have played a role initially in the calculation of department stores" (Benjamin 1999: 60).

[19] To avoid confusion, I refer to the novel as *The Ladies' Paradise* and the store as *La Bonheur des Femmes*.

sale everywhere at that price, will seem an extraordinary bargain, and will be sufficient to make up for the loss" (Zola 1883/1995: 39).

The climax of *The Ladies' Paradise* is the much-advertised and much-anticipated sale which generates a frenzy of buying:

> Outstretched hands were continually feeling the materials hanging at the entrance, a calico at thirty-five centimes, a wool and cotton grey material at forty-five centimes, and above all an Orleans cloth at thirty-eight centimes which was playing havoc with the poorer purses. There was much elbowing, a feverish scrimmage round the racks and baskets in which piles of goods at reduced prices laces at ten centimes, ribbons at twenty-five centimes, garters at fifteen, gloves, petticoats, ties, cotton socks and stockings were disappearing as if devoured by the crowd. In spite of the cold weather, the assistants who were selling to the crowd on the pavement could not serve fast enough. A fat woman screamed. Two little girls nearly suffocated (Zola 1883/1995: 239–40).

The force of Zola's work comes from the fact, that, at the time, all of this was new. The arrival of the *grand magasins* "changed everything" in the relationship between merchant and seller as well as between merchant and merchant. Price-wars, loss-leaders, promotional prices, sales—none of this had any precedent in the old world of haggling in small shops. A new urban pastime—shopping—was born. Previously, entering a Parisian shop implied an obligation to buy[20]—much as sitting at a table in a restaurant today implies an obligation to order—but the *grand magasins* adopted a policy of "free entry" by which people could wander about and simply browse or merely pass the time. The new retailers relied upon the power of their merchandising, the seduction of low prices, the very design of their buildings to drive customers into a sort of buying frenzy. However, Parisian consumers were not simply passive victims of the new technologies of retail seduction—Zola also chronicled the birth of what is now called the "strategic customer". When Madame Marty, on impulse, buys a red parasol at fourteen francs fifty, her friend, Madame Bourdelais chides her, "You shouldn't be in such a hurry. In a month's time you could have got it for ten francs. They won't catch me like that!" (Zola 1883/1995: 245).

Merchants portrayed their fixed price policies in high-minded terms: fixed prices were not only efficient, they promoted harmony. "New, fair and most agreeable relations were established between the purchaser and the seller," enthused John Wanamaker (1911). The sentiment is not entirely self-serving—with fixed pricing in place, merchants indeed no longer had to "compete with the customers", in Clifford Geertz's phrase. There is no question that an environment of continual haggling could lead to serious disagreements and even worse—the earliest meanings of the word "bargain" include "struggle" and "fight". The police in pre-revolutionary Paris continually worried that haggling over the price of bread between customers and bakery owners could lead to riots (Kaplan 1996). In *La Ventre de Paris*, a dispute between a merchant and a buyer threatens to turn into a general melee (Zola 1873/2007). The anthropologist Clifford Geertz described marketplace bargaining as "A personal confrontation between intimate antagonists" (Geertz 1978: 32). With fixed pricing the relationship between merchant and buyer was both less intimate and less antagonistic. Pricing had become impersonal.

---

[20] See Miller (1981: 24). The ubiquity of the "obligation to buy" in early eighteenth-century and seventeenth-century shops has been challenged by Walsh (1999).

2.5.4 Fixed pricing as impersonal

In *Looking Backward* (1888), Edward Bellamy described a retail store in the Utopian society of the distant future:

> Legends on the walls all about the hall indicated to what classes of commodities the counters below were devoted. . . . it is the business of the clerks to wait on people and take their orders; but it is not the interest of the clerk or the nation to dispose of a yard or a pound of anything to anybody who does not want it. . . . I saw then that there was fastened to each sample a card containing in succinct form a complete statement of the make and materials of the goods and all its qualities, as well as price, leaving absolutely no point to hang a question on. (Bellamy 1888/2005: 79–80)

To this extent—if in little else—Bellamy's vision has been realized. Retail stores in the early years of the second millennium are indeed characterized by standardized goods; clerks as order-takers rather than active seller; and marked, fixed prices. In fact, much retail trade has gone even further and eliminated the human element altogether. In the words of Stephen Gelber, "posted prices depersonalized the marketplace by making each customer a stranger and, by the same token, ensuring every stranger (customer) that he or she was not being cheated" (Gelber 2005: 121–2).

Depersonalization can be a signal of "fairness" in the sense of lack of discrimination among buyers. However, it is also a way that a retailer can discourage haggling. Consider the case of the airlines. By the 1960s many major passenger airlines were operating globally. Yet passenger reservations still required phone calls and faxes and the reservations themselves were typically stored in huge files full of index cards. It took an average of two hours to process a reservation and seats could not be sold more than 30 days prior to departure. In 1964, after six years of planning, design, and programming, American Airlines and IBM introduced the computerized Sabre. One purpose of the Sabre system was to provide a data storage and management system for flight reservations. The other purpose was to provide a pipeline by which prices, availabilities, and bookings could be transmitted instantaneously between the airlines and the growing global network of travel agents. As a consequence of this system, airline price distribution—and ultimately hotel, rental car, and cruise line price distribution—was fully mechanized. Prices could be set and updated centrally and immediately transmitted to travel agents worldwide—or at least those with a Sabre computer terminal (Barnes, Chapter 3).

The mechanization of pricing distribution for the airline was more than a simple technical breakthrough. As with the original institution of fixed prices by the early retailers Sabre *consciously and conspicuously* disempowered sales agents. Airline fares read from a computer screen were clearly non-negotiable—they were set by "the computer". Well into the 1960s, some customers were inclined to bargain over airline and hotel prices. This was a source of low-level stress for sales and travel agents. Sabre and competing automated distribution systems put an end to that—the human being audibly and visibly clicking the keys on his computer terminal was quite clearly a mere order-taker, not a price-setter. "I'm sorry but the computer won't let me do that", is an unanswerable response to any attempt to haggle. The Internet has extended this level of depersonalization to the pricing of almost everything imaginable.

2.5.5 Fixed pricing as normative

It is striking evidence of the triumph of retail fixed pricing that it has become strongly normative in industrialized societies. In retail markets, deviations from fixed pricing are often considered "unfair", even when potential buyers cannot fully articulate the reason why they consider them so (Haws and Bearden 2006). The fixed pricing norm has carried over from retail store purchases to automated selling. Even when there is no human being involved, customers expect machines to exercise "fair pricing". The ballyhoo over Coca Cola's expressed intentions to develop a vending machine that would change prices based on temperature is a perfect illustration. In a 1999 magazine interview, Douglas Ivester, CEO of Coca-Cola, expressed the opinion that,

> Coca-Cola is a product whose utility varies from moment to moment in a final summer championship, when people meet in a stadium to enjoy themselves, the utility of a chilled Coca-Cola is very high. So it is fair it should be more expensive. The machine will simply make this process automatic.[21]

Customers had a different view of "fairness" and complained vociferously. Coca-Cola dropped its plans and none of the vending machines have been deployed, almost a decade later.

When the on-line bookseller Amazon was suspected of charging different prices to its DVD customers based on their past buying behavior, many of its customers were outraged. "Amazon is over in my book!" was one of the more moderate on-line postings. In this case, a perceived deviation from fixed pricing was viewed as provocative and unfair. "I don't like the idea that someone is paying less than I am for the same product, at the exact same instant", as a reporter covering the Amazon story wrote.[22] Survey data have shown that most customers perceive paying a higher price than other customers as "very unfair" (Haws and Bearden 2006) and at least one empirical study has suggested that pricing differentials perceived as unfair by customers can lead to reduced demand (Anderson and Simester 2008).

Certainly, it has not always been the case that "fixed pricing" was viewed as normative. In pre-revolutionary Paris, the police insisted that bread shops allow haggling in order to benefit the working poor (Kaplan 1996: 88–9). Nor is it the case that all buyers necessarily preferred or welcomed fixed pricing. Daniel Defoe felt that it was the buyers, rather than the sellers, who wanted to bargain.[23] However, the idea that a fixed price is "more fair" than bargaining is an old one. Quaker commercial behavior was in line on the injunction from George Fox that "if a child were sent to their shops for anything, he was as well used as his parents would have been" (Kent 1990). The association of fixed prices with fairness was firmly established by 1907 when the *Baedeker's Guide to Paris* reassured British and American visitors that "The '*prix fixe*' system now obtains almost universally and, in the

---

[21] Ivester's statement was originally made in an interview with the Brazilian magazine *Veja* so he was referring to a soccer match. The quotation and more discussion of the reaction to the "temperature sensitive vending machine" can be found in Phillips (2005: 302–3).

[22] The quotes are from Phillips (2005: 302–3 and 312).

[23] "Indeed, it is the buyers that make this custom necessary; for they, especially those who buy for immediate use, will first pretend positively to tie themselves up to a limited price, and bid them a little and a little more, till they come so near the sellers' price, that they, the sellers, cannot find in their hearts to refuse it, and then they are tempted to take it, notwithstanding their first words to the contrary."

larger and more reputable establishments especially, strangers run little risk of being fleeced" (Baedeker 1907: 48).

Certainly the early American merchant princes advertised their fixed price policies in egalitarian terms. Rowland Macy, himself a Quaker, echoed George Fox's sentiment, "By adopting one price and never deviating, a child can trade with us as cheap as the shrewdest buyer in the country" (Scull 1967: 83). John Wanamaker crowed that "New, fair and most agreeable relations were established between the purchaser and the seller, the poor and the rich, the wise and the unwise—there was no favoritism" (Wanamaker 1911: 47). Many writers argued that fixed pricing was ethically superior to the bargaining modality that it replaced—to the extent that it provided moral justification for the wealth amassed by its pioneers: "Stewart, Wanamaker, Marshall Field, and a host of others who sprang up and flourished all over the country demonstrated that the retail merchant had a genuine and useful function to perform—fortunes awaited the merchant who served his customers by providing them with honest goods at honest prices.... And by becoming rich through honest methods they justified personal wealth as it had never been justified before" (Crow 1946: 151).

The rise of list pricing was accompanied by the increasing perception of haggling and bargaining as outmoded and déclassé. In Victorian England, "bargaining for necessities" was something one's servants did. In post-war America, buying wrapped meat at a fixed price was modern and middle class—haggling with the butcher was old-fashioned and lower class. This phenomenon is not confined to the developed world, in the 1970s, Ralph Beals noted that in Mexico, "many people aspiring to higher social status in the city and larger towns (feel) that bargaining is demeaning. Such buyers are much less apt to bargain or shop around for lower prices if they feel that the offering price is fair" (Beals 1975: 201). Fixed pricing, on the other hand, seems egalitarian by nature—it is well suited for the modern democratic world of commerce where customers from all classes may rub shoulders while buying groceries at Safeway or Whole Foods.

The upshot of almost 150 years of fixed pricing is that consumers in most Western economies not only expect fixed pricing, the process of bargaining or haggling often makes them uncomfortable. The word "haggling" itself has gained a pejorative connotation. "Besides, when you think about it, haggling is un-American" a 2007 *Business Week* article declared. The same article noted that 65 percent of all car buyers (and 72 percent of women) say they would rather not bargain when buying a car. "Negotiating price just isn't in our culture", according to a consultant who is working with automotive dealerships to develop "haggle-free" auto selling (*Business Week* 2007). Furthermore, fixed and fair prices seem to be part of the implicit contract that customers have established, at least mentally, with sellers. Bargaining can erode that understanding—"People soon lose confidence in a merchant with whom they can bargain, because they leave the store feeling that your goods are not worth what they paid for them" (Greenberg and Schindall 1946: 64–5).

2.5.6 The future of fixed pricing

Outside the developed economies, bargaining is still an everyday activity for much of the population. Very often, fixed price and bargaining modalities exist side-by-side. In 1983, Claire Robertson noted that, in Ghana, "Even in areas where one would not expect it, like imported goods, people occasionally bargained with storekeepers. . . . Bargaining is such a way of life in Ghana that it cannot be eradicated by such annoyances as price controls" (Robertson 1983: 479). An on-line guide to "Haggling and Bargaining in Gambia" recommends hard bargaining with all "market and street vendors" and at "goods shops" as well as whenever "hiring the services of local skilled craftsman such as a plumber, bricklayer or construction contractor." On the other hand,

> Do not bother haggling over prices charged in the supermarkets, restaurants, bars, night-clubs, and "Bitiks" as they tend to have fixed prices. Likewise don't bother with small items purchased from the local "Pular" corner shop such as a packet of razors, insect spray, fruits, peanuts, purified water bags, bread or coffee. However, if you are approached on the beach by a fruit seller or other hawker then do ask for a reduction. If you have bought a lot of items in bulk from a supermarket then it is worthwhile asking them to reduce their price as they are often willing to offer a discount particularly to valued customers. If your room lacks any promised facility or you are intending to stay over 2 weeks then it might be worthwhile asking for a reduction of room rates.[24]

This broad description is a credible characterization of markets in many non-industrialized economies in which fixed prices coexist with bargaining, just as they did in Paris prior to the advent of the *grands magasins*. As the relentlessly bargaining grocer, Madame François, complains in Zola's *The Belly of Paris*, "Oh, these Parisians! They'll haggle for an hour over half a sou and then go and spend everything in a bar" (1873/2007: 15). This passage implicitly contrasts the fixed pricing modality at the bar with the bargaining modality in the market. In "mixed" economies, natives know instinctively which transactions are customarily performed in which modality—visitors are often not sure. This can cause disorientation and anxiety for visitors—should I bargain or not? Have I gotten a good deal? The bargaining and haggling skills that used to be needed to negotiate everyday transactions are disappearing from developed economies.

It seems highly likely that the fixed price modality will continue to gain ground at the expense of bargaining as many of these markets become more integrated into the global economy. Bargaining is not only "inefficient", it disadvantages the foreign buyer. Clifford Geertz observes that information in the bazaar is "poor, scarce, maldistributed, inefficiently communicated and highly valued" (Geertz 1978: 21). Local sellers have much more information on cost, competing prices, and market conditions than foreign buyers. It is likely that the pressure to sell on global markets will lead to continued expansion of fixed pricing into these markets. Within developed economies, fixed pricing or "haggle-free pricing" is making inroads into such traditional bastions of bargaining as auto-selling and real estate.

Ultimately, fixed pricing should be considered one of the many innovations that both accompanied and enabled the rise of consumer capitalism. Fixed pricing was both more efficient (in terms of time and effort required) and more scalable than haggling. Fixed pricing was necessary for the development not only of the large department stores, but also for the later development of national and international chain retailing. Along with other elements of consumer capitalism, it has spread from its origins in America and Western Europe to industrial and industrializing nations worldwide.

---

[24] http://www.accessgambia.com/information/bargaining-haggling-tips.html. Last accessed January 3, 2008.

2.6 SUMMARY

Perhaps the most important message of this chapter is simply that *pricing has a history*—pricing modalities that we take for granted are not ahistorical and immutable, they have been strongly shaped by changes in technology, in institutions, and in broader societal attitudes. Pricing modalities can and will change—American retailers moved from bargaining to fixed pricing in less than two decades. Seemingly idiosyncratic or suboptimal modalities such as the upfront market for television advertising can persist and flourish through such major institutional changes as the end of the "big three networks" oligopsony and the rise of scores of competing channels. And, of course, the influence runs both ways. As list-pricing became dominant practice, it also became normative. The posted, fixed price—almost unknown in the United States before the Civil War—has become the standard for fairness in retail trade.

Once established, pricing modalities can be quite stable over long periods of time—hence the persistence of the upfront market for television advertising and the "single price" policy for movie theaters. Industry pricing modalities rarely seem to change due to a bold move on the part of one seller. In fact, attempts by a single seller to unilaterally change the pricing modality within an industry have had very mixed results. American Airlines is credited with successfully introducing advanced-booking discount fares into the airline industry. However, it spectacularly failed in its attempt to introduce a simplified fare structure in 1992 when competitors such as Northwest and Continental refused to go along (Barnes, Chapter 3). Stelios Haji-Ioannou, who founded easyJet, failed in his attempt to introduce more dynamic and differentiated pricing into movie theaters. Pricing modalities seem to come into being in times of institutional, technological, and regulatory changes. One example would be the origin of the television advertising upfront market in the switch from sponsored programming to slot sales in the mid to late 1950s. Over time, a modality becomes embedded in the structure of a market. Expectations, institutions, and infrastructure are built up to support the modality. In many cases, organizations not directly involved in the transaction develop an interest in the preservation of a particular structure—just as equity analysts have an implicit stake in the continuation in the upfront market.

It is important for pricing analysts, pricing vendors, consultants and even academics to recognize that they are part of this process. The more that an organization invests in developing expertise in a particular modality, the more invested they become in the continuation of that modality. The immense investment that commercial airlines put into developing automated reservation and yield management systems generated hundreds of millions of dollars in incremental revenue and profit. However, it also meant that the airlines were deeply invested (in both senses of the word) in a particular approach to managing prices in the marketplace—that of opening and closing discrete booking and capacity classes during the period of a flight booking. This may have left them more vulnerable to more nimble dynamic pricing employed by a new breed of low-cost competitors such as Southwest and easyJet.

Since pricing has a history, it has a future. As technologies, institutions, regulations, and societal attitudes change, so will pricing modalities. New modalities will arise in conjunction with new markets and market opportunities. A clear example of this is the "keyword auction" market for Internet advertising described by Vudali and Atherton (Chapter 7)—a market in which pricing rules are still in flux and the details of the final "equilibrium" modality are still undetermined. These situations present an opportunity for economists, sociologists, and historians to be "present at the birth" and gain a better understanding of how pricing modalities emerge, how they change, and how they become locked in. Ultimately, this should give us a better view of the complex and multi-form interactions among economic institutions and social and historical changes.

References

Ackroyd, P. (2000) *London: The Biography*. London: Chatto and Windus.

Allaz, B. and Vila, J.-L. (1993) "Cournot Competition, Forward Markets and Efficiency." *Journal of Economic Theory* 59/1: 1–16.

Allen, A. P. (2008) *The Ambassadors of Commerce*. London: T. Fisher Unwin.

Allen, B. and Hellwig, M. (1986) "Bertrand-Edgeworth Oligopoly in Large Markets", *Review of Economic Studies* 53/2: 175–204.

Anderson, E. T. and Simester, D. I. (2008) "Does Demand Fall When Customers Perceive that Prices are Unfair? The Case of Premium Pricing for Large Sizes", *Marketing Science* 27/3: 492–500.

Baedeker, K. (1905) *Baedeker's 1905 Guide to London*. Leipzig: Karl Baedeker Publishing.

——(1907) *Baedeker's 1907 Guide to Paris*. Leipzig: Karl Baedeker Publishing.

Beals, R. L. (1975) *The Peasant Marketing System of Oaxaca, Mexico*. Berkeley: University of California Press.

Bellamy, E. (1888/2005) *Looking Backward*. Edited with an introduction by Daniel H Borus. Boston: Bedford Books.

Benjamin, W. (1999) *The Arcades Project*, trans. Howard Eiland and Kevin McLaughlin. Cambridge, MA: The Belknap Press.

Bertrand, J. (1883) Review of "Theorie Mathematique de la Richesse Sociale", *Journal des Savants* 67/2: 499–508.

Boddy, W. (1990) *Fifties Television: The Industry and its Critics*. Urbana: University of Illinois Press.

Business Week (2007) "Car Dealers Stake Out Haggle-free Zones", October 23.

Camerer, C. F. (2003) *Behavioral Game Theory: Experiments in Strategic Interaction*. New York: Russell Sage Foundation.

Casson, L. (1974) *Travel in the Ancient World*. Baltimore: The John Hopkins University Press.

Castleman, H. and Podrazik, W. (1982) *Watching TV: Four Decades of American Television*. New York: McGraw-Hill.

Clark, T. D. (1944) *Pills, Petticoats and Plows: The Southern Country Store*. Indianapolis: The Bobbs-Merrill Co.

Crow, C. (1946) *The Great American Customer*. New York: Harper and Brothers Publishers.

Dana, Jr., J. D. (1998) "Advanced-Purchase Discounts and Price Discrimination in Competitive Markets", *Journal of Political Economy* 105/2: 395–422.

David, P. A. (1985) "Clio and the Economics of QWERTY", *American Economic Review* 75/2: 332–7.

David, P. A. (2000) "Path Dependence, its Critics and the Quest for 'Historical Economics'", in P. Garrauste and S. Ioannides (eds), *Evolution and Path Dependence in Economic Ideas: Past and Present*. Cheltenham: Edward Elgar.

Defoe, D. (1726) *The Complete English Tradesman*. London: Charles Rivington.

Diamond, J. (1997) "The Curse of QWERTY", http://www.geocities.com/malibumalv/curse.

Einav, L. (2007) "Seasonality in the U.S. Motion Picture Industry", *RAND Journal of Economics* 38/1: 127–45.

Ekelund Jr., R. B. and Hébert, R. F. (1999) *Secret Origins of Modern Microeconomics: Dupuit and the Engineers*. Chicago: University of Chicago Press.

Eliashberg, J., Elberse, A., and Leenders, M. A. A. M. (2006) "The Motion Picture Industry: Critical Issues in Practice, Current Research, and New Research Directions", *Marketing Science* 25/6: 638–61.

Emmet, B. and Jeuck, J. E. (1950) *Catalogues and Counters: A History of Sears, Roebuck and Company*. Chicago: University of Chicago Press.

The Emporium (1952) "How to Avoid Wasteful Markdowns" Pamphlet. San Francisco.

Ephron, E. (2003) "The Fascinating Story of the Upfront," reprinted in 2005 *Ephron on Media: Organized Crime Keeps Better Books*. New York: Ephron, Papazian, and Ephron, Inc., 6–12.

Fehr, E. and Schmidt, K. M. (1999) "A Theory of Fairness, Competition, and Cooperation", *Quarterly Journal of Economics* 114/3: 817–68.

Foreman, R. L. (1962) "The Dilemma of the TV Advertiser", *Television Quarterly* 1/1: 42–7.

Friedman, W. (2007) "Analysts still up on the upfront", *Variety*, May 4: 3.

Gallego, G., Huh, W. T., Kang, W., and Phillips, R. (2006) "Price Competition with the Attraction Demand Model: Existence of Unique Equilibrium and Its Stability", *Manufacturing and Service Operations Management* 8/4: 359–75.

Geertz, C. (1978) "The Bazaar Economy: Information and Search in Peasant Marketing", *American Economic Review* 68/2: 28–32.

Gelber, S. M. (2005) "Horseless Horses: Car Dealing and the Survival of Retail Bargaining", in P. N. Stearns (ed.), *American Behavioral History*. New York: NYU Press, 118–42.

Granovetter, M. (1985) "Economic Action and Social Structure: The Problem of Embeddedness", *American Journal of Sociology* 91/3: 481–510.

—— (1992) "Problems of Explanation in Economic Sociology", in N. Nohria and R. G. Eccles (eds), *Networks and Organizations: Structure, Form and Action*. Boston, MA: Harvard University Press, 453–75.

Greenberg, D. B. and Schindall, H. (1946) *A Small Store and Independence: A Practical Guide to Successful Retailing*. Fourth Printing. New York: Greenberg Printers.

Greif, A. (2006) *Institutions and the Path to the Modern Economy*. Cambridge: Cambridge University Press.

Haws, K. L. and Bearden, W. O. (2006) "Dynamic Pricing and Consumer Fairness Perceptions", *Journal of Consumer Research* 33/3: 304–11.

Heighton, E. J. and Cunningham, D. R. (1976) *Advertising in the Broadcast Media*. Belmont, CA: Wadsworth Publishing Co.

Henrich, J., Boyd, R., Bowles, S., Camerer, C., Fehr, E., Gintis, H., and McElreath, R. (2001) "In Search of Homo Economicus: Behavioral Experiments in 15 Small-Scale Societies", *American Economic Review* 91/2: 73–8.

—— —— —— —— —— and—— (eds) (2004) *Foundations of Human Sociality: Economic Experiments and Ethnographic Evidence from Fifteen Small-Scale Societies*. Oxford: Oxford University Press.

——————————————Alvard, M., Barr, A., Ensminger, J., Henrich, N. S., Hill, K., Gil-White, F., Gurven, M., Marlowe, F. W., Patton, J. Q., and Tracer, D. (2005) " 'Economic Man' in Cross-Cultural Perspective: Behavioral Experiments in 15 Small-Scale Societies", *Behavioral and Brain Sciences* 28/5: 795–855.

Hettinger, H. S. (1933) *A Decade of Radio Advertising.* Chicago: The University of Chicago Press.

—— and Neff, W. J. (1938) *Practical Radio Advertising.* New York: Prentice-Hall.

Hessel, E. (2007) "Why do Theaters Charge the Same Price for all Tickets?", *Forbes* January 29: 36.

Hopper, M. (1990) "Rattling SABRE—New Ways to Compete on Information", *Harvard Business Review*, 68/4: 118–30.

Kaplan, S. L. (1996) *The Bakers of Paris and the Bread Question 1770–1775.* Raleigh, NC: Duke University Press.

Kent, S. A. (1990) "The Quaker Ethic and the Fixed Price Policy", in W. H. Swatos, Jr. (ed.), *Time, Place, and Circumstance.* New York: Greenwood, 139–50.

Lazear, E. P. (1986) "Retail Pricing and Clearance Sales", *American Economics Review* 76/1: 14–32.

Leslie, P. (2004) "Price Discrimination in Broadway Theater", *RAND Journal of Economics* 35/4: 520–41.

Lewin, P. (ed.) (2002) *The Economics of QWERTY: History, Theory, and Policy Essays by Stan J. Liebowitz and Stephen E. Margolis.* New York: New York University Press.

Lotz, A. D. (2007) "How to Spend $9.3 Billion in Three Days: Examining the Upfront Buying Process in the Production of US Television Culture", *Media, Culture & Society* 29/4: 549–67.

McClellan, S. (2010) "Upfront Preview: Behind the Bust", *AdWeek* February 2: 16–17.

McMillan, J. (2002) *Reinventing the Bazaar, A Natural History of Markets.* New York: Norton.

Mashon, M. (2007) "NBC, J. Walter Thompson, and the Struggle for Control of Television Programming, 1946–58", in M. Hilmes (ed.), *NBC America's Network.* Berkeley: University of California Press.

Miller, M. B. (1981) *The Bon Marché: Bourgeois Culture and the Department Store, 1869–1920.* Princeton: Princeton University Press;

Norris, J. B. (1962) "One-Price Policy among Antebellum Country Stores", *Business History Review* 36/4: 455–8.

North, D. (1990) *Institutions, Institutional Change and Economic Performance.* Cambridge: Cambridge University Press.

Orbach, B. Y. (2004) "Antitrust and Pricing in the Motion Picture Industry", *Yale Journal of Regulation*, 21/2: 318–66.

—— and Einav, L. (2007) "Uniform Prices for Differentiated Goods: The Case of the Movie-Theater Industry", *International Review of Law and Economics*: 129–53.

Papadimitriou, C. (2007) "The Complexity of Finding Nash Equilibria", in N. Nisan, T. Roughgarden, È. Tardos, and V. Vazirani (eds), *Algorithmic Game Theory.* Cambridge: Cambridge University Press.

Petronius (1997) *The Satyricon*, trans T. G. Walsh. Oxford: Oxford University Press.

Phillips, R. L. (2005) *Pricing and Revenue Optimization.* Stanford: Stanford University Press.

Resseguie, J. (1965) "Alexander Tunney Stewart and the Development of the Department Store, 1823–1870", *Business History Review* 39/3: 301–22.

Riley, J. and Zeckhauser, R. (1983) "Optimal Selling Strategies: When to Haggle, When to Hold Firm", *Quarterly Journal of Economics* 98/2: 267–89.

Robertson, C. C. (1983) "The Death of Makola and Other Tragedies", *Canadian Journal of African Studies* 17/2: 469–95.

Sandoval-Strausz, A. K. (2007) *Hotel: An American History*. New Haven: Yale University Press.

Sawhney, M. S. and Eliashberg, J. (1996) "A Parsimonious Model for Forecasting Gross Box-office Revenues of Motion Pictures", *Marketing Science* 15/2: 113–31.

Scull, P. (1967) *From Peddlers to Merchant Princes: A History of Selling in America*. Chicago: Follet Publishing Company.

Spang, R. L. (2000) *The Invention of the Restaurant: Paris and Modern Gastronomic Culture*. Cambridge, MA: Harvard University Press.

Stauffer, T. (2007) "Movie-ticket Prices could Fluctuate as Airline, Hotel Fares Do", *Arizona Daily Star* January 6: B1.

Tardos, E. and Vazirani, V. (2007) "Basic Solution Concepts and Computational Issues", in N. Nisan, T. Roughgarden, È. Tardos, and V. Vazirani (eds), *Algorithmic Game Theory*. Cambridge: Cambridge University Press.

Tonning, W. A. (1956) "The Beginning of the Money-Back Guarantee and the One-Price Policy in Champaign-Urbana, Illinois, 1833–1880", *Business History Review* 30/2: 196–210.

U.S. Bureau of Labor Statistics (2007) "Consumer Expenditures in 2005". U.S. Department of Labor, Report 998. February.

Walsh, C. (1999) "The Newness of the Department Store: A View from the Eighteenth Century", in G. Crossick and S. Jaumain (eds), *Cathedrals of Consumption: The European Department Store 1850–1939*. Aldershot, UK: Ashgate.

Wanamaker, J. (1911) *The Golden Book of the Wanamaker Stores: Jubilee Year 1861–1911*. Privately published.

Weinstein, D. (2004) *The Forgotten Network: DuMont and the Birth of American Television*. Philadelphia: Temple University Press.

Wetherington, M. V. (1994) *The New South Comes to Wiregrass Georgia, 1860–1910*. Knoxville: University of Tennessee Press.

Yakubovich, V., Granovetter, M., and McGuire, P. (2005) "Electric Charges: The Social Construction of Rate Systems", *Theory and Society* 34/5: 579–612.

Zola, E. (1873/2007) *The Belly of Paris*, trans Brian Nelson. Oxford: Oxford University Press.

—— (1883/1995) *The Ladies' Paradise*, trans Brian Nelson. Oxford: Oxford University Press.

CHAPTER 3

··

AIRLINE PRICING

··

BRENDA A. BARNES

3.1 INTRODUCTION

"On my last flight, I sat next to a guy who paid $200 for his ticket. I paid $950. How can airlines charge different prices to different customers for the same seat on the same flight?"

"$50 to check baggage, $20 for extra leg room, $15 for a pillow, $25 to talk to an agent—what's next?"

"All the flights I've taken recently have been packed—how can the airlines not be making any money?"

"Why can't all airlines be like Southwest? Low fares, no baggage fees, flight attendants with a sense of humor—if they flew everywhere, I'd never take another airline!"

FOR most of its history, airline industry pricing has been the subject of relentless complaints, jokes, and debate. As former head of pricing and revenue management for a major US airline, I am often questioned by friends, relatives, and complete strangers about airfares. The highs, lows, loopholes, and lapses of airline pricing are prominently featured in travel TV, columns, blogs, and websites, all purporting to guide consumers to the elusive "lowest available" fare. The Internet has thrust the customer head first into the wild world of fare classes, rules, restrictions, terms, conditions, surcharges, fees, and footnotes, without the benefit of a translator, formerly referred to as a travel agent.

The media and public focus on airline pricing is just one indication of its significance in consumers' lives. In the 40 years since regulatory controls over industry pricing, scheduling, and route selection were removed, the number of passengers boarded on US airlines has increased nearly 270 percent. The average fare paid per mile flown has dropped from 8.49 cents to 4.19 cents per mile, and the average percentage of seats occupied has increased from 61.5 percent to 79.5 percent. These trends have been driven by increased price competition, the entrance of low-cost competitors, market expansion, and capacity increases (ATA 2009).

I'd like to thank Bob Phillips, Özalp Özer, Bob Coggin, and Bob Cross for their valuable input on this chapter. I'd also like to thank Barbara Amster, Bill Crown, and Ron Miller, formerly of American Airlines, as well as the rest of my former colleagues at American Airlines, Sabre, and Delta Air Lines, for teaching me virtually everything I know about airline pricing and revenue management.

Despite vast increases in service and a 50 percent decline in the average cost to fly, passengers do not believe that the formerly regulated airlines (the "legacy" carriers) provide good value. Customers see little difference between the airlines' product offerings. Leisure travelers consistently choose airlines based on price. Business travelers have become more price-sensitive as "perks" have become politically unpopular and economically impractical in a recessionary environment. Price long ago replaced service as consumers' primary airline selection criterion and steep discounting has become the norm.

In the late 1970s, airlines learned that superior price management can drive dramatic increases in profitability. Price management excellence creates a significant and sustainable competitive advantage. Gains from pricing and revenue management have accounted for some airlines' entire annual profits in some years, reflecting the slim margins of the industry.

The increased price transparency created by the Internet has directly exposed consumers to the complexity of airline pricing. On-line shoppers can now compare nearly every airfare of every domestic airline and most foreign carriers in "real-time". This transparency raises new questions in shoppers' minds, such as:

- Why do all airlines seem to file the same fares and change them so frequently?
- Why can't all airlines offer simple, low fares?
- What are all these new fees and what will I ultimately pay for my trip?
- What do all these convoluted fare rules and restrictions mean?

In this chapter, we will first introduce some essential airline pricing and revenue management (PRM) terms and concepts. We will then briefly review historical events that have shaped the field of airline PRM. We discuss current PRM practices, including strategy, tactics, processes, distribution, and systems. Finally, we will highlight trends that will impact the future practice of PRM.

We will focus on the current practices of the major US airlines, which include Delta Air Lines (DL), United-Continental Airlines (UA/CO), American Airlines (AA), and US Airways (US), and account for approximately 75 percent of US industry revenue, and the practices of the largest low-cost carriers, such as AirTran (FL), JetBlue (B6), and Southwest Airlines (WN). Detailed explanation of international pricing is beyond our scope. Metrics will be expressed in US dollars, cents, and miles.

3.2 BASIC CONCEPTS AND TERMINOLOGY

3.2.1 Origin and destination markets, legs, and metrics

Airlines sell tickets for transportation from an originating airport or city to a destination airport or city. Accordingly, an "origin and destination" (O&D) market is a pair of cities and/or airports. A passenger itinerary in an O&D market is comprised of either a single non-stop flight (a "local" itinerary) or a combination of non-stop flights (a "connecting" itinerary). A non-stop flight is called a flight "segment" or "leg".

An O&D market includes all passengers flown or revenue earned between a pair of airports or cities on any non-stop or connecting routing. For example, the New York-JFK

METRIC	CALCULATION	PRIMARY USAGE
Revenue Passenger Miles (RPMs)	Passengers Boarded * Miles Flown	Measures passenger demand/volume
Available Seat Miles (ASMs)	Available Aircraft Seats * Miles Flown	Measures capacity
Passenger Load Factor (LF)	(Passengers Carried * Miles Flown) ÷ (Available Seats * Miles Flown)	Capacity Utilization (standard definition)
Passenger Load Factor (LF)	Passengers Carried ÷ Available Seats	Capacity Utilization (alternative definition)
Passenger Yield (Yield)	Passenger Revenue ÷ Revenue Passenger Miles	Average fare paid per passenger per mile flown
Passenger Revenue per Available Seat Mile (PRASM) or Unit Revenue	Passenger Revenue ÷ (Available Seats * Miles Flown)	Revenue earned per unit of capacity
Passenger Revenue per Available Seat Mile (PRASM) or Unit Revenue	Yield ÷ Load Factor	Revenue earned per unit of capacity (alternate formulation)
Break-Even Load Factor (BELF)	BELF = Unit Cost / Passenger Yield	Load factor at which passenger revenue covers operating expenses
Operating Cost per Available Seat Mile (CASM) or Unit Cost	Operating Expenses ÷ (Available Seats * Miles Flown)	Costs per unit of capacity

FIGURE 3.1 Key performance metrics

to San Francisco market includes passengers on non-stop flights and connecting flights through many carriers' hubs, including Chicago, Denver, Dallas/Fort Worth, and Salt Lake City. Cities and airports are designated by standard three-letter codes, such as CHI for the city of Chicago, which includes both Chicago-O'Hare (ORD) and Chicago-Midway (MDW) airport. An O&D market may include all of the area airports in an origin or destination city, or only selected airports in either city. Passenger demand varies among airport pairs within a city pair so prices may vary accordingly.

Airlines and the Department of Transportation (DOT) refer to passenger volume (passenger "enplanements" or "boardings") as "traffic" or passenger demand. For revenue management purposes, PRM forecasts total demand, which includes both passengers boarded and customers who were unable or unwilling to purchase seats due to insufficient capacity at a particular price level. Customers turned away are referred to as "spilled" demand.

Airline traffic is measured by the number of paying passengers traveling one mile, called revenue passenger miles (RPMs). An aircraft carrying 100 passengers 1,500 miles carries 150,000 revenue passenger miles (RPMs). Average fare paid per mile is measured by passenger yield, which is total passenger revenue divided by RPMs.

Seat capacity offered for sale is measured by "available seat miles" (ASMs) or (available aircraft seats multiplied miles flown). The percentage of available capacity sold is the passenger load factor (RPMs divided by divide; ASMs) which can be calculated for any flight leg, combination of legs or the network. Revenue per unit of capacity (total operating revenue divided by ASMs) is a function of passenger yield and load factor. See Figures 3.1 and 3.2 for definition of key PRM revenue metrics.

Example based on US network airlines' 3Q10 financial results and operating statistics:

Total Passenger Revenue = $19.9 billion

Available Seat Miles (ASMs) = available seats flown * miles flown = 178 billion

Revenue Passenger Miles = total passengers carried * miles flown = 148 billion

LF = Revenue Passenger Miles/Available Seat Miles = 148 billion/178 billion = 83%

Revenue = RPMs * yield = 148 billion*.13 = $19.9 billion

Passenger Yield = Revenue/RPMs = ($19.9 billion/$148 billion) = 13.4 cents

(Psgr) Revenue per Available Seat Mile (RASM) = (Revenue/ASM) = ($19.9B/178B) = 11.2 cents

Alt: Revenue per Available Seat Mile (RASM) = Yield*LF = 13.4 cents * 83% = 11.2 cents

FIGURE 3.2 Revenue metric calculations

An airline sells a "fare product", defined as the price for air transportation in an O&D market subject to specific rules, restrictions, terms, and conditions. Although the same fares may initially be offered for non-stop and connecting itineraries in a market, the price for the most convenient non-stop flight is often much higher than the fare for a less convenient connecting flight. Airlines limit seats sold in advance at discounted fares on the most popular flights to ensure that later-booking passengers who are willing to pay higher prices can purchase seats closer to departure.

3.2.2 Point-to-point versus hub-and-spoke scheduling

"Point-to-point" flights are non-stop flights that are designed to primarily carry local passengers. Under Civil Aeronautics Board (CAB) regulation prior to 1978, airlines were awarded rights to fly routes on a non-stop basis. Longer distance passenger itineraries were typically comprised of connecting flight segments on two or more carriers. Ticket revenue was shared between the operating carriers.

Hub-and-spoke networks were developed after deregulation as airlines sought ways to grow and compete more effectively using their new freedom to determine routes, schedules, and fares. Carriers concentrated their flights and carefully timed flight arrivals and departures at hub cities to facilitate the transfer of passengers between flights. Hub-and-spoke networks allowed airlines to greatly expand service and achieve tremendous economies of scale. The percentage of passengers flying on connecting routings with one airline grew rapidly while inter-line traffic between carriers declined. Airlines also increased international service from major hubs and coordinated their schedules with global alliance partners.

Legacy airlines may also serve non-hub O&D markets on a point-to-point basis. For example, some carriers operate non-stop flights from larger spoke cities to popular leisure destinations primarily to fulfill frequent fliers' desires to redeem mileage awards. The majority of low-cost carriers rely primarily on point-to-point scheduling to avoid the cost of building and operating large hubs, although some concentrate flights in larger focus cities, such as New York for JetBlue. They have traditionally carried very little connecting traffic, although this has changed as their networks have grown.

3.2.3 Economics of airline pricing

Airlines use pricing and revenue management as primary tools to match supply and demand. Each airline seeks to sell its scheduled capacity at prices which will generate sufficient demand to ensure an adequate level of profit. An "adequate profit" level varies widely across carriers, depending on whether the airline is focused on short-term cash flow or longer-term capital needs. When launching new services, entering markets or increasing capacity, airlines may temporarily accept losses in the expectation of long-term profits (Doganis 2009).

Airline pricing is driven by certain characteristics of the industry's product and cost structure. Substantial, ongoing capital investments are required to acquire, maintain, and operate safe, modern aircraft and facilities. Total seat capacity is relatively fixed due to the cost and time involved in acquiring new aircraft. Schedules can be costly to change within 3 to 6 months of departure. Airlines also have high variable costs, led by labor and fuel. However, the costs of carrying an incremental passenger on a scheduled flight are very low. Longer-distance flights are generally less costly for an airline to operate than shorter flights. Since airline pricing is market-based rather than cost-based, the cost differences do not always correlate to fares. The objective in market-based pricing is to ensure total revenues cover fixed and variable costs, rather than requiring that individual customers or groups cover their own particular costs.

In addition, pricing and revenue management are based upon the premise that the airline product is highly perishable—once a flight has taken off, an empty seat has no value. As a result, struggling airlines have a tendency to price on a "marginal cost" basis. If a seat will otherwise go empty, a carrier may offer it for sale at a very low price, as long as the potential revenue exceeds the marginal cost of carrying the passenger.

For every flight, there is an average percentage of seats that must be occupied at which passenger revenues cover operating expenses, called the break-even load factor (BELF). The industry's average BELF increased from 65 percent in 2000 to over 85 percent in 2008 due to significantly higher fuel, labor, and security costs and a sharp decline in average fares (ATA 2010). As a result, while many flights may be sold out, many airlines still cannot sustain profitability. The sale of just one or two more seats on each flight, or a $1 change in the price of each seat sold, can determine profit or loss. This fact has led to an extremely competitive environment in which very small pricing differences may drive large market share shifts.

3.2.4 Pricing and revenue management

Pricing and revenue management include the strategies, tactics, business processes, decision models, data, and systems involved with: (1) designing, setting, and maintaining fare products; (2) determining and managing fare product availability; (3) distributing fare products and availability through various channels for reservations and ticketing. Pricing typically includes customer segmentation, product development, pricing strategy, fare management, and fare distribution for both published ("public" or "tariff") and unpublished ("private", "negotiated", or "off-tariff") fares. Revenue management (RM) refers to the decision models and processes that determine whether a fare product will be available for sale at any particular time prior to departure in each O&D market on each flight segment. RM includes demand forecasting, overbooking, inventory optimization, and related processes, originally called Yield Management.

3.2.5 Airline reservations and inventory systems

In the early 1960s, airlines became one of the first industries to have a centralized and automatically updated inventory repository, the computerized reservation system (CRS). AA and IBM jointly developed and introduced Sabre, the first CRS, in 1962. The system automatically reconciled reservations, recorded on passenger name records (PNRs), with seats sold and available for sale on each flight. IBM sold a similar system to PanAm, Delta, Eastern, TWA, and United. The airlines rapidly began to mine CRS data to predict customer behaviors, analyze flight patterns, identify market trends, and develop financial, forecasting, yield management, and other models. The CRS systems have since become comprehensive travel distribution companies called Global Distribution Systems (GDSs), which include Sabre, TravelPort (owner of Galileo, Apollo, and Worldspan) and Amadeus.

3.3 THE LEGACIES OF REGULATION

From the end of World War II through the late 1970s, the US commercial airline industry was regulated by the Civil Aeronautics Board (CAB). CAB controlled route selection, scheduling and princing for the growing industry. Even today, the industry's structure, pricing, costs, and competitive dynamics reflect the legacies of 30 years of government regulation.

Between 1949 and 1969, passenger volume grew at an average annual rate of 16 percent as aircraft safety, comfort, and technology improved. In 1970, passenger growth dropped abruptly to 1 percent and the average load factor dropped below 50 percent. Hundreds of new jumbo jets, such as the Boeing 747, went into service just as the economy plummeted into recession. Inflation-adjusted average fares declined by more than 25 percent during the 1960s despite strong demand due to increasing use of fare discounts (ATA 1970). Labor, fuel, and other costs rose sharply, contributing significantly to the deterioration in the industry's financial performance.

In the late 1970s, UA, AA, and others began installing their CRSs in travel agencies to improve agents' productivity and increase ticket sales. Airline owners of CRSs collected booking fees from other airlines' automated ticket sales and gave their own flights preferential display on agents' computer screens. Enabled by automation, travel agency sales grew from less than one-third to 56 percent of total reservations between 1967 and 1977.

As the airlines faced the challenges of excess capacity, rising costs, rapid growth, and declining fares, widespread public and government support for deregulation increased. In 1975, CAB reported that the industry was "naturally competitive, not monopolistic" (ATA 2010). Alfred Kahn, a Cornell University economist, noted that CAB's historical policies "tended to raise cost to the level of price" (Petzinger 1995). CAB's chairman recommended that the industry be deregulated and the agency be dissolved. CAB gradually eased pricing controls, authorizing fare discounts of up to 70 percent. Airline CEOs lobbied unsuccessfully against deregulation, worried that uncontrolled price competition and unrestricted market entry would ruin the so-called "world's greatest air transportation system".

On October 28, 1978, US President Jimmy Carter signed the Airline Deregulation Act removing regulatory restrictions on airline pricing, scheduling, market entry, and exit. Remaining regulatory authorities were transferred to the Department of Transportation (DOT). CAB's authority was phased out over four years and terminated on December 31, 1984.

The former regulated airlines became known as "legacy" carriers after deregulation. Their legacies included a bloated cost structure, particularly labor costs, which then represented 50 percent of the average airline's operating costs, and heavy infrastructure costs. Deregulation exacerbated the problem of excess capacity as carriers raced to capitalize on new growth opportunities and build dominant positions in hubs. Travel agency commission costs soared as the channel became the industry's largest source of revenue.

3.4 EFFECTS OF DEREGULATION

3.4.1 Network expansion and increased price competition

After deregulation, the legacy carriers established hub-and-spoke networks based on their geographic strengths. For example, Delta increased its dominance in Atlanta by adding spoke cities to compete more effectively with Eastern Airlines. Between 1978 and 1995, the number of average daily departures at small, medium, and large airports grew by 50 percent, 57 percent, and 68 percent respectively (GAO 1996). The percentage of total passengers traveling non-stop declined as an increasing number of markets and passengers were served through hub connections.

Carriers quickly learned that market share dominance created a disproportionate revenue advantage. The stronger the market presence, the greater the revenue advantage, a phenomenon known as the "S-curve" effect. The airlines rushed to achieve market, airport, city, and hub dominance to maximize S-curve benefits by increasing frequencies, capacity, and destinations.

The growth of hub-and-spoke networks greatly increased the complexity of airline pricing. The number of O&D markets to be priced increased exponentially as service to new spoke cities was added. Fare discounting flourished in the newly competitive environment. As new discount fares were created, the number of fare products in each O&D market grew from a few to a dozen or more. Airlines also designed more complicated rules and restrictions to segment customers more precisely and generate incremental revenues.

Hub-and-spoke scheduling further intensified competition by increasing service offerings in each market. Under regulation, only one or two non-stop carriers were typically authorized to serve each non-stop O&D market. With unrestricted market entry, a market could now be served by many carriers. For example, UA and AA were the only carriers authorized by CAB to fly the New York-JFK–Los Angeles (LAX) non-stop route. AA, UA, and other carriers added non-stop JFK–LAX service after deregulation. A growing number of passengers connected over various carriers' hubs from JFK to LAX. By the early 1990s, the JFK–LAX market had become one of the most competitive markets in the USA.

As a result of the growth in the number of discount fares and O&D markets, the Sabre CRS held approximately 45 million fares and processed 40 million changes per month by 1990 (Hopper 1990). More than 200,000 fares changed daily (Schmitt 1987).

3.4.2 Introduction of yield management

A major objective of deregulation was to stimulate competition, in part by reducing barriers to market entry for new carriers. Between 1977 and 1984, the number of new interstate carriers approved by CAB rose from 36 to about 120 (ATA 1975). The new entrant carriers could profitably offer far lower fares than the legacy carriers because they were not encumbered by pre-existing infrastructures and labor costs.

Southwest Airlines (WN), the original low-cost carrier, began operations in 1971 as an unregulated, intra-state carrier serving Dallas, San Antonio, and Houston, TX. The airline positioned itself as a convenient alternative to driving or taking the bus. WN offered frequent, point-to-point service in high-density markets using a single aircraft type with one class of service. It cross-utilized its employees; used aircraft and gates efficiently; served secondary airports; and offered "no-frills" service, providing no in-flight meals, assigned seating, or baggage transfers. The airline established and sustained an average unit cost advantage of more than 25 percent relative to the legacy carriers, giving it the flexibility to introduce fares that were at least 60 percent below prevailing market fares. When WN entered a market, its low fares consistently stimulated unprecedented amounts of leisure traffic, often tripling the market's passenger volume.

People Express (PEX) was a national low-cost carrier founded in 1981. PEX founder Donald Burr built a highly productive workforce by introducing cross-training, company stock, and profit-sharing for all employees. The carrier operated from Newark International Airport (EWR). PEX offered a single aircraft type, economy service, no galleys, high frequency, few amenities, and fast aircraft turnarounds, giving it a 45 percent cost advantage relative to the legacy carriers.

In its first four years of operation, PEX introduced service in smaller Northeastern, Florida, and trans-Atlantic markets with relatively weak competition. It targeted passengers who were willing to trade amenities for lower fares and those who previously traveled by car, bus, or train. PEX introduced fares typically 55–75 percent below pre-existing market fares and stimulated large amounts of new demand, sometimes tripling the market's passenger volume. The legacy airlines' initial pricing response to PEX was restrained. As long as PEX remained focused on its niche markets, the legacy carriers responded by offering a few seats on selected flights at deeply discounted fares in those markets.

In 1984, PEX expanded rapidly beyond its original niche into the legacy carriers' core markets, introducing non-stop flights in major transcontinental, Newark, and Florida markets. PEX boldly introduced $59 one-way fares, which were 25 percent below pre-existing fares, in the New York–Chicago market where AA and UA each operated 24 daily round-trip flights.

UA responded quickly by filing restricted $75 one-way fares in major Chicago–East Coast routes, requiring a 7-day advance purchase, Saturday night stay, and 60-day maximum stay, along with slightly higher unrestricted one-way fares.

AA had several years earlier introduced a restricted discount fare program, "Super Savers", as a way to respond to intense price competition from unscheduled charter operators while protecting revenue from business customers. Super Savers fares carried stringent restrictions, including a 30-day advance purchase and 7-day minimum stay requirement, designed to be acceptable to price-sensitive leisure passengers but unattractive to business customers. A certain number of seats were allocated on each flight to be sold at discount fares.

AA's management contemplated its options for responding to PEX incursions into its core markets. In order to broadly compete at PEX fares without incurring excessive losses, the airline needed to improve the accuracy of its flight-specific forecasts of business demand, which drove its discount seat allocations. If too many seats were sold in advance at the discounted fares, the airline might have to turn away higher-paying business passengers. If too few discount seats were sold and business demand failed to materialize, flights would depart with empty seats.

AA knew that the PEX reservation system allowed it to offer only one fare for each flight at any time, while Sabre could offer a variety of fares in each cabin on any flight at any time. AA could therefore segregate the seats it would offer at full fares into one booking class while offering deeply discounted fares to match PEX in a separate booking class. AA developed an enhanced discount allocation model to determine the number of seats to reserve for business passengers based on demand forecasts and Littlewood's Rule, an algorithm developed by British Airways' predecessor for determining the optimal number of discount reservations to accept to maximize revenue.

In January 1985, AA launched "Ultimate Super Savers", lowering fares by as much as 70 percent in many domestic routes, including markets where it competed with PEX. Fare restrictions included a 30-day AP requirement, non-refundability (to reduce no-shows), and a one-week minimum stay. At the same time, AA implemented its new discount allocation model to systematically control the availability of the discounted fares. AA's CEO, Robert L. Crandall, named the new program for managing discount fares "Yield Management" (YM).

Ultimate Super Savers was a tremendous success. While PEX carried only low-fare leisure passengers, AA carried a more profitable mix of business and leisure customers, offsetting its cost disadvantage with a higher average fare per passenger. PEX's performance deteriorated rapidly into bankruptcy. The airline was purchased by Texas Air in 1986. PEX Chairman Burr attributed the carrier's failure primarily to its inability to respond to AA's superior yield management and CRS capabilities (Cross 1997).

3.4.3 Growth of travel agency distribution

The CRS-owning carriers continued the competition to expand their subscriber bases. By 1983, approximately 65 percent of travel agency locations subscribed to a CRS, representing

88 percent of total domestic industry revenue. Apollo and Sabre held nearly 80 percent combined share of automated travel agency revenues. Travel agency issuance of total airline tickets increased to 86 percent in 1985 from 56 percent in 1977.

In the early 1980s, the non-CRS-owning airlines complained to the Department of Justice (DOJ) that they were at an unfair competitive disadvantage. CRS owners were accused of introducing "screen bias" that ensured that their own flights received preference in travel agent displays. Travel agents were much more likely to book flights from the first screen of a CRS display than they were to book flights appearing on later screens. CRS owners were perceived to have other unfair advantages, including access to travel agency booking data and a revenue-enhancing "halo" effect in markets where the CRS was dominant.

The DOJ and CAB issued new CRS regulations in 1984. The rules required that displays be based on certain objective quality of service criteria, such as price and schedule; system enhancements be offered to all airlines; all airlines be charged the same booking fees; and travel agency booking data be available to all subscribers for a fee.

The CRS systems were reprogrammed to display flights strictly according to price and schedule, allowing a non-owner's flight to display before the owner's flight if it was cheaper and met the passengers' schedule requirements. Despite substantial system changes, the non-CRS-owning carriers were not satisfied. Eleven airlines filed lawsuits charging that AA and UA possessed a monopoly over electronic booking of airline seats and were using their power to limit competition. As regulation and litigation costs reduced the advantages of ownership, the CRS-owning airlines divested their ownership interests (Copeland et al. 1995).

Following the airlines' divestments, the CRSs evolved into today's global distribution systems (GDS), independent companies that provide electronic marketplaces and products connecting travel agencies and suppliers, including most of the world's airlines, hotels, rental car companies, and cruise lines. The three largest GDSs today are Sabre, TravelPort (which owns Galileo, Apollo, and Worldspan), and Amadeus.

3.4.4 Industry structure

The development of hub-and-spoke networks, the entry and growth of low-cost carriers, mergers and acquisitions, advances in jet aircraft technology, and the expansion of overseas travel are among the forces that have shaped the post-deregulation airline industry. Deregulation fundamentally and dramatically changed the structure of the air transportation system as hubs were used to transfer more and more passengers between a rapidly growing number of spoke cities. The system infrastructure requirements also increased as air traffic control, terminals, gates, and passenger services became overwhelmed with the passenger growth enabled by airline expansion. Hub-and-spoke carriers, saddled with inflated pre-deregulation cost structures and entrenched infrastructures, have struggled for three decades to compete with lean, efficient, low-cost carriers that are unencumbered by these legacies of regulation.

The DOT classifies airlines by annual operating revenue. Airlines producing over $1 billion are categorized as "major", those generating $100 million to $1 billion per year as "national", and those producing less than $100 million as "regional" carriers. For our purposes, domestic airlines will be categorized as legacy airlines, regional carriers, and low-cost carriers.

3.4.4.1 *Legacy airlines*

The original trunk airlines that survived deregulation are referred to interchangeably as legacy, network, full-service, hub-and-spoke, or major carriers. As of May 2011, they included American Airlines, United Airlines (merged with Continental Airlines October 2010), Delta Air Lines (acquired Northwest Airlines in 2008), and US Airways. This group is often referred to as the "majors" with regard to pricing actions, although Southwest Airlines is also considered a major carrier by DOT. The major airlines have extensive networks with multiple hubs strategically placed to optimize connections. Smaller hub operators include Alaska Airlines and Hawaiian Airlines.

In the last decade, the network airlines have formed strategic alliances with foreign carriers in order to extend their global networks more profitably and rapidly than they could expand internationally with their own aircraft, given existing bilateral and US foreign ownership agreements. Most of the alliances began as "code-sharing" agreements, in which a carrier sells seats on flights operated by another airline using its own flight numbers and airline code (e.g., DL). Code-sharing provides significant screen display and other marketing benefits. When code-sharing, both carriers price seats to be sold on the same operating flight independently. Revenue earned is then shared between the carriers according to their agreement.

More recently, airlines have formed more integrated and expansive global alliances. The three major alliances are the Star Alliance, anchored by Lufthansa and United Airlines; oneworld, co-founded by American Airlines and British Airways; and SkyTeam, formed by Delta Air Lines and Air France KLM. All three alliances have been granted anti-trust immunity and are free to coordinate schedules, pricing, and inventory management.

The formerly regulated carriers are sometimes called "full-service" airlines to distinguish them from their "no-frills" low-cost competitors. Remaining "frills" on legacy airlines may include global market scope, frequent flier programs, lounge access, and premium classes of service. Increasingly, passengers on legacy carriers are being asked to pay for certain "frills", such as food and beverages, which were once complimentary, while some low-cost carriers are adding services, such as booking through travel agencies.

3.4.4.2 *Regional carriers*

Many small to medium-sized markets in the USA are served by regional carriers that operate jets or turbo-props with fewer than 100 seats. Several of these carriers are wholly owned subsidiaries of legacy carriers such as American Eagle (AMR Corp.) and ComAir (Delta). Others are independent, such as SkyWest. Most regional carriers have long-standing partnerships with the network airlines to provide connecting service from smaller spoke cities to the major hubs. Connecting service between the legacy and regional carrier is marketed, priced, and sold under the legacy carriers' airline code.

3.4.4.3 *Low-cost carriers (LCCs)*

All the carriers in the first wave of new market entrants after deregulation went bankrupt or were acquired by larger airlines by the mid-1980s. Since then, new low-cost carriers (LCCs) have taken advantage of the wide availability of trained staff, access to affordable aircraft,

Internet distribution, and high prevailing business fares to achieve better results. Low-cost airlines now carry more than 30 percent of domestic passengers, up from less than 10 percent in 1999 (Reed 2009).

Many of the newer LCCs are modeled on Southwest and primarily serve point-to-point markets, carry few connecting passengers, have substantial unit cost advantages, and offer simple, minimally restricted coach-only fares that undercut legacy carriers by 60–70 percent. Distribution is often limited to the airline's website and call center.

Increasingly, LCCs utilize hybrid versions of the original Southwest model which retain low-cost principles but add selected amenities to attract higher-paying travelers. For example, JetBlue operates at very low costs and offers highly competitive fares. However, JetBlue targets both price-sensitive business travelers and leisure travelers in its marketing, pricing, product design, and customer service policies. The carrier actively promotes innovative product features appealing to both segments, such as live satellite TV, while also offering extra legroom, free wireless service, and travel agency distribution to appeal to business customers.

3.5 THE AIRLINE PRICING PROCESS

Airline pricing and revenue management is comprised of strategic, tactical, and operational activities that typically occur over a 12-month period prior to a flight's departure. High-level strategies and key initiatives are developed and reviewed on an annual basis in accordance with the airline's corporate planning calendar. Regional and market group strategies and tactical initiatives are developed throughout the year as market and competitive conditions evolve, booking patterns emerge, and results are measured. Fare availability is reviewed at pre-determined dates prior to departure and may be adjusted more frequently closer to a flight's departure. Flights with early booking patterns, normally leisure markets, will be actively managed earlier than those with later booking patterns.

Competitive fares, market position, schedule changes, special events, seasonality, booking trends, and sales promotions, among other factors, are continuously monitored by pricing and RM teams. Fares and inventory levels are ideally set before a flight takes significant bookings so that revenue opportunities are identified before the window of opportunity passes. Rapid response to competitive action is imperative. The general steps of the airline pricing process are shown in Figure 3.3.

3.5.1 Airline product definition and customer segmentation

Airline customers sometimes perceive that they purchase a tangible product when buying an airline ticket, that is, a seat on a particular flight. In reality, the airline product is intangible. An airline sells air transportation service between two or more cities at a certain price with specified purchase requirements and restrictions. The airlines' service offerings, or "fare products", are targeted to various passenger segments based on the different values that customers attach to a seat on a particular flight. Fare products are designed to match

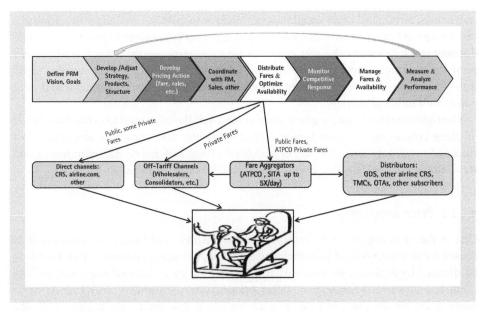

FIGURE 3.3 Airline pricing process

customers' booking patterns and travel preferences with their willingness-to-pay for certain product features, such as non-stop service and last-minute seat availability.

Segmented (or differentiated) pricing and the practice of RM help airlines manage distinct characteristics and challenges of the air transportation product:

1. the product is highly perishable—an empty seat has no value after the flight has departed;

2. the marginal cost to offer an additional unit for sale is relatively low;

3. prices are set and categorized into a pre-determined set of fare classes;

4. products are reserved in advance;

5. customer demand and behavior is uncertain;

6. prices are assumed to be held constant for the purpose of determining inventory availability.

Airline passengers have historically been segmented based upon their primary travel purpose: business or leisure. Within each of these broad segments, significant variations in booking patterns, travel preferences, and price sensitivity create the opportunity to target more precise sub-segments to drive incremental revenue. For example, although both corporate and independent business travelers' trip purpose is business, corporate fares are negotiated by a travel manager on behalf of the corporation, while independent business travelers generally purchase their own tickets on-line or through a travel agent.

For most of their history, airlines have used a restriction-based pricing model that evolved from AA's original "Super Savers" program. Restriction-based pricing uses rules, restrictions, terms, and other conditions of purchase to qualify a passenger to purchase a certain type of fare. For example, a leisure passenger may be qualified to purchase a certain discount fare if he reserves his seat 21 days in advance, purchases the ticket at least one day prior to departure, accepts a non-refundability condition, and stays over a Saturday night. Rules and restrictions are designed to exclusively target certain market segments and price points with minimal overlap.

The eight commonly used segmentation criteria and the rules used to define fares based on these criteria are discussed below. ATPCO currently maintains over 50 categories of rules and restrictions, including day of week/time of day, seasonality, minimum/maximum stays, stopovers, transfers, fare combinability, and blackout dates (ATPCO 2010).

3.5.1.1 Price sensitivity

One of the most important differences between business and leisure customers is their sensitivity to price, referred to as their price elasticity. Business customers' travel tends to be dictated by business requirements and reimbursed by a client or employer, making them less sensitive to changes in ticket prices. Leisure customers' travel tends to be more discretionary, planned further in advance, and paid for by the passenger. A one percent change in the price of a leisure ticket drives a much larger change in demand than a similar change in the price of a business ticket. As a result, it is much easier to stimulate leisure demand through short-term discounts, promotions, and permanent price reductions.

3.5.1.2 Time sensitivity

Business travelers have consistently demonstrated a willingness to pay more for the flight and airline that best meets their schedule requirements. Leisure passengers are more willing to accept less convenient flights in exchange for lower prices.

3.5.1.3 Time of booking

Longer (i.e., more restrictive) advance purchase (AP) restrictions are often required for discounted leisure fares, while later-booking business passengers can purchase full fare tickets up to the time of departure.

3.5.1.4 Flexibility

Refundability restrictions, change fees, and ticket reissue fees differentiate customers according to their flexibility requirements. Business travelers value the ability to change their travel plans, often at the last minute. Premium class and unrestricted economy fares primarily purchased by business travelers are fully refundable and can be changed at any time for free. Non-refundable discount tickets have been replaced in many markets by "reusable" tickets that can be reissued for travel within one year for payment of a fee and any fare difference.

3.5.1.5 *Trip duration*

Business trips tend to be much shorter than leisure trips. The legacy airlines traditionally used a minimum stay requirement, typically Saturday night, to segment customers based on their trip duration. As business fares increased relative to the lowest leisure fares, many businesses encouraged their employees to stay over Saturday night in order to qualify for discounted fares. Low-cost carriers generally do not require a minimum stay and legacy carriers have eliminated the requirement in many markets where they compete with LCCs.

3.5.1.6 *Affiliations and qualified groups*

Many travelers qualify for discounts based on their affiliation with an organization, group, or consortium. For example, government employees fly on discounted fares with minimal restrictions that are negotiated annually between the government and the airlines. Airlines also negotiate special unpublished fares with cruise lines and tour operators (see Lieberman, Chapter 12). These fares may be lower than the lowest published fares but are less likely to ignite price wars because the fare is not transparent to competitors.

3.5.1.7 *Loyalty*

Since the introduction of frequent flyer programs in the 1980s, customer loyalty—measured by miles flown—has become an important factor in customer segmentation. Frequent flier status may determine a passenger's access to benefits such as preferred seats and upgrades; change, baggage, and standby fee waivers; and priority security, boarding, and standby status.

3.5.1.8 *Distribution channel*

As Internet travel sales have grown and distribution channels have multiplied, booking channel has become an increasingly important segmentation criterion. Airlines' targeted incentives to first-time Internet users have driven rapid shifts from higher-cost booking channels, such as the GDS, to lower-cost on-line channels.

3.5.2 Dilution risk

Despite fare restrictions and inventory controls, customers do not always purchase the fare products targeted for their designated segments, resulting in revenue losses airlines call "dilution". If a business passenger purchases a $500 3-day advance purchase fare at 50 percent of the unrestricted coach fare when he would have been willing to pay the $1000 full fare, airline revenue has been diluted by $500. Longer advanced purchase requirements reduce the risk of dilution while shorter APs increase the risk.

In theory, customers can almost always be classified into smaller market segments to increase revenue. As stated by Robert L. Crandall, AA's CEO, "it is always in an airline's best interest to participate in every segment of the market, subject to having the capability to control seat inventory based on the value of the customer segment in relation to demand for all customer segments in the market" (Crandall 1998). In practice, however, setting and managing fares for every potential customer segment is impractical. Most airline reservation systems cannot control availability of fare products at the individual customer segment level. In addition, airlines must consider the costs of increased complexity associated with expanding the number of fare products.

3.5.3 Low-cost carrier and hybrid segmentation approaches

Low-cost carriers' customer segmentation and product design vary significantly from the legacy airlines' approaches. LCCs have used their ability to undercut existing fares to attract price-sensitive travelers when they enter a new market. Since they do not have an existing base of core business revenue to protect upon market entry, they have not needed the restrictions used by the legacy carriers to prevent business passengers from purchasing lower-priced leisure products.

Low-cost carrier customer segmentation is primarily based on a passenger's willingness to purchase a ticket in advance in exchange for a lower fare. LCCs tend to offer a small number of fare products in each market with minimal rules and restrictions. As a general rule, their RM requirements tend to be less complex than those of the legacy carriers.

Many LCCs use dynamic pricing to vary the prices on their flights according to demand. Rather than limiting the number of seats that can be sold at a discounted fare, the fare available for sale is changed to account for bookings to date and expected incremental demand. Some LCCs display only the lowest available fare for a flight on their websites. Others target price-sensitive business and leisure customers with a few differentiated fare products. For example, Southwest typically displays four fares, including its recently introduced Business Select product and three coach fares with various APs.

The incursion of LCCs into markets with traditional restriction-based fare structures has forced the legacy carriers to relax or remove many of the rules and restrictions that have historically been used to prevent business passengers from purchasing discounted leisure fares. The legacy carriers typically retain some higher fares with restrictions to preserve their ability to save seats for last-minute business demand. The resulting hybrid fare structure introduces greater dilution risk because of the co-existence of LCC-type fares and restriction-based fares in the same market. A legacy carrier's hybrid fare structure in an LCC-competitive market is shown in Figure 3.4.

3.5.4 The fare structure

An airline's fare structure defines the relationship between classes of service (i.e., First or Economy), categories of fare products (fare classes) within each class of service, and specific fare products within these categories. Aircraft may be configured with one, two, or three passenger classes of service (i.e., any combination of First, Business, and/or Economy or Coach Class). Fare classes (also called booking classes or booking codes) are single-letter codes that identify categories of fare products sold within each class of service. The codes also indicate the inventory booking class in the CRS that will be decremented when a seat is sold in the associated fare class. The airlines use a fairly standard system of single-letter

CARRIER	FARE PRODUCT	ONE-WAY FARE	BAG FEES	SELECTED BENEFITS, RULES & RESTRICTIONS
AA (American)	First Flexible	$1187	2 free bags/psgr	No change fees; standby permitted; no AP
AA	Economy Flexible	$860	2 free bags/psgr	No change fees; standby permitted; no AP
AA	Instant Upgrade	$491	2 free bags/psgr	No change fees; standby permitted; no AP
WN (Southwest)	Business Select	$209	2 free bags/psgr	Priority boarding/security; extra rewards pts; no change fees; free standby; no AP
WN	Anytime	$194	2 free bags/psgr	No change fees; free standby
AA	Economy Saver	$184	$25/1st checked bag $25/2nd checked bag	7-day AP; change fees $50-$150 plus fare difference
WN	Wanna Get Away	$140	2 free bags/psgr	7-day AP; standbys pay fare difference; no change fees
AA	Economy Super Saver	$140	$25/1st checked bag $25/2nd checked bag	7-day AP; change fees $50-$150 + fare difference

FIGURE 3.4 Hybrid fare structure—hypothetical market example

codes for the full (non-discounted) fare in each cabin: F for first, J or C for business, and Y for economy class. Although the full fare booking codes are relatively standard, discount fare class codes vary across carriers. Some CRSs limit fare class codes to a single letter, restricting the total number of fare classes that may be used.

Fare products within the fare classes are defined more precisely by 6–8 character alphanumeric codes called fare basis codes (FBCs). The first letter of the FBC is typically the booking class. FBCs may also identify some of the conditions associated with the fare, such as the AP, day of week, time of day, and/or seasonal application. For example, a discount fare with a FBC of MH7APX indicates that the fare must be booked in M class, purchased 7 days in advance and used for peak season travel. More comprehensive fare rules are filed and published with the fare.

3.5.4.1 Market example—non-LCC market

Figure 3.5 shows a simplified example of a network airline's published fare structure in November 2010 for the New York-La Guardia (LGA) to Dallas-Fort Worth (DFW) market. Within the coach cabin, the airline offers four regular fares: the full unrestricted fare booked in Y class, an "instant upgrade" fare booked in K class, and two regular discounted leisure fares booked in L and Q class, respectively. The instant upgrade K fare level is approximately 13 percent lower than the full Y fare and 30 percent lower than the full first class fare. It provides last-minute upgrades to first class if space is available and requires a 7-day AP.

FARE PRODUCT	FARE CLASS	FARE BASIS CODE	ADVANCE PURCHASE (AP)	FARE LEVEL	DISCOUNT OFF FULL FARE	DISCOUNT OFF NEXT HIGHER FARE	SELECTED BENEFITS, RULES & RESTRICTIONS
First Flexible (First Class)	F	FA2AA	N/A	$1528 (1-WAY)/ $3056 RT	N/A	N/A	No change/bag fee; free standby; refundable
Economy Flexible (Full Coach)	Y	YA2AA	N/A	$1228 (1-WAY)/ $2456 RT	20% off Full F	20% off Full F	No change/bag fees; free standby; refundable
Instant Upgrade (Economy to First or Business Class)	K	KA7UPPMR	7 DAYS	$1074 (1-WAY)/ $2148 RT	13% off Y; 30% if upgraded	13% off Y; 30% if upgraded	Standby upgrades; no bag/chg fee
Economy Saver (Regular Leisure Sell-up Fare)	L	LA7OERM5	7 DAYS	$973 RT*	60%	55%	RT purchase required; refundable; bag fees apply
Economy Super Saver (Regular Leisure Fare)	Q	QF21ERM1	21 DAYS	$513 RT*	79%	47%	RT purchase required; 1-night min stay; non-refundable; $150 change fee; bag fees apply
Net Saver (Winter Sale Fare)	M	MF14PROMO	14 DAYS	$342 RT*	86%	33%	RT purchase required; limited ticketing/travel periods, non-refundable; 1-night min; $150 change fee; bag fees apply

FIGURE 3.5 Legacy carrier fares in non-LCC market. (NY LGA–DFW sample fares)

The L class 7-day AP leisure fare is a "sell-up" fare, designed to attract passengers who are unable to book the lowest leisure fare, which is filed in Q with a more restrictive 21-day AP and more limited seat availability. The L fare, which requires round-trip (RT) purchase, is 60 percent below full Y and 55 percent below the next higher fare, the Instant Upgrade. The Q fare offers leisure customers an even better deal at 79 percent below full Y if they can meet the 21-day AP and round-trip purchase requirement.

The airline is also offering a short-term sale promotion for winter travel. The sale fare, filed in M class with a 14-day AP, is currently the best deal for leisure passengers who can meet the fare restrictions. It represents an 86 percent discount from full Y and a 33 percent discount from the regular Q fare. In addition to the AP, RT purchase, and non-refundability restrictions, the promotional fare has ticketing and travel time limits indicating that tickets must be purchased by November 22, 2010 for flights departing between December 1, 2010 and February 16, 2010.

3.5.4.2 Types of fare products

Fare products can be classified into four major categories: published, private, international, and interline fares.

Published ("tariff") fares are those that are made available to the general public through channels such as the airline's website, call centers, airports, ticketing offices, travel agencies (via the GDSs), and on-line travel agencies (OTAs). Published fares may be subject to commissions and booking fees.

Private ("unpublished", "negotiated", or "off-tariff") fares are distributed only to targeted customer segments through selected channels. They are typically sold through corporate travel agents, wholesalers, group sales departments, ticket consolidators, tour operators, cruise lines, and other specialty agencies. Airlines may utilize these channels to attract segments with year-round demand, such as corporate travelers; to fill excess capacity during slow periods; or to reach customer segments that primarily purchase through particular outlets, such as ethnic consolidators. In some market segments, it is common practice for the distributor and airline supplier to negotiate fares net of commissions. The distributor is then free (within contractual limitations) to mark up the net fare ticket for resale.

International fares for travel between the USA and other countries are governed by bilateral, multi-lateral, or "open skies" agreements. Bi- or multi-lateral agreements, where they still exist, specify how many airlines from each country can operate service, the routes and cities served, number of flights offered, and method for price determination. Carriers operating under regulatory constraints often negotiate code-share agreements to sell seats on partners' flights. Each partner airline schedules and prices their services independently.

More recently, open skies agreements have been negotiated between the USA and many other countries that remove regulatory limitations on carriers' rights to operate service between the respective countries. The agreements also eliminate legal constraints prohibiting coordination of fares, schedules, and routes between partners. The first open skies agreement was negotiated with the Netherlands in 1992, allowing Northwest Airlines and KLM to expand their pre-existing code-share agreement to form the first anti-trust immune global alliance. The US now has open skies agreements with over 90 foreign states, including a multi-lateral agreement with the EU.

When no code-sharing or open skies agreement exists, operating carriers negotiate the allocation of revenue through IATA, the international airline trade association.

Interline fares apply to itineraries that include segments operated under the codes of two or more carriers. Fares on such tickets are referred to as IATA, inter-line, or pro-rated fares. Itinerary pricing in the CRSs, GDSs, airline websites, and OTAs is governed by combinability and fare construction rules. Combinability indicates which fare products can be combined to create a multi-stop itinerary. Constructed fares also create multi-stop itineraries by combining a negotiated or published fare, such as a cruise fare, with add-on fares to multiple cities. Constructed fares are primarily used for unpublished products and in international markets. Unpublished fares typically represent a much larger percentage of tickets in international markets than in domestic markets.

Large airlines file fares for only a small percentage of possible itineraries because the potential number of combinations of O&D markets and fare products is unmanageable. Intermediaries, such as a GDS, use their own technology to search the airlines' fare and schedule data and construct a comprehensive, competitive, and feasible set of O&D market/fare product itineraries. The distributors strive to offer their customers the lowest available price on a valid itinerary in the requested market.

3.5.5 Strategic pricing

Pricing strategy determines how a carrier's products and pricing are defined and positioned vis-à-vis competitors. The airline's overall pricing strategy is aligned with the carrier's corporate, marketing, operating, customer, and financial strategies and based upon analysis of the competitive environment, the carrier's market position, customer and market segmentation, price elasticity, and the carrier's value proposition. Potential strategic initiatives are evaluated based on their contribution to the achievement of strategic goals and their estimated impact on system profitability.

The overall pricing strategy provides the framework for regional, market-specific, and competitor-specific strategies, initiatives, and tactics. Regional and market-specific strategies may vary considerably based on market objectives, competitive environment, market presence, quality of service (QSI), and other factors. At a macro level, markets can be categorized according to their relative yield performance (with higher yields indicating a business-oriented mix of passengers and lower yields suggesting a leisure-oriented passenger mix) and the carrier's market position. For example, the carrier's overall objective in markets where it earns high yields and holds a dominant market share will generally be to maximize yield and protect market share. However, where low-cost competition is a factor, the carrier might resist the temptation to raise fares to discourage customers from defecting to the LCC.

Pricing and revenue management has three "levers" with which to maximize revenue and contribution margin. The three levers are (1) strategic pricing initiatives, (2) tactical pricing actions, and (3) revenue management. Most often, a combination of one or more of these levers is used to achieve the desired impact. For example, when a short-term promotional sale fare is filed, RM reviews inventory levels to ensure the sale fare is available on all flights where bookings are lower than expectations for the targeted travel period.

Airlines are sometimes compelled to match competitive fares even though they may perceive a competitor's actions to be irrational. Because of leisure passengers' high price sensitivity, carriers nearly always match fare reductions initiated by competitors in order to avoid losing revenue. As AA's Crandall said in a 1992 interview: "People choose how to travel based on price and frequency. Now our business is the closest thing we have in this country to a perfect marketplace. The prices are always equal because there's nowhere to hide. You make one telephone call to your travel agent, and all of our prices come up on the computer. Anybody who offers a higher price for the same thing loses your business, so we all keep matching the competition" (Castro 1992).

3.5.6 Tactical pricing

Tactical pricing analysts monitor the competitive fare environment to identify opportunities to capture incremental revenue through pro-active fare initiatives or by responding to a competitor's actions. Efficient, accurate, and timely data retrieval, analysis, decision-making, implementation, and performance measurement are essential. Failure to respond quickly to fare changes can reduce revenue significantly due to price transparency and sensitivity. Pricing analysts continuously monitor and evaluate changes in competitors' fare levels, rules, restrictions, routings, promotional ticketing and travel periods, fees, surcharges and other relevant factors. Decision support systems assist analysts in retrieving, analyzing, and managing the vast amounts of fare data received and transmitted throughout the day. Analysts regularly monitor bookings and revenue performance in markets impacted by any significant fare change to evaluate the effectiveness of the action and identify any required adjustments.

The depth of analysis conducted to determine how a carrier will respond to a competitive fare action depends on its potential revenue impact and strategic importance, among other factors. Some pricing actions may be automatically submitted to distribution systems based on pre-determined heuristics. For example, fare changes impacting markets where the carrier is a small player and the competitor initiating the change is dominant may be matched automatically. Major competitive fare actions impacting large amounts of revenue, such as a system-wide fare increase or sale, require more detailed analysis.

A carrier's optimal price positioning in a particular market or set of markets is based on its overall pricing strategy, the competitive environment, its relative market position, the market's traffic composition (i.e., business versus leisure), and the airline's quality of service relative to competitors. Market-specific factors will determine whether fares in a market or group of markets should be (1) exactly competitive (i.e., match fare levels, rules, restrictions, and other terms), (2) lower than competitors (i.e., a larger discount) and/or less restrictive (i.e., a shorter AP or lower change fee), or (3) higher and/or more restrictive than other carriers.

Pricing decisions may be designed to achieve a targeted mix of leisure versus business passengers in a market. For example, an analyst may slightly increase fares or add an additional fare level to encourage passengers to "sell-up" to the higher fare level in conjunction with more restrictive inventory management tactics, thereby increasing the proportion of higher-paying passengers.

The Quality of Service Index (QSI) is widely used to estimate each carrier's expected share in a market by adjusting actual capacity share by factors influencing service quality, such as type of service (non-stop versus connecting), elapsed flight time, and time-of-day preferences. Each carrier's QSI share is compared to actual market share to determine whether a fare differential may be contributing to a smaller than expected share.

Revenue impact analysis is used to estimate the change in revenue resulting from a pricing change. The analysis estimates potential new demand, market share shift, demand shifts between fare products, and change in total market size expected from a price increase, decrease, or change in rules or restrictions.

Price elasticity varies significantly across fare products, customer segments, markets, and booking patterns. Late-booking customers paying higher fares are relatively inelastic, while elasticity is highest among early-booking leisure customers. Carriers often test market price elasticity in a small number of markets to refine estimates and assess competitive response prior to broad implementation of a fare initiative.

Game theory plays a significant role in airline pricing. Potential competitive responses are modeled to estimate their impact on revenue based on market testing, sensitivity analysis, and competitors' historical pricing behavior. Competitive response frequently determines whether a fare increase initiated by one carrier will remain in effect or be withdrawn. Fare reductions are generally matched in most markets but competitors' responses may vary widely with respect to market exclusions, rules, restrictions, ticketing and travel terms, and other conditions.

An important consideration in any pricing decision is whether seat availability for the impacted fare product(s) can be controlled as desired through the carrier's CRS. For example, two discount fares booked in Q class may receive the same inventory availability, despite significantly different fare levels, rules, and restrictions. An airline's ability to effectively manage availability of discount fares may be limited by its CRS capabilities, its RM system, business practices, contractual obligations, and/or organizational barriers.

3.5.7 Strategic pricing initiatives

Strategic pricing initiatives may be implemented system-wide (domestic, international, or globally), regionally (domestic North-East markets), in a group of markets (LCC-competitive markets), or in specific O&D markets (DFW–LAX). Three types of strategic pricing programs are particularly prevalent in the USA.

A *general fare increase* applies to a broad set of markets, such as all domestic markets. The intent is to raise the overall level of base published fares (and negotiated fares that are based on published fares). Some markets may be excluded from the initiative, most commonly those with low-cost competition. Fare increases may be fixed dollar amounts or distance-based.

For example, in mid-October 2009, AA initiated a mileage-based fare increase in all its domestic markets, including those with low-cost competition. AA raised fares between $4 and $16 round-trip on all domestic tickets. Within 24 hours, all of the legacy carriers had matched AA's initiative. Southwest Airlines increased fares across its route system by smaller amounts, but excluded its lowest leisure "Fun Fares" (Table 3.1).

Within two weeks, another round-trip fare increase of $10 in all domestic markets was implemented by most US carriers. AirTran soon initiated a smaller fare increase in its own markets. Legacy carriers matched not only in markets where they competed with AirTran but also in other domestic routes. As a result, the lowest round-trip domestic airfares were increased by up to $36 by the end of October in markets where all three fare increases applied.

Attempted general fare increases often fail because an airline cannot maintain a price premium without losing significant market share—sometimes within hours. The initiating carrier closely monitors competitive responses to determine if the increase is matched by all competitors. If one or more carriers do not match the increase within 24 hours, carriers that have already matched will usually revert to previous fare levels. In 2009, 11 attempts were made by major carriers to implement domestic system-wide fare increases; only four of

Table 3.1 Domestic ticket fare increases, October 2009

Distance	AA fare increase	LCC fare increase
0–450 miles	$2/$4 RT	$2/$4 RT
451–750	$5/$10	$3/$6
>750	$8/$16	$5/$10

these initiatives were matched by all other legacy carriers in at least two-thirds of their markets (Seaney 2010).

The most common type of large-scale pricing initiative is the *short-term seasonal sale*. System-wide short-term sales may be filed for travel during a specified period in all domestic routes or the airline's entire global network for a limited selling period ranging from a few hours to approximately two weeks. The initiating carrier sets the initial terms of the sale, including the fare discounts, rules, market scope, market exclusions, discount percentages, booking period, and effective travel period.

Competitors have the same options to respond to a short-term sale as they do to other pricing actions. A system-wide sale will rarely be ignored by a major competitor due to the risk of losing revenue and market share. If an airline believes the promotional discounts are too generous or the terms too lenient, the carrier may respond by filing a slightly higher fare, more restrictions, or additional market exclusions.

To illustrate how a sale initiated by one carrier can evolve once other airlines respond, assume Delta files a summer fare sale on Saturday, May 20 with discounts averaging 35 percent in all domestic markets, excluding markets with significant LCC competition. Terms include a 14-day AP requirement, ticketing by May 31 and travel completion by September 15. Delta's competitors are alerted of the sale when competitive fare data is received on Monday, May 22. Their evaluation of the fares, restrictions, and other terms of the sale will vary depending on their summer bookings, the sale's estimated revenue impact, their relative market positions, and other carrier-specific factors.

Most likely, the major network carriers will respond by matching the sale exactly in all of their domestic markets, excluding LCC markets. If a carrier wishes to change some aspect of the sale, its response will reflect the modifications. For example, AA reduced the AP requirement from 14 days to 7 days when it filed sale fares in its own markets in response to DL's sale. UA initially matched the discounts and terms of DL's sale; after AA's filing, DL, UA, and other majors reduced the AP to 7 days and extended the booking period to June 5.

After close of business on Monday, AirTran reduced its 3-day AP summer fares by 15 percent for tickets booked through June 5 on all its routes. Other LCCs matched AirTran's fares, except for Southwest. The majors then reduced their fares 15 percent in markets where they competed with the LCCs, retaining a 7-day AP and round-trip purchase requirement to limit business dilution.

Regional, market group, or competitor-specific initiatives target a subset of markets in the network that are of particular strategic importance, are underperforming, or have a significant impact on other markets. Such an initiative may be focused on building an airline's market position in a particular geographic area, such as the New York City region. Strategic initiatives have often been focused on improving the performance of a secondary hub, such as Continental's smaller hub in Cleveland or Delta's competing hub in Cincinnati.

Some initiatives target markets with certain competitive characteristics. An example would be the legacy carriers' evolving response to the growth of LCCs. In 1990, discount carriers (led by Southwest) carried about 7 percent of domestic passengers (Lee and Ito 2003). For the most part, the larger carriers either ignored the LCCs or matched their low fares selectively on a flight-specific basis. For example, a legacy carrier might match the LCC's fares on three of its twelve flight departures a day in a non-stop market that most closely matched an LCC's three flights in the market.

By 2002, Southwest's (WN's) market share had more than doubled to nearly 16 percent and total LCC share was 23.7 percent. As a result of diligent cost control, WN had maintained a 25 percent unit cost advantage relative to the major carriers' average unit cost. Between 1990 and 1998, passengers in WN markets paid approximately 54 percent less than passengers flying comparable distances in non-WN markets. The LCC's consistent pattern of doubling or tripling the market's size when it entered became known as the "Southwest Effect".

Given WN's early concentration in Texas, the airline initially overlapped most significantly with Continental (CO) and AA, serving markets representing 11 percent of each carrier's revenue in 1990. By 2002, all the legacy carriers except for US Air had low-cost competition in markets that generated more than 40 percent of their annual revenue. Two carriers, UA and AA, competed with LCCs on routes representing more than 60 percent of their annual revenue, particularly as WN's expansion into Chicago's Midway airport impacted their competing hubs at Chicago O'Hare. NW and US Airways were less impacted by LCCs in their major hubs although competition was growing.

The LCCs continued to expand into the network carriers' core markets, reducing market prices drastically. As the competitive threat from low-cost competition grew, the legacy carriers re-evaluated their pricing strategies. Their attempts to minimize damage by matching LCC fares on a few departures a day were no longer effective. However, matching the discounters' fares across-the-board seemed infeasible given the LCCs' average unit cost advantage of 25 percent or more (Kumar and Rogers 2000).

The legacy carriers analyzed their options for competing with the LCCs, which included abandoning the most price-sensitive leisure segment; continuing to match the LCCs selectively and limiting availability of the matching fares; or matching the LCCs' fares more broadly and gaining the benefits of the resulting demand stimulation, using fare rules and inventory controls to minimize business revenue dilution. Most of the legacy carriers eventually concluded that it was most profitable (and inevitable) over the long term to match any viable LCCs' fares with restrictions and inventory controls to prevent business dilution in competitive non-stop markets. The legacy airlines' competitive strategies continue to evolve as the LCCs' collective share of passengers carried in the top 1,000 O&D markets now exceeds 70 percent.

A fare increase will often be smaller in LCC-competitive markets because low-cost carriers are reluctant to raise fares. Similarly, short-term sales may not be filed in LCC markets because the fares are already so low.

3.5.7.1 Fare simplification

Within ten years of CAB's dissolution, 95 percent of total passengers flew on discounted fares averaging more than 60 percent below full economy fares. The number of markets to be priced and the fare types offered in each market continued to multiply, increasing the complexity and cost of distributing, maintaining, modifying, and promoting the airlines' products.

To combat the growing complexity and the deterioration of the airline's value proposition, AA developed a pricing program intended to simplify, rationalize, and improve customers' perceived value of its products. As leisure fares had dropped relative to the full coach fare, business customers complained that they were subsidizing leisure travel. In response, they "gamed" the system, circumventing fare rules to purchase restricted discount tickets.

On April 9, 1992, American implemented the Value Plan, replacing the multitude of existing fares with only four fares per market—first class, a 35–40 percent reduced unrestricted full coach fare, and two discount leisure fares priced to be competitive with the lowest fares in the market. Negotiated fares were to be eliminated once contractual obligations were fulfilled. The total number of published fares declined from approximately 500,000 to 70,000 (Silk and Michael 1993).

The Value Plan was promptly matched by all major airlines, with the exception of TWA and US Air, which undercut the Plan's lowest 21-day fares. Crandall expressed frustration: "This industry is always in the grip of its dumbest competitors....All I know is that we have no choice but to match whatever low fare anybody puts out there" (Castro 1992).

The Value Plan fare structure remained largely intact until Northwest filed a "buy one ticket, get one free" promotion on May 26, 1992 for summer travel. In retaliation for this challenge to its new fare structure, AA slashed leisure fares by 50 percent in all domestic routes. Other major carriers immediately matched. Reservations volume overwhelmed call centers and CRS systems. Competitive forces subsequently re-introduced complexity to the fare structure, nullifying the simplification effects of the Value Plan.

By the early 2000s, increased price transparency through the Internet exposed the relative complexity of the legacy carriers' fare structures compared with those of the LCCs. Delta made another ill-fated attempt to reduce pricing complexity in January 2005. DL reduced its domestic fare types to six in coach and two in first class, capped one-way fares at $499 for coach and $599 for first class, reduced last-minute fares by up to 50 percent, replaced the Saturday night stay requirement with a one-night minimum stay, and imposed a charge on agent-assisted bookings. Competitive factors eventually returned the average number of fares per market and fare levels to pre-simplification levels. DL's program—like American's Value Plan—ultimately failed due to lack of competitive support.

3.5.8 "A la carte" pricing and branded fare families

For much of the industry's history, the "all-inclusive" airfare included checked luggage, in-flight food and beverages, pillows and blankets, pre-assigned seats, and unlimited agent assistance with reservations, ticketing, check-in, and boarding. In the late 1990s, carriers began to cut back on such services to reduce costs. Despite these efforts, the industry lost more than $55 billion between 1999 and 2009 as it struggled to survive two recessions, terrorist attacks, two wars, increased price competition, and record oil prices. Domestic airfares declined 8.6 percent from a high of $340.11 in the fourth quarter of 2000 to $319.31 in the fourth quarter of 2009. Despite incremental fare increases, airfares have never recovered from their sharp decline after the September 11, 2001 terrorist attacks on the World Trade Center (IATA 2010).

As airlines search for new sources of revenue, they are increasingly unbundling the services they offer. "A la carte" or unbundled pricing separates the price paid for basic air transportation from the cost of ancillary services. Passengers pay only for the services they

	CHECKED BAGGAGE (PER BAG EACH WAY)	TICKET CHANGE	BOOKING W/AGENT	PREFERRED OR PRIORITY SERVICE (EACH WAY)	IN-FLIGHT FOOD/BEVERAGE	MISCELLANEOUS (EACH WAY)
AMERICAN	1ST $25, 2ND $35, 3-5 $100, 6+: $200	$150/ MAY VARY BY MARKET	$20-$30	"YOUR CHOICE" PRIORITY BOARDING/FLEX PKG; $9-$19	FOOD $3-$10; ALC BEV $6	PETS $100-$150 MINORS $100 SLEEP SET $9
CONTINENTAL	1ST $23-$25, 2ND $32-$35, 3-5 $50	$150	$20	FEES VARY FOR EXTRA LEGROOM	ALC BEV $6	PETS $125 MINORS $100 BLANKETS $0
DELTA	1ST $23-$25; 2ND $32-$35, 3RD $125, 4-10 $200	$150	$20-$35	N/A	FOOD $2-$8; ALC BEV $5-$7	PETS $125-$200 MINORS $100
UNITED	1ST $23-$25, 2ND $32-$35, 3RD $75-$85, 4+: $100	$150	$25-$30	"PREMIER" PERK PKGS START AT $9/FLT, $425 YR	FOOD $5-$9; ALC BEV $6	PETS $125-$250 MINORS $99
US AIRWAYS	1ST $23-$25, 2ND $32-$35, 3RD $75-$85, 4+: $100	$150	$25-$35	PREF SEAT $5	FOOD $3-$7 ALC BEV $7-$8	PETS $100 MINORS $100 SLEEP SET $12
AIRTRAN	1ST $15, 2ND $25, 3+: $50	$75	$15	RESERVED SEAT $6, EXIT ROW $20	ALC BEV $5-$6	PETS $69 (CABIN); MINORS $49-$69
JETBLUE	1ST $0, 2ND $30, 3+ $75	$100	$15	EXTRA LEGRM $10	FOOD $3-$7	PETS $100 (CABIN) MINORS $75 SLEEP SET $7
SOUTHWEST	2 FREE, 3-9 $50, 10+ $110	FREE (FLT CREDIT)	FREE	PRIORITY BOARDING $10	ALC BEV $5	PETS $75 (CABIN) MINORS $50
SPIRIT	1ST $15-45, 2ND $15-$25, 3-5 $85-$90 CARRY-ON: $20-$45	$100-$110	$5	EXIT ROW $20 PREMIUM $25 OTHERS $8-$15	FOOD $2-$5 REG BEV $2-$3 ALC. BEV $6	PETS $100 (CABIN) MINORS $100

FIGURE 3.6 Selected airline fees (US domestic routes, July 12, 2010)

Source: http://www.smartertravel.com; kayak.com supplier websites

use. Fees are added to the base fare for optional services the passenger selects. Premium class, full economy fare, and elite-level frequent travelers are often exempt from such fees.

Fees are somewhat less susceptible to price wars because they do not show up in GDSs and on-line travel agencies, making total fares more difficult to compare across carriers. The fees may be added to the base fare later in the booking process, at airport check-in, at the gate, or on-board, which means they may not be considered by the customer in her choice of flight. Therefore, the passenger may not know the all-inclusive fare until after the flight has been taken. Selected airline fees are shown in Figure 3.6.

In conjunction with à la carte pricing, carriers are discovering new ways of merchandising their products. Airlines are using branded fare families to target particular customer segments with fare products differentiated by price, restrictions, services, and features included in the fare and ancillary services available for an additional fee. Air Canada was the first international, full-service carrier to implement branded fares, launching the "Tango Fares" product line in 2006 in intra-Canadian markets. Passengers can select from a pre-determined set of economy fare products, ranging from "Tango", the lowest, most restrictive fare with fewest services included, to "Latitude", the highest, unrestricted coach fare which includes many added-value services, such as priority boarding and

FARE COMPONENTS (ONE-WAY)	TANGO	TANGO PLUS	LATITUDE	EXECUTIVE CLASS LOWEST	EXECUTIVE CLASS FLEXIBLE
FARES: YYZ–YVR (CAD)	$209	$274	$764	$949	$1888
REFUNDABILITY	NO	NO	YES	NO	YES
ANYTIME CHANGE FEE	$75 + FARE DIFFERENCE	$50 + FARE DIFFERENCE	FARE DIFFERENCE	$50 + FARE DIFFERENCE	FARE DIFFERENCE
AIRPORT STANDBY	NO	VARIES	YES	YES	YES
UPGRADE ELIGIBILITY	NO	W/UPGRADE CERTIFICATE	W/UPGRADE CERTIFICATE	N/A	N/A
PRIORITY CHECK-IN, BAGGAGE, BOARDING	NO	NO	YES	YES	YES
LOUNGE ACCESS	$45	$35	$30	FREE	FREE
MILEAGE EARNED	25%	100%	100%	150%	150%
COMPLIMENTARY CHECKED BAGS	2	2	2	3	3
ADVANCED SEAT SELECTION	FROM $15	YES	YES	YES	YES
PREPAID ONBOARD CAFÉ VOUCHER	$7	$7	YES	NO	NO
COMPLIMENTARY MEAL	NO	NO	NO	YES	YES

FIGURE 3.7 Air Canada "à la carte" fare structure (sample fares and fees as of August, 2010)

Source: Air Canada website, www.aircanada.com

assigned seating. Customers can then add optional services, such as lounge access. See example of Air Canada's fare structure in Figure 3.7.

Service fees can make a significant impact on the total airfare ultimately paid by the passenger. In the Toronto–Vancouver market, a recent fare quote for round-trip travel at the lowest available Tango fare was $548. If optional services were added, including a meal voucher, pre-assigned seating, a frequent flyer mileage bonus, and two checked bags, the total airfare would increase by $141 or 25 percent.

Low-cost carriers have embraced unbundled pricing. RyanAir introduced à la carte pricing to the UK and Europe upon its transition from full service to an LCC model in 1990. Dispensing with free in-flight amenities and other costly services in favor of lower fares, the popular carrier has become known for its exhaustive list of add-on fees (Kumar and Rogers 2000).

US LCCs tend to charge lower fees than the legacy carriers for services such as checked baggage and ticket changes. Spirit Airlines, which bills itself as an "ultra low cost carrier", has been particularly aggressive in charging fees for services other carriers provide for free, such as checked luggage, a second carry-on bag, and advance seat assignments. JetBlue appeals to a broader variety of customers by including a broad range of services in its base fare, including free wireless service, Direct TV, and one free checked bag. Southwest Airlines upholds its long-standing commitment not to add fees for services traditionally included in the fare by allowing each passenger to check two bags for free.

Southwest also offers a bundled business fare product which includes priority boarding and free drinks.

Legacy carriers have adopted the à la carte pricing model and branded fares more gradually, beginning with the introduction of a $25 fee for the second checked bag in 2005. Baggage fees have since risen to between $25–35 for the first and second bag checked. Reservation change fees, ticket reissue, and agent assistance fees have also become a major revenue stream.

Fees introduced more recently tend to be for value-added services often offered as packages, such as preferred seating, priority boarding, upgraded "sleep sets" and other convenience items. For example, UA recently introduced its "Premier Travel" option which includes extra legroom; priority boarding, security, and check-in; bonus frequent flier miles; and two free checked bags for a package price starting at $47.

As a result of these changes, airlines earned $7.8 billion from ancillary fee revenue in 2009, representing 6.5 percent of operating revenue for the 42 airlines reporting to DOT. Ancillary revenue was derived primarily from baggage fees, contributing $2.7 billion and reservation change fees, contributing $2.4 billion.

In addition to optional service fees, airlines use surcharges to recoup higher fuel expenses. Surcharges are added to the base fare and are subject to sales tax, while fees are quoted separately and are non-taxable. In 2008, legacy carriers imposed fuel surcharges of up to $150 round-trip on domestic tickets in response to a surge in the cost of jet fuel in the first six months of the year. As the average cost per barrel of jet fuel rose from $107 to $161, the average domestic carrier's fuel expense grew from less than 15 percent to more than 35 percent of total operating expenses (ATA 2009).

Fees and surcharges are widely perceived by airline customers to be back-handed ways for the airlines to raise fares. Passengers resent paying for product features and services that they feel entitled to receive as part of the base fare. Despite resistance, the trend toward unbundling continues.

A la carte pricing represents a profound change in airline customer segmentation, product design, merchandising, distribution, and service delivery. In most LCC-competitive markets, restriction-based segmentation is being replaced by a combination of simple advance purchase requirements, hybrid fare structures, dynamic pricing, and/or optional service fees. These changes in product, pricing, marketing, and merchandising strategies have wide-ranging impacts across the airlines, including RM, information technology, advertising, sales, branding, merchandising, customer service, distribution, operations, and revenue accounting.

Airlines have resisted pressure to provide intermediaries with the data required to quote optional fees, book optional services, and calculate total fares in an attempt to drive revenue to direct channels. As a result, GDS and online customers are often surprised at the final ticket price once all fees, surcharges, taxes, and other charges are tallied. Airlines are leveraging the pricing changes to improve distribution economics and to directly merchandise their products to customers by requiring optional services to be booked through a direct connection to the airline's CRS.

Global distribution systems and fare distributors have developed new capabilities to offer branded fares and ancillary services, assuming airlines agree to provide the required data. In an effort to reduce customer confusion, recent legislation will require that all fees and surcharges be disclosed at the time of booking in all distribution channels.

3.5.9 Pricing implementation and distribution

Once a carrier has decided to implement a pricing action, the fares and related rules must be loaded into the carrier's CRS and filed with industry fare aggregators. Airline fares and rules data are aggregated and distributed by two airline member-owned organizations. The Airline Tariff Publishing Company (ATPCO), owned by 16 major international airlines, is an airfare data provider for more than 500 airlines comprising 97 percent of worldwide industry revenue. SITA, owned by over 550 members of the air transport community, provides fares management and pricing services to approximately 180 airlines worldwide. ATPCO and SITA provide aggregated industry airfare data to the GDSs, airline CRSs, travel agencies, governments, and industry organizations.

Most domestic airlines use ATPCO's Government Filing System, the world's largest airfare database, to monitor and prioritize thousands of daily fare changes. ATPCO's products are used by carriers to file and update fares, rules, routing, surcharges, and other related data. Carriers file responses to competitors' fare changes very rapidly, usually within a few hours. Airlines can submit fare and rule changes to the fare aggregators up to eight times a day for a single market, a group of markets, or in larger batches.

Once fares have been submitted by the airline, ATPCO and SITA consolidate, process, and distribute the fares and associated data to their travel industry subscribers, such as the GDSs and airline CRSs. The new or revised fares are usually available in subscribers' systems within a few hours of filing. Once fare data are received by the GDS or other subscriber, it processes the data and builds itineraries to be displayed to its customers. The data are used by travel agents, consumers, and others for fare quotes, itinerary pricing, fare comparisons, booking, ticketing, and competitive analysis. The fare filing and distribution process is shown in Figure 3.3.

3.5.10 Changes in product distribution

As travel agency bookings grew to represent more than 85 percent of total reservations, GDS presence became an increasingly critical component of each airline's sales, marketing, and merchandising strategy. By the mid-1990s, distribution expense, including booking fees, travel agency commissions, and other incentive payments, had become the industry's third largest expense category after labor and fuel costs.

Although passengers booked by travel agents generally paid higher than average fares, agency-issued tickets were significantly more expensive to distribute than those sold through direct channels, such as the airlines' reservations call centers. Airlines paid a 10 percent base commission plus incentive-based overrides that in total represented almost 11 percent of total operating costs in 1993. The legacy airlines had historically been wary of reducing commission rates unilaterally due to fear of travel agency retribution and result- ing market share loss. However, carriers wished to reduce travel agents' control over the distribution. In the fall of 1994, Delta began reducing travel agent commissions, initially cutting international base commissions to 8 percent, then imposing a $50 maximum on domestic base commissions. The major airlines matched Delta's actions despite widespread protests from the travel agency community. As long as all carriers' base commission rates remained equal, no single carrier would bear the brunt of agency reactions.

Between 1999 and 2002, average annual payments from airlines to travel agencies dropped from $370 million to $159 million as carriers replaced flat commissions with incentives paid only to agencies meeting pre-defined revenue targets. Travel agents' leverage over airline suppliers continued to decline as marginal agencies failed to survive. On-line bookings grew from 7 percent in 1999 to 30 percent of total reservations in 2002. The legacy carriers saved over $200 million in distribution costs in the three years ending December 31, 2002 by reducing and eventually eliminating domestic base commissions.

As agencies' commission revenue declined, GDSs significantly increased their practice of rebating airline booking fees to travel agencies in order to retain loyalty and market share. Rebates paid by GDSs to travel agencies rose from $35 million in 1996 to $233 million in 2002 (GAO 2003).

As commissions dropped, booking fees became the focus of the airlines' distribution cost-cutting efforts. While CRS rules required that all airlines be charged the same fees, each GDS could set its own rates. Since travel agencies typically subscribed to a single GDS, nearly all carriers participated in all the major GDSs in order to get the broadest possible distribution. As a result, the GDSs had few constraints to keep them from raising booking fees. Average booking fees increased from $3.27 in 1996 to $4.36 per segment in 2002. As fees rose, airlines increasingly sought to bypass the GDS by establishing direct links between their CRS and the customer. The flow of payments between airline suppliers, intermediaries, and customers is illustrated in Figure 3.8.

During the same period, a powerful new channel, the Internet, was emerging that had enormous potential to change the dynamics of airline product distribution. By the late 1990s, the worldwide web created a real-time, direct-to-consumer, electronic marketplace for airline customers. For the financially struggling network carriers, e-commerce represented an opportunity to shift customers to a direct, low-cost channel with no commissions, incentives, or booking fees. Airlines had more experience than most companies with e-commerce because the CRS had provided an electronic marketplace with real-time pricing and inventory for more than 30 years.

The ability to reduce reliance on intermediaries, primarily travel agents, by increasing the number of customers using direct channels also brought the carriers much closer to their customers. Airlines could now more directly capture passenger shopping, booking, and ticketing data without going through the GDS or relying on reservation agents. This direct-to-consumer relationship enables more precise customer segmentation, targeted pricing, customized marketing, CRM initiatives, and collection of customer feedback.

Airlines rapidly developed their websites' capabilities to offer the same services as travel agencies, including schedule and fare comparisons, reservations, ticketing, itinerary changes, and cancellations. Electronic ticketing accelerated the conversion of customers from traditional to on-line channels.

The Internet opened up the "black box" of pricing, making the airlines' complex, rapidly changing fares much more transparent to customers. Since the first CRS was distributed to travel agencies in the late 1970s, agents have developed a wealth of knowledge about fare and schedule comparisons, tactics to find the lowest fare, fare categories, fare rules, and the unwieldy syntax used to create passenger records, book reservations, and issue tickets. Since the average passenger has no such knowledge, the airlines needed to find new ways to merchandise their products on-line that would not overwhelm, confuse, or

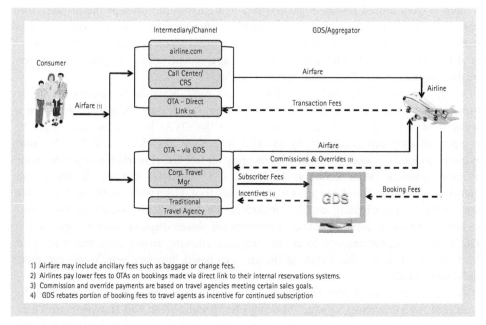

Intermediary/Channel   **GDS/Aggregator**

1) Airfare may include ancillary fees such as baggage or change fees.
2) Airlines pay lower fees to OTAs on bookings made via direct link to their internal reservations systems.
3) Commission and override payments are based on travel agencies meeting certain sales goals.
4) GDS rebates portion of booking fees to travel agents as incentive for continued subscription

FIGURE 3.8 Airline ticket distribution process

Source: US General Accounting Office (GAO-03-749 Airline Ticket Distribution 2003)

alienate customers. Southwest Airlines' simple fare displays became a model for other carriers.

Other companies were working to use the Internet as a platform for travel distribution. Microsoft launched Expedia.com, an on-line travel agency (OTA) in September 1996. Expedia became public in 1999 and reported its first profitable quarter in March 2001. Sabre and its partners launched Travelocity in March 1996. Travelocity merged with another leading OTA (Preview Travel) and became public in 2000. It is the third most-visited electronic commerce site in the world following Amazon.com and eBay.

Although booking and incentive schemes for OTAs were structured similarly to those used for travel agencies, the fees and average cost per booking are lower. OTA commissions were initially set at 5 percent with a $10 maximum per transaction. The airlines capped commissions at $10 per ticket for all airline tickets sold on-line or off-line during 2001, and some airlines—notably Northwest and KLM—eliminated commissions entirely for airline tickets sold on-line. In response, OTAs shifted their focus toward higher margin products, such as vacation packages and hotels, while adding service fees for bookings on non-commissionable airline tickets. Expedia emphasized a "merchant model", in which it purchased discounted airline seats and hotel rooms which it then marked up to sell to consumers.

Both OTAs featured on-line flight displays that emphasized price as the primary sort criteria, rather than quality of service, schedule, or brand, raising carriers' concerns that their product was being "commoditized". Price transparency intensified the airlines' tendency to match each other's lowest fares as uncompetitive fares might never be seen by the customer in an OTA's price-ordered display.

While the airlines expected to be able to shift most brand-loyal customers to their proprietary websites as their on-line capabilities improved, they knew there would be a segment of less brand-loyal customers drawn to the OTAs because of their desire to comparison-shop across carriers. In an effort to prevent Travelocity and Expedia from gaining too much market power in the emerging on-line travel market, a group of major airlines, including Delta, Continental, United, and Northwest Airlines, developed and launched an on-line travel agency, Orbitz.com, in 2001. Orbitz offered the best available fares from its participating carriers, including the lowest fares offered on their own websites. The site provided unbiased price-ordered screen displays. Orbitz bypassed the GDSs with direct connections to airline suppliers, allowing airline participants to avoid booking fees. It also offered state-of-the-art, web-based, low-fare search and itinerary-building technology.

Another significant development in online travel distribution in the late 1990s was the launch of two competing "opaque" booking sites, priceline.com and Hotwire.com. These sites mask the identity of the carrier and routing until a passenger has selected and purchased a flight that meets broadly defined requirements, such as desired origin, destination, and travel dates, at an agreed-upon price. The passenger trades the choice and certainty of carrier, departure time, routing, and flight duration for a fare that is lower than any available published fare.

Priceline.com, the first opaque site, has a "name your own price" model, whereby passengers enter the price that they're willing to pay for a round-trip flight between an origin and destination departing and arriving on specified dates during a relatively wide window, for example, between noon and 6.00 pm. The customer's bid is accepted if Priceline.com has an unpublished fare available from one of its airline suppliers that meets the customer's requirements and is equal to or below the customer's bid price. When a customer enters a bid, a credit card is required to purchase a confirmed seat. Hotwire's opaque business model also offers the customer lower prices in exchange for uncertainty. Both Priceline and Hotwire offer published fares and other travel products.

Airlines were initially fearful that participation in opaque sites would lead to a downward spiral of market prices. The key to preventing opaque fares from reducing published fares was to retain a high degree of uncertainty in the bidding process. As long as passengers cannot predict the carrier, flight, departure, and arrival time, a participating airline can generate incremental revenue from seats that would not otherwise be sold.

The GAO reported that bookings made through airline suppliers' Internet sites grew from 3 percent to 13 percent of total bookings between 1999 and 2002, while the percentage of total airline reservations made online grew from 7 percent to 30 percent. By 2002, the portion of airline tickets purchased through GDSs dropped to around 60 percent from a 1993 peak of 85 percent. During this time, the average cost per airline booking fell across all channels. Major airlines reduced their total distribution costs by approximately 26 percent between 1999 and 2002, or 44 percent on average per booking, driven by a 57 percent reduction in payments to travel agencies. In 2002, the average cost per airline ticket booked through a traditional travel agency was $30.66, through an OTA was $19.43, and through an airline website was $11.75 (GAO 2003).

Bookings through airline websites and on-line travel agents comprised more than 40 percent of domestic tickets sold in 2008 (Brunger 2010). The share of revenue booked through airline websites grew from 3 percent in 1999 to more than 33 percent in 2008. LCCs' proportion of sales booked on their own websites can be as high as 80 percent as many distribute their products primarily through their branded sites. On-line travel agencies represented 37 percent of total US travel bookings in 2008.

3.5.11 Impact of changes in product distribution on airfares

As Internet bookings grew, repercussions from travel agencies and corporate customers led the legacy carriers to agree to offer the same fares and inventory to "bricks and mortar" agencies as they offered through their own websites, eliminating "web only" specials. In return, the airlines negotiated lower GDS booking fees and a reduction in incentives paid by the GDSs to travel agencies. Most carriers now offer the same prices and inventory through all public channels, including OTAs, GDSs, and their branded websites.

Airline fares have declined substantially as the percentage of tickets sold over the Internet has increased. Fares dropped 24 percent in real dollars from the fourth quarter of 2000 to the fourth quarter of 2008. A recent study concluded that leisure travelers booking Continental Airlines through OTAs pay lower fares than customers booking through travel agents, despite having access to the same fares and availability (Brunger 2010). "Bricks and mortar" travel agencies continue to generate much higher valued bookings than OTAs, reflected in an average ticket price of $684 for GDS tickets versus $363 for OTA tickets in 2008 (Quinby and Merten 2009). Leisure passengers have shifted more quickly to Internet booking than business travelers, most likely because corporate negotiated fares are commonly managed through corporate travel agencies.

3.5.12 Impact of pricing and product changes on distribution

À la carte pricing is driving significant changes in airline distribution. Distribution systems require significant modification to allow carriers to offer and merchandise a broad range of unbundled products and branded fares. The shift to à la carte pricing has been called "the biggest change the air distribution channel has seen in years.... Exciting, scary, world-changing" (PhocusWright 2010).

ATPCO recently developed new products that allow carriers to automatically collect fees for ancillary services and differentiate their branded fare products. Many airlines have modified their websites to more effectively merchandise their branded fares by describing services and attributes included in each fare type versus those that are optional.

Many airlines have resisted distributing fee data to the GDSs, requiring that the information be directly accessed from their websites or reservation systems. As a result, the GDSs do not yet have the capability to accurately calculate, display, and distribute all-inclusive airfares, although they disclose all applicable fees and surcharges. In a widely-publicized dispute with the GDSs, AA has developed web-based technology allowing travel agents to book unbundled fares and optional services directly through its website. Other airlines are also seeking to reduce distribution costs. US Airways filed a lawsuit against Sabre for "monopolistic behavior". In a press release, US Airways said that "Sabre, which is a dominant distributor of airline fares and content to travel agents, has engaged in a pattern of exclusionary conduct to shut out competition, protect its monopoly pricing power, and maintain its technologically-obsolete business model" (US Airways, Inc. 2011)

3.6 Revenue management

Pricing and revenue management (PRM) seeks to maximize revenue by accepting the "right reservations at the right prices at the right time through the right channels". As discussed earlier, pricing determines which fare products an airline will offer. Revenue management (RM) determines how much of each fare product will be available for sale on each future flight at any point in time. RM affects yield by determining the mix of passenger reservations that will be accepted. RM also affects load factors by setting overbooking levels.

Pricing and revenue management may elect to change actual fares, inventory availability, or both, depending on the situation. In some cases, changing fares or fare rules may be the best strategy; in others, restricting or increasing availability may be better. The airline business is both seasonal and cyclical. Demand on a single flight can vary significantly from week to week, day to day, month to month, and year to year. RM forecasts the demand for each flight by fare type and O&D market. Holidays, special events, and peak times of year represent the best opportunities for RM to increase revenues by selectively accepting reservations. RM is also used to shift passengers from flights with excess demand to flights with less demand.

Since inventory changes are less visible to competitors than fare changes, network carriers have historically relied heavily on RM to achieve a revenue advantage. Carriers have traditionally not been able to easily access competitors' seat availability, while fare changes are visible within hours. For this reason, airlines have invested more heavily in improving revenue management than they have in pricing research.

3.6.1 Evolution of revenue management capabilities

As a result of heavy investment, airline RM capabilities have advanced significantly since deregulation. The legacy carriers have taken the lead in developing revenue management capabilities.

Inventory control refers to the mechanisms in the airline's CRS by which seat inventory is determined to be available for sale for a fare product or group of similarly-valued fare products. Inventory controls are sometimes called "capacity restrictions" because they restrict the sale of discount seats to a portion of the aircraft's total seat capacity.

An airline's internal CRS displays the total number of seats currently available for sale for each flight segment (the "authorization level") and the number of remaining seats available for sale in each O&D market/flight segment/fare class. A GDS can display inventory availability for up to 26 booking classes.

When a reservation is created, modified, or canceled, the passenger name record is created or updated in the airline's reservation system and the authorization level for a flight is updated. A CRS normally maintains current bookings and availability for a 330-day pre-departure booking window. For an airline of Delta's size, the CRS maintains detailed reservation and inventory records for more than 5,600 future flight departures per day. This means that more than 1.8 million scheduled departures are being managed at any time. Smaller airlines or LCCs may maintain fewer departure dates because of shorter booking windows.

Airline employees can access current reservations and seats available on a future flight departure through the CRS or the RM system. A reservation system's ability to process and maintain detailed flight information on each flight may be constrained by system archi-tecture, capacity, transaction volume, required response time, and reliability. Major changes to the existing CRS's are time-consuming and resource-intensive, partially due to the fact that systems are largely dependent on programs developed in the 1960s and 1970s. Airlines and GDS providers are now replacing these programs with more flexible web-based systems.

With the increase in discount fares and the expansion of hubs after deregulation, the potential number of different O&D market/fare product itineraries flowing over each flight leg grew dramatically. Discount allocation became increasingly complex. While carriers were originally allocating seats to just two categories of passengers on non-stop segments, they now had to allocate seat inventory among passengers requesting seats in ten or more fare classes of different values on dozens of competing local and connecting itineraries on each flight leg.

Hub expansion was the catalyst for the development of the next generation of RM, "origin and destination revenue management" or "network revenue management". In a hub-and-spoke network, the value of the reservation requests for seats on an individual flight segment varies greatly, depending on the passenger's itinerary (i.e., origin and destination) and the fare. Many connecting and local passengers compete for seats on a high demand flight segment. Network management considers the total value of a passen-ger's itinerary relative to competing requests for the impacted flight legs in accepting or denying reservation requests.

"Virtual nesting" was developed in the late 1980s as a first approach to network management. In virtual nesting, the potential combinations of itineraries and fare classes that could be sold on a particular flight leg are ranked in terms of their estimated revenue value. O&D market/fare class itineraries are assigned to 10–20 "virtual" inventory buckets of descending value, with market/fare classes of similar value grouped within the same bucket.

By grouping many O&D market/fare class itineraries into a smaller number of inventory buckets, virtual nesting eliminates the technical, operational, and financial challenges of maintaining separate inventory for all potential O&D market/fare class combinations. Seats are protected for sale in O&D markets/fare classes in higher valued inventory buckets, while seat availability is restricted for lower valued O&D markets/fares. Virtual nesting allows RM to consider the network contribution of itineraries of similar values grouped in one inventory bucket relative to those clustered in another bucket in accepting or denying reservations. Virtual nesting provided airlines with revenue boosts of up to 2 percent relative to previous methods of inventory control.

While virtual nesting is still in place at many airlines, the largest network airlines have deployed a more advanced method of inventory control called "origin and destination" revenue management. With O&D RM controls, availability is based on whether the value of a reservation request is higher than the expected opportunity cost of selling a seat to another passenger, called the "bid price". The bid price considers the value and expected demand for all itineraries that could potentially utilize seats on a particular flight segment.

Major CRS changes are required to implement O&D inventory controls using bid prices. Full bid price controls theoretically eliminate the need for nested fare classes, inventory buckets, and booking limits, replacing them with a basic "yes or no" response to an availability request. Carriers have used different methods for implementing network management which have required various degrees of CRS modification. Airlines that have implemented O&D controls with bid pricing have achieved 1–3 percent incremental revenue gains (Phillips 2005).

3.6.2 Revenue management concepts and models

The first revenue management discipline was overbooking—selling more tickets than there were physical seats on the aircraft in order to compensate for the tendency of customers to cancel or fail to show up ("no-show") for their reserved flights. After deregulation, the role of RM grew to include demand forecasting, discount allocation, and network (O&D) management.

Demand forecasting is the basis of all RM decisions. Demand on a single flight can vary significantly from season to season, week to week, day to day, month to month, and year to year. Airline passenger demand is heavily impacted by economic cycles, seasonality, holidays, special events, natural and man-made disasters, terrorism, operational disruptions, and a multitude of other factors. The passenger mix, in terms of trip purpose, connection versus local passengers, fare mix, and O&D itineraries, varies widely from market to market and flight to flight. RM forecasts the demand for each flight using up to 24 months or more of historical data.

Revenue management's demand forecast considers both actual seats sold historically on the flight and estimates of demand turned away due to capacity constraints. The demand forecasting model typically predicts the distribution of passengers by fare type based on the historical distribution of customers purchasing tickets at various price points on the flight. It also considers the "sell-up" rate, which is an estimate of how many passengers will buy a higher priced ticket when the fare they initially request is not available. RM also forecasts no-shows and cancellations based on history for the particular flight and recent flight patterns.

Airline demand forecasts have historically been based on time series models that incorporate seasonality and trends. Forecasts are typically updated at least once a day at approximately 15–20 specified points in time prior to the flight's departure. Forecasts are updated more frequently closer to departure as the pace of incoming bookings increases. Analysts can also adjust forecasts manually to reflect market variables that the forecast may not adequately reflect, such as a special event that moves from one city to another each year. Some carriers are replacing or supplementing time-series models with customer choice-based forecasting models.

Overbooking determines the total number of seats that will be authorized for sale on a flight for each cabin of service. Overbooking compensates for the fact that as many as half the passengers with confirmed reservations will either cancel their reservations or will not show up on the day of departure. No-shows and cancellations are impacted by relevant fare restrictions, such as non-refundability and change fees. In 1992, it was reported that overbooking generated 40 percent of revenue management benefits.

In general, airlines do not overbook First Class, conservatively overbook Business Class, and more aggressively overbook Coach Class. Some airlines, such as JetBlue, do not overbook coach class due to low no-show rates and customer service policies. The number of confirmed passengers that are denied boarding on a sold-out flight are called oversales or denied boardings (DBs). Since airline seats are perishable, empty seats at departure (referred to as "spoiled" seats) represent a lost revenue opportunity if the airline had the opportunity to sell the seats at some point during the flight's booking period.

The airlines' goal in overbooking is to maximize net revenue, or revenue minus esti- mated oversales and spoilage costs. Both overbooking and spoilage carry financial, oper- ational, and customer service risks. An overbooking optimization model balances the risks of oversales and spoilage to maximize expected revenue on a flight. Factors considered include aircraft capacity, forecasted demand by passenger type, average ticket price by passenger type, forecast cancellation and no-show rates, oversales and spoilage costs, and the likelihood that a turned-away reservation request will choose another flight on the same airline (recapture). The total number of seats to be sold (the authorization level) is determined by the overbooking model. For example, a flight with 200-seat capacity might have 230 seats authorized for sale.

Since the introduction of automated overbooking tools in the late 1970s, airlines have continued to improve overbooking. Demand, no-show, and cancellation rates and costs vary greatly across flights, markets, and customer segments. As a result, overbooking levels also vary significantly across the network, with authorization levels generally higher in business-oriented markets, where business passengers tend to no-show at higher rates, and lower in leisure-oriented markets, where reservations are more firm.

In some instances, a flight or sequential flights may become heavily overbooked due to flight cancellations, inclement weather, weight restrictions, operational issues, or other unpredictable events. RM will try to shift passengers to other flights prior to the departure date, if possible. RM analysts work with airport agents on the day of departure to retain as much revenue as possible by re-accommodating any oversold passengers on the airline's own flights, rather than sending them to other carriers.

Many carriers use an auction at the gate to manage heavily overbooked flights. The gate agent announces that the flight is overbooked and solicits volunteers who are willing to give up their seats and be confirmed on a later flight in exchange for a travel voucher. If volunteers are difficult to find, the voucher value will be increased until there are enough volunteers to avoid involuntarily denying any passengers from boarding (commonly referred to as "bumping"). Vouchers are less costly to airlines than cash payments because passengers don't always use the vouchers within the stated time limits. When the vouchers are redeemed, it is often for a ticket costing more than the voucher value, thereby generating incremental revenue.

The amount needed to persuade customers to willingly give up their seats on an oversold flight can escalate when many volunteers are needed. Delta Air Lines recently introduced an automated auction system that solicits passengers for oversold flights within 24 hours of check-in and asks them to enter the voucher value they would be willing to take in order to give up their seats. The gate agent then accepts the lowest bids from customers willing to give up their seats, as needed. In this way, the auction becomes less transparent to passengers, which may reduce the size of the needed voucher.

Setting overbooking limits too high will result in denied boarding costs. Denied boarding cost incorporates the value of any air, hotel, ground transportation, and meal vouchers, considering breakage (unused vouchers) and any incremental revenue generated upon voucher redemption. It also includes the cost of re-accommodating a passenger denied boarding on another flight, sometimes at full fare on another carrier. By law, domestic passengers involuntarily denied boarding are entitled to up to $1,300 in cash, depending on the length of delay. Involuntary boardings are exceptionally rare due to the effectiveness of the airlines' auction processes. According to DOT, only 65,000 or 1.09 passengers per 10,000 were involuntarily denied boarding on US carriers in 2010.

Spoilage results when overbooking is too conservative (low). The spoilage rate is the fraction of empty seats at departure that could have been booked. The spoilage cost is calculated by multiplying the number of spoiled seats by the estimated value of those seats. Spoilage tends to be more costly for airlines than oversales because of the high cost of turning away last minute, full fare customers. In practice, very few flights are completely sold out during the pre-departure booking period since the potential revenue to be gained warrants the risk of keeping full Y class seats available through departure.

Airlines supplement load factor with additional metrics for measuring overbooking effectiveness, including the number, rate, and cost of denied boardings and spoilage. The cost of a denied boarding (DB) increases with the number of oversold passengers on a flight. Some overbooking of coach class is almost always necessary to optimize a flight's revenue, given expected cancellations and no-shows. Figure 3.9 summarizes the key performance indicators used to measure overbooking performance.

Overbooking allows an airline to offer many more seats than it otherwise would be able to sell. Without overbooking, AA estimated that about 15 percent of seats would be unused on flights sold out at departure (Smith et al. 1992). Overbooking also increases the chance that business passengers with the highest time sensitivity will be accommodated on their desired flights.

Discount allocation is the process used to determine booking limits or "protection levels" to limit the number of seats available for sale at discounted fares. A booking limit is the number of seats available to a discount fare while a protection level is the number of seats reserved for future higher-fare customers. If a flight has a total authorization (overbooking) level of 100 seats, two fare types, and 50 seats reserved or "protected" for sale to high fare passengers, the booking limit for the discount fare is 50 seats.

Optimization models used in a virtual nesting environment for discount allocation are typically based on the concept of "expected marginal revenue" (EMSR). Forecasts by booking class are used to estimate the probability that selling a seat at a discounted fare

MEASUREMENT	METRIC	CALCULATION	PRIMARY USAGE
Overbooking	Spoilage	Number of spoiled (empty) seats on flights closed for sale during booking period	Assess impact of OB strategy on flight performance
Overbooking	Spoilage Rate	Ratio of number of spoiled seats to passengers boarded	Measure overbooking effectiveness
Overbooking	Spoilage Cost	No. of spoiled seats @ average fare when flight was closed for sale	Measure overbooking effectiveness, cost of overly conservative OB
Overbooking	Denied Booking Rate	No. of denied boardings per 10K passengers boarded	Measure voluntary DBs (internal) or involuntary DBs relative to competitors (DOT)
Overbooking	Denied Boardings – Voluntary	No. of passengers denied boarding (oversales) per oversold flight	Measure OB effectiveness & impact on customer service (internal)
Overbooking	Denied Boarding Cost - Voluntary	Avg cost per denied passenger, i.e., vouchers, reaccommodation cost, loss of goodwill	Calculation of future overbooking levels; compare to spoilage cost
Overbooking	Denied Boarding Cost - Involuntary	Reaccom w/in 2hrs: $400/per DB Reaccom in >2hrs; $800 per DB	Assess cost of involuntary denied boardings
Overbooking	Load Factor on Closed Flights	Weighted average final LF on flights sold out prior to departure	Measure OB error (too high or too low relative to flown LF)

FIGURE 3.9 Overbooking performance metrics

will displace a later-arriving, higher-fare passenger (typically business travelers). The optimal number of seats to protect for higher-valued passengers is the point at which the marginal revenue for preserving an additional seat for a projected higher-valued traveler is equal to the marginal revenue of selling a seat to a discount traveler. The decision to accept or deny a reservation request is based on the relative value of fares in each inventory bucket, the probability of future higher bookings and the probability that passengers who initially request a lower fare will purchase a ticket at a higher fare. (See Talluri, Chapter 26.)

The optimization model recommends booking limits and protection levels for each inventory bucket on each flight in the system. Once initial allocation levels have been set and loaded into the CRS, each flight is automatically re-optimized at approximately 15–20 fixed dates prior to departure. Revenue management typically begins monitoring and optimizing inventory availability many months in advance, particularly for high-demand or high-revenue flights.

RM analysts typically review only a relatively small subset of critical flights. Critical flights are the flights viewed as most likely to benefit from analyst intervention. Critical flights may be identified by heuristics, high forecasting errors, or opportunity for revenue improvement. They typically represent about 5–10 percent of all the flights in the system. Recommended booking limits for "non-critical" flights are typically automatically loaded from the RM system into the reservation system.

Analysts can manually adjust the forecasts or other model inputs and re-optimize discount allocations. Special events, holidays, and peak seasons with especially high demand may require an analyst to adjust forecasts to account for information not reflected in historical data. The highest demand flights and time periods offer the greatest opportunity for RM to improve the airline's bottom line.

Network management Several network carriers have implemented O&D (network) RM based on bid prices. Bid price controls set a threshold price such that a reservation request is accepted only if its expected revenue exceeds the threshold price and rejected otherwise (van Ryzin and Talluri 2004). A bid price essentially represents the opportunity cost of selling an additional seat on a particular flight segment. On connecting flights, the bid prices for each requested flight leg are added together to determine whether the request will be accepted.

In one method, bid prices are calculated by updating the O&D market/fare class effective revenue values and inventory bucket mappings used in virtual nesting. This method allows carriers to use existing virtual nesting-based control mechanisms in the CRS without having to forecast demand for every O&D/fare class combination. Bid prices are recalculated as frequently as possible for all flight legs in the system, based on current bookings, fares, and forecasts.

Another approach to implementing O&D RM relies on forecasting demand for each potential O&D market/fare class combination. This method allows calculation of bid prices directly for the highest volume O&D itineraries in the system. Bid prices are then used to accept or reject reservations as discussed above.

O&D RM may be more intuitive for users than virtual nesting once appropriate training and change management processes have been completed. By focusing on O&D markets rather than flight legs, it improves alignment between RM and pricing. Many of the largest US network carriers and several major international carriers have implemented some form of bid pricing, which remains the "state-of-the-art" RM approach today. Chapter 26 by Talluri discusses the calculation of bid prices in more detail.

3.6.3 Impact of hybrid fare structures on revenue management

Competition with low-cost carriers has driven major changes in the legacy carriers' fare structures. The legacy carriers have increasingly been compelled to match LCC fare levels and to reduce restrictions. A legacy carrier may publish higher fares along with LCC-competitive fares in the same markets to attract customers who are willing to pay to fly on a full-service network carrier. Competition with LCCs has thus resulted in "hybrid" fare structures in many markets.

The barriers that legacy airlines have constructed to target different customer segments with differentiated fare products are crumbling under competitive pressure. RM models have historically assumed that segment demands are independent and that customers can be effectively prohibited from "buying down" to lower fares by the use of fare restrictions. Relaxation or removal of pricing restrictions changes customer behavior—customer segment demands become interdependent. In many cases, the removal of restrictions allows customers to purchase lower-priced tickets. Such "buy down" can dilute revenue.

In a restriction-based fare structure, customers may purchase a fare product in the next higher fare class (i.e., "sell-up") if they cannot meet the restrictions of a lower fare. Airlines encourage passengers to purchase higher fares by restricting sales of discount fares. Sell-up is reduced when low, minimally restricted fares are available. RM models require adjustment to reflect the change in customer buying patterns when minimally restricted fares are offered in a hybrid fare structure (Ratliff and Weatherford 2010).

Airlines' forecasting models have traditionally not considered competitive schedules or fares. New customer choice-based forecasting models have been developed which assume dependent demand and incorporate current competitive fares and schedules. The new models utilize previously unavailable Internet customer shopping data to model customer choice among competitive flight options.

Optimization models using dependent demand forecasts have also been developed, tested, and evaluated. Less than 25 percent of carriers have modified their RM systems to reflect the virtual collapse of restriction-based segmentation in markets with low-cost competition. Most are still using simple heuristics to adjust RM models to reflect fare changes in these markets. Recent research has shown that carriers can achieve up to a 5 percent revenue improvement by replacing existing models with customer choice models (Ratliff and Weatherford 2010).

3.6.4 Revenue management systems

Airlines initially relied heavily upon individual analysts' market knowledge and experience to predict flight demand and set appropriate inventory levels. By the mid-1980s, most of the legacy airlines' networks had grown well beyond analysts' capabilities to manage flights effectively with manual and semi-automated methods. Several airlines introduced automated models and systems to forecast demand and optimize inventory availability by the late 1980s.

AA introduced its fully automated RM system, DINAMO (Dynamic Inventory Optimization and Maintenance Optimizer), for its domestic routes in 1988 (Smith et al. 1992). DINAMO reduced the proportion of flights requiring analyst review from 100 percent to approximately 5 percent. The system improved the airline's revenue by an estimated $1.4 billion in its first three years and was estimated to be worth $1 billion annually in 1998 (Cook 1998).

Other large carriers either internally developed or purchased RM systems from outside vendors, such as Sabre, DFI, Aeronomics, and PROS. Delta reported that it generated $300 million in incremental annual revenue in 1984 through yield management (Koten 1984). United, working with DFI, implemented its first automated RM system in the mid-1980s. All the major US carriers and many LCCs now use automated RM systems.

3.7 EVALUATING PRICING AND REVENUE MANAGEMENT PERFORMANCE

When fares were regulated and RM was limited to overbooking, airlines primarily used load factor (LF) to measure performance. The tendency to focus on maximizing load factor carried over into the early years after deregulation. Concerned about widespread discounting and the resulting decline in the average fare paid, legacy airlines eventually shifted their focus toward improving yield. In some cases, carriers began to over-emphasize yield, resulting in low LF flights with high yields. In contrast, airlines that still focused primarily on LF had full airplanes but low yields. Carriers shifted back and forth between LF and yield-focused strategies for many years before recognizing that the key to maximizing revenue was to balance the two metrics.

The most important metric currently used by airline managers to measure the effectiveness of PRM is Revenue per Available Seat Mile or RASM which is calculated as passenger revenue divided by available seats flown one mile or kilometer (available seat miles or ASMs). The components of RASM are yield and load factor, therefore changes in either or both metrics can drive RASM improvements or deterioration. Figure 3.1 shows the calculation of RASM. Year-over-year change in RASM is used by domestic carriers to monitor their revenue performance relative to the industry average. RASM helps an airline isolate factors impacting the industry as a whole versus the carrier in particular. For example, a strike will generally cause a carrier's RASM growth to be lower than the industry average. Historical RASM, LF, and yield trends are extensively used to adjust schedules, pricing, and RM strategies.

Pricing performance is difficult to isolate. It can drive RASM, load factor, and yield performance. Expected QSI share (versus actual share), GDS booking share, on-line booking share, and other competitive measures are commonly used to measure pricing performance. However, all of these metrics are also influenced by revenue management decisions.

RM effectiveness is generally measured by estimated revenue dilution and spoilage. Revenue dilution estimates require an estimate of how much higher-valued demand could have been accommodated if more discount passengers had been turned away. Spoilage measurements depend on whether a flight was closed for sale in discount fare categories with additional demand but departed with empty seats.

The widely accepted Revenue Opportunity Model (ROM) measures RM effectiveness. Traditional measures (LF, denied boardings, etc.) are affected by external factors such as schedule changes, fare changes, or competitive actions. ROM isolates the effect of RM from these external factors. ROM calculates the difference between the maximum revenue that could be achieved with perfect hindsight (i.e., accepting passengers from highest to lowest fare) and the minimum revenue that would be generated without RM controls (i.e., accepting passengers on a first-come, first-served basis). The difference between the maximum revenue and the minimum is the total revenue opportunity. The actual revenue is compared to the total revenue opportunity to determine the percentage of total opportunity achieved. For example, if the maximum revenue on a flight with "perfect RM" was estimated to be $30,000 and the minimum revenue with "no RM" was $10,000, the total revenue opportunity was $20,000. If actual revenue were $22,000, the carrier realized $12,000 or 60 percent of the total revenue opportunity. The percentage of revenue opportunity achieved can be used to monitor RM performance over time (Smith et al. 1992). Revenue opportunity lost can be decomposed into revenue lost through dilution and revenue lost through spoilage to help managers focus on corrective actions.

Forecasts always carry some degree of error, so RM closely monitors forecasts to detect any significant deviation from historical patterns that may require intervention to adjust the forecast based on current market trends or other information.

Other metrics measure the amount of revenue "leakage" (loss) caused by lack of adherence to pricing, inventory, or ticketing rules, such as advance purchase restrictions or refundability rules. If these rules are not enforced, months of RM effort may be wasted. In one year, Delta Air Lines recovered more than $300 million in lost revenues by more stringently enforcing cancellation policies, ticket change fees, advance purchase restrictions, and other rules. The key performance metrics used to measure RM performance are summarized in Figure 3.1.

3.8 CURRENT TRENDS IN AIRLINE PRICING AND RM

The majority of research and development in the PRM field over the past 30 years has focused on revenue management. RM's effectiveness is highly dependent on the accuracy of the underlying forecasting and optimization models. As a result, investments in improving RM models and related technology have historically been easy to justify and have yielded substantial incremental revenue benefits. Airlines have gained up to 11 percent improvement in revenue and profit through RM investments, more than the gains available through similar investments in other areas.

As the industry matured and price competition intensified, pricing became primarily focused on matching competitive fares. Since individual carriers have historically had little control over market prices, research and development dollars were perceived to be better spent on RM. However, recent changes in the fare environment are reducing the effectiveness of fare restrictions and current RM models. The Internet has made new data available for modeling consumer shopping and purchase behaviors which may be more useful in price optimization.

As a result of these changes, airlines, solution providers, and academics are increasingly directing their efforts toward pricing. Prior to the emergence of restriction-free fare structures, demand for different fare types was assumed to be independent and competition was not explicitly modeled. Research is increasingly focused on the development of customer choice models that more accurately reflect the current environment where customers choose from multiple flight options across different carriers and their decisions are impacted by the available alternatives. Though many airlines use automated tools to make the fare management process more efficient, accurate, and reliable, pricing decision support systems in place at major airlines are still relatively simplistic. Most airline systems do not yet have sophisticated elasticity modeling or price optimization models. R&D in this area is rapidly expanding. The trends discussed in this section will significantly impact airline pricing for the next 5 to 10 years.

3.8.1 Customer choice-based forecasting

Customer choice-based forecasting and optimization models have recently been developed that more effectively maximize revenue in an environment where a reduction in pricing restrictions has reduced the efficacy of traditional segmentation mechanisms. Most legacy carriers with significant low-cost competition are likely to convert their RM models to these methods within the next several years to take advantage of the estimated 5 percent incremental revenue opportunity.

3.8.2 Customer-centric pricing

Airline pricing and RM decisions have historically been made on a transaction-by-transaction basis. The decision to accept or deny a passenger reservation request is based primarily on the potential revenue of the particular request relative to other potential reservations, rather than the value a customer brings to the airline over the longer term. Frequent flier status may provide enhanced access to award, upgrade, and preferred seats, among other benefits, but status is generally based on mileage, as opposed to revenue collected from the customer.

Consolidated customer information is required to estimate customer lifetime value. In the past 10 years, carriers have created customer relationship management databases that include loyalty, booking, ticketing, revenue, shopping, and other customer data. These databases provide airlines with a more comprehensive understanding of the lifetime contribution of different customers, enabling strategies such as customized promotions, differential pricing, priority seat availability, and other customer service offerings. As these databases are expanded and enriched with on-line shopping data, this data will be increasingly used in pricing, RM, and related merchandising decisions.

3.8.3 Unbundled pricing and branded fare families

The transition from restriction-based pricing to unbundled pricing among legacy carriers shows no sign of slowing down. US airlines earned $7.8 billion in 2009 in ancillary revenues compared to $5.5 billion in 2008, an increase of nearly 42 percent. Ancillary revenue includes ticket change and baggage fees, but excludes fees for preferred seating, on-board food and beverages, entertainment, or other miscellaneous fees.

With the unbundling of fares, airlines have developed a new way of designing and merchandising the air transportation product and related services. With branded fare products and optional services, customers can effectively create a customized air product that best meets their particular requirements. Carriers are in effect "rebundling" the product into new packages that include particular services and product attributes designed to meet the needs of targeted customer segments. This bundled packaging approach is commonly used in many other industries, such as mobile telecommunications, and it is rapidly becoming the norm in the airline industry.

Air Canada was successful in introducing its à la carte pricing approach in part because Canada is a near-monopoly. In addition, the carrier carefully planned, analyzed, and launched the initiative with strong, cohesive marketing and communication. "We have been doing à-la-carte pricing for six years and it is popular with our customers. . . . About 47 per cent of our customers choose a higher fare product for its attributes—even with lower fares available" (Montie Brewer, CEO, Air Canada, April 2009) (Doganis 2009). US carriers, in contrast, have implemented new fees and increased others on an incremental basis. Adding fees in the US is more difficult because the market is far more competitive than Canada.

"Branded fare families" are created by re-bundling air transportation with selected services. US carriers have only introduced these once the "unbundling" process had already begun. This reduced the opportunity to communicate the benefits. Careless execution, poor marketing, and lack of communication could thwart the success of the unbundling strategy.

The history of the legacy airlines as full-service carriers creates a challenging dilemma. While low-cost airlines are perceived to deliver good value with few "frills", the legacy carriers are perceived to be "nickel and diming" consumers when they charge for services that were built into their products during the regulatory era. As noted by Michael Bell of Spencer Stuart in a 2009 article for Businessweek.com, "Despite being the most unionized airline in the U.S. and proudly offering nothing to eat or drink... Southwest enjoys outstanding customer service ratings and loyalty as well as the best financial returns in the industry" (Bell 2009).

The shift to unbundled pricing will drive broad changes to pricing and RM models and practices. For example, current RM models do not forecast demand for optional services or consider fees in evaluating the value of one itinerary versus another. Price elasticity estimates previously used for revenue analysis may no longer be valid as a $1 change in a fee may have a different effect on demand than a $1 change in the base fare. Newly "re-bundled" products will have different demand profiles than previous fare products. Pricing departments need to develop new ways of understanding how different customer segments value unbundled services and what they are willing to pay for optional services. With better knowledge of what the customer values, carriers can re-configure their products to offer more targeted packages of air transportation, features, and services.

Aggregation of CRM, loyalty, and RM data will be required to properly segment and value customer requests based on their propensity to select certain value-added features and services. The legacy airlines' current efforts to increase direct distribution coincide with the changes occurring in airline product design, merchandising, and distribution. With an increased volume of transactions coming through the Internet and direct links to the CRS, airlines will be able to use customer responses to different optional service combinations and price points to optimize product offerings to targeted customer segments.

3.8.4 Dynamic pricing

Dynamic pricing focuses on how changes in the price of a single fare product impact demand, considering consumer preferences, willingness-to-pay, and competitive factors. This contrasts with traditional RM, which considers how the availability of a fixed set of fare products within a single inventory class impacts demand. Researchers have recently become better able to test and simulate customer price sensitivity as a result of the greater availability of customer shopping, booking, ticketing, and competitive information from the Internet, enabling the development of new price optimization models. (See Aviv and Vulcano, Chapter 23.)

3.8.5 Price optimization

Price optimization models and systems focus on ensuring fares are set optimally based on customer willingness-to-pay, demand, and competitive fares. Research has recently focused on improving airlines' understanding of price elasticity. These findings can then be used in automated decision support models to help pricing analysts set fares that are more appropriate for each market segment.

3.8.6 Direct distribution

More than 40 percent of airline bookings are made on-line. Although on-line travel bookings are expected to grow at a slower rate over the next several years, airline website enhancements, GDS bypass, and other carrier-driven initiatives will continue to drive bookings and other transactions from traditional channels to the Internet. Although the average travel agency-booked ticket continues to generate a higher average fare than tickets booked through other channels, the LCCs have a double-digit distribution cost advantage relative to legacy carriers due to their greater reliance on direct channels.

In late 2010, AA removed its flights from Orbitz, due to the OTA's unwillingness to bypass the GDS and use the airline's direct link to access its flights, fares, and availability. Orbitz is owned by TravelPort, which also owns the Worldspan GDS used by Orbitz. Other OTAs supported Orbitz' stance by removing AA's flights from their systems or moving them to the bottom of screen displays. This is likely to be the initial skirmish in a long battle as airlines seek to reduce their distribution costs by moving bookings to less expensive channels.

The growth of XML messaging technology, more robust computing power, and lower connectivity costs have enabled carriers to build efficient direct links to their reservation systems. Carriers have requested that the GDSs integrate direct connections from their CRS systems into travel agency displays. So far, the GDSs have refused, although some appear ready to integrate Southwest Airlines' fares and availability in order to gain access to Southwest's flights.

By providing more direct links, carriers will be able to more effectively merchandise branded fare families and "upsell" passengers to purchase optional services. Airlines will be able to "push" targeted offers, including fares, features, and services, to customers, as opposed to relying on the GDS to pull together an offer based on the airlines' data. The GDSs may permanently lose access to the fares and availability of some carriers. Passengers' ability to shop and compare fares will be impaired if large carriers' flights and fares are not available through OTAs.

3.8.7 Alliance pricing and RM

Anti-trust immune alliances operating under open skies agreements will continue to grow. Direct mergers between US domestic and foreign-owned airlines are currently prohibited because of US foreign ownership laws. As a result, global alliances are likely to continue to be used to expand airlines' international networks. One of the biggest challenges in implementing and operating alliances is integrating the CRS and RM systems of the partners. The airlines today are not able to optimize combined revenue through their RM systems. Further research and systems development will be needed to allow alliance partners to maximize the value of their combined networks.

3.9 SUMMARY

Airlines have made significant strides in pricing and revenue management since gaining the freedom to set prices, select routes, and determine schedules more than three decades ago. The discipline has produced billions of dollars of incremental profit for the industry since yield management was introduced in the mid-1980s. While PRM benefits have not been able to completely offset the cost disadvantages of the legacy airlines, they have helped the survivors of deregulation stay aloft amidst an ever-growing list of low-cost competitors.

REFERENCES

ATA (1970) *ATA Annual Report*. Washington, DC: Air Transport Association.

—— (1975) *ATA Annual Report*. Washington, DC: Air Transport Association.

—— (2009) *Fares and Finance*. Washington, DC, http://www.airlines.org/economics/ finance/ PaPricesYield.htm.

—— (2010) *ATA Handbook*. Washington, DC, http://www.airlines.org/products/Airline-HandbookCh2.htm.

ATPCO (2010) *Glossary*. Washington, DC, http://www.atpco.net/atpco/products/glossary_ c.shtml.

Bell, M. (2009) "What You Can Learn from the Airlines", *Bloomberg Business Week* June 16, www.businessweek.com, accessed March 22, 2011.

Boeing (2009) http://www.boeing.com/commercial/products.html.

Brunger, W. (2010) "The Impact of the Internet on Airline Fares", *Journal of Revenue and Pricing Management* 9 (1/2): 66–93.

Castro, J. (1992) "ROBERT CRANDALL: This Industry Is Always in the Grip of Its Dumbest Competitors", *Time Magazine* May.

Committee for a Study of Competition in the U.S. Airline Industry, T. R. (1999) *Entry and Competition in the U.S. Airline Industry*. Washington, DC: Transportation Research Board.

Cook, T. (1998) "Sabre Soars", *ORMS Today* 25/3.

Copeland, D. G., Mason, R. O., and McKenney, J. L. (1995) "SABRE: The Development of Information-Based Competence and Execution of Information-Based Competition", *IEEE Annals of the History of Computing* 17/3: 30–56.

Crandall, R. L. (1998) "How Airline Pricing Works", *American Way Magazine* May 1.

Cross, R. G. (1997) *Revenue Mangement: Hard-Core Tactics for Market Domination*. New York: Broadway Books.

Doganis, R. (2009) *Flying off Course: Airline Economics and Marketing*, 4th edn. Abingdon: Routledge/CourseSmart.

GAO (1996) *AIRLINE DEREGULATION; Changes in Airfares, Service and Safety at Small, Medium-Sized and Large Communities*. Washington, DC: U.S. General Accounting Office.

—— (2003) *AIRLINE TICKETING: Impact of Changes in the Airline Ticket Distribution Industry*. Washington, DC: U.S. General Accounting Office.

Hopper, M. D. (1990) "Rattling SABRE—New Ways to Compete on Information", *Harvard Business Review* May–June: 118–25.

IATA (2010) Website facts and figures. Montreal: IATA, www.iata.org.

Koten, J. (1984) "In Airlines' Rate War, Small Daily Skirmishes often Decide Winners", *Wall Street Journal* August 24.

Kumar, N. and Rogers, B. (2000) "easyJet—The Web's Favorite Airline", *IMD—Institute for Management Development*. https://ecms.imd.ch/ecms/groups/cs_public/@i/@cs/@caid/@30873/@cimd_p129941/documents/cs_imd_p129941. hcst, accessed November 7, 2011.

Lee, D. and Ito, H. (2003) *Low Cost Carrier Growth in the U.S. Airline Industry: Past, Present and Future*. Providence, RI: Department of Economics, Box B, Brown University.

Petzinger, T. (1995) *Hard Landing*. New York: Random House.

Phillips, R. L. (2005) *Pricing and Revenue Optimization*. Palo Alto: Stanford University Press.

PhoCusWright (2010) *Travel Innovation and Technology Trends: 2010 and Beyond*. New York: PhoCusWright.

Quinby, D. and Merten, R. (2009) *The Role and Value of the Global Distribution Systems in Travel Distribution*. New York: PhoCusWright Inc.

Ratliff, R. M. and Weatherford, L. R. (2010) "Review of Revenue Management Methods with Dependent Demand", *Journal of Revenue and Pricing Management* 9/4: 326–40.

Reed, D. (2009) "Low-cost Airlines Grab 30% of Travel Market vs. Traditional Rivals", *USA Today* November 10.

Schmitt, E. (1987) "The Art of Devising Air Fares", *The New York Times* March 4.

Seaney, R. (2010) farecompare.com. April 8, http://rickseaney.com/timeline-2008-airfare-hike-attempts/.

Silk, A. J. and Michael, S. C. (1993) *American Airlines Value Pricing (A)*. Boston, MA: Harvard Business School Publishing.

Smith, B. C., Leimkuhler, J. F., and Darrow, R. M. (1992) "Yield Management at American Airlines", *Interfaces* 22/1: 8–31.

Star Alliance (2010) Star Alliance website. http://www.staralliance.com/en/.

US Airways (2011) "US Airways Files Antitrust Lawsuit against Sabre: Seeks to end Sabre's monopoly pricing power for airline ticket distribution and cites Sabre's anti-competitive and anti-consumer behavior", US Airways, Tempe, A2, April 21.

US Department of Transportation (2009) *Air Travel Consumer Report*. December. Washington, DC: US Department of Transportation.

van Ryzin, G. J. and Talluri, K. T. (2004) *The Theory and Practice of Revenue Management*. New York: Springer.

CHAPTER 4

....

ELECTRIC POWER
PRICING

....

ROBERT WILSON

POWER from electricity is so fundamental to a modern economy that it is commonly viewed as a necessity rather than an optional commodity or service. Its uses in residences, commerce, and industry include cooling and heating, lighting, motors, and electronic devices. Electric power is undifferentiated and available nearly constantly, but the diversity of its applications enables some differentiation of retail products and prices via conditions of delivery such as time, location, and reliability, and similar differentiation occurs in wholesale markets. Some countries allow competitive wholesale markets but fewer allow retail competition. Often the local utility is a regulated monopoly with an obligation to provide universal service according to the terms of an approved tariff, and vertically integrated except that major industrial customers can contract directly with independent generators. In the United States, retail operations (except for utilities owned by municipalities) are regulated locally by state agencies, while wholesale operations are regulated by the Federal Energy Regulatory Commission. Typically, a retail utility is allowed to recover its costs and a return on capital, and wholesale markets are conducted by a regulated system operator that manages the regional transmission grid. Regulations emphasize equal access on nondiscriminatory terms and penalize attempts to exploit market power. These features limit the scope for product and price differentiation to features directly related to the costs of fuel, generation, wholesale transmission, and retail distribution. Where non-utility providers are allowed, they resell power purchased in wholesale markets, and their products differ chiefly in how much risk of price variation is borne by retail customers.

4.1 BACKGROUND ON THE ELECTRIC
POWER INDUSTRY

....

The electricity industry is both capital and fuel intensive. It has a unique supply chain that runs from fuels (hydro, nuclear, coal, gas, oil, wind, etc.) to power plants adapted to use these fuels to generate power that is injected first into the high-voltage transmission grid and then into local distribution networks from which customers can withdraw power at low voltages. Each stage is managed according to strict engineering standards because the equipment is vulnerable to damage, and supply interruptions are costly to customers. Necessarily, power quality (e.g., voltage and frequency) is nearly uniform throughout, so apart from prices, a retail customer's main concern is availability. Power is essentially a flow since the few possibilities for storage are expensive, but generation and transmission capacities require large investments of capital. Generators' ratios of variable to capital and fixed costs differ greatly, and those using fossil fuels become less efficient as they near capacity, so generators are activated according to the merit order of their marginal costs. An important component is the cost of reserve capacity to meet contingencies. A generator designed for reserve duty or to meet peak loads is idle most of the time so its overall cost is minimized by a low investment in capacity even though this entails higher fuel costs when running. The marginal cost to serve night-time base loads is therefore much less than to serve peak loads (e.g., demands for cooling on a hot summer afternoon), and limited transmission capacity restricts imports from adjacent regions. Investments in generation capacity are often located to reduce congestion on transmission lines, and designed overall to match the mix of generation technologies to the mix of base and peak loads.

Aggregate demand grows steadily year-to-year but varies by business conditions, time of day, and weather. Demand is very inelastic in the short term within the usual range of prices, and it is insensitive to short-term price variations except for commercial and industrial customers with time-of-use meters. Favorable rates are offered mainly to those customers with steady demands that can be served with base-load generators that have low marginal costs, and to those customers who volunteer to curtail demand at times of peak loads, scarce supplies, or emergencies. For those customers requiring extremely high reliability, premium rates cover the costs of improved distribution and backup facilities. Customers respond slowly to long-term price trends, mainly via occasional purchases of new appliances and conversions to new technologies.

At the retail level, pricing by a regulated utility has two basic objectives. In the long term the aim is recover the capital costs of generators and transmission and distribution networks with lives measured in decades. Typically this is done via price components that recover costs amortized over many years so as to reduce the variability of prices paid by customers. In the short term the aim is to recover marginal costs that vary greatly between periods of base and peak loads. Thus many commercial and most industrial customers pay rates that vary with current prices in the wholesale market. Such time-of-use metering and pricing is rarely applied to residences and small commercial customers in the USA. However, it is prevalent in a few countries with deregulated retail markets (e.g., Scandinavia) where retailers offer service plans with options that vary according to how much a customer is exposed to variations in wholesale prices. Progress in implementing retail deregulation halted in the USA after the withdrawal, and in some cases financial collapse, of retailers during a period of extraordinarily high wholesale prices in California during 2000–01. Because power is essential, successful implementation requires suppliers of last resort in times when supplies are scarce or expensive, which in turn requires continued reliance on regulated utilities as major suppliers, especially to residences averse to price volatility.

4.2 PRICING IN WHOLESALE MARKETS

In some jurisdictions a regulated retail utility owns all the generation capacity. In some others it is the sole buyer in the wholesale market. In the latter case it typically contracts long term with independent generators for supplies in excess of its own generation, and it may also exchange supplies with other utilities in a wider region. This pattern of bilateral contracting is prevalent also in deregulated wholesale markets, and extends to contracting between industrial customers and generating companies. A great variety of contract forms and durations are used. Besides ordinary forward contracts that specify fixed quantities and prices, others are contracts-for-differences in which the parties mutually insure each other against variations in wholesale prices, call options, tolling agreements in which the buyer continually chooses the quantity, and "spark-spread" contracts in which buyers pay fuel costs.

In some countries, especially in Europe, wholesale markets are conducted by power exchanges in which standard bi lateral contracts with various terms (e.g., time, duration, location) are traded in auctions with offered bid and ask prices. Increasingly prevalent are special markets or contracts for "green" power from renewable sources. In those several jurisdictions in the USA managed by a regulated non-profit Independent System Operator (ISO), the ISO conducts multilateral markets. These are auctions in which demanders (utilities, other retailers, and exporters) submit bids to buy and sellers (generators and importers) submit offers to sell, each conditioned by the time of delivery and the location. The ISO uses sophisticated computer programs to maximize the gains from trade subject to constraints on transmission and reserve capacities needed to ensure reliability and security of the transmission grid. The end result is an array of market clearing prices for power— one price for each time period (an hour or as short as five minutes) and location in the grid. The difference between prices at two locations can be due to energy lost during transmission, or to congestion on the transmission lines between them. Also produced are prices for several categories of reserve capacity that depend on the delay in which they can be activated (e.g., in ten or thirty minutes). One such auction is held and accounts settled the day before delivery, and then a similar auction is repeated periodically during the day of delivery for adjustments to the day-ahead schedule to meet changing conditions. Some ISOs also conduct forward markets each season for reserve capacity, and forward markets each year for installed capacity deliverable several years later. Increasingly prevalent are bids from large industrial customers who offer reserve capacity via reductions of their loads when generation capacity is scarce. These markets supplement generators' income via demanders' payments for available capacity to meet contingencies. Market participants pay pro rata grid management charges that recover the ISO's costs, and charges that recover the amortized costs of transmission investments.

The volatility of daily prices encourages forward contracting. As mentioned previously, some European systems have established markets for standard bi lateral contracts based on posted bid and ask prices, and in the USA, trading in organized commodity exchanges is supplemented by private bi lateral relations and markets conducted by financial firms. In general, the main role of forward contracts is to hedge price risks. Buyers typically prefer short-term contracts and flexible quantities to the extent their needs are uncertain, and generators prefer long-term contracts for largely fixed quantities to provide steady income to payoff construction loans.

For a more detailed description of wholesale markets conducted by system operators, see Stoft (2002).

4.3 PRICING IN RETAIL MARKETS

The fundamental feature of electricity markets is volatility of prices and quantities. Power is homogeneous at any one time and location, but wholesale prices vary greatly by time, location, and events such as weather. Usually wholesale prices are highest when aggregate demand is greatest, but prices are occasionally high in the short term due to failures of generation or transmission facilities or to shortages of fuel, or over longer spans due to drought that depletes reservoirs. In many jurisdictions, within a typical year the highest wholesale spot price exceeds the lowest price by a factor of 500, and would be more if the ISO did not impose price caps on offers from suppliers. Aggregate demand varies regularly by time of day and randomly due to events such as weather, and also long term due to business cycles and demographic changes. Supply varies due to transmission congestion and occasional failures of generators and transmission lines, and also long term due to periodic droughts that limit supplies from hydroelectric dams. Moreover, supply costs vary in the short term due to winter cold that restricts supplies of natural gas and increases demand for gas-fired space heating, and also in the long term with variations in prices of fossil fuels.

The central problem of retail pricing is how to translate volatile wholesale prices into retail service plans acceptable to customers, many of whom are unwilling or unable to cope with variations in their monthly bills. This is a classic principal–agent problem in which customers want insurance against price volatility, but retailers want to sensitize customers to the costs that their demands impose. Regulated and municipal utilities have traditionally offered nearly complete insurance; that is, a utility's accumulated costs are capitalized and then recovered steadily over time from fixed prices charged to customers. Although this scheme mutes incentives to conserve power usage, it works well for customers severely averse to volatile prices, but others seek to obtain lower prices by bearing some price risks and moderating their usage when prices are high. Commercial and industrial customers are very heterogeneous in this respect. Some business and production operations can be curtailed or shut down when prices are high. Some applications are easily varied or usage delayed until prices subside—prominent examples are heating and cooling, because a heater or air conditioner can be off for some time before the temperature changes appreciably, and energy-intensive household tasks such as washing and drying can be deferred to the evening when prices might be lower.

Often the solution is to offer a tariff that includes a menu of options, among which each customer selects one based on its peculiar circumstances. The following options are listed roughly according to the price risk borne by the customer.

- Spot pricing, also called real-time pricing. In this case the retail price varies directly with the wholesale price. Spot pricing is limited chiefly by the scarcity of customers willing to bear all the volatility of wholesale prices. Historically it has been limited also by the costs of time-of-use metering and billing, but utilities' massive deployments of smart metering devices are removing that barrier.

- Curtailable or interruptible service. This case includes lower prices offered to customers willing to curtail or interrupt service when prices are high. A variant allows a customer to choose his priority of service, with lower prices charged for lower priorities.

- Time-of-use pricing. This case includes prices differentiated according to anticipated base and peak periods of aggregate demand, such as nights and weekends (base) and weekdays (peak) in areas where peak loads occur during weekdays. A variant identifies a peak period as contingent on a public announcement by the system operator.

In France, electricity tariffs use a unique approach to sensitizing customers to the costs their demands impose. Each customer pays a capacity charge based on its peak usage rate (the maximum number of kilo-Watts used at any one time during the year), plus an energy charge for the cumulative duration that each kilo-Watt is used. The capacity charges, and sometimes also the energy charges, increase nonlinearly to discourage customers from exacerbating peak loads, such as extravagant use of air conditioning.

In addition, significantly higher prices apply whenever the system operator announces the onset of an emergency. This tariff, called a Wright tariff, applies to each customer a microscopic version of the system's aggregate cost of providing capacity and energy produced from that capacity. A Wright tariff encourages customers to recognize the long-term costs of power production. Spot pricing is the other extreme in which customers are charged in each pricing period the short-term cost of power generation depending on the immediate circumstances. In principle, prices that reflect long-term or short-term costs can yield the same average net revenue overall, but a major difference is that spot prices are more volatile, yet provide stronger incentives for efficient usage depending on actual events.

The volume edited by Sioshansi (2008) includes several chapters that examine pricing in more detail.

4.4 THEORY OF ELECTRICITY PRICING

Pricing in wholesale markets managed by an ISO is justified by the implications of maximizing the gains from trade subject to constraints on transmission and reserve capacities. From the optimization one identifies the marginal cost of a withdrawal of energy at each location in the transmission system. This imputed marginal cost is then used as the price to settle the accounts of all parties who inject or withdraw energy at that location. Also obtained are the marginal values of reserve capacities that are then the prices paid for these supplemental services. For more details see Wilson (2002).

The theory of retail pricing draws on the literatures about product differentiation and about nonlinear pricing. The central consideration in both cases is heterogeneity among customers.

Product differentiation occurs in the design of menus of options such as spot pricing, curtailable service plans, and time-of-use pricing. The aim is to design products that best serve various types of customers. Their types differ chiefly in their willingness to bear price risk and their differing abilities to vary usage in response to varying prices. The typical result is that the menu enables each customer to choose its exposure to price risk, while also offering opportunities to moderate that risk by modifying its usage.

Nonlinear pricing occurs mainly in the tariffs of regulated utilities, such as the Wright tariff. Typically a menu of options is constructed as a family of two-part tariffs, for each of which the two components are a capacity charge for access and an energy charge for usage. Prices can increase with usage if the aim is to discourage heavy usage, or decrease if the aim is to encourage greater usage. The latter occurs mainly in the quantity discounts offered to large industrial customers. A prominent version is so-called Ramsey pricing, described in Wilson (1993), in which the schedule of nonlinear prices is designed to recover the utility's capital and fixed costs with the least distortion away from pricing according to marginal costs. However, simple Ramsey pricing is often inappropriate for electricity because it tends to tax most heavily those customers with inelastic demands, which in the case of electricity are mostly residences and small commercial customers whose political influence is sufficient to sway regulators against using Ramsey pricing. The usual solution is to apply variants of Ramsey pricing only to large customers.

4.5 FUTURE EVOLUTION OF ELECTRICITY PRICING

The evolution of electricity pricing will be affected by two developments. One near-term development is further deregulation, or "restructuring" as it is called in the industry. Regulated utilities will continue to serve risk averse customers, especially residences, by providing substantial insurance against volatile wholesale prices, and to be available as a supplier of last resort. But the role of lightly regulated power marketers will grow as more commercial and industrial customers opt to bear some price risk while moderating their usage in response to prices. Over the long term, a second development will lessen the role of product differentiation and strengthen the role of spot pricing. So-called "Smart Grid" technologies for system control, and customers' increasingly sophisticated smart meters, will increase the feasibility of spot pricing and more elaborate forms of product differentiation through load-control contracts. Customers will acquire monitoring and control devices that, in response to wholesale prices, enable continuous adjustments of power usage by various equipment and software in a factory, office, or home. Moreover, marketers will sell financial insurance against variations in wholesale prices. These developments are already under way in some countries, and are encouraged elsewhere by imperatives to reduce emissions from power plants.

REFERENCES

Stoft, S. (2002) *Power System Economics*. New York: Wiley-Interscience.
Sioshansi, F. (2008) *Competitive Electricity Markets*. Boston, MA: Elsevier.
Wilson, R. (1993) *Nonlinear Pricing*. New York: Oxford University Press.
—— (2002) "Architecture of Power Markets", *Econometrica* 70/4: 1299–340.

CHAPTER 5

HEALTH CARE PRICING IN THE UNITED STATES: THE CASE OF HOSPITALS

E. ANDREW BOYD

5.1 INTRODUCTION

In 2009, health care expenditures in the United States totaled $2.5 trillion—$8,086 for every person, and 17.6 percent of the US gross domestic product. Payment to hospitals amounted to $759 billion and represented the single largest expenditure in the health care system, outpacing number two—physician and clinical services—by more than $250 billion. Hospital payments alone account for over 5 percent of the US gross domestic product (US Centers for Medicare and Medicaid Services n.d.). By any measure, hospitals do a staggering amount of business. And all of their services must be priced.

Here we provide a brief overview of the issues and processes necessary for the reader to understand pricing in the US health care system in general, and hospital pricing in particular.

5.2 THE HEALTH CARE ENVIRONMENT AND THE ROLE OF HOSPITALS

Health care in the United States revolves around health care service providers, with a distinction made between physicians and facilities. Hospitals are the most common type of facility, providing operating rooms, beds, nursing, and an array of specialized treatment equipment. Physicians aren't employed by hospitals, but are paid directly by the patient or, more commonly, by the patient's insurance provider. Hospitals are paid for the use of their facilities, including support staff. Hospital administrators normally have specialized training in health care administration. Educational programs frequently include accounting and statistics, but quantitative problem solving skills such as those found in management science courses are rare.

Physicians have considerable flexibility in the hospitals they choose to work with. A hospital, on the other hand, only gets paid if physicians choose to use the hospital's facilities. It is therefore in a hospital's best interests to provide physicians with incentives. Incentives may include office space, the latest equipment, preferred time slots in operating facilities, and a staff attentive to physicians' needs. An affiliation with a highly regarded collection of physicians helps the reputation of the hospital in the eyes of patients. Hospitals associated with prestigious medical schools are a good example.

5.3 THE FLOW OF PAYMENT FOR RENDERED SERVICES

Very few people in the United States pay for their health care without some form of assistance. According to the US Census Bureau, 83.7 percent of the population had some form of insurance coverage in 2010. There are two primary sources of coverage: private commercial insurers and government programs. In 2010, 64.0 percent of the population had coverage with commercial insurers and 31.0 percent with government insurers.[1] The revenues flowing to hospitals mirror these amounts (US Census Bureau n.d.).

By far the largest and most well-known government programs are Medicare and Medicaid, two federal programs providing support for the elderly and disabled, and for the financially needy. Hospitals have no direct control over the fees paid by government programs. Lobbying efforts abound, however, since government programs account for such a large portion of most hospitals' revenue. This leaves commercial insurance contracts as the main source of revenue that hospitals have some control over.

Commercial health insurance is complicated by the fact that most insured individuals don't contract directly with an insurance company, but are covered by a sponsor. The most common sponsor is an individual's employer, with health insurance offered as part of a benefit package. The individual is usually required to supplement his or her payment to the insurance company. The typical chain of payment for an employer-sponsored individual is thus: (1) the employee pays the employer directly, indirectly, or both; (2) the employer supplements the employee contribution and pays the commercial insurer; (3) the commercial insurer pays the health care service provider whenever services are rendered. Price and negotiation come into play in both steps (2) and (3), giving rise to many interesting pricing problems. Here, we focus only on step (3), and in particular the case where the health care service provider is a hospital.

---

[1] There is overlap in the figures due to multiple sources of coverage and changes in coverage.

5.4 MOTIVATION OF THE PARTIES INVOLVED

The majority of hospitals in the United States are non-profit. According to the American Hospital Association, in 2009 only 20 percent of the registered community hospitals were for-profit (investor owned). Of the remaining hospitals, 22 percent were operated by state and local governments, and 58 percent were private non-profit (American Hospital Association n.d.). Private non-profit hospitals are typically associated with charities or medical schools.

The non-profit mindset effects how hospital administrators view their role in the world of health care. Their job is to determine "fair and reasonable charges" that will allow costs to be covered. They speak a language of services, charges, and reimbursements, not products and prices. Costs are important, and administrators will do what they can to contain them. But costs are not the overriding concern. Hospitals are in the business of saving lives, and cutting too deeply impacts a hospital's reputation and may lead to legal action if patients are adversely affected. Hospital pricing isn't the cut-throat activity found in many businesses. Even so, if a hospital cannot cover costs, it must close its doors. Administrators are very cognizant of the balance sheet even if the goal isn't to turn a hefty profit.

Commercial insurers are for-profit entities subject to market forces. They compete with one another to sell insurance contracts to employers/sponsors, and they seek low costs of service from health care service providers. Profit is the difference between what insurers collect in premiums and what they pay in claims. Commercial insurance in the healthcare industry differs somewhat from traditional insurance in that insurers only work with a preferred list of health care providers. When a homeowner makes a claim against an insurance policy, the claims investigator assesses the damage and provides market-based payment for repair. Homeowners are then free to contract with whatever repair company they choose. When an insured individual seeks medical treatment, he or she is limited to a network of preferred providers or, for higher out-of-pocket payments, the individual may seek treatment outside of the network. This *managed care* system provides commercial insurers with an opportunity to influence the prices charged by network providers. The larger the commercial insurer, the greater the influence. This has led to radical consolidation in the health care insurance industry.

A typical hospital may hold anything between a few dozen and a few hundred commercial insurance contracts in its portfolio, with most of the revenue coming from a handful of large contracts. Large contract negotiations may involve many people and weeks or even months of preparation, while small contracts may receive only a cursory review. A common practice is to write "evergreen" contracts—contracts that remain in place until one participant informs the other that it is time to renegotiate.

5.5 WHAT HOSPITALS SELL AND HOW THEY SELL IT

Contracts between hospitals and commercial insurers contain payment terms—prices. But before understanding how hospitals price, it is necessary to understand what they sell. From the perspective of pricing, hospitals deliver a remarkably complex product.

When a store charges $3 for a toothbrush that costs $2, the store nets $1 and the customer gets a toothbrush. When a hospital agrees to provide facilities and services for a heart bypass procedure, it doesn't know exactly what expenses it will incur. There are many different ways hospitals can price their services, and most have been tried at one time or another.

One method of pricing is to develop a very detailed price list covering everything from an hour of radiation therapy to administering an injection. The cost of a hospital stay is then simply the sum of the individual charges. When contracts for payment are based on detailed charge lists, commercial insurers typically seek a discount in return for including the hospital on their lists of preferred service providers. Contracts of this type are known as *discount-off-charges* contracts. As a result of the give and take of negotiations, the discrepancy between list charges and net charges after discounts has grown wildly. Discounts on the order of 50–60 percent are common, as hospitals set their prices at a level where they can make a positive return even after applying discounts. Pricing of this nature hurts individuals who do not have insurance coverage since they may be forced to pay inflated list prices. Recognizing this, many hospitals willingly reduce charges to individuals. Inflated list prices are common in industries where prices are set by negotiation. But the problem is especially disconcerting when people's health is at stake. Uninsured individuals who don't realize negotiation is acceptable may not get the care they need.

Discount-off-charges contracts have their roots in the non-profit history of the health care industry. Patients are given the treatment deemed necessary by physicians, accountants tally the expenses, and hospitals are reimbursed. One important consequence of discount-off-charges contracts is that they don't provide a strong incentive for hospitals to control costs. As a result, commercial insurance companies have sought to negotiate contracts that do provide incentives, such as *capitated* contracts.

Capitated contracts pay hospitals a fixed amount of money for every covered patient. If a patient doesn't need any treatment, the hospital pockets the entire payment. If a patient needs expensive treatment, the hospital incurs a loss. Capitated contracts provide a strong incentive for hospitals to operate cost effectively. They also shift risk from insurance providers to hospitals.

Per diem and *case rate* contracts offer two intermediate ways of defining payment for services. Commercial insurers still bear much of the risk, but hospitals are incentivized to operate cost effectively. Per diem contracts bundle services for which the hospital charges a daily fee. For example, a patient staying in an acute care facility might be charged $2,000 per day, while a patient staying in an intensive care facility might be charged $2,500. Hospitals have an incentive to operate cost effectively since they receive a fixed payment for each patient-day. However, the hospital receives more money when longer stays are required.

Case rate contracts structure payment around the specific ailment afflicting a patient. For example, if it is determined that a patient needs to have his or her spleen removed, a hospital receives a fixed payment associated with the case "splenectomy". Hospitals are again incentivized to keep an eye on costs, but payment is directly related to the number of patients a hospital treats for a given ailment.

In order to implement a case rate contract, hospitals and commercial insurance providers must agree on a list of billable cases. Specifically, there must be a list with the property that every patient can be classified into one or more cases on that list. If not, the hospital won't know what to charge when a patient walks out the door. Case rate contracts have the potential to become an administrative nightmare, especially if hospitals work with different case lists on different contracts. Fortunately, there's been considerable work done on developing standard sets of cases.

The earliest and most well-known classification system is that of *diagnosis related groups,* more commonly known as DRGs (Fetter 1991). The original DRGs were developed for Medicare, and were adopted by Congress as the basis Medicare payments in 1983. The present list of DRGs used by Medicare stands at just over 500. Many different variations on the DRG framework have been proposed and are in use today. While DRG classification systems have gained traction—in large part due to Medicare's ongoing use of the system— there are no defined standards uniformly adopted by commercial insurers and hospitals.

In summary, the services, or *products,* sold by the health care industry have the following distinguishing characteristics.

1. What products are sold, and how they are priced, is a result of negotiation.

2. There are many ways to define the products that hospitals sell. Among them:

   • as a detailed list of individual activities *(discount-off-charges)*;

   • no products; just a flat annual service fee per person *(capitated)*;

   • as daily usage of bundled services *(per diem)*;

   • as the resolution of a particular ailment *(case rate)*;

   • combinations of the above methods.

Capitated contracts are no longer widely used—the result of hospitals realizing they were assuming risk that should have been borne by commercial insurers. Hospitals typically prefer discount-off-charges contracts, since the contracts pay hospitals for any services rendered. Commercial insurers lean toward per diem and case rate contracts since they limit risk and provide good incentives for hospitals to keep their costs under control. At present, with the national emphasis on controlling health care costs, the general drift is toward per diem and case rate contracts. It is important to note, however, that there is no "standard" approach to contracting. The specific terms of a contract strongly depend on the parties involved in the negotiation.

5.6 PRICING AND QUANTITATIVE ANALYTICS

The flexibility in defining products creates complexity in health care pricing. This complexity has no obvious advantages from a social perspective. Administering contracts where there is no uniform industry pricing structure, and where the structure that exists is constantly changing, is costly. Health care pricing is confusing for service providers, commercial insurers, sponsors, and the insured. For individual parties, however, complexity provides opportunity.

Consider, for example, a hospital entering into a negotiation with a large commercial insurer. Furthermore, suppose the negotiation is initiated by the commercial insurer presenting a contract proposal to the hospital. How does the hospital go about evaluating the contract?

One very basic form of evaluation would be to take records from all of last year's patients and see how much the proposed contract would have generated with this set of cases—effectively, these patients times these terms equals this much money. But because there are so many ways contracts can be structured, and because hospital data are rarely if ever available in a database designed to support contract evaluation, just one evaluation of this sort can take weeks. What should be a relatively simple computational task is very difficult in practice for most hospitals. More often than not, the process is so arduous that even this basic level of analysis is not done.

Instead, hospital administrators rely on anecdotal quantitative analysis. If acute care facilities lost money last year, then the proposed contract must include an increase in payment for acute care. If the operating rooms were upgraded, the cost of operating room time must increase accordingly. Even anecdotal quantitative analysis isn't always used. Across the board percentage increases are common.

From the perspective of quantitative analytics, opportunities abound for those hospitals that address the data and computational issues. Rather than using last year's patient population to evaluate a contract, trends and changing population demographics could be used to forecast what the patient population will look like next year. Instead of simply evaluating contracts, optimization could be used to design contracts. By better understanding patient data, high return, low risk contracts could be structured that meet the demands of the negotiator across the table (Born 2004; Boyd 2007: ch.11).

5.7 CONCLUSIONS

Health care pricing in the United States is complex. Products can be defined in many different ways. Prices are negotiated. Data are not maintained in a way that promotes quantitative analysis. Health care administrators are not trained in the use of analytics.

None of these problems are insurmountable. For those who are willing to embrace the complexity of the system, the opportunities are enormous right now. Longer term, analytics won't flourish until a common infrastructure is established. Software vendors must develop systems specifically aimed at evaluating, monitoring, and designing health care contracts. But even more importantly, health care administrators need to be made aware of what analytics can provide. Analytics must be required in the educational curricula of health care administrators.

REFERENCES

American Hospital Association (n.d.) Fast Facts on U.S. Hospitals. http://www.aha.org/research/rc/stat-studies/fast-facts.shtml, accessed October 28, 2011.

Born, C. et al. (2004) "Contract Optimization at Texas Children's Hospital", *Interfaces* 34/1: 51–8.

Boyd, E. A. (2007) *The Future of Pricing: How Airline Ticket Pricing Has Inspired a Revolution.* New York: Palgrave Macmillan.

Fetter, R. B. (1991) "Diagnosis Related Groups: Understanding Hospital Performance", *Interfaces* 21/1: 6–26.

U.S. Census Bureau (n.d.) Coverage by Type of Health Insurance: 2009 and 2010. http://www.census.gov/hhes/www/hlthins/data/incpovhlth/2010/table10.pdf, accessed October 28, 2011.

U.S. Centers for Medicare and Medicaid Services (n.d.). National Health Expenditures 2009 Highlights. http://www.cms.hhs.gov/NationalHealthExpendData/downloads/highlights.pdf, accessed October 28, 2011.

CHAPTER 6

PRICING IN RESTAURANTS

SHERYL E. KIMES,
ROBERT PHILLIPS, AND
LISABET SUMMA

The waiter brings the check.
Otis P. Driftwood (*Grabbing the check.*): "Let me see that. $9.40? This is an outrage!"
(*Pushes the check to his dining companion.*) "If I were you, I wouldn't pay it."

Groucho Marx in *A Night at the Opera.*

6.1 INTRODUCTION

The restaurant business is a big business, in 2010 there were 945,000 restaurants in the United States employing 12.7 million people and with total revenue of $580 billion.[1] The restaurant business is also a risky business. Although the percentage varies from year to year, about a quarter of new restaurants fail in their first year and between 40–60 percent fail within the first three years of operation.[2] It is a highly competitive business—diners in urban areas such as New York, Paris, and Tokyo have thousands of restaurant options to choose from. Setting the right price can be critical to success—if prices are perceived as too high, customers will not patronize the restaurant, but if they are too low, the restaurant will go out of business.

This chapter discusses some of the challenges of restaurant pricing and reviews methods that restaurants use to set prices. We begin with a brief history of restaurants and present how restaurants are currently classified. In Section 6.3, we discuss the different approaches

---

[1] www.restaurant.org/research/facts, accessed October 26, 2011.
[2] Parsa et al. (2005) estimated the first-year failure rate of restaurants at 26.2% and the cumulative three-year failure rate at 59.7% based on Dun and Bradstreet data for 1996–99. Cline Group (2003) estimated a 23% first-year failure rate and a 44% failure rate for restaurants in the Dallas Texas telephone directory (1997–2002). At any rate, the widely quoted statistic that "90% of new restaurants fail in the first year"— repeated in advertisements for the reality television show *The Restaurant*—is inaccurate.

that restaurants use to set prices today. Next we discuss the psychology of restaurant prices and how it influences menu design and give an overview of how revenue management is applied in the restaurant industry. We conclude with a short discussion of opportunities for the future.

Our goal is to provide the interested reader with an overview of how restaurants set prices and an introduction to research in restaurant pricing. For this reason, we have focused primarily on issues specific to restaurant pricing. For example, restaurants often apply pricing and promotion tactics common to retailers such as couponing, low-pricing of "traffic-building" items, and other types of sales promotion. Discussions of such promotional tactics can be found in Blattberg and Briesch (Chapter 24). Finally, we do not provide recommendations on how a particular restaurant "should" price. Pointers for pricing menu items in a new restaurant can be found in any one of a number of restaurant management handbooks or textbooks such as Shock et al. (2003), Mill (2006), or Brown (2007).

6.2 HISTORY AND CURRENT CLASSIFICATION

As described in Casson (1994), there have been inns and taverns selling food, lodging, and beverages to travelers at a price since the time of ancient Egypt and Babylonia. They became commonplace during the Classical period as travel and trade expanded throughout the Mediterranean world. Notably, such inns and taverns were among the first to utilize a "list price" modality as described by Phillips (Chapter 2)—a sign from an inn of the Classical Period promises a price list inside (Casson 1994).

While inns and taverns catering to travelers date to very ancient times in the West, restaurants as a social destination for locals (as opposed to taverns and inns that catered primarily to travelers) arose in pre-revolutionary France. List prices were a logical evolution from the *menus de hote* used to inform dinner party guests of the dishes to be served (Spang 2000). Since that time, list pricing has remained the dominant mode of pricing in restaurants, with prices either printed in a menu (or displayed on a board) for all to see.[3] Diners generally take for granted that these are fixed prices, that the prices are generally the same for all diners (with the possible exception of senior citizen discounts and the use of coupons), and that bargaining is not likely to be effective. In this setting, the primary pricing problem faced by the restaurant operator is what prices to set for the dishes on the menu and how to update them over time.

Early menus used simplified pricing structures—for example a single price for all appetizers and another single price for all entrées—in order to facilitate calculation of the diner's total bill. With the advent of the cash register in the late nineteenth century, this was no longer an issue and restaurants could offer a wide variety of dishes on an *à la carte* basis. For example, the 1899 menu for *Delmonico* Restaurant in New York listed 208 items with some fine distinctions in price: "French coffee" for $0.15 versus "Turkish coffee" for $0.20 (Delmonico 1899).

---

[3] The historic exception was the use of "blind menus" at higher-end restaurants in which only the males in a dining party would be provided menus with prices—women (and children) would receive "blind menus" with no prices. The use of blind menus at *L'Orangerie* in Los Angeles was the subject of a discrimination lawsuit filed by Gloria Allred in 1980 (Allred 2000). Perhaps as a result, the use of "blind menus" is no longer common.

Over time, a wide variety of restaurants sprang up, serving different customer needs and market segments. Modern restaurants are commonly divided into five categories:

1. *Fine dining restaurants* are full service, sit-down restaurants serving food in a décor that is designed to create a luxurious ambiance. They have a relatively high average check per person. They are usually independent businesses with either a single location or a small number of locations. These restaurants vie for ratings in such publications as the *Guide Michelin*, the *Mobil Guide*, and others.

2. *Upscale casual restaurants* are also full service, sit-down restaurants with a comprehensive menu, but tend to be in a more casual setting. They have a fairly high average check per person and are the type of restaurant that people might visit once a month. They may be individual businesses or chains. Examples of upscale casual restaurant chains include Houston's, Legal Sea Food, and P.F. Chang's China Bistro.

3. *Casual restaurants* are full service, sit-down restaurants with a somewhat limited menu that is served in a casual setting. Their average check per person is moderate. These are the type of restaurants that people might visit once a month or more often. They are often part of a chain. Examples include TGIFridays and Chili's.

4. *Fast casual restaurants* are limited service restaurants with a fairly limited menu. They do not offer table service but they typically offer the opportunity to eat on the premises. The quality of food is considered higher, and the price point is typically higher than fast food restaurants. Examples include Chipotle and Panera Bread.

5. *Quick service (fast food) restaurants* have limited service and a limited menu. They emphasize speed of service and low price over atmosphere. They do not offer table service and a large fraction of diners are expected to take food to go, although some may eat the food on the premises. Many, although by no means all, quick service restaurants are chain operations. Examples include McDonald's, KFC, Jack in the Box, and Taco Bell.

The category of restaurant will influence how it sets prices. Broadly speaking, restaurants in the quick service and fast casual categories are serving customer segments who are both likely to be highly price-sensitive and who have the potential to be frequent patrons. More upscale restaurants—especially fine dining establishments—compete by providing a more luxurious dining experience for patrons who are likely to visit less often. As a result, they may experience somewhat less price-elastic demand. However, pricing is a critical element of success to restaurants in all categories.

6.3 How restaurants set prices

Broadly speaking, restaurant operators set prices in one of three ways: (1) cost-based, (2) demand-based, or (3) competition-based. We will discuss each in turn.

6.3.1 Cost-based pricing

Cost-based pricing is the most common pricing approach used by restaurants. With cost-based pricing, restaurants determine the food costs associated with each menu item and apply a multiplier (generally 3 or 4) to determine the price. Cost-based pricing is widely recommended by popular guides as a starting point for pricing. For example, one guide recommends "Multiply a menu item's cost by a factor of 3 to 7. If you are a value-oriented restaurant, then the multiples you use must be on the low side" (Shock et al. 2004: 91). Cost-based pricing does not typically consider demand. This may lead to prices being much lower than customers are willing to pay. In addition, cost-based pricing is not normally based on what the competition is charging.

Restaurants do not apply the same multiplier blindly to all dishes. Diners bring a set of pricing expectations every time they open a menu—and most restaurants seek to price so that these expectations are not violated. For example, most diners anticipate that entrées will be priced higher than appetizers which will be priced higher than desserts and salads. For this reason, the prices derived by multiples are typically only initial estimates that are tinkered with and adjusted before they can be considered menu prices.

Effective cost-based pricing requires, of course, accurate cost estimates which, in themselves, can be difficult to calculate. The cost of food served is typically determined by the recipes and the recipes are written by the chef. Historically, chefs primarily focused on creating the recipes and preparing the food. However, more and more chefs are being trained to understand the cost implications of the choices they make and to incorporate these into the recipes that they develop. While this might be seen as hindering creativity, in fact it is necessary in order to ensure that the items on the menu can be delivered within the price position of the restaurant.

In addition to the raw materials and the labor required to create the items on the menu, some restaurants offer additional items such as bread and condiments for free. Clearly, these items need to be factored into the cost of meals. The additional cost applied to items to account for these is sometimes called the *Q-factor*. In a typical high-end restaurant, particularly one baking its own rolls, the average Q-factor can be around $3.00 or more. A sophisticated restaurant will calculate and apportion a different Q-factor for each entrée. For example, an order of "hamburger with fries" will use more ketchup and other condiments on average than a "chicken Caesar salad" and, ideally, this should be reflected in the cost. However, most restaurants tend to calculate a common Q-factor and allocate it among entrées.

Cost-based pricing is admittedly, highly simplistic. For example, it does not include any costs for preparation time and labor. More sophisticated, "activity-based" costing approaches for restaurants have been proposed but are rarely used in practice (Raab and Mayer 2000). Given that the costing is used as a rough estimate to which simple multiples are applied in order to estimate prices, it may well be sufficient. However, Raab and Mayer (2007) claim that a more accurate activity-based approach to costing gives a very different view of item profitability than standard approaches.

We note that cost-based pricing in restaurants has the same drawbacks as it does in other businesses. First of all, a cost-based price does not necessarily have any relationship to what customers are willing to pay for the item. Secondly, it can lead to an illusion of profitability. Every item on a menu may have an impressive "contribution margin" defined as price minus food cost. But if demand is low or fixed costs are too high, the restaurant will still be unprofitable.

Restaurants are a highly dynamic business. In particular, it is critical for most restaurants to track the changing costs of the food that they purchase and, as necessary, to update prices on the menu to incorporate these changes. Furthermore, many restaurants like to update their menus periodically to drop some existing items and add new items. And, of course, many restaurants have daily specials that incorporate seasonally available meat or produce. Many restaurants print their own daily menus, which very much facilitates the updating process.

6.3.2 Demand-based pricing

Under demand-based pricing, a restaurant seeks to determine the right price for a menu item by understanding how price affects demand. Three approaches are commonly used to estimate the effect of price on demand: estimating customer willingness-to-pay, menu engineering, and price elasticity estimation. We will discuss each in turn.

6.3.2.1 Customer willingness-to-pay

A variety of methods have been suggested for determining customer willingness-to-pay. One of the most important is *price sensitivity estimation* (Lewis and Shoemaker 1997; Raab et al. 2009), a survey-based tool in which customers are asked four questions about a particular menu item or service:

- At what price do you consider the menu item to be cheap?
- At what price do you consider the menu item to be expensive?
- At what price do you consider the menu item to be too expensive, so expensive that you would not consider buying it?
- At what price do you consider the menu item to be too cheap, so cheap that you would question its quality?

The percentage of answers to these questions can be plotted to derive four curves as shown in Figure 6.1. The intersection of those who find a particular price "too cheap" and "not cheap" and the intersection of those who find a particular price "too expensive" and those who find it "not expensive" define two points. According to the advocates of this approach, there is a range of "acceptable prices" between those two points. This method has been adopted by Taco Bell and Marriott Hotels and Resorts in setting their price levels and also in assessing whether their current prices are too high or too low. We note that this is an approach that is also used in the hospitality industry to determine price ranges for room types (Shaw 1992).

An alternative approach to price sensitivity estimation is to use experimental pricing or price tests to determine customer willingness-to-pay. Under this approach, restaurants experiment with several different menu item prices and test customer response to those prices. For example, Kelly et al. (1994) conducted a study in a mid-scale restaurant in which they printed menus that had four different prices (one regular and three higher prices) for a popular fish dish. They randomly assigned the menus to customers and found that the sales of the fish dish did not vary by price level. This suggested that the restaurant could raise the price of that menu item without having to worry about a decrease in sales.

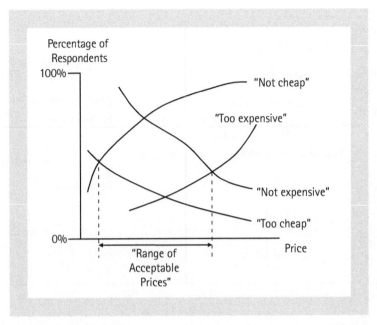

FIGURE 6.1 Determining the range of acceptable prices from a price-sensitivity estimation survey

6.3.2.2 *Menu engineering*

Many restaurants use *menu engineering* as a rough method for determining the relative price sensitivity of different menu items. Menu engineering includes information on menu item popularity (or menu mix share) as well as the contribution margin (most typically the price less the food cost) of each menu item. We note that this contribution margin will typically be greater than zero for most items, particularly if the restaurant has initially used a multiplier approach to setting prices. The menu is divided into categories (e.g., appetizers, entrées, and desserts) and the menu mix share and contribution margin are calculated for each menu item. Finally, the menu items are divided into four categories:

1. *Stars*: above-average menu mix share, above-average contribution margin;
2. *Cash Cows*: above-average menu mix share, below-average contribution margin;
3. *Question Marks*: below-average menu mix share, above-average contribution margin;
4. *Dogs*: below-average menu mix share, below-average contribution margin.

Once all menu items have been classified, strategies for each item can be developed. Many restaurants plot the menu items on a graph of the type shown in Figure 6.2 so that they can better visualize the relationships between items sold and contribution margin.

There are different strategies for each menu item classification.

1. Menu items that are classified as Stars are not only popular but also provide a good margin for the restaurant. Several strategies are typically used: (1) the menu item is highlighted on the menu or servers are asked to suggest this menu item when asked for recommendations, or (2) the price of the menu item is increased.

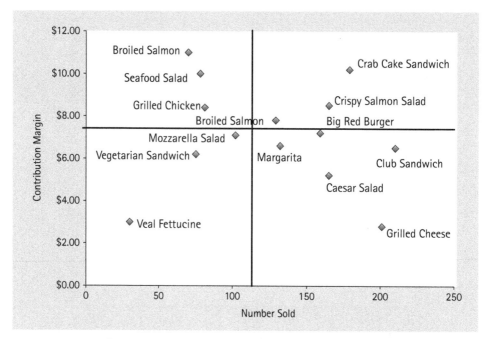

FIGURE 6.2 Contribution margin for menu items plotted as a function of number sold

2. Menu items that are classified as Cash Cows are popular but provide a below average margin for the restaurant. Several strategies are typically used: (1) the menu item is not featured on the menu since customers will most likely order the item anyway, or (2) the price of the menu item is increased because of its popularity.

3. Menu items that are classified as Question Marks are profitable for the restaurant but not particularly popular with customers. There are at least three possible reasons for this: (1) the menu item might be over-priced, (2) the menu item may be unappealing, and (3) the name of the menu item might be confusing or unappealing. Depending upon the reason, restaurants will either (1) drop the price a bit or (2) change the name.

4. Menu items that are classified as Dogs are not very popular and also don't provide much of a margin for the restaurant. The typical response is to drop these items off the menu, but care must be taken because they may appeal to certain customers.

Restaurants that use menu engineering typically review and analyze their menu on a regular basis (often monthly). Once they do their analysis, they will change the prices for a few menu items, reprint the menu and then monitor how the new prices are received. If the price turns out to be too high (demand drops off too much), they may drop the price to its previous level for the next period. Conversely, if demand does not fall too much, they may increase the price for the next period. This continuous review and adjustment allows restaurants to continually improve their pricing and track market trends. There are a number of commercial software packages for performing menu engineering, but many restaurants use simple Excel-based models.

6.3.2.3 *Measuring price elasticity*

Some restaurants (primarily larger chains) measure the price elasticity of each of their menu items and adjust their prices accordingly. Basically, price elasticity is measured by looking at changes in demand caused by changes in price. If sales of a menu item don't vary much even when the price changes, the item is considered to be inelastic, while if sales change quite a bit when the price changes, the item is considered to be elastic.

Price elasticity models can range from fairly simple calculations to sophisticated statistical models. For example, McDonald's works with a company called Revenue Management Solutions to set the menu prices at their outlets. Revenue Management Solutions (RMS) uses econometric models to estimate menu item price sensitivity. According to McDonald's, this has boosted profits at 7,000 US outlets in the past four years.[4]

6.3.3 Competitive pricing

Another approach is to set prices based on what the competition is charging. Restaurants will "shop" similar or nearby restaurants and try to position their prices relative to those restaurants. For example, a restaurant may decide that it does not want to have the highest prices in the market and may try to position itself as second highest. Or, a restaurant may decide that it wants to keep its menu prices on a par with that of the competition.

6.3.4 Summary

We note that, in practice, restaurants are not necessarily "pricing purists" but often use a combination of two or all three approaches. That is, a restaurant may use cost-based calculations to set the initial price for a menu item, but may then adjust these prices over time in response both to demand and to what competitors are charging.

While many restaurants seek to set prices to maximize the overall return from the menu, a further consideration in pricing is the recognition that the popularity of a restaurant is itself a factor in the customer experience. That is, most people enjoy eating in a restaurant that is well patronized than one that is cavernously empty. Furthermore, passers-by are more likely to choose a restaurant that is largely full than one that is empty or nearly so. This phenomenon was cited by the economist Gary Becker as providing the solution to a seeming puzzle—why very popular restaurants continued to turn away reservations rather than raise their prices until demand matched their limited capacity. Becker showed that, in the case in which overall demand positively influences the experience of other customers (and thus the total demand), it can be optimal for a restaurant to price lower than the tactically optimal price without the externality (Becker 1991).[5]

---

[4] http://www.tampabay.com/blogs/venturebiz/content/tampa-boasts-mcdonalds-menu-pricing-guru.
[5] Becker also considered in passing (1991: 1115) the possibility that a restaurant could become too crowded or popular and therefore deter some demand. This phenomenon had first been noted by Yogi Berra who, when asked why he no longer went to Ruggeri's, a St Louis restaurant, replied "Nobody goes there anymore. It's too crowded." (Berra 1998).

6.4 PSYCHOLOGY OF PRICES AND MENU DESIGN

As in other industries, pricing in restaurants has many psychological aspects. In particular, the way in which prices are presented on a menu has also been found to affect customer buying behavior. We discuss each of these in turn. A comprehensive review of psychological and behavioral influences on pricing can be found in Özer and Zheng (Chapter 20).

6.4.1 Psychology of restaurant pricing approaches

Restaurants use a variety of pricing approaches including decoy pricing and bundling to sell menu items. In addition, discounted prices are often used to help stimulate sales during low demand periods.

6.4.1.1 Decoy pricing

Restaurants often use *decoy pricing* to help make the prices of certain menu items seem more attractive (and thus increase sales). For example, a restaurant might put a very high priced wine on the menu. The purpose of that is not so much to sell that particular wine, but to make the other wine prices seem more reasonable and affordable. By providing the "decoy" wine, the restaurant can increase sales of other wines on the menu (Ariely 2008). This phenomenon may be related to the so-called "compromise effect" or "context effect", see Özer and Zheng (Chapter 20). One survey in the UK showed that 25 percent of diners will order the second cheapest wine in a category (Gaiter and Brecher 2004). A common explanation for the "second cheapest" wine purchase phenomenon is based on the fact that most purchases of wine by the bottle are done by a group. The person in the group choosing the wine wishes to be frugal but doesn't want to appear "cheap" or non-discriminating to others in the party. Thus, they choose the second cheapest wine in the category instead of the cheapest. While this explanation is commonly cited, to our knowledge it has not been empirically confirmed.

6.4.1.2 Bundling

Bundling is also commonly used in the restaurant industry. The basic idea of bundling is to combine multiple menu items into one price. The price of the bundle is typically lower than if the included menu items were purchased separately. In addition, a well-designed bundle might also include a menu item that people might not normally purchase (perhaps a dessert) and lead to incremental sales of that item. A discussion of strategies for creating and pricing bundles can be found in Oren (Chapter 22).

The most common examples of bundled pricing include *prix fixe* menus (multiple courses for one price), the "happy meal" type pricing commonly seen in fast food restaurants, and buffet or "all-you-can-eat" pricing. Bundled prices also allow a restaurant to effectively disguise their individual menu item prices. Because of this, the use of bundled pricing is even more common during slow economic times because it allows restaurants to offer lower prices without having to openly offer discounts.

6.4.1.3 Discounts and promotions

Restaurants also offer discounts and promotions to help build demand during slow periods. These discounts and promotions are intended to attract customers who might not otherwise have patronized the restaurant, while at the same time not offering these discounts to customers who were willing to pay the original, higher price. In order to do this, restaurants, like airlines and hotels, develop rate fences to make sure that they target the discounted prices at the right segment of customers (See Chapter 3 by Barnes and Chapter 26 by Talluri).

Typical rate fences include discounts targeted at particular age groups (i.e., children, senior citizens), certain days of the week (i.e., weekdays), certain meal periods (i.e., lunch), and certain time periods (i.e., happy hours). When developing these rate fences, restaurants need to be sure that customers perceive the rate fences as fair since pricing practices that are seen as unfair have been shown to lead to lower customer satisfaction and lower intent to return (Kimes and Wirtz 2003; Wirtz and Kimes 2007). As in other industries, rate fences that are framed as discounts are seen as more acceptable and fair than if framed as premiums (Özer and Zheng, Chapter 20). For example, if a restaurant states that prices are 20 percent lower on weekdays than on weekends, it will be perceived as more fair than if they said that weekend prices are 20 percent higher than weekday prices (Kimes and Wirtz 2003; Wirtz and Kimes 2007).

6.4.2 Menu design

Customers have been found to be affected by menu item descriptions, the last number of a price, by the use of currency symbols or words and by the placement and display of the menu item on the menu.

6.4.2.1 Menu item descriptions

Consumer purchase behavior and value and quality assessments can be affected by menu item labels and descriptions. In a test involving menus at a college faculty cafeteria, Wansink et al. (2001, 2005) found that descriptive labels can increase an item's purchase frequency as well as consumers' satisfaction towards the purchase. Wansink and his collaborators changed menu descriptions in a cafeteria on different days of the week. They monitored unit sales and surveyed purchasers. On some days items had extended descriptions such as "Traditional Cajun Red Beans and Rice" or "Grandma's Zucchini Cookies" and on other days they had short descriptions such as "Red Beans and Rice" or "Zucchini Cookies". On days when the extended description ("Grandma's Zucchini Cookies) was used, items had, on average, 27 percent higher sales than on days when the short description was used ("Zucchini Cookies"). In addition, survey participants who purchased the item with the extended description tended to rate their experience better on various scales (e.g., "This item was appealing to the eye") than those who had purchased it with the short description. Sales volume and expressed satisfaction were both increased by the extended description of the product.

6.4.2.2 *Last numbers of prices*

Other research has indicated that the attitude of value-oriented customers may be influenced by odd-numbered or "value" price presentations (Carmin and Norkus 1990; Naipaul and Parsa 2001). For example, Naipaul and Parsa (2001) found that restaurant customers thought that quick-service menus were more value-oriented when its prices ended in 9 than when the prices ended in 0 or 5. In the same study, customers felt that fine dining establishments were of higher quality when their menu prices ended with 0 than when their prices ended with 9. This is consistent with the penny-ending studies in other retail settings (see Özer and Zheng, Chapter 20).

6.4.2.3 *Currency symbols or words*

In addition, the presence or absence of a currency symbol or word has been shown to affect spending behavior. In a recent study (Yang et al. 2009), the average checks for customers who were presented menus without a currency symbol ($) or word (dollar) were significantly higher than for customers who were presented menus with a currency symbol ($) or word (dollar). Perhaps not coincidentally, many fine dining and upscale casual restaurants have begun omitting currency symbols and words from the prices on their menus. Thus, for example, a restaurant might list "Petrale Sole 26," rather than "Petrale Sole $26.00".

6.4.2.4 *Menu item location*

Popular menu design recommendations often focus on making sure customers know that certain products exist by drawing repeated attention to them or by making them more memorable. For example, items targeted for increased promotion through design are recommended to be: boxed or highlighted (Hunt-Wesson Foodservice 1999; Hug and Warfel 1991; Stoner 1986), placed at the top or bottom of a category list (Gallup 1987), or placed in areas of the menu where customers look the most frequently (Gallup 1987).

6.5 Revenue management

Revenue management, as described elsewhere in this handbook (see Talluri, Chapter 26), is also applied in the restaurant industry. As in the hotel and airline industries, restaurants manipulate price, length of customer usage, and space to maximize revenue given their constrained seating capacity. Revenue per available seat hour (RevPASH) is the typical performance measure. It can be calculated by multiplying the seat occupancy percentage by the average check per person. RevPASH can be increased by increasing seat occupancy or by achieving a higher average check per person or by doing both.

Seat occupancy can be increased in several ways including increased efficiency of the service delivery process (Sill and Decker 1999; Kimes 2004a), better table mix (Kimes and Thompson 2004, 2005), better use of reservations and wait lists (Bertsimas and Shioda 2003; Thompson and Kwortnik 2008; Kimes 2009), or by promotions designed to attract additional customers at certain times (Susskind et al. 2004).

Average price per person can be increased through many of the demand-based pricing methods and menu design techniques described in this chapter. Suggestive selling (in which the server suggests additional menu items) or upselling (in which the server suggests higher priced menu items) is also used to help increase the average check.

During slow periods, restaurants typically focus on attracting more customers (sometimes at a discounted price) to increase seat occupancy, while during busy periods, the focus is more on efficiency and maintaining high occupancy while achieving a reasonable average check per person. Regardless of the demand level, the intent of revenue management is always the same: to maximize RevPASH. For an overview of restaurant revenue management, see Kimes (2004b).

6.6 Opportunities for the Future

Pricing is universally considered of critical importance to the success of a restaurant, yet most restaurants continue to rely on "tried and true" methods of pricing. While we are unaware of any systematic study, we believe that most restaurants use some variation of cost-based pricing supplemented with competitive information. More sophisticated restaurants closely track sales and adjust prices upward or downward and drop items based on sales trends. In addition, restaurants use many of the same promotional tactics as other retailers including coupons, loyalty programs, and "specials" to lure customers, especially during less popular times. One gimmick, used by the London restaurant chain Belgo, is to charge customers an amount in British pounds equal to the time shown on their check for meals purchased from 5:00 to 6:30 on weeknights.[6]

Given the current situation, it would appear that there is an opportunity for restaurants to improve profitability through increased analytical sophistication. For example, it appears that only a small fraction of the 945,000 restaurants in the United States have developed an analytical understanding of customer response to their prices in a way that many large retailers now rely upon. Indeed, there have been few, analytic studies of price-sensitivity to menu prices. Only a handful of larger chains, such as McDonald's "optimizes" their prices (or even seeks to) using analytical software packages such as those used by many retailers and grocery stores. Even the most sophisticated restaurants tend to analyze the pricing and performance of individual items in isolation without considering how changing the price of one item might either support or cannibalize sales of other items. We believe that there is plenty of scope for increased adoption of analytic pricing and revenue management techniques in the future.

One area of recent research is reservation management. Reservations at popular restaurants are a "hot" commodity: so much so that companies such as withoutreservations.biz and Weekend Epicure reserved tables at popular restaurants under fictitious names and then sold those names to diners who want tables. The cost of a reservation was of the order of $35 to $40 (Alexandrov and Lariviere 2007). Furthermore, no-show and cancelation rates can be significant, ranging from 3 percent to 15 percent for an average restaurant (Bertsimas and

---

[6] http://www.belgo-restaurants.co.uk, accessed October 26, 2011.

Shioda 2003) to more than 40 percent on Valentine's Day or New Year's Eve (Martin 2001). Overbooking and active management of the reservation mix has the potential to increase utilization and revenue (Bertsimas and Shioda 2003), however higher-end restaurants are increasingly taking deposits with reservations in order to "hedge" against no-shows (Bauer 2011). This approach has something in common with partially refundable airline tickets (Barnes, Chapter 3) and other "service engineering approaches" (Gallego and Stefanescu, Chapter 28). Determining the right mixture of deposits and reservation policy to maximize profitability in different environments is an open area of research.

Finally, it should be noted that restaurants are in the unusual position of providing both a necessary good (nourishment) and an experiential good (dining out). Pricing is part of the overall customer experience and it interacts in complex ways with other parts of the experience. As noted above, how prices are presented on a menu can influence purchase decisions in unexpected ways. In addition, the prices themselves contribute to the overall "image" of a restaurant. While many aspects have been researched, it is not the case that the full interaction between pricing and customer behavior is fully understood. While many establishments are successfully using revenue management and other analytic approaches to improve profitability, most restaurants still consider pricing to be more art than science.

REFERENCES

Alexandrov, A. and Lariviere, M. A. (2007) "Are Reservations Recommended?" Center for Operations and Supply Chain Management, Kellogg School of Management, Northwestern University. Working Paper COSM-06-001 R1.

Allred, G. (2000) *Fight Back and Win: My Thirty Year Fight Against Injustice and How You can Win your own Battles.* New York: Regan Books.

Ariely, D. (2008) *Predictably Irrational: The Hidden Forces that Shape our Decisions.* New York: HarperCollins Publishers.

Bauer, M. (2011) "Restaurant No-Shows: What's a Restaurant to do?" *Inside Scoop SF.* http://insidescoopsf.sfgate.com/blog/2010/01/07/reservation-no-shows-whats-a-restaurant-to-do-2/.

Becker, G. (1991) "A Note on Restaurant Pricing and Other Examples of Social Influence on Price", *Journal of Political Economy* 99/5: 1109–16.

Berra, Y. (1998) *The Yogi Book: "I Didn't Really Say Everything I Said".* New York: Workman Publishing.

Bertsimas, D. and Shioda, R. (2003) "Restaurant Revenue Management", *Operations Research* 51/3: 472–86.

Brown, D. R. (2007) *The Restaurant Manager's Handbook.* Ocala, FL: Atlantic Publishing.

Carmin, J. and Norkus, G. X. (1990) "Pricing Strategies for Menus: Magic or Myth?" *Cornell Hotel & Restaurant Administration Quarterly* 31 /3: 44.

Casson, L. (1994). *Travel in the Ancient World.* Baltimore, MD: Johns Hopkins Press.

The Cline Group (2003) *Restaurant Start and Growth Magazine: Unit Start-up and Failure Study.* Parkville, MD: Specialized Publications/Cline Group.

Delmonico Restaurant menu for April 18, 1899. New York Public Library Digital Collection. Miss Frank E. Buttolph American Menu Collection (Digital ID 467783).

Gaiter, D. J. and Brecher, J. (2004) *Wine for Every Day and Every Occasion*. New York: HarperCollins.

Gallup Report (1987) "Through the Eyes of the Customer", *The Gallup Monthly Report on Eating Out* 7/3: 1–9.

Hug, R. J. and Warfel, M. C. (1991) *Menu Planning and Merchandising*. Berkeley, CA: McCutchan Pub. Corp.

Hunt-Wesson Foodservice (1999) *How to Turn Your Menu Into a Bestseller*. Fullerton, CA: Hunt-Wesson, Inc.

Kelly, T. J., Kiefer, N. M., and Burdett, K. (1994) "A Demand-Based Approach to Menu Pricing", *Cornell Hotel and Restaurant Administration Quarterly* 35/1: 48–52.

Kimes, S. E. (2004a) "Revenue Management: Implementation at Chevys Arrowhead", *Cornell Hotel and Restaurant Administration Quarterly* 44/4: 52–67.

—— (2004b) *Restaurant Revenue Management*. Center for Hospitality Research Report. Cornell University.

—— (2009) "Customer Attitudes Towards Restaurant Reservations Policies", *Journal of Revenue and Pricing Management* 10: 244–60.

—— and Thompson, G. M. (2004) "Restaurant Revenue Management at Chevys: Determining the Best Table Mix", *Decision Sciences Journal* 35/3: 371–91.

—— and —— (2005) "An Evaluation of Heuristic Methods for Determining the Best Table Mix in Full-Service Restaurants", *Journal of Operations Management* 23/6: 599–617.

—— and Wirtz, J. (2003) "When Does Revenue Management Become Acceptable?" *Journal of Service Research* 7/2: 125–35.

—— (2007) *Customer Satisfaction with Restaurant Seating Policies in Casual-Dining Restaurants*. Cornell University Center for Hospitality Research Report.

—— Chase, R. B., Choi, S., Ngonzi, E. N., and Lee, P. Y. (1998) "Restaurant Revenue Management", *Cornell Hotel and Restaurant Administration Quarterly* 40/3: 40–5.

Lewis, R. C. and Shoemaker, S. (1997) "Price-Sensitivity Measurement: A Tool for the Hospitality Industry", *Cornell Hotel and Restaurant Administration Quarterly* 38 /1: 44–54.

Martin, M. (2001) "Side Dish", *Riverside Time* May 2.

Mill, R. C. (2006) *Restaurant Management: Customers, Operations and Employees*, 3rd edn. Upper Saddle River, NJ: Prentice-Hall.

Naipaul, S. and Parsa, H. G. (2001) "Menu Price Endings that Communicate Value and Quality", *Cornell Hotel and Restaurant Administration Quarterly* 42/1: 26.

Parsa, H. G., Self, J. T., Njite, D., and King, T. (2005) "Why Restaurants Fail", *Cornell Hotel and Restaurant Administration Quarterly* 46/3: 304–22.

Phillips, R. L. (2005) *Pricing and Revenue Optimization*. Palo Alto, CA: Stanford University Press.

Raab, C. and Mayer, K. (2000) "Exploring the Use of Activity Based Costing in the Restaurant Industry", *International Journal of Hospitality and Tourism Administration* 4/2: 1–14.

—— and —— (2007) "Menu Engineering and Activity-Based Costing: Can They Work Together in a Restaurant?" *International Journal of Contemporary Hospitality Management* 19/1: 43–52.

—————— Kim, Y.-S., and Shoemaker, S. (2009) "Price-Sensitivity Measurement: A Tool for Restaurant Menu Pricing", *Journal of Hospitality and Tourism Research* 33/1: 93–105.

Shaw, M. (1992) "Positioning and Price: Merging Theory, Strategy, and Tactics", *Hospitality Research Journal* 15/2: 31–9.

Shock, P. J., Bowen, J. T., and Stefanelli, J. M. (2004) *Restaurant Marketing for Owners and Managers*. New York: John Wiley and Sons.

Sill, B. T. and Decker, R. (1999) "Applying Capacity-Management Science: The Case of Browns Restaurant", *Cornell Hotel and Restaurant Administration Quarterly* 40/3: 22–30.

Spang, R. L. (2000) *The Invention of the Restaurant: Paris and Modern Gastronomic Culture*. Cambridge, MA: Harvard University Press.

Stoner, C. L. (1986) "Menus: Design Makes the Difference", *Lodging Hospitality* 42/9: 70–2.

Susskind, A. M., Tsuchiya, E., and Reynolds, D. (2004) "An Evaluation of Guests' Preferred Incentives to Shift Time-Variable Demand in Restaurants", *Cornell Hotel and Restaurant Administration Quarterly* 45/1: 68–84.

Thompson, G. M. and Kwortnik, R. J. (2008) "Pooling Restaurant Reservations to Increase Service Efficiency", *Journal of Service Research* 10/4: 335–46.

Wansink, B., Painter, J., and van Ittersum, K. (2001) "Descriptive Menu Labels' Effect on Sales", *Cornell Hotel and Restaurant Administration Quarterly* 42/7: 68.

——— and —— (2005) "How Descriptive Food Names Bias Sensory Perception in Restaurants", *Food Quality and Preference* 16: 393–400.

Wirtz, J. and Kimes, S. E. (2007) "The Moderating Role of Familiarity in Fairness Perceptions of Revenue Management", *Journal of Service Research* 9/3: 229–40.

Yang, S., Kimes, S. E., and Sessarego, M. M. (2009) "Menu Price Presentation Influences on Consumer Purchase Behavior in Restaurants", *International Journal of Hospitality Management* 28/1: 157–60.

CHAPTER 7

PRICING OF ON-LINE DISPLAY ADVERTISING

MADHU VUDALI AND ANDY ATHERTON

This chapter addresses various aspects of Pricing and Yield Management (PYM) for On-line Display Advertising[1] from the perspective of an on-line publisher. Our primary focus will be on the pricing process and the techniques used to set and negotiate prices, but we will also discuss the broader role of yield management. Both play important and complementary roles in improving a publisher's financial performance.

7.1 OVERVIEW

We assume that the readers are familiar with the World Wide Web and the basics of web-browsing. However, we will start with some of the basics of display advertising to facilitate the pricing and yield management discussion later in the chapter.

7.1.1 The buyers (the advertisers)

Advertisers purchase display advertising directly or through an advertising agency[2] such as Digitas, Mindshare, or Universal McCann. Some companies have in-house advertising

This chapter relies heavily on examples and experience drawn from the work done by the authors at Yahoo!. The success of the PYM initiative at Yahoo! was the result of the innovation and hard work of many of our colleagues, too numerous to mention each by name. However, we would like to express our particular gratitude to Wenda Harris Millard, formerly Chief Sales Officer, Yahoo! and Todd Teresi, formerly Senior Vice President, Yahoo! Display Operations. During the course of implementing PYM at Yahoo!, we drove several significant changes to the sales process. We could not have succeeded without Wenda's active support and encouragement. We thank Todd for his vision to create the PYM department at Yahoo! and for his energetic sponsorship of various PYM projects and initiatives.

[1] Search Advertising with text ads is the other major on-line advertising market. Google is the dominant player in this market.

[2] There is another type of buyer in on-line advertising—the "ad network", which is an intermediary between advertisers/agencies and publishers. Ad networks are not the focus of this chapter. However, we will discuss their role later in the chapter.

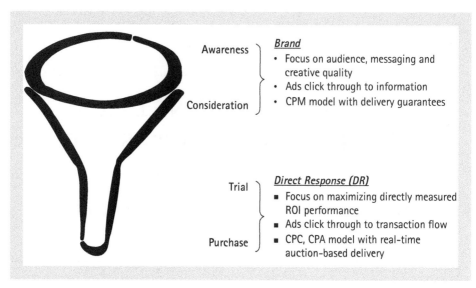

FIGURE 7.1 The marketing funnel

functions within their marketing departments but most advertisers outsource some portion of their advertising process to ad agencies. Ad agencies play a crucial role in the advertising ecosystem and in the media-buying process as they can leverage their expertise and scale. Agencies plan and execute the advertising campaigns as well as negotiate pricing on behalf of their clients. (For our discussion, we will use the terms advertisers and agencies interchangeably.)

Different advertisers have different objectives for their advertising campaigns. Similarly, an individual advertiser may have different objectives for different campaigns. Broadly advertising can be divided into Brand advertising and Direct Response (DR) advertising. Brand advertising is intended to drive awareness consideration and purchase intent, with a focus on audience, messaging, and the content/creative quality. DR advertising is intended to "close the sale" with a focus on maximizing the direct return-on-investment (ROI) on the current campaign. The two broad types of advertising are obviously and intimately related—brand advertising creates the awareness and consideration that direct response advertising capitalizes on to generate sales. Research from the Atlas Institute (a part of Microsoft Advertising) indicates that factoring every "consumer touch point" enables advertisers to be "more effective, more creative, and more relevant with their digital marketing" (Atlas Institute 2008). With respect to the common marketing notion of a "funnel", brand advertising is a "top of the funnel" function while DR advertising is a "bottom of the funnel" function as shown in Figure 7.1.

7.1.2 The sellers (the publishers)

On-line display advertising is primarily sold by publishers of web content.[3] There are different types of publishers in the display advertising market:

---

[3] Ad networks are sellers as well, as they aggregate and roll-up inventory from publishers.

- *Portals versus "verticals"*—AOL/MSN/Yahoo! are prime examples of portals that are one-stop-shops providing a variety of content and services to their users. Verticals, on the other hand, are specialist websites that focus on particular domains, and as such draw very domain-specific advertising; e.g., CNET.com for Technology. In contrast, a portal attracts a much more diverse group of advertisers due to the variety of its offerings.

- *"Pure play" versus Print/TV extension*—Yahoo! is an example of a "pure play" Internet publisher, which does not have any other affiliations. In contrast, MTV.com or NYTimes.com are extensions of their off-line TV and print publishing businesses, respectively. These publishers have the opportunity to offer advertising packages that bundle off-line and on-line media.

- *Head versus Tail*—About.com is an example of a "head" publisher with a large audience and variety of content/services for that audience. "Tail" publishers, on the other hand, are niche publishers with a small, devoted audience focused on narrow topics. Blogs are examples of the publishing tail. A key distinction between head and tail publishers is the degree and consistency of professional editorial quality control over their content. Tail publishers are by definition small and as a population have inconsistent quality control over their content. Brand advertisers are extremely sensitive to content quality when deciding where to place their ads and they do not have the time to perpetually review a constantly changing landscape of thousands of tiny publishers. Further, tail publishers do not have the scale to support a direct salesforce that packages and sells their inventory. They typically consign their inventory to third parties for ad sales. As a result, tail publishers typically attract advertising from ad networks representing DR advertisers who are much less sensitive to content quality.

7.1.3 The ads

When a user visits an on-line website such as Yahoo! Finance (finance.yahoo.com) to check her stock portfolio or to read the news on the website of *The New York Times* (www.nytimes.com), she is presented the content along with advertisements. These advertisements are typically called "banner ads". There are a variety of sizes for banner ads and each website makes a particular choice. The sizes are described using the dimensions of the area in pixels, for example 728 × 90, 300 × 250, or 160 × 600. The Interactive Advertising Bureau (IAB) at www.iab.net has industry-wide standards on its website. The delivery of the advertisement to the user is referred to as "ad-serving". Increasingly, when the ad is served, the user can interact with the ad to get a custom message and/or the ad transforms the content around it momentarily to grab the user's attention. These types of ad-formats are collectively called "rich media" and are unique to display advertising. Advertisers and publishers are continually evolving formats to better convey the marketing message.

7.1.4 The users

When a user browses a website, the website has knowledge of the user based on the information that is stored in the user's "cookie"—a text file that typically stores data such as history on user behavior and personally identifiable information on the user's computer. Typically, the information includes information such as the user's age, gender, and occupation that the user has chosen to disclose at the time of registration with the website. Collectively, these attributes are referred to as "demographic" attributes. In addition, the website can infer "geographic" attributes of the user's location such as country, state, DMA (designated marketing area), or ZIP code. Lastly, depending on the sophistication of the website, the website may be able to assign the user various "behavioral targeting" (BT) attributes based on her browsing patterns on the website. So, let us assume in the case of our user on Yahoo! Finance that the user is a female, aged 32, logged in from the city of San Francisco, California. Yahoo! would "know" all of this information when the user logs in to Yahoo!. Further, let us assume that Yahoo! assigns the user the BT categories of "Home Loans" and "Car Insurance" based on her browsing patterns. These attributes, along with the "context" (i.e., which Yahoo! page she's browsing), are the criteria by which Yahoo! determines to show an ad to her.

Each visit by the user generates an opportunity to show an ad—typically referred to as an "impression". The more users a website has and the more frequent their visits, the more the impressions. Ad impressions are the most basic form of inventory for the website. A publisher is trying to make the most revenue from this inventory. Note that the inventory is perishable. The publisher only has one opportunity to make the most of the impression at the moment when a user consumes a page; the impression cannot be stored for later use.

7.1.5 The campaigns

Depending on their objectives, advertisers want to target their ads to groups of users that fall within various combinations of contextual, demographic, geographic, and behavioral clusters. For example:

- A movie studio launching a new blockbuster might run an ad on the Front Page of Yahoo! without any targeting—i.e., to target all users—to maximize its "reach".
- A California-based bank looking to increase awareness and attract deposits might run an ad targeted at users over the age of 18 from the state of California that are browsing Yahoo! Finance.
- An auto-insurance company seeking new customers might target users who are assigned to the "Car Insurance Purchase Intent" BT category no matter where they are on Yahoo!'s many websites.

Note that a given user will simultaneously fall into multiple targeting clusters and hence will qualify for multiple ad-campaigns. Our San Francisco user will qualify to see the ads of campaigns of the three advertisers mentioned above when she visits various Yahoo! websites.

A common form of measurement for display advertising is impression delivery, which represents the number of times an ad is shown during the length of the campaign to the targeted audience. Along with impression delivery, reach and frequency metrics are typically used for brand advertising. "Reach" is the number of unique users ("UUs") that were exposed to the ad. "Frequency" is the number of times those users were exposed to the ad. Reach and frequency are typically expressed together, for example, 2 million UUs at a frequency of 5 per week. Advertisers running DR campaigns also attempt to measure the direct "performance" of the ads when they are shown, that is, clicks, sales transactions, or other valuable actions resulting from the ad. Before advertisers run each campaign they typically specify a measurement objective, such as ad impression, reach, clicks, and sales.

To summarize, a campaign is an advertising buy with a collection of specific requirements, typically expressed by some combination of the following attributes:

- context—type of content on the website the user is browsing;
- demographic—who the user is;
- geographic—where the user is located;
- behavior—what the user's interests are based on her online activity;
- flight—the start and end dates of the campaign;
- ad creative—ad sizes, images, artwork and related collateral, and media formats;
- goals—impression delivery, reach, clicks, or transactions.

7.2 BUYING MODELS

As mentioned previously, on-line display advertising is highly measurable—impressions, reach, frequency, clicks, for all campaigns, and transactions or other actions for DR campaigns. A publisher can ensure that a campaign gets the number of contracted impressions or reach. However, they cannot ensure how well the campaign performs, that is, how many clicks or transactions are generated. That depends on the ad, the offer, and the particular targeting chosen by the advertiser. This difference in accountability between the publisher and the advertiser has created two primary buying models—guaranteed and non-guaranteed.

In a guaranteed contract, the publisher agrees to sell a certain number of impressions to the advertiser at a certain price. *The industry standard unit of pricing is CPM (cost per thousand impressions).* This price is typically negotiated because the publisher wants a premium to provide the guarantee, which the advertiser may or may not be willing to pay. When a publisher enters a guaranteed contract, it ensures that the advertiser's campaign receives the number of impressions that was agreed upon by the two parties. There is an advertising industry practice called "makegood", which provides some compensation to the advertiser should the guarantee not be met. If the advertiser's campaign does not receive the agreed-upon impressions, then the parties can negotiate the makegood. Typically, the makegood takes the form of credit on a future campaign, or extension of the current campaign without charge. The publisher is not liable for how well the campaign "performs"—that is left to the advertiser. Guaranteed contracts are most similar to TV and print advertising and are preferred by brand marketers whose main objective is to maximize the reach of their brand messages with careful control of demographics and context.

In a non-guaranteed contract, the advertiser agrees to pay when a click or transaction is generated. *The unit of pricing is referred to as a CPC (cost per click), CPA (cost per action), or CPO (cost per order).* A publisher does not control, for example, the ad creative or the specific marketing message that an advertiser chooses to display and, therefore, whether the ad will get clicked or not. Hence, the publisher does not want to guarantee any type of performance. However, since the publisher only gets paid when the user takes some action on the ads, they try to optimize the ad-serving to maximize the number of actions. Non-guaranteed contracts are similar to search advertising and are preferred by advertisers with DR objectives. As in search advertising, the CPC/CPA that the advertiser wants to pay is up to them. The advertiser, typically, pays based on their return-on-investment or profit margin. From a publisher's standpoint, it is best to deliver non-guaranteed contracts using auctions, as the competition amongst advertisers nets the best monetization. The auction is conducted one ad impression at a time to maximize the *expected* revenue.

Some advertisers who are more price-sensitive and less delivery-sensitive may also buy impressions—not just clicks and actions—on a non-guaranteed basis. Non-guaranteed purchases allow for additional monetization when the publisher has excess supply after servicing guaranteed demand. Airlines handle their standby passengers in a similar fashion: standby passengers are seated after all regular fare passengers are seated allowing the airline to increase the revenue on the flight by filling an otherwise empty seat.

7.3 Pricing

This section describes the basics of pricing from a publisher's perspective and the factors that need to be considered to set and manage rates.

7.3.1 Rate card

The rate card is the set of prices that a sales representative uses to respond to a proposal from an advertiser. The rate card establishes the pricing guidelines for selling guaranteed contracts.

Most rate cards attempt to cover the suite of ad products—essentially a combination of the attributes that describe an ad campaign—that are available for purchase. However, highly customized advertising opportunities (e.g., a custom "microsite" hosted by the publisher for an advertiser) are typically negotiated on a one-off basis rather than priced on the rate card. A typical publisher has hundreds, if not thousands, of ad products that they can sell. Given the complexity and scale of ad products, most publishers rely on *attribute-based* pricing rather than individually price every single combination of attributes. This attribute-based approach is reflected in the rate card:

- "Base" prices: Prices for a limited set of ad products, which form the core of the publisher's offering. For example, combinations of context and ad-size (such as, "Finance/300 × 250" or "News/160 × 600") can have specific prices.
- Attribute mark ups: An incremental price (typically expressed as a %-mark up or an absolute $-mark up) for a product attribute, e.g., a 10% mark up for Age = "25–34".

This flexible segmentation of the rate card allows full leverage of the available data and helps focus the publisher's pricing efforts. In the absence of data, a publisher can focus analytic resources on base prices, while utilizing a consensus-based approach on determining attribute markups. With the accumulation of data and the analytics to process it, the publisher can choose a more sophisticated approach for determining prices.

7.3.2 List prices and floor prices

An externally published rate card typically has a list price at which negotiations can start with advertisers for guaranteed contracts. Often, there's a price below which the publisher is not inclined to offer a guarantee and would rather put the inventory out to auction and take their chances in the non-guaranteed market. We refer to this price as the "Floor Price". The floor price is the minimum price at which a guarantee is made.

The purpose of price optimization, then, is to create a set of floor and/or list prices that achieve the publisher's objectives. In practice, the publisher either chooses to optimize for floor or list price but not both. We recommend that the publisher optimize the price relative to which the customer's price elasticity is measured. (In our case, it was the floor price.) After determining one, the other is derived simply by using a formula. For example, list price is twice the floor price.

7.3.3 Inventory pooling

In many cases, the same impression can be used to fulfill multiple campaigns. Stated differently, the same source of supply can be used to fulfill multiple sources of demand. We will call this "inventory pooling". The pricing implication of inventory pooling is that the price for a given ad product is impacted by other ad products that use the same inventory. Recall our example of the user visiting Yahoo!'s websites. The price of the user's impressions when these impressions are part of the California regional campaign is different from the price that Yahoo! charges when the impressions are part of the "Car Insurance" BT category. Typically, the "BT impressions" are priced higher than "Geographic impressions". The price difference captures the relative value placed by advertisers on these two different ad products and the relative magnitude of their demand versus available supply.

Further, inventory pooling also has an impact on the availability of various ad products, and, by implication, on their prices. Let us say that 1 in 10 California users qualifies for a "Car Insurance" BT category. If we sold 10 million "California" impressions, then we will be depleting the supply pool of not just the 10 million "California" impressions but also potentially 1 million "Car Insurance" BT impressions. When setting prices, we will need to account for the overlap of these various ad products within a given inventory pool.

7.3.4 Non-guaranteed contracts

Non-guaranteed contracts in on-line display advertising present an alternate source of monetization to publishers. In general, non-guaranteed contracts are priced substantially less than guaranteed contracts: advertisers in the non-guaranteed market are more price-sensitive and the publisher has more flexibility. For example, if the non-guaranteed CPM is

$1.00, then any guaranteed contract should be priced *at least* $1.00 since the publisher is making a delivery guarantee to the advertiser. From a pricing standpoint, then, the non-guaranteed CPMs become the minimum prices that the publisher should charge for providing the guarantee. In price optimization, non-guaranteed CPMs can be treated either as opportunity costs for providing the guarantee or as minimum-price constraints. There is a potential substitution effect to consider as well: if the guarantee is priced too high, then advertisers may balk and take their chances in the non-guaranteed auction.

7.3.5 Perishable inventory

Ad inventory is perishable—the publisher has a limited time window to capitalize on the opportunity to serve the right ad to maximize revenue. When a user shows up on a site, the publisher has a few milliseconds to make a decision on what ad to serve to that user. *The opportunity to serve the ad cannot be stored for later use.*

Given the perishable nature of the inventory, then, every opportunity to ad-serve is an opportunity to make incremental revenue. All things being equal, it is better to show an ad than not. Since the marginal cost of ad-serving is negligible, the publisher should consider any demand with a CPM greater than $0.00.[4] However, the publisher should factor inventory pooling and non-guaranteed contracts for determining opportunity costs for pricing.

Additionally, as with airlines, perishable inventory implies that the "time to departure" also has an impact on pricing. For a given date in the future, if remaining inventory is less (more) than the expected amount for that date, then prices tend to increase (decrease) as the date approaches. Any unsold inventory on the date is monetized in the non-guaranteed spot market. As with airlines, on-line publishers need to estimate booking curves, in order to factor "time to departure" in pricing.

7.3.6 Booking curves

Advertising is reservation-based in a fashion similar to airlines and hotels and shares with those industries the concept of booking curves—how bookings materialize over time for a product. For example, for a given date in the future, there may be no bookings one year prior to the date, 10 percent of the total inventory booked nine months out, 20 percent booked six months out, 60 percent booked three months out, 75 percent booked the day before, and thereby leaving 25 percent of the inventory to be sold on that date in the non-guaranteed market. This booking pattern can vary by ad product. "Autos" inventory tends to be sold out sooner as car manufacturers lay out their promotional plans 12–18 months in advance. In contrast, generic inventory like "News" tends not to sell out in advance since such inventory is relatively abundant compared to demand and thus a substantial amount of such inventory is sold in the non-guaranteed market.

We note that booking curves at the detailed ad product level can be difficult to estimate due to data scarcity. Our experience is that it is best to estimate booking curves at some

---

[4] Most publishers show "house ads" (promotions for publisher products/services) rather than not show any ads.

logical aggregation of ad products. For example, it makes more sense to estimate a booking curve for "News" than it does for " News/Male/18–34/728 × 90."

Once we estimate the booking curves, we can adjust prices based on how the actual bookings for a delivery date deviate from the expected bookings for that delivery date. If the actual bookings are ahead of the expected bookings pace, then prices should be raised and vice versa.

7.3.7 Price optimization

A publisher's objective is to set prices to maximize profit. Since the marginal cost of serving an ad is negligible, maximizing revenue is equivalent to maximizing profit. In light of the various buying models, however, the publisher has to consider the expected revenue from all the demand sources when setting prices. More formally, the expected revenue per thousand impressions (RPM) is defined as yield. For guaranteed contracts, the CPM charged on the contract is the RPM. For non-guaranteed contracts, we can convert the CPC, CPA, or CPO that the advertiser is willing to pay into the equivalent RPM. For example, if there is a probability of 0.5 percent ("click-through rate" or CTR) for an ad to be clicked and the advertiser is willing to pay $1.00 per click, then the RPM for the non-guaranteed contract is $5.00.[5] We can now calculate the total yield by summing the yield from every contract that utilizes the inventory. Prices are optimized to maximize yield on the inventory.

Based on the preceding discussion, several factors at play determine pricing in display advertising. Price optimization for display advertising should consider:

- *Price elasticity*. Historical demand data and econometric analysis can inform the estimation of product price elasticities. Since advertising products are highly substitutable, we should also consider cross-product price elasticities.

- *Inventory forecasts*. Forecasts of traffic patterns for each ad product.

- *Inventory availability*. Amount of ad inventory remaining after factoring currently booked campaigns. Due to inventory pooling, a single booking can potentially deplete inventory from multiple ad products.

- *Booking curves* for each ad product or an aggregation thereof.

- *Opportunity costs*. Yield from alternate monetization opportunities.

Depending on the resources available to a publisher, price optimization can be done either in-house or out sourced to a software vendor focused on pricing for display advertising.

7.3.8 Negotiated pricing

Most on-line display media is sold via direct salesforces with negotiated pricing. An optimal rate card is a necessary foundation, but it is not sufficient to ensure the successful optimization of rates in individual transactions.

---

[5] With a CTR of 0.5%, we get 5 clicks by serving 1,000 impressions. Since the advertiser is willing to pay $1.00 per click, the total expected revenue is $5.00.

As discussed previously, inventory pooling implies that the sale of one ad product has an impact on the availability and pricing of other products that share the same inventory pool. A sales process where each sales region or sales channel makes their own pricing decisions can yield sub-optimal revenue outcomes as teams are competing for shared resources and are making independent decisions. In particular, this is true for making discounting decisions. Discounting decisions are key for large-volume transactions or for "upfront" deals, that is, when an advertiser is committing to a full-year media purchase. Given their size and span, these types of deals can affect the pricing for other advertisers.

Our approach at Yahoo! was to use a "Floor Price"—a price above which no approval was needed—with a centralized discount management process. The floor price approach allowed the distributed/decentralized sales teams to work autonomously from the headquarters. The rate card was updated frequently to get the latest data to inform the pricing decisions. When a proposal to an advertiser was below the floor price, it triggered an exception approval request. The same team that managed the rate card also managed the pricing exceptions. Some benefits of this centralized process are:

- Pricing exceptions are made from a "portfolio" perspective—each exception is evaluated for its impact on the entire portfolio not just on the particular ad product or sales region.

- Since it is the same team making the decisions each time, it created consistency/predictability within the process, potentially allowing for automation of some of the decisions down the road.

- Most importantly, it is a very valuable feedback mechanism—the pricing team has a first-hand view of how the rate card is received in the marketplace.

7.4 INVENTORY MANAGEMENT AND OVERBOOKING

Once a publisher has made commitments, he faces the problem of how to manage his inventory in the face of uncertain supply and potentially modified commitments. Managing these decisions carefully is critical for profitability. This section discusses two key techniques that a publisher can use to address this issue.

7.4.1 Delivery prioritization

For any given piece of inventory, it is possible to have multiple guaranteed and non-guaranteed contracts vying for delivery. Therefore, the ad server must be loaded with an intelligent set of prioritization rules if the optimal ad is to be selected for each serving opportunity (impression).

At a gross level, guaranteed contracts should take precedence in serving as publishers and advertisers are averse to makegoods. This prioritization is also very useful in informing the pricing of the guarantees, that is, non-guaranteed contracts provide the opportunity costs for serving guaranteed contracts first. Further, there is potential for substitution between guaranteed and non-guaranteed ad products, that is, if the guarantee were priced too high, then advertisers may take their chances in the non-guaranteed auction.

Secondly, because of inventory pooling, the ad server must consider inventory scarcity when managing delivery contention between guaranteed contracts. In our earlier example of the Yahoo! user, when the ad server receives an ad request for a user from California who belongs to the Car Insurance BT category, the ad server should serve a Car Insurance BT campaign before a California regional campaign (assuming both have been sold). This approach maximizes the likelihood of delivering on all guarantees. Further, it helps maximize revenue as scarcer inventory, such as impressions of Car Insurance BT category, tends to be priced higher than the more abundant inventory, such as impressions of California region. Finally, delivery of non-guaranteed contracts should be prioritized by yield.

7.4.2 Inventory buffering and overbooking

Publishers have to consider the possibility of advertisers canceling, delaying, or modifying their campaigns. Ad budgets are cut in harsh economic conditions; advertisers may adjust their budget allocations to various ad products mid-campaign. An additional complication in display advertising is the fact that demand is lumpy and variable—advertisers' demand is not for one ad impression but for a variable amount of impressions. The practical implication of this lumpiness is that it is easier analytically to deal with supply uncertainty than it is to deal with demand uncertainty. On the supply side, different ad products have different traffic patterns. For example, News video is very "bursty" while Finance is affected by external market conditions. In addition, the more specific the product definition, the greater the supply uncertainty for that product. For example, supply of "Female, 18–34" impressions is more certain than the supply of "Female, 18–34, San Francisco, BT/Car Insurance". A critical implication of the supply uncertainty is in making delivery guarantees. To minimize makegoods due to under-delivery, the publisher's inclination is to buffer the inventory predictions and provide a "safe" guarantee. The risk in this case is under-monetization due to excess inventory. On the other hand, if we allow overbooking, we risk under-delivery and makegoods. Different ad products lend themselves to different approaches. With unique products such as "Oscars Package" or "Front Page" inventory buffering is preferred as there are no readily available substitutes if there is under-delivery. With more generic products such as "Mail" or "Sports" overbooking is preferred although frequently not possible due to a supply/demand imbalance.

7.5 PRICING AND YIELD MANAGEMENT AT YAHOO!

This section describes our experience with PYM for the display advertising business at Yahoo! (2002–07). We will discuss the PYM project that was initiated in 2002 and fully incorporated into the operational processes by the end of 2003. In particular, we focus on the challenges of implementing a successful PYM program.

7.5.1 Project scope

The environment at Yahoo! prior to the initiation of the PYM project in 2002 could be summarized as follows:

- manual/subjective pricing;
- outdated paper rate card and discount schedule;
- business units competing with each other to get revenue by discounting;
- sales people negotiating internally with many parties;
- no standard data entry procedures;
- no central pricing authority;
- no price-based incentive structure for sales.

As a result, overall yield on the inventory was declining. The goal of the PYM project was to address all aspects of pricing and yield management to reverse the trend of declining yield.

The overall implementation took us one-and-half years to complete. However, we had interim deliverables, each of which improved the PYM practice within Yahoo!. In the first year, the centralized pricing and system-based price execution were created to facilitate clean data collection. We also worked with sales management to re design incentives for sales representatives to include price-based compensation. At the beginning of the second year, we launched a price optimization system, which we licensed from Rapt—a software vendor (now part of Microsoft). Throughout the implementation, we worked with sales teams on "change management" so that they were ready as and when the changes were being rolled out.

7.5.2 Implementation challenges

We briefly describe the challenges we faced as we implemented our PYM project. We believe that these are common challenges facing most practitioners and we offer some recommendations to overcome these challenges.

7.5.2.1 Planning and buy-in

Successful PYM efforts are complex initiatives that involve many people and technical systems. Careful planning and executive sponsorship is important. Management and practitioners should spend the time upfront to understand the entire problem that needs to be solved. Senior management and key stakeholder buy-in is critical in ensuring the success of the PYM initiative. Therefore, it is important to get agreement on the overall pricing vision and framework before addressing specific problem areas. Once the buy-in is obtained, the appropriate phasing of the project deliverables can be determined, with a focus on key leverage points. For example, poor pricing performance may be the result of poor price/policy enforcement. Correcting this discipline issue is necessary before investing in an econometric model for effective pricing. Knowing where to focus to get maximum leverage is critical. One or two quick, obvious wins can be very helpful in establishing the credibility necessary to move as quickly as possible with a PYM initiative.

7.5.2.2 Change management

Change management is one of the most difficult elements of any PYM program, particularly in the context of a direct, negotiated sales model. However, successful change management is also critical to the success of a PYM initiative when a salesforce is involved. A motivated, disciplined salesforce that understands the rationale behind pricing can vastly improve the bottom-line impact of pricing. An undisciplined or hostile salesforce can stop a PYM initiative in its tracks.

To facilitate change management, we recommend that practitioners assemble an advisory team of sales people to provide feedback and assist in communication. The PYM team should equip the sales team on the importance of pricing as well as being transparent about the decision-making process. Also, given the tactical nature of sales and operations, care must be taken to communicate system and process changes sufficiently in advance and follow up with feedback and review once the changes are in place.

Finally, change management takes time. The process should be started as early as possible and moves more quickly if the complete framework can be laid down first, followed by refinements in each area. For example, start building discipline by agreeing on a rate card and exception process then focus on optimizing rates and reducing exceptions over time.

7.5.2.3 Data quality

The price optimization problem in on-line display advertising is a fairly complex optimization problem and data requirements are substantial. Having consistent and coherent data to feed the pricing models is extremely important. Therefore, it is best to undertake price-optimization only when a sufficient amount of clean data is available.

From our experience, that is rarely the case at the beginning of a new PYM initiative. Undisciplined sales practices, incentive misalignment, or order entry errors can create severe data quality issues. Therefore, we recommend that substantial early effort be spent in making sure that gaps in data are addressed either via incentives to teams that generate the data and/or by system/process changes to capture data more easily. These efforts will build and clean the data asset over time.

7.5.2.4 Incentive alignment and compliance

When a direct salesforce executes prices, proper incentive alignment is critical to the success of any PYM initiative. Sales representatives are most often motivated by revenue attainment, not by price attainment. While many companies have a variety of sales incentives and policies, we will focus on how incentives can affect market feedback into pricing. For the sake of this discussion, we assume that there is already a commission plan in place to pay sales representatives for achieving their revenue quotas.

While a publisher could set floor prices optimally based on all the factors discussed previously, a customer might have a higher or lower willingness-to-pay than is indicated by the prices on the rate card. We illustrate this mismatch by two simple scenarios with associated incentive alignment suggestions:

- *Advertiser's willingness-to-pay is higher than floor price*: The sales representative can close the deal at the floor price without any negotiation. How does the sales representative "discover" the higher reservation price? One possibility is to provide an incentive on the price premium that a sales representative is able to command for a given set of products. If sales representative A sells product X at a higher price than sales representative B, then representative A gets a higher bonus than representative B.

- *Advertiser's willingness-to-pay is lower than floor price*: If the sales representative is penalized for lower prices, what incentive does she have to ask for a pricing exception to win the revenue? One possibility is to provide compensation "accelerators" on revenue achievement, i.e., any revenue above the quota has a higher commission. This will motivate sales representatives to bring forward a price exception for consideration—even if it is likely that the particular exception is not approved.

Note that under both scenarios, properly designed incentives provide valuable new data points for pricing analysis and optimization and improve the capability of the pricing methodology to adapt to changing market conditions.

7.5.3 Results

The results at Yahoo! for the PYM approach described were impressive. The PYM effort at Yahoo! reversed two years of steady CPM declines in the display advertising business; average display CPMs grew at a compound *quarterly* rate of 10 percent from Q103 to Q107, contributing an incremental $100M+ to EBITDA. These pricing improvements were achieved while revenue grew rapidly and substantially faster than the market overall; during this period Yahoo! gained approximately five points of market share (measured by revenue). As any PYM practitioner can attest, rapid and simultaneous growth in revenue, share, and pricing is quite a significant achievement.

7.6 CURRENT TRENDS AND CONCLUSION

The on-line media market is evolving rapidly as consumers increasingly shift their media consumption away from off-line media in favor of on-line alternatives. As this evolution unfolds, there are a number of significant trends at play, each with implications for on-line display advertising in general and publisher PYM efforts in particular.

7.6.1 Ad networks

On-line media is much less consolidated than off-line media, which continues to create opportunities for ad networks—intermediaries who aggregate supply and demand, increasing efficiency in a fragmented market.

There are a variety of ad networks, focusing on different aspects of the advertising business. Some of the focus areas and the ad networks that are addressing them are: *targeting technology* (such as Google Content Network—contextual targeting, Audience Science—behavioral targeting), *type of advertiser* (such as Advertising.com—DR, Brand.net—brand), *type of content* (such as Healthline—health, Fantasy Sports Ad

Network—fantasy sports), *demographics* (such as Glam Networks—women, Hispano-Click—Hispanics), and *ad format* (such as YuMe—video, AdMob—mobile).

From an advertiser's perspective an ad network is an efficient, aggregated source of ad inventory (supply) that also provides value-added services/products. For example, many ad networks track a user's activity across various sites so that they can predict her affinity for a particular ad and then use this data automatically to maximize campaign performance across a broad/diverse inventory mix.

From a publisher's perspective, an ad network aggregates advertiser budgets (demand). An ad network can provide a small publisher significant monetization of inventory without the need to invest in a salesforce. An ad network can provide a large publisher a valuable source of non-guaranteed demand to backfill for demand generated by its direct salesforce.

While ad networks can provide a valuable source of additional demand for a publisher, use of ad networks by publishers is not without risks. Most ad networks aggregate primarily DR demand, which generally offers dramatically lower yield to publishers. Ad networks can also generate channel conflict for publishers, interfering with their direct sales efforts.

Publishers should seek networks that represent brand advertising demand as well as DR and should carefully manage channel conflict with all indirect sales channels. Publishers can minimize channel conflict by only working with blind networks on a non-guaranteed delivery basis, while maintaining their creative standards (Atherton 2009).

7.6.2 Auctions/ad exchanges

Pioneered in search advertising, auctions have taken root broadly in display advertising. In display advertising, auctions have become the de facto mechanism for clearing excess inventory. Auctions are inherently non-guaranteed and are primarily used by DR advertisers and ad networks.

More recently, ad exchanges have been created to bring publishers and advertisers together in ad marketplaces. These exchanges are quite dissimilar to the typical commodities or futures exchange, which are characterized, for example, by standard contracts, clearinghouses, and margin requirements. In their current form, most ad exchanges are essentially collective auctions, which restrict their usage to DR advertisers and ad networks representing them. Publisher PYM teams should take advantage of auction capabilities to increase yield on excess inventory, where possible without generating channel conflict.

7.6.3 Supply/demand imbalance

As shown in Figure 7.2, the on-line brand advertising market is approximately one-third the size of the on-line DR advertising market. However, the overall brand advertising market is nearly twice as large as the overall DR market. Brand advertising is dramatically under-represented on-line (ThinkEquity Partners LLC 2007; Lehman Brothers 2008; DMA 2008).

DR advertisers have more readily adopted display advertising due to two primary factors: (1) their relative focus on measurability over content quality and control and (2) the operational efficiency available through DR-focused ad networks. Brand advertising has moved on-line slowly in large part because it has been a difficult, inefficient process for

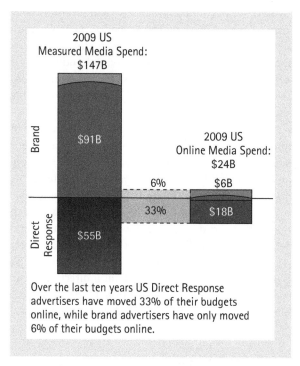

FIGURE 7.2 Relative sizes of brand and DR ad markets

Source: Brand.net analysis based on data from Barclays Capital, ThinkEquity Partners LLC, and DMA

brand advertisers and agencies to reach their target audiences in the highest-quality, contextually relevant environments they require.

Brand budgets are significantly lagging the shift of consumer audiences towards on-line media consumption. This lag has meant that there is far more display advertising supply than there is demand for it. Further, the existing demand is primarily DR, which is more price-sensitive than the media market at large. As a result, there is downward pressure on publisher yield. This pressure has intensified in recent years as ad networks have increased in scale and are able to supply more ad inventory to the market.

Given their focus on guaranteed delivery, brand advertisers tend to pay higher prices (to procure the guarantee). Publishers are advised to make every effort to attract brand advertising demand to drive revenue and improve yield. Brand-focused ad networks, such as Brand.net, can help in this regard.

The market for on-line display advertising is large and growing rapidly. Results at Yahoo! prove that a comprehensive, flexible, data-driven approach to PYM can provide tremendous upside for an on-line publisher. Optimal pricing is an important foundation for PYM, but a variety of other technical and operational issues must be addressed to ensure a successful program.[6]

---

[6] There is an excellent glossary of many of the terms that are referenced in this chapter (and more) at the IAB website at http://www.iab.net/media/file/GlossaryofInteractivAdvertisingTerms.pdf, accessed October 26, 2011.

REFERENCES

Atherton, A. (2009) "Eliminating Channel Conflict Between Publishers", Ad Networks. Media Post, 2/25. New York.

Atlas Institute (2008) *Engagement Mapping*. Seattle, WA: Atlas Institute.

Bain/Internet Advertising Bureau (IAB) (2008) *Digital Pricing Research*. New York: IAB.

Direct Marketing Association (DMA) (2008) *The Power of Direct Marketing*. New York: DMA.

Lehman Brothers (2008) Internet Data Book. New York: Lehman Brothers.

ThinkEquity Partners LLC (2007) *Online Advertising 2.0: The Opportunity in Non-Premium Display*. San Franscisco, CA: ThinkEquity Partners LLC.

CHAPTER 8

....

CONSUMER CREDIT PRICING

....

SIMON CAUFIELD

8.1 INTRODUCTION

....

Consumer credit takes several forms. It may be secured on the underlying asset, as in the case of mortgages, home equity, and auto loans; or unsecured as in credit cards and unsecured consumer loans. Customer interest rates may be fixed or variable over the life of the loan. The amount borrowed and term may be fixed as in loans or indefinite as in credit cards and lines of credit. There are also several forms of price. Although the interest rate generates most of the lender's revenue from credit, there are also fees. In credit cards, for example, fees may be charged for additional services such as getting cash from an ATM or using the card overseas; penalty fees may be charged for late payment and insufficient funds; and annual fees may be charged for owning the card. In this article, we use the term *rate* to mean interest rate only and will use *price* when including other fees.

The pricing challenges in consumer credit are somewhat different from most other industries. Neither revenues nor costs are known with certainty at the point of sale and both vary by customer. The impact of poor decisions is severe. Annual net interest revenue on an individual loan may be as little as 1 percent of the principal but if the customer defaults, costs may be up to the total amount outstanding. The credit crisis of 2007–09 cruelly exposed lenders that underestimated potential risks. Fifteen years of relatively stable economic conditions including falling interest rates and rising real estate prices resulted in optimistic estimates for both the probability of customer default and the likely loss given default.

Interest rates may be used in direct marketing as well as broadcast advertising where pricing cannot be tailored to different segments or individuals. The ideal rate differs at key stages of the customer relationship. That is because a lender's objectives may differ between acquisition and retention or the lender may be trying to stimulate dormant customers. In some sectors such as auto loans, the customer sale is complicated by the role of intermediaries who may be directly responsible for setting the ultimate price to the end customer. Pricing is also usually subject to regulation, for example the Fair Lending Act in the USA and Treating Customers Fairly (TCF) in the UK. Both of these regulations aim to restrict lenders from applying different policies to different customers.

Until the 1980s, banks and finance companies set only one price that applied to all customers for each product such as the interest rate on a home equity. There was no differentiation. The price was set to cover the cost of funds, expected credit losses, and operating expenses. A target return on capital was used to determine the margin. Prices were fine-tuned to achieve volume targets or to maintain a hierarchy in relation to key competitors. In this environment, prices would typically be set centrally, often by a pricing committee. Prices were not often changed. Relics of this simpler environment still exist. However, in the 1980s the industry started to develop more sophisticated methods of pricing which began to reflect the differences in costs between customers. Most lenders today use *risk-based pricing*, mathematical models which adjust rates to account for the fact that expected credit losses—caused by customers that default on their loan repayments—differ by customer type. The adoption of risk-based pricing was accelerated by the growth in direct distribution channels, such as direct mail for credit cards, where it was feasible to differentiate prices by customer segments. Over time, risk-based pricing models have evolved into product profitability models that estimate the total expected profitability of a loan over its life depending on the price. This evolution has required the development of forward-looking models for expected pre-payment and cross-sales by customer segment. Such advances have been facilitated by heavy investment in modern application processing systems and data warehouses, which have created rich datasets for use in the development of these models. However, the advance has left some important issues unresolved. For example, risk models are principally used in credit approval decisions—which are basically yes or no questions—and often are not precisely adapted for price setting. This creates some organizational challenges as these models tend to have been developed and owned by the finance and risk functions rather than Marketing or Pricing.

Whilst an important development, risk-based pricing is really just the consumer credit industry's name for what other industries know as cost-plus pricing. Compared to many other retail industries such as hotels, cruise lines, retail, rental cars, and passenger transportation, the consumer credit industry has been late in adopting price optimization (also known as profit-based pricing) solutions that take into account the impact of price on demand. This is surprising as lenders typically have far richer information on their customers to enable them to use price-demand modeling than most other industries. Early adopters within consumer credit achieved profit increases of up to 20 percent in 2004–07 and this is finally spurring faster penetration.

Looking forward, accelerating adoption of price optimization solutions and further advances in the modeling of losses and customer behavior suggest the need for pricing to become a specialist function within lenders' organizations. There should also be a dramatic change in the modeling of risk to overlay a more forward-looking perspective to the sophisticated analysis of historical data.

8.2 THE CHALLENGE OF PRICING IN
CONSUMER CREDIT

The key pricing challenge in consumer credit is that neither costs nor revenues are known at the point of sale. Consider, for example, a credit card. Competition has virtually eliminated annual fees for cardholders so revenue is comprised of:

- *Net interest revenue* is equal to the customer rate less cost of funds, on the balance that the customer does not payoff at the end of the month.
- *Interchange revenue, which is about 1 percent of customer purchases,* is paid by the acquiring bank that provides card acceptance services to a retailer out of fees paid by the retailer to the acquirer.
- *Assorted 'back-end' fees* are charged for cash advances, balance transfers by the customer from his account with another issuer, foreign exchange translation on payments in foreign currency, and penalty fees for late payment or if the customer has insufficient funds in his check account to pay the card issuer.

When the card issuer sets rates to attract new customers, it does not know how much any customer will use the card, the average balance that he or she will typically allow to revolve each month, or how much fee income it will receive from so-called back-end fees. In addition, the issuer does not know if the customer will default on his or her repayments and whether it will be able to recover the debt or have to write off some portion of the sum outstanding. These expected future revenues and costs are different for each individual customer and ideally should be reflected in the price of the product.

To attract new customers to its product, the issuer may have advertised its rates. For several years, issuers have used teaser rates and/or balance transfer campaigns to attract new card holders. Such strategies require that the issuer specify the introductory rate, the length of time it applies, and the so-called go-to rate after the introductory period expires. When the customer returns the application form, the issuer may opt to raise the rate on the riskier applicants based on credit checks and credit scores. This practice is constrained by regulation. In the UK, issuers are bound by "Treating Customers Fairly" regulation. Specifically, if an issuer advertises a specific customer interest rate, then 66 percent of customers must actually receive that rate or better. In the USA, lenders are constrained by Fair Lending regulation. This practice restricts lenders from treating customers differently by virtue of age, sex, or ethnicity. It also guards against "disparate impact" where segments of customers may receive different outcomes (in terms of access to credit, prices, etc.) even if the original treatment did not intentionally discriminate.

Like most businesses, consumer credit companies use pricing to achieve their revenue and profit objectives. However, the pricing function must also be mindful of other constraints such as portfolio limits. Most lenders set maximum limits on the proportion of their portfolio from riskier customers, asset classes, or geographic regions. Concentrated portfolios are considered risky. For example, UK mortgage lenders typically restrict loans above 90 percent loan-to-value (LTV) to a small proportion of the overall portfolio.

In addition, the issuer almost certainly will need to consider re-pricing the customer at the point of switchover from *intro* to *go-to rate* (after the introductory offer period has expired). Almost certainly, the competitive landscape will have changed since customer acquisition. The automatic rate increase may trigger customers to transfer their business to another lender. Hence, the issuer seeks to limit the attrition of profitable customers. Recently, issuers have discovered the value of periodic back-book re-pricing of individual customers to reduce attrition, stimulate dormant or low-usage customers, or to raise margins on less profitable customers. Sectors such as mortgage lending and auto finance face another complication: third-party brokers or intermediaries that complete the sale on behalf of the lender. Brokers usually have the stronger relationship with the customer and the lender must decide how much pricing discretion to grant.

This is the environment facing lenders in their attempts to set prices to attract and retain profitable customers, satisfy regulatory requirements, and manage portfolio composition. In the next section, we examine the various ways that lenders use to set prices.

8.3 Pricing consumer lending in practice

Lenders use four basic methodologies to set prices for consumer credit based on: volume, market, risk/cost, and profit, as outlined in Figure 8.1.

Most lenders use a combination of approaches. Over time, companies have also tailored each technique to suit their needs. The details often differ somewhat between lenders even if the principles are common.

To illustrate the four basic approaches, consider the credit card industry. Twenty to thirty years ago, credit cards were new and market growth was rapid. Prices comprised both an interest rate and annual fee. Each company would typically only offer one combination. The goal of most issuers was to use pricing to grow the number of new accounts rather than

Pricing Methodology	Objective	Advantages	Issues
Volume-based	To achieve a target market share or volume	• Simplicity	• Usually unscientific • Takes no account of profitability
Market-based	Setting prices based on key competitors	• Simplicity	• What should be the price differential? • Takes no account of profitability
Risk-based	To ensure prices cover expected future credit losses	• Ensures accounts are profitable	• What should be the margin over and above break-even? • Takes no account of demand
Profit-based	To maximise profits based on costs and demand	• Comprehensive • Profit-maximizing	• Requires investment in data, technology, and capabilities

FIGURE. 8.1 Four pricing methodologies

to maximize profitability on existing accounts. Competition was less intense than today and margins fatter. Lenders typically considered prices in a monthly process in which a committee would consider the previous month's business results and adjust prices depending on volumes. If new account openings were below budget, the interest rate would be reduced and vice versa. A pricing committee involving representatives from Risk, Finance, and Treasury would have the authority to sign-off pricing decisions to ensure alignment with funding, risk, and profit objectives at the portfolio and overall company level. This was a comparatively stable environment. Customer interest rates did not change every month and the annual fees rarely ever changed. There was little science behind pricing decisions and the views of the most powerful or vocal member of the committee could prevail. In this environment, volume-based pricing delivered fast growth and high profitability. Its drawbacks—lack of consideration of profitability or competitive response—did not matter at that time because growth rates and margins were high.

As the credit card market grew, it attracted new entrants and the early explosive growth rates slowed. As the market matured, companies could only grow rapidly by taking market share from competitors. In addition, incumbents with large books of existing accounts had to consider the trade-off between the growth of new accounts and the profitability of existing accounts. If prices were set to attract new customers, new account growth could remain high. However, lower margins would reduce profit from existing accounts.

By adopting market-based pricing, companies would benchmark themselves against competition. To sustain high growth, prices could be set in, say, the top quartile of competitors. If profit was the more important goal, the ranking could be below average. By including market and competitive considerations, market-based pricing was a useful enhancement to volume-based methodologies and remains a popular component of modern pricing. However, market-based pricing ignores the issue of how profitability is affected by price. This is particularly problematic if margins are slim. One CEO described market-based pricing as "tantamount to outsourcing the pricing decision to competitors. We consider pricing a core capability and such a vital driver of performance; outsourcing would be so foolish as to be virtually negligent."

As competition continued to grow and margins declined, it became increasingly important for issuers to distinguish between high and low margin customer segments. After the cost of funds, provision for expected future credit losses is the largest component of the total costs of maintaining a credit card account. Techniques such as credit scorecards for assessing credit risk had been developed to support decisions such as whether to approve or decline individual customer applications for new accounts and how large a credit line to grant. Risk-based pricing involved applying scorecards to pricing purposes. Mathematical models were built to translate externally provided credit scores into expected future credit losses. The models were based on internal and historical data on delinquencies, defaults, and write-offs by customer segment.

Risk-based pricing enables lenders to reduce prices for customer segments with lower-than-average expected future losses and still maintain the same level of margin and profit. Naturally, prices for higher risk customers are raised for the same reason. The adoption of risk-based pricing was a development of great importance for the industry and is still considered by many within the industry as highly sophisticated. However, this approach is really only the consumer lending industry's version of cost-plus pricing which has been common practice in many other industries for years. Whilst differentiating costs between customer segments, risk-based pricing does not inform the margin decision; namely how high should prices be set above costs. Many years after the adoption of risk-based pricing, most lenders used the same margin for all segments. However, risk-based pricing represented the first step towards a more sophisticated pricing environment. At first, it was used in direct marketing to differentiate prices by distribution channel and mailing list. From an era of one-size-fits-all, it now made sense to have different prices for different segments of customers based on their risk.

Of course, risk is neither the only driver of a credit card issuer's costs nor the only characteristic in which customer behavior varies substantially among segments. Issuers have extended risk-based pricing by building predictive models for new customer response rates, card usage, revolving credit balance, and customer attrition. These developments have created more and more sophisticated models for segmenting how profitability changes with price over the lifetime of the account.

Until quite recently, however, these techniques provided no guidance on the margin that should be charged over and above costs. Lenders continued to set a single margin for all customer segments. To determine what margin should be charged, many lenders are beginning to use *profit-based pricing*. Profit-based pricing or price optimization, as it is sometimes called, requires the inclusion of price in all individual models for profit drivers. Response rates at customer origination were the first to include price. More recently, transaction, borrowing, and attrition behavior models have been adapted to include price effects. This has led to a complete view of expected profits as a function of the customer and price. As prices are raised, net interest margin increases but response rates, usage, and average revolving balances decrease. Also attrition increases. There is an optimum price for each segment that maximizes the expected profit over the lifetime of the account. In my experience, the determination of optimum prices has enabled issuers to boost profits by 10–25 percent. Nomis Solutions, a company that licenses price optimization software to financial services companies, has case studies on its website: www.nomissolutions.com.

Generally the credit card industry has been fastest to adopt sophisticated pricing techniques but the state of adoption varies among companies. In the last 2–3 years, a few fast movers in other sectors of the consumer lending industry—especially in auto finance in the USA and unsecured consumer loans in the UK—have overtaken the credit card issuers in the development of profit-based pricing. In the next section, we examine some examples and describe current practices in more detail.

8.4 PRICING BACK-END FEES IN CREDIT CARDS

During the 1990s card issuers discovered that they could significantly improve card profitability by replacing annual fees with back-end fees for items such as delinquency (late payment), not having sufficient funds, foreign exchange translation for overseas purchases, and cash withdrawals. While customers were sensitive to the annual fee when choosing their card, they seemed impervious to fees that would not be incurred until much later, if at all. By eliminating the annual fee, issuers made their cards more attractive for new customers and were able to increase the volume of cards in force. By introducing an ever wider range of back-end fees and raising the fees over time, issuers could more than compensate for the lower annual fees per card. By the end of the 1990s, back-end fees grew to represent up to 30 percent of total revenue for some issuers.

Delinquency fees in the UK are capped by regulation at £12 per occasion. While other back-end fees have attracted scrutiny from the consumer finance media, it appears that the vast majority of customers are completely insensitive to their prices. In my experience, direct marketing response rates, spend, and revolve behavior are largely insensitive to the levels of back-end fees. So the pricing of back-end fees has become one of the purest forms of market-based pricing. Most competitors charge the same prices.

Since customers are insensitive and competition is weak, issuers would maximize profits by large increases in back-end fee prices. However, this risked unwanted scrutiny by the financial media and perhaps regulators. So the solution is to match the fees charged by the highest-priced competitors without exceeding them. In this way, an issuer reduces the risk of being singled out by the media or regulators.

Most issuers price back-end fees this way. From time to time, a few well-meaning issuers have tried to make a virtue of lower back-end fees and have heavily marketed such cards. However, few customers reward such altruism and the offers are eventually withdrawn by the issuers. There are also some issuers who match competitors somewhat inconsistently, arguing that it is risky to match the highest-priced competitor on every type of fee. The available evidence, however, suggests that matching highest-priced competitors is the most profitable strategy, even if it attracts a few complaints from individual customers.

8.5 PRICING UNSECURED PERSONAL LOANS IN THE UK

An unsecured personal loan in the UK is perhaps the simplest form of consumer credit. The amount borrowed, term, and interest rate are all fixed at origination. In addition, the only price to be set is the interest rate that the customer pays.

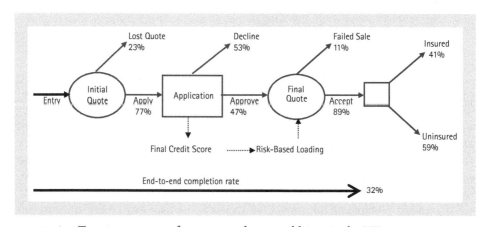

FIGURE. 8.2 Two-stage process for unsecured personal loans in the UK

Beginning with a customer's request for quotation, lenders follow one of two processes for quotation and application conversion. Figure 8.2 illustrates the two-stage process for a typical UK lender in 2004.

The lender provides an initial quote based on loan size. If the lender has advertised the interest rate, the quoted rate is the same as the advertised rate. If the customer rejects the price, it becomes a lost quote. If the customer accepts the initial quote, he or she proceeds to application. The lender then asks a series of questions (such as income, employment, household expenditure, outstanding debts, and credit history) in order to develop a credit score specific to the customer application. If this *application score* is higher than a pre-defined level, the lender approves the application and honors the initial price in the final quote. If the application score is below a threshold value, the lender will decline the application. If the score is between the two levels, the customer receives a final quote from 2–7 percentage points (200–700 basis points) higher than the initial quote reflecting the higher risk of default and loss. This premium is known as a *risk-based loading*. The customer may either accept or reject the final quote. Only some 32 percent of applicants make it successfully through the entire process. Some 41 percent of these customers also choose to pay extra for insurance that will repay the loan in the event of death, accident, disability, or unemployment.

The Treating Customers Fairly Act specifies that 66 percent of funded loans must match or beat the advertised rate. This is an onerous constraint. A study by one lender showed that meeting this constraint would reduce the maximum achievable average profitability per loan by 35 basis points. So naturally, issuers have responded to the regulation by excluding price from advertising material.

In the *one-stage process*, the customer does not receive an initial quote and instead proceeds directly to application scoring. Thereafter the process is the same as for the two-stage version. The one-stage process is becoming more common. It takes longer for the customer to receive a price quotation. However, approved customers only receive one price quote. The advantage for the lender is that the advertised rate constraint no longer applies.

Until the mid-2000s, individual lenders offered little price differentiation between customer segments. Customers for smaller loans paid more—most lenders used different rates for loan sizes of £1–3k, £3–5k, £5–7k, and above £7k which was the typical loan size used in advertising. There was no separate pricing function within the bank. Product management was responsible for recommending price changes to a pricing committee, which met monthly to review and approve recommendations. The decision support tools and information available to support pricing decisions were (1) competitor prices, (2) monthly and year-to-date sales volumes relative to target, and (3) a product profitability model. Profitability models allowed the user to change assumptions for credit loss but otherwise worked on an average loan and average customer. Prices did not change often.

Between 2003 and 2008, the pricing of unsecured personal loans in the UK changed dramatically and perhaps half of the leading issuers adopted price optimization. Product profitability models comprise modules for account net interest revenue, expected losses, expected pre-payment (early settlement), and expected take-up of creditor insurance. Expected profit is calculated as a function of loan size, term, channel, application score, and brand taking. A few sophisticated lenders have even adjusted their credit loss models to account for *adverse selection*—the phenomenon that customer credit quality deteriorates with higher prices—but this is still rare. Demand models have been developed to determine

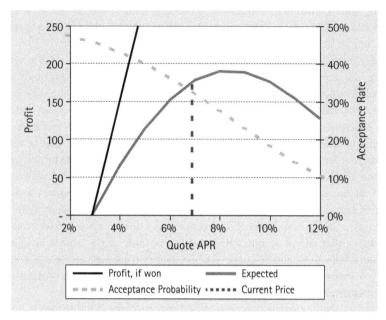

FIGURE. 8.3 Profit and probability of conversion versus APR

Note: Unsecured consumer loan, £7,000, 48-month term, call-center, new customers.

the impact of price on the probability that individual price quotations will convert into booked loans. Such models lead to the appreciation that loan size, channel, and credit score affect customer price sensitivity as well as profitability. Optimization software is used to set prices, by segment, that maximize profits by trading-off the profitability of individual loans (which rises with price) with the probability of quote conversion (which reduces with price).

The principles of price optimization are shown in Figure 8.3. The figure relates to a 4-year, £7,000 unsecured loan originated through a call-center by a first-time customer. The straight, near-vertical line describes the relationship between profits and interest rate if the customer accepts the rate quotation and is approved for credit. The sloping dotted line describes the relationship between the likelihood of customer acceptance and quoted rate. The solid inverted U-shaped line is the expected profit per loan at the point of quotation. It combines the profitability and probability of customer acceptance of the quote. The profit-maximizing rate is about 8.5 percent where the curve flattens out. This contrasts with the then current rate offered by the bank of about 6.8 percent (marked by the vertical dotted line). The impact on expected loan profit can be read on the left-hand vertical scale. Expected profit would increase from £175 to £190 per loan, an increase of 8.5 percent. The likelihood of conversion would fall from 32 percent to 25 percent.

Some lenders have increased the sophistication and benefits from optimization by developing models that relate advertised prices to the volume of requests for quotation received. Some also modeled price effects on pre-payment (early settlement). Business constraints to such as minimum volumes, portfolio composition limits, and even the 66 percent typical advertised APR regulation are applied to the optimization to ensure that prices are consistent with all the lender's goals. Pricing has become a specialist function and prices change more frequently. The pricing committee's responsibility has changed. It now reviews and approves the expected results of a package of price changes. It has the time to drill-down into the occasional segment price which may look like an outlier. Price optimization has improved personal loan profitability for most lenders who have adopted it by 20–30 percent.

8.6 MORTGAGE PRICING

Mortgages are amongst the more complex products for lenders to price. There are potentially thousands of product variations based on:

- fixed versus adjustable (variable) rate;
- different indices against which the adjustable rate is benchmarked;
- term over which the rate applies, including introductory term and total term of the mortgage;
- different customer segments; in the US prime, alt-A or near prime, and sub-prime; in the UK mainstream, buy-to-let, self-cert mortgages for the self-employed, and sub-prime;
- loan sizes, such as, in the USA "conforming" mortgages below about $417,000 are accepted by Fannie Mae and Freddie Mac (as of January 2008 for one-family homes, before the US Government's economic stimulus package). Non-conforming mortgages do not benefit from the implicit government guarantee of Fannie and Freddie and therefore carry a higher cost of funds. In the UK, there is no such distinction and customers taking larger loans tend to be both lower risk and more price-sensitive. So whereas larger loans are more expensive than smaller loans in the USA, the reverse is true in the UK.

Secondly, there is more than one price to set. In addition to the interest rate, a customer may choose to pay a fee to reduce the rate. In the USA, customers may pay "points" with each point costing 1 percent of the loan amount to reduce the rate. Lenders typically quote rates for 0, 1, and 2 points. In the UK, lenders quote both arrangement fee and rate which requires customers to perform some additional arithmetic to compare lenders and calculate which product is best for their circumstances. The customer also incurs closing costs (legal costs and valuation/survey fees in the UK). Sometimes these may be arranged by the lender and included in the offer but usually not.

Thirdly, most mortgages are originated through brokers although the larger banks may have a sizeable minority through their branch network and other direct channels. In the mortgage market, the convention is that the lender sets the price to the end customer and pays a commission to the broker out of its receipts. This is different from, say, the auto finance market where the lender quotes a wholesale or "buy" rate to the dealer who then sets the price to the end customer and takes most of the difference as a commission.

The presence of the broker creates several complications for the lender. Prices are more transparent and price discovery easier than in many other consumer credit businesses. Customers do not have to complete multiple application forms to obtain quotes from different lenders. The lender receives broker applications only from those customers that have already made a price comparison. In the mortgage market, if the price is uncompetitive, the volume of applications from the broker channel dries up very quickly. In other markets where price transparency is lower, pricing might have less impact on the volume of requests for quotation than the quote to loan conversion rate.

Modeling price effects in the mortgage market is complicated by the role of the broker in the sales process. And early attempts to model aggregate demand as a function of price were not very successful due to the large number of non-price factors that affect demand such as seasonality, cyclicality, day of the week, and advertising and promotional spending by competitors.

Finally, there are different business models. In the USA, a common practice is for lenders to securitize mortgages and sell them into the secondary market. Maximizing profits in this model requires volume. Those lenders that hold mortgage assets on their balance sheets have a short-term disadvantage in terms of funding. They also need higher prices to generate net interest revenue. In the UK, normal practice is to hold mortgages on the balance sheet. In the last few years, some aggressive lenders did securitize to fund lending but these lenders are the ones that suffered most during the credit crisis of 2007–09. Many such as Northern Rock, Bradford & Bingley, and the UK arm of GMAC Residential Finance are no longer in business.

For all these reasons, the state-of-the-art in mortgage pricing is somewhat behind that in other consumer credit sectors. Profitability models are used to ensure that prices meet minimum investment hurdle rates. Also modeling is used to predict pre-pay rates. Prices are typically set in relation to competition, funding costs, and volumes against budget. There has been little science applied to setting prices this way. Two key questions are the following. What are the most effective definitions of (1) absolute price and (2) price relative to competitors when it comes to modeling demand? For example, it is only recently that one of the largest UK lenders determined that a synthetic rate based on the fee amortized over the contractual term (25 years) added to the customer rate was more effective than a similar measure based on amortizing the fee over the special terms period. In addition, the best metric for the relative rate used the ratio of this synthetic rate to the synthetic rate of the third most aggressively-priced competitor. However, in its specialist businesses, it was the ratio to the average synthetic rate of the top five competitors that was most predictive.

Arguably more so than other finance businesses, mortgage lenders face the challenge of inconsistent objectives. The mortgage businesses in some larger financial groups experience periods in which top management's primary goal is volume and others in which it is profitability. In late 2006, for example, one of the UK's largest lenders raised prices aggressively in one segment of the market and saw volumes collapse. Believing that the competition would eventually follow, it held its position for nine months, but competitors did not raise prices to match. Instead, a new order was established and the incumbents were content to accept increased volumes at the same price. Eventually, the former market leader capitulated and re-entered the market segment with an aggressive set of rates designed not just to re-establish its former position but to claw back some of the lost volume. The market disorder created by this inconsistent price positioning led to erosion of brand value as it could no longer command its former market share at its former price position. In addition, the credit quality of mortgages written by this issuer was also lower. It is hard to imagine market leaders in consumer goods or retailing being so inconsistent with their price positioning.

Another challenge facing the mortgage business over recent years has been credit risk; specifically what allowance to make for credit losses. In the benign environment prior to 2007, delinquencies and defaults were lower than the long-term average. Risk models in consumer credit companies tend to rely on recent historical delinquency data to predict expected default. Therefore, the models tend to underestimate losses when defaults are low and overestimate risk when default rates are high. However, most risk professionals are too young to remember the previous cycle. Few companies have kept detailed delinquency and default data going back over a full economic cycle. Losses were almost non-existent for 15 years before 2008 because real estate prices rose so fast. There were few repossessions and almost no upside-down loans. In hindsight, it is evident that few lenders made sufficient allowance for risk in setting prices. The relative richness of delinquency data has enabled sophisticated modeling to measure fine distinctions between segments and credit scores on the basis of their relative probability of missing a payment. Few other industries have such rich data and this has created a huge demand for analysis. But the relative rarity of defaults requires much more data than is available to produce reliable models.

Modeling losses is even more difficult. Economic downturns causing losses on mortgage lending are rare but each one is different and this makes it extremely difficult to predict the severity of the next downturn. In hindsight, lenders have devoted relatively large efforts to building credit risk scorecards for default probability (using backward looking delinquency data) and so little effort on building models for loss given default. Surely, the credit crisis will lead to further efforts to translate credit scores based on historical data into forward-looking default probability. It will also lead to new initiatives to assess loss given default.

8.7 Pricing point of sale auto finance

As in mortgage lending, most auto loans are sold through intermediaries, either auto dealers or brokers. Unlike mortgage lending, however, auto dealers make loans to end customers and sell them to lenders. Dealers set interest rates to end customers; lenders set prices (called *buy rates*) to dealers at which they will buy loans. Lenders also pay dealers a commission based on the difference between buy rates and customer rates. In the UK, the *difference in charges* (DIC) commission is 80–100 percent of the difference in rates multiplied by the loan size and term (with a 3-year maximum). Typically dealers also receive a volume bonus paid as a fixed proportion of the loan. In the USA, dealer "participation" is typically 100 percent of the difference in charges but capped at a much lower level than in the UK.

There are important differences in both sales process and pricing practice between the USA and UK. In the UK, bureau credit scores are rare, not known by most customers and not typically used for pricing. Although rate cards are used by franchised dealers, others set customer rates by negotiation. Once the rate is agreed with the customer, the dealer—

usually the finance and insurance (F&I) specialist—completes an application on behalf of the customer and sends it to the lender for approval. In some larger dealerships, the application is sent to an internal department whose function is to redirect the application to the lender with the most attractive terms (for the dealer) for that individual application. Custom and practice, and systems constraints make it impossible for the lender to change the terms of the deal following underwriting so his options are limited to approving, declining, or conditionally approving, for example, subject to a larger down-payment.

Buy rates are based largely on loan-to-value (LTV) to reflect credit risk. Lenders set buy rates and volume bonuses in contract negotiations with dealerships. Contracts are typically for one year although lenders are increasingly trying to lock-in terms for 3 years. To support price negotiations, most lenders use a simple pricing tool that allows the account manager leading the negotiations to determine return on capital depending on input assumptions including loan volume, buy rates, volume bonus, and percentage of DIC. The pricing tool is effectively a cost plus pricing tool with a target margin set at the level of dealership.

Sales process and pricing practices are responsible for several problems in UK point of sale auto finance. Customers with weak negotiating skills (arguably most Brits) are disadvantaged and prices are only weakly correlated with risk. Both give rise to cross-subsidies between customers. Customer rates are high relative even to unsecured bank lending so point of sale finance as a proportion of all lending for auto purchases is declining. Dealers capture the majority of the total value per loan without bearing any credit risk or capital requirements. IT constraints, lenders' weak bargaining power, and inertia make the system difficult to change. The credit crisis of 2007–09 should create a once-in-a-lifetime opportunity to address these issues. Lenders could also learn much from best practices in the USA.

In the USA, the dealer's "participation" is capped so that the end customer rate is typically 200 basis points or less above the buy rate. Buy rates tables are based on both FICO and application credit scores. The dealer, or his F&I specialist, can make an initial quote to the customer based on his FICO score and also provide a maximum–minimum range. Automated systems such as Dealer Track and Route One enable a dealer to send a customer application to several different lenders and see competing quotes within 30 seconds. The dealer can accept one of these offers or can seek to negotiate a better rate with one or more lenders.

To support the pricing, many auto lenders have developed product profitability models at the level of individual applications. Whereas in the UK, expected loss calculations are based only on LTV, US lenders forecast losses for each loan that incorporate the customer credit score and, often, many other factors. Furthermore, US auto lenders have been among the fastest adopters of price optimization solutions of any consumer lenders. This has entailed developing price sensitive demand models for the volume of applications received and conversion rate of accepted applications into booked loans. Many lenders have also adapted their expected credit losses models to include price as a driver of risk in order to allow for adverse selection. The benefits have been substantial. For example, according to Tom Schwartz, Former VP of Operations Analytics, AmeriCredit—a US subprime auto lender—generated $18 million in profitability within one year of using the Nomis Solutions Price Optimizer and projected $40 million in increased profitability over three years. Quoted on the Nomis Solutions website (www.nomissolutions.com), he states "the

(Nomis) solution helped us improve our ability to execute on our pricing strategies and proactively manage the dynamic market." Recent advances include real-time price optimization solutions to support the booking call negotiation by trading-off the probability and profitability of conversion.

8.8 ISSUES IN PRICING DECISIONS

8.8.1 Product profitability

Accurately pricing consumer credit requires an incremental profit model to calculate the expected contribution to profit of a single loan dependent upon its APR, term, size, etc. However, whilst many lenders have developed product profitability models, it is surprising how few are well suited for the purpose of pricing decisions. Some have portfolio models that compute the expected profitability of a portfolio of many loans. Others have incremental models that inappropriately allocate fixed costs to individual loans in a way that can distort the pricing decisions. For example, marketing expenses are often misallocated. At the point when a customer requests a price quotation, the marketing costs have been incurred already. Such expenses are sunk costs at the point of decision and should be excluded. In contrast, deciding what price to advertise might justify including such costs. The key point is that the profitability model should include only those expenses that are truly incremental at the point of decision.

Profitability models are often developed by the finance function for specific applications. They may not be ideally suited for the specific requirements of pricing. Sometimes the finance function's need for reliability and compliance gets in the way of flexibility and adaptability. Pricing models should be consistent with finance models but need to be specifically adapted for their purpose.

8.8.2 Credit loss models and adverse selection

Credit models are typically developed by the risk function to address questions of credit acceptance, acquisition policy, and risk appetite. These models are not always ideally suited for pricing decisions. Amongst the challenges are:

- Because they are based on delinquencies and arrears rather than default or loss, risk models may not accurately capture the impact of credit risk on expected profitability. In the credit crisis of 2007–09, many formerly predictable relationships between delinquency, default, and loss became less reliable.

- Most loss models are based on historical data although their purpose is related to the risk that customers acquired in the near-future will subsequently default and cause losses. Some lenders, however, put only limited effort to "future proof" their models. In that sense, risk models are often better at assessing the risk of one application *relative* to another, or to a benchmark, than measuring risk *in absolute terms*. Actual loss experience depends so much on the future macroeconomic environment including inflation and interest rates, real estate prices, unemployment, and disposable income.

- Some lenders consider the credit approval decision at a different step in the process from the pricing decision. This challenge is common in auto lending, for example, when third parties are involved in the process. The information available is inevitably different. It is the credit risk team that develops risk models. So the risk model is designed for approval decisions. Ideally, the lender should change the process to take both approval and pricing decisions at the same point. Alternatively, it should develop two risk models; one for approval and one for pricing.
- Curiously, few lenders have developed risk models that incorporate price effects despite the fact that increasing price will lead to increased risk due to adverse selection. This effect is especially important in near-prime and sub-prime markets.

The benefits of accurate loss models are substantial so we would expect to see lenders increasingly develop loss models specifically for the purpose of pricing decisions rather than adapt the ones developed for acquisition decisions. A few lenders are beginning to implement profitability scorecards. These scorecards may be developed outside the risk function while remaining compliant with regulation. Adopting separate risk and profit scorecards allows lenders to manage risk appetite and profitability independently.

8.8.3 Relationship pricing

The industry has seen substantial improvements in both use of data and sophisticated decision support tools. Nonetheless, relationship pricing remains a huge challenge. Advocates would like individual product prices to reflect the full breadth and depth of the customer's relationship. That means individual product prices would not be the same across all customers. Many banks take the pragmatic view that developing better individual product pricing is necessary before relationship pricing could be contemplated. A few banks, however, offer discounts to existing profitable customers to encourage multiple product relationships. These discounts may take the form of 25–50 basis points better pricing across all product holdings depending on the number of products held. The incentive is often justified on the grounds that an existing customer may be highly profitable to the bank even after the discount or that it is more cost effective to sell additional products to existing customers rather than new customers. The right approach varies from company to company depending, in part, on the strength of its franchise. The arguments used to justify relationship discounts are often erroneous. In most circumstances, new to franchise customers are more price-sensitive than existing customers so a price discount should be more effective at attracting new customers than boosting profits from existing ones. In addition, although existing customers that qualify for the relationship discount may be highly profitable, incremental profit impact of the additional product is questionable. The generally lower price elasticity of existing customers suggests that discounts for existing customers will usually reduce profits. There may be situations where this general rule is incorrect. The most common is retention pricing. If, for example, the loss of a customer's mortgage would also lead to the loss of a home equity line, it would of course be rational to consider the profit contribution from both products in setting the price. However, the lender would want to determine the likelihood of also losing the home equity line before making the pricing decision.

8.9 Pricing and the credit crisis of 2007–09

Based upon the experience of Nomis Solutions, prices for consumer credit were generally too low prior to the financial crisis of 2007–09. That is, higher prices would have reduced lending volumes but increased profits. Nomis was involved in dozens of pricing projects from 2002 onwards; 80–90 percent of all the pricing changes made by Nomis's price optimization software were increases. Prices were low for two reasons. One is fairly obvious. Banks and finance companies underestimated the level of defaults and write-offs. The other is less obvious. They preferred higher volumes to higher profits. There were two explanations offered for this curious result. Product managers would say that they were simply following instructions from top management. They said top management believed that the loss of market share from raising prices would adversely affect the share price, even if profits were higher. The alternative explanation is that bonus arrangements accidentally or deliberately favored volume over shareholder value. This implies that financial companies were run for the benefit of the employees rather than the shareholders. Either way, it was a little known but important contributor to the credit crisis.

8.10 Future developments in pricing

Adoption of smart pricing, including price optimization solutions, was accelerating prior to the credit crisis. Pricing was becoming a specialized function and career path within early adopters. Resource levels allocated to pricing were growing in recognition of the substantial potential benefits. From a consumer perspective, lenders' increased focus on relationship management was creating a demand for individually negotiated prices from the more financially-sophisticated customers.

The credit crisis will accelerate some of these trends and may slow down others. Fewer players and reduced risk appetite will create an opportunity for the survivors to rebuild margins and profitability without smart pricing. The potential benefits, however, should be higher in a less competitive environment so the adoption of price optimization, for example, should continue to build after a period in which capital, funding, and re-organization are the immediate priorities. Relationship management and individual price negotiation may be delayed somewhat longer.

The credit crisis will surely increase the pressure for better risk models. Although some outside observers were critical of lenders' risk management processes, there had been little appetite for changing established practices. Losses were low and the personal risk of being the first amongst your competitor group to change established risk management practices considered high. After the crisis, it seems much clearer that models essentially built on historical data need to be future-proofed. However, memories are notoriously short. As real estate prices stabilize and the economy bottoms out, the old risk management techniques based on historical data may begin to overestimate future losses. So this may reduce the pressure for change. For the sake of next time, I hope not.

CHAPTER 9

···

WIRELESS SERVICES PRICING IN THE UNITED STATES

JON ZIMMERMAN

9.1 INTRODUCTION

···

The United States wireless industry has a number of characteristics that make the effective use of pricing critical for success. First and foremost, the industry is mature and highly competitive. Wireless penetration in the USA is approximately 90 percent and few new consumers enter the category each year. The industry is characterized by high defection and low loyalty. Customer churn at the major US wireless carriers ranges from 1 to 2.5 percent per month, and the average customer tenure at a given carrier is between one and three years. The carriers' primary product—bandwidth on their network—is a perishable commodity with finite capacity; customers are willing to pay different prices depending on how the commodity is made available (e.g., weekend versus weekday utilization, data versus voice); high fixed and variable costs; expensive distribution channels; and expensive recourse when there is insufficient availability. All of these factors make effective pricing critical in the long-term success of a wireless carrier.

Although pricing in the wireless industry shares many characteristics with traditional revenue management applications such as those in the airline industry, added complexities include modeling revenue and cost components that are dynamic and difficult to forecast, and a major focus on long-term customer cash flows rather than transactional revenue.

To illustrate this point, consider an airline pricing problem for a passenger who wants to fly from Seattle to San Francisco. A classic revenue management technique is to segment leisure and business travelers by offering two fares—$199 if the consumer is willing to stay over a Saturday night and $299 with no restrictions. In this case the revenue and cost components are well known, understood by both the customer and airline. The pricing decision is based on a single transaction and the airline maximizes revenue by capturing surplus from less flexible business travelers.

Now, consider a customer who is planning to subscribe to a wireless service. The wireless service provider, or carrier, is willing to include a free phone if the consumer signs a 2-year contract with a penalty for early termination of the service, or a phone at wholesale cost of $400 if the customer will not sign a contract. Then the carrier offers two calling plans, the first costs $40 per month and provides 600 minutes of airtime and will be charged a per-minute fee of $0.40 for any additional usage; the second costs $45 per month and provides 700 minutes of airtime and has an overage charge of $0.45 per minute. Neither the decision by the carrier of which plan to offer nor the decision by the customer whether or not to accept either plan is straightforward. In each case, the parties must forecast the long-term economic impact of their decisions.

For the airline, the focus is on a single transaction. For the wireless carrier the focus is on the ongoing potential revenue stream from each customer. The ultimate cash flow from each plan is difficult to estimate because cash flow depends on the subscribers' usage pattern *each month* as well as how long they remain a subscriber. The cash flow derived from any customer may range from unprofitable to highly profitable depending on the revenue and cost streams as well as the ultimate tenure of the customer. This comparison demonstrates the complexity faced by both wireless customers and pricing managers.

In the long run the goal of each carrier's pricing strategy in wireless telecommunications is to maximize the overall expected profitability of its customer base. In this context pricing tactics are used to grow the customer base through the acquisition of new-to-wireless subscribers or subscribers switching from a competitor; to increase the average revenue per user (ARPU) and increase the duration of the customer's relationship with the carrier, hereafter referred to as customer tenure.

As will be discussed, the decision about what rate plan to offer to which customers has major implications on the economics of an individual rate plan as well as on the mix of customers on different rate plans in the portfolio. Three essential analysis steps should be carried out to effectively maximize profitability: *determining customer segments*; *modeling rate plan economics*; and ultimately the *construction and management of a rate plan portfolio*. By following these steps the carrier attempts to maximize the overall discounted cash flows of the customer base. The remainder of this chapter focuses on describing each of these steps.

9.2 DISTRIBUTION CHANNELS

Wireless carriers sell their services through both *direct* and *indirect* channels. Direct sales channels, which are controlled by the carrier, exist both on-line through the carrier's website and off-line in the form of retail stores. Prices available through direct sales channels are communicated at point of sale and through national and regional advertising.

Indirect sales channels also exist both on-line and off-line. On-line, wireless services are sold by major retailers such as Amazon.com as well as by e-commerce sites dedicated to wireless such as www.wirefly.com. Similarly, large retailers such as Best Buy and dedicated wireless retailers sell wireless service off-line. In some cases, indirect dealers will have exclusive relationships with a single carrier, and in other cases, indirect dealers will simultaneously offer services provider by multiple carriers. Given the intense competition for market share, all US wireless carriers distribute their service through both direct and indirect channels; however, the ratio of direct to indirect sales varies widely by carrier.

There are two major reasons why carriers attempt to manage indirect sales. First, indirect sellers typically have some ability to manage the prices they offer by rebating commissions back to the customer. Since indirect dealers also advertise prices at both point of sale and through national and regional advertising, such advertisements can lead to customer confusion due to multiple price points for the same service in the market. In addition, the need to offer commission and other incentives to indirect dealers can make the indirect channel more expensive than direct channels, ultimately making the indirect channel less profitable for the carrier.

9.3 CUSTOMER SEGMENTATION

A critical role of the pricing manager is to design and evaluate rate plans by estimating cash flow scenarios under different usage and attrition patterns. As with pricing in many industries, identifying distinct customer segments is critical when developing an appropriate set of rate plans. In the wireless industry, various approaches are used to segment customers; two of the most important are *credit-based segmentation* and *usage-based segmentation*.

9.3.1 Credit-based segmentation

In the US wireless industry, customers are often offered a heavily subsidized handset when first subscribing for service. Depending on the wholesale cost of the handset, this approach can result in very high customer acquisition costs for the carrier. Thus, determining the likelihood that a customer will meet their monthly revenue commitment, or conversely, default on their contract, is very important. Hence, many wireless carriers segment customers by credit class. At the point of sale, the wireless provider checks the credit history of the potential subscriber, and based on the customer's creditworthiness, different rate plans will be offered that adjust the revenue and cost flows to minimize the likelihood of losing money on a customer. In the United States, for example, the credit-challenged have been one of the fastest growing wireless segments.

A special case of credit-based segmentation is that of minors without credit history. As wireless penetration has increased, the ability to acquire market share among teenagers has become important. By segmenting the credit-challenged segment itself, rate plans targeting youth have been created by offering "additional lines" for a fee on the rate plan of a creditworthy subscriber. These are typically called "family plans" because the primary subscriber is a parent and the added line is for one or more children.

9.3.2 Usage-based segmentation

Segmentation by usage is an obvious choice in wireless. There are many ways to segment customers by usage, ranging from the overall amount of usage, to the type and mix of usage (i.e., voice versus data services), to when the service is used (i.e., time of day). For example consumers can be divided into minimal, medium, and high usage types. Minimal usage customers may want to have a phone nearby in case of emergencies and expect to use the phone as little as 30 minutes per month. A medium usage segment may constitute customers who plan to use the service anywhere from 100 to 500 minutes per month. These customers plan to use the service to a limited degree but may also have a landline and separate service for business. A high-usage segment, on the other hand, may be consumers who are either replacing their landlines or using the phone for business. Pricing can be tailored to each of these segments by offering plans with different monthly recurring charges and corresponding amounts of included minutes. The effective cost per included minute can be tailored based on the segment's willingness-to-pay.

In addition to usage frequency, customers can be further segmented by when they use the service. For example, most business customers require the ability to use the service at all times of the day whereas customers who are using the service primarily for leisure may have more flexibility in when they use the service. Strategies such as differentiated pricing for peak and off-peak calling allow the carriers to use pricing as a tool to manage network utilization and to charge a higher average rate per minute for peak times.

Customers can also be segmented by usage type by considering their mix of usage across voice, data, and other ancillary services. In so doing, bundling and similar pricing tactics can be used to enhance revenue. For example, rate plans with lower rates for voice services when a data service is included allow the carrier to increase overall monthly revenue without cannibalizing voice-related revenue for customers who do not want data services.

There are many other segmentation schemes that can be considered given the myriad of components available to the pricing manager in constructing a rate plan. For example, early adopters who demand the latest types of handsets or the latest features and services may be identified as a segment. The ability to segment across many dimensions allows for the creation of more targeted price plans that maximize the profitability of an individual consumer.

9.4 WIRELESS PRICING STRUCTURES

It is common practice for wireless phone carriers to offer a wide variety of rate plans that are consistent with both usage-based and credit-based segmentation schemes. The two most common rate plan structures are "pre-paid" and "post-paid". Pre-paid rate plans were created to specifically address the issue of the payback period relative to the carrier's cost of acquisition. With credit-challenged customers, this problem can be particularly acute and these plans have become very popular both internationally and in the USA, where the percentage of pre-paid accounts grew to 50 percent of the subscriber base for some major carriers in 2008, five years after introduction. A typical pre-paid rate plan includes a wireless device possibly with a rebate or subsidy, and a set of pre-paid minutes. The price of the minutes varies based on the amount purchased. For example, subscribers of a pre-paid phone might have the option of purchasing 500 minutes of service for $50, 100 minutes for $25, or 50 minutes for $10. Once purchased, the pre-paid minutes may or may not expire depending on the carrier. In addition, a pre-paid plan often includes a commission or "spiff"[1] depending on the point of sale, some of which may be passed through to the subscriber.

Pre-paid plans have several advantages from a pricing perspective: acquisition costs and bad debt are minimized; and the carrier is usually able to charge higher per-minute rates if the plans are properly targeted at low credit segments with limited alternatives. The primary disadvantage of offering pre-paid is the uncertainty of the ongoing revenue stream. Without a contracted term of service and early termination fee, pre-paid customers have very low switching costs, and the customers attracted to these plans are often price-sensitive. For the carrier, this makes modeling expected cash flows from these plans extremely challenging. Unlike pre-paid rate plans, post-paid rate plans require customers to sign a service contract with a fee for early termination. In exchange they receive a highly subsidized handset. These rate plans are usually nonlinear and include the following components.

- *A monthly recurring charge* that includes a specified number (or bucket) of airtime minutes that the subscriber may use each month at no additional cost. It has been a common practice for monthly access charges to include different varieties of included minutes. Many popular plans provide minutes that can be used at any time of day. In addition, wireless service providers also sell plans with blocks of airtime divided up into peak and off-peak minutes. Peak minutes come at a premium and can be used from 7am to 7pm on weekdays. Weekends and evening hours are considered off-peak, and off-peak calls cost much less per minute.

- *Overage*, a per-minute charge for additional usage that is incurred once a customer exceeds their allotted number of minutes in a given month. Overage can be a significant source of revenue for a carrier, particularly in the first few months of service for a new subscriber before the subscriber either adapts her behavior to the constraints of the rate plan, or migrates to a rate plan that better matches her usage characteristics. Overage is also a key source of customer dissatisfaction and the effect of overage charges on customer churn must be considered in pricing decisions.

- *Additional line fees* that allow subscribers to add family members to their calling plan. These plans have become increasingly popular; particularly as cell phone usage has penetrated demographics that may lack the necessary credit history to subscribe for post-paid service. Wireless providers typically offer additional lines for a fixed monthly charge.

- *Ancillary services*, such as text messaging, email, data services, 411 and directory assistance, ring tones, and games have become an important source of revenue, particularly as handsets have become increasingly sophisticated. Carriers have utilized a wide variety of pricing schemes for value-added services, including per use, fixed fee, non-linear pricing schemes, and bundling. For example, by 2008 sales of ring tones in the USA generated over $500 million in revenue for carriers.

- *Early termination fees* that are charged if the customer breaks a contract prior to the service contract period (typically one–two years). The rationale behind the early

---

[1] A "spiff" is an upfront bonus paid by a wireless carrier directly to the seller upon the sale or activation of a specific service.

termination fee, which can range up to several hundred dollars, is that it is necessary to defray handset subsidies and other costs for signing up new customers. These fees have resulted in class-action lawsuits in the USA requiring that the fees be related to the actual cost of the phones or prorated relative to the percentage of the contract completed. Recently a number of US wireless carriers have settled these suits out of court without admitting wrongdoing, thereby preserving this important revenue stream.

An example of a typical post-paid rate plan is as follows: the subscriber is offered a choice of handsets at various price points, ranging from free to manufacturer suggested retail. The price of the handset depends on the term of the contract (i.e., one or two years) as well as the rate plan selected. A typical rate plan might include 1,000 minutes, free nights and weekends and limited data services with a per-use charge, an additional usage of $0.40 per minute, and cost around $40.

Nonlinear rate plans such as the example are designed to extract maximum consumer surplus given the variability in monthly usage (see Oren, Chapter 22). In months when the subscriber uses fewer minutes than included on the plan, the carrier collects the monthly recurring charge, and in months when the subscriber uses more minutes than expected, the carrier collects the overage charges. However, this pricing structure often leads to customer dissatisfaction; subscribers often feel they are "over-paying" when they leave minutes unused or incur overage charges in a given month. An effective pricing strategy must balance incremental monthly revenue against the churn due to ill-will resulting from the fact that the customer almost always over-pays either by not using all of their minutes or by incurring overage.

Carriers generally offer both a pre-paid rate plan and a variety of post-paid plans based on the number of included minutes, with the effective rate per minute decreasing as the monthly recurring charge and number of included minutes increases. As discussed below, this rate-plan provides an opportunity for the carrier to increase expected long-run cash flow by targeting rate plans to particular customer segments. Despite the complexity in selecting a plan that best matches their needs, many consumers who are offered post-paid plans prefer them to pre-paid because they reduce entry costs and are less expensive on a per-minute-of-use basis.

The diverse components that comprise an individual rate plan make it possible for wireless carriers to create a potentially unlimited number of rate plans. The potential combinations of handset offers, price points, contract terms, definitions of included minutes, and ancillary services allow wireless carriers to create a complex rate plan portfolio. Effectively managing this complexity is critical to successful pricing in the wireless industry. In the context of these pricing structures, there are a number of cost components that play a crucial role in pricing. The impact of these costs is relevant at different junctures in the customer lifecycle including subscriber acquisition costs, customer care costs, variable network costs, retention costs, and bad debt.

9.4.1 Subscriber acquisition costs

Subscriber acquisition costs vary widely depending on the sales channel and sales offering. Most carriers acquire customers via both direct and indirect channels. In both cases, paying commissions for new subscribers is a common practice. These commissions vary widely by carrier and by sales channel and may be as much as $100 per activation. Moreover, carriers often pay "spiffs", or cash bonuses, to sales agents depending on the type of rate plan selected by the customer, and the number of ancillary services added to the rate plan. A new activation typically has a spiff value of $20–30, as well as $10–15 per additional line activated and $1–5 for the sale of ancillary services such as data services.

Handset subsidies are the second major component of subscriber acquisition costs. In the USA, it has been common practice for the wireless carrier to provide highly subsidized phones to new subscribers. These subsidies take many forms, ranging from discounts to various types of rebates, and range in value depending on the type of handset and selected rate plan. It is not unusual for a carrier to offer one or more fully subsidized (i.e., free) phone on most rate plans, and average handset subsidies in excess of $100 are common.

9.4.2 Customer care costs

Wireless service customers can demand significant amounts of customer support. Wireless devices can be difficult to configure, and when problems occur, they can be difficult to diagnose (e.g., whether a problem is network or handset related). In addition, questions about monthly charges, requests for rate plan changes, and other inquiries are common. Although many wireless carriers have successfully automated some customer service interactions, high-touch interactions are common and wireless carriers maintain large customer support organizations.

An important consideration in wireless pricing is how the pricing will indirectly drive costs. Indirect costs, such as those related to customer service, are non-trivial. To illustrate this point, note that some pricing structures can lead to an increase in customer-support interactions, usually consisting of a call to a call center which costs the carrier approximately $10. A typical customer may have a support interaction once every two months or more. Many of these calls are billing (i.e., pricing structure) related such as the customer who does not understand their bill or may have experienced a "price shock" where charges were higher than expected due to overage or other charges, although some of these calls are also service-related (e.g., a problem with a handset, etc.)

9.4.3 Variable network costs

Network bandwidth has finite capacity and one of the most important aspects of the carrier's pricing decision is managing the opportunity cost associated with this capacity. Incremental costs such as customer support are small relative to the cost of building and maintaining the wireless network infrastructure. In developing a pricing strategy, it is important to understand and quantify the variable cost for subscribers on the network. Wireless carriers build their networks to handle a peak load in the various geographies that they serve. Beyond this peak level, customers experience degradation of service and, in extreme cases, a temporary loss of service.

Although network infrastructure can be viewed as a fixed cost, a key driver of the pricing strategy is to understand the usage patterns (total minutes of use as well as use at peak times) as well as the incremental cost due to a diminished level of service or the need for additional capital expenditures. For low-use customers who typically do not use network capacity at peak times, variable network costs approach zero. For high usage subscribers who demand network access at peak times, variable network costs can be significant.

For carriers to lack coverage in certain geographical regions is not uncommon. To provide nationwide service, carriers sign roaming agreements with competitors that allow their subscribers access to a competitor's network, for which the carrier pays a per-minute fee. In some cases, these fees are passed through to the subscriber as roaming charges. Typically, carriers expend significant effort to forecast "on-network" and "off-network" usage to understand the blended cost of providing nationwide service.

9.4.4 Retention costs

Retention costs are the direct and indirect costs associated with extending customer tenure. Customer retention is critical for wireless carriers since subscriber acquisition costs are usually high relative to the monthly recurring revenue. In the case of a typical post-paid rate plan, average revenue per user is about $60 per month whereas retention costs can exceed $400 over the lifetime of the customer. Like variable network costs, retention costs can be difficult to measure. For example, the portion of brand advertising that is targeted to the existing customer base to build brand loyalty is difficult to estimate as are other costs directed at improving the customer experience to reduce churn. There are a number of direct retention costs, such as handset upgrades and retention offers (e.g., discounted offers for contract renewals) that are easily quantified. In some cases, retention costs can rival subscriber acquisition costs in magnitude.

9.4.5 Bad debt

Bad debt includes credits, dunning costs, and other uncollectable revenue. In the case of post-paid wireless rate plans, consumers pay following usage and carriers face significant exposure to write-downs for uncollectable accounts. Depending on the credit segment, bad debt on post-paid plans, due to "involuntary churn" can be a significant cost.

9.5 MODELING RATE PLAN ECONOMICS

The typical wireless pricing structures allow flexibility in the development of a wide variety of rate plans. Most carriers develop a portfolio of pre-paid and post-paid rate plans that are consistent with their target customer segments and the competitive offerings in the market-place. Although the wireless carrier's ultimate goal is to determine how to create a portfolio of rate plans that maximizes the overall profitability of their customer base, it is easiest for discussion purposes to first consider the problem in the context of an individual customer's rate plan.

At the subscriber level, the goal is to maximize the profitability of each subscriber over their "lifetime", defined as their tenure with the carrier. Therefore, effective rate plan analysis requires modeling the revenue and cost components of a rate plan as well as how these components, and the customer's relationship with the carrier, evolve over time. Thus, the focus is on the dynamics of cash flows that are driven by the evolution of consumer behavior as their tenure changes as well as their propensity to *churn*.

Due to the competitive nature of the wireless industry, where customers defect at a rate of 1–2 percent per month, rate plan economics are highly sensitive to customer churn. High quality and differentiated services are obvious ways of extending customer tenure, and carriers have used many tactics, ranging from better network coverage to exclusive handsets (e.g., the iPhone on AT&T), to drive customer loyalty. In addition, pricing has also been an important tool to extend tenure directly through methods such as multi-year contracts and high early termination fees or indirectly through tactics that increase switching costs. In fact, understanding how the construction of rate plans changes the propensity for different customer segments to churn is perhaps the most important determinant of the profitability of the rate plan. The remainder of this section will discuss the basic modeling concepts for the estimation of financial and marketing impact in both pre-paid and post-paid rate plans.

9.5.1 Modeling pre-paid rate plans

Pre-paid rate plan analysis is challenging for a number of reasons. Although call patterns and the point of sale (i.e., direct or indirect channel) are known for past subscribers, little or no demographic information is available. Lack of information makes building predictive models difficult if not impossible. In addition, the lack of a contract and monthly billing makes it difficult to determine when a subscriber has defected to another carrier ("churned"), or whether a subscriber is "new" or simply an "existing" subscriber who has signed up again to take advantage of subsidies offered at acquisition. The most detailed information about a pre-paid subscriber is their usage pattern once they begin using the service.

To effectively estimate the future cash flows of a pre-paid pricing strategy, a model must, for a given offering, estimate the time between repurchases as well as the size of each repurchase. In addition, the model must also incorporate how these factors change as a function of customer usage and tenure. Finally the model must be flexible enough to perform sensitivity analysis on the effects of competitive changes in the marketplace and perturbations to elements of the carrier's own pre-paid offering.

A variety of stochastic modeling techniques are used to estimate the expected lifetime value of pre-paid subscribers. A relatively simple model conditions repurchase amount and frequency on the dollar amount of the previous purchase, the average time between purchases, and the time elapsed since first purchase. By using this model in conjunction with historical pre-paid usage and cost data, an expected lifetime value can be approximated for the typical pre-paid subscriber. This model can be used to create a basic pre-paid offering, which would include the subsidy and commission at acquisition, the set of refills available to the customer, as well as to evaluate modifications to an existing pre-paid structure.

Example decision: Consider a wireless carrier who is contemplating the addition of a new pre-paid refill card to their product line already consisting of two popular refill cards.

Currently the carrier offers refill-card 1 which costs the customer $10 and includes 50 minutes, and refill-card 2 at $20 that includes 150 minutes. Assume the newly proposed third refill card would have a cost of $15 that includes 90 minutes of service. How should the carrier model the impact of the proposed change?

One approach to analyzing this proposed addition is to create a stochastic model based on past customers' sequences of refills and to then estimate the effect on these sequences due to the introduction of a third refill option. In so doing, it is possible to understand the tradeoff in the effective revenue per minute for the new refill level relative to other changes in the frequency and likelihood of purchasing additional refills. If the change does not increase expected profitability over the lifetime of the customer then the carrier should not offer the additional refill. Although this example is relatively simplistic in that most carriers offer a large range of refills with a variety of per-minute rates, it provides an idea of the types of tradeoffs that must be considered.

9.5.2 Modeling post-paid rate plans

Post-paid analysis is similar to pre-paid analysis in that the ultimate goal is to model the expected lifetime value of subscribers. Modeling post-paid plans differs from modeling pre-paid plans for a number of reasons, including the ability to segment customers by usage or credit; the contract a customer signs at activation; the nature of billing; the increased opportunity to sell ancillary services; and the ability to make innovative pricing offers.

At its most simplistic, post-paid rate plan analysis looks very much like a standard cash flow analysis. The carrier incurs an acquisition cost when the subscriber begins service, and then the carrier collects revenue and incurs costs each month on a regular billing cycle. Once the discounted sum of the average revenue per user minus the average cost of service exceeds the acquisition cost the rate plan is profitable. Although this basic approach is quite simple, there are a number of complexities that must be incorporated to represent customer behavior. Sales channels, for example, can affect the economics of a post-paid rate plan. Wireless carriers utilize a variety of direct and indirect sales channels, including their own retail stores and website, as well as indirect off-line and on-line dealers. Although the sales channel commissions and spiffs paid by sales channel are relatively easy to incorporate, subsequent customer behavior may differ based on sourcing channel. For example, customers who purchase via indirect channels are often more price-sensitive than customers who buy directly from the carrier. As a result, these customers are more likely to churn when their contract concludes.

Due to competitive pressures, many rate plans are designed so that the discounted future monthly recurring charges offset the average acquisition costs around initial contract expiry. In this case, even if the cash flows in the first year are similar for customers across sales channels, the expected lifetime value of customers varies greatly based on how quickly they churn after contract expiry.

Similarly, handset pricing can affect customer acquisition cost, the customer's usage behavior, the tenure dynamics, and ultimately the expected profitability of customers who sign up for a particular rate plan. Carriers often provide larger subsidies for more sophisticated handsets with additional functionality such as email or Internet browsing because these handsets offer the opportunity for the carrier to charge for ancillary services. Since the wholesale cost of this handset is often higher than less sophisticated handsets, the carrier typically requires that the customer sign a longer-term contract to ensure sufficient tenure to recoup the acquisition cost.

The expected profitability of a customer who is offered a heavily subsidized and sophisticated handset depends on both customers' usage of voice services, and their propensity to pay for ancillary services. Depending on customers' propensity to add ancillary services, the expected monthly cash flows can vary dramatically. In addition, customers who demand higher-end handsets often have a propensity to desire the newest technology. Since the best opportunity to get the latest technology is to take advantage of competitors' activation subsidies, early adopters are often at higher risk of churning than other customers.

Credit history is also a common segmentation dimension for wireless carriers. A customer's credit history is usually a good indicator of her likelihood to meet her contractual obligations. In almost all cases, the net customer profitability is negative immediately after subscribing due to acquisition costs. Since it is common for subscriber acquisition costs to approach $500 and average monthly revenue to range from $50 to $60, many customers do not become profitable until their tenure approaches one year.

In addition to estimating the likelihood that a customer "voluntarily" churns at some point following the term of their contract, post-paid pricing analysis must also incorporate "involuntary" churn when a customer becomes delinquent on their bill. If this occurs early in the relationship, the carrier may not only fail to recoup acquisition costs, the carrier may also incur additional dunning costs if it attempts to aggressively collect delinquent revenue. Although involuntary churn is typically a small fraction of overall churn, it can be a major cost to carriers as lost acquisition costs and dunning costs typically outweigh any revenue ultimately recovered.

9.6 Pricing innovations

One of the most interesting exercises in wireless pricing analysis is modeling the effect of pricing innovations on expected cash flows. Wireless carriers have a great deal of flexibility in how minutes "included" as part of the monthly recurring charge are defined. For example, many carriers offer "free nights and weekends" whereby weekday usage after 7pm and before 6am are offered in addition to a bucket of "anytime" minutes. The definition of these minutes can have large impacts on voice-driven revenue and costs as well as customer tenure. In the case of "free nights and weekend", the carrier may forego overage, or airtime revenue, because customers are less likely to exceed their allotted minutes and they may inflict additional variable network costs as customers adjust their calling behavior and create peak loads on the network during free calling periods. However, the pricing plan may increase customer loyalty.

Two other examples of pricing innovations that had important impacts on customer profitability are "in-network" calling and "roll-over minutes". Much like "free nights and weekends", "in-network" plans treat calls made within the carrier's subscriber base as free. These plans may decrease revenue for a given subscriber, however this is often outweighed by the increased loyalty from that customer and network effects in attracting other subscribers.

"Rollover minutes", introduced by Cingular Wireless (now AT&T) in 2003 are unused, accumulated, included minutes that roll over from month to month. Subscribers can avoid airtime charges by using their accumulated rollover minutes. This pricing strategy increased "switching costs" as consumers did not want to walk away from unused minutes and led to a significant reduction in Cingular's monthly churn. Rollover minutes are interesting from a pricing perspective not only because they target tenure rather than monthly revenue to maximize long-term customer cash flows, but because they show the complex relationship between monthly recurring revenue and tenure. As pricing analysts at Cingular discovered, the majority of airtime revenue is received in the first two–three months of a customer's tenure as they adjust their usage to fit the constraints of the rate plan (and before they accrue rollover minutes). After this period, consumers rarely exceed their "free" minutes in any particular month and the rollover minutes are not used.

From Cingular's perspective, rollover minutes had little impact on monthly revenue but had measurable impacts on churn (and acquisition due to its uniqueness). Cingular's use of rollover minutes allowed for longer customer tenure and increased the net present value of future expected cash flows—an example of using innovative pricing tactics to drive customer lifetime value.

9.7 CONSTRUCTION AND MANAGEMENT OF RATE PLAN PORTFOLIO

Modeling the economics of individual pre-paid and post-paid rate plans is a demanding exercise. Wireless carriers generally create a portfolio of rate plans including a variety of pre-paid and post-paid plans, each with different monthly recurring charges and corresponding levels of included minutes. These plans are made available across many handsets with different levels of subsidy and related contractual terms. Finally there is usually a set of ancillary offers that the customer can choose for value-added services. Given the number of pricing attributes available to create unique rate plans, it is not uncommon for a wireless carrier to simultaneously offer hundreds of rate plans. This variety creates the "portfolio problem" of how to price a portfolio of different rate plans in the face of both cannibalization and external competition.

9.7.1 Migration and cannibalization

Creating a large set of rate plans appears like a reasonable way to tailor pricing to customer needs. However, ensuring that the right subscriber ends up using the right rate plan becomes difficult. One of the reasons is the nature of segmentation in the wireless industry. Consider, for example, the expected usage level. Misalignment between a customer's actual usage and the usage pricing component of her selected rate plan can lead to loss of potential profitability, due in some cases to increased churn and in other cases by curtailed usage. To illustrate the challenges, consider the following example:

Example decision: A wireless carrier who currently offers two post-paid rate plans: the first costs $20 per month and provides 400 minutes of airtime and will be charged a per-minute fee of $0.60 for any additional usage; the second costs $60 per month and provides 1,000 minutes of airtime and has an overage charge of $0.45 per minute. The carrier is contemplating the addition of a new rate plan that costs $40 per month and provides 600 minutes of airtime and a per-minute fee of $0.50 for overage. How should the carrier determine whether or not it would be profitable to add the new rate plan to its portfolio?

For this example the pricing analyst must evaluate whether the additional rate plan will increase the sum of expected customer lifetime values across all potential and existing subscribers. Potential subscribers are an important consideration in adding a new rate plan in that attracting new subscribers is one of the primary reasons for adding new rate plans. It is important to note the distinction between potential and incremental subscribers. It cannot be assumed that all subscribers who select a new rate plan are incremental. Some customers would have subscribed for service on another rate plan. In addition to overhead and administrative considerations, "cannibalization" is also an important factor to evaluate when increasing the number of rate plans in the portfolio.

To evaluate cannibalization the pricing analyst must estimate incremental demand for the new rate plan as well as the expected number of customers who would have subscribed for other rate plans who now select the new plan. Given these demand estimates, the pricing analyst must then model the customer lifetime value for incremental subscriber as well as the change in customer lifetime value (which can be positive or negative) for customers who would have subscribed for service with an alternate rate plan. As discussed in the previous section, the revenue, cost, and tenure characteristics vary for the same customer depending on the selected rate plan.

The effect of a new rate plan on the existing customer base must also be considered. When a new rate plan is offered, existing customers often "migrate" to the plan. Some customers who are subscribed to rate plans with lower monthly recurring charges may "upgrade" to the new plan and others on more expensive plans may "downgrade" to the new plan. In addition to the cannibalization of new subscribers from alternate rate plans, the migration of existing customers must be estimated along with the changes in customer lifetime value for customers who migrate from other plans. It is important to note that "downgrades" from rate plans at higher price points do not necessarily decrease customer lifetime value. In many cases, customers are "right-fitting" their rate plan to their desired usage. Although this may decrease monthly revenue due to a lower monthly recurring charge or less overage, it may increase the customer's lifetime value if it reduces churn. In the example above, the pricing analyst would need to model the dynamics of potential and existing subscribers, estimate the economics of each rate plan given the mix of customers subscribed to the plan, and ultimately estimate the long term profitability of the portfolio with and without the proposed new rate plan.

9.7.2 External competition

The goal of wireless pricing is to maximize the long-run profitability of the subscriber base. Pricing dynamics are a key driver of customer switching behavior and pricing decisions must in the context of the competitive environment. Each carrier in the marketplace is competing to attract switchers and to keep their own subscribers from churning. The pricing analyst must consider how competitors react to each potential pricing change to the portfolio because competitive response to pricing actions can have a large impact on the long-run economics of the firm.

For example, in the absence of competition a carrier may decide to add a new rate plan based on the assumption that incremental subscribers will offset the revenue lost from cannibalization and from migration within the existing base. If other carriers match the pricing change then incremental demand may be below forecast and the change may decrease the overall profitability of the subscriber base. In addition, if one or more carriers perceive a portfolio change as a threat, they may respond aggressively. As in most competitive industries, the risk of initiating a price war must be a careful consideration in tactical and strategic pricing decisions.

9.8 Pricing analysis tools

A common practice at major wireless carriers is to develop portfolio analysis tools to assess the impact of rate plan changes on profitability and to perform "what-if" analyses on underlying model assumptions.[2] A comprehensive set of demand, revenue, cost, churn, and migration forecasts are required to develop a baseline model of the current portfolio. To capture the portfolio dynamics, forecasts must be maintained for various combinations of customer segment and rate plan. Due to the potential complexity, it is critical to identify a customer segmentation scheme that captures the underlying portfolio dynamics without becoming explosive in terms of the number of forecasts that must be maintained.

Forecasts are developed using a number of approaches and rely on a variety of data sources, ranging from expert opinion to historic transactional data. Demand for existing rate plans by customer segment is typically estimated using a combination of "top-down" and "bottom-up" forecasts. Top-down forecasts are based on a number of inputs, including current market size and expected estimated growth; estimates of each carrier's propensity to capture new customers; and a "switching matrix" that describes the dynamics of how subscribers churn among competitors in the market. These forecasts are usually made at the monthly or quarterly level and provide a macro view of market demand. In conjunction with a top-down demand forecast, a "bottom-up" forecast is typically constructed using time-series approaches and historical activation data.

Producing good forecasts to drive portfolio simulation tools is challenging. In the case of "top-down" approaches that rely on a "Delphi" or "panel of experts", marketers infer demand for a new rate plan based on limited information from focus groups or consumer survey data. In the case of forecasts using historical data, errors often appear due to the difficulty in modeling changing competitive pressures that influence, for example, rates of

---

[2] References for a number of recent examples of published works in quantitative modeling of wireless subscriber behavior are included at the end of this chapter.

adoption. In the case of new rate plans, forecasts must be adjusted to account for anticipated incremental demand that the new rate plan will drive as well as for the anticipated cannibalization from subscribers who will select the new rate plan instead of an existing rate. A combination of expert opinion and analysis of behavior by customer segment when similar changes were made in the past can be used to estimate customer migration within the existing portfolio base.

In addition to demand and migration estimates, forecasts of revenues, costs, and usage by customer segment, rate plan, and tenure must be maintained in order to estimate the expected cash flows for the existing customers on various rate plans. For existing rate plans, these forecasts are generally constructed using historic transactional data as inputs. These forecasts are typically updated monthly or quarterly to capture underlying changes in behavior as different customer vintages progress through their tenure on plans. For example, customers who subscribed to a particular rate plan several years ago may behave differently than customers who have subscribed more recently when they are at the same point in their tenure on the plan. In the case of new rate plans, cash flows are more difficult to predict due to the lack of historical data. One common approach is to base usage on existing rate plans with similar characteristics and then estimate revenue and costs accordingly. It is important to note that when new rate plans are added to the portfolio, it is necessary to update cash flow estimates for existing rate plans as well because migration and cannibalization will change the mix of customers on existing rate plans, in turn changing the "blended" cash flow from customers who remain on these plans.

Finally, carriers must also forecast churn. Unlike other forecasts that are generated at the customer segment and rate plan level, churn is typically predicted at the customer level based on transactional and socio-demographic factors, including tenure, rate plan, recent usage and overage, contract status, and age of handset. Binary choice models, such as logit or probit models, can be utilized to estimate the propensity of individual customers to churn, and from these individual estimates, aggregate churn rates can be generated by rate plan and tenure. In the case of new rate plans it is necessary both to forecast churn for new subscribers to the new rate plan as well as the change in churn for customers on existing plans.

Using these forecasts along with the existing rate plan portfolio and customer base, the number of customers on each rate plan and the associated cash flows can be estimated for subsequent time periods and the expected net present value of the portfolio can be computed. By creating (or modifying) a rate plan, updating model drivers, creating new forecasts, and re-running the model, the effect of portfolio changes can be evaluated. When the expected net present value of the portfolio increases, then the carrier should consider the change subject to anticipated competitive responses.

The portfolio-based approach to modeling pricing changes has several benefits. First and foremost, it incorporates many of the complex dynamics that occur across rate plans when a change is made to the lineup of rate plans. Secondly, by modeling the change in future cash flows due to a rate plan change, this approach directly captures the long-run economics of pricing actions. Finally, this type of holistic modeling approach explicitly identifies the wide variety of model drivers (e.g., spill, migration, changes in cash flows across rate plans and churn behavior) and enables the analyst to perform sensitivity analysis on their assumptions.

9.9 FUTURE PRICING ANALYSIS CHALLENGES

At the inception of the wireless industry, pricing decisions were based on voice usage. As wireless technology has evolved, non-voice related applications such as text messaging, email, and web browsing have becoming increasingly important to wireless consumers. These services are major sources of revenue for wireless carriers and will require increasing amounts of network capacity. As a result, pricing decisions will become increasingly focused on a bundle of wireless applications rather than primarily on the number of included voice minutes. This will increase the combinatorial complexity of the rate plan portfolio, require the inclusion of new types of customer segments based on technology adoption and non-voice usage, and complicate the modeling of both rate plans and the portfolio.

In addition to pricing a more complex service offering, horizontal and vertical competition is likely to increase. To date, wireless service providers have not directly competed with handset providers, other broadband technologies, or providers of wireless content and applications. Wireless services providers have controlled pricing and the availability of handsets as well as access to network capacity. As wireless services evolve, it is possible that wireless carriers will face new forms of competition from Skype and other firms that are able to offer similar services using different technology.

As the industry evolves the overall pricing objective will likely remain the same, namely to maximize overall expected profitability by growing the customer base; increasing the average revenue per user; and increasing customer tenure. With increasing product complexity and growing competition, decisions about what rate plans to offer to which customers at what prices will continue to grow in complexity.

FURTHER READING

Huang, C.-I. (2008) "Estimating Demand for Cellular Phone Service under Nonlinear Pricing", *Quantitative Marketing and Economics* 6/4: 371–413.

Iyengar R., Jedldl, K., and Hohill, R. (2008) "A Conjoint Approach to Multipart Pricing", *Journal of Marketing Research* 45/2: 195–210.

Kim, S.-Y., Jung, T.-S., Suh, E.-H., and Hwang, H.-S. (2006) "Customer Segmentation and Strategy Development Based on Customer Lifetime Value: A Case Study", *Expert Systems with Applications* 31/1: 101–7.

Lambrecht, A., Seim, K., and Skiera, B. (2007) "Does Uncertainty Matter? Consumer Behaviors Under Three-Part Tariffs", *Marketing Science* 26/5: 598–710.

Murray, J. A. (2002) *Wireless Nation: The Frenzied Launch of the Cellular Revolution in America*. Cambridge, MA: Perseus.

Narayanan, S., Chintagunta, P. K., and Miravete, E. (2007) "The Role of Self Selection, Usage Uncertainty and Learning in the Demand for Local Telephone Service", *Quantitative Marketing and Economics* 5/1: 1–34.

Samanta, S. K., Woods, J., Ghanbari, M., and Rahman, Z. (2009) "Tariff Balancing for Increased Subscription and Revenue in a Mobile Network", *International Journal of Mobile Communications* 7/2: 213–31.

Shi, Mengze, Chiang, Jeongwen, and Rhee, Byong-Duk (2006) "Price Competition with Reduced Consumer Switching Costs: The Case of Wireless Number Portability in the Cellular Phone Industry", *Management Science* 52/1: 27–38.

CHAPTER 10

FOR WHAT IT'S WORTH: PRICING INTERNAL IT SERVICES

DIOGO RAU AND PAUL WILLMOTT

If the cliché "you get what you pay for" holds true, then businesses must get a great amount from information technology (IT). Often 3 percent to 7 percent of revenue, IT is not cheap. Yet business managers and end users routinely cite IT as a source of unending angst.

The pricing strategy for IT matches its history as a corporate function. In the infancy of information systems, IT groups—then termed Management Information Systems (MIS) departments—managed the mundane details of payroll, accounts receivable, and accounts payable. Like finance, legal, and human resources, IT was a shared service, the entire costs of which were paid by the corporate center. As applications expanded into logistics, sales, and other areas that touched individual businesses, IT's budget grew. But the pricing model remained unchanged: a shared resource, paid for by the corporate center. As individual businesses within the enterprise acted in each unit's best interest, demand for IT out-stripped supply.

Recognizing the shortcomings of the traditional approach, managers are starting to adopt new pricing mechanisms, in order to control and channel IT resources to the highest value projects. Managers realize that IT pricing is not just for accounting and budgeting; it is also a means to transform the way a company runs.

One mechanism is to focus on simply recovering the costs from the business units through allocations. This cost recovery can vary from simple mechanisms based on revenue or headcount to more complex consumption-based mechanisms. These methodologies all allocate cost post-consumption, thereby removing the element of predictability and thus control of costs from the buyer's side.

Another mechanism, rooted in market pricing mechanisms, distinguishes supply from demand. IT, acting as the supplier of IT services and products, sets a price for a product; the businesses, acting as buyers, decide the volume to buy. IT has an incentive to maintain cost efficiency. The business buyer has an incentive to constrain consumption. In theory, the "invisible hand" that Adam Smith described in the *Wealth of Nations* now improves the enterprise as a whole.

10.1 PRICELESS: WHAT MAKES PRICING IT DIFFICULT

Both the costs and the benefits of IT are generally difficult to assign. The difficulty in pricing IT costs stems from three factors: shared ownership of IT services, customization of IT services that have no equivalent market product, and a "long tail" of expenses over the life of those services.

Unlike end-user costs for telephones, computers, or productivity software that readily match an individual user, the majority of IT costs cannot be ascribed to a single user or even business unit. Multiple organizations will share hardware and applications for benefits of scale. Software vendors may sell a product for one organization and give away a product that benefits another organization. Maintenance costs, commonly termed "keep the lights on" can typically be over 50 percent of the budget. Included in this category are housekeeping expenses for maintaining data centers, the core financial and human resource applications, and other hard-to-allocate systems. To make matters more obscure, enterprises commonly capitalize hardware purchases and application development expenses. Hefty depreciation charges, typically 10–20 percent of the budget appear as an opaque financial mass.

IT is often a monopoly supplier, by design, providing personalized applications that are not available in the wider market. The buyer may have to pay whatever price IT demands. Since application development is usually customized, the buyer may not have a meaningful benchmark to understand the fair market cost of a project. In addition IT expenses last long after the project finishes. Each project that goes into service encumbers an unknown, unfunded liability. Hardware will need upgrades. Software will need patches. Defects will need fixes. The total cost of ownership can seem incalculable.

10.2 MUST, SHOULD, WOULD, COULD: DECOMPOSING PROJECTS ACCORDING TO VALUE

Measuring return on investment depends on a good definition of value. Classifying projects according to the value driver can help. Most IT projects fall into one of the following categories:

- *Compliance and risk mitigation*. Compliance with government regulations, such as Sarbanes Oxley or Basel II, often provides no easily quantifiable benefit for any part of the organization. Nevertheless, organizations often give this "benefit" the highest weighting, as implementation is mandatory.

- *Process efficiency.* Perhaps the most common motivation for IT projects over the last several decades, automating operations reduces labor and material costs in the business. The value is generally clear in the cost savings.

- *Revenue.* IT's contribution to revenue is often difficult to assign, but may have much higher impact than on costs. Better demand forecasting is one example. In most cases, the true revenue impact is not predictable with a great deal of accuracy.

- *Soft factors.* IT projects often improve a number of unquantifiable, or hard-to-quantify, strategic benefits. Flexibility is one of the most common motivations, such as the ability to support future acquisitions. Since the value is so challenging to measure, most organizations fund few, if any, projects on soft factors alone.

Estimating a hard return on investment in IT is impractical in many cases; the financial case alone is not a good enough criterion for investment in a single project. Lee and Özer (2007) described this phenomenon in estimating the value of RFID, the inventory tracking technology: it is notoriously difficult to ascribe its value to specific parts of an organization.

However, different economic models that guide the interaction between the business client and IT can improve the likelihood of investing in the "right" projects.

10.3 MARX OR FRIEDMAN? CHOOSING THE ECONOMIC MODEL

The economic model guides the behavior of businesses with IT. Frequently, a single organization will operate multiple economic models, depending on the desired behavior. There are two main considerations when deciding on the economic model: the payer for the IT services and the model by which the payer pays IT. Most organizations, 57 percent, operate with a budget centrally controlled by IT (CIO 2007).

The choice of payer can have a significant impact on value to the enterprise. If the corporate center pays, but lacks suitable controls, even business units acting rationally can destroy enterprise value, by inflating benefits and demanding as many projects and features as possible. Leaving business clients with the bill may not encourage the right behavior, either. Each business might shy from collaboration, choosing to retain independent IT groups. The enterprise would forego the scale benefits of sharing common resources, such as servers and help desks, and lose the ability to share data across businesses.

The choice of who pays influences, but does not set, the economic model for funding IT. Whenever the business does not "own" IT in its entirety, an economic model guides the interactions between the business client and IT. These models typically fall into one of four types:

- *Corporate-funded*—individual businesses do not pay for IT;
- *Cost-allocated*—businesses pay an assigned "tax" for IT services;

- *Consumption-driven*—businesses pay at prices set by IT;
- *Market-based*—businesses pay at prices set by the market.

Note that these models can coexist within a single organization. In fact, some organizations might choose to subdivide IT into "domains", each with a different model. For example, an enterprise might choose to provide core infrastructure and financial systems through corporate funding, while letting the business use a market-based approach for all other investments. We will treat "IT" as a single domain in the forthcoming sections for simplicity. But for IT organizations with multiple domains, the underlying principles apply equally well to each domain.

10.3.1 The corporate-funded model: priceless

In a corporate-funded model, IT is purely a cost center. The corporate center funds IT, and individual businesses do not see these charges on their books. Typically, the CFO and the CEO will set a top budget for IT and leave IT to decide what to invest, in some cases without much input from the business. This model works well for small companies and long-term capital projects.

The price to the business unit is effectively "free", even though the costs may be significant. But since the actual capacity to deliver is limited, demand for services nearly always exceeds the supply.

This pricing model motivates the businesses to compete for the "free" resources until the capacity is exhausted. Maximizing consumption will maximize profit for each business. Businesses will have long "wish lists". In fact, CIOs rated "the overwhelming backlog of requests and proposals" as the biggest barrier to job effectiveness, according to *CIO Magazine* (CIO 2005). Making the decisions even more difficult, clients may overstate the value of a project in order to encourage funding.

But this model may do more than simply obscure the financials of IT. Technology is a substitute for labor, and free technology can lead a business to over-automate. For example, a business in this model might demand automating an accounts receivable process—even if the costs far exceeded that investment.

With a free-spending buyer, the functioning of the enterprise economy depends on the supplier's behavior. Organizations in this model depend heavily on a prioritization process of business cases. Business units rarely make the ultimate investment decisions, hoping at best to influence the outcome.

At one large insurer with this model, IT organized a project portfolio during the annual IT budget review, and the CFO was the ultimate decision-maker. If a business unit asked for a project that was not on the list from IT, the CFO would entertain the proposal only if the business could make up for the cost elsewhere in the annual budget. While effective at managing demand, this approach could lead the company to be excessively conservative, missing lucrative opportunities whenever the upside was not certain.

The corporate-funded model can work well for long-term capital projects. When general managers at a decentralized manufacturing firm wanted to start building common platforms, the CFO offered a corporate-funded economic model for an enterprise resource planning (ERP) system. The economic case was strongly positive, but would have been exceedingly difficult for the general managers to find a fair way to fund.

10.3.2 The cost-allocated model: fair share

In the cost-allocated model, IT assigns each client a portion of the total expense. By explicitly paying for the resource, businesses expect a greater voice than in the previous model. As a result, this model is suited for projects that involve multiple businesses, and where the value is not apparent when considering only one business.

The cost-allocated model attempts to inspire common interests in the enterprise's IT strategy. IT is not a free resource, as in the corporate-funded model, but is instead a common resource. To pay for the shared resource, business units pay a "fair share" of the IT costs, essentially a tax. Rooted in the principle that the value and cost of IT are proportional to the organization's size, enterprises typically allocate costs to businesses using one or more size metrics. Typical metrics include revenues, staff, costs, and prior year IT spend.

Like teenagers splitting a check at a restaurant, each buyer tends to consume more than they admit—and then complain when the bill arrives. As a buyer, a rational business will eagerly promote projects that benefit its unit. Businesses may request more projects than needed, knowing that sibling businesses will subsidize the implementation costs. This behavior was termed "The Tragedy of the Commons" by ecologist Garrett Hardin (1968). Using the metaphor of herders sharing a common parcel of land for their cows to graze upon, he explains the tragedy: "Each man is locked into a system that compels him to increase his herd without limit—in a world that is limited".

The actual bills are often opaque. Figure 10.1 shows a typical invoice from IT to its business client based on the cost-allocation model. This invoice rolls up total charge, but leaves the business manager without a clear idea of how to manage consumption or price. Instead, a business manager may spend more time debating the accuracy or fairness of the allocation process.

With a stronger voice than in the corporate-funded model, the buyers will be cautious of enterprise-wide investments, given the incremental cost. They may bicker about what costs they drive and what value they receive. But they may be appropriately motivated to make sure these enterprise-wide investments, such as ERP systems, do deliver true value. Furthermore, buyers will often be averse to standardization whenever those standards delay delivery or increase cost, regardless of the long-term benefit to the enterprise.

As with the corporate-funded model, the functioning of the technology economy depends on the behavior of the supplier. This is especially important when the sizes of the business units are imbalanced. Small units may not receive sufficient attention from IT, given their smaller contribution. In most enterprises, investment committees guide the decision making to ensure projects use funding efficiently and maintain standards for the enterprise.

One software company using this model set up funding committees for each business. Having paid a "fair share" of the IT costs, each business unit expected and received representation on its committee. The IT representatives spanned multiple committees, to ensure funding of enterprise initiatives and consistency across the enterprise.

Perhaps the most critical design decision in this model is whether to permit incremental spending by a business, in addition to the allocated base. When the model permits additional spending, the business buyer expects a high degree of ownership of the incremental effort.

Invoice for Fixed Income division – period FY 2008		
Application development & maintenance		
Application labor		**Charge $ Millions**
Fixed income		100
Equity		50
...		–
Subtotal application development & maintenance		–
Infrastructure		
Area	**Product**	**Charge $ Millions**
Labor	Engineering and support labor	10
	Distributed computing labor	20
	End user technology labor	10
	Mainframe labor	10
	Infrastructure management labor	5
	...	–
	Total labor	**100**
Equipment	Mainframe	10
	Distributed computing	50
	Other	10
	...	–
	Total equipment	**100**
Other	. . .	50
Subtotal infrastructure		**250**
Division total		**400**

FIGURE 10.1 Typical IT invoice to business

A large wholesale bank used incremental spending to great benefit, keeping the cost-allocated portion to the projects that IT viewed necessary, while allowing the business to prioritize the applications it wanted to invest in. But the software company mentioned earlier experienced a less attractive result with incremental funding. In some cases, the business funded projects reasonably denied by the committee. Some groups also formed "shadow" IT teams to implement the projects, causing data stores and platforms to proliferate.

More than any of the other models, the cost-allocated approach requires a strong degree of collaboration between buyer and supplier to be successful. This collaboration ensures that the buyers (the businesses) give a clear indication of the worth of different IT projects, and the supplier has overall control over IT provisioning.

10.3.3 The consumption-driven model: pay-as-you-go

Many organizations are turning to a new pricing model that is consumption-driven. Termed "pay-as-you go", or more cheekily "pay-per-drink", this approach splits the total cost into a price per unit and a number of distinct units. As a result, this model motivates the buyer to constrain demand. Unlike the cost-allocated model, the buyer has a clear mechanism to change costs, through the number of units. This model relies on IT being able to commoditize its products and services.

IT sets the price per unit, in a monopolistic fashion. Prices are naturally a function of the IT organization's ability to deliver. But since the prices in this model are provided by IT before consumption, the prices become a function of the organization's ability to forecast demand and estimate future costs, both of which can be exceedingly difficult. Beyond these cost estimates, four important decisions remain for a consumption-based pricing model:

- *Fixed or floating?* IT can propose a fixed set of prices in advance of projects, or it can provide best estimates of effort. Floating methods risk overruns in the business client's budget but more easily accommodate changes during the project.

- *Marginal costs or average costs?* Prices based on marginal costs will provide a known, fixed overhead, and will be attractive to business clients. But marginal costs discount the true cost to the buyer.

- *Strategic pricing or actual costs?* IT can price products to motivate behaviors, such as offering lower rates for systems that stick to the architecture's preferred platform and higher rates for maintaining systems at end-of-life. Or IT can use strategic pricing to fund "skunk-works" projects.

- *Where to put the profits and losses?* If IT uses fixed, marginal or strategic pricing, the group will likely incur a profit or a loss. The profits or losses will often return to the corporate center, but could also return to the business or roll over for IT to the following year.

When executed well, the business client will not request as many projects as in the corporate-funded or cost-allocated models. At the same time, the buyer will be able to forecast IT expenses and model scenarios at different consumption levels. The business client will be inclined to join enterprise-wide efforts whenever the price justifies the value. Furthermore, the buyer will be motivated to ask for a low price.

But the model does not automatically compel IT to reduce its cost per unit, especially when demand is high. Other controls, such as measuring IT managers on cost efficiency, need to be in place. Furthermore, forecasting becomes an essential skill for IT to avoid oversupply. A glut of servers or application developers could leave IT with a cost overrun. Effective consumption-driven approaches depend on a clear definition of the unit available for purchase. A useful definition of *product* meets three criteria:

- packages individual cost elements into the smallest grouping that meaningfully meets business objectives;

- specifies a price that approximates unit costs, given a range of variability;

- measures usage through the simplest single metric that best approximates consumption.

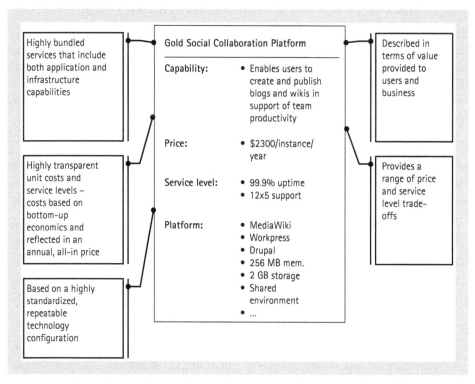

Highly bundled services that include both application and infrastructure capabilities

Highly transparent unit costs and service levels – costs based on bottom-up economics and reflected in an annual, all-in price

Based on a highly standardized, repeatable technology configuration

Gold Social Collaboration Platform

Capability: • Enables users to create and publish blogs and wikis in support of team productivity

Price: • $2300/instance/ year

Service level: • 99.9% uptime
• 12x5 support

Platform: • MediaWiki
• Workpress
• Drupal
• 256 MB mem.
• 2 GB storage
• Shared environment
• ...

Described in terms of value provided to users and business

Provides a range of price and service level trade-offs

FIGURE 10.2 Example of a clear product definition: A product is a bundled offering that can be understood by a business customer and delivered at a specified rate

Consequently, there is no useful definition of "product" that is universal to all organizations or even all business units. An organization focused on improving salesforce productivity might use a product definition such as "user licenses of customer relationship management software". But a manufacturing organization with few office staff might find this definition too granular for the business managers, instead preferring a higher-level definition of "desktop computer for office worker".

Figure 10.2 shows an example of a good product definition, specifying a product in terms of value to the user (collaboration tool that improves team productivity), at a clear price ($2,300/instance/year) with an unambiguous metric (each instance of the tool).

Product definitions are relatively easy for infrastructure items; numbers of servers, gigabytes of storage, or terabytes of data are easy to measure and to price. While this might be a suitable consumption-based model *within* IT—between an application team (an example of an application team is one that provides software to regulate payroll) and an infrastructure team (an example of an infrastructure team is one that provides end-user terminals)—these metrics will rarely be the best choice between IT and the business client. In a consumption-based model, metrics that tie to business objectives will meet the needs of the business client better—number of transactions executed, claims processed, customer records, or even "seats" (users of the application).

IT organizations can also vary the service levels to change behaviors rather than creating new products. The IT organization of one software company charges for hosting servers at a fixed cost regardless of the operating system version used. But servers on older operating systems receive reduced support (more than 24-hour response time), while those willing to test the next generation receive immediate support (under one hour). Using this type of product definition, the total number of products an IT organization offers will be small, generally fewer than 100 for most enterprises. Minimizing the size of the product offering is important to keep the accounting associated with the products unobtrusively small in energy and expense.

10.3.4 The market-based model: paying market rates

A market-based model allows business users to select external vendors, treating IT as one of several suppliers. In this model, more so than the pay-as-you-go model, there is reliance on commoditized IT products and services. In this case, the product/service should be packaged to be sold to a number of organizations.

The market for IT services sets the prices, rather than IT, as in the consumption-driven approach. When competing for a project, for example, IT may propose hourly rates of its full-time employees at rates comparable to those available externally. As a better-informed supplier, IT may be able to charge a small premium over market rates for the knowledge of the business and existing systems that it already holds. This model motivates the buyer to control usage as in the consumption-driven approach. But it also inspires the business to shop around projects to more vendors. This, in turn, compels IT to be more efficient.

Demand forecasting is not as essential as in the consumption-driven model. If fear of oversupply leads IT to instead undersupply, the business can turn to an external provider to make up the difference.

The enterprise, with IT, must set clear policies of what can go to market. While some organizations are willing to turn over all of its IT to an outsourced provider, other enterprises are committed to retaining some activities, to maintain trade secrets, customer privacy, or legal requirements. Furthermore, the enterprise needs strict architecture standards and guidelines if a variety of vendors will deliver.

Corporate governance rarely allows free reign to an invisible hand, even if it makes the enterprise more efficient. But as IT evolves from its role as an order-taking group managing information systems to a true enabler of the business, new pricing models should follow. Whether through an assigned tax, a monopolistic price list, or a true free market, enterprises can make a conscious choice in the partnership between business and IT. While only 52 percent of companies have a formal chargeback policy (Forrester 2009), this number is increasing, with half of those not doing so already either working on developing such a policy or considering one.

Whereas having IT simply respond to demand results in the unintended consequence of businesses pulling IT resources toward their own best interests, the natural byproduct of the right IT pricing model is more than just the channeling of IT resources to the best value projects—it's also the information that results from forcing the businesses to examine their IT projects in a new way. Through the right pricing, IT drives the businesses to examine metrics that will allow them to strategize better within the larger organization and derive the best value from their IT investment. IT pricing thus becomes a means of transforming the way a company runs, moving far beyond accounting and budgeting purposes.

Companies that see this and evolve their IT pricing out to the forefront now will position themselves to experience much greater success. Nevertheless, there is no "silver bullet" to find the right IT pricing. The optimum pricing model is dependent on the type of company and even on the type of projects, with each pricing model motivating different behaviors from both IT and businesses.

As technology evolves, there will be a corresponding change in the future of IT pricing mechanisms. Already, firms such as HP and Microsoft are offering services that would have traditionally fallen under the remit of internal IT organizations. For example, cloud computing offers the potential of computing services being provided externally. These external providers are likely to be strongest on commoditized IT services, where internal IT organization will compete with external vendors to provide the best value service. Also, as with new industries, new standards will evolve as industry-wide IT product catalogues are defined. This can only exert a downward pressure on the cost of IT, as industry IT suppliers achieve benefits of scale. On the other hand, internal IT organizations will gravitate toward products and services that differentiate them from the competition. We could then end up with a differential system comprised of a market-based model for commoditized products, a cost allocation model for internal services and a corporate-funded or cost-allocated model for organization-wide projects.

References and Further Reading

Appel, Andrew M., Arora, Neeru, and Zenkich, Raymond (2005) "Unraveling the Mystery of IT Costs", *McKinsey Quarterly* Fall.

CIO Magazine (2005) *State of the CIO 2006*. CXO Media.

CIO Magazine (2007) *State of the CIO 2008*. CXO Media.

Forrester (2005) *The State of IT Governance in Europe*. Cambridge, MA: Forrester Research, Inc.

Forrester (2009) *IT Chargeback Adoption: The Haves And Have-Nots*. Cambridge, MA: Forrester Research, Inc., July 29.

Gentle, M. (2007) *IT Success! Towards a New Model for Information Technology*. Chichester: John Wiley & Sons Ltd.

Hardin, G. (1968) "The Tragedy of the Commons", *Science* 162/3859: 1243–8.

Lee, H. and Özer, Ö. (2007) "Unlocking the True Value of RFID", *Production and Operations Management* 161: 40–64.

Symons, C., Leaver, S., and DeGennaro, T. (2009) *IT Chargeback Adoption: The Haves and Have-Nots*. Cambridge, MA: Forrester.

Weill, P. and Ross, J. (2004) *IT Governance: How Top Performers Manage IT Decision Rights for Superior Results*. Boston, MA: Harvard Business School Press.

CHAPTER 11

....

TELEVISION ADVERTISEMENT PRICING IN THE UNITED STATES

....

ROBERT PHILLIPS AND
GRAHAM YOUNG

Since the earliest days of television, American commercial broadcast networks have obtained the vast majority of their revenue from advertising. While this may not seem particularly remarkable, what is perhaps more interesting is that television advertisements in the United States are bought and sold in a highly idiosyncratic market whose structure appears to be unique. Specifically, 70–80 percent of broadcast network television advertising inventory is sold in a hectic two-week period known as the *upfront market*, while the remainder is sold during the balance of the year in the so-called *scatter market*. This chapter describes how television advertising is bought and sold in these markets, with an emphasis on pricing. We begin by presenting an overview of the American broadcast television industry, followed by a high level description of the upfront and scatter markets. We follow this with a more detailed description of how prices and products are developed and sold in both the upfront and scatter markets. We discuss the use of automated pricing and revenue management systems by the networks. We conclude with a short discussion of the changes that the industry is undergoing. Our primary focus throughout is on the United States, although we mention practices in a number of other countries.

The authors gratefully acknowledge the comments from Özalp Özer and two anonymous referees that led to significant improvements in the chapter.

11.1 STRUCTURE OF THE AMERICAN TELEVISION INDUSTRY

The structure of the American television industry is, in large part, a product of its history. Until the mid-1970s, three networks—ABC, CBS, and NBC—dominated commercial television. The vast majority of households received their television via antenna from a local broadcasting station. Cable television was developed in the 1950s primarily as a vehicle to deliver television to households that were not able to receive reliable broadcast signals either because of distance or because of topography. Initially, government regulation largely prohibited cable from competing with the established networks. A series of rulings by the Federal Communications Commission (FCC) in the 1970s released these restrictions and cable grew rapidly thereafter. Initially, cable's growth was driven by the fact that it delivered superior picture quality and reliability, but it was not long before new networks arose that used cable as the distribution channel for their own programming. HBO began showing "pay-for-view" movies on cable in the early 1970s and Ted Turner launched his independent cable network in 1976. Commercial satellite television became available as an option for many American households in the late 1980s.

All three of these delivery options—broadcast, cable, and satellite—are in use today. In 2008, approximately 61 percent of American households with television had wired cable access and another 28 percent had satellite dishes, leaving only 11 percent entirely dependent on broadcasts from terrestrial sources (Papazian 2009). Internet television (IPTV) is a small, but rapidly growing, fourth delivery channel.

As noted above, the bulk of the revenue received by commercial television networks comes from advertising. In fact, advertisers spend more money on television than any other medium. In 2008, national advertisers spent about $52 billion dollars on television advertising,[1] compared to about $21 billion on magazines and newspapers and about $4 billion on radio. Internet advertising—although growing fast—was about $12 billion, or less than 25 percent of the amount spent on television. Television advertising represents between 40 percent and 45 percent of national advertising media spend, a fraction that has remained roughly constant since 1980 (Papazian 2009; ProQuest 2010).

There are three major groups of players in the market for television advertising:

1. The *advertisers* are primarily major corporations, most of whom have multi-million dollar advertising budgets. In 2008, the top television advertiser was Procter and Gamble, who spent $2.04 billion on national ads. The remainder of the top five were AT&T, General Motors, Verizon Communications, and Toyota. Most—but not all—national advertisers are corporations. One of the largest non-corporate advertisers is the US Government, who spent $456 million on national TV ads in 2008. Political campaigns are also major purchasers of television advertising. In the presidential election year of 2008, political campaigns spent $1.3 billion on television advertising (ProQuest 2010).

---

[1] In addition to these national revenues, television stations received about $13 billion from local advertisers in 2009 (Papazian 2009; ProQuest 2009).

2. *Advertising agencies* work with their clients—the advertisers—to develop, implement, and evaluate television campaigns. This includes the production of the commercials and the negotiations with the networks for spots. Some of the top advertising agencies in terms of television spend include BBDO, Ogilvy & Mather, McCann-Ericson, and JWT (formerly J. Walter Thompson). Several agencies have combined into media buying groups to increase their purchasing power.

3. The *television networks* control one or more channels of distribution for national broadcasting. They also develop content (i.e., programming from the network's own or affiliated production studios) and/or license content from others (e.g., independent studios, Hollywood movies, or British television programs). There are two types of networks:

   - The *broadcast networks* in the United States currently consist of ABC, CBS, NBC, and Fox—sometimes called the "Big Four"—plus the much smaller CW network and two Spanish-language networks, Univision and Telemundo. Three of these networks—ABC, CBS, and NBC—date back to the earliest days of commercial television. Fox is a relative newcomer having begun service in 1986 and CW is even newer, having been formed from the merger of the WB and UPN networks in 2006. The Big Four are generalists in that they provide a wide variety of content—news, drama, sports, comedy, talk shows, etc.—to attract a broad and diverse viewing audience. While they have gradually been losing ground to cable networks, they are still the dominant powers in television.

   - The *cable networks* deliver their products entirely through cable and/or satellite—that is, they do not broadcast on the air waves. There are more than 100 cable networks in operation in the United States. As a rule, cable networks tend to be more specialized than the broadcast networks. They tend to specialize either in a particular type of content such as news (CNN, Fox News Channel), weather (the Weather Channel), or sports (ESPN, Fox Soccer Channel); or by targeting specific audience segments such as the "lesbian, bisexual and transgender audience" (LOGO) or children (Nickelodeon, Disney). In terms of total audience, the five most popular cable networks in 2010 were Nickelodeon, Nick at Nite, USA, Disney, and Fox News Channel (ProQuest 2010). While the advertisement-based model described in this chapter is used by the majority of cable networks, a handful of *premium pay cable networks* such as Showtime, HBO, and Starz rely entirely upon carriage fees in which viewers pay a monthly fee to access the channel. In return, the pay cable networks air programming free of commercial interruptions.

The interaction among the networks, the agencies, and the advertisers determines the price at which advertising inventory is bought and sold.[2] We now describe the nature of that inventory.

---

[2] In addition to the national market that we consider here, there are also *station markets* in which individual stations—which may or may not be affiliated with a broadcast network—primarily sell advertising time on local programming.

11.2 THE NATURE OF INVENTORY

An important characteristic of the television advertising market is that the inventory that the sellers control is not what buyers want to purchase. Specifically, each network controls *slots* in program breaks. Slots usually occur in increments of 60, 45, 30, and 15 seconds. While the network controls the slots and their placement within and between shows, what advertisers want to buy are *impressions* or *eyeballs*—the number of people viewing a commercial. Furthermore, advertisers are not just interested in how many people watched a commercial, they also are interested in *who* watched it. Thus, the rating services track many different viewer characteristics such as age and gender. The most sought-after demographic in prime-time is Adults 18–49.

The number of impressions generated by a spot is measured in different ways. The *reach* or *cume* (cumulative) of a commercial is the number of unique viewers who saw the commercial at least once over some predetermined period of time. The *frequency* is the average number of times that each viewer saw the commercial. The *gross rating points* measures the total number of times that the commercial was viewed. It can be computed as the product of the reach and the frequency. Thus, a commercial with a reach of 3 million during a week with a frequency of 3.2 would have a gross rating of 3.2 × 3 million = 9.6 million. Advertisers are often more interested in reach than in frequency for their commercials.

Measuring how many impressions are garnered by each advertisement is done by the *ratings agencies*, of which the dominant player in the United States is Nielsen Media Research (formerly A.C. Nielsen). Nielsen tracks the television viewing patterns of 25,000 *Nielsen households* in the United States using *set meters* that track what shows are playing on all television sets in those households at all times. Information from the set meters is transmitted nightly to Nielsen. In addition, members of the Nielsen households keep *viewer diaries* in which they are supposed to record which shows they watch every day. Using these data, Nielsen develops estimates of how many people from each demographic category are watching every show throughout the nation. While the accuracy of the Nielsen ratings has been disputed from time to time, the ratings are by far the most commonly used measure of performance in contracts between agencies and networks. More details on the ratings methodology used by A.C. Nielsen can be found on their website at http://www.nielsenmedia.com.

We note that the advent of video recording and services such as Tivo have made estimating viewership much more complicated since a significant number of viewers now watch a program on a delayed basis (or on a different screen, such as the Internet or smartphone). This has generated a confusing variety of ratings categories such as *Live, Live plus delayed viewing 3-days-later*, and *Live plus 7-days-later*. After a period of rating proliferation, the industry appears to be settling into a standard based on two measures: the number of viewers who watch a commercial live and those who watch it within three days of air, known as *C3*. However some advertisers will always require that a network use the Live rating alone. A retailer advertiser on Friday night for a weekend sale is not willing to pay for viewers who watch the show on a delayed basis on Sunday night.

The standard measure of price or cost in the television industry is the *CPM* or *cost per thousand impressions*. It is the total price paid for a slot (or set of slots) divided by the total audience for those slots measured in thousands. Thus, if a network receives $80,000 for a slot viewed by 10,000,000 people, the corresponding CPM is $80,000/10,000 = $8.00.

While advertising slots are the networks' bread-and-butter, there are also other programming attributes that can be sold such as sponsorships, exclusivity, and in-program product placement. These attributes generate only a tiny portion of total network revenue and we will not discuss them further.

11.3 STRUCTURE OF THE MARKET

The television season in the United States runs from September or October of one year through May of the following year.[3] New programs and new episodes of existing programs are typically scheduled to start at the beginning of the season. New episodes of a program will typically run for either half a season or for a full season—although an underperforming program can be cancelled at any time.

Advertising for a season is sold in two markets:

1. The *upfront market*[4] takes place in late May shortly after the networks announce their new programming for the upcoming season. During the upfront market, which typically lasts about two weeks, the networks and the agencies negotiate contracts for the majority of the anticipated advertising capacity for the next year. For example, during the 2010 upfront market, advertisers committed between $8.1 and $8.7 billion in sales to the broadcast networks (Steinberg 2010). This represented about 70 percent of the total revenue for the networks.

2. The *scatter market* refers to inventory sales after the upfront has occurred. A typical scatter buy contains much less inventory per proposal than an upfront buy. The scatter market is used by smaller advertisers who may be unable to make an upfront commitment, as well as by larger advertisers who wish to purchase additional advertising time on top of what they purchased in the upfront. In some years, advertisers have avoided upfront buying in the anticipation of saving money if scatter pricing falls below upfront pricing. This is generally a very risky bet since, in most seasons, scatter prices have turned out to be higher than upfront prices.

During the season, networks schedule and air commercials within and between their programs. As the seasons progress, Nielsen estimates viewership and demographics for each show. If a broadcaster meets or exceeds his agreement to an advertiser to deliver a certain number and type of audience, then no further action is necessary. If, however, the broadcaster fails to deliver the audience that was agreed upon in the upfront, then the broadcaster must re-negotiate the agreement or provide additional commercial spots until

---

[3] We note that the existence and timing of the television season varies from country to country. In Australia, there is no television season to speak of. In Japan, programming is typically scheduled in four 13-week seasons. The origins of the American television season are obscure, although there is some evidence that it was inherited from radio.

[4] While it is traditional to speak of the network prime-time upfront market as "the" upfront market, there are, in fact, several upfront markets. The cable networks hold an upfront market that typically starts slightly later and historically lasts a bit longer than the network upfront. In addition there are typically separate upfront markets for daytime television and for weekend children's television. In this chapter we focus on the prime-time upfront market.

Timing	Activity
Before May	*Networks* develop programs, create program schedule and estimate viewership for next season. Based on their estimates, they create upfront rate cards. *Agencies* work with advertisers to understand desired total impressions, demographics and budgets. Based on this information they allocate the budget among different media. They will also create a specific *television budget* specifying the total impressions, demographics, and timing desired from television advertisements.
May	*Networks* release schedules and, upon contracting, confirm viewership guarantees for the upcoming season to agencies.
End of May	**The up front market.** Agencies and Networks negotiate contracts under which 75–90% of anticipated inventory is sold.
Early June – onward	**The scatter market.** Networks sell the remaining inventory to advertisers. This inventory is typically sold with no guaranteed impressions.
September – the following September	**The season.** Networks schedule commercials and air them. Viewership for each commercial is measured by Nielsen. To the extent that upfront commitments for guaranteed impressions are not met, networks must either renegotiate or provide Audience Deficiency Units (ADUs).

FIGURE 11.1 Timing of major events in the market for television advertising

the agreed upon audience is delivered. We discuss this case in Section 11.6. The timing of the major events in the market is summarized in Figure 11.1.

11.4 PRICING IN THE UPFRONT MARKET

In some sense, "pricing" is performed (or at least considered) by a network throughout the entire process of program planning and schedule development. In particular, networks aim to plan a schedule that delivers the most valuable possible audience to prospective advertisers. They then estimate the audience that they anticipate for each show on the schedule. Based on this, the networks develop an upfront *rate card* that specifies prices for each combination of show, viewership, and demographic. While the rate card specifies the prices that the network would like to achieve, the actual prices will be determined through negotiation with the agencies during the upfront market. This section describes each of these steps in more detail.

11.4.1 Program scheduling and formatting

The first step in the planning process is the development of the programming schedule for the upcoming season. Each season is a mix of continuing programming—new seasons of existing shows—and new shows that will debut that season. Once the shows have been selected for a new season, they need to be scheduled. Program schedule development is a critical task for a network. Typically, program schedulers want to attract and retain viewers as the evening progresses. Audience levels also depend on other factors such as the day of week and the schedule of competing networks.

Once programs have been scheduled, they are formatted with breaks, called *pods*. Within each pod, a network will schedule commercial advertising, promotional content, and public service announcements. This process is called *formatting*. Formats may change prior to air time, but the initial format determines the number of commercial spots planned for each program and the non-commercial time allocated to internal promotions and public service announcements. This is the starting point for estimating how many impressions the upcoming season can deliver.

11.4.2 Estimating the audience

Once a schedule is complete and formatted, the network estimates the audience for each show. History can be used to generate accurate estimates for programs with consistent audiences such as continuing daytime soaps and children's shows. However, prime-time programming, especially for new shows, demonstrates tremendous variability in audience appeal. Estimating the audience for a new show is as much art as science.

The research department determines the expected number of viewers for any given program and estimates the ratings variability. These results are critical to the sales department, who sell the estimates to the agencies. If the network overestimates the audience, the network will have to compensate agencies with additional slots or other considerations as described in Section 11.6. However, if the network underestimates the audience, the advertiser is typically not charged for the excess viewers delivered. Thus an underestimate can result in the network giving away valuable inventory for free. As a result, the network must be extremely careful to understand the variability around the initial estimates or they will not be able to profit from successful shows while being penalized for shows that perform below expectation. This risk is somewhat mitigated by the fact that most audience guarantees are based on the total audience across all programs—that is, under delivery on one program may be balanced by over delivery on another.

11.4.3 Establishing the upfront rate card

After a network has estimated the audience for its shows, it calculates a target CPM for each *daypart*, where a daypart refers to a standard division of the broadcasting week. Some important dayparts are:

- Morning—7:00 am to 9:00 am, Mon.–Fri.
- Daytime—9:00 am to 4:30 pm, Mon.–Fri.
- Early fringe—4:30 pm to 8:00 pm, Mon.–Fri. 4:30 pm–7:00 pm, Sun.
- Prime time—8:00 pm to 11:00 pm, Mon.–Fri. 7:00 pm–11:00 pm, Sun.
- Late fringe—11:30 pm to 1:00 am, Mon.–Fri.

Once target CPMs by daypart have been established, each show will be "indexed" against its target CPM to determine a CPM rate for that show. As a general rule, a popular show can command higher-than-average CPMs than a less popular show because the reach of a popular program is greater than that of a less popular one. In addition, buyers in the upfront market often bid aggressively to ensure that they have exposure on shows that attract their desired demographics (Vogel 2007). However, even though a show is expected to do well in terms of total audience and demographics, it may not be attractive to some advertisers. Programming that pushes social norms in controversial areas such as religion, sex, or violence may be shunned by some advertisers. In contrast, returning shows may be more highly valued by advertisers for their loyal viewers. The sales team also considers the advertising demand for different days of the week. Additionally, even though a show may deliver a sizeable audience reach, it may be in a demographic that is not attractive to advertisers. For example, advertisers consider older viewers less valuable—perhaps because they have more established brand loyalties. All of these factors are considered as the network establishes a CPM for each show in the schedule.

The next step is to determine the impact of the base prices on advertisers. Since the bulk of advertising time is purchased by a relatively small number of advertisers, the network does not have total freedom in pricing. The network compares the reference CPM for the current season with the previous season's CPM to understand the effect on advertisers. The sales team calculates the expected impact of the reference CPM on each of the largest advertisers by examining the advertiser's buy of the previous year and mapping it into the current year's schedule. In other words, what would happen to the advertiser's budget/CPM if they bought exactly what they did the previous year at this year's rates? This may result in iterative price adjustments until the sales team is satisfied with the rate card.

Upfront rate card pricing differs by network and by country. In North America, a standard price is generally assigned to all spots in a given program/air date. At some networks, prices are the same for two or more episodes of the same show. At other networks, the price may vary for each episode. At some European networks, it is customary to further differentiate prices based on pod placement, with a premium being attached to the first and last slot in a pod (which have the most likelihood of being watched). In any case, the prices are published in the upfront rate card which typically forms the starting point for negotiation with the agencies.

11.4.4 Final pricing in the upfront market

While the networks estimate their audiences and establish their rate cards, the advertising agencies meet with their clients to understand their desires for the upcoming season. Specifically, the agencies develop a *budget* for each client specifying the number and type of impressions desired for each quarter. When the upfront market commences, the agencies present their desired CPMs and demographics for each advertiser to the networks. Based on the upfront rate card, the program schedule, and their audience estimates, the networks will respond to each budget with a *proposal* that proposes a programming mix. The agency evaluates the proposals and, typically, will request changes in the proposed programming mix—specifically movement among shows or among weeks. There may be two or three rounds of proposals and counter proposals before the agency and the network reach agreement on the mix for a particular client.

Once the advertising agency and the network have agreed on a proposed programming mix, they will negotiate over the price—the CPMs. The final prices and programming schedules are determined ultimately through negotiation. If demand by the agencies is higher than anticipated, then CPMs will be higher than the network anticipated; if demand is lower, then CPMs will be lower.

The upfront market can be extremely hectic—it requires both buyers and sellers to work long hours, often late into the night. This frantic negotiation process is prone to clerical errors that can lead to unintentional or mistaken offers. Finally, the upfront market requires both the advertising agencies and the networks to make firm contractual commitments under substantial uncertainty. Neither the networks nor the advertising agencies can accurately predict the performance of future programming. Some agencies have research departments who prepare their own performance estimates. These agencies will buy preferentially from networks who, they believe, have underestimated the performance of their programs.

The upfront market ends when supply meets demand: either the agencies are not willing to purchase any more upfront inventory and/or the networks are not willing to sell any more. In the 1960s, the upfront market lasted as much as eight weeks, but the particularly frantic upfront market of 2003 lasted only three days (Lotz 2007). While the networks and the agencies both carefully prepare for the upfront and the networks expend considerable time and energy in developing rate cards, it is important to recognize that the final prices are ultimately determined through negotiation. Estimates of the average upfront CPM received by the "Big Four" broadcast networks for different dayparts and demographics for the 2008–09 upfront are shown in Table 11.1.

Industry analysts closely observe the results of the upfront market. They pay particularly close attention to five metrics:

1. What was the total size of the upfront market?

2. How much total upfront revenue went to each network?

3. What fraction of their expected inventory did each network sell in the upfront?

4. What average CPM did each network receive?

5. How did the average CPM change relative to the previous year?

Performance relative to these metrics is used to judge the "health" of the advertising market as well as to measure the relative performances of the networks. For example, one analyst

Table 11.1 Estimates of the average upfront CPM (cost per thousand impressions in dollars) for the broadcast networks (ABC, CBS, Fox, and NBC) associated with different demographic categories for the 2008–09 television season

	Gender				Age categories		
	All homes	Adults	Men	Women	18–34	18–49	25–54
Morning	9.94	8.50	21.59	13.81	38.92	19.09	16.42
Daytime	6.00	5.46	–	7.48	15.99	10.53	11.33
Early fringe	10.12	7.39	17.24	13.59	42.81	19.61	18.27
Prime	23.22	16.80	35.52	25.85	48.43	29.60	30.68
Late fringe	18.75	14.61	34.67	30.55	38.49	23.33	26.95

Source: Adapted from Papazian (2009: 82)

Table 11.2 Estimated total prime-time upfront
commitments for ABC, CBS, Fox, and NBC by year

Year	Revenue ($ billions)
2007	7.60
2008	7.48
2009	6.52
2010	8.0–8.3 (est.)

Source: Schechner and Vranica (2010)

declared that CBS had been the most successful in the 2010 upfront market because, "They sold 80 percent of their inventory with CPM increases at 9 to 10 percent" (Vasquez 2010). Overall, the 2010 network upfront market was considered successful because, as shown in Table 11.2, total prime-time upfront sales for the Big Four broadcast networks increased significantly over previous years.

11.5 SCATTER MARKET PRICING

The networks develop an initial scatter market rate card at the same time as they develop the upfront rate card. Once the upfront market is complete, the network updates the scatter market rate card to reflect the anticipated inventory position after upfront sales. If a network exceeds its targeted upfront volume, less inventory than anticipated will be available for the scatter market, resulting in higher scatter prices. If upfront demand is lower than anticipated, a network may sell less inventory in the upfront and gamble that it will get higher rates in the scatter market. In a very difficult upfront, the network may elect to reduce the number of units offered for sale. This requires coordination with program development or finding an alternative use for the unit—for example, promotions or a public service announcement. It is generally believed that the networks want to manage their inventory so that scatter pricing is higher than upfront pricing in order to reward upfront buyers and maintain the structure of the market.

As scatter demand materializes, the networks will update their scatter rate cards. Higher than anticipated demand will increase scatter rates while lower demand will reduce scatter rates. A network will work with its customers to actively manage demand in the scatter market. For example, if a week is approaching during which inventory is undersold, a network may negotiate with existing customers with slots in future weeks to "pull their slots" forward in order to utilize the inventory and give the network additional time to find a buyer in the scatter market. Of course, incentives in the form of additional impressions or a move to higher-priced programming may be required to persuade advertisers to do this.

Audience measurements may also impact the scatter rate card. While ratings do not affect the number of units remaining available for sale, audience changes do affect the basic CPM equation. If the audience for a program is significantly lower than initially estimated, it results in pressure to reduce the scatter price. Conversely, surprise breakout hits reward the upfront buyers with cheaper CPMs while scatter buyers will pay more.

It should be noted that there is an important relationship between prices received in the scatter market and upfront pricing for the next season. Low scatter market prices are taken as a sign that demand will be weak in the upcoming upfront market and high scatter market prices are taken as a signal that upfront prices will be high. The latter situation was in play in the last quarter of the 2009–10 scatter market: "Scatter rates for prime-time TV spots this quarter are running 20% to 30% above the advance rates agreed to in last year's upfront, ad buyers say. Many media buyers and some marketers believe advertisers will avoid those premiums by buying more in advance, driving up upfront prices this year" (Schechner and Vranica 2010). This is another reason why the networks like to keep scatter rates high.

11.6 AUDIENCE GUARANTEES AND OPTION CUTBACKS

Since upfront purchases occur well before a program is aired, there is considerable risk that the promised impressions will not materialize as planned. In the early days of commercial television, this risk was borne by the agencies purchasing the inventory. In 1962, an advertising executive with BBDO compared purchasing time slots on television to "going to Las Vegas": "Last season two new half-hour situation comedies made their debut, each costing $57,000 per program. One got an audience of 5,159,000 homes per minute. The other delivered 14,070,000 homes per minute" (Foreman 1962: 44). He contrasted this situation unfavorably to advertising in newspapers and magazines in which case, "our advertiser knows how many people are going to get the magazines and the newspapers he buys. This is *guaranteed* him" (Foreman 1962: 33, emphasis in original). In response to similar complaints from advertisers and agencies, the networks ultimately agreed to guarantee impressions for upfront buys. The first guaranteed CPM deal was negotiated in 1967 between American Home Products and ABC (Ephron 2003: 9).

Guaranteed CPMs turned out to benefit both advertisers and networks. They benefited advertisers by taking the risk out of buying. They also benefited networks. Previously, advertisers had been very eager to buy the limited "real estate" in hit shows—especially those in the Nielsen "Top 10"—but were unwilling to buy slots at anything but bargain prices in less popular or new shows. By selling CPMs instead of slots, the networks could bundle and sell all of their inventory. In return, they guaranteed audience delivery. Guaranteed CPMs quickly became the industry standard and are currently the basis for the vast majority of upfront buys—and, in uncertain markets, even scatter buys.

With an audience guarantee, the network commits to steward contracts to deliver the audience that it originally promised. Upon completion of the upfront, the network removes units from scatter to cover the liability that could arise if the audience falls short of expectations. If the network's initial estimates are accurate, there is no impact on scatter inventory. When audiences are declining or individual shows do not perform as anticipated, a network may have to take many more units out of sale on the scatter market than they had planned. A unit removed from the scatter market in order to support a deficiency from the upfront market is called an *Audience Deficiency Unit (ADU)*. One might anticipate that reducing audience estimates would have a negative effect on scatter pricing—and it often does. In extreme cases, however, the removal of ADUs can reduce available scatter inventory, which can actually cause scatter rates to rise.

Although the advertiser receives an overall audience guarantee, the advertiser is not guaranteed to receive the same replacement programming mix originally outlined on the contract. This is not surprising when one considers that a show that fails to deliver the number of viewers expected may not have enough total audience in its season to satisfy upfront commitments, let alone the additional audience deficiency. As a result, the placement of ADUs becomes a source of further negotiation between network and agency. The network will try to deliver the audience with as little displacement of scatter business as possible, while the agency will strive to maximize the quality of programming received on behalf of its advertisers.

It should also be noted that the audience guarantee is not restricted to a specific season, but is generally guaranteed across the entire buy—typically a full year. As a result, a network that anticipates that viewership will increase may defer offering the ADUs until the later quarters of the contract. In practice, however, the network does not want to carry too much liability into later quarters, as viewership tends to fall in the summer—which normally represents the last quarter of the agreement. In extreme cases of audience deficiency, the agency and the network may agree to defer compensation until the following season.

In addition to guarantees, networks make a further concession to upfront advertisers. Normally the fourth quarter (late September through December) buy is firm, but beyond that, the agency has the flexibility to cancel a certain percentage of its upfront buy in each of the later quarters. This is called an *option cutback*. The initial scatter rate card is constructed with this in mind, but an unplanned change in the amount of returned inventory will cause a network to adjust scatter pricing. As actual program performance is measured, the network can anticipate the quantity of the cutback impact. If the network is performing better than its upfront estimates, it is likely to experience lower option cutbacks because the agencies are measured in part by the CPM they deliver to the advertiser. If the agency negotiated similar CPMs across its network buys, it will improve that metric by leaving more weight with the performing network and cutting back buys from underperforming networks.

It should be noted that the audience guarantees and option cutbacks create an asymmetry in the products sold that works in favor of the advertiser. In particular, if a spot overperforms (delivers more impressions than the network anticipated), then the advertiser reaps the benefit. If the spot underperforms, then the network is still obligated to provide "make-up" impressions in order to satisfy the audience guarantee. Since scatter market buys typically do not include guarantees, this is an additional incentive for advertisers to buy in the upfront.

11.7 ALTERNATIVE INVENTORY

Although not a major component of sales, the networks also sell other types of advertising inventory and services:

- *Direct Response (DR)* advertisements exhort the viewer to call a toll-free number to receive a special offer. They do not have any associated guarantees and are not placed in a fixed position until shortly before airtime. As a result, they are priced significantly below the rate card.

- *Per Inquiry (PI)* is an offshoot of Direct Response advertising that is priced according to the number of inquiries received by the advertiser's 800 number. The broadcaster has slightly more incentive to place the advertisement in a slot in which it will perform, since the broadcaster will ultimately earn more revenue with better performance. In practice, however, the per-inquiry rate is normally so low that it is not worth a lot of management time. Some networks also believe that offering PI and DR degrades the viewer perception of network quality. For this reason, they are typically only scheduled in lower-viewing overnight positions.

- *Video on Demand* is offered by many cable providers. The pricing model for video on demand is still in its infancy because issues are being resolved around audience measurement, whether the viewer will have the ability to fast forward through the ads and how flexible the cable company can be in changing the advertising content once promised delivery levels are attained.

- *Web TV*. Television programming is increasingly distributed via the Internet both directly from the networks' own sites and through services such as Hulu, a joint venture between NBC, ABC, and Fox. One advantage to the web as a distribution channel is that, using cookies, it is easy to identify the viewer—a key objective of the advertiser. On the down side, it is hard for the networks to make comparable money from Web TV (or IPTV) as from analog transmission. For this reason, some networks such as Viacom have pulled their programming from Hulu. As the Viacom CEO explained: "If they [Hulu] can get to the point where the monetization model is better, then we may go back" (Farrell 2010).

Finally, post-broadcast licensing of content on DVD has become an increasingly important source of revenue for the networks. It is difficult to estimate the magnitude of this revenue stream but it is worth noting that in 2009, about 20 percent of Netflix (annual revenue $1.6 billion) rentals were from content derived from television.

11.8 AUTOMATED PRICING AND REVENUE MANAGEMENT

Given the complexity of the pricing and placement issues faced by the networks—not to mention the financial stakes involved—it is not surprising that the networks have begun to invest in automated decision support systems to improve overall profitability but also to increase the efficiency and accuracy of previously manual processes. In this section, we give two examples of how automated systems have been used to support network pricing and revenue management decisions.

11.8.1 Automated scatter pricing

Since 1993, the Canadian Broadcasting Corporation (CBC) has automated its scatter rate card pricing using revenue management software provided by JDA. Each program/week start date is monitored to determine whether realized demand deviates from anticipated demand. Based on the direction and magnitude of the deviation, scatter prices are automatically adjusted either up or down. According to CBC, this system has enabled them to respond to market changes much more quickly. This in turn has allowed them to take the advanced (for North American networks) step of pricing each program/week start date individually. As a result, CBC's rate card reflects changes in short-term demand more accurately than a rate card predicated on pricing seasons or price periods.

11.8.2 Optimal placement

Placement is the process of scheduling advertisements into slots. Placement is first required during the upfront market when a network needs to determine which units (slots) to place against each advertising proposal that it receives. The advertiser provides broad guidance, which may include target CPM or total budget, flighting (the weight of audience desired by week), quarterly weights, and the type/mix of programming desired. Historically, placement has been a highly manual process—account executives or planners work until they find the first set of spots that approximately meets the advertiser's requirements. This task needs to be performed during the highly intense upfront market when the network is simultaneously negotiating with all of its customers. As a result, the initial placements have rarely been anything close to optimal and errors have been commonplace.

One American broadcast television network uses a commercial proposal optimizer developed by JDA. The system takes advantage of the computer's ability to generate and evaluate an extremely large number of candidate proposals before selecting the one that best fits available inventory to advertiser requirements. A key function of optimal placement is ensuring that slots that serve an attractive but narrow demographic are not allocated to proposals that could be satisfied by a much broader demographic. Optimal placement also balances overall load to ensure that, to the extent possible, the network does not oversell certain segments of inventory.

Optimal placement manages demand by channeling it to more appropriate programming, rather than artificially boosting price to force the resulting CPM to make the inventory less attractive to the advertiser. In an upfront, this reduces the necessity to change the rate card frequently. During the upfront, it is possible to sell billions of dollars in inventory in a period of two to three days. Without optimal placement, it is likely that some inventory will be sold out before the network has time to change the price.

Once the upfront market is complete, the network faces the problem of *final placement*—how to schedule commercials into slots in order to best meet contractual commitments. Placement is subject to a complicated set of business constraints—for example, two advertisements for a similar product offered by different advertisers cannot be shown in adjacent slots. Determining how to assign advertisements to slots to best meet contracted upfront obligations subject to these constraints presents a problem of great complexity (Bollapragada and Garbiras 2004; Brusco 2008). NBC is one of a handful of networks that use sophisticated software systems to support the placement process (Bollapragada et al. 2002).

11.9 THE FUTURE OF TELEVISION ADVERTISEMENT PRICING

The television advertising market is unquestionably in a state of flux. From the mid-1950s through the 1970s, the industry was a static oligopoly dominated by the "Big Three"—ABC, CBS, and NBC. Since the mid-1970s, two events have disrupted that once-comfortable triopoly. The first of these was the expansion of nationwide cable—and later satellite—service. This enabled the rise of scores of competing networks that were not reliant on a government grant of broadcasting frequency to deliver their products. The second, ongoing disruption is driven by the rise of the Internet, which has provided yet another channel for content delivery to the home—not to mention a strong competitor for viewer attention. As the Internet continues to gain traction, it has become almost commonplace to predict the demise of "television as we know it", the fall of the broadcast networks, and the loss of television's distinct identity and business model in the ultimate triumph of "media convergence". This may be true, but it is important to note the extent to which the television market has remained largely unchanged over the last half century. The broadcast networks still retain a high level of dominance: In 2008, 99 out of the top 100 highest rated shows in the United States aired on one of the Big Four broadcast networks (Papazian 2009). The upfront/scatter market structure has remained little changed since 1955 despite sporadic efforts by advertisers and agencies to "reform" it.[5] The rise of cable and satellite networks did not disrupt the upfront market—in fact, the cable networks started their own upfront market in imitation of the broadcast networks (Schneider 2002). While the cable networks sell a smaller fraction of their inventory during their upfront, the basic structure is the same as the network upfront.

Of course, the fact that the market for television advertising has not fundamentally changed in more than 50 years does not mean that it won't change in the future. The Internet may well be the force that finally disrupts the fundamental television business model—just as it has disrupted the video rental, newspaper, and recorded music industries. The Internet has two clear advantages for advertisers over traditional television. For one thing, the Internet enables advertisements to be targeted to individual customers much more selectively than television, based on information available through "cookies" (see Chapter 7 by Vudali and Atherton). Secondly, the Internet enables far more accurate real-time measurement of response to advertising via click rate measurements.

In response to the challenge of the Internet, there are many different initiatives underway to shape the "television of the future". One goal of many of these initiatives is to equip television with the same ability that the Internet enjoys: to target advertisements to individuals and immediately measure their responses. This so-called "addressability" feature is being actively pursued on a number of fronts. Google has partnered with

---

[5] In response to a CPM increase of 25% for the 1975–76 season, the largest television advertising agency J. Walter Thompson, decided not to bid in the upfront market. But the move backfired when the agency was forced to pay more for poorer slots in the scatter market (Ephron 2003: 8–9). A group formed by advertisers and media buyers in 2004 to reform the upfront market also failed to force any changes (McClintock 2004) as did a 2005 effort by Chrysler and other major buyers to replace the upfront with an e-Bay auction (McClellan 2010).

Echostar's Satellite Dish Network and Nielsen Corporation to provide addressability for Echostar's subscribers. Canoe Ventures was formed in 2008 as a joint effort by six major cable companies to enable addressability for cable subscribers (http://www.canoe-ventures.com). Google has developed set-top boxes in cooperation with Logitech and Sony that provide the same capabilities. Netflix is moving on-line and will be built into the upcoming Apple TV (*Economist* 2010). Which, if any, of these initiatives will blossom into the "television of the future" is far from clear.

There is one area in which television currently holds the advantage over the Internet. From dramas (*The Sopranos, MadMen*) to comedies (*30 Rock, The Simpsons*) to reality TV (*The Survivor, American Idol*)—network and cable TV have demonstrated an ability to consistently develop, produce, and deliver dramatic content—television shows—that millions of people want to watch. As of yet, there has been no Internet-specific video content that has come close to challenging the popularity of television. A 2010 Nielsen study showed that, on average, people only watch about three hours of on-line video per month as compared to 158 hours of television (*Economist* 2010).

Nonetheless, there is no question that the growing bandwidth and delivery quality of the Internet represent an existential threat to the existing television networks. Television networks may prove as durable as the Hollywood studios who found ways to weather similarly daunting challenges (including the rise of television) to emerge financially healthy and even globally dominant in the 1980s. Or, they may dwindle to irrelevance. In any case, the creativity and resilience of the networks will be sorely tested over the next decades.

The future of the upfront market is particularly in play. Some observers believe that the upfront market structure benefits the networks at the expense of advertisers and that the networks have utilized their market power to maintain the upfront structure (Ephron 2003). These observers believe that the upfront market creates an atmosphere in which advertisers will pay more than they otherwise would for inventory for fear of being shut out of popular shows and/or paying much higher rates on the spot market. To the extent this is true, the emergence of new competition should reduce the market power of the networks and reduce their ability to impose a market structure on advertisers. It will be fascinating to see if the upfront market endures the shifts of the next decade or if it is a casualty of increased competitive pressure from Internet-based entertainment sources.

We believe that the television advertising market is a very promising area for research. For example, the origin of the upfront/scatter market structure and the reason for its persistence is not well understood. Lotz (2007) views the upfront market as an "industrial norm" that persists due to its "ritual importance". Phillips (Chapter 2) argues that the upfront/scatter market structure is an example of historic "path-dependency". In his view, expectations surrounding the market make it difficult for one player to unilaterally defect without being punished—for example, a network that declined to sell on the upfront might be "punished" by equity analysts who suspect that it is trying to disguise an underperforming schedule. Some industry observers such as Ephron (2003) believe that the upfront benefits the networks and that the networks actively defend the structure. It is notable that the upfront/scatter market structure does not exist in markets that are superficially similar such as airlines and cruise lines. There are upfront markets in some other countries such as Canada, but they tend to be smaller. More research is needed to fully explain the origin and persistence of the upfront/scatter market structure.

Finally, there are many pricing and revenue management decisions faced by advertisers, agencies, and broadcasters that could be improved through the use of better analytics and decision support. As noted above, some networks have invested in automated systems to support scatter pricing and optimal placement. The problem of allocating advertising dollars among different media is a classic problem in the marketing literature—see Lilien et al. (1992) for an overview—and, indeed, many agencies and advertisers use optimization software to help them allocate their total spend both among media types (newspapers, television, Internet) and to allocate their television spend among networks (Ross 1998). There has been a smattering of papers in the management science literature addressing some of the pricing and revenue management problems faced by networks. Araman and Popescu (2010) model the optimal allocation of network inventory between the upfront and spot markets. Zhang (2006) and Kimms and Müller-Bargant (2007) address the problem of placing and scheduling advertisements within scheduled shows. Despite this work, many aspects of the pricing and allocation problems faced by networks and agencies remain as areas for further research.

References

Araman, V. F. and Popescu, I. (2010) "Media Revenue Management with Audience Uncertainty; Balancing Upfront and Spot Market Sales", *Manufacturing and Service Operations Management* 12/2: 190–212.

Blumenthal, H. and Goodenough, O. R. (2005) *This Business of Television*, 3rd edn. New York: Billboard Books.

Bollapragada, S. and Garbiras, M. (2004) "Scheduling Commercials on Broadcast Television", *Operations Research* 53/3: 337–45.

—— Cheng, H., Phillips, M., and Garbiras, M. (2002) "NBC's Optimization Systems Increase Revenues and Productivity", *Interfaces*, 32/1: 47–60.

Brusco, M. J. (2008) "Scheduling Advertising Slots for Television", *Journal of the Operational Research Society* 59/10: 1363–72.

The Economist (2010) "Haggling over the Remote", September 4: 69–72.

Ephron, E. (2003) "The Fascinating Story of the Upfront", reprinted in 2005 *Ephron on Media: Organized Crime Keeps Better Books*. New York: Ephron, Papazian, and Ephron, Inc., 6–12.

Farrell, M. (2010) "Dauman: Viacom Could Return to Hulu", *Multi-channel News* March 9. http://www.multichannel.com/article/449861-Dauman_Viacom_Could_Return_To_Hulu. php, accessed November 2, 2011.

Foreman, R. L. (1962) "The Dilemma of the TV Advertiser", *Television Quarterly* 1/1: 42–7.

Kimms, A. and Müller-Bargant, M. (2007) "Revenue Management for Broadcasting Commercials: The Channel's Problem of Selecting and Scheduling the Advertisements to be Aired", *International Journal of Revenue Management* 1/1: 28–44.

Lilien, G. L., Kotler, P., and Sridhar Moorthy, K. (1992) *Marketing Models*. Saddle River, NJ: Prentice-Hall.

Lotz, A. D. (2007) "How to Spend $9.3 Billion in Three Days: Examining the Upfront Buying Process in the Production of US Television Culture", *Media Culture Society* 29/4: 549–67.

McClellan, S. (2010) "Upfront Preview: Behind the Bust", *AdWeek* Feb. 2: 16–17.

McClintock, P. (2004) "Upfront reforms stalled", *Variety* April 29: 33.

Papazian, E. (ed.) (2009) *TV Dimensions 2009*. New York: Media Dynamics, Inc.

—— (2009) *Broadcasting & Cable Yearbook 2010*. New Providence, NJ: ProQuest, LLC.

ProQuest (2010) *Broadcasting & Cable Yearbook*. New Providence, NJ: ProQuest LLC.

Ross, C. (1998) "Optimizers and TV Upfront: How they Affect Ad Buying", *Advertising Age* June 29: 15–16.

Schechner, S. and Vranica, S. (2010) "Upfront Market Looks Primed for an Upswing", *The Wall Street Journal* April 26.

Schneider, M. (2002) "Upfront Sales Pump Nets", *Variety* June 2: 4.

Steinberg, B. (2010) "Broadcast Upfront Finishes Between $8.10 and $8.70", *Advertising Age* June 10, 2010. http://adage.com/article/special-report-upfront-2010/broadcast-upfront-fin-ishes-8-lb-8-7b/.

Vasquez, D. (2010) "In Sum, a Pretty Healthy Upfront Market", *Media Life* June 24: 12.

Vogel, H. L. (2007) *Entertainment Industry Economics: A Guide for Financial Analysis*, 7th edn. Cambridge: Cambridge University Press.

Zhang, X. (2006) "Mathematical Models for the Television Advertising Allocation Problem", *International Journal of Operations Research* 1/3: 28–44.

CHAPTER 12

....

PRICING IN THE
CRUISE LINE INDUSTRY

....

WARREN H. LIEBERMAN

Cruise line pricing challenges, tactics, and strategies differ greatly from hotels and other segments of the travel industry even though cruise ships are often described as floating hotels. Consider, for example, that hotels reporting annual *occupancy rates* of more than 70 percent are financial successes. The same is true for most airlines (although for airlines, it would be their utilization or *load factor*). When they have sustained occupancy rates of 80–90 percent, the profits of these firms are often enviable.

Successful cruise lines typically report utilization rates of at least 95 percent and the most financially successful cruise lines report utilization rates greater than 100 percent.[1] Empty cabins are not only problematic for the cruise line due to the potential loss of revenue, but for operational reasons as well. Many personnel on cruise ships depend on passenger gratuities for the bulk of their compensation; too many empty cabins can make it difficult for a cruise line to retain experienced employees and perhaps even more importantly, is also likely to have a negative effect on staff morale and consequently make the cruise a less pleasurable vacation for the passengers. The importance of filling every cabin makes pricing strategies and tactics especially critical for cruise lines.

I would like to express my great appreciation to Rod McLeod, Margarita Navarrete-Diaz, and Doug Santoni for reviewing this chapter and for providing me with a variety of ideas as well as many insightful recommendations for improving it. They were all very gracious in giving me more time than I had a right to ask of them. Having been a senior executive at several cruise lines during the past 40 years, Mr McLeod's knowledge of the industry is extraordinarily deep and broad. Beyond that, I have benefitted from the advice and guidance he has provided to me over many years. Not only did Ms Navarrete-Diaz offer her insights to me, but the friendship we have developed over the past 20 years has been extraordinarily valuable to me as well. I worked with Doug at American Airlines in the 1980s; having been with Royal Caribbean International for almost 20 years, he has witnessed and participated in much of the industry's evolution. To all three: Thank you! In addition, I would like to thank all of my colleagues at Veritec Solutions for allowing me the time to write this chapter; not only did it give me an opportunity to document some of my experiences over the past 20 years, it was a great deal of fun. Of course, any errors or inaccurate assertions remain my full responsibility.

[1] Cruise line occupancy rates are based on 2 passengers per cabin. As 3, 4, or 5 persons may occupy a cabin, occupancy rates can exceed 100 percent.

This chapter reviews some of the pricing challenges faced by major cruise lines and how they respond to these challenges. While the designation is somewhat arbitrary, our primary focus is on the "mass market" and premium cruise lines rather than specialty, deluxe, or luxury cruise lines. Mass market and premium cruise lines are sometimes grouped together and referred to as contemporary cruise lines. Carnival Cruise Lines, Royal Caribbean International, Disney Cruise Line, Norwegian Cruise Line, Holland America Line, Princess Cruises, and Celebrity Cruises are examples of cruise lines whose operations are consistent with the themes presented in this chapter.

The cruise industry, and the pricing strategies and tactics employed by cruise lines, have undergone considerable evolution during the past 40 years. In the 1970s, cruise lines generally published prices commonly known as brochure rate, list price, or full inclusive tariff (FIT) by departure date, port of embarkation, and the duration of cruise. These rates did not change during the booking period. Passengers frequently paid the brochure rate for a cruise. Pricing became more complex in the 1980s and increasingly dynamic in the 1990s, reflecting significant changes in the industry's operations.

Today, cruise lines initially set base rates that serve as initial selling rates. During the booking horizon, stateroom or cabin category prices are then adjusted for each cruise.[2] This chapter focuses on the process and decisions made to adjust cruise prices during the booking horizon rather than how the initial base prices are set. We also focus on the pricing practices of cruise lines with US-based cruises since over 80 percent of cruise embarkations in 2006 were from North American ports and 78 percent of the world's cruise passengers lived in the United States (BREA 2007).[3]

Understanding the nature of the industry's evolution provides insights into the pricing challenges currently faced by cruise lines. Consequently, prior to discussing specific pricing challenges and cruise line efforts, we begin with an overview of the recent evolution of the cruise industry and the business environment faced by cruise lines, with an emphasis on covering those aspects of the industry that influence pricing decisions.

12.1 CRUISE VACATIONS: THE MODERN ERA

Bob Dickinson and Andy Vladimir in their book *Selling the Sea* make a strong case that the modern cruising era began in the late 1960s or early 1970s (Dickinson and Vladimir 1997). After the television show *The Love Boat* premiered in 1977, cruise vacations became more popular. Their market appeal and sales opportunities greatly expanded. Perhaps 2 percent of the United States population had gone on a cruise 35 years ago (McLeod 2008), doubling to more than 4 percent by 1990 (CLIA 1990); today that figure is approximately 20 percent (CLIA 2008).

During the formative years, cruise operations underwent significant changes, some of which were to have significant and lasting (40 years and counting!) impacts on the pricing structure and approach of cruise lines. These included:

---

[2] The potential for price adjustments to shift demand between cruises on nearby departure dates is considered. When sufficiently deep discounts are offered, passengers who have already booked a cruise have been observed to cancel their reservations and switch to another departure date. In addition, offering deep discounts on a cruise may slow down the booking process for cruises on nearby dates.

[3] Europe and Asia are becoming increasingly important cruise markets.

- the cruise port with the greatest number of passenger embarkments in the United States shifted from New York to Miami, as the popularity of Caribbean cruise vacations began to dwarf the popularity of trans-Atlantic crossings;
- airline flights and cruises could be purchased as an integrated package; air/sea departments became critical within cruise lines;
- cruise line marketing shifted from a destination-focus to an experience-focus;
- active promotion of cruises began further out (i.e., relative to departure date);
- cruise lines adopted computer-based reservation systems;
- substantially larger ships were constructed;
- many cabins, not just a few suites, were designed with balconies;
- cruise lines offered enhanced on-board services, some available for a supplemental charge;
- total industry capacity increased dramatically.

For many, especially those who live in North America, the phrase *cruise vacation* is likely to spark images of warm, sunny beaches and Caribbean islands. In 2006, almost 56 percent of 9 million cruise passengers that embarked on cruises from US ports began their cruises from one of five Florida ports and sailed to various Caribbean islands. Approximately 1.9 million sailed from Miami and approximately 4.4 million sailed from three Florida ports: Miami, Port Canaveral, and Port Everglades. Indeed, more cruise passengers sailed from each of these ports than from any other US port.[4] The fourth largest cruise port in the United States was Galveston, Texas, where approximately 617,000 passengers began their cruise vacations. But Caribbean cruises out of Miami, or out of Florida ports were not always so dominant (BREA 2007).

The contemporary Caribbean cruise vacation product began to take shape in 1966 (Dickinson and Vladimir 1997). In that year, Arison Shipping Company formed a partnership with a Norwegian firm that owned the *Sunward*, a new ship. Under the name Norwegian Caribbean Lines (NCL), 3- and 4-day cruises to Caribbean islands were offered year round. Originally built to offer a cruise-ferry service in Europe, but unable to do so for a variety of reasons, the *Sunward* contained a roll-on roll-off cargo deck capable of transporting up to 500 cars. NCL added a second ship in 1968, the *Starward*; the *Starward* also had the capability to transport cars and cargo, although it had a more limited capacity of 250 cars. Caribbean cruising, as we know it today with ship design focused on providing for passenger entertainment was on the horizon but at this point wasn't quite the product with which we are now familiar.

Additional ships and cruise lines began sailing from Miami. A wider variety of cruise lengths were offered. Among them, 3-, 4-, and 7-day cruise vacations formed the staple of Caribbean cruising and were to become far more popular than trans-Atlantic voyages ever were. The Miami-based Caribbean cruise became the focal point of cruising in North America, although cruises from Los Angeles to the West Coast of Mexico, from Vancouver

---

[4] With approximately 457,000 cruise embarkations, Tampa, Florida was the seventh largest US port of embarkation and fourth largest in Florida. Including the embarkations from Florida's fifth largest port, Jacksonville, over 40 percent of the world's 12 million cruise embarkations were in Florida.

to Alaska, from New York to Bermuda, and cruises out of other Florida ports were also destined to grow in popularity.

As Miami-based Caribbean cruising proved to be popular, the number of cruise lines and ships serving this market grew rapidly. Cruise line executives realized that the local population was too small to provide enough passengers to fill the ships. New York City and the nearby cities in the northeast were large enough to provide a strong demand for the relatively modest number of trans-Atlantic voyages departing from New York City. Filling the berths on Miami-based cruises, however, required more passengers than Miami, or even Florida, could provide. Recognizing the need to broaden their marketing efforts and attract a significant number of passengers from outside of Florida, cruise lines began to include air transportation into their product offering. Recalling events in January 1971, Rod McLeod, a former Executive Vice President of Sales, Marketing, and Passenger Traffic for Royal Caribbean Cruise Line (RCCL), commented:

> We were reaching out for a new market and offering round-trip air from Los Angeles.... Our price, including all port charges, transfers, and a quick sightseeing tour of Miami and lunch on Key Biscayne before boarding the ship, was only $368! Since this price was only $50 or $60 higher than RCCL's brochure-cruise-price, it was a tremendous bargain by any standards. (Dickinson and Vladimir 1997)

The integration of air flights and cruises had begun.

12.2 AIR–SEA PRICING TAKES OFF

According to the Cruise Line Industry Association (CLIA), the number of worldwide cruise passengers grew from approximately 500,000 in 1970 to more than 12 million in 2006 (CLIA 2007). As noted previously, approximately 75 percent of the passengers in 2006 boarded cruises in North American ports and more than 80 percent lived in the United States. Approximately 60 percent traveled to their port of embarkation by air (BREA 2007). As the industry grew in the 1970s, 1980s and 1990s, so too did the importance of attracting passengers from cities throughout the United States.

Cruise lines tried a variety of pricing structures with varying results. Many, if not all cruise lines began to act as tour operators, packaging round-trip airfares, transfers between the airport and the ship, and hotel rooms for guests arriving the day prior to the cruise. Cruise line Air/Sea Departments became responsible for arranging air transportation for more and more passengers as the benefits of making integrated flight arrangements through the cruise line became apparent. Passengers benefited financially as the cost of getting to and from the cruise ship was often less when airline flights were arranged through the cruise line. In addition, when passengers booked an air–sea package through the cruise line, cruise lines assumed financial and logistical responsibility for transporting passengers to the ship even when flights were delayed, in some cases flying passengers to the ship's first port of call. In contrast, cruise lines did not assume any responsibility for getting passengers to the ship when they booked their own flights.

In many ways, the popularity of air–sea packages outpaced the ability of cruise lines to manage and price them. In the early 1990s, more than half the passengers on a 7-day Caribbean cruise might have purchased an air–sea package; an even greater percentage of the passengers on an Alaskan cruise were typically air–sea. The growth of the air–sea package raised new pricing questions:

- How should cruise-only prices relate to air–sea packages?
- Should the add-on for airfare depend on the gateway city (the city from which the passenger was flying from) and if so, how?
- When discounts were offered to air–sea passengers, should the price reduction be applied to the cruise or the flight cost?

As cruise executives struggled to address these questions, they generally adopted one of four pricing strategies:

- *Free airfare.* Advertise "free" airfare or "airfare included" in the cruise price, but provide a discount (often termed an allowance, credit, or deduction) from the all-inclusive price to those passengers who only wanted to book the cruise.
- *Air supplement.* Advertise a cruise-only price. Offer an optional air supplement for a specified set of cities. The supplement included round-trip airfare, ground transfers, and baggage transfer assistance. The air supplement was the same for passengers flying from any of the specified cities; for other gateway cities additional fees might apply and those fees could vary by gateway city.
- *Zonal fares.* Advertise a cruise-only price. Charge an airfare add-on for passengers who arrange their flights through the cruise line. Rather than charge a single air add-on for all cities or different add-ons for each gateway city, gateway cities were grouped into several zones. The airfare add-on to the port of embarkation was the same for all cities in the same zone.
- *Distinct air add-ons.* Advertise the cruise-only price and charge an air add-on, the amount of the air add-on varying by gateway city as well as by departure date.

Under all these strategies, the amount paid by the cruise line to the airline was generally not equal to the amount paid by the cruise passenger to the cruise line for the flight. Cruise lines typically negotiated contract airfares with each airline. The contract fares varied by gateway city, airline, and sometimes day of week. As passengers were not assigned to flights until after an air–sea rate was agreed to and the booking confirmed, cruise lines did not know the exact cost of transporting the passenger at the time of booking. Based on airline seat availability and the number of passengers flying out of a gateway city, cruise lines would frequently use multiple airlines from a gateway city (Lieberman and Dieck 2002).

During the past 20 years, most cruise lines have implemented at least two of the pricing strategies described above and some have probably tried three or all four strategies with varying levels of financial and marketing success. For example, a 1992–93 Carnival Cruise Lines brochure advertised a free round-trip airfare from over 175 cities to Miami, Los Angeles, or San Juan when taking a one-week cruise and a free round-trip airfare from over 150 cities to Miami or Orlando when taking one of their 3- or 4-day cruises. Passengers who purchased a cruise-only product were allowed to deduct $250 from the air-inclusive price when purchasing a 7-day cruise and $100 from the air-inclusive price when purchasing a 3- or 4-day cruise (Carnival Cruise Lines 1992). That pricing strategy was eventually abandoned.

When Disney Cruise Line (DCL) began offering 7-day vacations in 1998, a round-trip airfare was included for 114 airports in the United States and 3 Canadian airports. A $250 credit was granted to guests who provided their own air and ground transportation.[5] Within a few years, however, DCL no longer included airfare or ground transportation in its base price. As noted in its 2002–04 Vacations brochure, an airfare/ground transportation/baggage transfer add-on was available for 153 US airports with additional charges potentially applicable for other airports. Currently, DCL's charge for airfare varies by gateway city and departure date.

Offering free airfare is probably the easiest approach to market and communicate, but tends to limit a cruise line's ability to set cruise-specific prices that best attract the type and level of demand required. For example, as bookings are made for a cruise, stimulating demand in a particular city or set of cities is highly desirable. When free airfare is offered, cruise lines are more limited in their flexibility to use pricing to stimulate sales in these cities; this can be particularly problematic when sales need to be stimulated within a few weeks of departure.

Zonal fares are a middle ground. They are transparent, allowing potential customers to evaluate and compare the cost of a cruise vacation to other vacation options, without making a booking; but zonal fares are not quite as easy to communicate and market as free airfare. As with free airfare, zonal fares limit a cruise line's flexibility to use price reductions to stimulate cruise-only sales. Reductions in the cruise-only price can have the unintended consequence of stimulating sales from gateway cities that have high airfares and are subsequently less profitable for the cruise line. Limiting the number of air–sea packages that can be sold in a gateway city is one way of addressing this impact, but this requires a level of automation and management that was beyond the capabilities of many cruise lines in the 1980s and 1990s, when this pricing strategy enjoyed its greatest popularity.

Varying air add-ons by gateway city and day of departure provides a cruise line with the greatest flexibility in selling its product at profit-maximizing prices, but at the cost of significant added complexity. Potential air–sea cruise passengers are no longer able to easily estimate the cost of a cruise vacation from an advertisement; for example, specific travel dates and cruise departure date need to be provided to a cruise line or travel agent. Although cruise lines did not typically use this strategy in the 1980s and 1990s, this strategy is the most commonly used today.[6] Interestingly, the popularity of airline frequent flyer programs may have helped make this strategy more acceptable to cruise passengers. Compared to 1990, and certainly to 1980, many more cruise passengers redeem airline miles to procure their flights. (To be fair, it should be noted that American Airlines and United Airlines did not launch airline frequent flyer mileage programs until 1981). By the

---

[5] Initially, Disney Cruise Line's 7-day vacations combined a cruise of 3 or 4 days with a land vacation. Customers were referred to as *guests*, not as passengers. The air–sea price included ground transfers to and from *Walt Disney World Resort*, Port Canaveral, and the Orlando airport.

[6] In the 1980s and 1990s, cruise lines generally required reservations to be made through travel agents. Now, individuals can make reservations directly with cruise lines by phone or via their website. This has mitigated some of the complexity.

mid 1990s, cruise lines may have been making flight arrangements for almost 65 percent of their passengers; that fraction is likely now closer to 15 percent (McLeod 2008).

12.3 City-specific promotional fares

Migrating from the "one size fits all" strategy of having a single airfare add-on to a fully customized product where the airfare depends on the passenger's origin and travel dates allowed cruise lines to dramatically refine their pricing tactics. Promotional fares could now be directed at individual gateway cities or groups of cities without disrupting the integrity of the cruise line's pricing strategy.[7] For those cruise lines offering a Lowest Price Guarantee, this was especially valuable.

12.3.1 Lowest price guarantee

Those living near the ports from which cruise ships depart are geographically well positioned to take advantage of last-week or even last-minute discounting on cruise ships. Dickinson and Vladimir provide a wonderful description of last-minute pricing decisions (and we mean this literally) during the 1970s where "septuagenarians [were] milling about the embarkation area, bags in tow, hoping to take advantage of a standby rate or a last-minute cancellation." Additionally, embarkation supervisors and pursers "pocketed 'gratuities' in exchange for the cabin gratis or for a favorable rate", displaying entrepreneurial creativity (Dickinson and Vladimir 1997).

As more and larger cruise ships were built and operated, cruise lines placed higher importance on incentivizing passengers to book early. Without a sufficiently strong base of early bookings, deep discounting to fill a ship was often necessary and ultimately, a prescription for financial disaster.

To encourage early bookings, a few cruise lines, such as Princess Cruises and Holland America Line provided a "Lowest Price Guarantee". If the same product (e.g., cabin category, gateway city combination) was sold for a lower price on the same cruise at a later date, these cruise lines committed to refunding the difference to customers who booked earlier.

Distinguishing between the cruise-only and air–sea products, and setting airfare add-ons by gateway city, allowed these cruise lines enormous flexibility to offer discounts where and when they needed, with limited financial risk. For example, when booking levels were low on a departure, a review of the air–sea bookings for that departure enabled pricing and revenue management staff to identify those gateway cities from which air–sea passengers had booked; so discounted rates were only offered to air–sea passengers from other cities. If no air–sea passengers from Detroit had booked the departure, and the airfare from Detroit

---

[7] Cruise lines use a variety of tactics and strategies to sell their cabins for discounted prices. We use the term promotional fares as a broad reference to any of these options. Promotional fares may be highly targeted (e.g., to Florida residents, to passengers purchasing air travel from Detroit in conjunction with a cruise) or very broad. Some cabins on a cruise may be sold for full price while others are sold at discounted prices.

was $450, this essentially enabled the cruise line to discount the air–sea price for Detroit passengers by up to $450 without affecting air–sea bookings from any other gateway city or cruise-only bookings. Further, building up demand with such targeted discounts also meant that fewer deeply discounted cruise-only discounts would need to be offered closer in to a departure date.

In addition, depending on how much demand needed to be stimulated, opportunities existed for cruise lines to target air–sea promotions to those cities where they either had negotiated lower contract airfares, or in cases of cruise lines booking publicly available airfares, where those airfares were lowest.

12.4 WHEN IS A DISCOUNT NOT A DISCOUNT?

For the most part, people face, or artificially limit themselves to a relatively limited set of product choices when they travel. During the past 40 years, most airline flights have offered between two and four choices of cabin, such as Coach, Premium Coach, Business, and First Class. Given the price differential associated with these options, however, airline passengers rarely consider more than two of them and most only consider one when booking a flight. When renting a car, most customers typically consider no more than two or three car classes, although the rental car firm may offer 8–10 options. Even when booking a hotel room, no more than two or three choices tend to be considered by guests, even if the hotel offers 10–12 room categories.[8]

Cruise lines tend to classify their cabins in far more categories than other travel companies. We believe that many cruise passengers tend to weigh the advantages and disadvantages of more categories than they typically do when making their other travel choices. Excluding cabin categories that contain only 1 or 2 cabins, a large cruise ship is likely to have 15–25 different cabin categories, each with its own price.[9] Progressing from the least expensive cabin category on a ship to the most expensive, price differentials are frequently relatively small, ranging from perhaps just a dollar or two per day per person, up to perhaps $15 or $20 per day per person. Table 12.1 contains descriptions of the more common cabin categories for a particular ship (Royal Caribbean International 2008).[10] While many of the cabin categories are physically different from the others, this is not always the case. For example, Cabin Categories I and H are only differentiated by deck level.

Cruise lines have found that many customers have preferences and are willing to pay more for a wide variety of cabin features. Some of these features might be relatively easily anticipated, such as type of view (e.g., none, obstructed, small window, floor to ceiling window), whether or not the cabin has an outside balcony, and the size of the cabin.[11] Price

---

[8] These observations are based on our experience. More recently, some car rental firms seem to be borrowing from the cruise line playbook. Some rental locations offer as many as 25 car classes, although 15–20 of these may be *specialty* car classes containing only a single car model.

[9] The number of cabin categories on a ship has not always been as large as today. In 1990, for example, large ships generally had 10–15 cabin categories. Some newer ships have over 30 categories.

[10] Partial deck plan for the *Explorer of the Seas*.

[11] Lifeboats positioned outside cabins can obstruct views.

Table 12.1. Example cabin categories on a cruise ship

Cabin category	Cabin description	Accommodation description
D1, D2, D3	Superior ocean view stateroom	Two twin beds (can convert into queen-size), private balcony, sitting area, and a private bathroom. Rates vary from deck to deck (188 sq ft, balcony 50 sq ft). Some staterooms have a sofa bed.
E1, E2	Deluxe ocean view stateroom	Two twin beds (can convert into queen-size), private balcony, sitting area with sofa, and a private bathroom. Rates vary from deck to deck (173 sq ft, balcony 47 sq ft).
F0	Family ocean view stateroom	Two twin beds (can convert into queen-size), additional bunk beds in separate area, separate sitting area with sofa bed, and a private bathroom with shower (265 ft).
F	Large ocean view stateroom	Two twin beds (can convert into queen-size), sitting area with sofa, vanity area and a private bathroom (211 sq ft).
I	Ocean view stateroom	Two twin beds (can convert into queen-size), sitting area with sofa, vanity area, and a private bathroom (180 sq ft).
H	Ocean view stateroom	Two twin beds (can convert into queen-size), sitting area with sofa, vanity area, and a private bathroom (180 sq ft).
M, L, N, Q	Interior stateroom	Two twin beds (can convert into queen-size), sitting area with sofa, vanity area, and a private bathroom (160 sq ft).

differentials due to other cabin characteristics, such as a mid-ship versus end-of-ship location or deck level (large cruise ships generally have cabins on 5–9 decks) may be surprising to those who have not previously cruised. Consequently, booking a cruise vacation entails selecting from a portfolio of choices and prices.

Offering a portfolio of choices has enabled cruise lines to provide a wide variety of pricing incentives and promotions. Rather than simply lowering (or raising) prices, less transparent, but highly effective ways to manipulate demand and affect the net revenue received by the cruise line include offering Cabin Category Guarantees and Upgrades. While these techniques are available to—and are used by—travel companies such as car rental, hotels and resorts, tour operators, and even airlines, they tend to have more widespread application and offer greater value to the cruise lines because of the extent to which they have differentiated their physical product.

12.4.1 Cabin category guarantees

Although most reservations are for a specific cabin, some passengers may be allowed to book a cabin category instead. When passengers book a cabin category, they are guaranteed to receive a cabin in the designated category, or higher. This is called a *Cabin Category Guarantee*. The actual cabin and cabin category are selected at the cruise line's discretion prior to sailing.

For cruises where the lower priced cabin categories are fully booked, but higher cabin categories are not, selling guarantees helps a cruise line maintain integrity in its pricing structure and generate greater revenues. If demand is insufficient to sell-out the more expensive cabin categories, selling guarantees enables the cruise line to avoid explicitly discounting its premium cabins as it takes actions to ensure that the ship sails full. Depending on demand patterns, guarantees can be sold for selected lower priced cabin categories, even while additional reservations are accepted for the premium cabins at non-discounted prices to those who are willing to pay more to definitively secure such accommodations. Selling guarantees is essentially *overbooking* the lower cabin categories.

Selling guarantees allows the cruise line to maintain a high level of control over which of its guests are offered upgraded accommodations. For example, internal policies can be established to prioritize the order in which Cabin Category Guarantee bookings receive upgraded accommodations (e.g., those who have previously cruised with the cruise line might be rewarded for their loyalty). Cruise lines might even elect to offer upgrades to more valued customers who booked a specific cabin prior to upgrading customers who booked guarantees.

12.4.2 Upgrades

Guarantees do not require cruise lines to provide upgraded accommodations to a guest. By comparison, offering *upgrades* at the time of booking is a greater booking incentive, as passengers know for certain that they will be accommodated in a higher cabin category than the one for which they pay. When upgrades are offered, passengers may be informed that they will be upgraded to a specific cabin category or higher. Upgrades can be used strategically to encourage passengers to make purchases in higher categories than they otherwise might have done, lured by the promise of then being upgraded to an even better cabin.

For example, a cruise line might have several cabin categories for interior cabins (i.e., no window). Many passengers who book interior cabins choose to book the least expensive interior cabin category. Further, the price differential between the least expensive interior cabin category and the most expensive interior cabin category may be quite a bit less than the price differential between the least expensive cabin with a window and the least expensive interior cabin. Consequently, offering to upgrade those passengers who book a more expensive interior cabin category to a cabin with a window can induce some passengers to pay more for a cabin than they would otherwise have done.

Offering upgrades tends to have more financial risk for the cruise line than offering guarantees. Upgrades can dilute revenues when passengers who are willing to pay more for a more desirable cabin category elect to "buy down" from a higher cabin category to get the lower price, knowing that they will definitely be accommodated in a higher cabin category.

12.5 Case study: if there is no free lunch, who pays?

The prices offered by a cruise line are typically subject to extensive management review, analysis, and scrutiny. By comparison, internal *transfer pricing* decisions receive far less attention, yet can also have great impact on a cruise line's bottom line, especially for cruise lines that offer combined land and sea excursions. Sales responsibility for the land portion of purchases typically resides in a department other than the one responsible for the cruise portion. Each department's staff is likely to be evaluated and receive bonuses based on the financial performance of their operations. The dilemma: when land/sea packages are sold at a discounted price, how should the discounts be apportioned between the land and sea excursions? While it might not seem that such an internally focused decision would have an impact on customer purchases, it turns out that such decisions influence the sales process. Consider the case of a cruise line that operates cruises to Alaska.

In combination with the cruise, land tours in Alaska are offered. Passengers are thus able to take a 12-day cruise/tour, where they might take a 7-day north-bound cruise originating in Vancouver with its final stop in Anchorage, leave the ship to spend 5 days in northern Alaska, and then fly home. Or, passengers can fly to Anchorage, spend their first 5 days in northern Alaska, and then take a south-bound cruise from Anchorage to Vancouver.

For some cruise/tour dates, demand needs to be stimulated; discounts are offered. So whose budget does the discount go against? The cruise department's? Or the land tour department's? There are certainly many ways to carry out the allocation. In this case, the discount was applied to the land tour department's budget. Consequently, the land tour department had a strong incentive to avoid selling the discounted vacations, as increasingly large discount totals would have a negative impact on the department's staff compensation. Of course, if cruise/tours went unsold, this would also have a negative impact on the department's performance and staff compensation. So that was not a feasible option either.

Rather than bear the brunt of the impact of the transfer pricing policy, the land/tour department simply had cruise line staff try to sell the cruise/tours for the full price or only a small discount. In contrast, third-party tour companies were allowed to sell the cruise/tours for more heavily discounted prices. Not surprisingly, most of the cruise/tours were sold through these third-party companies rather than by the cruise line itself. This approach essentially gave the third-party tour companies effective responsibility for setting the price at which the cruise/tours were sold (e.g., the tour companies decided whether to give a customer the full benefits of the available discount). In addition, the cruise line also had to pay a sales commission for every cruise/tour sold by a third party; a commission that did not have to be paid when the cruise line's own agents made a sale. In short, the cruise line's transfer pricing policy did much to decrease the cruise line's revenues as well as increase its costs; not exactly a prescription for financial success.

Broadly speaking, the undesirable sales behavior noted above arose because individual and departmental goals were poorly aligned with corporate goals (e.g., maximizing profits). There are many ways to address such situations, although none are perfect. Consequently, a process of incremental improvement may provide the best strategy. For example, suppose monthly allowances for discounts were established. So long as the threshold was not exceeded, staff compensation would not be adversely affected. Financial incentives could be offered when the total volume of discounts in a month was less than specified thresholds. The monthly allowances might vary, based on the strength of market demand in combination with sales thresholds. The key point here is that internal company practices can—and for the above company, certainly did—have dramatic impacts on the prices being offered.

12.6 REVENUE MANAGEMENT

Although many valid definitions of revenue management have been proposed, Bob Cross provides one that is succinct yet comprehensive: "Revenue Management is the art and science of predicting real-time demand at the micromarket level and optimizing the price and availability of products" (Cross 1997). Although the reports and techniques used were rudimentary, cruise lines were certainly practicing revenue management in the mid 1980s. The primary state-of-the-art practices included *handicapping formulas* to predict the cancellation rates of group and individual bookings, booking pace information to inform decisions about what pricing initiatives should be implemented, and weekly information about the number of unsold cabins in each cabin category for all departures in the next 12 months, or even further into the future.

Compared with other segments of the travel industry, business processes initially adopted by cruise lines to make and execute revenue management decisions required much more time from senior management. Up until the early 1990s, it was a relatively common practice for the CEO or other Senior Executive to spend time, perhaps 45 minutes a week, working with each Ship Manager (each ship might have a different Ship Manager). They would review the booking status of each ship's departure over the next 12–18 months, the number of cabins still available for sale, and the fares offered. Using this information, they would identify what changes, if any, to make, including which promotions to launch, continue, or stop.

When a cruise line has no more than three or four ships, as was the case for the largest cruise lines until the mid-1980s, the above approach is feasible. Even with six or fewer ships it remains possible (whether or not it is desirable is another matter). But the practice does not scale well and as cruise lines began to operate more ships, responsibility for tactical pricing decisions was necessarily driven down to lower levels of the organization. A CEO simply does not have the time to meet with the staff managing ten ships to review the status of each future departure.

Cruise lines expanded at an accelerated pace during the 1990s and thereafter. Indeed, by early 2008, Carnival Cruise Lines operated 22 ships, Royal Caribbean International operated 21, Princess Cruises operated 16, Holland America Line operated 13, and Costa Cruises and Norwegian Cruise Line both operated 12 ships. Additional ships were also under construction for each of these lines.

In addition to the increasing number of ships, cruise ships were designed to accommodate far more passengers than ever before. "Revenue managing" larger ships is more complex than for smaller ships and typically requires more time and effort. In 1970, the largest cruise ship sailing year round to the Caribbean islands may have been the *Song of Norway*, a Royal Caribbean Cruise Line ship with a capacity of less than 1,000 passengers. By the early 1980s, ships able to accommodate as many as 1,500 passengers were sailing year round in the Caribbean. The era of the mega ship began when Royal Caribbean's *Sovereign of the Seas* departed on its maiden voyage out of Miami in 1988. The *Sovereign of the Seas* was capable of handling approximately 2,500 passengers. While some wondered whether a ship accommodating so many passengers was "too large", the *Sovereign* is dwarfed by the newest (and largest) ship cruising in the Caribbean, Royal Caribbean International's *Oasis of the Seas* which accommodates more than 6,000 passengers!

The extent to which this growth led (or perhaps required) the industry to transform its revenue management practices should not be underestimated. As cruise lines grew, the traditional ways in which they managed and adjusted their prices began to break down. Greater automation became necessary. These advances may have led some cruise industry executives to seek more systematic approaches to pricing. Other factors that may have prompted cruise executives to explore ways to enhance their revenue management capabilities were the decisions of some cruise lines to become public companies in the late 1980s and early 1990s as well as the widely reported success of airlines with innovative revenue enhancement strategies. Such developments led to greater pressures to maximize revenues and profits for each sailing, as more was as stake. Also, the greater potential revenue and profit made it easier and more important for cruise lines to invest in systems and strategies that were expected to help drive additional revenue and profits. Among these strategies, one of the most important was revenue management. Next we examine some of the specific advances that were made in this area.

12.6.1 Handicapping formulas

When a booking is received for a specific cruise departure, the cruise line estimates the likelihood that the booking will either *materialize* and yield passengers, or that the booking will cancel.[12] In the 1980s these estimates were typically based on a *handicapping formula*.

To understand how a handicapping formula works, it is important to know that every booking involved a sequence of required actions, typically requiring a payment or a communication. The following illustrates a typical sequence of events for a group booking:

- Within 1 month of the date of the group booking, an initial deposit of $25/person is required.
- A second deposit of $200/person is required by 5 months prior to departure.
- Final payment is due 60 days prior to departure; passenger names are to be provided at this time.

Of course, as one might imagine, payment due dates were often enforced loosely, or not at all, for the larger travel agencies and those agencies that provided a high volume of bookings to a cruise line.

A common cruise line practice to forecast the number of group passengers (known as the handicapping formula) was something akin to:

- When a group booking is initially received, forecast a 10 percent show-up rate.
- If any additional money is received when the initial deposit is due, revise the forecast to 35 percent.
- When the second deposit is received, revise the forecast to 85 percent.
- When final payment is received, revise the forecast to 100 percent.[13]

---

[12] Materialization forecasts are sometimes referred to as *show-up* forecasts.
[13] In some cases, the names of passengers might be supplied even prior to final payment. In such instances, cabins for these passengers might be allocated and a 100 percent show-up rate forecast for these cabins.

With respect to bookings by individuals, a typical policy was:

- Within a week of a reservation being made, a deposit of $200 per person is required. A grace period of up to four days may be granted if the deposit is not received by this time. If the initial deposit is not received by the end of the grace period, the reservation is cancelled.
- Final payment is due 4 weeks prior to departure.

Deposits were fully or partially refundable, depending on when the travel agent contacted the cruise line (in the late 1980s and early 1990s, virtually all cruise line bookings were made through travel agents).

For individual bookings, handicapping formulas might have forecast materialization at 100 percent after the initial deposit was received. This tended to be an overestimate of the actual materialization, as some bookings would typically be cancelled after the initial deposit was paid.

As cruise lines frequently offered greater discounts to groups, it was common practice for some travel agents to make group bookings on a speculative basis. Groups typically reserve cabins on sailings before individuals. High volume travel agents specializing in selling cruises would create "groups" in anticipation of having customers who would want to sail on the same departure. Doing so gave these travel agents greater flexibility in deciding what price to communicate to the passenger, as travel agents only needed to pay cruise lines the net amount due on a booking. Travel agent commissions and any discounts applying to the booking were not remitted to the cruise line.

Consequently, many group bookings would eventually yield no passengers or fewer passengers than the travel agent initially communicated to the cruise line. The handicapping formula described above reflects this as it initially predicts only 10 percent materialization. On a ship with 700 cabins, at various dates prior to departure, it would not be unusual for group bookings to be recorded for as many as 500 cabins, yet end up using only 150 or 200. Indeed, because the overall materialization rate for groups was so low, on many sailings the number of group cabin requests accepted by a cruise line could be larger than the number of cabins on the ship! To manage its inventory effectively, cruise lines had to forecast how many group passengers (and the number of cabins) would actually materialize from the group bookings.

The group handicapping formula was a rule-of-thumb that generally provided reasonable materialization estimates at an aggregated level for the year, but there were many individual sailings where it led to poor estimates and ultimately to drastic and undesirable pricing actions. Sometimes, higher than expected group materialization led to significant upgrading of group passengers; significant revenue dilution occurred as more expensive cabins could not be sold to customers prepared to pay for them. On occasions, less than expected group materialization led to high levels of discounting within a few months of sailing.

By 1988, some of the larger cruise lines recognized that they were significantly limiting their revenues and profits by continuing to rely on these rudimentary forecasting methods. Also, the introduction of larger ships resulted in a stronger emphasis on obtaining groups to ensure that these ships sailed full. Consequently, inaccurate estimates of group materialization were becoming more costly.

Some cruise lines began actively investing in designing and developing more advanced forecasting methods. Statistical models that considered the particular characteristics of group and individual bookings were developed. These models replaced the handicapping formulas that treated all group reservations and all individual reservations the same. Such models examine the specific composition of bookings on a ship and forecast group materialization based on factors such as type of group, travel agency, itinerary, season, and payment status. More accurate materialization forecasts of groups and individuals resulted, enabling better management and pricing of cabin inventory. These models are still state-of-the-art.

12.6.2 Early booking discounts

Early booking discounts were certainly available in the 1980s. Generally, these discounts were available to passengers who booked their cruise more than 12 months in advance. But booking early was no guarantee of getting a good price. Indeed, fare reductions far larger than the early booking discounts typically became available as the time to the cruise decreased.

As increasingly large discounts became more prevalent, savvy cruise passengers realized that bargains were to be had if they were willing to wait. And they waited. So much so, that cruise lines began to realize that something needed to be done. As early bookings dropped off and passengers demonstrated a greater willingness to book closer to departure date, cruise line staff grew increasingly nervous 6–9 months out, as they watched the number of unsold cabins on a cruise reach uncomfortably high levels. This led cruise lines to discount even further close in to departure, reinforcing the willingness of cruise line passengers to hold back on booking a cruise until closer to the departure date. A rather vicious cycle was taking hold and it did not bode well for the cruise lines.

Recognizing the benefits of getting passengers to book earlier, Royal Caribbean introduced its *Breakthrough Rates* program in 1992. Under this program, the lowest rates that were to be available for a cruise were offered when the cruise line began accepting reservations for that departure and over time, as sufficient bookings were received, the rates went up in pre-determined and specified increments. Communications from the company went out that booking earlier meant getting a better price. Other cruise lines soon adopted similar programs.

What was particularly innovative about the Breakthrough Rates program was that it began to systematize cruise line pricing tactics and discounting procedures. Potential customers received some assurance that fares would not decrease after they made their purchase, leaving them to feel foolish and regret having made the purchase. The new approach, however, made it even more important for cruise lines to manage their pricing decisions, as they were now faced with the decision of how deep a discount to provide to early booking customers and when those fares should be raised. Fortunately, for the cruise lines, their use of many cabin categories to sell cabins at a wide variety of prices, in combination with offering guarantees and upgrades on a selective basis (e.g., only in some markets) eased some of this pressure. Monitoring demand for each departure, cruise lines used these programs to stimulate demand when they mistakenly increased prices too quickly and inadvertently slowed demand for a cruise by more than anticipated. The integrity of the pricing structure was maintained, even while pricing promotions were offered.

12.6.3 Revenue management expands

By the mid to late 1990s, cruise lines were investing more resources towards improving their pricing decisions. Cruise lines were no longer willing to rely on manual review of booking activity reports as the primary basis for deciding where and when to direct promotional activity, as well as for determining the level of discounts to offer. Cruise lines undertook the design and development of data-driven models graphically depicting the historical impact of pricing actions on demand levels and quantifying response variation. State-of-the-art graphical interfaces supporting interactive queries at varying levels of detail were used.

These decision support tools provided great value helping cruise lines to better determine where and when to carry out promotions. By the late 1990s, virtually all the major cruise lines had launched revenue management initiatives. Some cruise lines focused on developing better descriptive decision support tools. Others were more ambitious, funding development efforts to more systematically review prices that included prescriptive tools providing recommendations of what actions to take.

As these decision support tools took greater hold in the industry, pricing analysts were given greater responsibility for making decisions. By 2000, pricing analysts at some cruise lines were using decision support tools recommending where and when price promotions should be launched or halted, as well as the magnitude of such promotions. The pricing decision support tools were far more advanced than those of 10 years earlier. In addition, pricing analysts also found themselves with greater responsibility and authority than ever before.

At many cruise lines, suggesting that the CEO or President meet with staff to discuss, review, and oversee specific tactical actions for each sailing would probably now be seen as a humorous and not too serious suggestion. But recall it was not too long ago that such meetings were common. Between the late 1980s and early 2010s, cruise line pricing strategies, tactics, organizational structure, and analytical methods have been greatly transformed.

12.7 SO WHAT ELSE IS THERE TO KNOW?

As is the case for many industries, there are a number of pricing issues specific to the cruise industry. To conclude this chapter, we present some curious and "fun" facts.

12.7.1 Lifeboat capacity

Occasionally, a ship departs with empty cabins despite there being sufficient demand to fill the ship. The maximum number of passengers legally allowed to sail on a cruise ship is generally less than the number of beds on the ship. Passenger capacity is limited by a ship's lifeboat capacity, which is generally more than the double occupancy carrying capacity. Many cabins, however, can accommodate 3, 4, or 5 passengers. Further, the fares for the third, fourth, and fifth person in a cabin are virtually always less what is paid for the first two passengers. Consequently, if too many reservations with three to five persons in a cabin are accepted, a cruise ship may have to sail with empty cabins. As this means reduced revenue, the number of bookings with more than two persons in a cabin needs to be closely monitored.

12.7.2 Fill the ship, but at what cost?

Transporting air–sea passengers to the port of embarkation at minimal cost while meeting customer service requirements involves many decisions (Lieberman and Dieck 2002). On one Caribbean cruise that had a number of empty cabins close to departure date, group sales was very proud of their ability to obtain a large group from Canada to occupy many of those cabins, although a fairly significant discount had to be given to the group. Unfortunately, group sales neglected to review the reservation request with the air–sea department. By the time the reservation was communicated to Air–Sea staff, the only seats still available on flights to transport the group were in first class. The cost of the group's airfare to the cruise line was greater than what the group paid to the cruise line for both airfare and the cruise. The cruise line must have hoped that those passengers spent a lot of money on board the ship!

12.7.3 It's a matter of perspective

Today, cabins with balconies are commonly found on newer ships. These cabins are priced at a premium relative to cabins without balconies. Passengers value having a private balcony and they are willing to pay extra for that privilege. While that may not be surprising, cruise line executives did not always have that perspective or understanding. In the mid-1990s, balconies were still relatively rare. When one cruise line introduced a new ship that had many cabins with balconies, the cabins with balconies were priced lower than cabins without. The logic governing this decision was based on the fact that the cabins with balconies were smaller than those without the balconies (the balconies were actually cut into the cabin space). Rather than consider the pricing issue from a customer value perspective, the cruise line approached it from an engineering perspective. Less interior cabin square footage meant charging a lower price. It was not long before the cruise line realized its mistake (with a little bit of help from pricing consultants) and reconfigured its pricing structure. Unfortunately for the cruise line's bottom line, although fortunately for many lucky passengers, the cabins with balconies did provide an incredible bargain for those who booked sailings before the pricing mistake was corrected.

REFERENCES

Business Research and Economic Advisors (BREA) (2007) *The Contribution of the North American Cruise Industry to the U.S. Economy in 2006*. Exton, PA: Prepared for Cruise Line International Association.

Carnival Cruise Lines (1992) *Carnival Cruise Lines Brochure. 1/2/92–6/11/93*. Miami: Carnival Cruise Lines.

Cross, R. G. (1997) *Revenue Management: Hard-Core Tactics for Market Domination*. New York: Broadway Books.

Cruise Lines International Association (CLIA) (1990) *The Cruise Industry: An Overview, Highlights Edition*. New York: CLIA.

—— (2007) *Cruise Industry Source Book, 2007 Edition*. Fort Lauderdale, FL: CLIA.

—— (2008) *2008 CLIA Cruise Market Overview, Statistical Cruise Industry Data Through 2007*. http://www.cruiseexperts.org./resources/file/US%202008%20CLIA%20stats.pdf, accessed November 1, 2011.

Dickinson, B. and Vladimir, A. (1997) *Selling the Sea*. New York: John Wiley & Sons.

Disney Cruise Line (1998) *Disney Cruise Line Brochure, April 1998–December 1998*.

—— (2002) *Disney Cruise Line Brochure, 2002–2004 Vacations*.

Lieberman, W. and Dieck, T. (2002) "Expanding the Revenue Management Frontier: Optimal Air Planning in the Cruise Industry", *Journal of Revenue and Pricing Management* 1/1: 7–24.

McLeod, R. (2008) Personal Communication.

Royal Caribbean International (2008) *Alaska 2009 Cruise & Cruisetour Vacation Planner*. Miami: Royal Caribbean International.

CHAPTER 13

....

LESS-THAN-
TRUCKLOAD PRICING

....

EDWARD KINTZ

This chapter reviews the pricing process in the less-than-truckload (LTL) motor carrier industry and the multiple factors that influence pricing decisions. First, we provide some background on the freight transportation industry contrasting the other modes to LTL. Following that we highlight the major legislation affecting pricing practices in the LTL industry. Next we review the LTL pricing process, examine the variables to consider when assessing a customers' contribution to system profits, and finish with a recap of the current challenges facing the motor carrier industry.

13.1 BACKGROUND TO THE TRANSPORTATION
INDUSTRY
....

Here we discuss the fundamental differences between the LTL industry and the other transportation industry segments, such as ocean, rail, full truckload, or express package. Understanding these differences provides a broader perspective on the characteristics that make the LTL industry and its pricing process unique.

Container ships or tankers are the most notable of ocean carriage and they handle most international trade. An ocean shipment may comprise multiple containers but typically there will be one shipment per container. If a customer does not have sufficient volume to fill a container they can tender traffic in less than container load shipments (LCL), however, this is a smaller segment of an ocean carrier's overall market. Ocean carriers utilize a combination of 20-foot and 40-foot containers that can be stacked up to seven high on a container vessel. A common unit of measure is the TEU, (i.e., a 20-foot equivalent unit). Shippers can contract directly with an ocean carrier or work with a non-vessel operating common carrier (NVOCC). An NVOCC, usually a freight forwarder, contracts capacity with ocean carriers then markets the space to their client base.

Rail transport can be an extension of ocean carriage by receiving cargo from the port for movement directly inland to a consignee or a logistics center for distribution to domestic markets. The combination of service from one transport mode to another is called inter-modal or co-modal. Rail traffic includes raw materials and general cargo (general cargo relates to goods packaged to some extent). A rail shipment can be an entire train movement, a combination of multiple rail cars within a train, or a single rail box or container car.

Full truckload (FTL), like less-than-truckload (LTL), is motor cargo, meaning it is transported over the road via motorized vehicle. FTL traffic generally consists of shipments that fill the entire volume or weight capacity of a trailer moving to a single consignee from a single shipper. Generally, shipments with weight in excess of 20,000 pounds are considered full truckload from a freight rate perspective. Depending on the density of the commodities shipped, the actual weight could be less than or far greater than 20,000 pounds. Some of the top FTL carriers in North America are Schneider National Inc., Swift Transportation, Werner Enterprises, U.S. Xpress Enterprises, and Landstar System.

The express package delivery sector has rules regulating the maximum size and weight of packages that can be carried. Multiple package shipments can range up to 500 pounds but the target market is single package shipments weighing 70 pounds or less. Depending on the urgency of the delivery service required, the market may be served via air or ground providers. Familiar package express companies include FedEx and UPS.

13.2 The less-than-truckload (LTL) industry

Less-than-truckload, as a rule, refers to traffic weighing less than 10,000 pounds. Traffic weighing 10,000 pounds and greater but less than 20,000 pounds is called *heavy LTL*. LTL by definition is the segment of the industry where shippers tender traffic in shipment quantities of less than a truck load. The top ten for-hire LTL carriers in the United States in 2009 are shown in Table 13.1.

Table 13.1 includes both regional and national carriers. The two have quite different business models. For example, the network of a regional carrier such as Saia is optimized for speed of service to provide customers with next day and second day delivery for a limited region of the country. In contrast, a national carrier such as Yellow Freight maintains service coverage that spans from coast to coast, border to border, and beyond. National carriers' networks are optimized to gain load efficiency and are typically designed in a "hub-and-spoke" structure. Traffic is picked up by drivers operating out of *end-of-line terminals* which deal directly with customers. From the origin terminal, freight is moved to the nearest hub or *breakbulk* terminal. At the breakbulk facility, freight from the hub's entire group of end-of-line terminals is consolidated into trailers then moved to the destination breakbulk. Freight is then transferred and loaded into trailers and moved to the destination end-of-line terminals. The end-of-line terminal operation delivers the freight to the customers. Although there are differences in network structure and service coverage each carrier's operational activities are very similar. The primary operational components as illustrated in Figure 13.1 include: (1) pick-up and delivery (P&D), (2) cross dock, (3) group linehaul, and (4) mainline linehaul.

Table 13.1 Top ten for-hire US LTL carriers, 2009

Carrier name	2009 revenue ($000s)
FedEx Freight	3,935,000**
YRC National Transportation	3,489,300
Con-way Freight	2,623,989
UPS Freight	1,886,000**
ABF Freight Systems	1,472,901
YRC Regional Transportation*	1,322,600
Estes Express Lines	1,247,677
Old Dominion Freight Line	1,245,005
Saia Inc.*	849,141
R + L Carriers*	728,379

* Regional Carriers
** Freight revenue only
Source: Transport Topics Online (2009)

P&D drivers operate routes within a terminal's coverage area. They perform the delivery and pick-up services and normally run the same routes every day in order to develop customer intimacy and route knowledge. The cross dock function is the transfer of shipments from one trailer to the next across the terminal's platform/dock. *Linehaul* is the movement of trailers from one terminal facility to the next. There is a distinction between group and mainline linehaul. *Group linehaul* is the movement between an end-of-line terminal and the origin hub or breakbulk terminal. *Mainline linehaul* is the movement between hub terminals.

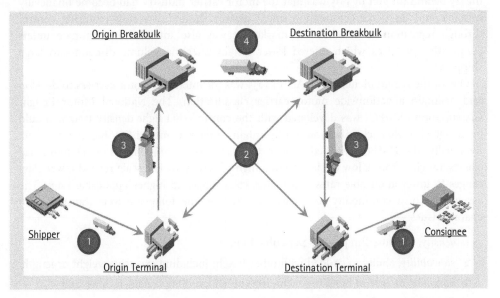

FIGURE 13.1 Primary operational components between shipper and consignee utilizing breakbulk

The best option to lower handling costs and expedite transit is for a carrier to load trailers "high and tight" meaning to maximum capacity from the origin terminal to the final destination terminal. Even though the transport is routed through the terminal network, freight handling at intermediate terminals is bypassed reducing costs and exposure to loss or damage. If the origin terminal does not have sufficient traffic to load a full trailer to the destination terminal, then the next best option is to load to the destination breakbulk terminal. The destination breakbulk terminal services multiple end-of-line terminals within a broader geographic market. If this is not possible, then the origin terminal will move the traffic picked up each day to their origin breakbulk terminal. Each origin break-bulk draws traffic from all the end-of-line terminals within its local geography. The objective is to load trailers to their optimal capacity, both cube and weight, and ship them to the furthest possible point in the network.

13.3 INDUSTRY LEGISLATIVE BACKGROUND

Over its history, the LTL industry has been subject to regulations that have played an important role in determining how prices are set. In this section we briefly review the major legislative actions which have shaped the industry. The initial legislation introduced to regulate the freight transportation industry in the United States was the Motor Carrier Act of 1935. Prior to 1935, rapid development of the national highway system provided shippers an alternative to rail transport. Cheap operating costs and low wages reduced the cost of entry and new motor carrier operations emerged introducing intense competition. This aggressive competitive environment resulted in a volatile system of rates and services. The theory behind the Act of 1935 was that the motor carrier industry had become financially unstable and the fierce competition might destroy the industry thus requiring control through regulation to stabilize the market. It was also intended to eliminate unfair competitive practices which offered lower freight rates via volume discounts to large shippers.

One of the requirements of the Act of 1935 was for interstate motor carriers to develop and maintain a nationwide motor carrier classification. The National Motor Freight Classification (NMFC) was developed with the concept that light density freight should be assigned higher classification ratings than similar commodities moving via rail. Eventually, the NMFC classified tens of thousands of commodities into 18 numerical classes, ranging from a low of class 50 to a high of class 500. The scale related lower class ranges to lower applicable rates and higher class ranges to higher applicable rates. The assignment of a commodity to a class is based on the following four transportation characteristics:

1. *density*, measured in pounds per cubic foot;

2. *stowability*, ability to co-load with other freight including excessive weight or length;

3. *handling*, or ease of handling including special handling considerations; and

4. *liability*, an item's susceptibility to loss or damage including the value of the item.

COMMODITY CLASSIFICATION STANDARDS BOARD VALUE GUIDELINES		COMMODITY CLASSIFICATION STANDARDS BOARD DENSITY GUIDELINES	
Class	Maximum Average Value Per Pound	Minimum Average Density (in pounds per cubic foot)	Class
50	$1.06	50	50
55	$2.06	35	55
60	$3.12	30	60
65	$5.17	22.5	65
70	$7.80	15	70
77.5	$10.39	13.5	78
85	$15.61	12	85
92.5	$20.78	10.5	93
100	$25.99	9	100
110	$28.60	8	110
125	$32.49	7	125
150	$39.02	6	150
175	$45.52	5	175
200	$52.02	4	200
250	$65.02	3	250
300	$78.01	2	300
400	$104.02	1	400
500	$130.04	Less than 1	500

FIGURE 13.2 Commodity Classification Standards Board value and density guidelines

Density is the predominant consideration in determining class. An example of the Commodity Classification Standard Board Density & Value Guidelines published by the National Motor Freight Traffic Association as of July 1, 2009 is shown in Figure 13.2.

The density guidelines are used in the assignment of classes where average density is representative or reflective of the range of densities exhibited. Furthermore, the density/class relationships set forth in the guidelines presume that there are no unusual or significant stowability, handling, or liability characteristics, which would call for giving those characteristics additional or different "weight" in determining the appropriate class. Value per pound is only one component of the liability characteristics. The value guidelines cannot be viewed as forming a matrix with the density guidelines, where one is measured against the other to arrive at the appropriate class representing an "average" of the two factors. Rather, the value guidelines provide an indication of the upper value limits associated with the various classes, as determined using the density guidelines. (National Motor Freight Traffic Association, Inc., 2009).

The NMFC also provides extensive direction on rules, packaging provisions, the uniform Bill of Lading, and the classification index, articles, headings, and participants. No other pricing medium includes all of these factors other than the NMFC. The general consensus is that eradicating the use of the NMFC within the LTL industry is extremely difficult if not impossible, until a more systematic and accurate method is devised to capture the cost and dimensional characteristics of freight tendered to LTL carriers.

Legislative activity continued through the years but arguably the next most important legislation affecting the industry was the Motor Carrier Act of 1980. The act significantly reduced the control of the Interstate Commerce Commission (ICC) over the trucking industry and truckers (Barrett 1980) and marked the beginning of deregulation of the LTL industry. Following the Motor Carrier Act of 1980, numerous legislative actions furthered deregulation. The Surface Transportation Board terminated its approval of all outstanding motor carrier bureau agreements under 49 U.S.C. 13703(c) in a decision served on May 7, 2007. Prior to this ruling, motor carriers had authority to enter into agreements with other carriers to collectively establish rates, classifications, mileage guides, rules, and rate adjustments for general application based upon industry average costs. This decision eliminated the protection of anti-trust agreements for the National Classification Committee (NCC) and ten other rate bureaus (Service Transportation Board Decision 2007). As a result, the legislative impacts on the motor carrier industry have come full circle. The industry is essentially operating in a state of deregulation, very similar to the time prior to the Motor Carrier Act of 1935.

13.4 LTL PRICING PROCESS

Pricing policy refers to how a company sets the price of its products or services based on costs, value, demand, and competition. Pricing strategy, on the other hand, refers to how a company uses pricing to achieve its strategic goals (Heil 2005).

Most carriers' pricing policy and strategy changed with the Motor Carrier Act of 1980. This law had far-reaching consequences, causing price competition and lower profit margins, forcing a search for efficiency in the industry (Lawdog 2000). One byproduct of the Act was the ability for LTL carriers to distinguish their respective portfolio of products and services from their competitors by marketing these services using pricing/cost differentials expressed in terms of a "discount" from the standard published rates. Today competitive discounting is a common practice.

During a period of economic expansion a market penetration strategy is suitable. When market conditions shift and the economy cannot sustain corporate revenue targets, carriers revert to more aggressive pricing strategies to fuel growth. Pricing policy is one of the principal mechanisms by which a carrier can execute its strategy. Consequently, pricing is one of the primary considerations in the integrated planning process and is used to help balance the conflicting objectives of growth versus profit. Figure 13.3 depicts the cycle and interaction between the main groups involved in the execution of a carrier's strategy.

A pricing department's goal is to provide dedicated decision support to sales and operations. To be effective, the pricing department needs to accomplish its directives

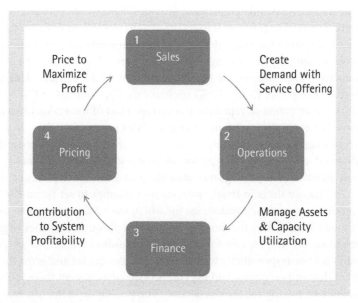

FIGURE 13.3 The carrier's strategy cycle

accurately and on time. Pricing terms can be stipulated in either a customer-specific pricing agreement for common carriage or a contractual agreement for contract carriage. For accurate rating, it is imperative the pricing provisions denoting the discount level, tariff base, coverage area, governing publications, and applicable special service charges are correctly transcribed into the rating system.

In general, large shippers put their traffic up for bid on a periodic basis to insure they maintain the most competitive price and service coverage available in the market. Typically, a large shipper will put its traffic up for bid annually. In these competitive bid situations, carriers will submit their proposed pricing terms and the shipper will evaluate the responses and make their selection. Numerous factors are considered in the selection of a carrier with bottom-line price being one of the most significant. The final negotiated terms are generally captured in a contractual agreement but it is not always the case. It is a customer's decision whether to use a contract or a common carrier agreement. Contracts by definition require bi lateral consideration but customers wield the ultimate power and control. Under contract carriage, all agreed transportation conditions are explicitly outlined. In addition to the rate and discount application, some of the most important contract items include: term and termination provisions, claims liability, substitute service conditions, and payment terms. Typically, corporate clients who command significant volumes of traffic also demand the deepest discounts. Common carrier agreements also reflect the specifically negotiated pricing terms and service coverage but refer to the carriers governing rules publications, common to all as referenced, for claims liability, payment terms, and so forth.

A contract (or a common carriage agreement), normally uses the standards provided in the NMFC and the Household Goods Mileage Guide as governing publications. The

Household Goods Mileage Guide publication provides the distance between points and is used when setting rates. The purpose is to incorporate standardized industry rules, as well as the classification system for use to determine the commodity class and associated class rate application. To simplify the pricing applications and rating, the practice of classification exceptions have been adopted by both customers and LTL carriers. This practice is commonly termed Freight All Kinds (FAK) applications. The intent of an FAK provision is to apply a single classification to represent the average class of the various commodities a customer ships. For example, a customer's commodities range from class 50 to class 100 with the average weighted class equating to 71. To simplify the rate application the parties agree to a discount off an FAK class 70 for all commodities between class 50 and 100. Carriers closely monitor FAK pricing since once the provisions are in place the freight mix may change. To manage shifts in freight mix, carriers attempt to set tiered FAK levels or place a cap on the commodity classifications for which the FAK provisions would apply.

Pricing requests funnel into the pricing department through the sales organization. Company salesmen are responsible for a defined portfolio of accounts or geographic coverage area. It is their responsibility to manage their sales quotas and grow the business. Considering the demand on quotas and the competitive environment there is constantly a significant volume of pricing requests generated. For pricing departments, managing the daily volume is a challenge. Processing guidelines are implemented to reduce the number of requests that require manual analysis. Requests for discounts below minimum guidelines are generally automatically approved and processed. The degree of scrutiny escalates along with the level of approval dependent upon specified criteria, namely, the level of discount, excess claim liability, monetary value of the opportunity and/or forecast contribution to system profitability. Usually approval for exceptions to specified guidelines is handled within the hierarchy of the pricing department. If sales should choose to challenge a decision they can escalate their objection up the sales organization. If agreement cannot be reached between the sales organization and the pricing department the final arbitrator will likely be the CFO. Depending on the circumstances, some pricing decisions may automatically escalate to the CFO or COO, for example, when the volume would demand dedicated capacity within the operation and the projected profit impact is negative. In special cases the decision may even raise to the CEO level.

Typical activities surrounding pricing decision support are shown in Figure 13.4. The primary activities include processing bid and pricing (discount) requests, analyzing the impact of pricing changes on customer profitability/system profits, managing the general rate increase, and assisting in the negotiations for rate increases with contract customers.

Additional filters are usually applied to ensure conformance to defined pricing policy. The usual check list would contain:

- commodity classification exceptions / FAK requests;
- net effective discount off the current tariff rate;
- absolute minimum charge levels;
- special service charge waivers or reductions;
- foreign/dated rate base and rate base comparison;
- fuel surcharge exemptions or reductions;
- lane balance / direct loading impacts;

- freight density / co-loadability;
- accounts receivable status;
- hidden costs;
- tier discount by lane/weight scale/inter-line service.

The objective of reviewing each pricing request against the items in a checklist is to protect the company's interest and impose discipline into the pricing process. Ultimately, pricing decisions are influenced by evaluating a combination of factors. The net effective discount is a metric used to evaluate the proposed net rate versus the most current rating tariff. Carriers manage multiple rating tariffs but one is usually set as the standard and used to benchmark discount levels. The lowest dollar amount a carrier will accept for handling a shipment is called the absolute minimum charge. Even if the base rate less discount is lower, the absolute minimum charge will apply. For example, assume a shipper negotiated a 65 percent discount with a $107.00 absolute minimum charge. If a shipment's pre-discount rate is $200 less the 65 percent discount the net charge equates to $70.00. This, however, is lower than the absolute minimum charge of $107.00, consequently the absolute minimum charge is applied. Hidden costs are those incurred by a carrier but not easily associated to a customer or a shipment. Examples include waiting in line for dock space to effect delivery, delays for paperwork at time of pick-up, increased cross dock handling due to the configuration of the shipment and shipping forms that are not stackable.

Given the time constraints and visibility associated with bid opportunities, it is necessary to have an effective sequence of events leading up to a bid submission. A bid review follows a similar pattern as regular pricing requests except for high-profile, large-dollar-value opportunities where senior management gets involved and more intense analysis is required.

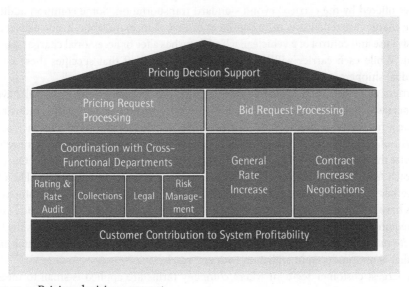

FIGURE 13.4 Pricing decision support

Fostering a spirit of teamwork and cooperation is also a vital component in working with cross-functional departments. Pricing departments collaborate with almost every part of the organization, most notably collections, claims, legal, and sales. They must facilitate conference calls or meetings with the other departments to resolve known issues. For example, when dealing with accounts with rating or collection challenges the pricing group must work with the collections and sales organizations, evaluate the situation, determine root cause and take corrective action. The analysis cannot be done in a silo, it requires coordination with cross-functional teams to make progress and solve issues.

Revenue management is another important area within the purview of the pricing department. The primary role of revenue management is to manage the revenue generating mechanisms to maximize system profit. This includes maintaining the proprietary rating tariff/s, the accessorial charges tariff, and evaluating the absolute minimum charge level to name a few. With regard to maintaining the rating tariff/s there are three primary factors influencing the application of rates—commodity classification, shipment weight, and distance. The tendency within the industry is to make rate adjustments by lane where a natural imbalance of trade exists or for high cost pick-up or delivery areas. Locations such as downtown Manhattan, Boston, Washington DC, and LA are often targeted first. With autonomous control, carriers adjust their tariff rates to support their operations. Rates continue to be applied on a hundred-weight basis. Eight distinct weight brackets comprise the rate scale ranging from minimum charge (MC), generally for shipments weighing less than 200 pounds, to a 10,000 pound rate scale, generally applied for shipments in excess of 10,000 pounds up to 20,000 pounds.

Along with the rating tariffs, revenue management is also responsible for the Rules and Special Service tariff, commonly referred to as the *accessorial charges* tariff. Standard transportation services include pick-up service at origin, transfer of lading to a terminal for loading onto linehaul equipment; over-the-road transport to the delivering terminal and transfer to a delivery truck for final delivery. The Special Service tariff covers all additional services offered by the carrier beyond standard transportation. Some common additional service charges are redelivery, reconsignment or diversion, extra labor, inside delivery, and exclusive use and control of a vehicle. Each of these has a fee or accessorial charge associated with it. While each carrier will have a Special Service tariff that specifies these charges, individual shippers may negotiate discounts to accessorial charges as well.

Carriers, as a rule, assess a general rate increase (GRI) annually. Some years will have two rate increases but this is not the common practice. In rare instances the industry has forgone a rate increase due to economic pressures. Carriers justify their rate increases on the basis of offsetting inflation and the higher cost of operations as well as the need to re-capitalize the fleet and network to maintain service standards and repair margin. Over time, with each GRI, carriers have modified their tariffs to achieve strategic goals. The consequence has been a proliferation of tariffs across the industry. Sophisticated shippers or agents have dealt with this issue by selecting one carrier's tariff or an industry-wide tariff as their required standard. One of the most prominent industry-wide tariffs in use is the SMC^3 *CzarLite rating tariff*, offered by the SMC^3 Company. *CzarLite* is a carrier-neutral base of rates that is not produced in affiliation with any carrier.

The largest customer segment where company tariffs are applied is small to medium-sized accounts. Unfortunately for the carriers this segment represents a dwindling percentage of revenue. Most carriers now bill less than half of their revenue from tariffs directly impacted by a GRI and roughly half of the GRI revenue is generated from a carrier's proprietary tariff. The remainder of revenue is generated from accounts with contractual agreements whose annual increases are negotiated individually.

13.5 PROFITABILITY ANALYSIS / CONTRIBUTION TO SYSTEM PROFIT

The ability to accurately determine a customer's contribution to total profit is essential when making a pricing decision. When attempting to improve yields outside of a general rate increase cycle, identifying customers with negative profit margins is vital. Given shrinking profit margins, carriers cannot afford errors. When negotiating increases they need to know when to hold strong and risk losing the business versus taking a softer approach so as not to lose freight that makes a positive contribution to profit.

On the surface developing transportation cost models may seem very straightforward. The basic activities are pick-up from shipper, handle freight cross dock, linehaul to destination, and final delivery to consignee. In reality, capturing and assigning costs by activity is a complex process. Operational considerations include directional movement of the traffic (i.e., moving equipment from a demand point to supply point or vice versa), direct loading impacts, capacity utilization, shipment density and co-loadability, and identifying slack capacity in pick-up and delivery routes. The synthesis of these variables requires sophisticated network algorithms, activity-based costing models, and management science to properly assign cost to a shipment. Capturing operational information at a shipment and customer level is crucial. Factoring all the costs, including the hidden costs, into the equation may be the difference between pricing profitably or not.

Contribution to profit has four primary components; revenue, variable operating cost, opportunity cost, and equipment movement cost. Only by explicitly computing each of these can the implications of gaining a customer's business be understood and the traffic priced to optimize the overall freight mix. While revenue and variable operating cost are relatively straightforward, opportunity cost and equipment movement costs are more complex to calculate and assign. Opportunity cost is useful when evaluating the cost and benefit of choices. Selecting between multiple customers' freight is a good example. One customer's freight mix may be tendered in cartons loose and complement the existing traffic in a lane and consequently not require equivalent capacity since cartons can be stacked on top of other traffic. A second customer's freight is tendered on pallets and drives the need for additional capacity since pallets require floor space on a trailer. Properly understanding the opportunity cost is important in this situation. For allocating equipment movement cost there are several factors to consider. Assigning the cost of moving a loaded trailer on a lane to the traffic aboard and allocating the cost of repositioning empty trailers in the network are key steps. Linehaul trailers have both a weight and cube constraint. The general freight characteristics today tend to cube out trailers more often then they weigh out. Meaning trailers are loaded to the maximum volume before they reach their weight capacity. Consequently, freight density is a primary component for allocating equipment movement cost. For empty repositioning this expense is typically regarded as a system expense and allocated using sophisticated network algorithms.

Profitability models are reflective of historical costs and seasonal effects on capacity utilization. Since productivity, capacity utilization, and freight mix are all dynamic, the ability to forecast what will happen rather than analyzing what has happened is where the real value is realized. Having a forecast capability enables a carrier to formulate strategy for the future as opposed to reacting to the past.

For the most part, motor carriage has been a very high-cost/low-margin business. Carriers must manage their cost, cash flow, and customer satisfaction to remain viable. The most successful carriers are those who focus to meet and exceed their customers' expectations. They leverage information management systems to keep ahead of their competition. They operate more efficiently by delivering actionable information to their drivers to eliminate waste and reduce cost while still providing high quality performance in the markets they service. Concentration on these strategic objectives helps differentiate them in the marketplace and affords them the opportunity to charge more for their services and achieve an above industry average return.

13.6 CHALLENGES FACING THE MOTOR CARRIER INDUSTRY

Economic cycles and escalating fuel costs have been the main two concerns facing the industry. Carriers have been very assertive in working to recover the increased cost of fuel through fuel surcharges. Fuel surcharges are listed in the Carriers Rules Tariff and applied for common carrier pricing agreements or specified in the pricing terms within a negotiated contract. Fuel surcharges are applied as a percent of revenue and as a rule indexed with the US DOE national average diesel price per gallon. They are increased at the time of a general rate increase or renegotiated on an annual basis when the contract term is near expiration. Shippers understand that fuel prices are a major component of operating cost but they are also working to keep costs down and at times the negotiation of fuel surcharges is contentious.

Carriers operate set terminal networks and adjust to swings in market demand by adjusting their rolling assets. Unfortunately for carriers, operational adjustments are not immediate and consequently carriers are exposed to periods of excess capacity when market demand is down or to the need to recapitalize when the market rebounds. Due to intense competition, during periods of excess capacity, carriers are inclined to price aggressively to maintain business levels. The bottom line effect is downward pressure on profit margins. When demand improves and capacity is at a premium carriers are able to price more conservatively and recover profits and increase operating margins. Ultimately those carriers which are adaptive, agile, and able to manage under uncertainty are the best positioned to withstand market changes and stay one step ahead of the competition.

Environmental challenges are also on the list of issues motor carriers must manage. The ecology is top of mind throughout the country with the "think green" campaigns and international concerns over global warming. Carriers have worked to optimize their pick-up and delivery routes to reduce miles driven. They also work to increase trailer load factor to reduce the number of schedules over the road as a means to reduce their carbon footprint. Anti-idling regulations and greater emissions controls continue to increase operating expenses and there is debate whether the cost of compliance may exceed the benefit.

13.7 CONCLUSION

Since 1980, the motor carrier industry has come full circle and is once again operating in a deregulated environment. Their anti-trust immunity for classifying goods has been eliminated. Ease of entry along with the capability to autonomously set rate and pricing levels has created a highly competitive environment. Creative pricing strategies will emerge as efforts to stabilize competitive pricing continue and carriers work to repair profit margins.

Carriers will continue to differentiate themselves by developing new service offerings, extended coverage areas and improved service. Niche carriers will try to expand their share of the shipper's wallet at the expense of the LTL market segment. Express package carriers will look to chip away at the lower weight bracket traffic, that is, less than 500 pounds, and truckload carriers and independents will chip away at the heavy LTL segment.

Both shippers and carriers will persist in their pursuit of simplified pricing. Even in a free market environment we believe that the pricing standard will continue to be built on the foundation established during the time of industry regulation. Shippers and third parties now have an equal voice regarding classification decisions but the format and function of the NMFC remains. Until someone develops a new pricing mechanism or tariff that considers all the characteristics of LTL freight, current industry pricing practices will remain relatively intact.

REFERENCES

Barrett, C. (1980) *Shippers, Truckers, and the Law: How to Live With the New Motor Carrier Act.* http://www.answers.com/topic/motor-carrier-act-1, accessed April 27, 2010.

Heil, K. rev. S. B. Droege (2005) *Pricing Policy and Strategy.* http://www.referenceforbusiness.com/management/OR-PR/Pricing-Policy-and-Strategy.html, accessed April 27, 2010.

Lawdog (2000) *History of Trucking Regulation at LAWDOG.* http://www.lawdog.com/transport/tp1.htm, accessed April 27, 2010.

National Motor Freight Traffic Association, Inc. (2009) *The Commodity Classification Standards Board—CCSB Density and Value Guidelines.* http://www.nmfta.org/Pages/CCSB.aspx, accessed May 14, 2010.

Service Transportation Board Decision (2007) *Investigation into the Practices of the National Classification Committee.* http://www.nitl.org/STBExparte656.pdf, accessed May 14, 2010.

Transport Topics Online (2009) *2009 Transport Topics 100.* http://www.ttnews.com/tt100/, accessed May 14, 2010.

CHAPTER 14

PRICING IN THE NORTH AMERICAN PROTEIN INDUSTRY

MICHAEL NEAL, ROBERT D. PIERCE,
MICHAEL FREIMER, AND SUSHIL VERMA

14.1 HISTORY AND STRUCTURE OF THE PROTEIN INDUSTRY

Protein production is the agricultural process of growing, harvesting, and processing animals for food. The protein industry includes production, processing, and marketing of animal-based protein at wholesale and retail. Some of the organizations formed to commercialize the harvesting and processing of animals are among the oldest continuously operating companies in the United States (Cargill 2008; Hormel 2008; John Morrell 2008; Smithfield 2008; Tyson 2008). Like other agricultural companies, the location and structure of many protein companies were dictated by the location of railheads during the development of the American West, and some of that historical influence remains. Insofar as ranching was one of the most important economic activities driving the opening of the West, the protein industry has ties to the American identity of the cowboy and the untamed West. Beef in particular carries a premium marketing position, apparently in part because of that emotional link.

The industry is organized around the species of animal to be processed, such as cattle, hogs, chicken, turkey, and lamb. Some large processing companies harvest multiple species, but usually within separate organizational divisions (Cargill 2008; Tyson 2008). Each of the species branches of the industry has similar stages of production, but the branches differ significantly in terms of the commercialization and the cost structure of the stages. The sizes of US domestic protein production by species are summarized in Table 14.1.

Table 14.1 2009 US production and processing data for selected species

Metric	Unit	Cattle and calves	Hogs	Sheep and lambs	Poultry
Cash receipts from farm marketings (2008)	B USD	48	16	0.45	NA
Population on farms (2009)	M Head	94.5	66.7	5.7	NA
Slaughter (2008)	M Head	35	116	2.6	9,075
Wholesale production (2008)	B lbs.	27	23	0.2	37.5
Packing and processing sales (2006)	B USD	97 (breakout by species NA)			46

Source: AMI (2009)

Production and marketing in any species require a series of steps:

- *Breeder:* maintaining breeding stock; producing juvenile stock;
- *Feeder:* raising of juveniles to harvest potential;
- *Packer:* harvesting; processing for wholesale;
- *Processor:* value-added processing; industrial processing;
- *Retailer.*

Packers are wholesale manufacturers in the protein industry and are the primary focus of this chapter. At each stage there is the potential to integrate or consolidate the industry. Corporations may be segmented by production stage, thereby creating an independent market for the animals or products between one stage and the next. Alternatively, two or more stages may be vertically integrated within a single corporation, bypassing the need to market the intermediate products. The corporations within a stage may exhibit different levels of consolidation, thereby altering the dynamics of competition and market behavior. Both vertical integration and consolidation differ widely between species and stages, resulting in highly complex market behavior. The effect of integration and consolidation on pricing will be explored by species in more detail below.

The protein industry has a long history of government regulation and reporting. All five of the major species (cattle, hogs, chicken, turkey, and lamb) are tracked and reported by the USDA (US Department of Agriculture) (AMS 2008a), though the level and mandate for participation in the reporting process vary across species. Live cattle and hog prices published by USDA are followed closely by the buyers and sellers. Georgia FOB (Freight On Board) dock prices published by the State of Georgia are the standard for chicken producers. For turkey and lamb, prices published by Urner Barry (an independent market research company) are given greater consideration. Figure 14.1 shows the recent history of the price index for each species.

Seasonality in domestic demand, supply levels, and export demand play active roles in the relative pricing of different proteins. Biology is also significant because some species retain a seasonal bias in reproductive and growth cycles. Information on live cattle prices goes back to the nineteenth century. Over much of that time, cattle prices have exhibited predictable decade-long cycles caused by the physical process of managing herd size. Beef,

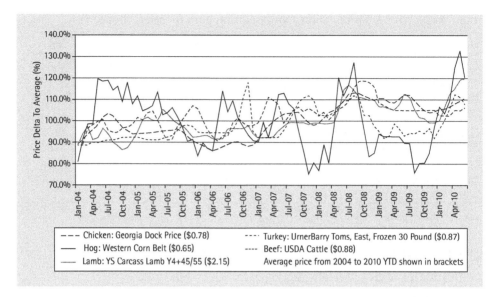

FIGURE 14.1 Historical key whole animal price indices

the natural product of raising cattle for food, has traditionally been priced in ratio to the live cattle price. Consequently beef has historically been a commodity with reasonably predictable prices. In the USA, beef has been the dominant or preferred protein for retail consumption, and the prices of other proteins have been positioned relative to beef. In more recent times, the linkages among growing constraints, live animal prices, wholesale prices, and retail prices have weakened. The causes of this phenomenon are related to the factors explored in this chapter, including advances in agricultural science, market consolidation, and the behavior of financial markets. The relationship among prices is shown in Figure 14.1. Prices have in general trended upwards, but species do not move together in price. Live cattle and hog prices, for example, often move in opposite directions due to differing market forces in the beef and pork industry.

14.1.1 Cattle

In some sense, beef is the original commercial protein. The health, safety, and economic imperatives entailed in butchering large animals such as cattle led to some of the earliest examples of industrial segmentation. Many large cities in Europe and the USA have neighborhoods or districts which have been associated with the industrial slaughter of cattle for hundreds of years. The challenges of raising cattle, moving them, butchering them, and marketing beef gave rise to economic specialization in the form of farmers, drovers, and butchers going back many hundreds of years (YBG 2010). This history, especially the association with the American West, together with the economic overhead of specialization has lent itself to a general domestic perception of beef as a premium product relative to other proteins. Moreover, the taste and texture variation across parts of the beef carcass has lent itself to the establishment of certain cuts, particularly steaks from the mid-section of the animal, as deserving an additional premium. Consequently, beef wholesalers can command a premium during robust economic times, but may suffer from consumer perceptions of high price during bad times.

The beef industry has remained vertically un-integrated to the present time. Each step in the process is performed by a different set of companies.

Breeders are referred to as "cow and calf" operations. "Cow" refers to an older female animal, which is used for breeding and dairy production, while "steers" (neutered males) and "heifers" (unbred females) are the predominant input to harvest for protein. Cows are harvested, but the resulting cuts are generally considered to be inferior quality relative to beef from steers and heifers due to the age and history of the animal. The meat is more often utilized in commodity trim and grind products (e.g., hamburgers) and commonly directed to industrial applications and foodservice (e.g., restaurants). Cow and calf operations remain highly segmented. In 1997, only 14 percent of cow and calf operations raised cattle as their primary source of income with a median herd size of about 300 animals, while 69 percent raised cattle as a source of supplementary income with 73 percent of these operators having herd sizes of less than 50 (APHIS 1997). As of 2007, the situation had not changed drastically, with the average operation having about 100 head (AMI 2009). Calves ready for feeding (i.e., fattening) may be delivered to feeders by individual contract, or may be centrally marketed. The USDA provides twice daily reports on the prices and quantities of marketings (i.e., live animal sales) and futures (AMS 2008b).

Feeders are more consolidated than breeders with the top 6 percent representing 49 percent of the marketed animals (AMI 2009). As with calves, fed cattle may be delivered to packers on individual contracts, or they may be regionally marketed at auction. Fed cattle purchases are reported by the USDA. In addition, there is an active futures market for fed cattle at the Chicago Mercantile Exchange (CME). The actual price paid by packers for individual head may be arrived at in a number of ways, including a flat rate, a formula to previous USDA prices, or on a grading grid. In the latter case, a premium may be paid for animals that have a particular attribute. Carcass attributes that may justify a premium or discount include genetics such as Angus, USDA Grade based on visible fat marbling of the rib-eye, yield grade based on total carcass fat, and carcass size. Large carcass size can cause extra processing costs or unsuitability for certain products because retail and foodservice operators control portion size by weight and cross-sectional area. For example, a 12-ounce steak from a large animal will be thinner and wider, causing it to cook faster, taste tougher, and take up a larger portion of the plate when served.

Packers are more consolidated than feeders, with the three largest representing a 70 percent market share. Starting in the 1960s, the packing industry was transformed from a predominantly harvesting function to a manufacturing function. Prior to the transformation, wholesale beef was sold as "sides", or half a carcass weighing 300 pounds or more. Large-scale butchering of the carcass is now performed on an assembly line in the packing plant. Nearly all wholesale beef is sold as "boxed beef" in relatively small pieces placed in convenient shipping containers weighing less than 70 pounds. The USDA reports wholesale sales by cut and pricing type, offering twice daily detailed aggregated transaction information (AMS 2008d). The USDA also offers daily reports of weighted average prices at the primal level (AMS 2008c). A "primal" refers to an anatomical section of the carcass which defines the origin and characteristics of a cut. Examples include the "chuck" or front shoulder yielding primarily roasts and ground beef, and the "rib" or middle section yielding primarily steaks. Reporting of wholesale transactions of beef products is mandatory in contrast to other species. While all transactions do not satisfy the categorization criteria of the USDA reports, the vast majority of wholesale beef sales are represented. This makes for a very competitive and transparent market, where buyers and sellers at every stage of the demand chain have access to timely market information.

14.1.2 Hogs

Wholesale manufacturing and marketing of pork products share many similarities with beef. However, the industry as a whole is significantly different, particularly on the production side. Hogs have a very different maturation process, which lends itself to a manufacturing approach to the breeding and feeding processes. In 2006, the top 4 percent of producers were responsible for half of the US hog supply (AMI 2009). Modern hog production takes place primarily indoors, occurs faster than beef, and results in a more uniform product. Hog carcasses do not have the variation that beef carcasses do. The distinguishing features of hog carcasses are mostly concerned with growing parameters (e.g., organic or antibiotic free), or carcass size which contributes to portion size control.

Pork packers are highly consolidated, with the top five representing 67 percent of market share (AMI 2009). The manufacturing nature of growing hogs has also contributed to significant vertical integration. For some large packers, the majority of the hogs they process are produced either by wholly owned subsidiaries or by growers under fixed long-term contracts. Some major pork packers remain un-integrated with producers, buying their hogs on the open market. The partial integration of the pork industry stands in contrast to beef, which is uniformly un-integrated, and chicken, which is uniformly integrated.

Many pork packers have invested heavily in value-added post-processing in contrast to beef packers who have made relatively few forays into post-processing. Several large pork packers in the USA own everything from farms to canning factories. Hence, cost structures are wildly dissimilar across the industry. Integrated packers benefit when live hog prices are high, while their un-integrated competitors gain advantage when hog prices are low. Consequently, the business interests of packers do not align as well as they do in the beef industry.

Third-party market reporting in the pork industry is similar to, but not as reliable as, reporting in the beef industry. The same entities play the same roles, namely the USDA and the CME, but on a smaller market share. The live hog price of the USDA and futures price of CME reflect those hogs which are available on the open market (AMS 2008e), and may not accurately reflect the cost structure of integrated producers. In addition, USDA reporting of wholesale pork products is voluntary (AMS 2008f). Anecdotes abound that voluntary price reports may include some manipulation, though there is little direct evidence. It is certain that the reports of wholesale pork products are much sparser than beef, and therefore much more volatile. Consequently, there is less confidence in pork market price reports, and the pricing of pork products at wholesale is not as transparent as beef.

Starting in 1987, US pork producers initiated a long-term marketing program labeling the product as the "other white meat" (Dougherty 1987). The intent of the program was to emphasize the healthiness of pork relative to beef, but has also served to bind consumer perceptions of pork to a chicken-like commodity. Hog genetics in the last several decades have been over-engineered so that fat content is extremely low while flavor has suffered. Again, this has created a perception of fresh pork as a commodity that has been difficult to market as a premium product, particularly in the competition for retail promotion volume and advertising space. While commodity pork typically competes more with chicken than beef at retail, pork generally cannot compete on a price per pound basis with industrialized chicken production. Consequently, packers have focused on value-added processing and branding as a primary vehicle for promotion and margin generation.

14.1.3 Chicken

Chickens are mostly hatched, raised, killed, and processed in enclosed factories using modern large-scale manufacturing principles. US chicken production in 2007 exceeded 8 billion birds. Chicken size has increased steadily over the years as a result of genetics and nutritional advances. Since 1940, the average chicken produced in American plants has doubled in size while the time and feed required to raise it has dropped by half. Inexpensive refrigerated transportation has contributed to vertical integration, production intensification, and consolidation of the chicken industry over the years.

Slaughtered chicken is sold in a variety of forms: fresh/frozen uncooked whole, fresh/frozen uncooked parts, sausages, ground chicken, pre-cooked breasts, rotisserie chicken, cooked wings, etc. Chicken has a smaller variety of cuts than other proteins, and some parts have historically had higher demand than others. Fresh chicken is sold whole for roasting and rotisserie purposes in retail and foodservice. Key fresh parts that are sold include breasts (whole, boneless/skinless), thighs (whole, boneless/skinless), drumsticks, leg quarters, and wings. Breasts have traditionally been the most valued part of chicken in the USA. They contain less fat and go by the name of white meat. Other chicken parts are called dark meat and are often the preferred form in Asia. Increasing consumption of animal protein in the emerging BRIC (Brazil, Russia, India, and China) economies has sent the demand for dark meat soaring, and as a result there is a surplus of white meat in the domestic markets.

There are three primary ways chicken is sold in the domestic and export markets: commodity whole/parts, fresh branded whole/parts, and branded and processed chicken products. The commodity market is fairly volatile and prices change on a daily basis. The USDA reports various domestic commodity markets on a daily basis, with Georgia FOB dock prices being the leading indicator. Fresh branded chicken prices offered by the manufacturers to the retailers are either tied to commodity market prices (in which case they vary day by day) or fixed at a list price for a longer period of time. Promotional vehicles such as ads, features, and temporary price reductions (TPRs) are common at the wholesale and retail level. Urner Barry collects and publishes manufacturer's price information on the branded side of the business on a weekly basis. IRI and Fresh Look (independent market research companies) track retail prices of fresh chicken products.

14.1.4 Turkey and lamb

Turkeys were domesticated over 500 years ago in Central America by the Aztecs and reached Europe in the early sixteenth century. Turkey is the fourth largest source of animal protein in the USA. In 2008, total turkey production stood at 6 billion pounds. Out of 265 pounds of the primary animal proteins (beef, pork, chicken, or turkey) consumed per capita in the USA, 20 pounds come from turkeys, of which more than 70 percent is consumed as sliced turkey breast meat. Turkeys are mostly raised by a network of growers under contract or owned by large vertically integrated corporations. The top three companies process half of the industry's total.

Female hens are smaller and largely sold as a whole bird, most often frozen, in the domestic market. Most shipments occur around Thanksgiving. "Toms" are larger male turkeys which supply the parts market. Manufacturers struggle to balance gender distribution with demand. Destroying eggs and poults (juvenile birds) are mechanisms to match supply with demand. Though not as fast growing as chickens, modern turkeys develop rapidly. Advances in nutritional science have increased the growth rate of birds. Toms can grow to 37 pounds in approximately 22 weeks. Turkeys are fed a diet consisting of grain, soybean meals for proteins, minerals, vitamins, and fat. Currently, 66 percent of the cost of raising turkey comes from corn. Recent increases in corn prices have left manufacturers struggling to pass corn prices through to their customers.

Turkey parts are sold in a variety of forms in retail, foodservice, institutional, and commodity markets. The chief forms are ground turkey breasts, sliced deli breasts, fresh breast cuts, turkey franks and sausages, turkey ham and bacon, and pre-cooked pan roasts. Commodity part prices are collected and reported by Urner Barry on a weekly basis.

Lamb is a minor source of protein in the USA, with a total domestic annual production of 160 million pounds translating to less than 1 pound of per capita consumption out of a total of 265 pounds. Limited market size, combined with a positive image of lamb meat causes lamb to fetch a high price per pound in the US market. There is an effort underway by Australian and New Zealand producers to develop the lamb market in the USA.

14.2 INDUSTRY CHALLENGES

Pricing in the protein industry is a very challenging task. Protein is a perishable good, so inventories must remain low. Government food safety mandates require extensive investments in capital equipment, so the overhead costs of meat processing plants, including refrigeration and maintenance, are very high. Prices are highly visible in the form of government reporting. As a result, feeders (suppliers) and retailers (customers) can infer packer margins. High fixed costs and the inability to hold inventory force continuous operation of facilities near capacity, and production output must be sold immediately. This causes packers to slash prices if inventory starts to build in order to clear the shelves for the next day's worth of production. The common (and only slightly hyperbolic) phrase used by sellers is: "sell it or smell it". This is a prescription for a high volume low margin business, driving highly elastic and dynamic prices. Next we review in more detail some of the challenges that protein companies face in establishing prices.

14.2.1 Market volatility and cost increases

The last decade has seen many changes to the way agricultural commodities are priced. Many factors have contributed to an unprecedented rise in price and the volatility of all agricultural commodities.

Protein is closely linked to other agricultural commodities. In particular, corn is the main feed used in growing livestock to harvest potential. Even where substitute grains exist, the linkage to corn remains strong because all grains compete for available acreage. President Bush's 2006 State of the Union address signaled a regulatory shift in the USA, emphasizing subsidized consumption of corn and oil seeds for energy including the production of ethanol and bio-diesel. This caused strong spikes in corn and soy prices in 2007 and 2008, and a corresponding rise in all other agricultural commodities. As a result of regulations and subsidies, volatility in energy commodities was directly linked to volatility in agricultural commodities including protein. The link is important because energy commodities have historically been more volatile than agricultural commodities.

The rise of a global economy has increased competition for agricultural commodities, including exports of protein, causing rises in global commodity prices. However, the relative strength of US exports also depends on the strength of the US dollar and the global economy, so foreign exchange volatility has been superposed on the general increase in prices.

Commodity protein sales are transparently reported, resulting in highly elastic prices and a low margin business. While these factors in and of themselves do not imply volatility, they suggest that producers with low margins have little ability to absorb volatility in their cost of goods. Hence, manufacturers try to pass on cost volatility, while retailers want stable pricing to offer to the consumer. This dynamic causes a tension between manufacturers and retailers.

Hedge funds have found that the seasonal structure of agricultural commodities represents an investing opportunity relative to financial securities, which are less pre-dictable. This speculation represents a shift in the way agricultural futures markets have operated. Traditionally, agricultural companies have used the futures markets to manage the risk of cash flows generated from buying and selling physical commodities. Hedge funds and speculators use the futures as a portfolio management tool. The increased scale of these investments has increased the efficiency of the market for agricultural futures, and therefore reduced the predictability of the underlying cash commodity prices. Companies in the protein supply chain have not welcomed this change in structure, because these companies benefit from stability in their operating expenses and revenues.

Other factors have also driven volatility. Market shocks occur often but unpredictably due to export market closures, disease outbreaks such as listeriosis (a bacterial infection affecting livestock and humans) or BSE (i.e., *mad cow disease*, a neurological disorder in cattle and humans), external market events (e.g., the corn run-up), and cultural movements such as the Atkins diet. Narrow margins in the industry mean that sudden shifts in demand can have significant impacts on profitability. For the most part, such events are not predictable. However, by acknowledging the volatility associated with these shocks and measuring the typical market response, the wholesale price setter can create a more robust plan that accommodates the shocks to some extent.

When margin is so low and cost is so volatile, it is risky to set a price "out front" (i.e., agreeing to a price today for delivery at some point in the future). Pricing errors often translate to losses quickly. Historically low margins together with a ratio model for prices (i.e., cut price to animal price) make it impossible to recover out front pricing errors in the spot market. Consequently, price setting in an organization is typically centralized with just a few senior individuals we refer to as *pricers*. The pricer's job is always to balance risks. There is risk in accepting a price that might turn out to be too low, but there is also a risk in turning down business because the impact could be greater later, if falling market prices and excess inventory together drive down revenue.

14.2.2 Protein as a salvage industry

The protein industry is sometimes referred to as a salvage industry. This phrase means that once an animal is harvested, the entire carcass must be sold in order to maximize (or salvage) the return on investment in the animal. In other words, packers buy the whole animal and sell component parts at significantly divergent prices. Hence, there is no obvious cost basis for individual pieces and no computable margin for most of the products a packer sells. All pieces must be sold, and the true margin on the carcass cannot be computed until the final part is sold.

The majority of the revenue realized from an animal comes from meat products, but every part of the carcass will be sold. The non-meat parts include hides, offal, and rendered products such as tallow, or blood and bone meal. For beef and pork, the revenue obtained from these non-meat items is collectively referred to as the "drop credit". The drop credit is an important component in the bottom line. Historically, the drop credit has been relatively stable, and has been positioned as an offset to fixed operating costs. This freed executives to focus on projected meat revenue as the basis for production decisions. Recent fluctuation in global markets competing for, or with, non-meat items has caused volatility, which in turn has required pricers to take a closer look at how drop credit items are priced.

The independent seasonality of different cuts also makes it difficult for packers to maintain profitability on an even keel. For example, stew meats (from the shoulder or rump of the animal) tend to peak in the winter, while grill meats (from the middle section of the animal) tend to peak in the summer. Since the middle meats are a smaller portion of the animal, but carry a much higher price, this leads to difficulties in "balancing" the revenue to cover the cost of the carcass. However, the complexity does not stop at seasonality, as independent cuts also have dynamics of their own, with certain cuts having unexpected peaks or valleys depending on how different retailers compete through promotions.

The complexity of balancing revenue leads pricers to make two simplifications with dubious validity. We will discuss more comprehensive solutions in later sections.

- The first simplification is to price using a "cost of meat" methodology. In this scenario, the reported market price of a USDA reported cut is viewed as a proxy for the "transfer cost" of purchasing the cut on the open market. The price charged is calculated as a markup to the transfer cost. There are several flaws to this approach. The reported market refers to sales already made, and not to the true marginal cost of an external purchase. More importantly, the salvage nature of the industry argues that the meat cost is actually sunk, and the sunk cost is at the whole animal level not the cut level. In other words, there is no actual cost attributable to each piece, and cost can only be attributed to the animal as a whole. Consequently, "cost based" pricing of individual cuts is artificial. This approach actually represents market pricing where the market may arbitrarily favor one product over another, and it does not necessarily lead to profitability based on a reliable cost of goods.

- The second simplification is "break-even" pricing, which is commonly referred to with the misnomer of "primal optimization". Break-even pricing refers to the practice of selecting a standard cut or primal piece for a specific portion of the animal—say a boneless loin—and pricing all other cuts in reference to the standard. Other cuts have different fabrication costs, and different byproducts, which have market value. The "break-even" or "primal optimization" calculation computes the price for a cut, say a bone-in loin, that should be charged so that the net revenue generated by the bone-in variation is the same as the net revenue generated by the boneless variation. De-boning a piece of meat yields a smaller product plus *credit* items such as trim, bone, and fat. Because the relative weight of the credit items can be large, the break-even price per pound for the bone-in and boneless products can be substantially different. Break-even pricing is not optimal in any sense since it ignores constraints (i.e., limitations to processing or supply) and market demand for different variations. For example, standing rib roasts (bone-in) might sell at a premium at Christmas while during the rest of the year, the boneless variation sells at a premium.

The salvage nature of the industry makes hedging difficult because orders are taken for products but futures markets operate at the level of the live animal. Individual product prices vary significantly relative to the market price of the live animal. The correlation coefficient between product prices and animal prices can range from negative to greater than 0.9. Hedging of long-term product contracts against live animal futures may actually add to the contract risk. In general, finding the right hedge position to offset risk for specific transactions is very difficult.

14.2.3 Retail consolidations and the "WalMart effect"

The "WalMart effect" is a popular term for the aggregation of negotiation power in the hands of consolidated retailers. WalMart is popularly believed to be responsible for holding some inflationary forces in check by aggressively using its massive buying power to hold down wholesale prices. Of course, WalMart is not alone in holding a consolidated position in retail. While assessing WalMart's net effect would be difficult, most manufacturers would say that their margin has eroded due to increasingly stiff negotiation by large retailers, distributors, and foodservice providers.

In general, consumer prices have been much less volatile than commodity costs. Some of this volatility is naturally absorbed as vendors add value to commodity material moving through the supply chain. However, for commodity items with a shallow supply chain, such as protein, processors are required to act as shock absorbers between the extreme volatility of commodities and the relatively stable prices at retail. In general, the risk of absorbing this kind of shock is at odds with the narrow margins realized in commodity production. In the past, hedging has been seen as an adequate mechanism to lay off a reasonable part of the risk. However, in the new volatile market, processors generally don't do a good job of getting a price premium to compensate for the added risk.

14.3 Pricing practices

There is a strong distinction in pricing practices between the two branches of the industry: commodity and value-added. The primary function of the packing industry has been to harvest animals and prepare meat for retail butchering or to sell to industrial processors. Industrial processors in turn take the wholesale meat and incorporate it into value-added or branded product offerings. For example, raw hog bellies can be preserved, sliced, and packaged for sale as bacon under a consumer recognized brand. Branded sales have historically garnered more margin than commodity wholesale. In recent years, there has been a move by packers to conduct more post-slaughter processing of their commodity material as an attempt to capture market share and margin from branded processors.

Methods and practices of pricing in the industry have developed from years of trading in a volatile market. Executives face the challenge of building a better connection between strategic objectives and tactical pricing methods. Executives have a great deal of influence on pricing by setting strategic goals, incentives, and production parameters. These strategic goals in turn influence the pricer's tactical decisions. In this section, we review industry standard pricing methodologies and some recent trends in strategic practices.

14.3.1 Commodity pricing

The high volatility and low margin of the commodity packer business make pricing a visible and risky responsibility. As a rule, pricing is handled as a trading operation, centered in the hands of a few experienced pricers. On a daily basis, the central trading desk evaluates the market, examines inventory and availability of product, sets price "trade" targets, and distributes a price list to the sales organization. Sales representatives interact with the customers, but any significant deviation from the preset trading levels must typically be approved by the trading desk. Trading prices may change several times each day.

Commodity sales have a number of tactical attributes by which prices are set and delivery is scheduled. There are four common pricing approaches:

- *Negotiated contracts* are fixed price for a fixed quantity to be delivered in a fixed timeframe.

- *Bookings* are approximate volumes to be delivered over a longer time interval at a fixed price.

- *Formula pricing* is an agreement that all orders in a specified timeframe and within a target volume window will be priced using a formula based on a mutually agreed upon index. Examples of indices that may be used include USDA reported wholesale spot prices, other third-party reports, and composite internal sales metrics.

- *Ceiling prices* are a negotiated upper bound on prices for a specified time interval. If the market price goes above the ceiling, the manufacturer is expected to honor orders at the ceiling price. This pricing mechanism is, essentially, an option granted by the manufacturer at no cost. Ceiling prices are unpopular with manufacturers, but are a fact of life because of the negotiating power of consolidated retailers.

The order horizon is the time between placement of an order and delivery. For negotiated contracts at fixed price, this is a very important dimension in the negotiations. The spot market is usually considered to be the final two or three weeks before production. Longer-term contracts represent a risk due to cost volatility. However, manufacturers cannot simply wait until the spot market to sell their goods. If they enter the spot market with less than a majority of their production sold, they will be forced to drastically cut prices in order to clear the excess inventory. Waiting to sell in the spot market carries additional risk because prices go down as often as they go up. Even in the spot market, uncertainty remains because reported spot market prices may vary several percentage points from day to day.

Contracts longer than eight weeks may be hedged in order to reduce risk. In this case, futures contracts on live animals will be taken out dollar for dollar to the contract value. This strategy operates under the assumption that the ratio between the product price and the live animal is predictable, so that hedging locks in a gross margin ratio. Unfortunately, this hedging strategy is far from perfect, and may actually increase risk in some cases because the assumption of correlation between the product and the live animal does not hold.

In the middle ground, so-called mid-term contracts operate in the three- to eight-week range. This is typical of promotional activity. Customers and packers will negotiate a wholesale price, which typically represents a "sharing" of the promotion budget. In other words, both wholesaler and retailer will take a margin reduction to ensure sufficient volume is available for the promotion.

Mid-term or promotional pricing is an important strategic element of the sales process. For most packers, the volume of long-term contracts with leadtimes greater than eight weeks is a relatively small share of the total volume. The mid-term represents the first time to effectively set a "position", meaning to affect significantly the volume of meat that needs to be sold in the spot market. While pricing in the three- to eight-week range represents a risk due to fluctuating commodity costs, the risk of taking a contract is balanced by the risk of having to sell an excessive volume on the spot market. Packers differ widely in the extent to which they take promotional business in the mid-term, ranging from a strong working relationship with retailers to a flat refusal to engage in forward sales.

Within the commodity segment of the business, there is a component that can be considered "branded" in the sense that the product is often marketed as a brand. We distinguish this case from the branded pricing discussion below and refer to it by the common industry term of *program* sales. Program sales include premium product that passes certain stringent grading criteria (e.g., USDA Prime), or product that has source attributes associated with genetics (e.g., Angus cattle), or growing methods (e.g., organic or antibiotic free). Program sales are typically conducted at a premium price, and the products typically demonstrate less elasticity and less volatility. However, the pricing mechanisms are similar to other fresh commodity products, because the perishable nature is the same.

14.3.2 Branded and promotional pricing

Value-added or branded products, aside from program sales, typically involve additional processing, so the product is differentiated from fresh in a noticeable way including appearance and taste. The product brand is typically associated with the distinctive taste.

A manufacturer often owns the brand, and invests considerable money and effort in building the brand. A well-known example of this is the Hormel company, whose SPAM and ham products are common household brands. Manufacturers occasionally cooperate with a major retailer or foodservice operator to develop a joint brand. A recent example of this is the Cargill Rancher's Reserve brand of beef, which is available exclusively through Safeway. The two main channels for sales of branded products are retail and foodservice. Each has distinctive pricing methods.

Prices of branded processed protein products are less volatile than fresh commodity products, primarily because the products are not as perishable. The additional processing of fresh meat into a branded product often extends its shelf life. Examples of processing include chemical preservation, canning, injection, and cooking. In addition, processing often utilizes frozen meat because the appearance of the final product may depend more on the processing and less on the freshness of the input material.

When sold to retailers, branded products behave similarly to consumer-packaged goods (CPGs). The manufacturer will typically establish a Manufacturer Suggested Retail Price (MSRP). The retailer will then decide an everyday consumer shelf price which may be less than the MSRP. The retailer may choose to publish the MSRP as a part of a price benchmarking strategy. The wholesale list price will be set in proportion to the MSRP, allowing both retailer and wholesaler a margin. MSRPs can be stable, though usually not as stable as the MSRPs of truly non-perishable CPGs.

For so-called *High–Low* retailers (in contrast to Every Day Low Price, or EDLP, retailers such as WalMart), consumer promotion is a lever the retailer can use to drive additional sales of a product. For high visibility products, retailers may discount below the wholesale cost to create a "traffic driver" or "loss leader". Traditionally, when a promotion of a branded product is offered, the retailer expects the manufacturer to share some of the margin loss in exchange for the increased volume. The mechanisms for doing this include special negotiated buys of a fixed volume at a fixed price, a flexible volume booking at a fixed price, and the use of *trade funds*—transfers of money from the manufacturer to the retailer to be used to buy down the list price to a reduced net price. These three pricing methods are essentially in order of increasing risk to the manufacturer and decreasing risk to the retailer.

In foodservice, branded protein products are often marketed through distributors. Distributor sales are perhaps the most complicated of all. While the pricing practice of setting a list price and offering trade funds to incent the distributor is superficially similar to the retail promotion scenario, in fact it is quite different. There is an extensive set of vehicles for delivery of trade funds including:

- *tiered volume target discounts*—the distributor receives a per unit discount when a target sales volume is achieved;
- *off-invoice rebates*—a negotiated per unit discount is rebated to the distributor off invoice, allowing the distributor to effectively price on an inflated invoice value;
- *earned income*—an off-invoice rebate given to distributors based on sales volume;
- *bill backs*—accounting method distributors use to reverse invoice the manufacturer for distribution services;
- *direct operator rebates and promotions*—deals the manufacturer makes with the end-use customer, cutting the distributor out of the promotional transaction.

In addition, *pay-to-play* marketing programs are common, in which manufacturers pay marketing funds directly to the distributor without a firm volume commitment in exchange.

14.3.3 Margin management

Most packers manage their bottom line by examining the *cutout*, or marginal revenue from a carcass, relative to the marginal cost of the carcass. In principle, the packer increases production as long as the difference between these measures is sufficient to cover fixed costs and provide a reasonable margin. When the net margin is projected to be negative, production will be reduced to the minimum necessary to meet existing orders. However, because of the salvage nature of the industry, this minimum may still mean that substantial amounts of meat need to be sold on the spot market at a loss. Each species presents challenges to balancing sales from different parts of the animal. For example, demand for grilling meats from the mid-section of the animal in the summer may outweigh demand for the end-meats. Unbalanced demand in the form of forward sales may force the packer to make sub-optimal production decisions.

Packers traditionally manage their Sales and Operations Planning (S&OP) process in weekly meetings that include executives, pricers, procurement, and plant operations. While this process includes the major players, it is still not perfect. One major difficulty is structuring salesforce incentives. Aligning salesforce incentives with overall profit is difficult because of the salvage nature of selling pieces of a total carcass. Traditional methods of creating salesforce incentives based on volume by weight or revenue do not work because of the extreme difference between the volume and price of various cuts. Establishing a transactional margin is difficult because of the uncertainty in establishing a true cost of a piece out of a total carcass. It is even difficult to create incentives based on indexing sales performance to external market metrics because of inventory position. For example, a sales representative may do an excellent job of clearing excess inventory by selling it at a slight discount to market instead of at a deep discount.

In recognition of these complexities, packers have begun to augment their traditional S&OP processes. In particular, it is becoming common to create an executive position responsible for Margin Management. This executive is charged with organizing sales and procurement strategy and salesforce incentives to align efforts in the organization to maximize bottom line margin dollars. Technological tools have also begun to play a role, as we discuss below.

14.3.4 Trend to de-commoditization (value-added products and services)

In a low margin, high volume industry with volatile costs, it is inevitable that companies' bottom lines will exhibit volatility, including intervals when net income is negative. Industrial processors producing value-added consumer products have traditionally made higher margins with less profit volatility.

Given the high level of capital investment that packers have already made in harvesting and processing equipment, packers may consider value-added post-processing as an efficient follow-on investment. In particular, they consider value-added products that are relatively close to the wholesale commodity. Typical products in this class include bacon, sausage, deli meats, packaged barbeque, preserved or cured meats, such as ham, and "enhanced" meats, such as those that have been smoked or injected. By eliminating the processor from the supply chain and producing the product close to the slaughter facility, packers can achieve efficiencies and economies of scale. Moreover, packers already have sales channels marketing direct to retail and foodservice through their fresh business. The challenge for the packer pursuing a value-added strategy is the unfamiliar process of building a consumer brand to compete with established brands.

Another trend is to reduce retail butchering of wholesale meat products. Maintaining a butchering facility in a retail store is no longer cost effective in many cases. High food safety standards, and the difficulty of hiring and retaining experienced and capable butchers are two primary contributors to this cost. As a consequence, packers have begun to offer shelf-ready products, where each sales portion is shrink wrapped, branded, and priced, ready to place in the retail meat case.

The end game in case ready service is *Vendor Managed Inventory*, which is common in the soft drink industry. Grocery retailers traditionally see the meat case as a primary traffic driver, and they are reluctant to relinquish control of it. However, there has been a movement towards establishing preferred vendor relationships between retailers and packers. Along with the reduction in retail butchers, the depth of experience in procuring and marketing specialized meat products has declined on the retail side. In general, packers perceive an opportunity to market their expertise through a cooperative process of planning sales and promotional events. One key to this process is having an unbiased projection of market behavior on which to base pricing and demand decisions, as discussed in the following section.

International markets represent an interesting example of another direction in which the retailer/packer relationship might evolve. Packers in the United Kingdom have not undergone the same level of consolidation as in the USA. However, retail consolidation is greater. This consolidation has led some packers to effectively become captive subsidiaries to a single large retailer, generating case-ready material to the retailer's specification, rather than having the packer take the lead in providing strategic planning.

14.4 TECHNICAL SOLUTIONS

Commodity protein pricing is in some respects similar to the revenue management problem faced by airlines, hotels, and rental car agencies (see Talluri, Chapter 26). Several conditions are required for classical revenue management models to apply: advanced bookings, an ability to segment customers by willingness-to-pay, and perishable and limited capacity or inventory. As described earlier, a large fraction of protein sales take place two or more weeks in advance of delivery. Prices are often negotiated, often with well-known, long-standing customers. This aspect differs somewhat from the airline or hotel scenario in which anonymous customers are offered a pre-determined price, which they either accept or reject. However, the negotiated aspect of the transaction facilitates segmentation, for example by customer size or region.

The "sell it or smell it" mantra of protein pricers emphasizes the perishability condition. High fixed costs mandate strict upper and lower bounds on production capacity, although there is typically some flexibility within these bounds. Unlike the hotelier who cannot easily add or remove rooms, protein manufacturers can slightly accelerate or delay the slaughter of animals and may be able to purchase additional material on the spot market. Unlike transportation or hospitality, there is a great deal of flexibility with respect to products that are produced from the supply of animals. Greater flexibility on the supply side of the business means that protein pricing models must explicitly incorporate manufacturing capacities and constraints.

Another issue that separates commodity protein pricing from airline pricing is that prices are set relative to a transparent reported market price (e.g., USDA cattle price). This relationship can be implicit, or explicit as in the case of a formula price. Furthermore, the price sensitivity of demand is *relative to the market price*. When the market price is increasing, a product's price and demand can simultaneously increase because the premium of the product price over the market price has declined. An important prerequisite to a price optimization model is, therefore, an accurate price forecast and an appropriate elasticity model.

In the next section we discuss issues of demand forecasting, both quantity and price, and describe an approach to modeling the price elasticity of demand. We build on these topics in the section on price optimization.

14.4.1 Forecasting price and demand

Commodity protein prices are set relative to a market price. Hence, a great deal of attention is paid to predicting the market price. A typical approach involves a time-series forecast that depends on past values of the time series (i.e., the series is auto-regressive) as well as other exogenous variables and external functions such as seasonality and trends. Time-series data can be drawn from the USDA or other organizations that aggregate protein price information. Exogenous variables might include futures prices, prices of other proteins, national freezer stocks, exchange rates, or other market data. Market emotion, the degree to which today's price is influenced by recent prices, is an important aspect of the protein industry and is captured in the autoregressive portion of the model. Since manufacturers view market turns as opportunities to make money, forecast accuracy is measured in terms of the timing and magnitude of market swings.

Price forecasts for individual products are based on the market price. The appropriate choice of market price depends on the particular product; the market price may be for the whole animal (e.g., hogs, cattle) or for individual primals (e.g., bellies, loins). The "market price" definition can be ambiguous since protein pricers consider a variety of data sources, including anecdotal evidence of their competitors' prices. An analysis of the correlation between various USDA time series and the historical product price can provide some guidance, as can an examination of the manufacturer's hedging strategy.

The relationship between product and market prices can be captured by either a multiplicative or an additive model. In the multiplicative case historical product prices are divided by the market price, and one forecasts the ratio of the two prices. Price ratios tend to be less volatile than the product prices, although they too have seasonal patterns and dynamics that must be captured. In the additive case, the market price is included in the product forecast model as an exogenous variable. This has the advantage that if the forecaster makes a poor choice for the reference market (i.e., one with a weak correlation to the product's price), a small coefficient will be estimated for the market term.

If price is to be used to balance demand for products across the whole animal, forecasts of the seasonal pattern of demand are also important. The quantity demanded is a function of the net price quoted, current history, trends, seasonality, and the customer's response to price and other marketing drivers. Price sensitivity is also measured relative to market. In this view, price sensitivity is the change in demand relative to the demand forecast caused by a change in price relative to price forecast. This sensitivity measure captures market drivers—other than price—that cause demand to vary. For example, consider a product that is popular during the winter holidays. The manufacturer may capitalize on this seasonal pattern by charging higher prices, so at first glance we see an inverted price-volume relationship: volume is increasing with price. By measuring price sensitivity relative to the forecasts we see what will happen if the manufacturer prices above or below the market during this period. According to such a model, elasticity is proportional to the ratio of price to reference price. Elasticity can vary seasonally, driven by variations in the reference forecast.

Many factors must be included to generate and calibrate a practical model for predicting supply and demand. The mechanics of producing and estimating demand models is well understood, and this section has outlined factors that should be considered for models to capture the dynamics of the protein industry.

14.4.2 Price optimization

Commodity protein prices can be deconstructed into three parts: the market price, a targeted deviation from the market price, and a demand-driven variation due to local conditions such as the firm's inventory position. The targeted deviation exists because the USDA specification seldom matches the exact product to be priced. Each manufacturer has hundreds of product variations, while the USDA regularly reports several dozen. At one extreme the product may be priced relative to the entire animal, or there may be a closer match (e.g., "bone-in sirloin 2.5–3.5#"). Even in this case, however, a difference in fat content may dictate a deviation from the market reference price. The deviation may also vary seasonally, as consumer preferences for different cuts change over the course of the year. Finally, the manufacturer's supply position is an overriding factor that determines whether the product price will be above or below the deviated market price. Since the product is perishable, a long position (i.e., extra inventory) drives the price down, and a short position drives the price up.

The forecast approach described above is designed to estimate the deviated market price without the effects of local conditions. Forecasts are based on historical transaction prices that incorporate *past* inventory and production considerations. In contrast, *projected* inventory and production plans are not incorporated into the forecast. Given enough history to capture seasonal effects, the price and quantity forecasts reflect an average inventory position at each time of the year. For example, if loins have historically been in short supply during the third week in December, historical prices during the same week would be higher, and historical demand would be lower than during other weeks. Price and demand forecasts also reflect this pattern. If this year's inventory position is particularly short, then the deviated price forecast needs to be adjusted upward. Since the manufacturer controls inventory and production plans, this forecast adjustment for local conditions is made as part of the optimization model. Price and demand forecasts are, therefore, the starting point for price optimization. An optimization model should combine supply and capacity limitations with price sensitivities to suggest deviations from the forecasted prices.

Simple revenue management models with uncoupled products are common and relatively easy to solve compared to the approach needed for the protein industry. When products compete for the same supply and capacity resources, their optimal prices must be determined jointly, and the problem becomes more difficult. The remainder of this section describes the elements of a simple model that can be applied in the protein industry. Below is a simple illustrative mathematical formulation of the problem:

$$\max_{p_1, \ldots, p_N} \sum_{i=1}^{N} p_i \cdot Q_i\,(p_i, t)$$

$$\text{subject to}: \sum_{i=1}^{N} a_{ij} \cdot Q_i\,(p_i, t) \le C_j, j = 1, \ldots, M.$$

where p_i denotes the product price, $Q_i(p_i, t)$ the market-aware demand forecast, N the number of products, M the number of resources, C_j the available capacity of resource j, and a_{ij} the amount of resource j consumed in producing a unit of product I.

Current orders play a role in determining available capacity and supply since sufficient material should be reserved to cover existing commitments. Since raw material is supplied at the level of the whole animal or major primals, supply constraints need to be constructed from the bill of materials (BOM) for each product:

$$\sum_{k=1}^{N} b_{ik} \cdot Q_i(p_i, t) \le S_k, k = 1, \ldots, L,$$

where L is the number of supply items, b_{ik} is the amount of supply item k required to produce a unit of product i as determined by product i's BOM, and S_k is the availability of supply item k. If the BOM has more than one level, then the model must also determine how much of each interim item to produce, and also include material balance constraints for these items. Capacity constraints may also be imposed at each stage of the BOM.

An additional complexity occurs when the same product can be sold through multiple channels, for example to retailers, foodservice companies, or an export market. In this case a distinct price forecast p_{fc}, quantity forecast $Q_c(p_c, t)$ and price sensitivity should be estimated for each channel c, and a price p_c should be set. Below is the single product case with a capacity constraint:

$$\max_{p_1, \ldots, p_U} \sum_{c=1}^{U} p_c \cdot Q_c\,(p_c, t)$$

$$\text{subject to}: \sum_{c=1}^{U} a \cdot Q_c\,(p_c, t) \le C,$$

where U is the number of channels.

In protein manufacturing, material must usually be sold quickly, clearing supply by the end of each week. Pricing decisions are consequently time dependent but separable across time. In other words, it is a reasonable assumption to set prices in one time period independent of decisions in other time periods. Each time period, of course, has distinct market conditions that influence the decision. When inventory can be held from one period to the next, as in the case of some frozen or processed products, then pricing decisions must be made jointly across time. For example, a low price in one period will reduce the availability of material in the next, increasing its optimal price. Material balance constraints should reflect this dependence across time.

In our experience, a price optimization model that has been appropriately constructed to support protein pricing decisions will have most of the features described in this section: multiple products that share common manufacturing resources and raw material supply, multi-level BOMs, multiple customer channels, products that can be stored and whose prices must be coordinated across time, and cost models of varying degrees of complexity. The solution to such a model comprises not only a set of optimal prices for each product, channel, and time period, but also an optimal product mix, that is, the amount we would expect to sell at each of those prices. The mix information is important since it reflects tradeoffs made with respect to limited capacity or supply.

SignalDemand, Inc. is a private software company that has implemented forecasting and optimization models similar to those discussed here across a significant market share of the beef and pork industry. The revenue impact on the bottom line of specific customer models is not publicly available. However, the impact on margin management processes, sales efficiency, and corporate profitability are reported as uniformly significant and positive (SignalDemand 2008).

14.5 Conclusion

In this chapter we have discussed many of the challenges facing the protein industry. The entire industry, from farm to store shelf, has been impacted by the increase in volatility and the price increases in agricultural commodities. The causes of price volatility are both internal to the companies in the protein supply chain, as well as in external market forces. Regardless of the volatility sources, the protein industry as a whole operates on thin margins, as protein has historically been an economic commodity. Consequently, price volatility of both cost and sales sides has a severe impact on the corporate bottom line.

We have reviewed some approaches that protein companies, and wholesale meat packers in particular, have applied to pricing. Rapid change has led to significant variation in practices across companies in the industry, with no single company having a uniformly successful methodology. The most innovative companies are applying a concerted approach to margin management, including changes to pricing policies and practices, industry consolidation, corporate organization, and adoption of novel software for price and supply chain optimization. Taken together, these evolving practices represent a strong and robust approach to risk mitigation and profitability.

References

Agricultural Marketing Service of the United States Department of Agriculture (AMS) (2008a) http://www.ams.usda.gov/AMSv1.0/, accessed December 1, 2008.

—— (2008b) "National Daily Feeder and Stocker Cattle AM summary", USDA Livestock & Grain Market News, http://www.ams.usda.gov/mnreports/LSDDFSS.pdf, accessed December 1, 2008.

—— (2008c) "National Daily Cattle and Beef Summary", USDA Livestock & Grain Market News, http://www.ams.usda.gov/mnreports/LSDDCBS.pdf, accessed December 1, 2008.

—— (2008d) "LM_XB403", USDA Livestock & Grain Market News, http://www.ams.usda.gov/mnreports/lm_xb403.txt, accessed December 1, 2008.

—— (2008e) "National Daily Hog and Pork Summary", USDA Livestock & Grain Market News, http://www.ams.usda.gov/mnreports/LSDDHPS.pdf, accessed December 1, 2008.

—— (2008f) "NW_LS500", USDA Livestock & Grain Market News, http://www.ams.usda.gov/mnreports/nw_ls500.txt, accessed December 1, 2008.

American Meat Institute (AMI) (2009) *Meat and Poultry Facts 2009*. AMI. Compiled statistics summarizing data publicly available from USDA and US Department of Commerce, pp. 1, 9, 10, 30, 33, 34.

Animal and Plant Health Inspection Service of the United States Department of Agriculture (APHIS) (1997) "Part 1: Reference of 1997 Beef Cow-Calf Management Practices", http://nahms.aphis.usda.gov/beefcowcalf/beef97/bf97pt1.pdf.

Cargill (2008) http://www.cargill.com/about/history.htm, accessed December 1, 2008.

Dougherty, P. H. (1987) "ADVERTISING; Dressing Pork for Success", *The New York Times* January 15, 1987. http://www.nytimes.com/1987/01/15/business/advertising-dressing-pork-for-success.html, accessed June 9, 2010.

Hormel (2008) http://www.hormelfoods.com/, accessed December 1, 2008.

John Morrell (2008) http://www.johnmorrell.com/about.aspx, accessed December 1, 2008.

SignalDemand (2008) http://www.signaldemand.com/, accessed December 1, 2008.

Smithfield (2008) http://www.smithfield.com/about/index.php, accessed December 1, 2008.

Tyson (2008) http://www.tyson.com/Corporate/AboutTyson/, accessed December 1, 2008.

York Butchers Gild (YBG) (2010) "History of the Butchers Gild", http://www.yorkbutchers-gild.com/pages/history.html, accessed June 9, 2010. There are many cultural references to butchering and droving as professions extending back to biblical times. Butchering as a guild profession in York is documented back to at least 1272.

CHAPTER 15

··

WINE PRICING IN THE UNITED STATES

··

WARREN BIDMEAD

15.1 OVERVIEW

Developing a pricing strategy for a wine brand or product is a complex process. Similar to making a bottle of wine, developing a pricing strategy is as much of an art as it is a science. It is less logical and quantitative, and more intuitive and qualitative than pricing strategies for many other agricultural-based consumer products. This is due to many variables including production techniques, packaging, location of the vineyards, and scarcity of grapes from many locations, consumer behavior, channel dynamics, and sales and marketing costs. Retail prices can range from under $1.00 per 750ml bottle to upwards of $1,000 per bottle. Few, if any, other agricultural products show this range of prices.

Wine is a naturally occurring byproduct of grapes. The juice of crushed grapes in combination with yeast and oxygen ferments and creates wine. All that is needed is a vessel to capture the juice. The consumption of wine can be traced to back to the Neolithic period, 7000 BC. In ancient Egypt, winemaking scenes appeared on tomb walls as part of a canonical set of provisions for the afterlife. In Mesopotamia wine was imported in jugs into ancient Sumer from the Zagros Mountains. The earliest civilizations managed many of the same considerations that are present in the industry today such as production, packaging, location of the vineyards, and consumer behavior, and it is likely that pricing was as variable then as it is now.

The production costs of grapes, barrels, and packaging combined with *value elements* help create an identity from which pricing is derived. Value elements include the location of the vineyards, the skill and reputation of the winemaker and producer, the quality of the packaging, critical acclaim, and the scarcity of the vintage and varietal. These elements, when combined with sales and marketing and general overhead, help form the basis for a price strategy for a brand. Different combinations of these variables lead to significant price variances from producer to producer as well as among different wines from the same producer.

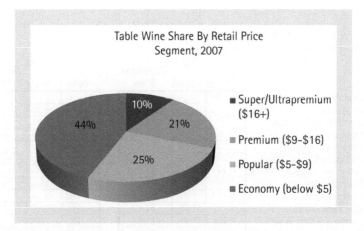

FIGURE 15.1 Table wine share by retail price segment, 2007

Source: Schmidt (2008)

Retail wine sales in the USA were $9.5 billion dollars in 2007 (Schmidt 2008: 8). Sales are growing at a rate of 4 percent annually.[1] Domestic wines make up 70.1 percent of wine consumed in the United States while imports make up 29.9 percent (Schmidt 2008: 23). The wine category can be segmented into four major pricing breaks and descriptions. *Economy* wines are those priced below $5 per 750 ml bottle, *popular* priced wines are priced from $5 to $9, *premium* priced from $9 to $16 and *ultra premium*, priced above $16. Volume by price break is shown in Figure 15.1. Growth is occurring across popular, premium, and ultra premium segments. Growth in the premium and ultra premium segments is good news for producers since margins are higher in these segments than in the economy segment. In the USA there are more than 3,000 wineries with the greatest concentration found in the west, especially California, Oregon, and Washington. Producers range in size from a few hundreds of cases produced annually to production of over 10 million cases annually (Figure 15.2).

15.2 Consumption Trends

Consumption of wine in the United States is growing at rates faster than other alcoholic beverages due to a number of factors. One of these is the purported health benefits of moderate consumption combined with an aging population that is aware of these benefits. Aggregate consumption in the USA was 294 million gallons in 2007, up from 234 million gallons in 2002, a 27% increase.[2] Gallons per adult in the USA is up from 2.8 gallons per adult consumed annually in 2002 to 3.0 in 2007 and is forecasted to increase to 3.3 gallons per adult in 2012.[3] While total US consumption ranks highly against other parts of the

---

[1] AC Nielsen Nitro   [2] Schmidt (2008: 11).   [3] Schmidt (2008: 19).

Leading Wine Suppliers, 2007
(Thousands of 9-Liter Cases and Millions of Dollars)

| | Volume | | | | Sales | | |
Supplier	Cases	Share	Cumulative Share		Dollars	Share	Cumulative Share
Constellation Wines	53,088	18.2%	18.2%		$1,790	18.8%	18.8%
E & J Gallo Winery	66,952	22.9%	41.1%		1,545	16.3%	35.1%
Foster's Wine Estates Americas	19,350	6.6%	47.7%		1,115	11.7%	46.8%
The Wine Group	36,460	12.5%	60.2%		1,115	11.7%	58.6%
Kendall-Jackson Wine Estates	5,107	1.7%	62.0%		385	4.1%	62.6%
W.J. Deutsch & Sons	9,740	3.3%	65.3%		370	3.9%	66.5%
Brown-Forman Beverages Worldwide	5,343	1.8%	67.1%		370	3.9%	70.4%
Trinchero Family Estates	10,163	3.5%	70.6%		360	3.8%	74.2%
Palm Bay International	5,450	1.9%	72.5%		290	3.1%	77.3%
Ste. Michelle Wine Estates	4,777	1.6%	74.1%		290	3.1%	80.3%
Diageo Chateau & Estate Wines	5,175	1.8%	75.9%		280	2.9%	83.3%
Banfi Vintners	6,735	2.3%	78.2%		240	2.5%	85.8%
Bronco Wine Co.	9,855	3.4%	81.5%		255	2.7%	88.5%
Moet Hennessy USA	1,565	0.5%	82.1%		220	2.3%	90.8%
Shaw-Ross International Importers	2,764	0.9%	83.0%		155	1.6%	92.4%
Total Leading Suppliers	242,524	83.0%	83.0%		$8,780	92.4%	92.4%
Others	49,566	17.0%	100.0%		$720	7.6%	100.0%
Total U.S.	292,090	100.0%			$9,500	100.0%	

Leading Wine Producers   Adams Handbook 2008

FIGURE 15.2 Leading wine suppliers, 2007 (thousands of 9-liter cases and millions of dollars)

world, per person consumption remains relatively low in comparison to other nations such as France at 14.6 gallons per person or Italy at 12.7 gallons per person. This creates a favorable environment for category growth, and the US market is viewed as a profitable growth opportunity market by many global producers. As a result price competition within the category is fierce, and the business of pricing a bottle of wine effectively is critical to deliver a profit.

15.3 DISTRIBUTION AND LEGAL CONSTRAINTS

For discussion purposes, distribution of wine can be classified in three major segments with each having their own pricing strategy and tactics—on premise, off premise and direct to consumer. On-premise sales are those in locations where wine is consumed on the premise of the retailer, such as a restaurant, bar, or special event venue. Off premise sales are retail sales where the wine is consumed away from the place of purchase, such as wine shops, grocery stores, liquor stores, and wholesale clubs such as Costco or Sam's Club. Also included in this description are on-line sales by a retail operator. Direct to consumer sales are those by a winery directly to a consumer either through a wine club or winery tasting room.

The sale of alcoholic beverages is tightly regulated and laws vary from state to state. The 21st Amendment to the Constitution repealed the 18th Amendment (Prohibition) and granted states the authority to regulate alcohol within their borders. The states adopted a three-tier system of beverage alcohol distribution, consisting of separate suppliers/manufacturers, wholesalers, retailers. This system was developed primarily to prevent perceived market abuse in which a producer could induce a retailer to carry a particular product to the exclusion of others. Other stated justifications for the three-tier system include facilitating the collection of taxes, promoting temperance, and making sure that only those who can purchase alcohol do so (licensed distributors selling to licensed retailers, no sales to minors, no sales in dry counties, no sales to intoxicated persons, no sales at times or days when they are not otherwise permitted, etc.). State laws (and federal laws to an extent) govern the relationships between the tiers. However, not all sales must pass through the three-tier system. Most notably, the right of producers to sell directly to consumers was upheld by the US Supreme Court in *Granholm vs. Heald* in 2005. However, state laws govern whether suppliers may *ship* wine direct to consumers, the requirements for shipping, and whether there are limits on the volume of wine that may be shipped.

Direct to Consumer sales are sales made directly by a winery to consumers. Typically these sales are made at the winery and are for personal consumption and not for resale. Many wineries have created wine clubs which allow purchasers to receive product on a subscription or ad hoc basis. Wine clubs can be very profitable since they allow the winery to avoid many distribution costs, and the wine club can be marketed cheaply through the Internet or winery website.

15.4 PRICING STRATEGY—WHOLESALE PRICING

For the purpose of this discussion, we will focus on wines with a retail price point between $5 and $16 per 750 ml bottle, the popular and premium price segments of the category, where the bulk of the volume in the USA is sold. This excludes economy wines where many of the pricing decisions are made strictly to provide acceptable margins for producer, distributor, and retailer.

The price of raw materials to produce a bottle of wine is a factor in developing a wholesale price. Grape costs vary from $200 per ton to more than $6,000 per ton. A commonly used industry rule of thumb is that grape cost per ton multiplied by 1 percent should roughly equate to the per bottle selling price, so the $200 per ton grapes should translate into a $2 bottle while $6,000 per ton grapes should translate into a $60 bottle.

Value is created through many elements beyond the production costs. Consumer perception, the location of the vineyards, the skill and reputation of the winemaker and producer, the quality of the packaging elements, critical acclaim, and the scarcity of the vintage and varietal are all elements that add value, and each plays a role in developing a price strategy. Packaging also supports pricing and quality cues, a bottle and label used for a $20 retail bottle will likely be of much higher quality than a $6 bottle.

Research has determined that price plays a role in the perception of value for the wine consumer. All things being equal, a consumer will derive greater enjoyment from a glass of wine if she believes that it is more expensive. A study was conducted where consumers were given samples of the same wine with the only variable being their knowledge of the retail price (Plassman et al. 2008). Consistently, the drinkers exhibited greater enjoyment and preferred the wines that they were told were more expensive even though it was the same wine. Thus, the perception of quality is supported by the price charged by the producer and the price is a key element within the brand's positioning for the target consumer.

Geography also plays a role in developing a pricing strategy. Winegrowing regions are classified by governmental agencies in an effort to assist buyers in understanding the taste and quality of the wine from that region. In France, wines are named after the region in which they are produced; a Burgundy can only be from the Burgundy region. This is known as the *Appellation Controllée* or AOC of the wine. In the United States, an American Viticultural Area (AVA) designation is used to define the growing region. Wine produced from appellations of higher quality and greater demand will command a premium in the marketplace. For instance, Cabernet Sauvignon grown in Napa Valley will command a premium relative to other appellations in California. This is due to the relative scarcity of grapes grown in this area, as well as a consumer perception of higher quality. Within an appellation such as Napa Valley, AVA designated districts such as Stag's Leap District and vineyards such as Usibelli Vineyards will command an even greater premium, again due to scarcity and perception of quality.

Critical acclaim influences price. A producer or winemaker that garners strong critical acclaim can usually command a premium in the marketplace (Mitham 2008). Consistent high scores from well-recognized critics, such as Robert Parker, or publications, such as *Wine Spectator*, generally allow a winery to price at a premium to competitive producers who have not earned similar acclaim. An example of this was the price premium commanded by Robert Mondavi Reserve Cabernet Sauvignon in the 1980s and 1990s. This wine consistently scored highly with critics and was able to command a premium compared to other Napa Valley Cabernet producers.

Red wines are typically more expensive to produce than white wines due to the additional barrel aging required to produce red wines, this adds carrying costs and costs of barrels and, as a result of the higher cost, most red wines are higher priced than white wines.

Table 15.1 compares the cost differences for a popular priced California appellated Chardonnay (Wine A) to a vineyard designated, award winning, ultra premium Chardonnay (Wine B) and compares the production costs and gross margin for each item.

As illustrated in Table 15.1, the more expensive wine B has significantly higher product and production costs but also has a much higher gross profit margin. The higher quality of the packaging materials of glass, label, closure, and carton supports the premium price charged for the $40 bottle and provides important quality cues for the ultra premium positioning.

Competitive set identification assists in developing a price identity for a wine brand. The identification and benchmarking of wines produced in a similar region for similar consumer targets is commonplace in the industry. Benchmarking takes places from both a sensory and business application, meaning taste plays a critical role in guiding a pricing plan. This analysis offers a competitive analysis and understanding of relative value within acceptable ranges. In practical terms, if one is developing a price strategy for a new brand of wine produced from Chardonnay vineyards in Sonoma County, one would identify all of

Table 15.1 Comparison of cost differences ($) for popular and ultra premium wines

	Wine	Glass	Label	Closure	Carton	Labor/ overhead	Total cost	Target wholesale price	Gross margin(%)
Wine A - $6 retail target	1.00	0.40	0.10	0.10	0.40	0.37	2.37	4	40.8
Wine B - $40 retail target	6.65	0.60	0.26	0.71	1.05	0.42	9.69	28	65.4

the competing production from the same and competing geographies and assess the competitors against the new brand being developed. A pricing matrix is typically created to identify retail price for the competitive items. This allows the producer to understand the range of acceptable prices, from which the producer can fine tune the price by accounting for production variables such as barrel aging time, vineyards, the primary sales channel, and the consumer target audience.

For wines sold in the popular and premium segments, typically red and white wines are priced at parity in an effort to encourage mass merchandising. Production cost differences are averaged to create a wholesale cost across varietals and color types within a brand. This allows the producer to offer multiple varietals of wine at a consistent price point and allows retailers to mass merchandise the brand at a common price point.

For premium and ultra premium wines, varietals within the same brand are typically priced differently due to two reasons. First, this price segment represents the premium level in the category and it is commonplace in this segment that a producer has some level of specialization. A producer that specializes in Pinot Noir may be able to command a premium due to the reputation of its best known varietal over a Pinot Gris produced by the same winery. The second reason is to exploit the production cost differential between red and white wines.

No discussion of wine pricing would be complete without mentioning the phenomenon of pricing for rare or cult wines. The pricing strategy for these brands is simple – price as high as the market will bear, and continually advance price with every vintage. In many instances the prices charged for these cult wines generate as much PR as the wines themselves and the purchasers are buying status goods for a collection or for resale through an auction house rather than a wine for consumption. Many of these sales are initially through the winery based on customer lists. The customer list forms the basis for product allocation and, due to the scarcity of these types of wines, consumers will buy to maintain their spot on the list. Needless to say, these wines are very profitable for the producer, with profits well in excess of $1,000 per case. One of the most famous examples of this phenomenon is Screaming Eagle, a highly acclaimed Napa Valley Cabernet Sauvignon. This wine is sold only through the winery's mailing list and to a limited number of retail locations. Those lucky enough to be on the mailing list can usually sell their wine at two or three times the winery's release price (Siles 2007). The place on the mailing list also has value; a spot on the Screaming Eagle list was priced on eBay at $2,650 although the seller's reserve was not met (Siler 2007).

15.5 Pricing tactics—off premise

The brand image and competitive set are key factors in developing and maintaining a retail price. While it is illegal for a producer to set the retail price, the pricing guideline developed by the producer usually is the price that will be found in the various off premise channels in the marketplace.

Retail pricing includes distributor and retailer margin requirements and state and local taxes. Distributor margins are set based on cost to serve plus the distributor profit requirements. These costs are not necessarily fixed and can vary from brand to brand based on item velocity. Much of this is negotiated between the distributor and producer, and brands of higher velocity may pay lower distribution-related expenses than lower velocity items.

Discounts and promotional pricing are common for most wine brands. More than 60 percent of the category volume is sold on some level of promotional discount, and promotional discounts take on a myriad of forms. The most common type of discount is commonly known as a *post off*. This stands for a posted or published off invoice discount, which is a flat amount offered off the invoice price of the item. Post offs are considered published deals, meaning that they are referenced in the distributors current pricing book. Typically these post offs are time bound.

Volume discounts can take the form of a negotiated amount based on a pre-set purchase requirement. This type of discount can be applied to the specific brand, a family of brands by the producer, or a one-time buy opportunity offered by the distributor. Volume discounts are fairly common where legal, allowing the producer to reflect cost savings associated with shipping larger amounts of product to a single customer.

The application of these discounts can result in significant pricing variances from retailer to retailer. A small liquor store may not have the same retail price on a bottle as a large chain operator. In an effort to keep some level of pricing consistency in the marketplace a producer or distributor may use additional discounts for smaller operators in an effort to build distribution and sales to all customers.

Other types of price promotion are *scan allowances* and *coupon discounts*. Scan allowances are a form of discount paid to retailers based on consumer pick-up rather than wholesale purchases. This type of discount is paid on the number of bottles scanned through the retailer's register and are based on a per bottle amount for a designated time period. Coupons are price promotion tactics used to provide rebates for purchases. Both of these types of tactics are used where legal for short-term volume increases.

15.6 Pricing tactics—on premise

The on-premise environment is considered critical to building a favorable brand image and building brand loyalty which can result in repeat sales. While only 22.7 percent of the category volume is sold on premise, 51.1 percent of the dollars sold is generated from the

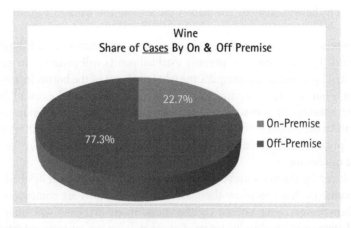

FIGURE 15.3 Wine sales: share of cases by on and off premise

Source: Schmidt (2008)

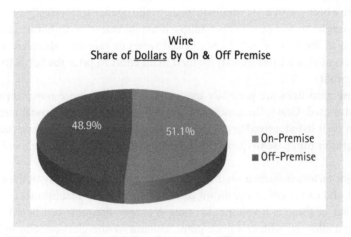

FIGURE 15.4 Wine sales: share of dollars by on and off premise

Source: Schmidt (2008)

on-premise sales (Figures 15.3 and 15.4). This means that much of the price identity for a brand can be formed in the on premise arena.

The on-premise environment represents a valuable trial venue for consumers to try new wines, and developing a pricing strategy that maximizes this opportunity is critical to long-term brand growth. Wine purchased by the glass is typically the least expensive method to try a wine. Therefore it drives needed trial of a brand. Additionally having a wine featured on the wine list of a leading restaurant helps a winery create a favorable image of their brand.

Pricing strategy in the on-premise environment is built on how the wine will be sold to the consumer, by the bottle or by the glass. It is estimated that about 80 percent of the volume sold on premise is sold by the glass; therefore gaining a by-the-glass feature (that is, being offered on the wine list "by the glass") can expose the wine to a greater number of drinkers.

The mechanics of setting a by-the-glass price for an on-premise establishment is fairly straightforward. Typically most on premise establishments will price by the glass using a formula of retail by-the-glass price equals the wholesale cost of the bottle. In a 750ml bottle, there are four 6-ounce pours; therefore the establishment will make the cost of the bottle on the first pour. Subsequent pours will help offset overhead costs and provide profit for the establishment. In practice, a bottle of wine with a wholesale price of $11 will translate into a by-the-glass price of $11. Given that there are four pours in the bottle, the bottle will generate $44 of revenue.

Wines featured by the glass move at significantly higher rates than by-the-bottle offerings, and because of this, special by-the-glass volume discounts are common where legal. Given the benefits of being offered by the glass, many wineries will offer additional promotional discounts specifically targeted to encourage on-premise establishments to offer their wines by the glass.

On-premise by-the-bottle pricing is typically based on a multiple of wholesale cost. Most restaurants charge three times to four times wholesale cost for wines offered on their wine list. Therefore a bottle with a $15 wholesale price to the retailer will typically be priced from $45 (3× wholesale) to $60 (4×). This multiple often decreases as the bottle wholesale cost increases, and in the case of very highly priced wines or rare and allocated wines, a 2× multiple or a cost plus a fixed fee may be used in an effort to price the bottle to maximize volume and profit.

While these guidelines are generally used in the industry, more novel approaches to pricing are also used. One is the concept of cost-plus pricing, where a restaurant will offer all bottles on their list at a fixed price above wholesale cost. This type of pricing typically results in a greater purchase frequency and allows the restaurant to move more expensive wines.

Three major factors influence what the consumer ultimately will pay in the on premise environment and can result in significant price variances from establishment to establishment. The first of these is a volume discount. Volume discounts can be offered by the producer in an effort to achieve a price point, either a by-the-glass price or by-the-bottle price. The discount is defined by volume purchased over a discrete time period. Volume discounts can also be family-based; meaning that total purchases made from a producer's entire portfolio or a subset of the portfolio earn a special promotional price. The second is a short-term promotional discount offered by either a producer or a distributor. Typically these short-term promotional discounts are offered for a limited time period in an effort to increase sales and are often coupled with promotional sales incentives provided by producers offered to distributor sales personnel. The third factor that can cause price variance is distributor markup. An example of the impact of discounting on pricing is illustrated in Table 15.2.

In the example in Table 15.2 customer A purchases the wine during a post off period with a 2-case discount applied, where customer B is buying 20 cases and featuring by-the-glass. Customer B's net bottle cost is 18 percent cheaper than customer A and in this example the saving is passed on in a by-the-glass special as well as a lower wine list price. Another opportunity for retailer B would be to maintain the $6 by-the-glass price and then price by the bottle at a higher price point in an effort to realize additional profit.

Table 15.2 The impact of discounting on pricing ($)

	Customer A		Customer B	
	Case	Bottle	Case	Bottle
Distributor list price	96.00	8.00	96.00	8.00
Discounts		—		—
Post off	6.00	0.50	6.00	0.50
Volume				
2-case buy	3.00	0.25		
20-case buy			12.00	1.00
BTG discount			6.00	0.50
Net	87.00	7.25	72.00	6.00
Wine list price at 3 × bottle		21.75		18.00
By the glass		Not offered		6.00

The growth of large national chain accounts has added additional complexity to pricing management. An account may want to feature a glass or bottle at a consistent price in outlets across multiple states. The impact of varying distributor margins and tax differential from state to state creates complexity for both the operator and producer. If legal, the price differential can be mitigated by additional marketing funding for the operator.

15.7 INCENTIVES

In addition to the post off and volume incentives to retailers, distributor incentives are offered to help push product into the on and off premise environments. These incentives can be short-term incentives based on a rate per case paid to distributor salespeople to place and sell additional cases. Incentives also can take the form of longer-term incentives paid to the distributor to achieve annual or semi-annual volume or sales goals. In rare instances, these incentives can find their way into the price charged to a retailer as a distributor may be inclined to add a discount in an effort to achieve a performance-based incentive offered by the producer.

15.8 PRICING MANAGEMENT

The myriad of discounts and promotions offered in the category require some level of technology to manage and account for the variances and ensure that distributors and customers receive the correct price based on the discounts earned. The management of this is done through the development of pricing structures for each market. Pricing structures capture all of the elements needed to determine a wholesale and retail price. This includes

FOB price, transportation charges, distributor margin, discounts and allowances to the distributor, retailer discounts and allowances, volume discounts, timing of discounts, taxes and retailer selling prices and margins. These structures are used to ensure that all deals are recorded and stated in the firm's enterprise software for billing and invoicing.

Category and competitive pricing is tracked on a regular basis to ensure that the pricing strategy is effective and competitive for the marketplace. This tracking can be through syndicated databases such as IRI or AC Nielsen or through observation by local distributors. Industry publications also provide insight into competitive pricing. On-line services such as Snooth.com and winesearcher.com also help track wine pricing.

15.9 SUMMARY

The competitive landscape of marketing wine requires effective pricing strategies. The growth of the marketplace combined with the myriad of competitive choices for the consumer force the wine marketer to develop and manage strategies far more aggressively in an effort to remain competitive. The use of a practical, customer-based approach supported by an in-depth understanding of the competitive set combines the art and science necessary to develop pricing strategies for the wine category.

Significant growth is forecasted for the wine category due to emerging markets in Asia as well as continued growth in the United States. The increased demand will be across all pricing segments and channels resulting in greater profit opportunities within the category. Marketers will need to make decisions based on channel profitability to maximize profits as supply is not forecasted to increase as much as demand in the short run. Therefore understanding the profit implications and how to effectively price and when to price promote will benefit the producer through this period.

REFERENCES

Mitham, Peter (2008) "Economists Question the Real Value of Wine", *Wines and Vines* August 19.

Plassman, H., O'Doherty, J., Shiv, B., and Rangel, A. (2008) "Marketing Actions can Modulate Neural Representations of Experienced Pleasantness", *Proceedings of the National Academy of Science* 105/3, January 22.

Schmidt, E. (ed.) (2008) *Adams Wine Handbook 2008*. Norwalk: The Beverage Information Group.

Siler, J. (2007) "Napa Valley Secret: A Fruitless Search For Rare Cabernet", *Wall Street Journal* April 26.

CHAPTER 16

PRICING AND SALES PRACTICES AT THE GRAND BAZAAR OF İSTANBUL

YOSUN DENIZERI

16.1 INTRODUCTION

The Grand Bazaar[1] of İstanbul, "Kapalıçarşı (kah-pah-luh chahr-shuh)" in Turkish, is probably the oldest and the largest covered market in the world. According to some sources, the location was used for trading as far back as the fifth century during the Byzantine Empire.[2] The current structure was built in the fifteenth century following the conquest of İstanbul[3] by the Ottoman Empire.[4] As is the case for the grand bazaars of Cairo, Tehran, and Tabriz, the Grand Bazaar of İstanbul has been a social, religious, and financial center as well as the main location for the trade of goods since it was established. It now spreads across 64 covered streets and consists of approximately 3,000 shops. The Bazaar has been the center of gold and foreign currency trade for centuries and has also acted as an auction house and clearing mechanism very similar to those in the modern trading floors.

---

[1] Bazaar is a permanent merchandizing area, marketplace, or street of shops where goods and services are exchanged or sold. Originating from ancient Islamic civilizations, the bazaar is the precursor for the modern day supermarket, flea-market, and shopping mall, and has had a great influence on the economic development and centralization in modern cities around the world.

[2] The Byzantine Empire or Eastern Roman Empire was the Roman Empire during the Middle Ages, centered on the capital of Constantinople, and ruled by emperors in direct succession to the ancient Roman emperors.

[3] İstanbul, called Constantinople at the time, was the imperial capital of the Byzantine/Eastern Roman Empire 395–1453 AD.

[4] The Ottoman Empire was a Turkish Empire that lasted from 1299 to 1922. At the height of its power (16th–17th century), it spanned three continents, controlling much of south-eastern Europe, western Asia and north Africa. The empire was at the center of interactions between the Eastern and Western worlds for six centuries.

FIGURE 16.1 Handmade ceramics sold at the Grand Bazaar (Photograph by Yosun Denizeri, 2008)

Today, the Grand Bazaar still continues to function as an independent foreign exchange and gold market and the daily exchange rates in the Bazaar are listed along with the regulated markets. Many merchants of the Bazaar are also wholesalers who sell to retailers across the country as well as overseas. It is still the go-to destination for gold, silver, and precious stones trade, and has daily visitor traffic of 250,000–400,000. Therefore, the business volume is not limited to what is seen in the small 50 sq feet stores. The Grand Bazaar is the most desirable retail location for jewelry, leather apparel and accessories, carpets, hand made textiles, and antiques. Therefore, the Grand Bazaar hosts some of the most expensive commercial real estate in İstanbul. At the time this article was written, the sales price of a small shop ranged between $2,300/sq. foot to $15,000/sq. foot. ($25,000/sq. meter to $160,000/sq. meter), with a typical 100 sq. feet (9.3 square meter) shop costing around $660,000.[5] Factors such as traffic and proximity to the main entrance gates play a

---

[5] Real estate prices based on May–June 2010 listings on real estate websites in Turkey.

role in the large range of prices; locations near the entrance gates cost significantly more than others located in smaller streets with less foot traffic.

As diverse as the layout of the Bazaar and the types of trade taking place are the pricing practices employed by different trades. As mentioned earlier, the Bazaar houses a variety of wholesale (business-to-business (B-to-B)), retail (business-to-consumer (B-to-C)), and auction transactions (B-to-B and B-to-C). In this chapter, we will focus on business to consumer (B-to-C) sales transactions, where the price is determined through negotiation between the individual buyer and the seller and is not determined by market rates (such as for gold jewelry) and wholesale contracts. The sales processes take from minutes to hours and often involve much dialogue between the merchant and the customer. During this process, the merchant gathers information about the customer and caters the selection of merchandise he shows to the customer's stylistic preferences and budget constraints. Price tags are not common outside commoditized products such as small ceramic bowls and souvenirs. The prices offered for the unique handmade products such as old carpets and decorative ceramics (see Figure 16.1) are often tailored to customers' willingness-to-pay and the likelihood of repeat business and referrals. Therefore, the local customers, due to their likelihood for referrals and repeat business are often offered discounts that are not readily available to tourists, thus leading to a perceived two-tier pricing system, "local versus tourist prices".

While Grand Bazaar tactics can come across as the legacy of the old world sales traditions and can be perceived as confusing at times, they are indeed in line with some of the most sophisticated sales and pricing techniques that are being adopted by retailers today. Bazaar merchants excel at the art and science of offering the right product to the right customer at the right price. They do that without help from a customer database, data-mining technology, or price optimization software.

In this chapter, we explore how the current selling and pricing tactics in the Bazaar have evolved throughout the centuries and highlight the aspects of the sales process that can be leveraged in the target pricing methodologies for retailers.

16.2 HISTORY OF THE GRAND BAZAAR

The Grand Bazaar was founded by the Sultan Mehmet the Conqueror in 1461, eight years after he conquered Constantinople and made it the imperial city of the Ottoman Empire. In those days, it was customary to set-up markets or other means of generating funds to sustain religious and public institutions such as mosques, hospitals, and schools. The Grand Bazaar was created as a source of income for the nearby church of Haghia Sophia[6] which was converted into a mosque. It was initially made up of two enclosed sections called

---

[6] Haghia Sophia, constructed 532–537 AD, is a former patriarchal basilica, later a mosque, now a museum. Famous in particular for its massive dome, it is considered the epitome of Byzantine architecture and was the largest cathedral in the world for nearly a thousand years and also the patriarchal church of the Patriarch of Constantinople and the religious focal point of the Eastern Orthodox Church.

Bedesten.[7] The *Inner Bedesten* was the place where the most expensive goods including jewelry, armor, and crystals were kept; they were protected from fire and burglary by the massive walls and the underground cells with iron gates. *Inner Bedesten* was also a safekeeping institution for the valuables of the rich and functioned as a bank. The Inner Bedestern Tradesmen were the wealthiest among the Bazaar merchants and were in the business of lending money to artisans and merchants, as well as others outside the Bazaar who would leave their valuables or title deeds as security. The Inner Bedesten was used regularly as an auction house. The second section was called *Sandal Bedesteni*,[8] and was more eclectic in terms of the goods sold. The *Sandal Bedesteni* was mostly known for textile production and trading and until the mid-nineteenth century it served as the center of the textile trade of the Ottoman Empire.

Over the centuries, the Grand Bazaar culture changed with the political, cultural, and economic changes in the country. During the rise of the Ottoman Empire (sixteenth–seventeenth centuries), the Bazaar was filled with exotic goods that came from all the different Ottoman territories in Africa, Arabia, and eastern Europe as well as those that came all the way from China and India through the Silk Road. The variety and the quality of these handmade goods such as Arabic spears, Persian daggers, Bahrain pearls, Ankara blankets, and Afghan shawls attracted customers from all over the empire territories as well as travelers from Europe. At that time, the Bazaar was not just a retail hub, but also a center for textile, metal, and jewelry production. All tradesmen, artisans, and merchants belonged to the guild system, which regulated all aspects of the production and sales process.

During the decline of the Ottoman Empire in the nineteenth century, the Grand Bazaar declined and was on the verge of being forgotten because it did not have the appeal required to compete with the modern-day department stores carrying European imports. During the post-World War II years of economic growth, once again the Grand Bazaar emerged as the destination for antiques, gold and diamond jewelry, and souvenirs. For our discussion, we will refer to the era corresponding to the rise of the Ottoman Empire as the *Classical Period* (fifteenth–mid-eighteenth century). During the Classical Period, the Bazaar was the show-room where East met West and was frequented by travelers from Europe and locals alike. The second period of interest is the last two centuries (mid-nineteenth century to the present day), which will be referred to as the *Modern Period*.

16.3 CLASSICAL PERIOD OF THE GRAND BAZAAR

During the Classical Period, the interior organization of the Bazaar was quite different than it is today. There were no shops with doors and windows. The Bazaar was made up of hundreds of open stalls; each about 6–8 feet in length and about 4 feet in depth, separated

---

[7] Bedesten is a domed masonry structure built for storage and safekeeping and is a common structure used in markets in the Middle East.

[8] Sandal is a type of fabric that is woven with silk and cotton yarns, which was probably the most popular type of textile sold there.

by curtains or wooden lattice partitions. There was a simple wooden sofa, a *divan*,[9] in front of each stall, where merchants spent most of their time. The customer sat on the divan next to the tradesmen and examined the goods while engaging in casual conversation, drinking coffee, or smoking the hookah. Celik Gulersoy describes the interior of the stalls as follows: "Some of the goods for sale were displayed in glass cases behind and around the *divan*, however, most of them were kept in drawers and were taken out one by one in a dazzling manner for those who were interested, appreciative and had enough gold coins" (Gulersoy 1980: 18).

In the Ottoman-Islamic culture of that period, putting up advertisements and signs to attract customers was considered boastful and not aligned with the principals of modesty and humility, therefore there were no advertisements, or even nameplates for the stalls. These beliefs also kept the artisans from signing their handicrafts (Gulersoy 1980: 19). At that time, all merchants and tradesmen were subject to the rules and regulations of the guild system which influenced all aspects of life in the Bazaar including artisanship training, rules for opening a shop, borrowing and lending, the employment of personnel, and pricing. Rules specific to each trade were determined by its corresponding guild. Each profession and trade of sufficient size had a guild. Each guild served as a licensed trade monopoly and the number of shops and stalls were fixed by the guild. As a requirement of the guild system, all stalls were grouped together by trade. "The regulation about each street being reserved for a certain trade was applied in such a strict fashion that, let alone selling a product outside the line of trade, one could not even put it on display on the shelves. Each good would be looked for in its rightful place, which made it convenient for the customers and eased the traffic flow in the Bazaar. The guilds were mutually exclusive; tradesmen who had a stall in one of the streets could not start one in another street or enter another trade" (Gulersoy 1980: 49).

Each guild had a representative in the government who dealt with matters related to pricing and taxation. The pricing system was generally cost-based and the unit cost rates were set by the government through the determination of a fixed cost rate for the raw materials and the labor fees. For instance a silver bowl's price would be determined by its weight, the cost of the silver, and the labor premium for that trade that was applied by weight.

The guild system declined towards the end of the nineteenth century amid the economic struggles and the political and military conflicts of the late Ottoman Empire and they were ultimately abolished in 1913. Today, there are a number of associations in the Bazaar, some organized by trade such as jewelry, antique dealers, but there are no such rules, regulations, and requirements as there were in the guild system of the Classical Period.

---

[9] A divan is a piece of couch-like sitting furniture. Originally, in the Orient (especially the Ottoman Empire), a divan was a long seat formed of a mattress laid against the side of the room, upon the floor, or upon a raised structure or frame, with cushions to lean against.

16.4 Modern Period

Starting in the second half of the nineteenth century, the Ottoman Empire started opening up to the West, and as the old traditions started fading, sales tactics began to evolve and change. The wooden divans and open stalls were considered outdated and during the renovation after the 1894 earthquake, the new shop system was introduced. The fronts of the stone stalls were covered with shop facades and the major streets acquired their present appearance during this period (Figure 16.2).

In the second half the nineteenth century, reduced import tariffs were granted to European countries resulting in the influx of large quantities of mass-produced imported goods at lower prices sold at modern department stores in the new, up-and-coming parts of the city. As a result, the demand for unique handmade merchandise declined. In the twentieth century, except for the Gold Market, which is still the center of gold wholesale and retail, the Grand Bazaar went from being the main shopping destination for İstanbulians' all kinds of needs, to an occasional shopping destination for carpets, antiques, and fine gold jewelry. (See Figure 16.3 for major differences between the Classical Period and the Modern Period.)

FIGURE 16.2 Textiles section of the Grand Bazaar (Photograph by Yosun Denizeri, 2009)

	Classical Period (16th–19th century)	Modern Period (Late 19th century-present day)
Vendors	Family-owned, in business for multiple generations Salespeople are owners Part of the guild system, following strict regulation Tradesmen and artisans located in the Bazaar Strong sense of community Co-location of merchants by trade	Small fraction are family businesses New businesses owners Salespeople are employees No more guild system Fewer artisans, mostly merchants Reputation is secondary, primary focus is short-term profitability Co-location to some degree, but not enforced
Customers	Ottoman elite Foreigners looking for exotic goods Locals from all walks of life looking for items for daily use and special occasions	Tourists Locals looking for antiques or items for special occasions
Merchandise	Unique, handmade Made to order Made by local artisans located in the Bazaar	Mass-produced Some made to order Local artisans disappearing except for goldsmiths and diamond cutters
Quality Assurance	Closely regulated by the guild Focused on customer satisfaction Guaranteed by reputation	Not regulated Most customers are focused on price
Competition	High sense of community Vendor referral within trade Low competition	Many fractions within each trade Vendor referrals across trades High competition
Sales Approach	Personalized Some level of middlemen involvement for foreigners Relationship building, value reputation and honor No hurry to make a sale	Personalized Aggressive sales tactics by some vendors Some transaction-based, opportunistic Some focused on lifetime customer value
Pricing	Prices published and regulated by the guild system, not much room for negotiation Bargaining unacceptable	Varies across vendors Bargaining is common

FIGURE 16.3 Comparison of the Classical Period with the Modern Period of the Grand Bazaar

16.5 GOODS TRADED IN THE BAZAAR

Since its beginnings the Bazaar played an important role in the trade of handmade goods between Asia and Europe as well as serving as the main retail outlet for local artisans. During the Classical Period, goods were brought from many different parts of the world and included Austrian crystals, French perfumes, Arabic spears, Tartar bows, Bahrain pearls, Indian diamonds, Ankara blankets, Afghan shawls, Indian muslin, Persian daggers, and exquisite Chinese silk. Each item had a story that was told during the conversations that took place on the divans of the stalls. However, the majority of the merchandise was produced locally by artisan workshops in or around the Bazaar. In addition to the rare and exotic merchandise, the shops also carried goods for the everyday needs of people from all walks of life. Men, women, children, and foreigners could find clothing and household goods with something for everyone's budget.

As noted before, the role of the Grand Bazaar as a primary shopping destination declined in the nineteenth century. The industrial revolution in Western Europe impacted the Grand Bazaar merchants in two ways:

- As mass-produced imports filled up the stores outside the Bazaar and tariff cuts led to lowering prices for imports, the demand for unique handmade items began to decline.
- British mills grew in production and started buying the best quality wool and silk from Anatolia.[10] As a result, the textile weavers in İstanbul had difficulty getting access to these raw materials.

The modern day Grand Bazaar still has many unique and exquisite products to offer along with more common goods that can be acquired anywhere else in the city. Today, the main merchandise categories are souvenirs and gifts, carpets, gold and silver jewelry, textiles, leather apparel and accessories. Some of these are still one-of-a kind, handmade items, but many are mass-produced in large workshops or factories. Finding a truly unique item at a fair price requires time, patience, and expertise. It is common to find stores that carry a great range of merchandise with prices that can range from $1 to $10,000. Today, each merchant offers all three categories of products summarized in Figure 16.4, however the ratio of transactions in each category varies by trade. Some merchants, such as those who sell textiles and souvenirs, have mostly mass-manufactured items. Others, such as the antique dealers, sell mostly unique items and still others, such as the ceramics merchants, sell a whole spectrum of products and are eager to offer custom-made products to meet customers' needs.

Almost every merchant offers an assortment of low-priced products. These are usually displayed in bulk in the shop window, or right at the entrance to the stores. Examples are small souvenirs, ceramics, scarves, leather wallets, and slippers. These products are the ones most likely to have price tags and the prices are usually well known by the merchants and the customers. Because these mass-produced items are usually the lowest price items in the store, the profit margins tend to be low as well. Therefore, the merchants are interested in getting a high turnover from this inventory. There is little room for bargaining on single unit

---

[10] Anatolia, also referred to as Asia Minor, the geographic area comprising most of the modern Republic of Turkey. The region is bounded by the Black Sea to the north, the Caucasus to the north-east, the Iranian plateau to the south-east, the Mediterranean Sea to the south and the Aegean Sea to the west. This region supplied the raw materials for the textile, carpet, and ceramic trades.

Type of product	Merchandise	Production method	Pricing	Inventory
Common	• Leather goods • Textiles • Souvenirs	• Mass-produced • Local or imported • Handmade or machine-made	• Price tags common • Cost-based pricing • Volume discount available	• High
Unique	• Gold and diamond jewelry • Old carpets • Antiques	• Hand made • Local	• No price tags • Customized	• Limited
Customized	• Ceramics • Gold jewelry • Leather apparel	• Handmade	• Customized Pricing	• Samples available • Made to order

FIGURE 16.4 Product categories sold in the Grand Bazaar in the Modern Period

purchases of these items, but the merchants are willing to give quantity discounts. The Bazaar merchants are often the suppliers of these common products to the retailers outside the Bazaar, so the Bazaar is the place for good bargains for large volume purchases. These types of products are also used to generate traffic: customers who are drawn to the good deals on these items walk into the store, giving the merchant opportunity to sell other products at higher prices.

Hand-woven carpets, decorative ceramic plates, tiles and fine silver jewelry are examples of the category of unique products. Samples of these products are displayed throughout the store and most of the inventory is stored at the back of the store and brought out during the sales process as the merchant develops an understanding of the customer's preferences in terms of style and price range. If the available products offered do not match the customer's needs, or the customer is looking for a truly unique product and has some flexibility on timing, then the merchant offers the option of *customization*. This third category is most common in products such as ceramic tiles used for decoration and jewelry that can be made to order in a matter of days.

16.6 BAZAAR MERCHANTS

During the Classical Period, the goods sold in the Bazaar were all handmade, and in many cases, the tradesmen and craftsmen producing these goods were located in the Bazaar. Many of the professions were passed from father to son. Due to the guild system, the community was close-knit with a strong sense of tradition and social ethics. During this period the largest category of tradesmen worked in apparel and textiles. Many of the tradesmen were highly specialized in the types of goods that they made and sold.

During that time, merchants and tradesmen were all bound by certain moral rules and ethical principles. The main principles have been summarized by Celik Gulersoy:

- *Sense of community*: Do not be envious of a neighbor's trade, on the contrary, be happy about it.

- *Indifference to profit*: Be content and make do with little. This attitude towards profit was demonstrated daily, especially in the morning, when a trader who had already made a sale would direct the next customer to a neighbor who had not yet had his first sale.

- *Single and consistent price point*: Bargaining was considered shameful.

The guild system also ensured consistent pricing practices within a trade. The pricing guidelines determined by the government were enforced by the guild system. Co-location of the tradesmen selling similar goods made it easy to monitor prices.

Another characteristic of merchants during the Classical Period was the high level of expertise and specialization in the goods they were selling. For many centuries, the merchants were closely involved in the creation of handicrafts such as textiles, ceramics, and jewelry, and some were artisans themselves. In the jewelry, business, it was very common for the merchants to be from families of goldsmiths and diamond cutters and the arts and handicrafts were passed on through the family for many generations. (See Figure 16.5 for a list of trades in the Classical Period.) Many craftsmen had workshops in the more secluded sections of the bazaar.

As can be imagined, the Grand Bazaar, with its maze of streets, the great number of merchants, and breadth of merchandise, could present a challenge for foreign travelers, who often did not know where to start. As McMillan puts it, "Information is the lifeblood of markets. Knowledge of what is available where and who wants it is crucial" (McMillan 2003: 44). This situation presented an opportunity for interpreters who knew their way around the Bazaar and spoke foreign languages. During the transition from the Classical Period to the Modern Period, as the Bazaar became a more competitive environment with more mass-produced goods and less demand, interpreters played an important role in the development of new sales tactics. Non-Muslim minorities such as Jews and Armenians were the initial information brokers in the Bazaar (Gulersoy 1980: 45). According to Ottoman law, these minorities could not serve in the military, therefore many of these families have been in a trade business for generations. Also, they attended private schools set up by foreign embassies or missionaries, where the main language of education was French, Italian, German, or English. Since they had the advantage of speaking multiple languages and had business connections, they assumed the role of interpreters and evaluators in trade deals with foreigners and acted as middlemen. Middlemen in the Grand Bazaar were recognized as a distinct trade group in the historical archives. In a way, they were the equivalent of "search engines" and they were an invaluable convenience for foreign customers who would be overwhelmed by the number of vendors and the variety of products on offer. In travelers' diaries we see references to these middlemen. They became skilled at studying the approaching foreigner's outfit, facial features, complexion, and weight to assess where he is from, how long he has been in İstanbul, what he is looking

Trade category	Tradesmen
Jewelry / Gold / Silver	Gold changers and goldsmiths, Jewelers, Renovators of old jewelry, Engravers, Embossers, Gold leaf artisans
Art / Decoration	Makers of reliefs, Calligraphers, Mother of pearl inlay artisans Ivory artisans, Miniaturists, Gilders, Spoon makers, Mirror makers
Metalwork and Armor	Knife makers and merchants, Repoussé workers, Scissor makers, Gun makers, Sword merchants, Helmet makers, Arrow and bow makers
Apparel and Textiles	Clothing merchants, Mohair, and alpaca merchants, Embroiderers, Textile artisans, Cobblers, Sole makers, Shawl makers, Lace makers, Quilt makers, Merchants of apparel accessories, Second-hand clothing dealers, Makers of silk textiles, Makers of wool textiles, Makers of cotton textiles, Makers of velvet, Silk robe tailors, Damask and Indian-striped fabric weavers, Waist-cloth makers, Felt makers, Brocade merchants, Fur merchants, Fabric dyers
Other	Second-hand book dealers, Makers of metal holders for porcelain coffee cups, Makers of pencil sharpeners, Second-hand dealers, Medicated toffee makers and herbalists

FIGURE 16.5 Categories of Bazaar merchants during the Classical Period

Source: Gulersoy (1980: 23–33)

for, and what he can afford. Based on this assessment, the middleman would direct the customer to the merchants where they would be likely to find something to their taste and budget. Since the local merchants did not speak European languages and few Europeans spoke Turkish, the middlemen would also negotiate on behalf of the customer and earn a commission from the sales (Gulersoy 1980: 45). Many of today's selling tactics are most likely the legacy of these middlemen.

Today the main category of trade still surviving from the Classical Period is that of the jewelers and diamond cutters. Outside the jewelry trade, merchants of the Modern Period are not usually part of the creative process nor do they have the same in-depth knowledge of the craft as their predecessors. Many shopkeepers are salaried employees rather than owners. Today, there are fewer merchant families who have been in the Bazaar for many generations than at any time in the past. However, the most reputable stores among the merchants continue to be those where the owners are personally involved in the creation of the goods and are in close partnership with the artisans. These merchants are experts in their field and are therefore good at estimating the labor and material costs of the goods. They can also offer customers options for tailor-made goods. For instance, in a situation where a customer does not find exactly what they are looking for in terms of design or proportions, a merchant selling ceramics can offer to have a piece custom-made for them. If the merchant is close to the creative process, he can tell the customer how many days it will take and how much it will cost to deliver the piece. Jewelry, carpet, and antique merchants are also often a great source of information about the product, its uniqueness, durability, and often the resale value as well. Often, they will offer to exchange the product in the future if the customer wants to upgrade to another style.

One of the traditions that still survives to some extent is the co-location of the vendors by product. Today's main sections are the Gold Market (Figure 16.6), the Silver Market, the Leather Market, and the Carpet Market. However, because the location of these stores is not regulated by guilds or any other institution, these stores are slowly dispersing among other sections. Although there are no regulations enforcing co-location, there is still an advantage to being located near other vendors selling the same goods. For the vendor, this proximity provides easy access to a customer segment that is looking for a particular type of product. For the customer, it minimizes search cost, and eases the traffic flow, dividing the crowds navigating through narrow streets across different sections. Given the maze-like nature of the Bazaar, this organization makes a significant difference to the shopping experience. For these reasons, co-location is likely to continue to a degree in the future.

The Gold market in the Bazaar is a good example of the co-location of merchants of the same trade. Customers shopping for gold jewelry have 300–400 stores to choose from.

FIGURE 16.6 View of the Gold market in the Grand Bazaar (Photograph by Yosun Denizeri, 2009)

Fortunately for the customer, almost all of them are gathered on a few streets, limiting the area they need to cover in their search. With such a large number of vendors and such a wide variety of goods offered, the search cost is rather high—a customer can easily spend hours, sometimes days, going from store to store and partaking in negotiations. In the absence of a website displaying the merchandise and rating the merchants, customers are left to word-of-mouth referrals from friends, family, or the travel agents. Therefore, local customers have the advantage of knowing the more established and reputable merchants in the Bazaar.

Today, the atmosphere of the Bazaar is rather different from the peaceful, dimly lit, humbly decorated stalls of the past. The constant chattering, merchants inviting customers to take a look inside, shop windows lit with dozens of light bulbs, big signs over the shops, and hundreds of goods on display in tiny windows create an intense shopping experience. Many merchants, however, still strive to re-create the peaceful environment of the past through the lighting and seating arrangements inside their stores. *Divans* are still an integral part of the décor in the carpet shops and they still serve their purpose of making customers feel relaxed and giving them a chance to catch their breath while the merchant determines the right product and the right price for that customer.

Some of the merchants who have been in business for many decades recall the days when they lived by the rule "My word is my contract". While the unwritten rules of trade are fading fast and the tradition of watching out for fellow shop owners is now rare, reputation is still important. There is still camaraderie among the traditional merchants running family businesses that have been around for many generations. These merchants are also the ones who tend to do most of the business with repeat customers or through referrals. The locals who are experienced Bazaar customers have loyalty to their favorite merchants. Most local customers tend to go directly to the merchants they know or those who are recommended by friends or family.

While a formal guild system does not exist, some of the merchants still carry on the strong sense of community and will refer their customers to other merchants of their caliber. Therefore, once a customer finds a fair and ethical merchant, they have access to a network of other merchants of similar caliber. Even if that merchant does not have what they are looking for, they will direct the customer to a fellow merchant who can help them. This referral network provides invaluable information for the customer and reduces the search cost.

16.7 SALES PROCESS

"The search for information is the central experience of life in the bazaar, it is the really advanced art in the bazaar, a matter upon which everything turns," said Clifford Geertz in his article on the bazaar economy (Geertz 1978: 28). This observation holds true for new customers and tourists in the Grand Bazaar. Geertz also adds, "The level of ignorance about everything from product quality and going prices to market possibilities and production costs is very high, and much of the way in which the bazaar functions can be interpreted as an attempt to reduce such ignorance for some, increase it for someone, or defend someone against it." In a similar manner to other bazaars, price tags are not common in the Grand Bazaar, therefore, comparison shopping is often complex and time consuming. However, it is not only the shoppers who are searching for information, the merchants often ask questions to assess the shopping habits and budgets of the customers. While the customers are looking for the best quality and best bargains, the merchants are looking for ways to assess customers' awareness of market prices, their spending limits and probability of repeat business. The shopping experience differs from that of the local customers who already have connections to the Bazaar merchants. Locals shoppers at the Bazaar go directly to the merchants they know and get preferred customer discounts.

In terms of the sales process, a shopper's experience in the Bazaar has changed significantly over the centuries. As mentioned above, in the Classical Period the merchants did not engage in aggressive selling or bargaining. They sat quietly on wooden divans in front of their shelves and cabinets. The most valuable objects were kept in drawers and were taken out one-by-one for those who inquired about them. Today, the market dynamics are more competitive. The Bazaar is not the only destination for shopping anymore and a significant portion of customers are tourists who do not have personal connections to merchants. Therefore, sales tactics can be more aggressive. For the merchant, the main challenge is to get the customer into the store so they can show them the more unique, higher priced products. Once the customer is engaged in a conversation with the merchant, the interactive sales process begins. The customer is offered refreshments and a place to sit and relax while a series of products are showcased. The products offered to the customer are selected in response to the customer's answers to a series of questions such as:[11]

- end use: everyday use at home, for decoration or special occasion, gift;
- occasion for purchase: special event such as graduation, engagement, wedding, new home, new baby, or business gift;
- spending range (budget);
- style or aesthetic preference: traditional, modern, unique.

In a way, these questions represent various nodes in the decision tree in the mind of the merchant. Answers to these questions narrow down the product offering and the price range, enabling the merchant to show the products that have the highest likelihood of meeting the customer's needs.

From the customer's point of view, the biggest concern is the lack of information about the fair price for an item and the quality. Therefore, the Bazaar provides an example of how market frictions arise from the uneven availability of information for new customers who do not have established relationships with the Bazaar merchants (McMillan 2002):

- search costs: the time, effort, and money spent learning what is available where and for how much;
- evaluation costs: arising from the difficulties buyers face in assessing quality.

---

[11] These are the most common and generic questions that came up in the interviews conducted with carpet, ceramic, and textile merchants and gold and silver jewelers. Information exchange is not limited to these and will have more specific elements applicable to the products in question.

Since the Bazaar is so big and has a range of merchants selling the same type of products, there is definitely a time cost associated with going from store to store to locate the products that appeal to customers. Not all of the products are always on display, especially the handmade carpets and kilims; they are usually piled up in the back room and are taken out ceremoniously one by one. This process can result in a customer spending hours in each store. Evaluation cost is another factor and becomes more significant for unique handmade items and antiques. For instance, in the case of hand-made carpets, usually, the older carpets are made with yarns dyed with plant extracts; these are more durable and therefore more expensive then new carpets, but it takes expertise to differentiate between them.

16.8 PRICING

One of the ways in which the Grand Bazaar resembles a traditional bazaar or market is the lack of information about pricing and the extensive use of customized pricing. Customers will see ticket prices only for the most inexpensive, highly commoditized items. Prices for higher value items are often determined through bargaining. Since most of the products are antiques and hand made goods such as jewelry, comparison shopping is not easy.

While there are opportunistic merchants who are looking for ways to take advantage of customers' lack of information, for the established Grand Bazaar merchants, the focus of the sales process is not the current transactions. For these merchants, the focus of the interaction is getting to know the customer and establishing a relationship to increase the probability of repeat business or referrals. A skilled merchant can quickly deduce a customer's price sensitivity from a series of questions that are sprinkled throughout the casual conversation about the customer's profession, family, residence, purpose of the shopping trip, etc. This process is an organic form of client relationship management at work.

The merchant usually starts with more expensive goods and will bring out less expensive alternatives in response to a customer's reaction. In the process of show and tell, the merchant asks questions that help them assess the lifetime value of the customer. The lifetime value is based on the following factors:

- *Frequency of shopping in the Bazaar*: This helps the merchant to assess the likelihood of repeat business. Locals have an advantage in this aspect. However, tourists or Turkish nationals living in other countries can qualify if they make frequent trips and can convince the merchant that they make regular purchases in the Bazaar.
- *Social network and connections*: A large social or professional network implies potential referrals from a satisfied customer.
- *Life stage and lifestyle*: Events such as an upcoming engagement or wedding or setting up a new home increase the probability of repeat business.
- *Level of product knowledge*: The customer's level of product knowledge and information on the market price for the product enables them to better assess the fair price and

gives the merchant an incentive to offer a fair price to earn customer loyalty in the long run.

There is neither a database nor a system involved in the pricing process. The initial price is typically based on cost-plus pricing that takes into account the labor that went into making, for example, goods such as ceramics and, in the case of jewelry, the daily market rate of silver or gold. A merchant's desire for repeat business may motivate him to offer lower prices to a local customer where there is a high probability of repeat business or potential referrals. If the merchant is convinced that that day's transaction is likely to be one of many to come, or the customer is already a frequent customer, he may offer a "friends and family" discount. Sometimes, he will also offer free gifts, such as bowls and coasters, as an expression of goodwill. That usually happens at the point when the customer is getting ready to pay the agreed upon price. The type of discount or gift is based on the merchant's assessment of the customer's needs and likes, and can vary across customers.

Establishing a good relationship with a merchant also benefits the customer on their next visit to the Bazaar, and they can save time by skipping the comparison-shopping process and go to the merchant they know. The customers with higher likelihood of repeat business represent a higher lifetime value for the merchant and this works to the advantage of local customers, therefore resulting in what is perceived as the dual price structure of "local price and tourist price".

In the case of handmade carpets, the pricing method varies depending upon whether the carpet is new or old. Carpet merchants usually have contracted workshops where they source made-to-order new carpets, so they are familiar with how much time it takes per square meter of any carpet ordered. The yarn used—wool, or silk—and the dyes used—organic or chemical—also play a role in setting the price. Good carpets appreciate in value by age. Older carpets are acquired through auctions or directly from the owners who have inherited them from their family. For older carpets, merchants base their pricing on demand in the market and refer to the Internet to get a feel for the going price for similar carpets in auctions around the world. The merchants take into account these resale values when they bargain on price and, often, will guarantee to buy the carpet back in a few years if the customer wants to exchange it for another.

Merchants who have been in this business for a long time are experts at setting fair market prices for the old carpets and are sought out by those looking to sell carpets. Therefore, when shopping for old carpets, it is extremely important to find a merchant with a reputation for being fair. If the customer knows what kind of carpet they are looking for, it also helps to do an Internet search and get an understanding of the going rates for similar carpets. Some old school merchants are offended when the customer tries to haggle for an unacceptable price and can decide that they do not want to do business with a customer who does not have sufficient appreciation for the quality of goods they are offering. Conversely, a merchant can also be extremely motivated to win over a customer who has done some research and can appreciate quality and craftsmanship. Such a merchant will spend time with the customer even if they do not intend to make a purchase that day. The merchant's intention is to establish a relationship with the customer so that they will come back at a future date when they are ready to make a purchase.

Pricing can be closely related to the supply and demand dynamics in the market for certain goods. One such category is antique textiles and clothing from the Ottoman period. These unique products are often acquired directly from families by agents who go from house to house looking for old but well-preserved outfits. The more unique and well-preserved the item, the higher the price. These merchants have in-house tailors who are skilled at restoration and can offer tailoring services to meet the customer's needs. Again, the focus is customer satisfaction and these merchants are similarly driven by maximizing repeat business and referrals to maximize lifetime value.

16.9 Conclusion

Today, the process of product offering and price setting in the Grand Bazaar is a combination of art and science. Understanding customer needs and tailoring the product offering to each individual customer is a skill that is developed through decades of experience and involves diligent data gathering through informal conversation. While price setting is a complex process that varies across different trades, the fundamental concept of assessing lifetime customer value and offering prices to maximize this value rather than the specific transaction is a common practice among the more established and successful merchants. Many of the tactics employed in the Bazaar can be a source of inspiration for retailers who are looking for ways to develop a more personal approach to product and promotional offerings. While there are no formal ways of monitoring prices and ethical trade as enforced by the guild system of the Classical Period, good reputation still goes a long way, and reputable merchants focus on earning repeat business and referrals. As McMillan says, "Concern for wider reputation provides a further incentive for honest dealing" (2002: 56). Although an on-line star-rating system for the Grand Bazaar merchants does not yet exist, it is likely that the informal information sharing will soon evolve into a more formalized system.

References

Geertz, C. (1978) "The Bazaar Economy: Information and Search in Peasant Marketing", *American Economic Review* 68: 28–32.
Gulersoy, C. (1980) *Story of the Grand Bazaar*. İstanbul: İstanbul Kitapligi.
McMillan, J. (2003) *Reinventing the Bazaar—A Natural History of the Markets*. New York: W. W. Norton & Company.

PART III

PRICING FUNDAMENTALS

CHAPTER 17

....

PRICE THEORY IN ECONOMICS

....

THOMAS A. WEBER

And there is all the difference in the world
between paying and being paid.
The act of paying is perhaps
the most uncomfortable infliction (. . .)
But being paid,—what will compare with it?
The urbane activity with which man receives money
is really marvellous.

HERMAN MELVILLE, MOBY DICK

17.1 ORIGIN OF VALUE AND PRICES

....

Price theory is concerned with explaining economic activity in terms of the creation and transfer of value, which includes the trade of goods and services between different economic agents. A puzzling question addressed by price theory is, for example: why is water so cheap and diamonds are so expensive, even though water is critical for survival and diamonds are not? In a discussion of this well-known "Diamond–Water Paradox", Adam Smith (1776) observes that

> [t]he word value, it is to be observed, has two different meanings, and sometimes expresses the utility of some particular object, and sometimes the power of purchasing other goods which the possession of that object conveys. The one may be called "value in use;" the other, "value in exchange." (Smith 1776: 31)

The author would like to thank Naveed Chehrazi, Martin Grossman, and several anonymous referees for helpful comments and suggestions.

For him, diamonds and other precious stones derive their value from their relative scarcity and the intensity of labor required to extract them. Labor therefore forms the basic unit of the exchange value of goods (or "items"), which determines therefore their "real prices". The "nominal price" of an item in Smith's view is connected to the value of the currency used to trade it and might therefore fluctuate. In this labor theory of value the Diamond–Water Paradox is resolved by noting that it is much more difficult, in terms of labor, to acquire one kilogram of diamonds than one kilogram of water.

About a century later, the work of Carl Menger, William Stanley Jevons, and Léon Walras brought a different resolution of the Diamond–Water Paradox, based on marginal utility rather than labor. Menger (1871) points out that the value of an item is intrinsically linked to its utility "at the margin". While the first units of water are critical for the survival of an individual, the utility for additional units quickly decreases, which explains the difference in the value of water and diamonds. Commenting on the high price of pearls, Jevons (1881) asks "[d]o men dive for pearls because pearls fetch a high price, or do pearls fetch a high price because men must dive in order to get them?" (1881: 102), and he concludes that "[t]he labour which is required to get more of a commodity governs the supply of it; the supply determines whether people do or do not want more of it eagerly; and this eagerness of want or demand governs value" (1881: 103). Walras (1874/77) links the idea of price to the value of an object in an exchange economy by noting that the market price of a good tends to increase as long as there is a positive excess demand, while it tends to decrease when there is a positive excess supply. The associated adjustment process is generally referred to as Walrasian *tâtonnement* ("groping"). Due to the mathematical precision of his early presentation of the subject, Walras is generally recognized as the father of general equilibrium theory.[1]

To understand the notion of price it is useful to abstract from the concept of money.[2] In a barter where one person trades a quantity x_1 of good 1 for the quantity x_2 of good 2, the ratio x_1/x_2 corresponds to his price paid for good 2. If apples correspond to good 1 and bananas to good 2, then the ratio of the number of apples paid to the number of bananas obtained in return corresponds to the (average) price of one banana, measured in apples. The currency in this barter economy is denominated in apples, so that the latter is called the *numéraire* good, the price of which is normalized to one.

The rest of this survey, which aims at providing a compact summary of the (sometimes technical) concepts in price theory, is organized as follows. In Section 17.2, we introduce the concepts of "rational preference" and "utility function" which are standard building blocks of models that attempt to explain choice behavior. We then turn to the frictionless interaction of agents in markets. Section 17.3 introduces the notion of a Walrasian equilibrium, where supply equals demand and market prices are determined (up to a common multiplicative constant) by the self-interested behavior of market participants. This

---

[1] The modern understanding of classical general equilibrium theory is well summarized by Debreu's (1959) concise axiomatic presentation and by Arrow and Hahn's (1971) more complete treatise. Mas-Colell (1985) provides an overview from a differentiable viewpoint, and McKenzie (2002) a more recent account of the theory. Friedman (1962/2007), Stigler (1966), and Hirshleifer et al. (2005) present "price theory" at the intermediate level.

[2] Keynes' (1936) theory of liquidity gives some reasons for the (perhaps somewhat puzzling) availability of money, which, after all, cannot be directly consumed, but provides a fungible means of compensation in exchange.

equilibrium has remarkable efficiency properties, which are summarized by the first and the second fundamental welfare theorems. In markets with uncertainty, as long as any desired future payoff profile can be constructed using portfolios of traded securities, the Arrow–Debreu equilibrium directly extends the notion of a Walrasian equilibrium and inherits all of its efficiency properties. Otherwise, when markets are "incomplete", as long as agents have "rational expectations" in the sense that they correctly anticipate the formation of prices, the Radner equilibrium may guarantee at least constrained economic efficiency. In Section 17.4 we consider the possibility of disequilibrium and Walrasian *tâtonnement* as a price-adjustment process in an otherwise stationary economy. Section 17.5 deals with the problem of "externalities", where agents' actions are payoff-relevant to other agents. The presence of externalities in markets tends to destroy the efficiency properties of the Walrasian equilibrium and even threaten its very existence. While in Sections 17.3 and 17.4 all agents (including consumers and firms) are assumed to be "price-takers", we consider strategic interactions between agents in Sections 17.6 and 17.7, in the presence of complete and incomplete information, respectively. The discussion proceeds from optimal monopoly pricing (which involves the problems of screening, signaling, and, more generally, mechanism design when information is incomplete) to price competition between several firms, either in a level relationship when there are several oligopolists in a market, or as an entry problem, when one incumbent can deter (or encourage) the entrance of other firms into the market. Section 17.8 deals with dynamic pricing issues, and in Section 17.9 we mention some of the persistent behavioral irregularities that are not well captured by classical price theory. Finally, Section 17.10 concludes and provides a number of directions from which further research contributions may be expected.

17.2 PRICE-TAKING BEHAVIOR AND CHOICE

Normative predictions about what agents do, that is, about their "choice behavior", requires some type of model. In Section 17.2.1, we introduce preferences and the concept of a utility function to represent those preferences. Section 17.2.2 then presents the classical model of consumer choice in terms of a "utility maximization problem" in an economy where agents take the prices of the available goods as given. In Section 17.2.3, we examine how choice predictions depend on the given prices or on an agent's wealth, an analysis which is referred to as "comparative statics". In reality it is only rarely possible to make a choice which achieves a desired outcome for sure. The effects of uncertainty, discussed in Section 17.2.4, are therefore important for our understanding of how rational agents behave in an economy. Decision problems faced by two typical agents, named Joe and Melanie, will serve as examples.

17.2.1 Rational preferences

An agent's preferences can be expressed by a partial order over a choice set X.[3] For example, consider Joe's preferences over the choice set $X = \{$Apple, Banana, Orange$\}$

---

[3] Fishburn (1970) and Kreps (1988) provide more in-depth overviews of choice theory.

when deciding which fruit to pick as a snack. Assuming that he prefers an apple to a banana and a banana to an orange, his preferences on X thus far can be expressed in the form

$$\text{Apple} \succeq \text{Banana},$$

$$\text{Banana} \succeq \text{Orange},$$

where $\succeq$ denotes "is (weakly) preferred to". However, these preferences are not complete, since they do not specify Joe's predilection between an apple and an orange. If Joe prefers an orange to an apple, then the relation

$$\text{Orange} \succeq \text{Apple}$$

completes the specification of Joe's preference relation $\succeq$ which is then defined for all pairs of elements of X. When Joe is ambivalent about the choice between an apple and a banana, so that he both prefers an apple to a banana (as noted above) *and* a banana to an apple (i.e., Apple $\succeq$ Banana and Banana $\succeq$ Apple both hold), we say that he is *indifferent* between the two fruits and write Apple $\sim$ Banana. On the other hand, if Apple $\succeq$ Banana holds but Banana $\succeq$ Apple is not true, then Joe is clearly not indifferent: he *strictly* prefers an apple to a banana, which is denoted by

$$\text{Apple} \succ \text{Banana}.$$

If the last relation holds true, a problem arises because Joe's preferences are now such that he strictly prefers an apple to a banana, weakly prefers a banana to an orange, and at the same time weakly prefers an orange to an apple. Thus, Joe would be happy to get an orange in exchange for an apple. Then he would willingly take a banana for his orange, and, finally, pay a small amount of money (or a tiny piece of an apple) to convert his banana back into an apple. This cycle, generated by the intransitivity of his preference relation, leads to difficulties when trying to describe Joe's behavior as rational.[4]

DEFINITION 1 *A rational preference $\succeq$ on the choice set X is a binary relationship defined for any pair of elements of X, such that for all $x, y, z \in X$: (i) $x \succeq y$ or $y \succeq x$ (Completeness), (ii) $x \sim x$ (Reflexivity), and (iii) $x \succeq y$ and $y \succeq z$ together imply that $x \succeq z$ (Transitivity).*

To make predictions about Joe's choice behavior over complex choice sets, dealing directly with the rational preference relation $\succeq$ is from an analytical point of view unattractive, as it involves many pairwise comparisons. Instead of trying to determine all "undominated" elements of Joe's choice set, that is, all elements that are such that no other element is strictly preferred, it would be much simpler if the magnitude of Joe's liking of each possible choice $x \in X$ was encoded as a numerical value of a "utility function" $u(x)$, so that Joe's most preferred choices also maximize his utility.

---

[4] When aggregating the preferences of a society of at least three rational agents (over at least three items), Arrow's (1951) seminal "impossibility theorem" states that, no matter what the aggregation procedure may be, these cycles can in general be avoided only by declaring one agent a dictator or impose rational societal preferences from the outside. For example, if one chooses pairwise majority voting as aggregation procedure, cycles can arise easily, as can be seen in the following well-known voting paradox, which dates back to Condorcet (1785). Consider three agents with rational preferences relations ($\succeq_1, \succeq_2$, and $\succeq_3$, respectively) over elements in the choice set $X = \{A, B, C\}$ such that $A \succ_1 B \succ_1 C$, $B \succ_2 C \succ_2 A$, and $C \succ_3 A \succ_3 B$. However, simple majority voting between the different pairs of elements of X yields a societal preference relation $\succeq$ such that $A \succ B$, $B \succ C$, and $C \succ A$ implying the existence of a "Condorcet cycle", i.e., by Definition 1 the preference relation $\succeq$ is intransitive and thus not rational.

DEFINITION 2 *A utility function* $u : X \to \mathbb{R}$ *represents the rational preference relation* $\succeq$ *(on X) if for all* $x, y \in X$:

$$x \succeq y \quad \text{if and only if} \quad u(x) \geq u(y).$$

It is easy to show that as long as the choice set is finite, there always exists a utility representation of a rational preference relation on X.[5] In addition, if u represents $\succeq$ on X, then for any increasing function $\varphi : \mathbb{R} \to \mathbb{R}$ the utility function $v : X \to \mathbb{R}$ with $v(x) = \varphi(u(x))$ for all $x \in X$ also represents $\succeq$ on X.

17.2.2 Utility maximization

If Joe has a rational preference relation on X that is represented by the utility function u, in order to predict his choice behavior it is enough to consider solutions of his *utility maximization problem* (UMP),

$$x^* \in \arg \max_{x \in X} u(x). \tag{1}$$

Let us now think of Joe as a consumer with a wealth w that can be spent on a bundle $x = (x_1, \ldots, x_L)$ containing nonnegative quantities x_l, $l \in \{1, \ldots, L\}$, of the L available consumption goods in the economy. We assume henceforth that Joe (and any other agent we discuss) strictly prefers more of each good,[6] so that his utility function is increasing in x. To simplify further, we assume that Joe takes the price p_l of any good l as given, that is, he is a *price-taker*. Given a price vector $p = (p_1, \ldots, p_L)$ he therefore maximizes his utility $u(x)$ subject to the constraint that the value of his total consumption, equal to the dot-product $p \cdot x$, does not exceed his total (positive) wealth w. In other words, all feasible consumption bundles lie in his *budget set*

$$B(p, w) = \{x \in \mathbb{R}_+^L : p \cdot x \leq w\}.$$

Joe's so-called *Walrasian demand* correspondence is

$$x(p, w) = \arg \max_{x \in B(p,w)} u(x). \tag{2}$$

---

[5] If X is not finite, it may be possible that no utility representation exists. Consider for example lexicographic preferences defined on the two-dimensional choice set $X = [0, 1] \times [0, 1]$ as follows. Let $(x_1, x_2), (\hat{x}_1, \hat{x}_2) \in X$. Suppose that $(x_1, x_2) \succeq (\hat{x}_1, \hat{x}_2) \overset{\text{def}}{\Longleftrightarrow} (x_1 > \hat{x}_1)$ or $(x_1 = \hat{x}_1$ and $x_2 \geq \hat{x}_2)$. For example, when comparing used Ford Mustang cars, the first attribute might index a car's horsepower and the second its color (measured as proximity to red). An individual with lexicographic preferences would always prefer a car with more horsepower. However, if two cars have the same horsepower, the individual prefers the model with the color that is closer to red. The intuition why there is no utility function representing such a preference relation is that for each fixed value of x_1, there has to be a finite difference between the utility for $(x_1, 0)$ and $(x_1, 1)$. But there are more than countably many of such differences, which when evaluated with any proposed utility function can be used to show that the utility function must in fact be unbounded on the square, which leads to a contradiction. For more details, see Kreps (1988). In practice, this does not lead to problems, since it is usually possible to discretize the space of attributes, which results in finite (or at least countable) choice sets.

[6] More precisely, it is sufficient to assume that Joe's preferences are "locally nonsatiated", meaning that in the neighborhood of any bundle x there is another bundle $\hat{x}$ (located at an arbitrarily close distance) that Joe strictly prefers. The consequence of this assumption is that Joe values any small increase of his wealth.

Depending on the uniqueness of the solutions to Joe's UMP, the Walrasian demand correspondence may be multivalued. Optimality conditions for this constrained optimization problem can be obtained by introducing the Lagrangian

$$\mathcal{L}(x, \lambda, \mu; p, w) = u(x) - \lambda(p \cdot x - w) + \mu x,$$

where $\lambda \in \mathbb{R}_+$ is the Lagrange multiplier associated with the inequality constraint $p \cdot x \leq w$ and $\mu = (\mu_1, \ldots, \mu_L) \in \mathbb{R}_+^L$ the Lagrange multiplier associated with the nonnegativity constraint $x \geq 0$. The necessary optimality conditions are

$$\frac{\partial \mathcal{L}(x, \lambda, \mu; p, w)}{\partial x_l} = \frac{\partial u(x)}{\partial x_l} - \lambda p_l + \mu_l = 0, \quad l \in \{1, \ldots, L\}. \tag{3}$$

Together with the complementary slackness conditions

$$\lambda(p \cdot x - w) = 0 \tag{4}$$

and

$$\mu_l x_l = 0, \quad l \in \{1, \ldots, L\}, \tag{5}$$

they can be used to construct Joe's Walrasian demand correspondence. For this, we first note that since Joe's utility function is increasing in x, the budget constraint is binding, that is, $p \cdot x = w$, at the optimum (Walras' Law). In particular, if Joe consumes positive amounts of all commodities, that is, if $x \gg 0$,[7] the complementary slackness condition (5) implies that $\mu_l = 0$ for all $l \in \{1, \ldots, L\}$, so that by (3) (with $\lambda > 0$) we obtain that

$$\mathrm{MRS}_{lj}(x) = \frac{\frac{\partial u(x)}{\partial x_l}}{\frac{\partial u(x)}{\partial x_j}} = \frac{p_l}{p_j}, \quad l, j \in \{1, \ldots, L\}, \tag{6}$$

where $\mathrm{MRS}_{lj}(x)$ is called the *marginal rate of substitution* between good l and good j (evaluated at x). Condition (6) means that the marginal rate of substitution between any two goods has to be equal to the ratio of the corresponding prices. It is interesting to note that Joe's marginal rate of substitution at the optimum would therefore be the same as Melanie's if she were to solve the same problem, even though her preferences might be very different from Joe's. In other words, *any* consumer chooses his or her Walrasian demand vector such that $L - 1$ independent conditions in eq. (6) are satisfied (e.g., for $i = 1, j \in \{2, \ldots, L\}$). The missing condition for the determination of the Walrasian demand correspondence is given by the budget constraint,

$$p \cdot x = w. \tag{7}$$

As an example, consider the case where Joe has a utility function $u(x) = x_1^{\alpha_1} x_2^{\alpha_2}$ for consuming a bundle $x = (x_1, x_2)$,[8] where $a_1, a_2 \in (0, 1)$ are constants. Then eqs (6) and (7) immediately imply Joe's Walrasian demand,

---

[7] We use the following conventions for inequalities involving vectors $x = (x_1, \ldots, x_L)$, $\hat{x} = (\hat{x}_1, \ldots, \hat{x}_L)$: (i) $x \leq \hat{x} \Leftrightarrow x_i \leq \hat{x}_i \, \forall \, i$; (ii) $x < \hat{x} \Leftrightarrow x \leq \hat{x}$ and $\exists \, j$ s.t. $x_j < \hat{x}_j$; and (iii) $x \ll \hat{x} \Leftrightarrow x_i < \hat{x}_i \, \forall \, i$.

[8] This functional form, first proposed by Cobb and Douglas (1928) for identifying "production functions" (cf. Section 17.3.2) rather than utility functions, is often used for its analytical simplicity and the fact that its parameters can easily be identified using data (e.g., by a linear regression).

$$x(p, w) = \left(\frac{\alpha_1 w}{(\alpha_1 + \alpha_2)p_1}, \frac{\alpha_2 w}{(\alpha_1 + \alpha_2)p_2} \right).$$

Note that the Lagrange multiplier λ for the UMP (2) corresponds to the increase in Joe's *indirect utility*,[9]

$$v(p, w) = \max_{x \in B(p,w)} u(x). \tag{8}$$

Indeed, by the well-known envelope theorem (Milgrom and Segal 2002) we have that

$$\frac{\partial v(p, w)}{\partial w} = \frac{\partial \mathcal{L}(x, \lambda, \mu; p, w)}{\partial w} = \lambda. \tag{9}$$

Lagrange multipliers are sometimes also referred to as "shadow prices" of constraints. In this case, λ corresponds to the value of an additional dollar of budget as measured in terms of Joe's utility. Its unit is therefore "utile" per dollar.

Let us now briefly consider the possibility of a *corner solution* to Joe's utility maximization problem, that is, his Walrasian demand vanishes for (at least) one good l. In that case, $\mu_l > 0$ and therefore

$$\text{MRS}_{lj}(x) = \frac{\lambda p_l - \mu_l}{\lambda p_j} = \frac{p_l}{p_j}\left(1 - \frac{\mu_l}{\lambda p_l}\right) < \frac{p_l}{p_j},$$

provided that $x_j > 0$, that is, Joe consumes a positive amount of good j.[10] Thus, Joe's marginal utility $\partial u(x)/\partial x_l$ for good l, which is not consumed, is lower relative to his marginal utility for good j that he does consume, when compared to a consumer (e.g., Melanie) who uses positive amounts of both good l and good j. The latter consumer's marginal rate of substitution is equal to the ratio of prices (p_l/p_j), whereas Joe's marginal rate of substitution is strictly less. This means that a consumer may choose to forgo consumption of a certain good if its price is too high compared to the price of other goods, so that it becomes "too expensive" to adjust the marginal rate of substitution according to the (interior) optimality condition (6).

17.2.3 Comparative statics

Samuelson (1941) describes "comparative statics" as the task of examining how a decision variable changes as a function of changes in parameter values. Examining the shifts of model predictions with respect to parameter changes is at the heart of price theory. We illustrate the main comparative statics techniques for the utility maximization problem. Consider, for example, the question of how Joe's Walrasian demand $x(p, w)$ changes as his wealth w increases. His demand $x_l(p, w)$ for good l is called *normal* if it is nondecreasing in w. If that demand is positive, the first-order condition (3) can be differentiated with respect to the parameter w (using eq. (9)) to obtain

---

[9] Joe's value function $v(p, w)$ is called "indirect utility" because he does usually not have a direct utility for the parameters p and w representing price and wealth, respectively, as they cannot be consumed directly. Yet they influence the problem and v can be thought of as representing a rational preference relation over different values of (p, w).

[10] Clearly, because his utility is increasing and his wealth is positive, he will always demand a positive amount of at least one good.

$$\frac{\partial x(p,w)}{\partial w} = (D^2 u(x(p,w)))^{-1} p \frac{\partial^2 v(p,w)}{\partial w^2} = (D^2 u(x(p,w)))^{-1} p \frac{\partial \lambda(p,w)}{\partial w}.$$

If u is strongly concave, then $\partial\lambda(p,w)/\partial w \leq 0$,[11] that is, the shadow value of wealth is decreasing as more and more wealth is added, since the individual's marginal utility for the additional consumption decreases.

REMARK 1 A good that is not normal, that is, for which demand decreases as wealth rises, is called *inferior*. Typical examples of such goods are frozen foods and bus transportation. In somewhat of a misnomer a normal good is referred to as a *superior* (or *luxury*) good if its consumption increases more than proportionally with wealth. Typical examples are designer apparel and expensive foods such as caviar or smoked salmon. In some cases the consumption of superior goods can drop to zero as price decreases. Luxury goods are often consumed as so-called *positional* goods, the value of which strongly depends on how they compare with the goods owned by others (Hirsch 1976; Frank 1985).

The change of the Walrasian demand vector with respect to a change in the price vector (*price effect*) is more intricate. It is usually decomposed into a *substitution effect* and a *wealth effect* (Figure 17.1). For example, if Joe notices a change in the price vector from p to $\hat{p}$, then the substitution effect of this describes how Joe's consumption vector changes if enough wealth is either added or subtracted to make sure that Joe's utility is the same before and after the price change. For example, if his utility level before the price change is U, then his *wealth-compensated* (or *Hicksian*) demand vector $h(p, U)$ is such that it solves the *expenditure minimization problem*

$$h(p,U) \in \arg \min_{x \in \{\xi \in \mathbb{R}_+^L : u(\xi) \geq U\}} \{p \cdot x\}.$$

The Hicksian demand $h(p, U)$ achieves the utility level U at the price p at the lowest possible expenditure. For example, if $U = u(x(p, w))$, where $x(p, w)$ is Joe's Walrasian demand vector, then $h(p, U) = x(p, w)$. If we denote the *expenditure* necessary to achieve the utility level U by $e(p, U) = p \cdot h(p, U)$, then one can (using the envelope theorem) show that $D_p e(p, U) = h(p, U)$ (Roy's identity) and from there deduce that for $w = e(p, U)$: $D_p x(p, e(p, U)) = \partial x(p, w)/\partial p + (\partial x(p, w)/\partial w)h(p, U)$, so that one obtains Slutsky's identity,

$$\underbrace{\frac{\partial x_l(p,w)}{\partial p_j}}_{\text{Price effect}} = \underbrace{\frac{\partial^2 e(p,u(x(p,w)))}{\partial p_l \partial p_j}}_{\text{Substitution effect}} - \underbrace{\frac{\partial x_l(p,w)}{\partial w} h_j(p,u(x(p,w)))}_{\text{Wealth effect}}, \quad l,j \in \{1,\ldots,L\}. \tag{10}$$

The (symmetric, negative semi-definite) matrix $S = \left[\frac{\partial^2 e(p,U)}{\partial p_l \partial p_j}\right]$ of substitution effects is referred to as *Slutsky matrix*.

REMARK 2 A *Giffen good* is such that demand for it increases when its own price increases. For example, when the price of bread increases, a poor family might not be able to afford meat any longer and therefore buy even more bread (Marshall 1920). It is necessarily an inferior good with a negative wealth effect that overcompensates the substitution effect, resulting in a positive price effect.[12] A related but somewhat different effect of increased consumption as a result of a price increase is observed for a so-called *Veblen good*

---

[11] The function u is strongly concave if its Hessian $D^2 u(x)$ is negative definite for all x.

[12] Sørensen (2007) provides simple examples of utility functions which yield Giffen-good effects.

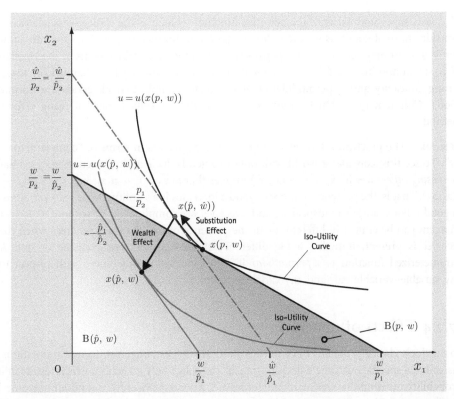

FIGURE 17.1 Price effect as a result of a price increase for the first good, i.e., a shift from $p = (p_1, p_2)$ to $\hat{p} = (\hat{p}_1, \hat{p}_2)$ (with $\hat{p}_1 > p_1$ and $\hat{p}_2 = p_2$), decomposed into substitution effect and wealth effect using the compensated wealth $\hat{w} = e(\hat{p}, u(x(p,w)))$.

(e.g., a luxury car or expensive jewelry). Veblen (1899: 75) pointed out that "[c]onspicuous consumption of valuable goods is a means of reputability to the gentleman of leisure." Thus, similar to positional goods (cf. Remark 1), Veblen goods derive a portion of their utility from the price they cost (compared to other goods), since that implicitly limits their consumption by others.

We have seen that situations in which the dependence of decision variables is monotone in model parameters are especially noteworthy. The field of *monotone comparative statics*, which investigates conditions on the primitives of a UMP (or similar problem) that guarantee such monotonicity, is therefore of special relevance for price theory (and economics as a whole). Monotone comparative statics was pioneered by Topkis (1968, 1998), who introduced the use of lattice-theoretic (so-called "ordinal") methods, in particular the notion of supermodularity.[13] Milgrom and Shannon (1994) provide sufficient and in some sense necessary conditions for the monotonicity of solutions to UMPs in terms

---

[13] For any two vectors $x, \hat{x} \in \mathbb{R}_+^L$, let $x \wedge \hat{x} = \min\{x, \hat{x}\}$ be their component-wise minimum and $x \vee \hat{x} = \max\{x, \hat{x}\}$ be their component-wise maximum. The choice set $X \subset \mathbb{R}_+^L$ is a *lattice* if $x, \hat{x} \in X$ implies that $x \wedge \hat{x} \in X$ and $x \vee \hat{x} \in X$. A function $u : X \to \mathbb{R}$ is *supermodular* on a lattice X if $u(x \vee \hat{x}) + u(x \wedge \hat{x}) \geq u(x) + u(\hat{x})$ for all $x, \hat{x} \in X$.

of (quasi-)supermodularity of the objective function, as long as the choice set is a lattice.[14] Consider normal goods as an example for monotone comparative statics. One can show that if u is strongly concave and supermodular, then the diagonal elements of the Hessian of u are nonpositive and its off-diagonal elements are nonnegative (Samuelson 1947). Strong concavity and supermodularity of u therefore imply that all goods are normal goods (Chipman 1977). Quah (2007) strengthens these results somewhat using ordinal methods.

REMARK 3 The practical interpretation of supermodularity is in terms of "complementarity". To see this, consider a world with only two goods. Joe's utility function $u(x_1, x_2)$ has *increasing differences* if $(\hat{x}_1, \hat{x}_2) \gg (x_1, x_2)$ implies that $u(\hat{x}_1, \hat{x}_2) - u(x_1, \hat{x}_2) \geq u(\hat{x}_1, x_2) - u(x_1, x_2)$. That is, the presence of more of good 2 increases Joe's utility response to variations in good 1. For example, loudspeakers and a receiver are complementary: without a receiver an agent can be almost indifferent about the presence of loudspeakers, whereas when the receiver is present, it makes a big difference if loudspeakers are available or not. A parameterized function is *supermodular* if it has increasing differences with respect to any variable–variable pair and any variable–parameter pair.

17.2.4 Effects of uncertainty

So far, Joe's choice problems have not involved any uncertainty. Yet, in many situations, instead of a specific outcome a decision-maker can select only an action, which results in a probability distribution over many outcomes $x \in X$, or, equivalently, a random outcome $\tilde{x}$ (or "lottery") with realizations in X. Thus, given an action set A, the decision-maker would like to select an action $a \in A$ so as to maximize the *expected utility* $\mathrm{EU}(a) = E[u(\tilde{x})|a]$. The conditional distributions $F(x|a)$ defined for all $(x, a) \in X \times A$ are part of the primitives for this expected-utility maximization problem,

$$a^* \in \arg\max_{a \in A} \mathrm{EU}(a) = \arg\max_{a \in A} \int_X u(x)dF(x|a).$$

For example, if Joe's action $a \in A = [0, 1]$ represents the fraction of his wealth w that he can invest in a risky asset that pays a random return $\tilde{r}$, distributed according to the distribution function $G(r) = P(\tilde{r} \leq r)$, then the distribution of his ex-post wealth $\tilde{x} = w(1 + a\tilde{r})$ conditional on his action a is $F(x|a) = G((\frac{x}{w} - 1)/a)$ for $a \neq 0$ (and $F(x|a = 0) = \delta(x - w)$ and δ is a Dirac distribution[15]), so that $\mathrm{EU}(a) = \int_{\mathbb{R}} u(x)dF(x|a) = \int_{\mathbb{R}} u(w(1 + ar))dG(r)$ for all $a \in A$ by simple substitution. The solution to Joe's classic *portfolio investment problem* depends on his attitude to risk. Joe's *absolute risk aversion*, defined by

$$\rho(x) = -u''(x)/u'(x),$$

---

[14] Monotone comparative statics under uncertainty is examined by Athey (2002); non-lattice domains are investigated by Quah (2007). The latter is relevant, as even in a basic UMP of the form (2) for more than two commodities the budget set $B(p, w)$ is generally not a lattice. Strulovici and Weber (2008, 2010) provide methods for finding a reparametrization of models that guarantees monotone comparative statics, even though model solutions in the initial parametrization may not be monotone.

[15] The (singular) Dirac distribution δ can be defined in terms of a limit, $\delta(x) = \lim_{\varepsilon \to 0+} (\varepsilon - |x|)_+/\varepsilon^2$. It corresponds to a probability density with all its unit mass concentrated at the origin.

is a measure of how much he prefers a risk-free outcome to a risky lottery (in a neighbor-hood of x). For example, in Joe's portfolio investment problem, there exists an amount $\pi(a)$ such that $u(E[\tilde{x}|a] - \pi(a)) = EU(a)$, which is called the *risk premium* associated with Joe's risky payoff lottery as a consequence of his investment action a. If Joe's absolute risk aversion is positive, so is his risk premium. The latter is the difference between the amount he is willing to accept for sure and the actuarially fair value of his investment under action a.

REMARK 4 In economic models, it is often convenient to assume that agents have *constant absolute risk aversion* (CARA) $\rho > 0$, which implies utility functions of the form $u(x) = -\exp(-\rho x)$ for all monetary outcomes $x \in \mathbb{R}$. The advantage is that the agents' risk attitude is then independent of their starting wealth, which insulates models from "wealth effects". Another common assumption, when restricting attention to positive wealth levels (where $x > 0$), is that agents have a *relative risk aversion* $\hat{\rho}(x) = x\rho(x)$ that is constant. Such agents with *constant relative risk aversion* (CRRA) $\hat{\rho} > 0$ have utility functions of the form

$$u(x) = \begin{cases} \ln x, & \text{if } \hat{\rho} = 1, \\ x^{1-\hat{\rho}}/(1-\hat{\rho}), & \text{otherwise.} \end{cases}$$

For more details on decision making under risk, see Pratt (1964) and Gollier (2001). An axiomatic base for expected utility maximization is provided in the pioneering work by Von Neumann and Morgenstern (1944).

17.3 PRICE DISCOVERY IN MARKETS

So far we have assumed that agents take the prices of all goods as given. Naturally, if goods are bought and sold in a market, prices will depend on the balance between demand and supply. Section 17.3.1 explains how prices are formed in a pure-exchange economy, in the absence of any uncertainty. Under weak conditions, trade achieves an economically "efficient" outcome in the sense that it maximizes "welfare", that is the sum of all agents' utilities. Under some additional assumptions, any efficient outcome can be achieved by trade, provided that a social planner can redistribute the agents' endowments before trading starts. In Section 17.3.2, we note that these insights carry over to economies where firms producing all available goods are owned and operated by the agents. Section 17.3.3 shows that these insights also apply in the presence of uncertainty, as long as the market is "complete" in the sense that all contingencies can be priced by bundles of available goods. Section 17.3.4 provides some details about "incomplete" markets, where this is not possible.

17.3.1 Pure exchange

Consider an economy in which N agents can exchange goods in a market at no transaction cost. Each agent i has utility function $u^i(x^i)$, where $x^i \in \mathbb{R}_+^L$ is his consumption bundle, and is endowed with the bundle $\omega^i \in \mathbb{R}_+^L$ (his *endowment*). At the nonnegative price vector p this agent's Walrasian demand $x^i(p, p \cdot \omega^i)$ is obtained by solving a UMP, where $p \cdot \omega^i$ is used as his wealth. The *market-clearing condition* that supply must equal demand yields

$$\sum_{i=1}^{N} x^i(p, p \cdot \omega^i) = \sum_{i=1}^{N} \omega^i, \tag{11}$$

and thus L relations (one for each good) that imply the price vector $p = (p^1, \ldots, p^L)$ up to a common multiplicative constant, for only $L - 1$ components in eq. (11) can be independent.

DEFINITION 3 *A* Walrasian equilibrium $(\hat{p}, \hat{x})$ *in a pure-exchange economy consists of an equilibrium price* $\hat{p} \in \mathbb{R}_+^L$ *and an equilibrium allocation* $\hat{x} = (\hat{x}^1, \ldots, \hat{x}^N)$ *such that*

$$\hat{x}^i \in \arg \max_{x^i \in B(\hat{p}, \hat{p} \cdot \omega^i)} u^i(x^i), \quad i \in \{1, \ldots, N\}, \tag{12}$$

and

$$\sum_{i=1}^{N} (\hat{x}^i - \omega^i) = 0. \tag{13}$$

As an example, let us consider Joe (= agent 1) and Melanie (= agent 2) with identical Cobb–Douglas utility functions $u^1(x_1, x_2) = u^2(x_1, x_2) = x_1^\alpha x_2^{1-\alpha}$, where $\alpha \in (0, 1)$ is a given constant. Suppose that Joe is endowed with the bundle $\omega^1 = (1, 2)$ and Melanie with the bundle $\omega^2 = (2, 1)$. The UMP (12) implies that agent i's Walrasian demand vector (or "offer curve" (OC) when viewed as a function of price) is

$$x^i(p, p \cdot \omega^i) = \left(\frac{\alpha p \cdot \omega^i}{p_1}, \frac{(1 - \alpha)p \cdot \omega^i}{p_2} \right).$$

From eq. (13) we obtain that $\alpha(p_1 + 2p_2)/p_1 + \alpha(2p_1 + p_2)/p_1 = 3$, so that the ratio of prices becomes $p_1/p_2 = \alpha/(1 - \alpha)$. By setting $p_1 = 1$ (which amounts to considering good 1 as the *numéraire*, cf. Section 17.1) we can therefore immediately determine a unique Walrasian equilibrium $(\hat{p}, \hat{x})$, where $\hat{p} = (1, (1 - \alpha)/\alpha)$ and $\hat{x}^i = x^i(\hat{p}, \hat{p} \cdot \omega^i)$ for $i \in \{1, 2\}$, so that $\hat{x}^1 = (2 - \alpha, 2 - \alpha)$ and $\hat{x}^2 = (1 + \alpha, 1 + \alpha)$. The distribution of resources in a two-agent exchange economy, such as in this example, can be conveniently displayed using the so-called Edgeworth–Bowley box diagram as shown in Figure 17.2.[16] The figure also shows that the intersection of the agents' offer curves lies on a "contract curve" which contains all "efficient" allocations as explained below.

The beauty of an exchange economy in which price-takers interact freely without any transaction cost is that a Walrasian equilibrium allocation cannot be improved upon in the following sense. A feasible allocation $x = (x^1, \ldots, x^N)$ is said to be *Pareto-efficient* (relative to the set X of feasible allocations) if there exists no other allocation $\hat{x} = (\hat{x}^1, \ldots, \hat{x}^N)$ in X at which all individuals are at least as well off as at x *and* at least one individual is better off. More precisely, x is Pareto-efficient if for all $\hat{x} \in X$:[17]

$$(u^i(x^i) \le u^i(\hat{x}^i) \ \forall i) \ \Rightarrow \ (u^i(x^i) = u^i(\hat{x}^i) \ \forall i).$$

Adam Smith (1776: book IV, ch. 2) pointed to an "invisible hand" that leads individuals through their self-interest to implement socially optimal outcomes. A key result of price

---

[16] A simple diagram of this sort was used by Edgeworth (1881: 28) to illustrate exchange allocations, and it was later popularized by Bowley (1924).

[17] For each Pareto-efficient allocation $x^* \in X$ there exists a vector $\lambda = (\lambda^1, \ldots, \lambda^N) \ge 0$ of nonnegative weights such that $x^* \in \arg\max_{x \in X} \left\{ \sum_{i=1}^{N} \lambda^i u^i(x^i) \right\}$. The last problem can be used to generate all such Pareto-efficient allocations by varying λ.

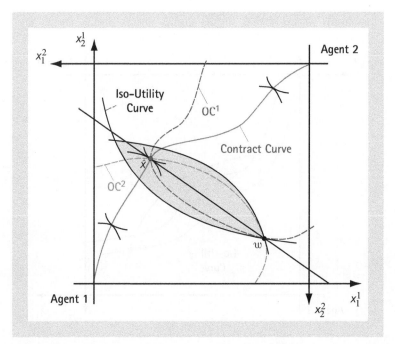

FIGURE 17.2 Offer curves (OC^1 and OC^2), Walrasian equilibrium, and Pareto-efficient allocations

theory is that Walrasian equilibria, even though merely defined as a solution to individual utility maximization problems and a feasibility constraint (supply = demand), produce Pareto-efficient outcomes.

THEOREM 1 (FIRST FUNDAMENTAL WELFARE THEOREM) *Any Walrasian equilibrium allocation is Pareto-efficient.*[18]

The intuition for the Pareto efficiency of a Walrasian equilibrium allocation is best seen by contradiction. Suppose that there exists an allocation $x = (x^1, x^2)$ that would improve Joe's well-being and leave Melanie at the utility level she enjoys under the Walrasian equilibrium allocation $\hat{x} = (\hat{x}^1, \hat{x}^2)$. By Walras' Law, for Joe allocation x^1 is not affordable under the equilibrium price $\hat{p}$, so that $\hat{p} \cdot x^1 > \hat{p} \cdot \hat{x}^1$. Furthermore, because Melanie is maximizing her utility in equilibrium, the alternative allocation x^2 cannot leave her with any excess wealth, so that $\hat{p} \cdot x^2 \geq \hat{p} \cdot \hat{x}^2$. Thus, the total value of the alternative allocation, $\hat{p} \cdot (x^1 + x^2)$, is *strictly* greater than the total value of the Walrasian equilibrium allocation, $\hat{p} \cdot (\hat{x}^1 + \hat{x}^2)$. But this contradicts the fact that the total amount of goods in the economy does not depend on the chosen allocation, so that the total value in the economy is constant for a given price. Hence, we have obtained a contradiction, which implies that the Walrasian equilibrium allocation must indeed be Pareto-efficient.

THEOREM 2 (SECOND FUNDAMENTAL WELFARE THEOREM) *In a convex economy it is possible to realize any given Pareto-efficient allocation as a Walrasian equilibrium allocation, after a lump-sum wealth redistribution.*

[18] The Pareto efficiency of a Walrasian equilibrium allocation depends on the fact that consumer preferences are locally nonsatiated (cf. footnote 6).

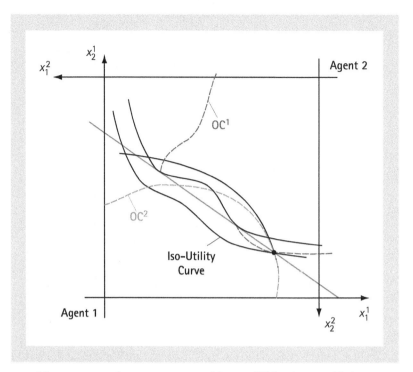

FIGURE 17.3 Nonconvex exchange economy without a Walrasian equilibrium

This important result rests on the assumption that the economy is convex, in the sense that each consumer's sets of preferred goods ("upper contour sets") relative to any feasible endowment point is convex. The latter is necessary to guarantee the existence of an equilibrium price; it is satisfied if all consumers' utility functions are concave.[19] Figure 17.3 provides an example of how in a nonconvex economy it may not be possible to obtain a Walrasian equilibrium: as a function of price, agent 1 switches discretely in his preference of good 1 and good 2, so that the market cannot clear at any price (except when all its components are infinity, so that agents simply keep their endowments).

The set of Pareto-efficient allocations in an economy is often referred to as the "contract curve" (or Pareto set; cf. footnote 17 and Figure 17.2). The subset of Pareto-efficient allocations which present Pareto improvements over the endowment allocation is called the *core* of the economy. While the first fundamental welfare theorem says that the Walrasian market outcome is in the core of an economy, the second fundamental welfare theorem states that it is possible to rely on markets to implement any outcome in the Pareto set, provided that a lump-sum reallocation of resources takes place before markets are opened.

[19] The proof of the second fundamental welfare theorem relies on the separating hyperplane theorem (stating that there is always a plane that separates two convex sets which have no common interior points). In an economy with production (cf. Section 17.3.2) the firms' production sets need to also be convex.

17.3.2 Competitive markets

The setting of the exchange economy in Section 17.3.1 does not feature any productive activity by firms. Consider M such firms. Each firm m has a (non-empty) production set $Y^m \subset \mathbb{R}^L$ which describes its production choices. For a feasible production choice $y^m = (y_1^m, \ldots, y_L^m)$, we say that firm m produces good l if y_l^m is nonnegative; otherwise it uses that good as an input. Thus, since it is generally not possible to produce goods without using any inputs, it is natural to require that $Y \cap \mathbb{R}_+^L \subseteq \{0\}$. This so-called *no-free-lunch* property of the production set Y^m means that if a firm produces goods without any inputs, then it cannot produce a positive amount of anything. Given a price vector p, firm m's profit is $p \cdot y$. The firms' *profit-maximization problem* is therefore to find

$$y^m(p) \in \arg\max_{y^m \in Y^m} \{p \cdot y\}, \quad m \in \{1, \ldots, M\}. \tag{14}$$

In a *private-ownership economy* each firm m is privately held. That is, each agent i owns the nonnegative share ϑ_m^i of firm m, such that

$$\sum_{i=1}^N \vartheta_m^i = 1, \quad m \in \{1, \ldots, M\}. \tag{15}$$

DEFINITION 4 *A Walrasian equilibrium $(\hat{p}, \hat{x}, \hat{y})$ in a private-ownership economy is such that all agents maximize utility,*

$$\hat{x}^i \in \arg\max_{x^i \in B(\hat{p}, \hat{p} \cdot \omega^i + \sum_{m=1}^M \vartheta_m^i (\hat{p} \cdot \hat{y}^m))} u^i(x^i), \quad i \in \{1, \ldots, N\},$$

all firms maximize profits,

$$\hat{y}^m \in \arg\max_{y^m \in Y^m} \{\hat{p} \cdot y\}, \quad m \in \{1, \ldots, M\},$$

and the resulting allocation is feasible,

$$\sum_{i=1}^N (\hat{x}^i - \omega^i) = \sum_{m=1}^M \hat{y}^m.$$

The two fundamental welfare theorems continue to hold in the more general setting with production. The existence of a Walrasian equilibrium is guaranteed as long as there are no externalities (cf. Section 17.5) and the economy is convex (cf. footnote 19).

17.3.3 Complete markets

The agents' consumption choice and the firms' production decisions are generally subject to uncertainty. As in Section 17.2.4, this may simply mean that agents maximize expected utility and firms expected profits. However, in many situations the agents can use a market mechanism to trade *before* a random state of the world realizes. Arrow (1953) and Debreu (1953) have shown that all the efficiency properties of the Walrasian equilibrium carry over to case with uncertainty, provided that "enough" assets are available, a notion that will be made precise in the definition of complete markets below (cf. Definition 5). For simplicity we assume that the uncertain state of the world, denoted by the random variable $\tilde{s}$, can have

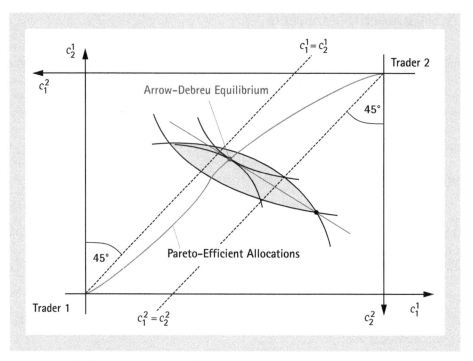

FIGURE 17.4 Market for contingent claims

realizations in the finite state space $S = \{s_1, \ldots, s_K\}$. Agent i believes that state s_k occurs with probability μ_k^i.

We now develop a simple two-period model to understand how agents (or "traders") can trade in the face of uncertainty. Consider Joe (= agent 1), who initially owns firm 1, and Melanie (= agent 2), who initially owns firm 2. The state space $S = \{s_1, s_2\}$ contains only two elements (i.e., $K = 2$). Let V^m be the market value of firm m in period 1. The monetary value of firm m in state s_k is ω_k^m. After trading of the firm's shares takes place in the first period, Joe and Melanie each hold a portfolio $\vartheta^i = (\vartheta_1^i, \vartheta_2^i)$ of ownership shares in the firms. In the second period all uncertainty realizes and each agent i can make consumption decisions using the wealth $w_k^i(\vartheta^i) = \vartheta_1^i \omega_k^1 + \vartheta_2^i \omega_k^2$ in state s_k, obtaining the indirect utility $v_k^i(w_k^i)$. Hence, in period one, the traders Joe and Melanie, can trade firm shares as follows. Each trader i solves the expected utility maximization problem

$$\hat{\vartheta}^i(V) \in \arg\max_{\vartheta^i \in B((V^1, V^2), V^i)} \left\{ \sum_{k=1}^K \mu_k^i v_k^i(w_k^i(\vartheta^i)) \right\}.$$

If in addition the market-clearing condition (15) holds, then the resulting equilibrium $(\hat{V}, \hat{\vartheta})$, with $\hat{V} = (\hat{V}^1, \hat{V}^2)$ and $\hat{\vartheta} = (\hat{\vartheta}^1(\hat{V}), \hat{\vartheta}^2(\hat{V}))$, is called a *rational expectations equilibrium*.[20] In this equilibrium, Joe and Melanie correctly anticipate the equilibrium market

---

[20] The concept of rational expectations in economics originated with Muth (1961), and the rational expectations equilibrium which is used here with Radner (1972).

prices of the firm when making their market-share offers, just as in the Walrasian pure-exchange economy discussed in Section 17.3.1.

In the last example, Joe and Melanie each owned a so-called *asset* (or *security*), the defining characteristic of which is that it entitles the owner to a determined monetary payoff in each state of the world. All that matters for consumption after the conclusion of trade in the first period is how much money an agent has available in each state. Thus, Joe and Melanie could come to the conclusion that instead of trading the firm shares, it would be more appropriate to trade directly in "state-contingent claims to wealth". If trader i holds a state-contingent claim portfolio $c^i = (c_1^i, \dots, c_K^i)$, then in state s_k that trader obtains the indirect utility $v_k^i(c_k^i)$. In the first period when trading in contingent claims takes place, the price for a claim to wealth in state s_k is p_k. Hence, each trader i has demand

$$\hat{c}^i \in \arg\max_{c^i \in B(p, p \cdot \omega^i)} \left\{ \sum_{k=1}^{K} v_k^i(c_k^i) \right\}, \quad i \in \{1, \dots, N\}, \tag{16}$$

that maximizes expected utility. Eq. (16) and the market-clearing relation

$$\sum_{i=1}^{N} (\hat{c}^i - \omega^i) = 0 \tag{17}$$

together constitute the conditions for a Walrasian equilibrium $(\hat{p}, \hat{c})$ in the market of contingent claims, referred to as *Arrow–Debreu equilibrium* (Figure 17.4). Using the insights from Section 17.2.2, note that the marginal rate of substitution between claims in state s_k and claims in state s_l equals the ratio of the corresponding market prices at an (interior) equilibrium,

$$\mathrm{MRS}_{kl}(c^i) = \frac{\mu_k^i v_k^i(c_k^i)}{\mu_l^i v_l^i(c_l^i)} = \frac{p_k}{p_l}.$$

This is independent of the agent i, so that after normalizing the market prices to sum to one, the prices $p_1, \dots, p_K$ define a probability distribution over the states of the world, which is referred to as *equivalent martingale measure*. While traders may disagree about their probability assessments for the different states of the world, they are in agreement about the equivalent martingale measure in equilibrium.[21]

It is possible to go back and forth between the market for firm shares and the market for contingent claims if and only if the system of equations

$$\underbrace{\begin{bmatrix} \omega_1^1 & \cdots & \omega_1^M \\ \vdots & & \vdots \\ \omega_K^1 & \cdots & \omega_K^M \end{bmatrix}}_{\Omega} \underbrace{\begin{bmatrix} \vartheta_1^i \\ \vdots \\ \vartheta_M^i \end{bmatrix}}_{\vartheta^i} = \underbrace{\begin{bmatrix} c_1^i \\ \vdots \\ c_K^i \end{bmatrix}}_{c^i}$$

possesses a solution, or, equivalently, if the *asset return matrix* Ω is of rank K.

---

[21] Aumann (1976) points out that, in a statistical framework, it is in fact impossible for agents to "agree to disagree" on probability distributions if all the evidence is made available to all agents. Naturally, without such information exchange, the agents' subjective probabilities may vary significantly.

DEFINITION 5 *(i) If the $K \times M$ asset return matrix Ω has rank K, then the market for contingent claims is called complete. (ii) A Walrasian equilibrium (p, c) in a complete market for contingent claims, satisfying eqs (16) and (17), is called an Arrow–Debreu equilibrium.*

The concept of completeness can easily be extended to multi-period economies (Debreu 1959), where time is indexed by $t \in \{0, 1, \ldots, T\}$. The state of the world $\tilde{s}_t$ at time $t \geq 1$ can depend on the state of the world $\tilde{s}_{t-1}$ at time $t - 1$. As the states of the world successively realize, they plow a path through an *event tree*. In a complete market it is possible to trade claims that are contingent on any possible path in the event tree.

17.3.4 Incomplete markets

If the market is not complete (in the sense of Definition 5(i)), the rational expectations equilibrium (also referred to as *Radner equilibrium*) may produce a Pareto-inefficient allocation. The reason is that if there are more states of the world than linearly independent assets, then it is generally not possible for agents to trade contracts that diversify the risks in the economy to the desirable degree. To see this, consider two risk-averse agents in an economy with two or more states, where there are no firms (or assets) that can be traded, so that there is no possibility for mutual insurance. The latter would be the Pareto-efficient outcome in an Arrow–Debreu equilibrium when contingent claims are available.

The consequence of market incompleteness is that agents in the economy cannot perfectly trade contingent claims. One can show that, in an economy with only two periods, a rational expectations equilibrium is "constrained Pareto-efficient", in the sense that trade in the first period is such that agents obtain a Pareto-efficient allocation in expected utilities, subject to the available assets.[22]

The question naturally arises as to how assets should be priced when markets are incomplete. The answer is that depending on the agents' beliefs in the market, a number of different prices are possible. In general, it is reasonable to assume that, as long as transaction costs are negligible, asset prices do not allow for *arbitrage* possibilities, that is, ways of obtaining a risk-free profit through the mere trading of assets. For concreteness, let us assume that there are three assets and that each asset $m \in \{1, 2, 3\}$ is characterized by a return vector $\omega^m = (\omega_1^m, \ldots, \omega_K^m)$ which specifies the payoffs for all possible states $s_1, \ldots, s_K$. In addition, suppose that the return vector of the third asset is a linear combination of the return vectors of the first two assets, so that

$$\omega^3 = \phi^1 \omega^1 + \phi^2 \omega^2$$

for some constants ϕ^1 and ϕ^2. If V^m is the market price of asset m, then clearly we must have that

$$V^3 = \phi^1 V^1 + \phi^2 V^2$$

in order to exclude arbitrage opportunities. In other words, if the state-contingent payoffs of an asset can be replicated by a portfolio of other assets in the economy, then the price of

---

[22] In multi-period (and/or multi-good) economies, rational expectations equilibria are not even guaranteed to be constrained Pareto-efficient (for details see, e.g., Magill and Quinzii 1996).

the asset must equal the price of the portfolio.[23] Accordingly, *no-arbitrage pricing* refers to the selection of prices that do not allow for risk-free returns resulting from merely buying and selling available assets.[24] But no-arbitrage pricing in an incomplete market alone provides only an upper and a lower bound for the price of an asset. Additional model structure (e.g., provided by general equilibrium assumptions or through the selection of an admissible equivalent martingale measure) is required to pinpoint a particular asset price. Arbitrage pricing theory (Ross 1976; Roll and Ross 1980) postulates that the expected value of assets can be well estimated by a linear combination of fundamental macro-economic factors (e.g., price indices). The sensitivity of each factor is governed by its so-called β-coefficient.

A rational expectations equilibrium in an economy in which the "fundamentals of the economy", that is, the agents' utilities and endowments, do not depend on several states, but consumptions are different across those states, is called a *sunspot equilibrium* (Cass and Shell 1983). The idea is that observable signals that bear no direct effect on the economy may be able to influence prices through traders' expectations. In the light of well-known boom–bust phenomena in stock markets, it is needless to point out that traders' expectations are critical in practice for the formation of prices. When market prices are at odds with the *intrinsic value* of an asset (i.e., the value implied by its payoff vector), it is likely that traders are trading in a "speculative bubble" because of self-fulfilling expectations about the further price development. Well-known examples of speculative bubbles include the tulip mania in the Netherlands in 1637 (Garber 1990), the dot.com bubble at the turn of last century (Shiller 2005; Malkiel 2007), and, more recently, the US housing bubble (Sowell 2010). John Maynard Keynes (1936) offered the following comparison:

> Professional investment may be likened to those newspaper competitions in which the competitors have to pick out the six prettiest faces from a hundred photographs, the prize being awarded to the competitor whose choice most nearly corresponds to the average preferences of the competitors as a whole; so that each competitor has to pick, not those faces which he himself finds prettiest, but those which he thinks likeliest to catch the fancy of the other competitors, all of whom are looking at the problem from the same point of view. It is not a case of choosing those which, to the best of one's judgment, are really the prettiest, nor even those which average opinion genuinely thinks the prettiest. We have reached the third degree where we devote our intelligences to anticipating what average opinion expects the average opinion to be. And there are some, I believe, who practise the fourth, fifth and higher degrees" (Keynes 1936: 156).

In this "beauty contest", superior returns are awarded to the trader who correctly anticipates market sentiment. For additional details on asset pricing see, for example, Duffie (1988, 2001).

---

[23] To see this, assume for example that the market price V^3 is greater than $\phi^1 V^1 + \phi^2 V^2$. Thus, if a trader holds a portfolio with quantities $q^1 = \phi^1 V^3$ of asset 1, $q^2 = \phi^2 V^3$ of asset 2, and $q^3 = -(\phi^1 V^1 + \phi^2 V^2)$ of asset 3, then the value of that portfolio vanishes, as $\sum_{m=1}^{3} q^m V^m = 0$. However, provided an equivalent martingale measure $p_1, \ldots, p_M$ (cf. Section 17.3.3) the total return of the portfolio, $\sum_{k=1}^{K} p_k V^m \omega_k^m q_k = p_k \omega_k^3 (V^3 - (\phi^1 V^1 + \phi^2 V^2))$, is positive for each state s_k.

[24] Another approach to asset pricing is Luenberger's (2001, 2002) zero-level pricing method, based on the widely used Capital Asset Pricing Model (Markowitz 1952; Tobin 1958; Sharpe 1964). It relies on the geometric projection of the prices of "similar" traded assets.

17.4 DISEQUILIBRIUM AND PRICE ADJUSTMENTS

In practice, we cannot expect markets always to be in equilibrium, especially when agents are free to enter and exit, economic conditions may change over time, and not all market participants possess the same information. Section 17.4.1 specifies a possible price adjustment process, referred to as "*tâtonnement*", that tends to attain a Walrasian equilibrium asymptotically over time. In Section 17.4.2, we summarize important insights about the strategic use of private information in markets, for example the fundamental result that trade might not be possible at all if all agents are rational and some hold extra information.

17.4.1 Walrasian *tâtonnement*

In real life there is no reason to believe that markets always clear. At a given price it may be that there is either excess demand or excess supply, which in turn should lead to an adjustment of prices and/or quantities. While it is relatively simple to agree about the notion of a static Walrasian equilibrium, which is based on the self-interested behavior of price-taking agents and firms as well as a market-clearing condition, there are multiple ways of modeling the adjustment dynamics when markets do not clear. Walras (1874/77) was the first to formalize a price-adjustment process by postulating that the change in the price of good $l \in \{1, \ldots, L\}$ is proportional to the *excess demand* z_l of good l, where (suppressing all dependencies from entities other than price)

$$z_l(p) = \sum_{i=1}^{N} \left(x_l^i(p) - \omega_l^i \right) - \sum_{m=1}^{m} y_l^m(p).$$

This leads to an adjustment process, which in continuous time can be described by a system of L differential equations,

$$\dot{p}_l = \kappa_l z_l(p), \quad l \in \{1, \ldots, L\}. \tag{18}$$

This process is commonly referred to as a *Walrasian tâtonnement*. The positive constants κ_l determine the speed of the adjustment process for each good l.[25] One can show that if the Walrasian equilibrium price vector $\hat{p}$ is unique, and if $\hat{p} \cdot z(p) > 0$ for any p not proportional to $\hat{p}$, then a solution trajectory $p(t)$ of the Walrasian *tâtonnement* (18) converges to $\hat{p}$, in the sense that

$$\lim_{t \to \infty} p(t) = \hat{p}.$$

As an illustration, we continue the example of a two-agent two-good exchange economy with Cobb–Douglas utility functions in Section 17.3.1. The *tâtonnement* dynamics in eq. (18) become

$$\begin{cases} \dot{p}_1 = 3 \, \kappa_1(\alpha(p_1 + p_2)/p_1 - 1), \\ \dot{p}_2 = 3 \, \kappa_2((1 - \alpha)(p_1 + p_2)/p_2 - 1), \end{cases}$$

[25] It may be useful to normalize the price vector $p(t)$ such that $p_1^2(t) + \cdots + p_L^2(t) \equiv 1$, since then $d(p_1^2(t) + \cdots + p_L^2(t))/dt = 2p(t) \cdot z(p(t)) \equiv 0$ (with $z = (z_1, \ldots, z_L)$). Under this normalization any trajectory $p(t)$ remains in the "invariant" set $S = \{p : (p_1)^2 + \cdots + (p_L)^2 = 1\}$.

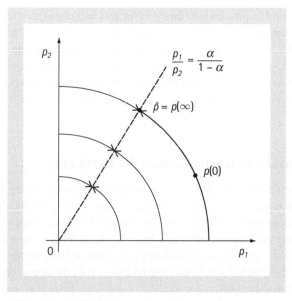

FIGURE 17.5 Walrasian price adjustment process with asymptotic convergence of prices

where $\kappa_1, \kappa_2 > 0$ are appropriate constants. It is easy to see that $p_1/p_2 < \alpha/(1-\alpha)$ implies that $\dot{p}_1 > 0$ (and that $\dot{p}_2 < 0$) and vice versa. In (p_1, p_2)-space we therefore obtain that a trajectory $p_2(p_1)$ (starting at any given price vector) is described by

$$\frac{dp_2(p_1)}{dp_1} = \frac{3 \,\kappa_2(\,(1-\alpha)(p_1+p_2)/p_2-1)}{3 \,\kappa_1(\alpha(p_1+p_2)/p_1-1)} = -\frac{\kappa_2}{\kappa_1}\frac{p_1}{p_2}.$$

It follows a concentric circular segment, eventually approaching a 'separatrix' defined by $p_1/p_2 = \alpha/(1-\alpha)$ (cf. Figure 17.5). We see that when the price of good 1 is too low relative to the price of good 2, then due to the positive excess demand, p_1 will adjust upwards until the excess demand for that good vanishes, which—by the market-clearing condition—implies that the excess demand for the other good also vanishes, so that we have arrived at an equilibrium.[26]

Walrasian price-adjustment processes have been tested empirically. Joyce (1984) reports experimental results in an environment with consumers and producers that show that for a single unit of a good the *tâtonnement* can produce close to Pareto-efficient prices, and that the process has strong convergence properties. Bronfman et al. (1996) consider the multi-unit case and find that the efficiency properties of the adjustment process depend

---

[26] A Walrasian equilibrium price is locally asymptotically stable if, when starting in a neighborhood of this price, Walrasian *tâtonnement* yields price trajectories that converge toward the equilibrium price. A sufficient condition for local asymptotic stability (i.e., convergence) is that the linearized system $\dot{p} = A$ $(p - \hat{p})$ corresponding to the right-hand side of eq. (18) around the Walrasian equilibrium price $\hat{p}$ is such that the linear system matrix A has only eigenvalues with negative real parts. In the example, we have that $A = 3\alpha \begin{bmatrix} -\alpha\kappa_1/(1-\alpha) & \kappa_1 \\ \kappa_2 & -\alpha\kappa_2/(1-\alpha) \end{bmatrix}$, the eigenvalues of which have negative real parts for all $\kappa_1, \kappa_2 > 0$ and all $\alpha \in (0,1)$. For more details on the analysis of dynamic systems, see, e.g., Weber (2011).

substantially on how this process is defined. Eaves and Williams (2007) analyze Walrasian *tâtonnement* auctions at the Tokyo Grain Exchange run in 1997/98 and find that price formation is similar to the normative predictions in continuous double auctions.

We note that it is also possible to consider quantity adjustments instead of price adjustments (Marshall 1920). The resulting quantity-adjustment dynamics are sometimes referred to as *Marshallian dynamics* (in contrast to the *Walrasian dynamics* for price adjustments).

17.4.2 Information transmission in markets

It is an economic reality that different market participants are likely to have different information about the assets that are up for trade. Thus, in a market for used cars, sellers may have more information than buyers. For simplicity, let us consider such a market, where cars are either of value 0 or of value 1, but it is impossible for buyers to tell which one is which until after the transaction has taken place. Let $\varphi \in (0,1)$ be the fraction of sellers who sell "lemons" (i.e., cars of zero value) and let $c \in (0,1)$ be the opportunity cost of a seller who sells a high-value car. Then, if $1 - \varphi < c$, there is no price p at which buyers would want to buy and high-value sellers would want to sell. Indeed, high-value sellers sell only if $p \geq c$. Lemons sellers simply imitate high-value sellers and also charge p for their cars (they would be willing to sell at any nonnegative price). As a consequence, the buyers stand to obtain the negative expected value $(1 - \varphi) - p$ from buying a car in this market, which implies that they do not buy. Hence, the market for used cars fails, in the sense that only lemons can be traded, if there are too many lemons compared to high-value cars (Akerlof 1970). This self-inflicted disappearance of high-value items from the market is called "adverse selection".

In the context of Walrasian markets in the absence of nonrational ("noise") traders, and as long as the way in which traders acquire private information about traded assets is common knowledge, Milgrom and Stokey (1982) show that none of the traders is in a position to profit from the private information, as any attempt to trade will lead to a correct anticipation of market prices. This implies that private information cannot yield a positive return. Since this theoretical no-trade theorem is in sharp contrast to the reality found in most financial markets, where superior information tends to yield positive (though sometimes illegal) returns, the missing ingredient are irrational "noise traders", willing to trade without concerns about the private information available to other traders (e.g., for institutional reasons).

What information can be communicated in a market? Hayek (1945: 526) points out that one should in fact consider the "price system" in a market as "a mechanism for communicating information". The price system is useful under uncertainty, since (as we have seen in Section 17.3) markets generally exist not only for the purpose of allocating resources, but also to provide traders with the possibility of mutual insurance (Hurwicz 1960). To understand the informational role of prices under uncertainty, let us consider a market as in Section 17.3.4, where N strategic traders ("investors") and a number of nonstrategic traders ("noise traders") trade financial securities that have state-contingent payoffs. Each investor i may possess information about the future payoff of these securities in the form of a private signal $\tilde{z}^i$, which, conditional on the true state of the world, is independent of any other investor j's private signal $\tilde{z}^j$. In the classical model discussed thus far, at any given market price vector p for the available securities, agent i has the Walrasian demand $x^i(p, \omega^i; z^i)$, which—in addition to his endowment ω^i—also depends on the realization z^i of his private signal. However, an investor i who conditions his demand only on the realized price and his private information would ignore the process by which the *other* agents arrive at their demands, which help establish the market price, which in equilibrium must depend on the full information vector $z = (z^1, \ldots, z^N)$. For example, if investor i's private information leads him to be very optimistic about the market outlook, then at any given price p his demand will be high. Yet, if a very low market price p is observed, investor i obtains the valuable insight that all other investors' signal realizations must have been rather dim, which means that his information is likely to be an extreme value from a statistical point of view. Grossman and Stiglitz (1980) therefore conclude that in a rational-expectations equilibrium each investor i's demand must be of the form $x^i(p, \omega^i; z^i, p(z))$, that is, it will depend on the way in which the equilibrium price incorporates the available information.[27] While in an economy where private information is freely available this may result in the price to fully reveal the entire information available in the market (because, for example, it depends only on an average of the investors' information; Leland and Pyle 1977), this does not hold when information is costly. Grossman and Stiglitz (1980) show that in the presence of a (possibly even small) cost of acquiring private information, prices fail to aggregate all the information in the market, so that a rational expectations equilibrium cannot be "informationally efficient".[28]

The question naturally arises of how to use private information in an effective way, especially if one can do so over time.[29] Kyle (1985) develops a seminal model of insider trading where one informed investor uses his inside information in a measured way over a finite time horizon so as to not be imitated by other rational investors. Another option an informed investor has for using private information is to sell it to other investors. Admati and Pfleiderer (1986) show that it may be best for the informed investor to degrade this information (by adding noise) before selling it, in order to protect his own trading interests.

---

[27] In an actual financial market (such as the New York Stock Exchange), investors can submit their offer curves in terms of "limit orders", which specify the number of shares of each given asset that the investor is willing to buy at a given price.

[28] In the absence of randomness a rational expectations equilibrium may even fail to exist. Indeed, if no investor expends the cost to become informed, then the equilibrium price reveals nothing about the true value of the asset, which produces an incentive for investors to become informed (provided the cost is small enough). On the other hand, if all other investors become informed, then, due to the nonstochastic nature of the underlying values, an uninformed investor could infer the true value of any security from the price, which in turn negates the incentive for the costly information acquisition.

[29] It is important to realize that while *private* information tends to be desirable in most cases (for exceptions, see Section 17.7.4), this may not be true for *public* (or "social") information. Hirshleifer (1971) shows that social information that is provided to all investors in a market might have a negative value because it can destroy the market for mutual insurance. To see this, consider two farmers, one with a crop that grows well in a dry season and the other with a crop that grows well in a wet season. If both farmers are risk-averse, then given, say, *ex ante* equal chances of either type of season to occur, they have an incentive to write an insurance contract that guarantees part of the proceeds of the farmer with the favorable outcome to the other farmer. Both of these farmers would *ex ante* be strictly worse off if a messenger disclosed the type of season (dry or wet) to them (while, clearly, each farmer retains an incentive to obtain such information privately).

REMARK 5 Arrow (1963) realized that there are fundamental difficulties when trying to sell information from an informed party to an uninformed party, perhaps foreshadowing the no-trade theorem discussed earlier. Indeed, if the seller of information just claims to have the information, then a buyer may have no reason to believe the seller.[30] The seller, therefore, may have to "prove" that the information is really available, for example by acting on it in a market (taking large positions in a certain stock), to convince potential buyers. This may dissipate a part or all of the value of the available information. On the other hand, if the seller of information transmits the information to a prospective buyer for a "free inspection", then it may be difficult to prevent that potential buyer from using it, even when the latter later decides not to purchase the information. Arrow (1973) therefore highlights a fundamental "inappropriability" of information.[31] Clearly, information itself can be securitized, as illustrated by the recent developments in prediction markets (Wolfers and Zitzewitz 2004). Segal (2006) provides a general discussion about the informational requirements for an economic mechanism (such as a market) if its purpose is to implement Pareto-efficient outcomes but where agents possess private knowledge about their preferences (and not the goods). □

17.5 EXTERNALITIES AND NONMARKET GOODS

Sometimes transactions take place outside of markets. For example, one agent's action may have an effect on another agent's utility without any monetary transfer between these agents. In Section 17.5.1, we see that the absence of a market for such "externalities" between agents can cause markets for other goods to fail. Similarly, the markets for certain goods, such as human organs, public parks, or clean air, may simply not exist. The value of "nonmarket goods", which can be assessed using the welfare measures of "compensating variation" and "equivalent variation", is discussed in Section 17.5.2.

17.5.1 Externalities

In Section 17.3 we saw that markets can produce Pareto-efficient outcomes, even though exchange and productive activity is not centrally managed and is pursued entirely by self-interested parties. One key assumption there was that each agent i's utility function u^i depends only on his own consumption bundle x^i. However, this may not be appropriate in some situations. For example, if Joe listens to loud music while Melanie tries to study for an upcoming exam, then Joe's consumption choice has a direct impact on Melanie's well-

---

[30] More recently, "zero-knowledge proof" techniques have been developed for (at least approximately) conveying the fact that information is known without conveying the information itself; see, e.g., Goldreich et al. (1991).

[31] For "information goods" such as software, techniques to augment appropriability (involving the partial transmission of information) have been refined. For example, it is possible to provide potential buyers of a software package with a free version ("cripple ware") that lacks essential features (such as the capability to save a file) but that effectively demonstrates the basic functionality of the product, without compromising its commercial value.

being. We say that his action exerts a (direct) *negative externality* on her. Positive externalities also exist, for example when Melanie decides to do her cooking and Joe loves the resulting smell from the kitchen, her action has a direct positive impact on his well-being.[32]

There are many important practical examples of externalities in the economy, including environmental pollution, technological standards, telecommunication devices, or public goods. For concreteness, let us consider two firms, 1 and 2. Assume that firm 1's production output q (e.g., a certain chemical)—due to unavoidable pollution emissions—makes firm 2's production (e.g., catching fish) more difficult at the margin by requiring a costly pollution-abatement action z (e.g., water sanitation) by firm 2. Suppose that firm 1's profit $\pi^1(q)$ is concave in q and such that $\pi^1(0) = \pi^1(\bar{q}) = 0$ for some $\bar{q} > 0$. Firm 2's profit $\pi^2(q, z)$ is decreasing in q, concave in z, and has (strictly) increasing differences in (q, z) (i.e. $\partial^2 \pi^2 / \partial q \partial z > 0$), reflecting the fact that its marginal profit $\partial \pi^2 / \partial z$ for the abatement action is increasing in the pollution level. Note that while firm 2's payoff depends on firm 1's action, firm 1 is unconcerned about what firm 2 does. Thus, without any outside intervention, firm 1 chooses an output $q^* \in \arg \max_{q \geq 0} \pi^1(q)$ that maximizes its profit. Firm 2, on the other hand, takes q^* as given and finds its optimal abatement response, $z^* \in \arg \max_{z \geq 0} \pi^2(q^*, z)$. In contrast to this, the socially optimal actions, $\hat{q}$ and $\hat{z}$, are such that they maximize joint payoffs (corresponding to "social welfare" in this simple model), that is:

$$(\hat{q}, \hat{z}) \in \arg \max_{(q,z) \geq 0} \{\pi^1(q) + \pi^2(q, z)\}.$$

It is easy to show that the socially optimal actions $\hat{q}$ and $\hat{z}$ are at strictly lower levels than the privately optimal actions q^* and t^*: because firm 1 does not perceive the social cost of its actions, the world is over-polluted in this economy; a market for the direct negative externality from firm 1 on firm 2 is missing.

A regulator can intervene and restore efficiency, for example by imposing a tax on firm 1's output q which internalizes the social cost of its externality. To accomplish this, first consider the "harm" of firm 1's action, defined as

$$h(q) = \pi^2(q, z^*(0)) - \pi^2(q, z^*(q)),$$

where $z^*(q)$ is firm 2's best abatement action in response to firm 1's choosing an output of q. Then if firm 1 maximizes its profit minus the harm $h(q)$ it causes to firm 1, we obtain an efficient outcome, since

$$\hat{q} \in \arg \max_{q \geq 0} \{\pi^1(q) - h(q)\} = \arg \max_{q \geq 0} \left\{\pi^1(q) + \max_{z \geq 0} \pi^2(q, z)\right\}.$$

Hence, by imposing a per-unit excise tax of $\tau = h'(\hat{q})$ (equal to the marginal harm at the socially optimal output $\hat{q}$) on firm 1, a regulator can implement a Pareto-efficient outcome.[33] Alternatively, firm 1 could simply be required (if necessary through litigation) to

---

[32] In contrast to the direct externalities where the payoff of one agent depends on another agent's action or choice, so-called "pecuniary externalities" act through prices. For example, in a standard exchange economy the fact that one agent demands a lot of good 1 means that the price of that good will increase, exerting a negative pecuniary externality on those agents.

[33] This method is commonly referred to as *Pigouvian taxation* (Pigou 1920).

pay the total amount $h(q)$ in damages when producing an output of q, following a "Polluter Pays Principle".[34]

The following seminal result by Coase (1960) states that even without direct government intervention, an efficient outcome may result from bargaining between parties, which includes the use of transfer payments.

THEOREM 3 (COASE THEOREM) *If property rights are assigned and there are no informational asymmetries, costless bargaining between agents leads to a Pareto-efficient outcome.*

The intuition for this result becomes clear within the context of our previous example. Assume that firm 1 is assigned the right to produce, regardless of the effect this might have on firm 2. Then firm 2 may offer firm 1 an amount of money, A, to reduce its production (and thus its negative externality). Firm 1 agrees if

$$\pi^1(\hat{q}) + A \geq \pi^1(q^*),$$

and firm 2 has an incentive to do so if

$$\pi^2(\hat{q}, \hat{z}) - A \geq \pi^2(q^*, z^*).$$

Any amount A between $\pi^1(q^*) - \pi^1(\hat{q})$ and $\pi^2(\hat{q}, \hat{z}) - \pi^2(q^*, z^*)$, that is, when

$$A = \lambda(\pi^1(\hat{q}) + \pi^2(\hat{q}, \hat{z}) - \pi^1(q^*) - \pi^2(q^*, z^*)) + (\pi^1(q^*) - \pi^1(\hat{q})), \quad \lambda \in [0, 1],$$

is acceptable to both parties. Conversely, if firm 2 is assigned the right to a pollution-free environment, then firm 1 can offer firm 2 an amount

$$B = \mu(\pi^1(\hat{q}) + \pi^2(\hat{q}, \hat{z}) - \pi^1(0) - \pi^2(0, z^*(0))) + (\pi^2(0, z^*(0)) - \pi^2(\hat{q}, \hat{z})), \quad \mu \in [0, 1],$$

to produce at the efficient level $\hat{q}$. The choice of the constant λ (or μ) determines which party ends up with the gains from trade and is therefore subject to negotiation.

Instead of assigning the property rights for pollution (or lack thereof) to one of the two parties, the government may issue marketable pollution permits which confer the right to pollute. If these permits can be traded freely between firm 1 and firm 2, then, provided that there are at least $\hat{q}$ permits issued, the resulting Walrasian equilibrium (cf. Section 17.3.1) yields a price equal to the marginal harm $h'(\hat{q})$ at the socially optimal output. Hence, efficiency is restored through the creation of a market for the externality.

The preceding discussion shows that without government intervention Adam Smith's "invisible hand" might in fact be absent when there are externalities. Stiglitz (2006) points out that "the reason that the invisible hand often seems invisible is that it is often not there." Indeed, in the presence of externalities the Pareto efficiency property of Walrasian equilibria generally breaks down. An example is when a good which can be produced at a cost (such as national security or a community radio program) can be consumed by all agents in the economy because they cannot be prevented from doing so. Thus, due to the problem with appropriating rents from this "public" good, the incentive for it is very low, a phenomenon that is often referred to as the "tragedy of the commons" (Hardin 1968). More precisely, a *public good* (originally termed "collective consumption good" by Samuelson (1954)) is a good that is *nonrival* (in the sense that it can be consumed by one agent and is still available for consumption by another agent) and *nonexcludable* (in the sense that it is not possible, at any reasonable effort, to prevent others from using it). Examples include

<hr>

[34] This principle is also called Extended Polluter Responsibility (EPR) (Lindhqvist 1992).

Table 17.1 Classification of goods		
Good	Excludable	Nonexcludable
Rival	Private	Common
Nonrival	Club	Public

radio waves or a public park. On the other hand, a *private* good is a good that is rival and excludable. All other goods are called *semi-public* (or *semi-private*). In particular, if a semi-public good is nonrival and excludable, it is called a *club good* (e.g., an electronic newspaper subscription or membership in an organization), and if it is rival and nonexcludable it is referred to as a *common good* (e.g., fish or freshwater). Table 17.1 provides an overview.

It is possible to extend the notion of Walrasian equilibrium to take into account the externalities generated by the presence of public goods in the economy. Consider N agents and M firms in a private-ownership economy as in Section 17.3.2, with the only difference that, in addition to L private goods, there are L_G public goods that are privately produced. Each agent i chooses a bundle ξ of the available public goods, and a bundle x^i of the private goods on the market. Each firm m can produce a vector y_G^m of public goods and a vector y^m of private goods, which are feasible if (y_G^m, y^m) is in this firm's production set Y^m. Lindahl (1919) suggested the following generalization of the Walrasian equilibrium (cf. Definition 4), which for our setting can be formulated as follows.

DEFINITION 6 *A Lindahl equilibrium $(\hat{p}_G, \hat{p}, \hat{\xi}, \hat{x}, \hat{y}_G, \hat{y})$ in a private-ownership economy, with personalized prices $\hat{p}_G = (\hat{p}_G^1, \ldots, \hat{p}_G^N)$ for the public good, is such that all agents maximize utility,*

$$(\hat{\xi}, \hat{x}^i) \in \arg \max_{(\xi, x^i) \in B((\hat{p}_G^i, \hat{p}), \hat{w}^i)} u^i(\xi, x^i), \quad i \in \{1, \ldots, N\},$$

where $\hat{w}^i = \hat{p} \cdot \omega^i + \sum_{m=1}^{M} \vartheta_m^i \left(\sum_{i=1}^{N} \hat{p}_G^i \cdot \hat{y}_G^m + \hat{p} \cdot \hat{y}^m \right)$, all firms maximize profits,

$$(\hat{y}_G^m, \hat{y}^m) \in \arg \max_{(y_G^m, y^m) \in Y^m} \left\{ \sum_{i=1}^{N} \hat{p}_G^i \cdot y_G^m + \hat{p} \cdot y^m \right\}, \quad m \in \{1, \ldots, M\},$$

and the resulting allocation is feasible,

$$\hat{\xi} = \sum_{m=1}^{M} \hat{y}_G^m \quad and \quad \sum_{i=1}^{N} (\hat{x}^i - \omega^i) = \sum_{m=1}^{M} \hat{y}^m.$$

It can be shown that the Lindahl equilibrium exists (Foley 1970; Roberts 1973) and that it restores the efficiency properties of the Walrasian equilibrium in terms of the two fundamental welfare theorems (Foley 1970).[35] Because of personal arbitrage, as well as the difficulty of distinguishing different agents and/or of price discriminating between them, it may be impossible to implement personalized prices, which tends to limit the practical implications of the Lindahl equilibrium.

REMARK 6 Another approach for dealing with implementing efficient outcomes in the presence of externalities comes from game theory rather than general equilibrium theory. Building on insights on menu auctions by Bernheim and Whinston (1986), Prat and Rustichini (2003)

---

[35] We omit the technical assumptions required for a precise statement of these theorems.

examine a setting where each one of M buyers ("principals") noncooperatively proposes a nonlinear payment schedule to each one of N sellers ("agents"). After these offers are known, each seller i then chooses to offer a bundle ("action") $x_i^j \in \mathbb{R}_+^L$ for buyer j. Given that buyers' utility functions can have full externalities, Prat and Rustichini show that there exists an equilibrium which implements an efficient outcome. Weber and Xiong (2007) generalize this finding under minimal assumptions to the fully general setting where both buyers and sellers care about every action taken in the economy. In this situation, prices become nonlinear functions of the quantities, effectively extending the traditionally "linear" notion of price (where twice as much of an item typically costs twice as much) in a full-information setting.[36] Jackson and Wilkie (2005) consider another generalization of Prat and Rustichini's results, allowing for side payments between different market participants.   □

REMARK 7 We briefly mention the possibility of central planning as an alternative to resource allocation through markets. While the "Chicago School" in economics with proponents such as Ronald Coase, Frank Knight, Friedrich von Hayek, George Stigler, Gary Becker, or Milton Friedman, tends to favor the use of markets for the allocation of resources, the above-mentioned possibility of market failure due to the lack of an invisible hand in the presence of externalities might call for a compromise between markets and government intervention. The main drawback of centrally managed economies stems from the difficulty of collecting and aggregating information at a center (Hayek 1945). Shafarevich (1980) and Stiglitz (1994) provide additional interesting perspectives.

REMARK 8 Related to the last remark, when a social planner has full authority, desirable allocations may be implemented using either permits or quotas.[37] The question of *what* allocations may be desirable invokes the problem of fairness, which may be addressed by what maximizes the sum of all agents' utilities (utiliarian solution; Mill 1863), what is best for the economically weakest agents (egalitarian solution; Rawls 1971), a robust intermediate allocation (relatively fair solution; Goel et al. 2009), or by what ensures that no agent would want to swap his allocation with another agent (envy-free solution; Foley 1967).

17.5.2 Nonmarket goods

For many goods, such as public parks, clean air, the Nobel memorial prize, human organs, or public offices, there are no well-defined markets. Yet, these goods may be of considerable value to some, so that the question begs of how one should determine the value of a *nonmarket good* to a given individual. In contrast to market goods, it is not possible to find an "objective" value by looking up the good's price. The good has no *a priori* price and its value, as we shall see below, depends on the individual with whom a transaction is to take place and possibly also on the direction of the transaction.[38]

A general way of thinking about a nonmarket good is in terms of a "change of state" between $s = 0$ and $s = 1$. In state 1 the good is present, whereas in state 0 it is absent. If x denotes a typical consumption bundle of market goods, then Joe's utility of x in state $s \in \{0, 1\}$

---

[36] In Section 17.7, we see that in the presence of information asymmetries nonlinear price schedules arise naturally.

[37] In the presence of uncertainty this equivalence may disappear, as noted by Weitzman (1974).

[38] For a recent survey on nonmarket valuation see Champ et al. (2003).

is $u_s(x)$. Thus, given a wealth of $w > 0$ and a price vector p for the bundle of conventional market goods, by eq. (8) Joe's indirect utility is

$$v_s(p,w) = \max_{x \in B(p,w)} u_s(x), \quad s \in \{0,1\}.$$

Hence, if Joe does not have the nonmarket good initially, he would be willing to pay any amount c that leaves him at the reduced wealth $w - c$ at least as well off as he was initially. Hence, the maximum amount Joe is willing to pay, given his initial wealth w, is

$$CV(w) = \sup \{c \in \mathbb{R}: v_1(p, w - c) \geq v_0(p, w)\}. \tag{19}$$

The welfare measure CV is called Joe's *compensating variation* or *willingness to pay* (WTP) for the change from $s = 0$ to $s = 1$. Conversely, if Joe initially has the nonmarket good, then the smallest amount he is willing to accept, given his initial wealth w, is

$$EV(w) = \inf \{e \in \mathbb{R}: v_0(p, w + e) \geq v_1(p, w)\}. \tag{20}$$

The welfare measure EV is termed *equivalent variation* or *willingness to accept* (WTA) for the change from $s = 1$ to $s = 0$.

As an example, we consider as "the" classical application of these welfare measures, proposed by Hicks (1939), the case where the change of state corresponds to a change in the market price from p to $\hat{p}$ (say, $\hat{p} \ll p$ in case of a price decrease). The equivalent variation measures how much Joe would be willing to give up in wealth in return for a change in the price vector from p to $\hat{p}$. From eq. (19) we obtain (dropping any subscripts) that

$$\underbrace{v(\hat{p}, w - CV(w))}_{=v(\hat{p}, e(\hat{p}, U))} = \underbrace{v(p, w)}_{=v(p, e(p, U))},$$

where $e(p, U) = w$ is Joe's expenditure on market goods necessary to attain the utility level $U = u(x(p, w))$ (cf. Section 17.2.3). Hence, $w - CV(w) = e(p, U) - CV(w)$ must be equal to $e(\hat{p}, U)$, so that

$$CV(w) = e(p, U) - e(\hat{p}, U). \tag{21}$$

In a completely analogous manner one finds that

$$EV(w) = e(p, \hat{U}) - e(\hat{p}, \hat{U}), \tag{22}$$

where $\hat{U} = u(x(\hat{p}, w))$ is the utility level at the new price $\hat{p}$.[39]

---

[39] It is interesting to note that the compensating and equivalent variations in eqs (21) and (22) depend only on the initial price p and the final price $\hat{p}$, not on the path from one to the other. This is in contrast to the change in *consumer surplus*, $\Delta CS(w) = \int_{\hat{p}}^{p} x(p(\gamma)) \cdot d\gamma$, which depends on the path γ taken. Taking classical mechanics as an analogy, the variation in potential energy when moving a rigid body between two points in a (conservative) gravitational field depends only on these two points. Similarly, the expenditure function can be viewed as a "potential function" that measures the variation of welfare for a price change only in terms of the beginning and ending prices. The underlying mathematical justification is that as a consequence of Roy's identity (cf. Section 17.2.3) the Hicksian demand is a gradient field (generated by the expenditure function), whereas Slutsky's identity (10) implies that (due to the wealth effect) Walrasian demand generally is not a gradient field, i.e. not integrable. (Integrability is characterized by the Frobenius theorem, whose conditions, $\partial x_i(p, w)/\partial p_j = \partial x_j(p, w)/\partial p_i$ for all i, j, are generally not satisfied for a given Walrasian demand.) It is easy to see that $\Delta CS(w)$ always lies between $CV(w)$ and $EV(w)$. Willig (1976) has shown that the difference between the two is likely to be small, so that the variation of consumer surplus (along any path) can often be considered a reasonable approximation for the welfare change. For more general state changes this observation becomes incorrect (see, e.g., Hanemann 1991).

There is a simple and exact relation between compensating and equivalent variation, provided that both are finite (Weber 2003, 2010), one being a shifted version of the other,

$$EV(w - CV(w)) = CV(w) \quad \text{and} \quad EV(w) = CV(w + EV(w)). \tag{23}$$

REMARK 9 Nonmarket goods are by definition traded using contracts rather than markets. The expense of writing such contracts can be substantial, implying a nonnegligible "transaction cost" (Coase 1937). Williamson (1975, 1985) points out that transaction costs are driven by the specificity and uncertainty attached to the items to be transacted, as well as the bounded rationality and opportunistic behavior of the contracting parties. Transaction cost economics also recognizes the fact that contracts are necessarily "incomplete" in the sense that not all possible contingencies can be captured and therefore all "residual claims" must be assigned to one party (Hart 1988; Hart and Moore 1990). Transaction cost economics can be used to help explain the boundary of the firm, which is determined by the decision of which goods and services are to be procured from within the firm and which from outside.

17.6 STRATEGIC PRICING WITH COMPLETE INFORMATION

So far, the price or value of a good has been determined in a nonstrategic way, either via an equilibrium in a competitive market with price-taking agents (cf. Section 17.3.2), or, for nonmarket goods, via indifference using Hicksian welfare measures (cf. Section 17.5.2). In general, the price can be influenced strategically by agents who have "market power". Section 17.6.1 deals with the case where there is one such agent and Section 17.6.2 with the case where there are several. In Section 17.6.3, we briefly discuss what a single strategic firm in a market can do to prevent competitors from entering that market.

17.6.1 Monopoly pricing

Consider a single firm that can set prices for its products and choose the best element of its production set Y (introduced in Section 17.3.2). We assume that it is possible to split the components of any feasible production vector $y \in Y$ into *inputs* z and *outputs* (or *products*) q, so that

$$y = (-z, q),$$

where $q, z \geq 0$ are appropriate vectors. Thus, in its production process the firm is able to distinguish clearly between its inputs and its outputs. The problem of finding the firm's optimal price is typically solved in a *partial equilibrium* setting, where for any price vector p that the firm might choose, it expects to sell to a demand $q = D(p)$.[40]

---

[40] In contrast to the *general equilibrium* setting in Section 17.3 we neglect here the fact that in a closed economy the agents working at the firm have a budget set that depends on the wages that the firm pays, which in turn might stimulate these agents' demand for the firm's output. The latter is often referred to as the *Ford effect*, for it is said that Henry Ford used to pay higher wages to his employees in order to stimulate the demand for Ford automobiles (Bishop 1966: 658).

Given a vector of input prices w, the firm's *cost* for producing an output q of goods is

$$C(q; w, Y) = \min\{w \cdot z: (-z, q) \in Y\}.$$

This cost corresponds to the minimum expenditure for producing a certain output q. It depends on the market prices of the inputs as well as on the shape of the production set. For convenience, it is customary to omit the parameters w and Y from the cost function $C(q)$. The firm's *monopoly pricing problem* is to solve

$$\max_p \{p \cdot D(p) - C(D(p))\}. \tag{24}$$

The first-order necessary optimality condition is

$$pD'(p) + D(p) - C'(D(p))D'(p) = 0, \tag{25}$$

so that in the case of a single product we obtain the *(single-product) monopoly pricing rule*[41]

$$\frac{p - \text{MC}}{p} = \frac{1}{\varepsilon}, \tag{26}$$

where $\text{MC}(p) = C'(D(p))$ is the firm's marginal cost, and $\varepsilon = -pD'(p)/D(p)$ is the *(own-price) demand elasticity* for the good in question. The value on the left-hand side is often referred to as the Lerner index (Lerner 1934). It represents the firm's market power: the relative markup a single-product monopolist can charge, that is, the Lerner index, is equal to the multiplicative inverse of demand elasticity. Note that the pricing rule (26) also implies that the firm chooses to price in the elastic part of the demand curve, that is, at a point p where the elasticity $\varepsilon > 1$.

When there are multiple products, the first-order condition (25) yields a *multi-product monopoly pricing rule* (*Niehans formula*, Niehans 1956) of the form

$$\frac{p_l - \text{MC}_l(p)}{p_l} = \frac{1}{\varepsilon_{ll}}\left(1 - \sum_{j \neq l} \varepsilon_{lj}\left(\frac{p_j - \text{MC}_j(p)}{p_j}\right)\left(\frac{p_j D_j(p)}{p_l D_l(p)}\right)\right),$$

where $\varepsilon_{lj} = -(p_l/D_j(p))\partial D_l(p)/\partial p_j$ is the elasticity of demand for good l with respect to a change in the price of good j. ε_{ll} is the own-price elasticity for good l, whereas ε_{lj} for $l \neq j$ is called a *cross-price elasticity*. When the demand for good l increases with an increase of the price for good j, so that $\varepsilon_{lj} < 0$, then good l and good j are *complements* and the markup for good l tends to be below the single-product monopoly markup (but the firm expects to sell more of both products). Conversely, if the demand for good l decreases with an increase in the price of good j, so that $\varepsilon_{lj} > 0$, then the two goods are *substitutes*, which tends to decrease the price of good l compared to what a single-product monopolist would charge.

An example of complementary goods are the different components of a drum set (e.g., a snare drum and a snare-drum stand). *Perfect complements* are such that one cannot be used without the other, such as a left shoe and a right shoe which are therefore usually sold together in pairs.

---

[41] Eq. (26) can also be written in the form $p = \text{MC}\frac{\varepsilon}{\varepsilon-1}$, which is sometimes referred to as the *Amoroso–Robinson relation*. Note also that the elasticity ε depends on the price, so one needs in general to solve a fixed-point problem to obtain the optimal monopoly price.

Price discrimination

The practice of selling different units of the same good at different prices to different consumers is called *price discrimination*. Consider, for example, Joe and Melanie's demand for movie tickets. If the seller could somehow know exactly how much each individual would want to pay for a ticket for a given movie (at a given movie theater, at a given time), *perfect* (or *first-degree*) *price discrimination* is possible and the seller is able to extract all surplus from consumers by charging each consumer exactly his willingness to pay. However, the willingness to pay for a good is in many cases private information of potential buyers and therefore not known to a seller, who therefore has to restrict attention to observable characteristics. For example, a movie theater may offer student tickets at a discounted price in order to charge prices based on an observable characteristic (possession of a student ID card).[42] This is called *third-degree price discrimination*. Lastly, if the seller cannot discriminate based on observable characteristics, then it may still obtain a separation of consumers into different groups through product bundling. For example, the movie theater may give quantity discounts by selling larger numbers of movie tickets at a lower per-unit price. Alternatively, it could offer discounts on tickets for shows during the day or on weekdays. This lets consumers select the product or bundle they like best. If Joe is a busy manager, then he might prefer the weekend show at a higher price, whereas Melanie may prefer to see the same movie at the "Monday-afternoon special discount price". The practice of offering different bundles of (similar) goods by varying a suitable instrument (e.g., quantity, time of delivery) is called *second-degree price discrimination* or *nonlinear pricing* (discussed in Section 17.7.1).

As an example of third-degree price discrimination, consider a firm which would like to sell a certain good to two consumer groups. The marginal cost of providing the good to a consumer of group i is equal to c_i. At the price p_i group i's demand is given by $D_i(p_i)$, so that the firm's pricing problem (24) becomes

$$\max_{p_1,p_2} \left\{ \sum_{i=1}^{2} (p_i - c_i)D_i(p_i) \right\}.$$

Thus, the firm applies the monopoly pricing rule (26) to each group, so that

$$p_i + \underbrace{\frac{D_i(p_i)}{D_i'(p_i)}}_{MR_i(p_i)} = \underbrace{c_i}_{MC_i} \tag{27}$$

for all $i \in \{1, 2\}$. Eq. (27) says that a monopolist sets in each independent market a price so as to equalize its marginal cost MC_i and its *marginal revenue* $MR_i(p_i)$ in that market.[43]

---

[42] In some jurisdictions it is illegal for sellers to price discriminate based on certain observable characteristics such as age, gender, race, or certain other characteristics. For example, in the USA the Robinson–Patman Act of 1936 (Anti-Justice League Discrimination Act, 15 U.S.C. §13) is a federal law that prohibits price discrimination between equally situated distributors.

[43] In general, a firm's marginal cost MC_i depends on the firm's output and thus also on its price, just as its marginal revenue does. The marginal revenue is defined as the additional revenue the firm obtains when adding an infinitesimal unit of output. That is, $MR_i = \partial(p_i D_i)/\partial D_i = p_i + (D_i/D_i')$, using the product rule of differentiation and the inverse function theorem. We quietly assumed that the firm's marginal revenue is increasing in price (i.e., decreasing in quantity for all but Giffen goods). This assumption is not always

17.6.2 Oligopoly Pricing

The presence of other firms tends to erode the market power of any given firm. The reason is that this firm needs to anticipate the actions of all other firms.

In general, we can think of each firm i as having a set A^i of possible actions (or strategies) available. The vector $a = (a^1, \ldots, a^N) \in A = A^1 \times \cdots \times A^N$, which represents the vector of actions of all N firms, is called a *strategy profile*. Each firm i's profit, $\pi^i(a)$, depends on its own action a^i and the vector $a^{-i} = (a^1, \ldots, a^{i-1}, a^{i+1}, \ldots, a^N)$ of all other firms' actions.

DEFINITION 7 *A (pure-strategy) Nash equilibrium of the simultaneous-move game*[44] *is a strategy profile* $\hat{a} = (\hat{a}^1, \ldots, \hat{a}^N) \in A$ *such that*

$$\hat{a}^i \in \arg\max_{a^i \in A^i} \pi^i(a^i, \hat{a}^{-i}), \quad i \in \{1, \ldots, N\}. \tag{28}$$

Depending on if the firms set prices or quantities in their strategic interactions, the game is referred to either as a Bertrand pricing game or as a Cournot quantity-setting game (Bertrand 1883; Cournot 1838). For simplicity, we restrict attention to the special case in which each firm is producing a single homogeneous product.

Bertrand competition

Consider the situation in which there is a unit demand and only two firms which compete on price, so that the firm with the lower price obtains all of the sales. Firm $i \in \{1, 2\}$ therefore faces the demand

$$D^i(p^i, p^j) = \begin{cases} 1, & \text{if } p^i < \min\{p^j, r\}, \\ 1/2, & \text{if } p^i = p^j \leq r, \\ 0, & \text{otherwise,} \end{cases}$$

as a function of its own price p^i and the other firm's price p^j (where $j \in \{1, 2\} \setminus \{i\}$). Firm i's profit is $\pi^i(p^i, p^j) = (p^i - c)D^i(p^i, p^j)$. If firm j charges a price p^j greater than the firms' common marginal cost c, it is always best for firm i to slightly undercut firm j. If $p^j = c$, then by also charging marginal cost firm i cannot earn a positive profit, so that it becomes indifferent between charging $p^i = c$ or any price that is higher than the other firm's price (and which therefore results in zero sales). The unique Nash equilibrium strategy profile is described by $\hat{p}^i = \hat{p}^j = c$: both firms sell at marginal cost and make no profits at all. The firms are "trapped" in their strategic interaction: they cannot take advantage of technological innovation, that is, cutting c in half has no effect on their profits (Cabral and Villas-Boas 2005). In particular, both firms charge marginal cost and dissipate all of their profits. None of the firms can make any money. It is interesting to note that the zero-profit outcome persists when we add firms with identical marginal costs, and even if the marginal

satisfied, neither in theory nor even empirically (Beckman and Smith 1993), but it ensures a convex optimization problem (with concave objective function). We refer to it as the "regular case", and return to this case in Section 17.7.3 to avoid technical complications.

[44] A *game* is a collection of a set of players, a set of strategy profiles, and a set of payoff functions (one for each player, that maps any strategy profile to a real number). A *simultaneous-move game* is a game in which all players select their strategies at the same time. More information on game theory and its applications can be found in Kopalle and Shumsky (Chapter 19).

costs decrease for all firms from c to $\hat{c} < c$. This pessimistic outlook changes somewhat when the marginal costs are different across firms. In that case, there is generally a continuum of Nash equilibria that allow for prices between the most efficient firm's marginal cost and the second-most efficient firm's marginal cost (minus epsilon).

The extreme price competition in a Bertrand oligopoly is softened when firms are selling differentiated products. Hotelling (1929) introduced a by now classical model where two different sellers of the same good are located at two points on a line segment while consumers are distributed on a line segment. Each consumer faces a "transportation cost" to go to one of the two sellers, which allows them to charge a price premium as long as their locations are different. This "spatial" model of product differentiation is "horizontal", since different consumers may have quite different preferences for what is essentially the same good (once it is purchased and brought back home). Shaked and Sutton (1982) allow for vertical product differentiation, which also softens price discrimination.[45] Another reason why Bertrand oligopolists may obtain positive markups in equilibrium is that firms may have capacity constraints (Osborne and Pitchik 1986), so that the demand needs to be rationed, which can lead to positive rents.

Cournot competition

If instead of price firm i chooses its production quantity q^i, and at the aggregate quantity $Q(q) = q^1 + \cdots + q^N$ the (inverse) market demand is $p(Q) = D^{-1}(Q)$, then its profit is

$$\pi^i(q^i, q^{-i}) = (p(Q(q^i, q^{-i})) - c^i)q^i.$$

Each firm i can then determine its optimal quantity (also referred to as its "best response") as a function of the vector q_{-i} of the other firms' actions. For example, when the inverse demand curve is linear, that is, when $p(Q) = a - bQ$ for some $a, b > 0$, then the N conditions in eq. (28) yield firm i's Nash equilibrium quantity,

$$\hat{q}^i = \frac{a - c^i + \sum_{j=1}^{N} (c^j - c^i)}{(N+1)b},$$

provided that all firms produce a positive quantity in equilibrium.[46] The aggregate industry output becomes

$$\hat{Q} = \frac{N(a - \bar{c})}{(N+1)b},$$

where $\bar{c}$ is the average marginal cost of active firms in the industry. As the number of firms in the industry increases, the equilibrium price $\hat{p} = p(\hat{Q})$ tends toward the average marginal cost.[47]

[45] Beath and Katsoulacos (1991) give a survey of the economics of product differentiation in a locational setting. Anderson et al. (1992) give a survey in an alternative, random discrete-choice setting.

[46] Firms that prefer not to produce anything will be the ones with the highest marginal costs. Thus, after labeling all firms such that $c^1 \le c^2 \le \cdots \le c^N$ we obtain that $\hat{q}^i = (a - c^i)/b - (1/(1 + |I|)) \sum_{j \in I} (a - c^j)/b$, where $I = \{i \in \{1, \ldots, N\}: (1+i)(a - c^i) > \sum_{j=1}^{i} (a - c^j)\}$ is the set of participating firms.

[47] In the symmetric case, when all the firms' marginal costs are the same, i.e. when $c^1 = \cdots = c^N$, the equilibrium market price therefore tends toward marginal cost as the number of firms in the market increases.

$$\hat{p} = \frac{(a/N) + \bar{c}}{1 + (1/N)} \to \bar{c} \quad (\text{as } N \to \infty).$$

As in Section 17.6.1, each firm's market power can be measured in terms of the relative markup it is able to achieve. The more firms in the industry, the closer the market price will approximate the industry's lowest (constant) cost, forcing companies with higher marginal costs to exit. Eventually, the relative markup will therefore approach zero.

A practical measure of the competitiveness (or concentration) of an industry is the Herfindahl–Hirschman index (HHI); it measures industry concentration as the sum of the squares of the firms' market shares $\sigma^i = \hat{q}^i/\hat{Q}$ (Herfindahl 1950; Hirschman 1964),[48]

$$\text{HHI} = \sum_{i=1}^{N} (\sigma^i)^2 \in [0,1].$$

REMARK 10 From an empirical point of view (see, e.g., Baker and Bresnahan 1988, 1992) it is useful to identify the relative markup in an industry and compare it to the extreme cases of perfect competition (zero relative markup) on one side, and the monopoly pricing rule in eq. (26) on the other side. For example, the pricing rule in a symmetric N-firm oligopoly is

$$\frac{p - c}{p} = \frac{\theta}{\varepsilon},$$

where $\theta = \text{HHI} = 1/N$ and ε is the demand elasticity (cf. Section 17.6.1). In a monopoly $\theta = 1$, and under perfect competition $\theta = 0$. Thus, an empirical identification of θ allows for a full "conjectural variation", as a priori it can take on any value between zero and one.

REMARK 11 In a Cournot oligopoly firms might be "trapped" in their competitive inter-action just as in the Bertrand oligopoly: it may be to all firms' detriment when costs decrease. This was pointed out by Seade (1985), who showed that an increase of excise taxes may increase all firms' profits in a Cournot oligopoly. The intuition for this surprising result is that a higher cost may shift firms' output into a less elastic region of the consumers' demand curve, so that the firms' resulting price increase overcompensates them for their increased cost.[49] In this (somewhat pathological) situation, the consumers therefore bear more than the change in total firm profits, in terms of their welfare losses.

17.6.3 Entry deterrence and limit pricing

In general it is unrealistic to assume that strategic actions in an industry are taken simultaneously. An incumbent firm in an industry can try to protect its monopoly position by discouraging entry by other firms, for example by pricing below the long-run average cost, a practice which is called *limit pricing*.[50] If some fixed cost is required to enter the

---

[48] The HHI is used by the antitrust division of the US Department of Justice. Markets where HHI $\leq$ 10% are generally considered as competitive (or unconcentrated). A market for which HHI $\geq$ 18% is considered uncompetitive (or highly concentrated). Mergers or acquisitions which stand to change the HHI of an industry by more than 1% tend to raise anti-trust concerns.

[49] As an example, one can set $N = 2$, $c^1 = c^2 = c$, and $p(Q) = 100 \, Q^{-3/2}$ in our model, and then consider the increase in marginal cost from $c = 10$ to $c = 20$, which proves to be beneficial for the firms.

[50] It is possible to consider limit pricing also in an oligopolistic setting (Bagwell and Ramey 1991).

industry, a potential entrant may therefore be discouraged. The flip side of this is of course that the mere existence of *potential* entrants tends to limit the pricing power of an incumbent monopolist firm as a function of the required upfront investment. If the latter is close to zero, the markup a monopolist can charge also tends to zero.

Sometimes there are other activities that a monopolist can pursue to keep out competitors, such as advertising and/or building a loyal consumer base. These so-called *rent-seeking* activities (Tullock 1980) are generally costly. In principle, the monopolist is willing to spend all of its extra profit (of being a monopolist instead of an oligopolist) pursuing wasteful rent-seeking activities to obtain the extra profit (Posner 1975). Naturally, if one includes the intermediaries providing rent-seeking services, such as search advertising, into the system, then these activities may (even though not fully efficient) not be completely wasteful (Weber and Zheng 2007).

Sometimes the incumbent may resort to threats that *if* a competitor should enter, *then* a price war would be started that would have detrimental effects on the entrant, as they would not be able to recoup any upfront cost (which is already sunk for the incumbent). However, at times such threats may not be credible. For example, if a large incumbent in telecommunications is faced with a small capacity-constrained entrant, it may be better for the monopolist to ignore the entrant, allowing it to obtain a small market share at discount prices while it still retains a lion's share of the market at monopoly prices. The accommodated entrant can then work on building its consumer base and increasing its capacity, and gradually become a more serious threat to the incumbent (Gelman and Salop 1983).

REMARK 12 It is not always in an incumbent firm's best interest to discourage entry by other firms. For example, when other firms' products are complements, their presence would in effect exert a positive externality on the incumbent which may prompt the latter to encourage the entry of such "complementors" (Economides 1996). For example, a firm that wishes to sell a certain computer operating system may want to encourage the entry of software companies in the market that directly compete with certain of its own products (e.g., browser software) but at the same time render the operating system more valuable to consumers.

17.7 STRATEGIC PRICING WITH INCOMPLETE INFORMATION

The optimal pricing problem becomes more delicate if there are informational asymmetries between a seller and potential buyers. For example, the buyer's utility function may be unknown to the seller, rendering it impossible to extract all surplus. In the resulting *screening problem*, the seller tries to optimally construct a menu of options for the buyer, so that the buyer through his selection of an option reveals his private information. Or, it may be that the seller has private information about the quality of the good that is being sold, and the resulting *signaling problem* is to convey that information in a credible manner to a potential buyer. When there are several different potential buyers with private information, the seller may be able to solve a *mechanism design problem* so as to extract surplus from the buyers or to implement an efficient allocation of the goods. Lastly, information asymmetries play a role when there are several sellers who may or may not have an incentive to share some of their private information.

17.7.1 Screening

Consider a seller who would like to sell a bundle of L products $x = (x_1, \ldots, x_L)$ (or, equivalently, a single product with L attributes; Lancaster 1966). If the seller charges a price p for this bundle, then the consumer's net utility is

$$u(x, \theta) - p,$$

where $\theta \in \Theta = [\underline{\theta}, \bar{\theta}] \subset \mathbb{R}$ represents the consumer's private information (e.g., the marginal utility) and $u : \mathbb{R}_+^L \times \Theta \to \mathbb{R}$ is his utility function. The problem the seller has is that each consumer type θ may have different preferences, so that it is generally impossible for him to extract all of a given consumer's surplus, since that surplus is by hypothesis unknown. In order to extract information from the buyer, the seller needs to offer a menu of bundles including a price $p(x)$ for each item on this menu.

The seller's problem is to design an economic *mechanism* $\mathcal{M} = (\hat{\Theta}, \rho)$ that consists of a "message space" $\hat{\Theta}$ and an 'allocation function' $\rho = (\xi, \tau)$ that maps each element $\hat{\theta}$ of this message space to a product bundle $\xi(\hat{\theta}) \in \mathbb{R}_+^L$ and a price (monetary transfer) $\tau(\hat{\theta}) \in \mathbb{R}$. Given such a mechanism $\mathcal{M}$, the sequence of events is as follows. The seller proposes $(\hat{\Theta}, \rho)$ to the buyer, meaning that she explains to the buyer that all product choices are coded by elements in the message space (e.g., using tags on items displayed in a store). By sending a message $\hat{\theta} \in \hat{\Theta}$ the buyer effectively points to the item he wants (including the almost always feasible choice of "no item", reflecting the buyer's voluntary participation in the mechanism), and has to pay the transfer $\tau(\hat{\theta})$ to the seller.

The problem of finding an optimal mechanism seems daunting, since there are in principle many equivalent ways to select a message and at least as many ways of defining an allocation function. The following trivial result, generally attributed to Gibbard (1973) and Myerson (1979), considerably simplifies the search for an optimal mechanism.

THEOREM 4 (REVELATION PRINCIPLE) *For any mechanism* $\mathcal{M} = (\hat{\Theta}, \rho)$ *there exists a "direct revelation mechanism"* $\mathcal{M}_d = (\Theta, \rho_d)$ *such that if an agent of type θ finds it optimal to send a message $\hat{\theta}$ under mechanism $\mathcal{M}$, he finds it optimal to send the fully revealing message θ under $\mathcal{M}_d$ and consequently obtains the identical allocation* $\rho_d(\theta) = \rho(\hat{\theta})$.

It is very easy and instructive to see why this result must hold. Under the mechanism $\mathcal{M}$ agent θ solves

$$\hat{\theta}^*(\theta) \in \arg\max_{\vartheta \in \hat{\Theta}} \{u(\xi(\vartheta), \theta) - \tau(\vartheta)\}. \tag{29}$$

Thus, by setting $\rho_d(\theta) = (\xi(\hat{\theta}^*(\theta)), \tau(\hat{\theta}^*(\theta)))$ the revelation principle follows immediately. The intuition is that the mechanism designer can simulate the buyer's decision problem and change his mechanism to a direct revelation mechanism accordingly.

By using the revelation principle, the seller can—without any loss in generality—consider only direct revelation mechanisms, for which $\hat{\Theta} = \Theta$ and $\hat{\theta}^*(\theta) = \theta$. To simplify the solution of the screening problem, we assume that $u(x, \theta)$ is increasing in θ, and that the Spence–Mirrlees "sorting condition"[51]

$$u_{x\theta}(x, \theta) \geq 0 \tag{30}$$

is satisfied for all (x, θ). The (direct) mechanism $\{\mathcal{M} = (\Theta, \rho)$ with $\rho = (\xi, \tau)$ is *implementable*, that is, it is a direct revelation mechanism, if $\hat{\theta}^*(\theta) = \theta$ holds for all $\theta \in \Theta$. The first-order necessary optimality condition for the corresponding "incentive-compatibility condition" (29) is

$$u_x(\xi(\theta), \theta)\, \xi'(\theta) = \tau'(\theta), \quad \underline{\theta} \leq \theta \leq \bar{\theta}, \tag{31}$$

and the second-order necessary optimality condition is

$$u_{x\theta}(\xi(\theta), \theta)\xi'(\theta) \geq 0, \quad \underline{\theta} \leq \theta \leq \bar{\theta}. \tag{32}$$

The seller's payoff from selling the bundle $x = \xi(\theta)$ to a consumer of type θ at the price $p(x) = \tau(\theta)$ under the implementable mechanism $\mathcal{M}$ is

$$\pi(x, \theta) + p(x).$$

Again, we assume that the seller's payoff satisfies a Spence–Mirrlees sorting condition, so that

$$\pi_{x\theta}(x, \theta) \geq 0$$

for all (x, θ). Given some beliefs about distribution of the (from her perspective random) consumer type $\tilde{\theta} \in \Theta$ with the cdf $F(\theta) = P(\tilde{\theta} \leq \theta)$, the seller's expected payoff is[52]

$$\bar{\pi}(\xi, \tau) = \int_{\underline{\theta}}^{\bar{\theta}} (\pi(\xi(\theta), \theta) + \tau(\theta)) dF(\theta)$$

$$= \int_{\underline{\theta}}^{\bar{\theta}} \Big(\underbrace{\pi(\xi(\theta), \theta) + u(\xi(\theta), \theta)}_{\text{Total Surplus}} - \underbrace{\frac{1 - F(\theta)}{F'(\theta)} u_\theta(\xi(\theta), \theta)}_{\text{Information Rent}} \Big) dF(\theta) \tag{33}$$

$$\underbrace{\qquad\qquad\qquad\qquad\qquad\qquad\qquad\qquad}_{\text{Virtual Surplus } (\equiv S(\xi(\theta), \theta))}$$

The previous relation shows that for each type θ the seller would like to maximize a so-called "virtual surplus" $S(\xi(\theta), \theta)$ which consists of the total surplus $W(\xi(\theta), \theta) = \pi(\xi(\theta), \theta) + u(\xi(\theta), \theta)$ minus a nonnegative "information rent". The latter

---

[51] Subscripts denote partial derivatives. For example, $u_{x\theta} = \partial^2 u / \partial x \partial \theta$.

[52] This identity is obtained, using eq. (31) and performing twice an integration by parts, as follows:

$$\int_{\underline{\theta}}^{\bar{\theta}} \tau(\theta) dF(\theta) = \int_{\underline{\theta}}^{\bar{\theta}} \left(\int_{\underline{\theta}}^{\theta} \tau'(s) ds \right) dF(\theta) = \int_{\underline{\theta}}^{\bar{\theta}} \left(\int_{\underline{\theta}}^{\theta} u_x(\xi(s), s)\xi'(s) ds \right) dF(\theta)$$

$$= \left(\int_{\underline{\theta}}^{\theta} u_x(\xi(s), s)\xi'(s) ds \right) F(\theta)\Big|_{\underline{\theta}}^{\bar{\theta}} - \int_{\underline{\theta}}^{\bar{\theta}} u_x(x(\theta), \theta)\xi'(\theta) F(\theta) d\theta$$

$$= \int_{\underline{\theta}}^{\bar{\theta}} (1 - F(\theta)) \left(\frac{du(\xi(\theta), \theta)}{d\theta} - u_\theta(\xi(\theta), \theta) \right) d\theta$$

$$= (1 - F(\theta)) u(\xi(\theta), \theta)\Big|_{\underline{\theta}}^{\bar{\theta}} + \int_{\underline{\theta}}^{\bar{\theta}} \left(u(\xi(\theta), \theta) - \frac{1 - F(\theta)}{F'(\theta)} u_\theta(\xi(\theta), \theta) \right) dF(\theta),$$

where the firm naturally sets $\xi(\underline{\theta})$ such that $u(\xi(\underline{\theta}), \underline{\theta})$ vanishes.

describes the discount that a consumer of type θ obtains compared to perfect price discrimination which the seller could implement under complete information (cf. Section 17.6.1).

Using basic insights from monotone comparative statics (cf. Section 17.2.3), it is possible to obtain a characterization of solutions to the seller's expected-profit maximization problem. Indeed, if we assume that π and u are supermodular, the hazard rate $h = F'/(1 - F)$ is nondecreasing, and u_θ is submodular, then the virtual surplus $S(x, \theta)$ is supermodular in (x, θ), so that the pointwise optimal solution $\xi(\theta)$ is nondecreasing in θ, and the second-order condition (32) is automatically satisfied. The first-order condition (31) was used to write the seller's expected profit in terms of virtual surplus (cf. footnote 52) and is therefore also satisfied. Hence, the optimal solution $\xi(\theta)$ to the seller's screening problem satisfies

$$S_x(\xi(\theta), \theta) = \pi_x(\xi(\theta), \theta) + u_x(\xi(\theta), \theta) - (u_{x\theta}(\xi(\theta), \theta)/h(\theta)) = 0 \qquad (34)$$

for all $\theta \in \Theta$ for which $x(\theta) > 0$. Realizing that $\tau(\underline{\theta}) = 0$, we obtain from eq. (31) that

$$\tau(\theta) = \int_{\underline{\theta}}^{\theta} u_x(\xi(\vartheta), \vartheta)\xi'(\vartheta)d\vartheta. \qquad (35)$$

Once (ξ, τ) have been obtained, the seller can use the so-called "taxation principle" (see, e.g., Rochet 1985) to determine the optimal nonlinear pricing scheme $p(x)$ for the different bundles $x \in \xi(\Theta)$:

$$p(x) = \begin{cases} \tau(\theta), & \text{if } \exists \, \theta \in \Theta \text{ s.t. } \xi(\theta) = x, \\ \infty, & \text{otherwise.} \end{cases} \qquad (36)$$

To understand the properties of the solution to the screening problem, we consider the example where $\pi(x, \theta) = -cx^2/2$ for some $c > 0$, $u(x, \theta) = \theta x$, and $F(\theta) = \theta$ on $\Theta = [0, 1]$, satisfying all of the above assumptions. The virtual surplus is $S(x, \theta) = -cx^2/2 + \theta x - (1 - \theta)x$, so that the optimality condition (34),

$$S_x(x, \theta) = -cx + \theta - (1 - \theta) = 0,$$

is satisfied for $x = \xi(\theta) \equiv (2\theta - 1)_+/c$. From eq. (35) we therefore obtain

$$\tau(\theta) = \frac{2}{c} \int_0^{\theta} 1_{\{\vartheta \geq 1/2\}} \vartheta d\vartheta = \frac{(4\theta^2 - 1)_+}{4c}.$$

The taxation principle (36) eliminates the type θ from the expressions for $\xi(\theta)$ and $\tau(\theta)$, returning the optimal nonlinear price,

$$p(x) = \begin{cases} (2 + cx)(x/4), & \text{if } x \in [0, 3/(4c)], \\ \infty, & \text{otherwise.} \end{cases}$$

In this example, we observe a number of regularities that remain valid for other parameterizations. First, the highest consumer type $\theta = \bar{\theta}$ obtains a product bundle $\bar{x} = \xi(\bar{\theta})$ that is efficient, in the sense that $\bar{x}$ maximizes $\pi(x, \bar{\theta}) + u(x, \bar{\theta})$, that is, the sum of the consumer's and the seller's payoff. In other words, there is "no distortion at the top". In general this is true because $S(x, \bar{\theta})$ is precisely the social surplus. Second, the lowest type $\theta = \underline{\theta}$ obtains zero surplus. In the example this is true for all $\theta \in [0, 1/2]$. In general, we have "full rent extraction at the bottom", because $u_\theta \geq 0$ would otherwise imply that one could increase the price for all consumers without losing any participation. In the terminology of Section 17.5.1 the low types through their presence exert a positive externality on the high types. Hence, a (first-order stochastically dominant) shift in the type distribution that increases the relative likelihood of high types versus low types tends to decrease the information rent they can obtain.

REMARK 13 The screening problem (first examined as such by Stiglitz 1975) has many applications, such as optimal taxation (Mirrlees 1971), the regulation of a monopolist with an unknown cost parameter (Baron and Myerson 1982), or nonlinear pricing (Mussa and Rosen 1978). The solution to the screening problem without the somewhat restrictive assumptions that guaranteed monotone comparative statics of the solution to eq. (34) needs the use of optimal control theory (Hamiltonian approach; Guesnerie and Laffont 1984). For $L = 1$, when the solution to eq. (34) would be decreasing, one needs to implement Mussa and Rosen's "ironing" procedure, which requires that $\xi(\theta)$ becomes constant over some interval, thus serving those consumer types with identical product bundles (typically referred to as "bunching"). For $L > 1$, the second-order condition (32) imposes only an average restriction on the slope, which allows avoiding inefficient bunching more easily. An extension of the model to multi-dimensional types θ is nontrivial, as it becomes more difficult to characterize the set of all direct revelation mechanisms over which the seller has to search for an optimal one (Rochet and Stole 2003).

17.7.2 Signaling

In the screening problem, the mechanism operator (referred to as *principal*), who is uninformed, has the initiative and designs the mechanism. If the party with the private information has the initiative, then it faces a *signaling problem*. For example, if Joe tries to sell his car, then it is reasonable to assume that he has important private information about the state of the car. However, if all he can do is "speak" to the prospective buyer, then (in the absence of any additional guarantees) the latter has no reason to believe what Joe says and can dismiss his sales pitch merely as "cheap talk" (Crawford and Sobel 1982; Farrell and Rabin 1996). However, the seller may be able to convey information when using a costly signal (Spence 1973). More precisely, the cost of the signal has to vary with the private information of its sender, for it to become informative. If each sender "type" sends a different message in such a "signaling game", then the signaling equilibrium is said to be "separating". Otherwise it is called "pooling" (or "semi-separating", if only a subset of types are separated).

Let us discuss a simple signaling game, adapted from Laffont (1989), to highlight the connection between signaling and screening.[53] More specifically, assume that a seller would like to sell a unit of a product of quality θ known only to him. The seller can offer an observable warranty level of e. Both buyer and seller know that the cost to a type-θ seller of

---

[53] The classic setting, explored by Spence (1973), deals with signaling in a labor market. A full analysis of signaling games is complicated by a generic equilibrium multiplicity, even in the simplest models. To reduce the number of equilibria, in view of sharpening the model predictions, a number of "equilibrium refinements", such as the "intuitive criterion" by Cho and Kreps (1987), have been proposed, with mixed success.

offering the warranty level e is $c(e, \theta)$, which is increasing in e. Suppose further that the cost satisfies the Spence–Mirrlees condition

$$c_{e\theta} \leq 0.$$

That is, the marginal cost c_e of providing a warranty decreases with the quality of the good. Let us now examine the seller's incentives to report the true quality value θ to the buyer, given that the buyer believes his message.[54]

If in a truth-telling (i.e., separating) equilibrium the buyer buys a unit amount $\xi(\theta) = 1$ at the price $\tau(\theta)$, then the seller's profit is

$$\pi(x, p, \theta) = \tau(\theta) - c(e, \theta).$$

The first-order condition for truth-telling is

$$c_e e' = \tau', \tag{37}$$

and the second-order condition

$$c_{e\theta} e' \leq 0. \tag{38}$$

If the quality of the good θ represents the gross utility for the product, then in a separating equilibrium the seller is able to charge a fair price $\tau(\theta) = \theta$, extracting all of the buyer's surplus. Hence, eq. (37) yields that

$$e'(\theta) = \frac{1}{c_e(e(\theta), \theta)}.$$

For example, let $\underline{\theta} = 1$, $c(e, \theta) = 1 - \theta e$. Then $c_e = -\theta$, and therefore $e' = -1/\theta$, and $e(\theta) = \ln(\bar{\theta}/\theta) + e(\bar{\theta})$. The notion of a "reactive equilibrium" (Riley 1979) implies that $e(\bar{\theta}) = 0$, and thus $e(\theta) = \ln(\bar{\theta}/\theta)$. There may be many other separating equilibria; there may also be pooling equilibria, in which the seller would offer any quality level at the same price.

REMARK 14 In the signaling model presented here, the warranty offered has no effect on the buyer's utility whatsoever. The only important feature is that the marginal cost of providing warranty depends monotonically on the types. This insight can be transferred to other application domains such as advertising. The latter—while still just a "conspicuous expenditure"—can become an informative signal about product quality if the firms' costs satisfy some type of relaxed Spence–Mirrlees condition (Kihlstrom and Riordan 1984). With multiple time periods to consider, even product prices can become signals (Bagwell and Riordan 1991), since a low-quality firm with a high price would face a much larger drop in sales than a high-quality firm, as the qualities become known to consumers. See Bagwell (2007) for an overview of the related economics of advertising. Kaya and Özer (Chapter 29) discuss signaling (and screening) in the context of supply-chain contracting.

17.7.3 Mechanism design

In the screening problem an uninformed party can design an economic mechanism to extract information from an informed party and implement its payoff-maximizing alloca-

---

[54] If the seller does not tell the truth under these circumstances, the buyer, of course, will not trust the seller in equilibrium. We omit the details for the precise specification of the equilibrium.

tion of resources.[55] An economic mechanism can generally involve more than one agent, in addition to the mechanism operator (principal). As a leading example, consider Vickrey's (1961) celebrated second-price auction. In that mechanism N bidders (agents) jointly submit their bids to the auctioneer (principal), who awards a single object to the highest bidder at a price equal to the second-highest submitted bid. It is easy to see that if every bidder $i \in \{1, \ldots, N\}$ has a private value $\theta^i \in \Theta \subset \mathbb{R}_+$ for the object, it is best for that bidder to submit his true value as bid b_i. This leads to a unique equilibrium "bidding function" $\beta : \Theta \to \mathbb{R}$ which describes each player i's bid, $b_i = \beta(\theta_i) \equiv \theta_i$, as a function of his type θ_i, independent of the players' beliefs.[56]

We illustrate the design of a mechanism[57] with the example of an optimal auction (Myerson 1981) that, on the one hand, parallels third-degree price discrimination (cf. Section 17.6.1), and, on the other hand, employs the same methods as our solution to the screening problem. Consider a seller who would like to sell a single indivisible item to either Joe (= agent 1) or Melanie (= agent 2) so as to maximize his expected revenues. As in the second-price auction, we assume that both Joe's and Melanie's value for the item is private. Suppose that this seller thinks that Joe's valuation θ_1 for the item is distributed with the cdf F_1 on the support $\Theta_1 = [\underline{\theta}_1, \bar{\theta}_1]$, while Melanie's valuation θ_2 is distributed with the cdf F_2 on the support $\Theta_2 = [\underline{\theta}_2, \bar{\theta}_2]$. Suppose further that the seller's opportunity cost for selling the item to agent i is $c_i \geq 0$.

Consider first the problem of how the seller would price to the two individuals so as to maximize expected profit from either of them, just as in third-degree price discrimination. At a price $p_i \in [0, 100i]$, the demand for the seller's good by individual i is $D_i(p_i) = 1 - F_i(p_i)$. Hence, the monopoly pricing rule (27) in Section 17.6.1 yields that the seller's optimal price r_i to agent i is such that marginal revenue equals marginal cost, that is,[58]

$$\text{MR}_i(r_i) = r_i + \frac{D_i(r_i)}{D_i'(r_i)} = r_i - \frac{1 - F(r_i)}{F_i'(r_i)} = c_i. \tag{39}$$

Let us now consider a mechanism-design approach for the optimal pricing problem. The revelation principle (Theorem 4) extends to the context of "Bayesian implementation", that is, situations with multiple agents, in the sense that it is possible for the principal to restrict attention to "direct revelation mechanisms" of the form $\mathcal{M} = (\Theta, \rho)$, where $\Theta = \Theta_1 \times \Theta_2$ is the type space, and $\rho = (\xi_1, \xi_2; \tau_1, \tau_2)$ the allocation function, with $\xi_i : \Theta \to [0, 1]$ the probability that agent i obtains the item and $\tau_i : \Theta \to \mathbb{R}$ the transfer that this agent pays to the principal.

---

[55] This allocation is referred to as "second-best", because it is subject to information asymmetries and therefore inferior in terms of the principal's expected payoff under the "first-best" allocation when information is symmetric. The latter is the case if *either* the agent is *ex ante* uninformed about his own type (so that the principal can extract all his expected surplus by an upfront fixed fee) *or* both parties are informed about the agent's type (so that the principal can practice first-degree price discrimination; cf. Section 17.6.1).

[56] Indeed, if—provided that all other bidders use the equilibrium bidding function β—bidder i chooses a bid b_i that is strictly less than his value θ_i, then it may be possible that another bidder j bids $\beta(\theta_j) \in (b_i, \theta_i)$, so that bidder i loses the object to a bidder with a lower valuation. If, on the other hand, bidder i places a bid $b_i > \theta_i$, then there may be a bidder k such that $b_k \in (\theta_i, b_i)$ forcing bidder i to pay more than his private value θ_i for the object. Hence, it is optimal for bidder i to set $b_i = \beta(\theta_i) = \theta_i$.

[57] The *design* aspect of mechanisms for resource allocation was highlighted by Hurwicz (1973).

[58] As in Section 17.6.1 (cf. footnote 43) we assume that we are in the "regular case", i.e. that the marginal revenue is increasing in price. If this assumption is not satisfied, an ironing procedure analogous to the one mentioned in Remark 13 needs to be performed (Bulow and Roberts 1989).

Given that agent j reports the true value θ_j, agent i finds it optimal to also tell the truth if

$$\theta_i \in \arg\max_{\hat{\theta}_i \in [\underline{\theta}_i, \bar{\theta}_i]} E[\theta_i \xi_i(\hat{\theta}_i, \tilde{\theta}_j) - \tau_i(\hat{\theta}_i, \tilde{\theta}_j)|\hat{\theta}_i, \theta_i] = \arg\max_{\hat{\theta}_i \in [\underline{\theta}_i, \bar{\theta}_i]} \{\theta_i \bar{\xi}_i(\hat{\theta}_i) - \bar{\tau}_i(\hat{\theta}_i)\},$$

for all $(\theta_1, \theta_2) \in \Theta$, where $\bar{\xi}_i(\hat{\theta}_i) = E[\xi_i(\hat{\theta}_i, \tilde{\theta}_j)|\hat{\theta}_i]$ is agent i's expected probability of obtaining the item when sending the message $\hat{\theta}_i$ and $\bar{\tau}_i(\hat{\theta}_i) = E[\tau_i(\hat{\theta}_i, \tilde{\theta}_j)|\hat{\theta}_i]$ is the resulting expected payment by that agent. Completely analogous to the implementability conditions (31) and (32) in the screening problem, we obtain

$$\theta_i \bar{\xi}_i'(\theta_i) = \bar{\tau}_i'(\theta_i), \quad \theta_i \in [\underline{\theta}_i, \bar{\theta}_i], \quad i \in \{1, \ldots, N\}, \tag{40}$$

and

$$\bar{\xi}_i'(\theta_i) \geq 0, \quad \theta_i \in [\underline{\theta}_i, \bar{\theta}_i], \quad i \in \{1, \ldots, N\}, \tag{41}$$

as implementability conditions for the principal's direct revelation mechanism.[59] The seller maximizes his profits by solving

$$\max_{\xi, \tau} \sum_{i=1}^{2} \int_{\underline{\theta}_i}^{\bar{\theta}_i} (\bar{\tau}_i(\theta_i) - c_i \bar{\xi}_i(\theta_i)) dF_i(\theta_i) = \max_{\xi} \sum_{i=1}^{2} \int_{\underline{\theta}_1}^{\bar{\theta}_1} \int_{\underline{\theta}_2}^{\bar{\theta}_2} (MR_i(\theta_i)$$
$$- c_i) \xi_i(\theta_1, \theta_2) dF_1(\theta_1) dF_2(\theta_2),$$

subject to $0 \leq \xi_1(\theta_1, \theta_2) + \xi_2(\theta_1, \theta_2) \leq 1$.[60] The optimal solution can be found by simply "looking hard" at the last expression. For a given type realization (θ_i, θ_j), the principal finds it best to place all probability mass on the agent with the largest difference between marginal revenue and marginal cost, as long as that difference is nonnegative. If it is, then it is better not to sell the item at all. Hence,

$$\xi_i^*(\theta_i, \theta_j) = \begin{cases} 1_{\{MR_i(\theta_i) - c_i > MR_j(\theta_j) - c_j\}} + (1_{\{MR_i(\theta_i) - c_i = MR_j(\theta_j) - c_j\}}/2), & \text{if } MR_i(\theta_i) \geq c_i, \\ 0, & \text{otherwise.} \end{cases}$$

To obtain a concrete result, let us consider the case where Joe's value is uniformly distributed on $\Theta_1 = [0, 100]$ and Melanie's value is uniformly distributed on $\Theta_2 = [0, 200]$, so that $F_i(\theta_i) = \theta_i/(100i)$. Furthermore, let $c_1 = c_2 = 20$. One can see that condition (41) is satisfied and that, in addition, condition (40) holds if we set[61]

---

[59] Differentiating eq. (40) with respect to θ_i we obtain $\bar{\xi}_i'(\theta_i) + \theta_i \bar{\xi}_i''(\theta_i) = \bar{\tau}_i''(\theta_i)$. On the other hand, the second-order optimality condition is $\theta_i \bar{\xi}_i''(\theta_i) - \bar{\tau}_i''(\theta_i) \leq 0$, so that (by combining the last two relations) we obtain inequality (41).

[60] The last identity is obtained, using eq. (40) and performing twice an integration by parts, as follows:

$$\int_{\underline{\theta}_i}^{\bar{\theta}_i} \bar{\tau}_i(\theta_i) dF_i(\theta_i) = \int_{\underline{\theta}_i}^{\bar{\theta}_i} \left(\int_{\underline{\theta}_i}^{\theta_i} s\bar{\xi}_i'(s) ds \right) dF_i(\theta_i) = \left(\int_{\underline{\theta}_i}^{\theta_i} s\bar{\xi}'(s) ds \right) F_i(\theta_i) \Big|_{\underline{\theta}_i}^{\bar{\theta}_i} - \int_{\underline{\theta}_i}^{\bar{\theta}_i} \theta_i \bar{\xi}_i'(\theta_i) F_i(\theta_i) d\theta_i$$

$$= \int_{\underline{\theta}_i}^{\bar{\theta}_i} (1 - F_i(\theta_i)) \theta_i \bar{\xi}_i'(\theta_i) d\theta_i = (1 - F_i(\theta_i)) \theta_i \bar{\xi}_i(\theta_i) \Big|_{\underline{\theta}_i}^{\bar{\theta}_i} - \int_{\underline{\theta}_i}^{\bar{\theta}_i} (1 - F_i(\theta_i) - \theta_i F_i'(\theta_i)) \bar{\xi}_i(\theta_i) d\theta_i$$

$$= -\underline{\theta}_i \bar{\xi}_i(\underline{\theta}_i) + \int_{\underline{\theta}_i}^{\bar{\theta}_i} \left(\theta_i - \frac{1 - F_i(\theta_i)}{F_i'(\theta_i)} \right) \bar{\xi}_i(\theta_i) F_i'(\theta_i) d\theta_i = \int_{\underline{\theta}_i}^{\bar{\theta}_i} MR_i(\theta_i) \bar{\xi}_i(\theta_i) dF_i(\theta_i),$$

where the firm naturally sets $\bar{\xi}_i(\underline{\theta}_i) = \bar{\tau}_i(\underline{\theta}_i) = 0$. The derivations are analogous to the ones in footnote 52.

[61] This is not the only way to satisfy eq. (40). For more details on Bayesian implementation, see Palfrey and Srivastava (1993) as well as Weber and Bapna (2008).

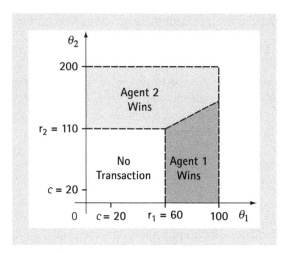

FIGURE 17.6 Allocations under the optimal selling mechanism

$$\tau_i^*(\theta_i, \theta_j) = 1_{\{MR_i(\theta_i) \geq c_i\}} \int_{\underline{\theta}_i}^{\theta_i} s \frac{\partial \xi_i^*(s, \theta_j)}{\partial s} ds = 1_{\{MR_i(\theta_i) \geq c_i\}} \int_{\underline{\theta}_i}^{\theta_i} s\delta(s - \theta_j - 50(i-j))ds$$

$$= \begin{cases} \theta_j + 50(i-j), & \text{if } \theta i \geq \max\{(c/2) + 50i, \ \theta_j + 50(i-j)\}, \\ 0, & \text{otherwise,} \end{cases}$$

where $\delta(\cdot)$ is the Dirac impulse distribution, which appears naturally as the (generalized) derivative of the indicator function (cf. footnote 15). In other words, the optimal selling mechanism for the principal is an auction where the winner is the agent with the highest marginal profit ($MR_i - c_i$), and the transfer is determined by the valuation of the losing bidder and the difference in their bids. In this asymmetric second-price auction, the optimal reserve price r_i for agent i is chosen such that $MR_i(r_i) = c_i$, that is, $r_i = (c_i/2) + 50i$, as already computed for the third-degree price discrimination in eq. (39) above: $r_1 = (c_1/2) + 50 = 60$ and $r_2 = (c_2/2) + 100 = 110$. Using the optimal auction mechanism, the firm obtains an expected profit of $E[\max\{0, MR_1(\theta_1) - c_1, MR_2(\theta_2) - c_2\}] = 2E[\max\{0, \theta_1 - 60, \theta_2 - 110\}] = 50.3\bar{6}$. The reason that the optimal auction seems to lead to a lower expected revenue than third-degree price discrimination is that the latter allows for items to be simultaneously sold to high-value types of both buyers ("markets"), whereas the former allocates one unit to either one of the two buyers ("agents"). The allocations resulting from the (asymmetric) optimal auction, for any $(\theta_1, \theta_2) \in \Theta$, are shown in Figure 17.6.

REMARK 15 The interpretation of the design of an optimal auction in terms of a third-degree monopoly pricing problem stems from Bulow and Roberts (1989). While Vickrey's second-price auction leads to a Pareto-efficient allocation *ex post* (i.e., the item ends up with the individual that has the highest value for it), Myerson's optimal auction may lead to an inefficient allocation, since it is possible that no transaction takes place even though an agent values the item above the seller's marginal cost.[62] This illustrates a fundamental

---

[62] The multi-unit generalization of the second-price auction is the Vickrey–Clarke–Groves (VCG) mechanism (Vickrey 1961; Clarke 1971; Groves 1973). Ausubel and Milgrom (2006) describe why the VCG mechanism, despite its many attractive features (such as truthful bidding strategies which are incentive-compatible in dominant-strategies, and *ex post* efficient allocations), is rarely used in practice.

conflict between efficient allocation and surplus extraction when information is asymmetric. Note that the expected-revenue difference between the Myerson and Vickrey auctions is small in the following sense: the expected revenues from a Vickrey auction with $N + 1$ *ex ante* symmetric bidders cannot be less than the expected revenue for an optimal auction with N *ex ante* symmetric bidders (Bulow and Klemperer 1996). For additional details on auction theory see, for example, Milgrom (2004). In many practical applications the principal also has private information, which complicates the mechanism design problem (Myerson 1983; Maskin and Tirole 1992).

17.7.4 Oligopoly pricing with asymmetric information

The most general strategic pricing problems arise when multiple sellers interact with multiple buyers in the presence of asymmetric information. An interesting case is the situation where the sellers observe different private signals about their demands and/or their own costs which they can choose to exchange with other sellers or not. Raith (1996) provides a model of information sharing when the sellers' payoffs are quadratic in their action variables, which encompasses the standard specifications of Cournot and Bertrand oligopolies with differentiated goods. A seller's incentive to reveal private information depends on the correlation of the signals (i.e., if seller i observes a high cost or a high demand, how likely is it that seller j has a similar observation?) and on the type of strategic interaction (i.e., does an increase in seller i's action tend to increase ("strategic complements") or decrease ("strategic substitutes") seller j's action?). For example, in a Cournot duopoly with substitute products, increasing firm i's output tends to decrease firm j's output, so that their actions are strategic substitutes. The firms' incentives to share information then increase as the correlation in their signals decreases. With very correlated signals, firm i does not expect to increase its payoffs by forcing its strategy to be even more negatively correlated with firm j's after information revelation than before. As signals are less correlated and the firms' products gain in complementarity, their strategic actions become more positively correlated *ex ante*, so that information sharing can profitably increase the precision of how the firms can take advantage of this implicit collusion against the consumers.

It is noteworthy that in an oligopoly setting it may be better for a seller to actually have less precise information if that fact can be made reliably known to others (Gal-Or 1988). Indeed, if in a Cournot oligopoly with substitute products a seller i does not know that uncertain market demand (common to all sellers) is likely to be low, then that seller will produce a larger output than sellers who are aware of the demand forecast, especially if those sellers know that seller i is uninformed. Thus, not having demand information helps a seller to credibly act "crazy" and thus to commit to an otherwise unreasonable action (an informed seller would never rationally opt to produce such a large output). Thus, while in single-person decision problems it is always better to have more information (with a partial information order induced by statistical sufficiency; Blackwell 1951), in strategic settings the value of additional information may well be negative.[63]

---

[63] Weber and Croson (2004) show that this may be true even in a bilateral setting where an information seller sells information to an agent with limited liability. The fact that too much information might induce

Another way for multiple buyers and sellers to interact is through intermediaries, who may be able to alleviate some of the problems that arise from asymmetric information. One can argue that most economic transactions are "intermediated", in the sense that a buyer who resells his item effectively becomes an intermediary between the party that sold the item and the party that finally obtains the item. Thus, retailers are intermediaries, wholesalers are intermediaries, banks are intermediaries, and so on. A necessary condition for a buyer and a seller to prefer an intermediated exchange to a direct exchange is that the fee charged by the intermediary does not exceed the cost of direct exchange for either of the two transacting parties. Thus, for the intermediary to have a viable business proposition it is necessary that the intermediation cost for a given transaction is less than the expected transaction cost the parties face in a direct exchange. As an example consider the market for used cars discussed at the beginning of Section 17.4.2. We saw there that if a buyer's expected value $1 - \varphi$ (where φ is the proportion of zero-value lemons in the market) is below the high-value seller's opportunity cost c, that is, if $1 - \varphi < c$, then the market fails, due to adverse selection. If an intermediary can observe and "certify" the quality of a seller's car at the intermediation cost κ, then the intermediary can charge the buyer a "retail price" $R \in \{R_L, R_H\}$ (with $R_L = 0$ and $R_H = 1$) and pass on to the seller a "wholesale price" $W \in \{W_L, W_H\}$ (with $W_L = 0$ and $W_H = c$), contingent on the observed value of the used car, such that all buyers and sellers are happy to use the intermediary. The intermediary is viable if and only if its expected revenues outweigh the intermediation cost, that is, if and only if

$$P(\text{Used Car is of High Value})(R_H - W_H) = (1 - \varphi)(1 - c) \geq \kappa.$$

Spulber (1999) provides an extensive discussion of market intermediation and different ways in which intermediaries can create value by effectively lowering the transaction cost in the market. More recently, the theory of intermediation has evolved into a "theory of two-sided markets", which emphasizes the intermediary's profit objective and the possibility of competition between intermediaries or "platforms" (Rochet and Tirole 2003).[64]

It is also possible to explicitly consider the competition between different economic mechanism designs as in Section 17.7.3 (Biais et al. 2000), with one of the main technical difficulties being that the revelation principle (Theorem 4) ceases to hold in that environment. For example, in the case of nonlinear pricing this leads to so-called "catalog games" (Monteiro and Page 2008).

REMARK 16 The source of incomplete information in a product market is in many cases directly related to a costly search process that limits the consumers' ability to compare

---

the agent to take overly risky actions, and thus perhaps be unable to pay the seller a pre-agreed *ex post* fee, is enough motivation for the seller to want to degrade the information before selling it, knowing well that its price decreases but that the increased likelihood of obtaining payment outweighs this loss.

[64] Rochet and Tirole (2005) point out that a "market is two-sided if the platform can affect the volume of transactions by charging more to one side of the market and reducing the price paid by the other side by an equal amount; in other words, the price structure matters, and platforms must design it so as to bring both sides on board."

different products. Weitzman (1979) points out that in an optimal sequential search a consumer should follow "Pandora's rule", trading off the cost of an incremental search effort against the expected benefit from that extra search over the best alternative already available. A particularly striking consequence of even the smallest search cost in a product market is the following paradox by Diamond (1971): if N symmetric firms are Bertrand-competing on price in a market for a homogeneous good and consumers can visit one (random) firm for free and from then on have to incur a small search cost $\varepsilon > 0$ to inspect the price charged by another firm, then instead of the Bertrand outcome where all firms charge marginal cost that would obtain for $\varepsilon = 0$ (cf. Section 17.6.2), one finds that all firms charge monopoly price. This rather surprising result will not obtain if consumers are heterogeneous in terms of their search costs (tourists versus natives) or their preferences (bankers versus cheapskates). Stiglitz (1989) provides a summary of the consequences of imperfect information in the product market related to search. See also Vives (1999) for a survey of oligopoly pricing under incomplete information.

17.8 DYNAMIC PRICING

For a seller with market power, the ability to adjust his prices over time is both a blessing and a curse.[65] On the one hand, the flexibility of being able to adjust prices allows the seller at each time t to incorporate all available information into his pricing decision. On the other hand, the fact that a seller has the flexibility to change prices at any time in the future removes his ability to commit to any particular price today. The following conjecture by Coase (1972) makes this last point more precise.[66]

THEOREM 5 (COASE CONJECTURE) *Consider a monopolist who sells a durable (i.e., infinitely lived) good to consumers with possibly heterogeneous valuations at times $t \in \{0, \Delta, 2\Delta, \ldots\}$ at the marginal cost $c \geq 0$. As $\Delta \to 0+$ the monopolist's optimal price $p_0(\Delta)$ at time $t = 0$ tends to his marginal cost, i.e., $\lim_{\Delta \to 0+} p_0(\Delta) = c$.*

When the length Δ of the time period for which a monopolist can guarantee a constant price decreases, the price it can charge drops. The intuition is that the monopolist at time $t = 0$ is competing with a copy of its own product that is sold at time $t = \Delta$. Clearly, when viewed from the present, that copy is not quite as good as the product now. However, that "quality" difference vanishes when Δ tends to zero. Thus, as $\Delta \to 0+$ arbitrarily many copies of virtually the same product will be available in any fixed time interval, so that the resulting perfect competition must drive the monopolist's price down to marginal cost.

The Coase problem, which arises from the lack of commitment power, can be ameliorated by renting the product instead of selling it, or by making binding promises about future production (e.g., by issuing a "limited edition"). Perishable products also increase the monopolist's commitment power (e.g., when selling fresh milk), as well as adjustment costs for price changes (e.g., due to the necessity of printing a new product catalogue). The

---

[65] For more details on dynamic pricing, see Aviv and Vulcano (this volume).

[66] The Coase conjecture was proved by Stokey (1981), Bulow (1982), and Gul et al. (1986) in varying degrees of generality.

ability to commit to a "price path" from the present into the future is a valuable asset for a seller; the question of commitment as a result of the consumers' option of intertemporal arbitrage (i.e., they can choose between buying now or later) must be at the center of any dynamic pricing strategy, at least in an environment where information is fairly complete. We note that the Coase problem is not significant in situations when consumers are nonstrategic (i.e., not willing or able to wait) or when goods respond to a current demand (e.g., for electricity). An intertemporal aspect is then introduced into a firm's pricing strategy mainly through its own cost structure, production technology, or changes in boundary conditions.[67]

Under incomplete information, buyers and sellers need to learn about their economic environment, which generally includes exogenous factors (such as technological possibilities, macro-economic conditions, and consumer preferences) or persistent endogenous information (such as past experience with products, reputations, and recent observable actions by market participants). All participants' beliefs may change from one time period to the next, based on their respective new information. At each time t, any agent trades off the value of additional costly information (important for improving decisions in the next period) against the benefit of using the available resources to directly augment current payoffs through non-informational actions. The difficulties of finding an optimal balance between exploration (i.e., the acquisition of new information) and exploitation (i.e., the accumulation of benefit) can be illustrated well with the so-called multi-armed bandit problem. In the simplest version of this problem a single agent can choose to pull one of several arms of a slot machine. Each arm pays a random reward with an unknown, stationary probability distribution. The agent weighs the current benefit of pulling a relatively well-known arm to gain a fairly certain reward against the possibility of experimenting with a new arm that could pay even better rewards. Gittins and Jones (1974) provide a surprisingly simple solution to what seems like a difficult dynamic optimization problem which for some time had a reputation of being unsolvable from an analytic point of view. Their solution shows that the problem can be decomposed so as to perform a separate computation of a *Gittins index* for each arm based on the available information for that arm. The Gittins index corresponds to the retirement reward (as a per-period payment in perpetuity) that would make the agent indifferent between stopping the experimentation with that arm or obtaining the retirement perpetuity instead. Given the vector of Gittins indices at time t, it is optimal for the agent to choose the arm with the highest Gittins index.

The fact that the Gittins indices can be computed separately for each arm allows for a use of this method in mechanism design, for example, in the construction of a mechanism that allocates an object of unknown value in different rounds to different bidders (Bapna and Weber 2006; Bergemann and Välimäki 2006). Based on their own observations, bidders can then submit bids which are related to the computation of their own Gittins index, the latter representing in effect the private types, the collection of which determines the socially optimal allocation at each point in time.

---

[67] For example, a firm may need to consider a production leadtime, the replenishment of inventories, a limited-capacity infrastructure (requiring "peak-load pricing"), or demand seasonality. Many of these issues have been considered in the operations management and public pricing literature; they are beyond the scope of this survey.

17.9 BEHAVIORAL ANOMALIES

A discussion of price theory could not be complete without the "disclaimer" that the self-interested *economic man* (or *homo economicus*) that appeared in all of the rational models in this survey is not exactly what is encountered in reality.[68] Individuals are generally subject to decision biases which may be psychological in nature or due to limited cognitive abilities (or both). The resulting "bounded rationality" leads human decision-makers to suboptimal decisions and to what Simon (1956) terms "satisficing" (rather than optimizing) behavior, which means that individuals tend to stop the search for better decision alternatives as soon as a decision has been found that promises a payoff which satisfies a certain aspiration level.

The behavioral anomalies encountered in practice are often too significant to be ignored in models, so that descriptive and normative models of bounded rationality increasingly influence and shape the evolution of economic theory (Thaler 1994; Rubinstein 1998; Kahneman and Tversky 2000; Camerer 2006). As an example for how decision-making can be biased by "mental accounting" (Thaler 1999), consider the following experiment by Tversky and Kahneman (1981), in which individuals were asked the following.

> Imagine that you are about to purchase a jacket for $125 (resp. $15) and a calculator for $15 (resp. $125). The calculator salesman informs you that the calculator you wish to buy is on sale for $10 (resp. $120) at the other branch of the store, located 20 minutes drive away. Would you make the trip to the other store? (Tversky and Kahneman 1981: 457)

The empirical observation in this experiment suggests that when individuals stand to save $5 from an original amount of $15 they are willing to travel to another store, but not if the original amount is $125. Thus, the same total amount of $5 tends to be aggregated into one mental account, which contains the total expense. This explains the decreasing marginal utility for a $5 savings in the base price of the item. The latter is explained by the empirical regularity that real individuals' utility functions for money tend to be convex for losses (implying "loss aversion") and concave for gains (implying "risk aversion"; cf. Section 17.2.4) (Kahneman and Tversky 1979). An individual with a utility function that, relative to the current wealth, exhibits both loss aversion and risk aversion, tends to avoid actions (i.e., lotteries) that change his *status quo*.

Related literature on the so-called *endowment effect* points to an important *caveat* when trying to identify a "behavioral anomaly" which may require the adjustment of economic theory. In a well-known experiment, Knetsch (1989) observes systematic differences between WTA and WTP when the welfare change is induced by the transfer of a nonmarket good. These empirical results, repeated in a variety of settings by other authors, suggest that a consumer's WTA tends to be larger than her WTP, a behavioral pattern that is generally referred to as the "endowment effect" or "status-quo bias". In Knetsch's experiment, one group of randomly selected subjects was given a coffee mug and another group of subjects a candy bar. No matter who was given the mug, the

[68] The term "economic man" dates back to Ingram (1888) who criticizes the work of Mill (1836) which—in Ingram's words—"dealt not with real but with imaginary men—'economic men' ... conceived as simply 'money-making animals' " (1888: 218); see also the discussion by Persky (1995). Behavioral issues in pricing are discussed further by Özer and Zheng (Chapter 20).

individuals' average WTAs tended to be much larger than their average WTPs, which has been commonly viewed as supporting evidence for the presence of an endowment effect. Yet, as the normative relation between WTA and WTP (i.e., the Hicksian welfare measures EV and CV) in eq. (23) shows, it is

$$\text{WTA}(w - \text{WTP}(w)) = \text{WTP}(w) \text{ and } \text{WTA}(w) = \text{WTP}(w + \text{WTA}(w)),$$

so that an identity between WTA and WTP is not actually required, even from a normative point of view, unless one makes sure that individuals are wealth-compensated as the previous identities indicate. More recently, Plott and Zeiler (2005) note (without alluding to the wealth-compensation issue) that the observed differences between WTA and WTP might disappear altogether if one controls for all possible biases in experimental settings, so that—as these authors point out—the endowment effect may be a mere artifact produced by observations under imperfect laboratory conditions. The controversy surrounding the endowment effect is symptomatic of the difficulties in separating implications of available normative models from behavioral anomalies that would require an extension of these models.[69]

17.10 OPEN ISSUES

The discussion in this survey has shown that the strategic and nonstrategic pricing of resources is complicated by the presence of externalities, asymmetric information, and behavioral anomalies. The following three axes will be instrumental in the further development of price theory.

First, as the growth of networks around us increases the "connectedness" of individuals, on the one hand new markets are created, but on the other hand the potential for direct externalities through actions taken by participants in these networks also increases. New economic theory is needed for the pricing and transfer of resources in networks which considers the informational, transactional, and behavioral aspects specific to the relevant networks.

A second fundamental driver for a change in the way price theory continues to develop is given by our transition to a "data-rich society", in the sense that firms (and individuals) are increasingly able to tap a variety of data sources for informing their decisions about the buying, selling, and pricing of resources. Consumers whose behavior can be tracked, firms whose products become customizable by informational components, and intermediaries that increase market transparency (up to a deliberate obfuscation point), imply reduced information rents. The countervailing trend is that a data-rich society allows for experimentation on an unprecedented scale. The resulting optimization of decisions increases the rents from information. It therefore becomes more critical to connect

---

[69] Weber (2010) shows that the endowment effect is unsurprising from a normative viewpoint, i.e., it is not necessarily a behavioral anomaly. For example, a "normative endowment effect" arises automatically if the welfare measures WTA and WTP are increasing in wealth. Weber (2012) provides a mechanism for eliciting the difference between WTA and WTP for any given individual.

economic models directly to data, blurring the boundaries of model identification and solution.

Lastly, with the advent of a data-rich society there remains the issue of "long-tails", that is, the fundamental impossibility to have well-defined beliefs about all relevant aspects of economic behavior. Low-probability, high-consequence events require decisions to be "robust", that is, valid under a range of possible scenarios.[70] One important aspect of robustness is an implementation of satisficing (cf. Section 17.9), where a simple expected-payoff objective is replaced by a "robustness criterion", such as a conservative worst-case value or a less stringent competitive-ratio criterion. Sample-sparse estimation is likely to become an important part of data-driven economic decision-making under uncertainty (Chehrazi and Weber 2010).

REFERENCES

Admati, A. R. and Pfleiderer, P. (1986) "A Monopolistic Market for Information", *Journal of Economic Theory* 39/2: 400–38.

Akerlof, G. A. (1970) "The Market for 'Lemons': Quality Uncertainty and the Market Mechanism", *Quarterly Journal of Economics* 84/3: 488–500.

Anderson, S., de Palma, A., and Thisse, J.-F. (1992) *Discrete-Choice Theory of Product Differentiation*. Cambridge, MA: MIT Press.

Arrow, K. J. (1951) *Social Choice and Individual Values*. New York: Wiley. (2nd edn: Cowles Foundation, Monograph 12, New Haven, CT: Yale University Press, 1963.)

—— (1953) "Le Rôle des Valeurs Boursières pour la Répartition la Meilleure des Risques", *Économétrie*, Colloques Internationaux du CNRS, XL, 41–8. (English translation: "The Role of Securities in the Optimal Allocation of Risk", *Review of Economic Studies* 31/2: 91–6. The paper was originally read at the *Colloque sur les Fondements et Applications de la Théorie du Risque* on May 13, 1952, in Paris, France.)

—— (1963) "Uncertainty and the Welfare Economics of Medical Care", *American Economic Review* 53/5: 941–73.

—— (1973) "Information and Economic Behavior", Lecture Presented to the Federation of Swedish Industries, Stockholm, Sweden. Reprinted in: *Collected Papers of Kenneth J. Arrow, Vol. 4*, Cambridge, MA: Belknap Harvard (1984) 136–52.

—— and Hahn, F. J. (1971) *General Competitive Analysis*. San Francisco, CA: Holden-Day.

Athey, S. (2002) "Monotone Comparative Statics Under Uncertainty", *Quarterly Journal of Economics* 117/1: 187–223.

---

[70] The second-price auction discussed in Section 17.7.3 is an example of a robust mechanism in the following sense. All bidders' equilibrium strategies (cf. footnote 56) are completely independent of their beliefs about the distribution of other bidders' valuations. In general, this is not the case. For example, if the auction were such that a winning bidder has to pay his bid (termed a first-price auction), then the equilibrium bid strategies become very sensitive to the beliefs about other players' types and to the players' common knowledge about these beliefs. This is to the extent that with asymmetric beliefs the first-price auction can yield inefficient allocations (although it is revenue-equivalent to the second-price auction in the symmetric case). The second-price auction, therefore, is in accordance with the so-called 'Wilson doctrine' (Wilson 1987), which calls for the design of distribution-free mechanisms. Auction pricing is discussed further by Steinberg (this volume).

Aumann, R. J. (1976) "Agreeing to Disagree", *Annals of Statistics* 4/6: 1236–9.

Ausubel, L. and Milgrom, P. R. (2006) "The Lovely But Lonely Vickrey Auction", in P. Cramton, Y. Shoham, and R. Steinberg (eds), *Combinatorial Auctions*. Cambridge, MA: MIT Press, 17–40.

Bagwell, K. (2007) "The Economic Analysis of Advertising", in M. Armstrong and R. Porter (eds), *Handbook of Industrial Organization, Vol. 3*. Amsterdam, NL: Elsevier, 1701–844.

—— and Ramey, G. (1991) "Oligopoly Limit Pricing", *RAND Journal of Economics* 22/2: 155–72.

—— and Riordan, M. H. (1991) "High and Declining Prices Signal Product Quality", *American Economic Review* 81/1: 224–39.

Baker, J. B. and Bresnahan, T. F. (1988) "Estimating the Residual Demand Curve Facing a Single Firm", *International Journal of Industrial Organization* 6/3: 283–300.

—— and —— (1992) "Empirical Methods of Identifying and Measuring Market Power", *Antitrust Law Journal* 61: 3–16.

Bapna, A. and Weber, T. A. (2006) "Efficient Dynamic Allocation with Uncertain Valuations", Technical Report 2006-03-31, Department of Management Science and Engineering, Stanford University, Stanford, CA.

Baron, D. P. and Myerson, R. B. (1982) "Regulating a Monopolist with Unknown Costs", *Econometrica* 50/4: 911–30.

Baumol, W. J. and Bradford, D. F. (1970) "Optimal Departures from Marginal Cost Pricing", *American Economic Review* 60/3: 265–83.

Beath, J. and Katsoulacos, Y. (1991) *The Economic Theory of Product Differentiation*. New York: Cambridge University Press.

Beckman, S. R. and Smith, W. J. (1993) "Positively Sloping Marginal Revenue, CES Utility and Subsistence Requirements", *Southern Economic Journal* 60/2: 297–303.

Bergemann, D. and Välimäki, J. (2006) "Efficient Dynamic Auctions", Cowles Foundation Discussion Paper 1584, Yale University, New Haven, CT.

Bernheim, B. D. and Whinston, M. D. (1986) "Menu Auctions, Resource Allocations, and Economic Influence", *Quarterly Journal of Economics* 101/1: 1–31.

Bertrand, J. L. F. (1883) "Théorie Mathématique de la Richesse Sociale, Recherches sur les Principes Mathématiques de la Théorie des Richesses", *Journal des Savants* 67: 499–508. (Review of the books by Walras (1874/77) and Cournot (1838).)

Biais, B., Martimort, D., and Rochet, J.-C. (2000) "Competing Mechanisms in a Common Value Environment", *Econometrica* 68/4: 799–838.

Bishop, R. L. (1966) "Monopoly Under General Equilibrium: Comment", *Quarterly Journal of Economics* 80/4: 652–9.

Blackwell, D. (1951) "Comparison of Experiments". Proceedings of the Second Berkeley Symposium on Mathematical Statistics and Probability, Berkeley, CA: University of California Press, 93–102.

Bowley, A. L. (1924) *The Mathematical Groundwork of Economics*. Oxford: Oxford University Press.

Bronfman, C., McCabe, K., Porter, D., Rassenti, S., and Smith, V. (1996) "An Experimental Examination of the Walrasian Tâtonnement Mechanism", *RAND Journal of Economics* 27/4: 681–99.

Bulow, J. (1982) "Durable Goods Monopolists", *Journal of Political Economy* 90/2: 314–32.

—— and Klemperer, P. (1996) "Auctions vs. Negotiations", *American Economic Review* 86/1: 180–94.

—— and Roberts, J. (1989) "The Simple Economics of Optimal Auctions", *Journal of Political Economy* 97/5: 1060–90.

Cabral, L. M. B. and Villas-Boas, M. (2005) "Bertrand Supertraps", *Management Science* 51/4: 599–613.

Camerer, C. F. (2006) "Behavioral Economics", in R. Blundel, W. K. Newey, and T. Persson (eds), *Advances in Economics and Econometrics, Vol. II.* Cambridge: Cambridge University Press, 181–214.

Cass, D. and Shell, K. (1983) "Do Sunspots Matter?" *Journal of Political Economy* 91/2: 193–227.

Champ, P. A., Boyle, K. J., and Brown, T. J. (2003) *A Primer on Nonmarket Valuation.* Dordrecht: Kluwer.

Chehrazi, N. and Weber, T. A. (2010) "Monotone Approximation of Decision Problems", *Operations Research* 58(4/2): 1158–77.

Chipman, J. (1977) "An Empirical Implication of Auspitz–Lieben–Edgeworth–Pareto Complementarity", *Journal of Economic Theory* 14/1: 228–31.

Cho, I.-K. and Kreps, D. M. (1987) "Signaling Games and Stable Equilibria", *Quarterly Journal of Economics* 102/2: 179–222.

Clarke, E. H. (1971) "Multipart Pricing of Public Goods", *Public Choice* 2/1: 19–33.

Coase, R. H. (1937) "The Nature of the Firm", *Economica* 4/16: 386–405.

—— (1960) "The Problem of Social Cost", *Journal of Law and Economics* 3/2: 1–44.

—— (1972) "Durability and Monopoly", *Journal of Law and Economics* 15/1: 143–9.

Cobb, C. W. and Douglas, P. H. (1928) "A Theory of Production", *American Economic Review* 18/1: 139–65.

Condorcet, M. J. A. N. De Caritat, Marquis de (1785) "Essai sur l'Application de l'Analyse à la Probabilité des Décisions Rendues à la Pluralité des Voix" (Essay on the Application of Analysis to the Probability of Majority Decisions), Imprimerie Royale, Paris, France. (Reprint: Providence, RI: American Mathematical Society, 1972.)

Cournot, A. (1838) *Recherches sur les Principes Mathématiques de la Théorie des Richesses*, Paris: Hachette.

Crawford, V. P. and Sobel J. (1982) "Strategic Information Transmission", *Econometrica* 50/6: 1431–51.

Cremer, H. and Thisse, J.-F. (1991) "Location Models of Horizontal Differentiation: a Special Case of Vertical Differentiation Models", *Journal of Industrial Economics* 39/4: 383–90.

Debreu, G. (1953) "Une Économie de l'Incertain", Working Paper, Électricité de France, Paris, France. (Published in 1960: *Économie Appliquée* 13/1: 111–16.)

—— (1959) *Theory of Value: An Axiomatic Analysis of Economic Equilibrium*, Cowles Foundation, Monograph 17. New Haven, CT: Yale University Press.

Deneckere, R. J. and McAfee, R. P. (1996) "Damaged Goods", *Journal of Economics and Management Strategy* 5/2: 149–74.

Diamond, P. A. (1971) "A Model of Price Adjustment", *Journal of Economic Theory* 3/2: 156–68.

Duffie, D. (1988) *Security Markets.* New York, NY: Academic Press.

—— (2001) *Dynamic Asset Pricing Theory* (3rd edn). Princeton, NJ: Princeton University Press.

Eaves, J. and Williams, J. (2007) "Walrasian Tâtonnement Auctions on the Tokyo Grain Exchange", *Review of Financial Studies* 20/4: 1183–218.

Economides, N. (1996) "Network Externalities, Complementarities, and Invitations to Enter", *European Journal of Political Economy* 12/2: 211–33.

Edgeworth, F. Y. (1881) *Mathematical Psychics: An Essay on the Application of Mathematics to the Moral Sciences*. London: C. Kegan Paul.

Farrell, J. and Rabin, M. (1996) "Cheap Talk", *Journal of Economic Perspectives* 10/3: 103–18.

Fishburn, P. C. (1970) *Utility Theory for Decision Making*. New York, NY: Wiley.

Foley, D. K. (1967) "Resource Allocation and the Public Sector", *Yale Economic Essays* 7: 45–98.

—— (1970) "Lindahl's Solution and the Core of an Economy with Public Goods", *Econometrica* 38/1: 66–72.

Frank, R. H. (1985) "The Demand for Unobservable and Other Nonpositional Goods", *American Economic Review* 75/1: 101–16.

Friedman, M. (1962/2007) *Price Theory*. London, UK: Aldine Transaction.

Gal-Or, E. (1988) "The Advantages of Imprecise Information", *RAND Journal of Economics* 19/2: 266–75.

Garber, P. M. (1990) "Famous First Bubbles", *Journal of Economic Perspectives* 4/2: 35–54.

Gelman, J. R. and Salop, S. C. (1983) "Judo Economics: Capacity Limitation and Coupon Competition", *Bell Journal of Economics* 14/2: 315–32.

Gibbard, A. (1973) "Manipulation of Voting Schemes", *Econometrica* 41/4: 587–601.

Gittins, J. C. and Jones, D. M. (1974) "A Dynamic Allocation Index for the Sequential Design of Experiments", in J. Gani, K. Sarkadi, and I. Vincze (eds), *Progress in Statistics*. Amsterdam, NL: North-Holland, 241–66.

Goel, A., Meyerson, A., and Weber, T. A. (2009) "Fair Welfare Maximization", *Economic Theory* 41/3: 465–94.

Goldreich, O., Micali, S., and Wigderson, A. (1991) "Proofs that Yield Nothing But Their Validity or All Languages in NP Have Zero-Knowledge Proof Systems", *Journal of the Association for Computing Machinery* 38/1: 691–729.

Gollier, C. (2001) *The Economics of Risk and Time*. Cambridge, MA: MIT Press.

Grossman, S. J. (1989) *The Informational Role of Prices*. Cambridge, MA: MIT Press.

—— and Stiglitz, J. E. (1980) "On the Impossibility of Informationally Efficient Markets", *American Economic Review* 70/3: 393–408.

Groves, T. (1973) "Incentives in Teams", *Econometrica* 41/4: 617–31.

Guesnerie, R. and Laffont, J.-J. (1984) "A Complete Solution to a Class of Principal–Agent Problems with an Application to the Control of a Self-Managed Firm", *Journal of Public Economics* 25/3: 329–69.

Gul, F., Sonnenschein, H., and Wilson, R. (1986) "Foundations of Dynamic Monopoly and the Coase Conjecture", *Journal of Economic Theory* 39/1: 155–90.

Hanemann, W. M. (1991) "Willingness to Pay and Willingness to Accept: How Much Can They Differ?" *American Economic Review* 81/3: 635–47.

Hardin, G. (1968) "The Tragedy of the Commons", *Science* 162/3859: 1243–8.

Hart, O. D. (1988) "Incomplete Contracts and the Theory of the Firm", *Journal of Law, Economics and Organization* 4/1: 119–39.

—— and Moore, J. (1990) "Property Rights and the Nature of the Firm", *Journal of Political Economy* 98/6: 1119–58.

Hayek, F. A. (1945) "The Use of Knowledge in Society", *American Economic Review* 35/4: 519–30.

Herfindahl, O. C. (1950) *Concentration in the U.S. Steel Industry*. Doctoral Dissertation, Department of Economics, Columbia University, New York.

Hicks, J. R. (1939) *Value and Capital*. Oxford: Clarendon Press.

Hirsch, F. (1976) *Social Limits to Growth*. Cambridge, MA: Harvard University Press.

Hirschman, A. O. (1964) "The Paternity of an Index", *American Economic Review* 54/5: 761–2.

Hirshleifer, J. (1971) "The Private and Social Value of Information and the Reward to Inventive Activity", *American Economic Review* 61/4: 561–74.

—— Glazer, A., and Hirshleifer, D. (2005) *Price Theory and Applications* (7th edn). Cambridge: Cambridge University Press.

Hotelling, H. (1929) "Stability in Competition", *Economic Journal* 39/153: 41–57.

Hurwicz, L. (1960) "Optimality and Informational Efficiency in Resource Allocation Processes", in K. J. Arrow and S. Karlin (eds), *Mathematical Methods in the Social Sciences*. Stanford, CA: Stanford University Press, 27–46.

—— (1973) "The Design of Mechanisms for Resource Allocation", *American Economic Review* 63/2: 1–30.

—— and Reiter, S. (2006) *Designing Economic Mechanisms*. Cambridge: Cambridge University Press.

Ingram, J. K. (1888) *A History of Political Economy*. New York: Macmillan.

Jackson, M. O. and Wilkie, S. (2005) "Endogenous Games and Mechanisms: Side Payments Among Players", *Review of Economic Studies* 72/2: 543–66.

Jevons, W. S. (1881) *Political Economy*. London: Macmillan.

Joyce, P. (1984) "The Walrasian Tâtonnement Mechanism and Information", *RAND Journal of Economics* 15/3: 416–25.

Kahneman, D. and Tversky, A. (1979) "Prospect Theory: An Analysis of Decision under Risk", *Econometrica* 47/2: 263–91.

—— and Tversky, A. (eds) (2000) *Choices, Values, and Frames*. Cambridge: Cambridge University Press.

Keynes, J. M. (1936) *The General Theory of Employment, Interest and Money*. London: Macmillan.

Kihlstrom, R. E. and Riordan, M. H. (1984) "Advertising as a Signal", *Journal of Political Economy* 92/3: 427–50.

Knetsch, J. L. (1989) "The Endowment Effect and Evidence of Nonreversible Indifference Curves", *American Economic Review* 79/5: 1277–84.

Kreps, D. (1988) *Notes on the Theory of Choice*. Boulder, CO: Westview Press.

Kyle, A. S. (1985) "Continuous Auctions and Insider Trading", *Econometrica* 53/6: 1315–35.

Laffont, J.-J. (1989) *The Economics of Uncertainty and Information*. Cambridge, MA: MIT Press.

Lancaster, K. J. (1966) "A New Approach to Consumer Theory", *Journal of Political Economy* 74/2: 132–57.

Leland, H. E. and Pyle, D. H. (1977) "Informational Asymmetries, Financial Structure, and Financial Intermediation", *Journal of Finance* 32/2: 371–87.

Lerner, A. P. (1934) "The Concept of Monopoly and the Measurement of Monopoly Power", *Review of Economic Studies* 1/3: 157–75.

Lindahl, E. (1919) *Die Gerechtigkeit der Besteuerung: eine Analyse der Steuerprinzipien auf der Grundlage der Grenznutzentheorie*, Hakan Ohlssons, Lund, Sweden. (Partially reprinted in 1958 as "Just Taxation: A Positive Solution", in R. A. Musgrave and A. T. Peacock (eds), *Classics in the Theory of Public Finance*, New York: St. Martin's Press, 168–76.)

Lindhqvist, T. (1992) "Extended Producer Responsibility", in T. Lindhqvist, *Extended Producer Responsibility as a Strategy to Promote Cleaner Products*, Seminar Proceedings, Department of Industrial Environmental Economics, Lund University, Lund, Sweden.

Luenberger, D. G. (2001) "Projection Pricing", *Journal of Optimization Theory and Applications* 109/1: 1–25.

—— (2002) "A Correlation Pricing Formula", *Journal of Economic Dynamics and Control* 26/7–8: 1113–26.

McKenzie, L. W. (2002) *Classical General Equilibrium Theory*. Cambridge, MA: MIT Press.

Magill, M. and Quinzii, M. (1996) *Theory of Incomplete Markets*. Cambridge, MA: MIT Press.

Malkiel, B. G. (2007) *A Random Walk Down Wall Street* (9th edn). New York: Norton.

Markowitz, H. (1952) "Portfolio Selection", *Journal of Finance* 7/1: 77–91.

Marshall, A. (1920) *Principles of Economics*. London: Macmillan.

Mas-Colell, A. (1985) *The Theory of General Economic Equilibrium*, Econometric Society Monographs. Cambridge: Cambridge University Press.

—— Whinston, M. D., and Green, J. R. (1995) *Microeconomic Theory*. Oxford: Oxford University Press.

Maskin, E. and Tirole, J. (1992) "The Principal–Agent Relationship with an Informed Principal, II: Common Values", *Econometrica* 60/1: 1–42.

Menger, C. (1871) *Grundsätze der Volkswirthschaftslehre: Erster, Allgemeiner Theil*. Vienna, Austria: W. Braumüller.

Milgrom, P. R. (2004) *Putting Auction Theory to Work*. Cambridge: Cambridge University Press.

Milgrom, P. and Segal, I. (2002) "Envelope Theorems for Arbitrary Choice Sets", *Econometrica* 70/2: 583–601.

Milgrom, P. R. and Shannon, C. (1994) "Monotone Comparative Statics", *Econometrica* 62/1: 157–80.

—— and Stokey, N. (1982) "Information, Trade, and Common Knowledge", *Journal of Economic Theory* 26/1: 17–27.

Mill, J. S. (1836) "On the Definition of Political Economy and on the Method of Investigation Proper to It", *London and Westminster Review*, October Issue. (Reprint: "Essay V" in J. S. Mill (1844) *Essays on Some Unsettled Questions of Political Economy*, London: Parker.)

—— (1863) *Utilitarianism*. London: Routledge.

Mirrlees, J. A. (1971) "An Exploration in the Theory of Optimal Income Taxation", *Review of Economic Studies* 38/2: 175–208.

Monteiro, P. K. and Page, Jr., F. H. (2008) "Catalog Competition and Nash Equilibrium in Nonlinear Pricing Games", *Economic Theory* 34/3: 503–24.

Mussa, M. and Rosen, S. (1978) "Monopoly and Product Quality", *Journal of Economic Theory* 18/2: 301–17.

Muth, J. F. (1961) "Rational Expectations and the Theory of Price Movements", *Econometrica* 29/3: 315–35.

Myerson, R. B. (1979) "Incentive Compatibility and the Bargaining Problem", *Econometrica* 47/1: 61–74.

—— (1981) "Optimal Auction Design", *Mathematics of Operations Research* 6/1: 58–73.

—— (1983) "Mechanism Design by an Informed Principal", *Econometrica* 51/6: 1767–98.

Niehans, J. (1956) "Preistheoretischer Leitfaden für Verkehrswissenschaftler", Schweizerisches Archiv für Verkehrswissenschaft und Verkehrspolitik 11: 293–320.

Osborne, M. J. and Pitchik, C. (1986) "Price Competition in a Capacity-Constrained Duopoly", *Journal of Economic Theory* 38/2: 238–60.

Palfrey, T. R. and Srivastava, S. (1993) *Bayesian Implementation.* Chur, Switzerland: Harwood Academic Publishers.

Persky, J. (1995) "The Ethology of Homo Economicus", *Journal of Economic Perspectives* 9/2: 221–31.

Pigou, A. C. (1920) *The Economics of Welfare.* New York: Macmillan.

Plott, C. R. and Zeiler, K. (2005) "The Willingness to Pay–Willingness to Accept Gap, the 'Endowment Effect,' Subject Misconceptions, and Experimental Procedures for Eliciting Valuations", *American Economic Review* 95/3: 530–45.

Posner, R. A. (1975) "The Social Costs of Monopoly and Regulation", *Journal of Political Economy* 83/4: 807–28.

Prat, A. and Rustichini, A. (2003) "Games Played Through Agents", *Econometrica* 71/4: 989–1026.

Pratt, J. (1964) "Risk Aversion in the Small and in the Large", *Econometrica* 32/1–2: 122–36.

Quah, J. K.-H. (2007) "The Comparative Statics of Constrained Optimization Problems", *Econometrica* 75/2: 401–31.

Radner, R. (1972) "Existence of Equilibrium of Plans, Prices, and Price Expectations in a Sequence of Markets", *Econometrica* 40/2: 289–303.

Raith, M. (1996) "A General Model of Information Sharing in Oligopoly", *Journal of Economic Theory* 71/1: 260–88.

Ramsey, F. P. (1927) "A Contribution to the Theory of Taxation", *Economic Journal* 37/145: 47–61.

Rawls, J. (1971) *A Theory of Justice.* Cambridge, MA: Harvard University Press. (Revised edition published in 1999.)

Riley, J. G. (1979) "Informational Equilibrium", *Econometrica* 47/2: 331–59.

Roberts, D. J. (1973) "Existence of Lindahl Equilibrium with a Measure Space of Consumers", *Journal of Economic Theory* 6/4: 355–81.

Rochet, J.-C. (1985) "The Taxation Principle and Multitime Hamilton-Jacobi Equations", *Journal of Mathematical Economics* 14/2: 113–28.

—— and Stole, L. A. (2003) "The Economics of Multidimensional Screening", in M. Dewatripont, L.-P. Hansen, and S. J. Turnovsky (eds), *Advances in Economics and Econometrics: Theory and Applications: Eighth World Congress*, Vol. I. New York: Cambridge University Press, 150–97.

—— and Tirole, J. (2003) "Platform Competition in Two-Sided Markets", *Journal of the European Economic Association* 1/4: 990–1029.

—— and —— (2005) "Two-Sided Markets: A Progress Report". Working Paper, Institut d'Économie Industrielle, Toulouse, France.

Roll, R. and Ross, S. A. (1980) "An Empirical Investigation of the Arbitrage Pricing Theory", *Journal of Finance* 35/5: 1073–103.

Ross, S. A. (1976) "The Arbitrage Theory of Capital Asset Pricing", *Journal of Economic Theory* 13/3: 341–60.

Rubinstein, A. (1998) *Modeling Bounded Rationality.* Cambridge, MA: MIT Press.

Samuelson, P. A. (1941) "The Stability of Equilibrium: Comparative Statics and Dynamics", *Econometrica* 9/2: 97–120.

—— (1947) *Foundations of Economic Analysis.* Cambridge, MA: Harvard University Press.

Samuelson, P. A. (1954) "The Pure Theory of Public Expenditure", *Review of Economics and Statistics* 36/4: 387–9.

Seade, J. (1985) "Profitable Cost Increases and the Shifting of Taxation: Equilibrium Responses of Markets in Oligopoly". Warwick Economic Research Paper No. 260, Department of Economics, University of Warwick, Warwick, UK.

Segal, I. (2006) "Communication in Economic Mechanism", in R. Blundel, W. K. Newey, and T. Persson (eds), *Advances in Economics and Econometrics, Vol. I.* Cambridge: Cambridge University Press, 222–68.

Shafarevich, I. R. (1980) *The Socialist Phenomenon.* New York: Harper and Row.

Shaked, A. and Sutton, J. (1982) "Relaxing Price Competition through Product Differentiation", *Review of Economic Studies* 49/1: 3–13.

Sharpe, W. F. (1964) "Capital Asset Prices: A Theory of Market Equilibrium under Conditions of Risk", *Journal of Finance* 19/3: 425–42.

Shiller, R. J. (2005) *Irrational Exuberance* (2nd edn). Princeton, NJ: Princeton University Press.

Simon, H. A. (1956) "Rational Choice and the Structure of the Environment", *Psychological Review* 63/2: 129–38.

Smith, A. (1776) *The Wealth of Nations.* Printed for W. Strahan and T. Cadell, London. (Reprint: New York: Modern Library, 1994.)

Sørenson, P. N. (2007) "Simple Utility Functions with Giffen Demand", *Economic Theory* 31/2: 367–70.

Sowell, T. (2010) *The Housing Boom and Bust* (Revised edn). New York: Basic Books.

Spence, A. M. (1973) "Job Market Signaling", *Quarterly Journal of Economics* 87/3: 355–74.

Spulber, D. F. (1999) *Market Microstructure: Intermediaries and the Theory of the Firm.* Cambridge: Cambridge University Press.

Stigler, G. J. (1966) *The Theory of Price.* New York: Macmillan.

Stiglitz, J. E. (1975) "The Theory of 'Screening,' Education, and the Distribution of Income", *American Economic Review* 65/3: 283–300.

—— (1989) "Imperfect Information in the Product Market", in R. Schmalensee and R. D. Willig (eds), *Handbook of Industrial Organization.* Elsevier, Amsterdam, 769–847.

—— (1994) *Whither Socialism?* Cambridge, MA: MIT Press.

—— (2006) *Making Globalization Work.* New York: Norton.

Stokey, N. L. (1979) "Intertemporal Price Discrimination", *Quarterly Journal of Economics* 93/3: 355–71.

—— (1981) "Rational Expectations and Durable Goods Pricing", *Bell Journal of Economics* 12/1: 112–28.

Strulovici, B. H. and Weber, T. A. (2008) "Monotone Comparative Statics: Geometric Approach", *Journal of Optimization Theory and Applications* 137/3: 641–73.

—— and —— (2010) "Generalized Monotonicity Analysis", *Economic Theory* 43/3: 377–406.

Thaler, R. H. (1994) *The Winner's Curse: Paradoxes and Anomalies of Economic Life.* Princeton, NJ: Princeton University Press.

—— (1999) "Mental Accounting Matters", *Journal of Behavioral Decision Making* 12/3: 183–206.

Tobin, J. (1958) "Liquidity Preference as Behavior Towards Risk", *Review of Economic Studies* 25/2: 65–86.

Topkis, D. M. (1968) *Ordered Optimal Solutions.* Doctoral Dissertation, Stanford University, Stanford, CA.

—— (1998) *Supermodularity and Complementarity.* Princeton, NJ: Princeton University Press.

Tullock, G. (1980) "Efficient Rent-Seeking", in J. M. Buchanan, R. D. Tollison, and G. Tullock (eds), *Toward a Theory of the Rent-Seeking Society*. College Station, TX: Texas A&M University Press, 97–112.

Tversky, A. and Kahneman, D. (1981) "The Framing of Decisions and the Psychology of Choice", *Science* 211/4481: 453–8.

Veblen, T. (1899) *The Theory of the Leisure Class: An Economic Study of Institutions*. New York: Macmillan. (Reprint: New York: Penguin, 1994.)

Vickrey, W. (1961) "Counterspeculation, Auctions, and Competitive Sealed Tenders", *Journal of Finance* 16/1: 8–37.

Vives, X. (1999) *Oligopoly Pricing*. Cambridge, MA: MIT Press.

Von Neumann, J. (1928) "Zur Theorie der Gesellschaftsspiele", *Mathematische Annalen* 100/1: 295–320.

—— and Morgenstern, O. (1944) *Theory of Games and Economic Behavior*. Princeton, NJ: Princeton University Press.

Walras, L. (1874/77) *Éléments d'Économie Politique Pure*. Lausanne, Switzerland: Corbaz. (English translation: *Elements of Pure Economics*, London: Allen and Unwin, 1954.)

Weber, T. A. (2003) "An Exact Relation between Willingness to Accept and Willingness to Pay", *Economics Letters* 80/3: 311–15.

—— (2010) "Hicksian Welfare Measures and the Normative Endowment Effect", *American Economic Journal: Microeconomics* 2/4: 171–94.

—— (2011) *Optimal Control Theory with Applications in Economics*. Cambridge, MA: MIT Press.

—— (2012) "An Augmented Becker–DeGroot–Marschak Mechanism for Transaction Cycles", *Economics Letters* 114/1: 43–6.

—— and Bapna, A. (2008) "Bayesian Incentive Compatible Parametrization of Mechanisms", *Journal of Mathematical Economics* 44/3–4: 394–403.

—— and Croson, D. C. (2004) "Selling Less Information for More: Garbling with Benefits", *Economics Letters* 83/2: 165–71.

—— and Xiong, H. (2007) "Efficient Contract Design in Multi-Principal Multi-Agent Supply Chains", *Proceedings of the 18th Annual Conference of the Production and Operations Management Society (POMS)*, Dallas, TX.

—— and Zheng, Z. (2007) "A Model of Search Intermediaries and Paid Referrals", *Information Systems Research* 18/4: 414–36.

Weitzman, M. L. (1974) "Prices vs. Quantities", *Review of Economic Studies* 41/4: 477–91.

—— (1979) "Optimal Search for the Best Alternative", *Econometrica* 47/3: 641–54.

Williamson, O. D. (1975) *Markets and Hierarchies: Analysis and Antitrust Implications*. New York: Free Press.

—— (1985) *The Economic Institutions of Capitalism*. New York: Free Press.

Willig, R. D. (1976) "Consumer's Surplus Without Apology", *American Economic Review* 66/4: 589–97.

Wilson, R. B. (1987) "Bidding", in J. Eatwell, M. Milgate, and P. Newman (eds), *The New Palgrave: A Dictionary of Economics, Vol. 1*. London: Macmillan, 238–42.

—— (1993) *Nonlinear Pricing*. Oxford: Oxford University Press.

Wolfers, J. and Zitzewitz, E. (2004) "Prediction Markets", *Journal of Economic Perspectives* 18/2: 107–26.

CHAPTER 18

....

MODELS OF DEMAND

....

GARRETT J. VAN RYZIN

18.1 INTRODUCTION

Demand models are essential for analytical pricing. They predict how a firm's pricing actions will influence demand for its products and services, which in turn determines revenues and profits. Here we review the most important demand models used in pricing practice and survey approaches to estimating these models.

The most widely used models of demand assume customers are *rational* decision-makers who intelligently alter when, what, and how much to purchase to achieve the best possible outcome for themselves. This is a quite plausible assumption. Moreover, an important consequence of this rationality assumption is that customer behavior can be "predicted" by treating each customer as an agent that optimizes over possible choices and outcomes. Optimization theory can then be used to model their behavior. These are the most widespread models used in pricing practice and the focus of this chapter. Other theories of customers from behavioral science depart from this classical rational view and examine important biases in buying decisions. These theories are covered in Chapter 20 of this handbook and are also discussed briefly below.

Because demand results from many individuals making choice decisions—choices to buy one firm's products over another, to wait or not to buy at all, to buy more or fewer units, etc.— we begin by looking at models of individual-choice behavior. When added up, these individual purchase decisions determine aggregate demand, so we next examine aggregate-demand functions and their properties. Finally, we survey how such models can be estimated from data.

18.2 CONSUMER THEORY

For completeness, here we briefly review the fundamentals of classical consumer theory from economics, highlighting the concepts and assumptions that are important for

This chapter is adapted from Talluri and van Ryzin (2004).

operational demand modeling. A complete treatment of consumer theory is given in Chapter 17 of this volume.

18.2.1 Choice and preference relations

What do we mean by choice? Formally, given two alternatives, a *choice* corresponds to an expression of preference for one alternative over another. Here, "alternatives" may refer to different products, different quantities of the same product, bundles of different products or various uncertain outcomes (such as buying a house at the asking price versus waiting and bidding in an auction against other buyers). Similarly, given n alternatives, choice can be defined in terms of the preferences expressed for all pairwise comparisons among the n alternatives.

The mathematical construct that formalizes this notion is a *preference relation*. Customers are assumed to have a set of *binary preferences* over alternatives in a set X; given any two alternatives x and y in X, customers can rank them and clearly say they prefer one over the other or are indifferent between them. This is represented by the notation $x \succeq y$. A customer strictly prefers x to y, denoted $x \succ y$, if he prefers x to y, but does not prefer y to x (that is, he is not indifferent between the two alternatives). Consider a complete set of all such pairwise binary preferences between alternatives in X with the following two properties:

- *Asymmetry* If x is strictly preferred to y, then y is not strictly preferred to x.

- *Negative transitivity* If x is not strictly preferred to y and y is not strictly preferred to z, then x is not strictly preferred to z.

Such a binary relation is called a preference relation. While asymmetry is a very plausible assumption, negative transitivity is not completely innocuous, and it is possible to construct natural examples of preferences that violate it. Still, preference relations form the classical basis for modeling customer choice.

The following is a common example of a preference relation:

Example 1 (ADDRESS MODEL) *Suppose we have n alternatives and each alternative has m attributes that take on real values. Alternatives can then be represented as n points, z_1, ..., z_n, in $\Re^m$, which is called the* attribute space. *For example, attributes could include color, size, indicators for features and price.*

Each customer has an ideal point ("address") $y \in \Re^m$, reflecting his most preferred combination of attributes (such as an ideal color, size, and price). A customer is then assumed to prefer the product closest to his ideal point in attribute space, where distance is defined by a metric ρ on $\Re^m \times \Re^m$ (such as Euclidean distance). These distances define a preference relation, in which $z_i \succ z_j$ if and only if $\rho(z_i, y) < \rho(z_j, y)$; that is, if z_i is "closer" to the ideal point y of the customer.

18.2.2 Utility functions

Preference relations are intimately related to the existence of utility functions. Indeed, we have the following theorem (see Kreps (1988) for a proof):

Theorem 1 *If X is a finite set, a binary relation $\succ$ is a preference relation if and only if there exists a function u: $X \rightarrow \Re$ (called a **utility function**), such that*

$$x \succ y \quad \textit{iff} \quad u(x) > u(y).$$

Intuitively, this theorem follows because if a customer has a preference relation, then all products can be ranked (totally ordered) by his preferences; a utility function then simply assigns a value corresponding to this ranking. One can think of utility as a cardinal measure of "value", though in a strict sense its numerical value need not correspond to any tangible measure. Theorem 1 applies to continuous sets X (such as travel times or continuous amounts of money) as well under mild regularity conditions, in which case the utility function $u(\cdot)$ is then continuous. Continuing our previous example:

Example 2 *Consider the address model of Example 1. Theorem 1 guarantees an equivalent utility maximization model of choice. In this case, it is easy to see that for customer y the continuous utilities*

$$u(z) = c - \rho(z, y),$$

where c is an arbitrary constant, produce the same preferences as the address model.

18.2.3 Consumer budgets, demand, and reservation prices

Demand can be derived once customers' preferences are known. Given a customer's preferences for bundles of n goods, a vector of market prices $\mathbf{p} = (p_1, \ldots, p_n)$ for these goods, and a level of monetary wealth (or *income*) w, we simply ask how our customer would "spend" his wealth? Let x_i denote the quantity of each good i consumed. We assume x_i are continuous quantities and our customer has a continuous utility function $u(\mathbf{x})$. Let $\mathbf{x} = (x_1, \ldots, x_n)$. The *consumer budget problem* can then be formulated as

$$
\begin{aligned}
\max \quad & u(\mathbf{x}) \\
\text{s.t.} \quad & \mathbf{p}^\top \mathbf{x} \le w \\
& \mathbf{x} \ge 0.
\end{aligned}
\tag{1}
$$

In other words, a customer's purchase quantities maximize their total utility subject to their limited wealth (income). The resulting optimal $\mathbf{x}^*$ is a customer's demand vector for the n goods at price vector $\mathbf{p}$.[1]

18.2.4 Reservation prices

A *reservation price*, denoted v_i, is the monetary amount a customer is willing to give up to acquire an additional marginal unit of good i. Reservation prices are also referred to as the customer's *willingness-to-pay*. One can show from the first-order conditions of the budget problem that if $x_i^* > 0$, then $v_i = p_i$. Thus, a customer's reservation price for goods that are *currently consumed* is simply the market price. The reasoning is intuitive; if our customer valued consuming an additional marginal unit of good i at strictly more than its market price, then he would be able to increase his utility by marginally reducing consumption of other goods and increasing his consumption of good i. Since our customer is maximizing utility, this cannot occur.

---

[1] The optimal consumption vector x^* may not be unique, in which case $x^*(\mathbf{p})$ is a demand correspondence rather than a demand function; see Chapter 17 for more details.

On the other hand, for goods i that are not being consumed, $x_i^* = 0$ and it follows from the first-order conditions of the budget problem that $v_i \leq p_i$. In other words, the customer's reservation price for initial consumption of good i is less than its current market price. Moreover, the customer would only change his allocation and buy good i if its price p_i dropped below his reservation price v_i.

As a practical matter, this formal theory of reservation prices is less important than the informal concept—namely, that a reservation price is the maximum amount a customer is willing to pay for an additional unit of good i and to entice a customer to buy good i, the price must drop below his reservation price. Still, the formal analysis highlights the important fact that reservation prices are not "absolute" quantities. They depend on customers' preferences, wealth, their current consumption levels, and the prices of other goods the customers may buy; change one of these factors, and customers' reservation price may change.

18.2.5 Preference for stochastic outcomes

Many choices involve uncertain outcomes, such as buying insurance, making investments, or even eating at a new restaurant. How do customers respond to such uncertainties? The theory of choice under uncertainty is a deep and extensive topic. Here, we outline only the main concepts.

Consider again a discrete set of n alternatives, $X = \{x_1, \ldots, x_n\}$. Let $\mathcal{P}$ be the class of all probability distributions $P(\cdot)$ defined on X. That is, $P \in P$ is a function satisfying $\Sigma_i P(x_i) = 1$ and $P(x_i) \geq 0$ for $i = 1, \ldots, n$. One can think of each P as a "lottery", the outcome of which determines which one of the alternatives the customer gets according to the distribution P.

What can we say about a customer's preference for lotteries? Specifically, when can we say that for any two lotteries P_1 and P_2, customers "prefer" one over the other (denoted by $P_1 \succ P_2$)?

To answer this question we need to make some assumptions on customer preferences. First, we will assume there exists a preference relation $\succ$ on the n different outcomes x_i as before. Second, for any two lotteries P_1 and P_2, consider a compound lottery parameterized by α as follows: (i) A coin is flipped with probability of heads equal to α; (ii) If the coin comes up heads, the customer enters lottery P_1, otherwise the customer enters lottery P_2. Denote this compound lottery by $\alpha P_1 + (1 - \alpha)P_2$. Note this compound lottery is also contained in the set $\mathcal{P}$ (i.e., $\mathcal{P}$ is a convex set). We then require the following consistency properties on a customer's preference for lotteries:

- *Substitution axiom* For all P_1, P_2, and P_3 in $\mathcal{P}$ and all $\alpha \in (0, 1)$, if $P_1 \succ P_2$, then $\alpha P_1 + (1 - \alpha) P_3 \succ \alpha P_2 + (1 - \alpha)P_3$.
- *Continuity axiom* For all P_1, P_2, and P_3 in $\mathcal{P}$ with $P_1 \succ P_2 \succ P_3$, there exist values $\alpha \in (0, 1)$ and $\beta \in (0, 1)$ such that $\alpha P_1 + (1 - \alpha)P_3 \succ P_2 \succ \beta P_1 + (1 - \beta)P_3$.

Roughly, the first axiom says that substituting a gamble that produces a strictly preferred collection of outcomes in the compound lottery should be preferred. The second axiom says that if a customer strictly prefers one gamble to another, then he should be willing to accept a sufficiently small risk of an even worse outcome to take the preferred gamble. We then have:

Theorem 2 *A preference relation on the lotteries $\mathcal{P}$ exists that satisfies the substitution and continuity axioms if and only if there exists a utility function $u(\cdot)$ such that $P_1 \succ P_2$ if and only if*

$$\sum_{i=1}^{n} u(x_i)P_1(x_i) > \sum_{i=1}^{n} u(x_i)P_2(x_i).$$

That is, if and only if the expected utility from lottery P_1 exceeds the expected utility of lottery P_2. In addition, any two utility functions u and u' satisfying the above must be affine transformations of each other; that is,

$$u(x) = cu'(x) + d,$$

for some real $c > 0$ and d.

This result is due to von Neumann and Morgenstern (1944) and the function $u(x)$ above is known as the *von Neumann–Morgenstern utility*. Essentially, this result allows us to extend utility as a model of customer preference to the case of uncertain outcomes, with expected utility replacing deterministic utility as the criterion for customer decision-making.

18.2.6 Risk preferences

An important special case of expected-utility theory is when outcomes correspond to different levels of wealth and lotteries correspond to different gambles on a customer's ending wealth level. We assume the wealth levels are continuous and that the customer has preferences for wealth that satisfy the conditions of Theorem 2. Also, assume the lotteries are now continuous distributions F on $\Re$.[2]

Consider now any given lottery F (a distribution on possible wealth outcomes) and let μ_F denote the mean of the distribution. A customer is said to have *risk-averse preferences* if he prefers the certain wealth μ_F to the lottery F itself for all possible lotteries F. That is, the customer always prefers the certainty of receiving the expected wealth rather than a gamble with the same mean. The customer is said to have *risk-seeking preferences* if he prefers the gamble F to the certain outcome μ_F for all F. Finally, he has *risk-neutral preferences* if he is indifferent between the lottery F and the certain reward μ_F.[3] Risk preferences are linked directly to concavity or convexity of the customer's utility function as shown by the following theorem:

Theorem 3 *A customer's preference $\succ$ for lotteries exhibits risk-aversion (risk-seeking) behavior if and only if his von Neumann–Morgenstern utility function $u(w)$ is concave (convex). His preference is risk-neutral if and only if $u(w)$ is affine.*

The reason is quite intuitive; with a concave utility function for wealth, a customer gains less utility from a given increase in wealth than he loses in utility from the same decrease in

---

[2] The extension of Theorem 2 to the continuous case requires some additional technical conditions that are beyond the scope of this chapter. See Kreps (1988).

[3] Note that a customer's preferences may not fall into any of these three categories. For example, many customers take out fire insurance, preferring a certain loss in premium payments every year to the gamble between making no payments but potentially losing their house, yet simultaneously play their local state lottery, which has an expected loss but provides a small probability of a large wealth payoff. Such behavior violates strict risk preference.

wealth. Hence, the upside gains produced by the volatility in outcomes do not offset the downside losses, and customers therefore prefer the certain average to the uncertain outcomes of the lottery. Since most customers have a decreasing marginal utility for wealth, risk aversion is a good assumption in modeling customer behavior.

Still, the concept of risk aversion has to be addressed with care in operational modeling. While it is true that most customers are risk-averse when it comes to *large* swings in their wealth, often the gambles we face as customers have a relatively small range of possible outcomes relative to our wealth. For example, a customer may face a price risk in buying a CD or book online. However, the differences in prices for such items are extremely small compared to total wealth. In such cases, the utility function may be almost linear in the range of outcomes affecting the decision, in which case the customer exhibits approximately risk-neutral preference.[4] Similar statements apply to firms. Generally, they are risk-averse too, but for decisions and gambles that involve "small" outcomes relative to their total wealth and income, they tend to be approximately risk-neutral. Hence, risk-neutrality is a reasonable assumption in operational models and, indeed, is the standard assumption in pricing practice.

18.3 DISAGGREGATE DEMAND MODELS

With the basic concepts of consumer theory in hand, we next look at approaches for modeling individual customer purchase decisions. Such models may be used on their own to predict individual purchase instances (e.g., the likelihood a customer buys when visiting a website) or as building blocks in aggregate demand models, which are discussed in the subsequent section. With the increased availability of individual customer level data and the trend toward making pricing more targeted, such disaggregate models of demand are increasingly being used directly in pricing practice.

18.3.1 An overview of random-utility models

The disaggregate demand models most commonly used are based on a probabilistic model of individual customer utility. This framework is useful for several reasons. First, probabilistic models can be used to represent heterogeneity of preference among a population of customers. They can also model uncertainty in choice outcomes due to the inability of the firm to observe all the relevant variables (other alternatives, their prices, the customer's wealth, and so on) or situations where customers exhibit *variety-seeking behavior* and deliberately alter their choices over time (movie or meal choice, for example). Finally, probabilistic utility can model customers whose behavior is inherently unpredictable—that is, customers who behave in a way that is inconsistent with well-defined preferences and who at best exhibit only a probabilistic tendency to prefer one alternative to another (see Luce 1959).

---

[4] Formally, one can see this by taking a Taylor series approximation of the utility function about the customer's current wealth w; the first-order approximation is affine, corresponding to risk-neutrality.

Specifically, let the n alternatives be denoted $j = 1, \ldots, n$. A customer has a utility for alternative j, denoted U_j. Without loss of generality we can decompose this utility into two parts, a *representative* component u_j that is deterministic and a *random* component, ξ_j (often assumed to have zero or constant mean for all j). Therefore,

$$U_j = u_j + \xi_j, \tag{2}$$

and the probability that an individual selects alternative j given a choice from a subset S of alternatives is given by

$$P_j(S) = P(U_j \geq \max\{U_i : i \in S\}). \tag{3}$$

In other words, the probability of selecting alternative j is the probability that it has the highest utility among all the alternatives in the set S. The set S (called the *choice set*) is a collectively exhaustive, mutually exclusive set of all the feasible alternatives considered by a customer when making a choice decision. It varies based on which alternatives a firm makes available (the *offer set*), the set of outside alternatives (competitors' offer sets or substitute options), and which subset of these internal and external alternatives a customer actually considers when making a choice (this may vary by customer segment). Identifying appropriate choice sets is a challenging modeling task. In operational modeling, a common simplification is to aggregate all competitor and substitute alternatives into a single generic "outside" alternative or "no purchase" alternative.

The representative component u_j is often modeled as a function of the relevant attributes of alternative j. A common assumption is the *linear-in-parameters* model

$$u_j = \beta^\top x_j, \tag{4}$$

where β is a vector of weights and x_j is a vector of attribute parameters for alternative j, which could include factors such as price, measures of quality, and indicator variables for product features.[5] Variables describing characteristics of the customer (segment variables) can also be included in x_j.[6]

This formulation defines a general class of random-utility models, which vary according to the assumptions on the joint distribution of the utilities $U_1, \ldots, U_n$. Random-utility models are no more restrictive in terms of modeling behavior than classical utility models; essentially, all we need assume is that customers have well-defined preferences so that utility maximization is an accurate model of their choice behavior. However, as a practical matter, certain assumptions on the random utilities lead to simpler models than others. We look at a few of these special cases next.

18.3.2 Binary probit

If there are only two alternatives to choose from (e.g., buying or not buying a product), the error terms ξ_j, $j = 1, 2$, are normally distributed random variables with mean zero and the

---

[5] Attribute parameters can also include transforms of attribute values, such as the natural log or square root.

[6] Specifically, the utility can also depend on observable customer characteristics, so for customer i the utility of alternative j is u_{ij}. For simplicity, we ignore customer-specific characteristics here, but they can be incorporated into all the models that follow.

difference in the error terms, $\xi = \xi_1 - \xi_2$, has variance σ^2, then the probability that alternative 1 is chosen is given by

$$P(\xi_2 - \xi_1 \leq u_1 - u_2) = \Phi\left(\frac{u_1 - u_2}{\sigma}\right), \tag{5}$$

where $\Phi(\cdot)$ denotes the standard normal distribution. This model is known as the *binary-probit* model. While the normal distribution is an appealing model of disturbances in utility (i.e., it can be viewed as resulting from the sum of a large number of random disturbances), the resulting probabilities do not have a simple closed-form solution.

18.3.3 Binary logit

The binary-logit model also applies to a situation with two choices, similar to the binary-probit case, but is simpler to analyze. The assumption made here is that the difference in the error terms, $\xi = \xi_1 - \xi_2$, has a *logistic* distribution—that is,

$$F(x) = \frac{1}{1 + e^{-\mu x}},$$

where $\mu > 0$ is a scale parameter. Here ξ has a mean zero and variance $\frac{\pi^2}{3\mu^2}$. The logistic distribution provides a good approximation to the normal distribution, though it has "fatter tails". The probability that alternative 1 is chosen is given by

$$P(\xi_2 - \xi_1 \leq u_1 - u_2) = \frac{e^{\mu u_1}}{e^{\mu u_1} + e^{\mu u_2}}.$$

18.3.4 Multinomial logit

The multinomial-logit model (MNL) is a generalization of the binary-logit model to n alternatives. It is derived by assuming that the ξ_j are i.i.d. random variables with a Gumbel (or double-exponential) distribution with cumulative density function

$$F(x) = P(\xi_j \leq x) = e^{-e^{-\mu(x-\eta)}},$$

where μ is a positive scale parameter and η is the mode of the distribution. The mean and variance of ξ_j are

$$E[\xi_j] = \eta + \frac{\gamma}{\mu}, \quad Var[\xi_j] = \frac{\pi^2}{6\mu^2},$$

where γ is Euler's constant ($= 0.5772\ldots$). The *standard Gumbel distribution* has $\eta = 0$ and $\mu = 1$, and since utility can be shifted and scaled without altering choice outcomes one often assumes disturbances have a standard Gumbel distribution in the MNL.

The Gumbel distribution has some useful analytical properties, the most important of which is that the distribution of the maximum of n independent Gumbel random variables is also a Gumbel random variable. Also, if two random variables ξ_1 and ξ_2 are independent and Gumbel distributed, then $\xi = \xi_1 - \xi_2$ has a logistic distribution. (See Ben-Akiva and Lerman (1985) and Train (2006) for details.)

For the MNL model, the probability that an alternative j is chosen from a set $S \subseteq \mathcal{N} = \{1, 2, \ldots, n\}$ that contains j is given by

$$P_j(S) = \frac{e^{\mu u_j}}{\sum_{i \in S} e^{\mu u_i}}. \tag{6}$$

If $\{u_j : j \in S\}$ has a unique maximum and $\mu \to \infty$, then the variance of the ξ_j, $j = 1, \ldots, n$ tends to zero and the MNL reduces to a deterministic model—namely

$$\lim_{\mu \to 0} P_j(S) = \begin{cases} 1 & \text{if } u_j = \max_{i \in S} \{u_i\} \\ 0 & \text{otherwise.} \end{cases}$$

Conversely, if $\mu \to 0$, then the variance of the ξ_j, $j = 1, \ldots, n$ tends to infinity and the systematic component of utility u_j becomes negligible. In this case,

$$\lim_{\mu \to \infty} P_j(S) = \frac{1}{|S|}, \quad j \in S,$$

which corresponds to a uniform random choice among the alternatives in S. Hence, the MNL can model behavior ranging from deterministic utility maximization to purely random choice.

Though widely used as a model of customer choice, the MNL possesses a somewhat restrictive property known as the *independence from irrelevant alternatives* (IIA) property; namely, for any two sets $S \subseteq \mathcal{N}$, $T \subseteq \mathcal{N}$ and any two alternatives $i, j \in S \cap T$, the choice probabilities satisfy

$$\frac{P_i(S)}{P_j(S)} = \frac{P_i(T)}{P_j(T)}. \tag{7}$$

Equation (7) says that the relative likelihood of choosing i and j is independent of the choice set containing these alternatives. This property is not realistic, however, if the choice set contains alternatives that can be grouped such that alternatives within a group are more similar than alternatives outside the group, because then adding a new alternative reduces the probability of choosing similar alternatives more than dissimilar alternatives, violating the IIA property. A famous example illustrating this point is the "blue-bus/red-bus paradox", (Debreu 1960):

Example 3 *An individual has to travel and can use one of two modes of transportation: a car or a bus. Suppose the individual selects them with equal probability. Let the set $S = \{car, bus\}$. Then*

$$P_{car}(S) = P_{bus}(S) = \frac{1}{2}.$$

Suppose now that another bus is introduced that is identical to the current bus in all respects except color: one is blue and one is red. Let the set T denote $\{car, blue\ bus, red\ bus\}$. Then the MNL predicts

$$P_{car}(T) = P_{blue\ bus}(T) = P_{red\ bus}(T) = \frac{1}{3}.$$

However, as bus's color is likely an irrelevant characteristic in this choice situation; it is more realistic to assume that the choice of bus or car is still equally likely, in which case we should have

$$P_{car}(T) = \frac{1}{2}$$
$$P_{blue\ bus}(T) = P_{red\ bus}(T) = \frac{1}{4}.$$

As a result of IIA, the MNL model must be used with caution. It should be restricted to choice sets that contain alternatives that are, in some sense, "equally dissimilar".

Despite this deficiency, the MNL model is widely used in marketing (see Guadagni and Little 1983). It has also seen considerable application in estimating travel demand (see Ben-Akiva and Lerman 1985). The popularity of MNL stems from the fact that it is analytically tractable, relatively accurate (if applied correctly), and can be estimated easily using standard statistical techniques.

18.3.5 Finite-mixture logit models

In the basic MNL model with linear-in-attribute utilities, the coefficients β in (4) are assumed to be the same for all customers. This may not be an appropriate assumption if there are different segments with different preferences. Moreover, as we have seen, the assumption leads to the IIA property, which may not be reasonable in certain contexts. If we can identify each customer as belonging to a segment, then it is an easy matter to simply fit a separate MNL model to the data from each segment. However, a more sophisticated modeling approach is needed if we cannot identify which customers belong to each segment.

Assume that customers within each segment follow an MNL model with identical parameters and that customers have a certain probability of belonging to a finite number of segments (called *latent segments*), which has to be estimated along with the MNL parameters for each segment. This results in the so-called *finite-mixture logit models*.

Assume that there are L latent segments and that the probability that a customer belongs to segment l is given by q_l. All customers in segment l are assumed to have utilities determined by an identical vector of coefficients β_l. Then the probability of choosing alternative j in this finite-mixture logit model is given by

$$P_j(S) = \sum_{l=1}^{L} q_l \frac{e^{\beta_l^\top x^j}}{\sum_{i\in S} e^{\beta_l^\top x_i}}, \quad j \in S.$$

The mixed logit is an important generalization of the MNL. Indeed, McFadden and Train (2000) show that any discrete choice model derived from random utility can be approximated arbitrarily closely by an appropriate finite mixing distribution. One can estimate the coefficients of the model (β_l and q_l, $l = 1, \ldots, L$) using, for example, maximum-likelihood methods as discussed below. This model often provides better estimates of choice behavior than the standard MNL model, at the expense of a more complicated estimation procedure. Also, the more segments included in the model, the more parameters there are to estimate and more data are required to get high-quality estimates.

18.3.6 Random-coefficients logit models

Another approach to modeling heterogeneity is to assume that each customer has a distinct set of coefficients β that are drawn from a distribution—usually assumed normal for analytical convenience—over the population of potential customers. This leads to what is called the *random-coefficients logit model*. The coefficients may also be correlated, both among themselves as well as with the error term, though we focus here on the simpler case where the coefficients are mutually independent.

Here again the utility of alternative j is given, similar to the MNL model, as

$$U_j = \boldsymbol{\beta}^\top \mathbf{x}_j + \xi_j, \quad j = 1, \dots, n.$$

But $\boldsymbol{\beta}$ is now considered a vector of random coefficients, each element of which is assumed to be independent of both the other coefficients in $\boldsymbol{\beta}$ and the error term ξ_j. Furthermore, the components of $\boldsymbol{\beta}$ are assumed to be normally distributed with a vector of means $\mathbf{b}$ and a vector of standard deviations $\boldsymbol{\sigma}$. The components of the random vector $\boldsymbol{\beta}$ corresponding to characteristic m, denoted β_m, can be decomposed into

$$\beta_m = b_m + \sigma_m \zeta_m,$$

where $\zeta_m, m = 1, \dots, M$ is a collection of i.i.d. standard normal random variables.

It is convenient to express the utility as a systematic part and a mean-zero error term as before. To this end, define the composite random-error term

$$\nu_j = \left[\sum_{m=1}^{M} x_{mj} \sigma_m \zeta_m\right] + \xi_j, \quad j = 1, \dots, n. \tag{8}$$

Then a customer's random utility is given by

$$U_j(\boldsymbol{\nu}) = \mathbf{b}^\top \mathbf{x}_j + \nu_j, \quad j = 1, \dots, n, \tag{9}$$

where ν_j is given by (8). Hence, the key difference between the standard MNL and the random-coefficient logit is that the error terms ν_j are no longer independent across the alternatives, and somewhat less importantly, they are no longer Gumbel distributed.

18.4 Aggregate demand models

It is often easier to model and estimate aggregate demand rather than individual customer-choice decisions. Depending on the model, this aggregate demand could be defined at the product, firm, or market level. If defined at the product or firm level, interactions with demand for other products (cross-elasticities) and dependence on historical demand or product attributes may have to be incorporated in the specification. In this section, we look at some commonly used aggregate-demand models.

Before doing so, however, note that aggregate demand models can be formed from disaggregate demand models simply by "adding up" the effect of many individual consumer choice decisions. For example, suppose we know that the probability that a given consumer purchases an alternative j from a set of alternatives S is $P_j(S)$. This probability could come from an MNL model, a mixed logit model, or a more complex discrete choice model. Suppose further that we know that N such customers will face the same choice. Then the aggregate expected demand for j is simply $D_j(S) = NP_j(S)$. Likewise, as we show below, aggregate demand models can often be interpreted as stemming from an underlying disaggregate demand model that is multiplied by a "market size" to produce aggregate demand. So in many ways the distinction between aggregate and disaggregate models is not sharp—both are ultimately trying to explain the same real-world demand. The choice of which approach to use depends on the data available, the pricing decision being addressed, and, to a very real extent, the preference of the model builder.

18.4.1 Demand functions and their properties

For the case of a single product, let p and $d(p)$ denote, respectively, the (scalar) price and the corresponding demand at that price. Also let Ω_p denote the set of feasible prices (the domain) of the demand function. For most demand functions of interest, $\Omega_p = [0, +\infty)$ but some functions (such as the linear-demand function) must be constrained further to ensure they produce nonnegative demand.

18.4.1.1 Regularity

It is often convenient to assume the following regularity conditions about the demand function:

Assumption 1 (Regularity: Scalar Case)

 (i) *The demand function is continuously differentiable on* Ω_p.

 (ii) *The demand function is strictly decreasing,* $d'(p) < 0$, *on* Ω_p.

 (iii) *The demand function is bounded above and below:*

$$0 \le d(p) < \infty, \quad \forall p \in \Omega_p.$$

 (iv) *The demand tends to zero for sufficiently high prices—namely,*

$$\inf_{p \in \Omega_p} d(p) = 0.$$

 (v) *The revenue function* $pd(p)$ *is finite for all* $p \in \Omega_p$ *and has a finite maximizer* $p^0 \in \Omega_p$ *that is interior to the set* Ω_p.

These are not restrictive assumptions in most cases and simply help avoid technical complications in both analysis and numerical optimization. For example, consider a linear demand model (defined formally in Section 18.4.3.1)

$$d(p) = a - bp, \quad p \in \Omega_p = [0, a/b]. \tag{10}$$

This is trivially differentiable on Ω_p, is strictly decreasing if $b > 0$, is nonnegative and bounded for all $p \in \Omega_p$, tends to zero for $p \to a/b$ and the revenue $ap - bp^2$, and has a finite maximizer $p^0 = \frac{a}{2b}$.

18.4.1.2 Reservation prices and demand functions

Demand functions can naturally be interpreted in terms of a reservation price model in which each customer is assumed to follow a simple decision rule: if his reservation price (or valuation) v equals or exceeds the offered price p, the customer purchases the product; otherwise, he does not purchase. Moreover, customers buy only one unit of the product. A customer's reservation price is specific to each individual and is normally private information unknown to the firm, though one may estimate a distribution of reservation prices across a population of customers. Let the probability that a customer's reservation price is below p be given by $F(p) = P(v \leq p)$. The derivative of $F(p)$ is denoted $f(p) = \frac{\partial}{\partial p} F(p)$.

Using this model, it is often convenient to express the demand function in the form

$$d(p) = N(1 - F(p)), \tag{11}$$

where $F(p)$ is the reservation price distribution and N is interpreted as the *market size*. $1 - F(p)$ is then the fraction of customers willing to buy at price p. For example, consider again the linear-demand function (10). This can be written in the form (11) if we define $N = a$ and $F(p) = pb/a$. Since $F(\cdot)$ is the probability distribution of a customer's reservation price v, reservation prices are uniformly distributed in the linear-demand-function case.

18.4.1.3 *Elasticity of demand*

The *price elasticity* of demand is the relative change in demand produced by a unit relative change in price. It is defined by

$$\varepsilon(p) \equiv \frac{p}{d} \frac{\partial d}{\partial p} = \frac{\partial \ln (d)}{\partial \ln (p)}.$$

Note that elasticity is defined at a particular price p.

To illustrate, for the linear-demand function (10), $\frac{\partial d}{\partial p} = -b$, so the elasticity is

$$\frac{p}{d} \frac{\partial d}{\partial p} = -\frac{bp}{a - bp}.$$

Products can be categorized based on the magnitude of their elasticities. A product with $|\varepsilon(p)| > 1$ is said to be *elastic*, while one with an elasticity value $|\varepsilon(p)| < 1$ is said to be *inelastic*. If $|\varepsilon(p)| = \infty$, demand for the product is said to be *perfectly elastic*, while if $|\varepsilon(p)| = 0$, demand is said to be *perfectly inelastic*.

Table 18.1 shows a sample of estimated elasticities for common consumer products. This table distinguishes between short- and long-run elasticities for products. For example, in the short term consumers cannot do much about an increase in natural gas prices; they might slightly decrease consumption by lowering thermostats, using supplementary heating sources, etc. Such behavior will not significantly affect demand for natural gas. However, a long-term increase in natural gas prices could easily cause consumers to replace gas furnaces with oil heating or other alternative energy sources, causing a much more significant loss in demand. This is consistent with the numbers: short-term elasticity for gas is much lower than the long-term elasticity (0.1 versus 0.5). While many factors affect elasticity, these estimates give some sense of the relative magnitudes of elasticities.

18.4.1.4 *Inverse demand*

The *inverse-demand function*, denoted $p(d)$, is the largest value of p which generates a demand equal to d—that is,

$$p(d) \equiv \max_{p \in \Omega_p} \{p : d(p) = d\}.$$

Given an inverse-demand function, one can view demand rather than price as the decision variable, since every choice of a demand d in the range of the demand function (domain of the inverse) implies a unique choice of price $p(d)$. This is often a useful transformation, as the resulting revenue and profit functions are usually simpler to work with, both analytically and computationally.

Equation (11) expressed in terms of the reservation-price distribution, $F(p)$, the inverse-demand function is defined by

$$p(d) = F^{-1}(1 - d/N),$$

where $F^{-1}(\cdot)$ is the inverse of $F(\cdot)$.

Table 18.1 Estimated elasticities (absolute values) for common products

Product	$|\varepsilon(p)|$
Inelastic	
Salt	0.1
Matches	0.1
Toothpicks	0.1
Airline travel, short-run	0.1
Gasoline, short-run	0.2
Gasoline, long-run	0.7
Residential natural gas, short-run	0.1
Residential natural gas, long-run	0.5
Coffee	0.25
Fish (cod) consumed at home	0.5
Tobacco products, short-run	0.45
Legal services, short-run	0.4
Physician services	0.6
Taxi, short-run	0.6
Automobiles, long-run	0.2
Approximately unit elasticity	
Movies	0.9
Housing, owner occupied, long-run	1.2
Shellfish, consumed at home	0.9
Oysters, consumed at home	1.1
Private education	1.1
Tires, short-run	0.9
Tires, long-run	1.2
Radio and television receivers	1.2
Elastic	
Restaurant meals	2.3
Foreign travel, long-run	4.0
Airline travel, long-run	2.4
Fresh green peas	2.8
Automobiles, short-run	1.2–1.5
Chevrolet automobiles	4.0
Fresh tomatoes	4.6

Source: Reported by Gwartney and Stroup (1997), collected from various econometric studies.

To illustrate, the inverse of the linear-demand function (10) is

$$p(d) = \frac{1}{b}(a - d),$$

and the set of feasible demands is $\Omega_d = [0, a]$.

18.4.1.5 Revenue function

The *revenue function*, denoted $r(d)$, is defined by

$$r(d) \equiv dp(d).$$

This is the revenue generated when using the price p and is of fundamental importance in dynamic-pricing problems. For example, the linear-demand function (10) has a revenue function

$$r(d) = \frac{d}{b}(a - d).$$

For most pricing models, it is desirable for this revenue function to be concave or at least unimodal, as in the linear example above. This leads to optimization problems that are numerically well behaved.

18.4.1.6 Marginal revenue

Another important quantity in pricing analysis is the rate of change of revenue with quantity—the *marginal revenue*—which is denoted $J(d)$. It is defined by

$$J(d) \equiv \frac{\partial}{\partial d} r(d) \tag{12}$$
$$= p(d) + dp'(d).$$

It is frequently useful to express this marginal revenue as a function of price rather than quantity. At the slight risk of confusion over notation, we replace d by $d(p)$ above and define the marginal revenue as a function of price by[7]

$$J(p) \equiv J(d(p)) = p + d(p)\frac{1}{d'(p)}. \tag{13}$$

Note that $J(p)$ above is still the marginal revenue with respect to quantity—$\frac{\partial}{\partial d} r(d)$—but expressed as function of price rather than quantity; in particular, it is not the marginal revenue with respect to price.[8]

Expressing marginal revenue in terms of the reservation-price distribution $F(p)$, we have that

$$J(p) = p - \frac{1}{\rho(p)}, \tag{14}$$

[7] By the inverse-function theorem, $p'(d) = 1/d'(p)$.
[8] The relationship between the marginal revenue with respect to price and quantity is as follows: since $r = pd$, then $\frac{\partial r}{\partial d} = d\frac{\partial p}{\partial d} + p$ and $\frac{\partial r}{\partial p} = p\frac{\partial d}{\partial p} + d$. Therefore, $\frac{\partial r}{\partial p} = \frac{\partial d}{\partial p}(p + d\frac{\partial p}{\partial d}) = \frac{\partial d}{\partial p}\frac{\partial r}{\partial d}$. (This also follows from the chain rule.)

where $\rho(p) \equiv f(p)/(1 - F(p))$ is the *hazard rate* of the distribution $F(p)$. To illustrate, consider the marginal revenue of the linear-demand function of (10) as a function of d,

$$J(d) = \frac{\partial}{\partial d}\left[\frac{d}{b}(a - d)\right] = \frac{1}{b}(a - 2d).$$

Substituting $d(p) = a - bp$ for d above we obtain the marginal revenue as a function of price

$$J(p) = \frac{1}{b}(a - 2(a - bp)) = 2p - \frac{a}{b}.$$

18.4.1.7 *Revenue maximization*

Maximizing revenue and profit is a central problem in pricing analysis. Assuming the maximizer is an interior point of the domain Ω_p, the *revenue-maximizing price* p^o is determined by the first-order condition

$$J(p^o) = 0.$$

Similarly, the revenue-maximizing demand, denoted d^o, is defined by

$$J(d^o) = 0.$$

They are related by

$$d^o = d(p^o).$$

For example, for the linear-demand function we have $J(p) = 2p - a/b$ so $p^o = \frac{a}{2b}$, an interior point of the set $\Omega_p = [0, a/b]$. The revenue-maximizing demand is $d^o = a/2$.

Note from (13) that since $J(p) = p\left(1 + \frac{d}{p}\frac{\partial p}{\partial d}\right)$, $\frac{\partial d}{\partial p} < 0$ (from Assumption 1, part (ii)), and $\frac{\partial d}{\partial p}\frac{p}{d} = \varepsilon(p)$ is the price elasticity, we have

$$J(p) = p\left(1 - \frac{1}{|\varepsilon(p)|}\right). \tag{15}$$

Thus, marginal revenue is positive (revenues are increasing in demand, decreasing in price) if demand is elastic at p (that is, if $|\varepsilon(p)| > 1$), and marginal revenue is negative (revenues are decreasing in demand, increasing in price) if demand is inelastic at p (that is, if $|\varepsilon(p)| < 1$). At the critical value $|\varepsilon(p^o)| = 1$, marginal revenue is zero and revenues are maximized.

When are these first-order conditions sufficient? If the revenue function is unimodal,[9] this suffices to ensure that the first-order conditions determine an optimal price. The following sufficient conditions on the reservation-price distribution ensure unimodality (or strict unimodality) of the revenue function (see Ziya et al. 2004):

Proposition 1 *Suppose that the reservation-price distribution $F(p)$ is twice differentiable and strictly increasing on its domain $\Omega_p = [p_1, p_2]$ ($F(p_1) = 0$ and $F(p_2) = 1$). Suppose further that $F(\cdot)$ satisfies any one of the following conditions:*

[9] A function $f(x)$ defined on the domain $[a, b]$ is said to be a *unimodal function* if there exists an $x^* \in [a, b]$ such that $f(x)$ is increasing on $[a, x^*]$ and $f(x)$ is decreasing on $[x^*, b]$; it is *strictly unimodal* if there exists an $x^* \in [a, b]$ such that $f(x)$ is strictly increasing on $[a, x^*]$ and $f(x)$ is strictly decreasing on $[x^*, b]$

(i) $r(d) = dp(d)$ is (strictly) concave on $d \in \Omega_d$.

(ii) $r(p) = pd(p)$ is (strictly) concave on $p \in \Omega_p$.

(iii) The absolute value of the elasticity $|\varepsilon(p)| = p\rho(p)$ is (strictly) increasing on $p \in \Omega_p$ and $\sup_{p \in \Omega_p} |\varepsilon(p)| > 1$.

Then the revenue function $r(p) = pd(p) = pN(1 - F(p))$ is (strictly) unimodal on Ω_p (equivalently, the revenue function $r(d) = p(d)d$ is (strictly) unimodal on $\Omega_d = [N(1 - F(p_1)), N(1 - F(p_2))]$. Moreover, the above three conditions are (respectively) equivalent to:

(i) $2\rho(p) \geq -\frac{f'(p)}{f(p)}$ for all $p \in \Omega_p$.

(ii) $\frac{2}{p} \geq -\frac{f'(p)}{f(p)}$ for all $p \in \Omega_p$.

(iii) $\rho(p) + \frac{1}{p} \geq -\frac{f'(p)}{f(p)}$ for all $p \in \Omega_p$

with strict inequality replacing equality for strict unimodality.

These conditions are intuitive. The first two state that if the revenue function is concave when parameterized either in terms of quantity (demand) or price, this implies unimodality of $r(p)$. For the third condition—that the magnitude of the elasticity, $|\varepsilon(p)|$ is increasing—recall the revenue is increasing in price when $|\varepsilon(p)| < 1$ and decreasing in price when $|\varepsilon(p)| > 1$; hence, it is clear that there is a revenue maximizing price if elasticity is monotone increasing. Ziya et al. (2004) show there are demand functions that satisfy one condition but not the others, so the three conditions are indeed distinct.

If there is a cost for providing the product—either a direct cost or opportunity cost—it is always optimal to price in the elastic region. To see this, let $c(d)$ denote the cost, so that $r(d) - c(d)$ is the firm's profit. Then the optimal price will occur at a point where $J(d) = r'(d) = c'(d)$. Assuming cost is strictly increasing in quantity, $c'(d) > 0$, the optimal price will be at a point where marginal revenue is positive—in the elastic region. Thus, it is almost never optimal to price in the inelastic region.[10]

18.4.1.8 Variable costs and profit maximization

The prior results on revenue maximization extend to the case where there are variable costs and the firm seeks to maximize profits (revenues minus costs). Let the cost of supplying d units of demand be denoted $c(d)$. We will assume this cost function is convex and continuously differentiable. Let $c'(d)$ denote the marginal cost (derivative of $c(\cdot)$). In this case, the optimization problem is

$$\max_d \{r(d) - c(d)\}, \tag{16}$$

and the first-order conditions for the optimal demand level are

$$J(d) = c'(d). \tag{17}$$

That is, the optimal volume of demand (and associated price) occurs at the point where marginal revenue equals marginal cost. For the constant marginal cost case

[10] The only exception is if the firm *benefits* from disposing of products—that is, if it has a negative cost. For example, this could occur if there is a holding cost incurred for keeping units rather than selling them. In such cases, it may be optimal to price in the inelastic region.

$c(d) = cd$, using (15) and rearranging, this optimality condition can be written in the convenient form:

$$\frac{p-c}{p} = \frac{1}{|\varepsilon(p)|}.$$

(18)

The left-hand side is simply the relative profit margin (profit as a fraction of price), and the left-hand side is the inverse of the elasticity. When costs are zero, the relative profit margin is always one, so the optimal price occurs when the elasticity is one, as we observed above. When marginal cost is positive, however, the relative profit margin will be less than one, so the optimal price occurs at a point where elasticity is greater than one (the elastic region).

18.4.2 Multiproduct-demand functions

In the case where there are $n > 1$ products, let p_j denote the price of product j and $\mathbf{p} = (p_1, \ldots, p_n)$ denote the vector of all n prices. The demand for product j as a function of $\mathbf{p}$ is denoted $d_j(\mathbf{p})$, and $\mathbf{d}(\mathbf{p}) = (d_1(\mathbf{p}), \ldots, d_n(\mathbf{p}))$ denotes the vector of demands for all n products. Again, $\mathbf{\Omega}_p$ will denote the domain of the demand function. We also use the notation $\mathbf{p}_{-j} = (p_1, \ldots, p_{j-1}, p_{j+1}, \ldots, p_n)$ to denote all prices other than p_j.

Paralleling the single-product case, the following regularity assumptions for the multiproduct-demand function help ensure the resulting optimization models are well behaved:

Assumption 2 (Regularity: n-Product Case) *For $j = 1, \ldots, n$:*

(i) $d_j(\mathbf{p})$ *demand is strictly decreasing in p_j for all $\mathbf{p} \in \mathbf{\Omega}_p$.*

(ii) *The demand function is continuously differentiable on $\mathbf{\Omega}_p$.*

(iii) *The demand function is bounded above and below:* $0 \leq d_j(\mathbf{p}) < +\infty$, $\forall \mathbf{p} \in \mathbf{\Omega}_p$.

(iv) *The demand function tends to zero in its own price for sufficiently high prices—that is, for all $\mathbf{p}_{-j}$,* $\inf_{p_j \in \ \Omega_p} d_j(p_j, \mathbf{p}_{-j}) = 0$.

(v) *The revenue function $\mathbf{p}^\top \mathbf{d}(\mathbf{p})$ is bounded for all $\mathbf{p} \in \mathbf{\Omega}_p$ and has a finite maximizer $\mathbf{p}^\circ$ that is interior to $\mathbf{\Omega}_p$.*

As in the scalar case, we let $\mathbf{p}(\mathbf{d})$ denote the inverse-demand distribution; it gives the vector of prices that induces the vector of demands $\mathbf{d}$. In the multiproduct case, this inverse is more difficult to define generally, and in most cases we simply assume it exists. (For the common demand functions to be defined below in Section 18.4.3, the inverse can be defined either explicitly or implicitly.) Likewise, we denote by $\mathbf{\Omega}_d$ the domain of the inverse-demand function, the set of achievable demand vectors $\mathbf{d}$.

The revenue function is defined by

$$r(\mathbf{d}) = \mathbf{d}^\top \mathbf{p}(\mathbf{d}),$$

which again represents the total revenue generated from using the vector of demands $\mathbf{d}$—or equivalently, the vector of prices $\mathbf{p}(\mathbf{d})$. Again, for numerical optimization, it is desirable if this revenue function is jointly concave.

The *cross-price elasticity* of demand is the relative change in demand for product i produced by a relative change in the price of product j. It is defined by

$$\varepsilon_{ij}(p) = \frac{p_j}{d_i}\frac{\partial d_i}{\partial p_j} = \frac{\partial \ln (d_i)}{\partial \ln (p_j)}.$$

If the sign of the elasticity is positive, then products i and j are said to be *substitutes*; if the sign is negative, the products are said to be *complements*. Intuitively, substitutes are products that represent distinct alternatives filling the same basic need (such as Coke and Pepsi), whereas complements are products that are consumed in combination to meet the same basic need (such as hamburgers and buns).

18.4.3 Common demand functions

Table 18.2 summarizes the most common demand functions and their properties. All these functions satisfy the regularity conditions in Assumptions 1 and 2, except for the constant-elasticity-demand function, which does not satisfy part (v) of either assumption as explained below.

Unfortunately, there are no hard and fast rules about which demand function to use in a given application. Any of the functions in Table 18.2 will work well in modeling modest price adjustments around a fixed price point; in this case only the local properties (slope) of the function matter. The models show greater difference when applied to a wider range of prices. Some, like the log-linear and logit model, have more reasonable properties when extrapolated to extremely high or low prices. Estimation concerns can also dictate the choice; the log-linear model, for example, is poorly suited to sparse demand applications since zero-demand observations cause problems when using the log-demand transformation typically required to estimate the model via regression. Simplicity and ease of use matter as well; the linear demand model remains quite popular in practice because it is both simple analytically and easy to estimate using regression. The intended use of the model is also important. For example, constant elasticity models are popular for econometric studies, but assuming elasticity is constant for all prices leads to highly unrealistic behavior in optimization models. In short, the best model to use in any given application depends on the characteristics of the demand, its ease of use and the intended purpose of the modeling effort; ultimately, it is more an engineering than a scientific choice.

18.4.3.1 Linear demand

We have already seen the case of a linear demand function in the scalar case. To summarize, it is

$$d(p) = a - bp,$$

where $a \geq 0$ and $b \geq 0$ are scalar parameters. The inverse-demand function is

$$p(d) = \frac{1}{b}(a - d).$$

The linear model is popular because of its simple functional form. It is also easy to estimate from data using linear-regression techniques. However, it produces negative demand values when $p > a/b$, which can cause numerical difficulties when solving optimization problems. Hence, one must typically retain the price constraint set $\Omega_p = [0, a/b]$ when using the linear model in optimization problems.

Table 18.2 Common demand functions

	$d(p)$	$p(d)$	$r(d)$	$J(d)$	$\|\varepsilon(p)\|$	p^0
Linear	$a - bp$	$\frac{1}{b}(a - d)$	$\frac{d}{b}(a - d)$	$\frac{1}{b}(a - 2d)$	$\frac{pb}{a-bp}$	$\frac{a}{2b}$
Log-linear (exponential)	e^{a-bp}	$\frac{1}{b}(a - \ln(d))$	$\frac{d}{b}(a - \ln(d))$	$\frac{1}{b}(a - 1 - \ln(d))$	pb	$\frac{1}{b}$
Constant elasticity	ap^{-b}	$\left(\frac{a}{d}\right)^{1/b}$	$a^{1/b} d^{1-1/b}$	$\left(1 - \frac{1}{b}\right)\left(\frac{a}{d}\right)^{1/b}$	b	$\begin{cases} 0 & b > 1 \\ +\infty & b < 1 \\ \text{all } p \geq 0 & b = 1 \end{cases}$
Logit	$N\frac{e^{-bp}}{1+e^{-bp}}$	$\frac{1}{b}\ln\left(\frac{N}{d} - 1\right)$	$\frac{d}{Nb}\ln\left(\frac{N}{d} - 1\right)$	$\frac{1}{b}\left(\ln\left(\frac{N}{d} - 1\right) - \frac{N}{d-N}\right)$	$\frac{bp}{1+e^{-bp}}$	No closed-form formula

Definitions: $d(p)$ = demand function, $p(d)$ = inverse demand function, $r(d)$ = revenue function, $r(d) = dp(d)$, $J(d)$ = marginal revenue $(J(d) = \partial r(d)/\partial d)$.
$\|\varepsilon(p)\|$ = elasticity $\left(\|\varepsilon(p)\| = \left\|\frac{p}{d}\frac{\partial p(d)}{\partial d}\right\|\right)$, p_0 is the revenue maximizing price.

In the multiproduct case, the linear model is

$$\mathbf{d(p)} = \mathbf{a} + \mathbf{Bp},$$

where $\mathbf{a} = (a_1, \ldots, a_n)$ is a vector of coefficients and $\mathbf{B} = [b_{ij}]$ is a matrix of price sensitivity coefficients with $b_{ii} \leq 0$ for all i and the sign of b_{ij}, $i \neq j$ depending on whether the products are complements ($b_{ij} < 0$) or substitutes ($b_{ij} > 0$). If $\mathbf{B}$ is nonsingular, then the inverse-demand function exists and is given by

$$\mathbf{p(d)} = \mathbf{B}^{-1}(\mathbf{d} - \mathbf{a}).$$

One sufficient condition for $\mathbf{B}^{-1}$ to exist is that the *row* coefficients satisfy (see Horn and Johnson 1994; Vives 2001):

$$b_{ii} < 0 \quad \text{and} \quad |b_{ii}| > \sum_{j \neq i} |b_{ij}|, \quad i = 1, \ldots, n. \tag{19}$$

Roughly, this says that demand for each product i is more sensitive to a change in its own price than it is to a simultaneous change in the prices of all other products. An alternative sufficient condition for $\mathbf{B}^{-1}$ to exist is that the *column* coefficients satisfy

$$b_{jj} < 0 \quad \text{and} \quad |b_{jj}| > \sum_{i \neq j} |b_{ij}|, \quad j = 1, \ldots, n. \tag{20}$$

Equation (20) says that changes in the price of product j impact the demand for product j more than it does the total demand for all other products combined. In the case of substitutes ($b_{ij} > 0$, $i \neq j$), this is equivalent to saying there is an aggregate market expansion or contraction effect when prices change (for example, the total market demand strictly decreases when the price of product j increases, and demand for product j is not simply reallocated one-for-one to substitute products).

18.4.3.2 *Log-linear (exponential) demand*

The log-linear—or exponential—demand function in the scalar case is defined by

$$d(p) = e^{a - bp},$$

where $a \geq 0$ and $b \geq 0$ are scalar parameters. This function is defined for all nonnegative prices, so $\Omega_p = [0, +\infty)$. The inverse-demand function is

$$p(d) = \frac{1}{b}(a - \ln(d)).$$

The log-linear-demand function is popular in econometric studies and has several desirable theoretical and practical properties. First, unlike the linear model, demand is always nonnegative so one can treat price (or quantity) as unconstrained in optimization problems. Second, by taking the natural log of demand, we recover a linear form, so it is also well suited to estimation using linear regression. However, demand values of zero are not defined when taking logarithms, which is problematic when sales volumes are low.

The multidimensional log-linear form is

$$d_j(\mathbf{p}) = e^{a_j + \mathbf{B}_j^\top \mathbf{p}}, \quad j = 1, \ldots, n,$$

where a_j is a scalar coefficient and $\mathbf{B}_j = (b_{j_1}, \ldots, b_{jn})$ is a vector of price-sensitivity coefficients. Letting $\mathbf{a} = (a_1, \ldots, a_n)$ and $\mathbf{B} = [b_{ij}]$, as in the linear model, and taking the logarithm, we have

$$\ln(\mathbf{d}(\mathbf{p})) = (\ln(d_1(\mathbf{p})), \ldots, \ln(d_n(\mathbf{p}))) = \mathbf{a} + \mathbf{B}\mathbf{p},$$

so again the log-linear model can be estimated easily from data using linear regression provided zero sales instances are not frequent.

The inverse-demand function can be obtained as in the linear case if $\mathbf{B}$ is nonsingular, in which case

$$\mathbf{p}(\mathbf{d}) = \mathbf{B}^{-1}(\ln(\mathbf{d}) - \mathbf{a}),$$

and one can again use the sufficient conditions (19) or (20) to check that $\mathbf{B}^{-1}$ exists.

18.4.3.3 Constant-elasticity demand

The constant-elasticity demand function in the single-product case is of the form

$$d(p) = ap^{-b},$$

where $a > 0$ and $b \geq 0$ are constants. The function is defined for all nonnegative p, so $\Omega_p = [0, +\infty)$. Since $\partial d/\partial p = -abp^{-(b+1)}$, the elasticity is

$$\varepsilon(p) = \frac{p}{d}\frac{\partial d}{\partial p} = -b,$$

a constant for all values p (hence the name). The inverse-demand function is

$$p(d) = \left(\frac{a}{d}\right)^{1/b}.$$

Note that because elasticity is constant, from (15) the marginal revenue will always be positive or will always be negative for all values of p (unless by chance $|\varepsilon(p)| = 1$, in which case it is zero for all values of p). Thus, this function usually violates Assumption 1, part (iv), because either the marginal revenue is always positive so $p_o = +\infty$ or the marginal revenue is always negative, so $p_o = 0$, both extreme points of the set Ω_p (unless, again, the elasticity is exactly one, in which case all values of p are revenue maximizing). From this standpoint, it is a somewhat ill-behaved demand model in pricing-optimization problems, though in cases where revenue functions are combined with cost functions it is less problematic.

The multiproduct constant elasticity model is

$$d_i(\mathbf{p}) = a_i p_1^{b_{i1}} p_2^{b_{i2}} \cdots p_n^{b_{in}}, \quad i = 1, \ldots, n,$$

where the matrix of coefficients $\mathbf{B} = [b_{ij}]$ defines the cross (and own) price elasticities among the products, since

$$\varepsilon_{ij}(\mathbf{p}) = \frac{\partial d_i/d_i}{\partial p_j/p_j} = b_{ij}.$$

Note that the inverse-demand function $\mathbf{p}(\mathbf{d})$ exists if the matrix $\mathbf{B}$ is invertible, since $(\log(d_1(\mathbf{p})), \ldots, \log(d_n(\mathbf{p}))) = \mathbf{a} + \mathbf{B}p$ (here $\mathbf{a} = (a_1, \ldots, a_n)$) and $\log(\cdot)$ is a strictly increasing function.

18.4.3.4 *Logit demand*

The logit demand function is based on the MNL model of Section 18.3.4. Since utility is ordinal, without loss of generality we can assume the no-purchase utility $u_o = 0$. The choice probabilities are then given by (6) with the no-purchase alternative having a value $e^{u_o} = 1$.

As mentioned, it is common to model the representative component of utility u_j as a linear function of several known attributes including price. Assuming u_j is linear in price and interpreting the choice probabilities as fractions of a population of customers of size N leads to the class of logit-demand functions.

For example, in the scalar case, we assume $u_1 = -bp$, and this gives rise to a demand function of the form

$$d(p) = N \frac{e^{-bp}}{1 + e^{-bp}},$$

where N is the market size, $1 - F(p) = \frac{e^{-bp}}{1 + e^{-bp}}$ is the probability that a customer buys at price p, and b is a coefficient of the price sensitivity. The function is defined for all nonnegative p, so $\Omega_p = [0, +\infty)$. The inverse-demand function is

$$p(d) = \frac{1}{b} \ln\left(\frac{N}{d} - 1\right).$$

Logit demand models have a desirable "S"-shape that many practitioners find appealing and intuitively plausible; the function in fact can be interpreted as resulting from a population of reservation prices that is approximately normally distributed around a mean value (the logistical distribution in the error term of the utility approximates a normal random variable).

In the multiple-product case, the demand function is given by

$$d_j(\mathbf{p}) = N \frac{e^{-b_j p_j}}{1 + \sum_{i=1}^{n} e^{-b_i p_i}}, \quad j = 1, \ldots, n,$$

where again $\mathbf{b} = (b_1, \ldots, b_n)$ is a vector of coefficients and

$$P_j(\mathbf{p}) = \frac{e^{-b_j p_j}}{1 + \sum_{i=1}^{n} e^{-b_i p_i}}$$

is the MNL probability that a customer chooses product j as a function of the vector of prices $\mathbf{p}$.

One potential problem with the MNL demand model is that it inherits the IIA property (7). This causes problems if groups of products share attributes that strongly affect the choice outcome. To illustrate what can go wrong, consider the cross-price elasticity of alternative i with respect to the price of alternative j, $\varepsilon_{ij}(\mathbf{p})$. This is given by

$$\varepsilon_{ij}(\mathbf{p}) = \frac{\partial \ln d_i(p)}{\partial \ln p_j}$$

$$= -p_j b_j \frac{e^{-b_j p_j}}{1 + \sum_{k=1}^{n} e^{-b_k p_k}}.$$

(21)

Notice that this cross-price elasticity is not dependent on i, and therefore cross-elasticity is the same for all alternatives i other than j.

The implications of this constant cross-price elasticity can be illustrated by an example of automobile market shares.[11] Consider a pair of subcompact cars and an expensive luxury car. If we lower the price of one of the subcompact cars by 10 percent, then (21) says that the percentage change in the demand for the other subcompact car will be the same as the percentage change in the demand for the luxury car (if the other subcompact car demand drops by 20 percent then the luxury car demand will also drop by 20 percent). Such behavior is not very realistic. This IIA behavior stems fundamentally from the i.i.d. assumption on the random-noise terms ξ's of the MNL model. (See Berry (1994) for a discussion, and a possible way around these restrictions on cross-price elasticities.)

18.4.4 Stochastic-demand functions

At disaggregate levels of modeling—for example modeling sales in a given store on a given day or an individual on-line shopper's decision to buy or not buy—demand outcomes are inherently uncertain. In such cases, stochastic demand models are required. We can convert a deterministic demand function $d(p)$ into a stochastic model of demand in a variety of ways. In the stochastic case, we let $D(p, \xi_t)$ denote the random demand as a function of the price p and a random-noise term ξ_t. The three most common random-demand models are discussed below.

18.4.4.1 Additive uncertainty

In the additive model, the demand is a continuous random variable of the form

$$D(p, \xi) = d(p) + \xi,$$

where ξ is a zero-mean random variable that does not depend on the price. In this case, the mean demand is $d(p)$, and the noise term ξ shifts the demand randomly about this mean.

Note that this additive disturbance has the property that the elasticity of demand depends on ξ. This follows since

$$\varepsilon(p, \xi) = \frac{p}{D(p, \xi)} \frac{\partial D(p, \xi)}{\partial p} = \frac{\varepsilon(p)}{1 + \xi/d(p)},$$

where $\varepsilon(p) = \frac{p}{d(p)} \frac{\partial d(p)}{\partial p}$ is the deterministic elasticity. So if a realization of ξ is less than zero, the elasticity of demand in the stochastic model is greater than the deterministic elasticity, and if the realization of ξ is greater than zero, it is smaller.

One potential problem with the additive uncertainty model is that demand could be negative if $d(p)$ is small and the variance of ξ is large. For this reason, the additive model should be used with caution in applications where the coefficients of variation for the demand uncertainty is high.

---

[11] If the population is homogeneous, the choice probabilities represent market share, and the MNL can be used to estimate market shares.

18.4.4.2 *Multiplicative uncertainty*

In the multiplicative model, the demand is again a continuous random variable but of the form

$$D(p, \xi) = \xi d(p),$$

where ξ is a nonnegative random variable with mean one that does not depend on the price p. In this case, the mean demand is again $d(p)$, and the noise term ξ simply scales the mean demand by a random factor. For the multiplicative model, the elasticity of demand for any given realization of ξ is the same as the deterministic elasticity, since

$$\varepsilon(p, \xi) = \frac{p}{d(p, \xi)} \frac{\partial d(p, \xi)}{\partial p} = \varepsilon(p),$$

where again $\varepsilon(p)$ is the deterministic elasticity. Thus, the random-noise term does not affect the elasticity of demand; it affects only the magnitude of demand.

Note that one can also combine the multiplicative and additive uncertainty models, leading to a demand function of the form

$$D(p, \xi) = \xi_1 + \xi_2 d(p),$$

where ξ_1 is a zero-mean random variable and ξ_2 is a nonnegative, unit-mean random variable.

18.4.4.3 *Poisson and Bernoulli uncertainty*

In the Bernoulli model, $d(p)$ is the probability of an arrival in a given period. So $d(p)$ is the probability that demand is one in a period, and $1 - d(p)$ is the probability that demand is zero. As a result, the mean demand in a period is again $d(p)$, and we can represent the demand as a random function

$$D(p, \xi) = \begin{cases} 1 & \xi \leq d(p) \\ 0 & \xi > d(p) \end{cases},$$

where ξ is a uniform $[0, 1]$ random variable.

For example, consider a situation in which the buyer in the period has a reservation price v that is a random variable with distribution $F(\cdot)$. If the firm offers a price of p, they will sell a unit if $v \geq p$, which occurs with probability $1 - F(p)$. This corresponds to setting $d(p) = 1 - F(p)$ above.

In the Poisson model, time is continuous, and $d(p)$ is treated as a stochastic intensity or rate. That is, the probability that we get a unit of demand in an interval of time $[t, t + \delta)$ is $\delta d(p) + o(\delta)$ and the probability that we see no demand is $1 - \delta d(p) + o(\delta)$ (all other events have probability $o(\delta)$).

The Poisson and Bernoulli models are useful for several reasons. First, they translate a deterministic demand function directly into a stochastic model, without the need to estimate additional parameters (such as variance). They also are discrete-demand models—as opposed to the continuous demand of the additive and multiplicative models—and more closely match the discreteness of demand in many pricing applications. At the same time, the Poisson and Bernoulli models assume a specific coefficient of variation, which may or may not match the observed variability. The additive and multiplicative models, in contrast, allow for different levels of variability in the model, as the complete distribution of the noise term can be specified.

18.4.5 Subrational behavior models

While rational behavior is the standard assumption underlying most of the theory and practice of pricing, it is far from being completely accepted as a model of how an actual customer behaves. Indeed, much of the recent work in economics and customer behavior has centered on explaining observed, systematic deviations from rationality on the part of customers. These theories are covered in detail in Chapter 20 of this handbook. Here we only give a brief overview of the main ideas and their implications for demand modeling.

Kahneman and Tversky (1979; Kahneman et al. 1982) famously showed that people exhibit consistent biases when faced with simple choices in an experimental setting. Their key insight is that most individuals tend to evaluate choice in terms of losses and gains from their status quo wealth, rather than evaluating choices in terms of their terminal wealth as in classical utility theory. They show customers have a tendency toward "loss aversion" rather than risk aversion, and they have a strong preference for certainty of outcomes when evaluating choices. Other experiments revealed that people put a much higher value on a product they already own than one that they do not own because giving up a product feels like a loss. This is known as the *endowment effect*. Another bias people exhibit is due to what is called *mental accounting*, in which customers tend to evaluate gains and losses for different categories of goods differently because they have "mental budgets" for each category of goods.

Subrational behavioral theory has potentially profound implications for tactical demand modeling and pricing optimization. For example, if customers base their purchase decisions on perceived losses and gains, imagine how this might affect retail pricing decisions. For instance, suppose sales of a product at its initial price are low. Currently, most tactical pricing models would interpret this as a clear pricing error; we simply priced too high. But such a high price might actually help, because once the price is reduced, customers will then perceive the reduction as a gain. Indeed, it may be optimal to set the initial price very high—or leave it high longer—because then the perceived gain once the price is lowered is that much greater. Such notions are of course part and parcel of the general marketing toolkit, but today they are applied quite crudely. The potential is to deploy these same concepts with the sort of precision and detail made possible by a model-based pricing system.

Do such findings mean that current demand models based on rational behavior are obsolete? Not exactly. In a gross sense, people do tend to behave in accordance with rationality assumptions; they buy more when prices are lower and less when prices are high. However, what this behavioral theory and supporting laboratory and real-world observation shows is that the axioms of rational behavior, plausible as they may be, do not apply uniformly and that there are situations in which deviations from rational behavior are systematic and substantial.

An immediate practical consequence of these findings is that one has to be keenly aware of the environment in which choices are made; the details of the buying situation matter in terms of customers' responses. How prices are presented, what "reference point" the customer perceives, the framing of the choice decision, their sense of "ownership" over the product—can all potentially influence their responses. While many of the tactics used to influence these factors lie in the domain of general marketing, the message that the choice environment can heavily influence purchase behavior is an important one for pricing modelers to heed. Moreover, such behavioral theories of demand are working their way into the operational pricing research literature, and it is likely that such ideas will influence analytical pricing practice more directly in the years ahead.

18.4.6 Strategic behavior models

Another important customer behavior that has important consequences for tactical pricing is the self-interested behavior of customers. Such considerations lead to the idea of *strategic customer models*, in which customers are viewed as utility maximizers who respond to a seller's actions and adjust their timing and channel of purchase in order to maximize their gains. Aviv and Vulcano (Chapter 23) provide a comprehensive overview of strategic behavior models; here, we briefly summarize the main ideas.

Building models of this sort requires expanding the customer's strategy space—that is, the range of alternatives available to them. So, for example, rather than viewing customers as arriving and making a choice decision on the spot, we model them as deciding when to arrive as well. If they anticipate that prices will be low in the future, this then creates an incentive for them to delay their purchases. Hence, our decisions on pricing or availability over time will affect the purchase strategies adopted by our consumers. From a modeling standpoint, such behavior can be considered to be a game between a firm and its customers; each strategy adopted by the firm induces a different strategy among its customers. The question then is: Which pricing strategy should we adopt to induce the most profitable equilibrium among customers? Equilibrium and game theory methods can be used to analyze such questions.

The outputs from such models can result in profoundly different pricing decisions. Take markdown pricing; a typical pricing optimization model upon seeing sluggish sales at the current price recommends a markdown. But what if demand is low early in the sales season precisely because customers anticipate the firm will mark down eventually? Does it really make sense then to lower prices, because doing so may simply reinforce their expectations and perpetuate a bad equilibrium? Perhaps a constant pricing policy, while less profitable in the short run, would train customers not to wait for markdowns. The resulting shift in their equilibrium behavior might then be more profitable in the long run.

While such considerations have intriguing implications and there has been considerable recent theoretical research on strategic consumer models (see Shen and Xu (2007) for a recent survey), to date they have yet to find their way into tactical pricing systems. There are several reasons for this. First, the area is young and most of the research work on the topic has appeared only in the last decade; new models and methods are still being developed and disseminated. Second, strategic behavior is complex to model and analyze. Most of the current research models are quite stylized—and even these highly pared-down models often require intricate equilibrium analyses to understand. Getting such models and analysis to the level of sophistication required for realistic operational pricing applications will be a significant challenge. Lastly, it is an open question how well one can identify and estimate strategic behavior in practice. It requires understanding customers' expectations of the future and their decision-making process over time. This significantly greater scope in the estimation and validation task is a potential practical limitation.

That said, strategic consumer models hold great potential to help temper the "overly myopic" nature of current tactical pricing systems, which can overweight short-term revenue gain at the expense of long-run customer reactions.

18.5 ESTIMATION AND FORECASTING

Estimating demand models and accurately forecasting the effect of pricing actions is critical to success in operational pricing. In many ways, though, this task is a standard one and system designers can avail themselves of a vast array of tools and techniques from statistical estimation and forecasting to accomplish it. Yet there are some unique challenges in demand model estimation which we highlight here. There are many excellent references on estimation and forecasting methods, so our focus here is on the key challenges involved in estimating demand models, the high-level design choice one must make in building an estimation and forecasting system and how demand estimation is executed in practice.

In operational pricing, estimation and forecasting are typically automated, transactional, and data-driven—as opposed to qualitative (such as expert opinion) or survey-based. This is due to the sheer volume of forecasts that have to be made and the tight processing time requirements of a real-time system. These practical constraints limit the choice of methods. They also limit the types of data that can reasonably be collected and the amount of time a user can spend calibrating and verify estimates and forecasts. Certain procedures, even if they give superior estimates, may simply not be viable options in practice because they take too long to run, require data that is too expensive to collect (e.g., surveys), or require too much expert, manual effort to calibrate.

Estimation and forecasting requirements are also driven by the input requirements of the optimization modules they feed. Many optimization models use stochastic models of demand and hence require an estimate of the complete probability distribution or at least parameter estimates (e.g., means and variances) for an assumed distribution. Besides producing estimates of price response and demand volume, many other features of the demand might need to be estimated—how it evolves over time, how it varies seasonally, from which channels and segments it arrives, how it responds to a promotions versus a regular price change—all of which are important in making good tactical pricing decisions.

Since no statistical model can incorporate all possible factors influencing demand, it is common practice to rely on analysts to monitor outside events and compensate for special events by adjusting forecasts appropriately through so-called *user influences*. In this sense, one should view estimation and forecasting in practice as a hybrid of automated, analytical inputs and human, subjective inputs.

We begin by looking at typical data sources and main design choices in estimation and forecasting. We then survey the main methodologies used, focusing again on those that are of special importance for demand estimation. Lastly, we discuss issues involved in implementing estimation and forecasting in real-world systems.

18.5.1 Data sources

Data is the life-blood of any estimation and forecasting system. Therefore, identifying which sources of data are available and how they can best be used is an important first step in approaching the problem.

The main sources of data in most pricing systems are transactional databases—for example, reservation and property management systems (PMSs) in hotels, customer relationship management (CRM) systems, enterprise resource planning (ERP) systems, and retail inventory and scanner databases. These sources may be centralized, independent entities shared by other firms in the industry (such as global distribution systems (GDSs) of the airline industry selling MIDT data), a centralized facility within a company that interfaces with several local systems (e.g., a retail chain's point-of-sale (POS) system linking all its stores), a local reservation system (a hotel PMS), or a customer-oriented database with information on individual customers and their purchase history (CRMs).

In addition to sales information, databases often store information on the controlling process itself. Examples of this kind of data include records of past prices, promotion activities and win/loss data on customized pricing offers. Inventory data are also provided by many retail POS systems, and these data are useful for correcting for stockouts and broken-assortments effects (e.g., missing color-size combinations).

Panel data, obtained from tracking purchases of a group of panelists over time, provide valuable information on cross-sectional and intertemporal purchase behavior. Such data are widely used in retail and media industries. A panel member's purchase data are also linked to promotions, availability, displays, advertising, couponing, and markdowns through the time of purchase, allowing for precise inferences on preferences and marketing influences. Many marketing research companies provide such panel data services.

A few auxiliary data sources also play an important role in pricing systems in some industries. For instance, currency exchange-rate and tax information is necessary to keep track of revenue value for sales in different countries. In the airline industry, the schedules and possible connections (provided by firms such as the official airline guide (OAG)) are required to determine which markets are being served. In broadcasting, ratings, customer location, and demographic information are required. A causal forecasting method may take into account information on the state of the economy, employment, income and savings rates, among other factors. Information on ad hoc events (special events) like conferences, sports events, concerts, holidays, is also crucial in improving the accuracy of forecasts.

Many retail pricing systems also use weather data, which are supplied by several independent vendors via daily automated feeds. Short-term weather forecasts guide discounting and stocking decisions. Weather data also play an important role in energy forecasting for electric power generators and distributors.

Macroeconomic data (such as gross national product (GNP) growth rates and housing starts) are rarely used in automated, tactical forecasting but frequently play a role in aggregate forecasts of factors such as competitors' costs, industry demand and market share, and broad consumer preferences. Statistics on cost of labor are published by the

Bureau of Labor Statistics (BLS) in the United States in a monthly publication called *Employment and Earnings*, which provides average hourly earnings for workers by product category. BLS also provides monthly producer price indexes on raw materials.

18.5.2 Estimation and forecasting design decisions

Before applying any analytical methods, there are a number of important structural design choices involved in developing an estimation and forecasting system. We discuss the main choices next.

18.5.2.1 Bottom-up versus top-down Strategies

Broadly speaking, there are two main ways to construct estimates and forecasts: bottom-up and top-down. In a *bottom-up forecasting strategy*, forecasting is performed at a detailed level to generate *subforecasts*. The end forecast is then constructed by aggregating these detailed subforecasts. In a *top-down forecasting strategy*, forecasts are made at a high level of aggregation—a *superforecast*—and then the end forecast is constructed by disaggregating these superforecasts down to the level of detail required.

Which strategy is most appropriate is not always clear-cut. The choice depends on the data that are available, the outputs required, and the types of forecasts already being made. Moreover, the "right" answer in most cases is that both strategies are required, because certain phenomena can only be estimated at a low level of aggregation, while others can only be estimated at a high level of aggregation. For example, seasonality is hard to identify at low levels of aggregation because the data are often so sparse that one cannot distinguish "peak" from "off-peak" periods. In fact, aggregate phenomena such as daily or weekly seasonalities, holiday effects, or upward or downward trends in total demand are—for all practical purposes—unobservable at the highly disaggregate level; one must look at aggregate data to estimate them. At the same time, if we aggregate across products or markets to understand seasonality, we may lose information about the difference in price sensitivity between product and markets. For this reason, using hybrid combinations of bottom-up and top-down approaches is the norm in practice.

18.5.2.2 Levels of aggregation

Which level of aggregation to use (whether arrived at from a top-down or bottom-up approach) is another important design decision. The choice here is not purely a matter of estimation; it is also highly dependent on the parameter requirements of the optimization model. For example in retailing, store-level pricing requires store-level estimates of demand and price sensitivity for each product, whereas a model that optimizes prices that are set uniformly on a chain-wide basis does not require such detail. If household purchase data (panel data) are available or if experiments or surveys can be conducted, then one can forecast based on models of individual purchase behavior and combine these to determine an aggregate demand function. However, if only aggregate POS sales data can be obtained, we might be limited to estimating an aggregate demand function directly.

In theory one would like the most detailed demand model possible—to know the response parameters of every customer even. That way, we can forecast at as detailed a level as we like and we don't lose information by assuming groups of customers or products have the same behavior. But as one moves down to finer levels of detail, the data become sparser (e.g., imagine the data a grocery store has available for total sales of a given product versus the data it has on a given customer's purchase of that same product)—and sparse data increase estimation error. There is a balance then between the *specification error* (error in the form of the model) introduced from aggregating potentially dissimilar entities together versus the *estimation error* (error in the parameter estimates of a given model) introduced by the limited data available from disaggregating entities. While there is theory from model selection in statistics to help guide this tradeoff (Burnham and Anderson 2002), in practice it's often a matter of extensive trial and error to determine which level of aggregation produces the most accurate estimate of demand.

18.5.2.3 *Parametric versus nonparametric models*

Estimators can be specified in one of two ways. The first is to assume a specific functional form and then estimate the parameters of this functional form. This approach is called *parametric estimation.* Alternatively, distributions or functions can be estimated directly based on observed historical data, without assuming any *a priori* functional form. This approach is called *nonparametric estimation.* Choosing between a parametric or nonparametric approach to estimation and forecasting is a key design decision.

While nonparametric methods are in a sense more general, they are not necessarily a better choice. Nonparametric estimates suffer from two serious drawbacks: First, because they do not use a functional form to "fill in" for missing values, they often require much more data than are available in many applications to obtain reasonable estimates of a distribution or demand function. Second, even with sufficient data, nonparametric estimates may not be as good at predicting the future, even if they fit the historical data well. Parametric models are better able to "smooth out" the noise inherent in raw data, which often results in a more robust forecast. There are intermediate approaches too. Neural networks are sometimes viewed as *semiparametric* methods, in that they assume a parametric form but it is a general and high-dimensional one that, as the size of the network increases, can provide a close approximation to a non-parametric model.

Parametric methods usually are more modest in their data requirements, have the advantage of providing estimates of demand that extend beyond the range of the observed data (allow for extrapolation), and are generally more robust to errors and noise in the data. The disadvantage of parametric techniques is that some properties of the distribution must be assumed—for example, that it is symmetric about the mean, has certain coefficients of variation, or has certain *tail behavior* (the characteristics of the demand distribution for extreme values of demand). Thus, parametric methods can suffer in terms of overall forecasting accuracy if the actual demand distribution deviates significantly from these assumptions (called *specification errors*).

18.5.3 Estimation methods

Here we briefly survey methods for estimation and discuss some of the theoretical and practical issues that arise.

18.5.3.1 *Estimators and their properties*

An estimator represents, in essence, a formalized "guess" about the parameters of the underlying distribution from which a sample (the observed data) is drawn. Estimators can take on many forms and can be based on different criteria for a "best" guess. We focus on parametric estimation.

For a parametric estimator, we assume that the underlying distribution of demand, Z, is of the form

$$P(Z \leq z \,|\, \boldsymbol{\beta}, \mathbf{y}) = F(z, \boldsymbol{\beta}, \mathbf{y}), \tag{22}$$

where $\mathbf{y} = (y_1, \dots, y_M)$ is a vector of M observed explanatory variables which includes, of course, prices (own and competitors)—but can also include other explanatory variables such as time, indicators of holiday events, lagged observations of Z itself, and so on. $\boldsymbol{\beta} = (\beta_1, \dots, \beta_M)$ is an M-dimensional vector of parameters that must be estimated from data. Z is often referred to as the *dependent* variable and the vector $\mathbf{y}$ as the *independent* variables. The density function of demand (if it exists) is denoted $f(z \,|\, \boldsymbol{\beta}, \mathbf{y}) = \frac{d}{dz} F(z, \boldsymbol{\beta}, \mathbf{y})$. For ease of exposition, we assume that the dimensions of $\boldsymbol{\beta}$ and $\mathbf{y}$ are the same, though this is not necessary. For example, this function may be one of the aggregate demand functions discussed above or a random utility model of individual purchase outcomes.

Alternatively we can express the relationship between the demand and the explanatory variables as consisting of two parts: a systematic (deterministic) component, $\zeta(\boldsymbol{\beta}, \mathbf{y}_k)$ (also called a *point estimate*), and a zero-mean error term, ξ_k, so that:

$$Z_k = \zeta(\boldsymbol{\beta}, \mathbf{y}_k) + \xi_k. \tag{23}$$

Assume we have a sequence of N independent observations $z_1, \dots, z_N$, with values for the explanatory variables represented by vectors $\mathbf{y}_1, \dots, \mathbf{y}_N$. The estimation problem, then, is to determine the unknown parameters $\boldsymbol{\beta}$ using only the sample of the N observations and the values of the explanatory variables corresponding to each observation.

As an example, consider the linear demand function with additive noise:

$$Z = \boldsymbol{\beta}^\top \mathbf{y} + \xi, \tag{24}$$

where ξ is an i.i.d. $N(0, \sigma^2)$ random noise term, independent of the explanatory variables $\mathbf{y}$. The distribution of Z in terms of (22) is then

$$F_Z(z \,|\, \boldsymbol{\beta}, \mathbf{y}_k) = P(Z \leq z \,|\, \boldsymbol{\beta}, \mathbf{y}) = \Phi\left(\frac{z - \boldsymbol{\beta}^\top \mathbf{y}}{\sigma}\right),$$

where $\Phi(\cdot)$ is the standard normal distribution.

18.5.3.2 *Properties of estimators*

If the set of N observations, $\mathbf{z}_N = (z_1, \dots, z_N)$, are considered independent realizations of Z, then an estimator based on these observations is a function of the random variables, $\hat{\boldsymbol{\beta}}(\mathbf{z}_N)$, and is therefore itself a random variable. What properties would we like this (random) estimator to have?

- **Unbiasedness** For one, it would be desirable if the expected value of the estimator equaled the actual value of the parameters—that is, if

$$E[\hat{\boldsymbol{\beta}}(z_N)] = \boldsymbol{\beta}.$$

If this property holds, the estimator is said to be an *unbiased estimator*, otherwise, it is a *biased estimator*. The estimator of the mth parameter, $\hat{\beta}_m$, is said to have a *positive bias* if its expected value exceeds β_m, and a *negative bias* if its expected value is less than β_m.
  If the estimator is unbiased only for large samples of data—that is, it satisfies

$$\lim_{N \to \infty} E[\hat{\boldsymbol{\beta}}(Z_N)] = \boldsymbol{\beta}$$

—then it is called an *asymptotically unbiased estimator*.

- **Efficiency** An estimator $\hat{\boldsymbol{\beta}}(Z)$ is said to be an *efficient estimator* if it is unbiased and the random variable $\hat{\boldsymbol{\beta}}(Z)$ has the smallest variance among all unbiased estimators. Efficiency is desirable because it implies the variability of the estimator is as low as possible given the available data. The Cramer–Rao bound[12] provides a lower bound on the variance of *any* estimator, so if an estimator achieves the Cramer–Rao bound, then we are guaranteed that it is efficient. An estimator can be inefficient for a finite sample but *asymptotically efficient* if it achieves the Cramer–Rao bound when the sample size is large.

- **Consistency** An estimator is said to be *consistent* if for any $\delta > 0$,

$$\lim_{N \to \infty} P(|\hat{\boldsymbol{\beta}}(Z_N) - \boldsymbol{\beta}| < \delta) = 1.$$

That is, if it converges in probability to the true value $\boldsymbol{\beta}$ as the sample size increases. Consistency assures us that with sufficiently large samples of data, the value of $\boldsymbol{\beta}$ can be estimated arbitrarily accurately.

Ideally, we would like our estimators to be unbiased, efficient, and consistent, but this is not always possible.

18.5.3.3 *Minimum square error (MSE) and regression estimators*

One class of estimators is based on the *minimum square error (MSE)* criterion. MSE estimators are most naturally suited to the case where the forecast quantity has an additive noise term as in (23). Given a sequence of observations $z_1, \ldots, z_N$ and associated vectors of explanatory variable values $\mathbf{y}_1, \ldots, \mathbf{y}_N$, the MSE estimate of the vector $\boldsymbol{\beta}$ is the solution to

$$\min_{\boldsymbol{\beta}} \sum_{k=1}^{N} [z_k - \zeta(\boldsymbol{\beta}, \mathbf{y}_k)]^2, \tag{25}$$

where the point estimate $\zeta(\beta, \mathbf{y}_k)$ is as defined in (23). The minimization problem (25) can be solved using standard nonlinear optimization methods such as conjugate-gradient or quasi-Newton. If the point estimate is linear so that

$$Z = \boldsymbol{\beta}^\top \mathbf{y} + \xi,$$

---

[12] See DeGroot (1985: 420–30) for a discussion of the Cramer–Rao bound.

and the error term ξ is a normal random variable that is i.i.d. with zero mean and constant variance for all observations, then the MSE estimate is known as the *ordinary least-squares (OLS) estimator*—or *linear-regression estimator*. Standard linear regression packages can be used to estimate such models. Because of its simplicity and efficiency, regression is widely used in price-based management for estimating price sensitivity, market shares, and the effects of various marketing variables (such as displays and promotions) on demand.

18.5.3.4 *Maximum-likelihood (ML) estimators*

While regression is based on the least-squares criterion, *maximum-likelihood (ML) estimators* are based on finding the parameters that maximize the "likelihood" of observing the sample data, where *likelihood* is defined as the probability of the observations occurring. More precisely, given a probability-density function f_Z of the process generating a sample of data Z_k, $k = 1, \ldots, N$, which is a function of a vector of parameters $\boldsymbol{\beta}$ and the observations of the explanatory variables, $\mathbf{y}_k$, the likelihood of observing value z_k as the kth observation is given by the density $f_Z(z_k \,|\, \boldsymbol{\beta}, \mathbf{y}_k)$ (or by the probability mass function if the demand distribution is discrete). The likelihood of observing the N observations $(z_1, \mathbf{y}_1), \ldots, (z_N, \mathbf{y}_N)$ is then

$$\mathcal{L} = \prod_{k=1}^{N} f_Z(z_k \,|\, \boldsymbol{\beta}, \mathbf{y}_k). \tag{26}$$

The ML estimation problem is to find a $\boldsymbol{\beta}$ that maximizes this likelihood $\mathcal{L}$. It is more convenient to maximize the log-likelihood, $\ln \mathcal{L}$, because this converts the product of the function in (26) to a sum of functions. Since the log function is strictly increasing, maximizing the log-likelihood is equivalent to maximizing the likelihood. This gives the ML problem:

$$\max_{\boldsymbol{\beta}} \sum_{k=1}^{N} \ln f_Z(z_k \,|\, \boldsymbol{\beta}, \mathbf{y}_k).$$

In special cases, this problem can be solved in closed form. Otherwise, if the density $f_Z(\cdot)$ (or probability mass function in the discrete case) is a differentiable function of the parameters $\boldsymbol{\beta}$, then gradient-based optimization methods can be used to solve it numerically.

ML estimators have good statistical properties under very general conditions; they can be shown to be consistent, asymptotically normal, and asymptotically efficient, achieving the Cramer–Rao lower bound on the variance of estimators for large sample sizes.

As an example, consider estimating the parameters of the MNL choice model described above. The data consists of a set of N customers and their choices from a finite set S of alternatives. Associated with each alternative j is a vector $\mathbf{y}_j$ of explanatory variables (assume for simplicity there are no customer-specific characteristics). The probability that a customer selects alternative i is then given by

$$P_i(S) = \frac{e^{\boldsymbol{\beta}^\top \mathbf{y}_i}}{\sum_{j \in S} e^{\boldsymbol{\beta}^\top \mathbf{y}_j} + 1}, \tag{27}$$

where $\boldsymbol{\beta}$ is a vector of (unknown) parameters. Let $c(k)$ be the choice made by customer k. The likelihood function is then

$$ \mathcal{L} = \prod_{k=1}^{N} \left[\frac{e^{\boldsymbol{\beta}^{\top} y_{c(k)}}}{\sum_{j \in S} e^{\boldsymbol{\beta}^{\top} y_j} + 1} \right], $$

and the maximum-likelihood estimate $\hat{\boldsymbol{\beta}}$ is then determined by solving

$$ \max_{\boldsymbol{\beta}} \, \ln \mathcal{L}. \tag{28} $$

While this maximum-likelihood problem cannot be solved in closed form, it has good computational properties. Namely, there are closed-form expressions for all first and second partial derivatives of the log-likelihood function, and it is jointly concave in most cases (McFadden 1974; Hausman and McFadden 1984). The ML estimator has also proven to be robust in practice.

18.5.3.5 *Method of moments and quantile estimators*

While MSE and ML are the most prevalent estimators in practice, several other estimators are also used as well. Two common ones are *method of moments* and *quantile estimators*.

In the method of moments, one equates moments of the theoretical distribution to their equivalent empirical averages in the observed data. This yields a system of equations that can be solved to estimate the unknown parameters $\boldsymbol{\beta}$.

Alternatively, we can use quantile estimates based on the empirical distribution to estimate the parameters $\boldsymbol{\beta}$ of a distribution. For example, we might estimate the mean of a normal distribution by noting that as the normal distribution is symmetric, the mean and median are the same. Hence, we can estimate the mean by computing the median of a sequence of N observations. More generally, one can compute a number of quantiles of a data set and equate these to the theoretical quantiles of the parametric distribution. In general, if m parameters need to be estimated, m different quantiles are needed to produce m equations in m unknowns (for a normal distribution, for example, one could equate the 0.25 and 0.75 quantiles of the data to the theoretical values to get two equations for the mean and variance). Quantile estimation techniques are sometimes preferred as they tend to be less sensitive to outlier data than are MSE and ML estimators.

18.5.4 Endogeneity, heterogeneity, and competition

In this section, we focus on a few estimation problems that are of particular importance for pricing applications—endogeneity, heterogeneity, and competition.

18.5.4.1 *Endogeneity*

The model (23) is said to suffer from endogeneity if the error term ξ is correlated with one of the explanatory variables in y. This is a common problem in pricing practice, both in aggregate-demand function estimation and in disaggregate, discrete-choice model estimation. For example, products may have some unobservable or unmeasurable features—quality, style, reputation—and the selling firm typically prices its products accordingly. So if there are two firms in the market with similar products and one has higher nonquantifiable quality, we may observe that the firm with the higher-quality product has both a larger market share and a higher price. A naive estimate based on market shares that ignores the unobserved quality characteristics would lead to the odd conclusions that higher price leads to higher market share. Or take the case of a model that ignores seasonality; demand is higher in a peak season and firms typically price high accordingly. Without accounting for the resulting correlation between the price and this unobserved seasonal variation in demand, we may again reach the false conclusion that high prices lead to high demand. Lastly, consider a car dealer who sizes up a customer based on the way they dress, act, and the information they reveal about their profession. Based on such information, the dealer may quote higher prices to customers who have higher willingness-to-pay, and hence only looking at transaction data we may conclude that higher prices "produce" higher probabilities of sale.

Econometricians call this problem *endogeneity* or *simultaneity*. The technical definition is that the random-error term in (23) is correlated with one of the explanatory variables, $E[\mathbf{Y}^\top \boldsymbol{\xi}] \neq 0$, or equivalently (in the case of linear regression) these vectors are not orthogonal. So while $\boldsymbol{\xi}$ is supposed to represent all unobservable customer and product characteristics that influence demand for a given set of explanatory variables $(Z \mid \mathbf{y})$, some of the explanatory variables $\mathbf{y}$ also contain information on the unobservable attributes through their correlation with $\boldsymbol{\xi}$. Such effects are a common problem in price elasticity estimation. Indeed, a recent meta-analysis of elasticity estimates by Bijmolt et al. (2005) showed that accounting for endogeneity was the single strongest determinant of price elasticity differences among a wide set of elasticity studies.

Econometric techniques for correcting for endogeneity fall under a class of methods called *instrumental-variables (IV) techniques*, attributed to Reiersøl (1945) and Geary (1949). Two-stage and three-stage least-squares methods (2SLS and 3SLS) are some of the popular IV techniques. Instrumental variables are exogenous variables that are correlated with an explanatory variable but are uncorrelated with the error term $\boldsymbol{\xi}$. If there are such IVs, we can use them to "remove" the problematic correlation between the independent variables $\mathbf{y}$ and $\boldsymbol{\xi}$.

For example, one often encounters endogeneity when estimating discrete-choice demand models such as the MNL model from aggregate data (prices correlated with unobservable product characteristics). However, the problem is hard to correct because the aggregate demand is a nonlinear function of the utilities of each product and the endogeneity is present in the equation for the utilities. So using any IV technique for correcting for endogeneity becomes computationally challenging, as pointed out by Berry (1994). Berry (1994) and Berry et al. (1995) recommend that for the case of discrete-choice models in an oligopoly setting, one use measures of the firm's costs and the attributes of the products of the other firms as IVs. See also Besanko et al. (1998) for estimating a logit model in the presence of endogeneity due to competition.

18.5.4.2 *Heterogeneity*

We have already examined a few models of heterogeneity—namely, the finite-mixture logit model and the random-coefficients discrete-choice model. Here, we discuss how to estimate these models.

Estimation of the finite-mixture logit model is relatively straightforward. First, we must determine the number of segments. If there is no *a priori* knowledge of the number, we iterate the estimation procedure, increasing or decreasing the number of segments in each round, using suitable model-selection criteria to decide on the optimal number of segments. For a given number of segments L, we find the parameters that maximize the log-likelihood function. Estimating the random-coefficient logit, likewise, can be done using maximum-likelihood methods, though it is more difficult in general than the standard multinomial logit.

One of the problems dealing with unobservable heterogeneity in the population is that we often have to assume a distribution of heterogeneity without having much evidence as to its specification. Many times, a distribution is chosen for analytical or computational convenience. Unfortunately, a situation can arise where two radically different distributions of heterogeneity equally support the same aggregate demand observations.

Heckman and Singer (1984) illustrate this overparameterization with the following example: Consider an aggregate-demand function based on a heterogeneity parameter θ. The variance on the distribution of θ represents the degree of heterogeneity. Let the demand for a particular value of θ be given by the distribution

$$G_1(z \mid \theta) = 1 - e^{-z\theta}, \quad z \geq 0, \theta > 0,$$

and let θ be equal to a constant η with probability 1 (essentially saying the population is homogeneous). The aggregate-demand distribution then is $F_1(z) = 1 - e^{-z\eta}$.

Consider another possible specification where

$$G_2(z \mid \theta) = 1 - \int_{z(2\theta)^{-0.5}}^{\infty} \frac{2}{\sqrt{2\pi}} e^{-w^2/2} dw, \quad z \geq 0$$

and the distribution of θ given by $\eta^2 e^{-\eta^3 \theta}$. This also turns out to lead to an aggregate-demand distribution given by $1 - e^{-z\eta}$. So based only on aggregate demand data, it is impossible to identify which specification is correct.

Nonparametric methods avoid the problem of having to specify a distribution, and Jain et al. (1994) follow this strategy. Assume that the coefficients of the MNL model β in (27) are randomly drawn from a discrete multivariate probability distribution $G(\Theta)$. That is, the kth customer is assumed to make his choice using $\tilde{\beta}_k$, whose components are drawn from $G(\Theta)$. $G(\cdot)$ is considered a discrete distribution with support vectors $\theta_1, \ldots, \theta_L$. They estimate the number of support vectors L, the location of the support vectors, and the probability mass θ_i associated with the ith support vector from observed data.

18.5.4.3 *Competition*

Accounting for the effects of competition when estimating demand models is another common and important challenge. The most direct approach—and one frequently used in practice—is simply to use competitors' prices as explanatory variables in a standard regression or discrete choice model of demand. The potential problem with this approach is that it implicitly assumes that competitors will not react to your price change—or alternatively, when a firm makes a price change, analysts have to manually estimate the reaction of competitors and input this set of prices into an industry model to determine demand.

Another strategy in such cases is to assume a model of competition between the firms, derive the equilibrium conditions implied by this model, and then estimate the parameters subject to these equilibrium conditions. We illustrate this approach with an example: Assume a homogeneous population of customers who choose among n products according to the MNL model. Then the theoretical share of product j is given as in Section 18.3.4,

$$P_j = \frac{e^{\beta^\top y_j}}{\sum_{i=1}^n e^{\beta^\top y_i}},$$
(29)

where price is one of the explanatory variables in y_j. One way to estimate the parameters β is by equating the observed market share to the theoretical equilibrium prediction. It is convenient to take logs in doing this, which yields the following system of equations relating market shares to choice behavior:

$$\ln P_j = \beta^\top y_j - \ln\left(\sum_{i=1}^n e^{\beta^\top y_i}\right), \quad j = 1,\dots,n.$$
(30)

Next assume that prices are formed by a Bertrand style competition in prices. Let c_j be the constant marginal cost of production for product j. The profit function for product j is given by

$$V_j(p_j) = (p_j - c_j)NP_j,$$
(31)

where N is the size of the population. Let β_p be the coefficient of price in (29). Differentiating (31) with respect to p_j and setting it to zero, we get the first-order equilibrium conditions,

$$(p_j - c_j)\beta_p P_j(1 - P_j) + P_j = 0, \quad j = 1,\dots,n.$$
(32)

The vector of parameters β is then estimated by attempting to fit a solution to (30) and (32) simultaneously. This can be done using, say, nonlinear least-squares estimation.

18.6 Conclusions

A model of demand is the heart and sole of an analytical pricing system. And constructing good ones is a complex task—requiring data sources, information technology for collecting and storing data, statistical estimations models, algorithms to process and analyze these data, and infrastructure for deploying model outputs—all of this is required to turn raw data, into actionable market decisions.

Modern pricing systems are arguably among the most advanced applications of business analytics today. Only the most sophisticated models used in financial markets (e.g., portfolio optimization, options pricing, etc.) and those in certain direct marketing settings (e.g., catalog retailing, credit cards, etc.) rival the complexity and sophistication of today's state-of-the-art pricing systems. But in absolute terms, there is still a long way to go. Pricing systems today use only a fraction of the relevant data that the present-day information-enabled business environment provides. And currently only the basic factors affecting demand are estimated from these data. Much more is possible. The behavioral economic and strategic consumer models emerging in the research literature are promising in terms of expanding the scope and sophistication of demand models, but more development will be needed to bring these ideas into practice.

More complex models of behavior will in turn drive the need for increasingly sophisticated optimization and estimation methods. There may come a time where the phenomenon and problems encountered become so complex that modeling itself becomes the main obstacle. In this case, it may be necessary to resort to more computational approaches like agent-based modeling and simulation to make progress. There will certainly be no shortage of interesting challenges in the years ahead.

18.7 Further reading

The books of Phillips (2005) and Talluri and van Ryzin (2004) provide comprehensive treatment of demand models and their application to tactical pricing and revenue management. The book by Nagle and Holden (2006) provides a good general management overview of pricing decisions. Two excellent and comprehensive references on discrete choice models are Ben-Akiva and Lerman (1985) and Train (2006). Both include extensive treatment of choice model estimation as well. Kök and Vaidyanathan (2009) provide a review of applications of demand models to retail assortment optimization. Shen and Xu (2007) provide a survey of recent research on strategic customer models. See also Ho and Su (2009) and Elmaghraby and Keskinocak (2003).

For details on estimating price-response functions and market-share models, see the following marketing science text books: Eliashberg and Lilien (1991), Wedel and Kamakura (2000), Hanssens et al. (1990), Cooper and Nakanishi (1988), Dasgupta et al. (1994), Hruska (1993), West et al. (1997), Hill et al. (1994), Zhang (1998), and Lee et al. (1994). See Berry (1994), Berry et al. (1995), Besanko et al. (1998), and Chintagunta et al. (1999) for estimation in competitive markets. The problem of endogeneity in estimation has received much recent attention in the marketing science literature spurred by the paper of Berry (1994). See also Chintagunta et al. (1999) and Villas-Boas and Winer (1999).

References

Ben-Akiva, M. and Lerman, S. (1985) *Discrete-Choice Analysis: Theory and Application to Travel Demand*. Cambridge, MA: MIT Press.

Berry, S. (1994) "Estimating Discrete-choice Models of Product Differentiation", *RAND Journal of Economics* 25: 242–62.

—— Levinsohn, J., and Pakes, A. (1995) "Automobile Prices in Market Equilibrium", *Econometrica* 63: 841–90.

Besanko, D., Gupta, S., and Jain, D. (1998) "Logit Demand Estimation under Competitive Pricing Behavior: An equilibrium framework", *Management Science*, 44: 1533–47.

Burnham K. P. and Anderson, D. R. (2002) *Model Selection and Multimodel Inference: A Practical-Theoretic Approach*, 2nd edn. New York: Springer-Verlag.

Chintagunta, P. K., Kadiyali, V., and Vilcassim, N. J. (1999) "Endogeneity and Simultaneity in Competitive Pricing and Advertising: A logit demand analysis". Technical report, Graduate School of Business, University of Chicago, January.

Cooper, L. G. and Nakanishi, M. (1988) *Market-share Analysis*. Norwell, MA: Kluwer.

Dasgupta, C. G., Dispensa, G. S., and Ghose, S. (1994) "Comparing the Predictive Performance of a Neural Network Model with some Traditional Market Response Models", *International Journal of Forecasting*, 10: 235–44.

Debreu, G. (1960) "Review of R. D. Luce, individual choice behavior: A theoretical analysis", *American Economic Review* 50: 186–8.

DeGroot, M. H. (1985) *Probability and Statistics*, 2nd edn. Reading, MA: Addison Wesley.

Eliashberg, J. and Lilien, G. L. (eds) (1991) *Management Science in Marketing*. Amsterdam: North Holland.

Elmaghraby, W. J. and Keskinocak, P. (2003) "Dynamic Pricing: Research overview, current practices, and future directions", *Management Science* 49/10: 1287–1309.

Fisher M., Kok, G., and Vaidyanathan, R. (2009) "Assortment Planning: Review of literature and industry practice", in N. Agrawal and S. Smith (eds), *Retail Supply Chain Management: Quantitative Models and Empirical Studies*. New York: Springer, 99–154.

Geary, R. (1949) "Determination of Linear Relations between Systematic Parts of Variables with Errors of Observation the Variance of which is Unknown", *Econometrica* 17: 30–58.

Guadagni, P. M. and Little, J. D. C. (1983) "A Logit Model of Brand Choice Calibrated on Scanner Data", *Marketing Science* 3: 203–38.

Gwartney, J. D. and Stroup, R. L. (1997) *Economics: Private and Public Choice*, 8th edn. Stamford, CT: Harcourt.

Hanssens, D. M., Parsons, L. J., and Schultz, R. L. (1990) *Market Response Models: Econometric and Time Series Analysis*. Norwell, MA: Kluwer.

Hausman, J. and McFadden, D. (1984) "A Specification Test for the Multinomial Logit Model", *Econometrica* 52: 1219–40.

Heckman, J. and Singer, B. (1984) "A Method for Minimizing the Impact of Distributional Assumptions in Econometric Models for Duration Data", *Econometrica* 52: 271–320.

Hill, T., O'Connor, M., and Remus, W. (1994) "Neural Network Models for Time Series Forecasting", *Management Science* 42: 1082–91.

Ho, T.-H. and Su, X. (2009) "Strategic Pricing Response and Optimization in Operations Management", in V. R. Rao (ed.), *Handbook of Pricing Research in Marketing*. Cheltenham, UK: Edward Elgar Publishing.

Horn, R. A. and Johnson, C. R. (1994) *Matrix Analysis*. Cambridge: Cambridge University Press.

Hruska, H. (1993) "Determining Market Response Functions by Neural Network Modeling: A comparison to econometric techniques", *European Journal of Operational Research* 66: 27–35.

Jain, D., Vilcassim, N. J., and Chintagunta, P. K. (1994) "A Random-coefficients Logit Brand-choice Model Applied to Panel Data", *Journal of Business and Economic Studies* 12: 317–28.

Kahneman, D. and Tversky, A. (1979) "Prospect Theory: An analysis of decision under risk", *Econometrica* 47: 263–92.

—— Slovic, P., and Tversky, A. (eds) (1982) *Judgement Under Uncertainty: Heuristics and Biases*. Cambridge: Cambridge University Press.

Kreps, D. M. (1988) *Notes on the Theory of Choice*. London: Westview Press.

Lee, K., Choi, T., Ku, C., and Park, J. (1994) "Neural Network Architectures for Short Term Load Forecasting", in *Proceedings of the IEEE International Conference on Neural Networks*, Orlando, FL: IEEE ICNN.

Luce, R. (1959) *Individual Choice Behavior: A Theoretical Analysis*. New York: Wiley.

McFadden, D. (1974) "Conditional Logit Analysis of Qualitative Choice Behavior", in P. Zarembka (ed.), *Frontiers in Econometrics*. New York: Academic Press, 105–42.

—— and Train, K. (2000) "Mixed mnl Models for Discrete Response", *Journal of Applied Econometrics* 15: 447–70.

Nagle, T. T. and Holden, R. K. (2006) *The Strategy and Tactics of Pricing: A Guide to Growing More Profitably*, 4th edn. Upper Saddle River, NJ: Pearson Education.

Phillips, R. L. (2005) *Pricing and Revenue Optimization*. Stanford, CA: Stanford University Press.

Reiersøl, O. (1945) "Confluence Analysis by Means of Instrumental Sets of Variables", *Arkiv for Mathematik, Astronomi och Fysik* 32.

Shen, Z. J. M. and Su, X. (2007) "Customer Behavior Modeling in Revenue Management and Auctions: A review and new research directions", *Production and Operations Management*, 16: 713–28.

Talluri, K. T. and van Ryzin, G. J. (2004) "Revenue Management under a General Discrete Choice Model of Consumer Behavior", *Management Science* January.

Train, K. E. (2006) *Discrete Choice Methods with Simulation*. Cambridge: Cambridge University Press.

van Heerde H. J., Bijmolt, H. A., and Pieters, R. G. M. (2005) "New Empirical Generalizations of the Determinants of Price Elasticity", *Journal of Marketing Research* 42: 141–56.

Villas-Boas, J. M. and Winer, R. S. (1999) "Endogeneity in Brand-choice Models", *Management Science* 45: 1324–38.

Vives, X. (2001) *Oligopoly Pricing: Old Ideas and New Tools*. Cambridge, MA: MIT Press.

von Neumann J. and Morgenstern, O. (1944) *Theory of Games and Economic Behavior*. Princeton, NJ: Princeton University Press.

Wedel, M. and Kamakura, W. (2000) *Market Segmentation: Conceptual and Methodological Foundations*, 2nd edn. Norwell, MA: Kluwer.

West, P. M., Brockett, P. L., and Golden, L. L. (1997) "A Comparative Analysis of Neural Networks and Statistical Methods for Predicting Consumer Choice", *Marketing Science* 16: 370–91.

Zhang, G., Patuwo, B. E., and Hu, M. Y. (1998) "Forecasting with Artificial Neural Networks: The state of the art", *International Journal of Forecasting* 14: 35–62.

Ziya, S., Ayhan, H., and Foley, R. D. (2004) "Relationships Among Three Assumptions in Revenue Management", *Operations Research* 52/5: 804–9.

CHAPTER 19

GAME THEORY MODELS OF PRICING

PRAVEEN K. KOPALLE AND ROBERT A. SHUMSKY

19.1 INTRODUCTION

In 1991, packaged-goods behemoth Procter & Gamble (P&G) initiated a "value pricing" scheme for sales to retailers. Value pricing was P&G's label for *everyday low pricing* (EDLP), a pricing strategy under which retailers are charged a consistent price rather than a high baseline price punctuated by sporadic, deep discounts. P&G had many reasons for converting to EDLP. Its salesforce had grown to rely on discounting to drive sales and the use of deep discounts had spiraled out of control, cutting into earnings (Saporito 1994). The discounts then created demand shocks, as both retailers and customers loaded up on products whenever the price dropped. This exacerbated the so-called bullwhip effect, as demand variability was amplified up the supply chain, reducing the utilization of distribution resources and factories and increasing costs (Lee et al. 1997).

Despite the costs of its traditional discounting strategy, the move to value pricing was risky for P&G. How would retailers, consumers, and competing manufacturers respond to P&G's EDLP program? For example, would competitors deepen their own discounts to pull market share away from P&G? Or would they also move to a low, consistent price? To accurately predict competitors' behavior, P&G would have to consider each competitor's beliefs about P&G itself. For example, it was possible that Unilever, a competing manufacturer, might increase its discounting if it believed that P&G was not fully committed to EDLP but otherwise might itself adopt EDLP. Therefore, P&G's decision on whether and how to adopt EDLP depended on the responses of its competitors, which, in turn, depended upon their beliefs about what P&G was going to do.

P&G's actions depended on Uniliver's, which depended on P&G's—a chicken-and-egg problem that can make your head spin. There is, however, an approach to problems like

We would like to thank Özalp Özer, Robert Phillips, and an anonymous referee for their helpful suggestions.

Table 19.1 Game types in this chapter

	Timing of actions	
Number of periods	Simultaneous	Sequential
One	Sections 19.2.1–19.2.4, 19.2.6	Section 19.2.5
Multiple	Sections 19.3.1–19.3.4	Sections 19.3.5–19.3.6

this that can cut through the complexity and help managers make better pricing decisions. That approach, game theory, was first developed as a distinct body of knowledge by mathematicians and economists in the 1940s and 1950s (see the pioneering work by von Neumann and Morgenstern 1944, and Nash 1950). Since then, it has been applied to a variety of fields, including computer science, political science, biology, operations management, and marketing science.

In this chapter, we first introduce the basic concepts of game theory by using simple pricing examples. We then link those examples with both the research literature and industry practice, including examples of how game theory has been used to understand P&G's value pricing initiative and the competitive response. In Section 19.2 we define the basic elements of a game and describe the fundamental assumptions that underlie game theory. In the remaining sections we examine models that provide insight into how games work (e.g., understanding various types of equlibria) as well as how competition affects pricing. The models may be categorized according to two attributes: the timing of actions and the number of periods (Table 19.1). In many of the models, competitors make simultaneous pricing decisions, so that neither player has more information about its competitor's actions than the other. In other games with sequential timing, one competitor sets its price first. Some games have a single period (we define a 'period' as a time unit in which each player takes a single action), while other games will have multiple time periods, and actions taken in one period may affect actions and rewards in later periods. Along the way, we will make a few side trips: a brief look at behavioral game theory in Section 19.3.2 and some thoughts on implications for the practice of pricing in Section 19.4.

This chapter does not contain a rigorous description of the mathematics behind game theory, nor does it cover all important areas of the field. For example, we will not discuss *cooperative* game theory, in which participants form coalitions to explicitly coordinate their prices (in many countries, such coalitions would be illegal). We will, however, say a bit more about cooperative games at the end of Section 19.2.6.

For a more complete and rigorous treatment of game theory, we recommend Fudenberg and Tirole (1991), Myerson (1991), and Gibbons (1992). For more examples of how practitioners can make use of game theory for many decisions in addition to pricing, we recommend Dixit and Nalebuff (1991). Moorthy (1985) focuses on marketing applications such as market-entry decisions and advertising programs, as well as pricing. Cachon and Netessine (2006) discuss applications of game theory to supply chain management. Nisan et al. (2007) describe computational approaches to game theory for applications such as information security, distributed computation, prediction markets, communications networks, peer-to-peer systems, and the flow of information through social networks. The popular press and trade journals also report on how game theory can influence corporate strategy. For example Rappeport (2008) describes how game theory has been applied at Microsoft, Chevron, and other firms. Finally, information intermediaries such as Yahoo! and Google employ research groups that develop game theory models to understand how consumers and firms use the web, and to develop new business models for the Internet.[1]

19.2 INTRODUCTION TO GAME THEORY:
SINGLE-PERIOD PRICING GAMES

A game is defined by three elements: players, strategies that may be used by each player, and payoffs.

DEFINITION 1 A game consists of players (participants in the game), strategies (plans by each player that describe what action will be taken in any situation), and payoffs (rewards for each player for all combinations of strategies).

In the value-pricing example above, the players might be P&G and Unilever, their strategies are the prices they set over time under certain conditions, and the payoffs are the profits they make under various combinations of pricing schemes. Given that each player has chosen a strategy, the collection of players' strategies is called a *strategy profile*. If we know the strategy profile, then we know how every player will act for any situation in the game.

When describing a game, it is also important to specify the information that is available to each player. For example, we will sometimes consider situations in which each player must decide upon a strategy to use without knowing the strategy chosen by the other player. At other times, we will let one player observe the other player's choice before making a decision.

When analyzing a game, there are two basic steps. The first is to make clear the implications of the rules—to fully understand the relationships between the strategies and the payoffs. Once we understand how the game works, the second step is to determine which strategy each player will play under various circumstances. This analysis may begin with a description of each player's optimal strategy *given* any strategy profile for the other players. The analysis usually ends with a description of *equilibrium* strategies—a strategy profile that the players may settle into and will not want to change. One fascinating aspect of game theory is that these equilibrium strategies can often be quite different from the best overall strategy that might be achieved if the players were part of a single firm that coordinated their actions. We will see that competition often can make both players worse off.

A typical assumption in game theory, and an assumption we hold in much of this chapter, is that all players know the identities, available strategies, and payoffs of all other players, as in a game of tic-tac-toe. When no player has private information about the game that is unavailable to the other players, and when all players know that the information is available to all players, we say that the facts of the game are *common knowledge* (see Aumann 1976 and Milgrom 1981 for more formal descriptions of the common knowledge

---

[1] See labs.yahoo.com/ and research.google.com/.

assumption). In some instances, however, a player may have private information. For example, one firm may have more accurate information than its competitor about how its own customers respond to price changes by the competitor. Such games of *incomplete information* are sometimes called *Bayesian games*, for uncertainty and probability are important elements of the game, and Bayes' rule is used to update the players' beliefs as the game is played. See Gibbons (1992) and Harsanyi (1967) for more background on Bayesian games.

We also assume that the players are rational, that is, that firms make pricing decisions to maximize their profits. Finally, we assume that each player knows that the other players are rational. Therefore, each player can put itself in its competitors' shoes and anticipate its competitors' choices. Pushing further, each player knows that its competitors are anticipating its own choices, and making choices accordingly. In general, we assume that the players have an *infinite hierarchy of beliefs* about strategies in the game. This assumption is vital for understanding why competitors may achieve the Nash equilibrium described in the next section. The assumption also highlights a key insight that can be developed by studying game theory—the importance of anticipating your competitors' actions.

19.2.1 A first example: pricing the UltraPhone and the Prisoner's Dilemma

Consider two players, firms A and B, that have simultaneously developed virtually identical versions of what we will call the UltraPhone, a hand-held device that includes technology for cheap, efficient 3-dimensional video-conferencing. Both firms will release their Ultra-Phones at the same time and, therefore, each has to set a price for the phone without knowing the price set by its competitor. For the purposes of this example, we assume both firms will charge either a High price or a Low price for all units (see Table 19.2). Therefore, the firms' possible actions are to price "High" or "Low", and each firm's strategy is a plan to charge one of these two prices.

To complete the description of the game, we describe the payoffs under each strategy profile. At the High price, the firms' unit contribution margin is $800/phone; at the Low price, the firms' unit contribution margin is $300/phone. There are two segments of customers for the UltraPhone, and the maximum price each segment is willing to pay is very different. The two million people in the "High" segment are all willing to pay the High price (but would, of course, prefer the Low price), while the two million people in the "Low" segment are only willing to pay the Low price. We also assume that if both firms charge the same price, then sales are split equally between the two firms. And we assume both firms can always manufacture a sufficient number of phones to satisfy any number of customers. Note that in this example, there is no reliable way to discriminate between segments; if the phone is offered for the Low price by either firm, then both the two million Low customers and the two million High customers will buy it for that Low price.

Given the information in Table 19.2, both firms ask, "What should we charge for our phone?" Before looking at the competitive analysis, consider what the firms should do if they coordinate—for example if they were not competitors but instead were divisions of one firm that is a monopoly producer of this product. The total contribution margin given the High price is 2 million × $800 = $1.6 billion. The margin given the Low price is

Table 19.2 Prices, margins, and segments for the *UltraPhone*

Price	Unit contribution margin at that price	Number in segment
High	$800	2,000,000
Low	$300	2,000,000

B Chooses...

		High	Low
A Chooses...	High	8, 8	0, 12
	Low	12, 0	6, 6

Table 19.3 The *UltraPhone* game. Entries in each cell are payoffs to A (first number in each cell) and to B (second number in each cell) in $100 millions

(2 million + 2 million) × $300 = $1.2 billion. Therefore, the optimal solution for a monopoly is to set prices to exclusively target the high-end market.

Now we turn to the competitive analysis—the game. The two competing firms, A and B, face the situation shown in Table 19.3, which represents a normal form of a game. The rows correspond to the two different strategies available to firm A: price High or Low. The columns correspond to the same strategies for B. The entries in the tables show the payoffs, the total contribution margins for firm A (the first number in each cell of the table) and firm B (the second number in each cell) in units of $100 million. If both price High (the upper left cell), then they split the $1.6 billion equally between them. If both price Low (bottom right cell), then they split the $1.2 billion. For the cell in the upper right, A prices High but B prices Low, so that B captures all of the demand at the Low price and gains $1.2 billion. The lower left cell shows the reverse.

Given this payoff structure, what should the firms do? First, consider firm A's decision, given each strategy chosen by B. If B chooses High (the first column), then it is better for A to choose Low. Therefore, we say that Low is player A's best response to B choosing High.

DEFINITION 2 A player's best response is the strategy, or set of strategies, that maximizes the player's payoff, given the strategies of the other players.

If B chooses Low (the second column), then firm A's best response is to choose Low as well. The fact that it is best for A to price Low, no matter what B does, makes pricing Low a particular type of strategy, a dominant one.

DEFINITION 3 A strategy is a dominant strategy for a firm if it is optimal, no matter what strategy is used by the other players.

Likewise, *dominated strategies* are never optimal, no matter what the competitors do.

Pricing Low is also a dominant strategy for B: no matter what A chooses, Low is better. In fact, the strategy profile [A Low, B Low] is the unique Nash equilibrium of this game; if both firms choose Low, then neither has a reason to unilaterally change its mind.

DEFINITION 4 The firms are in a Nash equilibrium if the strategy of each firm is the best response to the strategies of the other firms. Equivalently, in a Nash equilibrium, none of the firms have any incentive to unilaterally deviate from its strategy.

This is the only equilibrium in the game. For example, if A chooses High and B chooses Low, then A would have wished it had chosen Low and earned $600 million rather than $0. Note that for the Nash equilibrium of this game, both firms choose their dominant strategies, but that is not always the case (see, for example, the Nash equilibria in the game of chicken, Section 19.2.4).

Because we assume that both firms are rational and fully anticipate the logic used by the other player (the infinite belief hierarchy), we predict that both will charge Low, each will earn $600 million, and the total industry contribution margin will be $1.2 billion. This margin is less than the optimal result of $1.6 billion. This is a well-known result: under competition, both prices and industry profits decline. We will see in Section 19.3.1, however, that it may be possible to achieve higher profits when the game is played repeatedly.

This particular game is an illustration of a Prisoner's Dilemma. In the classic example of the Prisoner's Dilemma, two criminal suspects are apprehended and held in separate rooms. If neither confesses to a serious crime, then both are jailed for a short time (say, one year) under relatively minor charges. If both confess, they both receive a lengthy sentence (five years). But if one confesses and the other doesn't, then the snitch is freed and the silent prisoner is given a long prison term (ten years). The equilibrium in the Prisoner's Dilemma is for both prisoners to confess, and the resulting five-year term is substantially worse than the cooperative equilibrium they would have achieved if they had both remained silent. In the UltraPhone example, the Low–Low strategy is equivalent to mutual confession.

The strategy profile [A Low, B Low] is a *Nash equilibrium in pure strategies*. It is a *pure strategy* equilibrium because each player chooses a single price. The players might also consider a *mixed strategy*, in which each player chooses a probability distribution over a set of pure strategies (see Dixit and Skeath 1999: ch. 5, for an accessible and thorough discussion of mixed strategies). The equilibrium concept is named after John Nash, a mathematician who showed that if each player has a finite number of pure strategies, then there must always exist at least one mixed strategy or pure strategy equilibrium (Nash 1950). In certain games, however, there may not exist a pure strategy equilibrium and, as we will see in Section 19.2.4, it is also possible to have multiple pure-strategy equilibria.

19.2.2 Bertrand and Cournot competition

The UltraPhone game is similar to a *Bertrand competition*, in which two firms produce identical products and compete only on price, with no product differentiation. It can be shown that if demand is a continuous linear function of price and if both firms have the same constant marginal cost, then the only Nash equilibrium is for both firms to set a price equal to their marginal cost. As in the example above, competition drives price down, and in a Bertrand competition, prices are driven down to their lowest limit.

Both the UltraPhone example and the Bertrand model assume that it is always possible for the firms to produce a sufficient quantity to supply the market, no matter what price is charged. Therefore, the Bertrand model does not fit industries with capacity constraints that are expensive to adjust. An alternative model is *Cournot competition*, in which the firms' strategies are quantities rather than prices. The higher the quantities the firms choose, the lower the price. Under a Cournot competition between two firms, the resulting Nash equilibrium price is higher than the marginal cost (the Bertrand solution) but lower than the monopoly price. As the number of firms competing in the market increases, however, the Cournot equilibrium price falls. In the theoretical limit (an infinite number of competitors), the price drops down to the marginal cost. See Weber (Chapter 17) for additional discussion of Bertrand and Cournot competition.

Besides the assumption that there are no capacity constraints, another important assumption of Bertrand competition is that the products are identical, so that the firm offering the lowest price attracts all demand. We will relax this assumption in the next section.

19.2.3 Continuous prices, product differentiation, and best response functions

In Section 19.2.1 we restricted our competitors to two choices: High and Low prices. In practice, firms may choose from a variety of prices, so now assume that each firm chooses a price over a continuous range. Let firm i's price be p_i (i = A or B). In this game, a player's strategy is the choice of a price, and we now must define the payoffs, given the strategies. First we describe how each competitor's price affects demand for the product. In the last section, all customers chose the lowest price. Here we assume that the products are differentiated, so that some customers receive different utilities from the products and are therefore loyal; they will purchase from firm A or B, even if the other firm offers a lower price. Specifically, let $d_i(p_i, p_j)$ be the demand for product i, given that the competitors charge p_i and p_j. We define the linear demand function,

$$d_i(p_i, p_j) = a - bp_i + cp_j.$$

If $c > 0$, we say that the products are substitutes: a lower price charged by firm A leads to more demand for A's product and less demand for B's (although if $p_B < p_A$, B does not steal all the demand, as in Section 19.2.1). If $c < 0$, then the products are complements: a lower price charged by A raises demand for both products. In the UltraPhone example, the products are substitutes; product A and a specialized accessory (e.g., a docking station) would be complements. If $c = 0$ then the two products are independent, there is no interaction between the firms, and both firms choose their optimal monopoly price.

Now let m be the constant marginal cost to produce either product. Firm i's margin is therefore $(p_i - m)d_i(p_i, p_j)$. This function is concave with respect to p_i, and therefore the optimal price for firm i given that firm j charges p_j can be found by taking the derivative of the function with respect to p_i, setting that first derivative equal to 0, and solving algebraically for p_i. Let $p_i^*(p_j)$ be the resulting optimal price, and we find,

$$p_i^*(p_j) = \frac{1}{2b}(a + bm + cp_j). \tag{1}$$

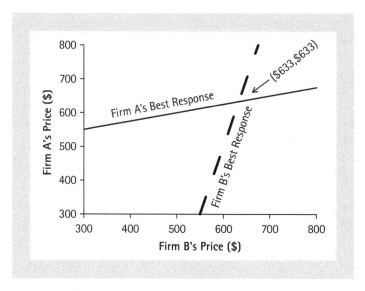

FIGURE 19.1 Best response functions in the *UltraPhone* pricing game with product differentiation

This optimal price is a function of the competitor's price, and therefore we call $p_i^*(p_j)$ the *best response function* of i to j; this is the continuous equivalent of the *best response* defined in Section 19.2.1. Figure 19.1 shows the two best response functions on the same graph, for a given set of parameters $a = 3,000$, $b = 4$, $c = 2$, and $m = \$200$/unit. For example, if Firm B sets a price of \$300, Firm A's best response is a price of \$550. From the function, we see that if the products are substitutes and $c > 0$ (as in this case), the best response of one firm rises with the price of the other firm. If the products are complements, the lines would slope downward, so that if one firm raises its prices then the best response of the competitor is to lower its price.

   The plot also shows that if Firm A chooses a price of \$633, then Firm B's best response is also \$633. Likewise, if Firm B chooses \$633, then so does Firm A. Therefore, neither firm has any reason to deviate from choosing \$633, and [\$633, \$633] is the unique Nash equilibrium. In general, the equilibrium prices satisfy equation (1) when i is Firm A as well as when i is Firm B. By solving these two equations we find,

$$p_i^* = p_j^* = \frac{a + bm}{2b - c}.$$

Note that as c rises, and the products move from being complements to substitutes, the equilibrium price declines.

   In this example, the firms are identical and therefore the equilibrium is symmetric (both choose the same price). With non-identical firms (e.g., if they have different parameter values in the demand function and/or different marginal costs), then there can be a unique equilibrium in which the firms choose different prices (Singh and Vives 1984). We will discuss additional extensions of this model, including the role of reference prices, in Section 19.3.3.

19.2.4 Multiple equilibria and a game of chicken

Now return to the UltraPhone pricing game with two price points, as in Section 19.2.1, although we also incorporate product differentiation, as in Section 19.2.3. Assume that 40 percent of the High-segment customers are loyal to firm A and will choose A's product even if A chooses a High price while B chooses a Low price. Likewise, 40 percent of the High-segment customers are loyal to firm B. The payoffs from this new game are shown in Table 19.4. If both firms price High or both price Low, then the payoffs do not change. If A prices High and B prices Low (the upper right cell), then A's margin is 40%×(2 million)× $800 = $640 million while B's margin is (60%×(2 million) + 2 million)×$300 = $960 million. The lower left cell shows the reverse.

The presence of loyal customers significantly changes the behavior of the players. If B chooses High, then A's best response is to choose Low, while if B chooses Low, A's best response is to choose High. In this game, neither firm has a dominant strategy, and [A Low, B Low] is no longer an equilibrium; if the firms find themselves in that cell, both firms would have an incentive to move to High. But [A High, B High] is not an equilibrium either; both would then want to move to Low.

In fact, this game has *two* pure strategy Nash equilibria: [A High, B Low] and [A Low, B High]. Given either combination, neither firm has any incentive to unilaterally move to another strategy. Each of these two equilibria represents a split in the market between one firm that focuses on its own High-end loyal customers and the other that captures everyone else.

This example is analogous to a game of "chicken" between two automobile drivers. They race towards one another and if neither swerves, they crash, producing the worst outcome—in our case [A Low, B Low]. If both swerve, the payoff is, obviously, higher. If one swerves and the other doesn't, the one who did not swerve receives the highest award, while the one who "chickened out" has a payoff that is lower than if they had both swerved but higher than if the drivers had crashed. As in Table 19.4, there are two pure strategy equilibria in the game of chicken, each with one driver swerving and the other driving straight.[2]

B Chooses...

		High	Low
A Chooses...	High	8, 8	6.4, 9.6
	Low	9.6, 6.4	6, 6

Table 19.4 Payoffs for the *UltraPhone* game with loyal customers, in $100 millions. Entries in each cell are payoffs to A, B

[2] There is also a mixed-strategy equilibrium for the game in Table 19.4. If each player randomly selects a High price with probability 0.2 and a Low price with probability 0.8, then neither player has any incentive to choose a different strategy.

The existence of multiple equilibria poses a challenge for both theorists and practitioners who use game theory. Given the many possible equilibria, will players actually choose one? If so, which one? Behavioral explanations have been proposed to answer this question—see Section 19.3.2. In addition, game theorists have invented variations of the Nash equilibrium to address these questions. These variations are called *refinements*, and they lay out criteria that exclude certain types of strategies and equilibria. Many of these innovations depend upon the theory of dynamic games, in which the game is played in multiple stages over time (see Section 19.3). The *subgame perfect equilibrium* described in the next section is one such refinement. Another is the *trembling-hand perfect equilibrium* in which players are assumed to make small mistakes (or "trembles") and all players take these mistakes into account when choosing strategies (Selten 1975; Fudenberg and Tirole 1991: sect. 8.4). For descriptions of additional refinements, see Govindan and Wilson (2005).

19.2.5 Sequential action and a Stackelberg game

In the previous section, we assumed that both firms set prices simultaneously without knowledge of the other's decision. We saw how this game has two equilibria and that it is difficult to predict which one will be played. In this section we will see how this problem is resolved if one player moves first and chooses its preferred equilibrium; in the game of chicken, imagine that one driver rips out her steering wheel and throws it out of her window, while the other driver watches.

For the UltraPhone competition, assume that firm A has a slight lead in its product development process and will release the product and announce its price first. The release and price announcement dates are set in stone—for example firm A has committed to announcing its price and sending its products to retailers on the first Monday of the next month, while firm B will announce its price and send its products to retailers a week later. It is important to note that these are the *actual* pricing dates. Either firm may publicize potential prices before those dates, but retailers will only accept the prices given by firm A on the first Monday and firm B on the second Monday. Also, assume that the one-week "lag" does not significantly affect the sales assumptions introduced in Sections 19.2.1 and 19.2.4. This sequential game has a special name—the Stackelberg game.

DEFINITION 5 In a Stackelberg game one player (the *leader*) moves first, while the other player (the *follower*) moves second after observing the action of the leader.

The left-hand side of Figure 19.2 shows the extensive-form representation of the game, with A's choice as the first split at the top of the diagram and B's choice at the bottom.

One can identify an equilibrium in a Stackelberg game (a Stackelberg equilibrium) by *backward induction*—working up from the bottom of the diagram. First, we see what firm B would choose, given either action by firm A. As the second tree in Figure 19.2 shows, B would choose Low if A chooses High and would choose High if A chooses Low. Given the payoffs from these choices, it is optimal for A to choose Low, and the Stackelberg equilibrium is [A Low, B High], with the highest payoff—$960 million—going to firm A. By moving first, firm A has guided the game towards its preferred equilibrium.

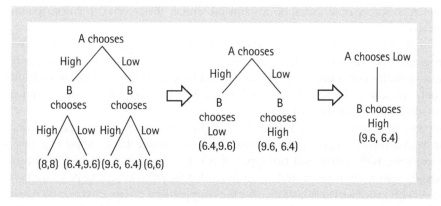

FIGURE 19.2 Analysis of the *UltraPhone* game with loyal customers and A as a first mover

It is important to note, however, that [A High, B Low] is still a Nash equilibrium for the full game. Suppose that firm B states before the crucial month arrives that *no matter what firm A decides*, it will choose to price Low (again, this does not mean that firm B actually sets the price to Low before the second Monday of the month, just that it claims it will). If firm A believes this threat, then it will choose High in order to avoid the worst-case [A Low, B Low] outcome. Therefore, another equilibrium may be [A High, B Low], as in the simultaneous game of Section 19.2.4.

But can firm A believe B's threat? Is the threat credible? Remember that A moves first and that B observes what A has done. Once A has chosen Low, it is not optimal for B to choose Low as well; it would be better for B to abandon its threat and choose High. We say that B's choices (the second level in Figure 19.2) are subgames of the full game. When defining an equilibrium strategy, it seems natural to require that the strategies each player chooses also lead to an equilibrium in each subgame.

DEFINITION 6 In a subgame perfect equilibrium, the strategies chosen for each subgame are a Nash equilibrium of that subgame.

In this case, B's strategy "price Low no matter what A does" does not seem to be part of a reasonable equilibrium because B will not price Low if A prices Low first; an equilibrium that includes B Low after A Low is not Nash. Therefore, we say that [A Low, B High] is a subgame perfect equilibrium but that [A High, B Low] is not.

19.2.6 An airline revenue management game

In the UltraPhone game, the two firms set prices, and we assume the firms can easily adjust production quantities to accommodate demand. The dynamics of airline pricing often are quite different. The capacity of seats on each flight is fixed over the short term, and prices for various types of tickets are set in advance. As the departure of a flight approaches, the number of seats available at each price is adjusted over time. This dynamic adjustment of seat inventory is sometimes called *revenue management*; see Talluri (Chapter 26) for additional information on the fundamentals of revenue management as well as Barnes

(Chapter 3), Kimes et al. (Chapter 6), and Lieberman (Chapter 12) for descriptions of applications.

Here, we will describe a game in which two airlines simultaneously practice revenue management. As was true for the initial UltraPhone example, the game will be a simplified version of reality. For example, we will assume that the single flight operated by each airline has only one seat left for sale. As we will discuss below, however, the insights generated by the model hold for realistic scenarios.

Suppose two airlines, X and Y, offer direct flights between the same origin and destination, with departures and arrivals at similar times. We assume that each flight has just one seat available. Both airlines sell two types of tickets: a low-fare ticket with an advance-purchase requirement for $200 and a high-fare ticket for $500 that can be purchased at any time. A ticket purchased at either fare is for the same physical product: a coach-class seat on one flight leg. The advance-purchase restriction, however, segments the market and allows for price discrimination between customers with different valuations of purchase-time flexibility. Given the advance-purchase requirement, we assume that demand for low-fare tickets occurs before demand for high-fare tickets. Customers who prefer a low fare and are willing to accept the purchase restrictions will be called "low-fare customers". Customers who prefer to purchase later, at the higher price, are called "high-fare customers".

Assume marginal costs are negligible, so that the airlines seek to maximize expected revenue. To increase revenue, both airlines may establish a *booking limit* for low-fare tickets: a restriction on the number of low-fare tickets that may be sold. (In our case, the booking limit is either 0 or 1.) Once this booking limit is reached by ticket sales, the low fare is closed and only high-fare sales are allowed. If a customer is denied a ticket by one airline, we assume that customer will attempt to purchase a ticket from the other airline (we call these "overflow passengers"). Therefore, both airlines are faced with a random initial demand as well as demand from customers who are denied tickets by the other airline. Passengers denied a reservation by both airlines are lost. We assume that for each airline, there is a 100 percent chance that a low-fare customer will attempt to purchase a ticket followed by a 50 percent chance that a high-fare customer will attempt to purchase a ticket. This information is summarized in Table 19.5.

The following is the order of events in the game:

1. Airlines establish booking limits. Each airline chooses to either close the low-fare class ("Close") and not sell a low-fare ticket, or keep it open ("Open"). In this revenue management game, the decision whether to Close or remain Open is the airline's strategy.

Table 19.5 Customer segments for the revenue management game

Fare class	Ticket price	Demand	
		Airline X	Airline Y
Low	$200	1 (guaranteed)	1 (guaranteed)
High	$500	Prob{0}=0.5	Prob{0}=0.5
		Prob{1}=0.5	Prob{1}=0.5

Y Chooses...

		Open	Close
X Chooses...	Open	200, 200	200, 375
	Close	375, 200	250, 250

Table 19.6 Expected payoffs for the airline revenue management game. Entries in each cell are payoffs to X, Y

2. A low-fare passenger arrives at each airline and is accommodated (and $200 collected) if the low-fare class is Open.

3. Each airline either receives a high-fare passenger or does not see any more demand, where each outcome has probability 0.5. If a passenger arrives, and if the low-fare class has been closed, the passenger is accommodated (and $500 collected).

4. A high-fare passenger who is not accommodated on the first-choice airline spills to the alternate airline and is accommodated there if the alternate airline has closed its seat from a low-fare customer and has not sold a seat to its own high-fare customer.

Table 19.6 shows the payoffs for each combination of strategies. If both airlines choose to keep the low-fare class Open, both book customers for $200. If both choose to Close, each has a 50 percent chance of booking a high fare, so that each has an expected value of $(0.5) \times \$500 = \$250$. In the upper right cell, if X chooses to Open and Y chooses to Close, then X books a low-fare customer for $200 while Y has a chance of booking a high-fare customer. That high-fare customer may either be a customer who originally desired a flight on Y (who arrives with probability 0.5) or a spillover from X (who also arrives, independently, with probability 0.5). Therefore, Y's expected revenue is $[1 - (0.5)(0.5)] \times \$500 = \$375$. The lower left cell shows the reverse situation.

By examining Table 19.6, we see that the only Nash equilibrium is [X Close, Y Close]. If one airline chooses to Close, then the airline that chooses Open foregoes the opportunity to book a high-fare customer.

Note that this game is not precisely the same as the UltraPhone game/Prisoner's Dilemma discussed in Section 19.2.1; the airlines could have had an even worse outcome with [X Open, Y Open]. The competitive equilibrium, however, is inferior in terms of aggregate revenue to the cooperative solution, just as it is in the Prisoner's Dilemma. In Table 19.6, the highest total revenue across both airlines—$575—is obtained with strategies [X Open, Y Close] or [X Close, Y Open]. The Nash equilibrium has an expected total revenue of $500.

There is another interesting comparison to make with the UltraPhone game. In that game, competition drove prices down. In this game, competition leads the airlines from an optimal coordinated solution [X Open, Y Close] or [X Close, Y Open] to the Nash equilibrium [X Close, Y Close]. Therefore, under the coordinated solution, one low-fare ticket is sold and one high-fare ticket may be sold. Under the Nash equilibrium, only high-fare tickets may be sold. Netessine and Shumsky (2005) analyze a similar game with two customer classes and any number of available seats, and they confirm that this general insight continues to hold; under competition, more seats are reserved for high-fare customers, while the number of tickets sold (the load factor) declines, as compared to the monopoly solution. The use of seat inventory control by the airlines and the low-to-high pattern of customer valuations inverts the Bertrand and Cournot results; competition in the revenue management game raises the average price paid for a ticket as compared to the average price charged by a monopolist.

In practice, however, airlines may compete on multiple routes, offer more than two fare classes, and do not make a single revenue management decision simultaneously. Jiang and Pang (2011) extend this model to airline competition over a network. Dudey (1992) and Martinez-de-Albeniz and Talluri (2010) analyze the dynamic revenue management problem, in which the airlines adjust booking limits dynamically over time. d'Huart (2010) uses a computer simulation to compare monopoly and oligopoly airline revenue management behavior. He simulates up to four airlines with three competing flights offered by each airline and six fare classes on each flight. The simulation also incorporates many of the forecasting and dynamic revenue management heuristics used by the airlines. The results of the simulation correspond to our models' predictions: fewer passengers are booked under competition, but with a higher average fare.

Of course, the airlines may prefer to collaborate, agree to one of the monopoly solutions, and then split the larger pot so that both airlines would come out ahead of the Nash outcome. In general, such collusion can increase overall profits, while reducing consumer surplus. Such price-fixing is illegal in the United States, Canada, the European Union, and many other countries. Occasionally airlines do attempt to collude and get caught, for example British Airways and Virgin Atlantic conspired to simultaneously raise their prices on competing routes by adding fuel surcharges to their tickets. Virgin Atlantic reported on the plot to the US Department of Justice, and British Airways paid a large fine (Associated Press 2007).

In the absence of such legal risks, a fundamental question is whether such collusion is stable when airlines do not have enforceable agreements to cooperate as well as explicit methods for distributing the gains from cooperation. As we have seen from the examples above, each player has an incentive to deviate from the monopoly solution to increase its own profits. In Section 19.3 we will discuss how repeated play can produce outcomes other than the single-play Nash equilibrium described above.

In certain cases in the United States, airlines have received permission from the Department of Justice to coordinate pricing and split the profits. Northwest and KLM have had such an agreement since 1993, while United, Lufthansa, Continental, and Air Canada began coordinating pricing and revenue management on their trans-Atlantic flights in 2009 (BTNonline.com 2008; DOT 2009). The ability of such joint ventures to sustain themselves depends upon whether each participant receives a net benefit from joining the coalition. Cooperative game theory focuses on how the value created by the coalition may be distributed among the participants, and how this distribution affects coalition stability. Such joint ventures, however, are the exception rather than the rule in the airline business and elsewhere, and therefore we will continue to focus on non-cooperative game theory.

19.3 DYNAMIC PRICING GAMES

Pricing competition can be viewed from either a static or a dynamic perspective. Dynamic models incorporate the dimension of time and recognize that competitive decisions do not necessarily remain fixed. Viewing competitive pricing strategies from a dynamic perspective can provide richer insights and, for some questions, more accurate answers, than when using static models. In this section we will first explain how dynamic models differ from the models presented in the last section. We will then describe a variety of dynamic models, and we will see how the price equilibria predicted by the models can help firms to understand markets and set prices. Finally, and perhaps most significantly, we will show how pricing data collected from the field has been used to test the predictions made by game theory models. First, we make clear what we mean by a dynamic game.

DEFINITION 7 If a game is played exactly once, it is a single-period, or a one-shot, or a static game. If a pricing game is played more than once, it is a dynamic or a multi-period game.

In a dynamic game, decision variables in each period are sometimes called control variables. Therefore, a firm's strategy is a set of values for the control variables.

Dynamic competitive pricing situations can be analyzed in terms of either continuous or discrete time. Generally speaking, pricing data from the market is discrete in nature (e.g., weekly price changes at stores or the availability of weekly, store-level scanner data), and even continuous-time models, which are an abstraction, are discretized for estimation of model parameters from market data. Typically, dynamic models are treated as multi-period games because critical variables—sales, market share, and so forth—are assumed to change over time based on the dynamics in the marketplace. Any dynamic model of pricing competition must consider the impact of competitors' pricing strategies on the dynamic process governing changes in sales or market-share variables.

In this section we will describe a variety of dynamic pricing policies for competing firms. See Aviv and Vulcano (Chapter 23) for more details on dynamic policies that do not take competitors' strategies directly into account. That chapter also describes models that examine, in more detail, the effects of strategic customers. Other related chapters include Ramakrishnan (Chapter 25), Blattberg and Briesch (Chapter 24), and Kaya and Özer (Chapter 29). This last chapter is closely related to the material in Sections 19.2.5 and 19.3.5, for it also describes Stackelberg games, while examining specific contracts between wholesalers and retailers (e.g., buy-back, revenue sharing, etc.), the effects of asymmetric forecast information, and the design of contracts to elicit accurate information from supply chain partners. For additional discussion of issues related to behavioral game theory (discussed in Section 19.3.2, below), see Özer and Zheng (Chapter 20).

19.3.1 Effective competitive strategies in repeated games

We have seen in Section 19.2.1 how a Prisoner's Dilemma can emerge as the non-cooperative Nash equilibrium strategy in a static, one-period game. In the real world, however, rarely do we see one-period interactions. For example, firms rarely consider competition for one week and set prices simply for that week, keeping them at the same level during all weeks into the future. Firms have a continuous interaction with each other for many weeks in a row, and this continuous interaction gives rise to repeated games.

DEFINITION 8 A repeated game is a dynamic game in which past actions do not influence the payoffs or set of feasible actions in the current period, that is, there is no explicit link between the periods.

In a repeated game setting, firms would, of course, be more profitable if they could avoid the Prisoner's Dilemma and move to a more cooperative equilibrium. Therefore, formulating the pricing game as a multi-period problem may identify strategies under which firms achieve a cooperative equilibrium, where competing firms may not lower prices as much as they would have otherwise in a one-shot Prisoner's Dilemma. As another example, in an information sharing context, Özer et al. (2011) discuss the importance of trust and determine that repeated games enhance trust and cooperation among players. Such cooperative equilibria may also occur if the game is not guaranteed to be repeated, but may be repeated with some probability.

A robust approach in such contexts is the "tit-for-tat" strategy, where one firm begins with a cooperative pricing strategy and subsequently copies the competing firm's previous move. This strategy is probably the best known and most often discussed rule for playing the Prisoner's Dilemma in a repeated setting, as illustrated by Axelrod and Hamilton (1981), Axelrod (1984), and also discussed in Dixit and Nalebuff (1991). In his experiment, Axelrod set up a computer tournament in which pairs of contestants repeated the two-person Prisoner's Dilemma game 200 times. He invited contestants to submit strategies, and paired each entry with each other entry. For each move, players received three points for mutual cooperation and one point for mutual defection. In cases where one player defected while the other cooperated, the former received five points while the latter received nothing. Fourteen of the entries were from people who had published research articles on game theory or the Prisoner's Dilemma. The tit-for-tat strategy (submitted by Anatol Rapoport, a mathematics professor at the University of Toronto), the simplest of all submitted programs, won the tournament. Axelrod repeated the tournament with more participants and once again, Rapoport's tit-for-tat was the winning strategy (Dixit and Nalebuff 1991).

Axelrod's research emphasized the importance of minimizing echo effects in an environment of mutual power. Although a single defection may be successful when analyzed for its direct effect, it also can set off a long string of recriminations and counter-recriminations, and, when it does, both sides suffer. In such an analysis, tit-for-tat may be seen as a punishment strategy (sometimes called a *trigger strategy*) that can produce a supportive collusive pricing strategy in a non-cooperative game. Lal's (1990a) analysis of price promotions over time in a competitive environment suggests that price promotions between national firms (say Coke and Pepsi) can be interpreted as a long-run strategy by these firms to defend market shares from possible encroachments by store brands. Some anecdotal evidence from the beverage industry in support of such collusive strategies is available. For example, a *Consumer Reports* article (Lal 1990b) noted that in the soft-drink market, where Coca Cola and PepsiCo account for two-thirds of all sales, "[s]urveys have shown that many soda drinkers tend to buy whichever brand is on special. Under the Coke and Pepsi bottlers' calendar marketing arrangements, a store agrees to feature only one brand at any given time. Coke bottlers happened to have signed such agreements for 26 weeks and Pepsi bottlers the other 26 weeks!" In other markets, such as ketchup, cereals, and cookies (Lal 1990b), similar arrangements can be found. Rao (1991) provides further support for the above finding and shows that when the competition is asymmetric, the national brand promotes to ensure that the private label does not try to attract consumers away from the national brand.

19.3.2 Behavioral considerations in games

We now step back and ask if our game theory models provide us with a sufficiently accurate representation of actual behavior. Behavioral considerations can be important for both static games and for repeated games, where relationships develop between players, leading to subtle and important consequences.

The assumptions we laid out at the beginning of Section 19.2—rational players and the infinite belief hierarchy—can sometimes seem far-fetched when we consider real human interactions. Given that the underlying assumptions may not be satisfied, are the predicted results of the games reasonable? When describing research on human behavior in games, Camerer (2003) states,

> game theory students often ask: "This theory is interesting ... but do people actually play this way?' The answer, not surprisingly, is mixed. There are no interesting games in which subjects reach a predicted equilibrium immediately. And there are no games so complicated that subjects do not converge in the direction of equilibrium (perhaps quite close to it) with enough experience in the lab. (Camerer 2003: 20)

Camerer and his colleagues have found that to accurately predict human behavior in games, the mathematics of game theory must often be merged with theories of behavior based on models of social utility (e.g., the concept of fairness), limitations on reasoning, and learning over time. The result of this merger is the fast-growing field of behavioral economics and, more specifically, behavioral game theory.

Behavioral game theory can shed light on a problem we saw in Section 19.2.4: when there is more than one equilibrium in a game, it is difficult to predict player behavior. Psychologists and behavioral game theorists have tested how player behavior evolves over many repetitions of such games. According to Binmore (2007), over repeated trials of games with multiple equilibria played in a laboratory, the players' behavior evolves towards particular equilibria because of a combination of chance and "historical events". These events include the particular roles ascribed to each player in the game (e.g., an employer and a worker, equal partners, etc.), the social norms that the subjects bring into the laboratory, and, most importantly, the competitive strategies that each player has experienced during previous trials of the game. Binmore also describes how, by manipulating these historical events, players can be directed to non-equilibrium "focal points", although when left to their own devices players inevitably move back to a Nash equilibrium.

Behavioral game theorists have also conducted laboratory tests of the specific pricing games that we describe in this chapter. For example, Duwfenberg and Gneezy (2000) simulated the Bertrand game of Section 19.2.1 by asking students in groups of 2, 3, or 4 to bid a number from 2 to 100. The student with the lowest bid in the group won a prize that was proportional to the size of that student's bid. Therefore, the experiment is equivalent to the one-period Bertrand pricing game of Section 19.2.1, in that the lowest price (or "bid" in the experiment) captures the entire market. This bid–reward process was repeated 10 times, with the participants in each group randomized between each of the 10 rounds to prevent collusive behavior—as described in the previous section of this chapter—that may be generated in repeated games with the same players.

No matter how many competitors, the Nash equilibrium in this game is for all players to bid 2, which is equivalent to pricing at marginal cost in the Bertrand game. Duwfenberg and Gneezy found that when their experiments involved two players, however, the bids were consistently higher than 2 (over two rounds of ten trials each, the average bid was 38, and the average winning bid was 26). For larger groups of 3 and 4, the initial rounds also saw bids substantially higher than the Nash equilibrium value of 2, but by the tenth round the bids did converge towards 2.

Camerer (2003) describes hundreds of experiments that demonstrate how actual player behavior can deviate from the equilibrium behavior predicted by classical, mathematical game theory. He also shows how behavioral economists have gone a step further, to explicitly test the accuracy of behavioral explanations for these deviations, such as bounded rationality or a preference for fairness.

A great majority of experiments conducted by behavioral game theorists involve experimental subjects under controlled conditions. Of course, actual pricing decisions are not made by individuals in laboratories, but by individuals or groups of people in firms, who are subject to a variety of (sometimes conflicting) financial and social incentives. Armstrong and Huck (2010) discuss the extent to which these experiments may be used to extrapolate to firm behavior. An alternative to laboratory experiments is an empirical approach, to observe actual pricing behavior by firms and compare those prices with predictions made by game theory models. We will return to the question of game theory's applicability, and see an example of this empirical approach, in Section 19.3.6. In addition, Özer and Zheng (Chapter 20) discuss many issues related to behavioral game theory.

19.3.3 State-dependent dynamic pricing games

State-dependent dynamic pricing games are a generalization of repeated games, in which the current period payoff may be a function of the history of the game.

DEFINITION 9 In a dynamic game, a state variable is a quantity that (i) defines the state of nature; (ii) depends on the decision or control variables; and (iii) impacts future payoffs (e.g., sales or profitability).

DEFINITION 10 In a state-dependent dynamic game, there is an explicit link between the periods, and past actions influence the payoffs in the current period.

In other words, pricing actions today will have an impact on future sales as well as sales today. We are taught early in life about the necessity to plan ahead. Present decisions affect future events by making certain opportunities available, precluding others, and altering the costs of still others. If present decisions do not affect future opportunities, the planning problem is trivial; one need only make the best decision for the present. The rest of this section deals with solving dynamic pricing problems where the periods are physically linked while considering the impact of competition.

Table 19.7 Static versus dynamic pricing example

	Static	Dynamic
Period 1 Equilibrium price	$2.00	$1.85
Period 2 Equilibrium price	$1.90	$1.80

In their pioneering work, Rao and Bass (1985) consider dynamic pricing under competition where the dynamics relate primarily to cost reductions through experience curve effects. This implies that firms realize lower product costs with increases in cumulative production. It is shown that with competition, dynamic pricing strategies dominate myopic pricing strategies.

Table 19.7 illustrates the impact of dynamic pricing under competition relative to a static, two-period competitive game.

In other words, while a static game may suggest an equilibrium price of, say, $2.00 per unit for a widget in the first period and $1.90 in the second period, a dynamic game would recommend a price that is less than $2.00 (say, $1.85) in period 1 and even lower than $1.90 (say, $1.80) in period 2. This is because a lower price in the first period would increase sales in that initial period, thus increasing cumulative production, which, in turn, would reduce the marginal cost in the second period by more than the amount realized under a static game. This allows for an even lower price in the second period. In such a setting, prices in each period are the control (or decision) variables, and cumulative sales at the beginning of each period would be considered a state variable that affects future marginal cost and, hence, future profitability.

Another pricing challenge involving state dependence is the management of *reference prices*. A reference price is an anchoring level formed by customers, based on the pricing environment. Consider P&G's value pricing strategy discussed earlier in the chapter. In such a setting, given the corresponding stable cost to a retailer from the manufacturer, should competing retailers also employ an everyday low pricing strategy or should they follow a High–Low pricing pattern? In addition, under what conditions would a High–Low pricing policy be optimal? The answer may depend upon the impact reference prices have on customer purchase behavior. One process for reference-price formation is the exponentially smoothed averaging of past observed prices, where more recent prices are weighted more than less recent prices (Winer 1986):

$$r_t = \alpha r_{t-1} + (1 - \alpha)p_{t-1}, \ 0 \le \alpha < 1,$$

where r_t is the reference price in period t, r_{t-1} is the reference price in the previous period, and p_{t-1} is the retail price in the previous period.

If $\alpha = 0$, the reference price in period t equals the observed price in period $t-1$. As α increases, r_t becomes increasingly dependent on past prices. Thus, α can be regarded as a memory parameter, with $\alpha = 0$ corresponding to a one-period memory. Consider a group of frequently purchased consumer brands that are partial substitutes. Research (Winer 1986; Greenleaf 1995; Putler 1992; Briesch et al. 1997; Kalyanaram and Little 1994) suggests that demand for a brand depends on not only the brand price but also whether that brand price is greater than the reference price (a perceived loss) or is less than the reference price (a perceived gain). It turns out that the responses to gains and losses relative to the reference price are asymmetric. First, a gain would increase sales and a loss would decrease sales. Secondly, in some product categories, the absolute value of the impact of a gain is greater than that of a loss, and in yet other categories, it is the opposite. In this scenario, since past and present prices would impact future reference prices, prices can be considered control variables and consumer reference prices would be state variables, which then impacts future sales. In a competitive scenario, this might lead to a dynamic pricing policy, and this rationale differs from other possible explanations for dynamic pricing, such as heterogeneity in information among consumers (Varian 1980), transfer of inventory holding costs from retailers to consumers (Blattberg et al. 1981), brands with lower brand loyalty having more to gain from dynamic pricing (Raju et al. 1990), and a mechanism for a punishment strategy (Lal 1990b).

Consider a dynamic version of the one-period model of Section 19.2.3. In this version, a brand's sales are affected by its own price, the price of the competing brand, and the reference price. Demand for brand i, $i = 1, 2$, in time t is given by:

$$d_{it} = a_i - b_i p_{it} + c_i p_{jt} + g_i(r_{it} - p_{it})$$

where $g_i = \delta$ if $r_{it} > p_{it}$, else $g_i = \gamma$.

Ignoring fixed costs, the objective function for each competitor i is to maximize the discounted profit stream over a long-term horizon—that is:

$$\max_{pit} \sum_{t=1}^{\infty} \beta^t (p_{it} - c) d_{it}$$

where,

t = time

β = discount rate (between 0 and 1)

p_{it} = price

c = marginal cost

d_{it} = demand for competitor i's product in time t

This problem can be solved using a dynamic programming approach (Bertsekas 1987) in a competitive setting, where each competitor maximizes not just today's profits but today's profit *plus* all the future profits by taking into consideration how today's pricing would impact tomorrow's reference price and, hence, tomorrow's profitability (Kopalle et al. 1996).

Of course, each player cannot ignore the actions of competing players when solving this optimization problem, and we are interested in the players' equilibrium behavior. The specific type of equilibrium we use here is the subgame perfect equilibrium we defined for the Stackelberg game in Section 19.2.5, but now applied to a more general dynamic game (also see Fudenberg and Tirole 1991). That is, a strategy is a subgame perfect equilibrium if it represents a Nash equilibrium of every subgame of the original dynamic game.

Now we discuss the results of this model and distinguish two possible cases. One is where customers care more about gains than losses—that is the impact of a unit gain is greater than that of a unit loss ($\delta > \gamma$). Such was the case in Greenleaf's (1995) analysis of peanut butter scanner data. In such a situation, in a monopoly setting Greenleaf (1995) finds that the subgame perfect Nash equilibrium solution is to have a cyclical (High–Low) pricing

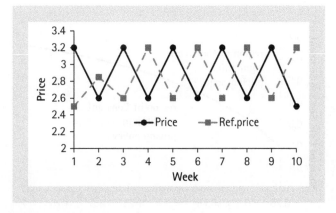

FIGURE 19.3 Equilibrium prices over time

strategy. In a competitive setting, Kopalle et al. (1996) extend this result and show that the dynamic equilibrium pricing strategy is High–Low as shown in Figure 19.3.

The other case is where customers are more loss averse (e.g., as found by Putler (1992) in the case of eggs)—that is, the impact of a loss is greater than that of a corresponding gain ($\gamma > \delta$). It turns out that the Nash equilibrium solution is to maintain a constant pricing policy for both competitors. These results hold in an oligopoly consisting of N brands as well. Table 19.8 shows the two-period profitability of two firms in a duopoly. The first and second numbers in each cell refer to the profit of Firm 1 and of Firm 2 over two periods. For both firms, constant pricing is the dominant strategy, and the Nash equilibrium is a constant price in both periods:

In the more general case, where some consumers (say, segment 1) are loss averse ($\gamma_1 > \delta_1$) and others (say, segment 2) are gain seeking ($\delta_2 > \gamma_2$), Kopalle et al. (1996) find that in a competitive environment, a sufficient condition for a cyclical pricing policy to be a subgame perfect Nash equilibrium is that the size of the gain seeking segment (i.e., non-loss-averse) segment is not too low. As seen in Figure 19.4, as the relative level of loss aversion in segment 1 increases, that is $(\gamma_1 - \delta_1)/(\delta_2 - \gamma_2)$ increases, the size of the gain seeking segment needs to be larger for High–Low pricing to be an equilibrium.

		Firm 2 Chooses...	
		Constant Pricing	High-Low Pricing
Firm 1 Chooses...	Constant Pricing	95, 95	100, 90
	High-Low Pricing	90, 100	90, 90

Table 19.8 Expected pay-offs for the reference price game. Entries in each cell are pay-off to 1, 2

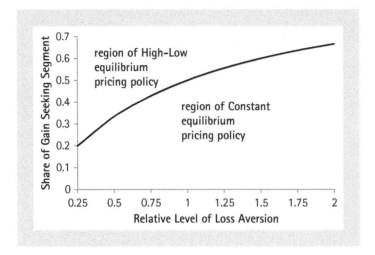

FIGURE 19.4 High-Low equilibrium pricing policy and share of gain seeking segment

Finally, note that reference prices may also be influenced by the prices of competing brands. The equilibrium solutions of High–Low dynamic pricing policies hold under alternative reference-price formation processes, such as the reference brand context, where the current period's reference price is the current price of the brand bought in the last period.

19.3.4 Open- versus closed-loop equilibria

Two general kinds of Nash equilibria can be used to develop competing pricing strategies in dynamic games that are state-dependent: open loop and closed loop (Fudenberg and Tirole 1991).

DEFINITION 11 In a state-dependent dynamic game, an equilibrium is called an open-loop equilibrium if the strategies in the equilibrium strategy profile are functions of time alone.

In a state-dependent dynamic game, an equilibrium is called a closed-loop or a feedback equilibrium if strategies in the equilibrium strategy profile are functions of the history of the game, that is, functions of the state variables.

The notation in dynamic models must be adapted to whether open- or closed-loop strategies are used. Let S_{it} represent the ith state variable at time t, and let P_c denote the pricing strategy of competitor c. The notation $P_c(t)$ indicates an open-loop strategy, while a function $P_c(S_{it}, t)$ is a closed-loop strategy.

With open-loop strategies, competitors commit at the outset to particular time paths of pricing levels, and if asked at an intermediate point to reconsider their strategies, they will not change them. In an open-loop analysis of dynamic pricing in a duopoly, Chintagunta and Rao (1996) show that the brand with the higher preference level charges a higher price. In addition, they find that myopic price levels are higher than the corresponding dynamic prices. The authors also provide some empirical evidence in this regard by using longitu-

Table 19.9 Open-loop equilibrium prices versus static model results

Retail margin	Brand	Dynamic model	Static model
40%	Yoplait	$0.46	$1.83
40%	Dannon	$0.61	$1.08
50%	Yoplait	$0.39	$1.72
50%	Dannon	$0.55	$1.05

dinal purchase data obtained from A. C. Nielsen scanner panel data on the purchases of yogurt in the Springfield, Missouri market over a two-year period. Their analysis focuses on the two largest, competing brands, Yoplait (6 oz) and Dannon (8 oz). The empirical analysis shows that (i) the dynamic competitive model fits the data better than a static model, and (ii) the preference level for Dannon is noticeably higher than that for Yoplait. The equilibrium retail prices per unit are given in Table 19.9 under two different margin assumptions at the retailer.

It turns out that the actual prices were fairly close to the equilibrium prices generated by the dynamic model, while the equilibrium static model prices are inflated relative to both the dynamic model as well as reality. Further, the higher preference level for Dannon is reflected in the higher pricing for the corresponding brand in the dynamic model results. The static model essentially ignores the evolution of consumer preference over time due to past purchases.

One drawback of open-loop Nash equilibria is that fixed, open-loop strategies cannot be modified on the basis of, say, current market share. Pricing managers, however, are unlikely to put their strategies on automatic pilot and ignore challenges that threaten their market positions. There are plenty of instances of companies and brands responding to competitive threats to their market shares—for example, the "leapfrog" pricing of Coke and Pepsi at stores, where Coke is on sale one week and Pepsi on sale the next. Closed-loop equilibria are more realistic than open-loop strategies because they do allow strategies to adjust to the current state of the market. Closed-loop equilibria, however, are harder to solve (Chintagunta and Rao 1996), and their analysis may require sophisticated mathematical techniques and approximations. For example, in an airline revenue management context, Gallego and Hu (2008) develop a game theoretic formulation of dynamically pricing perishable capacity (such as airplane seats) over a finite horizon. Since such problems are generally intractable, the authors provide sufficient conditions for the existence of open-loop and closed-loop Nash equilibria of the corresponding dynamic differential game by using a linear functional approximation approach to the solution. Dudey (1992) and Martinez-de-Albeniz and Talluri (2010) also describe dynamic revenue management games.

19.3.5 A dynamic Stackelberg pricing game

The Stackelberg game defined in Section 19.2.5 has been applied to the sequential pricing process involving manufacturers and retailers. Initial research on this problem has focused on static Stackelberg games (Choi 1991; McGuire and Staelin 1983; Lee and Staelin 1997; Kim and Staelin 1999). In this game, the manufacturers maximize their respective brand profits, while the retailer maximizes its category profits, which include profits from sales of the manufacturer's brand as well as other brands in that category. The decision variables are the wholesale and retail prices, where the manufacturer decides the wholesale price first and then the retailer determines the retail price. The models described in the references above, however, do not include promotional dynamics over time.

To see how promotional dynamics can affect the game, consider a manufacturer that sells a single product (product 1) to a retailer. The retailer sells both product 1 and a competing brand, product 2, to consumers. Let $\bar{p}_k$ be the retailer's regular, undiscounted price of product $k = 1, 2$, and let p_{kt} be the retailer's chosen price in period t. A promotion, a temporary price reduction in product k, can lead to an immediate increase in sales, which we will capture in the demand function d_{kt} defined below. The promotion, however, may also have a negative impact on sales in future periods because consumers buy more than they need in period t (stockpiling), the discount may reduce brand equity, and/or the discount may reduce the product's reference price. We represent this effect of promotions in future periods with the term l_{kt}, $k = 1, 2$:

$$l_{kt} = \alpha l_{k,t-1} + (1 - \alpha)(\bar{p}_k - p_{kt}),\ 0 \leq \alpha \leq 1.$$

We use l_{kt} in the following retail-level demand function, to capture this lagged effect of promotions on both baseline sales and price sensitivity. For $(j,k) = (1,2)$ or $(2,1)$,

$$d_{kt} = a_k - (\bar{b}_k + b_k l_{kt})p_{kt} + (\bar{c}_k + c_k l_{jt})p_{jt} - g_k l_{kt}. \tag{2}$$

The second term is the direct impact of product k's price on demand, where the price sensitivity is adjusted by the lagged effect of promotion, l_{kt}. The third term is the impact of product j's price on product k sales, adjusted by the effect of previous promotions for product j. The last term is the lagged effect of product k promotions on baseline sales of product k (baseline sales are sales that would occur when there are no promotions).

Now we describe the objective functions of the manufacturer and retailer . Within each period t the manufacturer first sets a wholesale price w_{1t} for product 1. Given marginal product cost c_1 and discount rate β (and ignoring fixed costs), the manufacturer's objective over a finite period $t = 1 \ldots T$ is,

$$\max_{w_{1t}} \sum_{t=1}^{T} \beta^t (w_{1t} - c_1) d_{1t}.$$

Note that d_{1t} depends upon the prices p_{1t} and p_{2t} that are chosen by the retailer in each period t after the manufacturer sets its wholesale price . The retailer's objective is,

$$\max_{p_{1t}, p_{2t}} \sum_{t=1}^{T} \beta^t \sum_{k=1}^{2} (p_{kt} - w_{kt}) d_{1t}.$$

Kopalle et al. (1999) describe a more general version of this game, with any number of retailers, any number of competing brands, and controls for seasonality, features, and displays. Their model also has an explicit term for the stockpiling effect, although when the model was fit to data, the direct stockpiling effect was not significant. Finally, the model in Kopalle et al. (1999) differs in a few technical details, for example the expressions above are in terms of the logarithm of demand and price.

This interaction between manufacturer and retailer is an example of a closed-loop, dynamic Stackelberg game.

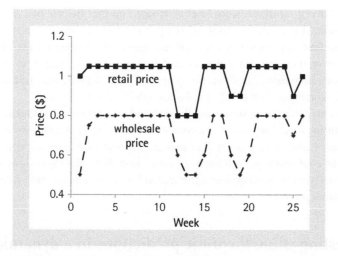

FIGURE 19.5 Equilibrium wholesale and retail prices

DEFINITION 12 In a dynamic Stackelberg game, the leader and the follower make decisions in each period and over time based on the history of the game until the current period.

In the one-period Stackelberg game of Section 19.2.5, the leader (in this case, the manufacturer) only anticipates the single response from the follower (the retailer). In this dynamic game, the leader must anticipate the retailer's reactions in all future periods. Also, in the one-period game the follower simply responds to the leader's choice—the decision is not strategic. In this dynamic game, when the retailer sets its price in period t, the retailer must anticipate the manufacturer's response in future periods. As in our previous dynamic games, one can solve this game using Bellman's (1957) principle of optimality and backward induction. This procedure determines the manufacturer's and retailer's equilibrium pricing strategies over time.

Before solving for the manufacturer's and retailers' strategies, Kopalle et al. (1999) estimate the parameters of the demand model, using 124 weeks of A. C. Nielsen store-level data for liquid dishwashing detergent. The results suggest that when a brand increases the use of promotions, it reduces its baseline sales; increases price sensitivity, thus making it harder to maintain margins; and diminishes its ability to use deals to take share from competing brands. Figure 19.5 shows a typical equilibrium solution for manufacturer's wholesale prices and the corresponding brand's retail prices over time in the game.

Kopalle et al. (1999) find that many other brands have flat equilibrium price paths, indicating that for these brands, the manufacturer and retailer should curtail promotion because the immediate sales increase arising from the deal is more than eliminated by future losses due to the lagged effects of promotions.

In practice, estimates of baseline sales and responses to promotions often ignore past promotional activity. In other words, the lagged promotional effects l_{jt} and l_{kt} in demand function (2) are ignored. To determine the improvement in profits due to using a dynamic model rather than a static model, one must compute the profits a brand would have had, assuming that it had estimated a model with no dynamic effects. Comparing the static and dynamic Stackelberg solutions, Kopalle et al. (1999) find that the use of a dynamic model leads to a predicted increase in profits of 15.5 percent for one brand and 10.7 percent for another. These findings further suggest that managers can increase profits by as much as 7–31 percent over their current practices and indicate the importance of balancing the tradeoff between increasing sales that are generated from a given discount in the *current period* and the corresponding effect of reducing sales in *future periods*.

Promotions may stem from skimming the demand curve (Farris and Quelch 1987), from the retailer shifting inventory cost to the consumer (Blattberg et al. 1981), from competition between national and store brands (Lal 1990a; Rao 1991), or from asymmetry in price response about a reference price (Greenleaf 1995). Kopalle et al. (1999) show that another explanation for dynamic pricing exists: the tradeoff between a promotion's contemporaneous and dynamic effects.

19.3.6 Testing game theoretic predictions in a dynamic pricing context: how useful is a game theory model?

Prior research has illustrated some of the challenges of predicting competitive response. For example, a change by a firm in marketing instrument X may evoke a competitive change in marketing instrument Y (Kadiyali et al. 2000; Putsis and Dhar 1998). Another challenge is that firms may "over-react" or "under-react" to competitive moves (Leeflang and Wittink 1996). Furthermore, it is unclear whether managers actually employ the strategic thinking that game theoretic models suggest. Research by Montgomery et al. (2005) indicates that managers often do not consider competitors' reactions when deciding on their own moves, though they are more likely to do so for major, visible decisions, particularly those pertaining to pricing. Therefore, it is reasonable to ask whether game theory models can be useful when planning pricing strategies and whether they can accurately predict competitor responses. Here we describe research that examines whether the pricing policies of retailers and manufacturers match the pricing policies that a game theory model predicts. The research also examines whether it is important to make decisions using the game theory model rather than a simpler model of competitor behavior, for example, one that simply extrapolates from previous behavior to predict competitor responses.

In one research study, Ailawadi et al. (2005) use a dynamic game theory model to consider the response to P&G's "value pricing" strategy, mentioned at the beginning of this chapter. The high visibility of P&G's move to value pricing was an opportunity to see whether researchers can predict the response of competing national brands and retailers to a major policy change by a market leader. The researchers empirically estimate the demand function that drives the model, substitute the demand parameters into the game theoretic model, and generate predictions of competitor and retailer responses. To the extent their predictions correspond to reality, they will have identified a methodological approach to predicting competitive behavior that can be used to guide managerial decision making.

Ailawadi et al. (2005) base their game theoretic model on the Manufacturer–Retailer Stackelberg framework similar to that of Kopalle et al. (1999), described in Section 19.3.5. Their model is significantly more comprehensive in that it endogenizes (1) the national brand competitor's price and promotion decisions; (2) the retailer's price decision for P&G, the national brand competitor, and the private label; (3) the retailer's private-label promo-

Table 19.10 Predictive ability of a dynamic game theoretic model versus a statistical model competition dynamics

	Dynamic game theoretic model			Statistical model of competition dynamics		
	Deal amount (%)	Wholesale price (%)	Retail price (%)	Deal amount (%)	Wholesale price (%)	Retail price (%)
% directionally correct predictions	78	71	78	52	48	55
% directionally correct predictions when actual values increased	79	50	87	46	25	64
% directionally correct predictions when actual value decreased	77	93	65	60	67	36

tion decision; and (4) the retailer's forward-buying decision for P&G and the national brand competitor. This model of the *process* by which profit-maximizing agents make decisions includes *temporal* response phenomena and decision making. In this sense, it is a "dynamic structural model". Such models are particularly well suited to cases of major policy change because they are able to predict how agents adapt their decisions to a new "regime" than are reduced-form models that attempt to extrapolate from the past (Keane 1997). However, they are more complex and present researchers with the thorny question of how all-encompassing to make the model.

To develop their model, Ailawadi et al. (2005) use the scanner database of the Dominick's grocery chain in Chicago and wholesale-price and trade-deal data for the Chicago market from Leemis Marketing Inc. Data were compiled for nine product categories in which P&G is a player. Dominick's sold a private label brand in six of these nine categories throughout the period of analysis. The number of brands for which both wholesale and retail data are available varies across categories, ranging from three to six. In total, there were 43 brands across the nine categories (9 P&G brands, 28 national brand competitors, and 6 private label competitors).

As seen in Table 19.10, their results show that a game theoretic model combined with strong empirics does have predictive power in being able to predict directional changes in wholesale deal amounts given to the retailer by the manufacturer, wholesale price, and retail price. The predictive ability of the directional changes ranges from 50 percent to 93 percent. The table shows that of the times when the game theoretic model predicted that competitors would increase wholesale deal amounts, competitors actually increased it 79 percent of the time. This compares with correct predictions of 46 percent for the statistical model of competitor behavior, which essentially is a statistical extrapolation of past behavior. The predictions of another benchmark model, where the retailer is assumed to be non-strategic, does no better with 46 percent correct predictions.

Their model's prescription of how competitors should change wholesale price and trade dealing and how the retailer should change retail price in response to P&G's value pricing strategy is a significant predictor of the changes that competitors and Dominick's in the Chicago market actually made. This suggests that, in the context of a major pricing policy change, managers' actions are more consistent with strategic competitive reasoning than with an extrapolation of past reactions into the future or with ignoring retailer reaction.

In the wake of its "Value Pricing" strategy, it turns out that P&G suffered a 16 percent loss in market share across 24 categories (Ailawadi et al. 2001). If P&G's managers had built a dynamic game theoretic model, they might have been able to predict (at least direction-ally) the categories in which the competitors would follow suit versus retaliate. This could have helped P&G to adopt a more surgical approach to its value pricing strategy instead of a blanket strategy that cut across many categories.

The above test was for a major policy change and the findings support the view of Montgomery et al. (2005) that when faced with highly visible and major decisions, especially with respect to pricing, managers are more likely to engage in strategic competitive thinking. It also supports the premise that when the agents involved are adjusting to a change in regime, structural models are preferable to reduced-form models. Other approaches such as the reaction function approach (Leeflang and Wittink 1996) or a simplified game theoretic model (for example, assuming that the retailer is non-strategic and simply uses a constant markup rule for setting retail prices) may have better predictive ability for ongoing decisions and week-to-week or month-to-month reactions where managers are less likely to engage in competitive reasoning.

19.4 IMPLICATIONS FOR PRACTICE

Firms have many opportunities to increase profitability by improving the way they manage price. Many need better systems, such as enterprise software to manage strategy effectively and optimize execution to support their decisions. Vendors provide tools that monitor customer demand and measure how price is perceived compared to other retailers, helping to optimize pricing. Assortment and space-optimization tools help retailers manage their merchandise and shelf space, but these tools lack sophisticated predictive analytics. Although retailers can access a range of data, such as point-of-sale, packaged goods product information, competitor prices, weather, demographics, and syndicated market data, they do not have the tools they need to integrate all these data sources to manage strategies and optimize price in a competitive setting. In particular, current pricing systems do not incorporate the strategic impact of pricing changes—the dynamics described by game theory. The flowchart of Figure 19.6 is adapted from Kopalle et al. (2008), and envisions a pricing system with modules that incorporate data-driven competitive analysis. In the diagram, the "Strategic Framework" module contains the underlying model of competition, and is driven by data on competitors.

The analysis conducted in the Strategic Framework module would focus on a variety of questions, guided by the models introduced in this chapter. In Table 19.11 we lay out the frameworks, using this chapter's taxonomy of models. For the simultaneous, one-shot

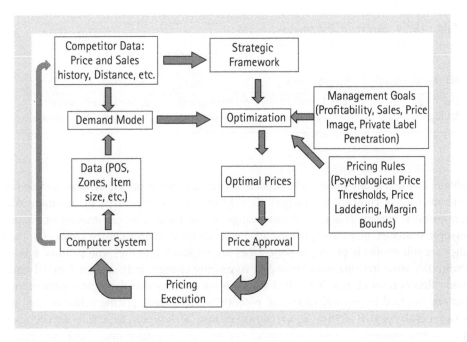

FIGURE 19.6 Pricing algorithm

pricing games in Box 1 (Nash games), the impact of product differentiation, and whether the products are substitutes or complements become important issues to consider. As discussed earlier in the chapter, there are advantages of moving first, thereby changing the game from a simultaneous to a sequential game. For the one-period sequential (Stackelberg) game in Box 2, while the questions for Box 1 are still relevant, it is also important for a firm to recognize whether it is a leader or follower. If it is a leader, it should anticipate the followers' reactions to its moves. If a follower, a firm should determine if it is advantageous to become a leader (sometimes it is not), and consider how.

Box 1's questions also apply to Box 3, which refers to simultaneous games over multiple periods. Here firms should also consider the degree to which their competitors take a strategic, forward-looking view. In addition, recall that in a retail application, the optimal strategy is determined by the degree to which reference prices influence customer purchasing behavior, as well as the strength of loss aversion among customers. Finally, we saw that when players repeat a game over multiple periods, trigger strategies (such as tit-for-tat) may be important. In Box 4, leaders in dynamic Stackelberg games should consider the impact of promotions on followers' actions and on future profits. In contrast to the single-period game, followers cannot ignore the future; they should consider the impact of their actions on leaders' actions in later periods.

For all of these environments (Boxes 1–4), fruitful application of game theory to pricing requires that a firm understand its competition's pricing strategy. For retailers in particular, the impact of competition has been well documented (Lal and Rao 1997; Moorthy 2005; Bolton and Shankar 2003; Shankar and Bolton 2004), but a lack of knowledge of their competitors' prices and strategies hinders retailers. Such knowledge is usually difficult to

Table 19.11 Strategic frameworks

Number of periods	Timing of actions	
	Simultaneous	Sequential
One	**Box 1:** Static (one-shot) Nash games	**2:** Stackelberg games
Multiple	**3:** Repeated and dynamic games	**4:** Dynamic Stackelberg games

obtain, and that is one reason why firms either (1) implement pricing systems that do not attempt to take competitor strategies directly into account (perhaps by assuming that competitors' current actions will not change in the future); or (2) implement simple, myopic strategies, given competitors' actions. If all firms in an industry choose (1), then they are still implicitly playing a game—they are responding to their competitors' actions indirectly, using information obtained by measuring changes in their own demand functions. Recent research has shown that strategies based on models that ignore competitors' actions can lead to unpredictable, and potentially suboptimal, pricing behavior (e.g., see Cooper et al. 2009). If all firms in an industry choose (2), however, the results depend upon the myopic strategy. If firms only match the lowest competitor price (and, say, ignore product differentiation), then firms simply drive prices down. There is a stream of research that shows that firms in an oligopoly who choose the "best response" to the current prices of their competitors will result in a sequence of prices that converges to the unique Nash equilibrium from the simultaneous game (Gallego et al. 2006).

The models and frameworks presented in this chapter are most useful when a firm can understand and predict its competitors' pricing strategies. With improving price visibility on the web and masses of data collected by retail scanners, there is much more data available about competitors. Market intelligence services and data scraping services collect and organize such information. Examples include QL2.com for the travel industries and Information Resources Inc. for the consumer packaged goods industry. In the retailing world, some firms use hand-held devices to track competitors' prices of key items.

It is difficult, however, to distill raw data into an understanding of competitor strategy. In some industries, conferences can serve to disseminate price strategy information. In the airline industry, for example, revenue management scientists attend the AGIFORS conference (sponsored by the Airline Group of the International Federation of Operational Research Societies) and share information about their pricing systems (this is not collusion—participants do not discuss prices, pricing tactics, or pricing strategies but do discuss models and algorithms). Consider another example from outside the airline industry: when one major firm implemented a revenue management system, they were concerned that their competitors would interpret their targeted local discounting as a general price "drop" and that a damaging price war would ensue. A senior officer of the firm visited various industry conferences to describe revenue management at a high level to help prevent this misconception on the part of the competitors. In the abstract, such information may be used to design pricing systems that are truly strategic.

Of course, game theory motivates us to ask whether providing information about our pricing system to a competitor will improve our competitive position. There are certainly games where knowledge shared between competitors can improve performance for both players: compare, for example, the one-shot Prisoner's Dilemma (with its equilibrium in which both "confess") with a repeated game in which competitors anticipate each others' strategies and settle into an equilibrium that is better for both.

In general, our hope is that this chapter will help nudge managers toward making analytics-based pricing decisions that take into account competitor behavior. Further, our view is that a significant barrier to the application of game theory to pricing is the extent to which mathematical and behavioral game theory, developed at the individual level, is not applicable to firm-level pricing decisions. In particular, a pricing decision is the outcome of group dynamics within the firm, which can be influenced by a range of factors that are different from factors that drive individual behavior. Recall from this chapter the research on individual behavior in laboratory pricing games (e.g., Duwfenberg and Gneezy 2000; Camerer 2003) as well as one attempt to empirically validate a game theory model of pricing at the firm level (Ailawadi et al. 2005). There has been little research in between these extremes. More work is needed to identify the general characteristics of firms' strategic pricing behavior, and we believe that there is a significant opportunity for research to bridge this gap.

References

Ailawadi, K., Kopalle, P. K., and Neslin, S. A. (2005) "Predicting Competitive Response to a Major Policy Change: Combining Game Theoretic and Empirical Analyses", *Marketing Science* 24/1: 12–24.

—— Lehmann, D. R., and Neslin, S. A. (2001) "Market Response to a Major Policy Change in the Marketing Mix: Learning from Procter & Gamble's Value Pricing Strategy", *Journal of Marketing* 65/January: 44–61.

Armstrong, M. and Huck, S. (2010) "Behavioral Economics as Applied to Firms: A Primer", CESifo Working Paper Series No. 2937, http://ssrn.com/abstract=1553645, accessed February 9, 2012.

Associated Press (2007) "British Airways and Korean Airlines Fined in Fuel Collusion", *The New York Times* August 2.

Aumann, R. (1976) "Agreeing to Disagree", *The Annals of Statistics* 4/6: 1236–9.

Axelrod, R. (1984) *The Evolution of Cooperation*. New York: Basic Books.

—— and Hamilton, W. D. (1981) "The Evolution of Cooperation", *Science* 211/4489: 1390–6.

Bellman, R. (1957) *Dynamic Programming*. Princeton, NJ: Princeton University Press.

Bertsekas, D. P. (1987) *Dynamic Programming: Deterministic and Stochastic Models*. Englewood Cliffs, NJ: Prentice Hall.

Binmore, K. (2007) *Does Game Theory Work?* Cambridge, MA: The MIT Press.

Blattberg, R. C., Eppen, G. D., and Lieberman, J. (1981) "Price-Induced Patterns of Competition", *Marketing Science* 8/Fall: 291–309.

Bolton, R. N. and Shankar, V. (2003) "An Empirically Derived Taxonomy of Retailer Pricing and Promotion Strategies", *Journal of Retailing* 79/4: 213–24.

Briesch, R. A., Krishnamurthi, L., Mazumdar, T., and Raj, S. P. (1997) "A Comparative Analysis of Reference Price Models", *Journal of Consumer Research* 24/2: 202–14.

BTNonline.com (2008) "Continental Plans UAL Joint Venture, Star Membership", June 19, http://www.btnonline.com/businesstravelnews/headlines/article_display.jsp?vnu_content_id=1003818864, accessed May 24, 2010.

Cachon, G. P. and Netessine, S. (2006) "Game Theory in Supply Chain Analysis", in Paul Gray (ed.), *TutORials in Operations Research*. Hanover, MD: INFORMS, 200–33.

Camerer, C. (2003) *Behavioral Game Theory*. Princeton, NJ: Princeton University Press.

Chintagunta, P. K. and Rao, V. R. (1996) "Pricing Strategies in a Dynamic Duopoly: A Differential Game Model", *Management Science* 42/11: 1501–14.

Choi, S. C. (1991) "Price Competition in a Channel Structure with a Common Retailer", *Marketing Science* 10/Fall: 271–96.

Cooper, W. L., Homem-de-Mello, T., and Kleywegt, A. J. (2009) "Learning and Pricing with Models that Do Not Explicitly Incorporate Competition". Working paper, School of Industrial and Systems Engineering, Georgia Institute of Technology, Atlanta, Georgia, http://www2.isye.gatech.edu/~anton/competitive.pdf, accessed February 9, 2012.

DOT (Department of Transportation) (2009) "Joint Application of Air Canada, The Austrian Group, British Midland Airways LTD, Continental Airlines, Inc., Deutsche Lufthansa AG, Polskie Linie Lotnicze LOT S.A., Scandinavian Airlines System, Swiss International Air Lines Ltd., TAP Air Portugal, United Airlines Inc. to Amend Order 2007-2-16 under 49 U.S. C. 41308 and 41309 so as to Approve and Confer Antitrust Immunity", Order: 2009-7-10, http://www.regulations.gov/fdmspublic/ContentViewer?objectId=09000064809eda55&disposition=attachment&contentType=pdf, accessed May 24, 2010.

d'Huart, O. (2010) *A Competitive Approach to Airline Revenue Management*. Unpublished Master's Thesis, Massachusetts Institute of Technology, Cambridge, MA.

Dixit, A. K. and Nalebuff, B. J. (1991) *Thinking Strategically: The Competitive Edge in Business, Politics, and Everyday Life*. New York: W. W. Norton & Company.

—— and Skeath, S. (1999) *Games of Strategy*. New York: W. W. Norton & Company.

Dudey, M. (1992) "Dynamic Edgeworth-Bertrand competition", *Quarterly Journal of Economics* 107: 1461–77.

Duwfenberg, M. and Gneezy, U. (2000) "Price Competition and Market Concentration: An Experimental Study", *International Journal of Industrial Organization*, 18: 7–22.

Farris, P. and Quelch, J. A. (1987) "In Defense of Price Promotions", MIT *Sloan Management Review* 29/Fall: 63–9.

Fudenberg, D. and Tirole, J. (1991) *Game Theory*. Cambridge, MA: The MIT Press.

Gallego, G. and Hu, M. (2008) "Dynamic Pricing of Perishable Assets Under Competition", *SSRN Working Paper*, http://ssrn.com/abstract=1308848, accessed February 9, 2012.

—— Huh, T., Kang, W., and Phillips, R. (2006) "Price Competition with the Attraction Demand Model: Existence of Unique Equilibrium and its Stability", *Manufacturing and Service Operations Management* 8: 359–75.

Gibbons, R. (1992) *Game Theory for Applied Economists*. Princeton, NJ: Princeton University Press.

Govindan, S. and Wilson, R. (2005) "Refinements of Nash equilibrium", in S. Durlauf and L. Blume (eds), *The New Palgrave Dictionary of Economics 2*. London: Palgrave Macmillan.

Greenleaf, E. A. (1995) "The Impact of Reference Price Effects on the Profitability of Price Promotions", *Marketing Science* 14/Winter: 82–104.

Harsanyi, J. (1967) "Games with Incomplete Information Played by Bayesian Players Parts I, II and III", *Management Science* 14/3,5,7: 159–82, 320–34, 486–502.

Jiang, H. and Pang, Z. (2011) "Network Capacity Management under Competition", *Comput. Optim. Appl.* 50: 287–326.

Kadiyali, V., Chintagunta, P., and Vilcassim, N. (2000) "A Manufacturer–Retailer Channel Interaction and Implications for Channel Power: An Empirical Investigation of Pricing in a Local Market", *Marketing Science* 19/2: 127–48.

Kalyanaram, G. and Little, J. D. C. (1994) "An Empirical Analysis of Latitude of Price Acceptance in Consumer Packaged Goods", *Journal of Consumer Research* 21/3: 408–18.

Keane, M. (1997) "Modeling Heterogeneity and State Dependence in Consumer Choice Behavior", *Journal of Business and Economic Statistics* 15/3: 310–27.

Kim, S. Y. and Staelin, R. (1999) "Manufacturer Allowances and Retailer Pass-Through Rates in a Competitive Environment", *Marketing Science* 18/1: 59–76.

Kopalle, P. K., Rao, A. G., and Assunção, J. L. (1996) "Asymmetric Reference Price Effects and Dynamic Pricing Policies", *Marketing Science* 15/1: 60–85.

—— Mela, C. F., and Marsh, L. (1999) "The Dynamic Effect of Discounting on Sales: Empirical Analysis and Normative Pricing Implications", *Marketing Science* 18/3: 317–32.

—— Biswas, D., Chintagunta, P. K., Fan, J., Pauwels, K., Ratchford, B., and Sills, J. (2009) "Retailer Pricing and Competitive Effects", *Journal of Retailing* 85: 56–70.

Lal, R. (1990a) "Price Promotions: Limiting Competitive Encroachment", *Marketing Science* 9/3: 247–62.

—— (1990b) "Manufacturer Trade Deals and Retail Price Promotions", *Journal of Marketing Research* 27/November: 428–44.

—— and Rao, R. C. (1997) "Supermarket Competition: The Case of Every Day Low Pricing", *Marketing Science* 16/1: 60–80.

Lee, E. and Staelin, R. (1997) "Vertical Strategic Interaction: Implications for Channel Pricing Strategy", *Marketing Science* 16/3: 185–207.

Lee, H. L., Padmanabhan, V., and Whang, S. (1997) "The Bullwhip Effect in Supply Chains", *MIT Sloan Management Review* 38/3: 93.

Leeflang, P. S. H. and Wittink, D. R. (1996) "Competitive Reaction Versus Consumer Response: Do Managers Overreact?" *International Journal of Research in Marketing* 13: 103–19.

McGuire, T. W. and Staelin, R. (1983) "An Industry Equilibrium Analysis of Downstream Vertical Integration", *Marketing Science* 2/2: 161–92.

Martinez-de-Albeniz, V. and Talluri, K. (2010) "Dynamic Price Competition with Fixed Capacities", Universitat Pompeu Fabra Department of Economics and Business, Working Paper 1205, http://www.econ.upf.edu/docs/papers/downloads/1205.pdf, accessed February 9, 2012.

Milgrom, P. (1981) "An Aximomatic Characterization of Common Knowledge", *Econometrica* 49/1: 419–22.

Montgomery, D. B., Moore, M. C., and Urbany, J. E. (2005) "Reasoning about Competitive Reactions: Evidence from Executives", *Marketing Science* 24/1: 138–49.

Moorthy, K. S. (1985) "Using Game Theory to Model Competition", *Journal of Marketing Research* 22: 262–82.

Moorthy, S. (2005) "A General Theory of Pass-Through in Channels with Category Management and Retail Competition", *Marketing Science* 24/1: 110–22.

Myerson, R. B. (1991) *Game Theory: Analysis of Conflict.* Cambridge, MA: Harvard University Press.

Nash, J. (1950) "Equilibrium Points in N-Person Games", *Proceedings of the National Academy of Sciences of the United States of America* 36/1: 48–9.

Netessine, S. and Shumsky, R. A. (2005) "Revenue Management Games: Horizontal and Vertical Competition", *Management Science* 51/5: 813–31.

Neumann, J. von and Morgenstern, O. (1944) *Theory of Games and Economic Behavior.* Princeton, NJ: Princeton University Press.

Nisan, N., Roughgarden, T., Tardos, E., and Vazirani, V. V. (eds) (2007) *Algorithmic Game Theory.* Cambridge, MA: Cambridge University Press.

Özer, Ö., Zheng, Y., and Chen, K.-Y. (2011) "Trust in Forecast Information Sharing", *Management Science* 57/6: 1111–37.

Putler, D. (1992) "Incorporating Reference Effects into a Theory of Consumer Choice", *Marketing Science* 11/Summer: 287–309.

Putsis, W. and Dhar, R. (1998) "The Many Faces of Competition", *Marketing Letters* 9/3: 269–84.

Raju, J. S., Srinivasan, V., and Lal, R. (1990) "The Effects of Brand Loyalty on Competitive Price Promotions", *Management Science* 36/3: 276–304.

Rao, R. C. (1991) "Pricing and Promotions in Asymmetric Duopolies", *Marketing Science* 10/Spring: 131–44.

—— and Bass, F. M. (1985) "Competition, Strategy, and Price Dynamics: A Theoretical and Empirical Investigation", *Journal of Marketing Research* 22/August: 283–96.

Rappeport, A. (2008) "Game Theory Versus Practice", *CFO Magazine* July 15.

Saporito, B. (1994) "Behind the Tumult at P&G", *Fortune* 129/5: 74.

Schelling, T. (1960) *The Strategy of Conflict.* Cambridge, MA: Harvard University Press.

Selton, R. (1975) "Reexamination of the perfectness concept for equilibrium points in extensive games", *International Journal of Game Theory* 4: 25–55.

Shankar, V. and Bolton, R. N. (2004) "An Empirical Analysis of Determinants of Retailer Pricing Strategy", *Marketing Science* 23/1: 28–49.

Singh, N. and Vives, X. (1984) "Price and Quantity Competition in a Differentiated Duopoly", *Rand Journal of Economics* 15/4: 546–54.

Varian, H. (1980) "A Model of Sales", *American Economic Review* 70/September: 651–9.

Winer, R. S. (1986) "A Reference Price Model of Brand Choice for Frequently Purchased Products", *Journal of Consumer Research* 13/2: 250–6.

CHAPTER 20

BEHAVIORAL ISSUES IN PRICING MANAGEMENT

ÖZALP ÖZER AND
YANCHONG ZHENG

20.1 INTRODUCTION

Economic systems are composed of and governed by human agents. Unlike physics where objects move and interact according to immutable laws, economic decisions are made by human agents with emotional concerns. Although neoclassical economic theories offer powerful tools to analyze, prescribe, and design efficient economic systems, we still observe market failures that cannot be explained by these theories. Thus, behavioral economics, which integrates insights from psychology with neoclassical economic theories, has become an important discipline that improves our understanding of observed market phenomena.

The history of behavioral economics can be traced back to the work of Nobel Laureate Herbert Simon. He develops a theory of bounded rationality, which suggests that most people are only partially rational and have limits in processing information as well as solving complex problems (Simon 1955). The studies of consumer choice and framing by Thaler (1980) and Tversky and Kahneman (1981) in the early 1980s have further prospered the progress in behavioral economics. Since then, numerous studies have been performed on topics ranging from individual choice to strategic interaction, corroborating that human decisions often deviate from the predictions of neoclassical economic theories. This chapter is dedicated to demonstrating how such human deviations affect pricing management in both areas of consumer pricing and pricing contracts among firms. We discuss an extensive spectrum of recent findings in behavioral economics, especially in a pricing context, and elaborate on the implications of these behavioral regularities for pricing strategies.

The authors are thankful to the anonymous reviewers, Rachel Croson, Warren Hausman, and Robert Phillips for their constructive comments. The authors also gratefully acknowledge financial support from National Science Foundation Grant No. 0556322 and No. 1002381.

How may psychology impact human decisions beyond neoclassical economic theories? Consider the following cases:

> Case 1: A gas station sells gas at $2.99 per gallon. Customers who pay with cash are offered a $0.10 discount per gallon.
> Case 2: A gas station sells gas at $2.89 per gallon. Customers who pay with credit cards are charged an extra $0.10 for each gallon.

It is not surprising to see that consumers perceive the pricing scheme in Case 2 to be more unfavorable than that in Case 1, since accepting the 10-cent surcharge in Case 2 induces more frustration than forgoing the 10-cent discount in Case 1. Indeed, no gas station adopts the surcharge scheme in Case 2. Further, the credit card industry insists that if retailers impose lower prices for cash payers than for credit card payers, the price differences should be described as cash discounts rather than credit card surcharges (Thaler 1980).

Another puzzling example is that the label "FREE!" appears irresistible to consumers. People often buy more than they want or need to obtain "FREE!" accessories or opt for "FREE!" shipping (Ariely 2010). An experiment by Shampanier et al. (2007) illustrates the power of "FREE!" on consumer choice. They offered two products: a Hershey's kiss and a Lindt truffle. The latter product has a much higher quality and higher market price. When the Hershey's is offered at 1¢ each and the Lindt at 15¢ each, 27 percent of the participants chose the Hershey's. However, when the Hershey's is offered free and the Lindt at 14¢ each, 69 percent chose the Hershey's. This sharp increase in the demand for Hershey's is inconsistent with rational behavior, since the same amount of discount (1¢) is offered for both products. A possible explanation for the power of "FREE!" is that a free item carries no risk or loss, and hence it appears disproportionately more attractive to consumers (who dislike bearing losses) compared to a discounted item with a positive price.

A third interesting phenomenon is the "sunk cost fallacy", presented by Thaler (1980) in the following instance:

> A family pays $40 for tickets to a basketball game to be played 60 miles from their home. On the day of the game there is a snowstorm. They decide to go anyway, but note in passing that had the tickets been given to them, they would have stayed home. (Thaler 1980: 47)

Neoclassical economists would consider such behavior irrational, as the already paid $40 is a sunk cost and should not affect the decision made on the day of the game. However, people often feel obliged to fulfill prepaid plans regardless of whether or not they want to, since otherwise they would experience the negative emotions from "wasting" resources.

To better understand how people make decisions and to prescribe better strategies, researchers have been using controlled laboratory experiments with human participation. In these experiments, people act as decision-makers in a specific context of interest. Researchers observe the participants' behavior and examine if and why (or why not) some pre-constructed hypotheses accurately predict human behavior. A frequent critique of this methodology is that experiments are not representative of the real world. We note that experiments are not designed to resemble reality. In contrast, they are designed to isolate the behavioral factors of interest so that these factors can be studied in the "cleanest" possible environment. In other words, the principle of a good experiment is to control for the factors that may serve as alternative explanations for the behavior but are not of interest in the investigation. We refer interested readers to Roth (1988) and Plott (1994) for more discussion about the role of laboratory experiments in advancing economic theories. Friedman and Sunder (1994) and Kagel and Roth (1997) provide more details about the proper design of an experiment.

Controlled laboratory experiments, field data, and theoretical models are complementary tools that help improve our understanding of human decision making. First, carefully calibrated laboratory experiments can help researchers study the effects of different possible factors one by one without being confounded by cross effects. The improved comprehension of these causal relationships enhances the development of innovative management tactics. These new tactics can be further tested in field experiments with more realistic market conditions. In addition, human-subject experiments can be used to verify whether predictions from normative models reflect actual behavior. Conversely, observed behavioral regularities shed light on how to incorporate critical behavioral factors into existing models. The resulting new theories thus enhance existing ones by providing better predictions about human decision making. Subsequently, these enhanced theories motivate the design of effective policies and strategies to better manage complex systems. We will emphasize the interplay among theory, experiments, and real-world practices throughout our discussion.

The rest of the chapter is organized as follows. In Section 20.2, we discuss some important theories regarding human decision making and social preferences, including the well-known "prospect theory." In Section 20.3, we focus on consumer pricing and investigate how different behavioral regularities affect a firm's marketing and pricing decisions. In Section 20.4, we discuss critical behavioral issues that impact the design and performance of pricing contracts among firms. In Section 20.5, we summarize our discussion and conclude by suggesting future research that considers behavioral issues in pricing management.

20.2 A BRIEF DISCUSSION OF RELEVANT BEHAVIORAL REGULARITIES

We discuss three main categories of behavioral theories that have potential impacts on pricing management. The first category studies individual choice theories, including choice under uncertainty and intertemporal choice. The second category focuses on how social preferences affect the outcome of interactions among human agents. The third category discusses bounded rationality in the sense that human agents are imperfect optimizers and their decisions are prone to errors, especially when they are facing complex decisions.

20.2.1 Individual choice theories

20.2.1.1 Prospect theory

Expected utility theory has long been used to explain individual choice under uncertainty. This theory, however, has been challenged by many observations related to consumer choice, such as the fact that people's risk attitude depends on whether the choice involves a gain or a loss. Consider the following scenarios of buying a computer online. In Scenario 1, you are offered to choose between a fixed discount and a bonus discount during checkout. If you choose the fixed discount, you save $100 instantly. If you choose the bonus discount, you have a 50 percent chance of saving $200 instantly and a 50 percent chance of saving nothing. Most people in this case choose the fixed discount. Now consider Scenario 2 in which you are offered to choose between a fixed payment and a bonus payment for a warranty upgrade you purchase for the computer. If you choose the fixed payment, you pay $100 for the upgrade. If you choose the bonus payment, you have a 50 percent chance of receiving the upgrade for free and a 50 percent chance of paying $200 for the upgrade. In this case, most people tend to choose the bonus payment. Are these choices consistent with expected utility theory? Note that Scenario 1 can be interpreted as choosing between a sure gain of $100 and a lottery that results in a gain of $200 or $0 with equal probabilities. Similarly, Scenario 2 can be viewed as choosing between a sure loss of $100 and a lottery that results in a loss of $200 or $0 with equal probabilities. Preferring the sure gain in Scenario 1 but preferring the lottery in Scenario 2 demonstrates an inconsistency in people's risk attitude. This inconsistency violates expected utility theory.[1]

Observed choice decisions that seem puzzling under expected utility theory have motivated economists to develop alternative theories for human decisions under uncertainty. The most important breakthrough in this field is "prospect theory" developed by Daniel Kahneman and Amos Tversky (Kahneman and Tversky 1979; Tversky and Kahneman 1992).[2] The key idea of prospect theory is that people evaluate an outcome based on the comparison of the outcome with some subjective reference point, rather than based on the absolute outcome itself. The evaluation of a lottery (or prospect) relies on a value function and a nonlinear probability weighting function, both of which are derived from experimental evidence. Figure 20.1 presents a typical value function and a typical probability weighting function used in prospect theory. From Figure 20.1(a) we note that the valuation of the outcome of a lottery is classified as gains or losses compared to the reference point. Losses loom larger in value than gains of equal magnitude, usually termed "loss aversion". In addition, people exhibit risk aversion in the gain domain (represented by the concavity of the value function) but risk seeking preference in the loss domain (represented by the convexity of the value function). In Figure 20.1(b), the dashed line is the 45° line (representing that equal weights are applied to all probabilities). The solid curve maps the actual probabilities to the weighted or perceived probabilities formed by human decision-makers. The solid curve being above the dashed line before their crossing point implies that people over-react to extreme events that have small probabilities. In contrast, the solid curve being below the dashed line after their crossing point suggests that people under-react to common events with large probabilities.

---

[1] Formally, let $u(\cdot)$ be an individual's Bernoulli utility function. Preferring the sure gain in Scenario 1 implies that $u(100) > 0.5 \times u(200) + 0.5 \times u(0)$, suggesting that $u(\cdot)$ is concave. Thus, expected utility theory predicts that $u(-100) > 0.5 \times u(-200) + 0.5 \times u(0)$, contrary to the fact that the lottery is preferred in Scenario 2.

[2] As an abuse of terminology, we do not distinguish between the original prospect theory and the improved "cumulative prospect theory" also developed by Kahneman and Tversky. The two versions only differ in the way that they weight probabilities. In the original prospect theory, weights are assigned to individual probabilities. In cumulative prospect theory, weights are assigned to cumulative probabilities, which makes the theory consistent with first-order stochastic dominance.

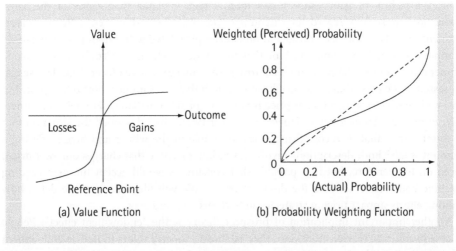

FIGURE 20.1 Typical value function and probability weighting function in prospect theory

The central ideas of reference-dependent utilities and loss aversion in prospect theory have led to the phenomenon of "framing effects"; that is, different presentations of the same choice problem may yield different or even reversed preferences. Consider the following problem studied by Tversky and Kahneman (1981):

> Scenario 1: "Imagine that the U.S. is preparing for the outbreak of an unusual Asian disease, which is expected to kill 600 people. Two alternative programs to combat the disease have been proposed. Assume that the exact scientific estimate of the conse-quences of the programs are as follows:
> - If Program A is adopted, 200 people will be saved.
> - If Program B is adopted, there is 1/3 probability that 600 people will be saved, and 2/3 probability that no people will be saved.
> Which of the two programs would you favor?"
> Scenario 2: (Same cover story with the following program descriptions)
> - "If Program C is adopted, 400 people will die.
> - If Program D is adopted, there is 1/3 probability that nobody will die, and 2/3 probability that 600 people will die.
> Which of the two programs would you favor?"

The results show that 72 percent of the participants in Scenario 1 chose A while 78 percent in Scenario 2 chose D. However, programs A and C are effectively identical and so are programs B and D. Tversky and Kahneman argue that the contradictory preferences for A and D are due to the tendency of risk aversion for gains and risk taking for losses, one of the key implications by prospect theory.

Our motivating example about gas stations charging different prices for cash payers and credit card payers in Section 20.1 is also a demonstration of framing effects. In that example, presenting the price difference as a surcharge for credit card payers induces a feeling of loss for consumers, whereas presenting the price difference as a discount for cash payers induces a feeling of gain. Since losses loom larger in value than gains of the same magnitude, consumers regard the discount frame more favorably even if the gas prices are identical in both frames. Consider another example related to the attempt by Coca-Cola Company to install a vending machine that automatically changes prices based on outside temperature. In 1999, the company's chairman and chief executive officer, Douglas Ivester, expressed in the press that a cold drink is more desirable in a summer sports championship final and hence charging a higher price is fair. This plan immediately outraged consumers (*San Francisco Chronicle* 1999). However, what if Ivester had described the situation in a discount frame; that is, a cold drink is less desirable in the winter and hence offering a discount is fair? Both descriptions involve a vending machine that charges different prices based on temperature, but it is possible that consumers would accept the new vending machine had Ivester adopted the discount frame. We will illustrate in more detail how framing effects impact pricing strategies in Sections 20.3 and 20.4.

Another important implication of prospect theory is the "endowment effect": People value a product or service more once they establish property rights to it. The endowment effect results in the buying–selling price gaps commonly observed in trading situations; that is, people state much lower buying prices (measuring their willingness-to-pay) than selling prices (measuring their willingness-to-accept) for a product. One possible reason for this phenomenon is loss aversion implied by prospect theory. Since sacrificing a pre-owned item is considered as a loss and buying a new item is considered as a gain, people tend to require a higher compensation for selling the item than they would be willing to pay for acquiring the same item. A large pool of experiments show that the endowment effect is evident for environmental and consumer goods (e.g., land and mugs) that are bought for use, and less evident for goods and lottery tickets that are bought for regular exchange (e.g., Knez et al. 1985; Kahneman et al. 1990; Boyce et al. 1992).

20.2.1.2 *Choice over time*

Consumer choice over time is another important area in economic studies. The standard normative models (e.g., Koopmans 1960; Fishburn and Rubinstein 1982) imply "exponential" discounting on individual's utility over time. Formally, exponential discounting suggests that a reward x received with a delayed period of t (or consumption x made in t periods from now) yields a present utility that is equal to $e^{-\beta t}u(x)$, where $u(\cdot)$ is the utility function and $e^{-\beta} \in [0, 1]$ is the discount factor. Several anomalies violate the exponential discounting framework. The first anomaly violates the assumption that people's implicit discount rate[3] is independent of time (i.e., β does not depend on t in the above model). There is evidence that people tend to be more patient about future delays than about immediate delays of the same length (e.g., Thaler 1981; Loewenstein 1988; Benzion et al. 1989). In other words, their implicit discount rate declines over time. For example, given the choice between receiving $100 today and receiving $105 in a week, most people prefer the former. In contrast, given the choice between receiving $100 in one year and receiving $105 in one year plus one week, most people prefer the latter. Exponential discounting, however, infers contradicting preferences in the two cases. Using the above model and let a period t

---

[3] The literature refers to the discount rate as "implicit" because it is inferred from people's choice decisions.

denote a day, preferring \$100 today over \$105 in a week infers the preference $u(100) >$ $\delta^7 u(105)$, where $\delta \equiv e^{-\beta}$ is the daily discount factor; but preferring \$105 in one year plus one week over \$100 in one year infers $\delta^{365} u(100) < \delta^{365+7} u(105)$. The key cause of such inconsistency lies in that exponential discounting models assume a constant discount rate over time. Hence, preference over temporal consumptions/rewards only depends on the absolute time difference between the options (i.e., the one week difference between the two choices in the above example).

People's impatience about immediate delays implies a present bias—they weight immediate rewards or costs much higher than a rational agent would do (O'Donoghue and Rabin 1999). Consider purchasing a magazine at the newsstand versus by subscription. If the magazine involves consumer learning (e.g., reading *Forbes*) and thus has delayed benefits compared to the time of reading (call it an "investment" magazine), purchasing at the newsstand causes consumers with a present bias to weight the current costs too high and the future returns too low. In contrast, purchasing by subscription delays both reading and returns to the future, thus diminishing the present bias. As a result, consumers have a lower willingness-to-pay at the newsstand than for subscription. Therefore, it is more profitable for publishers to sell investment magazines by subscription. Indeed, Oster and Morton (2005) empirically verify that the ratio of the subscription price (per issue) to the newsstand price is higher for investment magazines than for leisure magazines that offer immediate value at the time of reading, and investment magazines are sold by subscription more often than leisure ones. Similarly, consumers who exhibit a present bias (but may underestimate its effect on future behavior) prefer to pay for exercise through membership rather than on a per-visit basis, even though they would spend less in the latter case given their attendance frequency (DellaVigna and Malmendier 2006).

The next two anomalies have a close relationship with framing effects implied by prospect theory. One is called the "gain–loss asymmetry"—people discount gains at a higher rate than for losses of the same magnitude. Loewenstein and Prelec (1992) did the following experiment with two groups of MBA students, each group responding to one of the questions.

"Question 1. Suppose that you bought a TV on a special installment plan. The plan calls for two payments; one this week and one in six months. You have two options for paying:
A. An initial payment of \$160 and a later payment of \$110.

B. An initial payment of \$115 and a later payment of \$160.
Question 2. Suppose that you bought a TV on a special installment plan. The plan calls for two payments of \$200; one this week and one in six months. Happily, however, the company has announced a sale which applies retroactively to your purchase. You have two options:
C. A rebate of \$40 on the initial payment and a rebate of \$90 on the later payment.

D. A rebate of \$85 on the initial payment and a rebate of \$40 on the later payment."

They report that 54 percent of the participants chose A over B while 67 percent chose D over C, although A and C (B and D) yield the same results in terms of payments and delivery times. Note that the payment frame in Question 1 induces the participants to consider the choices in the loss domain. The rebate frame in Question 2 induces them to consider the options in the gain domain. The observed inconsistency in preferences suggests that the participants discount gains with a higher rate. Similar phenomena are observed in Thaler (1981) and Shelley (1993).

The gain–loss asymmetry suggests that consumers generally regard a benefit program with higher benefits realized earlier to be more favorable than one with higher benefits realized later, even if both programs offer the same total benefits. Consider a pizzeria designing a set of monthly coupons for the upcoming year. Each coupon is only valid for the specified month. The coupons provide different levels of benefits for consumers. For example, a "buy one, get one free" coupon provides the highest benefit, "25% off entire order" provides an intermediate benefit, and "free drink" provides the lowest benefit. The gain–loss asymmetry suggests that putting the higher benefits on the early months may render the coupons more appealing to consumers. This asymmetry also shows that consumers do not have a strong preference between a long-term payment scheme with higher payments at the beginning and one with higher payments towards the end. This result may explain why consumers accept financing programs that typically require high upfront payments.

The other anomaly related to framing effects is the "delay–speedup asymmetry"—people require a higher compensation for delayed consumption than they would be willing to pay for speeding it up; in addition, people demand a higher discount to expedite a future payment than they would be willing to pay to postpone a current payment. Benzion et al. (1989) show strong experimental evidence for this asymmetry. They use four scenarios to infer the participants' implicit discount rates: postpone/expedite a receipt, and postpone/expedite a payment. They find that discount rates are higher for (1) postponing (versus expediting) a receipt, and (2) expediting (versus postponing) a payment, controlling for the size of consumption/payment and the length of delay (also see Loewenstein 1988; Shelley 1993). These results have implications regarding the design of payment schemes. Consider a firm that has two alternatives for charging shipping: one provides a discount off the item price to postpone the shipping of the product, and the other requires a surcharge on top of the price to expedite shipping. Due to the delay–speedup asymmetry, the firm needs to offer a deeper discount than the surcharge it could demand to make consumers indifferent between the two options. Hence, the surcharge frame is a better option for the firm. This can be a potential reason why shipping costs are usually presented as surcharges for consumers.

Motivated by these observations, Loewenstein and Prelec (1992) follow an axiomatic approach to derive a "hyperbolic" discounting model. This model generalizes the traditional discounted utility theory and borrows insights from prospect theory. Formally, consider a sequence of dated consumptions denoted by $\{(x_i, t_i), i = 1, \ldots, n\}$, where x_i's denote the consumption levels and t_i's denote the consumption time. A consumer's utility of this sequence is equal to $U(x_1, t_1; \ldots; x_n, t_n) = \sum_{i=1}^{n} v(x_i)\phi(t_i)$. $v(\cdot)$ is the value function with the same structural properties as the one in prospect theory (see Figure 20.1a). $\phi(\cdot)$ is the discount function with a hyperbolic form: $\phi(t) = (1 + \alpha t)^{-\beta/\alpha}$, with $\alpha, \beta > 0$. The coefficient α shows the deviation from exponential discounting. In the limiting case, as α goes to zero, we revert to the standard exponential discount function: $\phi(t) = e^{-\beta t}$. Figure 20.2 provides some examples of the hyperbolic discount function with different values of α and β, as compared to the exponential discount function. To illustrate how the hyperbolic discounting model explains the aforementioned anomalies, consider for example the phenomenon that people are more patient about future delays. Suppose that an individual

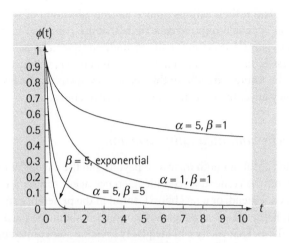

FIGURE 20.2 Examples of hyperbolic discount function

is indifferent between receiving q now and receiving x in t periods; that is, $v(q) = v(x)(1 + \alpha t)^{-\beta/\alpha}$. The question is under hyperbolic discounting, which choice the individual prefers if both rewards are delayed by s periods; that is, comparing $v(q)(1 + \alpha s)^{-\beta/\alpha}$ with $v(x)(1 + \alpha t + \alpha s)^{-\beta/\alpha}$. We know that $v(q)(1 + \alpha s)^{-\beta/\alpha} = v(x) [(1 + \alpha t)(1 + \alpha s)]^{-\beta/\alpha} < v(x) [(1 + \alpha t + \alpha s)]^{-\beta/\alpha}$ because $(1 + \alpha t)(1 + \alpha s) > 1 + \alpha t + \alpha s$. Therefore, the individual strictly prefers receiving x in $t + s$ periods to receiving q in s periods. This preference is consistent with the observation that people are more willing to wait when delays occur in the future. Similarly, the gain–loss asymmetry and the delay–speedup asymmetry can be explained by taking into account both the hyperbolic discount function and loss aversion implied by the value function (as in prospect theory).

The hyperbolic discounting model is shown to be consistent with empirical observations (e.g., Green et al. 1994; Kirby 1997). Laibson (1997) provides a discrete-time discounting structure that has the same qualitative properties as the above model while maintaining the analytical tractability of the exponential case. In his model, the utility of a sequence of consumptions x_t over the time horizon $t = 0, 1, \ldots, n$ is computed as $U(x_0, \ldots, x_n) = v(x_0) + \beta \sum_{t=1}^{n} \delta^t v(x_t)$, where $\beta, \delta \in (0, 1)$ are the discount factors and x_0 is the immediate consumption which is not discounted. Laibson's model is effective in explaining several economic phenomena including consumption discontinuities at retirement, consumer self-reported under-saving, and procrastination (e.g., Laibson 1998; O'Donoghue and Rabin 2001).

20.2.2 Social preferences

Neoclassical economic theories assume that decision-makers are self-interested agents who only care about their own payoffs. This assumption, however, has been seriously challenged by findings from psychology and experimental economics in the past few decades. Researchers find that human decisions are subject to emotional concerns, and these concerns have important economic implications (Fehr and Fischbacher 2002). For example, people feel bad if their actions induce uneven allocation of welfare in the group ("inequality aversion"); people respond to actions that are perceived to be kind in a kind manner ("reciprocity"); and even more surprisingly, people take actions that may put themselves in a worse economic position in the hope that others will honor their generosity and reciprocate in the future ("trust"). In this section, we focus on these social preferences and discuss how they affect the outcome of human interactions.

20.2.2.1 Reciprocity and inequality aversion

People are shown to care about both their own payoffs and the payoffs of relevant reference agents. Depending on the context, a relevant reference agent can be a trading partner, a colleague in a project, a friend, or a neighbor. Central in the preferences for reciprocity and inequality aversion is the idea that people are concerned about the fairness of the consequences of actions. Thus, reciprocity and inequality aversion sometimes appear intertwined when they are used to explain behavioral regularities. Although we do not attempt to distinguish them rigorously, we specify their distinctions whenever possible.

Let's first look at the preference for reciprocity. A reciprocal person reacts to actions perceived to be benevolent in a kind manner, and reacts to actions perceived to be malevolent in a hostile manner. Whether an action is considered benevolent or malevolent depends on one's interpretation of a fair outcome. This interpretation is determined by the equitability of the resulting payoff distribution. Preference for reciprocity has been tested in gift-exchange experiments and public goods games. The term "gift-exchange" follows from Akerlof (1982). He characterizes an employment opportunity offered by a firm as an offer to "exchange gifts" and considers effort levels exerted by workers as the size of the reciprocal gift. In a gift-exchange game, an employer offers a wage to an employee, and the employee in return selects an effort level that is costly. The higher the effort level, the better off the employer and the worse off the employee. The employer has no control on the effort level chosen by the employee. Thus, the gift-exchange game is a game with moral hazard[4] and no contract enforcement. Results from gift-exchange experiments show that the effort levels chosen by the employees are positively correlated with the wage levels received, which is evidence for reciprocity (e.g., Fehr et al. 1993; Fehr et al. 1998; Charness 2004).

Reciprocity is also shown to account for the conditional cooperation phenomenon observed in public goods games (e.g., Keser and van Winden 2000; Croson et al. 2005). In a linear public goods game with $N \geq 2$ players, each player is offered an endowment. Every player then determines how much of the endowment to contribute to a public project. The payoff for each player is equal to the remaining endowment plus a fraction (strictly between $1/N$ and 1) of the total contribution from all players. The unique Nash equilibrium in this game is for all players to free ride; that is, to contribute zero.[5]

---

[4] Moral hazard arises when a party in a transaction exerts unobservable actions that affect both parties' welfare.

[5] Formally, suppose that there are $N > 2$ players indexed by $i = 1, 2, \ldots, N$ and the marginal return of the public project is $1/2$. Let e_i be player i's endowment and x_i be player i's contribution. Player i's payoff is given by $\pi_i(x_i, x_{-i}) = e_i - x_i + (1/2)\sum_{j=1}^{N} x_j = e_i - (1/2)x_i + (1/2)\sum_{j \neq i} x_j$, where x_{-i} is a vector of the other players' contributions. The payoff function shows that player i has a dominant strategy of contributing zero regardless of other players' contributions. Therefore, the unique Nash equilibrium of the game is free riding.

Fischbacher et al. (2001) elicit players' decisions in a public goods game with the "strategy method": They ask each player to indicate how much s/he is willing to contribute for each of the possible average contributions from his/her group members. Their results show that about half of the participants are willing to contribute more if the average contribution from their group members increases, which can be viewed as reciprocal actions.

Although reciprocity arises from a recipient's viewpoint, the existence of a reciprocal agent can affect the motives of the first mover. For example, if a person knows that his partner in interaction has a strong preference for reciprocity, he will be induced to deviate from selfish actions in favor of his partner because he expects to be rewarded, or because he fears punishment if his partner considers his action to be unfair. The indirect influence of reciprocity on the first mover is further strengthened when the recipient has an explicit option to punish unfair actions, even if punishing is costly to the recipient (Fehr and Gächter 2000). Existing models of reciprocity include Rabin (1993), Dufwenberg and Kirchsteiger (2004), and Falk and Fischbacher (2006).

The idea of inequality aversion is motivated by behavior observed in ultimatum bargaining games. There are two players in this game, a proposer (he) and a responder (she). The proposer is provided with an endowment X, and he offers an amount $Y \in [0, X]$ to the responder. The responder then decides whether to accept or reject the offer. If she accepts, the payoffs for the proposer and the responder are $X - Y$ and Y, respectively. If she rejects, both parties receive zero. The unique subgame perfect Nash equilibrium is for the proposer to offer the smallest amount and the responder to accept any positive offer. However, numerous experiments show that proposers usually offer 40–50 percent of the endowment and responders reject offers that are below 20 percent about half of the time. These observations are very robust, irrespective of the stake size, culture, or gender (e.g., Roth et al. 1991; Forsythe et al. 1994; Eckel and Grossman 2001; see Camerer 2003 for a review).

Two explanations have been proposed for this behavior: (1) proposers make high offers because they fear rejections of low offers by responders, and (2) proposers make high offers because they are purely generous. The first explanation relates to the responder's preference for reciprocity: being given a low offer is considered mean and the responder punishes the proposer by rejecting it (also called "negative reciprocity"). The second explanation is a measure of the proposer's concern about fairness. To determine which explanation plays a major role, economists study the proposer's behavior in a variation of the ultimatum game; that is, the dictator game. In a dictator game, the proposer still makes an ultimatum offer, but the responder is forced to accept the offer (i.e., she cannot reject). In this game, the effect of the responder's reciprocity on the proposer's decision is eliminated, so the proposer's offer is purely driven by his own concern about fairness. Proposers in dictator games are observed to offer around 20 percent of the endowment, compared to 40–50 percent in ultimatum games. This result suggests that both the proposer's concern about fairness and the responder's preference for reciprocity jointly shape the proposer's behavior.

Motivated by the above results, Fehr and Schmidt (1999) develop a model of "inequality aversion". In their model, an individual's utility depends on both his own payoff and the difference between own and others' payoffs. Formally, consider a group of n individuals indexed by $i \in \{1, 2, \ldots, n\}$. Player i's utility over a monetary allocation $x = [x_1, x_2, \ldots, x_n]$ is equal to $U_i(x) = x_i - \frac{\alpha_i}{n-1} \sum_{j \neq i} \max \{x_j - x_i, 0\} - \frac{\beta_i}{n-1} \sum_{j \neq i} \max \{x_i - x_j, 0\}$, where

$\beta_i \leq \alpha_i$ and $0 \leq \beta_i < 1$ for all i. α_i is called the envy weight and β_i the guilt weight. The second term in the utility function incorporates the impact of being worse off than others, and the third term incorporates the impact of being better off than others. Two assumptions in Fehr and Schmidt's model form the foundation of inequality aversion: (1) people dislike inequity in payoff distributions, and (2) people are more averse to being worse off than being better off (by the assumption $\beta_i \leq \alpha_i$). By deriving the appropriate envy and guilt weights, their model is capable of explaining the major observations in ultimatum bargaining experiments, even when proposer competition and responder competition are considered. They also derive conditions under which free riding or cooperation may emerge in public goods games. Around the same time, Bolton and Ockenfels (2000) develop a similar model of inequality aversion, which they call the "ERC" (for Equity, Reciprocity, and Competition) model. In the ERC model, an individual cares about his own payoff and his relative share in the total group payoff. Hence, an individual's utility is given by $U_i(x) = u\left(x_i, x_i / \sum_{j=1}^{n} x_j\right)$. They assume that people have concave increasing utilities over monetary payoffs, and more importantly, people strictly prefer an even distribution of payoffs to any other distribution outcomes. That is, the utility function is assumed to be strictly concave in the second argument with a unique maximum achieved at $1/n$. This assumption suggests that people will be willing to sacrifice their own payoffs to move their relative share closer to the average. They show that the ERC model can explain observations from gift-exchange games, public goods games, and ultimatum bargaining and dictator games.

20.2.2.2 *Trust and reputation*

Trust is an important psychological state that has been extensively studied in various disciplines such as psychology, political science, and economics. In *The Silent Language* (1959), anthropologist Edward Hall argues that trust plays a stronger role than legal contracts in supporting cooperative relations. Economist Kenneth Arrow echoes Hall's thought in stating that trust is crucial for efficient economic transactions (Arrow 1972). Berg et al. (1995) present one of the first experiments that use an investment game to demonstrate the existence of trust induced by the investor's expectation of reciprocity from the trustee. The game is played as follows. An investor is endowed with X, and he decides to invest an amount $Y \in [0, X]$ at a rate of r; that is, the investment returns $(1 + r)Y$. The trustee, who is another party, then determines how much of the investment return will be repaid to the investor. If the trustee decides to repay Z, the payoffs to the investor and the trustee are $X - Y + Z$ and $(1 + r)Y - Z$, respectively. The value Y invested is a measure of the investor's trust, and the value Z repaid is a measure of the trustee's trustworthiness. The unique subgame perfect Nash equilibrium is for the investor to invest zero and the trustee to repay zero. In sharp contrast to this normative prediction, Berg et al. (1995) show that even if reputation, contract enforcement, and punishment are absent, investors invest about half of the endowment, and trustees repay about the same amount as what was invested. Later experiments with the investment game and its variations in different cultures and social groups suggest that the existence of trust and trustworthiness is a universal phenomenon (e.g., Croson and Buchan 1999; Fehr and List 2004; Holm and Nystedt 2005).

Researchers have strived to sort out the determinants of trust. For example, Eckel and Wilson (2004) find in their experiments that trusting behavior is not related to risky choices and risk preferences as suggested by Ben-Ner and Putterman (2001). They instead conclude that trust is determined by how a person judges her counterpart's trustworthiness. Bohnet and Zeckhauser (2004) identify that the psychological cost of being betrayed after trusting another individual is a major determinant that influences trusting behavior. They find evidence for betrayal aversion in different countries (Bohnet et al. 2008). According to Ho and Weigelt (2005), trust is induced by the expected future gains from trusting. Ashraf et al. (2006) find that another determinant of trust is unconditional kindness generated by social norms or values that an individual adheres to. Hong and Bohnet (2007) examine how people's social status affects three determinants of trust: risk preference, cost of being betrayed, and inequality aversion. They identify, for example, that for a "low" status group trusting behavior is primarily determined by inequality aversion, and for a "high" status group the primary determinant is betrayal aversion.

The above literature shows that trust encourages the trustor to voluntarily pass property rights to the trustee in the hope of future gains. Another group of studies demonstrates that trust also improves the efficacy of using costless, non-binding, and non-verifiable communication (termed "cheap talk" in the economics literature) to convey information among transactors. For example, Forsythe et al. (1999) show that buyers' trust in sellers' quality claims greatly increases the probability that trade happens and hence improves overall market efficiency, in a setting where the product quality is privately known to the seller and the parties transact only once. Gneezy (2005) demonstrates that people are averse to lying, especially when lying causes a huge loss to the party being lied to. Özer et al. (2011) study the capacity investment problem of a firm who solicits demand forecast information from his customer to determine capacity. They demonstrate a continuum of trust and trustworthiness between the firm and the customer, which facilitates forecast communication and enables a high market efficiency.

Reputation is an important factor that supports cooperative actions among human agents when they interact repeatedly. By studying the iterated Prisoner's Dilemma, both theoretical and experimental research show that reputation can be built through reciprocal strategies such as tit-for-tat,[6] and mutual cooperation can be sustained (e.g., Axelrod 1981; Andreoni and Miller 1993; Dal Bó 2005). Reputation is also considered as a driving factor that determines trust from an evolutionary perspective (Ben-Ner and Putterman 2001). Lewicki and Bunker (1995) show that trust develops from calculus-based to knowledge-based and finally to identification-based as parties gain more information about each other in the process of interpersonal interactions. Doney and Cannon (1997) study the trust-building process in a buyer–seller relationship. They demonstrate that repeated interactions help the seller establish his/her reputation of being credible and benevolent, and the buyer's past successful experience from trusting encourages future interactions with the seller. In recent years, reputation established through on-line feedback systems has become an essential element that facilitates transactions in electronic marketplaces such as eBay.

---

[6] Consider an iterated Prisoner's Dilemma in which each player can take either of two actions: cooperate or defect. With a tit-for-tat strategy, a player chooses to cooperate as long as the other player has been cooperating, and chooses to defect if the other player has defected.

20.2.3 Complexity and bounded rationality

Neoclassical economic theories assume that human agents are perfect optimizers—they can perfectly infer any information from what they observe, and they can solve any complex decision problems without errors. The reality, however, appears to be quite different from these assumptions. In this section, we discuss two models that describe the bounded rationality of human agents in the sense that they are not perfect optimizers: level-k thinking and quantal response equilibrium.

20.2.3.1 Level-k thinking

An important assumption in game theoretic equilibrium analysis is that players have infinite levels of reasoning. For example, in a two-person game, Player 1 (he) knows Player 2 (she)'s strategy and vice versa; Player 1 knows that Player 2 knows his strategy and vice versa; Player 1 knows that Player 2 knows that Player 1 knows her strategy and vice versa; continuing to infinity. Eventually, a Nash equilibrium arises at the fixed point of this reasoning process where Player 1 best responds to Player 2's strategy and vice versa. This infinite level of reasoning, however, is not always supported by experimental results, even in a dominance-solvable game.[7]

A game called the "p-beauty contest" is frequently used to study the level of iterated dominance that an individual practices (Nagel 1995). In this game, a group of players simultaneously pick a number in the interval [0, 100], and the player who picks a number that is closest to a multiple p of the average number wins a fixed prize. For example, if $p = 2/3$ and $\bar{x}$ is the average of the numbers picked by the players, the player who has picked a number that is closest to $2\bar{x}/3$ is the winner. By iterated elimination of dominated strategies, the unique Nash equilibrium in this game with $p < 1$ is to pick 0. In sharp contrast, players in experiments with $p = 2/3$ in Nagel (1995) choose 36 on average, with spikes at 33 and 22, and very few choose 0. If a player thinks that other players pick a number randomly, he expects an average of 50 and best responds by picking $50 \times (2/3) = 33$—this is the first level of iterated dominance. If a player thinks that other players all practice the first level of iterated dominance, he expects an average of 33 and best responds by picking 22—this is the second level of iterated dominance. Therefore, the above result suggests that most players in Nagel's experiment only practice up to two levels of iterated dominance.

The finite level of reasoning by human participants is also observed in Stahl and Wilson (1995), who introduce the term "level-k thinking". They differentiate people by their degree of sophistication in reasoning. A level-0 player is a "naive" type who picks choices randomly and equally likely. A level-1 player believes that other players are level-0 type and best responds to the level-0 type's strategy. Moving forward similarly, a level-k player believes that other players are of lower levels (i.e., a combination from level-0 to level-$(k - 1)$) and best responds to the lower-level types' strategies. Stahl and Wilson (1995) estimate that most players are level-1 or level-2 types. Ho et al. (1998) replicate Nagel's p-beauty contest with multiple values of p and apply level-k thinking to measure the depth of iterated dominance

---

[7] A dominance-solvable game is a game that can be solved by iterated elimination of strictly dominated strategies (see Gibbons 1992).

in their participants. They identify that the participants are spread from level-0 to level-3, with higher-level types hardly observed.

Level-k thinking is also used to explain the widely observed phenomenon of "winner's curse" in auctions—bidders bid too high compared to the equilibrium bids.[8] Crawford and Iriberri (2007) show that the winner's curse can be largely explained by the behavior of level-1 bidders, who assume that others bid randomly and best respond to such random bidding. The above results support that strategic thinking does exist in human reasoning, although with a limited level of sophistication compared to equilibrium analysis. Given its recent development, the application of level-k thinking in a pricing context still requires further exploration. As researchers put increasing attention on the interaction between firms and consumers, we expect that level-k thinking will become an important complement to standard equilibrium analysis for a better understanding of human decisions.

20.2.3.2 Quantal response equilibrium

Another assumption in normative decision theory that is frequently challenged is that people can perfectly solve decision problems without any errors. This assumption proved problematic as early as in Simon (1955). One important milestone in resolving this problem in a game theoretic setting is the "quantal response equilibrium" (QRE) introduced by McKelvey and Palfrey (1995). This model specifies that human decisions are prone to errors, although an action associated with a higher expected utility is more likely to be chosen. Under the QRE framework, a player does not follow his best response with certainty but makes mistakes by occasionally choosing worse responses. He expects others to make mistakes as well and evaluates the expected utility of an action given such expectation. Eventually, the choice distributions formed by the players' strategies turn out to be best responses to each other, given the underlying error structure. Hence, the QRE model still obeys the notion of infinite levels of reasoning in equilibrium analysis, but relaxes the perfect optimization assumption to be error-prone. This is different from level-k thinking, which assumes that players have limited levels of reasoning but at each level they are perfect optimizers.

McKelvey and Palfrey (1995) study a particular parametric class of QRE called the "logit equilibrium." To illustrate the idea, consider a game with 2 players indexed by $i = 1, 2$. Player i has 2 pure strategies (s_{i1}, s_{i2}). Let $(p_i, 1 - p_i)$ denote the mixed strategy that Player i follows; i.e., Player i plays strategy s_{i1} with probability p_i and s_{i2} with probability $1 - p_i$. Given the other player's mixed strategy p_{-i}, define Player i's expected payoff under a pure strategy s as $\bar{u}_i(s, p_{-i})$. Then the strategy profile $\{(p_1^*, 1 - p_1^*), (p_2^*, 1 - p_2^*)\}$ constitutes a logit equilibrium if $p_i^* = \exp\{\lambda \bar{u}_i(s_{i1}, p_{-i}^*)\}/[\exp\{\lambda \bar{u}_i(s_{i1}, p_{-i}^*)\} + \exp\{\lambda \bar{u}_i(s_{i2}, p_{-i}^*)\}]$ for $i = 1, 2$. Hence, p_i^* is the probability that Player i plays s_{i1} in equilibrium. The parameter λ is inversely related to the level of errors: $\lambda = 0$ implies that decisions are dominated by errors and players choose actions randomly; $\lambda = \infty$ implies no error and players choose the best-response action with certainty, i.e., reverting to standard Nash equilibrium. McKelvey and Palfrey provide a general formulation of the logit equilibrium for normal-form games. They

---

[8] See Steinberg (Chapter 27) for more discussion about the winner's curse.

apply this logit QRE model to show that behavior in several existing experiments is indeed a result of error-prone decision making. In addition, participants' estimated error rates (inverse of λ) decline with their experience, indicating learning. Recently, Baye and Morgan (2004) apply a similar logit QRE model that handles continuous strategy space to explain the widespread phenomenon of price dispersion in market environments approximate to Bertrand competition. We will illustrate in §4 how QRE explains some behavioral regularities in the context of pricing contracts among firms.

20.2.4 Summary

In this section, we discuss three categories within behavioral economics that are important to pricing management. The first category investigates how individuals make choices that involve risk and uncertainty, as well as choices that span over time. The main theories include prospect theory and the hyperbolic discounting model, which are foundations for some well-established behavioral observations such as loss aversion, framing effects, and the present bias. The second category demonstrates the impact of social preferences on human decisions in a strategic environment. We emphasize that human agents are not always self-interested decision makers who only care about their own payoffs. Their concerns for other people's welfare lead to behaviors such as reciprocity, inequality aversion, and trust. Finally, we discuss the boundedly rational nature of human decision making in the sense that human agents are subject to a limited level of sophistication in reasoning, and that their decisions are often prone to errors. The models of level-k thinking and quantal response equilibrium serve as effective alternatives to standard Nash equilibrium and capture such bounded rationality. In what follows, we examine how these behavioral regularities affect pricing strategies in two important areas: consumer pricing and pricing contracts among firms.

20.3 BEHAVIORAL ISSUES IN CONSUMER PRICING

Consumer pricing is the subject of many issues in pricing management, such as markdown and revenue management. Our discussion in this section is divided into three groups. The first group studies the interaction between individual choice theories and consumer pricing. We discuss how the framing/context of a choice problem and individual biases affect consumer preferences, as well as their implications for pricing management. In the second group, we focus on how consumers' fairness concerns affect firms' pricing strategies. Finally, we discuss the emerging phenomenon of consumer-to-consumer pricing in e-commerce and the role of reputation in the electronic marketplace.

20.3.1 Individual choice theories and consumer pricing

The efficiency of pricing strategies relies heavily on the understanding of consumer preferences. Solutions derived from models that assume consumers to be rational

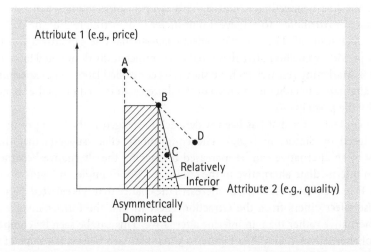

FIGURE 20.3 Demonstration of attraction effect and compromise effect (As an example, consider a higher value of Attribute 1 as a lower price and a higher value of Attribute 2 a better quality.)

expected-utility maximizers should be generalized to incorporate better characterizations of consumer preferences. The behavioral phenomena of context effects, reference pricing, and price presentation effects are important findings that improve our understanding of consumer choice behaviors.

20.3.1.1 Context effects

"Context effects" refer to the observation that adding a new alternative to or removing an existing alternative from the initial choice set may change a consumer's preference ranking for the other alternatives. This observation violates the axiom of "independence of irrelevant alternatives" in standard choice theories.[9] An example that has received considerable attention from marketing researchers is the "attraction effect" (Huber et al. 1982; Huber and Puto 1983). This effect shows that adding an alternative that is dominated by one alternative in all attributes but not by the other alternatives can increase the choice probability of the dominating alternative (a phenomenon also called "asymmetric dominance"). In addition, adding a "relatively inferior" alternative to a choice set also increases the choice probability of the superior alternative. Figure 20.3 demonstrates both ideas in the comparison of two alternatives A and B along two attributes 1 and 2. A higher value of either attribute is considered to be more favorable.[10] Observe that neither A nor B dominates the other because neither has higher values in both attributes. Alternatives in the slanted rectangular area are "asymmetrically dominated" by B—they are worse than B in both attributes but better than A in Attribute 2. Alternatives in the dotted triangular area are "relatively inferior" to B. For instance, we know that the line connecting A and C has a steeper

---

[9] The independence of irrelevant alternatives axiom postulates that an individual who prefers A to B in a choice set consisting of alternatives A, B, and C should still prefer A to B when C is removed from the choice set.

[10] We offer price as an example of Attribute 1 in Figure 20.3. Here, a higher value of Attribute 1 means a lower price.

slope than the line connecting A and B. This steeper slope implies that one needs to sacrifice more of Attribute 1 to achieve a unit increase of Attribute 2 in the A–C tradeoff than in the A–B tradeoff. The attraction effect suggests that one can attract consumers to prefer B by providing an alternative that is either asymmetrically dominated by or relatively inferior to B. Marketing researchers have shown by controlled laboratory experiments that adding an alternative in either the slanted or the dotted area indeed raises the chance that B is chosen by the participants.

Another context effect that has been widely acknowledged is the "compromise effect", first introduced by Simonson (1989). The compromise effect suggests that the choice probability of an alternative can be increased by making the alternative become a compromise/an intermediate alternative in the choice set. For example, in Figure 20.3, adding alternative D to the choice set of {A, B} increases the chance that B is selected. Note that the compromise effect differs from the attraction effect in that the former involves a more extreme alternative rather than an inferior alternative. This can be seen by comparing the positions of alternatives C and D in Figure 20.3. As discussed before, the slope of the A–C line is steeper than that of the A–B line, thus making C inferior to B. In contrast, D lies exactly on the line connecting A and B but at a farther out position than B, thus making D more extreme. As a simplified example, consider the comparison between two computers: A has 1G memory and costs $600, B has 2G memory and costs $800. The phenomenon that adding a third computer C which has 3G memory and costs $1,200 increases the sales of B exemplifies the attraction effect. This is because the A–C tradeoff requires a larger price increase to achieve a unit increase in memory than the A–B tradeoff: paying $300 versus $200 for every 1G extra memory. In contrast, if adding a third computer D that has 3G memory and costs $1,000 increases the sales of B, it is the compromise effect that is in effect: Both the A–D and the A–B tradeoffs require paying $200 for every 1G extra memory, but D is in a more extreme region (much better performance with a much higher price).

The compromise effect can be considered as a consequence of loss aversion implied by prospect theory (Simonson and Tversky 1992; Kivetz et al. 2004a). If the advantages (disadvantages) of an alternative relative to another alternative is viewed as gains (losses), the disadvantages of extreme alternatives (e.g., A or D in Figure 20.3) loom much larger than their advantages. In contrast, the compromise/intermediate alternative exhibits much smaller losses. Hence, a loss-averse consumer tends to prefer the intermediate alternative. Simonson and Tversky (1992) hypothesize this explanation as "extremeness aversion" and show that the degree of extremeness aversion is not necessarily equal for all attributes. In their experiments, they observe that low quality, low price products have a much smaller market share in three-option choice sets than in two-option choice sets, but this is not true for high quality, high price products. This result suggests that people are more averse to sacrificing quality than to paying a high price. In other words, there is strong extremeness aversion for quality, but little for price. One immediate implication from this observation is that adding a middle option between a low quality, low price product and a high quality, high price product is likely to draw market share towards the high end. This implication may explain why automotive companies provide luxurious add-ons to their base models to create mid-class vehicles, in addition to introducing the high-end models.

Quality and price are two common attributes that consumers consider in their purchasing decisions. Kivetz et al. (2004b) provide a real-life example of asymmetric dominance—subscription options for *The Economist*. There are three options for subscribing to the

Select your MacBook Pro.		
15-inch: 2.4GHz	15-inch: 2.53GHz	15-inch: 2.66GHz
Intel Core i5	Intel Core i5	Intel Core i7
4GB memory	4GB memory	4GB memory
320GB hard drive	500GB hard drive	500GB hard drive
SD card slot	SD card slot	SD card slot
Built-in battery (8-9 hour)	Built-in battery (8-9 hour)	Built-in battery (8-9 hour)
Intel HD Graphics	Intel HD Graphics	Intel HD Graphics
NVIDIA GeForce GT 330M with 256MB	NVIDIA GeForce GT 330M with 256MB	NVIDIA GeForce GT 330M with 256MB
$1,799.00	$1,999.00	$2,199.00

FIGURE 20.4: Example of compromise effect

Source: http://store.apple.com/us/, as of August 2010.

magazine: (1) $59 for an annual subscription of on-line access, (2) $125 for an annual subscription of the print edition, and (3) $125 for an annual subscription of both print edition and on-line access. Here, option (2) is asymmetrically dominated by option (3). Therefore, the attraction effect predicts that the presence of (2) increases consumers' choice for (3). This is indeed what happened in a controlled laboratory experiment conducted by the authors: 72 percent of the participants choose option (3) when (2) is present, compared to 43 percent when (2) is not present.

Attraction effects that involve the presence of a relatively inferior alternative are also commonly observed. For example, among the unlimited rental plans offered by Netflix (as of August 2010), the options of having 2, 3, and 4 DVDs at a time are priced at $13.99, $16.99, and $23.99, respectively. The presence of the $23.99 option presumably makes the $16.99 option more favorable to consumers. As another example, Amazon.com offers three different shipping options: standard shipping (delivery within 3–5 business days), two-day shipping, and one-day shipping. The price difference between two-day and one-day shipping is much larger than that between standard and two-day shipping for most products,[11] making the two-day shipping option more appealing to consumers. One implication of the attraction effect relates to product promotions. Consider a firm that has two brands of a product, one with standard quality and a low price, the other with premium quality and a high price. If the firm wants to shift consumer purchase to the premium brand, an effective strategy is to introduce a so-called "super-premium" brand, which is slightly better than the premium brand in quality but priced much higher. This type of practice is often seen in industries such as apparels, cosmetics, tourism, beverages, and electronics. Finally, the compromise effect can be regarded as a contributing factor to the common practice that sellers present products with increasing quality and increasing

[11] Consider apparels for example, standard, two-day, and one-day shipping cost $4.98, $8.98, and $17.98, respectively. See http://www.amazon.com/gp/help/customer/display.html/ref=hp_468520_continental?/nodeId= 468636, as of February 2012.

prices. Figure 20.4 presents an example from the Apple Store website. Note that if Apple charged $2,399 instead of $2,199 for the high-end model, it would create an attraction effect instead of a compromise effect for the middle option.

Understanding context effects is important from both a theoretical and an applied perspective. Due to their prevalence and robustness, context effects are considered as rules rather than exceptions in choice behavior. Several researchers attempt to revise traditional choice models to capture the above findings (e.g., Tversky and Simonson 1993; Kivetz et al. 2004a). The adoption of these models is likely to alter firms' pricing strategies for a product portfolio, as well as firms' decisions on how products and/or services should be bundled. From an applied perspective, context effects have important implications for new product positioning, product promotions, and comparative advertising. A better perception of context effects can also improve standard methods that practitioners use to predict consumer choice and market share.

20.3.1.2 *Reference-dependent preferences and reference pricing*

A key implication of prospect theory is that individual preferences are reference dependent. The reference point against which an individual evaluates different choices can be the status quo (Samuelson and Zeckhauser 1988), the current endowment (Kahneman et al. 1991), or the focal point in a comparison (Dhar and Simonson 1992). Dhar and Simonson (1992) show in their experiments that making a product (or service) become the focus of a binary comparison can increase the choice probability of the focal product. This phenomenon can be explained by loss aversion. When a product is framed as the focus of a comparison, it becomes a consumer's reference point. The product's advantages compared to the other product become losses if the consumer does not choose the focal product. Based on loss aversion, the advantages of the focal product appear more salient than its disadvantages. Hence, a loss-averse consumer is more likely to prefer the focal product. The impact of focal points on consumer choice supports the use of comparative advertising; that is, a product appears more attractive to consumers when its advantageous features are compared to a competitive product, rather than being displayed alone. For example, the Honda website provides consumers with a comparison tool to compare the price and features of a Honda vehicle with a competing model in the market. The comparison tool automatically highlights the aspects in which Honda has a competitive advantage, making them the focus of comparison.[12]

A phenomenon closely related to consumers' reference-dependent preferences is that consumers form internal reference prices for price judgments, which then influence their purchasing decisions (Monroe 1973). Researchers have demonstrated that for frequently purchased goods (e.g., groceries and daily care products), historical prices and promotions significantly impact consumers' reference prices, and the prices of more recent purchases have a stronger effect (Kalwani et al. 1990; Briesch et al. 1997). In addition, if consumers encounter more frequent or deeper discounts, they tend to set lower reference prices for future transactions (Kalwani and Yim 1992). Interestingly, the frame of the discounts is also shown to impact the reference prices. DelVecchio et al. (2007) experimentally verify that when discounts are deep, presenting them in a percentage-off frame (as opposed to a cents-

---

[12] See http://automobiles.honda.com/tools/compare/models.aspx, as of August 2010.

off frame) results in higher reference prices for transactions occurring after the promotion. This result may be attributed to the greater cognitive difficulty of calculating the final selling price based on a percentage-off discount. Nevertheless, more research has to be conducted before obtaining a conclusive result on how promotion frames affect reference prices. We conjecture that product categories and consumer demographics also affect the adoption of a certain frame. For example, the percentage-off frame is more common in the apparel industry, whereas the cents-off frame is prevalent in food and high-tech product retailing. Why different promotion frames are used and how they impact reference prices are interesting research questions to investigate.

Formation of reference prices varies across different product categories (frequently purchased goods versus durable products) and customer types (brand-loyal customers versus switchers). For example, for high-tech products (e.g., personal computers) whose attributes and technologies evolve rapidly, their reference prices are more affected by the price and technological level of competitive products at the time of purchase than by historical prices (Bridges et al. 1995). Compared to bargain hunters, brand-loyal customers value brand names more than low prices. Hence, brand-loyal customers tend to rely more on the current prices of their favorite brands than on historical prices to form their reference prices (Mazumdar and Papatla 1995). Researchers also notice that different external reference points provided by the retailers have different impacts on consumers' internal reference prices (Urbany et al. 1988). In the context of automobile sales, Bearden et al. (2003) find that given the same sale price, advertising the sales offer as a markup above the invoice price (or dealer cost) generates significantly higher reference prices than advertising the offer as a markdown from the manufacturer suggested retail price. As a result, consumers consider the offer a better deal in the invoice frame. As another example, Kamins et al. (2004) demonstrate that in an on-line auction, the final bid of an item is raised (decreased) when the seller specifies a reservation price (a minimum bid), compared to the case where no external reference point is provided. This result may explain why we see auction items in Internet marketplaces such as eBay are sometimes equipped with a "buy-it-now" price, which serves as a reservation price.

Econometric models that incorporate reference prices have been used to explain consumer decisions in brand choices, purchase quantities, and purchase timing (e.g., Winer 1986; Krishnamurthi et al. 1992; Bell and Bucklin 1999). Nevertheless, researchers warn that the effect of reference prices on consumer decisions claimed in the current literature may be confounded with consumer heterogeneity in price sensitivity, promotion expectation, and purchase timings (Bell and Lattin 2000; Lattin and Bucklin 1989; Chang et al. 1999). A more rigorous treatment should control for these heterogeneities to identify the pure effect of reference prices. Interested readers are encouraged to see Mazumdar et al. (2005) for a more comprehensive discussion about the current status and future direction of research in reference pricing.

20.3.1.3 *Price presentation effects*

Another field that receives considerable attention from both researchers and practitioners is the influence of price presentations on consumers' purchase decisions. One well-known example is the price-ending effect. The digits 0, 5, and 9 are the most frequently used rightmost (i.e., ending) digits in retail prices, with the digit 9 especially dominant for discounted prices (Twedt 1965; Kreul 1982; Schindler and Kirby 1997). In addition, using 9-ending prices can substantially increase retail sales compared to prices not ending in 9 (Anderson and Simester 2003). While the frequent use of 0 and 5 can be attributed to the high cognitive accessibility of round numbers (Schindler and Kirby 1997), the reasons for the pervasive existence of 9-ending prices are diverse (Stiving and Winer 1997). Some researchers suggest that consumers tend to round prices down and hence underestimate the magnitude of a 9-ending price (Lambert 1975; Schindler and Warren 1988). Lacking sufficient empirical evidence for this argument (Schindler and Kibarian 1993), a more accepted explanation is that consumers tend to compare two prices by processing the digits from left to right, and they overly emphasize the difference in the left digit. For example, a consumer may perceive the difference between $93 and $79 to be greater than that between $89 and $75, since the first pair involves a difference of 2 in the left digit and the second pair involves a difference of 1 (Monroe 1979: 47). Thomas and Morwitz (2005) experimentally verify that a 9-ending price induces consumers' perception of a larger discount when the left digit is reduced than when the left digit remains unchanged; for example the perceived discount value from $3.00 to $2.99 is larger than that from $2.80 to $2.79. These findings suggest that retailers are more inclined to set a 9-ending price when adding one cent to the price induces an increase in the left digit; for example setting a price of $7.99 occurs more often than setting a price of $7.89 (see Schindler and Kirby 1997). A third reason for the broad use of 9-ending prices is that consumers tend to believe 9-ending prices signal a good deal. For example, they believe that prices ending in 9 imply the product is on sale or the price is the lowest one among all. Schindler and Kibarian (1996) present an interesting case where 99-ending prices generate higher sales than both 88-ending and 00-ending prices, even though the 88-ending prices are better deals. Anticipating such consumer beliefs, retailers may intentionally use 9-ending prices to signal a low-price image for their products, even if these prices do not actually represent that the products are sold at competitively low prices (Schindler 2006).

Another interesting price presentation effect is the precision effect recently studied by Thomas et al. (2010). The precision effect suggests that consumers incorrectly perceive precise large prices such as $364,578 to have lower magnitudes than comparable round prices such as $364,000, even if the actual magnitude of the precise price is higher than that of the round price.[13] The authors argue that this effect is caused by people's lower confidence when processing large precise numbers (Kelley and Lindsay 1993), and their belief from prior experience that precise (round) numbers are prevalently used for presenting small (large) magnitudes (Dehaene and Mehler 1992). The authors experimentally verify that the precision effect does exist, but it can be moderated by increasing the participants' confidence or changing their prior experience with precise numbers. Specifically, when participants are told that most students accurately evaluate real estate prices even without experience in actual transactions (high confidence case), their perceived magnitudes for the precise and round prices are not different. In contrast, when participants are told that students without experience in real estate transactions usually could not

---

[13] The price precision effect focuses on "stand-alone" magnitude perceptions rather than comparative magnitude perceptions. That is, we are interested in how price precision affects consumers' judgment in whether $364,578 is high or low, rather than judging whether $364,578 is higher or lower than $364,000.

accurately evaluate the prices (low confidence case), the precision effect becomes significant. In addition, when participants are deliberately exposed to a scenario where large prices are precise and small prices are round, they do not exhibit the precision effect in subsequent price judgments. More importantly, the precision effect tends to increase consumers' willingness-to-pay. Based on an on-line experiment and field data from actual real estate transactions, the authors confirm that consumers presented with a precise list price are willing to pay (or actually pay) a higher final price than consumers presented with a round list price. Thus, the precision effect may be a plausible reason why real estate or automobile sellers often employ precise list prices.

20.3.2 Social preferences: fairness and consumer pricing

In 2000, Amazon.com infuriated its customers with a test of a dynamic pricing strategy (Streitfeld 2000). A customer who bought a DVD at $24.49 from the website rechecked the price of the same item a week later and found that the price had jumped to $26.24. As an experiment, he cleaned the cookies on his computer, which identified him as an old customer to Amazon, and checked the price again. It went down to $22.74. This customer spread the word on DVDtalk.com, and the response was immediate. Some bloggers complained, "This is a very strange business model, to charge customers more when they buy more or come back to the site more. ... This is definitely not going to earn customer loyalty." Others were outraged, "I find this extremely sneaky and unethical." "I will never buy another thing from those guys!!!" The uproar was a nightmare for Amazon.

Many other examples have demonstrated the aftermath of unfair pricing (Maxwell 2008). Why consumers perceive a price to be fair or unfair and how these perceptions affect purchasing behavior have long been among the most active and important topics in pricing management, for both researchers and practitioners. One of the earliest results in this field is the principle of *dual entitlement* suggested by Kahneman et al. (1986a). Dual entitlement specifies that consumers are entitled to a reference price and firms are entitled to a reference profit. Under dual entitlement, firms cannot arbitrarily raise prices to reap profits. Otherwise, consumers will consider the price change as violating their entitlement to the reference price and perceive it as unfair. The authors conducted the following two telephone surveys to identify the conditions under which a price increase by a firm is regarded fair or unfair by its consumers.

> Survey 1: "A store has sold out the popular Cabbage Patch dolls for a month. A week before Christmas a single doll is discovered in a storeroom. The managers know that many customers would like to buy the doll. They announce over the store's public address system that the doll will be sold by auction to the customer who offers to pay the most. Would you consider selling by auction as completely fair, acceptable, somewhat unfair, or very unfair?"

> Survey 2: "A landlord owns and rents out a single small house to a tenant who is living on a fixed income. A higher rent would mean the tenant would have to move. Other small rental houses are available. The landlord's costs have increased substantially over the past year, and the landlord raises the rent to cover the cost increases when the tenant's lease is due for renewal. Would you evaluate the price raise as completely fair, acceptable, somewhat unfair, or very unfair?"

In Survey 1, 74 percent of the respondents consider selling the doll by auction to be unfair. In contrast, 75 percent of the respondents in Survey 2 consider the price raise as acceptable or completely fair. These contrasting responses reflect a key aspect in dual entitlement: A price increase to cover higher costs is generally considered fair, whereas a price increase to exploit market demand and increase profit is considered unfair. For example, the soaring gas price in summer due to an increasing amount of traveling and car usages often induces widespread consumer complaints.

Dual entitlement also postulates that consumers' fairness concerns do not require firms to cut prices when costs decrease, as shown in Survey 3 below (Kahneman et al. 1986b):

> Survey 3: "Suppose a factory produces a particular table and has been selling it for $150 each. Suppose that the factory has now found a supplier who charges $20 less for the materials needed to make each table. Does fairness require the factory to change its price from $150? [Respondents who answered "yes" were now asked, "What is a fair price that it could charge?"] [All respondents were then asked the following question.] Imagine instead that the factory saved $20 on each table not by getting less expensive supplies but by inventing a more efficient way of making the tables. Does fairness require the factory to change its price from $150 in this case?"

Fewer than one-third of the respondents require that the price for each table should drop by $20, and about half of them feel it acceptable for the factory to keep the current price. Further, the responses do not change whether the cost reduction is due to a lower material cost or improved efficiency. These results thus illustrate another aspect of dual entitlement: while fairness permits firms to shift the losses due to increased costs to consumers, it does not require them to equivalently share the gains with consumers in the case of decreased costs.

The proposition by dual entitlement that consumers consider it fair for firms to keep the original price when costs decrease does not hold universally. Kalapurakal et al. (1991), for example, show that when consumers know the history of the firm's pricing behavior, a pricing rule governed by dual entitlement is considered less fair than a cost-plus rule in which a firm raises (cuts) its price when costs increase (decrease). They present the following scenario to their respondents:

> "A department store has been buying an oriental floor rug for $100. The standard pricing practice used by department stores is to price floor rugs at double their cost, so the selling price of the rug is $200. This covers all the selling costs, overheads, and includes profit. The department store can sell all of the rugs that it can buy. Suppose because of exchange rate changes the cost of the rug rises from $100 to $120, and the selling price is increased to $220. As a result of another change in currency exchange rates, the cost of the rug falls by $20 back to $100. The department store continues to sell the rug for $220."

This scenario is then contrasted to a scenario with a cost-plus pricing rule; that is, after the cost of the rug falls back to $100, the store reduces the price to $200. The respondents rated that the cost-plus pricing practice is much fairer than the pricing rule governed by dual entitlement. Similar results are reported in Dickson and Kalapurakal (1994). Since in reality consumers are likely to observe firms' pricing behavior and judge price fairness over time, the above result suggests that firms should not take the principle of dual entitlement for granted but should cautiously adjust their pricing practices according to the specific situations.

Are all cost changes treated equivalently by consumers? An experimental study by Vaidyanathan and Aggarwal (2003) shows that whether consumers consider a price increase justifiable depends on the type of cost that increases and the reason for the cost increase. Particularly, two contextual factors are shown to affect consumers' price fairness perceptions. The first factor is whether the cost increase is due to internal or external causes. If it is the firm (internal cause), but not the outside market conditions (external cause), that is responsible for the cost increase, the resulting higher price is viewed as less fair. For example, price increases due to increased managerial costs (e.g., to cover a government fine resulting from an accounting oversight) are considered less fair than price increases due to increased material costs. The second contextual factor is whether the cost increase is controllable. If the firm can control the cost increase but still raises the price to match the growing market price, consumers tend to view the resulting higher price as less fair. For example, consider a grocery store that observes an increased wholesale price for lettuce in the market due to a supply shortage. If the store grows its own lettuce (thus can control the cost) but still raises the selling price, the price increase is regarded as less fair. The above discussion suggests that consumers regard a price increase to be fair only when the cost increase is both due to external causes and beyond the firm's control. The absence of either factor may result in perceptions of an unfair price. The implications of these results are two-fold. From the firm's perspective, explicating the reasons for price increases can positively affect consumers' price fairness perceptions. Conversely, consumers should be wary of the cost justification of a price increase because firms may take advantage of the growing market price to raise their own price, especially when consumers have limited information about the firms' cost status. Recently, Bolton and Alba (2006) find that a price increase to cover increased costs directly related to the product (e.g., material costs) is considered to be fairer than a price increase to cover increased indirect costs (e.g., rent). Further, consumers are more willing to accept a rise in service price than in product price when an indirect cost increases. These results provide some guidance on how firms could adjust the product and service prices to cover cost changes while maintaining good fairness perceptions from their consumers.

Despite researchers' debates on its robustness, the dual entitlement principle serves as an important starting point for studying consumers' perceptions of a fair price. Two central elements in dual entitlement are the consumers' definition of a reference price and their perceptions of the firms' profit margins. The choice of the reference price forms the foundation for price comparisons.[14] A consumer may use three sources as reference points: the price that the consumer paid in the past, the price that a comparative other consumer paid, and the price offered by competitive sellers. All three sources have been shown to affect price fairness perceptions (Collie et al. 2002; Bolton et al. 2003; Ho and Su 2009). In addition, Ordóñez et al. (2000) suggest that when there exist multiple external reference prices, a consumer tends to compare his/her own price with each reference price independently. The disadvantages of the consumer's own price compared to the other prices turn out to be more salient in his/her fairness perception than the advantages, consistent with loss aversion in prospect theory. Xia et al. (2004) further propose that price compari-

[14] See Section 20.3.1.2 for more discussion on reference prices outside the scope of fairness judgments.

son with a comparative other has a greater impact on fairness perceptions than price comparison with one's own past.

Consumers' misunderstanding of the sellers' profit margins or costs is also well documented. Through a telephone survey, Bolton et al. (2003) show that consumers generally overestimate sellers' profits. For example, the respondents estimated an average of 27.5 percent profit margin for grocery stores, whereas the industry reports a 1–2 percent margin. In a series of laboratory experiments, the authors also demonstrate that people attribute the different prices observed in different types of stores (e.g., a department store versus a discount store) more to profit differences than to cost or service differences. In addition, when the participants are prompted to think about the detailed costs of a seller (e.g., by asking them to explicitly estimate labor costs or rent), they provide more realistic profit estimates and generally give higher fairness ratings. Nevertheless, similar to Vaidya-nathan and Aggarwal (2003), the authors observe that consumers do not view every cost equivalently. For example, fairness ratings increase more when markdown costs or rent are made salient, compared to when labor costs are made salient. In contrast, fairness ratings go down slightly when promotion costs are made salient. These results suggest that firms can potentially improve consumers' fairness perceptions by making their cost information more transparent. They should, however, be cautious in disclosing the "right" types of cost information.

Consumers' reference-dependent fairness perceptions and their frequent ignorance about a firm's true costs raise some warning for markdown practices. Consumers may take the markdown price during the sales season as the reference price and think that firms can still earn profits with these low prices. As a result, the regular prices seem exorbitant to consumers and generate feelings of being treated unfairly. In the long run, the markdown practice induces more consumer waiting, and it may even lead consumers to buy from other brands due to dissatisfaction. Consequently, the short-term goal of clearing end-of-season inventory by markdowns is likely to hurt the firm's long-term profit. A tactic called "price-match guarantee" is increasingly used by firms (e.g., Gap Inc., Best Buy)[15] to deter consumer waiting for markdowns. With this tactic, firms commit to compensating a consumer for the price difference if the purchased item is marked down within a certain time window.[16] Alternatively, firms can also try to educate consumers to learn that sale prices are generally below costs. Doing so helps consumers to better understand the firms' profit margins and consequently modify their fairness perceptions.

In addition to studying the drivers for consumers' price (un)fairness perceptions, understanding the consequences of these perceptions helps firms to react effectively. Evidence from experiments and field surveys shows that the perception of an unfair price may lead to consumers leaving the current buyer–seller relationship (Huppertz et al. 1978), customer complaints and dissatisfaction (Oliver and Swan 1989a,b; Herrmann et al. 2007), lower buying intentions (Campbell 1999; Maxwell 2002), and decreased demand and profit (Anderson and Simester 2006). Further, strong unfairness perceptions generate

---

[15] See http://www.gap.com/customerService/info.do?cid=40959&mlink=null,1981604&clink=1981604, http://www.bestbuy.com/site/Help-Topics/Bestbuy.com-Price-Match-Guarantee/pcmcat204400050011.c?id=pcmcat 204400050011, as of August 2010.

[16] Lai et al. (2010) analytically specify the conditions under which price-match guarantees can improve sellers' profits. Their model, however, studies rational expectation equilibria without incorporating fairness concerns.

anger among consumers. Angry consumers tend to revenge the unfair firm by spreading negative word of mouth. They may even switch to direct competitors despite the high switching costs in time and effort (Bougie et al. 2003). When consumers are faced with unfair prices, they not only seek to restore an equitable financial position, but they also take action to cope with their negative emotions such as disappointment, regret, or anger (Xia et al. 2004). Therefore, firms should be responsive once a sense of price unfairness arises among their consumers. Offering financial compensation such as refunds or gift certificates can help. Addtionally, firms should maintain a good customer service program to handle complaints respectfully and swiftly to soothe consumers' negative emotions.

Despite its long history, price fairness remains one of the top issues for both researchers and practitioners. Nowadays, customer-based price differentiation such as senior discounts and family specials are widely used in various industries without incurring many consumer complaints. Airline companies continue adopting revenue management programs to segment their customers (Phillips 2005). Different pricing strategies emerged in the e-commerce era and their impact on price fairness perceptions also attracts much attention. Explaining why a certain pricing strategy (especially one that employs price discrimination) works in some situations but not in others requires further studies of the interaction between fairness concerns and other factors such as transaction contexts, information structures, and consumers' cultural and social backgrounds. In addition, incorporating fairness into consumer pricing models is a relatively new research area (e.g., Rotemberg 2011). We believe that these future endeavors are essential for prescribing more effective pricing strategies under different market conditions.

20.3.3 Social preferences: reputation and consumer-to-consumer pricing

Internet trading involves sellers and buyers whose identities are private. Despite the lack of interpersonal contact as in traditional bricks-and-mortar markets, Internet trading has flourished in the past decade, partially attributed to the use of feedback systems that make sellers' reputation information accessible to potential buyers. We note, however, that reputation information derived from feedback is different from that gained in a long-term relationship in traditional markets. In fact, most Internet transactions are one-time exchanges between strangers (Resnick and Zeckhauser 2002). From a buyer's perspective, feedback in Internet markets provides information about a seller's reputation with respect to other buyers, whereas reputation information in a traditional market is generally derived from one's own experience. Researchers have been studying this distinction and the efficacy of feedback systems in promoting on-line trading.

Bolton et al. (2004) study buyer and seller behaviors, as well as trading efficiency in a controlled laboratory experiment that involves three different markets. In all three markets, the buyer decides whether or not to purchase from the matched seller. If the buyer chooses to purchase, s/he faces a moral hazard problem in which the seller can exploit the buyer's payment without shipping the product. In the *strangers market*, buyers and sellers are matched with each other at most once and they interact anonymously. No information about the sellers' shipping decisions in past transactions is revealed to the buyers. In the *feedback market*, although matching remains one-time and anonymous, a buyer has access to the complete history of the matched seller's past shipping decisions before s/he decides whether to purchase or not. Finally, in the *partners market,* matching is fixed and the pairs interact repeatedly with the buyers having access to the sellers' full shipping history. The strangers market represents the situation where no reputation can be established; the feedback market mimics Internet trading with perfectly reliable reputation information; and the partners market resembles traditional transactions.

The authors observe that trading is most efficient in the partners market, significantly less efficient in the feedback market, and least efficient in the strangers market. Buyers (sellers) are most trusting (trustworthy) in the partners market—the highest percentage of buyers (sellers) chooses to purchase (ship). The substantial increase in trading efficiency from the strangers market to the feedback market confirms the positive effect that feedback systems bring to trade. However, the substantial decrease in trading efficiency from the partners market to the feedback market shows the limitation of feedback systems in promoting transactions. There are two reasons for this limitation. The first reason lies in the fact that a buyer's trust in the feedback market generates a positive reputation of the seller for other buyers rather than for the buyer himself as in the partners market. Since the informational benefit from trusting is not gained by the buyer in the feedback market, the buyer has weaker incentive to trust; that is, he is less willing to engage in the transaction. The second reason is related to the fact that in the feedback market, a seller's reputation may be affected by the buyer's past experience with other sellers. A trustworthy seller appears to be less trustworthy for a buyer who is frequently exploited by previous sellers. Conversely, an untrustworthy seller may be trusted by a buyer who has had a good experience before. Imposing stricter control on buyer/seller identification in Internet trading is likely to help alleviate both effects.

The authors also find that negative feedback has a stronger impact than positive feedback, and so does recent feedback compared to old feedback. This observation suggests that an efficient feedback system should not solely rely on cumulative information. Instead, it should provide more recent and detailed information regarding positive and negative behaviors. This managerial insight has resulted in the evolution of feedback systems adopted by Internet trading sites such as eBay. In the eBay feedback system as of August 2010, overall rating is computed based on feedback in the last 12 months only. The system also shows the number of positive and negative feedback reports a buyer/seller receives in the last 1, 6, and 12 months. In addition, the detailed seller rating presents a seller's performance in four categories important to buyers: whether item description is consistent with actual quality, whether communication is easy and responsive, whether shipment is timely, and whether shipping and handling charges are reasonable.

Recently, Bolton et al. (2008) further study how the interaction between competition and reputation affects trading in the feedback market and the partners market.[17] They study two types of competition. Under *matching* competition, a buyer chooses from two sellers based on their reputation information in each transaction round. Under *price* competition, a buyer chooses between two sellers based on both reputation information and price offers. The authors observe that the introduction of either competition promotes buyer's trust and seller's trustworthiness in the markets, leading to improved trading efficiency. Nevertheless,

[17] Bolton et al. (2008) refer to the feedback market in Bolton et al. (2004) as the *strangers market.* We keep the terminology of the feedback market to prevent confusion.

the improvement in trading efficiency due to competition is much smaller in the partners market. This is because the existence of equally reputable sellers with competing prices reduces the buyers' tendency to partner with a seller and hence weakens the efficiency-enhancing effect of partnership. The authors also observe that reputation information is more salient than price offers in a buyer's choice.

Resnick et al. (2006) conducted a randomized controlled field study with an actual eBay seller to study how reputation affects on-line trading. The seller regularly auctioned vintage postcard lots on eBay and had a highly positive rating. In the experiments, the seller created several new identities without any feedback history and sold pairs of vintage postcard lots with either the established identity or a new identity, determined by a random device. The product description, terms of payment, shipping rules, and webpage demonstration were identical among all identities. Their results show that buyers' willingness-to-pay is on average 8.1 percent higher for the established identity than for a new one. The established identity outperforms the new identities in selling more units at or above the opening bids and enjoys higher end prices for the units sold. Their results and those discussed earlier suggest that in the electronic marketplace, reputation plays a more important role than offering competitive prices in affecting buyers' purchasing decisions. In other words, a well-established seller does not need to engage in a price war with newcomers. Rather, s/he should put the emphasis on maintaining a good reputation. Nevertheless, given the limited amount of studies in this field, more research is required to verify the robustness of these results in more diversified market environments.

20.3.4 Summary and future prospects

We discuss in this section how behavioral concerns (as opposed to pecuniary incentives) affect pricing for consumers. We determine that a buyer's purchasing decision is affected by the context in which s/he makes the decision, and a buyer's internal reference price as well as the presentation of prices often impact his/her willingness to purchase. Consumers' concerns for fairness shed light on how firms should interact with their customers to ensure long-term profitability. Finally, in the increasingly popular electronic marketplace, dissemination of reputation by feedback systems prospers trust and trustworthiness among transactors and improves trading efficiency.

There has been limited research combining the insights of behavioral economics with standard pricing models. Some examples along this line include Popescu and Wu (2007), Su (2009) and Nasiry and Popescu (2012). Popescu and Wu (2007) demonstrate that if consumers derive reference prices based on past transactions and if they are loss-averse, the optimal price path that a firm follows converges to a constant steady-state price in the long run. Su (2009) develops a model of consumer inertia to show that loss aversion, probabilistic weighting, and hyperbolic discounting all contribute to consumers' tendency to procrastinate buying, which in turn impacts a firm's dynamic pricing strategy. Nasiry and Popescu (2012) study the effect of consumer regret on a firm's advance selling strategy. They show that when consumers have uncertain and heterogeneous valuations for the product, firms can increase profits by taking advantage of consumers' anticipated regret of not buying in advance selling. One critical behavioral issue missing in the analytical research of consumer pricing is people's bounded rationality in solving complex decision problems. For example, level-k thinking and quantal response equilibrium can serve as alternatives to the rational expectations assumption to better predict consumer purchase decisions. We believe that capturing behavioral concerns in traditional pricing models opens a fruitful avenue for future studies.

20.4 BEHAVIORAL ISSUES IN BUSINESS-TO-BUSINESS PRICING CONTRACTS

Bilateral contracting has been an active research area in supply chain management in recent years. The topics in this field can be divided into two main streams. One stream studies the ability of different contracts to eliminate double marginalization (Spengler 1950) and coordinate the channel to achieve the centralized system outcome. These studies assume that supply chain members have access to the same information regarding their business parameters and market information. A large number of contract types have been investigated, including the buy-back contract (Pasternack 1985), two-part tariff (Moorthy 1987), quantity flexibility contract (Tsay 1999), sales-rebate contract (Taylor 2002), and revenue-sharing contract (Cachon and Lariviere 2005). Researchers show that these contracts induce supply chain members to effectively share inventory and demand risks to achieve channel coordination. The next research stream considers information asymmetry; that is, different supply chain members have access to different information. The focus of this stream is to develop analytical remedies and mechanisms to induce credible information sharing between supply chain partners. Employing principal–agent models, these studies result in pricing contracts that align the pecuniary incentives between supply chain partners. Consequently, credible information sharing and cooperation between the parties are enabled (e.g., Ha 2001; Corbett et al. 2004; Özer and Wei 2006). Kaya and Özer (Chapter 29) provide a comprehensive discussion on how pricing contracts enable risk and information sharing in a supply chain.

The above literature uses an analytical approach that assumes supply chain members to be self-interested and purely motivated by maximizing their own pecuniary payoffs. As discussed in Section 20.2, these assumptions do not always reflect human behavior. Recently, behavioral issues have gained popularity in operations management, leading to the new area of Behavioral Operations Management (BOM).[18] Studies in BOM include analyzing the behavioral causes of the bullwhip effect (Sterman 1989; Croson and Donohue 2006; Wu and Katok 2006) and examining how a single decision-maker's behavior deviates from theoretical predictions (Schweitzer and Cachon 2000; Bolton and Katok 2008; Su 2008). Researchers have also started to investigate behavioral issues in a strategic context where multiple decision-makers interact with each other (Cui et al. 2007; Chen et al. 2008; Özer et al. 2011). Since BOM is a relatively new research area, it has explored only part of the behavioral regularities discussed in Section 20.2. In what follows, we focus on three types of

---

[18] Interested readers are referred to Bendoly et al. (2006), Gino and Pisano (2008), and Bendoly et al. (2010) for a comprehensive discussion of recent developments and future trends in BOM.

behavioral issues: framing effects, social preferences, and bounded rationality in the sense that people are prone to decision errors.

20.4.1 Individual choice theories: framing effects and pricing contracts

Theoretical studies of pricing contracts have focused on investigating how various contracts affect firms' pricing, inventory, and quality decisions in different supply chain environments. Researchers have shown that multiple forms of contracts can coordinate firms' decisions and achieve full channel efficiency. They also derive conditions under which different contract types are theoretically equivalent, resulting in the same channel profit and profit distribution among supply chain members. Different types of contracts, however, impose different decision frames for supply chain members. Hence, framing effects implied by prospect theory (see Section 20.2.1.1) are likely to affect the performance of different pricing contracts.

Consider the two-part tariff in a manufacturer–retailer dyad facing deterministic linear demand. The manufacturer (she) produces at cost c and sells the product to the retailer. The retailer (he) sells to consumers at price p with demand $q = a - p$. The manufacturer offers a take-it-or-leave-it contract (in the form of a two-part tariff) to the retailer, and the retailer in response decides whether to accept or reject the contract. Under the two-part tariff, the manufacturer specifies a fixed fee F and a wholesale price w. If the retailer accepts the contract, he pays F upfront and is charged w for each unit ordered; that is he pays $F + wq$ when ordering q units. If he rejects, both parties earn zero payoffs. Ho and Zhang (2008) show that in equilibrium the two-part tariff can align the parties' incentives with the integrated channel's and hence coordinate the channel.

Note that the two-part tariff can be framed as an equivalent quantity-discount contract: The manufacturer charges the retailer a unit price of $(F/q) + w$ when q units are ordered. Since this quantity-discount contract is merely a different frame of the two-part tariff, both contracts generate identical outcomes and achieve full channel efficiency in theory. However, Ho and Zhang (2008) observe in controlled laboratory experiments that neither the quantity-discount contract nor the two-part tariff coordinates the channel, although the former achieves higher channel efficiency than the latter. A key observation that drives the inefficiency of both contracts is that the retailers reject the contracts more often than predicted, especially for the two-part tariff.

One reason for the different performance of the two mathematically equivalent contracts is due to loss aversion. According to prospect theory, people's utilities are reference-dependent and losses loom larger than gains. In the two-part tariff, the retailer views the fixed fee paid upfront as a loss and the subsequent revenue as a gain. In addition, a $1 fixed fee is mentally accounted more than a $1 revenue. Therefore, a loss-averse retailer obtains a utility of $(p - w)q - \lambda F$ when ordering q units. $\lambda \geq 1$ measures the retailer's degree of loss aversion: a higher λ corresponds to a retailer more averse to losses. Since the loss due to the fixed fee is more salient in the two-part tariff, the retailer is likely to experience a higher degree of loss aversion under this contract and be biased towards rejecting it. Ho and Zhang (2008) empirically show that the estimated value of λ is indeed significantly higher in the two-part tariff than in the quantity-discount contract.

The above result suggests that due to loss aversion, the framing of the two-part tariff affects the retailer's contract acceptance decision and hence the efficiency of the contract. One may wonder whether reducing the salience of the contract acceptance decision can mitigate this framing effect. Consider the following variation of the original setting. After the manufacturer offers the contract, the retailer is asked to determine the ordering quantity without being first asked explicitly whether he will accept or reject the contract. Note that the option of rejecting a contract remains valid (though implicit) because the retailer can order zero quantity. However, reducing the step of deciding contract acceptance suppresses the retailer's mental process of defining the gain–loss domains in his utility, thus alleviating the impact of loss aversion. An additional experiment conducted by Ho and Zhang (2008) confirms this argument.

Next we turn to two other coordinating contracts: the revenue-sharing contract and the buy-back contract. Suppose in a supplier–retailer dyad, the retailer (he) faces the news-vendor problem with exogenous stochastic demand and decides how much to order from the supplier. The supplier (she) is the Stackelberg leader who offers the contract: She determines the wholesale price w_{BB} and the buy-back rate b in a buy-back contract, or she determines the wholesale price w_{RS} and a revenue-sharing rate r in a revenue-sharing contract.[19] Cachon and Lariviere (2005) show that both contracts can achieve channel coordination with arbitrary division of channel profits between the parties. In addition, the two contracts are theoretically equivalent if the cost of units sold and unsold are the same under both contracts; that is, if $w_{BB} = w_{RS} + r$ and $w_{BB} - b = w_{RS}$.

If these two contracts are to coordinate the channel, w_{RS} is necessarily lower than w_{BB}. If the retailer faces a low demand and is not guaranteed a positive revenue (e.g., when the minimum demand is 0), the higher wholesale price paid upfront in the buy-back contract becomes a salient loss. Hence, loss aversion induces the retailer to order less in the buy-back contract than in the revenue-sharing contract and makes the buy-back contract less effective in coordinating the channel.[20] What if the retailer faces a high demand and is guaranteed a positive revenue (e.g., when demand is at least 50)? Now the shared revenue becomes a salient loss. Thus loss aversion renders the revenue-sharing contract less effective in coordinating the channel. A more interesting case is to frame a high demand as a low decision frame; for example by asking the retailer to order an amount in addition to the minimum demand of 50. Since the guaranteed 50 units is separated from the decision frame, prospect theory suggests that people will consider the utility from selling 50 units as the reference point for evaluating gains and losses. Therefore, the retailer's behavior in this high-demand-low-frame case is expected to be similar to that in the low-demand case. Through a controlled laboratory experiment, Katok and Wu (2009) provide empirical support for the above arguments.

---

[19] In a buy-back contract, the supplier charges w_{BB} for each unit ordered and offers the retailer a rebate b for each unsold unit. In a revenue-sharing contract, the supplier charges w_{RS} for each unit ordered and receives from the retailer a bonus r for each sold unit.

[20] A standard analysis of the newsvendor problem shows that double marginalization reduces channel efficiency by making the retailer order too few compared to the efficient level. Thus, an optimal coordinating contract must induce higher orders from the retailer.

20.4.2 Social preferences and pricing contracts

As seen in Section 20.2.2, the presence of social preferences mitigates people's self-interested motives and encourages cooperative actions. In this section, we discuss two effects of social preferences in the context of pricing contracts: how they alleviate double marginalization in a supply chain, and how they induce effective information sharing between supply chain members.

20.4.2.1 Social preferences and double marginalization

Consider a manufacturer–retailer dyad facing a deterministic linear demand. The manufacturer (she) determines a wholesale price w for selling a single product to the retailer. The retailer (he) then sets a retail price p and orders the demand $D(p) = a - bp$ with $b > 0$ from the manufacturer. In the unique subgame perfect Nash equilibrium, the manufacturer sets w higher than the marginal production cost, and the retailer sets p higher than the optimal retail price in a centralized channel (i.e., when both parties are consolidated into a single decision maker). The resulting channel efficiency is low. This phenomenon is an example of double marginalization: Both parties set a substantial profit margin to maximize their own payoffs without considering the externality of their actions to the other party and hence the entire supply chain. If one party exhibits some concern about the other party's welfare, double marginalization may be mitigated and even eliminated. One such other-regarding concern is the concern for fairness.

If, for example, the retailer is fair-minded, his fairness concern has two effects on the supply chain. First, the manufacturer may want to deviate from setting a high w given the fear that the fair-minded retailer may punish her by setting a high p that results in zero demand. Secondly, the fair-minded retailer may also want to lower p to both reward the manufacturer's fair action and achieve equitable outcomes between the two parties. Therefore, if the retailer's fairness concern is strong, these joint effects may be sufficient to eliminate double marginalization and achieve channel coordination. One way to model the retailer's fairness concern is to follow the model of inequality aversion by Fehr and Schmidt (1999). Assume that the retailer considers a fraction γ of the manufacturer's profit as the reference point for a fair outcome. The retailer's utility is given by

$$u(w, p) = \pi(w, p) - \alpha \max\{\gamma\Pi(w, p) - \pi(w, p), 0\} - \beta \max\{\pi(w, p) - \gamma\Pi(w, p), 0\},$$

where π and Π denote the profit function for the retailer and the manufacturer, respectively. $\alpha \geq 0$ is the retailer's envy weight (due to being worse than the fair outcome), and $\beta \geq 0$ is the retailer's guilt weight (due to being better than the fair outcome). This formulation is due to Cui et al. (2007). They provide analytical solutions for both parties' decisions under this setting. Their results coincide with the above intuitive arguments: (1) When w is sufficiently high, the retailer sets a high p to punish the manufacturer, even if doing so sacrifices his own payoff; (2) when w is sufficiently low, the retailer sets a low p to reward the manufacturer's generosity; and (3) when w is in the intermediate level, the retailer sets a price so that the channel achieves an equitable outcome from his perspective, that is, $\pi(w, p) = \gamma\Pi(w, p)$.

These results illustrate two contradicting effects of the retailer's fairness concern on double marginalization. When w is high, the retailer's fairness concern exacerbates double marginalization because he marks up the retail price to punish the manufacturer. Conversely, when w is low, the retailer's fairness concern alleviates double marginalization as he sets a low retail price to reward the manufacturer. Under the right conditions, the manufacturer is motivated by the reward to set a sufficiently low wholesale price that coordinates the channel. Additionally, when w is at the medium level, the fair-minded retailer voluntarily aligns his incentive with the manufacturer's by setting a retail price to achieve the equitable payoff $\gamma\Pi$. Consequently, the optimal wholesale price eliminates double marginalization by simultaneously maximizing the manufacturer's, the retailer's, and the channel profit. These results highlight that the simple wholesale price contract can be used as a coordinating mechanism and a favorable pricing strategy that fosters an equitable channel relationship. Cui et al. (2007) also discuss the case where both the manufacturer and the retailer are fair-minded. In that case, the simple wholesale price contract achieves channel coordination if the manufacturer can tolerate some level of payoff inequality.

Controlled laboratory experiments can be used to verify whether fairness concerns help coordinate a supply chain with human decision-makers. Keser and Paleologo (2004) study a dyadic supply chain with three characteristics: (1) Demand is stochastic, (2) the retail price is exogenously fixed, and (3) the retailer orders from the manufacturer who sets the wholesale price. Their results show a strong tendency for fairness in the supply chain: The manufacturers set wholesale prices that are significantly lower than the equilibrium price, leading to a more equitable profit split between the two parties. Nevertheless, the resulting channel efficiency is not better than the equilibrium prediction. One major reason for this outcome is that people have cognitive limitations in solving for the optimal ordering quantity and the optimal wholesale price in face of stochastic demand. We will discuss the impact of such cognitive limitations on contract performance in Section 20.4.3.

Fairness is only one type of preference that reflects one's care about others' outcomes. One can generalize these preferences (e.g., reciprocity, inequality aversion) to the preference for *relationship*, aggregating all social concerns for sustaining a good relationship with one's partner. As discussed earlier, the key for eliminating double marginalization under a wholesale price contract is that the supply chain partners care about each other's payoffs. Hence, one should expect that if the preference for relationship is prominent, channel coordination may be possible under simple pricing contracts. Contrary to the preference for relationship, the preference for *status* reflects motivational concerns that one desires to be outstanding relative to one's peers. The preference for status may induce competition in interactions (e.g., Loch et al. 2000; Huberman et al. 2004), and hence it is likely to aggravate double marginalization. Loch and Wu (2008) experimentally study the impact of both preferences on a supply chain by contrasting them to a control treatment where neither preference is salient. They follow the pricing game discussed at the beginning of this section but allow participants to interact repeatedly. In the control treatment, participants were randomly matched with each other and did not know their partners' identities throughout the experiment. In the *relationship* treatment, paired participants first met in person and talked, then engaged in the pricing game. In the *status* treatment, participants were matched as in the control treatment, but after each round of interaction, the person who achieved a higher profit than his/her partner was declared as the "winner" and announced (on the computer screen) within the corresponding pair. There is no payoff reward for being a winner.

The experimental results strongly support the idea that the preference for relationship (status) alleviates (exacerbates) double marginalization. Specifically, participants set much lower (higher) prices in the relationship (status) treatment compared to the control treatment. Hence, channel efficiency is improved by making the relationship concern salient but deteriorated if the status concern is emphasized. The results also reflect that people's concern for social preferences is separate from economic motives in shaping their decisions. In other words, these social considerations are not a result of expecting future economic gains, but a consequence of attaining self-valued social goals. The authors demonstrate this result by showing that pricing decisions made by a rational agent who cares about long-term profits cannot explain the experimental data. Another evidence is that long-term profits even decrease in the status treatment. Note that the status of being a "winner" in a round is not related to the participants' monetary payoffs at all but is just a symbol. Yet, the participants still compete by setting high margins for themselves to crave for the status symbol, even though doing so hurts both their own payoffs and channel efficiency.

20.4.2.2 *Trust and pricing contracts for credible information sharing*

A recent research trend in bilateral contracting in a supply chain is to develop effective mechanisms to ensure credible information sharing between supply chain partners. The resulting contracts are usually complex and costly to manage. Thus, researchers have started to investigate whether these contracts are necessary and/or implementable to induce credible information sharing.

Consider a manufacturer–retailer dyad in which the manufacturer (he) solicits demand forecast information from the downstream retailer (she) to determine production capacity. The parties interact under a wholesale price contract and face stochastic demand $D = \mu + \xi + \varepsilon$, where μ is the constant average demand, ξ is the retailer's private forecast information, and ε is the random market uncertainty. The retailer has better forecast information due to her proximity to the end market. After the retailer observes ξ, she submits a report $\hat{\xi}$ to the manufacturer. The manufacturer receives $\hat{\xi}$ and builds capacity K at cost c_K. Market uncertainty (and hence demand) is then realized. The manufacturer produces $\min(D, K)$ and sells to the retailer at price w. Finally, the retailer sells to the end market at price r. Note that $\hat{\xi}$ is not a binding order and does not impose any cost to the retailer. The manufacturer also cannot verify whether $\hat{\xi}$ is equal to ξ. Since the retailer is better off if the manufacturer builds higher capacity, she has an incentive to inflate her forecast in this cheap-talk forecast communication. Anticipating this incentive, the manufacturer would disregard the forecast report, leading to ineffective forecast sharing. Özer et al. (2011) indeed show that the only perfect Bayesian equilibrium in this forecast sharing game is uninformative.

In reality, however, some firms seem to effectively share forecast information via cheap talk, whereas others fail to do so. Why? Through a series of controlled laboratory experiments, Özer et al. (2011) determine that trust and trustworthiness among human agents are the key drivers for effective cheap-talk forecast sharing under a wholesale price contract. In particular, the retailers' reports are informative about their forecasts, and the manufacturers rely on the reports to determine capacity. Existing supply chain literature assumes that supply chain partners either fully trust each other and cooperate when sharing forecasts, or do not trust each other at all. Contrary to this all-or-nothing view, the authors determine that a continuum exists between these two extremes. They determine when trust matters in forecast information sharing, how trust is affected by changes in the supply chain environment, and how trust affects related operational decisions. For example, they show that trust and cooperation are affected more by changes in the capacity cost (which is a measure of the vulnerability due to potential loss from trusting) than by market uncertainty of the product.

The authors propose an analytical model of trust to capture both pecuniary and non-pecuniary incentives in the game theoretic model of cheap-talk forecast sharing. Specifically, the manufacturer's trust affects his belief update about the private forecast: Given $\hat{\xi}$, he believes that the private forecast has the same distribution as $\alpha\hat{\xi} + (1 - \alpha)\xi^T$, where ξ^T follows the same distribution as ξ but capped by $\hat{\xi}$. $\alpha \in [0, 1]$ measures the manufacturer's trust level: $\alpha = 1$ implies full trust on the report, whereas $\alpha = 0$ implies no trust and the manufacturer considers the report as an upper bound for the private forecast. The retailer's trustworthiness is characterized by a disutility of deception, modeled as $\beta|\hat{\xi} - \xi|$. $\beta \geq 0$ controls the retailer's incentive to misreport her forecast. A retailer with a higher β is more trustworthy because she experiences a higher disutility when giving the same amount of forecast distortion as one with a lower β. The new model enhances standard theory by effectively explaining the observed behavior.

These results have important implications for a firm's forecast management and contracting strategies. For example, in market conditions that foster trust and natural cooperation (e.g., when capacity cost is low), a simple wholesale price contract suffices to induce effective forecast sharing, and hence implementing complex contracts to ensure credible information sharing is unnecessary. Conversely, in situations where trust is not spontaneously formed (e.g., when both capacity cost and market uncertainty are high), firms should invest in either complex contracts or long-term trust-building relationships to improve forecast sharing. Sharing forecast for capacity investment is prevalent in the computing industry. For example, Hewlett-Packard's Imaging and Printing Group interacts with six major distributors. Its annual business volume amounts to $2 billion. A management project was dedicated to designing proper strategies and contracts to motivate credible forecast sharing from the distributors. HP reports that the above study has provided practical guidance for the group to develop effective forecast sharing programs with its distributors based on different product types.

20.4.3 Bounded rationality and pricing contracts

As discussed in Section 20.2.3, people have a limited level of sophistication in reasoning and are prone to decision errors. These cognitive limitations often lead to suboptimal decisions and hence affect the performance of a pricing contract. In this section, we discuss how bounded rationality affects the efficacy of pricing contracts in coordinating a supply chain.

Consider the quantity-discount contract in a manufacturer–retailer dyad facing a deterministic linear demand. The manufacturer (she) produces a product at cost c and sells to the retailer. The retailer (he) orders q from the manufacturer, resulting in a retail price $p = a - q$ for consumers. The manufacturer offers a one-block, two-block, or three-block contract to the retailer. A one-block contract simply specifies a wholesale price. A two-block contract employs incremental quantity discounts with parameters $\{x_1, w_1, w_2\}$ where $w_2 < w_1$; that is, the payment charged for q units is

$$T(q) = \begin{cases} w_1 \cdot q, & \text{if } 0 < q \leq x_1, \\ w_1 \cdot x_1 + w_2 \cdot (q - x_1), & \text{if } q > x_1, \end{cases}$$

Similarly, a three-block contract has two levels of incremental quantity discounts based on the order quantity. If the retailer accepts the contract, he chooses the order quantity, which determines both parties' payoffs. If he rejects, both parties earn zero payoffs. Lim and Ho (2007) show by standard game theory that the manufacturer can calibrate the contract parameters so that in both two-block and three-block contracts, (1) the retailer buys only from the last block (i.e., at the lowest price), and (2) full channel efficiency is achieved (versus 75 percent efficiency under a one-block contract).

Do these results reflect actual behavior? Lim and Ho (2007) experimentally test them with human participants and find that the answer is no. Particularly, the two-block contract does not achieve full channel efficiency, although it increases efficiency compared to the one-block contract. The three-block contract significantly outperforms the two-block contract and achieves 95 percent efficiency conditional on contract acceptance. These results are robust to the level of the participants' managerial experience (undergraduate versus MBA students), the stake size, the length of time for understanding the instructions, and individual versus group decision making.

One major reason why these contracts fail to coordinate the channel in the experiments is that the retailers often buy from blocks with higher prices than the last block, contrary to theory. This suboptimal behavior can be induced by the retailer's cognitive limitation in identifying the optimal block he should buy from. One way to characterize this cognitive limitation is to follow the quantal response equilibrium (QRE) model by McKelvey and Palfrey (1995).[21] For example, Lim and Ho (2007) specify that the retailer buys from the second block in a two-block contract with probability $e^{\gamma U_R^r} / \left(1 + e^{\gamma U_R^l} + e^{\gamma U_R^r}\right)$, where U_R^l and U_R^r are the retailer's utility of buying from the first and second block, respectively. $\gamma \geq 0$ measures how much the retailer is subject to decision errors: $\gamma = 0$ implies that the retailer makes choices randomly, whereas $\gamma = \infty$ implies that the retailer is a perfect optimizer. Lim and Ho (2007) show that the retailer's probabilistic choice of blocks is a key contributor to the worse performance of the two-block and three-block contracts compared to theory. These results emphasize that researchers should be cautious about non-pecuniary factors latent in people's utility functions, especially when their conclusions strongly rely on the assumptions of incentive compatibility and perfect payoff sensitivity.

Recently, researchers started to investigate the joint effects of social preferences and bounded rationality on the performance of pricing contracts. For example, a fair-minded retailer is likely to reject a contract offered by a manufacturer if the contract yields an unfair profit distribution between the two parties. This fairness concern and the retailer's occasional mistake of rejecting an optimal contract jointly influence contract acceptance rates and hence the efficiency of the contract. Pavlov and Katok (2011) present an analytical

---

[21] As discussed in Section 20.2.3.2, QRE postulates that people make mistakes when responding to others' actions (i.e., do not always best respond), although a response associated with a higher expected utility is chosen more frequently.

model that captures these issues. Their model suggests that if the retailer's fairness concern is private information, the optimal contract does not coordinate the channel due to a positive probability that the contract is rejected by the retailer. Further, if the retailer occasionally rejects an optimal contract due to decision errors, channel coordination is impossible even if the retailer's fairness concern is common knowledge. Supported by experimental observations, these theoretical results indicate that both incomplete information about fairness concerns and decision errors in contract acceptance are important reasons for the failure of a pricing contract to coordinate the channel.

20.4.4 Summary and future prospects

In this section, we discuss how behavioral regularities affect the performance of different pricing contracts. Theoretical results such as channel coordination by pricing contracts and equivalence between different coordinating contracts are not supported in experiments. Future opportunities for studying contract performance with controlled laboratory experiments abound. For example, a comprehensive study of different contract types can provide insights about which contract generates better outcomes under what conditions and hence can serve as a practical guide. Existing experiments have also not examined the negotiation process through which a contract is established. This can be done with an experiment that allows one party to repeatedly offer a contract to the other through an alternating bargaining process. Further, complex, nonlinear pricing contracts designed to ensure credible information sharing require contract designers to fully understand the implications of actions (e.g., imposing constraints on incentive compatibility and individual rationality in principal–agent models). It is doubted that these contracts can perform as well as predicted by theory when decision-makers are boundedly rational. Therefore, one should empirically verify if and how social preferences and/or individual decision biases render these contracts to achieve better or worse outcomes than simpler linear pricing contracts in different market environments.

Little research has fully explored the power of combining experimental studies with theoretical modeling. Pavlov and Katok (2011) and Özer et al. (2011) discussed above are two examples along this line. Additionally, Chen et al. (2008) study a manufacturer's strategy of managing his direct on-line sales channel and an independent bricks-and-mortar retail channel, when both channels compete in service. They consider a wholesale price contract between the manufacturer and the retailer, and characterize how the direct channel cost and the retailer inconvenience cost (e.g., traveling cost for store visits) affect the manufacturer's dual channel strategy. The authors experimentally verify that their model accurately predicts the direction of changes in the dual channel strategies adopted by the participants due to changes in the supply chain environment. The empirical support for their model suggests that the model can be employed in actual business environments to manage sales channels. We believe that combining experimental studies and theoretical modeling in a complementary fashion can help research in operations management to better prescribe effective pricing and contracting strategies for real-world applications.

20.5 CONCLUSIONS

Psychological and emotional concerns are integral parts of human decision making, and thus important driving factors for the efficiency of economic systems full of human agents. In this chapter, we describe how these concerns induce human decisions that deviate from the predictions of neoclassical economic theories, and how they impact a firm's pricing strategies. We discuss theories in behavioral economics ranging from prospect theory, hyperbolic discounting to social preferences and people's cognitive limitation in solving decision problems. These theories have critical impacts on pricing management in both areas of consumer pricing and pricing contracts among firms. For example, the reference-dependent nature of consumers' utilities advocates the use of comparative advertising; the framing and presentation of prices affect consumers' willingness-to-pay and their perception of whether they encounter a good deal; consumers' present biases influence the design of long-term payments, coupons, and discount schemes; their fairness concerns raise cautions for frequent markdown practices; and framing effects, social preferences, and people's cognitive limitation in making optimal decisions all contribute to varying performance of different pricing contracts.

Our discussion highlights the importance of considering behavioral issues, in addition to pecuniary incentives, in designing effective pricing mechanisms. As seen in the discussion, controlled laboratory experiments involving human participants are powerful tools for unraveling latent behavioral factors that impact decision making. Thus, an emerging area of interest is to use these small-scale experiments as first steps to guide more effective large-scale field experiments in the market (e.g., Charness and Chen 2002). Small-scale laboratory experiments can provide a deeper understanding of human responses to changes in the decision-making environment, offering useful guidance to developing innovative management tactics. Complementarily, large-scale market experiments have the advantage that they can investigate potential outcomes of candidate policies under realistic market conditions. In addition, future success in pricing management is likely to rely on better economic models that account for both pecuniary and non-pecuniary incentives in business transactions. Ultimately, we believe that incorporating behavioral issues in pricing management not only offers a fertile avenue for future academic research, but also provides practitioners with a scientific methodology for prescribing more effective and more pragmatic pricing strategies.

REFERENCES

Akerlof, G. (1982) "Labor Contracts as Partial Gift Exchange", *Quarterly Journal of Economics* 97/4: 543–69.

Anderson, E. and Simester, D. (2003) "Effects of $9 Price Endings on Retail Sales: Evidence from Field Experiments", *Quantitative Marketing & Economics* 1/1: 93–110.

—— and —— (2006) "Does Demand Fall When Customers Perceive that Prices Are Unfair? The Case of Premium Pricing for Large Sizes", *Marketing Science* 27/3: 492–500.

Andreoni, J. and Miller, J. (1993) "Rational Cooperation in the Finitely Repeated Prisoner's Dilemma: Experimental Evidence", *Economic Journal* 103/418: 570–85.

Ariely, D. (2010) *Predictably Irrational: The Hidden Forces That Shape Our Decisions*. New York: Harper Perennial.

Arrow, K. (1972) *The Limits of Organization*. New York: W. W. Norton & Company.

Ashraf, N., Bohnet, I., and Piankov, N. (2006) "Decomposing Trust and Trustworthiness", *Experimental Economics* 9/3: 193–208.

Axelrod, R. (1981) "The Emergence of Cooperation among Egoists", *American Political Science Review* 75/2: 306–18.

Baye, M. and Morgan, J. (2004) "Price Dispersion in the Lab and on the Internet: Theory and Evidence", *RAND Journal of Economics* 35/3: 449–66.

Bearden, W., Carlson, J., and Hardesty, D. (2003) "Using Invoice Price Information to Frame Advertised Offers", *Journal of Business Research* 56/5: 355–66.

Bell, D. and Bucklin, R. (1999) "The Role of Internal Reference Price in the Category Purchase Decision", *Journal of Consumer Research* 26/2: 128–43.

—— and Lattin, J. (2000) "Looking for Loss Aversion in Scanner Panel Data: The Confounding Effect of Price-Response Heterogeneity", *Marketing Science* 19/2: 185–200.

Ben-Ner, A. and Putterman, L. (2001) "Trusting and Trustworthiness", *Boston University Law Review* 81/3: 523–51.

Bendoly, E., Donohue, K., and Schultz, K. (2006) "Behavior in Operations Management: Assessing Recent Findings and Revisiting Old Assumptions", *Journal of Operations Management* 24/6: 737–52.

—— Croson, R., Goncalves, P., and Schultz, K. (2010) "Bodies of Knowledge for Research in Behavioral Operations", *Production & Operations Management* 19/4: 434–52.

Benzion, U., Rapoport, A., and Yagil, J. (1989) "Discount Rates Inferred from Decisions: An Experimental Study", *Management Science* 35/3: 270–84.

Berg, J., Dickhaut, J., and McCabe, K. (1995) "Trust, Reciprocity, and Social History", *Games & Economics Behavior* 10/1: 122–42.

Bohnet, I. and Zeckhauser, R. (2004) "Trust, Risk and Betrayal", *Journal of Economic Behavior & Organization* 55/4: 467–84.

—— Greig, F., Herrmann, B., and Zeckhauser, R. (2008) "Betrayal Aversion: Evidence from Brazil, China, Oman, Switzerland, Turkey, and the United States", *American Economic Review* 98/1: 294–310.

Bolton, G. and Katok, E. (2008) "Learning-By-Doing in the Newsvendor Problem: A Laboratory Investigation of the Role of Experience and Feedback", *Manufacturing & Service Operations Management* 10/3: 519–38.

—— and Ockenfels, A. (2000) "ERC: A Theory of Equity, Reciprocity, and Competition", *American Economic Review* 90/1: 166–93.

—— Katok, E., and Ockenfels, A. (2004) "How Effective Are Electronic Reputation Mechanisms? An Experimental Investigation", *Management Science* 50/11: 1587–602.

—— Loebbecke, C., and Ockenfels, A. (2008) "Does Competition Promote Trust and Trustworthiness in Online Trading: An Experimental Study", *Journal of Management Information Systems* 25/2: 145–70.

Bolton, L. and Alba, J. (2006) "Price Fairness: Good and Service Differences and the Role of Vendor Costs", *Journal of Consumer Research* 33/2: 258–65.

Bolton, L., Warlop, L., and Alba, J. (2003) "Consumer Perceptions of Price (Un)Fairness", *Journal of Consumer Research* 29/4: 474–91.

Bougie, R., Pieters, R., and Zeelenberg, M. (2003) "Angry Customers Don't Come Back, They Get Back: The Experience and Behavioral Implications of Anger and Dissatisfaction in Services", *Journal of the Academy of Marketing Science* 31/4: 377–93.

Boyce, R., Brown, T., McClelland, G., Peterson, G., and Schulze, W. (1992) "An Experimental Examination of Intrinsic Values as a Source for the WTA-WTP Disparity", *American Economic Review* 82/5: 1366–73.

Bridges, E., Yim, C., and Briesch, R. (1995) "A High-Tech Product Market Share Model with Customer Expectations", *Marketing Science* 14/1: 61–81.

Briesch, R., Krishnamurthi, L., Mazumdar, T., and Raj, S. (1997) "A Comparative Analysis of Reference Price Models", *Journal of Consumer Research* 24/2: 202–14.

Cachon, G. and Lariviere, M. (2005) "Supply Chain Coordination with Revenue-Sharing Contracts: Strengths and Limitations", *Management Science* 51/1: 30–44.

Camerer, C. (2003) *Behavioral Game Theory: Experiments in Strategic Interaction*. Princeton, NJ: Princeton University Press.

Campbell, M. (1999) "Perceptions of Price Unfairness: Antecedents and Consequences", *Journal of Marketing Research* 36/2: 187–99.

Chang, K., Siddarth, S., and Weinberg, C. (1999) "The Impact of Heterogeneity in Purchase Timing and Price Responsiveness on Estimates of Sticker Shock Effects", *Marketing Science* 18/2: 178–92.

Charness, G. (2004) "Attribution and Reciprocity in an Experimental Labor Market", *Journal of Labor Economics* 22/3: 665–88.

—— and Chen, K. (2002) "Minimum Advertised-Price Policy Rules and Retailer Behavior: An Experiment by Hewlett-Packard", *Interfaces* 32/5: 62–73.

Chen, K., Kaya, M., and Özer, Ö. (2008) "Dual Sales Channel Management with Service Competition", *Manufacturing & Service Operations Management* 10/4: 654–75.

Collie, T., Bradley, G., and Sparks, B. (2002) "Fair Process Revisited: Differential Effects of Interactional and Procedural Justice in the Presence of Social Comparison Information", *Journal of Experimental Social Psychology* 38/6: 545–55.

Corbett, C., Zhou, D., and Tang, C. (2004) "Designing Supply Contracts: Contract Type and Information Asymmetry", *Management Science* 50/4: 550–9.

Crawford, V. and Iriberri, N. (2007) "Level-*k* Auctions: Can a Nonequilibrium Model of Strategic Thinking Explain the Winner's Curse and Overbidding in Private-Value Auctions?", *Econometrica* 75/6: 1721–70.

Croson, R. and Donohue, K. (2006) "Behavioral Causes of the Bullwhip Effect and the Observed Value of Inventory Information", *Management Science* 52/3: 323–36.

—— and Buchan, N. (1999) "Gender and Culture: International Experimental Evidence from Trust Games", *American Economic Review* 89/2: 386–91.

—— Fatas, E., and Neugebauer, T. (2005) "Reciprocity, Matching and Conditional Cooperation in Two Public Goods Games", *Economics Letters* 87/1: 95–101.

Cui, T., Raju, J., and Zhang, Z. (2007) "Fairness and Channel Coordination", *Management Science* 53/8: 1303–14.

Dal Bó, P. (2005) "Cooperation under the Shadow of the Future: Experimental Evidence from Infinitely Repeated Games", *American Economic Review* 95/5: 1591–604.

Dehaene, S. and Mehler, J. (1992) "Cross-Linguistic Regularities in the Frequency of Number Words", *Cognition* 43/1: 1–29.

DellaVigna, S. and Malmendier, U. (2006) "Paying Not to Go to the Gym", *American Economic Review* 96/3: 694–719.

DelVecchio, D., Krishnan, H., and Smith, D. (2007) "Cents or Percent? The Effects of Promotion Framing on Price Expectations and Choice", *Journal of Marketing* 71/3: 158–70.

Dhar, R. and Simonson, I. (1992) "The Effect of the Focus of Comparison on Consumer Preferences", *Journal of Marketing Research* 29/4: 430–40.

Dickson, P. and Kalapurakal, R. (1994) "The Use and Perceived Fairness of Price-Setting Rules in the Bulk Electricity Market", *Journal of Economic Psychology* 15/3: 427–48.

Doney, P. and Cannon, J. (1997) "An Examination of the Nature of Trust in Buyer-Seller Relationships", *Journal of Marketing* 61/2: 35–51.

Dufwenberg, M. and Kirchsteiger, G. (2004) "A Theory of Sequential Reciprocity", *Games & Economics Behavior* 47/2: 268–98.

Eckel, C. and Grossman, P. (2001) "Chivalry and Solidarity in Ultimatum Games", *Economic Inquiry* 39/2: 171–88.

—— and Wilson, R. K. (2004) "Is Trust a Risky Decision?", *Journal of Economic Behavior & Organization* 55/4: 447–65.

Falk, A. and Fischbacher, U. (2006) "A Theory of Reciprocity", *Games & Economic Behavior* 54/2: 293–315.

Fehr, E. and Fischbacher, U. (2002) "Why Social Preferences Matter—The Impact of Non-Selfish Motives on Competition, Cooperation and Incentives", *Economic Journal* 112/478: C1–C33.

—— and Gächter, S. (2000) "Cooperation and Punishment in Public Goods Experiments", *American Economic Review* 90/4: 980–94.

—— and List, J. (2004) "The Hidden Costs and Returns of Incentives—Trust and Trustworthiness among CEOs", *Journal of the European Economic Association* 2/5: 743–71.

—— and Schmidt, K. M. (1999) "A Theory of Fairness, Competition and Cooperation", *Quarterly Journal of Economics* 114/3: 817–68.

—— Kirchsteiger, G., and Riedl, A. (1993) "Does Fairness Prevent Market Clearing? An Experimental Investigation", *Quarterly Journal of Economics* 108/2: 437–59.

—— Kirchler, E., Weichbold, A., and Gächter, S. (1998) "When Social Norms Overpower Competition: Gift Exchange in Experimental Labor Markets", *Journal of Labor Economics* 16/2: 324–51.

Fischbacher, U., Gächter, S., and Fehr, E. (2001) "Are People Conditionally Cooperative? Evidence from a Public Goods Experiment", *Economics Letters* 71/3: 397–404.

Fishburn, P. and Rubinstein, A. (1982) "Time Preference", *International Economic Review* 23/3: 677–94.

Forsythe, R., Horowitz, J., Savin, N., and Sefton, M. (1994) "Fairness in Simple Bargaining Experiments", *Games & Economic Behavior* 6/3: 347–69.

—— Lundholm, R., and Rietz, T. (1999) "Cheap Talk, Fraud, and Adverse Selection in Financial Markets: Some Experimental Evidence", *Review of Financial Studies* 12/3: 481–518.

Friedman, D. and Sunder, S. (1994) *Experimental Methods: A Primer for Economists*. New York: Cambridge University Press.

Gibbons, R. (1992) *Game Theory for Applied Economists*. Princeton, NJ: Princeton University Press.

Gino, F. and Pisano, G. (2008) "Toward a Theory of Behavioral Operations", *Manufacturing & Service Operations Management* 10/4: 676–91.

Gneezy, U. (2005) "Deception: The Role of Consequences", *American Economic Review* 95/1: 384–94.

Green, L., Fry, A., and Myerson, J. (1994) "Discounting of Delayed Rewards: A Life-Span Comparison", *Psychological Science* 5/1: 33–6.

Ha, A. (2001) "Supplier–Buyer Contracting: Asymmetric Cost Information and Cutoff Level Policy for Buyer Participation", *Naval Research Logistics* 48/1: 41–64.

Hall, E. (1959) *The Silent Language*. New York: Anchor Press.

Herrmann, A., Xia, L., Monroe, K., and Huber, F. (2007) "The Influence of Price Fairness on Customer Satisfaction: An Empirical Test in the Context of Automobile Purchases", *Journal of Product & Brand Management* 16/1: 49–58.

Ho, T.-H. and Su, X. (2009) "Peer-Induced Fairness in Games", *American Economic Review* 99/5: 2022–49.

—— and Weigelt, K. (2005) "Trust Building among Strangers", *Management Science* 51/4: 519–30.

—— and Zhang, J. (2008) "Designing Price Contracts for Boundedly Rational Customers: Does the Framing of the Fixed Fee Matter?" *Management Science* 54/4: 686–700.

—— Camerer, C., and Weigelt, K. (1998) "Iterated Dominance and Iterated Best Response in Experimental '*p*-Beauty Contests' ", *American Economic Review* 88/4: 947–69.

Holm, H. and Nystedt, P. (2005) "Intra-Generational Trust—A Semi-Experimental Study of Trust among Different Generations", *Journal of Economic Behavior & Organization* 58/3: 403–19.

Hong, K. and Bohnet, I. (2007) "Status and Distrust: The Relevance of Inequality and Betrayal Aversion", *Journal of Economic Psychology* 28/2: 197–213.

Huber, J. and Puto, C. (1983) "Market Boundaries and Product Choice: Illustrating Attraction and Substitution Effects", *Journal of Consumer Research* 10/1: 31–44.

—— Payne, J., and Puto, C. (1982) "Adding Asymmetrically Dominated Alternatives: Violations of Regularity and the Similarity Hypothesis", *Journal of Consumer Research* 9/1: 90–8.

Huberman, B., Loch, C., and Önçüler, A. (2004) "Status as a Valued Resource", *Social Psychology Quarterly* 67/1: 103–14.

Huppertz, J., Arenson, S., and Evans, R. (1978) "An Application of Equity Theory to Buyer-Seller Exchange Situations", *Journal of Marketing Research* 15/2: 250–60.

Kagel, J. and Roth, A. (1997) *The Handbook of Experimental Economics*. Princeton, NJ: Princeton University Press.

Kahneman, D. and Tversky, A. (1979) "Prospect Theory: An Analysis of Decision under Risk", *Econometrica* 47/2: 263–91.

—— Knetsch, J., and Thaler, R. (1986a) "Fairness as a Constraint on Profit Seeking: Entitlements in the Market", *American Economic Review* 76/4: 728–41.

—— —— and —— (1986b) "Fairness and the Assumptions of Economics", *Journal of Business* 59/4: S285–S300.

—— —— and —— (1990) "Experimental Tests of the Endowment Effect and the Coase Theorem", *Journal of Political Economy* 98/6: 1325–48.

—— —— and —— (1991) "Anomalies: The Endowment Effect, Loss Aversion, and Status Quo Bias", *Journal of Economic Perspectives* 5/1: 193–206.

Kalapurakal, R., Dickson, P., and Urbany, J. (1991) "Perceived Price Fairness and Dual Entitlement", *Advances in Consumer Research* 18/1: 788–93.

Kalwani, M. and Yim, C. (1992) "Consumer Price and Promotion Expectations: An Experimental Study", *Journal of Marketing Research* 29/1: 90–100.

—— —— Rinne, H., and Sugita, Y. (1990) "A Price Expectations Model of Customer Brand Choice", *Journal of Marketing Research* 27/3: 251–62.

Kamins, M., Drèze, X., and Folkes, V. (2004) "Effects of Seller-Supplied Prices on Buyers' Product Evaluations: Reference Prices in an Internet Auction Context", *Journal of Consumer Research* 30/4: 622–8.

Katok, E. and Wu, D. (2009) "Contracting in Supply Chains: A Laboratory Investigation", *Management Science* 55/12: 1953–68.

Kelley, C. and Lindsay, D. (1993) "Remembering Mistaken for Knowing: Ease of Retrieval as a Basis for Confidence in Answers to General Knowledge Questions", *Journal of Memory & Language* 32/1: 1–24.

Keser, C. and Paleologo, G. (2004) "Experimental Investigation of Supplier–Retailer Contracts: The Wholesale Price Contract", IBM research report, IBM Thomas J. Watson Research Center, Yorktown Heights, NY.

—— and van Winden, F. (2000) "Conditional Cooperation and Voluntary Contributions to Public Goods", *Scandinavian Journal of Economics* 102/1: 23–39.

Kirby, K. (1997) "Bidding on the Future: Evidence against Normative Discounting of Delayed Rewards", *Journal of Experimental Psychology: General* 126/1: 54–70.

Kivetz, R., Netzer, O., and Srinivasan, V. (2004a) "Alternative Models for Capturing the Compromise Effect", *Journal of Marketing Research* 41/3: 237–57.

—— —— and —— (2004b) "Extending Compromise Effect Models to Complex Buying Situations and Other Context Effects", *Journal of Marketing Research* 41/3: 262–8.

Knez, P., Smith, V., and Williams, A. (1985) "Individual Rationality, Market Rationality, and Value Estimation", *American Economic Review* 75/2: 397–402.

Koopmans, T. (1960) "Stationary Ordinal Utility and Impatience", *Econometrica* 28/2: 287–309.

Kreul, L. (1982) "Magic Numbers: Psychological Aspects of Menu Pricing", *Cornell Hotel & Restaurant Administration Quarterly* 23/2: 70–5.

Krishnamurthi, L., Mazumdar, T., and Raj, S. (1992) "Asymmetric Response to Price in Consumer Brand Choice and Purchase Quantity Decisions", *Journal of Consumer Research* 19/3: 387–400.

Lai, G., Debo, L., and Sycara, K. (2010) "Buy Now and Match Later: Impact of Posterior Price Matching on Profit with Strategic Consumers", *Manufacturing & Service Operations Management* 12/1: 33–55.

Laibson, D. (1997) "Golden Eggs and Hyperbolic Discounting", *Quarterly Journal of Economics* 112/2: 443–77.

—— (1998) "Life-Cycle Consumption and Hyperbolic Discount Functions", *European Economic Review* 42/35: 861–71.

Lambert, Z. (1975) "Perceived Prices as Related to Odd and Even Price Endings", *Journal of Retailing* 51/3: 13–22.

Lattin, J. and Bucklin, R. (1989) "Reference Effects on Price and Promotion on Brand Choice", *Journal of Marketing Research* 26/3: 299–310.

Lewicki, R. and Bunker, B. (1995) "Trust in Relationships: A Model of Development and Decline", in B. Bunker and J. Rubin (eds), *Conflict, Cooperation and Justice: Essays Inspired by the Work of Morton Deutsch*. San Francisco, CA: Jossey-Bass Publishers.

Lim, N. and Ho, T. (2007) "Designing Price Contracts for Boundedly Rational Customers: Does the Number of Blocks Matter?" *Marketing Science* 26/3: 312–26.

Loch, C. and Wu, Y. (2008) "Social Preferences and Supply Chain Performance: An Experimental Study", *Management Science* 54/11: 1835–49.

—— Huberman, B., and Stout, S. (2000) "Status Competition and Performance in Work Groups", *Journal of Economic Behavior & Organization* 43/1: 35–55.

Loewenstein, G. (1988) "Frames of Mind in Intertemporal Choice", *Management Science* 34/2: 200–14.

—— and Prelec, D. (1992) "Anomalies in Intertemporal Choice: Evidence and an Interpretation", *Quarterly Journal of Economics* 107/2: 573–97.

McKelvey, R. and Palfrey, T. (1995) "Quantal Response Equilibria for Normal Form Games", *Games & Economic Behavior* 10/1: 6–38.

Maxwell, S. (2002) "Rule-Based Price Fairness and Its Effect on Willingness to Purchase", *Journal of Economic Psychology* 23/2: 191–212.

—— (2008) *The Price is Wrong: Understanding What Makes a Price Seem Fair and the True Cost of Unfair Pricing*. Hoboken, NJ: John Wiley & Sons, Inc.

Mazumdar, T. and Papatla, P. (1995) "Loyalty Differences in the Use of Internal and External Reference Prices", *Marketing Letters* 6/2: 111–22.

—— Raj, S., and Sinha, I. (2005) "Reference Price Research: Review and Propositions", *Journal of Marketing* 69/4: 84–102.

Monroe, K. (1973) "Buyers' Subjective Perceptions of Price", *Journal of Marketing Research* 10/1: 70–80.

—— (1979) *Pricing: Making Profitable Decisions*. New York: McGraw Hill.

Moorthy, K. (1987) "Managing Channel Profits: Comment", *Marketing Science* 6/4: 375–9.

Nagel, R. (1995) "Unraveling in Guessing Games: An Experimental Study", *American Economic Review* 85/5: 1313–26.

Nasiry, J. and Popescu, I. (2012) "Advance Selling When Consumers Regret", forthcoming in *Management Science*.

O'Donoghue, T. and Rabin, M. (1999) "Doing It Now or Later", *American Economic Review* 89/1: 103–24.

—— and —— (2001) "Choice and Procrastination", *Quarterly Journal of Economics* 116/1: 121–60.

Oliver, R. and Swan, J. (1989a) "Consumer Perceptions of Interpersonal Equity and Satisfaction in Transactions: A Field Survey Approach", *Journal of Marketing* 53/2: 21–35.

—— and —— (1989b) "Equity and Disconfirmation Perceptions as Influences on Merchant and Product Satisfaction", *Journal of Consumer Research* 16/3: 372–83.

Ordóñez, L., Connolly, T., and Coughlan, R. (2000) "Multiple Reference Points in Satisfaction and Fairness Assessment", *Journal of Behavioral Decision Making* 13/3: 329–44.

Oster, S. and Morton, F. (2005) "Behavioral Biases Meet the Market: The Case of Magazine Subscription Prices", *Advances in Economic Analysis & Policy* 5/1: 1–30.

Özer, Ö. and Wei, W. (2006) "Strategic Commitments for an Optimal Capacity Decision under Asymmetric Forecast Information", *Management Science* 52/8: 1239–58.

—— Zheng, Y., and Chen, K. (2011) "Trust in Forecast Information Sharing", *Management Science* 57/6: 1111–37.

Pasternack, B. (1985) "Optimal Pricing and Return Policies for Perishable Commodities", *Marketing Science* 4/2: 166–76.

Pavlov, V. and Katok, E. (2011) "Fairness and Coordination Failures in Supply Chain Contracts", Working paper, The University of Auckland Business School, Auckland, New Zealand.

Phillips, R. (2005) *Pricing and Revenue Optimization*. Stanford, CA: Stanford University Press.

Plott, C. (1994) "Market Architecture, Institutional Landscapes and Testbed Experiments: Introduction", *Economic Theory* 4/1: 3–10.

Popescu, I. and Wu, Y. (2007) "Dynamic Pricing Strategies with Reference Effects", *Operations Research* 55/3: 413–29.

Rabin, M. (1993) "Incorporating Fairness into Game Theory and Economics", *American Economic Review* 83/5: 1281–302.

Resnick, P. and Zeckhauser, R. (2002) "Trust among Strangers in Internet Transactions: Empirical Analysis of eBay's Reputation System", in M. Baye (ed.), *The Economics of the Internet & E-Commerce*, Vol. 11 of *Advances in Applied Microeconomics*. Amsterdam: Elsevier Science, 127–57.

—— —— and Swanson, J. (2006) "The Value of Reputation on eBay: A Controlled Experiment", *Experimental Economics* 9/2: 79–101.

Rotemberg, J. (2011) "Fair Pricing", *Journal of the European Economic Association* 9/5: 952–81.

Roth, A. (1988) "Laboratory Experimentation in Economics: A Methodological Overview", *Economic Journal* 98/393: 974–1031.

—— Prasnikar, V., Okuno-Fujiwara, M., and Zamir, S. (1991) "Bargaining and Market Behavior in Jerusalem, Ljubljana, Pittsburgh and Tokyo: An Experimental Study", *American Economic Review* 81/5: 1068–95.

Samuelson, W. and Zeckhauser, R. (1988) "Status Quo Bias in Decision Making", *Journal of Risk & Uncertainty* 1/1: 7–59.

San Francisco Chronicle (1999) "Coke's Automatic Price Gouging", October 29.

Schindler, R. (2006) "The 99 Price Ending as a Signal of a Low-Price Appeal", *Journal of Retailing* 82/1: 71–7.

—— and Kibarian, T. (1993) "Testing for Perceptual Underestimation of 9-Ending Prices", *Advances in Consumer Research* 20/1: 580–5.

—— and —— (1996) "Increased Consumer Sales Response through Use of 99-Ending Prices", *Journal of Retailing* 72/2: 187–99.

—— and Kirby, P. (1997) "Patterns of Rightmost Digits Used in Advertised Prices: Implications for Nine-Ending Effects", *Journal of Consumer Research* 24/2: 192–201.

—— and Warren, L. (1988) "Effect of Odd Pricing on Choice of Items from a Menu", *Advances in Consumer Research* 15/1: 348–53.

Schweitzer, M. and Cachon, G. (2000) "Decision Bias in the Newsvendor Problem with a Known Demand Distribution: Experimental Evidence", *Management Science* 46/3: 404–20.

Shampanier, K., Mazar, N., and Ariely, D. (2007) "Zero as a Special Price: The True Value of Free Products", *Marketing Science* 26/6: 742–57.

Shelley, M. (1993) "Outcome Signs, Question Frames and Discount Rates", *Management Science* 39/7: 806–15.

Simon, H. (1955) "A Behavioral Model of Rational Choice", *Quarterly Journal of Economics* 69/1: 99–118.

Simonson, I. (1989) "Choice Based on Reasons: The Case of Attraction and Compromise Effects", *Journal of Consumer Research* 16/2: 158–74.

—— and Tversky, A. (1992) "Choice in Context: Tradeoff Contrast and Extremeness Aversion", *Journal of Marketing Research* 29/3: 281–95.

Spengler, J. (1950) "Vertical Integration and Antitrust Policy", *Journal of Political Economy* 58/4: 347–52.

Stahl, D. and Wilson, P. (1995) "On Players' Models of Other Players: Theory and Experimental Evidence", *Games & Economic Behavior* 10/1: 218–54.

Sterman, J. (1989) "Modeling Managerial Behavior: Misperceptions of Feedback in a Dynamic Decision Making Experiment", *Management Science* 35/3: 321–39.

Stiving, M. and Winer, R. (1997) "An Empirical Analysis of Price Endings with Scanner Data", *Journal of Consumer Research* 24/1: 57–67.

Streitfeld, D. (2000) "On the Web, Price Tags Blur", *Washington Post* September 27.

Su, X. (2008) "Bounded Rationality in Newsvendor Models", *Manufacturing & Service Operations Management* 10/4: 566–89.

—— (2009) "A Model of Consumer Inertia with Applications to Dynamic Pricing", *Production & Operations Management* 18/4: 365–80.

Taylor, T. (2002) "Supply Chain Coordination under Channel Rebates with Sales Effort Effects", *Management Science* 48/8: 992–1007.

Thaler, R. (1980) "Toward a Positive Theory of Consumer Choice", *Journal of Economic Behavior & Organization* 1/1: 39–60.

—— (1981) "Some Empirical Evidence on Dynamic Inconsistency", *Economic Letters* 8/3: 201–7.

Thomas, M. and Morwitz, V. (2005) "Penny Wise and Pound Foolish: The Left-Digit Effect in Price Cognition", *Journal of Consumer Research* 32/1: 54–64.

—— Simon, D., and Kadiyali, V. (2010) "The Price Precision Effect: Evidence from Laboratory and Market Data", *Marketing Science* 29/1: 175–90.

Tsay, A. (1999) "The Quantity Flexibility Contract and Supplier–Customer Incentives", *Management Science* 45/10: 1339–58.

Tversky, A. and Kahneman, D. (1981) "The Framing of Decisions and the Psychology of Choice", *Science* New Series, 211/4481: 453–8.

—— and —— (1992) "Advances in Prospect Theory: Cumulative Representation of Uncertainty", *Journal of Risk & Uncertainty* 5/4: 297–323.

—— and Simonson, I. (1993) "Context-Dependent Preferences", *Management Science* 39/10: 1179–89.

Twedt, D. (1965) "Does the '9 Fixation' in Retail Pricing Really Promote Sales?" *Journal of Marketing* 29/4: 54–5.

Urbany, J., Bearden, W., and Weilbaker, D. (1988) "The Effect of Plausible and Exaggerated Reference Prices on Consumer Perceptions and Price Search", *Journal of Consumer Research* 15/1: 95–110.

Vaidyanathan, R. and Aggarwal, P. (2003) "Who is the Fairest of Them All? An Attributional Approach to Price Fairness Perceptions", *Journal of Business Research* 56/6: 453–63.

Winer, R. (1986) "A Reference Price Model of Brand Choice for Frequently Purchased Products", *Journal of Consumer Research* 13/2: 250–6.

Wu, D. and Katok, E. (2006) "Learning, Communication and the Bullwhip Effect", *Journal of Operations Management* 24/6: 839–50.

Xia, L., Monroe, K., and Cox, J. (2004) "The Price is Unfair! A Conceptual Framework of Price Fairness Perceptions", *Journal of Marketing* 68/4: 1–15.

PART IV

PRICING TACTICS

PART IV

PRICING TACTICS

CHAPTER 21

....

CUSTOMIZED PRICING

....

ROBERT PHILLIPS

21.1 BACKGROUND AND INTRODUCTION

Consider the following three pricing situations:

- A global telecommunications company sells its services in North America. The company sells more than forty individual services including local, long-distance, data communications, and corporate network. Different customers request different levels and combinations of these services. The company sells its services on a contract basis, with the typical term of a contract being a year. An important segment of the company's business consists of customers with annual telecommunications bills of between $10,000 and $10 million. Customers in this segment are primarily large and medium-sized businesses, educational institutions, and various state and local government agencies. Prospective customers in this segment typically submit a Request for Quote (RFQ) to two or more telecommunications companies annually. Based on the bids received, they determine which company will be their service provider for the next year. Bids by competing telecommunications companies are usually specified as discounts from their standard list prices. The problem facing the company is what discount to quote in response to each RFQ (Phillips 2005: 264–5).

- The Soundco Radio Company sells aftermarket radios and CD players for automobiles. Its customers are regional and national electronics retailers, automotive stereo catalog sellers, and electronics wholesalers. The dealer base price for one of Soundco's most popular models, the CDR-2000 is $109. However, the average price actually paid by customers in 2007 was $67.50. The difference of $41.50 was due to a variety of discounts, promotions, and concessions that Soundco made on different deals. For example, while the average price paid by customers for the CDR-2000 was $67.50, there was a wide variation in actual price paid: about 18 percent of sales were at $55 or less while 17.5 percent were at $85 or more. Soundco wants to know if it is giving

I would like to thank Joe Nipko, Özalp Özer, Robin Raffard, and an anonymous reviewer for their thoughtful comments that led to improvements in this chapter.

the right discounts to the right customers to maximize profitability and, if not, how it should change its discounting (Marn et al. 2004: 31–3).

- A medical testing device company sells a gas chromatograph refill cartridge with a standard list price of $11.85. The refill cartridge is typically ordered in batches. Orders for fewer than 200 units are handled through the company's website or through a reseller with no discount. Large orders (more than 1,000 units) are negotiated by a national account manager, usually as part of a large, bundled sale. Orders for 200–1,000 units are handled by a regional sales staff that has considerable freedom to set discounts. Analysis of historical data showed that discounts ranged from 0 percent to more than 30 percent for some deals. The company wants to determine the "right" levels of discount to offer for various deals (Agrawal and Ferguson 2007: 220).

The three cases described above are examples of *customized pricing*. Customized pricing is most common in business-to-business settings, although it is also found in consumer lending and insurance. Customized pricing is defined by three characteristics:

1. Customers approach a seller. Each buyer describes a product, or set of products that she would like to purchase. Often this is specified in a Request for Proposal (RFP) or Request for Quote (RFQ) or, in the case of insurance or credit, an application. We call such an inquiry a *customer request*.

2. The seller must decide how to respond to each customer request. One possibility is not to respond—that is, pass up the opportunity for the business. If a seller does respond, he needs to determine what price to quote for each customer request. At the point the price is quoted, the seller knows the product(s) requested by the buyer, the channel through which the buyer approached, and at least some information about the buyer. Often in business-to-business settings, price is quoted in terms of a discount from a list price or tariff.

3. The seller has some freedom to quote different prices for different customer requests based on the products in the request, the sales channel through which the request is received, and the characteristics of the buyer.

Each customer request can be characterized by the characteristics of the order (e.g., the number and configuration of products ordered), the channel through which the request was received (e.g., Internet versus direct sales), and the characteristics of the customer making the request (e.g., large manufacturer in the north-east versus small distributor in the south-west). The problem facing the seller at any time is what price to quote for the request currently under consideration. In the extreme, the seller could quote a different price for each request—this would approach the ideal of "one-to-one" pricing. More typically, the seller differentiates prices by a finite set of combinations of order characteristics, customer characteristics, and channel. For example a seller might define five order-size tiers, with increasing levels of discount by order-size. We use the term *pricing segment* to denote each combination of order characteristic, customer characteristic, and channel for which a seller can set a price.

This chapter focuses on the use of mathematical analysis by a seller to set and update the prices for a finite set of pricing segments. The idea of using mathematical analysis to optimize prices in this fashion is relatively new. Several authors such as Friedman (1956),

Gates (1967), and Morin and Clough (1969) describe models in which price is the only criterion used to select a supplier. Talus Solutions was the first company to develop a software system to optimize customized prices (Boyd et al. 2005). The first detailed treatment of an optimization approach to customized pricing for segmented markets is chapter 11 in Phillips (2005). Agrawal and Ferguson (2007) apply a similar analytical approach to two examples of what they call *customized-pricing bid–response models* *(CPBRMs)* and compare the performance of segmented and unsegmented approaches.

21.2 BUSINESS APPLICATION OF
CUSTOMIZED PRICING

A stylized view of the customized pricing sales process is shown in Figure 21.1. Prospective customers approach a seller one-by-one through different channels. Each customer describes her desired purchase to the seller. Based on the combination of the desired purchase, the channel, and the characteristics of the customer, the seller chooses the price to offer. Once the price is known, the customer decides whether or not to purchase from the seller. The seller knows the characteristics not only of the seller's own customers and their purchases, but also the characteristics of those potential customers who did not purchase from him—that is *lost sales*. Typically the majority of a seller's lost sales went on to purchase from a competitor, although some portion of the lost sales may have decided not to purchase at all.

In many business-to-business markets, a purchase is often initiated when a buyer sends an RFP or an RFQ to one or more competing suppliers describing the buyer's needs for goods or services. Each supplier receiving the RFP or RFQ needs to decide whether or not to bid for the business. A supplier may decide not to bid if they feel that they cannot satisfy the requirements of the buyer, or if they feel that their probability of making the sale is not high enough to justify bidding, or for other reasons. If a supplier does bid, he needs to choose a price. At the highest level, the tradeoff in determining the price is straightforward—if the seller sets the price high, he will make a high profit if he wins, but has a low probability of winning; if he sets the price low, he will make less profit if he wins, but he has a higher probability of winning. The price that maximizes his expected profit optimally balances these two effects.

Customized pricing is commonly used for products that are highly configured. Heavy trucks are a good example. The 2008 Model 388 Day Cab heavy truck sold by Peterbilt allows the customer to choose his desired options for thirty-four different components of the truck ranging from the rear-wheel mudflap hangers which can be straight, coiled, or tubular to fifteen different choices for rear axles to seven different transmissions to the choice between an aluminum or a steel battery box.[1] Multiplying the number of options in the Peterbilt list would imply that they could combine in 75×10^{16} possible ways—each corresponding to a different truck. In practice, not all combinations are feasible and the

---

[1] From the Peterbilt website at http://www.peterbilt.com/trad388dc.4.aspx, as accessed in November, 2008.

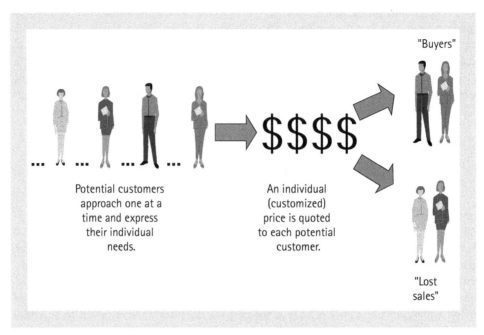

FIGURE 21.1 A stylized view of the customized pricing sales process

actual number of possible trucks is smaller—probably by two or three orders of magnitude. Each of the options has a list price and the sum of the list prices for the chosen options plus a base price is the "list price" for the configured truck. However, in the vast majority of cases, heavy trucks are sold at a discount from this list price. The customized pricing problem is what discount to apply for each quote.

Highly configurable products such as heavy trucks lend themselves to customized pricing for a number of reasons. First of all, configurability usually implies the existence of a large number of potential products—as in the case of Peterbilt. One heavy truck manufacturer claimed in conversation that no two customers had ever independently ordered exactly the same truck. This means that there is a lot of potential to segment based on product dimensions. Secondly, configurable products and services are usually "big ticket" items that often involve considerable interaction between the buyer and the seller during the sales process. This provides an opportunity for customer-based price differentiation. Finally, options often vary widely in their profitability to the seller. This variation gives an additional motivation for price differentiation. In the case of Peterbilt, a truck built of highly profitable options provides much more scope for possible discounting than a less profitable configuration.

The stylization of customized pricing in Figure 21.1 should not be interpreted to imply that sellers are passively waiting for customer requests to arrive. On the contrary, the vast majority of sellers will be actively engaged in marketing their products and services through advertising and brand support as well as soliciting business through direct and indirect sales channels. These sales and marketing activities are often critical in generating business, however they largely (if not entirely) represent "sunk" costs by the time the final

Table 21.1 Information required for an on-line auto insurance application with GEICO

Name	Zip code	Address
Currently insured?	Insured with GEICO in last 6 months?	Date of birth
Gender	Marital status	Student?
Employment status	Age drivers license first obtained	Education level
Industry	Veteran?	Field of occupation
Accidents/Violations/Thefts/Suspensions ?	Current Insurance Company	Years with current company

Source: www.geico.com, August 2008

price is quoted. Sales and marketing activities influence the volume of customer requests that a seller receives and the willingness-to-pay of potential buyers. A company with strong sales and marketing will have more opportunities to bid and will be able to bid successfully at higher prices than a competitor with weaker sales and marketing. The goal of a customized pricing process should be to enable a supplier to determine the best price to bid for each customer request given the supplier's strengths and weaknesses relative to the competition.

Customized pricing is most commonly associated with business-to-business markets: most consumer products and services are priced using list prices combined with various promotions. However, customized pricing is also common in consumer and small business loans and insurance. Both lenders and insurance companies typically require applications from prospective customers describing both the desired product (e.g., size and term of loan) as well as information about the prospective borrower themselves. Table 21.1 lists the information required for an on-line application for auto insurance from the insurance company GEICO's website—www.geico.com.[2] GEICO uses the information received with a customer's application to determine whether or not they will offer insurance to that customer.[3] GEICO can use the information on these applications not only to determine which customers to accept, but the rate that they want to quote to each customer. Mortgages, home equity loans, student loans, and auto loans all use a similar process of customer approach followed by an application with significant disclosure. Loan prices can depend both on characteristics of the lending product such as term and size of loan and on characteristics of the customer—particularly the lender's estimation of the customer's creditworthiness. Thus, customers with better credit history are likely to be offered lower rates for auto loans than those with poor credit. For a fuller discussion of the application of customized pricing to consumer credit markets see Caufield (Chapter 8).

---

[2] Accessed on November 4, 2008.

[3] In the words of Stiglitz and Weiss (1981), both insurance and consumer credit are *rationed*. There are customers to whom it is unprofitable to extend credit at any price due to adverse selection in the face of private information held by the customers. The same holds true of insurance markets as noted by Akerlof (1970).

21.3 FORMULATING AND SOLVING THE
CUSTOMIZED PRICING PROBLEM

The level and type of pricing segmentation that a seller uses is a major determinant of the effectiveness of customized pricing. If a seller differentiates price by five order size tiers, six regions, and three channels, then the seller has $5 \times 6 \times 3 = 90$ pricing segments. If the lender decided to increase the number of order size tiers to 10, then the number of pricing segments would increase to 180. If, in addition, he decided to differentiate pricing between existing and new customers, then the number of pricing segments would double to 360. For many sellers, particularly those with highly configurable or bundled products, the number of pricing segments can be very large. One mortgage lender in the United States manages over two million prices at any one time. The number of pricing segments is a measure of the amount of price differentiation being employed by a lender—the more pricing segments, the greater the level of differentiation.

To formalize the customized pricing problem, let N be the number of pricing segments. For each segment i, the customized pricing problem is to determine a price p_i for $i = 1, 2, \ldots, N$. Define D_i as the number of customer requests that will be received in segment i during some future period. For the moment, we assume that D_i is independent of price, p_i. Define $\rho_i(p_i)$ as the bid–response function for segment i—that is, for a segment i, $\rho_i(p_i)$ is the fraction of customers in the segment that will purchase if the seller bids at price p_i. Define $f_i(p_i)$ to be the incremental profit function for segment i as a function of price. Then, the Unconstrained Customized Pricing Problem is:

$$\max_p \sum_{i=1}^{N} D_i \rho_i(p_i) f_i(p_i) \tag{1}$$

$$\text{s.t. } p > 0 \tag{2}$$

where $p = (p_1, p_2, \ldots, p_N)$. In (1), the objective is to maximize the total expected profit from all customer segments. We will discuss later the situation in which a seller wishes to pursue other objectives for some or all segments.

We note that this formulation of the problem is quite general with respect to the level of segmentation. Setting $N = 1$ corresponds to a single price for all customers. At the other extreme, a seller could define a separate segment for every possible combination of customer characteristics, channel, and product. For example, a heavy truck manufacturer might wish to set a different discount for an order of 39 trucks than for one of 40 trucks or 38 trucks. By defining segments ever more finely, the seller can approach the limit of "market-of-one" pricing. As an example, each piece of information shown in Table 21.1 is a potential pricing dimension for GEICO. If GEICO used all possible values of all of these dimensions in setting their prices, then it would come close to "market-of-one" pricing.

Effective customized pricing involves solving the problem in (1) for every possible bid request. As shown in Figure 21.2, this requires five steps:

1. *Segmenting the market.* This involves establishing a set of *pricing segments,* each of which, in theory, could be charged a different price.

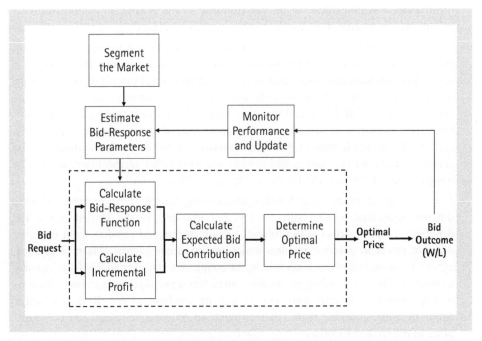

FIGURE 21.2 Steps in the customized pricing process

Source: Phillips (2005)

2. *Estimating bid–response functions.* For each pricing segment, a bid–response curve needs to be estimated that predicts the probability that an order in that segment will accept a bid as a function of price.

3. *Calculating incremental profit.* For each bid request, the incremental profit that the seller expects to realize if he wins the bid needs to be determined as a function of price.

4. *Optimizing.* Given the bid–response function and incremental profit function for a given bid, the bidder needs to determine the price that is most likely to help him achieve his goals. Often—but not always—the goal is to maximize expected profitability.

5. *Monitoring and updating.* As bid results are received, the seller needs to monitor the results relative to expectation. Based on the results, he may need to update the market segmentation and/or the parameters of the bid–response functions.

We discuss each of these steps in more detail in the following subsections.

21.3.1 Segmenting the market

In theory, a seller would want to segment his market as finely as possible in order to maximize his profitability. In practice, several factors limit the amount of market segmentation that a particular market can support. The most important of these factors are:

- *Informational limits.* A seller can only differentiate prices based on information available at the time of a bid. Even if a seller believes that, say, a customer's annual income has a strong influence on her response to his pricing, he cannot use that information in pricing if he does not know it when he is bidding.

- *Infrastructure limitations.* It is not uncommon that the IT infrastructure supporting pricing limits the level of differentiation that a seller can support. For example, a seller's pricing execution system may only support up to three pricing dimensions with five values per dimension. In this case, the seller cannot support more than $5^3 = 125$ pricing segments. Infrastructural limits are very real barriers to pricing differentiation for many companies. In some cases, they can be relaxed by investing in improved IT systems, however, changes to price distribution and bid evaluation systems can be expensive and time-consuming and the benefits from better segmentation need to be weighed against the cost and time of changing systems.

- *Legal and regulatory limits.* Laws and regulations may limit the types and levels of price differentiation that a seller can employ. For example, in the United States, the Robinson–Patman Act of 1936 prohibits manufacturers and resellers from charging different prices to different retailers under certain circumstances (Marn et al. 2004: 257–8). Laws and regulations on pricing differentiation can vary widely from country to country. The Fair Lending Act in the United States prohibits lenders from discriminating among prospective borrowers strictly on the basis of age (Ross and Yinger 2002). In contrast, setting loan APR's on the basis of age is both legal and commonplace in the United Kingdom.

- *Simplicity and transparency.* A seller may refrain from extensive price differentiation because he believes that there is value in maintaining a simple pricing structure that is fully disclosed to all customers, particularly when the product is sold through intermediaries. Resellers and intermediaries often express a desire for "simple" pricing, although evidence is often lacking that they are willing to accept higher prices for a simpler structure.[4]

- *Arbitrage.* The ability of a seller to differentiate pricing among different customers may be limited due to the potential for arbitrage—customers offered a low price could purchase more than they need and resell the surplus to other customer segments, undercutting the seller. The threat of arbitrage is particularly great for standardized products with low transportation costs. It often limits the extent to which companies selling easily transportable products can charge different prices through different channels, to different customer segments, or to different countries. Services and highly customized products are not as subject to arbitrage and often support higher levels of customer segmentation.

- *Fairness concerns.* A seller may be reluctant to differentiate prices along a certain dimension due to concerns about fairness. These concerns can be of two types: the seller may believe that differentiating price along a certain dimension is unfair. Alternatively, the seller may be concerned that differentiating along a certain dimen-

---

[4] The passenger airlines present a case of an industry in which customers have often complained about the complexity of the fare structure, but there is no evidence that any group of customers systematically chooses higher priced flights offered by airlines with simpler fare structures. The perception that customers—especially intermediaries—will reject complex or non-transparent pricing remains quite high in many industries, often with little or no concrete evidence.

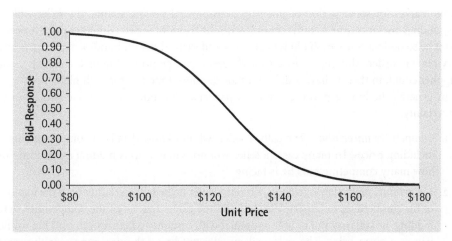

FIGURE 21.3 An example bid–response curve

sion may be perceived by customers as unfair. This could lead to resentment on the part of the customers and, ultimately, lower demand. See Maxwell (2008), Phillips (2005: ch. 13), and Özer and Zheng (Chapter 20) for some of the "perception of fairness" issues encountered in pricing.

Due to these limitations most sellers operate in a world of finite customer segmentation well below the theoretical limit of one-to-one pricing.

21.3.2 Estimating the bid–response function

A key element in customized pricing is the supplier's uncertainty about how a prospective buyer will respond to a bid price. Presumably a supplier who bids on a piece of business believes that he has a non-zero probability of winning—otherwise he would not waste the time and effort to bid.[5] It is also reasonable to assume that the seller's estimate of the probability that his bid will win should be a decreasing function of price—that is, the higher the price that he bids, the lower his probability of winning. For each bid, the *bid–response function* specifies the seller's probability of winning as a function of the price that he bids. A typical bid–response function is shown in Figure 21.3. In this figure, the horizontal axis is price, the vertical axis is the probability of winning the bid and the bid–response function is a decreasing function of price.

The bid–response function shown in Figure 21.3 is analogous to the more familiar "price-response" or "demand" curves found in many discussions of price theory such as Phillips (2005) and van Ryzin (Chapter 18). The bid–response function represents the seller's probability that he will win a particular bid as a function of price while a demand curve represents the total demand that a seller would expect to receive if he posted a fixed price in

---

[5] This is not strictly true. A supplier might decide to make a bid that he knows will not win simply to signal his willingness to do business with the buyer in order to be included in future bid opportunities. Or he might decide to bid to "keep the competition honest"—that is, to provide the buyer with some leverage that the buyer could use to force a competitor to lower his price.

some market for some period of time. In a customized pricing setting, the seller will be responding one-at-a-time to different bids with the freedom to set a different price for each bid if he so desires. Since each bid is likely to be different (different bundles of products and services on order, different customers, different competitors, different channels), the supplier could, in theory, have a different bid–response function for each bid.

In general, the bid–response curve for a particular bid must incorporate two types of uncertainty:

1. *Competitive uncertainty.* Typically a seller will not know details of competing bids— including prices. In many cases a seller will not know who is bidding against him or how many competing bids he is facing.

2. *Uncertainty on buyer preferences.* Even if a seller knew with certainty both the identity of his competitors on a particular bid *and* the prices that all of the competitors were bidding, he still may not be able to predict with certainty whether or not his bid would win at a given price. The seller will usually not know the preferences or the exact process by which the buyer will choose a winning bid. In most cases, the buyer is not certain to choose the lowest-price bid.[6]

We can conceive of many different ways in which a seller might estimate the bid–response curve for a particular customer request. For a particularly important bid, a seller might invest considerable time and effort in preparing its bid. For example, a large airline seeking to purchase aircraft for its fleet is likely to solicit proposals from both Boeing and Airbus. If the order is sufficiently large, both manufacturers will devote substantial amounts of time and thought to all elements of their proposals—including price. Typically each manufacturer will convene an internal group of people who have knowledge of the particular deal, experience with the customer, understanding of the competition, and experience with similar bidding situations in order to derive the best possible understanding of how the potential customer is likely to respond to the price associated with the deal. When a sale involving hundreds of millions or billions of dollars is at stake, it is not unusual for companies to devote many man-months—even man years—to developing their proposals. The ultimate price offered in the proposal will be determined as the result of long discussions, competitive role playing, and complex calculations. The final price for the transaction may only be determined after many rounds of negotiation.

While each very large customer request can be treated as unique and subjected to in-depth analysis, there are many situations in which the following three conditions hold:

1. The seller makes many relatively small quotes—in many cases thousands or tens of thousands—during the course of a year.

2. The seller retains historic "win/loss" data. That is, the seller retains full information on the details of each quote including the product requested, the customer, the channel, the price quoted, and the outcome of the bid—that is, if the business was won or lost.

[6] As an exception, some government procurements are required by law to select the lowest-price bid. As a result, government RFPs tend to be exceptionally detailed in order to minimize non-price differences among bids.

3. The seller offers a menu of standardized products. This is in contrast to fully customized services such as architecture, construction, or management consulting where each job is unique and it is difficult to establish comparability.

Under these three conditions, a seller can use statistical regression to estimate bid–response functions that can be used to determine the optimal prices for all pricing segments.

When the rate of incoming customer requests is high, it is typically too expensive or difficult for the seller to devote substantial amounts of time or effort to analyzing each deal. Auto F&I (finance and insurance) executives requesting a quote for an auto loan typically require a response within a few seconds. Given that an auto lender may be receiving hundreds or thousands of such requests daily it is infeasible for them to convene a corporate task force to determine the rate to quote for each one. They need a more rapid and automated approach. Fortunately, a high rate of incoming quotes usually implies a large volume of historical data that can be used to estimate stable and predictive bid–response functions that can be applied to future bids.

If sufficient historic win/loss data is available, a bid–response function can be estimated based on historical win/loss data using techniques of *binary regression*. The *target* data for binary regression consist of ones and zeroes. In estimating the coefficients of a bid–response function, the target data are the history of "wins" and "losses" that the seller has experienced in the past. In this case, a one can be used to indicate a win and a zero a loss. The *covariates* of the model include all of the other information available with the past bids including the price, the characteristics of the product or products ordered, the characteristics of the customer, and which channel the request was received through. Table 21.2 illustrates the bid history data available for a manufacturer of printer ink cartridges. This manufacturer sells three grades of cartridge—silver, gold, and platinum—to four types of customers: resellers, government agencies, educational institutions, and retailers. The manufacturer has kept track of the outcome of each bid and the amount

Table 21.2 Sample historic bid data available to a printer ink cartridge seller

| No. | W/L | Price | Request characteristics | | Customer characteristics | | |
			Grade	Size	New?	Type	BusLevel
1	W	$7.95	S	1,259	N	Res	0
2	L	$9.50	P	655	E	Gov	$153,467
3	L	$9.75	P	790	E	Gov	$1,402,888
4	W	$8.50	G	840	N	Ret	0
5	L	$8.47	G	833	E	Ret	$452,988
6	L	$9.22	P	540	E	Edu	$55,422
7	W	$8.61	G	850	N	Ret	0
...	...	...	...	...	...	...	...

"No." is an arbitrary bid number. W indicates that the bid was won, L that it was lost. "Price" is the unit price bid. "Grade" indicates the grade of the product ordered: S = Silver, G = Gold, P = Platinum. "Size" is the number of units in the order. N indicates a new customer, E an existing customer. The seller services four types of customer: Res = Reseller, Gov = Government, Ret = Retailer, Edu = Educational Institution. "Business Level" is the total amount of business sold to this customer over all business lines in the previous 12 months.

of business that it has done with each customer over the previous year. This information has been stored in a database and can be retrieved in a format similar to that shown in Table 21.2.

The challenge facing the cartridge manufacturer is how to use the data in Table 21.2 to estimate bid–response functions. This typically requires four steps: (1) segmenting the market, (2) determining the model structure, (3) estimating the coefficients of the model based on historic data, and (4) measuring the quality of the model. This is a classical problem of model specification and estimation—not different in principle from similar problems faced in promotion response estimation as discussed in Blattberg and Briesch (Chapter 24). We will give a broad introduction to some of the issues involved in developing bid–response models, more detailed discussions of statistical modeling can be found in any standard text on statistical modeling.

Model specification and model estimation typically proceed iteratively—that is, market segments and model structure will often be sequentially "tweaked" until the model fit meets some criteria or until additional tweaking fails to make improvements. To illustrate this process, consider the example shown in Table 21.2 and define the following notation:

- GRADES = 1 if Grade is Silver, 0 otherwise; GRADEG = 1 if Grade is Gold, 0 otherwise; GRADEP = 1 if Grade is Platinum, 0 otherwise;
- *PRICE* = price;
- *SIZE* = order size;
- *NEW* = 1 if customer is new, *NEW* = 0 if customer is existing;
- RES = 1 if the customer is a reseller, 0 otherwise; GOV = 1 if the customer is a government agency, 0 otherwise; RET = 1 if the customer is a retailer, 0 otherwise; and EDU = 1 if the customer is an educational institution, 0 otherwise;[7]
- *BUSLEVEL* = total amount of business done in the last 12 months.

A bid–response model using this data would specify the probability of winning a bid as a function of the price p and all of the other information available with the order. For the printer cartridge manufacturer, this information is grade, size, customer status, customer type, and level of business sold to the customer. Denote all of these non-price characteristics as a vector x. One extremely popular function for bid-response modeling (and, in fact, for binary response models in general) is the *logit* function, which is given by:

$$p(p, x) = 1/\left(1 + e^{g(p, x)}\right) \tag{3}$$

---

[7] The variables indicating which grade and type the order falls into are called *categorical variables*. Since, by assumption, the order can only be for one grade of cartridge, then exactly one of GRADES, GRADEG, and GRADEP can be 1 with the other two 0. A similar property holds for the variables indicating type. Experienced modelers will recognize that, when there are $n \geq 2$ categorical variables, only $n - 1$ need to be included in the model since the value of the missing variable can be inferred from the values of the others. For example, in the example, if GRADES and GRADEG are both equal to zero, than GRADEP must equal one. If either GRADES or GRADEG are equal to one, then GRADEP must equal zero. This means that *GRADEP* = 1 − *GRADES* − *GRADEG*. In other words, GRADEP is *co-linear* with GRADES and GRADEG and does not need to be included as an explanatory variable. In what follows, we will ignore this and continue to include all of the variables in the model formulation.

where $g(p, x)$ is an affine function of price and the (possibly transformed) non-price characteristics of a bid. The logit function is popular both because it is easily tractable and because statistical packages such as SAS and R include extensive support for it. The logit is a member of a larger category of statistical models known as *Generalized Linear Models* (GLMs). Other commonly used GLM forms include the probit and the linear.

Once the choice has been made to use the logit, the next step is to estimate the coefficients of the variables in the function $g(p, x)$. One obvious choice is simply to include all of the available variables in their raw form. In the case of the printer cartridge manufacturer, this would result in a specification of the form:

$$
\begin{aligned}
g(p, x) = \quad & \beta_0 \\
& + \beta_1 \times PRICE \\
& + \beta_2 \times GRADES + \beta_3 \times GRADEG + \beta_4 \times GRADEP \\
& + \beta_5 \times SIZE \\
& + \beta_6 \times NEW \\
& + \beta_7 \times RES + \beta_8 \times GOV + \beta_9 \times RET + \beta_{10} \times EDU \\
& + \beta_{11} \times BUSLEVEL.
\end{aligned}
\tag{4}
$$

Equations 3 and 4 specify a *statistical model* for bid response. Once a model has been specified, the next task is to determine the values of the coefficients—in this case, the values of β_0 through β_{11}—that best fit the historic data. This is a standard problem of binary regression which we will not address in detail here except to note that most common statistical packages such as SAS and R include routines for estimating the coefficients of a logit model. They will also calculate various measures of statistical fit such as Concordance and the Akaike Information Criterion (AIC) that estimate how well the chosen model actually fits the data. How binary regression can be used to estimate the coefficients for a logit bid–response model is discussed in more detail in Phillips (2005: 284–7). Some good additional references on the properties and estimation of GLMs are McCullagh and Nelder (1989), Lindsey (2000), and Dobson and Barnett (2008).

Equation (4) is not the only possible formulation of a bid–response model using the data from Table 21.2. For example, (4) includes the term $\beta_5 \times SIZE$. This term specifies the effect of order size on the probability that the seller will win a bid, all else being equal. In many situations, order size has a strong influence on the probability that a bid will be won at a particular price—typically, customers placing larger orders tend to be more price-sensitive. The model specified in Equation (4) represents this dependence as linear in the size of the order. In many cases—particularly when order size can span a very large range—the strength of bid–response may be more closely correlated with the *logarithm* of order size. This would suggest a model in which the term $\beta_5 \times SIZE$ is replaced with $\beta_5 \times \log(SIZE)$. The supplier might also want to consider a model in which the product of price and order size influences the probability of winning a bid, in which case he could add an additional term of the form $\beta_{12} \times PRICE \times SIZE$. Determination of the best statistical model for bid–response is partly art and partly science. The process usually proceeds by sequentially trying different models and keeping the one that best fits the data. By sequentially comparing alternative models and choosing winners, an experienced modeler can usually develop a predictive and stable model.

We note that the statistical procedure described here is only one possible approach to estimating the bid–response curve and, indeed, is only feasible when the seller has retained historic win/lose information *and* there are sufficient historic data to support the estimation. Our experience has been that when these two conditions are satisfied, standard binary regression approaches such as maximum likelihood estimation can deliver stable, significant, and highly predictive estimates of the bid–response curve. However, there are a number of factors that can confound the estimation, particularly the presence of *endogeneity*. Endogeneity occurs when the price offered to a customer is influenced by variables correlated with his price sensitivity that are not included in the data. For example, a car salesperson may use how well a customer is dressed as an indication of the willingness of the customer to accept a higher price. To the extent the salesperson is correct, the price offered to customers is not independent of their willingness-to-pay, and as a result binary regression will tend to underestimate price sensitivity. The effect of endogeneity can be significant.[8] To the extent that the magnitude of endogeneity is understood, the regression can be adjusted to account for it. Alternatively, random price tests can be used to generate observations that are free from any potential taint of endogeneity.

There are also cases in which sufficient historic data may not be available (as in the introduction of a new product) or in which the seller has not preserved a record of wins and losses. In these cases, alternative approaches such as judgmental estimation of the bid–response curves must be used. In any case, the initial estimation of the bid–response curve should always be updated over time as customer response to new bids is observed.

21.3.3 Calculating incremental profit

The objective function in the Unconstrained Customized Pricing Problem in eq. (1) specifies that the seller is seeking to maximize total expected profit, which is calculated as the product of the probability of winning a bid and the incremental profitability if the bid is won. *Incremental profitability* is calculated as the total expected profitability of the seller if the bid is won minus the expected profitability if the bid is lost. In many cases, the incremental profitability of a transaction is simply the price charged minus the unit cost, that is, $f_i(d, p) = d(p - c_i)$ where p is the price charged, c_i is the unit (incremental) cost per sale in segment i, and d is the order size. This definition of incremental profitability assumes that unit cost is fixed and independent of both the selling price and the number of units sold. In this case, the unit cost c_i should be calculated so that the total cost of the order dc_i is equal to the difference between the total cost that the company will incur if it makes the sale minus the total cost that the company will incur if it doesn't make the sale.

There are cases where the simple linear relationship $f_i(d, p) = d(p - c_i)$ does not apply. In some cases, a seller is bidding to provide an unknown level of products or services to a buyer for future business. For example, UPS competes with FedEx in the package express business. Typically a potential customer will request bids from both companies. A typical bid by UPS or FedEx would be to serve all of the package express business generated by that customer for the coming year. At the time of the bid, neither UPS nor FedEx nor the customer can perfectly forecast its shipping needs for the next year. In this and similar

---

[8] In a meta-analysis of price-estimation studies, Bijmolt et al. (2005) found that the treatment of endogeneity had a major effect on the estimates of price elasticity across industries.

cases, incremental profitability is a random variable and optimization is over expected incremental profitability.

The level and composition of products or services that will be demanded from a supplier under a contract may not only be uncertain, they may depend on the price. For example, many manufacturers contract with less-than-truckload (LTL) trucking companies such as Roadway or Yellow Freight to transport their products to distributors or retailers. A common practice is to choose two or three LTL companies as *preferred suppliers* from ten or more who bid on an annual contract. Under this arrangement, the shipper commits to use one of the preferred suppliers for every shipment. The shipper may also guarantee a minimum level of business to each preferred supplier. However, when it comes to the time to move a particular shipment, the shipper is more likely to choose the supplier who has bid the lowest price for that type of shipment. Even if a trucking company wins the right to be a preferred supplier, the amount of business that it will receive will be a decreasing function of price. More detail on the LTL trucking industry can be found in Kintz (Chapter 13).

Finally, in consumer credit markets incremental cost is typically an *increasing* function of price due to *adverse selection*. This means that, as the prices offered by a lender increase, the loss rates for the loans that it funds will also increase. This will occur even if the lender does not change its underwriting guidelines—that is, it does not change the criteria by which it chooses which applicants it will lend to. As the prices offered by a lender rise relative to the competition, customers with a lower probability of default will defect to other lenders at a higher rate than those with a higher probability of default—who have fewer alternatives. A similar phenomenon occurs in insurance markets. In these cases, the unit cost of serving segment i, c_i cannot be treated as a constant, but must be represented as a function of price—that is, as $c_i(p)$. More detail on the effect of adverse selection on pricing in consumer lending can be found in Phillips and Raffard (2010).

21.3.4 Optimization

Once the bid–response function and the incremental profit function have been determined for each pricing segment, the next step is to determine the optimal price for each segment. If the seller is seeking to maximize expected profitability and does not wish to apply any constraints, then this is equivalent to finding the set of prices that solves the optimization problem in eq. (1). Since this problem is separable, the optimal price for each segment can be determined independently. The optimization problem for a single segment is illustrated graphically in Figure 21.4. In this figure, the dashed downward-sloping curve is the bid–response function and the upward sloping solid line is the incremental profit function. The product of bid–response and incremental profit is expected profit which is the hill-shaped curve in Figure 21.4. In the absence of any constraints, a seller who seeks to maximize expected profit would choose the price at the "top of the hill", labeled p^* in Figure 21.4.

For most realistic bid–response curves and incremental profit functions, expected profitability is well behaved in the sense that it is a smooth function of price with a single peak.[9] This is the case in Figure 21.4. This means that, in the absence of constraints, the

---

[9] Most standard bid–response functions such as probit, logit, or linear satisfy a property known as the Increasing Failure Rate (IFR) property (Barlow and Proschan 1965). If the bid–response functions $\rho_i(p)$ demonstrate the *Increasing Failure Rate* (IFR) property *and* all the incremental profit functions $f_i(p)$ are

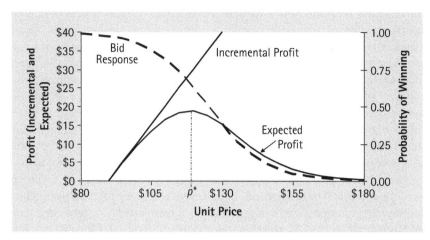

FIGURE 21.4 Calculating expected profitability as a function of price. Expected profitability is the product of bid–response and incremental profit. The profit-maximizing price is shown as p^*.

optimal price can be calculated using standard "hill-climbing" approaches such as gradient ascent.

21.3.4.1 *Optimality condition*

While the unconstrained customized pricing problem in eq. (1) can be easily solved using numerical techniques, it is useful to observe that the optimal price for a segment obeys a standard price-optimality condition. For each segment, define the *bid price elasticity* as the percentage change in the probability of winning a bid divided by the percentage change of price:

$$\varepsilon_i(p) = p\left|\rho_i'(p_i)p_i/\rho_i(p_i)\right|. \tag{5}$$

$\varepsilon_i(p_i)$ in eq. (5) is the analog of the familiar concept of *own-price elasticity* which is defined as the percentage reduction in demand resulting from a 1 percent increase in price. It should be noted that, in the unconstrained case, eq. (5) implies that the optimal price for segment i must satisfy:

$$\varepsilon_i(p_i^*) = \frac{f_i'(p_i^*)p_i^*}{f_i(p_i^*)}. \tag{6}$$

Note that if $f_i(p_i) = p_i - c_i$—that is, incremental profit is equal to price minus unit cost— then condition (6) reduces to

$$\varepsilon_i(p_i^*) = p_i^*/(p_i^* - c_i).$$

increasing, continuous, and concave, it can be shown that a unique optimal price will exist for each segment. This uniqueness property was apparently first identified by the econometrician Theil (1948) in his Master's Thesis.

This is the "elasticity equals the reciprocal of unit margin" condition for price optimality (See Phillips 2005: 64–5 and van Ryzin Chapter 18). Equation (6) is the extension of this well-known condition to the case in which incremental profit is a more complex function of price.

21.3.4.2 *Constrained problems*

The optimization problem in eq. (1) is unconstrained. In most business applications, the seller will wish to set constraints on prices. Examples of typical constraints include:

- *Bounds:* Typically, user-specified upper and lower bounds, p_i^+ and p_i^- are applied on each price by specifying constraints of the form $p_i^+ \geq p_i^*$ and $p_i^* \geq p_i^-$ for each segment i. Price bounds can be applied for a number of different reasons. They may be used in order to maintain some level of price stability by making sure that the new price does not deviate too much from a previous one. For example, an auto manufacturer may want to make sure that the per-unit price quoted to its fleet customers for an order is never more than 10 percent higher than the last price quoted previously to the same customer. Bounds are also applied to ensure that recommended prices are within the region of statistical reliability of the bid–response curve calculation. In other cases, regulations may require a cap on the maximum rate that can be quoted to a particular pricing segment. For example, usury laws in some states specify a maximum interest rate that can be charged for consumer loans.

- *Monotonicity constraints:* In many cases, sellers want to ensure that prices consistently increase or decrease along certain dimensions. A seller might want to ensure that, for otherwise identical customer requests, the unit price bid for a larger order should never be higher than the unit price bid for a smaller order—otherwise customers could get a lower price by breaking a large order into several smaller orders. As another example, sellers often require that an order from an existing customer should never be priced higher than an identical order from a new customer.

- *Business performance constraints:* A seller may wish to maintain certain minimum levels of total sales or revenue, even at the expense of profitability. Management might give a directive such as; "we want to maximize contribution, but we can't allow sales to fall below $10 million for our flagship product during the next quarter or analysts are likely to downgrade our stock." This can be imposed by adding a constraint of the form:

$$\sum_{i \in I} D_i \rho_i(p_i) p_i \geq \$10,000,000$$

where I is the set of segments that include the flagship product.

- *Price banding:* A seller may want prices in a particular region or through a particular channel to maintain some relationship to prices in other regions or channels. For international companies, such price bands are often necessary to prevent arbitrage. A semiconductor manufacturer may need to specify that chips cannot be sold in Brazil for less than 2 cents per unit less than they are sold in the United States, otherwise it would be profitable for arbitrageurs to purchase chips at the lower price in Brazil and resell them in the United States.

- *Channel constraints:* Sellers often wish to maintain relationships among the prices charged through different channels. For example, a seller might want to ensure that the price quoted through the Internet for a customer request should never be higher than the price quoted for the same request received through a call center.

Each of the conditions described above can be imposed by adding one or more constraints to the optimization problem specified in eq. (1). From a technical point of view, adding constraints usually makes the pricing optimization problem harder to solve. However, as long as the constraints define a convex feasible region, standard solution approaches can be used to solve for optimal prices. From a business point of view, adding and managing constraints can be more problematic. In particular, care needs to be taken that users do not over-constrain the problem.

21.3.5 Monitoring and updating

As shown in Figure 21.2, an effective customized pricing process needs to include a mechanism for monitoring the market and updating prices over time. No matter how carefully crafted, a set of prices cannot be optimal forever. Prices need to be adjusted in response to changes in the macroeconomic environment, changes in costs, shifting customer preferences, and competitive actions. Depending upon the market and velocity of transactions, prices might need to be updated daily, weekly, or monthly. Most companies using an analytical approach to customized pricing update prices on a fixed periodic basis with interim *ad hoc* changes in response to external events.

Not only prices, but model coefficients also need to be updated. That is, the values of β_0, $\beta_1, \ldots, \beta_{11}$ estimated by the printer cartridge manufacturer for the model in eq. (4) will need to be monitored periodically and refined. Typically, model coefficients are updated much less frequently than the prices themselves. Prices need to be changed whenever market conditions change, costs change, or the business goals and constraints change. Depending upon the market, coefficients might be updated monthly, bi-monthly, or even semi-annually. A seller should periodically monitor the performance of the statistical model relative to actual results. If the predictions of his model begin to deviate significantly from reality, then it is a good idea to re-estimate the coefficients.

One way to update the coefficients is to append the most recent win/loss observations to the data file and re-run the regression. This is typically done with weighting the most recent observations more heavily than the historic data. Alternatively, various *Bayesian approaches* can be used. With Bayesian updating, new observations are used directly to update the values of the parameters[10] Updating is particularly important early in the adoption of an analytic approach in order to ensure that the initial set of coefficients has been estimated accurately. It is also important in markets with rapidly changing costs.

---

[10] Gill (2008) provides an introduction to the use of Bayesian statistics.

21.4 ENHANCEMENTS AND EXTENSIONS

The previous sections have described the application of an analytical approach to customized price optimization in the "plain vanilla" case in which the seller seeks to maximize expected profitability, each customer request contains only one product, the prices offered by competitors are not available, and the bid price is not negotiated. In most real-world applications, one or more of these conditions will not hold. We now briefly discuss the effects of relaxing these conditions.

21.4.1 Alternative objective functions

The customized pricing problem as specified in eq. (1) maximizes expected contribution. This is consistent with a corporate goal of maximizing expected short-run profitability. However, it is often the case that a seller might wish to maximize expected *revenue* rather than expected profitability for one or more segments. For certain segments, a seller may wish to hold or increase its market share for strategic reasons and is willing to give up some profitability to do so. In that case, the objective function in (1) would be replaced with:

$$\max_p \left[\sum_{i \in I_1} D_i \rho_i(p_i) f_i(p_i) + \sum_{i \in I_2} D_i \rho_i(p_i) p_i \right].$$

where I_1 is the set of pricing segments for which expected contribution is to maximized and I_2 is the set for which revenue is to be maximized.

Maximizing revenue always results in lower prices than maximizing profitability. Intuitively, this occurs because the "profit-maximizing price" is an increasing function of the unit cost and the revenue-maximizing price is the same as the profit-maximizing price with a unit cost of 0. When unit cost is greater than 0, the additional revenue generated by the revenue-maximizing price comes at the expense of profitability—this is often described as "buying market share". One way to visualize the tradeoff between contribution and revenue (or market share) is through the use of an *efficient frontier* as illustrated in Figure 21.5. The efficient frontier shows all of the combinations of prices at which profit is maximized subject to achieving at least a certain level of revenue. Points inside the frontier can be achieved by changing prices; points outside the frontier cannot be achieved by changing prices. It could be argued that a firm would always wish to be operating at a point on the efficient frontier. If it is operating inside the efficient frontier, it could increase both revenue and profitability simply by changing prices. Thus, a firm currently operating at Point A in Figure 21.5 could achieve the same level of profitability but higher revenue by moving to Point B. Alternatively, it could maximize profitability at the same level of revenue by moving to Point C. Points between B and C on the efficient frontier all represent points at which the firm could increase both revenue and profitability relative to operating at Point A.

The efficient frontier enables the seller to calculate how much profit it would lose by meeting any particular revenue target. This can be a valuable insight since it allows management to set revenues with a full understanding of the implications for reduced profit.

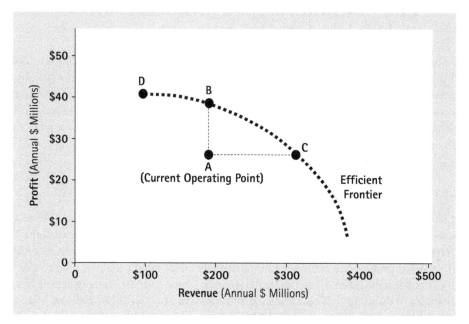

FIGURE 21.5 An efficient frontier. The frontier represents all points at which profit is maximized subject to a minimum revenue requirement or, equivalently, revenue is maximized subject to a minimum profit constraint. The firm is currently operating within the frontier at Point A. Point B maximizes profit at current revenue and Point C maximizes revenue at current profit. Any point on the frontier between B and C achieves both higher profit and higher revenue than Point A. Point D maximizes Profit, but at lower revenue than Point A.

21.4.2 Incorporating competitive information

So far, we have ignored competition. At first glance, this might appear to be a major lapse. After all, most companies would likely nominate "what the competitor is charging" as a major determinant of whether or not they will win a bid. In fact, there is no theoretical difficulty in incorporating competitive prices into the bid–response function. If competitive prices are known at the time bids are made, they can (and should) be incorporated into the bid–response function. To see how this is done, assume that the printer cartridge seller has two competitors. Let p_A denote the price bid by the first competitor and p_B the price bid by the second competitor. Then, the model specified in eq. (4) could be supplemented with the two additional terms $\beta_{12} \times p_A$ and $\beta_{13} \times p_B$. The values of β_{12} and β_{13} can be determined using regression in the same fashion as the other coefficients and used as predictors for future bid–response.

The rub is that in the majority of customized pricing settings, competing prices are typically not known when the price for a bid must be determined. A seller responding to an RFP or an on-line order inquiry will typically not know the identity or even the number of competitors he is facing—much less what prices they are bidding. In fact, in most cases, the seller will not have full information about competitive pricing even if he wins a bid. Thus, there will be little or no competitive price information in the historical win/loss data. In this case, the best option open to the seller may be to use a bid–response model that does not explicitly include competitive pricing terms.

Note that excluding competitive pricing terms from the bid–response curve is not the same as "ignoring competition". Rather, it is equivalent to assuming that *competitors will set prices in the future in the same way as they have done in the past*. Even though they do not contain explicit competitive price terms, the bid–response curves implicitly incorporate within them the effect of past competitive pricing. The results of running a regression may be to show that a particular segment seems to be highly price-sensitive. This could be because customers in that segment are intrinsically more sensitive to price. However, it could also indicate that one or more competitors typically price "aggressively" (i.e., low) in this segment. As long as competitive pricing in this segment does not change, the predicted level of price sensitivity should be stable and predictive of the future. If a competitor changes its pricing strategy for a segment—say by raising price, a supplier will find that it is winning more deals in that segment than it forecasted. This should be a trigger to re-estimate the model coefficients. The updated coefficients will reflect the new competitive strategy.

21.4.3 Segment selection

The formulation of the Unconstrained Customized Pricing Problem in eq. (1) implicitly assumes that some price will be quoted to all customer segments. There are situations in which this is not the case, that is, the seller does not want to sell to every segment. The most obvious case is lending and insurance—as noted before, due to risk, there are some customers who are unprofitable at any price and therefore cannot obtain credit at all. However, there are other cases in which a seller might not wish to sell to every potential customer segment. It may be unprofitable to sell certain items through certain channels or to certain regions. It is not uncommon to set minimum order size restrictions on small, inexpensive items and so on. This suggests that the formulation of the Unconstrained Customized Pricing Problem in eq. (1) should be expanded to enable simultaneous pricing and segment selection:

$$\max_{p,x} \sum_{i=1}^{N} D_i x_i \rho_i(p_i) f_i(p_i)$$
$$\text{s.t. } p > 0$$
$$x \in \{0, 1\}$$
(7)

where $x = (x_1, x_2, \ldots, x_n)$ is a vector such that $x_i = 1$ means that the seller should sell into customer segment i and $x_i = 0$ means that he should not sell into that segment. The unconstrained version of the problem shown in (7) is not difficult to solve: simply solve the Unconstrained Customized Pricing Problem in (1) and set $x_i = 1$ for all segments whose maximum profit is greater than 0 and set $x_i = 0$ for all segments with maximum profit less than 0. A similar approach can be used when the only constraints are price bounds. However, if there are many constraints applied, the problem can become quite difficult because the constraints may force some segments to be served at unprofitable prices in order to meet the constraints.

21.4.4 Multi-dimensional prices and bundled products

In many cases, there is more than one "price" required for a bid. In the United States, lenders typically charge a number of upfront fees to obtain a mortgage. In addition, the mortgage may have "points" associated with it, where the points are a fee paid by the borrower expressed as a percentage of a loan. Points can enable a borrower to obtain a lower APR by paying a fee expressed as a percentage of the amount they wish to borrow. For example, a \$100,000 mortgage might be available at 7.9 percent with \$1,000 in fees and 0.5 points. The 0.5 points would be an additional fee of 0.5 percent $\times$ \$100,000 = \$500. Since fees and points are usually rolled into the initial balance, the borrower is actually borrowing \$101,500 at a 7.9 percent APR and her monthly payment is computed accordingly. All three components—APR, fixed fees, and points—are part of the "price" of the mortgage. All three can influence the buyer's decision whether or not to accept the mortgage as well as the seller's profitability if the mortgage is chosen.

As another example, many business-to-business service providers such as telecommunications companies price based on an "n-part" tariff in which the total cost to the buyer is based on a periodic base price plus a usage cost that depends on the level of service used—the higher the level of service, the lower the per-unit usage cost. Typically the per-unit cost is a step-function of usage, thus the charge might be a base cost of \$100 per month plus \$.02 per minute for the first 300 minutes per month, \$.015 per minute for the next 100 minutes, and \$.01 per minute for any usage above 400 minutes. A bid must specify the base cost as well as all the per-unit costs as well as the breakpoints. In theory, a supplier could specify a personalized n-part tariff for each bid. In practice, most sellers tend to maintain a few standard tariff structures. When they bid, they specify the tariff structure and a discount to be applied. The problem facing the bidder is to determine which structure and what level of discount to bid for each request.

Another example of multi-dimensional pricing is provided by business-to-business software licenses that often specify timed payments. For example, a software license might specify a payment to be made upon signing, a further payment to be made upon installation, and additional support and maintenance fees to be paid annually for five years. Each of these payment amounts is a component of the overall "price".

There are several approaches to optimizing multi-dimensional prices. One is to compute an "aggregate price" which ideally reflects the metric that buyers are using to choose among bids. For example, it is not unreasonable to assume that borrowers use monthly payment as the "pricing metric" that they use to compare alternative mortgages. A lender might then consider monthly payment to be a logical choice for the "aggregate price" of a mortgage. A software company might consider the Net Present Value of payments to be the aggregate price of its software. Let $p = (p_1, p_2, \ldots, p_m)$ be the elements of price and let $q_i(p)$ be the aggregate price for segment i. Then, the customized pricing problem with aggregate prices can be written:

$$\max_{p} \sum_{i=1}^{N} D_i \rho_i(q_i(p)) S_i(p)$$

where $S_i(p) : \mathcal{R}^m \to \mathcal{R}^1$ is a function that specifies incremental profitability for segment i as a function of the various price elements. The aggregate price can be used as an explanatory variable within binary regression in order to estimate the bid–response functions $\rho_i(q_i(p_i))$.

While the aggregate price approach has the advantage of being simple, it assumes that buyers in all segments are indifferent among options with the same aggregate price. However, in most cases, it is likely that different buyers weight price elements differently and that no single aggregate price measure holds for all buyers. For companies purchasing software licenses, some may face short-run budget constraints that make them very sensitive to the upfront cash outlay while other buyers may be quite willing to accept a higher upfront cash payment in return for a lower overall cost of ownership. This suggests the alternative approach of including each pricing dimension independently in the regression and allowing the regression to determine their weights. For the software license example, p^1 might be the upfront cash payment, p^2 the total license fee, and p^3 the annual support and maintenance. By including p^1, p^2, and p^3 as covariates in the binary regression, the seller could, in theory, determine how different segments weight each of the pricing elements in their pricing decisions and determine the corresponding bid–response curves as a function of all three elements.

As usual in regression, the best approach will depend upon the situation. The aggregate price approach is more parsimonious because it collapses all of the pricing elements into a single aggregate price. However, as discussed, the aggregate price chosen may not accurately reflect how buyers actually compare alternatives. Several different aggregate prices may need to be considered. While the approach of incorporating all of the pricing elements in the regression is more flexible, it also has drawbacks. It requires much more data for stable estimation since a coefficient needs to be estimated for each pricing element. Choosing among approaches may require several rounds of trial-and-error and comparison of the results of different approaches.

21.4.5 Bundled products

A problem similar to multi-dimensional pricing is faced by sellers who are selling bundled products or highly configured products. In many cases, a price (possibly quoted as a discount from list price) must be quoted individually for every element of the order. For example, automotive fleet RFPs often include several different types of vehicles—for example, 10 cars, 5 pick-up trucks, and 5 panel vans. If the bid is indivisible—that is, the buyer firmly commits to purchase all of the vehicles from the same seller—then the best strategy is to determine the optimal price to quote for the entire bid. If, on the other hand, the bid is divisible in the sense that the buyer may choose to purchase the cars from one supplier, the trucks from another, and the panel vans from a third; then the optimal strategy is to treat the bid as three independent bids—that is, determine the optimal bid for the cars, the optimal bid for the pick-up trucks, and the optimal bid for the panel vans. While these two extreme cases are straightforward, many bidding situations fall between these extremes. In particular, a buyer may express a preference for purchasing from a single supplier but reserve the right to purchase from two or more. In this case, the allocation of the total price among the vehicle categories becomes important—the price allocated to each vehicle category may need to be chosen to be "competitive"—that is not too far out-of-line with expected competitive bids. More discussion of bundled pricing can be found in chapter 11 of Phillips (2005) as well as in Oren (Chapter 22) and Gallego and Stefanescu (Chapter 28).

21.4.6 Negotiated deals

The discussion so far has assumed a "take it or leave it" pricing situation—that is, the buyer describes her needs, sellers quote their prices, and the buyer then chooses which seller (if any) from which to purchase. The price quoted by each seller is final—the only decision facing the buyer is which bid (if any) to accept. While this reasonably characterizes many customized pricing situations, there are cases in which the final price is the product of one or more rounds of negotiation between the buyer and the seller. The prevalence of negotiation in customized pricing differs widely from industry to industry and even from segment-to-segment within an industry. For example, in the US auto lending market, negotiation is relatively rare in prime markets but almost universal in sub-prime markets. Negotiation is generally more common for larger deals. It is also more common in face-to-face selling situations (whether direct or indirect) than telesales or Internet channels. For those situations in which negotiation is likely, an effective approach should provide more than simply a single optimal price—it should also provide some guidance regarding an acceptable range of prices and, ideally, some idea of the tradeoffs between price and other aspects of the deal.

A common approach to support negotiated pricing is to use the expected profit function to help define a range of acceptable prices. The basic idea is illustrated in Figure 21.6. Here, the unit price that maximizes expected profit is $150, at which price the expected profitability from the bid under consideration is $15,000. A lower price and an upper price have been set so that the expected profitability is $13,500 at both p_L and p_U. At any price between p_L and p_U, the expected profit will be within 10 percent of the optimum. This range along with the target price can be used by the seller to guide sequential rounds of negotiation and ensure that the final outcome is within a desired range.

The approach illustrated in Figure 21.6 is often used to support a combined centralized/ decentralized approach to negotiated pricing. The target price p^* and the upper and lower

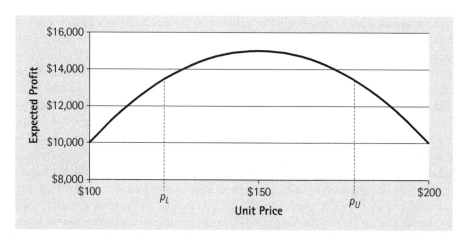

FIGURE 21.6 Setting bounds for guide price negotiation.

Note: p_L and p_U are the prices at which expected profit is $13,500: 10% lower than the optimal expected profit of $15,000 which is achieved at $p^* = $150. Any price between p_L and p_U will result in expected profit within 10% of the optimal.

bounds p_L and p_U can be calculated centrally consistent with corporate goals and business constraints. The local sales person has the freedom to negotiate the best price he can within the specified bounds. This approach can deliver the best of both worlds: all of the data available to the corporation are used to calculate the bid–response curves and set pricing ranges for each segment based on overall corporate strategy while local knowledge of individual customers can be used to negotiate the best deal within the specified range. In many cases, the local sales person will have specific customer or competitive knowledge of the deal under consideration that can lead to better overall performance than using the same optimal price for all deals within a segment.

Of course, in many negotiated settings, price is not the only element of the deal in play. An auto lender might be willing to offer a lower APR if the borrower is willing to put more money into the down payment. A heavy truck manufacturer might be willing to lower the price if the buyer agrees to purchase an extended warranty. An enterprise software vendor selling a multi-year license deal might be willing to lower the price if the buyer agrees to pay more cash up front. Complex negotiations can involve multiple rounds of give and take and a full discussion of the "art and science of negotiation" is well beyond the scope of this section—Raiffa et al. (2003) provide an introduction to the topic. However, the analytic concepts behind price optimization can also provide invaluable guidance to negotiation. In particular, they give insight into the central questions: If we change this non-price characteristic of the deal, what will be the effect on incremental profitability? How, then, should we change price in order to maximize expected profitability given the new profitability level? A number of customized pricing optimization software systems enable users to perform these computations in order to help support the negotiation process.

21.5 THE FUTURE OF CUSTOMIZED PRICING

The primary focus of this chapter has been on the technical and mathematical aspects of pricing optimization. The problem is of sufficient complexity that, for sellers selling multiple products to many different customer segments, automated software systems are often used to set customized prices and update them over time. Whether or not the size and complexity of the customized pricing problem facing a seller is sufficiently great to justify implementing a software system, many companies have the opportunity to improve their pricing by implementing a consistent process of learning and improvement such as the one illustrated in Figure 21.2.

Of course, the primary motivation for adopting an analytical approach to customized pricing is usually to increase profitability. The package shipper UPS reported a profitability increase of more than $100 million per year in North America through the use of a software system to optimize customized prices (Boyd et al. 2005). The sub-prime auto lender AmeriCredit saw a $4 million increase in profitability within three months of implementing a customized pricing optimization system (Phillips 2010). Results such as these provide strong motivation for companies utilizing customized pricing to invest in improving both the processes and the systems that they use to set prices. There is at least anecdotal evidence that an increasing number of firms using customized pricing are applying analytic approaches to setting their prices. The *Wall Street Journal* described the benefits resulting from the introduction of more analytical approaches to customized pricing at industrial parts manufacturer, Parker Hannifin (Aeppel 2007). A number of companies such as Nomis Solutions and Zilliant offer automated pricing optimization solutions to companies facing customized pricing situations.

Customized pricing also offers a number of promising research opportunities. Relative to its importance in the economy, it has been relatively less studied than other pricing modalities such as auctions or list pricing. There are at least two promising areas for future research. One is the estimation of customer price-sensitivity information from historical data, especially the elimination of endogeneity effects as described in Section 21.3.2. The identification and use of instrumental variables to address endogeneity as in Berry et al. (1995) holds promise but its use has not been documented in a customized pricing setting. The other area for additional research is in the area of optimal segmentation—when the ability to segment is limited, how should a seller choose and price to segments in order to maximize expected profitability? Both of these represent areas where research break-throughs could lead to substantial improvements in practice.

References

Aeppel, T. (2007) "Seeking Perfect Prices, CEO Tears up the Rules", *The Wall Street Journal* March 27.

Agrawal, V. and Ferguson, M. (2007) "Bid–Response Models for Customised Pricing", *Journal of Revenue and Pricing Management* 6/3: 212–28.

Akerlof, G. A. (1970) "The Market for 'Lemons': Quality Uncertainty and the Market Mechanism", *Quarterly Journal of Economics* 84/3: 488–500.

Barlow, R. E. and Proschan, F. (1965) *Mathematical Theory of Reliability*. New York: John Wiley and Sons, Inc.

Berry, S., Levinsohn, J., and Pakes, A. (1995) "Automobile Prices in Market Equilibrium", *Econometrica* 63/4: 841–90.

Bijmolt, T. H. A., van Heerde, H. J., and Pieters, R. G. M. (2005) "New Emprical Generaliza-tions of the Determinants of Price Elasticity", *Journal of Marketing Research* 42: 141–56.

Boyd, D., Gordon, M., Anderson, J., Tai, C., Feng, Y., Kolamala, A., Cook, G., Guardino, T., Purang, M., Krishnamurthy, P., Cooke, M., Nandiwada, R., Monteiro, B., and Haas, S. (2005) *Manugistics Target Pricing System*. US Patent No: 6963854.

Dobson, A. J. and Barnett, A. (2008) *An Introduction to Generalized Linear Models*, 3rd edn. Boca Raton, FL: Chapman and Hall/CRC.

Friedman, L. (1956) "A Competitive Bidding Strategy", *Operations Research* 4/1: 104–12.

Gates, M. (1967) "Bidding Strategies and Probabilities", *Journal of the Construction Division, Proceedings of the American Society of Civil Engineers* 93/1: 75–107.

Gill, J. (2008) *Bayesian Methods: A Social and Behavioral Sciences Approach*, 2nd edn. Boca Raton, FL: Chapman and Hall/CRC.

Lindsey, J. K. (2000) *Applying Generalized Linear Models*. New York: Springer.

McCullagh, P. and Nedler, J. A. (1989) *Generalized Linear Models*, 2nd edn. Boca Raton, FL: Chapman and Hall/CRC.

Makridakis, S., Wheelwright, S. C., and Hyndman, R. J. (1998) *Forecasting: Methods and Application*, 3rd edn. Boston, MA: John Wiley and Sons.

Marn, M. V., Roegner, E. V., and Zawada, C. C. (2004) *The Price Advantage*. Hoboken, NJ: John Wiley and Sons.

Maxwell, S. (2008) *The Price is Wrong: Understanding what makes a Price Seem Fair and the True Cost of Unfair Pricing*. Hoboken, NJ: John Wiley & Sons.

Morin, T. L. and Clough, R. H. (1969) "OPBID: Competitive Bidding Strategy Model", *Journal of the Construction Division, Proceedings of the American Society of Civil Engineers* 95/1: 85–106.

Phillips, R. L. (2005) *Pricing and Revenue Optimization*. Stanford, CA: Stanford University Press.

—— and Raffard, R. (2010) "Price-driven Adverse Selection in Consumer Lending", Working paper 2011-3. Columbia Center for Pricing and Revenue Management. Available at < http://www7.gsb.columbia.edu/cprm/sites/default/files/files/2011-3-Price-Driven-Adverse-Selection%281%29.pdf.

Raiffa, H., Richardson, J., and Metcalfe, D. (2003) *Negotiation Analysis: The Science and Art of Collaborative Decision Making*. Cambridge, MA: Harvard University Press.

Ross, S. L. and Yinger, J. (2002) *The Color of Credit: Mortgage Discrimination, Research Methodology, and Fair-Lending Enforcement*. Cambridge, MA: MIT Press.

Stiglitz, J. E. and Weiss, A. (1981) "Credit Rationing in Markets with Imperfect Information", *American Economic Review* 71/3: 393–410.

Theil, H. (1948) "A Static Theory of Entrepreneurial Behavior". Master's Thesis, University of Amsterdam, Amsterdam (in Dutch).

CHAPTER 22

··

NONLINEAR PRICING

··

SHMUEL S. OREN

22.1 INTRODUCTION

··

While basic economic theory characterizes products as homogeneous commodities that are traded at uniform unit prices so that purchase price is proportional to purchase quantity, real products and services are more complex. Quantity metrics, to the extent they are meaningful, represent only one dimension upon which purchase prices are based. Nonlinear pricing is a generic characterization of any tariff structure where the purchase price is not strictly proportional to some measure of purchase quantity but also reflects other characteristics of the product, the purchaser, the purchase as a whole, its timing and any contractual terms imposing restriction on the purchase and its subsequent use. A fundamental aspect of nonlinear pricing methodology is the systematic exploitation of heterogeneity in customer preferences with respect to purchase characteristics and the explicit modeling targeting the preference structures underlying such heterogeneity. In that respect, nonlinear pricing theory differs from revenue management, which recognizes customer heterogeneity but typically models it as a random phenomenon. A key assumption of nonlinear pricing is the existence of identifiable differences among customers that affect their choices in a systematic way. Furthermore, it is assumed that these differences among customers are either directly observable or that customers can be sorted by observing measurable characteristics of the customer or her purchases.

Nonlinear pricing is motivated by several goals such as: efficient use of resources, cost recovery by a regulated utility, exercise of monopoly power, obtaining competitive advantage, rewarding customer loyalty, as well as social goals such as subsidies to the poor and discounts to service persons in uniform. Being able to sell identical or similar products or services at different prices to different customers has powerful ramifications and can lead to win–win outcomes from the customers' and the sellers' perspectives.

To illustrate such potential benefits let us consider the classic case of a homogeneous commodity sold by a monopoly supplier at a uniform unit price. The demand for the commodity is characterized by a simple downward sloping demand function. Such a demand function does not distinguish between multi-unit purchases by a single customer

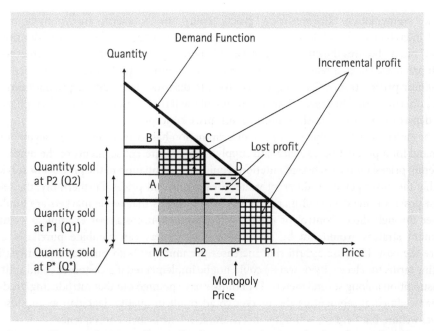

FIGURE 22.1 Increased monopoly profits (incremental minus lost) and social welfare gain (area ABCD) through bifurcated pricing

or single unit purchases by many customers. In making its pricing decision, the monopoly supplier must trade off increased profits from selling additional units by lowering the price against the lost profits from existing sales. Consequently, the monopoly supplier will set a price above marginal cost, which is suboptimal from a social welfare[1] perspective (since it excludes some customers who are willing to pay more than the product costs). If the monopoly supplier were able to segment the demand and charge two prices for the same product as illustrated in Figure 22.1, more demand valuing the product above marginal cost would be served ($Q_1 + Q_2 > Q^*$), increasing social welfare. Furthermore, the original monopoly profit $(P^* - MC) \cdot Q^*$, could increase, if the incremental profit exceeds the lost profit (as in Figure 22.1), resulting in a "win–win" proposition.

The difficulty in implementing such market segmentation based on customers' willingness-to-pay is that such information is typically private. Furthermore, such price discrimination would require some means of preventing the high paying customers from purchasing the product at the low price.

Nonlinear pricing, which implements the basic idea illustrated above in a variety of contexts, encompasses basic principles of price discrimination, product differentiation, and

[1] Social welfare (also referred to as social surplus) measures the total benefit to society from production and consumption of a good or service. It is defined as the total benefit from consuming the good or service (as reflected by customers' willingness-to-pay) less the production cost. Social welfare is also the sum of the consumer surplus and producer surplus. The consumer surplus measures the net benefit to consumers from the good or service and is defined as the aggregate willingness-to-pay minus payment. The producer surplus measures producers' total profit (i.e., revenue less production cost) from selling the good or service. Since payments for the good or service constitute a transfer from consumers to producers, prices only affect social surplus to the extent that they affect production or consumption quantities.

market segmentation. However, for all practical purposes, these terms are synonymous and used interchangeably. Unfortunately, the negative connotation of the term "discrimination" often obscures the efficiency gains and Pareto improvement that can be achieved by such practices. For that reason many important contributions to the theory and practice of nonlinear pricing (e.g., Wilson 1993) have tried to disassociate nonlinear pricing from the price discrimination interpretation and the use of the term "Nonlinear Pricing" emphasizes the departure from the classical uniform unit price concept.

The classic economic theory of price discrimination has focused on how to segment the demand for a product or a service and supply them to different segments of the market at different prices. Often, such segmentation requires differentiation of the product or services so that the buyer perceives different values for the different prices. Furthermore, the seller must possess some degree of market power which means that resale markets are limited, either through direct control or due to high transaction costs. For example a volume discount strategy would not be sustainable if customers can combine purchases and share the cost. Likewise a tariff that increases per unit cost with purchase quantity (like lifeline tariffs for electricity or water) could not be implemented if a customer could split its consumption among several meters. Economists have pointed out that introducing product variants aimed at segmenting the market could result in quality degradation and loss of social welfare but here we will not concern ourselves with such consequences.

The principles of price discrimination were introduced by Pigou (1920) who distinguished between three basic forms of price discrimination:

- First degree (Direct) discrimination where prices are based on the purchasers' willingness-to-pay.
- Second degree (Indirect) discrimination where prices are based on some observable characteristics of the purchase (e.g., volume), which is correlated with the customer's preferences.
- Third degree (Semi-direct) discrimination where prices are based on some observable characteristics of the buyer (e.g., geographic location or age).

To illustrate the difference between Semi-direct and Indirect price discrimination consider the example of a children's menu in a restaurant which under a semi-direct discrimination policy can be ordered only by children. By contrast, an indirect discrimination approach would offer on the menu discounted small portions of assorted items that are unlikely to be ordered by an adult but without prohibiting such orders. Nonlinear pricing falls under the category of indirect or second degree discrimination. The efficiency properties of such practices stem from the fact that they induce customers to sort themselves and reveal private information that leads to improved production and allocative efficiencies.[2]

Necessary conditions for sustainability of price discrimination strategies are various forms of nontransferability conditions. In the case of indirect discrimination the demand must be nontransferable, meaning that one type of purchase, for example high end wine bottles, cannot be met through decanting of discounted jug wine of the same brand. Such a

---

[2] Production efficiency refers to the extent to which a good or service is produced at least cost while allocative efficiency refers to the extent to which a good or service is allocated to its highest valued use.

possibility would undermine a volume discount strategy. Likewise, semi-direct discrimination requires nontransferability of the product, for example a discounted senior ski ticket cannot be used by a non-senior person. Nontransferability of products (or services) is relatively easy to enforce. Airline restrictions on transfer of tickets represent a classic example of such practices. Nontransferability of demand is harder to enforce but can be facilitated by technological constraints, product differentiation (sometimes at a cost), search cost, and transactions costs. The requirement for a Saturday night stay is an example of product differentiation for the purpose of discriminating between business and recreational travelers at the expense of unutilized plane capacity on Saturdays. Frequent travelers were able for a while to overcome this restriction through overlapping back to back bookings but the airlines were able to curb such practices using sophisticated monitoring of reservations (see Barnes Chapter 3).

Direct discrimination is rare since it requires both types of nontransferability as well as information regarding the customer's preferences and the states of nature upon which such preferences may depend. Nevertheless, pricing of services based on the value of a transaction, for example sale of real estate or pricing of personal services, comes close to direct price discrimination.

In this chapter we will focus primarily on indirect price discrimination, which underlies most of the commercially motivated nonlinear pricing schemes. An exception that will be discussed is Ramsey pricing which discriminates among customer types (e.g., industrial versus residential customers). The objective of such pricing is to achieve cost recovery in regulated utilities with concave cost structures with least efficiency losses due to deviation from marginal cost pricing (known as second best policies).

From an economic theory perspective, the design of nonlinear pricing schemes as indirect price discrimination mechanisms falls into the general category of mechanism design and agency theory (e.g., Tirole 1988) where the seller can be viewed as the principal who designs an incentive scheme that will induce desired purchase behavior by its customers who are the agents.

An indirect price discrimination mechanism must first identify target characteristics, which differentiate customers and develop a sorting mechanism that separates customers according to the target characteristic such as quantity choice, time of use, time value, or level of use. In order to implement such a mechanism we must have disaggregated demand data specifying customer preferences with regard to various product attributes. Assembling such data requires that at a minimum we are able to specify the following aspects:

- What is a customer? (For instance regarding frequent flyer plans, the customer and the billing account may not be the same.)
- Dimension of the tariff (physical units, number of transactions, dollar amount)
- Units of purchase (kWh, KW, metric cube)
- Quality dimensions (time of use or interruptibility for electricity service, advance reservation, and flexibility for airline tickets)
- Method of billing (low daily rate with mileage charge versus flat daily rate with unlimited miles). Terms of the contract and method of billing may be sometimes interpreted as quality attributes.

In the following we will discuss in more detail five generic nonlinear pricing schemes that will illustrate the underlying theory and practical applications of such methods:

- Bundling
- Quantity discounts
- Ramsey pricing
- Quality differentiation
- Priority pricing and efficient rationing

The objective of this chapter is neither to be exhaustive in surveying nonlinear pricing practices and methods nor to be comprehensive in terms of the theoretical foundation of the nonlinear pricing methods discussed and the related literature. For an extensive treatment of nonlinear pricing the reader is referred to Wilson (1993) that provides a deep analysis of such methods along with a detailed bibliographic survey and historical review of the area. This chapter is written primarily as a tutorial with the objective of conveying the philosophical basis for nonlinear pricing and highlighting thematic application areas, key ideas, and the basic methodologies used in designing such tariff structures.

22.2 BUNDLING

Bundling is the most basic form of nonlinear pricing and indirect price discrimination which segments the market by offering commodities either separately or in a bundle which is offered at a price below the sum prices of the components. There is a fine line between bundling and "tying" which is illegal in the USA. Under tying, customers are forced to buy one thing as a condition for being able to buy another popular or essential product or service. Companies often use tying as a mechanism to monitor usage of the essential product, which will enable them to discriminate based on usage. For instance IBM used to force their customers who bought IBM computers to buy only IBM punch cards. By controlling the price of the punch cards they were effectively able to charge for their computers different prices based on use. Similarly Xerox was forcing their customers to use only Xerox toner in their copiers and more recently HP was trying to force their customers to buy HP maintenance services for their HP computers. These practices are now considered illegal.

By contrast, bundling refers to the practice where products or services are sold together as a package providing a discount relative to component pricing. Pure bundling means that only the package is offered whereas mixed bundling means that both the package and the components are available. To see how bundling can be beneficial consider the following example adapted from Stigler (1963). Suppose that we have two products X and Y and two types of customers A and B. The products are unique and are produced by a monopoly supplier at zero marginal cost. Table 22.1 summarizes the willingness-to-pay (WTP) of each customer type for each of the products and the resulting market outcomes. We observe that by offering the bundle the monopolist is able to increase its profits from $19 to $20, by exploiting the negative correlation in preference among the two customer types.

Table 22.1 Mixed bundling example

	WTP by A	WTP by B	Monopoly price	Profit
Product X	$8.0	$7.0	$7.0	$14.0
Product Y	$2.5	$3.0	$2.5	$5.0
Bundle X+Y	$10.5	$10.0	$10.0	$20.0

When we have a continuum of customers that are characterized by their willingness-to-pay for products X and Y we can identify the regions in which consumers will buy the separate products and the bundle as illustrated in Figure 22.2. We denote the prices and corresponding costs of the component products X and Y as P_X, P_Y, C_X, C_Y respectively, and the bundle price for one unit of X and one unit of Y as P_b. Furthermore we consider the case where a customer will only consider buying at most one unit of each product (e.g., travel and lodging for a vacation). If a bundle is not offered then customers in the area AJEC would buy only product Y since their willingness-to-pay for product X is less than its price. Likewise, customers in the area KEGM would only buy product X and customers in the area JEK would buy the two products since their willingness-to-pay for each product exceeds the price. With the bundle we increase sales of the two products by essentially offering them at a discount through the bundle to customers who buy both. We are also

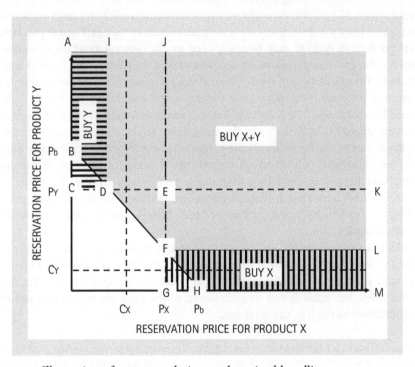

FIGURE 22.2 Illustration of customer choices under mixed bundling

able to sell the bundle to customers in the area DEF who would not buy anything if the bundle was not offered. The optimal price for the bundle and the component products can be determined by formulating an optimization problem that will maximize the seller's profit given the distribution of customers' willingness-to-pay for the two products. Since offering the bundle at a price that equals the sum of the components is a feasible solution of such optimization, mixed bundling is guaranteed to yield at least as much profit as simple linear pricing of the component products.

While the analysis of bundling can be extended to more than two products the graphical representation gets messy and we will not pursue it any further for bundling arbitrary products. However, we can analyze in more generality special kinds of bundles consisting of multiple units of the same product. In such a case the bundling strategy is referred to as quantity discounts.

22.3 QUANTITY DISCOUNTS

In order to analyze quantity discount strategies, we have to extend our concept of a demand function to capture the divergence among customer types with regard to purchasing of multiple units of a product. If we assume that all units are sold at the same price, as in basic economic theory, we do not care if ten units are purchased by ten different customers or by one customer. However, if we want to use purchase quantity as a means for screening customers by type, a more disaggregated demand model is needed. We can do it by defining a demand profile, $N(q, p)$, that describes how many customers will buy q units or more of the product at unit price p. Alternatively, we may think of each incremental unit of purchase as a separate product so $N(q, p)$ may be interpreted as the demand function describing the demand for the qth unit purchased by a customer as a function of the price charged for the qth unit. This will allow us to set the price of each incremental unit of purchase separately and obtain a price function, $p(q)$, which specifies the marginal price for the qth unit purchased by a customer.[3] In practice, volume discounts take the form of block declining tariffs characterized by break points at discrete quantity levels as shown in Figure 22.3.

The lower part of the figure shows the marginal unit price, which changes as purchase quantity increases while the upper part shows the cumulative payment as function of quantity. Note that we can also have a fixed charge such as a monthly fee for phone service on top of which we have a per-minute charge, which declines with usage. A two-part tariff consisting of a fixed charge and a constant per unit charge is simply a declining block tariff with a single block.

In order to sustain such a pricing scheme it must be impossible or costly for buyers to get together and buy a larger quantity at a discount and split it among themselves. Often, when dealing with packaged goods like cereal not all quantities are available and the supplier offers just a few box sizes. If you look, however, at the price per ounce you will note a quantity discount as the box size increases.

---

[3] Volume discounts are specified sometimes in terms of a uniform price $P(q)$ applied to all the units purchased, which is declining with purchase quantity. Such a uniform price can be interpreted as the average price corresponding to the marginal price function $p(q)$ and calculated as $P(q) = \frac{1}{q} \int_0^q p(\alpha)d\alpha$.

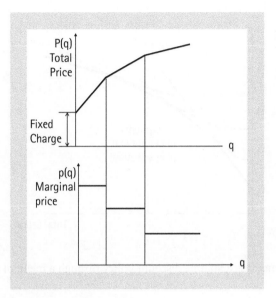

FIGURE 22.3 A block declining tariff structure

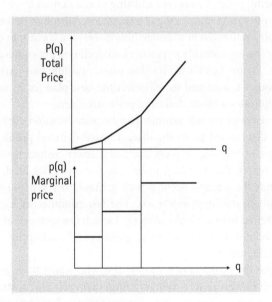

FIGURE 22.4 A block increasing tariff structure

For some commodities, such as electricity or water, where the objective of price discrimination is to promote conservation and "tax the rich", the marginal price function is actually increasing with quantity as shown in Figure 22.4.

The lower consumption blocks that are billed at a lower per unit price are sometimes called "life line" rates. In such cases it will be to the advantage of a household to get two

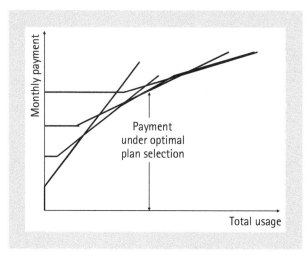

FIGURE 22.5 Implementing a volume discount policy through a menu of optional two-part tariffs

water or electricity meters and pretend to be two households, hence it is essential in order to sustain such a pricing policy to prevent splitting of the demand.

In many cases quantity discount pricing is implemented through optional two-part tariff contracts. For example, in the case of a mobile phone service a consumer can choose among several plans with increasing monthly payments and declining per minute cost (for minutes above the free ones). Figure 22.5 illustrates that when multiple two-part tariff options are offered and the customer is assumed to self-select the best plan for its usage rate then the entire price menu replicates a block declining price structure.

For analytical convenience we will assume that the price function $p(q)$ is continuous and show how it can be determined given the disaggregated demand profile $N(q, p)$. We also assume that for any quantity q, $N(q, p)$ is declining in p (fewer customers will buy the qth unit as the unit price increases, that is $\partial N(q, p)/\partial p < 0$. For any price level, p, the number of customers who will buy the qth unit declines with q, that is, $\partial N(q, p)/\partial q < 0$ and the rate of decline decreases with p, $\partial^2 N(q, p)/\partial q \partial p > 0$. The last condition is a common technical assumption (often referred to as a "single-crossing") which guarantees that demand functions for different units q will not cross. Under the single-crossing[4] assumption, the profile $N(q, p)$ will look as shown in Figure 22.6.

Let us now consider the problem of a monopolist who wants to determine a unit price function $p(q)$ that will maximize its profit assuming that each unit costs c to produce. For simplicity, let us assume that q can only take integer values. The profit of the monopolist is given by:

$$\pi = \sum_{q=1}^{Q} N(q, p(q))(p(q) - c)$$

[4] The term "single-crossing" refers to the fact that any monotone function of p will cross the demand function corresponding to any unit q at most once.

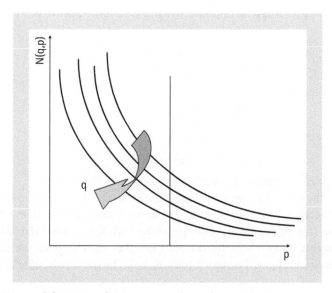

FIGURE 22.6 Demand functions for incremental purchase units

We note, however, that this profit function is separable with respect to q so in order to maximize this function with respect to $p(q)$ we need to maximize each of the terms. Thus the necessary conditions for maximum profit are:

$$\frac{\partial}{p(q)} \{N(q, p(q))(p(q) - c)\} = 0 \text{ for } q = 1, 2, 3, \ldots$$

This gives the optimality condition:

$$(p(q) - c) \cdot \frac{\partial N(q, p(q))}{\partial p(q)} + N(q, p(q)) = 0$$

We can define the elasticity of demand for the qth unit as:

$$\varepsilon(q) = -\frac{\partial N(q, p(q))/\partial p(q)}{N(q, p(q))/p(q)} = -\frac{\partial N(q, p(q))/N(q, p(q))}{\partial p(q)/p(q)}$$

Then the optimality condition becomes:

$$\frac{p(q) - c}{p(q)} = \frac{1}{\varepsilon(q)}$$

The, so-called, "inverse elasticity rule" implied by this optimality condition is that the optimal "percentage markup" for each incremental unit should be inversely proportional to the demand elasticity for that unit. The intuitive justification for this rule is that high demand elasticity entails stronger response (i.e., larger demand decrease) to the same percentage increase in price. Thus, a monopoly, that must tradeoff between reduced sales versus increased profit per sale in choosing the optimal markup, will opt for a lower percentage markup when demand is more elastic.

Let us consider now a special case where $N(q, p) = a \cdot p^{-\eta q}$, $a > 0$, $\eta > 1$
For this case

$$\varepsilon(q) = -\frac{-a \cdot \eta \cdot q \cdot p^{-\eta q - 1}}{a \cdot p^{-\eta q}/p} = \eta \cdot q$$

$$\frac{c}{p(q)} = 1 - \frac{1}{\eta q}$$

$$p(q) = \frac{c\eta q}{\eta q - 1}$$

as $q \to \infty$ $p(q) \to c$

The resulting price function will have the form shown in Figure 22.7.

To illustrate the win–win aspect of volume discounts, consider now a special case of the above where customers can only buy either one or two units of a product, the disaggregated demand profile $N(q, p)$ is as in the example above with the demand elasticity parameter $\eta = 2$ and marginal cost $c = 1$. In this case the monopoly will charge for the first unit $p_1 = 2$ and sell the second unit at a discounted price $p_2 = \frac{4}{3}$. The monopoly seller's total profit in this case is:

$$profit = N(1, p_1) \cdot (p_1 - c) + N(2, p_2) \cdot (p_2 - c) = a \cdot (2c)^{-2}(c) + a \cdot \left(\tfrac{4}{3}c\right)^{-4}\left(\tfrac{1}{3}c\right)$$

$$= \tfrac{a}{4}\left(1 + \tfrac{27}{64}\right) = 0.36a$$

and the corresponding total number of units sold is:

$$units = N(1, p_1) + N(2, p_2) = a \cdot (2c)^{-2} + a \cdot \left(\tfrac{4}{3}c\right)^{-4} = 0.56a$$

For comparison, suppose that the monopoly seller could not use volume discounts because it was unable to restrict resale (i.e., buyers that only want one unit can form coalitions and buy two units at discounted prices and then split them). In that case, the monopoly seller would set a uniform price for all units treating the demand as a single demand function given by:

$$x(p) = N(1, p) + N(2, p) = a \cdot (p^{-2} + p^{-4})$$

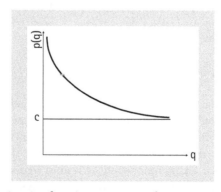

FIGURE 22.7 Optimal unit price function versus purchase quantity

The optimal monopoly price is still given by the inverse elasticity rule:

$$\frac{p - c}{p} = \frac{1}{\varepsilon}$$

Except that here the elasticity is based on the aggregate demand function $x(p)$ so

$$\varepsilon = -x'(p) \cdot p/x = \frac{2p^2 + 4}{p^2 + 1}$$

To determine the price, we solve the equation:

$$\frac{p - 1}{p} = \frac{p^2 + 1}{2p^2 + 4}$$

which reduces to the polynomial equation $p^3 - 2p^2 + 3p - 4 = 0$ having a root at $p = 1.65$. Thus, instead of pricing the first purchase unit at $p = 2$ and the second unit at 1.33, the monopoly seller will price all units at $p = 1.65$. The total demand corresponding to that price is $x(1.65) = 0.5a$ and the total profit is given by $0.5a(1.65 - 1) = 0.325a$. So the ability to discriminate based on purchase quantity increases the monopolist profit by about 11 percent and increases social welfare since more customers who value the product above its marginal cost of production will be able to enjoy it although some will pay more for it (those who only buy one unit). It should be noted, however, that price discrimination does not always result in increased social welfare. As shown by Varian (1985), under fairly general conditions, a necessary condition for a social welfare increase due to price discrimination is an increase in output (or consumption). Thus, to the extent that a nonlinear pricing scheme could result in reduced consumption such a strategy would also reduce social welfare.

22.4 RAMSEY PRICING

As mentioned in the introduction, Ramsey pricing is a form of semi-direct price discrimination. Its purpose is to enforce a total profit constraint while incurring the least social cost. It is presented here because, in spite of the different motivation and apparent philosophical differences, the methodology used to derive Ramsey pricing and the end results bear remarkable similarity to those presented in the previous section in deriving optimal volume discount schedules.

Here instead of differentiating among the demands for the first, second, and third ... unit of consumption the regulated monopoly seller (with the blessing of the regulator) differentiates among the demand of different customer classes; say, commercial and residential. This type of price discrimination was common in the old days when AT&T had a monopoly over long-distance phone service. Suppose that the demand functions for phone call units in each customer class are given by $x_c(p)$ and $x_r(p)$, respectively.

Again if the monopoly wants to maximize total profit and is able to charge different prices to the two customer classes then the problem is separable and the optimal price charged to each class is determined by the inverse elasticity rule:

$$\frac{p_c - c}{p_c} = \frac{1}{\varepsilon_c} \text{ and } \frac{p_r - c}{p_r} = \frac{1}{\varepsilon_r},$$

where ε_c and ε_r denote the elasticity of the corresponding demand functions, $x_c(p)$ and $x_r(p)$.

The example given in the previous subsection for price discrimination between the first and second unit of purchase can be relabeled to reflect discrimination between commercial and residential demand for long distance phone calls since the commercial demand function is in general less elastic than residential demand just as the demand for the first unit of purchase was assumed to be less elastic than that for the second unit. Thus, by discriminating between the two classes of service the monopolist's profits go up, total usage increases and therefore social welfare increases (because we assume constant unit cost). Furthermore the residential customers will end up paying less for their calls while commercial customers pay more.

When the seller is a regulated monopoly (as AT&T was), the regulator may put a limit on the profits that the monopoly can earn based on the cost of investment made by the regulated monopoly in building the infrastructure. This is called rate of return regulation where the monopoly profits are limited to an annual percentage return on investment cost. In such a case, the regulated-monopoly-pricing problem is formulated as one of maximizing social welfare subject to a profit constraint.

As explained in the introduction, the social welfare resulting from consuming an incremental unit of a product or service (i.e., the surplus to society) is given by the difference between the consumers' willingness-to-pay for that unit (given by the inverse demand function $P(x)$ in Figure 22.8) and the unit's production cost c. This difference, which varies with the total consumption level x, is represented by the vertical slices shown in Figure 22.8. The purchase quantity of the product or service offered at a uniform price p^* is given by

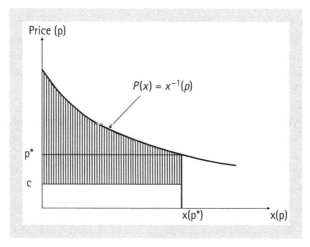

FIGURE 22.8 Illustration of social value resulting from consumption at unit price p^*

$x(p^*)$ at which point consumers' willingness-to-pay $P(x(p^*)) = p^*$. Hence the aggregate social welfare is given by the area between the marginal cost c and the willingness-to-pay function $P(x)$ to the left of $x(p^*)$, as shown in Figure 22.8.

In our setting we assume that commercial and residential customers have willingness-to-pay functions $P_c(x)$ and $P_r(x)$ respectively, and the monopoly supplier is regulated so that its net profit is set to a predetermined value π (e.g., based on some allowed rate of return on capital investment). Then the optimization problem for setting the socially optimal prices p_c and p_r for the two customer classes, subject to the regulated profit constraint is:

$$\max_{p_c,\ p_r} \left\{ \int_0^{x_c(p_c)} (P_c(x) - c)dx + \int_0^{x_r(p_r)} (P_r(x) - c)dx \right.$$

Subject to: $x_c(p_c) \cdot (p_c - c) + x_r(p_r) \cdot (p_r - c) = \pi$

To solve this problem we write the Lagrangian:

$$L(p_c, p_r, \lambda) = \int_0^{x_c(p_c)} (P_c(x) - c)dx + \int_0^{x_r(p_r)} (P_r(x) - c)dx + \lambda\{x_c(p_c) \cdot (p_c - c)$$

$$+ x_r(p_r) \cdot (p_r - c) - \pi\}$$

This Lagrangian is separable so the optimality conditions are given by

$$\frac{\partial}{\partial p_i}\left\{ \int_0^{x_i(p_i)} (P_i(x) - c)dx + \lambda \cdot x_i(p_i) \cdot (p_i - c)\right\} = 0 \quad i = \{c, r\},$$

and the profit constraint. This reduces to:

$$(p_i - c) \cdot x_i'(p_i) + \lambda \cdot (p_i - c) \cdot x_i'(p_i) + \lambda \cdot x_i(p_i)\} = 0 \quad \text{for} \quad i = \{c, r\},$$

which can be rewritten as

$$\frac{p_i - c}{p_i} = \frac{\lambda/(\lambda + 1)}{\varepsilon_i} \quad i = \{c, r\}$$

The above result tells us that the optimal regulated monopoly prices should be set so that the percentage markup in each customer group is proportional to the inverse elasticity. In other words, the more elastic the demand is, the lower the markup should be (price that the market will bear). The Lagrange multiplier factor $\lambda/(\lambda + 1)$, which scales the percentage markup, is determined so the profit constraint is satisfied.

In other words the ratio of percentage markup rule among classes of customers in the regulated monopoly problem is the same as in the profit maximizing monopoly problem (and the same as in an oligopoly) but the prices are different because of the profit constraint. This pricing rule is called the *Ramsey pricing* rule. The intuition behind this rule is that social welfare is affected by consumption. Transfer of money between members of society does not affect the social welfare of society as a whole. Therefore, if we need to generate a certain level of profit so as to recover the supplier's investment costs and fair return on capital, we charge more to those customers whose demand will be affected the least by a higher price.

22.5 QUALITY DIFFERENTIATION

In this section, we will discuss nonlinear pricing that is based on differentiating products or services so as to exploit customers' heterogeneous preferences for specific product attributes. Such differentiation can be based on exogenous product characteristics such as speed, convenience, and packaging, or can be induced through pricing that results in self-segmentation or rationing schemes that create supply uncertainty for the service or product.

22.5.1 Pricing exogenous quality attributes

Quality differentiation in the context of nonlinear pricing is done through unbundling quality attributes of products or services for which customers have heterogeneous preferences, for the purpose of market segmentation and indirect price discrimination. Typical unbundled attributes include product features, packaging, distribution channels, or delivery conditions such as time of use, class of service in airlines, speed of delivery in mail service, bulk versus retail.

The basic idea is to capitalize on the dispersion in customer preferences (i.e., willingness-to-pay for the different attribute levels) and create an offering that gives customers a tradeoff between attribute level and price. In general not all customers rank attribute options in the same way. For example, choice between points of delivery will be ranked differently by customers based on where they live. Similarly time of use of a service may be ranked differently by different customers. Location and time of use fall under the general category of locational attributes. On the other hand, attributes such as speed of mail delivery, priority of service in a queue, or comfort levels in a plane are ranked the same by all customers even if they differ in how much they are willing to pay for different levels of these attributes. Attributes for which customers have the same preference rankings are called "quality attributes". A general property of quality attributes is that they are "downward substitutable", that is, you can always use a higher quality level to serve demand for a lower quality level. For instance, a 2 GHz processor can always replace a 1 GHz processor in a computer and a first class seat in a plane can be used to accommodate a customer that paid for a coach seat.

We characterize the quality dimension by a parameter, s, so that a larger value of s represents higher quality. For example, s may represent speed of delivery for mail service (defined as the inverse of time en route), or the speed of memory chips. In general, quality can be multi-dimensional, reflecting different aspects of a product or service affecting customers' preferences. In this chapter, we restrict ourselves to a single quality dimension to simplify the exposition. The demand function is characterized by a function, $N(s, p)$ that

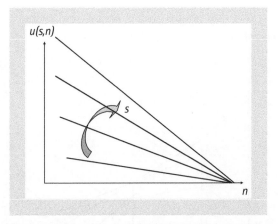

FIGURE 22.9 Illustration of inverse demand function (utility) for different quality levels

defines the demand function for quality s as function of price, if that was the only product quality offered. Alternatively, we can arrange the units of demand in decreasing order of willingness-to-pay and define the inverse demand function, $u(s, n)$, so that $N(s, u(s, n)) = n$.

Figure 22.9 illustrates the inverse demand functions for different quality levels. We assume that the inverse demand functions satisfy the following properties:

$$\frac{\partial u(s, n)}{\partial n} < 0, \quad \frac{\partial u(s, n)}{\partial s} > 0, \quad \frac{\partial u(s, n)}{\partial s \partial n} < 0.$$

These inequalities imply that willingness-to-pay for any quality level decreases with n (we sort the customers so that this is true). Willingness-to-pay by any customer n increases with quality and the sensitivity of customers to quality decreases with n. The last condition is again a "non-crossing" condition ensuring that the demand functions for different quality levels do not cross. The commonly used multiplicative utility function form $u(s, n) = g(s) \cdot w(n)$, where $g(s)$ is increasing and $w(n)$ is decreasing, is a special case that satisfies these properties. Figure 22.9 illustrates the case where $w(n)$ is linear.

Suppose that a discrete set of quality levels, $s_1 > s_2 > , \ldots > s_k$, is being offered at prices, $p_1 > p_2 > , \ldots > p_k$. Thinking of each unit n of demand as a separate customer, we can write the so-called self-selection and individual rationality conditions for customer n as:

$$i(n) = \arg \max_i \{u(s_i, n) - p_i\}$$

and

$$u(s_{i(n)}, n) - p_{i(n)} > 0$$

These conditions state that each customer n selects the quality level $i(n)$ that maximizes his surplus (defined as utility minus price) provided that the surplus is positive otherwise no product is chosen yielding zero surplus. These conditions are illustrated graphically in Figure 22.10.

The customers will divide themselves among the different product qualities by selecting the quality that maximizes their surplus. Thus the demand for each quality level s_i is given

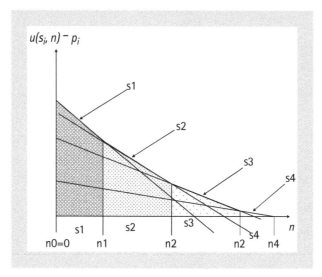

FIGURE 22.10 Customers' maximum surplus for different quality levels

by the difference, $(n_i - n_{i-1})$, where the boundary points, n_i, are defined by the indifference relations $u(s_i, n_i) - p_i = u(s_{i+1}, n_i) - p_{i+1}$, $i = 1, 2, \ldots k$, and the individual rationality condition $u(s_i, n_i) - p_i \geq 0$. We may assume that s_{k+1} is a default free quality level for which the utility of all customers is zero. The above model characterizes the demand function and cross substitution among the different quality levels. A monopoly offering a product line consisting of quality levels $s_1 > s_2 >, \ldots . > s_k$ with corresponding unit costs $c_1 > c_2 >, \ldots . > c_k$ can determine the profit-maximizing prices for each quality level by solving the optimization problem:

$$\max_{p_1, p_2, \ldots, p_k} \sum_{i=1}^{k} (n_i - n_{i-1})(p_i - c_i)$$

s.t.

$$u(s_i, n_i) - p_i = u(s_{i+1}, n_i) - p_{i+1}, i = 1, 2, \ldots, k$$

$$u(s_i, n_i) - p_i \geq 0, i = 1, 2, \ldots, k$$

The above framework can also be used to solve the problem of a supplier that wants to introduce a new product offering a new quality level in a market that is already divided between existing quality levels serving the demand. For example, it would apply to a provider of two-day delivery service in a market already served by cheap US Postal Service and FedEx, which offers next day delivery at a much higher price. In that case, the supplier of the new service can solve the above optimization problem to determine its optimal price, while taking the prices of the existing quality levels as given. Interestingly, he only needs to consider the qualities adjacent to his since all the other terms in the objective function and constraints are not affected by his decision and will drop out of the optimization.

Pricing of a product line consisting of quality-differentiated products has been extensively addressed in the revenue management (RM) literature. However, the traditional RM approach usually characterizes the demands for different product variants or quality levels as exogenous independent stochastic processes. Modeling cross-substitution among different products based on the underlying customer choice behavior is a relatively recent trend in the RM literature, pioneered by Talluri and van Ryzin (2004). While these efforts have yet to make the connection and capitalize on the rich literature on multiproduct pricing, in marketing science and economics, this is a promising development. Characterizing the customer preference structure underlying the demand for variants of differentiated products is essential for understanding the impact of relative prices and how a new entry might impact an existing product line.

22.5.2 Price induced endogenous qualities

Differential quality of service can sometimes be created by inducing customers to sort themselves through differential pricing in situations where quality is affected by the demand, for example through congestion. To illustrate such phenomena, consider a situation where 100 customers need to be served, each taking 1 minute. All arrive at once and are served at random by two servers that charge $2 per customer. Assume this is the prorated cost of providing the service which in total costs $200. The average waiting time of each customer is 25 minutes. Let us assume now that the customer population consists of 75 students whose time is worth $6/hour and 25 professors whose time is worth $60/hour. Table 22.2 summarizes the costs and benefits incurred by each of the customer types, the supplier, and society as a whole under the random service policy.

Suppose now that we offer service at one server for free while the other server charges $10 per customer. We do not restrict access to any of the servers but provide a forecast of an equilibrium average waiting time of 12.5 minutes for the $10 server and 37.5 minutes for the free server. Customers will self-select which server they want to use based on the calculation in Table 22.3. Accordingly, students will self-select the free line while professors will select the $10 server, so the waiting time forecast will be realized and everyone is better off than before.

Price induced quality differentiation is common in pricing products and services where customers incur personal cost in addition to the tariff (e.g., waiting time cost). It has been proposed, for instance, as a mechanism for increasing the utilization of underutilized carpool lanes on the freeways by allowing drivers to buy permits for these lanes at high prices (in addition to permits for carpools and gasoline efficient cars). To some extent such

Table 22.2 Costs under uniform price

	Students	Profs	Supplier	Society
Cost	$6 \times 25/60 = \$2.5$	$60 \times 25/60 = \$25$	$200	
Charge	$2	$2	($200)	
Total	$4.50	$27	0	$4.5 \times 75 + 27 \times 25 = \$1012.5$

Table 22.3 Cost distribution and service qualities under differential pricing

| | Students | | Professors | | Supplier | Society |
	Serv A	Serv B	Serv A	Serv B		
Cost	$6 \times 12.5/60$ $= \$1.25$	$6 \times 37.5/60$ $= \$3.75$	$60 \times 12.5/60$ $= \$12.5$	$60 \times 37.5/60$ $= \$37.5$	$200	
Charge	$10	0	$10	0	($250)	
Total	$11.25	$3.75	$22.50	$37.50	($50)	$3.75 \times 75 + 22.5 \times 25$ $-50 = \$793.75$

a policy is implicitly implemented through enforcement policies that determine the probability of a citation for illegal use of carpool lanes, setting the price to the expected value of the fine. Student nights at movie theaters at reduced ticket prices is another example of price induced quality.

22.5.3 Rationing-based quality differentiation

When the supply of a product is limited by scarcity or limited capacity, it is possible to use supply uncertainty as a mechanism for quality differentiation. Such an approach is particularly useful when the demand function is such that using a single price will result in monopoly prices that underutilize available supply. This may occur when the profit function as a function of supply quantity is non-monotone so that the monopoly supplier may be induced to withhold available capacity.

Consider a promoter of a rock concert in a sports arena that can accommodate 10,000 people. The cost of putting up the event is $300,000. Market research data suggest that the market for such an event consists of two segments. There are about 5,000 customers in the area who will pay up to $100 per ticket and another 55,000 potential customers who are willing to pay up to $20 per ticket. It is impractical to have assigned seats so a simple option is to have a uniform price for all tickets. If the price is set at $100 per ticket 5,000 tickets will be sold at a net profit, after covering expenses, of $200,000. The corresponding social welfare as measured by willingness-to-pay minus cost is also $200,000. Alternatively, if ticket prices are set so as to fill up the venue they can be sold at $20 on a first come first serve basis over the Internet. This pricing scheme will make some people happy but will result in a $100,000 loss for the promoter. Furthermore, at $20 per ticket the chance of any customer getting a ticket is on average 1/6 so the expected social welfare of such a strategy is $(5000 \times 100 + 55,000 \times 20)/6 - 300,000 = -\$33,000$. Clearly the first option of pricing the tickets at $100 is superior both from a profit-to-promoter and a social welfare perspective. However, the thought of having half the venue empty while there are 55,000 potential customers out there willing to pay $20 per tickets is bothersome.

Figure 22.11 illustrates the demand function and revenue function, which create the dilemma faced by the promoter. The important aspect of that revenue function is its non-concavity in the region where the available capacity falls.

The solution to the promoter's dilemma is to introduce two types of tickets: reserved tickets at $90 and lottery tickets at $20. All the reserved tickets can then be sold in advance

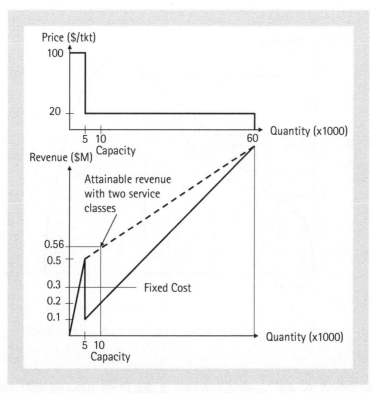

FIGURE 22.11 Demand and revenue functions for tickets

to the customers who are willing to pay $100 while the rest of the tickets are released on the Internet the day before the show at $20 with an average probability of 1/11 of getting one. For this to work, however, one must assure nontransferability of the demand of the potentially high paying customers, that is induce such customers not to opt for the cheap tickets. This is guaranteed by the above prices since $100 - 90 > (100 - 20)/11$ so that a customer whose willingness-to-pay is $100 will maximize his/her expected utility by purchasing the reserved ticket, while customers who are willing to pay $20 will compete for the standby tickets (perhaps we should give them a break and sell the tickets for $19.) With this strategy the promoter can increase its profits and the social welfare by $100,000 and make some additional customers happy.

Ferguson (1994) provides an elegant proof showing that the above approach will increase the monopolist profit whenever the profit function is non-concave and the capacity limit falls in a rising non-concave portion of the profit. Figure 22.12 illustrates the profit as a function of quantity sold at a single price taking into consideration that the price that will sell quantity q is given by the inverse demand function $P(q)$. The dashed line shows the attainable profit when we introduce a second offering with uncertain delivery.

To achieve the higher profit we will offer q_1 units with guaranteed supply at a price p_1 and offer the remaining $Q - q_1$ units on a lottery basis at a price $p_2 = P(q_2)$. The quantities q_1 and q_2 are exactly the tangency points on the curve. This can be proven by starting with

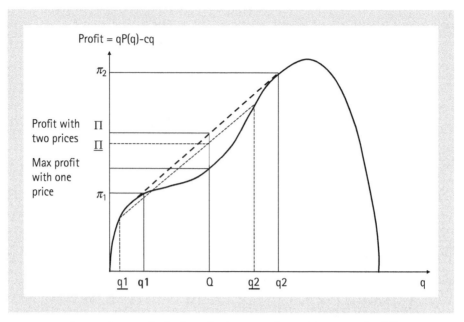

FIGURE 22.12 Improving profits by introducing a product with uncertain delivery

arbitrary quantities, $\underline{q}_1$ and $\underline{q}_2$, and maximizing the profit function with respect to these quantities. The tangency condition follows from the optimality conditions. Given the above structure, the probability that a standby customer gets the product is given by $r = (Q - q_1)/(q_2 - q_1)$ so now we can calculate p_1 so that the first q_1 customers will prefer the guaranteed supply option, that is, $P(q_1) - p_1 \geq r \cdot (P(q_1) - p_2)$. The monopolist will want to set p_1 as high as possible. Thus, $p_1 = (1 - r) \cdot P(q_1) + r \cdot P(q_2)$ and the corresponding total profit, assuming a unit cost c, is therefore:

$$\Pi = p_1 \cdot q_1 + p_2 \cdot (Q - q_1) - c \cdot Q = p_1 \cdot q_1 + r \cdot p_2 \cdot (q_2 - q_1) - c \cdot Q$$

$$[(1 - r) \cdot P(q_1) + r \cdot P(q_2)] \cdot q_1 + r \cdot P(q_2) \cdot (q_2 - q_1) - c \cdot Q$$

Therefore, $\Pi = (1 - r) \cdot \pi_1 + r \cdot \pi_2$

where r is such that $Q = (1 - r) \cdot q_1 + r \cdot q_2$

The above derivation is valid for arbitrary values of q_1 and q_2, not just the tangency points (see dashed lines in Figure 22.12) but it is easy to see from the figure (or prove algebraically) that choosing the tangency points maximizes the supplier's profits. We may further conclude that such a strategy is beneficial only if the available capacity falls in a region where the profit function is increasing and there is a gap between the profit function and its concave hull. Under such circumstances, a single product with uncertain delivery will suffice to attain the potential profit, given by the concave hull of the original profit function at full capacity utilization.

22.6 PRIORITY SERVICE PRICING AND EFFICIENT RATIONING

In the previous section we introduced the idea of quality differentiation through uncertain supply when capacity is scarce and fixed. This basic concept is expanded by *priority pricing*. This pricing mechanism is a quality differentiation and enables an efficient rationing in situations where supply is both scarce and uncertain. It enables customers to pay different prices based on the order in which they are served or probability of getting the product. In the case of electricity supply, for instance, customers can sign up for an option of being curtailed when supply is scarce in exchange for a discount on their electricity bills. Another example of priority pricing is the practice of the discount clothing store Filene's Basement, which posts on each item a series of increasing percentage discounts on the item and the date on which each discount level will go into effect. Customers must trade off the option of a larger discount against the probability that someone else will purchase the item they want.

The basic principle is that an efficient priority-pricing scheme will result in customers being served in order of willingness-to-pay. Therefore, under efficient rationing the qth unit of demand is served if and only if the available supply is q or larger. Therefore, the probability that the qth unit is served $r(q) = 1 - F(q)$ where $F(q)$ denotes the cumulative probability that the available supply level is q. We assume now that each unit of demand corresponds to a customer demanding one unit and the inverse demand function representing the willingness-to-pay of customer q for the product is given by $v(q)$. Since the demand is monotone in q we can, without loss of generality, characterize customers in terms of their valuation v and define directly the probability of service for a customer with valuation v as $r(v) = 1 - F(q(v))$ where $q(v)$ is the demand at price v. Since the supplier does not know how much a particular customer is willing to pay for the product all he can do is set prices based on probability of delivery or equivalently the place in line for delivery. Thus, the price structure will be of the form $P + p(r)$ where P is a uniform fixed charge applied to all customers and $p(r)$ depends on the probability of service selected by the customer. The challenge here is to design the price function to induce each customer v to select her designated efficient service priority $r(v)$. The self-selection condition and individual rationality condition for customer q are:

$$\max_r \{r \cdot v - P - p(r)\}$$

$$r \cdot v - P - p(r) \geq 0$$

Customers whose optimal r does not satisfy the second condition will not buy the service. We assume in the above formulation that a customer pays even if she does not get the service but the formulation can be easily changed so that payment is made only if service is obtained.

The first order necessary condition for the customer's self-selection is: $dp(r)/dr = v$ and we want to induce the customer to select $r = r(v)$. We will determine the price function $p(r)$ indirectly by first defining $\hat{p}(v) = p(r(v))$. Thus,

$$\frac{d\hat{p}(v)}{dv} = \frac{dp(r)}{dr} \cdot \frac{dr(v)}{dv} = v \cdot \frac{dr(v)}{dv}$$

so,

$$\hat{p}(v) = \int_o^v \omega \cdot dr(\omega) = v \cdot r(v) - \int_o^v r(\omega)d\omega$$

The price function can now be obtained as $p(r) = \hat{p}(v(r))$ where $v(r)$ is the inverse of the function $r(v)$. Note that the expected social surplus from offering priority $r(v)$ to the customer with valuation v is given by $v \cdot r(v)$. Out of this total surplus the supplier collects $P + \hat{p}(v)$. From the individual rationality condition a customer will buy only if,

$$v \cdot r(v) - P - \hat{p}(v) = \int_o^v r(\omega)d\omega - P \geq o$$

Thus, the fixed charge can be mapped onto a cutoff value v_0 so that

$$P = \int_o^{v_0} r(\omega)d\omega$$

Customers with valuation below v_0 are excluded and $r(v_0)$ is the lowest probability of service being offered. The consumer surplus to a customer with valuation v under this scheme is

$$CS(v) = \int_{v_0}^v r(\omega)d\omega$$

Figure 22.13 illustrates the distribution of surplus between the supplier and the customer.

So far, we have characterized the pricing scheme that will induce efficient rationing through self-selection. The only degree of freedom in that price structure is the fixed charge, P, which determines the cutoff level for customers that will be served. This level can be set based on the objective of the supplier, whether it is to maximize social welfare, recover the supply cost, or maximize profit in the case of a monopoly.

To illustrate the implications of the above results we now specialize them to the case where the probability of supply is described by a uniform distribution on $[o, Q]$,

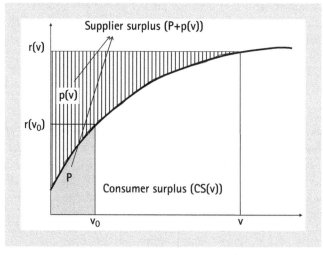

FIGURE 22.13 Allocation of the social surplus $v \cdot r(v)$ due to serving a unit with valuation v

that is, $F(q) = q/Q$ and the inverse demand function is given by $v(q) = 1 - q/Q$. This implies that the probability of having enough supply to serve a customer with valuation v under an efficient rationing scheme is $r(v) = v$. Plugging this into the above results gives:

$$\hat{p}(v) = v \cdot r(v) - \int_0^v r(\omega)d\omega = v^2 - \frac{v^2}{2} = \frac{v^2}{2}$$

Hence $p(r) = r^2/2$, $P = v_0^2/2$ and the fraction of served demand is $q_0/Q = 1 - \sqrt{2P}$. The total supplier revenue is given by

$$\Pi = P \cdot q_0 + \int_0^{q_0} p(r(v(q)))dq = P \cdot q_0 + \int_0^{q_0} \frac{(1 - q/Q)^2}{2} dq = P \cdot q_0 - \frac{Q}{6}[1 - \frac{q}{Q}]^3|_0^{q_0}$$

$$= P \cdot Q\left(1 - \sqrt{2P}\right) - \frac{Q}{6}\left[\left(\sqrt{2P}\right)^3 - 1\right] = Q \cdot \left[P - \frac{4}{3}P\sqrt{2P} + \frac{1}{6}\right]$$

Maximizing the profit with respect to P yields $P = 1/8$ and consequently $q_0/Q = 1/2$, that is, the optimal strategy of a monopolist is to price out half of the demand by imposing a fixed charge $P = 1/8$ and a priority charge $p(r) = r^2/2$ for values of r between 0.5 and 1. The monopolist profit will then be $\Pi = \frac{5Q}{24}$

The total social welfare is given by

$$SW = \int_0^{q_0} v(q) \cdot r(v(q))dq = \int_0^{q_0} (1 - q/Q)^2 dq = -\frac{Q}{3}[1 - \frac{q}{Q}]^3|_0^{q_0} = \frac{Q}{3}\left[1 - \left(\sqrt{2P}\right)^3\right].$$

Thus the social welfare under a monopoly regime is $SW_m = \frac{7Q}{24}$ and consequently the total consumer surplus is $CS_m = \frac{Q}{12}$.

A social welfare maximizing entity, however, will impose no fixed charge so that no customer is excluded (this is often called Universal Service), achieving a social welfare of $SW = \frac{Q}{3}$ but customers will still be charged a priority price $p(r) = r^2/2$, which yields a profit of $\frac{Q}{6}$ (substitute $P = 0$ in the profit formula above). An interesting question is whether a universal service scheme with priority pricing is better for consumers than free universal service with random rationing. To address this question we compare the individual consumer surplus for both cases. With free random rationing, every customer has a probability $R = 1/2$ of being served and there is no charge. In that case, a customer with valuation v gets an expected benefit of $v/2$. With priority service, a customer with valuation v gets an expected consumer surplus of $v \cdot r(v) - p(r) = v^2/2$ (since under efficient rationing $v = r$). Thus the net gain in consumer surplus from priority pricing for a consumer with valuation v is $v(v - 1)/2$ which is negative for all v in the interval $[0, 1]$ so all customers are worse off.

If the social welfare maximizer is a cooperative that returns all profits to the consumers as a uniform dividend, then allocating the profit of $\frac{Q}{6}$ to the Q units of consumption results in a dividend of $\frac{Q}{6}$ per unit and a net consumer surplus gain (over the free universal service approach) of $v^2/2 - v/2 + 1/6$. This net gain attains its minimum at $v = 1/2$. In other words, the least advantaged customer is the one with valuation $1/2$ who will receive the same service reliability of $1/2$ with both approaches. For that customer, the net gain in consumer surplus is $\frac{1}{8} - \frac{1}{4} + \frac{1}{6} = \frac{1}{24}$. Therefore, all customers are better off with the revenue neutral priority service approach. The above result was shown by Chao and Wilson (1987) to be true in general not just for uniform distributions.

The social welfare for free universal service with a single priority of service (i.e., uniform service) is given by:

$$SW_1 = \int_0^Q R \cdot v(q)dq = Q_2^{\frac{1}{2}} \cdot \frac{v^2}{2}\Big|_0^1 = \frac{Q}{4}$$

Hence, the social welfare loss due to inefficient rationing of a uniform service is $\frac{Q}{3} - \frac{Q}{4} = \frac{Q}{12}$ which represents a 25 percent efficiency loss.

So far, we have considered a continuum of priorities but in practice we may be able to segment customers into a limited number of discrete priorities. One question is how much of the welfare gains from priority service we lose if we only have a discrete number of priority classes. We start by segmenting the customers into two halves $v \in [0, \frac{1}{2}]$ and $v \in [\frac{1}{2}, 1]$, and offer to the first (lower valuation group) probability of service $R_1 = \frac{1}{4}$ and to the second (higher valuation group) probability of service $R_2 = \frac{3}{4}$. This is feasible since the average probability of service across all customers is $\frac{1}{2}$ which is how much the system can provide. To enforce such market separation through self-selection we will charge the low priority group a uniform price p_1 and the high priority group a higher price p_2. Incentive compatibility and individual rationality conditions require that:

$$\text{for } v \in [0, \frac{1}{2}], v \cdot R_1 - p_1 \geq 0 \text{ and } v \cdot R_1 - p_1 \geq v \cdot R_2 - p_2$$

$$\text{for } v \in [\frac{1}{2}, 1], \ v \cdot R_2 - p_2 \geq 0 \text{ and } v \cdot R_2 - p_2 \geq v \cdot R_1 - p_1$$

Since the lowest value customer in the low priority group has valuation zero we must have $p_1 = 0$. Then we can determine p_2 by applying the incentive compatibility condition to the boundary customer with valuation $v=1/2$ who will be indifferent between getting the higher reliability at the higher price or the lower reliability at the lower price. Thus, $\frac{1}{2} \cdot \frac{1}{4} - p_1 = \frac{1}{2} \cdot \frac{3}{4} - p_2$, which results in $p_2 - p_1 = \frac{1}{2}(\frac{3}{4} - \frac{1}{4}) = \frac{1}{4}$ so $p_2 = \frac{1}{4}$. One can easily verify that these prices satisfy the incentive compatibility and individual rationality constraints above.

Now let us calculate the social welfare of the two priority schemes and compare it to the free universal service approach and the continuous priority pricing. Denote the social welfare corresponding to the continuous priorities as $SW_\infty = \frac{Q}{3}$ (infinite number of priorities), and as shown above, for the single priority $SW_1 = \frac{Q}{4}$.

For the two priority cases, the social welfare is given by:

$$SW_2 = \int_0^{Q/2} R_2 v(q)dq + \int_{Q/2}^Q R_1 v(q)dq = Q\left[\frac{1}{4} \cdot \frac{v^2}{2}\Big|_0^{1/2} + \frac{3}{4} \cdot \frac{v^2}{2}\Big|_{1/2}^1\right] = \frac{10Q}{32}$$

Thus the relative welfare loss of the two priority cases as compared to the single priority case is:

$$\frac{SW_\infty - SW_2}{SW_\infty - SW_1} = \frac{\frac{Q}{3} - \frac{10Q}{32}}{\frac{Q}{3} - \frac{Q}{4}} = \frac{1}{4} = \frac{1}{2^2}$$

In other words, going from one to two priorities reduced the welfare loss by a factor of 4. Using the approach described above it is possible to extend the result to n priorities and show that for the special case studied above the relative welfare loss for n priorities is $1/n^2$. In simple terms, the above implies that with two priorities we can capture 75 percent of the welfare gains achievable with an infinite number of priorities and with three priorities 91

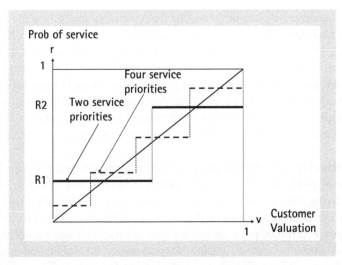

FIGURE 22.14 Priority service pricing with discrete priority levels

percent of the achievable gain. Figure 22.14 illustrates the market segmentation with discrete priority service. Note that in deriving the welfare loss above we assumed equal partitioning of the demand into priority classes which is optimal when the valuations are uniformly distributed. In general, however, the optimal partitioning may be non-uniform and can be optimized to achieve maximum efficiency gains. Chao and Wilson (1987) have shown that in general the welfare loss with n discrete priority levels is of order $1/n^2$.

22.7 Concluding remarks

In this chapter, we described various nonlinear pricing schemes that exploit disaggregated demand data and revealed heterogeneity of customers' preferences. The common theme in the methodological treatments presented is a strong emphasis on modeling the preference structure that underlies the demand heterogeneity. This approach is based on a vast literature in economics of information and game theory dealing with price discrimination, mechanism design, principal agent theory, and incentives. For ease of presentation, all examples and theory were presented for the cases where a customer's heterogeneity can be characterized by a single dimension. However, the theory can be generalized to multi-dimensional customer types as shown in Wilson (1993).

The above approach differs from the growing body of literature on revenue management that takes the heterogeneous demand as given (but subject to stochastic variations) and focuses instead on more detailed modeling on the supply side which is typically modeled simplistically in the aforementioned economics literature. Supply side aspects, such as inventories and the news-vendor problem, have been typically abstracted in the economics literature dealing with mechanism design and in the nonlinear pricing literature. On the other hand, by not modeling the underlying structure of the demand side, the revenue management literature has been limited in addressing the problem of cross-impact among existing products and pricing of new products attempting to penetrate existing markets. Recent work by Talluri and van Ryzin (2004), Su (2007), and by Lutze and Özer (2008) are good examples of an emerging trend to bridge the gap between the two approaches. Such research should continue to develop models that have realistic representations of supply side aspects along with a fundamental representation of preference structures and incentives on the demand side, which drive the demand for diverse products and services.

From a practical applicability perspective, sophisticated nonlinear pricing schemes have become technologically feasible in many service industries due to the proliferation of advanced metering and control technologies at low cost. In the electric power industry, for instance, we are witnessing massive deployment of smart meters that will facilitate demand response through price incentives and contracted load control options that enable differentiation of service quality. Opportunities for facilitating load response through nonlinear pricing schemes have also spurred new business opportunities for retail intermediaries (often referred to as aggregators) that package load control options into wholesale products that are offered to the grid operator as operating reserves or offered into the balancing market auction (see Chapter 4 by Wilson). In the airline industry, nonlinear pricing has been common and enabled by the technological advances in online reservation systems (see Chapter 3 by Barnes). Likewise telecom services such as mobile phone services are provided with a multitude of billing and service options (see Chapter 9 by Zimmerman). Nonlinear pricing methods have also become more prevalent in retail over the past two decades largely due to sophisticated scanning and penetration of radio-frequency identification (RFID) tagging that supports modern inventory management and automatic "markdown" policies.

Given the technical feasibility of nonlinear pricing approaches, an open question for practitioners is how much differentiation is appropriate when taking into account the ability of consumers to process information and possible adverse reaction to what may be perceived as unstable prices. Some pricing policies such as real time pricing of electricity face political scrutiny and in the telecom industry we are witnessing a return to tariffs that provide unlimited service at flat rates. Theoretical models of customer choice, traditionally used in the economics and marketing literature, often assume that customers are perfectly rational and have unlimited computational capabilities. However, a growing literature in behavioral economics (see Camerer et al. 2004 and Chapter 20 by Özer and Zheng) suggests that customers' rationality and ability to determine their optimal choice are limited while human judgment is affected by numerous biases that can be manipulated. Future research on nonlinear pricing accounting for customers' preferences and strategic choice behavior should attempt to integrate new empirically validated models of choice behavior emerging from the rapidly growing field of behavioral economics. Such research will hopefully provide insight and practical guidance with regard to tradeoffs between the pursuit of efficiency versus realistic limitation on product variety and pricing complexity in designing nonlinear pricing schemes.

22.8 BIBLIOGRAPHICAL NOTES

The purpose of this section is to provide a brief historical perspective and some key references that were omitted in the text for sake of continuity. This bibliographic review is by no means comprehensive and the reader is referred to the book by Wilson (1993) for a more complete review of the literature.

The theory of price discrimination dates back to Pigou (1920). Cassady (1946a,b), Phlips (1983), and Varian (1985) provide detailed reviews and interpretations of the theory and practice of price discrimination. The example of bundling given in this chapter is due to Stigler (1963). The analysis of two-product bundling with continuous willingness-to-pay is due to Adams and Yellen (1976). Optimal two-part tariffs, which represent the simplest form of quantity-based nonlinear pricing, were analyzed by Oi (1971) and many others. The analysis of nonlinear pricing for continuous quantities has been influenced primarily by Mirrlees' (1971) work on optimal taxation, which is rooted in the work of Ramsey (1927). A sample of key contributions and expositions addressing the optimal structure of quantity-based nonlinear tariffs under alternative competitive conditions, their welfare implications and various extensions of the theory include: Brown and Sibley (1986), Goldman et al. (1984), Katz (1982), Mirman and Sibley (1980), Oren, Smith, and Wilson (1983, 1984, 1985), Roberts (1979), Spulber (1981), Stiglitz (1977), Willig (1978). The derivation of quantity-based nonlinear tariffs using profile function, used in this chapter, is due to Wilson (1993). This derivation is more transparent since it avoids the use of customers' utility functions parametric on customer type, which is the common approach in the literature. Laffont et al. (1987) and Oren et al. (1985) developed special cases of nonlinear pricing when customers' types are multi-dimensional. Early contributions to nonlinear pricing in the management science and marketing science literature began in the mid-1980s, including Jucker and Rosenblatt (1985), Monahan (1984), Moorty (1984), Lal and Staelin (1984), Braden and Oren (1994). One of the early contributions to the analysis of quality differentiated nonlinear pricing is Mussa and Rosen (1978) which focuses on the welfare implication of such differentiation by a monopoly supplier. Subsequent work by Oren et al. (1982a, b, 1987), Chao et al. (1986), and by Smith (1986, 1989) emphasizes the development and applications of quality differentiated price schedules, particularly in the context of electric power service and high tech products. The recent books by Talluri and van Ryzin (2005) and by Phillips (2005) provide an extensive review of the alternative treatment of quality differentiated pricing in the growing revenue management literature. Marchand (1974) and Tschirhart and Jen (1979) describe the early analysis of interruptible electricity pricing. The concept of priority pricing has been introduced by Harris and Raviv (1981) and extended by Chao and Wilson (1987) with a special emphasis on application to the electric power service. Wilson (1989a) generalized the idea of priority service to a general theory of efficient rationing and Wilson (1989b) combines the concepts of priority service with Ramsey pricing.

References

Adams, W. and Yellen, J. L. (1976) "Commodity Bundling and the Burden of Monopoly", *Quarterly Journal of Economics* 90: 475–98.

Braden, D. J. and Oren, S. S. (1994) "Nonlinear Pricing to Produce Information", *Marketing Science* 13/3: 310–26.

Brown, S. J. and Sibley, D. S. (1986) *The Theory of Public Utility Pricing*. Cambridge: Cambridge University Press.

Camerer, C. F., Lowenstein, G., and Rabin, M. (2004) *Advances in Behavioral Economics*. Princeton, NJ: Princeton University Press.

Cassady, R. (1946a) "Some Economics of Price Discrimination under Non-perfect Market Conditions", *Journal of Marketing* 11: 7–20.

—— (1946b) "Techniques and Purposes of Price Discrimination", *Journal of Marketing* 11: 135–50.

Chao, H. P. and Wilson, R. B. (1987) "Priority Service: Pricing, Investment and Market Organization", *American Economic Review* 77: 899–916.

—— Oren, S. S., Smith, S. A., and Wilson, R. B. (1986) "Multi-Level Demand Subscription Pricing for Electric Power", *Energy Economics* 8: 199–217.

Ferguson, D. G. (1994) "Shortages, Segmentation and Self-selection", *The Canadian Journal of Economics* 27/1: 183–97.

Goldman, M. B., Leland, H. E., and Sibley, D. S. (1984) "Optimal Nonuniform Pricing", *Review of Economic Studies* 51: 302–19.

Harris, M. and Raviv, A. (1981) "A Theory of Monopoly Pricing Schemes with Demand Uncertainty", *American Economic Review* 71: 347–65.

Jucker, J. V. and Rosenblatt, M. (1985) "Single-Period Inventory Models with Demand Uncertainty and Quantity Discounts: Behavioral Implications and New Solution Procedures", *Naval Research Logistics Quarterly* 32: 537–50.

Katz, M. L. (1982) "Nonuniform Pricing, Output and Welfare under Monopoly", *Review of Economic Studies* 50: 37–56.

Laffont, J.-J., Maskin, E., and Rochet, J.-C. (1987) "Optimal Nonlinear Pricing with Two-Dimensional Characteristics", in T. Groves, Radner R. and, S. Reiter (eds): *Information, Incentives and Economic Mechanisms*. Minneapolis, MN: University of Minnesota Press, 256–66.

Lal, R. and Staelin, R. (1984) "An Approach for Developing an Optimal Quantity Discount Policy", *Management Science* 30: 1524–39.

Lutze, H. and Özer, Ö. (2008) "Promised Lead Time Contracts under Asymmetric Information", *Operations Research* 56/4: 898–915.

Marchand, M. G. (1974) "Pricing Power Supplied on an Interruptible Basis", *European Economic Review* 5: 263–74.

Mirman, L. J. and Sibley, D. S. (1980) "Optimal Nonlinear Prices for Multiproduct Monopolies", *The Bell Journal of Economics* 11: 659–70.

Mirrlees, J. A. (1971) "An Exploration in the Theory of Optimal Taxation", *Review of Economic Studies* 38: 175–208.

Monahan, J. P. (1984) "A Quantity Discount Pricing Model to Increase Vendor Profits", *Management Science* 30(6): 720–6.

Moorty, K. S. (1984) "Market Segmentation, Self-Selection, and Product Line Design", *Marketing Science* 3: 288–307.

Mussa, M. and Rosen, S. (1978) "Monopoly and Product Quality", *Journal of Economic Theory* 18: 301–17.

Oi, W. J. (1971) "A Disneyland Dilemma: Two-Part Tariffs for a Mickey Mouse Monopoly", *Quarterly Journal of Economics* 85: 77–96.

Oren, S. S., Smith, S. A., and Wilson, R. B. (1982a) "Linear Tariffs With Service Quality Discrimination", *The Bell Journal of Economics* 13/2: 455–71.

—— —— and —— (1982b) "Nonlinear Pricing in Markets with Interdependent Demand", *Marketing Science* 1/3: 287–313.

—— —— and —— (1983) "Competitive Nonlinear Tariffs", *Journal of Economic Theory* 29/1: 49–71.

—— —— and —— (1984) "Pricing a Product Line", *Journal of Business* 57/1: S73–S99.

—— —— and —— (1985) "Capacity Pricing", *Econometrica* 53/3: 545–67.

—— —— and —— (1987) "Multiproduct Pricing for Electric Power", *Energy Economics* 9/2: 104–14.

Phillips, R. (2005) *Pricing and Revenue Optimization*. Stanford, CA: Stanford University Press.

Phlips, L. (1983) *The Economics of Price Discrimination*. Cambridge: Cambridge University Press.

Pigou, A. C. (1920) *The Economics of Welfare*. London: Macmillan Press Ltd. 4th edn 1932.

Ramsey, F. P. (1927) "A Contribution to the Theory of Taxation", *Economic Journal* 37: 47–61.

Roberts, K. W. S. (1979) "Welfare Considerations of Nonlinear Pricing," *Economic Journal* 89: 66–83.

Smith, S. A. (1986) "New Product Pricing in Quality Sensitive Markets", *Marketing Science* 5/1: 70–87.

—— (1989) "Efficient Menu Structures for Pricing Interruptible Electric Power Service", *Journal of Regulatory Economics* 1: 203–23.

Stigler, G. J. (1963) United States v. Loew's, Inc.: A note on Block Booking, Sop. Ct. Rev. 152.

Spulber, D. (1981) "Spatial Nonlinear Pricing", *American Economics Review* 71: 923–33.

Stiglitz, J. E. (1977) "Monopoly, Nonlinear Pricing and Imperfect Information: The Insurance Market", *Review of Economic Studies* 44: 407–30.

Su, X. (2007) "Intertemporal Pricing with Strategic Customer Behavior", *Management Science* 53/5: 726–41.

Talluri, K. T. and van Ryzin, G. J. (2004) "Revenue Management under General Discrete Choice Models of Consumer Behavior", *Management Science* 50/1: 15–33.

—— and —— (2005) *The Theory and Practice of Revenue Management*. New York: Springer Press.

Tirole, J. (1988) *The Theory of Industrial Organization*. Boston MA: MIT Press.

Tschirhart, J. and Jen, F. (1979) "Behaviour of a Monopoly Offering Interruptible Service", *Bell Journal of Economics* 10: 244–58.

Varian, H. (1985) "Price Discrimination and Social Welfare", *American Economic Review* 75: 870–5.

Willing, R. D. (1978) "Pareto-Superior Nonlinear Outlay Schedules", *The Bell Journal of Economics* 9: 56–69.

Wilson, R. B. (1989a) "Efficient and Competitive Rationing", *Econometrica* 57: 1–40.

—— (1989b) "Ramsey Pricing of Priority Service", *Journal of Regulatory Economics* 1: 189–202.

—— (1993) *Nonlinear Pricing*. New York: Oxford University Press.

CHAPTER 23

DYNAMIC LIST PRICING

YOSSI AVIV AND
GUSTAVO VULCANO

23.1 INTRODUCTION

Dynamic list pricing (DLP) belongs to the broad field of revenue management (RM), a practice that emerged more than three decades ago in the airline industry, and since then has been expanding into other business areas such as hospitality, car rental, retailing, and financial services. Under DLP, sellers use prices as a mechanism to control demand and maximize revenues; hence, DLP is considered to be a *price-based* RM strategy. As a complement to this type of strategies, some companies adopt *quantity-based* RM strategies, which take menus of prices as given, but adjust the amount of capacity allocated to each price-point. In some industries, one observes a mixed use of price-based and quantity-based RM. For example, traditional airlines tend to use capacity-control-based RM, while low-fare carriers are more prone to use prices as the control mechanism. In general, price-based RM is more suitable for businesses that have more price flexibility than quantity flexibility. For instance, a large fraction of retail operations (e.g., apparel or computer games) deals with long production and delivery leadtimes, and relatively short selling seasons. Thus, it is often very costly, or impossible, to readjust inventory during the selling season. Consequently, the retailers' best RM strategy is based on their ability to adjust prices, in a way that extracts the maximum consumer surplus. Some recent studies show that despite significant improvements in reducing supply chain costs via improved inventory and logistics management, the competitive advantage provided by scientific (or *smart*) pricing, is considered to be the fastest and most cost-effective way to increase profits (Phillips 2005). Analysts and vendors tout a 1 percent to 3 percent boost in overall sales, and in some cases a 10 percent rise in gross margins for companies that employ price-optimization technology (Sullivan 2005).

Traditionally, organizations have followed static-pricing policies over relatively long selling periods. Obviously, this simplest form of pricing mechanism is easy to implement. But no less importantly, in the past, firms did not possess the capability to plan, execute, and take advantage of dynamic pricing strategies. However, in recent decades, companies across many industries have witnessed a significant advance in the ability to collect and store consumer demand data—and the cost of acquiring and maintaining such information has been rapidly declining over time. IT decision-support applications have also grown in sophistication, which together with smaller transaction costs associated with changing prices (specially for e-tailers), the use of take-it-or-leave-it prices adjusted over time has become an increasingly popular practice. Indeed, changing prices is often easy and relatively costless, since it just requires changing price tags, signage, and modifying fields of a database. While there has been an exponential expansion in the use of on-line auctions by e-tailers in the late 1990s and early 2000s, conventional list pricing mechanisms are finding their ways back into these environments. Consider, for instance, eBay, which allows for auctions with "buy-now" options. Some companies even favor the use of plain fixed prices to any dynamic price schemes.

Talluri and van Ryzin (2004: section 5.1) identify three canonical examples of dynamic pricing and the qualitative factors driving them:

- *Style-goods markdown pricing*, implemented by retailers of innovative, style, and/or seasonal goods with the objective of clearing excess inventory before the end of the relatively short season (e.g., apparel, sporting goods, high-tech, grocery). The main incentives for price reductions in such cases are product perishability, the need for learning about consumers' willingness-to-pay (firm sets high price for all items initially, the items first gone are the ones with highest reservation-values among consumers), market segmentation (time-sensitive versus price-sensitive customers), and the fact that demand is more price-sensitive during peak periods like Christmas (e.g., see Warner and Barsky 1995).

- *Discount airline pricing*, where the trend of the price pattern is usually upward-biased. This is justified by the increasing willingness-to-pay of passengers as the flight day approaches.

- *Consumer-packaged goods promotions*, which are short-run, temporary price reductions. Given that customers are aware of past prices, promotions impact their subjective "reference price" for the product. Since customers may buy in advance, short-run increases in demand due to promotions may come at the expense of reduced future demand.

The purpose of this chapter is to provide a survey of the large body of modeling-based research in dynamic, pricing. We next look at the main characteristics of the market framework that condition the type of dynamic pricing problem a firm faces.

1. *Myopic versus strategic customers.* A myopic customer is one who simply buys a given product at the first time the price drops below his willingness-to-pay, without considering future prices. Conversely, a strategic (or forward-looking) customer factors into his decision the future path of expected (or pre-announced) prices. Depending on the specific practical setting, a seller may face some combination of strategic as well as myopic customers. For example, when customers do not have sufficient time (e.g., when buying a gift at a last moment) or information to predict future prices and availability, they are likely to behave myopically. In contrast, when the product is expensive and durable, and customers are patient in timing their purchases, they are more likely to exhibit strategic behavior.

2. *Replenishment versus no replenishment of inventory.* The ability of the seller to procure and receive additional units of capacity during the selling horizon may play an important role in the model setup. A model of pricing of replenishable capacity typically includes two dynamic control variables: inventory and pricing. Such a model may include procurement costs that may or may not vary over time. The case of non-replenishable capacity is simpler, with only one type of decision involved (pricing), and inventory procurement costs can be considered as "sunk costs" when it comes to the identification of optimal dynamic pricing policies.

3. *Infinite versus finite-population models.* In infinite population models, the distribution of customers and their willingness-to-pay is not affected by the past history of observed demand. Alternatively, there could be a finite (possibly random) number of customers with heterogeneous willingness-to-pay values. If one of the customers purchases, he is removed from the population of potential customers. The latter is the so-called "durable-goods assumption" in economics, because it considers the life of the product being longer than the time horizon over which the retailer makes price changes.

4. *Monopoly versus competitive models.* Until recently, most of the pricing models used in RM have been monopoly models, in which the demand a firm faces is assumed to depend only on its own price and not on the price of its competitors. Capturing oligopolistic effects is one of the current trends in RM, inspired by the narrow margins and the stiff competition in retail operations. The abundance of airline alliances and their need for well-designed coordination mechanisms has also contributed to this new line of research.

5. *Independent versus choice-based demand models.* Traditionally, RM models (both price-based and quantity-based) have assumed that the demand for different products is mutually independent, implying that there is a stream or subset of customers associated with one specific product. It is not hard to argue that customers behave in a more complex way, and in fact the sales that a firm observes are a function of the different products made available to the customer base at different points in time during the selling season. One of the current trends in the RM literature is the development and analysis of models that explicitly capture customer choice behavior.

The organization of the chapter proceeds as follows. In Section 23.2 we discuss the foundations of DLP: single-product models with finite and non-replenishable capacity. We briefly touch upon a model variant that allows for replenishable inventory. Section 23.3 is devoted to multiple products generated from a given set of limited resources. These two sections establish the basic framework for price-based RM, and together form what we would characterize as *traditional dynamic pricing*. We present and briefly discuss several mathematical models of single and multiproduct pricing. These traditional models assume that the firm is either a monopolist or operates in a market with imperfect competition, and, therefore, has the power to influence the demand by varying the price. Costumers are myopic, and most of the models assume that they come from an infinite population. The demand for different products is typically mutually independent. Two surveys published almost simultaneously (Elmaghraby and Keskinocak 2003 and Bitran and Caldentey 2003) provide a comprehensive study of the early and follow-up literature until the early 2000s. In

Talluri and van Ryzin (2004: ch. 5), the reader can find a discussion of several discrete-time counterparts of the aforementioned model formulations.

The remainder of the chapter is presented in slightly less technical fashion, and focuses on recent and current trends in DLP. Section 23.4 brings in the forecasting process. Often, retailers of seasonal, short lifecycle products face a significant level of uncertainty about demand. However, as they observe the sales of their product, they can update their demand forecast, and improve their pricing. A complicating factor in the pricing decision process is that retailers may need to consider the influence of pricing on learning. We introduce models that embed demand learning processes into the dynamic control system, and discuss the value of active versus passive learning. In Section 23.5 we survey models that capture the important phenomenon of strategic waiting. In response to the extended practice of markdowns, justified by the traditional models mentioned above, consumers have been trained to strategize over the timing of their purchases and buy on sale. This higher market sophistication requires a refinement of the usual markdown practice that preserves the advantage of price discrimination but mitigates the downside of the con-sumers' forward-looking behavior. We survey a large body of research on this phenomenon that has emerged in recent years. Section 23.6 is devoted to other behavioral considerations and their impact on the pricing practice, including the influence of the product assortment on the purchasing decisions, and psychological biases (e.g., the effect of past prices in setting expectations for future prices). Finally, in Section 23.7 we conclude and discuss directions for future research.

23.2 ELEMENTARY MODELS OF DYNAMIC PRICING

Revenue management systems are based on the fundamental principles of market segmen-tation and price discrimination, both of which have been extensively studied in the economics literature. When these two concepts are applied to tactical business manage-ment settings with limited sales horizon and limited capacity, they gain an operational flavor. For this reason, the large majority of the academic research on RM resides in the field of Operations Management. Earlier papers on dynamic pricing, which consider non-replenishable capacity and price-dependent demands includes, in chronological order: Lazear (1986), Gallego and van Ryzin (1994), Feng and Gallego (1995), Bitran and Mond-schein (1997), Bitran et al. (1998), Smith and Achabal (1998), and Zhao and Zheng (2000).

Lazear (1986) studies the benefit of intertemporal pricing with a simple and insightful dynamic programming model. Since his model involves demand learning, we defer the discussion to Section 23.4. As an outstanding representative of the early literature, in the next subsection we discuss in detail the influential paper by Gallego and van Ryzin (1994). This paper not only strikes a good balance between model sophistication and intuitive appeal, but it effectively conveys a compelling set of managerial insights, and an expandable building-block for further research. Indeed, this paper has engendered a significant level of interest in the operations management community.

23.2.1 A fundamental intensity-control, single-product model

Gallego and van Ryzin (1994) model arrivals as a homogeneous, time-invariant, Poisson process with intensity $\lambda(p) \in \Lambda$, nonincreasing in p. They define a *regular demand function* under the following mild technical requirements:[1] (1) there is a one-to-one correspondence between prices and demand rates so that $\lambda(p)$ has an inverse $p(\lambda)$; (2) the associated revenue rate $r(\lambda) = \lambda p(\lambda)$ is continuous, bounded, and concave, and satisfies $\lim_{\lambda \to 0} r(\lambda) = 0$; and (3) it has a finite least maximizer defined by $\lambda^* \triangleq \min\{\lambda : r(\lambda) = \max_{\lambda \geq 0} r(\lambda)\}$.

They proceed by formulating an intensity-control (see Brémaud 1980), continuous-time problem where the firm initially keeps C units of inventory to deplete over a selling horizon of length T. Letting N_s denote the cumulative number of items sold up to time s, the realization of a demand unit at time s is reflected by a sample-path derivative $dN_s = 1$. If so, the firm sells one item and collects revenue p_s. The price p_s must be chosen from a set of allowable prices $\mathcal{P}$, which is linked to Λ (i.e., $\Lambda = \{\lambda(p) : p \in \mathcal{P}\}$). Denote $\mathcal{U}$ the class of all non-anticipating pricing policies satisfying

$$\int_0^T dN_s \leq C.$$

Index t runs backward in time. Let c denote the number of remaining units of inventory at the beginning of period t, and $J_u(c, t)$ be the expected revenue during a selling horizon $t > 0$, that is,

$$J_u(c, t) = E_u\left[\int_0^t p_s dN_s\right],$$

with boundary conditions

$$J_u(c, 0) = 0, \ \forall c; \quad \text{and} \quad J_u(0, t) = 0, \ \forall t.$$

The firm's problem is to find a pricing policy u^* that maximizes the total expected revenue generated over the horizon of length T, denoted $J^*(C, T)$, that is

$$J^*(C, T) = \sup_{u \in \mathcal{U}} J_u(C, T).$$

The authors derive the Hamilton–Jacobi–Bellman (HJB) equation to get sufficient conditions that a policy u^* must satisfy. Since by selecting intensity λ, an item is sold over a small period of length δt with probability $\lambda \delta t$, by the Principle of Optimality,

$$J^*(c, t) = \sup_\lambda \{\lambda \delta t(p(\lambda) + J^*(c - 1, t - \delta t)) + (1 - \lambda \delta t)J^*(c, t - \delta t) + o(\delta t)\}.$$

Using $r(\lambda) = \lambda p(\lambda)$, dividing by δt, and taking limit as $\delta t \to 0$, they obtain

$$\frac{\partial}{\partial t}J^*(c, t) = \sup_\lambda \{r(\lambda) - \lambda(J^*(c, t) - J^*(c - 1, t))\}, \tag{1}$$

for all $c \geq 1$ and $t > 0$, with boundary conditions $J^*(c, 0) = 0$, and $J^*(0, t) = 0$. The interchange of *sup* and *lim* can be justified formally using Brémaud (1980: Theorem II.1), where general intensity control problems are studied. A solution to equation (1) is the optimal

---

[1] See also Chapter 18 by van Ryzin.

revenue $J^*(c, t)$, and the intensities $\lambda^*(c, t)$ that achieve the supremum form an optimal intensity control. Moreover, they prove that under the demand regularity condition, there exists a unique solution to equation (1), and that the optimal intensities satisfy $\lambda^*(c, s) \leq \lambda^*$, for all c and for all $0 \leq s \leq t$. The following intuitive structural results were also validated formally from their model:[2]

(P1) For a given time t, the optimal price decreases as the inventory c increases in order to induce more demand to clear the units.

(P2) For a given inventory level c, the optimal price increases if there is more time t (i.e., opportunities) to sell.

(P3) A higher inventory level c and/or longer remaining selling horizon t leads to higher expected revenues.

Although obtaining a closed-form solution $\lambda^*(c, s)$ is impossible for arbitrary regular demand functions, they managed to find an analytical expression for the exponential demand function $\lambda(p) = ae^{-bp}$, with $a, b > 0$. They show that the price describes a sawtooth pattern with decaying trend: After each sale, the price jumps and then decreases until another sale is made, at which point the price takes another jump. The upward jumps are explained by the higher prices posted by the firm when selling fewer items over a given interval t. To be precise, we are comparing the effect of having c units over a horizon t, versus $c - 1$ units over $t - \delta t$. The reduction of inventory by one unit is significant relative to the instantaneous decrement of the horizon length. The decaying price between sales can be considered a price promotion and follows from the fact that $\lambda^*(c, t)$ is decreasing in t for a fixed c (recall that the time index runs backward).

An important and undesirable feature of the optimal price is that it changes continuously over time. Seeking to circumvent this and obtain a more practical, stable pricing policy, Gallego and van Ryzin (1994) study a fluid-type approximation of the problem where demand is set constantly at its mean rate. Its formulation is as follows:

$$J^D(c, t) = \max_{\{\lambda_s \in \Lambda\}} \int_0^t r(\lambda_s) ds$$

subject to

$$\int_0^t \lambda_s ds \leq c.$$

It turns out that in this limiting model, the optimal policy is to set a fixed price throughout the selling horizon. The asymptotic fixed price (FP) is given by

$$p^D \triangleq \max\{p^0, p^*\}, \tag{2}$$

where $p^0 \triangleq p(c/t)$ is the run-out price, and p^* is the price associated to the least maximizer λ^* of $r(\lambda)$. Furthermore, the optimal revenue

$$J^D(c, t) = t \min\{p^* \lambda(p^*), p^0 \lambda(p^0)\}$$

satisfies $J^*(c, t) \leq J^D(c, t)$.

---

[2] These properties also hold under other models that we present later, as pointed out by Elmaghraby and Keskinocak (2003).

Gallego and van Ryzin also consider a refinement of this heuristic by choosing an optimal (single-period) fixed price (OFP); that is, the one maximizing $pE[\min\{c, N_{\lambda(p)t}\}]$, where N_α denotes a Poisson random variable with mean α. They prove that both policies are asymptotically optimal if the volume of expected sales is large.[3] Their numerical examples show that even for moderate expected volume of sales both fixed-price heuristics (and specially OFP) perform quite well. In addition, they analyze the case where only a finite set of prices is allowed. The deterministic solution in this case is also asymptotically optimal and consists of two consecutive price points from the grid (assuming prices are ordered increasingly), used for αt and $(1 - \alpha)t$ units of time, respectively, where α is given by the solution to a linear program.

Of course, the natural discussion that arises is: Why do we need to use dynamic pricing when a constant fixed price is nearly optimal, and by far easier to implement? It does not involve any monitoring of the inventory level and remaining time, and by definition the price adjustment cost is zero. As Gallego and van Ryzin point out, offering multiple prices can at best capture only second-order variations in revenue due to the statistical variability of demand. However, given the narrow margins and the cost structure of retailers that relies significantly on fixed costs, these incremental revenues might translate into significant profits.

Their paper also presents few departures from the basic setting. The first one is about modeling demand as a compound Poisson process, where they manage to verify the near-optimality of a fixed-price policy. The second one is a case where demand depends both on the price p and elapsed time s in a multiplicative way, so that $\lambda(p, s) = \lambda(p)g(s)$, $0 \leq s \leq t$. For example, if the peak demand occurs at the middle of the season, then $g(s)$ may be a concave function peaking near that time. They prove that under this nonhomogeneous, time-variant demand case where the ratio between demand intensities for any two prices is constant over the entire horizon, the formulation can be reduced to the basic formulation, so that all the previous results hold.

23.2.2 Extensions to the fundamental single-product problem

23.2.2.1 Accounting for customer reservation prices

Bitran and Mondschein (1997) build upon Gallego and van Ryzin (1994) by endogenizing the dynamics of how customers make purchasing decisions. They consider a nonhomogeneous Poisson process with rate λ_t, and a time-dependent valuation distribution F_t, so that the demand process for a given pricing policy is a nonhomogeneous Poisson process with intensity $\lambda(p, t) = \lambda_t(1 - F_t(p))$. In this regard, the demand is a function of the price through the distribution of the reservation prices.

Bitran and Mondschein start by discussing what they label as a *continuous-time model*, which is indeed a discrete-time model with small time periods of length δt that admit at

---

[3] More precisely, this occurs in two limiting cases: (i) the number of items is large ($c \gg 1$) and the horizon is long enough ($c < \lambda^* t$); or (ii) there is the potential for a large number of sales at the revenue maximizing price ($\lambda^* t \gg 1$), and there are enough items in stock to satisfy this potential demand ($c \geq \lambda^* t$).

most one arrival in each period. For a planning horizon of length L, the discrete number of periods is $T = L/(\delta t)$. The stochastic dynamic programming formulation is given by:

$$J(c, t) = \max_{p \geq 0} \{ m_t(1 - F_t(p))(p + J(c-1, t-1)) + (1 - m_t(1 - F_t(p)))J(c, t-1) \},$$

with boundary conditions

$$J(0, t) = 0, \ \forall t, \quad \text{and} \quad J(c, 0) = 0, \ \forall c; \quad \text{and where } m_t = \int_t^{t+\delta t} \lambda_\tau d\tau.$$

If the reservation price distribution is invariant with time, properties (P1)–(P3) above hold, and the optimal price follows a sawtooth pattern such as the one described for Gallego and van Ryzin (1994). On the other hand, when the reservation price varies with time, the optimal price can increase from one period to another even for a constant inventory level. First-order conditions for the stochastic dynamic program can be derived by balancing the expected benefit associated with marginally increasing the price (i.e., $(1 - F_t(p))dp$), and the expected loss associated with not selling the unit, which is partly offset by the possibility of selling it in the future (i.e., $[p - (J(c, t-1) - J(c-1, t-1))] f_t(p)dp$). In the latter, $F_t(p + dp) - F_t(p) \approx f_t(p)dp$ is the probability that a customer is willing to buy at p but not at $p + dp$. In the general case, this balance is posed as

$$[p - (J(c, t-1) - J(c-1, t-1))] f_t(p) = 1 - F_t(p). \tag{3}$$

The optimal pricing policy can be found by solving the nonlinear equation (3) backward in the time indices. Indeed, a necessary condition for a price p to be optimal is

$$p - \frac{1 - F_t(p)}{f_t(p)} = J(c, t-1) - J(c-1, t-1). \tag{4}$$

The left-hand side in (3) is the so-called *virtual value* of a consumer with reservation value p and is central to the design of revenue-maximizing auctions (see Steinberg Chapter 27). The quantity $(1 - F_t(p))/f_t(p)$ is the *information rent* that a customer retains due to the asymmetry of information. Thus, the optimal policy prices at a level $p^*(c, t)$ where the virtual value of a consumer with willingness-to-pay $p^*(c, t)$ matches the marginal value of capacity.

Arguing that retail stores revise their pricing policies periodically, Bitran and Mondschein consider the case where price can be altered at most K times during the selling horizon. They formulate a dynamic program which involves solving a unidimensional nonlinear program at each of the K stages. The state variable is defined by a pair of values: the inventory level, and the previous period's price—assuming the latter belongs to a discrete set. Under this model, it is also optimal to set a fixed-price policy when the initial capacity is large and the reservation price distribution is invariant with time. They present computational experiments with decreasing price paths, planning horizon of $L = 2$ weeks, $K = 4$, $\lambda_t = 70$, and reservation prices following a Weibull distribution with different variances. Two important outcomes of their experiments are:

- The impact of imposing a nonincreasing price path constraint on the total expected profit is relatively minor (less than 0.7%).

- The maximum revenue gap observed between a continuous and a periodic review pricing policy is relatively small (at most 2.2%).

In addition, the cases with high reservation price variance lead to higher profits than the cases with low reservation price variance.

Finally, they study a pricing strategy with pre-announced fixed-discount per period. Their analysis shows that this policy, in general, leads to a significant loss in expected profits that can scale up to 20 percent.[4] The authors alert that retail stores should evaluate the implicit benefits of this simplified markdown policy (e.g., a larger flow of customers and savings associated with advertising) very carefully before using it.

A takeaway of this paper is that uncertainty in demand for new products (represented numerically through a high-variance Weibull distribution) leads to higher prices, larger discounts, and more unsold inventory. Other observations are that higher levels of inventories lead to lower prices, and longer planning horizons lead to higher prices.

23.2.2.2 *Other important extensions and variations*

Partly justified by the limiting regime results of Gallego and van Ryzin (1994) that show the asymptotic optimality of the policies that allow at most one price change, Feng and Gallego (1995) study the optimal stopping time problem for using an initial price; that is they identify the time when the seller has to adjust it to either a given lower (as it is typically in retailing) or higher (e.g., airlines) second price. In their model, there is a pre-specified set of allowable prices. Under relatively mild conditions, they show that it is optimal to decrease (respectively, increase) the initial price when the remaining season length falls below (resp. above) a time threshold that is a function of the number of units in stock. For both cases, the time thresholds are monotonically increasing in the time-to-go. One clear benefit of their approach is that the sequence of thresholds is precomputable for any pair of prices, and is applied dynamically afterwards. A follow-up paper by Feng and Xiao (2000) extends the results to more than two prices, and provides an analytical optimal solution.

In an interesting piece of practice-oriented research, conducted in cooperation with a large retail company in Chile, Bitran et al. (1998) study the problem of coordinating markdown sales among multiple stores, in the spirit of Bitran and Mondschein (1997). Two common practices for allocating inventories to stores are: (1) an initial allocation without further redistributions, (2) an initial assignment and further reallocations to respond to demand and sales imbalances. The authors develop heuristics for solving the associated dynamic programming models for both settings. These heuristics are based on the optimal pricing policies for simpler problems where there is either no price change or at most one change is allowed during the planning horizon. The results show that the heuristics' performance are close to the optimum, and significantly better than the retailer practice by that time.

Smith and Achabal (1998) develop a deterministic continuous demand model for clearance pricing policies, and test it on three major retail chains. Its novelty is the introduction of inventory level as another factor that influences demand (jointly with time and price), with the objective of capturing the adverse effect of low inventory levels. Their goal is to determine the optimal inventory level C and the optimal price markdown path for a

---

[4] This seems to be related to the myopic characteristic of the consumers, since a pre-announced fixed-discount policy is convenient when the seller faces forward-looking consumers, as discussed later in Section 23.5.

product across a short life cycle (see Ramakrishnan Chapter 25 for an in-depth discussion of this paper). Smith and Achabal establish that the optimal price trajectory exactly compensates for the effects of reduced inventory, independent of the form of inventory sensitivity. Inventory sensitivity implies that prices should be set higher before the clearance period begins, and then reduced more sharply during the clearance period. For some products, it is optimal to leave some quantity of merchandise unsold at the end of the season, especially if it has a salvage value.[5]

Zhao and Zheng (2000) adopt Bitran and Mondschein's (1997) demand model. Recall that under the specific time-variant demand model presented by Gallego and van Ryzin (1994) where $\lambda(p, s) = \lambda(p)g(s)$, it could be established that for a given number of items the optimal price decreases over time (see (P2) above). However, (P2) may fail for a general case, but does hold under the following sufficient condition of the reservation price distribution: For any p_1, p_2 with $p_1 > p_2$, the conditional probability that the customer is willing to pay p_1 given that he would buy at p_2, that is, $(1 - F_t(p_1))/(1 - F_t(p_2))$ is increasing in t. In other words, (P2) holds if the probability that a customer is willing to pay a premium decreases over time. This condition seems to hold for most fashion goods but not for travel services, which would explain the opposite price trends often observed in these two industries.

23.2.3 Joint dynamic pricing and inventory management

When the production or procurement strategy allows for product replenishment, then the interesting problem that arises is how to coordinate pricing and inventory decisions. The traditional literature on inventory management (e.g., Karlin and Carr 1962) typically assumes that the price charged remains constant throughout the horizon. Given the nature of this chapter, we focus here on the case where the control variable *price* can be adjusted dynamically.

In their exhaustive survey, Elmaghraby and Keskinocak (2003) classify the literature on joint pricing and inventory management in three categories:

1. Models where the seller faces an uncertain demand, has convex production, holding and ordering cost, and unlimited production capacity (e.g., Zabel 1972; Thowsen 1975; Federgruen and Heching 1999).

2. Models that extend the previous ones by incorporating a fixed ordering cost (e.g., Chen and Simchi-Levi 2004a,b), or limited production capacity (e.g., Chan et al. 2005).

3. Models with deterministic demand (e.g., Rajan et al. 1992).

We will concentrate on the first category here, and refer the reader to Chen and Simchi-Levi Chapter 30 for deeper discussion. The three papers in this group look at the problem of a seller facing a stochastic demand $D(p_t)$, where the control p_t is updated periodically over time. As Elmaghraby and Keskinocak (2003) point out, the demand model can be viewed as lumping together the individual (Poisson) arrivals in Gallego and van Ryzin (1994) and

---

[5] We point out here that Smith and Achabal (1998) do not consider strategic consumers. In Section 23.5 we discuss the issue of capacity/inventory management under forward-looking consumers.

Feng and Gallego (1995) over the length of a period, such that all of the demand that occurs in the same period sees the same price.

In each period, the seller must decide on the new inventory level y_t before demand is realized, and incurs three possible types of costs: (1) a convex production cost, (2) a convex holding cost, and/or (3) a convex ordering cost. The main result of this stream of literature is that for a broad range of settings (including variations on demand, cost structure, lost sales or backlogging, and zero or positive production/procurement leadtime), a so-called *basestock, list price* policy (BSLP) is optimal. This policy is defined by two critical, time-dependent values p_t^* and y_t^*; if the inventory is above y_t^*, the firm orders nothing and selects an inventory-dependent price below p_t^*, which is decreasing in the inventory on hand; if the inventory is below y_t^*, the optimal policy is to order up to y_t^* and price at p_t^*. Thus, once the inventory level drops below y_t^* (i.e., once the system reaches steady state), the optimal policy is to use a fixed-price and a fixed base-stock level in each period.

Zabel (1972) studies a finite horizon, lost sales setting with zero leadtime, convex production cost, and linear holding cost. When the seller faces an additive, downward-sloping linear demand curve of the form $D_t(p) = u(p) + \eta_t$, where $u(p)$ is deterministic and η_t is a noise term, Zabel finds that: (1) the optimal price p_t^* is a decreasing function of the on-hand inventory right after ordering, y_t, (2) after ordering, given an on-hand inventory level of y, the optimal price with t periods left is greater than with $t-1$ periods left (i.e., $p_t^*(y) > p_{t-1}^*(y)$), and (3) the optimal production amount is increasing in the remaining time for any given initial inventory level x, that is, $y_t^*(x) > y_{t-1}^*(x)$. Note that (1) and (2) are parallel to (P1) and (P2), respectively, of Gallego and van Ryzin (1994).

Thowsen (1975) extends these results to the case where the seller admits backorders, incorporates the possible deterioration of inventory over time, and allows for the possibility that payments for demands are not received until after the order is placed. Thowsen finds that BSLP is optimal for fully backlogged demand, linear production costs, convex holding and stockout costs, and finite $E[\eta]$. Thowsen also finds a BSLP policy to be optimal when partial backlogging is allowed, provided that production and stockout costs are linear, holding costs are convex, and η is drawn from a family of distributions where $E[\eta] = 0$.

23.2.3.1 *A pricing/inventory system for a general stochastic demand model*

Federgruen and Heching (1999) extend the demand models of the previous two papers to more general stochastic functions. Specifically, demand in each period is a random variable $D_t(p, \eta_t)$ having expectation $d_t(p) = E[D_t(p, \eta_t)]$, with $d_t(p)$ being decreasing in p and having inverse $p_t(d)$. Other relatively mild technical conditions apply (e.g., uniformly bounded variance, and concavity in price p). The random revenue in each period is $R_t(d, \eta_t) = p_t(d)D_t(p_t(d), \eta_t)$. They also assume that prices p_t belong to a bounded range $\mathcal{P}$.

The inventory/pricing model assumes a per unit ordering cost c_t, and a convex cost $h_t(x)$ on the ending inventory x in period t which typically accounts for both holding and backordering costs (e.g., $h_t(x) = a \max\{x, 0\} + b \max\{-x, 0\}$, where a and b are unit holding and backlog costs).

In order to avoid fairly technical details of Federgruen and Heching (1999), we include here the slightly simplified version of the problem discussed in Talluri and van Ryzin (2004:

ch. 5). The profit optimization problem for the finite-horizon case can be formulated as follows:

$$J(x, t) = \max_{y \geq x,\, d \geq 0} E[R_t(d, \eta_t) - c_t(y - x) - h_t(y - D_t(d, \eta_t)) + J(y - D_t(d, \eta_t),\, t - 1)],$$
$$= \max_{y \geq x,\, d \geq 0} \{r_t(d) - c_t(y - x) + G_{t-1}(y, d)\}, \tag{5}$$

with boundary conditions $J(x, 0) = 0$, $\forall x$, and where

$$r_t(d) = E[R_t(d, \eta_t)], \quad \text{and}$$
$$G_{t-1}(y, d) = E[J(y - D_t(d, \eta_t),\, t - 1) - h_t(y - D_t(d, \eta_t))].$$

It can be proved that: (1) $G_t(y, d)$ is jointly concave in y and d, (2) $J(x, t)$ is concave in x, (3) $\frac{\partial}{\partial d} G_t(y, d)$ is increasing in y, and (4) $\frac{\partial}{\partial y} G_t(y, d)$ is increasing in d.

Properties (3) and (4) imply that G_t is supermodular.[6] Let y_t^* and d_t^* denote the maximizers of eq. (5) without the constraint $y \geq x$; i.e., (y_t^*, d_t^*) solve

$$\max_{y \in \mathcal{R},\, d \geq 0} \{r_t(d) - c_t(y - x) + G_{t-1}(y, d)\}. \tag{6}$$

Assume further an interior optimal solution for y and d so that, by joint concavity of $G_t(y, d)$, the necessary and sufficient conditions for y_t^* and d_t^* are then

$$c_t = \frac{\partial}{\partial y} G_{t-1}(y_t^*, d_t^*)$$
$$r_t(d_t^*) = -\frac{\partial}{\partial d} G_{t-1}(y_t^*, d_t^*)$$

If there are several pairs fulfilling these equations, pick the $(y_t^*, -d_t^*)$ that is lexicographically largest.

Since the inner function in eq. (6) is jointly concave in (y, d), (y_t^*, d_t^*) is the optimal decision pair when $x \leq y_t^*$. Similarly, it can be seen that for $x > y_t^*$, it is optimal to choose $y = x$.[7] They conclude in particular that $y(x)$ is nondecreasing in x. Note that the expression in brackets in (6) is supermodular in (y, d), because the first two terms depend on just one of these parameters. Moreover, it is concave in d, and so the optimal demand $d(y)$ is unique. Supermodularity implies that the optimal demand is nondecreasing in the state variable y, which is in turn nondecreasing in x, and hence the optimal demand $d(x)$ is nondecreasing in x. All in all, the BSLP that we introduced earlier in the section is optimal.

Federgruen and Heching also study the case where prices are only allowed to decrease over time and the case of an infinite horizon formulation. For the former, they show the optimality of a modified BSLP policy, defined for period t by: (a) If the price in previous period $t + 1$, p_{t+1}, verifies $p_{t+1} \geq p_t^*$, implement the usual BSLP; otherwise, (b) if $p_{t+1} < p_t^*$, compute the optimal inventory level $\hat{y}(p_{t+1})$, where $\hat{y}(p_{t+1})$ is the largest maximizer of (6)

---

[6] A function $f: \mathcal{R}^2 \to \mathcal{R}$ is *supermodular* when it satisfies increasing differences in (y, d); i.e., for all $y_1 > y_2$, $f(y_1, d) - f(y_2, d)$ is nondecreasing in d.

[7] If for $x > y_t^*$, a decision pair (y, d') is chosen with $y > x$, then for the pair (y, d'') on the line connecting (y_t^*, d_t^*) with (y, d'), the inner function in (6) evaluated at (y, d'') is higher than evaluated at (y, d').

for a fixed $d = d_t(p_{t+1})$. If $x_t \leq \hat{y}(p_{t+1})$, bring the inventory level up to $\hat{y}(p_{t+1})$ and set price p_{t+1}. If $x_t > \hat{y}(p_{t+1})$, then stay at x_t and charge $p^*(x_t) \leq p_{t+1}$.

For an infinite horizon, BSLP remains optimal when maximizing expected discounted profits. For average long-run profits where prices are allowed to freely move, BSLP is again optimal. But if prices should not increase over time, then the seller's optimal strategy is to charge a fixed static price p in all periods and follow a simple order-up-to policy with target level $y^*(p)$.

23.3 MULTIPRODUCT DYNAMIC PRICING

The practice of dynamic pricing executed over a single product certainly has limitations, since there are applications where pricing decisions are inherently linked over multiple products. One factor that leads to this multidimensional problem is the demand correlation between substitute or complement products. Another one is that products may be attached to joint capacity or inventory constraints. For example, in the case of airlines, a product may be defined as an itinerary–fare-class combination spanning more than one leg in the network (e.g., a flight with a stopover). Here, the acceptance of a specific product will imply the consumption of one unit of capacity in all the legs involved. Also, in some production/ inventory problems, resources are components that can be assembled into a certain number of variations in a product line. The problem is to price the product line to maximize the revenue from a given initial stock of raw components. In this section, we look at multiproduct models and methods.

We start by discussing the fundamental paper of Gallego and van Ryzin (1997), which extends their earlier model to this more challenging setting. Next, we introduce the work by Kleywegt (2001)—deterministic optimal control formulation; Liu and Milner (2006)— multi-item pricing with a common pricing constraint; and the simplifying framework of Maglaras and Meissner (2006).

23.3.1 A fundamental multiproduct, multi-resource model

Gallego and van Ryzin (1997) model demand as a multidimensional, controlled Poisson process with intensity $\lambda(p, s)$, $\lambda : \mathcal{R}^{n+1} \rightarrow \mathcal{R}^n$, where $p \in \mathcal{R}^n$ is the vector of prices charged at time s. This Poisson process further satisfies a generalization of the conditions for a regular demand function described in Section 23.2.1 (i.e., $\lambda(p, s)$ has an inverse for a given s, the revenue rate $r(\lambda, s) = \lambda^\top p(\lambda, s)$ is continuous, bounded, and concave, and there exists a null price $p_\infty^j(s)$ that allows the turning off of the demand for product j at any time). The counting process N_s^j denotes the number of product j sold up to time s.

There are m resources involved in the production of the n products. The initial stock of resources is $C = (C_1, \ldots, C_m)$, the planning horizon has length T, and an integer matrix $A = [a_{ij}] \in \mathcal{Z}^{m \times n}$ describes the consumption rates or bill of materials for all n products. A demand for product j is realized at time s if $dN_s^j = 1$, in which case the firm takes a_{ij} units of each resource i, $i = 1, \ldots, m$, out of its capacity or inventory, produces the product, and provides it to the customer in return for a revenue of p_s^j.

As in the case of a single product, prices are chosen using a nonanticipating pricing policy $p_s = p(\lambda_s, s)$. The vector of prices p_s must be chosen from a set $\mathcal{P}(s)$ of allowable prices. Equivalently, prices may be chosen via nonanticipating intensities $\lambda_s = \lambda(p_s, s)$. The set of allowable intensities is denoted by $\Lambda(s) = \{\lambda(p, s) : p \in \mathcal{P}(s)\}$, where $\Lambda(s)$ is assumed to be convex for all s.

The class of all nonanticipating pricing policies is denoted by $\mathcal{U}$, and satisfies

$$\int_0^T A \, dN_s \leq C$$

This constraint acts to stop the demand process for a product j when the firm lacks sufficient resources to provide it. Thus if resource i is exhausted at time s, the prices of all products j consuming resource i are increased to $p_\infty^j(s)$. Pricing policies are nonanticipating in the sense the price at time s can depend only on s and on the realization of sales up to (but not including) time s. Since policies could depend on the actual realization of past demand, the price p_s and the corresponding demand intensity λ_s are random. In addition, both price vector p_s and demand vector λ_s are random.

The formulation of the optimization problem is analogous to the single product one. Given a pricing policy $u \in \mathcal{U}$, a vector x of initial stock resources, and a sales horizon $t > 0$, the expected revenue is represented by

$$J_u(x, t) = E_u\left[\int_0^t p_s^T dN_s\right].$$

The firm's problem is to find a pricing policy u^* that maximizes the total expected revenue, denoted $J^*(C, T)$, that is,

$$J^*(C, T) = \sup_{u \in \mathcal{U}} J_u(C, T). \tag{7}$$

The HJB sufficient conditions for optimality state that

$$\frac{\partial}{\partial t} J^*(x, t) = \sup_{\lambda \in \Lambda(x, t)} \left\{ r(\lambda, t) - \sum_{j=1}^n \lambda^j (J^*(x, t) - J^*(x - A^j, t)) \right\},$$

where

$$\Lambda(x, t) = \Lambda(t) \cap \{\lambda : \lambda^j = 0 \text{ if } a_{ij} > x_i \text{ for some } i\}$$

denotes the set of allowable intensities in state x at time s and A^j denotes the jth column of A. J^* satisfies the boundary conditions:

$$J^*(x, t) = 0, \; \forall t, \quad x : x_i < a_{ij} \quad \text{for some } i, \text{and for all } j = 1, \ldots, n;$$
$$J^*(x, 0) = 0, \; \forall x.$$

As noticed for the single product case, in general it is difficult to find closed form solutions for such systems of differential equations. Although some of them can be solved numerically, the solutions tend to lead to continuous price decreases between sales and price jumps immediately after each sale.

In order to overcome this limitation, Gallego and van Ryzin (1997) propose the following deterministic analog to problem (7). At time zero, the firm has a supply vector C of continuous quantities, and faces a horizon of length T to sell continuous amounts of products. Demand and price vectors are deterministic. The firm's problem is to maximize the total revenue generated over $[0, T]$ given C, denoted $J^D(C, T)$:

$$J^D(C, T) = \max \int_0^T r(\lambda_s) ds,$$

subject to

$$\int_0^T A\lambda_s ds \leq x,$$

$$\lambda_s \in \Lambda(s), \quad 0 \leq s \leq T.$$

The solution (if one exists) is a function $\lambda_D(s) : [0, T] \to \mathcal{R}^n$. Such problems can be analyzed through the calculus of variations. In particular, in the time-invariant case (i.e., where $r(\lambda, s) = r(\lambda)$ and $\Lambda(s) = \Lambda$), the above problem reduces to a convex programming problem in $\mathcal{R}^n$ and solutions are always constant intensities (prices) over $[0, T]$. One can allow Λ to be nonconvex in this case. For instance, when Λ is discrete, the deterministic problem reduces to a linear program with decision variables being the amount of time each discrete price (intensity) is offered over $[0, T]$. The resulting solution is a set of piecewise constant intensities.

Note that the optimal revenue in the deterministic problem can be expressed as

$$J^D(x, t) = \sum_{j=1}^n \bar{p}^j \alpha^j,$$

where

$$\alpha^j = \int_0^t \lambda_D^j(s) ds,$$

is the total quantity of product j sold under the optimal policy, and

$$\bar{p}^j = \frac{\int_0^t p_D^j(s) \lambda_D^j(s) ds}{\int_0^t \lambda_D^j(s) ds}$$

is the weighted average price obtained for product j. Here, the price path $P_D(s)$ is the inverse of the demand path $\lambda_D(s)$.

The first theorem in Gallego and van Ryzin (1997) proves that the deterministic problem provides an upper bound to the stochastic problem; that is $J^*(x, t) \leq J^D(x, t)$. Next, they examine two heuristics suggested by the solution to the deterministic problem, which turn out to be asymptotically optimal:

- *Make-to-stock policy*: Since in the deterministic problem we know exactly the quantity of each product to be sold under any given policy, it is possible to anticipate production and hold inventories of finished products rather than hold inventories of resources. Taking the optimal deterministic demand path $\lambda_D(s)$ and price path $p_D(s)$, they define

$$z^j = \left\lfloor \int_0^T \lambda_D^j(s)\mathrm{d}s \right\rfloor = \lfloor \alpha^j \rfloor,$$

where $\lfloor x \rfloor$ stands for the largest integer less or equal to x.

The policy is: Preassemble z^j units of product $j = 1, \ldots, n$ and place the products in separate inventories. Price products at $p_D(s)$, $0 \le s \le T$ and sell them until the product inventories are exhausted or deadline T is reached, whichever comes first.

As Gallego and van Ryzin observe, there is no need to physically preassemble products in this heuristic, we only need logically reserve resources for specific products. However, the policy takes away both price flexibility and product-mix flexibility.

- *Make-to-order policy*: Here, the firm prices products according to deterministic prices $p_D(s)$, $0 \le s \le T$, and then simply satisfies requests on a first-come-first-serve basis. It rejects requests for a product j when the inventory of one or more of its resources i drops below a_{ij}.

The numerical experiments that the authors report indicate that performance of both heuristics is good, even for instances where sales volumes are moderate. Gallego and van Ryzin (1997) also present an extension of the model where they allow overbooking and no-shows.

23.3.2 Other important contributions

In this section we discuss a few other relevant papers on the multiproduct dynamic pricing problem. The models are introduced extending the notation of Section 23.3.1.

23.3.2.1 *Multiple customer classes*

Kleywegt (2001) studies a deterministic optimal control formulation of a pricing problem for the multiproduct, multi-resource setting. In addition to capturing cancelations and no-shows, the main novelty of his model is the introduction of customer classes. In a sense, the formulation can be seen as a preliminary, deterministic approach for customer choice-based pricing models.

Here, there are K customer classes, with $\lambda_k(t)$ representing the arrival rate per unit time of requests for class k customers at time t, and $h_{jk}(t)$ being the probability that a class k customer who makes a request at time t purchases product j if product j is offered. The value $\mu_{jk}(t)$ stands for the rate at which class k customers who have purchased a unit of product j cancel their purchases at time t. Let q_{jk} denote the probability that a class k customer who has purchased a unit of product j does not cancel the purchase at the last moment.

The controls are as follows. For each product $j = 1, \ldots, n$, class $k = 1, \ldots, K$, and time $t \in [0, T]$, let $u_{jk}(t) \in [0, 1]$ denote the fraction of class k requests to whom product j is offered at time t. The state of the system is described by a vector $y(t)$, with initial value $y(0) = y_0 \ge 0$. The value $y_{jk}(t)$ represents the cumulative amount of product j that has been sold to class k customers up to time t.

Because of cancelations and no-shows, the constraint associated with the limited amount x_i of each resource i is only enforced at terminal time T, allowing for overbooking at times

$t < T$. Let $Q \in \mathcal{R}^{n \times (nK)}$ denote the matrix with entry q_{jk} in row j and column jk. Then, entry j of vector $Qy(T)$ is equal to the quantity of product j that has to be supplied to customers after no-shows have been deducted. Entry i of vector $AQy(T)$ is the quantity of resource i that is needed to supply the products that are eventually sold. Hence, the constraints associated with the limited amount of resources are given by $AQy(T) \leq C$.

We let $p_j(t)$ denote the net revenue associated with selling a unit of product j at time t, and let $b_j(t)$ denote the net refund if the sale of a unit of product j is canceled at time t. The net refund given to a no-show for a unit of product j is therefore $b_j(T)$.

At any time $t \in [0, T]$, revenue from sales of product j to customers of class k is earned at rate $p_j(t)\lambda_k(t)h_{jk}(t)u_{jk}(t)$ per unit time, and refunds are paid due to cancelation of sales of product j by customers of class k at rate $b_j(t)\mu_{jk}(t)y_{jk}(t)$ per unit time. The amount $y_{jk}(t)$ of product j that has been sold to class k customers increases due to additional sales at rate $\lambda_k(t)h_{jk}(t)u_{jk}(t)$ per unit time, and decreases due to cancelations at rate $\mu_{jk}(t)y_{jk}(t)$ per unit time.

The objective is to maximize the total profit accumulated over the selling horizon. The control space $\mathcal{U}$ is the set of Lebesgue measurable functions, and the state space $\mathcal{Y}$ spans the space of absolutely continuous functions $y : [0, T] \to \mathcal{R}^n$. In symbols,

$$J(C, T) = \sup_{y \in \mathcal{Y}, \, u \in \mathcal{U}} \int_0^T g(y(s), u(s), s)\mathrm{d}s - Z(y(T))$$

subject to

$$y(t) = y_0 + \int_0^t f(y(s), u(s), s)\mathrm{d}s, \quad \text{for all } t \in [0, T] \tag{8}$$

$$AQy(T) \leq C$$

$$\sum_{j=1}^n u_{jk}(t) \leq 1, \quad k = 1, \ldots, K, \; \forall t \in [0, T] \tag{9}$$

Here, the profit rate function g is given by

$$g(y, u, t) = \sum_{j=1}^n \sum_{k=1}^K [p_j(t)\lambda_k(t)h_{jk}(t)u_{jk} - b_j(t)\mu_{jk}(t)y_{jk}]$$

The terminal cost function Z is given by

$$Z(y) = \sum_{j=1}^n \sum_{k=1}^K b_j(T)(1 - q_{jk})y_{jk},$$

where $1 - q_{jk}$ is the no-show probability of a class k customer who has purchased a unit of product j.

The transition rate function f that describes the evolution between states y is defined as

$$f_{jk}(y, u, t) = \lambda_k(t)h_{jk}(t)u_{jk} - \mu_{jk}(t)y_{jk}$$

Kleywegt (2001) shows that for each $u \in \mathcal{U}$, equation (8) always has a solution $y \in \mathcal{Y}$, and that if the problem is feasible, the optimal control problem is finite. Given the complexity of the formulation, the author proposes a Lagrangian relaxation that consists of bringing constraints (9) into the objective function, and discusses a numerical solution procedure for it, as well as an associated Lagrangian dual problem with its solution approach.

23.3.2.2 *Common pricing constraint*

Liu and Milner (2006) study a multiproduct, single-resource problem under a common pricing constraint to meet a heterogeneous demand. Their model is inspired by the fashion retail industry where a firm may carry the same product in an assortment of sizes and colors. The actual demand for variants of the product will often differ from an initial forecast, leaving relatively higher inventories of one variant versus another. Theoretically, the retailer would want to differentially price the variants in order to sell the items to achieve highest expected revenues. However, for the sake of fairness in customer perceptions, the retailer may decide to avoid such practice.

The paper is related to the aforementioned Bitran et al. (1998) (single-item pricing for multiple retail stores, see Section 23.2.2.2). In that article, each store sells to a different customer class, but all stores must use the same price. If we take a store as a product variant, the model by Liu and Milner (2006) matches the case in Bitran et al. (1998) where inventory cannot be transhipped between stores. Nevertheless, Liu and Milner (2006) differs from Bitran et al. (1998) in that the former authors consider a continuous time stochastic model and pursue an analytical approach, while most of the results in the latter are based on heuristics and simulations.

The model assumes independent Poisson arrival processes for the n products, with nonhomogeneous demand rates $\lambda^j(p_s)$ and associated counting process N_s^j. The arrival streams for the different products are splits from a common arrival rate $\lambda(p_s)$ via weights w^j that accounts for the probability that an arriving customer prefer product j, with $\sum_{j=1}^n w^j = 1$.

If $y_j(t)$ is the total number of items j sold up to time t, then $y_j(t) = \min\left\{N_t^j, C_j\right\}$, where C_j is the initial inventory level for those items. Define again $\mathcal{U}$ as the class of all non-anticipating pricing policies that satisfy

$$\int_0^T dy_j(s) \leq C_j, \quad j = 1, \ldots, n,$$

$$\int_{t_1}^{t_2} dy_j(s) \leq \int_{t_1}^{t_2} dN_s^j, \quad \text{for all } t_1 < t_2, \ t_2 \in [0, T], \quad j = 1, \ldots, n.$$

Let $J_u(x, t)$ be the expected revenue under policy $u \in \mathcal{U}$, that is,

$$J_u(x, t) = \mathrm{E}_u\left[\int_0^t p_s dy(s)\right],$$

with $J_u(x, 0) = 0$ for all x, and $J_u(0, t) = 0$, for all t, and let $J^*(C, T)$ be the associated maximum revenue over $[0, T]$

Let $I(x)$ be the set of products with $x_j > 0$. The HJB conditions for optimality state that

$$\frac{\partial}{\partial t}J^*(x,\ t) = \sup_{\lambda \in \Lambda(x,\ t)} \left\{ \sum_{j \in I(x)} w^j\big(r(\lambda) + \lambda\big(J^*(x - e_j,\ t) - J^*(x,\ t)\big)\big) \right\}, \tag{10}$$

where e_j is the unit vector that has a 1 in position j, and zero elsewhere. Liu and Milner prove that the optimal revenue $J^*(x, t)$ is increasing in x_j and t, and concave in $t \in [0, T]$. The optimal solution $\lambda^*(x, t)$ (respectively, price $p^*(x, t)$) is unique for each $t \in [0, T]$, and it is strictly decreasing (respectively, increasing) in t.

In contrast to the single-product model, the price here may decrease with a reduction in inventory because now, as the inventory levels of the product mix change, the price needs to account for the whole assortment. However, when just one product remains in stock, the optimal policy is in fact the one characterized by Gallego and van Ryzin (1994).

As noticed by Gallego and van Ryzin (1994), it is difficult to solve (10) analytically even for the single-product case, except for the exponential demand function. In order to circumvent this, Liu and Milner (2006) consider the analogous model where the demand is a deterministic function of the price. The control problem is formulated as

$$J^D(x,\ t) = \max_{\lambda_s} \int_0^T p(\lambda_s)\left(\sum_{j=1}^n \lambda_s^j\right)ds$$

subject to

$$\int_0^T \lambda_s^j \le x_j, \quad j = 1,\ \ldots,\ n,$$

$$\lambda_s^j \le w^j \lambda_s, \quad j = 1,\ \ldots,\ n,\ s \in [0,\ T],$$

with boundary conditions $J^{D*}(x, 0) = 0, \forall x$, and $J^{D*}(0, t) = 0, \forall t \in [0, T]$. Assume w.l.o.g. that x_j/w^j is increasing in j, and that the ratios are different (otherwise, those products with equal ratios can be pooled in a single supra-product). They prove that since the demand weights are constant with respect to price, the items are depleted in order $j = 1, \ldots, n$. Then, the problem boils down to determining a set of times $\tau = \{\tau_1, \ldots, \tau_n\}$ to deplete the n items, with $\sum_{j=1}^n \tau_j = T$. Here, τ_j represents the time between when the $(j-1)$th product is depleted, and when the jth is depleted. The authors show that the deterministic control problem above can be reduced to a convex optimization problem over the values τ. Once they find the vector τ^*, the optimal prices are calculated in closed-form and satisfy $p_1 \ge p_2 \ge \cdots \ge p_n$.

For the particular case of two products, that is, $n = 2$, Liu and Milner show that $J^*(x_1, x_2, T) \le J^{D*}(x_1, x_2, T)$. Next, they consider a restricted stochastic version of the problem where a single price change (markdown) is allowed at an arbitrary time τ, for given prices p_1 and p_2, $p_1 > p_2$, which provides a lower bound for the maximum revenue. Let $J(x, T; \tau)$ be the expected revenue given by using p_1 from time zero to τ, and p_2 from τ to T, for some $\tau \le T$. Let $N_1^j(t)$ be the total number of arrivals for product j before changing the price, and $N_2^j(t)$ be the total number for item j after changing the price. As before, arrivals are Poisson. Hence,

$$J(x, T; \tau) = (p_1 - p_2)\mathrm{E}\left[\sum_{j=1}^{n} \min\{x_j, N_1^j(\tau)\}\right]$$

$$+ p_2 \mathrm{E}\left[\sum_{j=1}^{n} \min\{x_j, N_1^j(\tau) + N_2^j(T - \tau)\}\right] \qquad (11)$$

Let

$$J(x, T) = \sup_{\tau} \mathrm{E}[J(x, T; \tau)],$$

be the expected revenue under an optimal policy, with τ belonging to the set of stopping times including those based on observed demand. They show that the optimal markdown time is given by a time threshold policy based on multidimensional inventory levels. If the time remaining is less than the threshold, then it is optimal to switch price immediately. The thresholds are not necessarily increasing in time, and determining them precisely implies solving a set of hard partial differential equations. The authors propose two approximations to simplify the calculations.

Observe that the stochastic problem (11) is dependent on values for p_1 and p_2. The dual of this problem is to determine prices p_1^* and p_2^* that maximize the expected revenue given a time τ when the prices will be switched, that is,

$$J'(x_1, x_2, T; \tau) = \max_{p_1, p_2} \mathrm{E}\left[(p_1 - p_2)\sum_{j=1}^{2} \min\{N_1^j(\tau), x_j\}\right.$$

$$\left. + p_2 \sum_{j=1}^{2} \min\{N_1^j(\tau) + N_2^j(T - \tau), x_j\}\right]. \qquad (12)$$

Under the assumption of Poisson arrivals with price-dependent arrival rates, since $r(\lambda)$ is continuous, bounded, and concave, the problem is a convex program and can be readily solved. But because it is dependent on a switching time, simultaneously solving for a price vector and a threshold policy is difficult.

Finally, Liu and Milner (2006) develop four heuristics for the stochastic common pricing problem, and apply them to the two-item case. The best performance is reported for a heuristic that uses the optimal switching time determined by the deterministic control problem, and the prices obtained by solving (12) (when solved using that stopping time as input).

23.3.3 A unifying framework for price- and quantity-based RM

The conceptual boundaries between price-based and quantity-based RM mentioned in Section 23.1 are diluted in the paper by Maglaras and Meissner (2006). They show that the aforementioned multiproduct dynamic pricing problem of Gallego and van Ryzin (1997) (for the single resource case), and the capacity control problem of Lee and Hersh [1993] can be recast within a common framework, and be treated as different instances of a single-product pricing problem for an appropriate concave revenue function.

The main idea is to decouple a revenue maximization problem in two parts: First, at each point in time the firm selects an aggregate capacity consumption rate from all products, and second, it computes the vector of demand rates to maximize instantaneous revenues subject to the constraint that all products jointly consume capacity at that rate.

Maglaras and Meissner start discussing a single resource, multiproduct setting. The random demand vector in period t, denoted by $\xi(t, \lambda)$, is Bernoulli with probabilities $\lambda(t) = \lambda(p(t))$, $\mathbb{P}(\xi_j(t, \lambda) = 1) = \lambda^j(p(t))$, and $\mathbb{P}(\xi_j(t, \lambda) = 0) = 1 - \lambda^j(p(t))$, for all $j = 1, \ldots, n$. Treating the demand rates λ^j as the control variables (prices are inferred via the inverse regular demand relationship), the discrete time formulation of the dynamic pricing problem of Gallego and van Ryzin (1997) is

$$V^{DP}(C, T) = \max_{\{\lambda(t),\, t=1,\ldots,\, T\}} \mathrm{E}\left[\sum_{t=1}^{T} p(\lambda(t))^\top \xi(t, \lambda) \right]$$

subject to

$$\sum_{t=1}^{T} e^\top \xi(t, \lambda) \le C,$$

$$\lambda(t) \in \Lambda, \quad \forall t \in [0, T],$$

where e is a vector of ones, C is a scalar, and Λ is a convex set. A slight simplification of the capacity control problem formulated by Lee and Hersh (1993) can be stated as follows. Price vector p and demand rate vector $\lambda = \lambda(p)$ are fixed. Given prices $p^1 \ge p^2 \ge \cdots \ge p^n$, the firm decides what fraction of a product unit to accept at any given time through a control $u_j(t) \in [0, 1]$. In symbols,

$$V^{CC}(C, T) = \max_{\{u(t),\, t=1,\ldots,\, T\}} \mathrm{E}\left[\sum_{t=1}^{T} p^\top \xi(t, u\lambda) \right]$$

subject to

$$\sum_{t=1}^{T} e^\top \xi(t, u\lambda) \le C,$$

$$u_j(t) \in [0, 1], \quad \forall t \in [0, T],$$

where $u\lambda$ above denotes the vector with coordinates $u_j\lambda^j$, $j = 1, \ldots, n$.

Maglaras and Meissner proceed to reduce both formulations to a common one in terms of the aggregate capacity consumption. When indices run backward in time, the HJB equation associated with the dynamic pricing problem $V^{DP}(C, T)$ is

$$J(x, t) = \max_{\lambda \in \Lambda} \left\{ \sum_{j=1}^{n} \lambda^j [p^j(\lambda) + J(x - 1, t - 1)] + (1 - e^\top \lambda) J(x, t - 1) \right\}, \tag{13}$$

with boundary conditions

$$J(x, 0) = 0, \ \forall x, \quad \text{and} \quad J(0, t) = 0, \ \forall t. \tag{14}$$

Letting $\Delta J(x, t) = J(x, t-1) - J(x-1, t-1)$ denote the marginal value of capacity as a function of the state (x, t), problem (13) can be written as

$$J(x, t) = \max_{\lambda \in \Lambda} \left\{ r(\lambda) - \sum_{j=1}^{n} \lambda^j \Delta J(x, t) \right\} + J(x, t-1),$$

$$= \max_{\rho \in \Psi} \{ R^r(\rho) - \rho \Delta J(x, t) \} + J(x, t-1), \tag{15}$$

where $\rho = \sum_{j=1}^{n} \lambda^j$ is the aggregate rate of capacity consumption, $\Psi = \left\{ \rho : \sum_{j=1}^{n} \lambda^j = \rho, \lambda \in \Lambda \right\}$, and where

$$R^r(\rho) = \max_{\lambda \in \Lambda} \left\{ r(\lambda) : \sum_{j=1}^{n} \lambda^j = \rho \right\} \tag{16}$$

is the maximum achievable revenue rate subject to the constraint that all products jointly consume capacity at a rate ρ. This is a concave maximization problem over a convex set, and its solution is readily computable. The optimal vector of demand rates, denoted by $\lambda^r(\rho)$, is unique and continuous in ρ.

Similarly, the HJB equation associated with $V^{CC}(C, T)$ is

$$J(x, t) = \max_{u_j \in [0, 1]} \left\{ \sum_{j=1}^{n} \lambda^j u_j [p^j + J(x-1, t-1)] + (1 - u^\top \lambda) J(x, t-1) \right\}$$

$$= \max_{u_j \in [0, 1]} \left\{ \sum_{j=1}^{n} \lambda^j u_j p^j - u^\top \lambda \Delta J(x, t) \right\} + J(x, t-1) \tag{17}$$

$$= \max_{0 \le \rho \le \sum_{j=1}^{n} \lambda^j} \{ R^a(\rho) - \rho \Delta J(x, t) \} + J(x, t-1),$$

where the boundary condition is given by (14), $\rho = u^\top \lambda$, and

$$R^a(\rho) = \max_{u} \left\{ \sum_{j=1}^{n} u_j \lambda^j p^j : u^\top \lambda = \rho, u_j \in [0, 1] \right\}$$

is the maximum revenue rate when the capacity is consumed at a rate equal to ρ.

The preceding analysis illustrates that both problems can be reduced to appropriate single-product pricing problems, highlighting their common structure and enabling a unified treatment. For both (15) and (17) the optimal control $\rho^*(x, t)$ is computed from

$$\rho^*(x, t) = \arg\max_{\rho \in \Psi} \{ R(\rho) - \rho \Delta J(x, t) \},$$

where $R(\rho)$ is a concave increasing revenue function.

Using the properties of $R(\rho)$, it holds that $\rho^*(x, t)$ is decreasing in $\Delta J(x, t)$. From here, using an induction argument in t gives that $\Delta J(x, t)$ is decreasing in x and increasing in the remaining time t. Given the relation between p, λ, and ρ (i.e., intuitively, a decreasing ρ implies a decreasing λ^j, which in turn implies an increasing price p^j), these monotonicity results about the marginal value of capacity can be seen as the discrete-time counterparts of results (P1) and (P2) for the single product case in Section 23.2. Maglaras and Meissner show how structural results for the pricing and capacity allocation policies can be recovered from their formulation. In addition, they provide an important qualitative insight of the results for this unifying framework: The translation of the capacity consumption rate to a set of product-level controls that jointly maximize the instantaneous revenue rates defines an *efficient frontier* for the firm's optimal pricing and capacity control strategies. This frontier captures in a tractable way the interactions between products due to cross-elasticity effects and the joint capacity constraint.

In order to come up with simple and implementable heuristics for the joint pricing and capacity control problem, the authors also study a *fluid* model with deterministic and continuous dynamics, obtained by replacing the discrete stochastic process by its rate, which now evolves as a continuous process. It is rigorously justified as a limit under a law-of-large-numbers type of scaling as the potential demand and the capacity grow proportionally large. The formulation is consistent with the limiting regimes presented by Gallego and van Ryzin (1994, 1997).

Let $a_j > 0$ be the rate at which a unit of product j consumes capacity, and denote by a the vector $(a_1, \ldots, a_n)$ (this corresponds to one row of the matrix A introduced in Section 23.3.1, that is, a is the bill of materials for a multiproduct, single-resource problem). The consumption rate is redefined as $\rho = a^\top \lambda$. The system dynamics are given by

$$\frac{d}{dt} x(t) = - \sum_{j=1}^{n} a_j \lambda^j(t), \quad x(0) = C, \quad \text{and boundary condition } x(T) \geq 0.$$

The firm selects a demand rate $\lambda^j(t)$ at each time t. The fluid formulation of the single resource case is the following:

$$\max_{\{\lambda(t), \, t \in [0, \, T]\}} \int_0^T R(\lambda(t)) dt$$

subject to

$$\int_0^T a^\top \lambda(t) dt \leq C$$

$$\lambda(t) \in \Lambda, \quad \forall t.$$

Following the unifying approach, they can reduce the multiproduct problem to an appropriate single-product one, and thus solve it in closed form. Specifically, recalling the definition of the aggregate revenue function $R^r(\rho)$ in (16) and its associated optimal demand rate vector $\lambda^r(\rho)$, adjusted now for the fact that $\rho = a^\top \lambda$, the fluid formulation can be rewritten as

$$\max_{\{\rho(t), \, t \in [0, \, T]\}} \int_0^T R^r(\rho(t)) dt \tag{18}$$

subject to

$$\int_0^T \rho(t) dt \leq C$$

$$\rho(t) \in \Psi, \quad \forall t.$$

Let $\rho^0 = C/T$ be the run-out capacity consumption rate, and $\rho^* = \arg \max_\rho R^r(\rho)$ be the unconstrained maximizer. Then, the optimal solution to (18) is to consume capacity at a constant rate ρ^D given by

$$\rho^D = \min \{\rho^0, \ \rho^*\}, \quad \forall t,$$

the corresponding vector of demand rates is $\lambda^r(\rho^D)$, while the price vector is $p(\lambda^r(\rho^D))$, both of them being constant over time. Note the analogy with the result in equation (2) for the single-product framework.

Based on the solution of the fluid formulation, Maglaras and Meissner analyze three heuristics: (1) a static pricing heuristic (which corresponds to the make-to-order heuristic of Gallego and van Ryzin 1997), (2) a static pricing heuristic applied in conjunction with an appropriate capacity allocation policy, and (3) a *resolving* heuristic that reevaluates the fluid policy as a function of the current state (x, t). They show that the three heuristics are asymptotically optimal under fluid scaling, but their numerical results give a better support for heuristics (2) and (3).

23.4 Dynamic pricing with learning

One interesting attribute of innovative, short lifecycle products, is that the level of demand uncertainty is high; yet, some of the uncertainty can be resolved as sales begin. The purpose of this section is to survey a part of the DLP literature that deals with the aspect of demand *learning* in dynamic pricing settings. We conclude this section discussing models of intertemporal consumers' valuations.

23.4.1 Early models of pricing with demand learning

Lazear (1986) considers a model of a firm that sells a *single* unit of a product to a single customer (i.e., demand, rather than inventory, is restricted). The firm does not know the customer's valuation, v, but can characterize its uncertainty by a probability distribution F, with a corresponding density function f. Now, suppose that the firm can sell the product over a sequence of two periods, as follows. In the first period, the firm offers an initial price (p_1); if the customer does not purchase the product, then the firm can offer the product at a different price, p_2, in the second period. The customer is assumed to purchase the product at any given time if the price falls below the valuation v.

Obviously, under the above conditions, the firm is able to update its belief about the customer's valuation, if the customer did not purchase the product at the price p_1. Moreover, it is noteworthy that the initial price influences the ability of the firm to learn about the customer's valuation. The dynamic pricing problem faced by the firm is given in the following equation (with a slight modification of the original work):

$$\max_{p_1, p_2} \{p_1 \cdot \bar{F}(p_1) + p_2 \cdot F(p_1) \cdot \bar{F}_2(p_2|p_1)\}.$$

The first term in the expression refers to the expected revenues collected in the first period. The second term includes the probability of no sale in the first period, multiplied by the price p_2, and the likelihood that the customer who has not purchased at p_1 will buy the product at the price p_2. For the special case in which the prior distribution F is Uniform[0, 1], Lazear shows that the optimal solution is $p_1 = \frac{2}{3}$, and $p_2 = \frac{1}{3}$. The expected revenue in this case is 1/3.

Lazear compares the latter dynamic model to a fixed-price benchmark case, in which the firm can only post a single price throughout the sales horizon. When F is uniform, the optimal price is given by

$$\arg \max_p \{p \cdot (\bar{F}(p))\} = \arg \max_p \{p - p^2\} = \frac{1}{2},$$

yielding an optimal revenue of 1/4. As can be expected, the ability to change a price during the season is beneficial to the firm, allowing it to increase its expected revenues from 1/4 to 1/3.

In the rest of the paper, Lazear considers variants of the above model. For example, in one of the models, the firm is faced with a fixed population of N customers, among which one group shares the same valuation ν (called "buyers") and one group has a valuation of zero (called "shoppers"). The probability that a given customer is a "shopper" (i.e., not interested in the product) is θ. The probability of a sale in the first period is hence $(1 - \theta^N) \cdot \bar{F}(p_1)$. The posterior probability of making a sale in the second period (if no sale was made during the first period) is $(1 - \theta^N) \cdot \bar{F}_2(p_2 \mid p_1)$. For instance, when the value of θ is 0, the model becomes equivalent to the initial model described above. For a positive θ, the ability of the seller to learn about the valuation ν is limited, but increases in N. Consequently, one observes that when N is large, prices start high (because there is an increased chance to capture "buyers" in each period) and discounts are deeper (because learning is more effective; hence if units were not sold in the first period, the firm can learn with high confidence that the value of ν is small).

Pashigian (1988) extends the analysis of Lazear to multiple units, and similarly to the previous paper's result he argues that when demand (product valuation) uncertainty increases, the markdowns tend to grow. He concludes that in markets that introduce an increasing number of fashion-type products, we should expect to see an increase in the level of markdowns. Indeed, based on data from the fashion industry, Pashigian finds empirical support for his argument.

Balvers and Cosimano (1990) study an active learning setting in which a firm faces a linear demand curve, but with unknown slope and intercept. The model is set as a periodic-review control problem in which price is the only control variable. Using historical prices and actual demand quantities, the seller updates her belief about the actual demand curve parameters. Since no inventories are allowed to be carried over from one period to another, production is always set to be equal to the price-induced demand. The inventory aspect is hence significantly different than that typically studied in RM systems: consecutive decision periods depend on each other solely through learning. Balvers and Cosimano argue that the optimal prices are relatively stable over time ("price stickiness"). They suggest that this phenomenon occurs because price changes add uncertainty to the decision process, as well as hinder the learning process, and therefore they are generally not desirable. We refer the reader to their literature review for a discussion of papers on active learning through pricing in competitive environments. Braden and Oren (1994) study a pricing problem for a firm that sells products to customers with different tastes that vary according to an index whose value is unknown. They show that it is optimal in their setting to follow a policy that maintains the *separation principle*, where the estimation problem of learning the parameters characterizing customer heterogeneity can be separated from the control problem of determining appropriate volume discounts to exploit that heterogeneity (e.g., see Bertsekas 2005: ch. 5): The control of prices can be achieved in a way that does not need to consider the evolution of information, provided the learning about the unknown demand parameter is done periodically, prior to each decision.

23.4.2 Models with capacity considerations

The papers surveyed below consider the aspect of demand learning in settings with finite capacities. Aviv and Pazgal (2005a) extend the work of Gallego and van Ryzin (1994) by considering uncertainty about the arrival rate. Similarly to the models in the latter paper, a seller has a limited capacity of C units that needs to be sold over a finite horizon of length T. Demand for the product occurs in single units, governed by a Poisson process with an intensity rate denoted by λ. However, the value of λ is *unknown* to the seller, who only has a prior belief about its value in the form of a Gamma distribution with a positive shape parameter m_0 and a positive scale parameter θ_0. Specifically,

$$f(\lambda|m_0, \theta_0) = \frac{\theta_0(\theta_0\lambda)^{m_0-1}e^{-\theta_0\lambda}}{\Gamma(m_0)}, \quad \lambda \geq 0$$

The customers' purchasing decisions are price-dependent, and assumed to be characterized by a purchasing probability function $\alpha(p) \in [0, 1]$ that is decreasing in price and is known to the seller. Hence, for any given price p, the sales rate is given by $\lambda \cdot \alpha(p)$. In the main part of their paper, they assume $\alpha(p) = e^{-ap}$, where a is a known non-negative scalar.

The key feature of Aviv and Pazgal's model is that the seller is able to learn about the store traffic intensity rate through the history of prices and sales. In fact, utilizing the statistical properties of the Gamma-Poisson model (i.e., a Poisson process driven by a parameter that has a Gamma distribution), they show that at any point of time s during the sales season, the seller's belief about the value of λ continues to be characterized by a Gamma distribution with parameters (m_s, θ_s), where

$$\theta_s = \theta_0 + \int_0^s \alpha(p(u))du; \quad \text{and} \quad m_s = m_0 + N_s, \tag{19}$$

and where N_s is equal to the number of sales realized up to time s. Let $J_p(C, t, m, \theta)$ be the expected store revenue under the given pricing policy p, when t time units are left to the end of the horizon. Also, let p^* be the optimal pricing policy such that

$$J_{p^*}(C, t, m, \theta) = \sup_{p\in\mathcal{P}} J_p(C, t, m, \theta) = J^*_{C, m}(t, \theta)$$

At each point in time, the seller needs to strike an optimal balance between setting the price too low risking loss of revenue, versus setting a high price and lowering the purchase probability as well as the likelihood of a reduction in the uncertainty about demand.

The authors report on several interesting results. First, in Theorem 4 of their work, and similarly to Gallego and van Ryzin (1994), it is shown that optimal prices jump upward immediately after sales, whereas, in between sales, the optimal price declines. The jump in prices immediately after sales is due to two reasons: there are less units to sell, and hence more time to experiment with higher prices. Additionally, the occurrence of a sale raises the seller's belief that the market condition is good (i.e., higher λ value). Secondly, optimal prices tend to be higher with higher levels of uncertainty about the market condition. In other words, when faced with uncertainty, the seller should ask for a high price betting on a strong market, particularly when the sales season is long enough to recover if conditions are not as favorable. Thirdly, like (P3) in Section 23.2, the optimal expected revenue increases as a function of the length of the sales season and the number of units available for sale, but in a *diminishing rate*. These results should be taken into account when the retailer has some influence over the length of the selling season and the initial inventory level.

In the second part of their paper, Aviv and Pazgal compare the expected revenues under the optimal pricing policies with alternative policies, such as fixed price schemes, certainty-equivalent heuristics, and a naive policy that completely ignores the uncertainty about the market condition. They argue that when the market is characterized by high levels of uncertainty, ignoring the uncertainty or using (even the) best fixed-price policy could be bad. In the latter case, the percentage loss in expected revenues (sub-optimality gap) grows larger when the season is longer. This result contrasts the observation made by Gallego and van Ryzin (1994), according to which fixed-price policies tend to perform very well in the case of full information about the market condition. Consequently, the authors conclude that the benefits of dynamic pricing strategies could be critical in settings with high but resolvable initial uncertainty about the market size. Finally, the authors argue that it is not necessary to perfectly solve the complex dynamic pricing decision problem by taking into account the impact of pricing on the learning process ("active learning"). They find that while it is vital for learning to take place, it is quite reasonable to adopt a "passive learning" approach in which the seller updates her belief about the market condition as time progresses, but at each moment the price is set as if the market condition is known and equal to its current estimate. Thus, prices are not used proactively to affect learning, but nevertheless they are used in the learning mechanism to update the belief about the market condition. The authors develop and test a simple certainty-equivalent heuristic to this end.

Aviv and Pazgal (2005b) continue with the same line of the previous work, introducing two additional forms of uncertainty. Recall that in Aviv and Pazgal (2005a) the purchasing probability $\alpha(p)$ was given and known. In other words, that model assumes that while there is uncertainty about the market size, there is complete certainty about the sensitivity of customers to pricing. Obviously, this assumption does not hold in many practical settings (see, e.g., Johnson (2001), for a discussion of the toy industry). Aviv and Pazgal model the joint uncertainty about the market size and sensitivity to prices via a set of K scenarios, Ω. Specifically, a scenario of type $k \in \Omega$ (also called state k) is characterized by a discrete, price- and period-dependent probability function b_k, where $b_k(d \mid t, p)$ is the probability that the demand during period t of type k is d, given that a price p was set for this period. Additionally, each state k is characterized by a Poisson arrival process with a given rate $\lambda_k > 0$. Unlike the previous paper, the current model is periodic, with the seller specifying prices over T periods of time. The second type of uncertainty introduced in this paper has to do with the dynamics in the market. Often, demand for retail goods depends on changes in basic economic variables that describe either the economy as a whole, or the state of the specific industry. The authors model this dynamics as a sequence of (possibly random) transitions between states, governed by a Markov chain. To reflect settings in which the retailers do not fully observe the exact core state of the demand environment, the authors use a partially observed Markov decision process (POMDP) framework. A POMDP is a sequential decision problem, pertaining to a dynamic setting, where information concerning the state of the world is incomplete. One of the key findings of their research is that pricing should be primarily driven by the level of inventory and time-to-go, whereas the influence of pricing on learning should not be a concern. For example, the authors also found that limited look-ahead policies may work well when inventory is unlimited. However, when inventory is limited, the sub-performance of such policy can be as bad as 30 percent.

Recently, Araman and Caldentey (2009) proposed a model of dynamic pricing in which a retailer sells a finite, perishable capacity to a customer population that is driven by a price-sensitive Poisson process. Similarly to Aviv and Pazgal (2005a), they assume that the Poisson process depends on an unknown parameter, and that the retailer has a prior belief in its value. This belief evolves over time, as prices and sales realize. However, in contrast to the mainstream literature on dynamic pricing models, the main feature of this paper is that it allows the retailer to consider the opportunity cost—given by the long-term average discounted profit that the retailer can gain if she stops selling the current product and starts selling a different assortment. The authors formulate the retailer's problem as an intensity control problem, where the retailer's task is to maximize her long-term average profit. Unfortunately, the intensity control problem is hard to solve and, therefore, the authors propose a simple approximation to compute the value function and a close-to-optimal pricing strategy. They show that the approximation performs exceptionally well, with a relative error of 1 percent, strikingly better than that of a myopic policy which exhibits an average error of 30 percent.

Boyaci and Özer (2010) consider a capacity planning strategy in which a manufacturer collects purchase commitments from customers prior to determining his production capacity. The manufacturer's problem is stated as a dynamic planning process that consists of T periods. During each of these periods, customers may place advance orders (commitments to purchase), and thus the manufacturer can learn about demand over time. The manufacturer has only one opportunity to invest in capacity before the regular sales season starts. In other words, the manufacturer needs to decide in which period to stop offering advance sales and move on to building capacity. The advantage of postponing the capacity decision is that the manufacturer can learn more about demand. However, postponement results in increasing capacity buildup costs. The authors study two pricing systems: An exogenous pricing scenario, in which the manufacturer follows a predetermined sequence of prices for the advance sales periods as well as the regular selling season. The second system uses an optimal pricing strategy in which the manufacturer jointly determines the optimal levels of capacity and the advance and regular sales prices.

For the exogenous pricing scenario, the authors show (Theorem 1) that a state-dependent control band policy is optimal. Under this policy, the capacity decision is made when the cumulative commitments fall within a given range (control band). To understand the rationale behind this policy structure, note that if the cumulative commitments are too low, then it makes sense to continue acquiring information so as to further resolve market uncertainty. When the cumulative commitments are sufficiently high (i.e., strong market potential), the manufacturer may gain from an opportunity to sell at a different price point by postponing the capacity investment decision for another period. Interestingly, even when commitments carry no predictive power (i.e., when future demand uncertainty cannot be resolved based on the observations of commitments), it can be optimal to continue offering advance sales. This is because the aggregate demand uncertainty (and hence mismatch costs) is reduced due to the observations of the early demand. For the joint capacity and price optimization scenario, the authors characterize the optimal strategy. In particular, they show (Theorem 5) that the structure of the optimal policy continues to possess a state-dependent control band form, as mentioned above.

Using a numerical study, Boyaci and Özer gauge the expected value of the dynamic planning strategy. They show that it is beneficial to a manufacturer when demand uncertainty is high, when customers anticipate capacity shortage in the market, capacity is costly but the timing of construction does not influence this cost in a significant way, commitments have moderate predictive power, and price sensitivity is relatively low. The authors further argue that these conditions are prevalent in industries such as high technology, apparel, and pharmaceuticals.

23.4.3 Heuristics for dynamic pricing systems with learning

Carvalho and Puterman (2005) develop and compare several heuristic pricing policies. For a two-period model, they construct a Taylor expansion of the reward function to explain the tradeoff between short-term revenue maximization and future information gains. The authors use the latter result to develop a "one-step look-ahead" policy for a periodic-review pricing control.

Bertsimas and Perakis (2006) present a set of optimization models in which sellers consider the joint problem of learning and pricing. In the first part of their work, they consider the case of no competition, assuming that the monopolist faces an uncertain demand that follows a linear form of the type

$$d_t = \beta^0 + \beta^1 p_t + \varepsilon_t$$

The parameters β^0 and β^1 are unknown, and the noise ε_t is normally distributed with mean zero and standard deviation σ. The authors develop a Kalman filter recursive algorithm for computing the least-squares estimates of the unknown parameters, as well as the residual level of uncertainty about these parameters' values. Since the Kalman filter algorithm is Markovian, the authors are able to embed it within a dynamic program which represents the seller's revenue maximization problem. As expected, the dynamic program is multidimensional (in fact, its underlying state is eight-dimensional), making it practically intractable. As a result, the authors pursue alternative (approximate) models of lower dimensionality. They first propose an approximation that results in a dynamic problem with five dimensions. They then propose two easily-solvable models which are based on the idea of separating the demand estimation from the pricing problem. The first heuristic is similar in spirit to the certainty-equivalent heuristics employed by Aviv and Pazgal (2005a, 2005b): The firm computes the estimates of the β parameters at the beginning of each period, and then solves a one-dimensional dynamic pricing problem under the assumption that the β-estimates are the real values of the unknown parameters. The second heuristic is based on the deterministic counterpart of the model; that is, the same model with all ε_t assumed to be equal to their mean value (zero). Here, again, the β values are re-estimated at the beginning of every period, and they are assumed to be the true values, before solving the deterministic problem. The authors conduct numerical studies of the above heuristics, as well as a myopic heuristic, and find that, often, the former heuristics significantly outperform the latter one.

In their second part of the paper, Bertsimas and Perakis consider a competitive oligopolistic environment. In this case, a firm needs to learn not only about their own demand function, but also about their competitors' demand functions. The demands are assumed to be linear, as before, but now they are functions of all firms' prices: for firm k, the demand is given by

$$d_{k,t} = \beta_{k,t}^o + \sum_{l \in \{-k\}} \beta_{k,t}^l p_{l,t} + \beta_{k,t}^k p_{k,t} + \varepsilon_{k,t}$$

Under the assumption that price elasticities vary slowly as a function of time, the authors propose a learning mechanism and, again, embed it into a set of approximate dynamic programs.

Farias and van Roy (2010) study a dynamic pricing model of a vendor with limited inventory, faced with customers that arrive according to a Poisson process with an uncertain rate. Customers' reservations prices are independent of each other and have a distribution F with non-decreasing hazard rate. Let N_t represent the number of purchases up to time t, and τ_0 the time at which the last unit is sold. The authors argue that the seller's expected revenue is given by

$$E\left[\int_{t=0}^{\infty} e^{-\alpha t} p_t dN_t \right] = E\left[\int_{t=0}^{\tau_0} e^{-\alpha t} p_t \lambda \bar{F}(p_t) dt \right],$$

where α is the seller's discount rate. To solve the seller's expected revenue maximization problem, one could set up a dynamic program that is identical to that of Aviv and Pazgal (2005a). First, the authors establish the same updating (learning) scheme property as in the latter paper; see (19) above. Similarly to Aviv and Pazgal, they also infer the HJB equation for this dynamic optimization problem. The authors then present three heuristics. The first, *certainty-equivalent heuristic*, is identical to that proposed by Aviv and Pazgal (2005a): At each point of time, the seller updates the expected value of the arrival rate, conditioned on the sales and price history. Then, the seller assumes that this expected value is the actual value of the arrival rate λ, and solves the dynamic pricing problem (see the discussion about Gallego and van Ryzin (1994) in Section 23.2). The second, *greedy pricing heuristic*, is identical to that proposed by Araman and Caldentey (2009). The third, *decay balancing heuristic*, introduced by the authors, is based on a computationally efficient algorithm which utilizes the solution to the original problem without uncertainty about the arrival rate. Furthermore, it is based on an approximation to the value function which takes into account the changes in the inventory levels, as well as the current estimate and residual uncertainty about the arrival rate. The authors find that the decay balancing performs close-to-optimal even in problems with high levels of uncertainty about the arrival rate, and that their resulting price paths are intuitively appealing (in contrast, e.g., to abnormal behavior that the certainty-equivalent and the greedy heuristics might exhibit).

Besbes and Zeevi (2009) develop two models of dynamic pricing, that primarily differ from each other on the basis of the structure of the uncertainty. The first model reflects settings in which the demand function does not admit any known parametric representation. For this case, the authors propose a pricing algorithm that is driven by two tuning parameters. One parameter specifies the length of the "exploration period" (during which prices are primarily driven by their ability to provide the seller with the ability to learn about demand). After that period, the seller shifts the focus to "exploitation"; that is, focusing less on the impact of prices on learning. The other tuning parameter specifies the number of prices to be tested during the exploration period. In the second model, the authors consider a situation in which the seller knows the parametric structure of the demand function; however, she does not know the values of some of this function's parameters. A very similar algorithm to the one proposed for the non-parametric case is suggested. In fact, the only change in the algorithm is that now the seller can utilize the known parametric structure to infer accurate information about the demand, using only a small number of test prices. To test the performance of the above pricing heuristics, the authors use the *regret* measure—the loss in revenues benchmarked against the maximal revenues that could be gained under the case of full information (i.e., if the demand function was known prior to the beginning of the sales season). The authors derive lower bounds on the regret, which allows them to gauge the effectiveness of their algorithms.

Recently, Levin et al. (2009) studied a dynamic pricing with learning model for a seller that faces strategic customers. In the learning procedure, the seller deploys an *aggregating algorithm* (AA)—a method for online learning developed by Vovk (1990). Upon learning, which is done periodically, the seller utilizes a simulation-based procedure in order to determine the price for the product. In order to reflect the strategic consumer behavior, the authors propose a game-theoretical consumer choice model, in which customers weigh the benefits of an immediate purchase versus a wait-for-discount action. The model assumes that consumers exhibit some limited rationality in their choices. The authors argue that the above pricing procedure is efficient, relatively general, and independent of specific distributional assumptions.

23.4.4 Models of intertemporal valuations with learning

In this last section, we survey models in which learning does not occur on the seller's side. Instead, when the consumers need to make their purchase decisions, they are uncertain about their own valuation for consuming the product at a future date. For example, consider a customer that plans to purchase a ticket for a concert that will take place in a few months. This person is not even sure about his future state (e.g., health, expected conflicts, mood) at the time of the concert. In this type of situation, a consumer faces two sources of uncertainty: first, his own random value for the capacity (which will be realized later), and secondly, the availability of capacity at the time of use.

Png (1989) proposes a two-period model of pricing and capacity sizing in a market where a known number of risk-averse customers are *ex ante* uncertain about their valuation for use of capacity. As unused capacity has no salvage value, the seller maximizes profit by economizing on capacity through overbooking. Because customers are risk-averse, they seek insurance, which is provided in a form of the ability to reserve a unit of capacity.

The seller is risk-neutral and the natural provider of insurance. But provision of insurance is complicated since each customer's realized valuation is private information that is difficult for third parties to verify. Hence, the seller needs to elicit this information.

Png shows that the optimal pricing strategy takes the form of a reservation that the seller offers at no charge. The reservation is designed so that the customer exercises it only if his value for the capacity is high. It provides each customer with full insurance against unavailability of capacity but only partial insurance against uncertainty in valuation. The paper provides rationality for why airlines, hotels, and car rental agencies take reservations free of charge. The reason is that the price of the reservation is also the payment by the customer in the event that his valuation is low. A full-information insurance contract would call for the seller to compensate the customer in that event. But in the absence of full information, such a contract would draw speculators to place reservations for the sake of the compensation. Png argues that the best policy is not to charge the customer for the reservation.

Shugan and Xie (2000) also note that the separation between the purchase and consumption times creates uncertainty about a buyer's own utility. They explore the desirability and implications of this separation; namely, should a service provider strategically influence time-separation? The authors show that service providers can earn more profit by advance selling than only spot pricing at the time of consumption. Interestingly, in the special case in which buyers are homogeneous with respect to valuations in the advance-purchase period (but not the consumption period), advance pricing can provide profits equal to the profits from near perfect (i.e., first-degree) price discrimination in the consumption period.

In a follow-up paper, Xie and Shugan (2001) show that the additional profits under advance selling come from more buyers being able to purchase. They find that although optimal advance prices can be at a discount to the spot price, sometimes a premium is optimal. Premiums are optimal when capacity is large (but limited) and marginal costs are not too large. Buyers advance purchase at a premium to spot prices when capacity is limited and spot prices are low (they point out that this is not about a risk premium, since risk aversion is not required). If the order of arrivals does not respect the low-before-high willingness-to-pay assumption, premium advance pricing could be optimal.

Xie and Shugan also notice that binding capacity constraints can impact the profitability of advance selling in opposite ways. On one hand, capacity constraints create seller credibility. Buyers believe that spot prices will be high when they know spot capacity is limited (and perhaps, even more limited by advance sales). On the other hand, when capacity is limited, the need to increase sales from discounted advance prices diminishes. They also show that buyer risk aversion can sometimes increase the profitability of advance selling. Consistent with Desiraju and Shugan (1999), they identify benefits from limiting advance sales when: (1) selling to early arrivals would leave insufficient capacity in the spot period for high-valuation arrivals, (2) the optimal spot price is high, and (3) marginal costs are sufficiently small to make advance selling profitable.

Gallego and Şahin (2010) also consider the case in which customer's valuations for a product are not fully revealed until the end of the selling horizon (i.e., booking process). The models that they explore also account for inter-temporal uncertainty in valuations, which allows an explanation and quantification of why forward price discounts are needed to induce customers to buy early. Moreover, modeling uncertainty in valuations leads to innovative product design ideas that are appealing to customers and to service providers, like offering call options on capacity that include low-to-high pricing as a special case. In a two-period model, the call option involves an option price paid in period 1 for the right to purchase a unit of capacity in period 2 at a specified strike price. Call options would be exercised only by option holders whose realized valuations in period 2 exceed the strike price. They show that including call options strictly and significantly improves expected revenues over traditional low-to-high pricing for all capacity levels that are likely to arise in practice.

In addition, Gallego and Şahin provide structural results for a fluid approximation of a two-period model with finite capacity and Poisson arrivals, including closed-form, distribution-free, bounds for the strike price and the optimal revenue. They also show that the solution to the fluid model is asymptotically optimal for the stochastic problem with overbooking, and extend the analysis to a multi-period setting.

23.5 DYNAMIC PRICING WITH FORWARD-LOOKING CONSUMERS—STRATEGIC WAITING

In this section, we survey an important recent stream of research in RM; namely, dynamic pricing under strategic consumer behavior. Often, sellers are faced with customers who may time their purchases in anticipation of future discounts. When customers exhibit such strategic behavior, the seller's ability to employ effective price segmentation is adversely affected. For example, in his famous paper, Coase (1972) considers a monopolist that sells a durable good to a large set of consumers with different valuations. In a benchmark case that represents an ideal setting for the seller, Coase considers a seller that employs *perfect segmentation* by charging each customer his own valuation. This is illustrated by a dynamic pricing process in which the seller initially charges a high price from the high-valuation customers; then, the seller sequentially reduces the prices to capture customers with smaller valuations. Such strategy is named *price-skimming*, and if it works as perfectly as planned, it results in extracting all of the consumer surplus. However, Coase argues that if high-valuation customers anticipate a price decline, they might wait for a price reduction rather than buy at premium prices. Under such behavior, Coase shows that in equilibrium, the seller effectively sells the product at marginal cost. This relatively simple model demonstrates that the consequences of strategic behavior could be dramatic.

Coase suggests a number of ways for the seller to avoid this phenomenon. For example, the seller can make a special contractual arrangement with the purchasers not to sell more than a given quantity of the product. In fact, this idea is close in spirit to the subject of *capacity rationing* we discuss later; see, for example, Liu and van Ryzin (2008a). Alternatively, the seller could offer customers to buy back the product if it was offered in the future at a lower price. This idea is very similar to the subject of *internal price guarantees* that we also survey later. The seller could also lease the product for relatively short periods of time and, for instance, announce that she would not change the rental price during the lease period.

As we previously discussed, the presence of *inventory constraints* brings up many interesting points. For example, when supply is limited, strategic customers need to consider not only future prices, but also the likelihood of stockouts. Consequently, one may expect that strategic consumer behavior will not have a significant impact on the retailer's revenue, since the shortage risk that customers face serves as a deterring factor against waiting for price discounts. However, this logic is incomplete, as argued by Aviv and Pazgal (2008): When inventory is low, the seller typically wants to charge a higher initial price as a "betting strategy". Essentially, the betting is made in an attempt to capture high margins from high-valuation customers who may visit the store. If such customers do not arrive, the seller can then reduce the price, and is still likely to sell its product, since the inventory quantity is small. However, if customers understand this strategy, and anticipate that the seller will sharply reduce prices later, they will feel inclined to wait. In summary, low inventory levels may increase the stockout probability, but may also increase the expected depth of discount.

23.5.1 Early models with no inventory considerations

Stokey (1979) considers a monopolist selling a product to customers by announcing a continuously declining price scheme over a finite horizon of length T. As in most papers with strategic consumers, time indices run forward so that from now onwards, we set $t = 0$ and $t = T$ as the beginning and end of the horizon, respectively. All customers are present at the store from $t = 0$ until the end of the season (or until they purchase a unit of the product; whichever occurs first). The interest (time-discount) rate, δ, is fixed and assumed to be equal for the customers and the seller.

Customers are heterogeneous in their reservation prices ν, distributed according to a density function f over the range $[0, \bar{\nu}]$, with F denoting the cumulative distribution. All customers share a common utility function $U(t, \nu)$, where t is the purchasing time. The utility function satisfies the conditions: $U(0, \nu) = \nu$, $\partial U/\partial t < 0$, $\partial U/\partial \nu > 0$, and $\partial^2 U/\partial \nu \partial t < 0$. The customer's *net welfare gain* is then defined by

$$W(t, \nu) = U(t, \nu) - e^{-\delta t} p(t).$$

Strategic behavior is considered in the following way. For any given announced price schedule $(p(t) : t \in [0, T])$, when should a customer with reservation ν buy the product (if at all)? In its main part, the paper explores the case of zero production costs. Stokey presents the first- and second-order conditions on the optimal timing of purchase. She then shows that purchase timings are nonincreasing in ν; namely, a customer with a given valuation never buys before someone else who values the product more. There could be situations in which a set of customers with sufficiently high valuations (i.e., above a certain threshold ν_0) will buy the product immediately at the beginning of the sales period. Similarly, there could be a portion of the population, with sufficiently low valuations (i.e., below a certain threshold ν_2) that will never buy the product. Let $\tau(\nu)$ denote the optimal purchasing time for a customer with valuation ν. Note that the monopolist is expected to gain a discounted profit[8] of $e^{-\delta \tau(\nu)} \cdot p(\tau(\nu))$ from any customer with valuation $\nu \in [\nu_2, \bar{\nu}]$. The monopolist is hence interested in solving the following problem:

---

[8] Profit and revenues can be used interchangeably since production costs are assumed to be equal to zero.

$$\max_{(p(t):t\in[0,\,T])} \pi(p(t)) \stackrel{\Delta}{=} \int_{v_2}^{\bar{v}} e^{-\delta\tau(v)} \cdot p(\tau(v))dF(v)$$

One of the interesting results obtained by solving the latter problem, is that the discount rate does not change the optimal sales pattern. In other words, while the prices vary as a function of δ, the occurrences (i.e., timing) of sales remain identical. Stokey explains this result as driven by the assumption that production is immediate, and bears no cost. It is also shown that the impact of starting the sales season at a later time, has a very simple effect on the sales pattern. Essentially, all of those customers who would have purchased the product between the original start-of-season time and the new one, would purchase the product at the new start time. The remainder of the sales pattern (i.e., to the end of the season) will stay unaltered. Perhaps more interestingly, Stokey shows that when the monopolist shortens the sales season, the optimal sales pattern remains unchanged within the length of the new season. Nonetheless, the optimal price schedule must be changed. She hence concludes that it is crucial for the monopolist to know how long she can sell the product, so that pricing can be set appropriately.

One model extension in Stokey's paper is worth mentioning. This is a special case in which the utility function takes the form $U(t, v) = g(t) \cdot v$, where $g(t)$ is a positive and declining function of time. In other words, customers experience the same rate of decline in the utility over time. Under this case, it is shown that all sales take place at the very first moment of the season, with the seller charging a price $p(0) = g(0) \cdot v_2$, where v_2 is the optimal valuation cutoff point. The implication of the latter result is that price discrimination is not possible (note that segmentation still takes place, in the form of targeting customers with valuations in the range $[v_2, \bar{v}]$ only). Furthermore, the quantity of sales is independent of the interest rate, the final sales date, and even the function $g(t)$. Instead, it only depends on the distribution of valuations in the population. We refer the interested reader to the paper for model extensions that explore settings with positive production costs.

Landsberger and Meilijson (1985) analyze a simplified version of Stokey (1979), in which a customer with valuation v gains a net utility of

$$W(t, v) = (v - p(t)) \cdot e^{-\delta t}$$

when buying the product at time t. This is equivalent to the case $g(t) = e^{-\delta t}$ in Stokey's terms. Recall that Stokey's finding is that price discrimination is *not* profitable under these conditions. However, here the authors assume that the consumers and seller have different discount rates. Landsberger and Meilijson demonstrate that in order to profitably employ price discrimination, the seller needs to postpone price discounts to the extent that it will not be beneficial for customers to wait (given the discount rate δ). In return, high-valuation customers will buy earlier, whereas lower valuation customers will wait. Now, a critical question obviously comes up: Can the seller get any value from the lower valuation customers? Stokey has already answered this question in a special condition; namely, with the seller facing the same discount rate as the customers, she cannot gain any value from future sales, hence targeting a portion of the customer population at the very beginning of the sales season, and not selling to the other portion. Here, Landsberger and Meilijson show that price discrimination could be profitable, but if and only if the seller's discount rate is sufficiently lower than the customers' discount rate.

Besanko and Winston (1990) introduce a game theoretic model of a monopolistic seller facing a market of strategic consumers with heterogeneous valuations. The distribution of these valuations is uniform over the interval $[0, \bar{v}]$. Customers know their individual valuations, but the monopolist is only privy to the statistical distribution characteristics. The population size is known and equal to N; in fact, all customers are present in the "store" from the beginning of the game. The monopolist has T periods of time to set the price, with p_t denoting the price in period t. The seller's production capacity is unlimited, so any desired quantity can be produced at any period, at cost c per unit (where $c < \bar{v}$).[9] The customers and the seller are assumed to have the same time discount factor δ.

Besanko and Winston look for a subgame perfect equilibrium, in which the seller makes the optimal pricing decision in each given period, and customers respond by making their best purchasing decisions. The authors first establish that in response to a given seller's pricing scheme, it is optimal for customers to follow a *threshold-type* purchasing policy, characterized by a sequence of thresholds $\{v_t\}$. Specifically, in period t, all customers still at the store with valuations larger or equal to v_t purchase the product and leave, whereas all other customers (i.e., with valuations below v_t) stay at the store. Besanko and Winston "guess" that prices and thresholds in subsequent periods are set in a way that makes a customer with valuation v_t indifferent between: (1) purchasing the product immediately and gaining a surplus of $v_t - p_t$; and (2) waiting for the next period and gaining a *discounted* surplus of $\delta \cdot (v_t - \tilde{p}_{t+1})$ (where $\tilde{p}_{t+1}$ is the *anticipated* price in following period, $t + 1$). Next, for a given purchasing policy $\{v_t\}$ that satisfies the latter conditions, the authors study the seller's best pricing scheme.

Let $p_t^*(v_{t-1})$ be the seller's equilibrium pricing strategy at time t, when faced with all remaining customers with valuations $[0, v_{t-1}]$. The authors propose the following dynamic program which represents the seller's equilibrium discounted profit over periods t through T, in a recursive fashion. Assuming that $H_{t+1}^*(v_t)$ has already been solved, they seek:

$$H_t^*(v_{t-1}) = \max_{p_t, v_t} \left\{ (p_t - c) \cdot \frac{v_{t-1} - v_t}{\bar{v}} \cdot N + \delta H_{t+1}^*(v_t) \right\}$$

s.t.

$$v_t \leq v_{t-1},$$
$$v_t - p_t = \delta \cdot \left(v_t - p_{t+1}^*(v_t) \right)$$

with $v_0 = \bar{v}$. The dynamic program stated above serves as a basis for calculating a subgame perfect Nash equilibrium for the game (we refer the reader to Proposition 1 in Besanko and Winston (1990) for the specific technical details). The authors show that in the above type of equilibrium, prices monotonically decline over time; in other words, *price skimming* arises in equilibrium.

To analyze the consequences of strategic consumer behavior, Besanko and Winston propose a benchmark model in which all customers are myopic. It is easy to see that when customers are myopic, the purchasing threshold in period t is simply $v_t = p_t$. Consequently, the seller's optimal pricing policy is provided by a solution to the dynamic program

---

[9] From now onwards, and consistently with the literature discussed in this section, c will refer to unit cost.

$$H_t(v_{t-1}) = \max_{p_t : p_t \leq v_{t-1}} \left\{ (p_t - c) \cdot \frac{v_{t-1} - p_t}{\bar{v}} \cdot N + \delta H_{t+1}(p_t) \right\}$$

Comparing the two models, Besanko and Winston show that with myopic consumers, the price is always higher in any given state than it is with strategic consumers. In other words, the first-period price with myopic consumers is higher than the first-period price with strategic consumers. It is noteworthy, however, that because the time paths of sales in the two cases differ, it is possible that the price with myopic consumers will fall below the price with strategic consumers in later periods. Two other interesting observations are made in the paper. First, the authors illustrate a situation in which a seller that commits to a price path that is based on the myopic case, and use it when customers are actually strategic, might significantly hurt her expected profit. Second, the authors argue that for any v, $H_t^*(v)$ is increasing in t (recall time indices run forward in this setting). In contrast, $\hat{H}_t(v)$ (the optimal expected profit in the myopic case) is decreasing in t. Consequently, starting in any state v, a monopolist prefers a shorter time horizon if faced with strategic consumers, but a longer time horizon if faced with myopic consumers. The intuition behind this is that the shorter is the time horizon, the smaller is the power of strategic consumers. In contrast, with myopic consumers, the monopolist prefers a longer time horizon because it gives her more flexibility in setting prices over time and hence extracting more revenues.

Finally, we direct the reader to Stokey (1981), Conlisk et al. (1984), and Sobel (1984) for additional references on the above line of literature.

23.5.2 Models with limited inventories

In this section, we survey the use of different strategies that have been proposed (and in some cases, implemented) in order to mitigate the adverse impact of consumer strategic behavior.

23.5.2.1 The use of markdowns: Contingent versus pre-announced discounts

Aviv and Pazgal (2008) consider a seller that has Q units of an item, available for sale during a sales horizon of length H. The sales season $[0, H]$ is split into two parts, $[0, T]$ and $[T, H]$, for a given fixed value T. During the first part of the season, a premium price p_1 applies, and during the second phase of the season a discount price p_2 is offered (where $p_2 \leq p_1$). The seller's objective is to set the premium and discount prices in order to maximize the expected total revenues collected during the sales horizon. An important feature of their model is that it includes two types of demand uncertainty: the total market size, and the time of arrivals. Specifically, it is assumed that customers arrive at the store following a Poisson process with rate λ. Customers' valuations of the product vary across the population, and decline over the course of the season according to

$$v_j(t) = v_j \cdot e^{-\delta t}$$

for every customer j. Specifically, customer j's base valuation v_j is drawn from a given continuous distribution form F. Then, depending on the particular time of purchase t, the realized valuation is discounted appropriately by a known exponential decline factor $\delta \geq 0$, fixed across the population. Customers who arrive prior to time T behave according to the following strategy: A given customer j, arriving at time t, will purchase immediately upon arrival (if there is inventory) if two conditions are satisfied about his current surplus $v_j e^{-\delta t} - p_1$: (1) it is non-negative; and (2) it is larger or equal to the expected surplus he can gain from a purchase at time T (when the price is changed to p_2). Of course, the latter expected surplus depends on the customer's belief about p_2 as well as the likelihood that a unit will be available to the customer. If the customer purchases a unit, he leaves the store immediately. Otherwise, the customer stays until time T. At time T, the seller observes the purchases, or equivalently, her level of inventory. She then determines the discounted price p_2, which depends on the remaining inventory at time T.

When the discount is announced at time T, all existing customers with valuations larger or equal to p_2, attempt to purchase a unit (if still available). In case there are fewer units than the number of customers who wish to buy, the allocation is made randomly. After time T, new customers may still arrive; they buy according to whether or not they can immediately gain a non-negative surplus.

Aviv and Pazgal identify a subgame-perfect Nash equilibrium for the game between the customers and the seller. Note that the seller's strategy is characterized by the initial premium price p_1 and the discounted price menu $\{p_2(q)\}_{q=1}^Q$. The customers' strategy is one that prescribes purchasing decisions for every possible pair of individual arrival time t, and base valuation v. They first study the best response of the customers to a given seller's pure strategy of the form $p_1, p_2(1), \ldots, p_2(Q)$. The response strategy is based on a competitive situation that exists among consumers, which arises due to the fact that an individual consumer's decision impacts the product availability for others. It is shown that a time-dependent threshold policy emerges. Specifically, a customer arriving at any given time $t < T$ will purchase an available unit immediately upon arrival if his valuation is at least as high as the threshold value at time t. Otherwise, the customer will revisit the store at time T, and purchase an available unit if his valuation is larger than or equal to the discounted price posted. Next, the seller's strategy is studied; namely, the best contingent pricing $\{p_2(1), \ldots, p_2(Q)\}$ in response to a given purchasing strategy, and a given initial premium price p_1. Finally, in order to maximize the expected total revenue over the sales horizon, the seller needs to pick the best premium price p_1.

In order to measure the benefit of price segmentation, Aviv and Pazgal consider the expected increase in revenues obtained by moving from an optimal static-pricing strategy (π_F^*), to a two-price strategy. Like Besanko and Winston (1990), they also consider benchmark models in which all customers are myopic. Their findings are summarized next: In general, the benefit of price segmentation appears to be very significant under the case of myopic customers. Unlike the case of myopic customers, they show that strategic customer behavior clearly interferes with the benefits of price segmentation. Strategic consumer behavior suppresses the benefits of segmentation, under medium-to-high values of heterogeneity and modest rates of decline in valuations. An underlying reason for this is that when the rate of decline in valuation is small, customers are patient in waiting for the discount time. Not only that, but unlike the case of fixed-price strategies, customers rationally expect discounts to take place. However, when the level of consumer heterogeneity is small, the rate of decline is medium-to-high, and the time of discount can be optimally chosen (in advance) by the seller, segmentation can be used quite effectively even with strategic consumers. The rationale for the result is that under these conditions, there is typically a little difference in price valuations at the time of discount. Hence, the discount price is generally set in a way that does not offer a substantial surplus to consumers.

The seller cannot effectively avoid the adverse impact of strategic behavior even under low levels of initial inventory. When the initial inventory level is low, the seller expects customers to be more concerned about product availability at discount time, and thus act in a similar way to myopic customers. However, for myopic consumers the seller should benefit from high-price experimentation. In other words, the seller would set a high price for the initial period of time in order to bet on collecting large revenues, speculating that a small number of unsold units can be easily sold at the end of the season. But high-price experimentations (which practically means high expected discounts) in the case of strategic consumers could drive customers to wait even if the availability probability is relatively low. Thus, high-price betting cannot be sustained in equilibrium.

When the seller incorrectly assumes that strategic customers are myopic in their purchasing decisions, it can be quite costly, reaching up to 20 percent loss of potential revenues. When the level of heterogeneity is large, misclassification results in offering high discounts. Now, if valuations do not decline significantly during the horizon, strategic customers would most likely wait. The dependency of the sub-optimality gap on the rate of decline in valuations works in two different ways. On one hand, when it is small, customers are typically more inclined to wait, but their valuations do not decline significantly. When the rate of decline is high, fewer customers will decide to wait, but the rapid decline in these customers' valuations would hurt the seller's ability to extract high revenues at time of discount. Finally, when customers' valuations are homogeneous and the decline rate is large, strategic customers do not have a substantial incentive to wait, and so misclassification is not expected to lead to significant loss.

In addition to the model described above, Aviv and Pazgal also consider a two-period pricing problem in which the seller commits upfront to a fixed price path (p_1, p_2). Interestingly, sellers such as Filene's Basement (e.g., see Bell and Starr 1994), Land's End, and Syms have used this method for pricing some of their products. Consider for a moment the case of myopic customers. Clearly, in such settings, a fixed discount is generally not optimal. The seller could obviously increase her expected revenues by waiting until time T and *then* determine the best price discount according to the remaining amount of inventory on hand. The same logic does not straightforwardly apply in face of strategic customers. In fact, under strategic consumer behavior there could be cases in which announced pricing schemes may perform better than contingent pricing policies. This is because the seller could possibly discourage strategic waiting if it can credibly commit to a smaller discount than otherwise expected by consumers.

The authors find that announced fixed-discount strategies perform essentially the same as contingent pricing policies in the case of myopic consumers. However, they suggest caution in interpreting this result. First, they consider the *optimal* announced discount. If a seller picks an arbitrary discount level, the sub-performance with respect to contingent pricing can be very high. Secondly, announced discounts prevent the seller from acting upon *learning* about demand. Under strategic consumer behavior, they found that announced pricing policies can bring an advantage to the seller (up to 8.32 percent increase in expected revenues), compared to contingent pricing schemes. Particularly, they observed that announced pricing schemes are advantageous compared to contingent pricing schemes under the following conditions: (1) The number of units are sufficiently high; (2) the level of heterogeneity in base valuations is high; (3) the discounts are offered at a late part of the season; and (4) the rate of decline in valuations is at a medium level. The underlying reason for the better performance of announced discount strategies, is that a credible pre-commitment to a fixed discount level avoids the situation in which customers rationally expect the seller to (optimally) offer large discounts. Interestingly, they found that in those cases that announced discount strategies offer a significant advantage compared to contingent pricing policies, they appear to offer only a minimal advantage in comparison to fixed pricing policies.

23.5.2.2 *Capacity rationing*

Liu and van Ryzin (2008a) propose a model for examining the potential value of *rationing strategies*. Under such strategies, a seller deliberately understocks a product, hence creating a shortage risk for customers. As a consequence, this motivates high-valuation customers to purchase early in the season at premium prices. In their model, a (monopoly) firm pre-announces a single-markdown pricing policy over two periods: A premium price p_1 for the first period, and a discounted price, p_2, for the second period. Similarly to some of the models surveyed in the previous section, this situation represents a setting in which the seller is able to make a price commitment. The market size, denoted by N, is deterministic, and consists of strategic consumers that are present at the store from the beginning of the horizon. Consumers have heterogeneous valuations that are independently drawn from a known distribution F, and they enjoy a utility of $u(v - p)$ when they have valuation v and purchase a unit at price p. The model assumes that the market size is large enough so that strategic interaction between customers can be ignored. The firm seeks to maximize profits by choosing its stocking quantity (capacity) at the beginning of the sales season.

When making their purchasing decisions, customers weigh the immediate utility $u(v - p_1)$ (reflecting a "buy now" choice), against the expected utility that they can gain in the second period. But to calculate the latter value, the customers need to multiply the utility $u(v - p_2)$ by the likelihood that a unit will be available. This probability, denoted by q, is assumed to be estimated exactly at the same value by all customers. It follows that, for any given q, the customers optimally follow a threshold policy with a parameter $v(q)$. This threshold value is implicitly defined by the equation

$$u(v - p_1) = q \cdot u(v - p_2)$$

Consequently, customers with valuations larger than $v(q)$ buy in period 1; the other customers wait for period 2.

The firm needs to determine its optimal capacity C, by taking into account the per-unit procurement cost c (assumed to be lower than p_2). But before we get into showing the formulation of the firm's decision problem, it is important to consider the connection between the capacity choice and the customers' behavior. Liu and van Ryzin show that under rational expectations:

$$q = \frac{C - N \cdot \bar{F}(v(q))}{N \cdot (F(v(q)) - F(p_2))}$$

the probability q is referred to as the *fill rate*. Note that $N \cdot \bar{F}(\nu(q))$ represents the number of customers who purchase the product (or more precisely, attempt to) in period 1. The term $N \cdot (F(\nu(q)) - F(p_2))$ is equal to the number of customers who are still in the market at the beginning of period 2, and have valuations that are at least as high as the discounted price p_2. Given prices p_1 and p_2, the firm's profit maximization in terms of ν and C is formulated as

$$\max_{\nu, C} \{N \cdot (p_1 - p_2) \cdot \bar{F}(\nu) + (p_2 - c) \cdot C\}$$

s.t.

$$u(\nu - p_1) = \frac{C - N \cdot \bar{F}(\nu(q))}{N \cdot (F(\nu(q)) - F(p_2))} \cdot u(\nu - p_2)$$

$$p_1 \leq \nu \leq \bar{\nu}$$

where $\bar{\nu}$ is an upper bound on the customers' valuations. Let us now follow the special case studied in that paper, where F is uniform over $[0, \bar{\nu}]$, and the utility function takes the form $u(\nu) = \nu^\gamma$ ($0 < \gamma < 1$). The parameter γ corresponds to the degree of risk aversion (lower values of γ correspond to more risk aversion). Under these assumptions, the authors show that the potential value of rationing depends on the number of high-valuation customers in the market (reflected by the parameter $\bar{\nu}$). Specifically, with a sufficiently large number of high-valuation customers in the market, it makes sense to adopt a rationing policy; otherwise, the firm should serve the entire market at the low price. The intuition behind this observation is simple. Note that by increasing the degree of rationing (i.e., less capacity brought to market), the firm induces higher demand in period 1 at the expense of missing the opportunity to serve some demand in period 2. Therefore, if the number of high-valuation customers in the market is small, the benefits gained in period 1 cannot justify the loss incurred in period 2. The authors find that when the firm can optimally select the prices, rationing is always an optimal strategy, for any value of $\bar{\nu}$. Liu and van Ryzin also explore the way in which the level of risk aversion γ influences the value of capacity rationing. They argue that when γ approaches 1 (i.e., customers becoming risk-neutral), the rationing risk that is needed in order to induce segmentation is very high. In other words, the planned leftover capacity level for period 2 should practically be set to 0 as γ approaches 1. Consequently, when the market consists of a sufficiently large number of high-valuation customers, it is optimal for the firm to serve the market only at the high price in period 1; otherwise, the firm serves the entire market at the low price only.

Liu and van Ryzin also study a model of oligopolistic competition. For the sake of brevity, we refer the interested reader to their paper for technical details (see Liu and van Ryzin 2008a: section 4.4). They show that competition makes it more difficult to support segmentation using rationing, and explain this as follows. When competing against a large number of other firms, a focal firm is very limited in her ability to create a sense of shortage risk. Thus, by reducing its capacity, a focal firm severely influences her own ability to serve demand, rather than drive high-valuation customers to buy at high prices. Particularly, the authors prove that there exists a critical number of firms beyond which creating rationing risk is never a sustainable equilibrium. Thus, rationing is more likely to be used in cases where a firm has some reasonable degree of market power.

Gallego et al. (2008) study a two-period pricing problem, in which a seller can offer all or some of her unsold inventory for sale in the second period, at a discount. The seller has a fixed capacity of C units. The market consists of N potential customers, each of which is characterized by a pair of valuations, v_1 and v_2, for a purchase of the product in periods 1 and 2, respectively. The valuations are private information, and the seller only knows their statistical distribution. The seller announces the prices in advance (p_1 and p_2). While there could be some customers with a second-period surplus ($v_2 - p_2$) larger than the first-period surplus ($v_1 - p_1$), customers may still be concerned about waiting, since the product might be in shortage. Hence, customers need to develop a rational estimate of product availability during the second period; this likelihood is denoted by q. Hence, a customer seeks to purchase in the first period if $v_1 - p_1 \geq q \cdot \max(v_2 - p_2, 0)$, in the second period if $q \cdot \max(v_2 - p_2, 0) \geq \max(v_1 - p_1, 0)$, but does not purchase if $v_1 < p_1$ and $v_2 < p_2$. Under these conditions, the optimal equilibrium policy is for the seller to set a single price, and not to restrict demand in the second period.

The authors show that when some of the above assumptions do not hold, different results can be expected. For instance, if the prices are exogenously given, the seller may want to control revenues, by creating a sense of shortage among the strategic consumers; hence, possibly limiting the second-period sales. If the market consists of myopic customers, the seller may want to use a discounting policy; this is because segmentation may become an effective tool. Additionally, under demand uncertainty (i.e., unknown value of N), it may be beneficial for the seller to utilize a markdown policy. The reason for that is that markdown pricing can be used as a contingent policy: The seller can experiment with a high price in the first period. If demand is high, the seller can enjoy high revenues. If demand happens to be low, the seller has an opportunity to gain better revenues by charging a lower price.

23.5.2.3 *The use of a* Quick Response *strategy*

Cachon and Swinney (2009) explore a two-period model that allows for dynamic planning of pricing and inventory. The price for the first period, p_1, is exogenously given. In the second period, the product is sold at a given markdown price p_2. The retailer's objective is to maximize her expected profit by selecting the optimal sale price and the initial level of inventory. The unit cost for the retailer is c.

The total number of customers that may purchase during the first period is random and denoted by D. Customers are heterogeneous in terms of their behavior. A portion of the customers ($\gamma \cdot D$) are strategic, and the remainder ($(1 - \gamma) \cdot D$) are myopic consumers that exist in the market in the first period only. All customers have the same (known) valuation in the first period, equal to v_1 ($v_1 \geq p_1$). The valuations of strategic customers in the second period changes in a random manner, assumed to be uniformly distributed between $[\underline{v}, \bar{v}]$ (where $\bar{v} \leq p_1$). It is assumed that strategic consumers know their individual second-period valuations in advance, from the beginning of period 1. In addition to the above mix of customers, the model introduces a third group of *bargain hunters*. These customers arrive only in period 2, and in large numbers; they are all assumed to share the same common valuation, v_2. The value of v_2 is assumed to be lower than the cost c, meaning that targeting this set of customers could be used as a mechanism for salvaging unsold inventory.

The retailer's and customers' actions are driven by a rational expectation equilibrium, as described below. First, in contemplating a "buy now vs. buy later" decision, a customer needs to assess the likelihood of getting a unit in period 2. Of course, this likelihood is influenced by the retailer's level of inventory, which is not directly observed. Hence, let $\hat{Q}$ be the customers' (common) belief about the initial stocking level of the retailer. Similarly, in order for the retailer to set the optimal inventory quantity, she needs to be able to anticipate the way in which customers make their purchasing decisions. Let $\hat{v}$ represent the belief that describes customers' threshold policy. The authors identify a subgame perfect Nash equilibrium with rational expectations to the game. Such equilibrium is denoted by (Q^*, v^*) and needs to satisfy a set of three conditions. First, the retailer is assumed to act optimally under her belief about the consumer behavior. In other words,

$$Q^* \in \arg\max_{Q \geq 0} \pi(Q, \hat{v})$$

where $\pi(Q, \hat{v})$ is equal to the retailer's expected profit under a given choice of initial inventory Q, and if all customers behaved according to the purchasing threshold policy $\hat{v}$. Secondly, the consumers' purchasing policy should be optimal if the seller indeed picks the initial quantity $\hat{Q}$. Let $v^*(Q)$ denote an optimal threshold policy for a known inventory Q. Then this condition is reflected by $v^* \in v^*(\hat{Q})$. Thirdly, the beliefs need to be consistent. In other words, $\hat{Q} = Q^*$, $\hat{v} = v^*$.

Cachon and Swinney show that if the demand is sufficiently large, the retailer should set the highest price that clears the existing inventory. If the demand is in some medium level, the retailer needs to optimally pick a price that maximizes the revenues collected from the remaining strategic customers. Typically, this will result in partial sales of the existing inventory. Finally, if the demand is at a relatively low level, the retailer should price at an inventory clearance price of v_2, making the product attractive to the large set of bargain hunters. The authors also show (Theorem 1) that the retailer orders less with strategic consumers compared to the case where she faces myopic customers only. To explain this, note that by lowering its initial inventory, the retailer raises the expected price in the second period, consequently inducing some strategic consumers to purchase at the full price. In other words, this behavior can be viewed as an act of capacity rationing. It is noteworthy to consider the authors' statement vis-à-vis this result:

> Other [researchers] have also found that the presence of strategic consumers causes a firm to lower its order quantity [e.g., Su and Zhang (2008)—discussed below—and Liu and van Ryzin (2008a)]. However, the mechanism by which this result is obtained is different: they depend on rationing risk, whereas in our model the result is due to price risk—strategic consumers expect they will receive a unit in the markdown period, but they do not know what the price will be. (Cachon and Swinney 2009: 505)

This observation is quite important in appreciating the value of the second model of Cachon and Swinney that we next present.

Consider now a situation in which the retailer can replenish her inventory at the beginning of period 2, after observing the demand D. Such type of replenishment option is generally feasible when the supply side (in terms of procurement, production, and delivery) is sufficiently responsive. Thus, the authors use the title *Quick Response* to reflect this situation. The analysis of the quick response setting appears to be very similar to that of the previous model. But, more importantly, the authors show that for a given value of $\hat{Q}$, the customers' behavior does not change in comparison to the situation with no replenishment opportunity. The driver of this result is that in both cases (with or without quick response), strategic customers can gain positive surplus in period 2 only if the demand happens to be sufficiently low. If that happens, then the retailer will not exercise the quick response option anyway. But the reader should not be confused. As can be expected, the retailer will not order the same number of units (Q) under both cases; we anticipate the initial order quantity to be lower with quick response, since the retailer can always order more later. In other words, the customers' behavior in equilibrium will be different (in general), depending on the feasibility of a quick response delivery. The authors also argue (Theorem 2) that quick response enables the retailer to increase the sense of rationing risk among strategic consumers, by ordering less. By driving strategic customers to purchase at the premium price p_1, the retailer gains an increased profit. Not only that, but with quick response, the retailer has an option to better match the supply with demand after observing D. Based on a numerical analysis, Cachon and Swinney note that the profit increase due to quick response can be dramatically higher when a retailer faces strategic consumers, than under settings with myopic customers only. This observation is key to the understanding of the potential benefits of quick response systems, and the ways in which they depend on consumer behavior.

   In the last part of their paper, Cachon and Swinney (2009) report on some results related to the question of whether or not a price commitment can perform better than subgame perfect dynamic pricing. It is noteworthy that unlike the model of Aviv and Pazgal (2008) (who studied a similar type of question), the current model assumes that the initial price is set exogenously, and so commitment here is on the markdown price p_2 only. Another important difference, is that in the first period, all strategic and myopic customers share the same valuation, v_1. It is for these reasons that Cachon and Swinney could argue that if the retailer had to commit to a discount, it would be optimal to not mark down at all; in other words, the retailer should use a static pricing policy, equal to the exogenously set price p_1. In settings with no quick response, making a "no markdown" commitment is beneficial only when the newsvendor critical ratio $(p_1 - c) / (p_1 - v_2)$, is sufficiently high. This is because the gain $(p_1 - c)$ from inducing purchase during period 1 outweighs the loss due to the inability of the retailer to salvage inventory at price v_2 in case of a low demand realization. When the retailer has quick response capability, static pricing tends to be more beneficial. The reason behind this is that quick response reduces the likelihood of having significant leftovers, and thus the loss due to price commitment (or, alternatively viewed—the likelihood of a need for inventory clearance) is not high.

23.5.2.4 *Strategic behavior under newsvendor-type settings*

Su and Zhang [2008] propose an extension of the traditional newsvendor inventory model, to incorporate the impact of strategic consumer behavior. In their setting, a single seller makes a choice of the capacity Q to bring to the market, as well as the price (p_1) to charge during the main season. Per unit cost to the seller is c, and at the end of the season the seller must set the price to p_2 (not a decision variable). Demand, denoted by D, is a random variable and is interpreted as the total mass of infinitesimal consumers in the market. The random variable D follows a distribution G. Consumers' valuations for the product are fixed at v. It is assumed that $p_2 < c < v$. Customers' purchasing behavior is assumed to be governed by a threshold policy with a reservation price r. Specifically, if $r \geq p_1$, they all attempt to buy immediately at price p_1; otherwise, they all wait for the salvage price.

It is noteworthy that the level of inventory, picked by the seller, is not observable to the customers. Similarly, the reservation price r is known to the customers, but not directly observed by the seller. Thus, Su and Zhang propose to study a rational expectation equilibrium in which estimates of these values are formed by the seller and customers. Specifically, the seller forms a belief ξ_r about the customers' reservation price, while the customers form a belief ξ_{prob} about the probability of availability on the salvage market (which obviously depends on the seller's choice of Q). Based on these expectations, customers need to compare between the surplus gained by a "buy now" decision (i.e., $v - p_1$), and the expected surplus to be gained by waiting (i.e., $(v - p_2)\xi_{prob}$). Since r has an interpretation of an indifference point (between a "buy now" or "wait"), it is easy to see that

$$r(\xi_{prob}) = v - (v - p_2)\xi_{prob}$$

(where r is stated as a function of the customers' belief ξ_{prob}). From the seller's perspective, it is obviously optimal to set the price to be equal to the customers' reservation price. However, since this value is not observed, we can write, for the moment, $p_1 = \xi_r$. The optimal quantity (for any given price p_1) is given by

$$Q(p_1) = \arg\max_Q \{\Pi(Q, p_1)\},$$

$$\text{where } \Pi(Q, p_1) = (p_1 - p_2) \cdot E[\min\{D, Q\}] - (c - p_2)Q.$$

The authors show that a rational expectation equilibrium is given by the solution to the equation $p_1 = v - (v - p_2) G(Q(p_1))$. They further show that it is optimal for the seller to lower her stocking quantity under strategic consumer behavior, again enforcing the use of capacity rationing as a strategy.

Next, Su and Zhang consider two types of commitments that can be made by the seller: a capacity commitment, and a price commitment. The first commitment represents a situation in which the seller can order Q units and convince customers that this is indeed the quantity level. In this case, there is no need for the customers to form a rational expectation about ξ_{prob}, as they can simply calculate the availability probability via $G(Q)$. The seller will then price

$$p_q(Q) = v - (v - p_2)G(Q),$$

where the subscript q stands for *quantity*. Consequently, the seller's optimal quantity decision is given by Q_q^*, the maximizer of the expected profit

$$\Pi_q(Q) = (p_q(Q) - p_2) E[\min\{D, Q\}] - (c - p_2)Q$$
$$= (v - p_2)\bar{G}(Q)E[\min\{D, Q\}] - (c - p_2)Q.$$

Let us now look at their model of price commitment. Here, it is easy to verify that the seller should commit not to reduce the price; that is, use a static price of v. Given this commitment, all customers attempt to buy the product at price v, and hence the expected profit is given by $\Pi_p(Q) = vE[\min\{D, Q\}] - cQ$. Su and Zhang show that price commitment may increase the seller's profit when the production cost c is relatively low and when the valuation v is relatively high. However, there exist situations in which price commitments are not desirable. This happens when the valuation v is relatively small. The intuition behind this is similar in spirit to that argued by Cachon and Swinney (2009); see above.

Su and Zhang (2009) propose a similar newsvendor-type model as in the previous setting, but with a slightly different feature. Here, instead of strategic customers contemplating between a "buy now" versus a "wait" decision, they are contemplating whether to "go to the store", or not. A "go to the store" action involves a search cost, which could be justified if the surplus from a purchase exceeds this value. However, customers face uncertainty about product availability, and so they risk losing the search cost if they came to the store and did not find an item available. The authors explore the outcome of the rational expectation game. The setting of the game is very similar to the aforementioned framework: The seller announces a price and selects a capacity (not directly observed by customers), and customers form a belief about the likelihood of finding a product available (this likelihood is not directly observed by the seller).

This paper also discusses two commitment strategies that the seller can use to improve expected profits. When capacity commitment can be made, it can be very valuable in that it encourages customers to spend the search cost and visit the store. This effect increases expected profit margins, and leads the seller to set a higher capacity. As a consequence, with higher inventory, the customers indeed experience a higher level of product availability. A second type of mechanism studied in this paper is an availability guarantee. Here, the seller promises to compensate consumers, ex post, if the product is out of stock. They find that the seller has an incentive to over-compensate consumers during stockouts, relative to the benchmark case under which social welfare is maximized. Finally, the authors argue that first-best outcomes (i.e., those achieved under the benchmark case) do not arise in equilibrium, but can be achieved when the seller uses some combination of commitment and availability guarantees.

23.5.2.5 The impact of inventory display formats: One-by-one versus All

Yin et al. (2010) propose a game-theoretical model of a retailer who sells a limited inventory of a product over a finite selling season by using one of two inventory display formats: Display All (DA) and Display One (DO). Under DA, the retailer displays all available units so that each arriving customer has perfect information about the actual inventory level. Under DO, the retailer displays only one unit at a time so that each customer knows about product availability but not the actual inventory level.

The key purpose of this paper is to understand whether strategic consumer behavior can be controlled via the inventory display format. Specifically, can a display format that conceals inventory information be used as a tool to influence customers' perceptions about the shortage risk (if they decide to wait for a discount)? The authors find that a change from DA to DO, even without a change of the price path, can never worsen the retailer's expected revenue. This observation supports the underlying hypothesis that the DO format increases the perceived level of shortage risk, and hence drives high-valuation customers to purchase the product at the premium price. When the optimal price path is used in each format, the advantage of using DO obviously increases. In particular, the results suggest that price modification typically plays a larger role than merely changing the display format. The marginal benefits of DO tend to be the largest when there is a sufficiently large spread in customers' valuations, the proportion of the high-valuation class in the population is at a modest level, and the customers' arrival rate is within a medium range relative to the initial inventory level. Interestingly, a move from DA to DO appears to be far from eliminating the adverse impact of strategic consumer behavior.

The authors also find that under modest-to-high store traffic rates and sufficient spread in valuations, the marginal benefit of DO can vary dramatically as a function of the per-unit cost to the retailer. When the retailer's per-unit cost is relatively high, but not too high to make sales unprofitable or to justify exclusive sales to high-valuation customers only, the benefits of DO appear to be at their highest level, and could reach up to a 20 percent increase in profit. This result is of particular interest, since high per-unit costs in our model can also reflect retail environments in which strategic customers weigh-in the possibility of alternative purchases if they wait for clearance sales and the item they wanted is out of stock. Finally, Yin et al. argue that by moving from DA to DO, while keeping the price path unchanged, the volatility of the retailer's profit decreases.

23.5.2.6 *Price guarantees*

In the retail industry, many companies offer some form of price guarantee to encourage customers not to delay their purchases; see Arbatskaya et al. (2004). One such offering, called *internal price-matching guarantee*,[10] reflects a situation in which a retailer ensures that a customer will be reimbursed the difference between the current purchase price and any lower price the retailer might offer within a fixed future time period. The following two papers propose models of this kind.

Png (1991) considers a monopolist that sells a limited capacity of size C, $0 < C < 1$, to customers whose valuations are either low (ν_l) or high (ν_h; $\nu_h > \nu_l$). A random portion $x \in [0, 1]$ of the customers belongs to the high-valuation class; x follows a given statistical distribution Φ. There are two periods in the interaction between the seller and customers. If at any time there is excess demand, the available units are allocated at random. All customers are present at the store from the beginning of period 1. To study the equilibrium in the game, it is useful to begin from the second period, where it is clear that the price $p_2 = \nu_l$ should be set. Going back to the first period, consider the customers' choice. Suppose that a high-valuation customer decides to purchase the product in period 1. Then, the likelihood of having access to the product is given by

$$\sigma_1(C) = \Phi(C) + \int_C^1 \frac{C}{x} \, d\Phi(x)$$

and therefore, the expected utility for buying in advance is $(\nu_h - p_1) \cdot \sigma_1(C)$. The latter value is based on an implicit assumption that all other high-valuation customers will act in the same way as that of the "focal" customer. Now, let us consider the situation in which just the "focal" customer deviates from the buy-now action, and decides to wait for period 2. In this case, he will receive the product in the second period with probability

---

[10] An alternative offering, called an *external price-matching guarantee*, is also popular in practice. There, the retailer offers to match the price advertised by any other retailer at the time of purchase. Nonetheless, our focus in this section is on internal price-matching mechanism only.

$$\sigma_2(C) = \int_0^C \frac{C-x}{1-x} d\Phi(x)$$

and hence his expected utility will be $(v_h - v_l) \cdot \sigma_2(C)$. Png argues that in order to maximize revenue, the seller should set the first period price p_1 so that each high-valuation customer will be indifferent between buying immediately and waiting. In other words,

$$p_1(C) = v_h - (v_h - v_l) \frac{\sigma_2(C)}{\sigma_1(C)}$$

The seller's expected revenue is given by

$$R(C) = v_l \cdot E[\max(C - x, 0)] + p_1(C) \cdot E[\min(x, C)]$$

In his second model, Png (1991) considers a *most-favorable-customer* (MFC) protection plan. Under this policy, the seller promises customers who buy early that they will receive a refund to cover for any subsequent price cut. Let $\hat{p}_1$ and $\hat{p}_2$ denote the prices in the first and second periods, respectively. It is clear that for high-valuation customers, the best strategy is to purchase in the first period. This is because when customers buy early, they increase their likelihood of product availability and they have nothing to lose on price. Therefore, it is optimal for the seller to set $\hat{p}_1 = v_h$. Given this choice, the low-valuation customers will wait until period 2. Consequently, there are two cases that need to be analyzed: $x \geq C$ and $x < C$. The first case is simple, since all units are purchased by the high-valuation customers, and the seller's profit is given by $v_h \cdot x$. In the second case, the seller faces the following tradeoff in setting $\hat{p}_2$. If $\hat{p}_2$ is set to v_l, the seller can extract a revenue of $v_l \cdot (C - x)$, but will need to refund the high-valuation customers. Or, more simply, the seller will effectively charge all customers the price v_l, and gain a revenue of $v_l \cdot C$. If $\hat{p}_2$ is set to v_h, then the seller's revenue is $v_h \cdot \min(C, x) = v_h \cdot x$ (in view of $x < C$). The seller's revenue under the second case is therefore $\max(v_l \cdot C, v_h \cdot x)$, and therefore the total expected revenue with an MFC provision is equal to

$$\hat{R}(C) = E[\max\{v_l \cdot C, v_h \cdot \min(x, C)\}]$$

A key result in Png's paper is that the seller always (weakly) prefers to guarantee MFC treatment to first period buyers and sell over two periods than to sell in one period only (see Proposition 1 in his paper). He explains the intuition behind this finding, by arguing that selling over two periods enables the seller to collect and use information about the customer demand. Formally, this type of advantage is described in the following inequality

$$\hat{R}(C) = E[\max\{v_l \cdot C, v_h \cdot \min(x, C)\}] \geq \max\{v_l \cdot C, E[v_h \cdot \min(x, C)]\}$$

with the right-hand side representing the maximal expected revenues that can be gained under a fixed-price policy. Another important observation made by Png, has to do with the comparison between MFC and no-MFC policies. He finds that MFC protection is the favorable choice for the seller when the capacity is large. The logic behind this result is that when capacity is high, customers have high confidence that waiting will not significantly harm their likelihood of receiving the product at v_l (under the no-MFC policy). Therefore, customers will wait for the second period, resulting in minimal expected revenues. Png also finds that when customers are more uncertain about the degree of excess demand in the first period, they tend to buy early at the high price. As a consequence, such customer base is a good candidate for price-discrimination, and no-MFC is the right choice for the seller.

Xu (2011) studies the optimal choice of internal price matching policies, to which she refers by the term *best-price policies* (BP). Unlike Png (1991) just discussed, Xu characterizes the best choice of policy parameters; namely, the time window during which the BP applies, and the portion of the price difference that is refunded (*refund scale*). The models of this paper are set on the basis of the following assumptions. A seller and customers interact over an infinite horizon, with the seller essentially being able to continuously change prices.[11] Customers are either high-valuation or low-valuation, and they all have the same discount rate (the seller, too, shares the same discount factor). At some point (and only one point) of time the valuations of all customers jump simultaneously into a lower state, according to some probabilistic mechanism. This *random-shock* phenomenon is embedded in the model in order to represent situations in practice where a product is going out of fashion, or becomes obsolete. The main model in the paper considers the case where the seller offers a BP policy, and cannot commit to prices. Two benchmark models are also analyzed: A case in which no BP is offered, but the seller can commit to prices (prices are contingent on the information history), and a case in which no BP is offered and the seller cannot make a price commitment. Xu finds that a finite and positive BP policy can be optimal for the seller, when a sharp drop in valuations can occur. In other words, BP policies can be effective for retailers whose products may go out of fashion or become obsolete. The seller's equilibrium profit under the optimal BP policy falls between the profits of the two benchmark models. In general, the optimal BP policy cannot achieve the profit that can be gained with full commitment because of the uncertainty in the time of demand drop, and the fact that a BP policy cannot be contingent on the event of demand drop (since such event is unverifiable and non-contractible).

Lai et al. (2010) consider a *posterior price matching policy*, a marketing policy offered by a seller to match the lower prices if the seller marks down within a specified time. In their model, the market consists of high-end (valuation $= v_H$) and low-end (valuation $= v_l$; $v_l < v_H$) consumers. They assume that the number of low-end consumers in the market is infinite, and that there is a large volume of potential high-end consumers, such that an individual consumer has a negligible effect on demand. The total volume of high-end consumers, denoted by λ, is unknown in advance, but can be characterized by a known distribution G, with a mean μ and a standard deviation σ. Information about the actual value of λ is gained via sales observations during the first period. In the second period, the high-end customer's valuations decline from v_H to v_h (where $v_l \le v_h \le v_H$). In contrast, the low-end consumer's valuations remain constant over the two periods. Among the high-end consumers, a fraction γ is strategic, whereas the rest are myopic. Strategic customers always request a refund, whereas only a fraction of the myopic customers do so. The seller determines whether or not to offer a posterior price matching (denoted by a binary variable v), sets the first-period price (p_1), and invests in inventory (Q). These decisions are made before the market volume is realized. The unit acquisition cost, c, satisfies the condition $v_l < c < v_H$.

Lai et al. employ a dynamic procedure to evaluate the outcome of the two-period interaction between the seller and the customers. Consider first the model without posterior price matching. Here, the authors show that in picking the second-period price (p_2), the

---

[11]   The paper assumes that the price-change points are confined to the time epochs $t = 0, \Delta, 2\Delta, \ldots$, but it then focuses on the limiting case $\Delta \to 0$.

seller can restrict her attention to two values: ν_h and ν_l; namely, either sell exclusively to strategic customers, or mark down further and clear the inventory. If the price ν_h is set, the seller needs to infer the size of the market from the sales volume observed in the first period. The authors show the way in which this inference is done, and consequently, how the optimal second-period price is set on the basis of the first-period demand realization. They also describe the customers' best response in equilibrium, and finally the way in which the seller optimally sets the first-period price and the inventory quantity Q.

In a setting where a posterior price matching policy is offered, it is also useful to consider the values ν_l or ν_h for p_2. However, the seller may want to consider charging $p_2 > \max \{p_1, \nu_h\}$. The rationale behind the latter price possibility is as follows: If a price $p_2 > \nu_h$ is expected, then the non-strategic customer is expected to wait for period 2. Then, setting the price below p_1 is ineffective since it will result in myopic high-end customers asking for a refund. When the seller perception about the delay probability (i.e., q^s) is sufficiently small, the best pricing in period 2 is to either clear leftover inventory ($p_2 = \nu_l$) or price above $\max \{p_1, \nu_h\}$. It is only when q^s passes a certain threshold that it is worthwhile to consider the price $p_2 = \nu_h$; see Proposition 5 in Lai et al. (2010). Interestingly, when it comes to the purchasing behavior of customers, the authors state (Lemma 4): The unique purchasing equilibrium is to buy immediately; that is, $q^o = 0$. It is easy to see the reasoning behind this result. For a focal strategic customer, the posterior price matching policy enables the obtainment of a refund if prices decline. Furthermore, the likelihood of obtaining a unit can only decline from period 1 to period 2. As a consequence of this observation, it is easy to verify that the optimal first-period price is $p_1^o = \nu_H$. As can be seen, the seller's first-period price and the customers' waiting strategy are both independent of γ—the fraction of strategic customers. The fraction γ influences the salvage value of the leftover inventory in a monotonic way. The larger is γ, the larger are the refunds in case of inventory clearance. Consequently, the authors show that the seller's equilibrium inventory level Q^o and her optimal expected profit are both monotonically decreasing in γ; see Proposition 8 in their paper.

Based on the above analytical findings and further numerical analysis, the authors conclude that price matching policies eliminate strategic consumers' waiting incentive and thus allow the seller to increase the price in the regular selling season. When the market consists of a sufficiently large fraction of strategic consumers with declining valuations (over time), the matching policy can be very effective. In contrast, price matching policies can be detrimental when there are only a few strategic consumers in the market, or if the strategic consumers' valuations do not decline much during the sales horizon. Finally, they find that the ability to credibly commit to a fixed price path is not very valuable when the seller can implement price matching.

23.5.2.7 *Allowing time-based binding reservations*

Osadchiy and Vulcano (2010) consider a monopolist endowed with an initial inventory Q who operates a *selling with binding reservations* scheme.[12] Strategic consumers arrive continuously during a finite horizon of length T. Upon arrival, each consumer, trying to maximize his own utility, must decide either to buy at the full price and get the item immediately, or to place a non-withdrawable reservation at a discount price and wait until

---

[12] Their model extends Elmaghraby et al. (2009), who studied the case $Q = 1$.

the end of the sales season when the leftover units are allocated according to a time-based priority rule. Even though their theoretical framework allows for different priority rules, they focus the discussion on the more realistic first-come-first-served case. The model is similar to the aforementioned one by Aviv and Pazgal (2008). The main departure is that while most papers in the literature (like the ones discussed in this section) assume random rationing when demand exceeds supply, Osadchiy and Vulcano concentrate on the impact of allocating excess units by prioritizing early arrivals who place reservations.

The game between the seller and the consumers is of the Stackelberg-type, with the seller being the leader, and the consumers being the followers. The seller announces the initial inventory, the full and discounted prices, and the length of the horizon, and consumers engage in a non-cooperative game. The authors prove the existence of a Bayesian-Nash equilibrium in this game, in which a consumer places a reservation if and only if his valuation is below a function of his arrival time. The computation of this consumer's strategy is intensive, and provably convergent under specific conditions (see Osadchiy and Vulcano (2010) for technical details). To overcome this limitation, the authors formulate an asymptotic version of the problem where demand and capacity grow proportionally large. This limiting regime leads to a simple closed-form solution, which is then used as an approximate equilibrium for the original problem. Their computations show that this heuristic is accurate for medium to large-size problems.

Finally, through an extensive numerical study, they compare the performance of the reservation scheme against the *preannounced discount* pricing policy under random rationing of Aviv and Pazgal (2008) discussed above. Osadchiy and Vulcano find that the mechanism with first-come-first-served reservations weakly dominates *preannounced discount*, and may exceed its revenues by more than 12 percent.

A critical feature for achieving higher revenues than *preannounced discount with random rationing* is that the seller's discount factor be lower than the consumers' discount factor, and that (1) the ratio between the number of units put up for sale and the expected demand is moderate, and/or (2) the heterogeneity of the consumers' valuations is moderate to high. The authors also study the impact of the presence of myopic consumers in the market, which naturally favors the seller. Interestingly, the revenue advantage of the reservation mechanism is still preserved in this case.

23.5.2.8 *Other contributions*

Elmaghraby et al. (2008) consider a setting in which a seller uses a pre-announced markdown pricing mechanism to sell a finite inventory of a product. The key differentiating feature in their model is the consideration of multi-unit demand. Specifically, the seller's objective is to maximize expected revenues by optimally choosing the number of price steps over the season, and the price at each step. An m-step markdown scheme is specified by a declining sequence of prices $\{p_k\}_{k=1}^m$. Demand is deterministic, and is driven by N customers with valuations $\{v_1, \ldots, v_N\}$, where $v_1 > v_2 > \ldots > v_N$. Furthermore, every customer j wishes to purchase up to D_j units of the product. The buyers are present at the store from the start of the selling period until its end (or until all the units have been sold or their demands have been satisfied).

Note that when charging a price p for the product, the highest possible demand under myopic behavior is given by $D(p) \overset{\Delta}{=} \sum_{\{j | v_j \geq p\}} D_j$; the authors refer to this quantity as the market demand at price p.

The purchasing process works as follows. At any given step k (i.e., when the price p_k is offered), buyer j submits a quantity bid q_{jk}, indicating the number of units he wishes to buy. Clearly, since inventory is limited, the seller might not be able to supply all the quantity requested. If so, the seller implements a random rationing rule as follows: Randomly pick a bidder j and assign him the minimum of q_{jk} and the remaining inventory. If there are remaining units, again randomly choose another bidder, and repeat this procedure until the inventory is exhausted. Let $\bar{q}_{jk}$ be the number of units actually awarded. Note that the surplus gained by customer j is given by $\Pi_j = \sum_{k=1}^m (v_j - p_k) \cdot \bar{q}_{jk}$, whereas the seller's revenue is given by $\Pi_S = \sum_{k=1}^m \sum_{j=1}^N p_k \bar{q}_{jk}$.

In their first, *complete information* model (CI), the authors consider a setting where the seller knows the customers' valuations and demands. They show that the optimal markdown has two steps, and that buyers submit all-or-nothing bids, that is, they submit either all or none of their demands at a price step. In addition, under this policy structure, the optimal price for the second step, p_2^*, is equal to the valuation of some customer; that is, $p_2^* = v_j$ for some j. Furthermore, in an effective optimal markdown, there is no scarcity at the high price (i.e., $D(p_1) < Q$), but there is scarcity at the low price (i.e., $D(p_2) > Q$), motivating the high types to buy at p_1, in order to avoid a shortage risk.

In the second, *incomplete information* model (IV), each customer's valuation is *private information* (drawn randomly from nonoverlapping valuation intervals). The distribution of the valuations is assumed to be common knowledge. For the IV case, the authors restrict their focus to the class of markdown policies that prescribe at most one price step in any one valuation interval. They find that, within this class, the optimal markdown has very few steps, and that the seller should never use more than three price steps. Similarly to the CI case, it is optimal for the customers to submit all-or-nothing bids at each price step.

In their conclusions, Elmaghraby et al. (2008) point out that there is a common intuition behind the first step prices under CI and IV. The ratio of a consumer's expected unmet demand to his total demand if he chooses to bid at p_2 can be perceived as a measure of scarcity, which the seller can use to induce purchases at the first step. Hence, the seller can charge a premium proportional to the scarcity that is equal to the maximum additional amount (above p_2) per unit the customer is willing to pay to secure his demand by bidding at p_1.

Su (2007) presents a pricing control model in which consumers are infinitesimally small and arrive continuously according to a deterministic flow of constant rate. The customer population is heterogeneous along two dimensions: valuations and degree of patience (vis-à-vis waiting). The seller has to decide on pricing and a rationing policy which specifies the fraction of current market demand that is fulfilled. Given these retailer's choices, customers decide whether or not to purchase the product and whether to stay or leave the market. The paper shows how the seller can determine a revenue-maximizing selling policy in this game. Su demonstrates that the heterogeneity in valuation and degree of patience jointly influence the structure of optimal pricing policies. In particular, when high-valuation customers are proportionately less patient, markdown pricing policies are effective. On the other hand, when the high-valuation customers are more patient than the low-valuation customers, prices should increase over time in order to discourage waiting.

23.6 DYNAMIC PRICING UNDER OTHER

BEHAVIORAL CONSIDERATIONS

In the previous two sections we surveyed papers that deal with more complex demand models than the ones in the early literature, incorporating behavioral features like learning and strategic waiting. There are other behavioral features that have recently enriched the dynamic pricing literature, like consumer choice behavior, and the inclusion of psychological factors and biases that may have important pricing implications.

23.6.1 Consumer choice behavior

Most of the RM models that account for customer choice behavior are inscribed within what we define in Section 23.1 as quantity-based RM, where capacity availability is the main control variable. Within this context, the design of specific approximation methods for choice-based, network RM was pioneered by the work of Gallego et al. (2004), who propose an LP formulation, the so-called *choice-based deterministic LP* (CDLP), further studied by Liu and van Ryzin (2008b). But to our knowledge, the literature on price-based RM accounting for choice behavior effects is limited. Two papers that belong to this narrow stream are Boyd and Kallesen (2004) and Zhang and Cooper (2009). They both focus on airline business contexts.

Motivated by the expansion of low-fare airlines offering undifferentiated pricing structures, and the consequent reaction of traditional carriers creating new fare structures in which the main differentiating element between classes is just price, Boyd and Kallesen (2004) suggest a new approach for modeling passenger demand. They coin the terms *yieldable* and *priceable* demand. To illustrate, they present the following simple example: Consider one flight with two classes H (high) and L (low). Under a *yieldable* model of demand, an H-type passenger is specifically interested in the H class, and will purchase that product even when the L class is open. Under a *priceable* model of demand, the H passenger is primarily concerned with price and will purchase an L-class ticket in case it is available. Boyd and Kallesen then raise the following important question: Are airline fare classes different products (yieldable) or different prices for the same product (priceable)? When fare class restrictions are negligible and the distribution environment presents fares transparently, the priceable demand model is appropriate. When fare class restrictions are significant or the distribution environment promotes segmentation by allowing passengers to see only those fares an airline wants them to see, the yieldable demand model is appropriate. Boyd and Kallesen point out that yieldable and priceable demands are extremes of a continuum, and that real demand probably lies somewhere in between. They acknowledge though that an overall shift toward priceable demand could be observed in the airline industry, and discuss the impact that this mixed demand model could have on the forecasting and optimization modules of an RM system. They note that without accounting for the buy-down behavior of priceable demand, passenger willingness-to-pay will be underestimated, and carriers will charge less for their tickets than the market is willing to bear. They conclude, cautioning: When priceable demand is accounted for, the net effect is to keep revenues from spiralling downwards by better limiting the availability of low-fare seats (see Cooper et al. (2006) for models of spiral-down effects).

Zhang and Cooper (2009) analyze the joint pricing problem for multiple substitutable flights between the same origin and destination as an MDP. The booking horizon is divided into T discrete time periods. In each period t there is one customer arrival with probability λ_t, and no customer arrival with probability $1 - \lambda_t$. There are n parallel flights offered, with limited capacities. The prices of the flights are denoted by a vector $p = (p_1, \ldots, p_n)$. The allowable prices for flight i are in the set $\mathcal{R}_i = \{\rho_0, \rho_{i,1}, \rho_{i,2}, \ldots, \rho_{i,k_i}\}$, where k_i is a constant for each i, and $\rho_0 > \rho_{i,1} > \rho_{i,2} > \cdots > \rho_{i,k_i}$. The price ρ_0 is a null price added to model cases when flight i is not offered any more. Let $\mathcal{R} = \mathcal{R}_1 \times \cdots \times \mathcal{R}_n$. Customers choose among the flights or purchase nothing. Given a price vector p in period t, and given that a customer arrives in period t, the probability that a customer purchases a ticket on flight i is $P_t^i(p)$. They use $P_t^o(p)$ to denote the probability that an arriving customer does not make a purchase. For each t and p, the choice probabilities satisfy: (1) For all i, if $p_i = \rho_0$, then $P_t^i(p) = 0$; otherwise, $P_t^i(p) \geq 0$, and (2) $\sum_{i=0}^{n} P_t^i(p) = 1$.

Let the state $x = (x_1, \ldots, x_n)$ be the vector whose ith entry is the number of unsold seats on flight i. Let $\mathcal{R}(x) = \{p : p_i \in \mathcal{R}_i \text{ if } x_i > 0, \text{ and } p_i = \rho_0 \text{ if } x_i = 0\}$ be the set of allowable price vectors given state x. Note that when there is no remaining capacity on flight i, the only allowable price is ρ_0, that is, the flight is closed. For each i, let ε_i be the n-vector with the ith component 1 and zeroes elsewhere. For a function $V(\cdot)$ of n variables, define $\Delta_i V(x) = V(x) - V(x - \varepsilon_i)$. Let $V_t(x)$ be the maximum expected revenue from periods $t, t + 1, \ldots, T$, given the state at time t is x. For each t and x, the optimality equation for the MDP is

$$
\begin{aligned}
V_t(x) &= \max_{p \in \mathcal{R}(x)} \left\{ \lambda_t \sum_{i=1}^{n} P_t^i(p)[p_i + V_{t+1}(x - \varepsilon_i)] + \left[1 - \lambda_t + \lambda_t P_t^o(p)\right] V_{t+1}(x) \right\} \\
&= \max_{p \in \mathcal{R}(x)} \left\{ \lambda_t \sum_{i=1}^{n} P_t^i(p)[p_i - \Delta_i V_{t+1}(x)] \right\} + V_{t+1}(x),
\end{aligned}
\tag{20}
$$

with boundary condition $V_T(x) = 0$, for all x.

This MDP has n-dimensional state and action spaces, and the computational effort to solve it is overwhelming for all practical purposes. Regarding structural properties, it is not generally true here that for an optimal policy $\{p_t^*(x)\}$, $p_{t,\,i}^*(x) \geq \Delta_i V_{t+1}(x)$ for all i, that is, it is not necessarily true that the optimal price in period t should exceed the marginal value of capacity for all i.

In order to overcome the curse of dimensionality, the authors proceed by developing and analyzing a variety of bounds and heuristics. First, they propose three pooling-based heuristics: (1) *price pooling*, where the same price is quoted on all the flights, (2) *inventory pooling*, where they aggregate the capacity of the n flights in one super-flight, and where the prices on different flights in the original problem are viewed as prices for different classes on the pooled flight, and (3) *inventory and price pooling*, where they add up the capacities of all the flights to form a single flight and assume that a single price is quoted in every period.

Next, they derive separable upper and lower bounds for the value function of the original problem, based upon solutions of one-dimensional MDPs. These bounds and one-dimensional problems suggest two other families of heuristics: *value* and *policy* approximation heuristics. In their numerical experiments, these heuristics work well, performing better than the pooling-based heuristics, especially under asymmetry among flights in terms of demand load and customer preferences. One of the insights that emerges from their study is that the revenue loss from instituting a single-price policy can be quite significant. Zhang and Cooper caution against the impact that this could have in other industries, like fashion retailing, as described by Bitran et al. (1998) (see Section 23.3.2.2 above).

They also examine via numerical experiments periodic price change policies. The results reveal that for practically implementable choices of such time points, the revenue loss from these policies in comparison to an optimal policy is small. This observation gives good support for practically implementable airline systems that modify prices only at certain pre-specified times, such as after daily database updates.

23.6.2 Reference price effects

The literature covered so far views consumers as rational agents who make decisions based on current prices (myopic consumers) or in anticipation of future prices (strategic consumers). However, in markets with repeated interactions (e.g., frequently purchased consumer goods), customers' purchase decisions are also conditioned by past observed prices. As customers revisit the firm, they develop price expectations, or reference prices, which become a comparative benchmark against the current prices. Prices above the reference price appear to be "high", and prices below the reference price are perceived as "low". The latter effect increases short-term demand, but it also decreases consumers' price expectations, and hence their willingness-to-buy the product at a higher price in the future. For the seller, this implies that extra gains today may be achieved at the expense of a profit loss in the future.

Popescu and Wu (2007) consider the dynamic pricing problem of a seller in a market where demand is a function of current and past prices, captured by an internal consumer's reference price. As the firm manipulates price p, consumers form a reference price r which is adjusted over time. Purchase decisions are made by assessing prices as discounts or surcharges relative to the reference price, in the spirit of *prospect theory* (see Kahneman and Tversky 1979; Tversky and Kahneman 1991; and Özer and Zheng Chapter 20). An important building block of this theory is the mental accounting framework (see Thaler 1985), which states that the total utility from purchasing a product is defined as the sum of the acquisition utility (i.e., the monetary value of the deal) and the transaction utility (i.e., the psychological value of the deal), determined by the difference $r - p$. It is well acknowledged by behavioral theories, based on empirical studies, that surcharges loom larger than discounts of the same magnitude (loss aversion).

Popescu and Wu (2007) formulate an infinite horizon dynamic programming model in which a revenue maximizing monopolist faces a homogeneous stream of repeated customers. The seller decides in every period what price $p \in \mathcal{P}$ to charge, where $\mathcal{P}$ is a bounded interval. The authors do not make inventory considerations. The per-period revenue is

$$\Pi(p, r) = pD(p, r), \quad \text{where} \quad D(p, r) = D(p, p) + R(r - p, r).$$

The first demand term, $D(p, p)$, stands for the regular demand at price p related to the acquisition utility; the second term, $R(r - p, r)$, is the differential demand at price p (or *reference effect* on demand) due to the reference price being r instead of the actual p.

It is related to the transaction utility. Popescu and Wu make the following regularity assumptions on the total demand $D(p, r)$: It is nonnegative, bounded, and continuous, decreasing in price p and increasing in r. The reference effect $R(x, r)$ is increasing in x, for $x = r - p$.

For an initial reference price r_0, and for indices running forward in time, the firm's long term, discounted revenue optimization problem is

$$V(r_0) = \sup_{p_t \in \mathcal{P}} \sum_{t=0}^{\infty} \alpha^t \Pi(p_t, r_t)$$

$$\text{s.t.} \quad r_t = \theta r_{t-1} + (1 - \theta) p_{t-1}, \quad t \geq 1,$$

for a discount factor $\alpha \in (0, 1)$. The constraint of this dynamic program reflects the exponential-smoothing-type of updating mechanism for the current reference price r_t, after customers observed the last price p_{t-1} charged by the firm. The parameter $\theta \in [0, 1]$ captures how strongly the reference price depends on past prices. Lower values of θ represent a shorter-term memory. Since revenues per stage are bounded, the value function is the unique bounded solution of the Bellman equation

$$V(r) = \sup_{p_t \in \mathcal{P}} W(p, r), \quad \text{where} \quad W(p, r) = \Pi(p, r) + \alpha V(\theta r + (1 - \theta)p).$$

A consequence of the demand regularity assumptions above is that short-term revenue $\Pi(p, r)$ and the value function are increasing in r, that is, larger reference prices are preferable for the firm. Since the action set $\mathcal{P}$ is compact and all functions are continuous, there exists an optimal stationary pricing policy that solves the Bellman equation. That is, there exist $p^*(r) = \arg\max_p W(p, r)$. The pricing path $\{p_t^* : t = 0, 1, \ldots\}$ is computed sequentially as $p_t^* = p^*(r_t^*)$, where the state variable is updated in each period via the reference price formation mechanism $r_t^* = \theta r_{t-1}^* + (1 - \theta) p_{t-1}^*$. The reference price $\{r_t^* : t = 0, 1, \ldots\}$ is the sequence of *perceived prices* or *price expectations*. A steady state p^{**} is one from which it is suboptimal to deviate, that is, $p^*(p^{**}) = \theta p^{**} + (1 - \theta) p^*(p^{**}) = p^{**}$, so the optimal price path starting at $r_0 = p^{**}$ is constant. Popescu and Wu proceed by investigating when such a steady state exists, and characterizing stability and monotonicity properties of the price and reference price paths. The results critically depend on consumer's reaction to discounts and surcharges.

The authors provide an exhaustive study of the complete spectrum of behavioral biases: loss neutral, loss seeking, and loss aversion cases. The analysis requires several technical (though plausible) assumptions. Overall, their results indicate that managers who ignore long-term implications of their pricing strategy (due to consumer memory and anchoring effects), will consistently price too low and lose revenue. They also show that cyclical high–low pricing policies can be explained by loss seeking behavior, when consumers react more to discounts than surcharges. Otherwise, the optimal pricing strategies converge in the long run to a constant price. The value of the steady state price decreases with customers' memory and with the sensitivity to the reference effect, all else being equal. Popescu and Wu conclude that higher loss aversion leads to higher pricing flexibility in the sense of a wider range of steady state prices.

Dependence of demand on past prices determines prices to vary over time, and in particular leads to skimming and penetration type strategies. They show that in general, customers' perception of prices follows a monotonic trajectory. If customers have short-term memory or they are increasingly sensitive to reference prices, then the pricing trajectory is also monotonic. While cyclical high–low pricing is optimal in certain cases, their extensive numerical simulations show that monotonic policies are more typical.

23.6.3 Consumer inertia

Su (2009) proposes a model of *consumer inertia* to describe the consumers' tendency to refrain from making any purchase. The decision-making problem of "purchasing now" or "wait" is described via a utility U representing the consumer's expected utility from buying now, and U' standing for the expected utility from waiting. The consumer will purchase as long as $U \geq U' + \Gamma$, with $\Gamma \geq 0$. Note that $\Gamma = 0$ corresponds to the forward-looking consumer behavior analyzed in Section 23.5.

The *trigger increment* Γ is consistent with the idea of loss aversion of Section 23.6.2. When consumers are loss-averse, the possibility of *ex post* losses generates purchase inertia. For example, under valuation uncertainty, making an advance purchase is associated with the possibility of incurring a loss if valuations turn out to be low. This potential loss generates an increased tendency to wait.

The model is as follows. A monopolist is endowed with an initial inventory Q to sell over two periods. The total market size D is random with distribution G. A fraction λ_i of customers arrive in period i, with $\lambda_1 + \lambda_2 = 1$. Among the early arrivals, a fraction γ of them are inertial with trigger increment Γ, and the remaining $\bar{\gamma} = 1 - \gamma$ are rational (i.e., with $\Gamma = 0$). Each consumer's valuation is independently distributed and takes values v_h with probability θ, and v_l with probability $\bar{\theta} = 1 - \theta$. Early arrivals face uncertainty in their valuation, which are realized in period 2. Consumption takes place at the end of the horizon, no matter when the purchase occurs. Valuations for period 2 arrivals are realized instantaneously. The seller chooses prices dynamically to maximize revenues. In period 2, all consumers are willing to buy at prices $p_2 \leq v_l$, but only high valuation consumers are willing to buy at $p_2 \in (v_l, v_h]$. There is a common discount factor δ for all consumers.

The seller first chooses a price $p_1 \in [\delta v_l, \delta v_h]$. Total market demand D is realized and period 1 arrivals decide whether to purchase the product. The seller observes sales and sets the period 2 price, p_2, which could be v_l or v_h. Let π be the probability of $p_2 = v_l$. Next, random valuations of period 1 arrivals (who did not buy in period 1) are realized, and then period 2 consumers arrive. Based on p_2, all remaining consumers then choose whether to purchase the product (subject to availability), and period 2 sales occur. In the event of scarcity, period 1 arrivals receive units with higher priority (note that this is different from Osadchiy and Vulcano (2010), where their continuous time model allows the definition of a total order among arrivals).

Taking the arrivals in period 1, consider first the rational consumers. Their valuation will be realized in period 2, with expected value $v = \theta v_h + \bar{\theta} v_l$. Therefore, under price p_1, the utility from purchasing in period 1 is $U = \delta v - p_1$. If the consumer does not purchase, the price in period 2 will be low with probability π and high with probability $\bar{\pi} = 1 - \pi$. The consumer receives a positive utility in period 2 only if the price falls and his valuation is v_h. Hence, a consumer's expected utility from waiting until period 2 is $U' = \delta \pi \theta (v_h - v_l)$. This utility implicitly assumes that the product is available in period 2, which is proved to be the case in equilibrium. In summary, rational consumers will purchase in period 1 as long as $U \geq U'$, that is, they will buy if $p_1 \leq \delta(\nu - \pi\theta(\nu_h - \nu_l))$.

The analysis for period 1 inertial consumers is similar. But given the condition that they buy in period 1 if and only if $U \geq U' + \Gamma$, they will buy when $p_1 \leq \delta(\nu - \pi\theta(\nu_h - \nu_l)) - \Gamma$. The parameter Γ is assumed to be small enough so that the right-hand side above is positive (otherwise, inertial consumers never buy in period 1 and can be treated as period 2 consumers).

Su proceeds to show how purchase inertia may arise in the presence of several well-studied behavioral biases, including prospect theory. In particular, he specifies the value of Γ as a function of the underlying parameters of these behavioral models.

The optimal pricing strategy is determined via backward induction. For period 2, suppose that a fraction λ_M of the market has decided to purchase in period 1, a fraction λ_H is present in period 2 with high valuations, and a fraction λ_L is present in period 2 with low valuations, with $\lambda_M + \lambda_H + \lambda_L = 1$. The number of units sold in period 1 is given by $Z = \min\{\lambda_M D, Q\}$. Su shows that a threshold pricing policy is optimal. In particular, suppose that $(\lambda_H + \lambda_L)\nu_l \geq \lambda_H\nu_h$. Then, for a realization z of the random variable Z, the optimal pricing policy in period 2 is

$$p_2^* = \begin{cases} \nu_h, & z \geq q \\ \nu_l, & z < q, \end{cases} \quad \text{where} \quad q = \frac{\lambda_M \nu_l Q}{\lambda_M \nu_l + \lambda_H \nu_h}, \quad q \in (0, Q),$$

and the probability that a low price will be charged in period 2 is

$$\pi = G\left(\frac{\nu_L Q}{\lambda_M \nu_l + \lambda_H \nu_h}\right).$$

On the other hand, when $(\lambda_H + \lambda_L)\nu_l < \lambda_H\nu_h$, the optimal period 2 price is $p_2^* = \nu_h$. In words, when the low valuation ν_l is sufficiently high relative to ν_h, then the seller should charge a high price in period 2 if more than q units were sold in period 1, and charge a low price otherwise. On the contrary, if ν_l is sufficiently low relative to ν_h, the seller charges a low price in period 2. As Su points out, the structure is intuitive: When demand is high (as suggested by high sales in period 1), the price should be kept high; but when demand is low, there should be a discount.

For period 1, the seller faces different possible scenarios to set p_1, including dynamic pricing neglecting or accounting for inertia, and static pricing (where the seller makes no sales in period 1, and sets $p_2 = \nu_h$ or $p_2 = \nu_l$). For the latter, he proves that charging a static low price ν_l always yields a lower profit compared to a dynamic pricing strategy.

Among the three remaining strategies (dynamic pricing accomodating/neglecting inertia, and static high prices—selling only in period 2), Su cites Xie and Shugan (2001) to support the dominance of dynamic pricing when the capacity Q is not too small. His analysis then focuses on this favorable case for dynamic pricing, showing that consumer inertia has implications on seller's revenues. While the depth of inertia Γ certainly hurts the seller, the effect of the breadth γ of inertia is mixed. The depth of inertia exerts a downward pressure on profits because prices must be lowered by Γ to trigger purchases from inertial consumers. On the other hand, the breadth of inertia has two separate effects: When inertial consumers delay purchases, demand is lowered in period 1, but at the same time the increased demand in period 2 lowers the chances of a price drop and thus increases the willingness-to-pay of rational consumers in period 1; thus, the net effect on seller's revenues of an increase in the fraction γ of inertial consumers may be positive or negative.

Su (2009) concludes the paper suggesting managerial policies that may influence inertial effects, including the use of refundable purchases and returns policies (to mitigate potential consumer losses), and the use of flexible payment options (to lower the "perceived payment" at the time of transaction).

23.7 CONCLUSIONS AND DIRECTIONS
FOR FURTHER RESEARCH

Information systems and technology serve critical roles in enabling revenue management processes. Enterprise transactional IT systems provide the means for sellers to gather and share demand and sales information. They also facilitate the process of price adjustment. Additionally, analytical IT applications provide the means for devising optimal pricing schemes. The evolution of these systems has engendered an increasing attention to the potential of dynamic pricing. Indeed, there is a broad consensus that formal pricing is a fast and cost-effective lever to increase profits. In fact, even in the electronic markets that have witnessed an exponential growth in on-line auctions, there has been a recent trend to resort to more traditional pricing mechanisms.

In this chapter, we surveyed a broad set of representative papers on dynamic pricing, which highlights the contribution of foundational as well as recent research in this area. Given the trends in IT and enterprise systems that we described above, we argue that there is a growing need for further influential research in this field, which can drive new business models and innovative product designs and pricing schemes.

One line of research, that deserves further attention, is the consideration of choice behavior effects on dynamic pricing. In particular, we see interesting research and practical opportunities in developing dynamic pricing policies for the standard network RM problem (multi-resource, multiproduct). The curse of dimensionality of the associated dynamic program requires the use of approximations and heuristics to come up with implementable policies.

The narrow margins inherent in retail operations invoke the need for creative business models and pricing schemes that mitigate the behavior of increasingly sophisticated consumers. Some of the examples that we reviewed include the rationing of capacity, the employment of price and capacity commitments, the offering of price matching policies, the control of the quantity of merchandise displayed, and the use of binding reservations. Developing other innovative pricing schemes and testing their viability empirically is another promising stream of research.

Most of the research surveyed in this chapter refers to monopolistic settings. Capturing oligopolistic effects is another encouraging line of research, inspired by the narrow margins and the stiff competition in retail operations, and by the widespread evolution of airline alliances and its calls for coordination mechanisms.

Finally, the combination of posted prices with other selling mechanisms such as auctions (e.g., see Caldentey and Vulcano 2007; Gallien and Gupta 2007) or negotiations (e.g., Bhandari and Secomandi 2011) deserve a thorough exploration. In particular, the simultaneous use of dynamic pricing with these alternative mechanisms may uncover interesting revenue opportunities.

References

Araman, V. and Caldentey, R. (2009) "Dynamic pricing for nonperishable products with demand learning", *Operations Research* 57: 1169–88.

Arbatskaya, M., Hviid, M., and Shaffer, G. (2004) "On the incidence and variety of low price guarantees", *Journal of Law and Economics* XLVII: 307–32.

Aviv, Y. and Pazgal, A. (2005a) "Dynamic pricing of short life-cycle products through active learning". Working paper, The John M. Olin Business School, St Louis, MO: Washington University.

—— and —— (2005b) "A partially observed Markov decision process for dynamic pricing", *Management Science* 51/9: 1400–16.

—— and —— (2008) "Optimal pricing of seasonal products in the presence of forward-looking consumers", *Manufacturing and Service Operations Management* 10/3: 339–59.

Balvers, R. and Cosimano, T. (1990) "Actively learning about demand and the dynamics of price adjustments", *The Economic Journal* 100/3: 882–98.

Bell, D. and Starr, D. (1994) "Filene's basement". Harvard Business School Case 9-594-018.

Bertsekas, D. (2005) *Dynamic Programming and Optimal Control*, vol. 1, 3rd edn. Belmont, MA: Athena Scientific.

—— and Perakis, G. (2006) "Dynamic pricing: A learning approach", in S. Lawphongpanich, D. Hearn, and M. Smith (eds), *Mathematical and Computational Models for Congestion Charging*, vol. 101 of *Applied Optimization*, pages 45–80. Springer, June.

Besanko, D. and Winston, W. (1990) "Optimal price skimming by a monopolist facing rational consumers", *Management Science* 36: 555–67.

Besbes, O. and Zeevi, A. (2009) "Dynamic pricing without knowing the demand function: Risk bounds and near-optimal algorithms", *Operations Research* 57: 1407–20.

Bhandari, A. and Secomandi, N. (2011) "Technical note: Revenue management with bargaining". Tepper School of Business, CMU. *Operations Research* 59/2: 498–506.

Bitran, G. and Caldentey, R. (2003) "An overview of pricing models for revenue management", *Manufacturing and Service Operations Management* 5: 203–29.

—— and Mondschein, S. (1997) "Periodic pricing of seasonal products in retailing", *Management Science* 43: 64–79.

—— Caldentey, R., and Mondschein, S. (1998) "Coordinating clearance markdown sales of seasonal products in retail chains", *Operations Research* 46: 609–24.

Boyaci, T. and Özer, Ö. (2010) "Information acquisition for capacity planning via pricing and advance selling: When to stop and act?" *Operations Research* 58: 1328–49.

Boyd, A. and Kallesen, R. (2004) "The science of revenue management when passengers purchase the lowest available fare", *Journal of Revenue and Pricing Management* 3/2: 171–7.

Braden, D. and Oren, S. (1994) "Nonlinear pricing to produce information", *Marketing Science* 13/3: 310–26.

Brémaud, P. (1980) *Point Processes and Queues: Martingale Dynamics*. New York: Springer-Verlag.

Cachon, G. and Swinney, R. (2009) "Purchasing, pricing, and quick response in the presence of strategic consumers", *Management Science* 55/3: 497–511.

Caldentey, R. and Vulcano, G. (2007) "Online auction and list price revenue management", *Management Science* 53/5: 795–813.

Carvalho, A. and Puterman, M. (2005) "Learning and pricing in an internet environment with binomial demands", *Journal of Revenue and Pricing Management* 3: 320–36.

Chan, L., Simchi-Levi, D., and Swann, J. (2005) "Pricing, production and inventory strategies for manufacturing with stochastic demand and discretionary sales", *Manufacturing and Service Operations Management* 8: 149–68.

Chen, X. and Simchi-Levi, D. (2004a) "Coordinating inventory control and pricing strategies with random demand and fixed ordering cost: The infinite horizon case", *Mathematics of Operations Research* 29: 698–723.

—— and —— (2004b) "Coordinating inventory control and pricing strategies with random demand and fixed ordering cost: The finite horizon case", *Operations Research* 56: 887–96.

Coase, R. (1972) "Durability and monoploy", *Journal of Law and Economics* 15: 143–9.

Conlisk, J., Gestner, E., and Sobel, J. (1984) "Cycling pricing by a durable goods monoploy", *Quarterly Journal of Economics* 99: 489–505.

Cooper, W., Homem-de-Mello, T., and Kleywegt, A. (2006) "Models of the spiral-down effect in revenue management", *Operations Research* 54/5: 968–87.

Desiraju, R. and Shugan, S. (1999) "Strategic service pricing and yield management", *Journal of Marketing* 63: 44–56.

Elmaghraby, W. and Keskinocak, P. (2003) "Dynamic pricing in the presence of inventory considerations: Research overview, current practices and future directions", *Management Science* 49: 1287–309.

—— Gulcu, A., and Keskinocak, P. (2008) "Designing optimal pre-announced markdowns in the presence of rational customers with multi-unit demands", *Manufacturing and Service Operations Management* 10/1: 126–48.

—— Lippman, S., Tang, C., and Yin, R. (2009) "Pre-announced pricing strategies with reservations", *Production and Operations Management* 18: 381–401.

Farias, V. and van Roy, B. (2010) "Dynamic pricing with a prior on market response", *Operations Research* 58: 16–29.

Federgruen, A. and Heching, A. (1999) "Combined pricing and inventory control under uncertainty", *Operations Research* 47/3: 454–75.

Feng, Y. and Gallego, G. (1995) "Optimal starting times for end-of-season sales and optimal stopping times for promotional fares", *Management Science* 41: 1371–91.

—— and Xiao, B. (2000) "Optimal policies of yield management with multiple predetermined prices", *Management Science* 48: 332–43.

Gallego, G. and Şahin, O. (2010) "Revenue management with partially refundable fares", *Operations Research* 58: 817–33.

—— and van Ryzin, G. (1994) "Optimal dynamic pricing of inventories with stochastic demand over finite horizons", *Management Science* 40: 999–1020.

—— and —— (1997) "A multi-product dynamic pricing problem and its applications to network revenue management", *Operations Research* 45: 24–41.

—— Iyengar, G., Phillips, R., and Dubey, A. (2004) Managing flexible products on a network. Technical Report CORC TR-2004-01, Department of Industrial Engineering and Operations Research, Columbia University.

—— Phillips, R., and Sahin, O. (2008) "Strategic management of distressed inventory", *Management Science* 17: 402–15.

Gallien, J. and Gupta, S. (2007) "Temporary and permanent buyout prices in online auctions", *Management Science* 53/5: 814–33.

Johnson, M. (2001) "Learning from toys: Lessons in managing supply chain risk from the toy industry", *California Management Review* 43/3: 106–24.

Kahneman, D. and Tversky, A. (1979) "Prospect theory: An analysis of decision under risk", *Econometrica* 47/2: 263–91.

Karlin, S. and Carr, C. (1962) "Prices and optimal inventory policies", in K. Arrow, S. Karlin, and H. Scarf (eds), *Studies in Applied Probability and Management Science*. Stanford, CA: Stanford University Press, 159–72.

Kleywegt, A. (2001) "An optimal control problem of dynamic pricing". Technical report, School of Industrial and Systems Engineering, Atlanta, GA: Georgia Institute of Technology.

Lai, G., Debo, L., and Sycara, K. (2010) "Buy now and match later: Impact of posterior price matching on profit with strategic consumers", *Manufacturing and Service Operations Management* 12: 33–55.

Landsberger, M. and Meilijson, I. (1985) "Intertemporal price discrimination and sales strategy under incomplete information", *The RAND Journal of Economics* 16: 424–30.

Lazear, E. P. (1986) "Retail pricing and clearance sales", *American Economic Review* 76: 14–32.

Lee, T. and Hersh, M. (1993) "A model for dynamic airline seat inventory control with multiple seat booking", *Transportation Science* 27: 252–65.

Levin, Y., Levina, T., McGill, J., and Nediak, M. (2009) "Dynamic pricing with online learning and strategic consumers: An application of the aggregating algorithm", *Operations Research* 57/3: 327–41.

Liu, B. and Milner, J. (2006) "Multiple-item dynamic pricing under a common pricing constraint". Working paper, Joseph L. Rotman School of Management, Toronto, ON: University of Toronto.

Liu, Q. and van Ryzin, G. (2008a) "Strategic capacity rationing to induce early purchases", *Management Science* 54/6: 1115–31.

—— and —— (2008b) "On the choice-based linear programming model for network revenue management", *Manufacturing and Service Operations Management* 10: 288–310.

Maglaras, C. and Meissner, J. (2006) "Dynamic pricing strategies for multiproduct revenue management problems", *Manufacturing and Service Operations Management* 8: 136–48.

Osadchiy, N. and Vulcano, G. (2010) "Selling with binding reservations in the presence of strategic consumers", *Management Science* 56: 2173–90.

Pashigian, P. B. (1988) "Demand uncertainty and sales: A study of fashion and markdown pricing", *American Economic Review* 78: 936–53.

Phillips, R. (2005) *Pricing and Revenue Optimization*. Palo Alto, CA: Stanford University Press.

Png, I. P. L. (1989) "Reservations: Customer insurance in the marketing of capacity", *Marketing Science* 8/3: 248–64.

—— (1991) "Most-favored-customer protection vs. price discrimination over time", *Journal of Political Economy* 99: 1010–28.

Popescu, I. and Wu, Y. (2007) "Dynamic pricing strategies with reference effects", *Operations Research* 55: 413–29.

Rajan, A., Rakesh, and Steinberg, R. (1992) "Dynamic pricing and ordering decisions by a monopolist", *Management Science* 38: 240–62.

Shugan, S. and Xie, J. (2000) "Advance pricing of services and other implications of separating purchase and consumption", *Journal of Service Research* 2/3: 227–39.

Smith, S. A. and Achabal, D. (1998) "Clearance pricing and inventory policies for retail chains", *Management Science* 44: 285–300.

Sobel, J. (1984) "The timing of sales", *Review of Economics Studies* 15: 353–68.

Stokey, N. (1979) "Intertemporal price discrimination", *Quarterly Journal of Economics* 93: 355–71.

—— (1981) "Rational expectations and durable goods pricing", *Bell Journal of Economics* 12: 112–28.

Su, X. (2007) "Intertemporal pricing with strategic consumer behavior", *Management Science* 53/5: 726–41.

—— (2009) "A model of consumer inertia with applications to dynamic pricing". Haas School of Business, Berkeley, CA: University of California. *Production and Operations Management* 18/4: 365–80.

—— and Zhang, F. (2008) "Strategic customer behavior, commitment, and supply chain performance", *Management Science* 54/10: 1759–73.

—— and —— (2009) "On the value of commitment and availability guarantees when selling to strategic consumers", *Management Science* 55/5: 713–26.

Sullivan, L. (2005) Fine-tuned pricing. Information Week, August 15.

Talluri, K. and van Ryzin, G. (2004) *The Theory and Practice of Revenue Management*. Boston, MA: Kluwer Academic Publishers.

Thaler, R. (1985) "Mental accounting and consumer choice", *Marketing Science* 4/3: 199–214.

Thowsen, G. (1975) "A dynamic nonstationary inventory problem for a price/quantity setting firm", *Naval Research Logistics Quarterly* 22: 461–76.

Tversky, A. and Kahneman, D. (1991) "Loss aversion in riskless choice: A reference dependent model", *Quarterly Journal of Economics* 106/4: 1039–61.

Vovk, V. (1990) "Derandomizing stochastic prediction strategies", *Machine Learning* 35: 247–82.

Warner, E. J. and Barsky, R. B. (1995) "The timing and magnitude of retail store markdowns: Evidence from weekends and holidays", *Quarterly Journal of Economics* 110: 321–52.

Xie, J. and Shugan, S. (2001) "Electronic tickets, smart cards and online prepayments: When and how to advance sell", *Marketing Science* 20/3: 219–43.

Xu, Z. (2011) "Optimal best-price policy", *International Journal of Industrial Organization* 29/5: 628–43.

Yin, R., Aviv, Y., Pazgal, A., and Tang, C. (2010) "Optimal markdown pricing: Implications of inventory display formats in the presence of strategic consumers", *Management Science* 55: 1391–408.

Zabel, E. (1972) "Multiperiod monopoly under uncertainty", *Journal of Economic Theory* 5: 524–36.

Zhang, D. and Cooper, W. (2009) "Pricing substitutable flights in airline revenue management", *European Journal of Operational Research* 197/3: 848–61.

Zhao, W. and Zheng, Y.-S. (2000) "Optimal dynamic pricing for perishable assets with nonhomogeneous demand", *Management Science* 46: 375–88.

CHAPTER 24

SALES PROMOTIONS

ROBERT C. BLATTBERG AND
RICHARD A. BRIESCH

24.1 INTRODUCTION

Over the last three decades, there have been numerous academic papers in economics, psychology, and marketing regarding the topic of sales promotions. Practitioners and consulting firms have made significant progress in applying and, in some cases, extending models from the academic community. Portions of this growth can be attributed to the increased managerial importance of sales promotions, as consumer packaged goods (CPG) companies allocate more than 50 percent of their marketing budgets and 13 percent of their revenues to sales promotions (ACNielsen 2002; Gómez et al. 2007). Part of this growth is also driven by the wider availability of data, particularly point of sale (POS) data from supermarkets and other retailers, which has allowed academics and practitioners to model and optimize sales promotions. This chapter is designed to assist managers in understanding the current state of the art of promotional modeling, its managerial applications, and to identify future issues that need to be addressed.

Before going further, it is useful to define *sales promotions*. Blattberg and Neslin (1990) define a sales promotion as "an action-focused marketing event whose purpose is to have a direct impact on the behavior of the firm's customer". There is also an important distinction to be made between sales promotions and a permanent price reduction. Sales promotions are temporary and a "call-to-action". If customers do not take advantage of promotions within specified timeframes, they will lose the benefit offered by the promotions. Sales promotions are almost always combined with some type of communication (e.g., a retailer ad) that the price is reduced and that the time period is limited (price is reduced only up to some point in time). Long-term price reductions may be accompanied by a price reduction signal (e.g., Walmart rollbacks in the USA) but the time period is "until further notice". A consumer can wait to make a purchase when price is reduced without a time limit with the only risk being that the consumer may not accurately estimate when the

The authors would like to thank William Dillon, the Editors, and an anonymous reviewer for their helpful comments and suggestions for this chapter.

price will increase. The distinction between sales promotions and permanent price reductions leads to differences in consumers' responsiveness to price changes and buyer (retailer) behavior to trade promotions.

The remainder of this chapter is organized as follows. In the next section, we provide a description of the major types of sales promotions offered. Section 24.3 provides a discussion of the behavioral underpinnings of sales promotions. Specifically, several theories are provided that explain why consumers respond more strongly to sales promotions than to a price decrease and shows the benefits to managers of understanding why sales promotions are used. Section 24.4 provides a description of how promotions affect sales, with a discussion of the sources of incremental volume associated with a promotion. These sources of the incremental volume dramatically affect the profitability of the promotion for both the manufacturer and retailer. Section 24.5 discusses strategic issues associated with sales promotions, and provides insight into why firms may still offer promotions even when they are unprofitable. Section 24.6 provides an overview of empirical methods used to estimate sales promotions models. Section 24.7 discusses emerging issues related to sales promotions. Finally, we conclude with a section focused on managerial implications and emerging managerial issues in sales promotions.

24.2 Description of types of promotions

Sales promotions are designed for different purposes and different target audiences: retailer, trade, and consumer. *Retailer promotions* are offered by retailers to consumers to increase sales for the item, category, or store. *Trade promotions* are offered to members of the channel distribution (called the trade) and are designed to stimulate the channel members to offer promotions to consumers (retailer promotions) or the channel member's customers. *Consumer promotions* are offered directly to consumers by manufacturers and are designed to stimulate the consumer to make a purchase at some point close to the time of the receipt of the consumer promotion. Figure 24.1 shows the interrelationship between the types of promotions.

Because of the growth of the Internet, *Internet promotions* have become prevalent for both consumer and retail promotions. We separate out these promotions because the medium is interactive and offers new capabilities to firms through the vast information now being provided to manufacturers and retailers.

24.2.1 Retailer promotions

The key elements of a retailer promotion are price discounts, the medium in which price discounts are offered, communications of sales promotions, and the objectives of the promotion.

Price discounts can take different forms ranging from straight price discounts to buy one get one free (BOGOs), to frequent shopper card discounts, to buy A and get a discount on B (bundled promotion). Commonly used discounts are listed in Table 24.1 with a brief description of each.

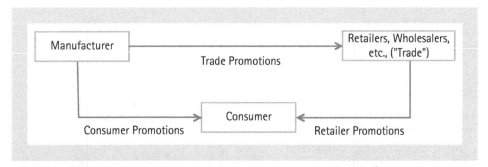

FIGURE 24.1 How trade promotions affect sales

Different types of price discounts have different levels of effectiveness and result in different types of behavior. For example, three for $2 has a greater impact on sales than a price discount of $0.67 because consumers tend to purchase three units. Rebates result in "breakage" which means consumers respond to the rebate but do not send in the requisite documentation to receive the rebate. Figure 24.2 reproduces a figure from Chandon et al. (2000) that measures consumers' perceptions of different types of discounts on two dimensions: utilitarian (monetary savings, improved product quality, and shopping convenience) and hedonic (the opportunities for self-expression, entertainment, and explor-

Table 24.1 Common types of retailer discounts

Type of retail promotion	Description
Price reduction	Retailers temporarily decrease prices on product.
Retailer coupon	Retailers issue coupons for product in their advertisement or on the shelf.
Free goods	The consumer receives free goods as the discount. It includes buy one get one free (or buy X get Y free), as well as promotions where goods in complementary categories are given away (e.g., salsa for tortilla chip purchase).
Sweepstakes	The consumer is entered into a contest where they have the chance of winning cash or other prizes.
Free trial	Consumers are given free samples of the product to encourage purchase of a new product.
N-for	The retailer offers a discounted price for the purchase of a set number (N) of items purchased, e.g., three for $1.
Discount card	Consumers sign up for a card that tracks their purchases. In return, the retailer provides discounted prices on some items in the store only for those consumers with the card.
Rebates	Consumers receive notices of a rebate at the shelf or display and then mail in proof of purchase and the rebate form.
Bundled promotion	The retailer gives the consumer a discount for purchasing products from complementary categories (e.g., hamburgers and ketchup).

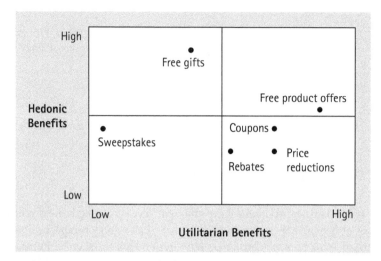

FIGURE 24.2 Consumer perceptions of sales promotion types

Source: Chandon et al. (2000)

ation). Interestingly, they find that non-monetary promotions work better for hedonic products, whereas monetary promotions work better for utilitarian products.

The next issue is what medium the retailer uses to provide price discounts. One option is simply to offer a discount in the store. Alternatives include frequent shopper card discounts available at the store or redemption cards sent to the shopper's home to be redeemed on the next visit. The relative merit of the medium chosen depends upon the retailer's objective. Frequent shopper discounts reward "regular shoppers". Mailed discount cards drive shoppers into the store. These media vehicles are not mutually exclusive.

Communication of the promotion is very important. Retailers use in-store signage, displays and periodic (weekly) fliers / feature advertising to communicate discounts. Obviously, it is very important to communicate price discounts so shoppers recognize them. For large discounts, retailers will have some form of display. For small discounts they will use in-store signage (e.g., shelf tags). Manufacturers often fund retailer communications through cooperative advertising funds which we cover in the next section.

The retailer can have different objectives associated with promotions. One of the most common is to generate traffic (customers visiting the store). The choice of the products/ brands offered on the promotion and the level of discount offered greatly influences the amount of traffic generated. Products/brands that have high penetration levels and high frequency of purchase are often very good traffic generators for grocery, drug, and mass retailers. Obviously, the greater the discount level offered, ceteris paribus, the more traffic that is generated by the promotion.

Besides traffic generation, another key objective of promotions is to sell excess merchandise that is caused by overstocking. After Christmas or a major holiday, promotions to clear unsold holiday merchandise are very common. Airlines have unsold seats during a specific day, week, or season and offer special promotions to sell those seats because they are "perishable". For a more complete discussion of this area, see Chapter 25 by Ramakrishnan. Promotions have other purposes beyond just driving customers into the store and selling unsold, perishable inventory. They can be used to increase category profitability by switching consumers from lower to higher margin products or they can be used to generate trials for a new product or a product category that has low penetration levels. (For a more comprehensive list of retailer promotional goals, see Blattberg and Neslin 1990.)

In summary, retail promotions are a very powerful sales tool. Many retail promotions are driven by trade promotions offered to the retailer by manufacturers and they are described in the next section.

24.2.2 Trade promotions

Trade promotions are used by manufacturers to achieve objectives such as generating a price decrease by retailers to consumers or gaining distribution for a new product.[1] Manufacturers offer retailers trade promotions to stimulate them to offer retail price discounts and communicate the discounts to consumers. Trade promotions use various price discounting mechanisms and incentives to gain price discounts, displays, in-store communications, and space in the retailers' advertisements.

Trade promotions have specific objectives and forms of incentives offered to the retailer. Typical trade promotion objectives are shown in Table 24.2. The mechanisms by which these objectives are met are embedded in the type of trade promotion offered and the requirements placed on the retailer. The issue of channel coordination is covered in more detail by Kaya and Özer in Chapter 29.

There are a number of types of trade promotion incentives offered by manufacturers. We cover the most common types: off-invoice, scan-back, accrual funds, and slotting fees.

The most widespread trade promotion is *off-invoice promotions* in which the manufacturer offers a discount to the channel (e.g., retailers) so that the channel will offer a price discount to the consumer. This type of promotion has two key issues: pass-through and forward buying. *Pass-through* is defined as the amount of the discount that the channel passes along to the consumer in the form of consumer discounts. *Forward buying* occurs when the retailer buys more during the promotional period than they intend to sell to consumers. They may either stockpile the additional inventory to sell in later periods at the regular price, or *divert* (i.e., resell) the excess inventory to other retailers. Some or the entire

Table 24.2 Typical trade promotion objectives

Gain or maintain distribution
Obtain temporary price discount
Display product
Include product in retailer's advertisements
Gain market share from competition
Increase sales
Reduce inventory
Sell off old or obsolete inventory

---

[1] For trade promotions we are going to focus on manufacturer to retailer promotions. There are also trade promotions designed for wholesalers to offer incentives to retailers.

stockpiled product is then sold at regular prices. This leads to lower profitability of the manufacturer's trade promotion.

To overcome some of the problems associated with off-invoice promotions, manufacturers have developed several alternative trade promotions. One is called a *scan-back promotion* in which the manufacturer offers the retailer payment for all the units sold during a specific week at a pre-specified discount to the consumer. It is measured using the retailer's scanner (point of sale or POS) system. The advantage of this type of trade promotion offer is that the manufacturer pays only for those units sold on promotion and not additional units purchased by the channel at the discounted price. The disadvantages are that it requires obtaining the unit sales from the retailer's POS system and that it requires the manufacturer to rely on the accuracy of the system and the honesty of the retailer. In markets that do not have POS systems, scan-back promotions cannot be used.

An alternative to scan-back promotions, also designed to limit forward buying and diverting, is *accrual funds* which are based on the number of units sold in a prior period to determine next period's funding level. Accrual funds generally are allocated jointly by the retailer and manufacturer to meet certain sales and profit objectives in the relevant spending period.

For most trade promotions that offer price discounts to the retailers, allowances are offered for feature advertising (ads by the retailer identifying the price discounts) and display. These funds are generally called *cooperative funds* and are used to entice the retailer to communicate the price discount on the manufacturer's products and to put up special displays in the retailer's stores to communicate that the product is available at a discount. Retailers often have "price lists" in which they indicate to manufacturers exactly how much it costs for a specific size ad and for a specific display type.

A variant of cooperative funds is for manufacturers and retailers to market and jointly promote the product. A retailer may decide to run a Fourth of July day special and contacts manufacturers to receive funds to partially pay for their ad and displays linked to the holiday.

Slotting fees are another form of trade promotion with a very different objective—gaining distribution for a new product or additional SKUs. The retailer charges the manufacturer a slotting fee to cover the cost of stocking and managing a manufacturer's new product introduction. The original purpose of slotting fees was to cover the retailers' new product introductory costs such as removing products from the shelf and replacing them with the new items, reclamation costs of the old items that were removed, the inventory risk of carrying new items if they do not sell, and the warehousing and administrative costs of adding new items. Slotting fees are very controversial and have been studied by regulatory agencies who argue in some cases that slotting fees limit competition from smaller manufacturers and for smaller brands being introduced. Table 24.3 provides a more comprehensive list of trade promotion types.

24.2.3 Consumer promotions

Consumer promotions are promotions from a manufacturer directly to consumers. In the USA the most common forms are *rebates* and *coupons*. In other countries, *contests* and *sweepstakes* are more prevalent. More and more consumer promotions are being offered on the Internet.

The purpose of consumer promotions is for a manufacturer to communicate a discount directly to the consumer and avoid intermediaries (e.g., retailers) who may not provide the discount the manufacturer wants. In the design of consumer promotions, the critical

Table 24.3 Trade promotion vehicles

Off-invoice	Discounts offered from the invoice price on all units sold to the retailer over a specified time period.
Accrual funds	Funds paid by the manufacturer to the retailer based on the prior period's unit sales movement.
Scan-back	Discounts offered based on units sold through the point of sale register rather than on units purchased by the retailer.
Count-recount	System used to pay retailers based only on units sold. Similar to scan-back promotions except the manufacturer does the counting in the retailer's (or wholesaler's) warehouse. Used when POS data are not readily available.
Co-op advertising	Manufacturer funds to support retailer advertising for the manufacturer's product(s).
Display allowances	Manufacturer funds to support displays put up by the retailer.
Bill backs	Similar to off-invoice funds except the retailer must provide proof that specific actions have taken place such as an ad was run by the retailer containing the manufacturer's products. Used to ensure compliance by the retailer.
Slotting fees	Manufacturer funds to cover the retailer's costs of new product introductions.
Free goods	Extra cases offered to the retailer by the manufacturer often for new products to induce the retailer to stock the items for which the free goods are offered.
Floor plan	Financing offered by the manufacturer to retailers or dealers to cover the financial inventory carrying cost of the retailer or dealer.
Financial terms	Terms to provide incentives to retailers to stock items and not have to carry the financial cost of inventory.

decisions are medium, redemption system, restrictions, and breakage. The medium used varies by type of consumer promotion. Print and the Internet are very common media used for consumer promotion because the promotion can be printed. Handouts, on-pack, and in-pack promotions are also used.

With the redemption system it is very important to avoid fraud. Coupons in the USA are managed through a complex clearing house system. Rebates are often sent to clearing houses as well. The difficulty is that retailers can misredeem the discount delivery vehicle (e.g., coupon) without a redemption, that is submit coupons for redemption that were not submitted by consumers with purchases. In the USA, misredemption of coupons is a serious problem. Misredemption and fraud are reasons that consumer promotions can be ineffective. Many consumer promotions have restrictions to limit long-term liability. Statements such as "good until June 30, 2010" restrict the term of the promotion. Restrictions can also take the form of "only one per customer" though those are very difficult to enforce.

One of the advantages of consumer promotions is *breakage*, which is the difference between the number used to induce a purchase and the number redeemed. Breakage is very common for product rebates. Consumers need to send in a proof of purchase (receipt) and the rebate document to a specific address. Many consumers will purchase based on the rebated price (retail price minus the rebate) but fail to send in the rebate because of the time required or the loss of the purchase receipt or rebate form. Breakage can increase the profitability of consumer promotions because it results in a higher *net* price.

Consumer promotions have significant advantages and disadvantages relative to trade/ retailer promotions. The primary advantage is that the manufacturer has control over the offer received by the consumer. When a promotion is offered through the retailer, generally the manufacturer does not have control over the price being offered to the consumer, though this varies by country. The primary disadvantages are the low redemption rates (free-standing insert coupons in the USA average about 1.5–2.5 percent redemption rates) and the cost of distributing the offer.

24.2.4 Internet promotions

Retailers and manufacturers can use the Internet as a vehicle for targeting and reaching customers with promotions. Unlike direct mail, the Internet is a virtually zero-cost communication vehicle. If a customer is willing to provide his or her e-mail address, then the firm selling the goods or services can reach the customer at a low cost. Offering highly targeted promotions which were very expensive using mail or other distribution systems becomes almost costless when using the Internet. The other important method for the distribution of discounts using the Internet is websites. Many manufacturers or third-party sites offer consumers discounts on purchases of products. Consumers can print coupons, use codes, or other mechanisms to obtain discounts.

The implication of a low-cost communication vehicle for offering targeted promotions combined with a wealth of consumer information available on the Internet is that the types of promotions will be much more selective. This means a critical research area is to determine the value of targeted promotions versus mass promotions (see e.g., Rossi et al. 1995). Models are also needed to determine what types of offers should be provided to different segments of the market. Whether firms will ever be able to offer one-on-one promotions is an open question because of the cost and sophistication required to provide the relevant analytics.

One issue that emerges with promotional targeting is "fairness". If one consumer receives a different promotion than another and each learns about the other's promotional offer, the consumer receiving the less favorable promotion is likely to be very upset and may stop purchasing from the company. Thus, the type of promotional offers used to target individual consumers is very important. For example, with frequent flyer programs, the flyer has to earn the benefits received. For frequent flyer and similar programs (e.g., hotels) different customers receive different offers based on "earning" the reward. For further discussion of the consumers' perception of fairness, see Chapter 20 by Özer and Zheng.

24.3 BEHAVIORAL UNDERPINNINGS OF SALES PROMOTIONS

There is a stream of research that is important in understanding why promotions exist— the psychological marketing literature. Three foundational articles provide the basis for this stream of research and provide relevant managerial implications.

24.3.1 Smart shopper

Schindler (1998) observes that price promotions are able to generate consumer responses that are far greater than the economic value of the money saved. In other words, one can look at the difference between a promotional price reduction and a regular price reduction and the response to the promotion, beyond just the temporal nature of the promotion, is far greater than the strict price reduction effect. Schindler posits the effect as consumers' perceiving themselves as "efficient, effective and smart shoppers". He argues that because consumers feel that their actions are perceived to be responsible for obtaining discounts, this will increase the noneconomic component of the discount.

24.3.2 Transactional utility

A related explanation is offered by Thaler (1985) who introduced the concept of transaction utility. Transaction utility is defined as the gain (loss) of utility when the consumer pays less (more) than the reference price of the product. The reference price is not the same as the actual price of the product but the price the consumer believes the good is worth or the price the consumer would expect to pay for the good. Positive transaction utility occurs when the reference price is above the actual price paid. If promotions produce transactional utility, then the firm is better off using promotions than simply lowering regular price. The outcome will be a higher response to the promotion than to an equivalent reduction in the everyday regular price. One of the key differences between Schindler's and Thaler's theories is the notion of reference price, or the perceived value of the good.

24.3.3 Reference price

One of the earliest studies of reference price was Winer (1986) who defined reference price as a function of past brand and category prices and estimated an empirical choice model that demonstrated that the reference price effect could be measured. Reference price effects have been reliably found in experimental data (Niedrich et al. 2001; Janiszewski and Lichtenstein 1999; Van Ittersum et al. 2005; Chernev 2006). Some research suggests that consumers use both internal (memory-based) as well as external (stimulus-based) reference prices (Mazumdar and Papatla 2000). Howard and Kerin's (2006) findings suggest that reference prices may be context specific, so different internal reference prices may be invoked when a product is advertised in the retailer's ad compared to when it is not.

These foundational articles also explain the finding that more frequent promotions reduce reference price (Blattberg et al. 1995). This change in reference price, in turn, can reduce the incremental sales associated with the promotion (Nijs et al. 2001; Krishna et al. 2002). However, Srinivasan et al. (2004) find some evidence against this generalization. They find that manufacturer revenue elasticities are higher for frequently promoted products and retailer revenue elasticities are higher for brands with frequent and shallow promotion, for impulse products, and in categories with a low degree of brand proliferation. This latter finding may be consistent with the results of Alba et al. (1999) who find that the depth of promotion dominates the frequency of promotion in the formation of reference prices when prices have a simple bimodal distribution.

The key insight from this discussion of reference price is that heavily promoted products tend to lose "brand equity" through a decrease in the amount a consumer is willing to pay for the product (Winer 2005). One interesting qualification is that when the variance of the deal discount increases, the reference price also increases, even though the average deal discount remained constant (Krishna and Johar 1996). A managerial implication is that brands should have multiple discount levels and sellers should vary the levels of the discount so consumers are less able to predict future savings.

When we combine the various behavioral theories, we begin to understand that promotions behave differently than long-term price reductions. Further, the frequency of promotions can affect reference price (lower it) which can make promotions less effective. Managers must consider the frequency and timing of their promotions and their impact on promotional effectiveness.

24.4 How promotions affect sales

There has never been debate about the foundational finding in the literature—sales promotions are associated with large increases in consumer sales. The question this raises is "what are the sources of incremental volume?"

In general, the sources of volume from a sales promotion come from one or more of the following sources: (1) customers switching their purchases from other brands (*brand switching*), (2) current consumers purchasing a greater quantity of the brand for inventory (*stockpiling*), (3) current consumers accelerating their purchase of the good (*purchase acceleration*), and (4) new consumers entering the market (*primary demand expansion—also called category expansion*).

24.4.1 Brand switching

Earlier studies show that a very high percentage of incremental promotional volume comes from switching. For example, Gupta (1988) showed that 84 percent of incremental sales was from switching. Other estimates have ranged from 43.8 percent to 93.9 percent (Bell et al. 1999).

More recently in a study across many categories, van Heerde et al. (2003) found that the percentage of the incremental volume attributable to brand switchers was only about one-third of the total incremental volume. They show that the difference in the percentage in their study versus previous studies arises from the fact that previous studies had not accounted for category growth in their calculations and hence overestimated the percentage attributed to brand switching. Van Heerde et al.'s findings have been supported by another study using store-level data (Pauwels et al. 2002).

For manufacturers, incremental volume coming from brand switching can be highly profitable because it is volume that the brand would not otherwise have. However, for retailers, incremental promotional volume from brand switching may or may not be profitable depending upon the brands it comes from and their profitability. Because brand does not expand category volume, it is far less advantageous to a retailer than to a manufacturer.

24.4.2 Purchase acceleration and stockpiling

When a promotion is run, consumers can react by changing their purchase timing by purchasing earlier than they normally would (purchase acceleration) and/or by purchasing

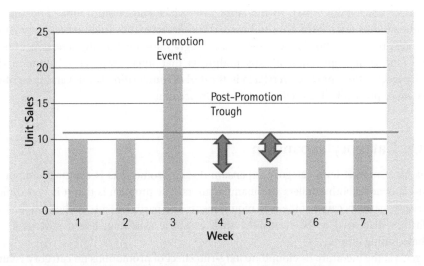

FIGURE 24.3 Post-promotion dip with stockpiling/acceleration effects

more units than they would normally purchase (stockpiling). Managers generally believe that purchase acceleration and stockpiling do not expand demand and are detrimental to both retailers and manufacturers. However, in categories in which consumption can expand due to product availability (e.g., candy), increasing a household's inventory of the product or moving their purchase forward can increase consumption and long-run sales. Purchase acceleration for services such as oil changes can also increase long-term sales. Studies have found that promotions can increase consumption in categories where the consumption rate is related to the amount of the product consumers have in their pantry (Ailawadi and Neslin 1998; Nijs et al. 2001), especially when the promotions involve strong brands (Sun 2005). For instance, two categories that exhibit this pantry effect are carbonated beverages and ice cream. Bell et al. (1999) quantified the proportion of the increase in sales due to a promotion that is attributable to purchase acceleration and increases in purchase quantity and found it ranged from 0.7 percent to 42.3 percent, with an average of 10.6 percent across thirteen categories.

Because purchase acceleration and stockpiling shift consumer purchases, we would expect to see a post-promotion dip after a promotion. Figure 24.3 shows the expected pattern with a promotion in week three. The "trough" or dip after the promotion occurs in weeks four and five, and is indicated by the arrows below the normal or baseline sales. During this trough, the additional units purchased during the promotion are consumed.

It is also possible to have a pre-promotion dip. In Figure 24.3, the sales in week two would then be less than the average due to consumers anticipating the promotion. Van Heerde et al. (2000) found evidence of pre-promotion dips as well as post-promotion dips.

Blattberg et al. (1995) summarized the literature and stated that post-promotional dips are rarely seen in store-level data. This seems paradoxical, as consumers should be consuming their inventory after a promotion instead of purchasing additional quantities. Subsequently, several papers investigated this issue and found either strong evidence of post-promotional dips (van Heerde et al. 2000) or qualified support of post-promotional dips (Mace and Neslin 2004). In the latter case, Mace and Neslin (2004) find that the promotional dips are related both to brand/UPC characteristics (high-priced, high-share, frequently promoted) and store trading area demographics (older customers, larger households). One clear implication of this finding is that inter-temporal substitution (i.e., quantity acceleration) may be overstated in the deal decomposition studies and promotions can be more profitable if this effect is taken into account.

24.4.3 Category expansion

The issue of market-level category expansion due to promotions is extremely important because it benefits both retailers and manufacturers. The problem is that it is very difficult to measure, partly because of the data requirements and partly because of the complexity of the factors that need to be controlled such as store switching, brand switching, and purchase timing effects.

In general the literature has found no long run effect of promotions on category volume, although short-term effects do exist (Ailawadi and Neslin 1998; Nijs et al. 2001). In a recent study of the effects of promotions at CVS Drug Stores, Ailawadi et al. (2007) find that 45 percent of the increase in sales due to promotions is attributable to category expansion effects. However, this may just be store switching rather than category expansion. While the literature does not find long-term category expansion effects, much more work needs to be conducted on this topic. It is a fundamental issue in determining the economic return from promotions.

24.4.4 How different sources of volume payout for retailers and manufacturers

There has been limited research into the profitability of promotions, in part, due to the lack of available cost data. However, several papers have studied the impact of promotions on revenues and profits. Srinivasan et al. (2004) find that promotions generally are profitable for manufacturers, but are not beneficial to retailers even when cross-category and store-traffic effects are considered. Similarly, in a study of promotions at CVS, Ailawadi et al. (2007) find that more than 50 percent of the promotions are not profitable. Further, in a field test, they determined that CVS could increase their profitability by $52 million if they eliminated promotions in the fifteen worst performing categories. A way to summarize the results above is to see how different sources of volume affect manufacturers' and retailers' profitability as shown in Table 24.4.

Manchanda et al. (1999) found large effects in complementary categories, and one study quantified these effects as 23–67 percent of profits and 33–40 percent of quantity in complementary categories are due to promotions (Niraj et al. 2008). However, these effects appear to be related to the categories and retailer brands, but not to national brands. Specifically, these effects do not appear to persist across categories for national brands (Russell and Kamakura 1997).

As noted above, one key objective of promotions is to drive incremental customers to the store, which, if true, would have a strong impact on the profitability of promotions.

Table 24.4 Effects of source of incremental volume on profitability of promotions

Source	Manufacturer	Retailer
Brand switching	Highly profitable if increased quantity covers cost of promotion.	Profitable if consumers purchase higher margin item.
Purchase acceleration and/or stockpiling	Mostly unprofitable. Can be profitable if stockpiling increases consumption or takes purchases from competitors.	Mostly unprofitable. Can be profitable if increase future demand or consumption.
Category expansion	Profitable if incremental volume covers cost of promotion.	Generally profitable.

Practitioners believe that a large percentage of store traffic is due to *feature advertising*. Feature advertising is defined as print media advertising by the retailer that highlights a set of products offered on promotion during the current week. While recent results do seem to indicate that some consumers respond to feature advertising (Briesch et al. 2009; Srinivasan and Bodapati 2006), they may be "cherry-picking" the featured items (i.e., only buying these featured items) which can reduce the profitability of the promotions (Fox and Hoch 2005; Rhee and Bell 2002). An intriguing finding is that assortment and distance are more important factors than price and promotions in store-choice decisions (Briesch et al. 2009).

In general there is limited empirical research showing what causes promotions to be profitable and when promotions are profitable. The presence of retailer and manufacturer promotions would suggest they are profitable; otherwise they would stop using them. However, there may be forces other than profitability driving the use of promotions. The next section discusses some of these issues and the strategy of promotions.

24.5 PROMOTIONAL STRATEGIES

This section looks at how retailers and manufacturers design promotional strategies. We begin with retailers and then turn to manufacturers.

24.5.1 Retailer promotional strategies

Many retailers use a merchandising system called "category management" designed to assist them develop pricing, promotions, item selection, space allocation, displays, and retailer advertising tactics. A category is defined as a set of products which consumers perceive to be close consumption substitutes. For example, peanut butter and jelly are in separate categories because they are substitutes, but not close substitutes. However, Jif and Peter Pan peanut butter are within the same category.

Some retailers use tactical guidelines based on the category roles to set their promotional strategies. Examples of category roles are "traffic" or "flagship". When the category role is to generate traffic (i.e., bring customers into the retailer's store), then promotions are likely to be deep, frequent, and less profitable for the category. The retailer is not setting promotional profitability as its objective but rather the power of the category to draw customers into the store. An example of a traffic-generating category in grocery stores is carbonated beverages.

For categories classified as flagship (large and profitable categories), the retailer will still promote but the depth of the promotional discount is lower and promotions will be evaluated based on how profitable they are. Examples of flagship categories in grocery stores are cookies and crackers.

How retailers promote categories influences the manufacturer's payout from their trade promotions. For categories with low volume and limited importance for the retailer, trade promotions will likely be less effective. For example, shoe polish is probably never or infrequently promoted by the retailer. Why should a manufacturer offer a trade promotion in that category? It is unlikely to have a positive payout. Thus, in designing a trade promotion strategy, a manufacturer must understand the retailer's category strategy.

Another strategic issue facing retailers is which brands to promote within a category. Retailers consider the brand's market share and consumer purchase behavior in deciding which brands to promote. Strong brands with high brand equity are likely to be promoted aggressively by the retailer. Weak brands, even in traffic-generating categories, are likely to receive less promotional push by the retailer. Again, in assessing its trade promotion strategy the manufacturer must understand how the retailer is likely to promote its brand and why.

24.5.2 Manufacturers promotions as a competitive tool

In considering how promotions are used by manufacturers as a competitive tool, we have identified two key strategic approaches. First, when manufacturers are battling each other through the use of promotions, an important consideration is whether the manufacturers are in a Prisoner's Dilemma. Secondly, manufacturers can use promotions to limit private label encroachment into a category.

24.5.2.1 Prisoner's Dilemma

Probably the most common strategic issue facing manufacturers is determining the likely competitive response to its promotion. Generally, a manufacturer should assume that a competitor is likely to respond and match its promotion. A simple way to capture the likely outcome is to create a two-by-two payoff matrix as shown in Table 24.5. For an explanation of such payoff matrices, see Chapter 19 by Kopalle and Shumsky. The matrix can have special properties depending upon what happens in the industry. We will concentrate on the payout when both manufacturers either promote or do not promote.

If the payout is higher for both firms when each competitor promotes than if they do not promote, then promoting can benefit both competitors. This is shown in Table 24.5a. This is a rarely discussed outcome in the marketing promotional literature because it is believed that promotions do not expand long-term total demand. However, as we discussed earlier, if promotions have a psychological advantage and cause consumers to have a greater response than a price reduction, then promotions can expand the market and consumption. Thus, the outcome that both firms are better off can definitely occur in the real world.

Table 24.5(a) Payoff tables—Higher payoff for firms with promotions

		Manufacturer A	
		Do not promote	Promote
Manufacturer B	Do not promote	8/8	12/5
	Promote	5/12	10/10

Notes: Values in cells represent profits for manufacturer A/manufacturer B

Table 24.5(b) Payoff table—Lower payoff for firms with promotions

		Manufacturer A	
		Do not promote	Promote
Manufacturer B	Do not promote	10/10	12/5
	Promote	5/12	8/8

Notes: Values in cells represent profits for manufacturer A/manufacturer B.

The more common view in the marketing literature is that the outcomes on the diagonals are as shown in Table 24.5b in which there is a higher payout when neither firm promotes than when they both promote. This is the classic Prisoner's Dilemma. Both firms promote because they are afraid their competitor will promote. Thus, promotions actually decrease profitability in the market and both firms are worse off.

In developing a promotional strategy it is extremely valuable to study what the likely payout matrix is and whether promotions actually increase "industry" profits. Unfortunately, little research has studied the actual frequency of the two cases described above in Table 24.5a and 24.5b. Procter and Gamble (P&G) tried an off-diagonal strategy, characterized by what they called "value pricing", designed to lower prices and reduce offering trade promotions. The strategy failed miserably because their competitors continued to promote and the outcome was a decrease in share for P&G. Ultimately, P&G reintroduced trade promotions on their brands.

24.5.2.2 *Competitive encroachment*

A number of papers (e.g., Lal 1990; Rao 1991) explore the extent to which price promotions are a way to limit competitive encroachment. Specifically, national brands (higher quality brands) will promote to reduce encroachment by private label brands (lower quality brands). Rao assumes that there are two firms in the market with one being a national brand and one being a private label brand. There are two segments of consumers: segment A consists of shoppers with no brand preference who purchase the lowest price brand; segment B shoppers rely on both price and brand preference. Segment B shoppers only purchase if the lower-quality brand has a large enough discount relative to the national brand. Given this setup, the manufacturer sets a single regular price and determines the number of promotions and the depth of the promotions. Rao shows that the strategies the two firms use are: (1) the national brand sets its regular price directed to its natural franchise (segment A) and (2) the private label sets its regular price to reduce the promotional encroachment by the national brand (segment B). The role of promotions is to "enforce the regular prices" and to decrease the incentive of the private label to reduce its price too much.

Lal (1990) makes a slightly different argument for price promotions. He assumes that there are three brands competing in the market—two national brands and one private label brand. Each national brand has a loyal segment, where loyal consumers will purchase their favorite brand as long as the price is below their reservation price. The private label brand does not have a loyal segment. Finally, there is a "switching segment" which purchases the brands based upon their relative prices. Lal shows that, under these assumptions, promotions are a way for the national brands to implicitly collude against the private label brand to limit its market share. He finds some empirical support for this theory.

Using a game-theoretic approach Agrawal (1996) examines the optimal advertising and promotional strategies when two manufacturers sell their products through a common retailer. Agrawal finds that advertising can be viewed as a defensive strategy to retain a loyal customer base, whereas promotions (i.e., trade deals) are an offensive strategy to attract competitors' loyal customers. In this case, it is optimal for a stronger brand to take an offensive strategy and offer more trade deals, whereas a weaker brand should adopt a defensive strategy. Additionally, Agrawal finds that the retailer should promote the stronger brand more frequently but with smaller discounts than the weaker brand.

All of these papers implicitly assume that cross-promotional effects are asymmetric. This assumption—higher quality/price brands are less vulnerable to price increases and gain more in category incidence and choice for price decreases than lower quality/price brands—has been supported in the empirical literature (Sivakumar and Raj 1997). However, it has been qualified in three important ways: (1) the effect depends not only on the price/quality tier, but on brand positioning advantage (over/under priced relative to competition) (Bronnenberg and Wathieu 1996); (2) promotions can diminish differentiation of high-tier brands, which would tend to diminish the asymmetric effects (Heath et al. 2000); and (3) when absolute effects (i.e., the change of share of the competing brand (not percentage) divided by the change in price (not percentage)) are considered instead of elasticities, the asymmetric relationship changes with smaller brands having an advantage over the larger brands (Sethuraman et al. 1999; Sethuraman and Srinivasan 2002). This area has high potential for future research because it examines the competition between national and store brands, which has grown in importance (Sethuraman 2009).

24.5.3 Manufacturers/retailers use promotions as a price discrimination mechanism

Even if we ignore the strong consumer response to promotions, several articles have argued that promotions can exist because they are a price discrimination tool. Specifically, promotions allow manufacturers and retailers to charge different prices to different consumers. In this section, we discuss several ways that promotions can be used to discriminate between consumers.

24.5.3.1 *Informed versus uninformed consumers*

Under the assumption that there are two types of consumers—informed and uninformed—it is optimal for retailers to offer promotions so that the uninformed consumers do not learn which store offers the lowest prices (Varian 1980). Informed consumers are assumed to know the prices at all stores in a given period; whereas uninformed consumers select stores at random. If the store does not randomize (promote) its prices, then the uninformed consumers would learn which store has the lowest price after several shopping trips and only visit the store with the lowest prices. Therefore, by randomizing (offering promotions), the firm can increase its profits (and prices) so the uninformed consumers never know which store has the lowest prices.

24.5.3.2 *Value of time*

A second explanation for why manufacturers offer coupons is based on heterogeneity in the value of time across consumers (Narasimhan 1988). The general idea is that a consumer is maximizing his or her utility which consists of consuming the good and "consuming" leisure time (called L). The consumer must spend a certain amount of time in order to clip and use the coupon, and saves S by using the coupon. The higher the value of S, the more of the good the consumer can use and hence the higher the consumer's utility.

However, the time to clip and use the coupon comes from the time devoted to leisure. Thus the tradeoff the consumer is making is reducing L, leisure time, which has some utility to the consumer and using it to redeem coupons which provides a saving. Because different consumers have different costs associated with L, firms can price discriminate between consumers with different value of time using coupons.

24.5.3.3 *Intertemporal discrimination*

Intertemporal discrimination has many forms and is covered more fully in Chapter 23 by Aviv and Vulcano and Chapter 25 by Ramakrishnan. However, we include a brief description and example for completeness. Assume that there are two segments of consumers: (1) consumers who cannot stockpile a good (i.e., their quantity purchase is limited to a single period), and (2) consumers who can stockpile for multiple periods.

When a promotion is offered, both segments can take advantage of the price discount. However, the segment which can stockpile the good purchases enough of the good for multiple periods; whereas the other segment only purchases for one period. Therefore, in the second period when there is no discount, the segment which cannot stockpile pays a higher price for the good. The same logic applies to households with different consumption rates, where the consumption rate determines the number of periods in which the household can stockpile the good.

24.5.4 Trade deals increase efficiency

Many marketing managers worry about the efficiency of the distribution channels. Generally, an efficient channel has the goal of all members aligned so that they are all working to maximize the system profits. Implicit in this definition is the notion that the actions of the channel members are coordinated. While the issue of channel contracts is covered in more detail in Chapter 29 by Kaya and Özer, we briefly cover the issue here for completeness. The problem can be viewed as one where the manufacturer and retailer have different objectives within a category for a market. For instance, as a manufacturer, Coca-Cola would like all carbonated beverage sales to be one of their products. However, the retailer would like to sell all of the carbonated products in the market, regardless of the manufacturer (ignoring margin considerations). Channel coordination and efficiency mechanisms align the retailer's goals and actions with the manufacturer's goals, in this case Coca-Cola.

Drèze and Bell (2003) examine scan-back promotions and compare them to off-invoice promotions and show that retailers strictly prefer off-invoice promotions to scan-back promotions. However, they also show that manufacturers can design scan-back promotions so that the retailer is indifferent between off-invoice and scan-back promotions. The result is that the manufacturer is better off, and the manufacturer can use scan-back promotions to align the retailer's actions with the manufacturer's profit goals.

Taylor (2002) examines a more general situation under which the manufacturer enters into a contract with the retailer where the manufacturer provides rebates to the retailer on the units sold beyond a target level. He finds that when retailer actions do not influence consumer demand, this contract is sufficient for channel coordination. However, when retailer actions do influence consumer demand, this target rebate contract does not coordinate the channel. To align the retailer's and manufacturer's objectives, the manufacturer must also allow the retailer to return unsold units.

A second trade dealing mechanism which can impact efficiency is *slotting fees*. While there has been a limited amount of analytical research into slotting fees, the key question is: "Do slotting fees increase efficiency in the marketplace or do they hinder competition in the market place?" (Bloom et al. 2000). The argument for hindering competition is that slotting fees greatly increase the costs of introducing new products and may make it economically infeasible for small and medium-sized firms to gain widespread distribution of their products. That said, new product introductions are inherently risky with one in three launched products unsuccessful (Cooper 2001). Therefore, one reason why slotting fees may increase market efficiency is that slotting fees transfer some of the risk of new product introductions from the retailer to the manufacturer by covering some of the potential lost opportunity costs and administrative and operating costs associated with the failed introduction.

Aydin and Hausman (2009) analytically examine this situation. Specifically, they assume there is some demand uncertainty which causes the retailer, but not the manufacturer, to incur inventory holding costs. They show that the manufacturer may offer to pay slotting fees to the retailer to ease the inventory costs so that the retailer will choose a larger assortment. Therefore, slotting fees can provide channel coordination in terms of providing optimal assortment to the consumer.

The empirical results addressing this issue are mixed. Sudhir and Rao (2006) find that slotting fees tend to increase efficiency in the marketplace, whereas Bloom et al. (2000) find that while slotting fees are a method to shift the risk of new product introductions to manufacturers, they are also applied in a discriminatory manner against manufacturers. Bloom et al.'s results tend to support the finding that slotting fees may hinder competition by making it difficult for smaller manufacturers to obtain widespread distribution.

24.6 EMPIRICAL MODELS OF PROMOTIONS

One of the reasons for the growth in promotional activity in the 1980s was the ability to measure the impact of promotions on sales. This section reviews the data available to model promotions, provides a description of the basic models and their purpose and ends with some of the more advanced issues, procedures, and rationale for addressing them.

24.6.1 Data to model promotions

There are two types of data critical for modeling sales promotions: sales and causal promotional data. The data sales data available for modeling promotions cover three types: (1) point of sale (POS) obtained from retailers' scanners, (2) panel data from a sample of consumers, and (3) customer purchase data. The other required data are causal data which include promotional discounts, presence of feature advertising, and displays.

24.6.1.1 *POS and causal data*

POS data are currently available for most consumer packaged goods categories in the USA and other developed countries because Nielsen and IRI collect both POS sales data and causal data. For categories other than packaged goods (e.g., durable goods), the problem for manufacturers is the availability of data both at the POS level and causal data because very few third parties collect and sell the data.

Retailers have the potential to have both POS and causal data for any type of business as long as they have scanners. However, in order to develop promotional models, they must collect and maintain the causal data which they often do not do. For retailers POS data provide much of the sales information that they need with the exception being individual purchase behavior. The disadvantage is retailers need to create causal databases and maintain them which, as stated earlier, many do not.

For manufacturers, the advantages of POS data are accuracy, ease of modeling, and wide availability through third-party data collection sources for some categories such as consumer packaged goods categories. The disadvantages are that consumer behavior cannot be modeled directly, and with some exceptions, categories outside consumer packaged goods are not readily available to manufacturers and causal data are not always maintained.

24.6.1.2 *Panel data*

The second source of data is panel data collected from consumers who shop a category or groups of categories. A sample of consumers is chosen to be part of the panel. All of their purchases are recorded by the panel member and maintained in a database. The problem is the causal data. Because each consumer shops at a different set of stores, there is no easy way to maintain and collect all of the causal data from all of the competing stores.

Panel data provide advantages to manufacturers because, in many categories, panel data can be collected when retailers are not willing to provide POS data. The problems with panel data are causal data and sample size limitations. Many panels are too small to capture accurate data at a local market level where promotional competition is occurring.

24.6.1.3 Purchase data

Purchase data maintained by Internet retailers and direct-to-consumer manufacturers can be highly accurate and provide significant insight into a consumer's purchase behavior and sensitivity to promotions. Purchase data is by far the best source of sales data. If the firm keeps accurate promotional history including non-responses to promotions, then the firm has potentially a highly accurate, detailed dataset which can be used to model individual promotional response behavior.

24.6.2 POS promotional models

POS promotional models have been utilized since the 1980s by both academics and practitioners (see, e.g., Blattberg and Neslin 1990 for a summary). The basic model used is:

$$\ln S_t = \alpha + \beta_1 P_t + \beta_2 D_t + \beta_3 FA_t + \beta_4 DISP_t + e_t$$

where S_t = unit sales at time t, P_t is the regular price at time t, D_t is the promotional discount at time t, FA_t is feature advertising (0, 1) at time t, and $DISP_t$ (0, 1) is presence of a display at time t and e_t is the error term at time t. By separating price from promotional discount, the modeler is assuming that promotions have a differential effect (usually assumed to be greater) from a price reduction.

This basic model has been revised and restructured in many ways both in terms of inputs such as by type of display and feature advertising, transforming it into a share model, and using reference prices and their variants. One key addition is capturing the post-promotion dip discussed earlier. By adding lagged promotion variables, dummy variables, or other indicator variables, the modeler can then estimate the total impact of promotions (Neslin 2002; van Heerde et al. 2002; van Heerde and Neslin 2008).

Using POS sales data from retailers and causal data from data suppliers such as Nielsen, the model's parameters are estimated. Once completed the firm can estimate sales with and without promotions, what impact different promotional discount levels have on sales, and how much feature ads and displays increase sales. A manufacturer can then optimize its trade promotion offer to retailers based on the likely impact it will have on both sales and profits.

Several issues arise with this basic model in practice. First, the likelihood of multi-collinearity that results from feature advertising, displays, and price discounts being offered simultaneously. This has posed problems to modelers for years and no simple solution exists. Only through experimentation and detailed store-level data can better estimates be obtained. For practitioners it is critical to test for multicollinearity to ensure that the model estimates for feature ad, display, and price discount have the appropriate precision.

A second issue is determining how to incorporate the promotional discount. If one uses a semi-log model, the effect of a promotion accelerates with the size of the discount, implying that smaller discounts will have limited sales effect. Some attempts have been made to incorporate S-shaped curves in modeling the promotional discount, implying a ceiling on sales after some promotional level is reached. This may not seem plausible but at some point consumers reach a saturation level in the quantity they can purchase. Other functional forms can be used depending upon the expected promotional effect being modeled. Should the discount be captured using a percentage or an absolute level? Little evidence is available to guide this decision.

Another issue is how to link the retail promotional model with trade promotions so that manufacturers can maximize their trade promotions. If the trade promotion offers a specified amount for a feature ad, does the retailer offer the manufacturer a feature ad? What is the relationship between manufacturer spending and receiving ads and discounts from the retailer? The requirement is to create a "linking" model which shows how various types of trade deals lead to specific retailer promotional actions which then lead to increases in sales.

Fourth is modeling category sales to estimate how category sales increase and which brands gain and lose sales when a given item is promoted. Many of the models in the marketing literature concentrate on brands or SKUs. However, retailers concentrate on brand and SKU impact, category sales, and category profit increases. Within a category certain brands are more likely to respond to promotions, will have a greater impact on category expansion and will cannibalize the sales of other brands including private label. Retailers need to understand the category dynamics of promotions to design their promotional strategies.

Fifth is determining the appropriate aggregation level. There is a major question in the real-world regarding the use of store-level data versus retailer-level or market-level data. Generally it is believed that using store-level data is better but much of the available level data have been aggregated to the retailer level.

In summary, the basic POS model and its variants have been a "workhorse" used by researchers, practitioners, and consultants to study the effects of promotions on sales. It has led to many manufacturers and retailers improving the effectiveness of their sales promotion tactics.

24.6.3 Promotional models using panel data

POS promotional models provide managers with the level of incremental sales but offer limited insight into the sources of volume. Promotional models using individual purchase history data can provide insights into how consumers are responding to promotions.

The types of promotional questions models can answer using individual purchase data are: (1) what are the sources of incremental volume? (2) which types of consumers are responding to promotions such as non-brand purchasers? (3) do promotions induce consumers to purchase resulting in future purchase loyalty? (4) is volume coming from competitive retailers or merely from the retailer's current customers?

For almost three decades marketing academics have modeled promotions using panel data starting with Guadagni and Little's (1983) path breaking article using a logit model to capture promotional effects. Later, Gupta (1988) used various models to decompose the promotional spike into its components.

One of the first promotional models was developed by Gupta (1988). We will not cover his model explicitly but will show the general form of the model. Specifically, define as Q_{scjt} the unit sales in store s ($s = 1..S$) in period t ($t = 1..T$) for item j ($j = 1..J$)[2] in category c ($c = 1..C$). Then Gupta's model can be written as:

$$Q_{scjt} = \sum_{h=1}^{H} Pr(y_{hst} = 1)Pr(y_{hct} = 1|y_{hst})Pr(y_{hbt} = 1|y_{hst}, y_{hct})q_{hbt}$$

where H is the number of households, $Pr(y_{hst} = 1)$ is the probability that store s is visited by household h in period t (i.e., where to shop?), $Pr(y_{hct} = 1|y_{hst})$ is the probability that household h purchased in category c, conditioned on visiting store s (i.e., when to buy?), $Pr(y_{hjt} = 1|y_{hst}, y_{hct})$ is the probability that item j was selected by household h, conditioned on being in store s and purchasing in category c, and q_{hbt} is the quantity that the household purchased conditioned on selecting brand b in category c in store s in period t (i.e., how much to buy?). Models are then created for each component of the above equation.

The probabilities in the above equations are all modeled through "utility" functions, where the utility function consists of a "deterministic" component (i.e., observed variables like price and feature advertising) and a "random" component (or "error term" as in the sales models above). In these types of models, it is assumed that a consumer is most likely to select the alternative with the highest utility. Therefore, the probabilities associated with the alternatives are proportional to their relative utilities. The specific assumptions made about the random component then define the form of the model. For instance, when the random component is assumed to have a normal distribution, a probit model results; and when the random component is assumed to have a Gumbel distribution, a logit model results. Both of these models are estimated through Maximum Likelihood techniques.

24.6.3.1 *Quantity Model*

Mela et al. (1998) provide a quantity model for household purchases. Their model has a form similar to:

$$\ln(q_{hsjt}) = \beta_{0hj} + \beta_{1h}f_{sjt} + \beta_{2h}D_{sjt} + \beta_{3h}(1 - d_{sjt}) + \beta_{4h}inv_{ht} + \beta_{5h}loy_{hjt} + \beta_{6h}w_{hjt} + \varepsilon_{sjt}$$

where and D_{sjt} (0, 1) is the presence of a display for brand j at time t in store s, d_{sjt} is the promotional discount percentage for brand j in period t at store s, and inv_{ht} represents the household's inventory of the category in period t, loy_{hjt} represents household h's loyalty to brand j in period t, w_{hjt} is a selection correction term (similar to a tobit model) because this model is conditioned on choice and incidence, and ε_{sjt} is the error term. While Mela et al. used a constructed inventory variable, more recently some authors have argued that this constructed variable can introduce bias into the model and as an alternative have suggested using three observed variables (lag quantity, time since last purchase, and their interaction) instead (Erdem et al. 2003; Hendel and Nevo 2006). Finally, consumer loyalty is included in the model because the literature has shown that consumers may purchase more of their favorite brand when it is on promotion (cf. Mela et al. 1998), for which they used a smoothed brand loyalty term (Guadagni and Little 1983).

---

[2] We use the term "item" here instead of brand, stock-keeping unit (SKU) or even brand-size as these different types of items imply different aggregation levels. Aggregation of SKUs is discussed in the section on data issues below.

24.6.3.2 *Purchase incidence model*

There are two basic forms of the incidence model depending upon whether or not choice is also modeled. When choice is included, and only one category is considered in the model, then incidence is modeled as a separate alternative (also called the *outside good*, or *no-purchase option*). For example, if we assume that a consumer's decision to purchase in a category is independent of the other categories, conditioned on the consumer being in a specific store, we can write the utility for category incidence as:

$$U_{cht} = Z_{ht}\beta_{1h} + X_{ct}\beta_{2h} + \varepsilon_{cht}$$

where Z_{ht} represents household-specific factors like consumer inventory levels and/or time since the household last purchased in the category (Briesch et al. 2008; Manchanda et al. 1999), X_{ct} represents category-specific factors like merchandising and price (Manchanda et al. 1999; Niraj et al. 2008), and ε_{cht} represents the random component or error term. This model allows managers to determine how in-store merchandising activity affects the consumer's purchase timing decision, after controlling for consumer's inventory levels and interpurchase time. As noted above, as the utility increases (decreases), the consumer is more (less) likely to purchase within the category.

While it is beyond the scope of this chapter to discuss all of the variants of incidence models (see Seetharaman et al. (2005) for a discussion of this literature), we provide a model of cross-category incidence based upon the model in Niraj et al. (2008), where they study cross-category purchase incidence. This behavior is very important to managers, as it affects the profitability of promotions. Specifically, managers may offer a promotion where they lose money on pasta, but because consumers also buy pasta sauce, complementary category sales can make the promotion profitable. Their joint category incidence model has the form:

$$U_{10ht} = X_{1t}\beta_{11h} + X_{2t}\beta_{12h} + \varepsilon_{10ht}$$
$$U_{01ht} = X_{1t}\beta_{21h} + X_{2t}\beta_{22h} + \varepsilon_{01ht}$$
$$U_{11ht} = X_{1t}\beta_{11h} + X_{2t}\beta_{12h} + X_{1t}\beta_{21h} + X_{2t}\beta_{22h} + \gamma_{11h} + \varepsilon_{11ht}$$
$$U_{00ht} = \varepsilon_{00ht}$$

where U_{10ht} represents the indirect utility for household h in period t of purchasing in the first category, but not the second category, U_{01ht} represents the indirect utility of purchasing in the second category but not the first category, U_{11ht} represents the indirect utility of purchasing in both categories, and U_{00ht} represents the utility of purchasing in neither category. The Xs represent predictor variables for incidence in each category (e.g., category price, display, and feature activity). When the merchandising variables are included as part of the Xs, then this model accounts for cross-category effects as the merchandising activity in one category is included in the indirect utility of the other category. This effect has been called *purchase complementarity/substitution*, that is, the categories are purchased together (complementarity) or exclusive of each other (substitution) (Sun 2005). γ_{11h} represents the additional utility the household receives for purchasing in both categories.

24.6.3.3 *Brand choice models*

Brand choice models normally assume that consumers have exogenously decided where to shop and when to shop, although these models have been extended to include incidence as well (see Chandukala et al. (2007) for a good review of the assumptions, trends, and construction of choice models). Choice models address the important question: given the merchandising effects in the store, which brand (or SKU) does the consumer select? Assuming that household h is presented with J alternatives ($j = 1..J$) in period t ($t = 1..T$), the choice model can be written as:

$$U_{hjt} = v_{hjt} + \varepsilon_{hjt}$$

$$v_{hjt} = \beta_{ohj} + X_{jt}\beta_h$$

where U_{hjt} is the indirect utility household h places on alternative j in period t, v_{hjt} is called the systematic component of utility and ε_{hjt} is the random component. X_{jt} then represents the predictor variables for choice, for example price, display, feature advertising, etc.

Note that the competitive pricing effects are not included in the indirect utility, as they are captured indirectly through consumers selecting one alternative from all of the alternatives. This effect is seen more clearly when we write out the logit model as:

$$P(y_{hjt} = 1) = \exp(v_{hjt})/\left(\sum_{i=1}^{J} \exp(v_{hjt})\right)$$

where $P(\cdot)$ represents the probability that household h selects alternative j in period t. Because choice is conditional on incidence, only variables that are alternative-specific are included in the model. Variables common to all alternatives (e.g., consumer inventory levels) are not identified.

24.6.4 Individual-level promotional models using firm purchase history data

The next frontier in promotional modeling is using actual individual-level purchase histories rather than panel data. Two sources now exist. First, retailers offer frequent shopper cards that record all purchases from the retailer by SKU and trip. Second, some direct-to-consumer sellers capture all of their customers' purchase histories. These companies range from on-line retailers such as Amazon to telecommunication companies such as Verizon or AT&T. When a promotion is run, the firm can analyze what the impact is on the acquisition of new customers, retention rates, spending levels, and long-term purchase behavior.

New models are being developed to analyze these data such as hazard models with explanatory variables to capture retention rates, logit models to estimate the responsiveness of current customers to promotions for additional products, and customer equity models to compute the long-term value of promoted versus not-promoted customers.

Hazard models study the likelihood a customer will defect given the customer has continued to be a customer up until a promotion occurs. This allows us to address key issues such as how does a promotion change the likelihood a customer will defect? How does the customer acquisition method affect the hazard rate (defection rate)? (See, e.g., Gupta et al. 2004; Jain and Singh 2002; Thomas 2001; Blattberg et al. 2008.)

The availability of better data allows the firm to develop data-driven analytical decisions regarding promotions. For example, one of the age-old promotion questions is does a promotion cause customers to require lower prices in order to continue purchasing from the company if their initial purchase is on promotion. Long-historical data series enable firms to answer this question. Panel data, because of the limited samples sizes and problems with the accuracy and availability of causal data, cannot easily answer many of the key individual behavior questions. Long individual purchase history data can address these questions.

Another area in which individual purchase histories can help a firm is in segmenting customers based on their promotional sensitivity. Models can be used to estimate each individual's sensitivity to promotions and then, using the results, the firm can segment customers so that different promotional offers can be provided based on their promotional sensitivity.

The two potential problems with individual purchase history data are the lack of promotional histories and the failure to model non-response to promotions. Surprisingly, many firms do not maintain accurate promotional histories by customers. This limits the firm's ability to develop these models. The models built must also include all promotions offered to the customer and then model the non-response as well as the response.

24.6.5 Modeling issues

In this section we briefly discuss modeling issues associated with sales promotions.

24.6.5.1 *Consumers have different promotional responsiveness*

Most researchers and managers believe consumer segments respond differently to promotions. Models need to be able to capture heterogeneity in consumer response to promotions otherwise the estimated parameters may be biased and provide nonsensical results (Allenby and Rossi 1999). There are two fundamental types of consumer heterogeneity—response and structural. Response heterogeneity assumes that consumers use the same model of choice, but differ in their parameters (e.g., the βs in the above equations). The parameters can be assumed to have either a continuous or discrete distribution. Research suggests that both provide reasonable estimates (Andrews et al. 2002). From a practical standpoint, discrete distributions (i.e., consumer segments are estimated) are more useful, but require the model to be estimated assuming that the researcher knows the true number of segments. To determine the "best" number of segments, the model must be estimated multiple times—a separate estimation for each different number of segments in the market. These estimation results are then compared and one final number of segments is selected based upon some information criteria (Kamakura and Russell 1989; Dayton and McReady 1988).

When a continuous distribution is used, the coefficients can either be estimated using Bayesian Methods (see, e.g., Rossi et al. 1995) or through classical econometric techniques. In the Bayesian methods, Markov Chains are used to get simulation-based estimates of the coefficients and their distributions (Rossi and Allenby 2003). Classical econometrics also use simulation-based techniques to estimate the parameters through a technique called Simulated Maximum Likelihood Estimation (SMLE). The basic idea is that the distribution of the parameters is assumed beforehand, and this distribution is numerically integrated during the estimation process (Train 2003).

Structural heterogeneity assumes that differences in consumer response among segments are best modeled using structurally different models for each segment. If the consumer segments are defined beforehand, estimating structural heterogeneity is straightforward. However, if the underlying consumer segments are not pre-identified, this type of model requires discrete heterogeneity. If the researcher is using POS data, several methods for estimating discrete segments at the aggregate-level have been proposed (Besanko et al. 2003; Bodapati and Gupta 2004).

24.6.5.2 *Modeling using aggregate POS or panel data*

Does aggregating household panel data to the retailer level produce any biases in the estimates? Gupta et al. (1996) examined this issue and found that when similar models were used for both the panel and store data, while the price elasticities were statistically different, they would not significantly change managerial decisions, that is, they were not managerially different. This finding is consistent with a meta-analysis of price elasticities which finds no significant difference between POS and panel data elasticities (Bijmolt et al. 2005). The decision about the aggregation level seems to be driven by whether or not the aggregation-level can answer the research question and not by biases introduced by the level of aggregation.

24.6.5.3 *Can brands, SKUs, or brand sizes be pruned from the data?*

In modeling panel data, it is common for researchers to eliminate SKUs to be able to efficiently estimate the model parameters. We note that this issue only applies to models that are constructed as choice models as opposed to models constructed as sales models. Zanutto and Bradlow (2006) found that the missing data introduced by deleting SKUs, brand sizes, or brands can lead to severe parameter bias in the estimation. The magnitude of the bias is related to the pruning method selected, whether or not the model is misspecified, and the relative fit of the model (models with better fits having lower bias).

24.6.5.4 *Can SKUs be aggregated to a higher level?*

Andrews and Currim (2005) found that significant biases can result from aggregating SKUs to the brand level in choice models. They recommend that, whenever possible, modeling should be done at the level where the marketing mix decisions are made. For instance, in soft goods, such as clothing, groups of SKUs (e.g., shirts from the same manufacturer that only differ in size) have the same prices. This bias was found to be related to linearly aggregating (taking a simple average over the SKUs) continuous variables from different SKUs. On the other hand, when marketing mix decisions are made at a level higher than the SKU level (e.g., prices are set at the brand-level for multiple flavors), estimation issues are introduced into SKU-level models because several predictors have high (or perfect) correlation.

24.6.5.5 Can households be removed from panel data estimation?

When households are removed using a random selection technique (e.g., to generate a hold-out sample) no biases are expected to be generated although the model loses power due to the smaller sample size.

Gupta et al. (1996) identify two general methods used to *non-randomly* exclude households from panel data: (1) household selection and (2) purchase selection. Under household selection, all purchases from those households that only purchase the selected items are included in the estimation. Under purchase selection, all purchases of the selected items are included (regardless of the household purchase history). They find that household selection can create severe biases in the parameter estimates when a large portion of the households are excluded. Kim and Rossi (1994) show that parameters will be biased towards higher price sensitivity when the sample is restricted to high purchase frequency or high volume households.

24.6.5.6 How should zero sales of an item be handled?

This question has two components. First, if no observations are recorded and the analyst does not have pricing information, what price should be used in this period (even as a competitive price predictor)? Second, should the observation with zero sales be included in the estimation?

Erdem et al. (1999) investigate the first issue and find that imputing prices (and/or coupons) can create severe biases in the estimated parameters. They recommend integrating out the missing price data over the observed distribution. A clear drawback to this method is the computational resources required to estimate the model. Some, but not all, of this problem can be alleviated when the analyst has separate information about the retailer pricing behavior. For instance, if the analyst knows that the retailer only changes prices once a week (say Friday), then missing prices within that week (say Wednesday) can be imputed from the other prices within the week.

Briesch et al. (2008) investigate the second issue within a choice context. They show that even when price information is accurate and complete, the parameter estimates can be biased when the zeros are improperly included or excluded. The general idea is that when the zeros are due to exogenous factors like the item being out of stock, then the zero should be excluded from the estimation. However, when the zeros are due to endogenous factors (e.g., promotion of a competing item), then the item should be included in the estimation. They develop models, based on the literature on choice sets (Bronnenberg and Vanhonacker 1999), that reduce the bias from the zeros.

24.7 EMERGING ISSUES

There are a number of issues in the promotion literature that have emerged over the last few years that require further research.

24.7.1 Overstock promotional clearance strategies

An emerging issue that has been previously researched but is important for soft goods and hard goods but less important for packaged goods is how to price overstocked goods. Lazear (1986) developed a theory of temporal promotions which assumed that a segment of consumers were fashion-driven and would pay more because they could receive the goods if they purchased early while another segment of consumers waited for lower prices and took the risk that the product would be available. For firms trying to manage overstocks and perishable inventory, an important issue becomes how many consumers are in the "wait and see" segment and how many want to ensure the availability of the merchandise (Gallego et al. 2009). For a more complete review of this literature, see Chapter 23 by Aviv and Vulcano.

The emerging issue is how consumer expectations enter the process. The pricing literature has developed models which begin to take into account consumer expectations regarding future prices. If a firm is known to price lower in the future for the same product, then consumers have an incentive to act strategically and delay their purchase (Soysal 2007; Su 2007; Aviv and Pazgal 2008; Boyaci and Özer 2010).

An important and related research area is the accuracy of consumer expectations with respect to promotions. Sun (2005) studies this issue and concludes that consumers can accurately anticipate promotions. However, further research into this area is needed. Obviously, this has great significance to managers at both manufacturers and retailers.

24.7.2 Promotions for non-packaged goods companies

Much of the promotional research in marketing has been for high-velocity packaged goods products because of the availability of the data. However, promotions are very important in many other industries such as the fashion and durable goods (e.g., electronics and automobiles). Automobiles highlight a very important issue discussed in the last section which is the impact of promotions on consumer expectations and the timing of purchases. Promotions have become very common in the automotive industry and the consumer has learned to wait to purchase based on when the promotions will occur. This raises issues about what "reference price" consumers use for a car. Because consumers have learned to purchase only when there is a promotion, managing production, inventories, and list price have become very complex (Busse et al. 2007).

For electronics and fashion, the promotional issues are linked to seasonal product change over holiday seasons and other peak selling seasons. An age-old question is: "When is the optimal time to offer promotions—during the peak season or the non-peak season?" The obvious answer is to offer them in the non-peak season but there are numerous promotions made during the peak season (Chevalier et al. 2003).

24.7.3 How do promotions affect the lifetime value of a customer within loyalty programs?

Loyalty programs using frequent shopper cards are now widespread in retailing. These programs rely heavily on promotions but do these programs increase the loyalty and lifetime value of a customer? There is limited research on this topic. Lal and Bell (2003) find that frequent shopper programs increase causal shoppers (often called cherry pickers) while subsidizing loyal customers. Loyalty because of the promotional strategy used by retailers may not actually produce the desired goal of increasing loyalty.

This raises many questions that have been asked and some addressed about promotions. In the 1980s and 1990s many anti-promotional advocates who believed that advertising was a preferred marketing expenditure argued that promotions reduced brand equity and loyalty. Dodson et al. (1978) raised this issue and found in laboratory studies that promotions decreased brand loyalty. However, others such as Johnson (1984) using real-world (not laboratory-generated) data, found that brands that increased promotions did not exhibit decreased brand loyalty. The empirical findings on this issue are mixed and this topic still remains highly controversial. The advent of retail loyalty data provides another opportunity to assess whether promotions can be used to increase or decrease loyalty.

24.7.4 Linking psychological theories of promotions and quantitative research

There needs to be a greater link between psychological theories such as smart shopper and transactional utility with empirical research. How do smart shoppers learn to be "smart shoppers?" Do they simply respond to promotions that provide reference prices? How large is transaction utility and under what conditions does it occur?

24.8 CONCLUSIONS AND SUMMARY

In this chapter we covered the important topic of sales promotions from the consumer, strategic, and empirical perspectives. From a consumer standpoint, the behavioral theories of transaction utility, smart shopper, and reference price provide insight into why consumers respond strongly to promotions rather than to a price decrease.

It is important for the managers to know the source of the incremental volume from a promotion, as this plays a major role in determining promotional profitability for both the manufacturer and retailer. When the source of the volume is brand switching, the promotion can be very profitable for the manufacturer, but is only profitable for the retailer when consumers are switching to higher margin items. For many categories, when the source of the incremental volume is purchase acceleration and stockpiling, then sales promotions will not be profitable for manufacturers unless they lead to increased consumption. Consumers will simply change their purchase timing, particularly loyal customers. When the source of the incremental volume is an increase in the number of consumers purchasing in the category, sales promotions can be profitable for both the retailer and manufacturer. An important and unresolved issue is, when promotions draw new consumers into the category (or increase consumption of the category), can sustained promotional activity keep these new consumers purchasing in the category and/or maintain the increased consumption rate of current consumers? If so, promotions could expand the overall category and lead to increased manufacturer and retailer profitability.

Strategically, there are many reasons sales promotions exist. First, trade deals can help coordinate activities within a marketing channel, ensuring that the participants are striving to maximize profitability for all firms. Secondly, sales promotions can be used as a competitive tool to temporarily steal market share from competitors, to protect one's own market share, or to prevent new entrants and/or store brands from gaining significant market share. Thirdly, sales promotions can be used to price discriminate against some consumers, raising the overall profitability of the firm. For instance, shopper cards are a mechanism where retailers can reward loyal consumers by providing discounts on certain merchandise. Similarly, coupons are a mechanism where manufacturers and retailers can provide discounts to targeted consumers—those who have the time to clip and redeem coupons.

The Internet provides new challenges and opportunities for sales promotions. The detailed consumer information as well as accurate causal information allows researchers to examine individual purchasing behavior. This type of data can provide better insights into consumer behavior and decision making.

The Internet raises a host of questions about consumer behavior, and ultimately firm profitability. For instance, given the new types of communication vehicles (e.g., e-mail, banner ads, partner links, keywords), which are more effective in attracting new customers? Specifically, how do they affect traffic (clicks, unique visits, new users)? How do they affect conversion rates? How do these different mechanisms affect brand image and loyalty? Given the "ease" of information search, are consumers more or less price-sensitive? Are they more or less brand/site loyal? How large is the spike in traffic/sales associated with these promotions? Are consumers more likely to cherry pick on promotions? How large are their basket sizes relative to "brick and mortar" retailers? From which specific channels do Internet retailers compete or take sales? Is it mass retailers or catalogue retailers? Even if large spikes in sales/traffic are observed due to Internet promotions, how much of this spike is due to purchase acceleration, quantity acceleration, and brand switching?

Promotions have been one of the most researched elements of the marketing mix. There are still many interesting and challenging issues facing managers. The growth of real-time sales data coupled with accurate promotional histories opens the future in which real-time on-line promotions will become the norm. This leads to opportunities for sales promotion researchers and practitioners to develop new methods, tactics, and strategies.

REFERENCES

ACNielsen (2002) *ACNielsen 2002 Trade Promotion Practices Study*. Available at: http://www2.acnielsen.com/pubs/2003_q2_ci_tpp.shtml.

Agarwal, D. (1996) "Effect of Brand Loyalty on Advertising and Trade Promotions: A Game Theoretic Analysis with Empirical Evidence", *Marketing Science* 15: 86–108.

Ailawadi, K. L. and Neslin, S. A. (1998) "The Effect of Promotion on Consumption: Buying it More and Consuming it Faster", *Journal of Marketing Research* 35: 390–8.

—— Harlam, B. A., Cesar, J., et al. (2007) "Quantifying and Improving Promotion Effectiveness at CVS", *Marketing Science* 26: 566–75.

Alba, J. W., Mela, C. F., Shimp, T. A., et al. (1999) "The Effect of Discount Frequency and Depth on Consumer Price Judgments", *Journal of Consumer Research* 26: 99–114.

Allenby, G. M. and Rossi, P. E. (1999) "Marketing Models of Consumer Heterogeneity", *Journal of Econometrics* 89: 57–78.

Andrews, R. L. and Currim, I. S. (2005) "An Empirical Investigation of Scanner Data Preparation Strategies for Consumer Choice Models", *International Journal of Research in Marketing* 22: 319–31.

—— Ainslie, A. and Currim, I. S. (2002) "An Empirical Comparison of Logit Choice Models with Discrete Versus Continuous Representations of Heterogeneity", *Journal of Marketing Research* 39: 479–87.

Aviv, Y. and Pazgal, A. (2008) "Optimal Pricing of Seasonal Products in the Presence of Forward-looking Consumers", *Manufacturing & Service Operations Management* 10: 339–59.

Aydin, G. and Hausman, W. H. (2009) "The Role of Slotting Fees in the Coordination of Assortment Decisions", *Production and Operations Management* 8: 635–52.

Bell, D. R., Chiang, J., and Padmanabhan, V. (1999) "The Decomposition of Promotional Response: An Empirical Generalization", *Marketing Science* 18: 504–26.

Besanko, D., Dube, J.-P., and Gupta, S. (2003) "Competitive Price Discrimination Strategies in a Vertical Channel Using Aggregate Retail Data", *Management Science* 49: 1121–38.

Bijmolt, T. H. A., van Heerde, H. J., and Pieters, R. G. M. (2005) "New Empirical Generalizations on the Determinants of Price Elasticity", *Journal of Marketing Research* 42: 141–56.

Blattberg, R. C. and Neslin, S. A. (1990) *Sales Promotions: Concepts, Methods and Strategies.* Englewood Cliffs, NJ: Prentice Hall.

—— Briesch, R. A., and Fox, E. J. (1995) "How Promotions Work", *Marketing Science* 14: G122–G132.

—— Kim, B.-D., and Neslin, S. A. (2008) *Database Marketing: Analyzing and Managing Customers.* New York: Springer Verlag.

Bloom, P. N., Gundlach, G. T., and Cannon, J. P. (2000) "Slotting Allowances and Fees: Schools of Thought and the Views of Practicing Managers", *Journal of Marketing* 64: 92–108.

Bodapati, A. V. and Gupta, S. (2004) "The Recoverability of Segmentation Structure from Store-Level Aggregate Data", *Journal of Marketing Research* XLI: 351–64.

Boyaci, T. and Özer, Ö. (2010) "Information Acquisition for Capacity Planning Via Pricing and Advance Selling: When to Stop and Act?" *Operations Research* 58: 1328–49.

Briesch, R. A., Dillon, W. R., and Blattberg, R. C. (2008) "Treating Zero Brand Sales Observations in Choice Model Estimation: Consequences and Potential Remedies", *Journal of Marketing Research* 45: 618–32.

—— Chintagunta, P. K., and Fox, E. J. (2009) "How Does Assortment Affect Grocery Store Choice?" *Journal of Marketing Research* 46/2: 176–89.

Bronnenberg, B. J. and Vanhonacker, W. R. (1999) "Limited Choice Sets, Local Price Response, and Imputed Measures of Price Competition", *Journal of Marketing Research* 33: 163–73.

—— and Wathieu, L. (1996) "Asymmetric Promotion Effects and Brand Positioning", *Marketing Science* 15: 379–94.

Busse, M. R., Simester, D., and Zettlemeyer, F. (2007) " 'The Best Price You'll Ever Get' The 2005 Employee Discount Pricing Promotions in the U.S. Automobile Industry". NBER Working Paper No. 13140.

Chandon, P., Wansink, B., and Laurent, G. (2000) "A Benefit Congruency Framework of Sales Promotion Effectiveness", *The Journal of Marketing* 64: 65–81.

Chandukala, S. R., Kim, J., Otter, T., et al. (2007) "Choice Models in Marketing: Economic Assumptions, Challenges and Trends", *Foundations and Trends® in Marketing* 2: 97–184.

Chernev, A. (2006) "Articulation Compatability in Eliciting Price Bids", *Journal of Consumer Research* 33: 329–41.

Chevalier, J. A., Kashyap, A. K., and Rossi, P. E. (2003) "Why Don't Prices Rise During Periods of Peak Demand? Evidence from Scanner Data", *American Economic Review* 93: 15–37.

Cooper, R. G. (2001) *Winning at New Products: Accelerating the Process from Idea to Launch.* Cambridge, MA: Perseus Books Group.

Dayton, C. M. and McReady, G. B. (1988) "Concomitant-Variable Latent-Class Models", *Journal of American Statistical Association* 83: 173–8.

Dodson, J. A., Tybout, A. M., and Sterntha, B. (1978) "Impact of Deals and Deal Retraction on Brand Switching", *Journal of Marketing Research* 15: 72–81.

Drèze, X. and Bell, D. R. (2003) "Creating Win–Win Trade Promotions: Theory and Empirical Analysis of Scan-Back Trade Deals", *Marketing Science* 22: 16–39.

Erdem, T., Keane, M. P., and Sun, B. (1999) "Missing Price and Coupon Availability in Scanner Panels: Correcting for the Self-Selection Bias in Choice Model Parameters", *Journal of Econometrics* 89: 177–96.

—— Imai, S., and Keane, M. P. (2003) "Brand and Quantity Choice Dynamics Under Price Uncertainty", *Quantitative Marketing and Economics* 1: 5–64.

Fox, E. J. and Hoch, S. J. (2005) "Cherry-Picking", *Journal of Marketing* 69: 46–62.

Gallego, G., Phillips, R., and Sahin, O. (2009) "Strategic Management of Distressed Inventory", *Production and Operations Management* 17: 402–15.

Gómez, M. I., Rao, V. R., and McLaughlin, E. W. (2007) "Empirical Analysis of Budget and Allocation of Trade Promotions in the US Supermarket Industry", *Journal of Marketing Research* 44: 410–24.

Guadagni, P. M. and Little, J. D. C. (1983) "A Logit Model of Brand Choice Calibrated on Scanner Data", *Marketing Science* 2: 203–38.

Gupta, S. (1988) "Impact of Sales Promotions on When, What, and How Much to Buy", *Journal of Marketing Research* 25: 342–55.

—— Chintagunta, P. K., Kaul, A., et al. (1996) "Do Household Scanner Data Provide Representative Inferences From Brand Choices: A Comparison With Store Data", *Journal of Marketing Research* XXXIII: 383–98.

—— Lehmann, D. R., and Stuart, J. A. (2004) "Valuing Customers", *Journal of Marketing Research* 41: 7–18.

Heath, T. B., Ryu, G., Chatterjee, S., et al. (2000) "Asymmetric Competition in Choice and the Leveraging of Competitive Disadvantages", *Journal of Consumer Research* 27: 291–308.

Hendel, I. and Nevo, A. (2006) "Sales and Consumer Inventory", *The RAND Journal of Economics* 37: 543–61.

Howard, D. J. and Kerin, R. A. (2006) "Broadening the Scope of Reference Price Advertising Research: A Field Study of Consumer Shopping Involvement", *Journal of Marketing* 70: 185–204.

Jain, D. and Singh, S. S. (2002) "Customer Lifetime Value Research in Marketing: A Review and Future Directions", *Journal of Interactive Marketing* 16: 34–46.

Janiszewski, C. and Lichtenstein, D. R. (1999) "A Range Theory Account of Price Perception", *Journal of Consumer Research* 25: 353–68.

Johnson, T. (1984) "The Myth of Declining Brand Loyalty", *Journal of Advertising Research* 24: 9–17.

Kamakura, W. A. and Russell, G. (1989) "A Probabilistic Choice Model for Market Segmentation and Elasticity Structure", *Journal of Marketing Research* 26: 379–90.

Kim, B.-D. and Rossi, P. E. (1994) "Purchase Frequency, Sample Selection and Price Sensitivity", *Marketing Letters* 5: 57–67.

Krishna, A. and Johar, G. V. (1996) "Consumer Perceptions of Deals: Biasing Effects of Varying Deal Prices", *Journal of Experimental Psychology* 2: 187–206.

—— Briesch, R., Lehmann, D., et al. (2002) "A Meta-Analysis of the Impact of Price Presentation on Perceived Savings", *Journal of Retailing* 78: 101–18.

Lal, R. (1990) "Price Promotions: Limiting Competitive Encroachment", *Marketing Science* 9: 247–62.

—— and Bell, D. R. (2003) "The Impact of Frequent Shopper Programs in Grocery Retailing", *Quantitative Marketing and Economics* 1: 179–202.

Lazear, E. P. (1986) "Retail Pricing and Clearance Sales", *American Economic Review* 76: 14–32.

Mace, S. and Neslin, S. A. (2004) "The Determinants of Pre- and Postpromotion Dips in Sales of Frequently Purchased Goods", *Journal of Marketing Research* 41: 339–50.

Manchanda, P., Ansari, A., and Gupta, S. (1999) "The 'Shopping Basket;' A Model for Multicategory Purchase Incidence Decisions", *Marketing Science* 18: 95–114.

Mazumdar, T. and Papatla, P. (2000) "An Investigation of Reference Price Segments", *Journal of Marketing Research* 37: 246–58.

Mela, C. F., Jedidi, K., and Bowman, D. (1998) "The Long-Term Impact of Promotions on Consumer Stockpiling Behavior", *Journal of Marketing Research* 35: 250–62.

Narasimhan, C. (1988) "A Price Discrimination Theory of Coupons", *Marketing Science* 3: 128–47.

Neslin, S. A. (2002) *Sales Promotion (Relevant Knowledge Series)*. Cambridge, MA: Marketing Science Institute.

Niedrich, R. W., Sharma, S., and Wedell, D. H. (2001) "Reference Price and Price Perceptions: A Comparison of Alternative Models", *Journal of Consumer Research* 28: 339–54.

Nijs, V. R., Dekimpe, M. G., Steenkamp, J. B., et al. (2001) "The Category-Demand Effects of Price Promotions", *Marketing Science* 20: 1–22.

Niraj, R., Padmanabhan, V., and Seetharaman, P. B. (2008) "A Cross-Category Model of Households' Incidence and Quantity Decisions", *Marketing Science* 27: 225–35.

Pauwels, K., Hanssens, D. M., and Siddarth, S. (2002) "The Long-Term Effects of Price Promotions on Category Incidence, Brand Choice and Purchase Quantity", *Journal of Marketing Research* XXXIX: 421–39.

Rao, R. C. (1991) "Pricing and Promotions in Asymmetric Duopolies", *Marketing Science* 10: 131–44.

Rhee, H. and Bell, D. R. (2002) "The Inter-Store Mobility of Supermarket Shoppers", *Journal of Retailing* 78: 225–37.

Rossi, P. E. and Allenby, G. M. (2003) "Bayesian Statistics and Marketing", *Marketing Science* 22: 304–28.

—— McCulloch, R. E., and Allenby, G. M. (1995) "Hierarchical Modelling of Consumer Heterogeneity: An Application to Target Marketing", in K. Singpurwalla (ed.), *Case Studies in Bayesian Statistics*. New York: Springer Verlag, 323–50.

Russell, G. J. and Kamakura, W. A. (1997) "Modeling Multiple Category Brand Preference with Household Basket Data", *Journal of Retailing* 73: 439–61.

Schindler, R. M. (1998) "Consequence of Perceiving Oneself as Responsible for Obtaining a Discount: Evidence for Smart-Shopper Feelings", *Journal of Consumer Psychology* 7: 271–392.

Seetharaman, P. B., Chib, S., Ainslie, A., et al. (2005) "Models of Multi-Category Choice Behavior", *Marketing Letters* 16: 239–54.

Sethuraman, R. (2009) "Assessing the External Validity of Analytical Results from National Brand and Store Brand Competition Models", *Marketing Science* 28: 759–81.

—— and Srinivasan, V. (2002) "The Asymmetric Share Effect. An Empirical Generalization on Cross-Price Effects", *Journal of Marketing Research* 39: 379–86.

—— —— and Kim, D. (1999) "Asymmetric and Neighborhood Cross-Price Effects: Some Empirical Generalizations", *Marketing Science* 18: 23–41.

Sivakumar, K. and Raj, S. P. (1997) "Quality Tier Competition: How Price Change Influences Brand Choice and Category Choice", *Journal of Marketing* 61: 71–84.

Soysal, G. P. (2007) "Demand Dynamics in the Seasonal Goods Industry: An Empirical Analysis", *Kellogg School of Management*. Evanston: Northwestern University.

Srinivasan, S., Pauwels, K., Hanssens, D. M., et al. (2004) "Do Promotions Benefit Manufacturers, Retailers, or Both?" *Management Science* 50: 617–29.

Srinivasan, V. and Bodapati, A. V. (2006) "The Impact of Feature Advertising on Customer Store Choice". Stanford University Graduate School of Business Research Paper No. 1935. Stanford University.

Su, X. (2007) "Intertemporal Pricing with Strategic Customer Behavior", *Management Science* 53: 726.

Sudhir, K. and Rao, V. R. (2006) "Do Slotting Allowances Enhance Efficiency or Hinder Competition", *Journal of Marketing Research* XLIII: 137–55.

Sun, B. (2005) "Promotion Effect on Endogenous Consumption", *Marketing Science* 24: 430–43.

Taylor, T. A. (2002) "Supply Chain Coordination under Channel Rebates with Sales Effort Effects", *Management Science* 48: 992–1007.

Thaler, R. (1985) "Mental Accounting and Consumer Choice", *Marketing Science* 61: 427–49.

Thomas, J. S. (2001) "A Methodology for Linking Customer Acquisition to Customer Retention", *Journal of Marketing Research* 38: 262–8.

Train, K. E. (2003) *Discrete Choice Methods with Simulation*. Cambridge: Cambridge University Press.

van Heerde, H. J. and Neslin, S. A. (2008) "Sales Promotion Models", in B. Wierenga (ed.), *Handbook of Marketing Decision Models*. New York: Springer, 107–62.

—— Leeflang, P. S. and Wittink, D. R. (2000) "The Estimation of Pre- and Postpromotion Dips with Store-Level Scanner Data", *Journal of Marketing Research* XXXVII: 383–95.

—— —— and —— (2002) "How Promotions Work: SCAN*PRO-Based Evolutionary Model Building", *Schmalenbach Business Review* 54: 198–220.

—— Gupta, S., and Wittink, D. R. (2003) "Is 75% of the Sales Promotion Bump Due to Brand Switching? No, Only 33% Is", *Journal of Marketing Research* 40: 481–91.

Van Ittersum, K., Pennings, J. M. E., Wasnink, B., et al. (2005) "The Effect of Primed and Framed Reference Points on Product Attribute Importance", *Advances in Consumer Research* 32: 113–14.

Varian, H. R. (1980) "A Model of Sales", *The American Economic Review*: 651–9.

Winer, R. S. (1986) "A Reference Price Model of Brand Choice for Frequently Purchased Products", *Journal of Consumer Research* 13: 250–56.

—— (2005) *Pricing (Relevant Knowledge Series)*. Cambridge, MA: Marketing Science Institute.

Zanutto, E. L. and Bradlow, E. T. (2006) "Data Pruning in Consumer Choice Models", *Quantitative Marketing and Economics* 4/3: 267–87.

CHAPTER 25

....

MARKDOWN
MANAGEMENT

....

RAMA RAMAKRISHNAN

25.1 INTRODUCTION

Marking prices down to stimulate demand and move inventory is an age-old retail practice. Large and small retailers alike use markdowns to manage the flow of merchandise through their stores. The effectiveness and efficiency with which merchandise is cleared via markdowns has a significant impact on retailer profitability, particularly for retailers of seasonal or short lifecycle merchandise (Smith and Achabal 1998).

Traditionally, retailers have used simple rules-of-thumb to manage markdowns. Such approaches may have been adequate for a single-store retailer. But as the number of stores grows into the hundreds, managing markdowns across all stores and for thousands of stock-keeping units (SKUs) in a way that systematically maximizes revenue calls for a qualitatively different approach. This approach is called *Markdown Optimization*.

This chapter covers markdown optimization. After motivating the need for effective markdown management, we describe the nature of the markdown optimization problem highlighting the key metrics that need to be optimized and the business rules and operating practices that constrain markdown decisions. We discuss traditional markdown management methods and highlight their shortcomings. Modern markdown optimization methods developed to address these shortcomings rely on two key building blocks: demand models and optimization algorithms. We describe how to build and estimate demand models. We then describe several optimization approaches and offer guidelines on how to select the appropriate one. We conclude by describing how to measure the benefits of markdown optimization.

25.2 BACKGROUND AND PROBLEM DEFINITION

Markdowns are generally applied to clear the remaining inventory of seasonal or discontinued products. In both cases, there are two fundamental reasons why markdowns are necessary (see Phillips 2005: ch. 10, for a detailed discussion).

First, the value of the inventory often decreases with time and if prices don't fall commensurately, shoppers will not be compelled to buy. This reduction in value can happen for a variety of reasons. The "fashion appeal" of an item may decrease towards the end of the season. Fashion-conscious buyers with high willingness-to-pay may not perceive the merchandise as fresh or new. Another reason is that the time left in the season to make use of the item gets shorter every day. Buying a cashmere sweater in September is a lot more useful than buying it in March. Finally, some products are discontinued when newer models are expected to arrive. Consumers may be unwilling to buy a discontinued product.

Secondly, the physical space occupied by this merchandise in the stores needs to be made available for other seasonal merchandise or newer models. Unless the inventory of current season merchandise is cleared, next season's merchandise will not be available for consumers to buy. Selling current season merchandise in a timely fashion also generates working capital that can be used to fund future purchases.

The reasons driving retailers to mark down prices have gotten stronger over the years as product lifecycles have shortened. The financial impact of effective markdown management is also significant. Selling an item at a 30 percent discount is vastly preferable to selling the same item to a "jobber" at an 80 percent discount. For retailers with a significant percent of revenue from seasonal merchandise, reducing the overall markdown discount rate by even a few percentage points can have a significant effect on overall margin and earnings. For example, at ShopKo, markdown optimization software deployed on 300 merchandise groups showed a 14 percent increase in revenue for those groups (Phillips 2005: 259). A women's specialty apparel retailer in the United States reported a 4.8 percent revenue improvement over traditional markdown management strategies by using a markdown optimization algorithm (Heching et al. 2002). Recently, Wall Street has also noticed the impact of effective markdown management on retailers' profitability. To estimate earnings and stock performance, equity analysts routinely discuss markdown rates and related metrics with retail CFOs and CEOs during quarterly earnings calls.

25.2.1 The markdown optimization problem

Consider an item that has a specified number of weeks left in its selling season. The markdown optimization problem for the item consists of choosing discount levels (or, equivalently, price points) for every week in the selling season to meet a business goal such as maximizing profit subject to various business rules affecting the timing and depth of the chosen discounts. Figure 25.1 illustrates two markdown price paths. In practice, for a single item, millions of such price paths are possible and it is not straightforward to find the one with the maximum revenue. In fact, even assessing the likely revenue from a given price path is a formidable forecasting problem.

25.2.1.1 Problem objective

The objective of markdown optimization is typically to maximize the revenue from the inventory of a product over its remaining life. Note that revenue and gross margin dollars are equivalent when the merchant already owns the inventory of the item, in which case the

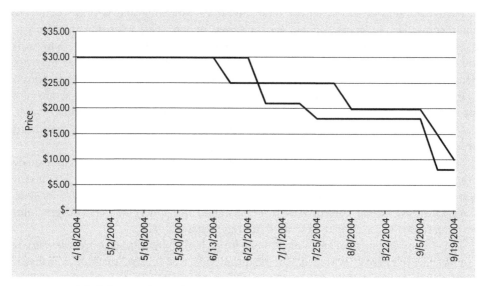

FIGURE 25.1 Markdown price paths

inventory cost is "sunk". Hence, maximizing revenue is equivalent to maximizing gross margin and we assume in this chapter that the retailer is maximizing revenue.

25.2.1.2 *Business rules and operating practices*

Markdown decisions are subject to a number of constraints or business rules. These rules have evolved over time to ensure that markdown decisions do not lead to undesirable consequences for various constituencies, including customers, merchants, and store personnel. Below we describe some common rules (Phillips 2005) and describe the business justifications for them:

- *Price ladders*: This rule is very common. Discounts or prices need to be on a *ladder* where the "rungs" of the ladder are discrete percentage points (e.g., a 4-rung discount ladder can be 20%, 40%, 60%, and 90%) or discrete price points (e.g., a 4-rung price ladder can be $14.99, $9.99, $6.99, and $4.99). Markdown recommendations need to be one of the points on the price ladder. Some retailers have price ladders with many rungs (e.g., every 99c ending from $29.99, to $4.99) while others have shallow ladders. Ladders vary across merchandise types. Ladders have evolved as a means to keep pricing simple for both the retailer and the shopper. Further, many retailers believe that shoppers respond favorably to "magic price endings" such as prices ending in 0.99 or 0.97, rather than arbitrary prices. (See the discussion in Chapter 20 by Özer and Zheng.)

- *Minimum price reduction rule*: This rule sets the smallest price reduction that will be allowed as an item's markdown recommendation. This rule is frequently applied to just the *first* markdown recommendation. One reason for this rule is the belief that too small a percentage price reduction does not make a difference to the customer's perception of value. Other reasons involve minimizing the workload for store personnel and merchants. In the stores, changing the markdown price (known as "retagging") is a manual operation and store managers like to minimize the labor involved. In headquarters, merchants or planners manually review and approve markdown recommendations before they are sent to the stores. This rule helps to make sure that they are not overwhelmed with markdown recommendations.

- *Maximum price reduction*: This rule sets the maximum recommended price reduction. This rule is often driven by two reasons. First, a very high percentage price reduction conveys a "this item is a loser" signal to the shopper and may harm the brand image. Secondly, the merchant who bought the item in question typically holds out hope that the item is a "late bloomer" and will live up to its promise soon. Therefore, the merchant would like to give the item a chance to sell strongly and "prove itself" rather than institute a large price cut and admit defeat. Merchants frequently apply this rule to the *first* markdown recommendation.

- *Maximum sell-through at exit date*: This rule stipulates that a certain percentage of the inventory must be left unsold at the end of the item's defined selling season in order to send inventory to outlet stores. While outlet stores were historically used only to dispose of unsold merchandise from the regular stores, they have evolved to become profit centers in their own right and need assured inventory.

- *No-touch period at season start*: This rule prevents markdowns from starting too early and forces the system to wait for several weeks before recommending a markdown. There are three reasons for this rule. First, merchants often want to ensure that the item has adequate time on the shelf to prove its worth. They also want to prevent unanticipated events in the first few weeks (e.g., a hurricane that dramatically decreases store traffic) from influencing the first markdown decision. Secondly, merchants want to maintain the value of the item in the perception of the shopper for several weeks. Finally, merchandise typically arrives at stores over a few weeks (i.e., not all in the same week). The no-touch rule ensures that all the stores get the item before any markdowns are announced.

- *No-touch period between markdowns*: This rule prevents markdowns that are too close to each other. Since every markdown involves "touching" the price tag of an item, store management wants to avoid touching the same item every week. This rule also reduces end-user workload by limiting the number of recommendations that need to be reviewed every week.

- *Maximum number of markdowns*: This rule limits the total number of markdowns for an item over its selling season. The rationale is to limit the store re-tagging workload per item and to limit the recommendation review workload for the merchant.

- *Markdown blackout period*: This rule stipulates that no markdowns can be done during certain weeks of the calendar, so as to lessen the re-pricing workload for store personnel during busy holiday periods.

- *Promotions*: When a promotion is planned for a future week, this rule will either prevent a markdown from being executed that week or set a maximum limit on the depth of a markdown for that week. The main reason is to make sure that shoppers coming into the store in response to the promotion don't see a lower ticket price on the item than was shown in the ad for the promotion.

- *Collections price-together*: Multiple items may be grouped together by the merchant (e.g., all items of the same brand from within a class) and all items in the group need to be priced together. This could mean that all the items need to have the same exact percentage discount or it could mean that the markdown *timing* needs to be the same across the items but the percentage discounts could vary.

25.2.2 Traditional approaches to markdown optimization

Retailers have been marking down merchandise for decades if not centuries. Over time, they have developed several heuristic approaches (Friend and Walker 2001) to setting markdowns. These approaches fall into two broad categories: Approaches dependent only on time and those dependent on time and inventory levels.

A common example of an approach from the first category is:

When the item enters the last 20 percent of its life, mark it down by 30 percent. When it enters the last 10 percent of its life, mark it down by 50 percent.

This rule-of-thumb may be expressed in weeks of life, rather than in percentage terms, but in any event, it does not take inventory levels into account. It also does not distinguish between slow and fast sellers. What it does offer is the ability to mark down hundreds or thousands of items efficiently. Retailers realize, of course, that this approach is a bit too simplistic and that is why the second approach evolved (Table 25.1).

This approach is an improvement: it takes the remaining inventory into account and compares it with the time remaining. If there is "enough" time left and the inventory isn't "too high", no markdowns or shallow markdowns are recommended. On the other extreme, if there is "too much" inventory left and there is hardly any time left, a deep markdown is recommended. The markdown percentages are derived from the retailers' intuition and experience, rather than from formal modeling.

The biggest shortcoming of this approach is that it ignores the rate of sale of the item. So, some retailers have incorporated the rate of sale of the item as well. Retailers also calculate a "weeks of supply" metric, that is, divide the inventory level by a recent average of weekly sales units. This metric can be used instead of the actual inventory level (Table 25.2).

The evolution of these approaches can be taken further. For example, rather than just rely on recent, *raw* rates of sale to calculate the weeks-of-supply, we could adjust the rates of sales to take out the effect of factors specific to only those weeks (e.g., what if a major holiday occurred last week?) to arrive at a "normal" rate of sale. Going further still, we could adjust this normal rate of sale to take into account seasonal factors in the remaining life of the item.

Table 25.1 Recommended markdown table—weeks of life

	Weeks left: 0–20% of life	Weeks left: 20–50% of life	Weeks left: over 50% of life
Less than 20% of starting inventory left	20%	No markdown	No markdown
Between 20–50% of starting inventory left	40%	20%	No markdown
Over 50% of starting inventory left	60%	40%	20%

Table 25.2 Recommended markdown table—rate of sale

	Less than 3 weeks left in the season	Between 3–6 weeks left in the season	Over 6 weeks left in the season
Less than 3 weeks of supply left	20%	No markdown	No markdown
Between 3–6 weeks of supply left	40%	20%	No markdown
Over 6 weeks of supply left	60%	40%	20%

Stepping back and looking at this progression, it becomes clear that we are getting closer and closer to a sales-forecast-based markdown decision-making system. Modern markdown optimization methods take this evolution to its logical conclusion.

25.2.3 Modern markdown optimization: two building blocks

Retailers make markdown decisions every day. These decisions interact with consumer behavior, competitive behavior, and environmental factors to determine the financial outcome for the retailer. An effective system that helps retailers make the *best* markdown decisions needs to answer two fundamental questions:

- What is the likely outcome (in unit sales and financial metrics) of a specific markdown decision?
- Of all the markdown decisions that can be made now, which decision maximizes the financial metric of interest (typically, revenue) over the life of the item?

To answer the first question accurately and reliably, a demand model is necessary. To answer the second question with confidence, an optimization algorithm is necessary. The optimization algorithm needs the demand model to assess the financial "worthiness" of every markdown decision it considers. Having one without the other isn't enough to get the job done. Demand models and optimization algorithms are both necessary for rigorous markdown optimization. They form the two critical building blocks of modern markdown optimization systems. We will discuss each in turn.

25.3 MARKDOWN DEMAND MODELS

Demand for merchandise is influenced by many factors. Ultimately, demand for an item is the result of numerous consumers deciding whether to buy the item. An individual consumer's decision is subject to several factors, many of which are idiosyncratic and specific only to that customer and possibly specific to that point in time. We assume that these idiosyncratic factors "cancel out" for the most part during the aggregation process.

Once the idiosyncratic factors wash out, we are left with *systematic* factors that drive demand. A systematic factor exerts a *common* influence on the *majority* of consumers. The effect of a systematic factor does not "cancel out" across consumers because this influence is common across all consumers. Instead, the effect tends to be cumulative, and hence significant and measurable. We refer to these systematic factors as *demand drivers*.

25.3.1 Demand drivers

What are the important demand drivers in markdown optimization? Before we answer this question, it is worth pointing out that in any discussion with retailers, several factors will be suggested as being important. While many of these are indeed significant, it is often the case that retailers' information systems either do not keep track of them or it is prohibitively expensive to extract, clean, and combine this data with sales, pricing, and inventory data.

For example, consider the fixture on which a sweater is placed. It is reasonable to expect that the nature of this fixture has a systematic influence on the consumer's decision to buy. Contrast a table fixture that is easily accessible to the consumer and allows a full frontal display of the sweater to a "rounder" where the sweater is displayed sideways. It is more likely that a consumer will buy the sweater from the table than from the rounder (other things being equal). Unfortunately, at the time of this writing, item-level fixture data are not easily available in retailers' systems, making it difficult if not impossible to include the "fixture" as a demand driver in markdown optimization.

Given these issues regarding data availability, we modify our earlier question: What are the important demand drivers in markdown optimization for which data are obtainable? The following demand drivers have withstood the test of time and have proved their usefulness in real-world markdown optimization: price discount, seasonality, promotion indicators, inventory level, and product lifecycle. We will discuss each of these in turn.

25.3.1.1 Price discount

Not surprisingly, price discount is a very significant demand driver. The higher the discount, the greater the effect on demand. The magnitude of the price discount is usually combined with a price elasticity parameter to mathematically represent the effect of a price cut on demand.

Figure 25.2 provides a common way to visualize the effect of prices on sales. We plot the % price reduction against the % change in sales (other things being equal) for different merchandise categories. The change in an item's demand in response to a price cut (i.e., the item's price elasticity) typically varies by merchandise type. In Figure 25.2, we observe that a 50 percent price cut triggers a 300 percent increase in sales for Women's sandals but "only" a 175 percent sales increase for Men's boots. Price elasticity can also vary by geography—stores in upscale neighborhoods may have lower price elasticity than stores in other locations. Moreover, one can argue that the item's age may also have an impact on its price elasticity. Early in its life, the item is "in fashion" and not shopworn while late in the season, its fashion appeal may have tapered off and due to its long presence on the shelf, it may have a "tired" look. For these reasons, the price elasticity later in the season can be lower than earlier in the season. However, detecting these differences is challenging and often leads to approximations in how price elasticity is estimated and used.

25.3.1.2 Seasonality

Seasonality captures the change in consumer demand from week to week due to, for example, seasonal changes or holidays. Seasonality can have a dramatic impact on demand and is comparable to price discounts in its importance. Seasonality usually varies by merchandise type and by geography as well. For instance, demand for cashmere sweaters is low from

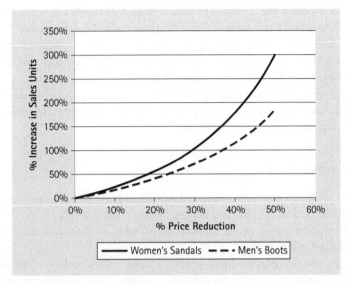

FIGURE 25.2 The effect of price reduction on sales

Reprinted with permission from *The Journal of Marketing*, published by the American Marketing Association, Chandon P, Wansink B, and Lawrent G. (2000), 'A benefit congruency framework of sales promotion effectiveness' 64:65–81.

March through July. It rises from August through October, stays at the same level through Christmas and falls back down to zero by February. Back-to-school merchandise, on the other hand, tends to exhibit dramatic sales spikes over a 6–8-week period of the year in the USA. This period corresponds to different calendar dates depending on the geography.

Figure 25.3 shows seasonality curves for coffee and ice cream. Coffee has stable seasonal demand throughout the year except for an increase at the end of the year. In contrast, ice cream has a pronounced surge in demand during the summer months. Seasonality is numerically represented as a unit-less, multiplicative index with the "average week" presumed to have a seasonal index of 1.0.

Holidays deserve special mention. Holidays such as Easter, Christmas, and Thanksgiving in the USA generate tremendous store traffic and capturing their effects accurately is important. Some of these holidays "move" from year to year. Easter, for example, falls between late March and early April depending on the lunar cycle. In forecasting demand, it is important to move the seasonal factor for every holiday according to where exactly it falls in the forecast period.

25.3.1.3 *Promotion indicators*

A promotion for an item affects demand for that particular item and draws traffic to the store, generating demand for all items. The promoted item may be a substitute for other items, which it cannibalizes, and it may be a complement with other items, in which case increasing its demand will increase their demand.

Merchandise can be promoted in numerous ways, depending only on the creativity of the retailer (see Chapter 24 by Blattberg and Briesch.) Apart from the standard "%-off" and

"$-off" promotions, there are "combo" promotions such as the BOGO (buy-one-get-one) and "$X off if the purchase exceeds $Y". Coupons may be layered on top of these promotions as well. Advertising in newspaper inserts and other media may support these price reductions. There may be supporting signage in-store as well, often accompanied by premium positioning in the high-traffic lanes of the store.

Quantifying and capturing the effects of promotions is a formidable challenge. Hence, we often include in the demand model only promotional events that are likely to have a substantial impact on items under consideration.

25.3.1.4 Inventory level

Clearly, if there is no inventory of an item at a store for a particular time period, sales won't be observed. But inventory's impact on demand goes far beyond this obvious relationship. As the level of inventory drops below a certain threshold level, demand starts to drop, often precipitously for several reasons.

First, when an item occupies one fixture, while a "sister item" (perhaps a different color of the same style) occupies five similar fixtures in the vicinity of the first item, it is possible that shoppers will be drawn to the five-fixture item rather than the one-fixture item, as long as the item's other attributes are equally attractive. Thus, the "fixture density" may affect demand.

Secondly, as the inventory drops below a certain point, the remaining units become harder to find, particularly if they have been misplaced by browsing shoppers. In addition,

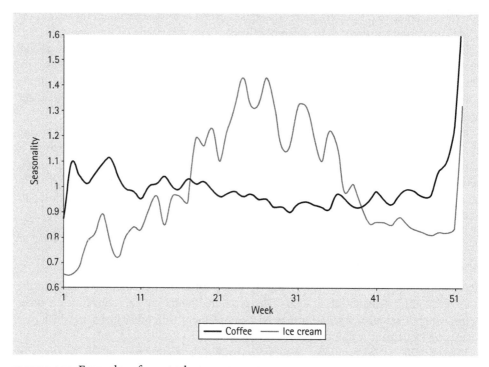

FIGURE 25.3 Examples of seasonal curves

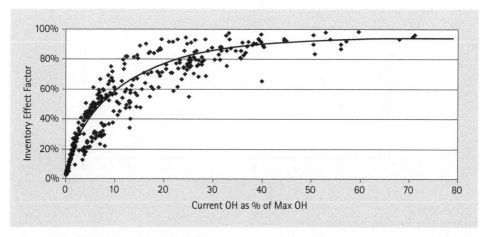

FIGURE 25.4 The inventory curve effect

some merchandise may have a natural minimum purchase quantity in the consumer's mind and if the inventory visible to the shopper is below this level, the shopper won't purchase. Table napkins are an example—shoppers may be looking for a minimum purchase of a set of four or eight.

Finally, demand is typically modeled at a level higher than SKU and if the actual mix of SKUs in the inventory of an item doesn't match the preference of the shopper, demand will fall. A "pink cashmere sweater" may be defined as an *item* with 5 different *sizes* (XS, S, M, L, XL) included. If, at a particular store, there are no XS and S units in stock, even if the total inventory of pink cashmere sweaters is high, demand will be negatively affected.

For these reasons, modeling the effect of low inventory levels on demand is an important component of markdown management. Figure 25.4 illustrates the dampening effect of decreasing inventory levels on sales: The inventory effect factor (y-axis) is a multiplier on sales and the on-hand inventory (OH) as a percentage of the maximum OH decreases from 100 percent.

25.3.1.5 Product lifecycle

A typical product lifecycle for a short sales season resembles a bell-shaped curve. After the item first appears in the store, demand starts to climb up from zero as shoppers "discover" the item. The demand keeps rising till shoppers lose interest and turn to other, newer items (see Figure 25.5 for an illustrative example). If the item is deemed "hot" from a fashion perspective, the demand can rise dramatically for several weeks. At some point, the popularity of the item peaks and the fall can be dramatic and precipitous. Since items vary in their appeal, product lifecycles come in different shapes.

The product lifecycle curve is a function of the *age* of the item and not of calendar time. Accordingly, the x-axis represents the item's age. Note that the product lifecycle effect exists without any changes in pricing, promotions, inventory levels, or seasonal factors, i.e., the product lifecycle is *independent* of the other demand drivers.

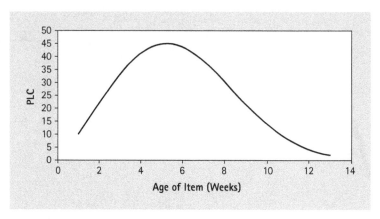

FIGURE 25.5 Product lifecycle curve

25.3.2 Functional forms for demand drivers

A demand model is typically defined at the level of "item" and "location". The item could be an individual SKU (e.g., pink XL cashmere sweater) or it could be a group of SKUs such as *style* (e.g., pink cashmere sweater) in which case the label "item" refers to all SKUs that belong to the group. Similarly, "location" can indicate a specific store, the entire chain (i.e., all stores), or a group of stores (i.e., a region). Items are typically defined at the style/region, style/chain, or in some cases at the style/store level. Without loss of generality, we define the item at the style/region level for the rest of this discussion. Note that the style/store and style/chain cases can be modeled by simply setting the store count to 1 or "all stores" in the demand model.

The *demand model* for a given item in week w can be written as:

$$D_w = PLC_w \cdot PD_w \cdot INVEN_w \cdot SEAS_w \cdot PROMO_w$$

In this multiplicative formulation, demand in week w is assumed to be the product of a *natural product lifecycle demand PLC* and a set of multipliers, each of which represents the *incremental* effect of a demand driver for that week w. Thus, the natural demand *PLC* is the demand for the item when there is no price discount, the inventory level is adequate, there is no holiday and no promotion. We define the following quantities:

D_w = demand in week w, measured in units per store (this is what we want to forecast)
PLC_w = natural product lifecycle demand in week w, measured in units per store
PD_w = price discount effect in week w
$SEAS_w$ = seasonality effect in week w
$INVEN_w$ = inventory effect in week w
$PROMO_w$ = promotion effect in week w

All the variables except D_w and PLC_w are unitless multipliers. This multiplicative demand model formulation is common in the econometric and marketing science literature and is called the *log-log* or *loglinear* model (Greene 2003). It is also widely used in practice (Leeflang et al. 2000; Hanssens et al. 2001). Each of the demand drivers is represented in the demand model by an *algebraic expression* (or *functional form*). Each such expression will have at least one *parameter* and may have one or more *variables*. Next we examine how each of the effects is algebraically represented.

25.3.2.1 *Incremental effect of Price Discount (PD)*

Let the planned price for an item in week w be P_w and the full-price be P_o. There are two common functional forms used to represent the price discount effect:

$$\text{Exponential form: } PD_w = e^{\gamma\left(1-\frac{P_w}{P_o}\right)}$$

$$\text{Power-law form: } PD_w = \left(\frac{P_w}{P_o}\right)^{-\gamma}$$

In both cases, as P_w decreases (i.e., the discount gets deeper), PD_w increases. The parameter γ appears in both forms and is related to the price elasticity—the percentage change in quantity resulting from a 1 percent increase in price. $-\gamma$ is the price elasticity for the power law form, and $-\gamma \cdot \frac{P_w}{P_o}$ is the price elasticity for the exponential form.

25.3.2.2 *Incremental effect of Seasonality (SEAS)*

Every week w in a given year has a Seasonality/Holiday effect. The simplest (and most common) way to represent these effects is via 52 (one for each week of the year) *dummy variables*:

$$SEAS_w = e^{\beta_1\delta_1(w)+\beta_2\delta_2(w)+\cdots+\beta_{52}\delta_{52}(w)} \text{ for } w = 1, 2, \ldots 52$$

β_w is the seasonality parameter for week w of the year. $\delta_t(w)$ is a 0–1 dummy variable that takes on the value 1 if $t = w$ and 0 otherwise. For any particular week w, exactly one of the 52 δ variables will be one, and the remaining 51 will be zero. For example, for week 23,

$$SEAS_{23} = e^{\beta_1\delta_1(23)+\beta_2\delta_2(23)+\cdots+\beta_{52}\delta_{52}(23)} = e^{\beta_{23}\delta_{23}(23)} = e^{\beta_{23}}$$

25.3.2.3 *Incremental effect of Inventory (INVEN)*

Let I_w be the available inventory in week w. There are many functional forms used to represent the effect of inventory. Smith and Achabal (1998) describe an exponential form and a piecewise linear form:

$$INVEN_w = e^{-\mu\cdot\max(0,1-\frac{I_w}{F})}$$
$$INVEN_w = 1 - \mu \cdot \max(0,1 - \frac{I_w}{F})$$

The parameter F is called "fixture fill". The idea is that F units of inventory are needed to make the fixture on which the merchandise is displayed look "full". If the inventory level drops below this level, demand is reduced. The parameter μ lies between 0 and 1 and measures the rate at which demand is dampened as the inventory level decreases from F to 0. Note that in both forms, if I_w is greater than or equal to F, there is no effect on demand since $INVEN_w = 1$. The piecewise linear form is shown in Figure 25.6.

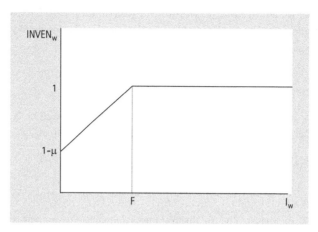

FIGURE 25.6 The piecewise linear inventory effect

In practice, it is advantageous to slightly modify these forms. Let I_0 be the starting inventory level. For items with short lifecycles, there is usually just *one* delivery of inventory to the stores and hence I_0 will also be the maximum inventory over the item's selling season. The modified forms are:

$$INVEN_w = e^{-\mu \cdot \max(0,1-\frac{I_w}{\lambda I_0})}$$

$$INVEN_w = 1 - \mu \cdot \max(0,1 - \frac{I_w}{\lambda I_0})$$

The parameter λ measures the threshold inventory level as a percentage of the starting inventory I_0. This small modification allows us to estimate the inventory effect by pooling historical data from items with very different sales and inventory levels.

25.3.2.4 *Incremental effect of Promotions (PROMO)*

As discussed earlier, promotions can occur in numerous variations and there may be complex relationships in how demand for one item affects demand for another. When the primary objective in demand modeling is to support markdown optimization (and not for promotions decision-support and other uses), a simple modeling approach is often sufficient.

In practice, promotions are typically modeled using the same dummy variable approach that we used for modeling the seasonality demand driver.

$$PROMO_w = e^{\alpha X(w)} \text{ for } w = 1, 2, \ldots 52$$

The parameter α measures the effect of promotions and $X(w)$ is a 0–1 dummy variable that takes on the value 1 if there was a promotion on week w and 0 otherwise. If the item is promoted with a price change *together with* supporting advertising, then the effect of the price change will be captured in *PD* (the price effect) but the residual effect due to the advertising will be captured in *PROMO*. We discuss how to estimate α from historical data later in the chapter.

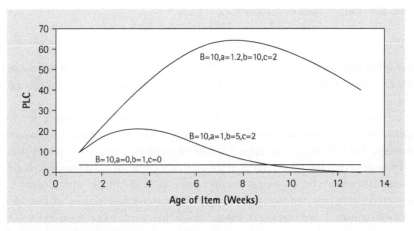

FIGURE 25.7 Product lifecycle curves

25.3.2.5 *Incremental effect of Product Lifecycle (PLC)*

There are many ways to model the PLC curve. Here we discuss a functional form due to Woo et al. (2005). Let t be the age of the item measured in weeks at week w. Then,

$$PLC_w = Bt^a e^{-\left(\frac{t}{b}\right)^c} \text{ for } w = 1, 2, \ldots 52$$

This formulation has one variable t and four parameters B, a, b, and c. The parameter B is related to the *scale* of the natural demand. If the item in question had a *constant* natural rate of sale (e.g., 5 units per week), then by setting $a = c = 0$ and $b = 1$, we get a constant value for the product lifecycle effect:

$$PLC_w = B/e$$

The parameter b is related to the peak of the curve. As the parameters B, a, b, and c take on different values, different lifecycle curves are generated (see Figure 25.7). Thus, this formulation is flexible enough to capture a wide range of unimodal lifecycle curves. It is important to keep in mind that the variable t is the age of the item in weeks and not the calendar week w. When forecasting the demand for an item for week w, the age of the item at that week needs to be calculated and then used in the formula for PLC_w.

25.3.3 The complete demand model

In the previous section, we described functional forms to represent each demand driver. Each form included at least one parameter. In this section, we describe how to estimate the values of these parameters from retailers' historical data. Once parameters are estimated, forecasting demand for an item for a particular week is simply a matter of "plugging in" the values of the estimated parameters and that week's variables into the demand model. By substituting the functional forms for each demand driver into

$$D_w = PLC_w \cdot PD_w \cdot INVEN_w \cdot SEAS_w \cdot PROMO_w,$$

we obtain the complete demand model:

$$D_w = Bt^a e^{-\left(\frac{t}{b}\right)^c} \cdot e^{\gamma\left(1-\frac{p_w}{p_0}\right)} \cdot \left(1 - \mu \cdot \max(0,1 - \frac{I_w}{\lambda I_0})\right) \cdot e^{\beta_1 \delta_1(w) + \beta_2 \delta_2(w) + \cdots + \beta_{52}\delta_{52}(w)} \cdot e^{\alpha X(w)} \qquad (1)$$

We have arbitrarily chosen the exponential form for *PD* and the modified piecewise linear form for *INVEN*. The basic estimation approach is the same even if other functional forms are used.

The complete demand model has 60 parameters: 52 for seasonality, 4 for product lifecycle, 1 for price discount, 2 for inventory effect, and 1 for promotions. However, the model as specified above has an extra "degree of freedom": given any set of parameter values, by multiplying the parameter B by an arbitrary constant k, and multiplying each of the 52 seasonality terms by $1/k$, we get another demand model that is equivalent to the first demand model but has one fewer parameter. To remove this degree of freedom, it is customary to constrain the average of the 52 seasonality terms to be equal to 1.0. This also supports the intuition that, for an "average" week, the seasonality factor is 1.0, i.e., there is no seasonality effect.

Since the demand model is defined at the item/week/store-group level, the historical data needed to estimate these parameters is also at that level. It is customary to work with at least 104 weeks (i.e., two years) of data. For each item/week, we need the following data: sales units, sales dollars (i.e., revenue), full price, list price, inventory units, calendar week, and promotions indicator.

For an item with two years of data, we have 104 observations to work with. But we have to estimate 60 parameters! Using 104 observations to estimate 60 parameters (an observations/parameters ratio of 1.76) will lead to unreliable parameter estimates. In addition, the one-item-at-a-time approach overlooks the fact that many items may have the same seasonal pattern and the same price elasticity. By *pooling* data from many items, we can exploit this commonality and increase the ratio of observations to parameters, resulting in more reliable estimates.

At the same time, we have to be careful about which items we pool. If we force very different items to share the same seasonality, the forecast accuracy will be low. Only items that behave similarly in their sales patterns should be pooled. This is where the retailer's *merchandise hierarchy* comes in. Retailers organize their merchandise using the merchandise hierarchy. Items that are similar in important ways are grouped together.

For example, a hierarchy common amongst apparel retailers is Chain, Division, Department, Class, Subclass, Style, Color, and Size. A hierarchy is best visualized as an upside-down tree with Chain at the root (on top) and Sizes at the leaves (on the bottom). Chain represents the whole company. At the Division level there may be three members (e.g., Men's, Women's, and Home). The Women's division may be divided into six to eight Departments (e.g., Outerwear). Each Department is divided into tens of Classes (e.g., Sweaters). Each Class is divided into Subclasses (e.g., Cashmere Sweaters), and each Subclass is divided into Styles (e.g., Brand ABC Cashmere Sweater). Styles may be further divided into Colors and Colors into Sizes.

How do we use the merchandise hierarchy for pooling? A common approach in practice is to pool the items in a *class* or *department* together and jointly estimate their parameters (see Hanssens et al. 2001: 119). Since the items in a class or department are by definition similar, we would expect that they would have similar seasonality. We may also postulate that their price elasticity parameters and their promotions parameters are the same.

In practice, the greatest improvement in the observations-to-parameters ratio comes from making the seasonalities common. If a class has m items, then the number of observations is $104m$. If we were to use distinct parameters for each item, there would be no benefit for pooling because the number of parameters would be $60m$ and the ratio would still be $104m/60m = 104/60 = 1.76$. But if we were to assume that there is only one set of 52 seasonality parameters for all the m items, then the ratio would be $104m/(52 + 8m)$. If $m = 10$, the ratio is 7.9 and for $m = 100$, it is 12.2. In practice, it is common to go a step further and start by assuming that all the parameters except the PLC scale parameter B are shared by the items. Since different items sell at different rates, we would expect that any parameter that is sensitive to the magnitude of the sales rate of the items should be item-specific. In our formulation, B is the only such parameter—all the other parameters are unitless. Therefore, it is a reasonable starting point to assume that they are all common to the items in a class or department. In this scenario, the observations/parameters ratio becomes $104m/(59 + m)$, with a value of 15 for $m = 10$ and a value of 65 for $m = 100$. This is a substantial improvement.

The pooling approach is not a panacea. It can cause difficulties when the retailer places dissimilar items in the same class. For example, orange-colored and red-colored candy may be placed in the same "Flavored Candy" class but orange-colored candy may have a big sales spike around Halloween but red-colored candy may not. By forcing them both to share the same seasonality, the model will underestimate demand for orange candy and overestimate demand for red candy around Halloween. Similarly, consider a class that contains low-priced and high-priced items. A 20 percent price cut for a $1.99 item in the class may not elicit a strong sales response while the same 20 percent price cut for a $49.99 item may result in a sales spike. Using the same price elasticity parameter for both items will result in forecast errors.

These issues are addressed in practice by first estimating all of the parameters except the scale parameter B at the class level and then evaluating the forecast accuracy. Items with high forecast errors are checked to see if they are different enough from the other items in the class. These exceptional items are given their own parameters, the estimation approach is run again, the new parameters are used to generate forecasts, the forecast accuracy is evaluated and the process is repeated. This iterative process continues till a satisfactory level of forecast accuracy is reached.

25.3.4 Estimating parameters for the demand model

The demand model in the form shown in equation (1) is non-linear in the parameters and cannot be estimated using linear regression techniques. However, a special case of the model can be solved by linear regression.

25.3.4.1 Linear estimation

We make two simplifications to the demand model in eq. (1) to get the special case. First, we assume that the effect of low inventory levels, i.e., the inventory effect, is ignored.

Secondly, we assume that the product lifecycle curve is flat, i.e., a straight line. These assumptions give us the simplified demand model:

$$D_w = B \cdot e^{\gamma\left(1-\frac{p_w}{p_0}\right)} \cdot e^{\beta_1\delta_1(w)+\beta_2\delta_2(w)+\cdots+\beta_{52}\delta_{52}(w)} \cdot e^{\alpha X(w)}$$

Taking the logarithm of both sides gives:

$$\ln(D_w) = \ln(B) + \gamma\left(1 - \frac{p_w}{p_0}\right) + \beta_1\delta_1(w) + \beta_2\delta_2(w) + \cdots + \beta_{52}\delta_{52}(w) + \alpha X(w) \quad (2)$$

Equation 2 is linear. Hence, one can use least-squares regression to estimate the parameters. The input dataset will have an observation for each item/week in the class or department under consideration.

Consider the following example. Item #2343 sold 100 units across a group of 10 stores during the week ending 1/11/2008. Every week is assigned a number from 1 through 52. Since 1/11 is the first full week of 2008, we refer to it as week 1. Assume that the total sales were $5213 and the full price for the item that week was $64.99. Suppose further that no promotion was in effect that week. This sales information represents one data point and will be recorded as:

$$D_1 = 100/10 = 10 \text{ (units per store)}, P_0 = \$64.99, P_w = \$5213/100 = \$52.13, \delta_1(1)$$
$$= 1, \delta_2(1) = \ldots = \delta_{52}(1) = 0 \ X(1) = 0.$$

All observations for all items/weeks in the dataset are fed into a linear regression. An important point here is that each item in the regression will have its own intercept or scale factor $\ln(B)$. Also, to remove the extra degree of freedom in the parameters, we can simply fix *one* of the 52 seasonality terms at 1.0, run the regression, and then multiply each of the 52 terms by an appropriate constant so that the average is 1.0. The regression generates values for all the parameters (along with confidence intervals and other statistical information). These parameter values are plugged back into the model to enable forecasting. Note that if m items participated in the regression, m scale parameters B, 52 seasonality parameters, 1 price elasticity parameter, and 1 promo effect parameter will be generated by the regression.

25.3.4.2 *Nonlinear estimation*

The general demand model is nonlinear in its parameters. To estimate the parameters, a nonlinear least-squares minimization method such as the Levenberg–Marquardt algorithm (Press et al. 1992) can be used. If the dataset is not too large, the estimation can be performed using the Solver function in Microsoft Excel.

The approach underlying nonlinear least-squares minimization is intuitive. The values from each observation are plugged into the right-hand side (RHS) of eq. 1, the resulting expression is subtracted from the sales units per store corresponding to that observation, and squared. These squared expressions are added across all the observations to create an objective function. The values of the parameters that, jointly, minimize this objective function are found using a nonlinear minimization algorithm. If there are constraints on the parameters (e.g., $0 \leq \lambda \leq 1$), these are taken into account as well by the optimizer. When solving the general model, three more data sets are needed for each observation: the inventory levels I_0 and I_w, and the age of the item t.

25.3.4.3 *Common pitfalls in demand model estimation*

While there are numerous pitfalls in parameter estimation and demand modeling, issues stemming from data quality and collinearity account for a disproportionate share.

25.3.4.3.1 *Data quality*

Experienced modelers and analysts know that data quality is a critical, if unglamorous, aspect of modeling and optimization. This certainly holds true for markdown optimization. Common data issues in fitting retail demand models are:

- Inventory levels may be reported as negative. Unfortunately, this is not uncommon. Leaving negative observations out of the dataset is often a good approach.

- Sales units may be reported as negative. This can happen when merchandise returned by customers are subtracted from the actual sales units and reported, i.e., *net sales units*, rather than *gross sales units*, are reported. In this situation, determining how many units were actually sold becomes impossible. Leaving negative sales observations out of the dataset is a good approach.

- Full prices may not be available. Without knowing the full price P_o of an item, it is impossible to calculate the price discount. One way to handle this issue is to set P_o equal to the maximum value of the "ticket price" of the item across all the weeks of data for the item. If the ticket price is not available, P_o can be set to the maximum of the "average sales price" (i.e., recall that average sales price = sales dollars/sales units) across all the weeks of data for the item. Since employee discounts and coupons can make the average sales price in any given week smaller than the ticket price of the item, this method isn't perfect.

- If there are no sales in a particular week (possible for very expensive items), that observation may not be reported at all, even though it is a valid and potentially useful one for estimation purposes. In this case, sales need to be inferred from the observations from the weeks on either side of the zero-sales week.

- Sometimes, the inventory units reported to be in-stock at a group of stores is less than the number of stores in the group! When this happens, the original inventory units should be replaced with the store count.

The data issues described above are not an exhaustive list but they give a sense for the types of data issues the analyst must be mindful of during the estimation process.

25.3.4.3.2 *Collinearity*

Collinearity occurs when two or more of the independent (i.e., the RHS) variables in a regression are correlated. It can also occur when a variable takes on a very narrow range of values in the data and it is thus collinear with the constant term. In either case, unreliable and inaccurate parameter estimates may result, leading to poor forecasts. Collinearity between demand drivers can occur in several ways:

- *Limited number and range of price discounts (from markdowns and temporary promotions)*: If only a few weeks exist in the data where price discounts are observed, or if the price discounts are in a narrow range, then it is difficult to accurately gauge the magnitude and sign of the price elasticity parameter. In the extreme case, where items in a class were always sold at full price, assessing price elasticity is impossible.

- *Inventory and markdowns*: For a short lifecycle item, the inventory level decreases as the season progresses. Markdowns happen during the latter part of the season when inventory is low leading to collinearity between the *INVEN* and *PD* drivers.

- *Promotions and holiday/seasonality*: Merchandise is promoted heavily during holidays and if promotions for a class of items fall mainly during holiday weeks, then it is difficult to separate the effect of the promotion from the holiday-seasonality for that week.

There is no hard and fast rule for addressing collinearity. If a variable exhibits very little variation in the data, it may be best to filter out the variable from the estimation. If a pair of variables is highly collinear, pick one for the estimation and leave the other one out. For example, if a promotion is almost always coincident with a specific week of the year, leave the promotion variable out and estimate just the seasonality for that week. This means that the demand model cannot be used to predict the effect of running that promotion on some other week in the future, but it is better to decline to forecast than to produce a forecast that is based on flawed parameter estimates.

25.3.5 Using the demand model for forecasting

In this section, we describe the use of the demand model for making forecasts. The use of the model differs slightly between new items and returning items.

25.3.5.1 *Returning items*

"Returning items" or "seasonal basics" refer to items that are carried in the stores every year but not necessarily throughout the year. For example, for the Fall season, these items may return to stores in July/August of every year and be cleared out by November. Since these items have a defined lifecycle, they need to be marked down and cleared out by the end of their life to make room for other seasonal merchandise.

Using the demand model for forecasting returning items is relatively straightforward. Consider an item A that belongs to Class C. Since it is a returning item, its historical data, along with the data from other items in Class C, must have been previously used to estimate parameters. Recall that item A has its own scale parameter B (to make this clearer, we have designated this parameter as B_A in the demand model equation below) but all the other parameters are at the class level, i.e., they are the same for all the items in C.

Generating the forecast for a particular week w as a function of the price P_w that is being planned for that week involves solving demand model (1) using the scale parameter for item A and the other parameters for class C. We can write this as:

$$D_w = B_A \cdot t^a e^{-\left(\frac{t}{b}\right)^c} \cdot e^{\gamma\left(1 - \frac{P_w}{P_0}\right)} \cdot \left(1 - \mu \cdot \max\left(0,1 - \frac{I_w}{\lambda I_0}\right)\right)$$
$$\cdot e^{\beta_1 \delta_1(w) + \beta_2 \delta_2(w) + \cdots + \beta_{52} \delta_{52}(w)} \cdot e^{\alpha X(w)}$$

where:

t—item A's age during week;

P_o—item A's full price;

P_w—price planned for item A during week w;

I_o—starting inventory level for item A;

I_w—inventory level of item A at the beginning of week w (we describe below how to calculate this quantity);

$\delta_i(w) = 1$ for $i = w$, o otherwise (for $i = 1, \ldots 52$);

$X(w)$—promotional indicator for week w (set to 1 if there is a promotion planned for week w, o otherwise).

We are now ready to generate a forecast (assume, temporarily, that the quantity I_w is available). Since all the other inputs into the model are parameters that have already been estimated, producing a forecast is simply a matter of solving the demand model equation. Note that the generated forecast is *units/store* of item A. To convert it into an absolute forecast, it needs to be multiplied by the *store count*, the number of stores that will be carrying item A during week w. If this is not obtainable from the retailer, an approximation can be used.[1]

We now describe how to calculate I_w. First calculate D_1. Note that this is easy to do since I_1 is simply I_o. Now, since $I_2 = I_1 - D_1$, D_2 can be calculated. Continuing this process forward, we arrive at I_w. Any inventory additions during a week can be added to the inventory position at the start of the next week. We calculate the demand for each week from week 1 up through week $w - 1$, and update the starting inventory position for the following week, using it to forecast demand for that week, and so on.

25.3.5.2 *New items*

Forecasting demand for a new item is slightly more complicated than forecasting demand for a returning item. Since the item is new, there are no historical data and therefore, it is not included in the parameter estimation that was run for its class. Consequently, the item does not have a scale parameter B in the parameter database. However, we know which class the new item belongs to because when a new item comes into existence, its position in the merchandise hierarchy (its subclass, class, department, and division membership) is defined by the retailer. Therefore, we can use the parameters associated with that class in the demand model for the new item and generate forecasts.

Note that once the scale parameter is computed, the rest of the forecasting process for new items is identical to the process for returning items. Then how do we get a scale parameter for the new item? There are two possibilities. We can "copy" the scale parameter of a returning item (typically in the same class as the new item) that is very similar to the new item. Such items are called "like items" or "sister SKUs". This notion of similarity is based on subjective considerations and the choice of like-item is typically made by the end-

---

[1] In practice, for short lifecycle merchandise, in the first few weeks of the life of the item, all the stores that will ever carry the item would have received it. Hence, using the store count at the end of the first few weeks as the on going store count for the rest of the season is often adequate.

user of the forecast. A variant of this idea is to use the average of the scale parameters of all the returning items in the new item's class.

Alternatively, we can wait for the first few weeks of the current season to unfold and use the sales data of the new item from those weeks to estimate its scale parameter (the next section on "Forecast updating" describes how this is done). This can be used, along with the class-level parameters calculated during the earlier parameter estimation process, to generate forecasts for the rest of the season. Waiting for a few weeks before generating forecasts and markdown price recommendations is acceptable in practice since markdown price decisions are typically executed in the latter, "clearance" part of the item's lifecycle.

25.3.5.3 Forecast updating

In the previous discussion, we have described how to use class-level parameters and the item-level scale parameter to generate forecasts. We have implicitly assumed that parameters, once estimated or computed, are unchanging and are used as-is for generating forecasts. As the season unfolds, however, fresh sales data become available with every passing week and using these current-season observations to update parameters can improve the forecasts.

Updating parameters optimally requires balancing two things: the benefits of picking up demand changes early with the costs of picking up random fluctuations. Updating too often or the wrong parameters can lead to "forecast whipsaw" from week to week. Updating too infrequently can lead to forecast errors as selling patterns change. In practice, we have found that updating the scale parameter B every week, and updating the other parameters far less frequently (e.g., twice a year) has resulted in good forecast accuracy without whipsawing.

To update the scale parameter in a particular week, consider the complete demand model in eq. 1 and assume that n weeks have elapsed and so we have n observations. For the first observation, we plug in the values of all the associated variables and the class-level parameters into the RHS of the equation, substitute the per-store sales units (i.e., D_1) on the LHS of the equation, and solve for B. Call this B_1. Repeat this process for the remaining observations, yielding $B_2, \ldots, B_n$.

These estimates can be combined in different ways to produce the updated scale parameter. The simplest option is to average the n values. Alternately, they can be exponentially smoothed or modeled as a time-series. In practice, the simple average is usually adequate since, even if the resulting estimate of B isn't quite right in one week, we will be able to change it during the following week's update.

25.4 DETERMINING OPTIMAL MARKDOWN PRICES

We have described how to build and calibrate a demand model. In this section, we show how to use a demand model to optimize markdown decisions. We note that our demand models were deterministic—that is, we did not estimate any uncertainty around our demand forecasts. We continue that philosophy in this section.

25.4.1 Optimization using mathematical programming

Mathematical programming (MP) involves the use of mathematical optimization techniques based on linear algebra, calculus, and combinatorics. Linear programming (LP), integer programming (IP), and nonlinear programming (NLP) are the three most important forms of mathematical programming. In using these techniques, the challenge lies in formulating or framing the markdown problem in an appropriate format so that commercially available or open-source solvers can be used to solve the problem and generate markdown recommendations.

The MP formulations presented in this section are based on the assumption that the inventory effect (i.e., the *INVEN* term) is absent from the demand model. The inventory effect introduces additional complexity to the optimization process and we would like to start with the simpler case first. We will later describe approaches based on dynamic programming and exhaustive search that incorporate the inventory effect.

We first describe a simple NLP formulation of the markdown optimization problem. We then describe an IP formulation of the problem that is flexible enough to handle the business rules discussed earlier. This makes the formulation more realistic but this added realism comes at a price: the IP formulation is significantly more difficult to solve than the simple NLP formulation.

25.4.1.1 A nonlinear programming model

At the simplest level, the markdown optimization problem consists of finding prices p_1, $p_2, \ldots p_T$ such that total revenue is maximized, total sales do not exceed inventory, and the prices $p_1, p_2, \ldots p_T$ are nonincreasing and never drop below a salvage price p_s. We assume that inventory left over at the end of period T (labeled as I_l) can be sold at a salvage price of p_s. Before we express this algebraically, we rewrite the demand model for notational convenience. The demand model without the *INVEN* term is:

$$D(p_w) = D_w = PLC_w \cdot PD_w \cdot SEAS_w \cdot PROMO_w$$

Writing it out in full, we get:[2]

$$D_w = B \cdot t^a e^{-\left(\frac{t}{b}\right)^c} \cdot e^{\gamma\left(1 - \frac{p_w}{p_0}\right)} \cdot e^{\beta_1 \delta_1(w) + \beta_2 \delta_2(w) + \cdots + \beta_{52}\delta_{52}(w)} \cdot e^{\alpha X(w)}$$

Note that p_w is the only decision variable on the right-hand side. Without the inventory effect term, the demand for any week w is completely determined by our choice of price p_w because all other variables are exogenously given. Thus, we can express the demand model as

$$D_w(p_w) = C_w e^{-\frac{\gamma}{p_0}p_w},$$

where C_w is a constant for each week.

---

[2] Note that we have arbitrarily chosen the exponential form for PD_w. The optimization approaches described below do not change materially if the power-law functional form is chosen instead.

We can now write the markdown optimization problem as:

$$\max_{p_1, p_2, \ldots, p_T} \sum_{w=1}^{w=T} p_w D_w(p_w) + p_s I_l \tag{3}$$

subject to

$$\sum_{w=1}^{w=T} D_w(p_w) + I_l = I_0$$

$$p_w \geq p_{w+1} \text{ for } w = 1, 2, \ldots T - 1$$

$$p_T \geq p_s$$

$$I_l \geq 0$$

The *objective function* in (3) is to maximize total revenue calculated as the sum of revenue from units sold during the T weeks plus the revenue from selling leftover units at the salvage price. The first constraint ensures that what is sold in each period plus what is salvaged is equal to the starting inventory. Optimal prices should be decreasing over time and be higher than or equal to the salvage price. Finally, the leftover inventory cannot be negative. While small instances of this optimization problem can be solved using standard nonlinear program solvers, solving large instances efficiently may require considerable tuning of the algorithms and taking advantage of problem structure.

As observed earlier, (3) is a deterministic formulation. It assumes that the forecasts have no error. In practice, of course, forecasts will have error. An easy way to mitigate the effect of uncertain demand in the optimization process is to re-solve the problem every week: at the beginning of every week, use the inventory level at that point in time as the starting inventory level, and determine the optimal prices for the remaining weeks. Not surprisingly, this weekly re-optimization of prices typically improves upon the "optimize once and forget about it" approach.

Furthermore, the formulation in (3) does not incorporate any of the business rules discussed earlier. While the Collections Price-Together rule (and its variants) introduces complexity that is beyond the scope of this article, all but three of the other rules presented earlier can easily be added as constraints to the NLP formulation. The exceptions are the "Price Ladder" rule, the "No-Touch Period between Markdowns" rule and the "Maximum Number of Markdowns". The "Price Ladder" rule can be approximated by solving the NLP and "rounding" the optimal prices to the nearest points on the price ladder. However, there are no easy ways to make the solution satisfy the "No-Touch Period between Markdowns" and "Maximum Number of Markdowns" rules.

25.4.1.2 *An Integer Programming model*

We assume a T-week planning period with n prices $p_1 > p_2 > \ldots > p_{n-1} > p_n$ on the price ladder (for convenience, we assume that the full price p_0 of the item is equal to the first price p_1). We define a decision variable x_{iw} which is equal to 1 if price p_i on the price ladder is chosen for week w and 0 otherwise. To ensure that exactly one price from the price ladder is chosen for each week, we include the constraints:

$$\sum_{i=1}^{n} x_{iw} = 1 \text{ for } w = 1, \ldots, T \tag{4}$$

The demand and revenue functions for each week can be written as *linear* functions of the variables x_{iw}. Let D_{iw} and R_{iw} be the demand and revenue, respectively, if price p_i is chosen from the price ladder for week w., that is

$$D_{iw} = C_w e^{-\frac{\gamma}{p_0}p_i} \text{ and } R_{iw} = p_i D_{iw} \text{ for } i = 1, \ldots, n$$

Constraint (4) ensures that exactly one of the prices $p_1, \ldots, p_n$ will be chosen for week w. As a result, $D_w(p_w)$ can be written in terms of D_{iw} and x_{iw}:

$$D_w(p_w) = \sum_{i=1}^{n} D_{iw} x_{iw}$$

The revenue $p_w D_w(p_w)$ for each week can now be written as $\sum_{i=1}^{n} R_{iw} x_{iw}$.

Note that both the demand and revenue for each week are now linear functions of the 0–1 variables x_{iw}. Now we can write an Integer Programming formulation of the basic markdown management problem:

$$\max \sum_{w=1}^{w=T} \sum_{i=1}^{n} R_{iw} x_{iw} + p_s I_l$$

subject to

$$\sum_{w=1}^{w=T} \sum_{i=1}^{n} D_{iw} x_{iw} + I_l = I_0$$

$$\sum_{i=1}^{n} x_{iw} = 1 \text{ for } w = 1, \ldots T$$

$$x_{j(w+1)} \leq 1 - x_{iw} \text{ for } w = 1, \ldots T - 1; i = 2, \ldots n; j = 1, \ldots n - 1; j < i$$

$$x_{iw} \in \{0,1\} \text{ for } w = 1, \ldots T \text{ and } i = 1, \ldots n$$

$$I_l \geq 0$$

The constraint set $x_{j(w+1)} \leq 1 - x_{iw}$ ensures that the prices chosen are nonincreasing. Note that if $x_{iw} = 0$ for any i and w, the constraint becomes $x_{j(w+1)} \leq 1$, which is redundant given that all the variables x_{iw} have to be either 0 or 1. If $x_{iw} = 1$ for any i and w, price p_i has been chosen from the price ladder for week w. With $x_{iw} = 1$, the constraint becomes $x_{j(w+1)} \leq 0$, which implies $x_{j(w+1)} = 0$ for all $1 \leq j < i$ in week $w + 1$, i.e., prices higher than p_i in the price ladder cannot be chosen the next week. Next we show how additional business rules can be incorporated in the IP formulation.

- *Minimum price reduction rule*: For every price p_i on the price ladder, this rule dictates that if p_i is in force for week w, the next markdown price chosen cannot be p_{i+1}, $p_{i+2}, \ldots p_{i+r}$. This rule can be modeled similar to the "prices should be nonincreasing" constraint:

$$x_{j(w+1)} \leq 1 - x_{iw} \text{ for } w = 1, \ldots T - 1; i = 1, \ldots n; j = i + 1, \ldots, i + r$$

- *Maximum price reduction rule*: This constraint is similar to the minimum price reduction constraint. For every price p_i on the price ladder, if p_i is in force for week w, the next markdown price chosen cannot be p_{i+r}, p_{i+r+1}, $\ldots$ p_n. The constraints are:

$$x_{j(w+1)} \leq 1 - x_{iw} \text{ for } w = 1, \ldots T - 1; i = 1, \ldots n; j = i + r, i + r + 1, \ldots, n$$

- *Maximum sell-through at exit date rule:* Suppose the maximum sell-through at the exit date has to be less than or equal to a defined quantity. This rule implies that the leftover inventory I_l has to be larger than or equal to a minimum quantity $I_{\min}$.

$$I_l \geq I_{\min}$$

- *No-touch period at season start rule:* Suppose weeks $w = 1, 2, \ldots, r$ are "no-touch", then we set the price for those weeks to be the starting price p_1 by adding the constraints:

$$x_{1w} = 1 \text{ for } w = 1, 2, \ldots, r$$

- *No-touch period between markdowns rule:* This rule stipulates that if a markdown is taken in week w, there cannot be any markdowns for r weeks after week w. Let's assume that the markdown price chosen on week w is p_i. This implies that $x_{iw} = 1$ and $x_{i(w-1)} = 0$. Therefore, we need to force $x_{i(w+j)} = 1$ for $j = 1, \ldots, r$ whenever $x_{iw} - 1$ and $x_{i(w-1)} = 0$. This is how:

$$x_{i(w+j)} \geq x_{iw} - x_{i(w-1)} \text{ for } j = 1, \ldots, r; i = 2, \ldots, n; w = 2, \ldots, T$$

- *Maximum number of markdowns rule:* To model this constraint, we introduce a new 0–1 variable y_i for $i = 2, \ldots n$. If price point p_i is chosen for *any* week w, y_i will be 1; if p_i is never chosen, y_i will be 0. We force y_i to conform to this definition with these constraints:

$$y_i \geq x_{iw} \text{ for } w = 1, \ldots, T; i = 2, \ldots, n$$
$$y_i \leq \sum_{w=1}^{T} x_{iw}$$

Let's see how these constraints work. If p_i is never chosen, then $x_{iw} = 0$ for all w; in this scenario, the first set of constraints become redundant and the second constraint forces y_i to be 0. If p_i is chosen, then at least one of the variables x_{iw} will be 1; in this scenario, the first set of constraints will force y_i to be 1 and the second set will be redundant.

The number of markdowns is equal to the number of price points from $p_2, \ldots, p_n$ that are chosen at least once during the T weeks (note that since p_1 is assumed to be the full-price p_0, it is not counted as a markdown). Since y_i measures if p_i is *ever* chosen, the number of *chosen* price points from $p_2, \ldots, p_n$ is simply $\sum_{i=2} y_i$. Now it is easy to model the Maximum Number of Markdowns rule:

$$\sum_{i=2}^{n} y_i \leq M$$

- *Markdown blackout period rule:* Let's assume that week w is blacked out. To ensure that no new markdowns are recommended during week w, we add these constraints:

$$x_{i(w-1)} = x_{iw} \text{ for } i = 1, \ldots, n.$$

These constraints simply force the price chosen in week w to be identical to what was chosen in week $w - 1$, thereby avoiding any price change (i.e., a new markdown) in week w.

- *Promotions rule:* In the case where this rule prevents a markdown from being executed in a particular week, it can be modeled as a markdown blackout period rule. In the case where this rule sets a maximum limit on the depth of a markdown for a particular week, it can be modeled as a special case of the maximum price reduction rule.

The IP formulation of the markdown optimization problem is quite general in the sense that all of the rules except for the "Collections Price Together" rule can be incorporated. The IP formulation can be solved by commercially available integer programming solvers such as ILOG CPLEX or Dash Optimization's Xpress-MP. However, IP models are often very difficult to solve and various problem-specific features have to be exploited to achieve acceptable performance in practice.

25.4.2 Optimization using Dynamic Programming

In this section, we describe a Dynamic Programming (DP) approach to markdown optimization. DP is a natural choice for the analysis of multi-stage pricing problems and most of the published academic work in this area uses the DP framework. Researchers have formulated and solved different versions of the markdown pricing problem, with varying assumptions on the nature of the demand model, the presence or absence of pricing ladders, the presence or absence of price monotonicity, and so on. Many of the assumptions behind DP formulations tend to be restrictive in practice but the insights derived from the analysis are nevertheless useful in the design of practical markdown optimization solutions. A brief sampling of published work in this area includes Bitran and Mondschein (1997), Feng and Xiao (2000), Gallego and van Ryzin (1994), Mantrala and Rao (2001), Smith and Achabal (1998), and Zhao and Zheng (2000).

An advantage of DP is that, under certain assumptions on the demand model and constraints, the optimal solution takes the form of a policy that is easy to implement and exceedingly fast in practice. However, DP can be computationally expensive and the addition of just one new business rule can render a formulation impractical to solve within acceptable run times. First, a few definitions:

- The state variable for the DP is the pair (I, p) where I is the current inventory and p is the current price.
- We represent the price ladder with the set $P = \{p_1, p_2, \ldots, p_n\}$ with $p_1 > p_2 > \cdots > p_{n-1} > p_n$. Unsold inventory can be salvaged at a price $p_s < p_n$.
- We define the value function $V_t(I, p)$ as the maximum revenue attainable when there are t weeks left to go and the system is in state (I, p).

With these definitions in place, we can write down the basic DP optimality equation:

$$V_t(I, p) = \underset{p' \in P, p' \leq p}{Max} (p' \cdot \min(I, D_t(p')) + V_{t-1}(Max(0, I - D_t(p')), p')$$

The boundary conditions are:

$$V_0(I, p) = Ip_s \text{ for } I \geq 0 \text{ and } p \in P$$

$$V_t(0, p) = 0 \text{ for } t = 1, 2, \ldots, T \text{ and } p \in P$$

To solve this DP, we start at the end of the planning period and recursively calculate the value function backwards for all possible values of the state variable (I, p) at every week t. This, of course, can be computationally formidable. For example, if an item has a 20-week selling season, a price ladder with 10 price points and 1,000 units of starting inventory, the values and associated optimal decisions at 200,000 states will have to be calculated! In practice, various computational "tricks" are employed to speed up the algorithm.

This formulation can be converted into a *stochastic* optimization problem in a straightforward manner. We re define $D_t(p)$ as a random variable with a known distribution (rather than a point forecast of demand); and $V_t(I, p)$ as the maximum *expected* revenue attainable when there are t weeks left and the system is in state (I, p).

With these definitions, we can compute the markdown decisions that maximize the *expected* revenue by rewriting the optimality equations as follows:

$$V_t(I,p) = \max_{p' \in P, p' \le p} E[p' \cdot \min(I, D_t(p')) + V_{t-1}(\text{Max}(0, I - D_t(p')), p')]$$

$E[.]$ is the expected value operator. The boundary conditions are unchanged from the deterministic formulation. The stochastic formulation is more computationally difficult than the deterministic formulation since the expectation operation has to be evaluated at each state over the distribution of demand for every feasible price point at that state.

Some of the rules discussed earlier can be easily accommodated into the DP formulation (e.g., the minimum price reduction rule) but others cannot be (e.g., the maximum number of markdowns rule) without expanding the state variable. Enlarging the state variable is very detrimental to computational performance so adding constraints must be done with caution.

The formulation in its current form assumes that the DP is run once, the optimal policy for each state and time period is stored in a database, and at each week of the item's selling season, the optimal decision is simply "looked up" based on the current state and price point. The formulation is thus an "optimize once" approach and doesn't take advantage of any updating we may do to the demand model's parameters as sales data come in.

One way to extend the DP approach to take advantage of demand updating is to run the DP algorithm from scratch at the beginning of every week using the updated demand model. The optimal price recommendation for that week is used but the rest of the DP solution (for future time periods) is not used. This is repeated at the start of every week. While this approach takes advantage of demand updating, it loses one of the primary advantages of DP, namely, optimizing once, storing the output, and very efficiently looking at the solution every week based on the state. Researchers have tried to incorporate "demand learning" into the formulation of the DP itself so that the advantages of DP are not lost (see Bitran and Wadhwa (1996) for an example of this approach).

The formulation described above treats time as discrete and solves for the optimal price at each discrete time point. But it is possible to adopt a continuous-time perspective and solve for the *optimal price trajectory* as a function of time and inventory level. See Feng and Xiao (2000) and Smith and Achabal (1998) for examples of this approach. Under certain assumptions, continuous-time formulations have closed-form analytic solutions which can be used to approximate the discrete-time solution.

25.4.3 Optimization using exhaustive search

For a given *fixed* set of business rule types, the aforementioned methods work well: by exploiting the mathematical structure of the problem, the resulting algorithms can be fine-tuned to perform well. However, the introduction of a *single* new business rule type may necessitate a complete re-design of the formulation and/or lead to a slowdown in computational performance that is so drastic that the underlying algorithms have to be completely rethought.

In practice, this lack of flexibility to accommodate new business rules is a drawback. While most retailers follow similar business rules, almost every retailer has unique rules. We describe an approach in this section that handles new business rule types without difficulty. It is based on the simple idea of exhaustive search (taken from artificial intelligence) and has proven to be very effective at solving large and complex instances of markdown optimization problems in practice.

The exhaustive search algorithm is illustrated in Figure 25.8. For simplicity, assume that there are two weeks left in the season and the current price point is p_1. For week 1, we can stay at p_1 or drop down to p_2 or p_3. For week 2, we have three price choices if we chose p_1 for week 1, two choices if we chose p_2 for week 1, and just one choice if we chose p_3 for week 1. Thus, there are five price paths that satisfy the "prices should be nonincreasing" constraint. The exhaustive search algorithm evaluates all these price paths either *implicitly or explicitly* and picks the one with the maximum revenue.

The key is the *implicit* evaluation or elimination of price paths from consideration. If every complete price path needs to be evaluated *explicitly*, the algorithm's performance will not be acceptable since the number of feasible price paths becomes astronomical for even moderately sized problems. Implicit enumeration/evaluation addresses this problem. How? By building candidate price paths *one week at a time and constantly looking* for opportunities to eliminate them from further consideration (thereby saving time).

Here are a couple of examples of how this "early elimination" (also called "pruning") works. Suppose that the algorithm is working with a partial price path with "revenue-so-far"

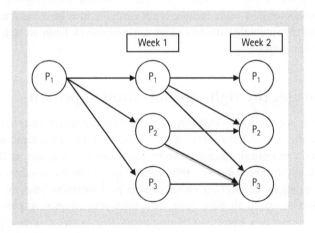

FIGURE 25.8 Exhaustive search

of R, current price point of p and inventory-remaining I. For the next week, assume a feasible price point is chosen. *If the resulting demand is more than remaining-inventory, then the price path need not be explored further*, since there's no inventory available to satisfy the demand from future price actions. In practice, if deep markdowns are chosen early in the season, many price paths containing them will run out of inventory well before the end of the season and can hence be pruned.

Assume that the current inventory I is all sold at the current price p. The revenue Ip from doing so, combined with the "revenue-so-far" of R, is an *upper bound* on the maximum revenue attainable from this price path. *If this upper bound $Ip + R$ is less than the revenue of the best price path found so far, then this partial price path can be eliminated from further consideration since it can never be the optimal solution.* By implementing such pruning strategies, substantial performance gains can be achieved, rendering the exhaustive search approach competitive with other approaches.

Given the simple, iterative nature of the algorithm, it is not hard to see how the exhaustive search approach can handle new business rule types without the need for significant rework. Consider, for example, the maximum number of markdowns rule. It is easy to accommodate this rule: as the algorithm builds a candidate price path, after every week, it compares the number of markdowns taken so far in the price path to the maximum and if the maximum has been reached, the prices for the remaining weeks are fixed at the current price, the revenue and demand numbers are updated, the price path is deemed complete and the algorithm moves on to the next candidate price path. Readers are invited to verify for themselves how the other business rule types can be accommodated within the exhaustive search framework.

There's a further positive aspect to handling new business rule types in exhaustive search. In general, business rules tend to make sets of price paths infeasible and thus reduce the size of the "search space", making it easier and faster for the algorithm to find the optimal price path. As was seen in our brief discussion about handling the maximum number of markdowns business rule, the rule actually *helped* the algorithm complete the evaluation of the price path *early*. In other words, all the extensions to the partial price path that involved taking markdowns and thereby exceeding the maximum were not considered by the algorithm at all, thanks to the rule. Thus, the exhaustive search algorithm framework not only accommodates new business rule types easily, it runs faster as a result! We also note that exhaustive search algorithms can be run every week from scratch, so as to take advantage of demand updating.

25.4.4 Choosing the right optimization approach

We described four approaches to optimization but there are many other approaches such as genetic algorithms, simulated annealing, tabu search, ant colony optimization, etc. How should one choose an optimization approach? There are two key factors that are worth considering carefully in choosing an optimization approach: the need to accommodate changes to the problem description either due to new business rules or new demand model forms, and the need to have "fast" run-time performance in practice. There is tension between these two objectives. Recognizing this tradeoff, a few guidelines are offered below.

If new business rules are unlikely to be added over time and the chosen demand model is considered reliable, then Integer Programming based approaches may be appropriate. There will be upfront effort needed to model all the existing business rules and to "tighten" the structure of the IP formulation so that fast performance can be achieved. Once that has been done, the system can be deployed and ongoing effort will be minimal as long as new business rules are not added and there is no substantive change to the demand model (note that some changes to the demand model can be handled easily—for example using the power-law instead of the exponential law for the price effect—but others cannot be, for example including a term for the inventory effect). Finally, algorithm-specific software development will be minimal since commercial IP solvers can be used for this purpose. However, application-specific software development—moving data to/from databases, user-interaction screens, etc.—may still be substantial.

If, however, new business rules or demand models will have to be supported over time (either because the system is built by a software vendor targeting multiple retailers or because the retailer anticipates significant change in their business), then exhaustive search may be better. Amongst all the algorithmic approaches we have seen, the exhaustive search framework makes the fewest assumptions about the problem structure and is therefore least likely to be "defeated" by a new business rule or demand model. On the other hand, building a robust and scalable exhaustive search algorithm takes significant effort and software engineering expertise.

25.5 Measuring the benefit of markdown optimization

The methodologies underpinning modern markdown optimization—demand models and optimization algorithms—are very different from the traditional methods used by retailers. This leads to a common question: how do we know that markdown optimization is better than what we have always done? More specifically, what's the *incremental benefit* of markdown optimization over traditional approaches? How do we quantify this benefit accurately? In this section, we discuss the challenges in accurately answering these questions and describe approaches used in practice to gauge the incremental benefit of markdown optimization.

25.5.1 Challenges in measuring benefit

In many types of decision-support systems, quantifying the benefit is straightforward. For example, for a new truck-route-optimization system (that promises least-cost schedules), it is straightforward to compare the total cost (e.g., a function of miles-traveled) of the optimal route generated by the new system with the cost of the solution from the old system/method. Similarly, for a new workforce scheduling system, it is easy to compare the total labor cost of the optimal schedule generated by the new system with the cost of the solution from the old system/method.

In these two cases, the benefits are easy to measure because the costs with and without the system are deterministic. In markdown optimization, however, the revenue from any markdown solution is determined in large part by how consumers will react. Since there is tremendous uncertainty in how consumers will react to different markdown solutions, it is not straightforward to compare two markdown solutions. For example, consider an item from last season that was managed traditionally and received two markdowns (30 percent off and 50 percent off) 5 and 8 weeks into the season. The revenue generated was $3,400. Now we run the same data (i.e., inventory level, price ladder, selling season, etc.) through a markdown optimization system. The new system recommends three markdowns (20 percent, 40 percent, 60 percent) 4, 7, and 9 weeks into the season. How can we tell what the revenue would have been if the three-markdown solution had been implemented last season? How do we know that it would have been more than $3,400? The markdown optimization system can certainly *predict* the revenue for the optimal solution but it is only a prediction and, as such, will have forecast error. Therefore, assessing the incremental benefit by comparing a predicted revenue number that includes forecast error to the actual revenue will lead to a benefits estimate that also includes error.

What is the difference between the route-optimization example and the markdown optimization example? The route-optimization objective was *completely* determined by the chosen route (and other factual data, such as cost of fuel, cost of labor, etc.). The objective *was not influenced by random factors* stemming from the chosen route. In contrast, the revenue from any chosen markdown solution is dependent on how consumers react to the price cut and other random factors. Thus, determining the benefit of new markdown management methods is not a straightforward exercise. Nevertheless, various approaches have been developed in practice to estimate, at least approximately, the incremental benefit of markdown optimization systems.

25.5.2 Measuring prospective benefit with test-and-control experiments

How can a retailer estimate the likely benefit from implementing a proposed markdown system? One way is to run an experiment: First, pick a department and randomly choose half the stores from the chain as the "test stores". The remaining stores are the "control stores". Next, use the markdown optimization system to manage markdowns in the test stores, and the traditional system to manage markdowns in the control stores. Finally, compare the key metrics for test and control stores and assess the benefit.

Since this is a controlled experiment, many sources of variation can be prevented from biasing the results. However, subtle sources of bias can still creep in and "pollute" the experiment. For example, as the experiment unfolds, the results from the test and control stores are visible to the merchant/planner teams responsible for the merchandise. If, for the same item, the test stores are doing better than the control stores (or vice versa), the winning strategies may be "copied over", thereby biasing the performance numbers. In the parlance of clinical trials in medicine, the merchants/planners are not *blinded* to the experiment's ongoing statistics and therefore they may bias the conduct of the experiment either intentionally or inadvertently. Finally, running an experiment (particularly one that involves hundreds of stores) is quite invasive and demands significant effort from the retail organization. The various functions that need to cooperate such as merchandising, planning, and store operations may have to be incented to participate in the experiment and to exert the care that is needed to produce robust results. Nevertheless, *if done well*, the test-and-control approach can generate reliable results.

25.5.3 Measuring retrospective benefit

Once a retailer has adopted a markdown management system, how can it estimate the *retrospective* benefit from the system? Two approaches are commonly used in practice: benefit comparison across time, and benefit comparison across items with varying recommendation acceptance. These methods are far from perfect but they are intuitive and provide at least an approximate way to estimate the benefit.

25.5.3.1 *Benefit comparison across time*

In this approach, the *aggregate* performance of a merchandise group is compared *before and after* the markdown optimization system was deployed. Since merchandise for which markdowns are applied have short lifecycles and tend to change significantly from year to year, it does not make sense to perform benefit analysis at the item level—therefore benefits are estimated at a more aggregate level such as department or class.

To make the basic idea concrete, let's consider the Women's Cashmere Sweaters class and assume that the Fall 2007 season was the first season when markdowns were managed with the help of a markdown optimization system. Markdowns in the Fall 2006 season were managed with the traditional method. To compare the performance of the Class between 2007 and 2006, several metrics are commonly used: sales (in monetary terms or in units), gross margin (in monetary terms or percentage) percentage sell-through, percentage revenue capture—defined as the actual revenue realized divided by the revenue if the entire inventory were sold at full price.

A simple side-by-side comparison of these metrics from year to year is not advisable. From 2006 to 2007, the underlying business may have changed significantly. For example, there may have been a strategic decision to bring in lower price-point items, or to flow the merchandise to the stores earlier than usual, or to deliver to the stores more frequently, or to increase the percentage of fashion-forward items in the class, to increase the length of the selling season by a few weeks, to allow the price to break (i.e., the first markdown) earlier than usual, to increase the frequency and depth of promotions, and so on. The macro-economic environment may have changed as well with an impact on consumer spending.

To at least partially account for these changing factors, the side-by-side comparison analysis can be done on various *slices* of the merchandise in the Class. If the price-point range of the items in the Class changed from Fall 2006 to Fall 2007, then slicing the merchandise into different price groups (e.g., Good-Better-Best, Less than $9.99—$10.00 to $19.99—$20.00 to $39.99—Over $39.99) would be helpful. The Fall 2006 and Fall 2007 metrics can now be compared side-by-side for each price group to see if the change in metrics was uniform across all the groups or if the new system helped certain groups at the expense of other groups.

If the length of the selling season or the timing of store deliveries changed between the two seasons, then slicing the merchandise into groups defined by the In-Store-Date and Exit-Date (e.g., "In-Store Oct Weeks 1–2, Exit Date Dec Weeks 2–3" would represent all the items that hit the shelves in the first two weeks of October and were cleared during the second and third weeks of December) would be helpful. The Fall 2006 and Fall 2007 metrics can now be compared side-by-side for each group to see if the change in metrics was uniform across all the groups or if the new system helped certain groups at the expense of other groups. Similar slices can be created to address other variations in the external environment from season to season.

Finally, it is worth noting that since there are inherent tradeoffs between the different metrics, looking for all the key metrics to be "better" with markdown optimization is not appropriate. For example, a very high sell-through rate can be achieved by marking prices down heavily but this will result in lower gross margin percentage and revenue capture percentage.

25.5.3.2 *Benefit comparison across items with varying recommendation acceptance*

This approach takes advantage of the fact that markdown management end-users (i.e., typically, merchants and planners) do not accept every recommendation made by a new markdown optimization system. It is common for a significant proportion of recommendations to be either ignored or to be modified every week. This lack of complete acceptance is due to several reasons.

First, the optimization system does not capture the effect of every factor that can influence an item's selling pattern. For example, the end-user may choose to ignore a deep-markdown recommendation for an item early in its life because he/she knows that the recent low sales rate for the item was caused by severe weather that resulted in abnormally low store traffic for a region. Secondly, it takes time for users to become familiar with and build trust in the workings of any new system. The rate of acceptance tends to rise with increasing familiarity and trust. Finally, when any complex new system is deployed, there is typically a "shake out" period in the beginning where issues stemming from the system's setup and configuration in the retailer's business environment are identified and addressed. During this period, the performance of the system can be uneven and end-users, accordingly, use the recommendations cautiously.

Varying levels of recommendation acceptance suggests the following approach to benefit estimation: Create two pools of items—one pool made up of items with a high degree of accepted markdowns and the other pool made up of items with a low level of acceptance. Compare the two pools side-by-side on the key metrics described earlier. For example, if the revenue capture percentage and the gross margin percentage metrics are significantly higher for the "high acceptance" pool relative to the "low acceptance" pool, that suggests that the markdown optimization system is improving performance.

Note that the differences in the metrics across the two pools cannot be due to factors that are *common* to all the items. The differences must be due to either random variation or to factors that affect one pool but not the other. The effect of random variation will be negligible since each pool has many items and item-level random errors will cancel out in the aggregation. What's left is the effect of factors that affect one pool but not the other. By definition, one of these factors is the rate of recommendation acceptance. The key assumption in this approach is that the "rate of recommendation acceptance" is the only one—or at least the dominant one.

One way to remove the need for this assumption is to list the various candidate factors that may be affecting one pool but not the other and then estimate a regression model using all these factors (and, of course, the "rate of markdown acceptance" factor) as independent variables and a key financial metric (e.g., revenue capture percentage or gross margin percentage) as the dependent variable. If the "rate of markdown acceptance" independent variable has a significant and positive coefficient, it is reasonable to infer that the markdown optimization system has a beneficial effect. The magnitude of the coefficient can be used to quantify the financial benefit of the new system. Further, by linking the rate of recommendation acceptance with increases in gross margin percentage, retail management may be able to motivate end-users to increase their use of the system.

25.6 Summary

In this chapter, we have described an analytical approach for effective markdown management. This approach, called markdown optimization, rests heavily on two pillars: demand models and optimization algorithms. Demand models predict sales as a function of planned markdown pricing actions and other factors. Optimization algorithms use this cause–effect capability of demand models to efficiently evaluate all valid markdown pricing actions and pick the best one.

This approach to markdown management makes it possible for retailers to profitably and efficiently set markdown prices for their SKUs across thousands of stores, comprehensively taking into account all the key demand drivers as well as business rules and operating practices. With the shortening of product lifecycles and ever-mounting competitive pressure on retailers, markdown optimization will become an increasingly indispensable tool for retailers. For the reader interested in learning more about the academic work in the "dynamic pricing" area in general, and markdown pricing in particular, a good starting point is the survey chapter by Aviv and Vulcano (Chapter 23) and Elmaghraby and Keskinocak (2003). For the reader interested in more details on the business context around markdown management and a fairly non-technical introduction to markdown optimization, chapter 10 in Phillips (2005) is an excellent source.

References

Anderson, E. and Simester, D. (2003) "Mind Your Pricing Cues", *Harvard Business Review*, September.

Bitran, G. R. and Mondschein, S. V. (1997) "Periodic Pricing of Seasonal Products in Retailing", *Management Science* 43: 64–79.

Bitran, G. R. and Wadhwa, H. (1996) "A Methodology for Demand Learning with an Application to the Optimal Pricing of Seasonal Products". MIT Sloan Working Paper.

Elmaghraby, W. and Keskinocak, P. (2003) "Dynamic Pricing in the Presence of Inventory Considerations: Research Overview, Current Practices, and Future Directions", *Management Science* 49: 1287–309.

Feng, Y. and B. Xiao. (2000) "Optimal Policies of Yield Management with Multiple Predetermined Prices", *Management Science* 48: 332–43.

Friend, S. C. and Walker, P. H. (2001) "Welcome to the New World of Merchandising", *Harvard Business Review*, November.

Gallego, G. and van Ryzin, G. (1994) "Optimal dynamic pricing of inventories with stochastic demand", *Management Science* 40: 999–1020.

Greene, W. H. (2003) *Econometric Analysis*. Upper Saddle River, NJ: Prentice Hall.

Hanssens, D. M., Parsons, L. J., and Schultz, R. L. (2001) *Market Response Models*. Norwell, MA: Kluwer Academic Publishers.

Heching, A., Gallego, G., and van Ryzin, G. (2002) "Mark-Down Pricing: An Empirical Analysis of Policies and Revenue Potential at one Apparel Retailer", *Journal of Revenue and Pricing Management* 1: 139–60.

Leeflang, P. S. H., Wittink, D. R., Wedel, M., and Naert, P. A. (2000) *Building Models for Marketing Decisions*. Norwell, MA: Kluwer Academic Publishers.

Mantrala, M. K. and Rao, S. (2001) "A Decision-Support System that Helps Retailers Decide Order Quantities and Markdowns for Fashion Goods", *Interfaces* 31: 146–65.

Phillips, R. (2005) *Pricing and Revenue Optimization*. Stanford, CA: Stanford Business Books.

Press, W. H., Teukolsky, S. A., Vetterling, W. T., and Flannery, B. P. (1992) *Numerical Recipes in C*. Cambridge: Cambridge University Press.

Smith, S. A. and Achabal, D. D. (1998) "Clearance Pricing and Inventory Policies for Retail Chains", *Management Science* 44: 285–300.

Woo, J., Levy, M., and Bible, J. (2005) "Inventory and Price Decision Support". United States Patent # 6910017.

Zhao, W. and Y.-S. Zheng. (2000) "Optimal Dynamic Pricing for Perishable Assets with Nonhomogeneous Demand", *Management Science* 46: 375–88.

CHAPTER 26

REVENUE MANAGEMENT

KALYAN TALLURI

26.1 INTRODUCTION

Revenue management (RM, sometimes also called *yield management*) is a form of price discrimination popularized by the airline and hotel industries. Some salient features of these industries are:

- a fixed capacity that they cannot change easily in the short term;
- high fixed costs and very low marginal costs;
- sale ahead of actual resource usage, in the form of reservation contracts;
- highly perishable inventory; for instance, unsold seats are worthless once the flight departs;
- demand that can vary by large amounts from one day to another;
- a heterogeneous customer population with different purchase preferences and willingness-to-pay;
- anonymous sales, so customers can be classified into segments very imperfectly, often based only on the timing of their purchase.

All these characteristics have influenced the development and practice of RM, which at a high level can be described as mechanisms to charge different prices for different customer segments for the consumption of the same product.

RM has become a business necessity for many industries that share at least some of the above characteristics. To see why, consider the following simple example. Say a flight has 80 seats in one single (coach) compartment. The main operating costs of the flight are the crew and fuel costs that the airline incurs irrespective of the flight's occupancy, and let's say they add up to $10,000. Transporting an additional passenger costs very little, so assume marginal cost per passenger is 0.

Suppose there are two types of customers, leisure and business, willing to pay at most $100 and $300 respectively for the flight and the market for a specific day has 60 of the former and 30 of the latter. If the firm were to charge a single price, it would be either $100 or $300, yielding revenues of $8,000 and $9,000 respectively. The firm would make a loss no matter what price it charges, making the route unprofitable to operate. If, however, it knows that leisure customers tend to book early and business customers closer to departure, it could create a product at a price of $100 with the restriction that the product has to be purchased at least two weeks prior to departure, and a full-fare product of $300 with no such advance-purchase restrictions, limit sales of the $100 tickets to 50 passengers (as we are aware that there are 30 passengers willing to pay higher, we reserve 30 for them) and conceivably capture a revenue of $14,000.

In practice the segments do not separate so perfectly, or indeed have valuations so clearly defined, but it is not hard to see that even done imperfectly, RM brings considerable revenue benefits to the firm. The above example also illustrates the main elements of RM tactics: identify customer purchase characteristics, set different prices for different segments, and control the sale of inventory based on forecasts for that day's inventory. Other industries that share the above-mentioned characteristics have also developed their variations of the basic RM theme.

This chapter gives an introduction to the models and algorithms behind many RM software implementations. RM can very well be implemented without any models, tools, or software of course, but the size and scale of the controls would require a prohibitive amount of manpower and effort. Take for instance a hotel—it needs to control bookings for stays in the future, which usually means a year's worth of inventory to control each day. Even if there are two or three segments, the manager or analyst has to come up with forecasts, prices, and controls for each of the segments for each one of these future days. If one were to do something more sophisticated and control by length of stay, the problem size really blows up.

This is where RM models and software come in handy. By controlling a large chunk of the inventory automatically they can free up the manager to concentrate only on exceptions or special days, improving the overall revenue performance. Many believe that by being dispassionate and risk neutral, a well-designed RM system obtains better revenue than the average RM analyst. In any case, it appears a combination of good modeling and RM software combined with manual oversight leads to significant revenue maximization.

This chapter is organized as follows: We describe the RM process in Section 26.2, describing product design and broader managerial and competitive RM concerns. In Section 26.3 we describe models and algorithms for single-resource revenue management, the operational control of sales for a single resource. In Section 26.4 we discuss network revenue management which is concerned with controlling the sale of products that consume multiple resources (such as multi-night stays for hotels). In Section 26.5 we discuss some auxiliary operational issues of RM, and finally conclude with some suggestions for further reading.

26.2 RM PROCESS

The RM process consists of a set of strategic and tactical decisions. The strategic decisions, made infrequently and often as a response to competitive moves, involve product design and pricing, and occasionally, global policies on sale controls such as price-matching (automatically match the competitor's current price). The more tactical operational decisions (i.e., decisions taken on a day-to-day basis) involve setting controls on the sale of the remnant inventory. We look at each in turn below.

26.2.1 Product design and pricing

The basic premise of RM is to sell the same physical inventory (say seats within the coach cabin for an airline, or cars in a certain category for a rental car company, or hotel rooms of a certain type for a hotel) to different customer segments at different prices. Attractive as this proposal may appear to the manager of a hotel or an airline, it raises two important implementation issues: (1) why would any customer buy the same product at a higher price when he could have bought at a lower one?, and (2) how can the firm know which customer belongs to which segment?

The second point is apt, as in most RM industries sales are anonymous and even if customers could be identified (say by web cookies, or customer registration), quoting different prices based on personal identification would constitute first-degree price discrimination, a practice that is illegal in many countries, and even if not, is bound to generate bad publicity and customer rejection.

RM price discrimination relies on designing many different products off the same physical inventory by adding restrictions on their sale and letting customers choose their most adequate price–product combination. To give an example, consider an airline that knows that many of its business customers have a strong preference for flexibility and are willing to pay more for the ability to change their reservation at any time. It could design two products, one a non-refundable $100 ticket and another one at $300 with no restrictions. So the price-sensitive leisure customer, for whom the restriction is probably irrelevant or non-binding, buys the cheap fare, whereas a customer traveling for business might find the restriction on the cheaper fare too odious and purchase the costlier fare product. So the products are the same physically (same flight, same compartment) and yet they are not (different conditions, different prices).

It helps that business customers tend to be much less sensitive to price than leisure customers (if not the firm would see little benefit in this exercise) as they can write it off as a business expense, or the trip is for making a sale, or even better, is being paid by the client.

It is worth emphasizing that in the above example each segment self-selects the product designed for them. It would of course be too much to hope that each segment selects their targeted product perfectly; there would always be some business customers (say someone self-employed or a small-business owner) who risks the possibility that he may not be using the ticket. But even if the restriction prevents 70 or 80 percent of business customers buying at $100, it would lead to a significant increase in revenues.

RM product design, then, is to come up with innovative ways of creating sale products. The guiding principle is that less restrictive products should be priced more and there be a correlation between willingness-to-pay and the restrictions. For instance, if in the above example business customers were as price-sensitive as the leisure customers, there is little point in creating a restricted product for the leisure customers.

There are many conditions and restrictions that one can potentially use in the design. In addition to the cancelation penalties mentioned above, Saturday-night stay requirements, cancelation and change penalties, and advance-purchase requirements are the most common dimensions of segmentation in the hotel and airline industries. In the hotel industry, because the rooms differ physically, further differentiation based on type of room as well as bundling with other services (gym, free breakfast) is a common practice.

RM product design is more art than science and it is difficult to say anything that applies to all firms, or even firms within an industry. Whether the firm (or industry) can sustain a segmentation depends on local demand characteristics, customer preferences, product differentiation, as well as competitive offerings. The airline industry at one point seemed to have reached an equilibrium where all the major carriers offered these differentiated products with more or less matching requirements. However, with the advent of budget carriers this equilibrium appears broken and the practice now, in many local point-to-point markets, is to control sales based solely on time-of-purchase—RM without any explicit product design, sometimes called restriction-free RM.

26.2.2 Fixing prices

Once the products are created with their restrictions and conditions, the second step is to set prices for them. One thing to note here is that we assume the firm fixes the prices for the RM products and then optimizes the resource allocations for the products. The firm exerts control on sales by limiting the amount of inventory it is willing to sell at each price point. This sometimes is referred to as "quantity-based" RM, as opposed to dynamic pricing or "price-based" RM where the firm changes the prices taking into account remaining inventory and demand. In this article we concentrate on quantity-based RM.

At first glance it may appear that the firm is limiting its options by fixing prices for a period of time, but it can effectively mimic dynamic pricing if it chooses to. Consider for instance the RM practiced by many budget airline carriers. They fix a set of discrete price points (say $20, $25, ...) and decide (on a flight-by-flight basis) which price point is open (available for sale) for a flight at every point in time. Since the product is not differentiated, consumers see changing prices for the same flight over time. This can be considered dynamic pricing (changing prices) or quantity-based RM (opening and closing classes). It can effectively fetch the same revenue as dynamic pricing as the discretization can be made as fine as one wants.

How to fix the prices then? Let's recall the "classical" theory from basic economics: get an idea of the price–demand curve (for a given segment) and find the price-point (subject to a capacity constraint) that maximizes revenue.

Two important complications arise. First, in RM the firm is constantly re-allocating a fixed capacity across many products, each intended for different segments. So, capacity allocated to a product changes by day and over the sale period. As the RM process first fixes prices and then allocates capacity, and the latter changes dynamically and for different days of inventory, it is not easy to determine the optimal capacity-constrained prices. Secondly, the optimal price is dependent on the prices of current market offerings. If the competition is practicing RM also, the prices for competing products are also changing constantly, making the price-setting part even more difficult to optimize.

One way around these difficulties is to set a series of price points for each product. This allows the firm to raise or lower the price by opening or closing the sales at a price point based on current market conditions or its forecast of demand for a particular day's inventory. The primary functionality of pricing moves to the operational, and more responsive, period of capacity control. Of course, this equivalence between changing prices and controlling inventory is valid only if sales are controlled in real-time by a centralized reservation or sale approval system.

Given that the firm is effectively setting a price for each RM product at any given point in time, this process of setting prices and controlling allocations may sound like a rather round-about way of doing things. Historically, the practice originated when airlines and hotels published prices in catalogs and mailed them to far-flung travel agents across the globe.[1]

These days, as more and more sales occur over the Internet[2] and the ability to control in real-time is increasing,[3] the persistence of this practice may be dismissed as a vestige of habit, but it does have some benefits. First, keeping prices to a set of discrete price points makes the process easier to manage (no agonizing over whether one should have charged $20.75 instead of $20.25) without losing too much in revenue. Secondly, even if the firm has the ability to change prices minute-by-minute, data and computational requirements may prevent it doing so. Setting upper limits on the amount of inventory the firm is willing to sell at each price point provides a sort of protection in case there is a surge of demand. This allows the firm to observe demand for a certain period of time while protecting itself from selling too much in the periods between re-optimizations.

26.2.2.1 *Segmentation effectiveness*

The idea behind designing a menu of RM products is that the firm offers a subset of them at any point in time and the customer selects the product intended for him. So in our prototypical example, the business customer purchases the restriction-free product while the leisure customer purchases the cheaper fare and accepts the restrictions on itinerary or cancelation penalties. Presumably the conditions are too onerous for the business customer to purchase the cheaper product, even though it is being offered at the same time. But the interactions between segments and products can get quite complicated.

Under the ideal scenario there is a one-to-one mapping between the RM products and the segment purchases,[4] *if* all the products were offered throughout the sale period. But RM

---

[1] The catalogs had just one price for each product. Travel agents would check if the itinerary met all restrictions and price the product by a complicated set of rules.

[2] The EyeforTravel Research, European Online Travel Report 2008 estimates that nearly 40% of airline sales in Europe are on-line and growing at a rate of 10% per year at the expense of off-line sales. Similarly, the eTRAK Full Year 2009 report on hotel bookings by channel estimates that 54% of all CRS bookings come from the on-line channel.

[3] Currently there are a few vendors that sell real-time dynamic pricing engines, often rules based, that can set prices or make decisions in real-time based on the characteristics of the booking request. It has to be noted however that unless the booking request comes directly to the firm's own server, the ability to make real-time decisions is limited.

[4] There could be more products than segments (of course, depending on what we mean by segment in the first place); whether effective or not, there is nothing stopping the firm from doing so. The definition of a "segment" itself is quite nebulous, so one may be tempted to back-define a segment based on the restrictions of the product they purchased, but that does not help us much in pricing or product design. For simplicity we assume that we first define what the segments are, with an identifiable price–demand curve, and then design one product for each segment.

controls may limit the sale of some items, and what happens then? If the RM control closes the sale of the cheaper restrictive product, a small proportion of leisure customers might just go on to purchase the unrestricted product. This is called *upsell* in marketing parlance. From the firm's point of view this is perfectly acceptable and indeed is something it would like to see more of, but it complicates the definition of a segment and the estimation of the demand from each segment.

From a purely modeling point of view, to make the RM control optimization problem easier, one could make a simplistic assumption that the restrictions are so designed and the price ranges for each segment are so separate that segments *only* purchase their intended product. So if the restricted product is not available, the leisure customer would find the price of the unrestricted product too high and not purchase (he travels on another flight, or on another day, or just cancels his trip). Likewise no business customer would purchase the lower price unrestricted product (called *dilution* or *downsell* in RM lingo). This assumption is sometimes called the *independent-class* or *perfect segmentation* assumption.

26.2.2.2 *Incentive compatibility*

In the previous section, we discussed segmentation effectiveness and how, as customers self-select, dilution may occur. Such dilution of course is not just dependent on the restrictions but also the prices the firm puts on the various products. Pricing a menu of products is tricky. The firm has to take the valuations (also called willingness-to-pay) for all the products into consideration and set prices to minimize dilution. Economists call this incentive-compatibility (*IC*): the prices are so designed so that the net utility for a segment is maximized by the product the firm designed for it.

We explain the concept using the simple example of Figure 26.1 that illustrates the valuations of consumers a and b for the two products X and Y. There are two customers a and b whose valuations for two products X and Y are as shown in Figure 26.1. There is one unit of X and Y and the firm's multiproduct pricing problem is to set prices p_X and p_Y.

The two customers are assumed to purchase the product that gives them the maximum net utility; that is their valuation for the product minus the price they pay for it. So if the firm were to naively price $p_X = 700$ and $p_Y = 100$, it would be advantageous for a to buy product Y, undermining the firm's segmentation plans. The optimal set of prices would be to set $p_X < 600$ and $p_Y = 100$, that is reduce the price of X enough to make a prefer X.

26.2.3 Control process

The role of daily RM operations is to monitor demand, competitor actions and adjust forecasts, and set controls that open or limit the sale of inventory to a particular RM product for a particular day in the future. Occasionally new RM products may be introduced, or prices adjusted (often as a competitive response), but by and large this is done manually and serves as inputs to RM software, so we assume from now on that both the products and prices are fixed (in the short term).

RM software and models usually work in two steps:[5] (1) forecasting the demand for each RM product for a specific day, and then (2) optimizing the controls given the forecasts.

---

[5] Methods that merge these two steps, called distribution-free or adaptive methods, have also been proposed in the literature, see van Ryzin and McGill (2000), but the dominant paradigm is still to separate the two steps.

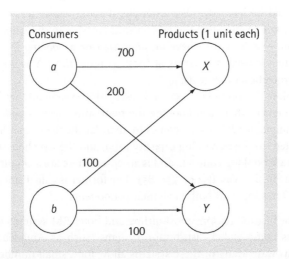

FIGURE 26.1 How much two customers, *a* and *b*, are willing to pay for two products, *X* and *Y*

The forecasting part is designed to obtain the best unbiased estimates of the future demand while the optimization part is to find the revenue-maximizing set of controls given the firm's estimates of future demand. We discuss next some common forms of controls used in RM systems.

26.2.3.1 Control systems

The control decision at any point in time is whether to accept a booking request for a particular RM product given the amount of time and inventory left and forecasts of future demand for the other (higher priced) products. However, in practice it is often infeasible to optimize the controls continuously because of two reasons: (1) it may be prohibitively expensive computationally to process all the data and run an optimization algorithm to evaluate each booking request, and (2) the actual sale may happen through a channel owned by a third party, such as a central reservation system, and it becomes too expensive and time-consuming to exchange messages for each transaction.

So a number of control forms have been developed in RM industries, which in turn have influenced the development of models and optimization algorithms. We briefly describe the most popular ones:

- *Nested allocations* or *booking limits:* All the RM products that share inventory are first ranked in some order, usually by their price.[6] Then the remaining capacity is allocated to these classes, but the allocations are "nested", so the higher class has access to all the inventory allocated to a lower class. For example, if there are 100 seats left for sale, and there are two classes Y, B with Y considered a higher class, then an example of a nested

---

[6] It is common to sometimes group different products under one "class" and take an average price for the class. In the airline industry for instance, the products, each with a fare basis code (such as BXP21), are grouped into fare classes (represented by an alphabet, Y, B, etc.)

allocation would be Y100 B54. For example, if 100 Y customers were to arrive, the controls allow sale to all of them. If 60 B customers were to show up, only 54 would be able to purchase. B is said to have an *allocation* or a *booking limit* of 54. Another terminology that is used is in terms of (nested) *protections*: Y is said to have (in this example) a protection of 46 seats.

The allocations are posted on a central reservation system and updated periodically (usually overnight). After each booking the reservation system updates the limits. In the above example, if a B booking comes in, then (as the firm can sell up to 54 seats to B) it is accepted, so the remaining capacity is 99, and the new booking limits are Y99 B53. Suppose a Y booking comes in and is accepted, there are a couple of ways the firm can update the limits: Y99 B54 or Y99 B53. The former is called *standard* nesting and the latter *theft* nesting, and both have their proponents.

- *Bid prices:* For historic reasons most airline and hotel RM systems work with nested allocations, as many global distribution systems (such as Amadeus or Sabre) were structured this way. Many of these systems allow for a small number of limits (10 to 26), so when the number of RM products exceeds this number, they somehow have to be grouped to conform to the number allowed by the system.

  The booking limit control is perfectly adequate when controlling a single resource (such as a single flight leg) independently (independent of other connecting flights for instance), but we encounter its limitations when the number of products using that resource increases, say to more than the size of inventory. Consider network RM, where the products are itineraries, and there could be many itineraries that use a resource (a flight leg)—the grouping of the products *a priori* gets complicated and messy (although it has been tried, and is sometimes called *virtual nesting*).

  A more natural and appropriate form of control, especially for network RM, is a threshold-price form of control called *bid price* control. Every resource has a non-negative number called a bid price associated with it. A product that uses a combination of resources is sold if the price of the product exceeds the sum of the bid prices of the resources that the product uses. The bid prices are frequently updated as new information comes in, or as the inventory is sold off.

26.3 SINGLE-RESOURCE RM

We consider the problem of controlling the sale of inventory of a single resource in isolation. That is, by concentrating on a single-resource we are ignoring the fact that the demand for the flight is affected by the controls and prices on adjoining flights and reciprocally, the controls for this flight affect the demand on adjoining flights. While the model optimizes a single resource in isolation, there is no reason that the data inputs for the model cannot take into account information from other related resources—the demand the firm observes for adjoining resources (for example, other flights in the market for an airline) can (and ought to) influence its forecasts for the resource.

We model demand, and control, at the level of *booking classes*, or simply *classes*. Different RM products may be grouped into classes for operational convenience or control system limitations. If such is the case, the price attached to a class is some approximation or average of the products in that class.

From now on we assume that each booking request is for a single unit of inventory. We also ignore the fact that customers reserve and then cancel or no-show. This simplifies the description and the modeling. Operational models incorporate both multi-unit bookings, group bookings, and adjust the controls as well for anticipated cancelations and no-shows.

26.3.1 Independent class models

We begin with the simplest customer behavior assumption, the independent class assumption. Recall that this means we are assuming demand is identified with each class (that has a fixed price) and customers purchase only their class, and if that class is not available for sale, then they do not purchase anything. The goal of the optimization model is to find booking limits that maximize revenue.

26.3.1.1 *Ordered arrivals*

In this section we assume that demand comes ordered by classes, in the order of their fares.[7] This conforms to the situation where the classes have progressively looser advanced purchase requirements and the prices increase as the restrictions come down.

Let's first consider the two-class model, as it is similar to the well-known *newsboy problem* in inventory theory. There are two classes, with associated prices $f_1 > f_2$ and the resource has an inventory of r_0. Assume that the demand for class 2 arrives first. Demand for class j is a random variable, denoted by D_j. How many units of inventory should the firm protect for the later-arriving, but higher-value, class 1 customers? The firm has only a probabilistic idea of the class 1 demand (the problem would be trivial if it knew this demand with certainty).

The firm has to decide if it needs to protect r units for the late-arriving class 1 customers. It will sell the rth unit to a class 1 customer if and only if $D_1 \geq r$, so the *expected marginal revenue* from the rth unit is $f_1 P(D_1 \geq r)$. So the firm accepts a class 2 request if f_2 exceeds this marginal value, or equivalently, if and only if

$$f_2 \geq f_1 P(D_1 \geq r). \tag{1}$$

The right-hand side of (1) is decreasing in r. Therefore, there will be an optimal protection level, denoted r_1^*, such that we accept class 2 if the remaining capacity exceeds r_1^* and reject it if the remaining capacity is r_1^* or less. Formally, r_1^* satisfies

$$f_2 < f_1 P(D_1 \geq r_1^*) \quad \text{and} \quad f_2 \geq f_1 P(D_1 \geq r_1^* + 1). \tag{2}$$

We next consider the general case of $n > 2$ classes. Again, we assume that demand for the n classes arrives in n stages, one for each class, with classes arriving in increasing order of their revenue values. Let the classes be indexed so that $f_1 > f_2 > \cdots > f_n$. Hence, class n (the lowest price) demand arrives in the first stage (stage n), followed by class $n-1$ demand in stage

---

[7] Robinson (1995) shows that the ordering can be arbitrary and not necessarily by fares.

$n-1$, and so on, with the highest price class (class 1) arriving in the last stage (stage 1). Since there is a one-to-one correspondence between stages and classes, we index both by j.

This problem can be formulated as a dynamic program in the stages (equivalently, classes), with the remaining capacity r being the state variable. At the start of each stage j, the demand $D_j, D_{j-1}, \ldots, D_1$ has not been realized.

Let $V_j(r)$ denote the value function at the start of stage j. Once the value D_j is observed, the value of a binary decision variable y (whether to accept or not) is chosen to maximize the current stage j revenue plus the revenue to go, or

$$f_j y + V_{j-1}(r - y),$$

subject to the constraint $0 \leq y \leq \min\{D_j, r\}$. The value function entering stage j, $V_j(r)$, is then the expected value of this optimization with respect to the demand D_j. Hence, the Bellman equation is

$$V_j(r) = E\left[\max_{0 \leq y \leq \min\{D_j, r\}} \{f_j y + V_{j-1}(r - y)\}\right], \tag{3}$$

with boundary conditions

$$V_0(r) = 0, \quad r = 0, 1, \ldots, C.$$

The values y^* that maximize the right-hand side of (3) for each j and x form an optimal control policy for this model.

The dynamic program (3) is easy to program and computationally tractable for the capacities one encounters in practice as the state-space consists of the capacity of a single resource.

26.3.1.2 *EMSR heuristic*

The expected marginal seat revenue (EMSR) heuristic[8] for solving the single-resource problem is based on an approximation that reduces the problem at each stage to two classes: the demand from future classes is aggregated and treated as one class with a revenue equal to the weighted-average revenue.

Consider stage $j+1$ in which the firm wants to determine protection level r_j. Define the aggregated future demand for classes $j, j-1, \ldots, 1$ by

$$S_j = \sum_{k=1}^{j} D_k,$$

and let the weighted-average revenue from classes $1, \ldots, j$, denoted $\bar{f}_j$, be defined by

$$\bar{f}_j = \frac{\sum_{k=1}^{j} f_k E[D_k]}{\sum_{k=1}^{j} E[D_k]}, \tag{4}$$

where $E[D_j]$ denotes the mean of class j demand. Then the EMSR protection level for class j and higher, r_j, is chosen by (2) so that

---

[8]   The heuristic we describe is sometimes referred to as EMSR-b heuristic as there was an earlier version called EMSR-a.

$$P(S_j > r_j) = \frac{\bar{f}_{j+1}}{\bar{f}_j}. \tag{5}$$

It is common when using EMSR to assume demand for each class j is independent and normally distributed with mean μ_j and variance σ_j^2, in which case

$$S_j = \mu + z\sigma,$$

where $\mu = \sum_{k=1}^{j} \mu_k$ is the mean and $\sigma^2 = \sum_{k=1}^{j} \sigma_k^2$ is the variance of the aggregated demand to come at stage $j+1$ and $z = \Phi^{-1}(1 - \bar{f}_{j+1}/\bar{f}_j)$ and $\Phi^{-1}(\cdot)$ is the inverse of the standard normal c.d.f. One repeats this calculation for each j.

The EMSR heuristic is very popular in practice as it is very simple to program and is robust with acceptable performance (Belobaba 1989).

26.3.1.3 *Unordered arrivals*

In this section we relax the assumption about the order of demand classes, and allow for any arbitrary ordering. On the other hand, we assume that we can estimate the mix of the classes at each point in time, or alternately the booking patterns for each class.

The model is time-based. There are T total periods and t indexes the periods, with the time index running forward ($t = 1$ is the first period, and $t = T$ is the last period). By making the number of periods sufficiently high, we assume that at most one arrival occurs in each period. The probability of an arrival of class j in period t is denoted $p_{j,t}$. The assumption of at most one arrival per period implies that we must have $\sum_{j=1}^{n} p_{j,t} \leq 1$.

Let r denote the remaining capacity and $V_t(r)$ denote the value function in period t. Let $F(t)$ be a random variable, with $F(t) = f_j$ if a demand for class j arrives in period t and $F(t) = 0$ otherwise. Note that $P(F(t) = f_j) = p_{j,t}$. Let $y = 1$ if the firm accepts the arrival (if there has been one) and $y = 0$ otherwise. We suppress the period subscript t of the control as it should be clear from the context. The firm wants to maximize the sum of current revenue and the revenue to go, or

$$F(t)y + V_{t+1}(r - y).$$

The Bellman equation is therefore

$$
\begin{aligned}
V_t(r) &= E\left[\max_{y \in \{0,1\}} \{F(t)y + V_{t+1}(r - y)\}\right] \\
&= V_{t+1}(r) + E\left[\max_{y \in \{0,1\}} \{(F(t) - \Delta V_{t+1}(r))y\}\right],
\end{aligned}
\tag{6}
$$

where $\Delta V_{t+1}(r) = V_{t+1}(r) - V_{t+1}(r-1)$ is the expected marginal value of capacity in period $t+1$. The boundary conditions are

$$V_{T+1}(r) = 0, \quad x = 0, 1, \ldots, C,$$

and

$$V_t(0) = 0, \quad t = 1, \ldots, T.$$

So if a class j request arrives, so that $F(t) = f_j$, then it is optimal to accept the request if and only if

$$f_j \geq \Delta V_{t+1}(r).$$

Thus, the optimal control can be implemented using a bid price control where the bid price is equal to the marginal value,

$$\pi_t(r) = \Delta V_t(r). \tag{7}$$

Revenues that exceed this threshold are accepted; those that do not are rejected.

This bid price control can easily be converted to a booking limits control for each period t. Suppose at time t we calculate $\pi_t(r)$ for all r. The protection for class j is at the point r where $\pi_t(r) = f_{j+1}$ (or 0 if there is no such point r).

It is natural and intuitive that the value of additional capacity at any point in time would decrease as capacity increases and the marginal value at any given remaining capacity r would decrease with time (because as time elapses, there are fewer opportunities to sell the capacity). This could be stated as follows: The increments $\Delta V_t(r)$ of the value function $V_t(r)$ defined by (6) satisfy $\forall r, t$:

  (i) $\Delta V_t(r+1) \leq \Delta V_t(r)$,
  (ii) $\Delta V_{t+1}(r) \leq \Delta V_t(r)$.

26.3.2 Discrete-choice model

The independent class assumption is a gross simplification of customer behavior. Even if there is a one-to-one correspondence between classes and segments it is very likely that no price-restriction combination achieves perfect segmentation. Customers clearly buy-down and buy-up from the intended class for their segment. Such behavior of course is a function of the restrictions and the price differentials between the classes. In this section, we consider RM under a discrete choice model of consumer behavior which attempts to incorporate such behavior by modeling customer purchase probabilities as a function of product characteristics.

As before, time is discrete and indexed by t, with the indices running forward in time ($t = T$ is the period of resource usage) and in each period there is at most one arrival. The probability of arrival is denoted by λ (note that now this is not tied to a product purchase), which we assume, for ease of exposition, is the same for all time periods t. There are n classes, and we let $\mathcal{N} = \{1, \ldots, n\}$ denote the entire set of classes. We let choice index o denote the no-purchase choice; that is, the event that the customer does not purchase any of the classes offered. Each class $j \in \mathcal{N}$ has an associated price f_j, and without loss of generality we index classes so that $f_1 \geq f_2 \geq \cdots \geq f_n \geq 0$. We let $f_o = 0$ denote the revenue of the no-purchase choice.

In each period t, the seller chooses a subset $S_t \subseteq \mathcal{N}$ of classes to offer. When the set of classes S_t is offered in period t, the probability that a customer chooses class $j \in S_t$ is denoted $P_j(S_t)$. $P_o(S_t)$ denotes the no-purchase probability.

The probability that a sale of class j is made in period t is therefore $\lambda P_j(S_t)$, and the probability that no sale is made is $\lambda P_o(S_t) + (1 - \lambda)$. The choice probabilities $P_j(S)$ define a probability function, that is, for every set $S \subseteq \mathcal{N}$, the probabilities satisfy

$$P_j(S) \geq 0, \quad \forall j \in S$$

$$\sum_{j \in S} P_j(S) + P_o(S) = 1.$$

As before, let t denote the current period, and r the number of remaining inventory units. Define the value function $V_t(r)$ as the maximum expected revenue obtainable from periods $t, t+1, \ldots, T$ given that there are r inventory units remaining at time t. Then the Bellman equation for $V_t(r)$ is

$$
\begin{aligned}
V_t(r) &= \max_{S \subseteq \mathcal{N}} \left\{ \sum_{j \in S} \lambda P_j(S)(f_j + V_{t+1}(r-1)) + (\lambda P_o(S) + 1 - \lambda) V_{t+1}(r) \right\} \\
&= \max_{S \subseteq \mathcal{N}} \left\{ \sum_{j \in S} \lambda P_j(S)(f_j - \Delta V_{t+1}(r)) \right\} + V_{t+1}(r),
\end{aligned}
\tag{8}
$$

where $\Delta V_{t+1}(r) = V_{t+1}(r) - V_{t+1}(r-1)$ denotes the marginal cost of capacity in the next period, and we have used the fact that for all S,

$$\sum_{j \in S} P_j(S) + P_o(S) = 1.$$

The boundary conditions are

$$V_{T+1}(r) = 0, \quad r = 0, 1, \ldots, C \tag{9}$$

$$V_t(0) = 0, \quad t = 1, \ldots, T. \tag{10}$$

The dynamic programming recursion (8) can be solved easily for the capacities one encounters in practice. The marginal value functions $\Delta V_t(r)$ can be shown to be decreasing in t for a fixed r and increasing in r for a fixed t, so the results can be translated to either a bid price control or a booking limits control.

26.4 Network RM

In the airline, railway, cruise line, and hotel industries, the products are a bundle of inventory from multiple resources. For instance, an airline sells an itinerary consisting of two flights with a connection at a hub. A hotel sells a multi-night stay that uses a hotel room during consecutive nights. Figure 26.2 shows how these products can be represented on a network.

When products are sold as bundles, the lack of availability of any one resource in the bundle limits sales of the product. This creates interdependence among the resources, and

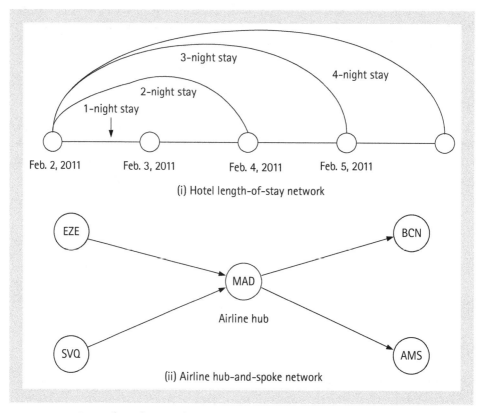

FIGURE 26.2 Examples of network RM: (i) hotel length-of-stay network and (ii) airline hub-and-spoke network

hence, to maximize total revenues, it becomes necessary to jointly manage (coordinate) the capacity controls on all resources.[9] In the airline industry, this problem is also called *the passenger-mix problem* or *O&D (origin–destination) control*, and in the hotel industry, *length-of-stay control*.

26.4.1 Notation, controls, and dynamic program

A product is a combination of resources and a price, along with the associated restrictions and conditions. (For example an itinerary-fare class combination for an airline network.) As before, we assume that the booking horizon begins at time 0 and all the resources are consumed instantaneously at time T. Time is discrete and assumed to consist of T intervals, indexed by t. We make the standard assumption that the intervals are fine enough so that at most one customer arrives in each period.

---

[9] As in all quantity-based RM, we assume here that prices are fixed for all the products and that we manage only the *allocation* of the resources to the different products.

The underlying network has m resources and n products. The current capacity on resource i at time t is r_i and the vector of capacities $\vec{r}$, and let the initial set of capacities at time o be $\vec{r}_o$. Products are indexed by j and resources by i. The revenue from product j is f_j (assume $f_j \geq o$). A resource i is said to be in product j ($i \in j$) if j uses resource i. We represent this by $a_{i,j} = 1$ if $i \in j$, and $a_{i,j} = o$ if $i \notin j$, or alternately with the o–1 incidence vector $\vec{a}_j$ of product j. An arrival is a purchase request for a product in a specific interval of time.

In period t, a request for product j appears with probability $p_{j,t}$. Our assumption of at most one arrival per unit time translates to $\sum_i p_{j,t} \ll 1$. We will assume that the demands for the different products are independent of each other, independent across time and across products.

26.4.1.1 *Controls*

For a capacity vector $\vec{r}$ at time t, define the set of all "acceptable" products as $\mathcal{A}_{\vec{r}} = \{j | \vec{a}_j \leq \vec{r}\}$. The control at time t consists of *opening* a subset of products; that is, given the vector $\vec{r}$ of remaining capacity at time t, and based on its forecasts of demand to come, the firm is willing to sell only a certain subset of products; alternately the firm *closes* some products for sale.

Let $\mathcal{Y}_{\vec{r}}$ denote the collection of all subsets of $\mathcal{A}_{\vec{r}}$, that is, the feasible controls. For a $y \in \mathcal{Y}_{\vec{r}}$, define $\vec{y}_{\vec{r}}$ as the o–1 incidence vector of the elements of y (a vector of size n, the number of products).

26.4.1.2 *Optimal dynamic program*

The dynamic program to determine optimal controls $\vec{y}_{\vec{r}}^*$ is as follows. Let $V_t(\vec{r})$ denote the maximum expected revenue to go, given remaining capacity $\vec{r}$ in period t. Then $V_t(\vec{r})$ must satisfy the Bellman equation

$$V_t(\vec{r}) = \max_{y \in \mathcal{Y}_{\vec{r}}} \left\{ \sum_j p_{j,t}\{f_j y_{j,t} + V_{t+1}(\vec{r} - y_{j,t}\vec{a}_j)\} \right\} \tag{11}$$

with the boundary condition

$$V_{T+1}(\vec{r}) = o, \forall \vec{r}. \tag{12}$$

$V^*(\vec{r}_o)$ then denotes the optimal value of this dynamic program for the given initial capacity vector $\vec{r}_o$.

26.4.2 Approximation methods

The dynamic program (11) is intractable even for small networks, as the state-space is the set of all possible capacity vectors less than or equal to the initial capacity vector $\vec{r}_o$. Moreover, a large number of networks have to be optimized during a small time-window; for instance, an airline has to optimize networks for a number of future days, and the entire optimization process has to be completed in a few hours during the night.

A number of approximation methods have been proposed in the literature. The methods are based on the following strategy: formulate an upper bound on the optimal value function $V^*(\vec{r}_o)$ and use the approximation to generate (bid price) controls. In general, the tighter the upper bound, the better the quality of the controls. Of course, there is a tradeoff—the more sophisticated methods such as the Lagrangian method and the affine-relaxation method are computationally demanding.

26.4.2.1 Deterministic linear program

One of the earliest methods proposed for generating network bid prices is a simple and compact linear program that generally goes by the name of Deterministic Linear Program (DLP). Here we relax the number of customers we accept to be fractional, so the decision variable $y_{j,t}$ is a continuous variable that is only required to be less than or equal to the expected demand in that period.

The method consists in solving the following linear program ($r_{i,o}$ is the capacity of resource i at time o):

$$\max \quad \sum_{j,t} f_j y_{j,t}$$

$$(DLP) \quad \text{s.t.} \quad \sum_t \sum_j a_{i,j} y_{j,t} \leq r_{i,o} \quad i = 1, \ldots, m \tag{13}$$

$$0 \leq y_{j,t} \leq p_{j,t}$$

and using the dual prices as the bid prices for control. We formulated (DLP) with variables explicitly indexed by time. This is done purely for expository purposes and to use a common notation with the Lagrangian heuristics we shall describe shortly. Notice that we can group together all the variables corresponding to a product j, and the probabilities $p_{j,t}$ into an aggregate demand estimate for class j, $S_j = \sum_t p_{j,t}$. This greatly reduces the size of the problem.

DLP is quite popular as it is very easy to program and can be solved quickly using any off-the-shelf LP software package. Its performance is quite reasonable, and often serves as the benchmark method in simulation comparisons.

26.4.2.2 Randomized linear program

Consider a simulation where we generate N instances from the demand data: each instance consists of a collection of (generated) samples, one for each product, generated from its demand distribution. Let $p_{j,t}^k = 1$ if j is generated at time t in instance k and o otherwise. Each generated instance k leads to a perfect-hindsight linear program $PHLP^k$ as follows.

$$\max \quad \sum_{j,t} f_j y_{j,t}^k$$

$$(PHLP^k) \quad \text{s.t.} \quad \sum_t \sum_j a_{i,j} y_{j,t}^k \leq r_{i,o} \quad i = 1, \ldots, m \tag{14}$$

$$0 \leq y_{j,t}^k \leq p_{j,t}^k$$

The randomized linear programming (*RLP*) method takes the average of the dual prices of $PHLP^k$ as the bid prices.

26.4.2.3 *Decomposition methods*

Another approach to network RM that is quite popular in practice is to first solve a relatively simple heuristic such as DLP or RLP and then use the bid prices generated by the method to decompose the network problem into tractable resource-level problems.

We need to somehow map the network-level products to resource-level products. The bid prices generated in the first phase help us do this mapping. Consider a product that spans two resources and has a price of \$200. Say the bid price of the first resource is 50 and the second resource is 100. Then the product is decomposed into two products, one using just the first resource with price \$200 − 100 = \$100 and the second using just the second resource with price \$200 − 50 = \$150 (other price mappings are possible). The resulting problem breaks up into resource-level RM problems and can be solved either by dynamic programming or even using a heuristic such as the EMSR.

Taking this idea one step further, we can iterate using the resulting decomposition. Start off with a set of bid prices generated using DLP or RLP, do a decomposition and solve the resource-level problems to get a new set of bid prices, and repeat the process till it converges according to some criterion. Such methods are popular in implementations as they have turned out to be robust with good revenue performance in simulations.

The resource-level dynamic programs yield bid prices that are then applied to control the network booking requests.

26.4.2.4 *Lagrangian methods*

The Lagrangian relaxation method of this section formalizes the decomposition methods and give the optimal way of decomposing the dynamic program. Simulation results show it to be one of the most promising methods proposed in the literature.

Let the decision variable $y_{i,j,t} = 1$ if the firm accepts a request for product j on resource i in period t and o otherwise. Let $\vec{e_i}$ be a m dimensional vector with 1 in position i and o elsewhere.

Augment the set of legs by a dummy resource ι with infinite capacity, and set all products to use one unit of this dummy resource ι. To keep the notation simple we assume that $y_{\iota,j,t}$ is an extra, dummy, unrestricted variable whose sole purpose is to impose the condition that the firm either accepts a product or rejects it on all the resources that the product uses.

The optimality condition (11) can be written as

$$V_t(\vec{r}) = \max \quad \sum_j p_{j,t}\left\{ f_j y_{\iota,j,t} + V_{t+1}\left(\vec{r} - \sum_{i \in j} y_{i,j,t}\vec{e_i} \right) \right\}$$

$$(DP) \quad \text{s.t.} \quad y_{i,j,t} \leq r_i \ \forall j, \forall i \in j \tag{15}$$

$$y_{\iota,j,t} - y_{i,j,t} \leq 0 \ \forall j, \forall i \in j$$

$$y_{i,j,t} \in \{0,1\}.$$

Notice that the constraints are constraints of a recursive dynamic program, so the variable $y_{i,j,t}$ has to be interpreted as a state-dependent variable and strictly speaking ought to be written as $y_{i,j,t,\vec{r}}$, that is, one for each possible state $\vec{r}$ at time t, i and j, as there are a set of constraints for all possible states in the future. We suppress $\vec{r}$ from the indexing when it is clear from the context.

Now relax the constraints of the form $y_{i,j,t} - y_{i,j,t} \leq 0$ with a set of Lagrange multipliers $\lambda = \{\lambda_{i,j,t}\}$ to break it up into resource-level dynamic programs:

$$V_t^\lambda(\vec{r}) = \max \sum_j \{p_j,_t f_j y_{i,j,t} - \sum_{i \in j} \lambda_{i,j,t} y_{i,j,t} + \sum_{i \in j} \lambda_{i,j,t} y_{i,j,t} +$$
$$p_{j,t} V_{t+1}^\lambda \left(\vec{r} - \sum_{i \in j} y_{i,j,t} \vec{e}_i \right) \}$$

s.t.

(LR_t^λ) $\qquad \qquad y_{i,j,t} \leq r_i \ \forall j, \forall i \in j$ $\qquad \qquad \qquad$ (16)

$\qquad \qquad \qquad \qquad y_{i,j,t} \in \{0,1\}.$

So, a relatively small set of Lagrange multipliers, that do not depend on the state (capacity vector) but just on the time and product, are used for all future time periods, reducing the state-space of the multipliers. Once relaxed, the problem decomposes into resource-level problems with much smaller state-spaces. Define the *LR* bound $LR = \min_\lambda V_0^\lambda(r_0)$. That is, we find the best set of Lagrangian multipliers, and one can show that this forms an upper bound on the dynamic program (*DP*).

In Talluri (2008) the *LR* bound is strengthened, combining it with parallel sample generation and partial relaxations.

26.4.2.5 *Affine relaxation methods*

The dynamic program (11) can be formulated as a linear program, albeit with a prohibitively large set of variables and constraints, as follows. The decision variables are $V_t(\vec{r})$, one for each possible state vector $\vec{r}$ at time t.

$$V^*(\vec{r}_0) = \min_{t, V_t(\vec{r})} \quad V_0(\vec{r}_0)$$
$$\text{s.t.} \quad V_t(\vec{r}) \geq \sum_{j \in y} p_{j,t} \{f_j y_{j,t} + V_{t+1}(\vec{r} - y_{j,t} \vec{a}_j)\} \quad \forall t, \vec{r}, y \in \mathcal{Y}_{\vec{r}} \qquad (17)$$

The linear program (17) has an exponential number of variables (the decision variables are the value functions defined for all possible feasible state vectors) and constraints and is completely impractical.

The idea now is to at least reduce the number of constraints by imposing a functional form on the value functions. The affine relaxation imposes a specific affine functional form on the variables:

$$V_t(\vec{r}) \approx \theta_t + \sum_i r_i v_{i,t}, \quad \forall t, \vec{r}. \qquad (18)$$

So the number of variables is reduced to the number of resources multiplied by the number of periods. The number of constraints, however, remains very large, but techniques such as column-generation can be brought to bear on a solution. A rough interpretation of $V_{i,t}$ is that it represents the marginal value of resource i at time t. Substituting (18) into (17) gives the linear program

$$\min_{\theta, v_{i,t}} \quad \theta_0 + \sum_i r_{i,0} v_{i,0}$$

(AR) s.t.

$$\theta_t - \theta_{t+1} + \sum_i \left(r_i v_{i,t} - v_{i,t+1} \left(r_i - \sum_{j \ni i, j \in y} p_{j,t} \right) \right) \geq \sum_{j \in y} p_{j,t} f_j \quad \forall t, \vec{r}, y \in \mathcal{Y}_{\vec{r}}$$

$$v_{i,t} \geq 0$$

The affine relaxation bound can be easily strengthened (Farias and Roy 2007; Meissner and Strauss 2008; Talluri 2008) by using the following approximation instead of (18):

$$V_t(r_t) \approx \theta_t + \sum_i \sum_{r=1}^{r_{i,t}} v_{i,t,r}, \quad \forall t, r_t. \tag{19}$$

Solving (AR), however, is quite complicated, as the column-generation requires solving an integer program; in the choice-version one has to solve a nonlinear mixed integer program.

26.4.3 Choice-based deterministic linear programming (CDLP)

Most network RM implementations have been under the independent class assumption. The problem is quite challenging as it is and, given the time and data requirements, there are few known large-scale implementations using more realistic customer behavior models. Indeed, even research into richer network RM models is relatively new. We present below the choice-based deterministic linear program (CDLP) that uses the discrete choice model of customer behavior that we introduced earlier.

Let $N = \{1, 2, \ldots, n\}$ be the set of n products and o represent the no-purchase option. If the firm offers a set S, customers are assumed to purchase product j with probability $P_j(S)$. If S is the set offered, let $R(S) = \sum_{j \in S} f_j P_j(S)$ representing expected revenue if the firm offers S and let $Q_i(S)$ represent the probability of using a unit of capacity on resource i given the offer set S.

Let decision variables $t(S)$ represent the fraction of time we offer S. If we assume that the choice probabilities are time-homogeneous then the order by which the firm offers the sets S is immaterial, so we can formulate an approximation to (11) as follows:

$$\max \quad \sum_S R(S) t(S) T$$

$(CDLP)$ s.t. $\displaystyle\sum_t \sum_{S \subseteq N} Q_i(S) t(S) T \leq r_{i,0} \quad \forall i$

$$\sum_{S \subseteq N} t(S) \leq 1 \tag{20}$$

$$0 \leq t(S) \quad \forall S \subseteq N$$

In contrast to the linear program (DLP), $(CDLP)$ has an exponential number of variables, but we can use column-generation techniques to solve it approximately. The solution of $(CDLP)$ gives marginal values (dual values) which can be used in decomposition heuristics as for the independent-class case.

The choice probabilities are usually assumed to be generated by a simple model—usually as a mixture of multinomial-logit distributions, where the mixture probabilities represent different

customer segments in the population. Each customer segment has a distinct set of parameters and consideration set. The column-generation however is non-trivial, in fact shown to
be NP-hard (Bront 2009) whenever the consideration sets of the customer segments
overlap.

Estimation of the choice probabilities and solving the problem within operational time
windows are also significant obstacles, and this is an active area of ongoing research.

26.5 Issues

This review did not cover a number of issues that are important in practice. We briefly
comment on some of these.

26.5.1 Competition

The models we have discussed ignored competition. They can be viewed as operational
models that aim to calculate the firm's best response function to the current market
situation. So the effects of competitor actions are assumed to be built in to the demand
forecasts, but the models neither anticipate nor model competitor behavior. For a tactical
model this is quite adequate—the plan is to solve the model frequently, and the firm will
react as and when the market changes. Our goal is to make operational decisions for the
short term rather than predict equilibrium strategies over the long run.

That said, one can ask how market information is being incorporated into the above
models. The implicit assumption is that the demand forecasts for an RM product reflect the
current competitive offerings. In fact, many operational implementations do not explicitly
do so but just reflect it weakly by adjusting demand forecasts based on observed demand.

The discrete choice model of Section 26.3.2 can easily be extended to incorporate
competition by augmenting the state vectors. But such models would be limited operation-
ally as critical competitor information is private. For instance, even though there are many
web service companies that supply competitor prices now, the remaining capacity for a
competing flight is likely to remain unobservable.

Dynamic pricing with fixed capacities is studied in the economics literature as
Bertrand–Edgeworth competition. It lacks a static equilibrium, but under the assumptions
of price-insensitive customers, one can show that there is a unique subgame-perfect Nash
equilibrium (see Martínez de Albéniz and Talluri (2011) for a review of this stream of
research).

26.5.2 Data

RM is distinguished by its use of models and algorithms to control inventory. They are
by definition based on data and their performance is influenced by the quality of the
input data.

Most RM implementations use just historic sales data. At the minimum, such data should contain the following fields for each individual purchase: time of booking, price paid, time of purchase (this can differ from the time the booking was made), date of the resource usage (for example, flight-departure date for an airline, starting date of the stay for a hotel), resources used (for example, number of nights stay), changes, and cancelation information. In addition, auxiliary information about additional customer spend, channel, etc. are often stored, and even used by some forecasting methods. Airlines and hotels store much of this information in PNR (Passenger Name Records) databases.

A recent development is the availability of current competitor prices for competing offerings. This is in large part due to Internet sales. Data firms scan Internet sites and clean and parse the data and sell it to the companies for a service fee. These services have become very popular and most hotels and airlines subscribe to them. There are a few known RM implementations which even use this data directly in their algorithms, but by and large the reports are used for manual oversight or control.

26.5.3 Estimation and forecasting

The forecasting task for models using the independent class assumption is conceptually quite simple: forecast the future demand-to-come from now till the time of resource usage for each class. The independent class assumption makes this task relatively simple. The demand for each class is completely independent of the controls as well as the demand for other classes. So it is reasonable to assume that historic demand for that resource and class gives a good indication of future demand. Time-series methods, that account for trends and seasonality, are often employed for this purpose. The historic demand is usually filtered to forecast by day-of-week or by proximity to some event (Easter, Christmas, etc.). The techniques used are quite standard and the reader can refer to any book on forecasting to get an idea on how to proceed.

Estimating discrete choice models is more complicated. We were deliberately vague in our description of the model on the dependent variables in estimating the choice probabilities. These generally include price, but could potentially include other characteristics such as day-of-week, season, restrictions, etc. Maximum-likelihood estimation is often employed to estimate the parameters. Details are again standard and can be found in a reference book such as Ben-Akiva and Lerman (1985).

One notable feature of RM estimation and forecasting is the emphasis given to correcting for unobservable demand and behavior. A firm's historic data usually include only purchases. When a class is closed, the firm obtains no information on all the customers who *would* have bought the product if it were open. So forecasting based only on observations biases the forecasts. Similarly, in discrete choice models not accounting for unobservable no-purchases gives biased estimates. Many RM implementations use the EM algorithm (see McLachlan and Krishnan 1997) to correct for such unobservable data.

26.5.4 Overbooking

Many RM industries are bookings-based. Customers are actually purchasing a reservation contract that guarantees inventory for them for some future date. Invariably there will be customers who find after their purchase that they cannot fly on a given date or make the trip after all. Depending on the product restrictions they may be able to change or cancel their reservation and get a refund back. For the firm this opens up inventory that it had previously considered sold. So RM has to take into account such *cancelations*.

Some customers may not notify the firm that their plans have changed (often because they bought non-refundable tickets and there is no point in doing so), and just do not show up on the date they were supposed to use the resource. Such customers are called *no-shows*.

Overbooking is a practice of taking more bookings than capacity would allow anticipating that a certain fraction of the customers would cancel or no-show. This leads to better capacity utilization, especially on high-demand days when the marginal value of each unit of inventory is very high. The firm, however, has to be prepared to handle a certain number of customers who are denied service, even though they have paid for the product and have a reservation contract. In many industries the benefits of better capacity utilization dominate the risk of denying service, and overbooking has become a common practice.

So all the RM models and algorithms that we have discussed have been generalized to incorporate cancelations and no-shows. The simplest approach is to follow a two-step approach: first set an overbooking limit which determines by how much the firm is willing to overbook at each point in time, and then run the standard RM model or algorithm. The forecasting part estimates cancelation and no-show probabilities along with the demand.

26.6 FURTHER READING

At the time of this writing, there are two technical books dedicated to the topic of RM: Talluri and van Ryzin (2004b) and Phillips (2005). In addition, many new books on supply-chain management, such as Cachon and Terwiesch (2006), include a chapter on RM. For the reader interested in a quick introduction to single-resource RM, I recommend Netessine and Shumsky (2002) which is available on the Internet at http://archive.ite. journal.informs.org/Vol3No1/NetessineShumsky/.

The two-class model of Section 26.3.1.1 is due to Littlewood (1972) and is one of the earliest known models for RM, and its generalization to n classes via the EMSR heuristic is due to Belobaba (1987). This in turn influenced the more rigorous dynamic programming formulations of Brumelle and McGill (1993), Curry (1990), and Wollmer (1992). Talluri and van Ryzin (2004a) introduced the discrete choice model of RM.

Network RM remains a very active area of research. It was first studied by Simpson (1989) who proposed the DLP and by Williamson (1988). The dynamic programming formulation of RM and its properties were first studied in Talluri and van Ryzin (1999a), and the RLP method in Talluri and van Ryzin (1999b). Topaloglu (2009) proposed the Lagrangian method and Adelman (2007) the affine relaxation method, and Liu and van Ryzin (2008) the choice LP formulation based on earlier work by Gallego et al. (2004).

REFERENCES

Adelman, D. (2007) "Dynamic bid-prices in revenue management", *Operations Research* 55/4: 647–61, July.

Belobaba, P. P. (1987) "Air Travel Demand and Airline Seat Inventory Management". PhD thesis, Flight Transportation Laboratory, Cambridge, MA: MIT.

—— (1989) "Application of a probabilistic decision model to airline seat inventory control", *Operations Research* 37: 183–97.

Ben-Akiva, M. and Lerman, S. (1985) *Discrete-Choice Analysis: Theory and Application to Travel Demand*. Cambridge, MA: MIT Press.

Bront, J. J. M., Méndez-Díaz, I., and Vulcano, G. (2009) "A column generation algorithm for choice-based network revenue management", *Operations Research* 57/3: 769–84.

Brumelle, S. L. and McGill, J. I. (1993) "Airline seat allocation with multiple nested fare classes", *Operations Research* 41: 127–37.

Cachon, G. and Terwiesch, C. (2006) *Matching Supply with Demand*. New York: McGraw-Hill.

Curry, R. E. (1990) "Optimal airline seat allocation with fare classes nested by origins and destinations", *Transportation Science* 24: 193–204.

Farias, V. F. and van Roy, B. (2007) "An approximate dynamic programming approach to network revenue management". Technical report, Massachussetts, MA: Sloan School of Management, MIT.

Gallego, G., Iyengar, G., Phillips, R., and Dubey, A. (2004) "Managing flexible products on a network". Technical Report TR-2004-01, New York: Dept of Industrial Engineering, Columbia University.

Littlewood, K. (1972) "Forecasting and control of passenger bookings", in *Proceedings of the Twelfth Annual AGIFORS Symposium*, Nathanya, Israel.

Liu, Q. and van Ryzin, G. (2008) "On the choice-based linear programming model for network revenue management", *Manufacturing and Service Operations Management* 10/2: 288–310.

McLachlan, G. L. and Krishnan, T. (1997) *The EM Algorithm and Extensions*. New York: Wiley.

Martínez de Albéniz, V. and Talluri, K. T. (2011) "Dynamic price competition with fixed capacities", *Management Science* 57(6): 1078–93.

Meissner, J. and Strauss, A. K. (2008) "Network revenue management with inventory-sensitive bid prices and customer choice". Technical report, Lancaster University, Department of Management Science.

Netessine, S. and Shumsky, R. A. (2002) "Introduction to the theory and practice of yield management", *INFORMS Transactions on Education* 3/1: September.

Phillips, R. (2005) *Pricing and Revenue Optimization*. Stanford, CA: Stanford Business Books.

Robinson, L. W. (1995) "Optimal and approximate control policies for airline booking with sequential nonmonotonic fare classes", *Operations Research* 43: 252–63.

Simpson, R. W. (1989) "Using network flow techniques to find shadow prices for market and seat inventory control". Technical Report Memorandum, M89-1, Flight Transportation Laboratory, Cambridge, MA: MIT.

Talluri, K. T. (2008) "On bounds for network revenue management". Technical Report WP-1066, UPF.

—— and van Ryzin, G. J. (1999a) "An analysis of bid-price controls for network revenue management", *Management Science* 44: 1577–93.

Talluri, K. T. and van Ryzin, G. J. (1999b) "A randomized linear programming method for computing network bid prices", *Transportation Science*, 33: 207–16.

—— and —— (2004a) "Revenue management under a general discrete choice model of consumer behavior", *Management Science*, January.

—— and —— (2004b) *The Theory and Practice of Revenue Management*. New York: Kluwer.

Topaloglu, H. (2009) "Using Lagrangian relaxation to compute capacity-dependent bid prices in network revenue management", *Operations Research* 57: 637–49.

van Ryzin, G. J. and McGill, J. I. (2000) "Revenue management without forecasting or optimization: An adaptive algorithm for determining seat protection levels", *Management Science* 46: 760–75.

Williamson, E. L. (1988) "Comparison of optimization techniques for origin–destination seat inventory control". Master's thesis, Flight Transportation Laboratory, Cambridge, MA: MIT.

Wollmer, R. D. (1992) "An airline seat management model for a single leg route when lower fare classes book first", *Operations Research* 40: 26–37.

CHAPTER 27

....

AUCTION PRICING

....

RICHARD STEINBERG

27.1 INTRODUCTION

....

Why auction? The primary reason is that the seller is sufficiently unsure of the valuations of
the potential buyers that he requires additional information before he can allow the sale of
the items to take place. Two additional reasons are the speed and transparency of the
auction process. Formally, we define an *auction* as a procedure to: (1) elicit information
from potential buyers regarding their valuations for a specified set of items available for
sale; and (2) based on this information, determine an allocation of the items to the potential
buyers along with the individual payments required from each.[1]

This chapter is dedicated to the memory of Michael H. Rothkopf, a true leader in the development of
auction pricing.

   The author would like to thank Lawrence Ausubel, Michael Ball, Octavian Carare, Peter Cramton, Robert
Day, George Donohue, Guillermo Gallego, Karla Hoffman, Peter Key, Thomas Kittsteiner, Paul Klemperer,
Evan Kwerel, Ailsa Land, Edward Lazear, Preston McAfee, Paul Milgrom, Michael Ostrovsky, David
Parkes, Martin Pesendorfer, Stephen Rassenti, Tuomas Sandholm, Itai Sher, Tunay Tunca, and Robert
Wilson, as well as the editors, Özalp Özer and Robert Phillips, for comments. However, the accuracy of the
material in this chapter, and the views expressed herein, are the responsibility of the author alone. The
author would also like to thank Paul Milgrom and the Department of Economics, Stanford University, for
inviting him to be Visiting Scholar for Stanford University's Fall term 2008, during which time much of the
work on this chapter was completed.

[1] The basic auction terminology is fairly obvious, but for completeness we specify that: the potential
buyers who chose to submit their information are called the *bidders*; the information provided by a bidder is
his *bid*; the party who elicits the information from the bidders and allocates the items to them is the
auctioneer, whom we will not usually distinguish from the *seller* (in practice, the former typically works on
behalf of the latter); the bidders who are allocated one or more items are the *winners*. A bid includes both a
set of items and the associated *bid price* (which may in fact be a set of prices), but we follow the common
practice of also using the term "bid" to refer to the bid price alone. A bidder's *valuation* is the maximum
amount he is willing to pay; there are a number of equivalent terms for valuation, including *value*,
willingness-to-pay, and *reservation price*, but not *reserve price*, which is the minimum price at which the
auctioneer is willing to sell. Two bidders are said to be of the same *type* if they have identical information,
beliefs, and preferences relevant to their decision making. A *reverse auction*, also known as a *procurement
auction*, is one in which the auctioneer is a buyer and the bidders are sellers. The theory for reverse auctions
is fundamentally the same as for *forward auctions*, the latter term being used when necessary to distinguish
the more familiar type of auctions from reverse auctions.

An auction can be used to sell a single item, or multiple units (i.e., a number of identical items), or multiple items (i.e., a number of items, generally nonidentical). Not all auctions are for discrete indivisible goods, like paintings or cattle, but can also be for divisible goods like electricity or the right to emit carbon dioxide. Auctions have been in existence since the fifth century BC (if we are to believe Herodotus), and the variety of items sold throughout history is staggering. For a detailed treatment of the institutional aspects of auction markets up until the mid-1960s, see Cassady (1967). For a more informal exposition, but one that is current to the mid-1980s, see Learmount (1985).

We present here a non-technical but rigorous tutorial on the state-of-the-art of auction theory, with an eye toward the real world of pricing. We include some historical details, since knowledge of the evolution of the ideas surrounding auctions is essential to understanding both the modern theory and any current applications. For the most part our presentation is structured by topic, rather than by paper. The significant exception is our discussion in Section 27.3 of the preeminent paper of Vickrey (1961) that established the field.

Five auction topics are not covered here (except in passing), since each comprises an area that is now so extensive as to require a major review of its own: sequential auctions, on-line auctions, procurement auctions, experimental methods, and empirical approaches. For sequential auctions, see Krishna (2010: ch. 15); Krishna's presentation is mathematical, however his chapter notes constitute an excellent non-technical overview. For on-line auctions, see Ockenfels et al. (2006); for procurement auctions, see Bichler et al. (2006); and for on-line procurement auctions, see the special issue of *Production and Operations Management* edited by Bichler and Steinberg (2007). For experimental methods, see Kagel and Levin (forthcoming); and for empirical approaches, see Athey and Haile (2006) and Hendricks and Porter (2007).

27.1.1 Efficiency versus optimality

Let us begin by immediately clearing up a common point of misunderstanding about auctions when discussed by non-economists, viz., the meaning of the word "efficient". This important term in the auction lexicon does not mean revenue-maximizing or cost-minimizing. An auction is said to be *efficient* if it allocates the items to those who value them the most *ex post*. In contrast, an auction is said to be *optimal* if it results in the most profitable allocation for the seller, for example if it maximizes expected revenue or minimizes expected cost. Efficient auctions are not necessarily optimal. Optimal auctions are not necessarily efficient.

Which is the proper goal of an auction, efficiency or optimality? Optimality seems more natural in many circumstances, but efficiency might be the appropriate objective, for example, in the case of auctions used to facilitate the transfer of public resources to the private sector. Thus, when Vice-President Al Gore opened the first series of US spectrum license auctions on December 5, 1994, he proclaimed their purpose as being "to put licenses into the hands of those who value them the most" (White House 1994). The fact that these nine auctions ultimately raised $20 billion (Cramton 1998) was presumably just a convenient truth.

27.1.2 Terminology

As mentioned above, the primary reason items are priced via an auction rather than other methods is that the seller is sufficiently unsure of the valuations of the potential buyers that he has an incentive to elicit additional information from them. This is an example of *information asymmetry*, that is, there is information available to one or more parties that is not available to others. In fact, William Vickrey shared his 1996 Nobel Prize in Economics for "fundamental contributions to the economic theory of incentives under asymmetric information" (Royal Swedish Academy of Sciences 1996).[2]

27.1.2.1 *Private values*

A specific case of information asymmetry is an auction in which each bidder knows his own value of the item at the time of the bidding; this is called a *private values* setting. In this scenario no bidder knows with certainty the valuations of the other bidders but, even if he were to learn what they are, this would not alter his valuation. An *independent private values* setting is a private values setting in which the bidders' values are independent random variables.

Independent private values is both the most unrealistic auction setting and the one most studied by economists. Milgrom (2004) provides an honest assessment of the situation:

> Relaxing the private-values and independence assumptions raises a host of new issues....
> Bidders' ignorance of their values leads us to study what information bidders are likely to acquire, whether they will share this information or keep it secret, and whether the auctioneer can improve the outcome by gathering and disseminating information on its own. The independence assumption is an essential premise of...the revenue equivalence theorems. Relaxing this assumption forces us to reevaluate the most basic results of auction theory. (Milgrom 2004: 157)

That being said, it is nevertheless common to add two further assumptions to the independent private values model. First, the bidders are *symmetric*, that is, the bidder types are not only independent but identically distributed according to some continuous density. Secondly, the bidders are *risk neutral*, that is, each seeks to maximize his expected profit, also called his *bidder surplus*, the difference between his valuation and the price he pays. All these assumptions are so standard, beginning with the seminal paper of Vickrey (1961), that the independent private values model with symmetric, risk-neutral bidders is often referred to as the *benchmark model* (see, e.g., Milgrom 2004). One hastens to add that the benchmark model does lend considerable insight into more general and applicable auction settings.

27.1.2.2 *Common value and the winner's curse*

Let us leave aside, for now, the benchmark model. It is possible, and in fact not unusual, that a bidder's precise valuation for an item is unknown to himself at the time of the

---

[2] Four other auction theorists have been awarded the Nobel Prize in Economics: Vernon L. Smith, "for having established laboratory experiments as a tool in empirical economic analysis, especially in the study of alternative market mechanisms" (awarded 2002); and Leonid Hurwicz, Eric S. Maskin, and Roger B. Myerson, "for having laid the foundations of mechanism design theory" (2007).

bidding. However, he may have some private information that is correlated with the item's true value to him; this information is called his *signal*. An example of a signal would be an expert opinion or a test result. From an information standpoint, the opposite of the private values model is the *common value model*, the scenario in which all bidders have the same valuation for the item, but where this valuation is unknown to the bidders at the time of the bidding. In a common value setting, different bidders in general have different signals.

What is arguably the most influential paper on common value auctions is not a theoretical analysis by an auction theorist ensconced in academia, but rather is a thought piece by three petroleum engineers employed by the Atlantic Richfield Company. In their paper "Competitive Bidding in High-Risk Situations", E. C. Capen, R. V. Clapp, and W. M. Campbell (1971) describe what has become known as the *winner's curse*.[3] As might be expected, the value of an oil exploration lease depends on how much oil is under the particular tract covered by the lease. Capen and his colleagues ask the reader to play a little game they call a "think sale". Think of yourself as a manager whose task is to set bids on parcels in an impending sale. On any of your parcels, you will have a consensus property value put together by your experts. Allow that *on average*, your value estimates are correct. However, your opponents *on this particular tract* will have better or worse information—that is, information that is either more accurate or less accurate than yours. Thus, there will be quite a divergence of opinions as to the tract's value, where some bidders have overestimated the true value of the parcel, and others have underestimated it. Capen et al. (1971) ask:

> Can we not then conclude that he who thinks he sees the most reserves, will *tend* to win the parcel in competitive bidding? This conclusion leads straightway to another: *In competitive bidding, the winner tends to be the bidder who most overestimates true tract value.* (Capen et al. 1971: 643)

In other words, winning against a number of rivals in a common value auction implies that your value estimate is in fact an overestimate, conditional on the event of winning. In fact, this happens not only in a "pure" common value setting. As long as there is *any* common value component to the bidder valuations—that is, the general model of interdependent values discussed immediately below—then you are at risk of falling victim to the winner's curse. This raises the question: In formulating a bid, how do you avoid being cursed by this "adverse selection" effect? Capen et al. suggest placing "a lower bid than one might come up with otherwise", that is, to engage in *bid shading*, a strategy that is in fact backed up by theory.

Competitive bidding becomes especially interesting when one of the parties knows the value of the item with certainty and the others do not. Consider the following refinement of the above scenario. You are bidding against another company that already owns oil rights to a contiguous parcel and therefore, by drilling "offset control wells" on the boundary, the other company has obtained nearly perfect information on the value of the rights on the parcel in which you are both interested. Your company is not so fortunate in that it has no contiguous parcel, and therefore only has imperfect seismic and other information on which to act. How should you bid? Actually, this question applies more generally to the case

---

[3] Despite a great many citations, the phrase "winner's curse" does not appear anywhere in the paper of Capen et al. (1971). The term appears on page 1078 of Oren and Williams (1975), who attribute it to a conference presentation of Capen, Clapp, and Campbell.

where your opponent does not have perfect information, just better information than you. This question, motivated by a case study of two major oil companies bidding via a sealed tender for rights to an offshore parcel, was considered by Wilson (1967, 1969). His analysis of it, together with the highly influential (though unpublished) PhD dissertation of Armando Ortega-Reichert (1968), opened up the entire field of common value auctions.

27.1.2.3 *Interdependent and affiliated values*

A general model lying between the two extreme settings of private values and common value allows each bidder's value to be a function of his own signal as well as the signals of all the other bidders, which are typically unknown to him. This setting is called *interdependent values*. This setting models the familiar situation in which a bidder's precise valuation is unknown at the time of the auction but would be affected by information available to other bidders.

An important special case, introduced by Milgrom and Weber (1982), is that of *affiliated values* in which the winning bidder's payoff depends upon his personal preferences, the preferences of others, and the intrinsic qualities of the item being sold. This is a strong form of positive correlation that allows for both private values uncertainty and common value uncertainty. Affiliation between two given bidders implies that if one bidder has a high estimate of value, it is more likely that the other bidder's estimate of the value is high. Klemperer (2004a: ch. 1) provides the following intuition: "[Y]our value for a painting may depend mostly on your own private information—how much you like it—but also somewhat on others' private information—how much they like it—because this affects the resale value and/or the prestige of owning it."

27.2 THE FOUR BASIC AUCTIONS

The four basic auctions are the English auction, the Dutch auction, the Vickrey auction, and the first-price sealed-bid auction. Each of these, in its simplest form, is an auction for a single item. Although economists tend to be more interested in efficiency than revenue, one of the first results in auction theory, which is due to Vickrey (1961), is that under the benchmark model the expected revenues of the four basic auctions are identical (see Section 27.3.3).

The English and Dutch auctions are both *dynamic auctions*, that is, they provide multiple opportunities for bidders to bid, where some information about the bidding is generally revealed to the bidders during the course of the auction. Thus, bidders have the opportunity to adjust their subsequent bids accordingly; this process is called *price discovery*.

27.2.1 The English auction

The *English auction* is an ascending-bid auction. Bidders submit successively higher bids for the item until no bidder is willing to bid higher. The last bidder to bid wins the item and pays the amount of his last bid.

The English auction is probably the format most people think of when they think of auctions, especially for auctions of fine art, and indeed, almost all fine art is auctioned via the English auction. The major auction houses are the English firms Christie's and Sotheby's. Beggs and Graddy (2009) explain how art auctions work. If someone wishes to sell a piece of art, an expert at the auction house will provide advice on the likely valuation of the piece, and together the seller and the expert will agree on a secret reserve price. Prior to the auction, information on the piece is published in a presale catalogue, which includes a low- and a high-price estimate for the work; the low estimate is invariably set at or above the secret reserve price. Bidding starts low, and the auctioneer subsequently calls out higher and higher prices. When the bidding stops, the item is said to be "knocked down". However, not all items that are knocked down are in fact sold. If the bidding does not reach the level of the secret reserve price of the item, it will go unsold, in which case it will be put up for sale at a later auction, sold elsewhere, or taken off the market. Tunca and Wu (2009) report that for industrial procurement, buyers most often use a reverse English auction.

It is probably impossible to determine when the English auction was first used, although Herodotus in his *Histories*, circa 440 BC, describes an English auction that even allowed for negative prices, that is subsidies.[4] This was at least a thousand years before the word "English" existed in any form. In fact, the term "English auction" is surprisingly recent, as the earliest known reference (Charlton 2008) appeared in *The Times* (London) in 1891: "All fish shall be sold by English auction" (*The Times* 1891). One may hypothesize that the term arose to distinguish the auction format that had been common in England for many years from the relatively recent arrival of the Dutch auction (see Section 27.2.2).

Three interesting variations on the English auction are the *candle auction*, the *Japanese auction*, and the *silent auction*.

27.2.1.1 *The candle auction*

In a *candle auction*, a short burning candle is used to determine the stopping time of the auction, at which time the highest bidder wins the item at his bid price. In his famous diary, Samuel Pepys (1926) reports observing a candle auction on two occasions for the sale of ships by the British Admiralty. The first time was on 6 November, 1660:

> From thence Mr. Creed and I to Wilkinson's, and dined together, and in great haste thence to our office, where we met all, for the sale of two ships by an inch of candle (the first time that ever I saw any of this kind), where I observed how they do invite one another, and at last how they all do cry, and we have much to do to tell who did cry last. (Pepys 1926)

By "cry", Pepys means "cry out"; the English auction is also called an *open outcry* auction. The second entry was on 3 September, 1662:

> After dinner by water to the office, and there we met and sold the Weymouth, Success, and Fellowship hulkes, where pleasant to see how backward men are at first to bid; and yet when the candle is going out, how they bawl and dispute afterwards who bid the most first.
>   And here I observed one many cunninger than the rest, that was sure to bid the last man and to carry it; and enquiring the reason, he told me that just as the flame goes out the smoke

---

[4] This auction described by Herodotus, the earliest auction known, served an important societal function. For more details, see Herodotus (1914: para. 196). This is also discussed in Cassady (1967: ch. 3).

descends, which is a thing I never observed before, and by that he doth know the instant when to bid last—which is very pretty. (Pepys 1926)

As Klemperer (2004b) points out, this is the first recorded instance of *sniping*—withholding one's true bid until shortly before the closing of the auction in the hope that it will be too late for other bidders to respond.

In England, the transition from candle auction to English auction began in the late eighteenth century. In 1778, two advertisements appeared in *The Times* side by side. The first was headed "Sales by Candle" and lists "The following GOODS, viz., 124 Chests of East India Indigo, 1 Barrel of French ditto, 2650 Pounds of Nutmegs, 239 ditto Mace..." The second advertisement was headed "Sale by Auction" for "All the Genuine HOUSEHOLD FURNITURE, China, Books, an Eight Day Clock, and other Effects of Mr. White, deceased" (*The Times* 1778). Here "by Auction" refers specifically to the English auction. The candle auction was in use in England as late as the early nineteenth century, as can be seen from a notice of a sale by candle in *The Times* in April 1825 (*The Times* 1825).

27.2.1.2 *The Japanese auction*

The *Japanese auction* is a variant on the English auction in which the bid price is raised continuously by the auctioneer, where each bidder must meet the current price to stay in the auction, and where all bidders are aware at all times as to the number of active bidders. Milgrom and Weber (1982: sect. 5) analyze the English auction using the Japanese variant.

An important feature that distinguishes it from the standard English auction is that the Japanese variant precludes *jump bids*. Jump bids are bids that exceed the minimum required increment, often significantly so. Avery (1998) points out that a jump bid can serve to discourage competition, for two related reasons. First, it suggests that the jump bidder values the item more than anyone else. Second, if the jump bidder drops out in favour of your later bid, his action is strong evidence that you have overbid.

In an implementation of the Japanese auction known as the *button auction*, bidders hold down a button to show that they are active as the auctioneer steadily increases the price; when the price exceeds a bidder's valuation, the bidder releases the button, which locks to prevent him from pressing it again. Another variation is where the bidders are assembled in a room and are asked to stand at the beginning of the auction, and to sit as the price is raised above their valuation. The last bidder to remain standing pays the current price.[5]

27.2.1.3 *The silent auction*

One generalization of the English auction for multiple items is the *silent auction*. In a silent auction, the multiple items are auctioned simultaneously, where all items are on display to all bidders—which might in fact be a description or photograph of the item. All bidders are permitted to bid on any number of items. As the name implies, there is no "oral outcry". Next to each item is a piece of paper, called a bid sheet, which specifies the minimum price,

---

[5] Auctions are popular in Japan, notably for the selling of fish, but the auctions used in Japan are not Japanese auctions. The Tsukiji fish market, the largest wholesale fish market in the world, uses the standard English auction. Nevertheless, "Japanese auction" is now a useful term to distinguish this variant of the English auction.

that is, the auctioneer's reserve price, and the minimum amount that the existing high bid must be raised for the new bid to be valid, that is the *bid increment*. There may also be an estimate of the value of the item. An interested bidder can decide whether he wishes to increase the *standing high bid* by writing his name and the new bid on the item's bid sheet. Bidding on all items closes simultaneously according to a common clock.

Silent auctions are typically used when there is a charitable or public goods component to the seller's revenues. In a charity auction, this component is often the donation or reduced cost to the charity of the items for sale at the auction. Charity auctions are commonly employed in church sales. In cases where the winner reneges, the auctioneer will typically allocate the item to the second-highest bidder at his bid price and then attempt to shame the high bidder into donating the difference.[6]

At silent auctions, it is not uncommon to observe the following behavior (Milgrom 2004: sect. 7.2). Very close to the announced ending time, there is someone who approaches a table, lifts the pencil and slowly writes his name and bid as the bell rings announcing the end of the auction. Often, this is the only bid the bidder ever makes for the item. The bidder's intent is to keep the price as low as possible and then place a bid only when no one has any time left to respond. In other words, this is another instance of sniping, although that term is rarely, if ever, used to describe this behavior in a charity auction context.

Sniping is not very harmful at charity auctions, Milgrom points out, since bidders might be happy to pay a higher price to acquire what they want, having contributed more to a worthy cause. However in on-line auctions, where people may not be feeling as charitable as at a church sale, this tactic can be a more serious issue. For more on sniping, see Ockenfels et al. (2006: sect. 4).

27.2.2 The Dutch auction

The *Dutch auction* is a descending-bid auction, where the auctioneer starts at a high price and announces successively lower prices. The first bidder to bid wins the item and pays the price current at the time of his bid. The Dutch auction is often referred to as the *descending clock auction* since, although it can be conducted orally, it often employs a clock, with the clock hand starting at a high price determined by the auctioneer, and dropping until a buyer stops the clock by pushing a button to bid for a lot at the price determined by the clock hand.

The Dutch auction is not only of conceptual interest; in terms of quantity of items sold and magnitude of revenues generated, it is one of the most significant auctions in the world today. Cassady (1967) reported Dutch auctions being used throughout Europe, in certain Middle Eastern countries, and in particular for the sale of fish in both Hull, England and in Israel. It has been used in Australia at the Sydney Fish Market since 1989. But the most famous application of the Dutch auction is, of course, the selling of flowers in the Netherlands. On January 1, 2008, the two great Dutch flower auction cooperatives, the Aalsmeer Flower Auction and FloraHolland, merged to become the new FloraHolland. According to a press release (FloraHolland 2008), during 2007 exporters, wholesalers, florists, and major

---

[6] Popkowski Leszczyc and Rothkopf (2010) studied motives and bidding in charity auctions by conducting field experiments consisting of simultaneous charity and non-charity auctions for identical products on an Internet auction site. Among their results, they found that auctions with 25% of revenue donated to charity had higher *net* revenue—after the charitable donation was subtracted—than non-charity auctions.

retailers bought 11 billion cut flowers and 1.2 billion house and garden plants from the Aalsmeer Flower Auction and FloraHolland. The total 2007 turnover of flowers and plants for the soon-to-be-merged cooperatives was in excess of €4 billion ($6.2 billion).

The day-to-day working of the Dutch flower auctions, which are auctions for multiple units, is explained by van den Berg et al. (2001). The wall in front of the auctioning room contains a large board with a "clock" and an electronic display of the properties of the product to be auctioned, as well as the minimum price. The clock is actually a circle of small lamps, each corresponding to a given monetary value. Once the clock is set in motion, consecutive lamps light sequentially clockwise, corresponding to a decrease in the value. Just prior to the start of the auction, the flowers or plants are transported through the room and a few items are shown to the buyers. The auctioneer decides on a starting position for the clock that corresponds to an "unreasonably high" price for the product, and sets the clock in motion. The value drops continuously until some buyer stops the clock by pushing a button, where the value indicated by the clock at that moment is the price he is to pay for a single item. The buyer then announces how many units he wants to purchase, where a unit is a fixed amount of items for the product, for example it might be 120 flowers. The identity of the buyer is shown on the electronic display. If he does not purchase the entire lot, the clock is re-set to a high value and the process starts again for the remaining units; this continues until the entire lot is sold. If the clock passes the minimum price, the remainder of the lot is destroyed. Van den Berg et al. (2001) report that the average duration of a single auction transaction is a couple of seconds.

27.2.2.1 An historical note

There exists a general consensus that the term "Dutch auction" derives from its use in the Dutch flower auctions and that these were originally devised by farmers in Holland during the 1870s (see, e.g., Learmount 1985: 74); however, this consensus is incorrect. There is no doubt that the term goes back decades earlier. In March 1830, the *Virginia Literary Museum & Journal of Belles-Lettres, Arts, Sciences &c.* (an ephemeral weekly in publication for a year at the University of Virginia) published a short story entitled "The Country Belle" (K 1830).[7] The story tells of a Miss Patty Starkie who, upon leaving boarding school, had prescribed a number of qualifications she required in a husband. Unfortunately, "it always happened that some one of these essentials was wanting, or was not possessed in sufficient quantity". Consequently:

> After a few years Miss Patty began to relax from the strictness of her conditions, and to follow the example of a Dutch auctioneer, whose practice is to set up his wares at the highest price, and thence bid downwards til he meets with a purchaser; but, unfortunately, however she fell in the price, it was always above the rate of the market, and the goods remained on hand; or to speak without a figure, she continued Miss Patty Starkie still, until the time of which we speak, when she had reached the sober and discreet age of thirty five. (K 1830)

We should point out that the term "Dutch auction" is sometimes used by practitioners to refer to some variation of the "uniform-price auction" (discussed in Section 27.3.2), such as the "Dutch auction" tender offer for common stock, and the eBay "Dutch auction" for

---

[7] "K" is probably George Tucker, the journal's editor.

auctioning multiple units on the Internet. In this chapter, the term *Dutch auction* will always refer to the descending-bid auction described above.

27.2.2.2 *The slow Dutch auction and markdown management*

Just how important is speed in determining the outcome of the Dutch auction? We will see in Section 27.3 that one of Vickrey's key results is the revenue equivalence between the Dutch auction and the "first-price sealed-bid auction" (discussed in Section 27.2.3). However, Lucking-Reiley (1999) reports results of field experiments of various auction formats on the Internet for collectable cards ("Magic: The Gathering"), and found that the Dutch auction earned approximately 30 percent more revenue than the first-price sealed-bid auction. Lucking-Reiley suggests that the longer timescales in these on-line auctions may be a factor, viz., days and hours, versus minutes and seconds. Carare and Rothkopf (2005) present both decision-theoretic and game-theoretic models that support this assertion. They find that bidders in such Dutch auctions, when faced with a positive cost of returning to the auction site, prefer to purchase the object sooner at a higher price so as to economize on the cost of return. Therefore, when transaction costs are accounted for, these Dutch auctions yield, on average, higher revenue than first-price sealed-bid auctions.

Thus, a distinction can be made between two types of Dutch auction according to their speed: the *descending clock auction* described earlier, and the *slow Dutch auction* considered by Lucking-Reiley and Carare and Rothkopf. The slow Dutch auction is similar to the retail pricing policy in which a merchant holding a fixed inventory of a perishable good or a fashion good finds it advantageous to *mark down*—discount—his stock rather than allowing it to depreciate or go out of style, and thus subjects it to increasingly deeper discounts until either the inventory of the product is completely sold or a final sell-by date is reached. This policy was made famous by Filene's Basement, a chain of department stores in the Boston area. In Filene's Basement, the price tag on each item is marked with the date it arrives on the selling floor. The longer an item remains unsold, the more the price is automatically reduced; first 25 percent then 50 percent and finally 75 percent of the original price; what is not sold is donated to charity.[8] Determining an optimal markdown policy is known as the *markdown management problem*. We refer the interested reader to Chapter 25 by Ramakrishnan.

The close connection between markdown pricing and the Dutch auction was first pointed out by Lazear (1986). Specifically, he observes that when markdown pricing is employed such that the reduction in price is small each time, and such that the number of potential buyers is sufficiently small that they may behave strategically with respect to the waiting time, then this procedure is essentially the Dutch auction. Lazear shows that "bargain basement" behavior can be predicted and that the price cutting rule can be specified, and he addresses the question of when a rigid rule of this sort is an optimal pricing policy. Under the assumption that all bidders have the same valuation, Lazear finds that both the initial price and the speed of the fall in price increase as the number of customers per unit of time increases, and as prior uncertainty about the value of the good increases.

Gallego et al. (2008) observe that in fashion retailing, stores often schedule the markdown of products to occur at the same times each year, hence shrewd customers quickly learn that

---

[8] Ironically Filene's Basement, which had been operating under Chapter 11 bankruptcy court protection, was itself sold at auction in June 2009.

they are likely to save if they are willing to wait. In effect, such sellers are training customers to wait. Gallego et al. investigate how this training effect might change the seller's optimal markdown policy and, in particular, whether a seller would be better off allowing merchandise to perish rather than selling it at a discount. Like Lazear, they abstract to a two-period model, where inventory perishes at the end of the second period. However, unlike Lazear, who considered the case when all customers have the same valuation for an item but the seller is *ex ante* uncertain whether that valuation is low or high, Gallego et al. assume that the customers follow a distribution of willingness-to-pay. They find that the seller's optimal equilibrium policy is to set a single price for both periods and to not restrict second-period sales, even if customer willingness-to-pay is lower in the second period than the first.

27.2.3 The first-price sealed-bid auction

In the first-price sealed-bid auction, bidders simultaneously submit sealed bids for the item; the highest bidder wins the item, and pays the amount of his bid. Klemperer (2004a: ch. 5) mentions that an advantage of the first-price sealed-bid auction is that it does not disincentivize anyone from entering the bidding, in contrast to the English auction, in which a weaker (potential) bidder knows that a stronger bidder can always re-bid so as to top his bid. But, as Klemperer explains, this advantage also highlights a disadvantage of the first-price sealed-bid auction, viz., it allows bidders with lower valuations to occasionally beat opponents with higher valuations, and thus is more likely to lead to inefficient outcomes.

Applications of first-price sealed-bid auctions come in two forms: the "buy" format, where bidders are purchasers and the high bid wins, and the reverse (i.e., procurement) format, where bidders are suppliers and the low bid wins. Vickrey (1961) provides as examples the sale of property and the underwriting of securities in the former case, and bidding for construction contracts in the latter.

McAfee and McMillan (1987) state that first-price sealed-bid auctions are sometimes used in the sale of artwork and real estate, but that they are of greater quantitative significance for government contracts, including mineral rights in government-owned land, as in the paper of Capen et al. (1971) discussed in Section 27.1. McAfee and McMillan wrote: "For many government contracts, firms submit sealed bids; the contract is required by law to be awarded to the lowest qualified bidder." This situation still holds widely in the United States. Zullo (2006), for example, examined public–private contracting in Wisconsin, and found that the state's Department of Transportation (DOT) has a well-developed system for competitive bidding on road and bridge construction. Before the Wisconsin DOT issues a request for proposals, DOT engineers estimate the cost of a project and prepare detailed specifications based on both experience and industry standards. Then bidders respond with proposals, and the lowest bid is selected. However, the DOT has, in effect, a reserve price: If proposals deviate significantly from the DOT estimate, the project is either re-evaluated or cancelled.[9]

---

[9] Although "lowest qualified bidder" is the *de facto* standard for state construction auctions in the United States, other countries take a more heterodox view. For example, in Italy, Portugal, Peru, Korea, Denmark, and Taiwan, the standard practice is to *exclude* the lowest bid, as well as the highest, and award the contract to the bid coming closest to the average of the remaining bids. See Lambropoulos (2007).

27.2.4 The Vickrey auction

The Vickrey auction is a second-price sealed-bid auction, where bidders simultaneously submit sealed bids for the item. The highest bidder wins the item and pays the amount bid by the second-highest bidder. The auction is named after William Vickrey who developed the theory behind it in his celebrated 1961 paper in the *Journal of Finance*.

It is easily seen that in the Vickrey auction it is a dominant strategy for a bidder to bid his true value.[10] A bidder has no incentive to bid lower than his value, since such a bid will not affect the price he pays if he wins, and could lose him the item that he might have otherwise won at an acceptable price; the bidder also has no incentive to bid higher than his value, since this will win him the item he would have otherwise lost only in the case where he will be required to pay more than his value. This truth-telling property is called *incentive compatibility*. Thus, the Vickrey auction always awards the item to the bidder who values it the most, that is, it is efficient.

An important way of viewing the Vickrey auction is that *the winning bidder pays the opportunity cost of winning the item*. That is, he pays the incremental value that would be derived by assigning the item according to the next-best use among the bidders. In this way, a winning bidder achieves a profit equal to his incremental contribution to total value. Of course, in an auction with a single item, this next-best use is to assign it to the second-highest bidder, and the incremental value is the second-highest bid. However, viewing the Vickrey auction in terms of opportunity cost allows for the possibility that the auction could be generalized for multiple items. We will return to this idea in Section 27.5.5.

With regard to theory, Vickrey was a pioneer; with regard to practice, there were forerunners. In 1797 Goethe devised a second-price auction with a reserve price in order to sell a manuscript to a single bidder (Moldovanu and Tietzel 1998), while stamp auctioneers have been using second-price sealed-bid auctions since 1893 (Lucking-Reiley 2000).

The Vickrey auction was employed by the government of New Zealand in 1989–90 in the first spectrum auction ever held (see Section 27.4). Unfortunately, the New Zealand auction was not ideally designed for achieving efficiency, and evidence suggests that the outcome was indeed inefficient (see Milgrom 2004: sect. 1.2.2). To make matters worse, the auction was dreadful in terms of generating revenue (see Mueller 1993). Fifteen years after the auction, in what some might describe as quintessential political understatement, the New Zealand Ministry of Economic Development (2005) issued a report stating: "The results of the second price tenders held in New Zealand attracted some criticism as the return to the Crown was below what some people considered to be the true value of the spectrum." The Ministry attributed the disappointing revenue to three factors: (1) very thin markets, (2) lack of information concerning the value of the spectrum, and (3) "instances where only nominal bids were placed and no reserves were set, meaning that some licences were essentially given away." We will discuss weaknesses of the Vickrey auction in Section 27.5.5.

Vickrey's paper is significant for both the depth and breadth of the contributions it makes, and is required reading for anyone interested in auction pricing. We thus discuss it in some detail in the next section.

---

[10] A *dominant strategy* for a bidder is one that is at least as good as any other strategy for that bidder, no matter how the other bidders may bid.

27.3 ANALYZING AUCTIONS

"Counterspeculation, Auctions, and Competitive Sealed Tenders" (Vickrey 1961) is the foundation paper of auction theory. In this remarkable work, Vickrey analyzed the four basic auction types under the benchmark model.[11] In the following subsection, we present a concise summary of his analysis.

27.3.1 Analyzing the four basic auctions (benchmark model)

- *The English auction and the second-price sealed-bid (Vickrey) auction.* In an English auction, a bidder has a dominant strategy to continue bidding up until the point at which the price reaches his valuation. The bidder with the highest valuation will win the item and pay a price just above the second-highest bidder valuation. A sealed-bid procedure that is strategically equivalent to the English auction is where the winner pays the price of the second-highest bid, since it will be a dominant strategy for a bidder to bid his valuation. The intuition is as follows. Bidding in an English auction will stop at a level approximately equal to the second highest value among the values that the bidders place on the item, since at that point there will be only one interested bidder left; the object will then be purchased at that price by the bidder to whom it has the highest value.

- *The Dutch Auction and the first-price sealed-bid auction.* In the Dutch auction, the first and only bid is the one that concludes the auction. Each bidder, in attempting to determine at what point he should be prepared to make a bid, will need to take into account whatever information he possesses concerning the probable bids by others. Under the benchmark model for the Dutch and first-price sealed-bid auctions, the unique equilibrium strategy determines how players should shade their bids, depending on their beliefs about the distribution of other bidders' bids. Thus, a bidder has no dominant strategy. The first-price sealed-bid auction is strategically equivalent to the Dutch auction. Therefore, a bidder in the Dutch auction should wait until the price falls to what he should have bid if he were participating in a sealed-bid auction.

- *Revenue comparisons among the four auctions.* The English and Dutch auctions can be shown to produce the same average expected price and thus the same expected profit to both the seller and to the bidders, respectively. Thus, all four auctions produce the same expected profit to the seller and to the bidders, respectively. However, in order to maximize his expectation of profit, a bidder in the first-price auction, as in the Dutch auction, must concern himself not only with his own valuation, but also with his estimates of the valuations of other bidders as well as the bidding strategies that he thinks they will follow, which can involve a considerable amount of expenditure of bidder resources. In contrast, the second-price method makes any such general market appraisal—as in the English auction—entirely superfluous.

The four basic auctions under the benchmark model are summarized in Table 27.1.

---

[11] It should be said that, until the appearance of his paper, "sealed-bid tenders" were not considered to be auctions. Vickrey himself described them in his paper as "not ... auctions as such" (p. 20).

Table 27.1 The four basic auctions

	Bidding procedure	
Dominant strategy exists?	Dynamic	Sealed-bid
Yes	↑ English ≡	Vickrey
No	↓ Dutch ≡	first-price sealed-bid

27.3.2 Other contributions of Vickrey

Probably due to the considerable significance of his main results, the other contributions of Vickrey's paper are often overlooked. Five other topics were covered by Vickrey in this paper: shill bids, third-price auctions, the second-price Dutch auction, multiple-unit ascending auctions, and multi-unit sealed-bid auctions.

- *Shill bids.*[12] Vickrey was aware that the second-price method may not be "automatically self-policing to quite the same extent as the first price method", and that a shill could be employed by the auctioneer to jack up the price by putting in a bid just under the top bid.

- *Third-price auctions.* What would be the equilibrium strategy in a *third*-price sealed-bid auction? Bid somewhat *higher* than one's valuation, since the danger of the payment exceeding the valuation is offset by the increased probability of gains in cases where the second-highest bid exceeds this value but the third-highest bid falls below it. Beginning with Vickrey, anyone who has ever discussed third-price auctions has felt an understandable obligation to mention that they are a theoretical construct of no known practical significance.

- *The second-price Dutch auction.* An interesting variation on the Dutch auction would be where the winner pays the second-highest bid price rather than the first, so as to make it equivalent to the second-price sealed-bid auction. The clock mechanism could be altered so that the first button pushed would pre-select the signal to be flashed, but there would be no indication until the second button is pushed, stopping the clock, indicating both the price determined by the second button and the winner determined by the first.

This idea was followed up forty-eight years later by Mishra and Parkes (2009) who, under the assumption of private values, introduced a "Vickrey-Dutch" auction for two different environments: (1) multiple items with buyers each having demand for a single item; and (2) multiple units with buyers each having non-increasing marginal values for additional units. Both variants of the Mishra and Parkes auction retain the advantages of the Dutch auction of speed and elicitation (which the authors show via simulation), and inherit the Vickrey property of supporting truthful bidding that terminates in an efficient allocation (which they show analytically).

---

[12] For readers outside of North America: The term *shill* refers to a seller's accomplice posing as a customer.

- *Multiple-unit ascending auctions.* In the multiple-unit generalization of the English auction, each bidder is interested in at most one unit. There are two variations. In the first, m units are offered simultaneously, and each bidder is permitted to raise his bid, even when this does not make it the high bid. When no bidder wishes to raise further, one unit is awarded to each of the m highest bidders, who pay the same price equal to the $m + $1st highest bid. The result is *Pareto optimal*, that is, no one could be made better off without someone else being made worse off. This is a *uniform-price auction*. In the second variation, the assumption is that there may be minor quality differences among the items, in which case they can be auctioned off successively. In this variation, bidders will need to bid strategically.

- *Multiple-unit sealed-bid auctions.* Vickrey describes bonds as often being sold in multiple-unit sealed-bid auctions, with bids accepted from highest to lowest until all units are allocated. He discusses the two variants, in which bidders are asked either to: (1) pay their bid, or (2) pay a uniform price set to the price of the last accepted bid. In the uniform-price case, Vickrey advises that it be set to the first bid rejected rather than the last bid accepted. There is still a debate on as to which of the two variants is best for selling government securities, *pay-your-bid* or *uniform-price*.

The US Treasury currently uses multiple-unit sealed-bid auctions to sell Treasury bills, notes, bonds, and TIPS (Treasury Inflation-Protected Securities) in order to determine their rate or yield. Each year, the Treasury conducts approximately 200 public auctions and issues more than $4.2 trillion in securities. All Treasury auctions operate as follows. Each bidder specifies an amount (up to 35 percent of the issue amount) and the yield that is acceptable to him. At the close of an auction, the Treasury accepts competitive bids in ascending order in terms of their yields, until the quantity of accepted bids reaches the offering amount. All successful bidders receive the same yield at the highest accepted bid, that is, the last bid accepted.

27.3.3 Optimal auctions

Which auction should a seller use so as to maximize his expected revenue? This is the *Optimal Auction Problem*. As discussed earlier, Vickrey showed in his classic 1961 paper that the four basic auctions under the benchmark model yield the same expected revenue to the seller. What could be described as the "Fundamental Theorem of Auctions" is a significant generalization of Vickrey's result, and is called the *Revenue Equivalence Theorem*. The result is due to Myerson and, independently, to Riley and Samuelson:[13]

Revenue Equivalence Theorem (Myerson 1981, Riley and Samuelson 1981)
Consider auctions in which the item goes to the bidder with the highest signal and in which any bidder with the lowest-possible signal expects zero profit. Assume that bidders are risk-neutral and that each has a private signal independently drawn from a common, strictly increasing continuous distribution. Then every auction yields the same expected revenue, and results in each bidder making the same expected payment as a function of his signal.

---

[13] There are various formulations of the revenue equivalence theorem, which differ primarily in their degree of generality, and which can be described collectively as the "revenue equivalence theorems".

Note that the theorem only specifies that the potential buyers have private *signals*, not private *values*. So, this result applies far more generally than to the private values setting considered by Vickrey (1961).

Myerson also showed that any of the four standard auction formats, together with an appropriately chosen reserve price, is an optimal auction. That is, no other auction format can result in a higher expected revenue for the seller. The necessity of a reserve price was dramatically demonstrated by the New Zealand auction (discussed in Section 27.2.4).

Virtually all subsequent work on optimal auctions has built on Myerson's paper. Independently, Riley and Samuelson (1981) established the Revenue Equivalence Theorem under somewhat less general conditions. However, unlike Myerson, they also considered the case of risk-averse bidders.

27.3.3.1 *The linkage principle*

The Revenue Equivalence Theorem requires the strong assumption that each bidder's private information is independent of his competitors' private information. This leads to the question of what can be said under the more realistic assumption that the bidders have "affiliated values" (discussed above in Section 27.1.2). Milgrom and Weber (1982: Theorem 21) show that for bidders with affiliated values, the English auction generates higher average prices than the Vickrey auction.

Klemperer (2004a: ch. 1) provides the following intuition. The winning bidder's surplus is due to his private information. The more that the price paid depends on others' information, the more closely the price is related to the winner's information, since information is affiliated. Now in an English auction with common value elements—the interdependent values model—the price depends on all other bidders' information, while in a Vickrey auction, the price depends on only one other bidder's information, so it follows that the English auction generates higher average prices than the Vickrey auction. Similarly, when bidders have affiliated values and are risk neutral, the Vickrey auction generates higher average prices than the Dutch and first-price sealed-bid auctions, which ignore all information except for the value of the winning bid. Klemperer points out that this general principle will imply the following practical rule of thumb: If the seller has access to any private source of information, it would be in his interest to reveal it honestly, as it is likely to result in higher revenue to him.

This general principle, that expected revenue is raised by linking the winner's payment to information that is affiliated with the winner's information, is sufficiently important to have a name:

The Linkage Principle (Milgrom and Weber 1982)
On average, a seller in an auction will enhance his revenue by providing the bidders with as much information as possible about the value of the item.

One consequence of the Linkage Principle, pointed out by Klemperer (2004a: ch. 1), is that if the winner's value can be observed (even imperfectly) after the conclusion of the auction, then the seller can earn more revenue by making the winner's payment depend on this observation.

The Linkage Principle, useful as it is, does come with one important caveat: It is only guaranteed to hold in the case of a single item; there are counterexamples for the case of multiple units. See Perry and Reny (1999) for a full discussion.

27.3.3.2 Optimality and information structure

Most of the literature on mechanism[14] design maintains the assumption of Myerson (1981) that the information held by market participants is exogenous. However, there are many auctions in which the precision of the information available to the buyers is at least partially controlled by the seller. For example, in US offshore "wildcat" oil tract auctions[15] the firms involved in bidding are permitted to gather information about the lease value and their drilling costs prior to the sale using seismic information, but no on-site drilling is allowed. In contrast, in US offshore "drainage" oil leases, some bidders are intentionally given access to superior information by allowing them prior drilling in the area. It would be helpful to know what information structures maximize the seller's revenues.

This question was taken up by Bergemann and Pesendorfer (2007), who consider the joint decision problem of a seller who wishes to sell an object to one of multiple bidders with private valuations, where the seller can decide (1) the accuracy by which bidders learn their valuation, as well as (2) to whom to sell at what price. Bergemann and Pesendorfer show the existence of an optimal information structure, characterize properties of optimal information structures, and illustrate that the case of Myerson (1981) emerges as a special case when the seller informs the bidders perfectly. Bergemann and Pesendorfer provide other examples in which the seller can control the precision of the information available to the buyers: wholesale used car auctions, licensing for motion pictures, and competition of brokers for the trade of a large portfolio on behalf of an institutional asset manager.

27.4 THE SIMULTANEOUS ASCENDING AUCTION

A new form of mechanism for auctioning *multiple items* appeared on the scene in 1994, the *simultaneous ascending auction* (SAA). This auction was designed for use by the US Federal Communications Commission to allocate licenses for the right to use bands of the electromagnetic spectrum. The simultaneous ascending auction is unique among auction mechanisms in that it was conceived for a very specific application and developed over a short period of time. Paul Milgrom and Robert Wilson, in consultation with John McMillan and Preston McAfee, developed and proposed this auction procedure, quite literally, over a period of a few weeks (Milgrom 2004: xi). This is all the more extraordinary in that the SAA has proved to be the most influential new auction design of the past century.

---

[14] Auctions comprise a subset of a class of objects called *mechanisms*, a topic that is beyond the scope of this chapter. Presentations of mechanisms and mechanism design can be found in Krishna (2010) and Milgrom (2004).

[15] These auctions were also discussed in the paper of Capen et al. (1971) considered in Section 27.1, above.

Cramton (2006) points out that auctions have become the preferred method of assigning spectrum—not only in the United States, but also in Europe and around the world. Since 1994 there have been over 80 *spectrum auctions* in the USA alone, mainly for Personal Communications Services (PCS) and Advanced Wireless Services (AWS), most of which have made use of the simultaneous ascending auction. Klemperer (2004a: ch. 5) reports that the early auctions in Europe for third generation (3G) mobile wireless licenses (Austria, Germany, Italy, the Netherlands, Switzerland, and the UK in 2000; Belgium, Denmark, and Greece in 2001) raised in total almost $100 billion (or over 1.5 percent of GDP). Hazlett (2008) reports that the US auctions alone—this is prior to the 700 MHz auction in mid-2008—raised in excess of $25 billion. The 700 MHz auction raised over $19 billion. Cramton (2006) observes that the SAA has been refined and extended to the sale of divisible goods in electricity, gas, and environmental markets.[16]

27.4.1 How the SAA works

The SAA proceeds by discrete rounds, where multiple items are auctioned simultaneously, each with its own price. Each bidder is free to bid in a round on any number of items, subject to: (1) a minimum bid increment; (2) an *activity rule* that restricts the pace of the bidding; and (3) an allowance for *bid withdrawal*, whereby players can withdraw their bids subject to a payment equal to the difference between the withdrawn bid and the bid that replaces it. The auction terminates when a round completes in which no new bids have been submitted on any item. The winner on each item is the high bidder on that item, who is required to pay his bid.

The minimum bid increment is typically specified as a percentage of the current price, and is subject to change throughout the auction. Minimum bid increments assure that the auction concludes in a reasonable amount of time.

The activity rule determines the bidder's current *eligibility*, which is the maximum quantity of items on which he may bid. Thus, the activity rule requires bidders to maintain a minimum level of bidding activity during the course of the auction where, as the auction progresses, the level of activity increases. The activity rule forces a bidder desiring a large quantity of items to bid for a relatively large quantity earlier in the auction, thus preventing against the "snake in the grass" strategy, in which a bidder maintains a low level of activity early in the auction and then greatly expands his demand late in the auction. The activity rule also promotes price discovery.

The bid withdrawal rule[17] facilitates the realization of bidder *synergies*, the situation in which a bidder has a higher valuation for a particular set of items than the sum of their values to him individually, that is the items in the set are *complements*. Thus, the bid withdrawal rule mitigates what is known as the *exposure problem*, in which a bidder is exposed to a possible loss by bidding on a set of items where his bid price accounts for synergistic gains that he might not achieve.

The simultaneous ascending auction can be seen to be a generalization of the silent auction, albeit with an electronic bid sheet.

---

[16] See Wilson (1979) for the classic paper on auctions of divisible goods.
[17] The bid withdrawal rule was proposed by Preston McAfee.

27.4.2 Development of the spectrum auctions

In 1985, a report entitled "Using Auctions to Select FCC Licensees" was issued by the Federal Communications Commission's Office of Plans and Policy (Kwerel and Felker 1985). Although the basic idea had been around for some time—in 1959 Ronald Coase famously proposed a general regime of spectrum property rights (Coase 1959)—the Kwerel–Felker paper can be credited as being the key document that successfully advocated the utilization of auctions for the allocation of spectrum licenses. Prior to this date, it had been generally accepted that there were only two ways to assign radio and television licenses.

The first method was *comparative hearings*. Depending on your point of view, comparative hearings meant that licenses were: (1) assigned by the statutory standard of "public interest, convenience or necessity" (Communications Act of 1934), or (2) "simply handed to politically preferred parties" (Hazlett 2008). In any event, comparative hearings suffered from being very slow, as well as being wasteful of resources and lacking transparency. The method was cumbersome and eventually led to a large backlog of unassigned licenses.

In the early 1980s, these drawbacks led to the replacement of comparative hearings by a system that could work quickly: *lotteries*. As Milgrom (2004) explains, the lotteries did speed up the license approval process, but the fact that lottery winners were permitted to resell their licenses meant that a huge number of new applicants—many of whom were speculators with no interest in the telephone business—were randomly rewarded with windfalls in the form of licenses worth millions of dollars. Huge amounts of resources were again wasted, and the resulting chaos delayed the introduction of nationwide mobile telephone services in the United States. A new method to allocate licenses was needed desperately.

Finally, eight years after the appearance of the Kwerel–Felker paper, Congress passed the 1993 Omnibus Budget Reconciliation Act, which gave the FCC authority to use competitive bidding to choose from among two or more mutually exclusive applications for an initial license. Kwerel (2004) reports in the foreword to Milgrom's book that one of the first auction design issues that the FCC considered was whether to use an ascending- or sealed-bid mechanism. If precedent were the guide, a sealed-bid design would have certainly won the day, since the Federal government already made use of simple sealed-bid auctions, especially for offshore oil and gas leases. Kwerel explains that the FCC chose the ascending bid mechanism because they believed that providing bidders with more information would likely increase efficiency. Complete details of the development of the auction are provided in Kwerel's foreword.

27.4.2.1 *An historical note*

Although it is generally accepted that the concept of auctions for radio and television licenses was first thought of by a law student named Leo Herzel who proposed it in the *University of Chicago Law Review* in 1951 (see, e.g., Hazlett 2008), the idea had in fact appeared the previous year in the *American Journal of Economics and Sociology* in a short note by Will Lissner, the journal's editor (Lissner 1950). Lissner discusses the decision by the government of South Vietnam to license gaming (i.e., gambling) houses: "As a matter of social policy the licenses had to be limited. Who was to get the privilege? Persons favored by the politicians? No, an auction was held on Nov. 27, 1948 at which the privilege of opening gaming houses in the Saigon-Cholon region went to the highest bidders." Lissner ends with an admonishment regarding a missed opportunity for another type of government auction closer to home, describing the status quo as follows: "Radio and television channel licensees in the United States enjoy as their private income the unearned income produced by their privilege."

27.4.3 The clock auction

The *clock auction* is an ingeniously simple variant on the SAA. Each item has its own associated upward-ticking clock, which is controlled by the auctioneer and indicates the current price for the item, where the clock price for that item applies to all the available units. The clocks are started at low prices, that is, the reserve prices. Each round, bidders are given a fixed amount of time to submit their bids for items they would like to purchase at the current clock prices. Where there is excess demand for an item, the price for that item ticks upward. A new round is started, and the auctioneer requests new bids. When demand equals supply on all items, the auction ends. A significant positive feature of the clock auction is that it obviously precludes the possibility of jump bids, the occurrence of which can forestall or signal competition.

There are two main variants of the clock auction. The first, called the "combinatorial clock auction", was developed during 1999 by David Porter, Stephen Rassenti, Anil Roopnarine, and Vernon L. Smith (2003). At the time, they were testing versions of the Federal Communication Commission's "simultaneous multiple round (SMR) auction"—the original term for the SAA—on hundreds of auction participants. Porter and his colleagues had four objectives in mind: efficiency in achieving all gains from exchange, task simplicity for the bidders, efficacy in handling complexity in the allocation problem, and computational feasibility. An important component of the combinatorial clock auction is that a final phase is required when, after a particular clock price increases, for example from $90 to $100, the demand for that item at the higher price—$100—becomes less than is available. In such cases where there is excess supply for at least one item, and demand exactly equals supply for all the other items, the auctioneer must solve an integer programming problem to find the allocation of items that maximizes his revenue. This integer programming problem is called the "winner determination problem" and is discussed in more detail in Section 27.5.2 below.

The second variant of the clock auction, called the "dynamic clock auction", is due to Ausubel and Cramton (2004). The key difference here is the allowance of *intraround bids*, in which bidders express their demands in each round at all possible combinations of prices between the start-of-round price to the end-of-round price. Thus, in the combinatorial clock auction of Porter et al. (2003) where the price increased from $90 to $100 in a round, a bidder was only able to express the quantity he desired at $90 and at $100. However, in the dynamic clock auction of Ausubel and Cramton, a bidder expresses his desired quantity at *all* prices between $90 and $100. This feature eliminates the need to solve an integer programming problem at the end of the auction.

Although Porter et al. slightly anticipated Ausubel and Cramton in their development of a clock auction, the latter authors admit that the idea goes all the way back to Walras

(1874: Lesson 12), who introduced a theoretical process to study price adjustments in a market involving a number of different commodities. A fictitious auctioneer announces a set of prices for each of the commodities, bidders respond by reporting the quantity of each item they wish to purchase at these prices, and the auctioneer increases or decreases the price on each item according to whether the excess demand is positive or negative. This iterative process, called *tâtonnement* (literally, "groping") continues until a set of prices is reached at which excess demand is zero, and trade occurs only at the final set of prices. Of course, the clock auction is not identical with Walrasian *tâtonnement*. In both types of clock auction, the prices can only rise; in Walrasian *tâtonnement*, the prices can both rise and fall, and in general there can be no guarantee of convergence, as the procedure may cycle indefinitely.

When should the clock auction be employed rather than the SAA? Milgrom (2004: sect. 7.2) explains that when there are a few homogeneous classes of items, each with many goods, the clock can run much faster than the standard SAA; further, it leads to the same near-competitive outcomes with *straightforward bidding*, that is the strategy in which a bidder bids the minimum amount in each round so as to maximize his surplus under the current prices. The earliest practical use of the clock auction is the Electricité de France (EDF) power plant auctions, which employed a dynamic clock auction (Ausubel and Cramton 2004). EDF's use of clock auctions began in 2001, and they have been successfully used by the company in 42 quarterly auctions, selling in total some €10 billion of electricity contracts as of December 2011 (Ausubel 2012).

27.4.4 Further reading

The spectrum auctions are ongoing, and the definitive history of these auctions is yet to be written. However, the reader wishing to acquire a good overview with a minimum of technical detail is directed to the following program of readings: McMillan (1994, 1995), McAfee and McMillan (1996), Cramton (1997, 2006), and Hazlett (2008). Klemperer (2004a: chs 5 and 6) discusses the "third generation" (3G) mobile telecommunication (UMTS) auctions held in 2000 and 2001, where ch. 5 focuses on the European auctions overall, and ch. 6 presents a first-hand account of designing the British 3G auction. For a technical presentation of the simultaneous ascending auction in the context of the spectrum auctions, see the book by Milgrom (2004).

27.5 COMBINATORIAL AUCTIONS

A *combinatorial auction* is an auction in which bidders can place bids on combinations of items, called *packages*, rather than just on individual items. Combinatorial auctions can also include the possibility of *Boolean bids*, package bids joined up by the Boolean connectives: AND, OR, and NOT. Note that the combinatorial clock auction, despite its name, is not a true combinatorial auction, as it does not allow package bids.

Although combinatorial auctions have been discussed in the literature for almost thirty years, most expositions of auctions by economists have little or no mention of them. The reason for this is clear: Combinatorial auctions are cross-disciplinary, requiring an understanding not only of economics but of combinatorial optimization as well. In addition, economists tend to seek equilibrium results, and finding an equilibrium in a combinatorial auction is a daunting task.[18]

Combinatorial auctions provide fertile ground for future research in, and applications of, auction pricing. One important caveat from Milgrom (2004: xiii): "Unlike auctions for a single object, in which efficiency and revenue objectives are usually at least roughly aligned, multi-item auctions can involve radical trade-offs between these two objectives."

27.5.1 Airport time slots

Just as the work of William Vickrey (1961) is widely accepted as the foundation paper in auctions, a strong claim can be made for the work of Stephen Rassenti, Vernon L. Smith, and Robert L. Bulfin (1982), "A Combinatorial Auction Mechanism for Airport Time Slot Allocation", as being the foundation paper in combinatorial auctions. Rassenti and his co-authors considered a topic that was, and is, real and urgent: the allocation of airport runway slots at congested airports.

It is certainly obvious that, when an airline requires a take-off slot for a flight at the originating airport, it also requires a landing slot at the terminating airport and, in cases where there are interconnecting legs, there will also be demands for take-off and landing slots at the intermediate airports. Rassenti et al. addressed the problem of designing a combinatorial sealed-bid auction to serve as the primary market for allocating airport slots for which individual airlines would submit package bids.

Rassenti et al. first formulated the auctioneer's problem as an integer programming problem, which they recognized as a variant of the *set-packing problem*. They next provided an algorithm that yields an allocation to packages that maximizes efficiency and determines individual slot resource prices, which are then used to price packages to winning bidders not exceeding the amount they bid. Finally, the authors conducted a series of experiments where students were paid according to how well they did in the auction.

As pointed out in the introductory chapter of Cramton et al. (2006), the paper of Rassenti et al. is significant not only for being the first on combinatorial auctions, but also for introducing many of the key ideas in the field. These include the mathematical programming formulation of the winner determination problem, the connection between the winner determination problem and the set packing problem, and the related issue of computational complexity. The paper described Boolean bids. It made use of techniques from experimental economics for testing combinatorial auctions. It raised the issue of incentive compatibility in combinatorial auctions. Even the very term "combinatorial auction" was introduced in this paper, as was "smart" exchange or market, a now-standard term. For the intriguing story of the origins of combinatorial auctions arising from airline deregulation in the USA, see Smith (2006). For more on auctions for airspace system resources, see Ball et al. (2006).

---

[18] I am grateful to Itai Sher for this additional point.

27.5.2 The winner determination problem

The idea of a combinatorial auction is simple enough, viz., to allow package bids in addition to individual bids. However, one rather significant problem arises, the notorious *Winner Determination Problem* (*WDP*). This is the auctioneer's problem of labeling bids as either winning or losing so as to maximize the sum of accepted bids, under the constraint that each item can be allocated to at most one bidder. This is a computationally intractable problem, since the WDP is equivalent to the *weighted set packing problem* in combinatorial optimization, and thus is *NP-hard*. What this means in practice is that, for realistically sized problems, the computational burden can be—astonishingly enough—beyond the capability of any existing computer.[19] For more details on the Winner Determination Problem, see Lehmann et al. (2006).

Another difficulty that arises in combinatorial auctions is known as the *threshold problem*. This is where the allowance for package bidding can favour bidders seeking larger packages, since bidders on smaller packages may not have the resources individually to overtake a large package bid, or may not have the ability to coordinate with each other in order to do so.

27.5.3 Combinatorial auctions in practice

Combinatorial auctions have been proposed for assigning universal service support for competing telephone companies (Kelly and Steinberg 2000). They have been used for truckload transportation in the USA (Caplice and Sheffi 2006), bus routes in London (Cantillon and Pesendorfer 2006), school milk programs in Chile (Epstein et al. 2002), and industrial procurement worldwide (Bichler et al. 2006). They were used in the allocation of spectrum in the USA in 2008 and in Britain in 2009.

Most of this probably would not have happened if it were not for the paper of Rassenti et al. (1982). But again, practice preceded theory. Twenty-seven years earlier, auction firm executive Louis McLean (1955) in his article, "Auction Anecdotes", retailed a number of stories about auctions involving lawyers, where three of his stories describe bankruptcy auctions allowing for *entirety bids*. An entirety bid is a package bid on all the items in the auction, where the highest entirety bid wins only if it exceeds the sum of the bids on the individual items. Auctions incorporating entirety bidding are still in common use today, especially for bankruptcy and real estate sales.

Below, we discuss three practical combinatorial auction designs.

27.5.4 Practical combinatorial auction designs

27.5.4.1 The ascending proxy auction

In an *ascending proxy auction*, each bidder reports his preferences for packages or contracts to an electronic *proxy agent* that subsequently bids on the bidder's behalf. Preferences for

---

[19] In some restricted cases the problem becomes tractable, but the restrictions required are invariably draconian. See Rothkopf et al. (1998).

packages or contracts can be much more than reservation prices. A contract could specify, for example, price, quality, and closing date.

The ascending proxy auction works as follows. In each round, if a given bidder is not among the provisional winners, the proxy agent submits the bid that the bidder most prefers according to his reported preferences. The auctioneer then considers all bids from the current and past rounds and selects his most preferred feasible collection of bids according to his objective, under the restriction that accepted bids can include at most one bid from each bidder. The auctioneer's selected bids become the new provisional allocation, the associated bidders are designated provisional winners, and the process repeats until no new bids are submitted.

A simple version of the proxy auction is used on most auction websites—most notably eBay—although a significant difference is that, for the Internet proxy auctions, there is only a single item, and the preferences and contracts consist only of a reservation price for the single item. Milgrom (2004: 52) notes that eBay uses the same rules that describes the outcome of a Vickrey auction for a single good. He points out that the English auction with proxy bidders and the second-price auction are strategically equivalent. For more on ascending proxy auctions, see Ausubel and Milgrom (2006b).

27.5.4.2 *The clock–proxy auction*

The *clock–proxy auction* is, as the name implies, a hybrid between the clock auction and the ascending proxy auction; it was proposed by Ausubel et al. (2006). The auction operates in two phases, where the first phase is a clock auction, in which the bidders directly submit bids, and the second phase is a proxy round, where bidders have a single opportunity to input proxy values, which is then run as a proxy auction. The conclusion of the proxy phase concludes the auction.

In the clock–proxy auction, bids are kept active throughout the auction, that is, no bid withdrawals are permitted. Specifically, bids from the clock phase are also treated as package bids in the proxy phase. All bids are treated as mutually exclusive, that is, as XOR bids. There are activity rules within the clock phase, and between the clock and proxy phases.

What are the advantages of the clock–proxy auction? The clock phase is simple for bidders and provides for price discovery. The proxy phase facilitates efficient allocations and competitive revenues, as well as reducing opportunities for collusion. The clock–proxy auction design has been tested successfully in the field; see Ausubel and Cramton (2004) for more details. It has been further developed and adopted for spectrum auctions in the UK.

27.5.4.3 *PAUSE: Progressive Adaptive User Selection Environment*

Is it possible to design a combinatorial auction mechanism that permits all package bids, yet is computationally tractable for the auctioneer? As demonstrated by Kelly and Steinberg (2000), the answer is yes. By transferring the computational burden of evaluating a package bid to the bidder submitting the bid, the auctioneer no longer faces the Winner Determination Problem. Although in theory a bidder might face a computationally intractable problem, in practice the bidder may have, for some of his bids, a relatively easy problem, and a basic principle in auctions has been that the task of finding an appropriate bid is the responsibility of the bidder. The Kelly–Steinberg design is called PAUSE (Progressive Adaptive User Selection Environment).

PAUSE proceeds in stages. In stage 1, a simultaneous ascending auction is held for all the items, thus facilitating price discovery. After stage 1, bidders can realize their synergies via package bidding. However, the bids on packages cannot be submitted in isolation: each bidder is required to submit them as part of a *composite bid*, which is a set of non-overlapping package bids (including possibly individual bids) that cover *all the items in the auction*. Of course, a bidder will generally be interested in bidding only on a subset of the items in the auction—and in any given round, perhaps only a subset of these. A composite bid consists of the bidder's own bids, together with previously-submitted bids—including composite bids—by any of the bidders.

The following example should make this clear (Figure 27.1). There are six items in the auction: α, β, γ, α', β', γ' (Figure 27.1a). Stage 1 ended with a bid of 5 on each item, respectively, by bidders A, B, C, D, E, F, and consequently a revenue to the auctioneer from these six bids totalling 30 (Figure 27.1b).

In the current round, there are standing bids of 11 by bidder A on the package $\alpha\alpha'$, 20 by bidder B on package $\beta\beta'$, and 14 by bidder C on package $\gamma\gamma'$, with revenue to the auctioneer from these three bids totalling 45 (Figure 27.1c).

Now, two composite bids are submitted simultaneously from Bidders A and B. Bidder A has a high valuation for the package $\alpha\beta\gamma$. His composite bid consists of a bid from himself of 35 on the package $\alpha\beta\gamma$, together with the earlier bids of 5 each on α', β', and γ',

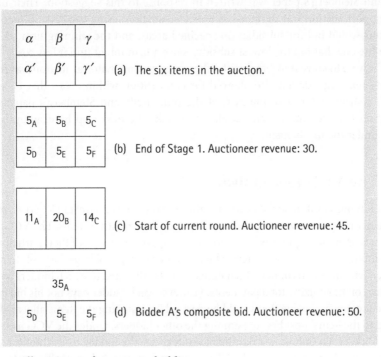

FIGURE 27.1 Illustration of composite bidding

respectively, from bidders D, E, and F, with revenue to the auctioneer of 50 (Figure 27.1d). Bidder B's composite bid (not shown) consists of a bid from himself of 35 on the package $\alpha\alpha'\beta\beta'$, together with the earlier package bid of 14 on $\gamma\gamma'$ from bidder C, with revenue to the auctioneer of 49. Thus, the auctioneer chooses bidder A's composite bid. The auction progresses from there, with bidders submitting composite bids of increasingly higher revenue until the auction terminates.

Composite bidding has three important consequences: (1) the auctioneer is relieved of the computational burden of the winner determination problem (since he needs only choose the highest valid composite bid); (2) each losing bidder can compare his bids with the winning composite bid to see why he lost; and (3) at the conclusion of the auction, no bidder—winning or losing—would prefer to exchange his allocation with that of another bidder. These features are called, respectively: (1) *computational tractability*, (2) *transparency*, and (3) *envy-freeness*.

Kelly and Steinberg introduced the PAUSE mechanism for a specific application in the USA arising from the *Telecommunications Act of 1996*, one of whose requirements was that regulators consider ways to reform the method of providing *universal service* subsidies for high-cost areas. This refers to the situation that had been in place in the USA for many years, in which telephone companies were granted a monopoly to provide telephone service within their operating region, but had a concomitant responsibility to provide basic telephone service to everyone, no matter how costly. This was mitigated by a provision in which the telephone companies would receive subsidies for designated "high cost areas". Around the time of the passage of the Act, several parties advocated that "competitive bidding"—auctions—be used to determine universal service subsidies.

Kelly and Steinberg's paper was written in response to this suggestion. Their universal service support auction was designed as a reverse auction, using the PAUSE mechanism, where firms would bid for subsidies on specified areas, and the winning firm on an area would be the one that bid the lowest subsidy. Since a firm might find it less costly to serve an area if it were to serve it together with other areas, a combinatorial auction was required. Kelly and Steinberg's design also allowed for competition within areas, that is "multiple winners", a strong interest of the FCC at the time. Kelly and Steinberg's paper focused primarily on the auctioneer. Land et al. (2006) take the next step by examining bidder behavior under the mechanism.

27.5.5 The VCG mechanism

The most famous combinatorial auction is the *Vickrey–Clarke–Groves* (*VCG*) *mechanism*, which is a natural generalization of the Vickrey auction to multiple items. The VCG, like the Vickrey auction itself, requires winners to pay the opportunity cost of their participation. It works as follows. Bidders report their valuations for every possible package of items to the auctioneer, who then determines which items are to be allocated to which bidders by solving the problem of maximizing total payments. However, each bidder pays not his bid price but rather the incremental value that would be derived by assigning the items allocated to him according to the items' next best use among the other bidders. Under the VCG mechanism, as in the Vickrey auction, it is a dominant strategy for the bidder to truthfully report his values. For a lucid presentation of the VCG formula, see Ausubel and Milgrom (2006a).

As the name indicates, the Vickrey–Clarke–Groves mechanism evolved from three sources: William Vickrey's (1961) famous paper on auctions, Edward H. Clarke's (1971) work on the pricing of public goods, and Theodore Groves's (1973) contribution to the theory of teams. These three papers were written independently—there are no cross-citations among them—and it is clear that neither Clarke nor Groves had an auction *per se* in mind. Clarke's idea was to propose a solution to the "revealed preference problem" for public goods, a situation in which individuals are induced to hide or understate their true preferences in order to improve their individual welfare while foregoing jointly available potential gains. Groves studied the problem of inducing members of an organization to behave as if they formed a team, where the team head's incentive problem is to choose a set of employee compensation rules that will induce his sub-unit managers to communicate accurate information and take optimal decisions. These two methods merged to become the "Clarke–Groves demand-revealing mechanism" for public goods, which later became the "Vickrey–Clarke–Groves mechanism" or, more simply, the "VCG mechanism". Often, the VCG mechanism is itself referred to as the Vickrey auction.

27.5.5.1 *Weaknesses of the VCG mechanism*

The VCG mechanism has some impressive theoretical strengths. However, its list of weaknesses is distressingly long. In his afterword to his survey of auction theory, Klemperer (2004a) emphasizes that the Vickrey auction is usually impractical even in those private-value contexts in which it is (in theory) efficient. Here is Klemperer's litany of VCG woes:

> Policy makers usually find a Vickrey auction very hard to understand and operate; it often results in bidders with high values paying less for objects than bidders who win identical objects but have lower values for them (which seems strange and unfair to many people); it offers unusual opportunities for collusive behavior which are also hard to guard against; and it sometimes yields low revenues. Furthermore, it is not efficient (and may perform very badly) if bidders are risk-averse or have budget constraints or have common-value elements to their valuations. (Klemperer 2004a: 64)

That the VCG sometimes yields low revenues is a problem of sufficient concern that it has a name: *revenue deficiency*. These low revenues can, in fact, be as low as zero!

As Ausubel and Milgrom (2006a) explain in their felicitously-titled work, "The Lovely but Lonely Vickrey Auction", its weaknesses go a long way to explaining why the VCG mechanism, "so lovely in theory", is "so lonely in practice". On their own list they include the auction's vulnerability to the use of multiple identities by a single bidder. This problem can be described as "shill bids by a bidder", in contrast to "shill bids by the auctioneer" (discussed above in Section 27.3.2). More formally, this ruse is known as *false name bidding* or *pseudonymous bidding* (Yokoo 2006). Yokoo states that, while many auction researchers have discussed problems arising from collusion, compared with collusion a pseudonymous bid is easier to execute on the Internet, since getting another identifier such as an e-mail address is cheap. But Day and Milgrom (2008) point out that the problem is broader than just anonymous Internet auctions. In the US spectrum auctions, several of the largest corporate bidders—including AT&T, Cingular, T-Mobile, Sprint, and Leap Wireless—had at times either contracts with, or financial interests in, multiple bidders bidding in the same auction. As Day and Milgrom explain, this allowed for strategies that would not be possible for a single, unified bidder.

Rothkopf (2007) includes among his "Thirteen Reasons Why the Vickrey–Clarke–Groves Process is Not Practical" two additional weakness not mentioned above: the possibility of alternative equilibria, and problems associated with the disclosure of valuable confidential information.

We next show that, by compromising the loveliness of the Vickrey auction, it became lonely no more.

27.5.5.2 *The generalized second-price auction*

The world's most frequently employed auction is unknown to the overwhelming majority of people who open the auction each day. This probably includes you. Each time you enter a search term into Google, you initiate an auction among a subset of Google's advertisers. The underlying auction mechanism used by Google—and by Yahoo and by most other search engines—is what Edelman et al. (2007) refer to as the *generalized second-price (GSP) auction*. According to Google's June 2009 quarterly report filed with the US Securities and Exchange Commission, over 97 percent of the company's $11.03 billion revenue for the 6-month period ending June 2009 came from advertising, that is, the GSP auction.

Your Google search term generates a page of links most relevant to the search term. No auction is involved here. However, in addition, the right side of your screen displays a list of paid advertisements, called *sponsored links*, that is, web links to advertisers who wish to target ads to you as a consequence of you entering that key word. There are a limited number of positions for sponsored links on the web page. Now, if you are sufficiently interested in a sponsored link that you decide to click on it, this will have two immediate effects: (1) you will be sent to the advertiser's web page, and (2) the advertiser will be charged a fee by Google, viz., the advertiser's individual *price-per-click*. The assumption is that, the higher up on the list a sponsored link appears, the more likely you are to click on it. Some type of *sponsored search auction* is employed to determine the allocation of the ad positions to advertisers and their individualized price-per-click bid price, conditional on your key word. As mentioned above, the mechanism used most often is the generalized second-price auction.

The GSP auction works essentially as follows. For a specific keyword, advertisers submit bids stating their maximum willingness-to-pay each time a user clicks on their sponsored link. The advertiser who bids highest is allocated the first sponsored link position, but his price-per-click is set at the bid price of the second-highest bidder. The advertiser who bid the second-highest price-per-click is allocated the second sponsored link position and pays the third-highest bid price as his price-per-click, and so forth.[20]

The GSP auction obviously generalizes the second-price auction in the sense that if there were only one sponsored link position, then the GSP auction would coincide with the original Vickrey auction. Further, the GSP auction has the feature that a bidder's payment does not directly depend on his own bid. However, as shown by Edelman et al., the GSP

---

[20] This description is in fact a simplification. Google, as well as most other search engines, currently multiply bids by "quality scores", which are often closely related to how good/clickable, the ad is. More detail is provided by Edelman et al. (2007: 257) and Varian (2007).

auction is (not surprisingly) not equivalent to the VCG mechanism. In particular, unlike the VCG, the GSP generally does not have an equilibrium in dominant strategies, and truth-telling is not an equilibrium of GSP. Varian (2007) provides empirical evidence, based on a random sample of 2,425 auctions involving at least five ads each on a particular day, that the equilibria of the GSP auction describe reasonably accurately the properties observed in Google's sponsored search auction.

27.6 SUMMARY AND FUTURE DIRECTIONS

The starting point of auction theory is Vickrey's seminal work, the significance of which has less to do with proposing the Vickrey auction than with founding a field that has now matured to the point where it can explain the limitations of the Vickrey auction. In summary, what basic lessons does that field provide to someone who wishes to engage in auction pricing?

First, know your objective. If it is efficiency, then go ahead and use the Vickrey auction, but be well aware of its weaknesses, too. If your objective is optimality, keep in mind that a slow Dutch auction will likely earn you more revenue than a first-price sealed-bid auction. Whatever your objective, always set a reserve price. If you choose to use a sealed-bid auction, don't even consider a third-price (or fourth- or fifth- etc. price) auction. If you are selling a single item and you want to maximize revenue, reveal any private information you may have, as this will likely yield you more. And if the winner's value can be observed to any extent after the auction's close, than you will probably do better still by making the payment dependent on this observation. In selling multiple items, you may wish to use the simultaneous ascending auction, but when there are only a few kinds of items, each with many units available, an ascending clock auction would probably run faster. If you suspect that some bidders might have significant synergies for at least some of the items, then a combinatorial auction would likely be best of all.

What are the important future directions in auctions? I suggest three:

- *Combinatorial auctions.* The future of auctions is combinatorial auctions. This is due to a convergence of two factors. First, as auctions have increasingly been put into practice, the limits of the usefulness of standard (i.e., non-combinatorial) auctions has been reached for most purposes, since the existence of bidder synergies is so common in many cases. Second, the Internet has made it no longer necessary for the bidders to be assembled in a single location, and at the same time makes the logistics of bid submission relatively easy, even with a large number of items and many bidders. Such large auctions are more likely to involve synergies. However, it is the appropriate choice of combinatorial auction that is the key question here. Testing and evaluation of combinatorial auction procedures is what is now needed.

- *Tie bids.* There is a dirty little word in the world of auctions, and that word is *tie*. Vickrey casually dismissed the issue: "In the case of tie bids we can assume the tie to be broken by a random drawing giving each tied player the same probability of winning." Alas, this obvious procedure, now called *the standard tie-breaking rule*, is not always sufficient to ensure an equilibrium. Under interdependent values, *special tie-breaking rules* might be required. For example, tied bidders might be asked to bid in a second-price auction. In practice, tie-breaking has often been effected via *time stamps*, that is where preference is given to a bid submitted earlier. Time stamps had been used in the US spectrum auctions, but the FCC reverted to the standard tie-breaking rule after observing the alarming practice of bidders rushing to submit their bids in an effort to win ties. Other tie-breaking rules can be more surprising. At the Tsukiji Fish Market in Tokyo, ties are often broken with a quick round of rock–paper–scissors. In Florida, current statutes require that, in any state procurement auction, ties are broken by giving preference to a business that certifies that it has implemented a drug-free workplace program. Well worthwhile would be further study regarding appropriate tie-breaking rules in theory and in practice.

- *Institutional aspects of auctions.* As we have seen, auctions currently have enormous impact in the pricing of fine art (English), spectrum (simultaneous ascending, combinatorial), Internet advertising (generalized second-price), Treasury securities (multiple-unit sealed-bid), and perishable products such as flowers and fish (Dutch). They are a key tool in industrial procurement (English, combinatorial) and government contracting (first-price sealed bid, other sealed-bid). Of course, auctions play a highly significant role in many other areas of commerce. It is this author's hope that some reader of this chapter will embark on an updated study of the institutional aspects of auction procedures and processes, as it would be of considerable value to both the academic and business communities to have a twenty-first-century *tour d'horizon* of what Cassady called "this fascinating method of selling and price making".

For further reading on auctions, three books comprise the gold standard: Krishna (2010), Klemperer (2004a), and Milgrom (2004). All three books provide the rigorous theory; however, the Klemperer and Milgrom volumes are ultimately aimed at applications, especially spectrum allocation, with Milgrom focusing on the American and Klemperer on the European auctions. Milgrom's book also discusses combinatorial auctions, a topic covered thoroughly in the integrated multi-authored book edited by Cramton et al. (2006).[21]

References

Athey, S. and Haile, P. A. (2006) "Empirical Models of Auctions", in R. Blundell, W. K. Newey, and T. Persson (eds), *Advances in Economics and Econometrics, Theory and Applications: Ninth World Congress, Volume II.* Cambridge: Cambridge University Press, 1–45.

Ausubel, L. M. (2012) Private communication, February 6.

—— and Cramton, P. (2004) "Auctioning Many Divisible Goods", *Journal of the European Economic Association* 2/2–3: 480–93.

---

[21] The choice from among four major publishers for the book *Combinatorial Auctions* was determined by the book's editors via auction, where bids were publisher offers to set the retail price of the book, and the publisher offering the lowest price would be selected the winner (MIT Press).

—— and Milgrom, P. (2006a) "The Lovely but Lonely Vickrey Auction", in P. Cramton, Y. Shoham, and R. Steinberg (eds), *Combinatorial Auctions*. Cambridge, MA: MIT Press, 17–40.

—— and —— (2006b) "Ascending Proxy Auctions", in P. Cramton, Y. Shoham, and R. Steinberg (eds), *Combinatorial Auctions*. Cambridge, MA: MIT Press, 79–98.

—— Cramton, P., and Milgrom, P. (2006) "The Clock–Proxy Auction: A Practical Combinatorial Auction Design", in P. Cramton, Y. Shoham, and R. Steinberg (eds), *Combinatorial Auctions*. Cambridge, MA: MIT Press, 115–38.

Avery, C. (1998) "Strategic Jump Bidding in English Auctions", *Review of Economic Studies* 65/2: 185–210.

Ball, M. O., Donohue, G. L., and Hoffman, K. (2006) "Auctions for the Safe, Efficient, and Equitable Allocation of Airspace System Resources", in P. Cramton, Y. Shoham, and R. Steinberg (eds), *Combinatorial Auctions*. Cambridge, MA: MIT Press, 507–38.

Beggs, A. and Graddy, K. (2009) "Anchoring Effects: Evidence from Art Auctions", *American Economic Review* 99/3: 1027–39.

Bergemann, D. and Pesendorfer, M. (2007) "Information Structures in Optimal Auctions", *Journal of Economic Theory* 137/1: 580–609.

Bichler, M. and Steinberg, R. (eds) (2007) Special Issue on E-Auctions for Procurement Operations, *Production and Operations Management* 16/4.

—— Davenport, A., Hohner, G., and Kalagnanam, J. (2006) "Industrial Procurement Auctions", in P. Cramton, Y. Shoham, and R. Steinberg (eds), *Combinatorial Auctions*. Cambridge, MA: MIT Press, 593–612.

Cantillon, E. and Pesendorfer, M. (2006) "Auctioning Bus Routes: The London Experience", in P. Cramton, Y. Shoham, and R. Steinberg (eds), *Combinatorial Auctions*. Cambridge, MA: MIT Press, 573–92.

Capen, E. C., Clapp, R. V., and Campbell, W. M. (1971) "Competitive Bidding in High-Risk Situations", *Journal of Petroleum Technology* 23: 641–53.

Caplice, C. and Sheffi, Y. (2006) "Combinatorial Auctions for Truckload Transportation", in P. Cramton, Y. Shoham, and R. Steinberg (eds), *Combinatorial Auctions*. Cambridge, MA: MIT Press, 539–72.

Carare, O. and Rothkopf, M. (2005) "Slow Dutch Auctions", *Management Science* 51/3: 365–73.

Cassady, R., Jr. (1967) *Auctions and Auctioneers*. Berkeley and Los Angeles: University of California Press.

Charlton, M. (2008) *Oxford University Press*, private communication, July 15 and 21, 2008.

Clarke, E. H. (1971) "Multipart Pricing of Public Goods", *Public Choice* 11: 17–33.

Coase, R. H. (1959) "The Federal Communications Commission", *Journal of Law and Economics* 2: 1–40.

Cramton, P. (1997) "The FCC Spectrum Auctions: An Early Assessment", *Journal of Economics and Management Strategy* 6/3: 431–95.

—— (1998) "The Efficiency of the FCC Spectrum Auctions", *Journal of Law and Economics* 41/2: 727–36.

—— (2006) "Simultaneous Ascending Auctions", in P. Cramton, Y. Shoham, and R. Steinberg (eds), *Combinatorial Auctions*. Cambridge, MA: MIT Press, 99–114.

—— Shoham, Y., and Steinberg, R. (eds) (2006) *Combinatorial Auctions*. Cambridge, MA: MIT Press.

Day, R. and Milgrom, P. (2008) "Core-Selecting Package Auctions", *International Journal of Game Theory* 36/3,4: 393–407.

Edelman, B., Ostrovsky, M., and Schwarz, M. (2007) "Internet Advertising and the General-ized Second-Price Auction: Selling Billions of Dollars Worth of Keywords", *American Economic Review* 97/1: 242–59.

Epstein, R., Henriquez, L., Catalán, J., Weintraub, G. Y., and Martinez, C. (2002) "A Combina-torial Auction Improves School Meals in Chile", *Interfaces* 32/6: 1–14.

FloraHolland (2008) "Smooth integration after merger: FloraHolland satisfied with annual figures for 2007", Press release, Aalsmeer, the Netherlands, May.

Gallego, G., Phillips, R., and Sahin, O. (2008) "Strategic Management of Distressed Inven-tory", *Production and Operations Management* 17/4: 402–15.

Groves, T. (1973) "Incentives in Teams", *Econometrica* 41/4: 617–31.

Hazlett, T. W. (2008) "Optimal Abolition of FCC Spectrum Allocation", *Journal of Economic Perspectives* 22/1: 103–28.

Hendricks, K. and Porter, R. (2007) "An Empirical Perspective on Auctions", in M. Arm-strong and R. Porter (eds), *Handbook of Industrial Organization*, Vol. 3. Amsterdam: Elsevier, 2013–143.

Herodotus (1914) *Histories, Book I (Clio)* (G. C. Macaulay, trans). London: Macmillan.

K (1830) "The Country Belle", *Virginia Literary Museum & Journal of Belles-Lettres, Arts, Sciences &c.* 1/40: 632–40.

Kagel, J. H. and Levin, D. (forthcoming) "Auctions: A Survey of Experimental Research, 1995–2010". In J. Kagel and A. Roth (eds), *Handbook of Experimental Economics, Vol. 2*. Princeton, NJ: Princeton University Press.

Kelly, F. and Steinberg, R. (2000) "A Combinatorial Auction with Multiple Winners for Universal Service", *Management Science* 46/4: 586–96.

Klemperer, P. (2004a) *Auctions: Theory and Practice*. Princeton: Princeton University Press.

—— (2004b) "An Early Example of 'Sniping' in an Auction", *Journal of Political Economy* 112/3.

Krishna, V. (2010) *Auction Theory*, 2nd edn. San Diego, CA: Academic Press.

Kwerel, E. (2004) Foreword to P. Milgrom, *Putting Auction Theory to Work*. Cambridge: Cambridge University Press, xv–xxii.

—— and Felker, A. (1985) "Using Auctions to Select FCC Licensees". Office of Plans and Policy Working Paper No. 16, Federal Communications Commission, Washington, DC, May.

Lambropoulos, S. (2007) "The Use of Time and Cost Utility for Construction Contract Award under European Union Legislation", *Building and Environment* 42/1: 452–63.

Land, A., Powell, S., and Steinberg, R. (2006) "PAUSE: A Computationally Tractable Combinatorial Auction", in P. Cramton, Y. Shoham, and R. Steinberg (eds), *Combinatorial Auctions*. Cambridge, MA: MIT Press, 139–57.

Lazear, E. P. (1986) "Retail Pricing and Clearance Sales", *American Economic Review* 76/1, 14–32.

Learmount, B. (1985) *A History of the Auction*. Iver, UK: Barnard & Learmount.

Lehmann, D., Müller, R., and Sandholm, T. (2006) "The Winner Determination Problem", in P. Cramton, Y. Shoham, and R. Steinberg (eds), *Combinatorial Auctions*. Cambridge, MA. MIT Press, 297–317.

Lissner, W. (1950) "Taxing Privilege in South Viet Nam", *American Journal of Economics and Sociology* 9/4: 444.

Lucking-Reiley, D. (1999) "Using Field Experiments to Test Equivalence Between Auction Formats: Magic on the Internet", *American Economic Review* 89/5: 1063–80.

—— (2000) "Vickrey Auctions in Practice: From Nineteenth-Century Philately to Twenty-First-Century E-Commerce", *Journal of Economic Perspectives* 14/3: 183–92.

McAfee, R. P. and McMillan, J. (1987) "Auctions and Bidding," *Journal of Economic Literature* 25/2: 669–738.

—— and —— (1996) "Analyzing the Airways Auction", *Journal of Economic Perspectives* 10/1: 159–75.

McLean, L. (1955) "Auction Anecdotes", *The Shingle* (Philadelphia Bar Association) 18/3: 65–70.

McMillan, J. (1994) "Selling Spectrum Rights", *Journal of Economic Perspectives* 8/3: 145–62.

—— (1995) "Why Auction the Spectrum?" *Telecommunications Policy* 19/3: 191–9.

Milgrom, P. R. (2004) *Putting Auction Theory to Work.* Cambridge: Cambridge University Press.

—— and Weber, R. J. (1982) "A Theory of Auctions and Competitive Bidding", *Econometrica* 50/5: 1089–122.

Mishra, D. and Parkes, D. C. (2009) "Multi-Item Vickrey-Dutch auctions", *Games and Economic Behavior* 66/1: 326–47.

Moldovanu, B. and Tietzel, M. (1998) "Goethe's Second-Price Auction", *Journal of Political Economy* 106/4: 854–9.

Mueller, M. (1993) "New Zealand's Revolution in Spectrum Management", *Information Economics and Policy* 5/2: 159–77.

Myerson, R. B. (1981) "Optimal Auction Design", *Mathematics of Operations Research* 6/1: 58–73.

New Zealand Ministry of Economic Development (2005) "Spectrum Auction Design in New Zealand", Radio Spectrum Policy and Planning, Resources and Networks Branch, November.

Ockenfels, A., Reiley, D. H., and Sadrieh, A. (2006) "Online Auctions", in T. J. Hendershott (ed.), *Handbook of Information Systems and Economics,* vol. 1. Amsterdam: Elsevier Science, 571–628.

Oren, M. E. and Williams, A. C. (1975) "On Competitive Bidding", *Operations Research* 23/6: 1072–9.

Ortega-Reichert, A. (1968) "Models for Competitive Bidding under Uncertainty", PhD dissertation, Department of Operations Research, Stanford University, Stanford, CA.

Pepys, S. (1926) *The Diary of Samuel Pepys.* Edited by M. Bright and H. B. Wheatley. London: George Bell & Sons.

Perry, M. and Reny, P. J. (1999) "On the Failure of the Linkage Principle", *Econometrica* 67/4: 895–900.

Popkowski Leszczyc, P. T. L. and Rothkopf, M. H. (2010) "Charitable Motives and Bidding in Charity Auctions", *Management Science* 56/3: 399–413.

Porter, D., Rassenti, S., Roopnarine, A., and Smith, V. (2003) "Combinatorial Auction Design", *Proceedings of the National Academy of Sciences* 100/19: 11153–7.

Rassenti, S. J., Smith, V. L., and Bulfin, R. L. (1982) "A Combinatorial Auction Mechanism for Airport Time Slot Allocation", *Bell Journal of Economics* 13/2: 402–17.

Riley, J. G. and Samuelson, W. F. (1981) "Optimal Auctions", *American Economic Review* 71/3: 381–92.

Rothkopf, M. H. (2007) "Thirteen Reasons Why the Vickrey–Clarke–Groves Process is Not Practical", *Operations Research* 55/2: 191–7.

—— Pekec, A., and Harstad, R. M. (1998) "Computationally Manageable Combinational Auctions", *Management Science* 44/8: 1131–47.

Royal Swedish Academy of Sciences (1996) Press release, Stockholm, Sweden, October 8.

Smith, V. L. (2006) Foreword to P. Cramton, Y. Shoham, and R. Steinberg (eds), *Combinatorial Auctions*. Cambridge, MA: MIT Press, xi–xv.

The Times (London) (1788) February 5: 4.

—— (London) (1825) April 29: 4.

—— (London) (1891) September 14: 12.

Tunca, T. I. and Wu, Q. (2009) "Multiple Sourcing and Procurement Process Selection with Bidding Events", *Management Science* 55/5: 763–80.

van den Berg, G. J., van Ours, J. C., and Pradhan, M. P. (2001) "The Declining Price Anomaly in Dutch Dutch Rose Auctions", *American Economic Review* 91/4: 1055–62.

Varian, H. R. (2007) "Position Auctions", *International Journal of Industrial Organization* 25/6: 1163–78.

Vickrey, W. (1961) "Counterspeculation, Auctions, and Competitive Sealed Tenders", *Journal of Finance* 16/1: 8–37.

Walras, Leon (1874) *Eléments d'economie politique pure; ou, théorie de la richesse sociale. (Elements of Pure Economics; or, The Theory of Social Wealth)*. Lausanne: Corbaz.

White House (1994) "Vice President Gore Opens First FCC Broadband Spectrum Auction", Office of the Vice President, press release, Washington, DC, December 5.

Wilson, R. B. (1967) "Competitive Bidding with Asymmetric Information", *Management Science* 13/11: 816–20.

—— (1969) "Competitive Bidding with Disparate Information", *Management Science* 15/7: 446–8.

—— (1979) "Auctions of Shares", *Quarterly Journal of Economics* 93/4: 675–89.

Yokoo, M. (2006) "Pseudonymous Bidding in Combinatorial Auctions", in P. Cramton, Y. Shoham, and R. Steinberg (eds), *Combinatorial Auctions*. Cambridge, MA: MIT Press, 161–87.

Zullo, R. (2006) "Public–Private Contracting and Political Reciprocity", *Political Research Quarterly* 59/2: 273–81.

CHAPTER 28

....

SERVICES ENGINEERING: DESIGN AND PRICING OF SERVICE FEATURES

....

GUILLERMO GALLEGO AND CATALINA STEFANESCU

28.1 INTRODUCTION

....

US airlines achieved a startling turnaround in 2009. Profits rose to $2.3 billion after a loss of $3.3 billion the year before. Also during 2009, the airlines collected $2.7 billion in baggage fees (US Bureau of Transportation Statistics 2010). In other words, by charging separately for a service once associated with the price of a ticket, the airlines turned a potential loss into a profit. Unbundling baggage handling from ticket prices also served consumers. By ensuring the industry's financial health, it allowed airlines to offer a wider selection of flights. It also helped carriers keep ticket prices low, directly benefiting those who chose to take carry-on luggage instead of checking their bags.

Unbundling is an example of the rapidly emerging field of services engineering. Services engineering involves designing and pricing derivative services to appeal to broader markets and to improve resource utilization. Other examples include:

- companies that offer discounts to customers who book a ticket, hotel room, and car at the same time;
- tour operators that substitute similar hotels based on their price and availability;
- providers that offer discounts conditional on their right to recall the service or offer an alternate service;
- rental companies that sell excess cars on name-your-own-price (bidding) websites; and
- staffing agencies that offer options to provide a given number of programmers for large projects.

The resemblance between the terms "services engineering" and "financial engineering" (and use of the word "derivative") are not accidental. Services engineering strives to create equivalents of such financial derivatives as options, puts, calls, bundling, and unbundling to modify a core service. Like financial engineering, services engineering is a strategic tool that helps service providers design portfolios of offerings to manage risk, improve resource utilization, and boost revenues. Service providers can use services engineering to design and price derivative services to segment markets in order to offer differentiated products and reach customers that otherwise would not be interested in the company's offerings. Customers benefit from a wider range of services and price points, enabling them to tailor their purchases to their budget. Services engineering[1] is a strategic tool that can lead to significant increases in profits and market share.

So what, exactly, is services engineering? In essence, it involves the virtual or operational modification of an underlying service. Virtual modifications are real (non-financial) options that affect the fulfillment or consumption of a service. Service providers can use them to mitigate supply or demand risk. For example, a company may obtain fulfillment options from customers that allow it to substitute one room for another or place a customer on one of several flights. It can then sell this flexibility in the form of consumption options to customers willing to pay a higher price for the right to decide which room or flight they want at the last minute. Real options can also be used to sell recurrent services to customers with heterogeneous usage rates, and form the basis for contracts with access fees and limited usage allowances.

Operational modifications involve adding (bundling) or removing (unbundling) ancillary services from core services. This creates varied versions of the service that appeal to different market segments. Bundling involves selling two or more services in packages that appeal to a range of market segments that value these service combinations differently. Unbundling consists of separating service features and charging separate prices for each. Both approaches can be used in "versioning", offering a line of services distinguished from one another by their combination of features as well as usage or purchasing restrictions that differentiate their quality.

In addition to helping manage resources and risk, customer segmentation using derivative products enables service providers to reap many of the advantages of secondary markets. Sellers can usually limit the resale of services in secondary markets, since unlike physical products, services cannot be stored and must be used by a certain date and time. A particular case are "experience goods" (Nelson 1970), which include healthcare, travel, entertainment, and performing arts. These products are highly intangible and cannot usually be experienced or tested before purchase. This limits opportunities for temporal arbitrage and secondary market resale of these products, although a flourishing secondary market for event tickets has emerged in spite of preventive efforts of primary providers and lawmakers (Happel and Jennings 1989).

From a marketing perspective, services engineering is analogous to the problem of developing the rules of a transaction game (Shugan 2005). By attempting to match most efficiently the needs and preferences of all partners in the transaction (buyers and sellers), the design of services determines both the likelihood of desirable outcomes and whether players will choose to play.

---

[1] Services engineering is a broad term used by different communities. IBM, for example, uses the phrase Service Science, Management, and Engineering (SSME) to describe an interdisciplinary approach to the study, design, and implementation of service systems. IBM global services provide call centers and tech support, so the study of stochastic networks is also a part of the concept. From a computer science perspective, services engineering concerns the development of software engineering methodologies including the specification, modeling, and architecture and verification functions.

This chapter addresses these issues in depth. In Section 28.2, we discuss virtual service modifications, a variety of real options that improve profits by segmenting customers. These include fulfillment options, consumption options, and real options for access services. In Section 28.3, we investigate operational service modifications. These include bundling, unbundling, and versioning. We also introduce concepts from financial engineering to illuminate the problem of designing and pricing bundles. In Section 28.4, we discuss ways to apply services engineering to revenue management and customer relationship management. We discuss our conclusions in Section 28.5.

28.2 REAL OPTIONS

Services engineering strategies based on real options can be classified in three broad categories. These consist of fulfillment options for the seller, consumption options for the buyer, and options used for accessing services. In this section we discuss these three categories, providing definitions and actual or potential applications.

28.2.1 Fulfillment options

Fulfillment options reflect seller rights to use different fulfillment alternatives. Some examples are upgrading, upselling, and bumping customers. Fulfillment options are designed to broker flexibility between flexible buyers with low willingness-to-pay and inflexible buyers with high willingness-to-pay. Fulfillment options reduce imbalances between demand and capacity, so they are particularly useful when capacity is limited and customers have heterogeneous consumption flexibility. The use of options may result in demand induction as customers who would otherwise not have considered buying the product respond to incentives. This can be helpful for companies even when capacity is ample. The use of options, however, may also result in demand cannibalization if customers form expectations about the likelihood of different fulfillment alternatives. Consequently, the design of fulfillment options must carefully trade off the benefits with the potential downside.

28.2.1.1 Callable services

Callable products have been proposed by Gallego et al. (2008) as a strategy for a company to maximize revenue from selling constrained capacity to customers with large heterogeneity in their willingness-to-pay. This is particularly relevant when selling in a market where customers with higher reservation prices arrive later than customers with lower reservation prices, as is the case in the leisure, entertainment, and travel industries. The concept is also useful in supply chain settings where there are customers who are willing to pay a significant premium for shorter order fulfillment leadtimes. Customer heterogeneity in willingness-to-pay for different fulfillment leadtimes gives rise to advance demand information, which helps the producer better plan for its inventory and distribution system; see Fisher (1997), Chen (2001), Gallego and Özer (2001), Özer (2003) and references therein.

A callable service embeds an option for the provider to recall the capacity at a pre-specified price before the service is delivered. Callable services are either sold at a discount or with an enticing recall price premium in order to compensate the customer for the potential inconvenience of having the service recalled; they can also be sold without a discount and with a small recall price when demand greatly exceeds supply. Callable services are appealing to customers with relatively low service valuations, or those with flexible consumption timing. For example, a cruise line could sell discounted callable cabins to flexible, price sensitive customers and later recall them if and when full rate demand exceeds available capacity. For this to work, the recall price needs to be, of course, lower than the full rate. A customer whose service is recalled may be offered an alternative service and a compensation. In the context of supply chain management, callable services may be sold to customers with predictable demands who operate with low margins. The predictability of their demands allows them to opt for lower prices and long leadtimes, while their low margins make a modest recall premium attractive. The flexibility gained by selling callable services can be used to accommodate the needs of customers with unpredictable demands who operate with high margins, as those customers are usually willing to pay a significant premium for shorter delivery leadtimes.

Callable services can also be an effective tool to prevent or mitigate the formation of secondary markets. In the entertainment industry, for example, primary providers of premium events often run out of capacity early on, with tickets later selling at much higher prices in the secondary market. By selling callable services when tickets first become available for sale, primary providers can discourage arbitrageurs from loading themselves with capacity that may later be recalled. In addition, selling callable services allows the primary provider to participate in the secondary market by recalling previously sold capacity as needed.

Gallego et al. (2008) show that, under mild conditions, callable products are a riskless source of additional revenue to the capacity provider and can be a win–win strategy for the provider and for both low and high valuation customers. They also show that callable products may induce demand from customers who may find the recall price just attractive enough to purchase a product that otherwise they would have not purchased. The concept of callable services is related to the strategy of *contingent pricing* (Biyalogorsky and Gerstner 2004), arising in transactions where the price is contingent on whether the seller succeeds in obtaining a higher price for the service during the period between sale and fulfillment. They show that contingent pricing increases the efficiency of resource allocation since the service is eventually sold to the customers with the highest reservation price.

28.2.1.2 *Flexible services*

A flexible service is a virtual offer involving the guarantee of receiving one out of a set of several alternative services, typically substitutes (Gallego and Phillips 2004). The seller decides the exact assignment close to or at the time of fulfillment on the basis of demand information acquired during the selling process. Flexible services are often, but not necessarily, sold at a discount in order to compensate the customer for the uncertainty of the final service assignment. For example, a customer may advance purchase a flexible airline ticket that guarantees air transportation between London and New York on a certain date in one of the three morning scheduled flights. The day before travel, the airline assigns the customer to one of these flights based on the realized demand. Since the airline is free to assign passengers who have purchased the flexible service to any of the three morning flights, the airline can do better at accepting higher fare requests for these flights. Although flexible services are similar to callable services, they expose customers to different forms of uncertainty. While the flexible product guarantees fulfillment within a set of pre-specified alternatives, buyers of callable services are not guaranteed the delivery of the service. Flexible products are also close to the opaque services discussed later in this chapter.

Flexible services can also be sold without an upfront discount when customers have a preference for a specific choice, with compensation occurring only if the customer is fulfilled with an alternative. The concept of flexible services can be pushed further to encompass conditional upgrades in the form of free put options on higher quality services. For example, at the time of purchase, a customer who selects a $100 standard room over a $150 deluxe room with an ocean view, may be enticed to agree to pay an extra $15 per night for the deluxe room if he is given an upgrade at the time of check-in. This is a flexible service sold at $100 per night, where the alternatives are the standard room and the deluxe room with the customer agreeing to pay $15 per night if he is upgraded. If the customer agrees, then the provider has the right but not the obligation to sell the deluxe room for $115 per night.

Flexible services are commonly used in industries such as Internet advertising, tour operators, and air cargo. They are also used in electricity markets where customers may agree to have a device that can remotely and intermittently shut down their air conditioners in exchange for a discount on their monthly fees. The concept of flexible services has parallel implications in supply chain management. In this setting some customers will be willing to accept a larger variance in leadtimes in exchange for a lower price, and this may allow the provider to offer more predictable leadtimes to customers willing to pay for it.

Although the main purpose of selling flexible and callable services is to improve capacity utilization by reducing the imbalance between capacity and demand, they also have the potential benefit of inducing new demand for the provider's services. When the price for the flexible or callable service is sufficiently low, it may attract customers who otherwise would not be interested in any of the provider's services at their full price. On the other hand, flexible and callable services may cannibalize demand from customers who would have otherwise advance purchased one of the specific alternatives. The key here is to carefully limit the number of services sold in order to avoid buying more flexibility than is needed.

The pricing of flexible services is an interesting research topic. Post (2010) proposes offering a large set of alternative services and then charging customers to reduce the consideration set. Customers are allowed to eliminate all but three alternatives and are guaranteed to receive one of the non-eliminated alternatives. As customers pay to eliminate undesirable alternatives, they are essentially paying to reduce consumption risk. When the price is right, the revenues from eliminated alternatives can be a significant source of profit for the provider. Some airlines have implemented the pricing strategy suggested by Post's company Sigma-Zen. Germanwings, for example, proposes blind bookings that typically consist of eight or more destinations within a certain theme such as "culture" or "sun and beach" at deeply discounted prices (typically €20), giving potential customers the ability to remove from the choice set all but three destinations at a cost of €5 for each removed destination.

Flexible services are related to *probabilistic goods* which are offers involving the probability of obtaining any one of a set of multiple distinct services. Fay and Xie (2008) show that, by introducing buyer uncertainty in the service assignment, a probabilistic selling strategy may increase capacity utilization through reducing the imbalance between capacity and demand. Unlike selling flexible services, however, in probabilistic selling the service assignment is confirmed immediately after the purchase, and before the seller has acquired any new information about demand.

28.2.1.3 *Upgrades and upsells*

Upgradeable services are an alternative mechanism for reducing capacity and demand imbalance and improving capacity utilization (Biyalogorsky et al. 2005). They are relevant for capacity providers who offer several services differentiated by their quality attributes. The seller of an upgradeable service has the option of replacing it at the time of fulfillment with a more desirable substitute from a pre-specified set of alternatives. Gallego and Stefanescu (2007) study different upgrade mechanisms and show that, as implicit price reductions, upgrades and upsells help balance demand and supply by shifting excess capacity from higher to lower quality services. Upgrades are frequent in package delivery and other transportation activities that offer priority options at differentiated prices, and in the semiconductor manufacturing industry where fast chips are sometimes used to fulfill demand for slower chips. They are also common in the leisure, travel, and entertainment industries, where the more desirable alternative could be a larger hotel room, a higher flight cabin class, or a better concert or theater seat. Upgrades can also be used by other providers of services such as web-farms that offer different service qualities with promised up-times. Customers who opt out from paying a premium for gold service may still receive a high level of service except for peak demand periods.

Besides offering free upgrades, companies sometimes entice customers to buy up to a more desirable service by offering attractively priced substitutes at the time of fulfillment. This upsell practice is common for car rental companies, hotels, and airlines. When the customer agrees to an upsell, he pays less than the full price for the more desirable service, but more than the price of the less-desirable service initially chosen.

While upgrades are frequently practiced by primary providers of capacity, resellers often also have an additional incentive to use upgrades extensively. The resellers' profit margins on different services are usually heterogeneous; in particular, resellers may sell both their own services and services on commission from other providers. In these situations resellers have an incentive to fulfill demands with desirable substitutes bringing higher commissions, thus effectively offering an upgrade. This often happens in on-line brokering of perishable capacity, such as in the secondary market of event tickets, and to a lesser extent with on-line travel agents that carry large inventories. The practice is also pervasive in standard retail environments where customers are steered to higher margin products through coupons or recommendations.

Gallego and Stefanescu (2007) show that access to commission services can significantly improve the reseller's profits even though direct sales of such services only account for a small profit increase. This is due to the fact that resellers can divert demand from the primary provider's services to their own services with higher margins, by enticing customers to upgrade or upsell. However, an excessive use of upgrades may result in low net sales of services belonging to primary providers, damaging their long-term relationship with the reseller. This can be avoided by agreeing to minimum sale volumes of any given service sold on commission.

The efficient design of upgrade and upsell mechanisms provides a rich topic for future research. One issue to be investigated is the definition of the alternative service sets for each upgradeable service, so that certain fairness criteria are met. Another issue is the optimal timing of upgrades and upsells over the selling horizon; companies have an incentive to delay upgrade decisions until more demand information has been acquired closer to fulfillment time, but doing so motivates customers to delay purchases and thus increases demand uncertainty. More research is also needed on the link between the timing and design of upgrades and the customer's expectation formations, as frequently upgraded services may become more attractive and induce customers to deliberately purchase lower quality services, further increasing the imbalance between demand and supply.

A related research topic of a more strategic nature is optimal capacity design that anticipates the use of upgrades. If the capacity provider knows that a higher quality service can be used to fulfill demand for an inferior service, he may decide to increase the capacity of the higher quality service at the expense of the lower quality service. This is particularly true if the difference in cost is small. As an example, car rental companies routinely buy more full size than compact cars. Capacity providers need to balance this additional flexibility against the extra cost and potential for customer expectation formation, when deciding the optimal capital allocation between different service quality levels.

28.2.1.4 Bumping customers

Bumping customers from a previously purchased service involves assigning them at consumption time a different service or no service at all. The probability of bumping is not explicitly priced into the service cost and sometimes customers are bumped against their will, therefore bumping is strictly a fulfillment option on the part of the capacity provider, rather than a service design feature.

Bumping is often a consequence of *overbooking* (taking more bookings than available capacity), a strategy frequently used by hotels, airlines, and other service providers as a way of hedging against cancellations and no-shows. Airlines, for instance, bump travelers by finding volunteers to give up their seats in exchange for cash and/or loyalty points and alternative accommodation. Bumping also occurs in supply chains when manufacturing or transportation is purposely delayed in order to accommodate emergency orders for higher margin products or customers. Such delays cause production and distribution disruptions downstream that can be mitigated by selling callable or flexible products.

When the bumping costs to the provider are smaller than the difference between the lowest and the highest price, the company may continue selling high price services after demand has exceeded capacity, since it is feasible to free capacity by bumping low price customers without hurting revenues. However, when customers are involuntarily denied there are also indirect costs in terms of ill-will. Airlines try to avoid ill-will by holding auctions to identify volunteers willing to take a different flight in exchange for suitable compensation, for example coupons for future flights; see Phillips (2005: 208–9). However, bumping costs have increased in some industries due to regulation; for example, the Denied Boarding Compensation Regulation for airlines has been active in the European Union since February 2005, limiting the benefits and the applicability of bumping beyond what is needed to hedge against cancellations and no-shows. This shift paves the way for callable services that give capacity providers the flexibility of the bumping strategy without the ill-will of involuntarily denied customers.

28.2.1.5 *Opaque services*

Most of the fulfillment options discussed so far pertain to primary providers of capacity. In contrast, opaque services are mechanisms that allow flexibility to brokers selling capacity from different providers, often without revealing their sources. For opaque services, the identity of the service providers and some other service attributes are concealed from consumers until after purchase (Fay 2008). For example, the opaque service may be accommodation in a certain city during a specified period of time, but the alternative hotels may be hidden from potential buyers. Primary capacity providers prefer to keep their identities opaque in order to mitigate demand cannibalization and potential adverse impact on brand image. The customer pays a discounted price for the opaque service and, once the purchase is completed, the reseller can assign to the customer any specific service that meets the revealed characteristics. Opaque selling is used in the travel industry by Hotwire and Priceline through which the customers can, for example, book a room from Hilton, Sheraton, or Marriott and the hotel identity is only revealed after purchase. The pricing models of the two firms are different—Hotwire offers a posted price for the opaque service, while Priceline uses the "Name Your Own Price" model where the customers place binding bids for the opaque service.

Jiang (2007) argues that opaque selling is a form of price discrimination through which firms can segment the market by charging a discounted price in the opaque market and a published full price in the full information market. Fay (2008) shows that opaque selling may lead to market expansion and reduce price rivalry, except in the case of industries with little brand loyalty.

From the customer's perspective, opaque services are similar to probabilistic goods (Fay and Xie 2008) and flexible services, since in all these cases the customer faces uncertainty about which service he will eventually receive. The difference is that in the case of flexible services and probabilistic goods the customer knows the exact set of alternatives, and in the case of opaque services he does not.

Due to different incentives, flexible services are designed to be mostly sold by primary capacity providers, while opaque services are designed to be mainly offered by capacity brokers. Primary providers could also sell opaque services; however, since in this case all the alternatives in the opaque set would belong to the same capacity provider, the opaque services cannot be too deeply discounted without having a negative impact on the brand image. For example, upscale hotel chains with several hotels in the same city may be reluctant to offer a deeply discounted opaque service consisting of rooms in any of their hotels when the difference between the opaque price and their full published price is too large. This creates an incentive for primary capacity providers to offer flexible rather than opaque services.

Similarly, flexible services could also be sold by capacity brokers by revealing the set of alternatives. However, primary providers may be unwilling to supply services if their identity is revealed, for example due to the existence of higher published prices for these services in the full information market. This creates an incentive for capacity brokers to offer opaque rather than flexible services.

Several topics for future research here include the tradeoff between the opaque price and the amount of information revealed prior to the purchase, the optimality of opaque selling under competition between several resellers of opaque services, and opaque selling strategies under models of customer learning and expectation formations.

28.2.2 Consumption options

Consumption options reflect buyer rights and are designed to preserve or enhance consumption flexibility. Some examples are refundability and exchangeability features. Consumption options are particularly relevant for services where advance booking is involved. Customers' service valuation typically changes over time. When purchase and consumption decisions are separated in time, buyers may not know at the time of purchase which alternative they will prefer at the time of consumption. Some of these customers may be willing to pay a premium to preserve choice flexibility. Indeed, Guo (2006) shows that buyer uncertainty about service valuation offers an incentive to reserve consumption flexibility by purchasing multiple items, a practice prevalent in many retail settings (for example, packaged goods). When the service price is high enough to preclude the purchase of multiple items, consumption flexibility can alternatively be ensured through the built-in features of the service itself. These consumption options allow the seller both to segment the customers according to their uncertainty about future service valuations, and to customize the services to better fulfill buyers' preferences.

28.2.2.1 *Optional services*

Optional services offer customers a menu of pre-specified alternatives to be selected at a given future period for consumption. For example, a customer could buy an optional opera ticket that would allow him to see a performance on either evening between April 13–15. Within a certain time period (say, a day) before the earliest performance date, the customer would have to decide on the chosen date and inform the theater of his choice. While the customer may be able to achieve the same outcome by buying just one refundable ticket for the most likely performance date and exchanging it later for a different date if the need arises, he would not have the guarantee of finding capacity still available for the alternative performance dates at the time of the decision. Therefore, optional services add value by offering the guarantee that a seat would be available, and can thus be sold at a premium over individual service prices.

From the customer's perspective, optional services are the mirror image of flexible services from the capacity provider's perspective. As in the case of callable and refundable services, the cost is incurred here by the party who has more flexibility—the buyer in the case of optional services sold at a premium, and the seller in the case of flexible services sold at a discount.

The choice of the alternative set for an optional service can belong both to the provider and to the customer. The seller may offer a "set menu" of optional services, or the buyer may build his own optional service at the time of purchase (and only a subset of the company's services may be available for inclusion in an optional service, as in the case of upgrades). Letting the customer design his own optional service makes more sense, and an interesting research question here is to optimize the price of optional services when they can be hedged by selling flexible and callable services.

28.2.2.2 Refundability options

A service can be fully, partially, or not at all refundable. For example, a partially refundable train or airline ticket may be sold as an (x, p, t) option where x is a non-refundable deposit that gives the right to the customer to travel by paying p at time t before departure. Ignoring the time-value of money, this option is equivalent to a total fare $x + p$ where p is refundable if the customer decides not to travel for any reason. The special cases $(x, 0, 0)$ and $(0, p, 0)$ correspond to non-refundable and fully refundable fares. Gallego and Sahin (2007a) show that the use of partially refundable fares can significantly increase revenues over the best capacity allocation between non-refundable and fully refundable fares. They also show that, properly used, options are socially optimal and provide a mechanism to allocate surplus between the consumers and the capacity provider. This result extends to the sale of different quality goods. In the supply chain management context, refundability options can be used as procurement options to hedge against uncertain demand. If demand turns out to be high then the options are exercised, otherwise the only cost is the non-refundable part. Gallego and Sahin (2007b) show that partially refundable fares are the only equilibria for the Stackelberg game between two providers. Moreover, they prove that the revenues obtained by using partially refundable fares Pareto-dominate the revenues from fully refundable fares.

Refundable services contracts can be used as an alternative to spot pricing to sell recurrent services with random costumer valuations and costs. Repair services are a good example. They are typically sold at spot prices or through warranties. Spot prices correspond to a contract of the type $(0, p(Z))$, where $p(Z) > Z$ is the repair price for a failure of random cost Z. Traditional warranties are of the form $(x, 0)$, where x is paid upfront to fully cover any qualified failure over a certain time horizon $[0, T]$. User heterogeneity makes traditional warranties expensive for low usage customers. This results in selection bias towards higher usage customers, which requires traditional warranties to be priced high (Hollis 1999). A "first-best" upper bound on expected profits from heterogeneous customers can be theoretically achieved if different options of the form (x_k, Z) were sold to customers with different usage rates. Here x_k is the upfront price paid by segment k customers that gives them the right to obtain repair services over $[0, T]$ at the actual random cost Z rather than at spot prices $p(Z)$. Unfortunately it is not possible to offer the menu (x_k, Z) without violating incentive compatibility constraints which are designed to make sure that customers prefer buying the contract designed for them. It is possible, however, to offer an optimal contingent contract where customers pay r upfront for the right to repair the *next* failure at the random cost Z. The upfront payment r is refundable up to the point of the next failure. By selecting r appropriately, it is possible to achieve the first-best expected profits, see Gallego (2010), when customers' valuations are identically distributed and failure rates are heterogeneous. The key here is that r is designed to make it incentive compatible for customers to re-purchase the contingent contract after each failure. Customers with higher failure rates naturally pay more as they have to buy the contract more frequently.

28.2.2.3 *Exchangeability options*

A service can be fully, partially, or not at all exchangeable. Usually, exchangeability is not restricted in terms of alternatives, but it is subject to available capacity. The customer may need to pay a fixed exchangeability fee, plus the difference in price between the service bought initially and the desired service. An exchangeable service is thus sold as an (x, p, t) option where x is the exchangeability fee, p is the price of the original alternative chosen, and t is the time before fulfillment when the option expires. For example, a customer may pay p for a theater ticket for a performance on 15 April, with the option of exchanging it later (say, until 13 April) against a fee of x for a performance of the same play on a different day. The customer will also have to pay any difference in price between the ticket originally chosen and the new alternative. The special cases $(0, p, 0)$ and (∞, p, t) correspond to fully exchangeable and non-exchangeable services.

There are close links between exchangeability, refundability options, and optional services. A refundable service is also exchangeable, since the customer is reimbursed for the original purchase and may always choose to buy another service. The converse is not always true; a service can be fully exchangeable and non-refundable, as in the case, for example, of some train and airline tickets. Exchangeable services also differ from optional services; unlike optional services, where the customer buys the option of consuming any service of his choice from a set of alternatives without further cost, exchangeable services do not guarantee either that capacity for the desired alternative will be available, or that the price will be the same. To our knowledge, no research exists on the optimal design and pricing of broad service menus with different exchange options and fees.

28.2.3 Real options for access services

A particular case of real options inherently designed into services consists of access plans for services. One example is a three-part tariff (x, c, p), where customers pay a regular (e.g., monthly) access fee x that covers an allowance c of a certain number of units access, after which they pay variable costs p depending on usage. The tariff (x, c, p) is commonly used in cell phone plans, the tariff (x, c, ∞) corresponds to calling cards, and the tariff $(x, \infty, 0)$ is practiced by gyms and golf club memberships that provide unlimited usage but may charge for ancillary services. The tariff $(x, 0, p)$ is common for warehouse clubs where the access fee gives the right to purchase goods at discounted price p. Certain professional or social clubs memberships are also of this form.

The real options embedded in access services induce an admission control problem for customers as they decide on usage levels, and can shape their purchasing and consumption behavior. For example, in the case of cell phone plans the customers' admission control problem consists of deciding whether or not to engage in a call at any time. Once the allowance is exhausted, the decision is simple because a customer would make or take a call only if its value exceeds the marginal cost p. However, prior to exhausting the allowance the problem of admitting calls is very similar to the admission control problem known as revenue management, practiced by providers of perishable capacity, as their decisions are made in terms of the remaining capacity and time-to-go. Notice that the admission control policy that the customers would use as a result of solving their admission control problem affects the total volume of calls. This itself depends on the parameters of the calling plan. By modeling the customers' expected utility of a plan $U(x, c, p)$ and taking into account the distribution of customers in the population, providers can design a menu of tariffs (x_i, c_i, p_i), $i = 1, \ldots, n$ to maximize expected revenues subject to incentive compatibility and capacity constraints. The tariffs employed may be driven by optimality conditions or by business rules. For example, they can share a common value of p as is the case when selling cell phone plans.

The design and pricing of limited warranties also share similar features through embedded real options. Limited warranties allow a limited number of claims, and require customers to solve an admission control problem to decide whether or not to claim a failure. The solution to this problem allows issuers to understand their customers' expected costs and to design and price a menu of warranties with varying deductibles, co-pays, or claim limits. These warranty services would appeal to customers with different usage and therefore different failure rates. Since customers self-select from the menu of available warranties according to their estimated usage, these policies help avoid the problem of traditional warranties which lose money on high-usage customers if priced low, and lose market share if priced high. Notice that these types of warranties are related to three-part tariffs, in that they have an access fee and an allowance (number of claims) but they do not have a constant variable cost for failures out-of-warranty.

Residual value warranties are contracts with a refund schedule that depends on the number of failures that are claimed (Gallego et al. 2010). For example, the contract may offer a refund only if there are no claims, or offer a smaller refund if there are just one or two claims. Residual value warranties allow the providers to appeal to a large share of the market with one single service. Indeed, the net cost of these policies is low for low-usage customers (as they receive larger refunds) and higher for high-usage customers, again avoiding the problem of traditional warranties. The admission control problem for customers who purchase residual value warranties is to maximize the expected refund net of the cost of failures paid out-of-pocket. At the time of a failure, the customers should compare the out-of-pocket repair cost with the marginal cost to the refund schedule. Notice that these contracts are also related to three-part tariffs with options, in that they have an access fee, either a finite or an infinite allowance, and a refund schedule that depends on the number of claims.

The pricing and design of access services with real options should take into account the insights from the behavioral economics literature on customers' valuation processes, and their implicit models and biases. Some relevant references are the contract design article by DellaVigna and Malmendier (2006), the article on tariff-choice biases by Lambrecht and Skiera (2006), and the book by Rubinstein (1988) that attempts to model bounded rationality.

28.3 BUNDLING, UNBUNDLING, AND VERSIONING

Operational strategies for derivative services include bundling, unbundling, and versioning the service by adding or removing some of its features or by imposing usage or purchasing restrictions. In this section we discuss and illustrate these three strategies.

28.3.1 Bundling

Bundling is the practice of selling two or more services in a package. This is essentially a segmentation strategy based on the fact that varying customer segments have different valuations for combinations of services. Bundling is practiced across a wide range of services and it is often used as a strategic competitive tool (Stremersch and Tellis 2002). Internet service providers offer bundles of web access, e-mail, search and instant messaging software, and web hosting. A premium bank account is typically a bundle of separate savings and checking accounts, debit and credit cards, access to investment advice, retirement plans, insurance cover, and currency transactions (Koderisch et al. 2007). Restaurants offer fixed-price menus which are bundles of appetizers, main courses, and desserts that cost less than ordering à la carte[2] or may contain items not found on the regular menu. Orchestras, theaters, and sports teams bundle different concerts, performances, or games tickets into season tickets. In the pharmaceutical industry, firms bundle their branded products with generics which are then sold to managed care buyers. In the transportation industry, any round trip ticket is effectively a bundle of two one-way tickets. Transportation companies offer bundles of different travel-related services such as airport transfers, car rental, hotel accommodation, or activities at the destination such as museum visits and tour guides.

Properly priced, bundles can lead to increased sales and reduced costs. Producers often have decreasing costs through economies of scale from increased sales, and through economies of scope from bundling interrelated services. The savings are higher when bundling products with low marginal costs and high development costs such as software or information goods (Bakos and Brynjolfsson 1999), than when bundling products with high marginal costs such as consumer durables. Cost savings are also relevant for consumers who face less choice complexity and may prefer the convenience of buying the bundle. Harris and Blair (2006) find that the consumers' preference for acquiring the bundle versus buying individual items is greater in the cases when choosing the bundle reduces search effort, particularly among consumers less motivated to process information.

In practice, there are two main forms of price bundling (Adams and Yellen 1976). In *pure bundling* only the bundle is offered for sale and the component services cannot be bought individually. For example, European ski resorts during peak season only offer one-week accommodation packages, and weekend or single night accommodation in most hotels cannot be purchased separately. Pure bundling is often used to achieve certain strategic objectives. Microsoft created a pure bundle of its Internet Explorer software with its

---

[2] These bundles may have a quantity discount component built into them.

Windows operating system—this was a major issue in the Microsoft anti-trust case, but it allowed the company to increase its share of the web-browsing market from 7 percent in mid-1996 to more than 90 percent in 2007. In the pharmaceutical industry, Pfizer planned to bundle its new heart treatment drug Torcetrabip with Lipitor, the company's best selling cholesterol-lowering drug (*New York Times*, March 7, 2005), and this pure bundling strategy would effectively extend the patent of Lipitor. Pure bundling is also sometimes used to sell distressed inventory whose potential to be sold at a normal price has passed or will soon pass. For example, by offering a pure bundle of hotel rooms and air tickets, capacity providers can sell distressed inventory at a lower price without offering that price to customers who are only interested in the hotel or in the air tickets.

In *mixed bundling* both the bundle and the individual services are offered for sale. Often, consumers pay the full price for a first "leader" product (usually an innovative product) and receive a discount for additional (usually mature) products. *Value-added bundling* is a variation on mixed bundling; instead of offering a discount on the bundle, the firm builds-in an additional feature that is attractive to price-sensitive customers and that may be sold only with the core service (for example, car vacuuming as an add-on service to a car wash). Consumer rebates can also be seen as a special form of mixed bundling; with the aim of fostering customer loyalty, companies sometimes offer consumers a rebate on the total sales across all company's products in a certain time frame. Fuerderer et al. (1999) note that these sales rebates can be seen as a mixture of bundling and nonlinear pricing.

The bundle design and pricing problem consists of determining which attributes or components are included in each bundle, and pricing each bundle optimally to maximize profits; see Oren Chapter 22. Customers are often assumed to be utility maximizers who select among the bundles and the no-purchase alternative. In addition, bundle prices need to be constrained in order to be efficient, in the sense that customers cannot reconstruct them at a lower price by purchasing more primitive bundles (Hanson and Martin 1990).[3] The efficiency constraint greatly complicates the bundle design and pricing problem.

When customers have utilities that are linear in the attributes, Gallego (2009) shows that bundles are efficient if and only if there exists a positive vector of attribute prices. This reduces the problem to that of designing the bundles (i.e., choosing the individual service components) and pricing their components. Then bundle prices are simply the sum of the prices of the component services. As an example, consider the case of four market segments $l = 1, \ldots, 4$ with sizes λ_l and valuations v_{li} for three attributes $i = 1, 2, 3$. The attribute costs are c_i, $i = 1, 2, 3$. The values of the parameters are as given in Table 28.1. If bundling is not allowed, the provider needs to optimize the price of each attribute and allow customers to select à la carte the attributes they desire. The optimal à la carte attribute prices can be shown to be given by the vector $q = (4, 10, 40)$. Given these prices, customers select attribute i if and only if $v_{li} > q_i$, $l = 1, 2, 3, 4$. Customers in segments $l = 1, 2, 3, 4$ will thus buy the bundles $(1, 1, 1)$, $(1, 0, 1)$, $(0, 1, 0)$, and $(0, 1, 1)$ respectively, paying 54, 44, 10, and 50

---

[3] The efficiency constraint may be relaxed if there are significant costs associated with reproducing bundles (Harris and Blair 2006). For example, a customer flying from Berlin to San Francisco may be presented with several connecting itineraries. Each connecting itinerary is essentially a bundle of the different flight legs involved. It is sometimes possible for a customer to pay less by separately buying the flight legs, but this involves higher search and transaction costs. In this case bundles may be purchased even if they can be reproduced at a lower price, because of the convenience factor and because being presented with a single bundle price lowers price sensitivity (Yadav and Monroe 1993).

Table 28.1 Four market segments, three attribute example

I	v_{i1}	v_{i2}	v_{i3}	λ_i
1	5	12	45	100
2	4	8	40	120
3	3	10	0	150
4	0	11	43	120
c	3	8	30	

for them. Under this pricing scheme the provider's profit is \$4,360, and market segments 1 and 4 enjoy surpluses of 8 and 4 respectively. When bundling the services as described in Table 28.2, it is possible to reduce the surplus of market segments 1 and 4 to zero by giving up the profits from market segment 3. This results in a 22.5 percent improvement in profits. The internally consistent vector of attribute prices is now $q' = (8, 18, 36)$, so the price of any of the offered bundles is just the sum of the attribute prices. However, customers should not be allowed to buy à la carte at q' as this results in very low profits of \$2,040 and defeats the purpose of bundling.

Hanson and Martin (1990) develop a bundle design and pricing model that can accommodate multiple components and a range of cost and reservation price conditions. Mussa and Rosen (1978) study the problem of nonlinear pricing and product line design in a monopolist setting, and Rochet and Chone (1998) extend this analysis to the multi-dimensional case where consumer types have different distributions. In a different stream of literature, behavioral research has investigated how consumers evaluate bundles. Most of the studies focus on how bundles are processed, particularly from a prospect theory or mental accounting perspective. Yadav and Monroe (1993) show that presenting customers with a single bundle price lowers price sensitivity and increases purchase likelihood, while Johnson et al. (1999) find that consumers perceive multiple savings in the bundle as more favorable than a single saving. The firm should therefore give customers a single bundle price rather than a list of separate service prices, and it should present the bundle discount as multiple savings. This strategy may affect not just consumers' purchasing decisions, but also their consumption behavior; Soman and Gourville (2001) show that customers who buy a bundle at a single bundled price consume less than those who buy when presented with separate service prices. This finding may in turn have implications for overbooking policies in the travel and leisure industries. For example, the seller could improve the forecasts of cancellations and no-shows based on information relative to the bundles sold, and therefore adjust the overbooking levels accordingly.

Table 28.2 Efficiently priced bundles

I	y_{i1}	y_{i2}	y_{i3}	price	profits
1	1	1	1	62	2,100
2	1	0	1	44	1,320
4	0	1	1	54	1,920
total					\$5,340

The problem of optimal bundle pricing is implicitly linked to the question of estimating the customers' valuation of bundles. This in turn is an area of research with strong links with behavioral economics, a branch of economics that applies research on human cognitive and emotional factors to understand how consumers make decisions and how these affect market prices. The primary concerns are with bounded rationality (Simon 1987) and with integrating psychology and economic theory. This subfield owes much to prospect theory developed by Kahneman and Tversky (1979) who compared cognitive models of decision making under risk and uncertainty with economic models of rational behavior.

Ariely (2008) claims that people are not only irrational but predictably so, and gives several pricing examples where people act irrationally in a predictable way. One of these examples deals with the price for *The Economist*, a popular British magazine. *The Economist* offers a paper-only subscription, an Internet-only subscription, and a bundle consisting of both subscriptions. The price of the bundle equals the price of the paper subscription and it is significantly higher than the price of the Internet subscription. In experiments with students, Ariely noticed that excluding the paper-only option biases the decision towards the cheaper Internet subscription, while the presence of the paper-only option biases the choice towards the bundle. From this experiment, Ariely developed and tested the hypothesis that people can be influenced in their choice between alternatives *A* and *B* by adding an alternative that is slightly inferior to the one the experimenter wants people to select. In *The Economist* example, adding the inferior paper-only subscription led to a bias toward the bundle. While this seems an ingenious way of steering predictably irrational customers towards buying the bundle, the strategy of offering the paper-only subscription and the bundle at the same price is actually consistent with pricing under the multinomial choice model in the likely case that the marginal cost of offering the Internet-only subscription is zero (Gallego and Stefanescu 2007). Offering a free product with the sale of another can be an effective way to increase sale volumes without discounting either of the products. Apple practices this by offering a free iPod Touch with the purchase of a MacBook laptop. In principle, some of Ariely's research can be used to design and price bundles taking into account irrational consumer behavior; see Özer and Zheng Chapter 20.

28.3.2 Unbundling

Unbundling is the strategy of separating the base service from the supplementary options and charging separate prices for each part of the service. For example, on-line music services such as iTunes unbundle by letting customers buy individual songs rather than complete CDs (Winer 2005). Airlines routinely unbundle luggage handling services from the ticket offers. In the finance industry, the unbundling practice of stripping bonds into a series of zero coupon bonds has met with great success. In the software industry, the SPSS software package was unbundled in the mid-1980s, allowing customers to purchase individual SPSS modules. Humphrey (2002) also describes the unbundling practices at IBM. Unbundling is primarily motivated by psychological research showing that unbundled prices may sometimes result in higher service valuations and greater purchase likelihood (Chakravarti et al. 2002).

28.3.3 Versioning

Service versioning is an operational strategy whereby the firm offers a product line based on different versions of a core service (Kahin and Varian 2000). More specifically, lowering the quality of a product to sell it to different customers is a part of this strategy also known as product damaging or product crimping (Deneckere and McAfee 1996; McAfee 2002). The objective is to appeal to price-sensitive customers who would not normally purchase the product at its regular price.

Examples of lowering product quality are slowing the speed of computer chips in semiconductor manufacturing, slowing the mail delivery, or offering uncomfortable seats for transportation,[4] entertainment, or sporting events. In the early 1990s IBM introduced an E model of its laser printer that printed at half the speed of the regular model. In industries that practice advance selling, lowering service quality can be achieved by imposing purchase timing restrictions (e.g., some tickets can only be bought two weeks before the event). In the transportation industry, lowering service quality usually involves imposing travel restrictions in the form of minimum, maximum, or mandatory stays. It should be noted that fare design in the airline industry mostly centered on service versioning by imposing fences such as advance purchasing and Saturday night stays on low fares. The ultimate outcome of these strategies is a product line with a range of "inferior" to "superior" products which is very common. There is a vast literature on this topic that includes tactics such as selling different grades of gasoline, different printer types, different classes of rental cars, paperback versus hardback books, different qualities of liquor, etc. even when some of the products sold as "inferior" are identical or damaged versions of the "superior" product, see Phillips (2005: 82–3).

The notion of versioning can be combined with the concepts of bundling and unbundling. As an example, let us reconsider the unbundling of luggage services that helped airline profitability in 2009. Airlines could version luggage handling by selling a premium service that gives luggage priority and thus decreases pick-up time at destinations. As another example, consider Southwest Airlines versioning of the plane boarding process. As many airlines do, Southwest gives free priority boarding to elite members. However, Southwest also sells boarding priority to non-elite passengers. Buying this priority is important since Southwest uses an open seating system instead of pre-assigning seats. Passengers arrange themselves into queues at the airport and take their preferred open seat once aboard. Queue A boards first, then B, and then C. Within each queue, passengers board according to a pre-assigned number; they also queue in specially designed areas which helps to speed up boarding. "The slight rush by passengers to claim a seat once they are on the plane actually speeds the process along", says CEO Gary C. Kelly (*New York Times* 2007). Currently Southwest ranks ninth out of 18 airlines in on-time arrivals (US Department of Transportation 2010), which helps to reduce the cost of airline delays currently estimated to be $32 billion per year (*Washington Post* 2010).

---

[4] The nineteenth-century French economist Emile Dupuit wrote about third-class carriages built without roofs that "what the company is trying to do is prevent the passengers who can pay the second-class fare from traveling third class; it hits the poor, not because it wants to hurt them, but to frighten the rich" (Ekelund 1970).

28.4 APPLICATIONS: REVENUE MANAGEMENT AND CUSTOMER RELATIONSHIP MANAGEMENT

Designing service features for market segmentation is often used in both revenue management (RM) and in customer relationship management (CRM). In this section we discuss actual and potential applications of service feature designs for both RM and CRM. We then point to some opportunities at the intersection of customer relationship and revenue management (CR^2M).

Revenue management refers to techniques to optimally or near-optimally allocate capacity among different fare classes to maximize expected revenues from perishable resources; see Talluri Chapter 2. Revenue management originated in the airline industry but its use has spread to hotels, car rental, restaurants, and other industries where capacity is reserved. In the airline industry the resources are the seats over the network. There may be several fares associated with an itinerary. A fare is a combination of a price and a set of restrictions such as advance purchase, Saturday night stay, and limited seat selection. This is in essence service versioning with the caveat that demands are random and the allocation to lower fares needs to be done before observing demand for higher fares. In addition, the very realization of demand depends on the admission control policy used. This is because as fares are closed customer demand may shift to other fares or may be lost. Cancellations and no-shows complicate the problem and are mitigated by the systematic use of capacity overbooking. At a strategic level RM is also about designing fares and setting competitive prices. Fare designs based on service versioning combined with overbooking and capacity allocation together provided a successful formula for airlines and other industries practicing RM. However, the presence of low cost carriers (LCCs) that do not impose purchase restrictions is dramatically diminishing the benefits of RM for competing traditional carriers.

It is therefore critical for the airline industry to find new ways to segment customers based on attributes other than purchase restrictions. One initiative that is gaining traction with some providers is the unbundling of the core service (transportation from an origin to a destination) from ancillary services such as luggage handling, meals, mileage accrual, or advance seat selection. These providers are now selling these services à la carte. On the other hand, airlines such as Air Canada cater to different market segments through bundles of branded services such as Tango, Tango Plus, Latitude, and Executive. Unbundling and bundling ideas are also used in the rental car industry. For example, mileage may be unbundled in situations where roads are harsh, while insurance may be mandatory for certain destinations. In addition, cars can be bundled with gas and features such as GPS or satellite radios. Hotels sometimes include breakfast and transportation, but may unbundle gym access and luggage storage for deeply discounted fare bookings.

Real options can also be used in RM to segment customers. On the fulfillment side, overbooking and upgrades are practiced in a variety of industries that practice RM. Opaque services are successfully used to sell distressed inventories, often as standalone services but also in bundles that combine air transportation with hotels and car rentals. On the consumption side, refundability and exchangeability options are often used in a crude way by the airlines, most of which only sell fully refundable or non-refundable fares.

Designing and pricing partially refundable fares, however, may be a profitable way to help customers manage consumption risk. Such fares are currently offered by some train companies including the Deutsche Bahn and the French SNCF. Exchangeability fees tend to be fixed, but there is the potential to make them fare class dependent. As an example, Air Canada has lower exchangeability fees on their highest priced bundles. Flexible services are used in a variety of industries, most prominently in cargo but also in car rentals (a class of cars is booked, any of which can be used to fulfill the request). Tour operators sell tours where a certain hotel class is promised, together with a list of possible hotels that can be used to fulfill the contract. In advertising, most ads are sold as flexible services as advertisers pay for impressions but publishers decide where ads are placed. Callable services, called preempting, are often used in Internet advertising where cost per action (CPA) or per click (CPC) are discounted in contracts that allow publishers to choose not to deliver ads if more valuable future contracts are formed. Callable services have the potential to reduce over-booking costs and improve capacity allocation in the travel industry. They may also help mitigate the formation of secondary markets in the entertainment industry.

Customer relationship management is the practice of tracking customer behavior in order to develop marketing programs bonding consumers to a brand, with the goal of maximizing long-term profitability. CRM strategies include tailoring the service delivery process to the specific preferences of individual customers, and developing customized marketing communications. CRM is particularly common in the hospitality industry where hotels endeavor to foster customer loyalty. CRM techniques are also used in the gaming industry to identify individual preferences, demographics, gaming propensity, psycho-graphic profiles and other behavior measures of casino customers that allow casinos to assess a customer's overall profitability. On this basis of expected profitability, casinos can customize service features such as discounted rooms, upgrades, complimentary airport transportation, free meals and drinks, and other ancillary services. Offering discounts and free services can create tension with RM systems designed to myopically extract the maximum expected profit from limited resources. To resolve this tension, RM systems need to incorporate the expected customer lifetime value.

A successful implementation is reported in Metters et al. (2007) who discuss the case of Harrah's Entertainment, the current CR^2M leader in the gaming industry. Their "Total Rewards" program tracks customer play across all properties and captures detailed customer information used to compute the lifetime value. The company uses around 100 customer segments based on lifetime values and varies the rates and room availabilities, rewards, and promotional messages by segment. This practice has increased revenue per room across the hotel chain by 15 percent, compared to an average 3–7 percent in other industries. Metters et al. (2007) note that the goal of Harrah's is to have a full hotel with an average room rate of $0/night, while the bulk of the revenue is generated by gambling. CR^2M strategies have also been explored in the airline industry, for example by using customer no-show information to improve forecasts of seat availability on a given flight. Jonas (2001) notes that CR^2M for airlines could add from 4–33 percent in incremental revenue, with an estimated average of 8 percent.

Substantial benefits can be derived from CR^2M in several industries. The main idea is to manipulate the mix of services and prices offered by the seller based on the characteristics of individual customers (in particular on their specific profitability) rather than on customer segments. The scant literature on CR^2M focuses mostly on applications in specific industries. Lieberman (2002) discusses the integration of revenue management with personalized marketing techniques. Noone et al. (2003) investigate the relationship between CRM and RM in the hospitality industry. Using the lifetime/profitability approach to customer segmentation, they identify appropriate customer segments for targeting with CRM techniques and outline a supporting RM strategy for each segment, including traditional RM, lifetime value-based pricing, availability guarantees, and short-term and ad hoc promotions. Hendler and Hendler (2004) provide an overview of CRM in gaming, and discuss how RM may be implemented in casinos alongside CRM to decide on effective room allocation and to maximize the overall property revenue. They note that allocating rooms is a main challenge for RM in gaming, where hotels must ensure that rooms are available for the most profitable segments but assessing customer profitability is not trivial. As Pilon (2008) points out, customer-centric RM would be discriminatory at the service availability level, since availability would depend on the profitability of the customer requesting the service, including his propensity of ancillary spend.

CR^2M is greatly facilitated by electronic commerce. In particular, electronic booking engines have the advantage of easy upselling (the situation where the seller offers service additions, including free upgrades) and cross-selling (when the seller offers service alternatives). In addition, the seller may offer customized subscriptions based on profiling (some examples are patronage programs used by leading cultural venues such as opera houses and concert halls). One of the main challenges in implementing CR^2M in an electronic commerce framework lies in finding techniques for handling multiple profiles that arise, for example, when customers browse for tickets without logging through registered profiles. This is a special case of the broader issue of correctly identifying customers who enter a transaction through different channels than those used for the loyalty programs, leading to the need to develop models for multi-channel shopping.

Great potential lies also at the intersection of supply chain management and $CR^2 M$. We have previously discussed the practice of customizing prices to preferred leadtimes. This is an example of a broader strategy that incorporates contract designs, shared forecasting, and capacity planning. For more insights, see Özer and Wei (2006) and Boyaci and Özer (2010).

28.5 CONCLUSIONS AND FUTURE RESEARCH

In this chapter, we discussed services engineering strategies that are or could be used successfully to increase profits and market share in a broad range of industries. Real options, bundling/unbundling, and versioning help broaden and segment markets. For providers, services engineering strategies promise to boost market share and improve capacity utilization and profits. Customers could benefit from a greater array of customized services that align better with their specific consumption needs and willingness-to-pay. Table 28.3 shows how these strategies could apply to industries as varied as travel and leisure, digital media and gaming, and utilities and pharmaceuticals (Tran 2010).

Many challenges remain before we see widespread implementation of robust services engineering strategies. From the technical perspective, the most important challenges involve information technology, forecasting, and pricing. Most companies lack the appropriate

Table 28.3 Design and pricing of service features by industry

	Real options									Product redesign			CRM
	Callable products	Flexible products	Upgrades/ Upsells	Bumping	Opaque products	Optional products	Refundability	Exchange-ability	Access	Bundling	Unbundling	Versioning	
Travel	P	X	X	X	X	P	X	X	X	X	X	X	X
Leisure	P	X	X	X	X	P	X	X	X	X		X	P
Hotel & hospitality	P	P	X	X	X	P	X	X	P	X	X	X	X
Entertainment tickets	P	P	X		P	P	P	P	X	X		X	X
Internet advertising	X	X	X		X		X			X			P
Technology		P	X		P		X		X	X	X	X	P
Digital media & gaming									X	X	X	X	P
Utilities		X							P				
Transport & supply chain	X	X	X	X	P	X	X	X		X	X	X	P
Insurance		X							X	X	X	P	P
Finance		X			P	X			X	X	X	X	
Pharmaceuticals			X		P		P			X		X	
Car rental	P	P	X	X	X		X	X	X	X	P	X	P
Club memberships			X		X				X	X	X	P	P

Key: X = In use; P = Possible opportunity

information technology to implement many derivative services. For example, the airline industry has not yet adopted ticket options mainly because its legacy systems are unable to handle the data requirements. Similarly, corporations need to update their accounting systems to recognize adequately nontraditional revenue streams. Optimally pricing new offers also presents hurdles, due to both the increased complexity of service features and the need to develop more sophisticated models of market demand. Demand forecasts, after all, are essential components of pricing models. In the case of non-traditional services, such forecasts may be difficult to construct without relevant past sales data.

Fortunately, the growth of Internet sales has greatly facilitated data collection and management through automated tools, enabling more complex and accurate demand modeling at lower levels of aggregation. In the past, many industries based their pricing strategies on models of aggregate demand at different pricing levels, assuming that demand from one segment of the market was independent of the other. With the availability of customer-level purchase data, these models are being replaced slowly by dependent demand models that account for consumer choice and can predict a customer's purchase likelihood based on buyer and service characteristics (Talluri and van Ryzin 2004; Gallego et al. 2006; Liu and van Ryzin 2008; Gallego et al. 2009).

Of course, providers must not only predict demand but generate it as well. In terms of marketing, they must help consumers understand how engineered services help them manage consumption risk and put a value on their own consumption flexibility. As in the financial industry, intermediaries—think of them as brokers—may play a critical role in educating customers. These intermediaries may help customers understand how to align derivative services with their needs, as well as provide tools for sophisticated customers to self-select services. Some potential customers may initially balk at price segmentation strategies. Brokers must find creative ways to frame engineered services by discussing their consumer benefits while explaining their potential costs.

Many of these challenges were first faced by firms that embraced financial engineering during its incipient stages. They went on to overcome many of these implementation issues. Today, financial engineering benefits both practitioners and consumers by spreading market risk and allowing capital to flow more efficiently. Services engineering can achieve similar improvements in risk reduction and demand generation, benefiting providers and consumers alike. As in the case of financial engineering, however, there are also the underlying dangers of the inappropriate use of some of these strategies. By studying the lessons of the 2007–9 credit crisis, future services engineers may learn how to better manage derivatives and prepare for potential extreme events.

One promising area of future research lies in the use of services engineering to design and price large service contracts. These might include outsourcing information technology or payroll, or setting up service call centers, or hiring temporary workers for large projects. Negotiations for such large deals may last many months and involve a delicate balancing act. On one hand, service providers must manage the sales funnel to maximize profit from conversion (or similar objectives). On the other, they must be able to allocate resources, including employees and contractors, in order to ramp up quickly once they close on a deal. Real options on projected resource requirements, including both equipment and personnel, can help fulfill such large deals without forcing service suppliers to overinvest in capacity. The pricing of a deal can be tied to fulfillment flexibility, customer options, and quality of service guarantees.

REFERENCES

Adams, W. J. and Yellen, J. L. (1976) "Commodity Bundling and the Burden of Monopoly", *Quarterly Journal of Economics* 90: 475–98.

Ariely, D. (2008) *Predictably Irrational*. London: Harper Collins.

Bakos, Y. and Brynjolfsson, E. (1999) "Bundling Information Goods: Pricing, Profits and Efficiency", *Management Science* 45: 1613–30.

Biyalogorsky, E. and Gerstner, E. (2004) "Contingent Pricing to Reduce Price Risks", *Marketing Science* 23: 146–55.

—— Weiss, D., and Xie, J. (2005) "The Economics of Service Upgrades", *Journal of Service Research* 7: 234–44.

Boyaci, T. and Özer, Ö. (2010) "Information Acquisition for Capacity Planning Via Pricing and Advance Selling: When to Stop and Act?", *Operations Research* 58/5: 1328–49.

Chakravarti, D., Krish, R., Paul, P., and Srivastava, J. (2002) "Partitioned Presentation of Multicomponent Bundle Prices: Evaluation, Choice and Underlying Processing Effects", *Journal of Consumer Psychology* 12: 215–29.

Chen, F. (2001) "Market Segmentation, Advanced Demand Information, and Supply Chain Performance", *Manufacturing and Service Operations Management* 3: 53–67.

Della Vigna, S. and Malmendier, U. (2006) "Paying Not to Go to the Gym", *American Economic Review* 96: 694–719.

Deneckere, R. and McAfee, R. P. (1996) "Damaged Goods", *Journal of Economics and Management Strategy* 5: 149–74.

Ekelund, R. (1970) "Price Discrimination and Product Differentiation in Economic Theory: An Early Analysis", *Quarterly Journal of Economics* 84: 268–78.

Fay, S. (2008) "Selling an Opaque Product Through an Intermediary: The Case of Disguising One's Product", *Journal of Retailing* 84: 59–75.

—— and Xie, J. (2008) "Probabilistic Goods: A Creative Way of Selling Products and Services", *Marketing Science* 27: 674–90.

Fisher, M. (1997) "What is the Right Supply Chain for Your Product?" *Harvard Business Review* March–April: 105–16.

Fuerderer, R., Herrmann, A., and Wuebker, G. (1999) *Optimal Bundling: Marketing Strategies for Improving Economic Performance*. Berlin: Springer.

Gallego, G. (2009) "Design and Pricing of Efficient Bundles". Working paper, Columbia University.

—— (2010) "Contingent Contracts for Repeated Services". Working paper, Columbia University.

—— and Özer, Ö. (2001) "Integrating Replenishment Decisions with Advance Demand Information", *Management Science* 47: 1344–60.

—— and Phillips, R. (2004) "Revenue Management of Flexible Products", *Manufacturing and Service Operations Management* 6: 321–37.

—— and Sahin, O. (2007a) "Revenue Management with Partially Refundable Fares", *Operations Research* 4: 817–33.

—— and —— (2007b) "Duopoly Competition with Partially Refundable Fares". Working paper, Columbia University.

—— and Stefanescu, C. (2007) "Upgrades, Upsells and Pricing in Revenue Management". Working paper, London Business School.

Gallego, G., Iyengar, G., and Phillips, R. (2006) "Revenue Management of Callable Products in a Network". Working paper, Columbia University.

—— Kou, S. G., and Phillips, R. (2008) "Revenue Management of Callable Products". *Management Science* 54: 550–64.

—— Lin, L., and Ratliff, R. (2009) "Choice-Based EMSR Methods for Single-Leg Revenue Management with Demand Dependencies". *Journal of Revenue and Pricing Management* 8: 207–40.

—— Hu, M., Wang, R., Ward, J., Beltran, J., and Shailendra, J. (2010) "No Claim? Your Gain: Price Discrimination Through a Residual Value Warranty". Working paper, Columbia University.

Guo, L. (2006) "Consumption Flexibility, Product Configuration, and Market Competition", *Marketing Science* 25: 116–30.

Hanson, W. A. and Martin, R. Kipp (1990) "Optimal Bundle Pricing", *Management Science* 36: 155–74.

Happel, S. and Jennings, M. (1989) "Assessing the Economic Rationale and Legal Remedies for Ticket Scalping", *Journal of Legislation* 16: 1–14.

Harris, J. and Blair, E. A. (2006) "Consumer Preference for Product Bundles: The Role of Reduced Search Costs", *Journal of the Academy of Marketing Science* 34: 506–13.

Hendler, R. and Hendler, F. (2004) "Revenue Management in Fabulous Las Vegas: Combining Customer Relationship Management and Revenue Management to Maximise Profitability", *Journal of Revenue and Pricing Management* 3: 73–9.

Hollis, A. (1999) "Extended Warranties, Adverse Selection and Aftermarkets", *Journal of Risk and Insurance* 66: 321–43.

Humphrey, W. (2002) "Software Unbundling: A Personal Perspective", *IEEE Annals of the History of Computing* 24: 59–63.

Jiang, Y. (2007) "Price Discrimination with Opaque Products", *Journal of Revenue and Pricing Management* 6: 118–34.

Johnson, M. D., Herrmann, A., and Bauer, H. H. (1999) "The Effects of Price Bundling on Consumer Evaluations of Product Offerings", *International Journal of Research in Marketing* 16: 129–42.

Jonas, D. (2001) "Carriers Melding Revenue Management and CRM Systems", *Business Travel News* March 26: 18–19.

Kahin, B. and Varian, H. R. (eds) (2000) *Internet Publishing and Beyond: The Economics of Digital Information and Intellectual Property*. Cambridge, MA: The MIT Press.

Kahneman, D. and Tversky, A. (1979) "Prospect Theory: An Analysis of Decision Under Risk", *Econometrica* 47: 263–91.

Koderisch, M., Wuebker, G., Baumgarten, J., and Baillie, J. (2007) "Bundling in Banking—A Powerful Strategy to Increase Profits", *Journal of Financial Services Marketing* 11: 268–76.

Lambrecht, A. and Skiera, B. (2006) "Paying Too Much and Being Happy About It: Existence, Causes and Consequences of Tariff-Choice Biases", *Journal of Marketing Research* 43: 212–23.

Lieberman, W. H. (2002) "Revenue Management: What Lies Ahead?" *Journal of Revenue and Pricing Management* 1: 189–95.

Liu, Q. and van Ryzin, G. (2008) "On the Choice-Based Linear Programming Model for Network Revenue Management", *Manufacturing and Service Operations Management* 10: 288–310.

McAfee, R. P. (2002) *Competitive Solutions: The Strategist's Toolkit*. Princeton, NJ: Princeton University Press.

Metters, R., Crystal, C., Ferguson, M., Harrison, L., Higbie, J., Ward, S., Barfield, B., Farley, T., Kuyumcu, A., and Duggasani, A. R. (2007) "The 'Killer Application' of Revenue Management: Harrah's Cherokee Casino & Hotel". Working paper, Emory University.

Mussa, M. and Rosen, S. (1978) "Monopoly and Product Quality", *Journal of Economic Theory* 18: 301–17.

Nagle, T. and Holden, R. (1995) *The Strategy and Tactics of Pricing*. Upper Saddle River, NJ: Prentice Hall.

Nelson, P. (1970) "Information and Consumer Behavior", *Journal of Political Economy* 78: 311–29.

New York Times, September 20, 2007. http://www.nytimes.com/2007/09/20/business/20air.html.

Noone, B. M., Kimes, S. E., and Renaghan, L. M. (2003) "Integrating Customer Relationship Management and Revenue Management: A Hotel Perspective", *Journal of Revenue and Pricing Management* 2: 7–21.

Özer, Ö. (2003) "Replenishment Strategies for Distribution Systems Under Advance Demand Information", *Management Science* 49: 255–72.

—— and Wei, W. (2006) "Strategic Commitments for an Optimal Capacity Decision Under Asymmetric Forecast Information", *Management Science* 52: 1239–58.

Phillips, R. (2005) *Pricing and Revenue Optimization*. Palo Alto, CA: Stanford University Press.

Pilon, R. (2008) "Integrating RM and CRM—A Myth or a Must?", AGIFORS RM & Cargo Conference, Tahiti.

Post, D. (2010) "Variable Opaque Products in the Airline Industry: A Tool to Fill the Gaps and Increase Revenues", *Journal of Revenue and Pricing Management* 9: 292–9.

Rochet, J. C. and Chone, P. (1998) "Ironing, Sweeping, and Multidimensional Screening", *Econometrica* 66: 783–826.

Rubinstein, A. (1988) *Modeling Bounded Rationality*. Zeuthen Lectur Book Series, Karl Gunnar Persson, editor. Cambridge, MA: MIT Press.

Shugan, S. (2005) "Marketing and Designing Transaction Games", *Marketing Science* 24: 525–30.

Simon, H. (1987) "Behavioural Economics", *The New Palgrave: A Dictionary of Economics* 1: 221–24.

Soman, D. and Gourville, J. T. (2001) "Transaction Decoupling: How Price Bundling Affects the Decision to Consume", *Journal of Marketing Research* 38: 30–44.

Stremersch, S. and Tellis, G. J. (2002) "Strategic Bundling of Products and Prices: A New Synthesis for Marketing", *Journal of Marketing* 66: 55–72.

Talluri, K. and van Ryzin, G. (2004) "Revenue Management Under a General Discrete Choice Model of Consumer Behavior", *Management Science* 50: 15–33.

Tran, A. (2010) "Service Engineering Applications". Summer Project, Columbia University.

US Bureau of Transportation Statistics (2010) Profitability: http://www.transtats.bts.gov/Data_Elements.aspx?Data=6 and Baggage Fees (Table 1C): http://www.bts.gov/press_releases/2010/bts021_10/html/bts021_10.html.

US Department of Transportation (2010) Air Travel Consumer Report.

Washington Post (2010) "Air travelers found to lose billions to delays", October 19.

Winer, R. (2005) *Pricing*. Cambridge, MA: Marketing Science Institute.

Yadav, M. S. and Monroe, K. B. (1993) "How Buyers Perceive Savings in a Bundle Price: An Examination of a Bundle's Transaction Value", *Journal of Marketing Research* 30: 350–8.

CHAPTER 29

PRICING IN BUSINESS-TO-BUSINESS CONTRACTS: SHARING RISK, PROFIT, AND INFORMATION

MURAT KAYA AND ÖZALP ÖZER

29.1 INTRODUCTION

The success of a product in today's global marketplace depends, to a large extent, on the activities of firms in the product's supply chain and their processing of information. Multiple firms manage today's global supply chains. Each firm sets strategic and operational goals to maximize its own profit by using local information such as cost structures, profit margins, and forecasts. Hence, effective management of supply chains requires firms to synchronize and coordinate the decentralized operations and information. Many experts have heralded advances in information technology and Internet infrastructure, both of which enable better visibility and information sharing, as the key to effective management of supply chains. Suppliers and manufacturers can share private information regarding, for example, costs or forecasts. But will they want to? Firms may be reluctant to collect, process, and share information because of conflicting incentives. For example, the informed firm may have an incentive to distort or hide information to gain strategic advantage. Incentive problems in supply chains can be attributed to not being able to share risks and information credibly (see, e.g., Özer 2006).

In this chapter, we discuss how *pricing terms* in business-to-business (B2B) contracts can be used to align incentives, and share risks, profits, and information between the members

The authors are grateful to an anonymous reviewer, Tamer Boyaci, Jingyun Li, Robert Phillips, and Yanchong Zheng for their constructive comments. The authors also gratefully acknowledge financial support from National Science Foundation Grant No. 0556322 and No. 1002381.

of a supply chain. In addition to price-related terms (e.g., the wholesale price that the retailer pays per unit of purchase to the manufacturer), the contracts we study might also include certain quantity-related terms (such as the number of units that can be returned to the manufacturer). We show that the pricing terms in a B2B contract are much more than a pricing scheme. They may serve a strategic purpose by helping reallocate risks and profits, and by enabling credible information sharing among supply chain members. As a result, decisions can be coordinated to synchronize information, material, and financial flows in a supply chain.

A contract is a document that describes, prior to the trade, the terms of a binding agreement specifying the process through which the amount of trade and cash flows are determined after the trade (Tirole 1988). The contract terms include who decides on what, such as capacity investment, and how the resulting profits are to be shared. The study of B2B contracts requires one to explicitly state the sequence of events, decisions, and resulting cash flows. The contract terms can be negotiated through an iterative process or they could be offered by one party to another as a take-it-or-leave-it offer. Note, for example, that by offering to pay full credit for any unsold unit, a manufacturer can signal to his retailer that he expects high demand for the product. Such an action may induce the retailer to carry a large inventory of the manufacturer's product. Hence, the process by which parties agree on contract terms affects the equilibrium outcome. For an academic survey of contracting among firms in a supply chain, and for detailed technical discussion, we refer the reader to the surveys by Cachon (2003) and Chen (2003).

Supply chains today are subject to many risks, including financial, operational, security, and environmental risks. The management of such risks has recently gained much attention due to globalization, outsourcing, and lean manufacturing trends. Our focus in this chapter, however, is not on supply chain risk management, but on how pricing terms in B2B contracts can be used to share two important operational risks in supply chains: *inventory risk* and *capacity risk*. To illustrate inventory risk, we study a manufacturer's relation with its downstream supply chain partner, a retailer who sells the manufacturer's product to satisfy uncertain consumer demand. We discuss the role of different B2B contracts on the retailer's product availability level and on her product pricing policy. To illustrate capacity risk, we study the manufacturer's relation with its upstream supply chain partner, a supplier who needs to build capacity to supply a critical component to the manufacturer. We also discuss how pricing terms can be used to elicit strategic information from supply chain partners.

Inventory risk is born out of a possible mismatch between the inventory/production level and uncertain demand. A firm may incur overage cost; that is excess inventory cost when demand turns out to be lower than anticipated. The firm may also incur underage cost; that is inventory shortage cost, when demand is higher than anticipated. Excess inventory cost includes the costs of physically holding inventory, the opportunity cost of the funds tied to inventory, and the costs related to devaluation of the inventory. The latter is particularly important in fashion and high-tech industries. Cost of shortage includes the lost profit margin and the cost of lost consumer goodwill. For an HP inkjet printer, for example, foregone profit from future ink cartridge sales and the cost to HP's brand loyalty might be higher than the lost profit margin on the printer itself. The consequences of inventory-demand mismatch can be significant. For example, Cisco had to write down $2.25 billion worth of inventory when demand for telecom and networking equipment plunged in the crisis of 2001. In the 1994 holiday season, IBM could not meet all the demand for its newly introduced Aptiva line of PCs. This caused IBM to miss millions of dollars in revenue in addition to losing consumer goodwill.[1]

Capacity risk is about matching the capacity with uncertain demand. Capacity decisions are often made well ahead of the selling season. Forecasting demand before the selling season is often very difficult. As a result, a supply chain builds either excessive or insufficient capacity relative to demand realization. Semiconductor firms, for example, were forced to operate at 50 percent capacity during the years 2002 and 2003 due to lower than anticipated demand (Chopra and Sodhi 2004). There exists an incentive conflict because the costs, which are often significant, and benefits of capacity accrue to different members of a supply chain. Manufacturers are known to inflate forecasts to make their suppliers invest in larger capacity (Lee et al. 1997; Cachon and Lariviere 2001; Özer and Wei 2006). Anticipating this, a supplier often discounts the manufacturer's forecast and builds conservative capacity. This capacity constraint might cause significant loss of sales if demand turns out to be high. For example, Boeing's suppliers could not satisfy the firm's large orders in 1997 due to capacity shortage, because the suppliers did not find Boeing's optimistic forecasts credible (Cole 1997). Ignoring the incentives and capacities of the upstream supply chain members can ruin even the best marketing strategy. For example, in 2003, Motorola was unable to satisfy the demand for its hot-selling camera phones due to shortages in the camera components.[2] Singhal and Hendricks (2002) estimate that a firm will suffer an average of 7.5 percent reduction in stock price when it announces a supply chain delivery–production problem. We discuss how a manufacturer can share the capacity risk of its supplier and how it can convey its *private* demand forecast information credibly by using pricing terms in B2B contracts.

Uncertainty in consumer demand is the main driver behind both inventory risk and capacity risk. This is why we use the *newsvendor model* to study the roles of B2B contracts in addressing these risks. Matching inventories or capacity to meet uncertain demand is difficult even for a single decision maker. The problem is exacerbated when the benefits and costs of inventory (or capacity) are shared between firms. Which firm owns the inventory of unsold units? Who is to blame when a manufacturer loses sales because its supplier did not have sufficient capacity? Note that certain other operational risks can also be studied in the context of these two risks. For example, *yield risk* can be modeled as part of capacity risk. *Leadtime risk* can be part of inventory risk when one considers multiple selling seasons. Also note that the inventory or capacity risks would apply to other linkages in supply chains than the ones we consider in this chapter. For example, inventory risk may be observed in the relation between a supplier and a procure-to-stock manufacturer, or between a distributor and a retailer. The requirement is that the downstream firm procures to stock and faces uncertain demand.

Certainly, a real B2B contract would have many more terms and would be more complicated than the contracts we consider here. We focus on elementary B2B contract forms and illustrate their implications to highlight some key issues that a manager should consider when designing their terms. Nevertheless, the fundamental principles discussed in

---

[1] *Wall Street Journal*, October 7, 1994.
[2] www.electronicsweekly.com, Thursday December 4, 2003.

this chapter can be used to design contracts that can help mitigate the adverse affects of other supply chain risks as well.

The rest of the chapter is organized as follows. In Section 29.2 we discuss how B2B contracts can be used to reallocate inventory risk in a supply chain. We illustrate how this reallocation affects stocking decisions and resulting profits. We also introduce the key terms and definitions in this section. In Section 29.3 we investigate how a contract between a manufacturer and a retailer can affect the retailer's pricing decision. In Section 29.4 we discuss how B2B contracts can be used to allocate capacity risk. In Section 29.5 we study how B2B contracts can be used to credibly share information. In particular, we focus on forecast information sharing. In Section 29.6 we discuss potential implementation issues. In Section 29.7 we conclude with a discussion on possible extensions and research opportunities.

29.2 Inventory risk sharing through B2B contracts

Before beginning our discussion on B2B contracts, we first study the inventory risk that an individual firm faces. Consider a firm that sells a product in a single selling season. Due to the possibility of obsolescence or the nature of the business, the firm does not have the ability to store inventory from one selling season to the next. Furthermore, the single selling season is not long enough to place a second order; that is, there is only one opportunity to stock inventory. In other words, the production or replenishment leadtime is longer than the selling season itself. Hence, the firm has to order and stock inventory prior to the selling season. Alas! Demand is also uncertain. How many units should the firm order before the selling season starts?

Firms from various industries face such notoriously difficult decisions. A newsvendor located at the corner of a street has to decide how many copies of a particular magazine issue she has to stock. A garment retailer who sells fashion products with a short selling season has to decide how many units to stock in its retail stores. A toy manufacturer has to decide how many units to manufacture in Asia and ship to North American retailers who sell during the Christmas season. A grocery store that has to sell some of its products on a given day is another example.

All these firms face a fundamental tradeoff. At the end of the selling season, if the realized demand turns out to be less than the available inventory, the firm needs to salvage leftover inventory at a discounted price.[3] For certain products, the firm may even have to pay a disposal fee for leftover inventory. However, if realized demand exceeds the available inventory, then the firm loses customers and hence the opportunity to make more money. In addition, the customers may choose to do business with their competitors in the following sales season.

---

[3] Chapter 25 of this handbook discusses the related problem of "markdown management" where a firm determines the optimal discounting policy to maximize revenue when selling a fixed quantity of perishable products.

Historically, this inventory management problem under demand uncertainty was motivated with a *newsvendor* narrative. We follow the tradition here and describe the newsvendor problem. Consider a newsvendor who prints/produces newspapers at unit cost c and sells them for p per unit throughout the day.[4] She can salvage unsold copies at v per unit.[5] Demand D for newspapers is uncertain. However, the newsvendor estimates that during any given day μ people on average buy the newspaper.

The newsvendor has to decide how many copies to print prior to a given day (sales season). She owns both the printing (manufacturing) facility and the distribution operations. In other words, the supply chain for the newspaper is *vertically integrated*. The newsvendor sets the production quantity to maximize the integrated supply chain's (*integrated firm's*) expected profit. An obvious solution alternative is to print μ copies, the average demand. Note, however, that not having a copy when a customer wants it costs the newsvendor $c_u = p - c$. We refer to this cost as the *cost of underage*. Having an unsold copy at the end of the day costs the newsvendor $c_o = c - v$. We refer to this cost as the *cost of overage*. Intuitively, the newsvendor should buy more than the average demand when the cost of underage is higher than the cost of overage. This observation suggests that the optimal number of copies to stock should depend on the costs of overage and underage.

The cost of underage represents the marginal benefit of having one more unit of inventory in stock when needed. Assume that the newsvendor is already committed to producing and stocking Q units in the morning. During the day, if she has one more unit of paper in stock, she may earn $c_u = p - c$. From historical data, the newsvendor estimates that demand during a given day exceeds Q units with probability $1 - F(Q)$, where $F(Q)$ is the probability that random demand D is less than or equal to Q. Hence, the expected marginal benefit of stocking one more unit is $c_u(1 - F(Q))$. On the other hand, the marginal cost of having one more unit of inventory in stock when it is not needed is $c_o F(Q)$. The optimal stocking quantity should strike a balance between the marginal benefit and the marginal cost of having an additional unit. The newsvendor can increase her production and stocking quantity one unit at a time until the marginal benefit of doing so is equal to the marginal cost; that is, until $c_u(1 - F(Q)) = c_o F(Q)$. Rearranging the terms, we arrive at the *critical ratio*:

$$\text{Set } Q \text{ such that } F(Q) = \frac{c_u}{c_u + c_o},$$

where $c_u/(c_u + c_o) = (p - c)/(p - v)$. This condition can be interpreted as follows. At the beginning of the selling season, set the stocking quantity such that the probability of satisfying all demand during the season (i.e., the probability of no stockout) is equal to the critical ratio $\frac{p-c}{p-v}$. Let Q^I denote the optimal stocking quantity that satisfies the above condition. The superscript I denotes the integrated firm. We have

$$Q^I = F^{-1}\left(\frac{p - c}{p - v}\right).$$

---

[4] For ease of reference, we summarize the notation in Appendix A.
[5] We assume $v < c$. Otherwise, the newsvendor would produce an infinite number of newspapers.

where $F^{-1}(\cdot)$ is the inverse cumulative distribution function of demand D.[6] The demand distribution information can be obtained from historical demand data and forecast errors.

So far, we determined the newsvendor's optimal production and stocking quantity Q^I through a marginal cost–benefit analysis. We can obtain the same solution by analyzing the newsvendor's *expected profit* from producing and stocking Q units. Note that if random demand D is realized as d units and the newsvendor produces Q units, she sells $\min(Q, d)$ units. Her *payoff* from producing and stocking Q units is

$$\pi^I(Q, d) = p \min(Q, d) + v(Q - \min(Q, d)) - cQ$$
$$= (p - v) \min(Q, d) - (c - v)Q.$$

If the newsvendor could produce after observing demand, then she would have produced and stocked $Q = d$ units, without facing any risk of excess or shortage. This quantity would maximize her payoff. However, demand is uncertain at the time when the newsvendor decides how much to produce. In this case, she can produce to maximize her expected profit

$$\Pi^I(Q) = (p - v)E[\min(Q, D)] - (c - v)Q, \tag{1}$$

where $E[\cdot]$ denotes expectation with respect to uncertain demand D. The expected sales is given by $E[\min(Q, D)] = \int_0^Q xf(x)dx + \int_Q^\infty Q f(x)dx$, where $f(x)$ is the probability density function of the random variable D. The function $\Pi^I(Q)$ is concave because its second derivative is negative. Hence, from the first-order condition, we determine the optimal production and stocking quantity as

$$Q^I = F^{-1}\left(\frac{p - c}{p - v}\right). \tag{2}$$

Note that this quantity is the same as the one obtained through the marginal cost–benefit analysis.

29.2.1 The wholesale price contract

Suppose that the newsvendor decides to focus only on the distribution of newspapers. To do so, she sells her printing machines and outsources production to a manufacturer who produces at cost c per unit and charges w per unit. In other words, the newsvendor *disintegrates* the firm, outsources manufacturing, and establishes a supply chain by agreeing on a *wholesale price contract* to buy the printed papers from the manufacturer. Under this agreement, the newsvendor (the retailer[7]) decides how much to order from the manufacturer and stock; that is the stocking quantity Q. The manufacturer produces Q units and satisfies the retailer's order prior to the sales season. The retailer sells the product at a unit price p during the sales season. The retailer salvages[8] any unsold newspaper at v per unit. Information, including the cost and demand parameters, is common to both firms

---

[6] We assume $F(\cdot)$ to be strictly increasing, hence its inverse function exists.

[7] When the newsvendor is only in charge of the distribution, we refer to her as the retailer.

[8] In some cases the manufacturer may salvage unsold units. Here, we assume that the salvage value is the same for both firms. Hence, the retailer is assumed to salvage unsold units to avoid additional transportation cost.

(i.e., there is no private information). For a given stocking quantity Q, the manufacturer's, the retailer's, and the total supply chain's expected profits are

$$\Pi_m^w(Q) = (w - c)Q, \tag{3}$$

$$\Pi_r^w(Q) = (p - v)E[\min(Q, D)] - (w - v)Q, \tag{4}$$

$$\begin{aligned}\Pi_{tot}^w(Q) &= \Pi_m^w(Q) + \Pi_r^w(Q) \\ &= (p - v)E[\min(Q, D)] - (c - v)Q.\end{aligned} \tag{5}$$

Notice first that the manufacturer's profit is certain once the retailer submits her order Q. It does not depend on the realization of demand. The retailer decides how much to order by maximizing her expected profit in (4). The retailer's optimal stocking (or, order) quantity is obtained by an argument similar to the one presented in the previous section. It is given by

$$Q^w = F^{-1}\left(\frac{p - w}{p - v}\right). \tag{6}$$

We observe the pivotal role of B2B pricing on the outcome of the relation between the firms. The wholesale price w affects the retailer's stocking quantity choice, and the stocking quantity, in turn, determines the expected sales of the retailer and the expected profits of both firms. Given this pivotal role, what wholesale price should the contract dictate, and who should set this price? The retailer's expected profit in (4) is higher with a lower wholesale price w. So, if the retailer could dictate the wholesale price, then she would set it equal to the unit production cost c such that the manufacturer is left with zero profit. Hence, when $w = c$, the retailer's profit is equal to total supply chain profit in (5). The manufacturer's profit in (3) is higher with a higher wholesale price up to a certain value. It decreases if the wholesale price is too high because then the retailer orders less. Hence, if the manufacturer dictates the wholesale price, he would not necessarily set $w = p$. Instead, he would choose the wholesale price w^* to maximize his expected profit $(w - c)Q^w$. In reality, neither party is likely to exert unidirectional pricing power on the other. Often, parties iterate over a bargaining process and agree on a wholesale price. Given the above discussion, this agreed-upon wholesale price would be between the production cost c and the sales price p; that is, $w \in (c, p)$. Figure 29.1 illustrates the expected profits as a function of the wholesale price w when the retailer orders Q^w units. We refer the reader to Lariviere and Porteus (2001) for a more detailed discussion of the wholesale price contract.

29.2.2 Double marginalization, coordination, and channel efficiency

Next we compare the solution we obtained for the *disintegrated (decentralized)* supply chain under a wholesale price contract with the vertically integrated firm solution (centralized solution). Four groups of observations are worth emphasizing. First, comparing (2) and (6) reveals that $Q^I > Q^w$ because $c < w$. The retailer orders a quantity less than the integrated firm's optimal quantity (unless $w = c$). As a result, the retailer is more likely to run out of stock, and consumers are more likely to face shortages. But why does the retailer order and stock less than the integrated firm? The answer lies in the difference between the

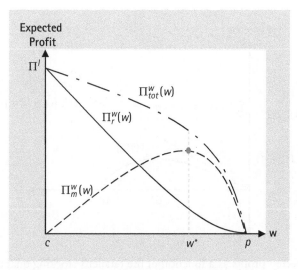

FIGURE 29.1 Expected profits as a function of the wholesale price

underage/overage costs that the retailer and the integrated firm face. The cost of underage for the retailer, $p - w$, is less than that of the integrated firm, $p - c$. Note that the cost of underage is equal to the profit margin for the retailer or for the integrated firm. The cost of overage for the retailer, $w - v$, is higher than the integrated firm's cost, $c - v$. Hence, the retailer's profit margin is lower than that of the integrated firm's, while facing a higher cost of excess inventory. Consequently, it is optimal for the retailer to stock less inventory under a wholesale price contract compared to the integrated firm. This is related to what is known as *double marginalization* (Spengler 1950).

Second, comparing (1) and (5) reveals that the expected total supply chain profit is equal to the integrated firm's expected profit for a given stocking quantity Q; that is, $\Pi^I(Q) = \Pi^{tot}(Q)$. This equivalence is not surprising. Payments between the retailer and the manufacturer cancel out when computing the total supply chain profit. Hence, the stocking quantity Q^I, which maximizes the integrated firm's expected profit also maximizes the expected total profit in the disintegrated supply chain. Figure 29.2 illustrates the expected profits in (3), (4), and (5) as a function of the retailer's stocking quantity for a given wholesale price w.

The above discussion leads to the third group of observations. The total supply chain expected profit when the retailer orders Q^w is less than the integrated firm's expected profit because $Q^w < Q^I$; that is, $\Pi^I(Q^I) > \Pi^I(Q^w) = \Pi_{tot}^w(Q^w)$. Note that the retailer's objective is to maximize her own expected profit, not the expected total supply chain profit. Hence, under a wholesale price contract she orders Q^w instead of Q^I units. The difference between the integrated firm's optimal expected profit and the disintegrated supply chain's total expected profit, $\Pi^I(Q^I) - \Pi_{tot}^w(Q^w)$, measures the magnitude of *channel (or, supply chain) inefficiency*. This difference measures how much money the manufacturer and the retailer leave on the table. Note that the existence of pricing (i.e., the wholesale price) between the firms causes inefficiency in the supply chain. If the firms cooperate and the retailer stocks Q^I units instead of Q^w, the total expected profit would be higher, and equal to that of the integrated firm's optimal expected profit. With a proper B2B contract mechanism, the firms

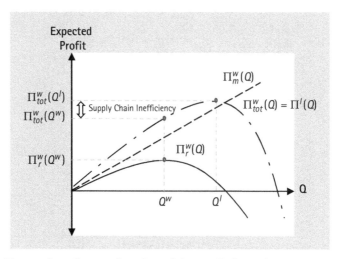

FIGURE 29.2 Expected profits as a function of the retailer's stocking quantity

can share this extra money and achieve an improvement over what they earn under the existing wholesale price agreement. Such a contract mechanism would be mutually beneficial for both parties and create a *win–win* situation. We call a contract *Pareto improving* if it increases one firm's profit without decreasing the other's profit under a pre-existing agreement. Without a proper mechanism, however, voluntary cooperation is not possible because the retailer's expected profit is lower if she orders Q^I units; that is, $\Pi^r(Q^w) \geq \Pi^r(Q^I)$. The manufacturer (or a third party) may enforce the retailer to stock the integrated firm's optimal quantity Q^I. However, enforcements that lack proper incentives are hardly sustainable. The key is to provide a mechanism that *aligns* the retailer's objective with the supply chain's objective such that the retailer voluntarily sets her stocking quantity equal to Q^I. We have seen that the wholesale price contract, with its single pricing term, is not sufficient for this purpose.

The final set of observations are based on comparing the *payoffs*.[9] Note that payoffs do not depend on demand distribution and they are helpful in identifying the firms' incentives. Figure 29.3(a) illustrates the firms' payoffs as a function of demand realization d for a given stocking quantity Q. The manufacturer's payoff is always nonnegative while the retailer faces the risk of a negative payoff. This is because the manufacturer produces to order whereas the retailer procures to stock. When demand turns out to be larger than the stocking quantity (i.e., when $d > Q$), the retailer's reward for carrying an extra unit of inventory $(p - w)$ is less than the integrated firm's reward $(p - c)$. This is because the manufacturer also benefits from the sale of that extra unit. Hence, the retailer's *upside potential* is lower than the integrated firm's. When demand turns out to be lower than the stocked quantity (i.e., when $d \leq Q$), the retailer's loss for carrying an extra unit of inventory

---

[9]   The payoff functions provide the profit values for a given realization of the random demand; i.e., when $D = d$. For example, the retailer's payoff with a wholesale price contract is $\pi_r^w(Q, d) = (p - v)\min(Q, d) - (w - v)Q$. Recall that we use the symbol π to denote payoffs and the symbol Π to denote expected profits.

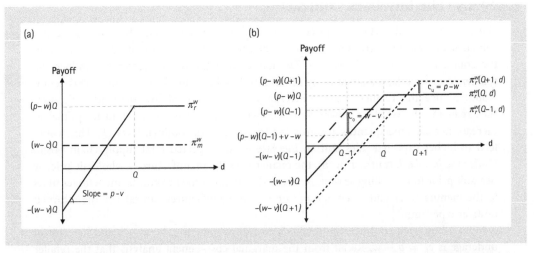

FIGURE 29.3 Payoffs as a function of demand realization with a wholesale price contract; (a) the firms' payoffs; (b) the retailer's payoffs under stocking quantities $Q - 1$, Q, and $Q + 1$

$(w - v)$ is higher than the integrated firm's loss $(c - v)$. The retailer's *downside risk* is higher than the integrated firm's. Note that the manufacturer does not face downside risk, because he produces to order. He only faces the risk of losing the upside potential. The above discussion suggests that the risk of inventory excess (downside risk) is not shared properly in a disintegrated supply chain under a wholesale price contract. Figure 29.3(b) compares the retailer's payoff under stocking quantities $Q - 1$, Q, and $Q + 1$, and illustrates her cost of underage and overage.

The pricing terms in B2B contracts can be used to reallocate risk and profit between the manufacturer and the retailer. By doing so, the firms can align the retailer's (the decision-maker's) incentive and objective with those of the integrated firm's. We say that the disintegrated supply chain achieves *coordination* if the expected total supply chain profit under the contract is equal to the integrated firm's optimal expected profit. In this case, the firms do not leave money on the table. Note, however, that a contract could still be beneficial and effective even if it does not help coordinate the supply chain. We measure a B2B contract's *efficiency* by the ratio of the total supply chain expected profit under the contract to the integrated firm's optimal expected profit (i.e., $(\Pi_r + \Pi_m)/\Pi^I$). If this ratio is equal to one, the supply chain is coordinated and the expected total supply chain profit is maximized. If it is less than one, there is room for improvement.

Effective B2B contracts would lead to high channel efficiency while allowing *flexibility* to share the benefit of efficiency. Channel efficiency (or, contract efficiency) does not indicate how the total profit is shared. For example, a wholesale price contract with w close to c would be efficient but it leaves almost no profit to the manufacturer. Next, we discuss a variety of B2B contract forms that achieve coordination through redistributing the risk of excess inventory and shortage. These contracts modify the underage and overage costs of the retailer, hence her critical ratio, through their pricing terms. They are designed to induce the retailer to order and stock Q^I units by aligning her objective with the integrated firm's objective.

29.2.3 The buy-back contract

We have seen that the wholesale price, as the single pricing term in the B2B contract, is not sufficient to coordinate the supply chain. Here, we introduce a second pricing term into the contract: The *buy-back price, b*. The idea is that the manufacturer can induce the retailer to order a larger quantity by offering to buy back any leftover units. This action would reduce the retailer's excess inventory risk in case of low demand realization (i.e., reducing the retailer's downside risk). Hence, the retailer would find it optimal to increase her stocking quantity towards the integrated firm optimal level Q^I. This would lead to higher expected sales and an increase in the expected total supply chain profit. Under the *buy-back contract* (w, b), the retailer pays the manufacturer a wholesale price w per unit prior to the selling season. At the end of the season she returns any leftover units to the manufacturer and receives b per unit. The manufacturer can salvage the returned units at v per unit.[10]

With a buy-back contract, the retailer's cost of overage is $c_o = w - b$ and her cost of underage is $c_u = p - w$. Recall from the marginal cost–benefit analysis that the retailer should order and stock such that the probability of not stocking out is equal to the critical ratio. Thus, the retailer should optimally order

$$Q^b = F^{-1}\left(\frac{c_u}{c_u + c_o}\right) = F^{-1}\left(\frac{p - w}{p - b}\right), \tag{7}$$

which is larger than the Q^w value in (6). The contract parameters can be set such that it is optimal for the retailer to order Q^I. This can be achieved by setting the parameters (w, b) such that the retailer's critical ratio is equal to the integrated firm's critical ratio; that is, such that $\frac{p-w}{p-b} = \frac{p-c}{p-v}$. Rearranging the terms, we obtain the following relationship between the price parameters w and b of a *coordinating* buy-back contract

$$b^b = \frac{p(w + v - c) - vw}{p - c}. \tag{8}$$

Note that the coordination relation is independent of the demand distribution. This allows a coordinating contract to be designed without market demand information.

Next we investigate the expected profits under the buy-back contract to clarify why the above condition on contract parameters helps achieve supply chain coordination (or, channel coordination). For a given stocking quantity Q, the manufacturer's, the retailer's, and the total supply chain's expected profits are

$$\Pi_m^b(Q) = (w - c)Q - (b - v)E[Q - \min(Q, D)],$$
$$\Pi_r^b(Q) = pE[\min(Q, D)] + bE[Q - \min(Q, D)] - wQ$$
$$= (p - b)E[\min(Q, D)] - (w - b)Q, \tag{9}$$
$$\Pi_{tot}^b(Q) = (p - v)E[\min(Q, D)] - (c - v)Q.$$

The retailer's optimal stocking quantity Q^b can be determined by solving $\max_Q \Pi_r^b(Q)$. This quantity is equal to the one in (7). Note that the expected total supply chain profit function in (9) is equal to the integrated firms' expected profit function in (1). Hence, if the retailer

---

[10] We assume $b > v$. Otherwise, the retailer has no reason to return unsold units and the buy-back contract would simply be equivalent to the wholesale price contract.

orders Q^I units, then the expected total supply chain profit would be maximized. Thus, any (w, b^b) pair that satisfies (8) helps achieve channel coordination.

In addition to maximizing the expected total supply chain profit through coordination (i.e., maximizing the size of the pie), the pricing terms of the buy-back contract also allow the manufacturer and the retailer to share the total supply chain profit in any way they want (i.e., sharing the pie). Note that if the contract parameters w and b satisfy

$$(p - b) = \theta(p - v) \quad \text{and} \quad (w - b) = \theta(c - v) \tag{10}$$

for some θ, then we have $\Pi_r^b(Q) = \theta\Pi_{tot}^b(Q)$. The retailer decides how much to order by solving $\max_Q \Pi_r^b(Q)$ or, equivalently $\max_Q \theta\Pi_{tot}^b(Q)$. Because θ is a constant, the retailer's optimal stocking quantity coincides with the supply chain optimal stocking quantity Q^I, and hence the supply chain is coordinated. We can obtain (8) also by solving the two equations in (10) simultaneously. Note also that θ represents the retailer's share of the total supply chain profit in a coordinating buy-back contract. Plugging the coordinating b^b from (8) in (10), we find

$$\theta = \frac{p - w}{p - c}. \tag{11}$$

By setting (w, b^b) according to (8), the manufacturer and the retailer achieve channel coordination and determine how the total profit should be shared. In other words, a coordinating buy-back contract works as a *profit sharing scheme* between the manufacturer and the retailer.

The coordinating buy-back contract is not unique. Any (w, b^b) pair that satisfies (8) coordinates the supply chain and achieves the maximum possible expected supply chain profit. Different (w, b^b) pairs, however, determine how this profit and associated inventory risk is shared between the two firms. At one extreme is the coordinating buy-back contract $(w = c, b^b = v)$, for which the retailer's share of the supply chain profit is 100%; that is, $\theta = 1$. With this contract, the manufacturer's unit profit margin and his expected profit is zero. All supply chain profit and all inventory risk is assigned to the retailer. At the other extreme is the coordinating contract $(w = p, b^b = p)$, for which the retailer's share of the supply chain profit is $\theta = 0$. With this contract, the retailer's profit margin is zero; however, she can return unsold units at full price. All supply chain profit and all inventory risk is assigned to the manufacturer.

The continuum of coordinating buy-back contracts (w, b^b) between these two extremes allows *arbitrary* profit and risk sharing. Note from (8) and (11) that a higher buy-back price b^b is coupled with a higher wholesale price in a coordinating contract, and such a contract leads to a lower profit share for the retailer. If the retailer wants more protection against excess inventory risk (in the form of a higher buy-back price), she needs to pay a higher wholesale price and forego part of her share of the supply chain profit. In other words, the coordinating buy-back contract assigns the retailer (or the manufacturer) higher expected profit in exchange for accepting higher excess inventory risk.

Arbitrary profit and risk sharing is an important feature of the buy-back contract. It can enable firms to achieve strict Pareto improvement; that is, improve both firms' expected profits relative to the status quo. If the status quo is a wholesale price contract, switching to a coordinating buy-back contract increases the expected total supply chain profit. Which coordinating contract (w, b^b) is to be chosen depends on the relative bargaining power and the firms' profits in the status quo. For example, for the manufacturer to switch to a

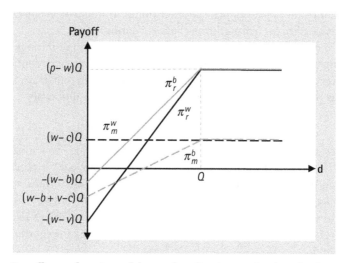

FIGURE 29.4 Payoffs as a function of demand realization with a buy-back contract

buy-back contract, the benefit from the retailer's increased stocking quantity to the manufacturer should outweigh the costs that the manufacturer undertakes due to assuming a portion of the inventory risk.

Figure 29.4 illustrates the firm's payoffs as a function of demand realization d for a given stocking quantity Q. The figure compares the payoffs between a wholesale price contract (the darker line) and a coordinating buy-back contract (the lighter line). For demand realizations lower than the stocking quantity Q, we observe how the buy-back contract transfers part of the retailer's excess inventory risk to the manufacturer. The contract enables the retailer to share her downside risk with the manufacturer. For demand realizations higher than Q, the payoffs under the two contracts overlap because there is no excess inventory to be bought back. Hence, overall, moving from a wholesale price contract to a buy-back contract would induce the retailer to carry more inventory.

Buy-back contracts are very popular in the book publishing industry. Around 30–35% of new hardcover books are returned to their publishers (Cachon and Terwiesch 2006). To minimize transportation costs, a bookstore often ships back not the book itself, but only its cover to prove that the book was not sold. Buy-back contracts are sometimes referred to as *returns policies*. A publisher can also use a buy-back contract to signal to the retailer the high demand potential for the product. A manufacturer working with multiple retailers may want to buy back unsold units with the purpose of redistributing them to retailers that need additional units. Alternatively, a manufacturer may buy back unsold units to prevent them from being sold at deep discounts, which would damage his brand image. We refer the reader to Padmanabhan and Png (1995, 1997) for further discussion of the buy-back contract.

29.2.4 The revenue sharing and rebate contracts

The buy-back contract achieved coordination through a contract parameter (buy-back price) related to the retailer's unsold product quantity. Another approach is to contract on the retailer's sales quantity. Here we discuss two contracts that use this approach.

Consider a contract with parameters (w, f). The retailer pays to the manufacturer w per unit ordered prior to the selling season. During the selling season the retailer sells the product at price p per unit. At the end of the season, for each unit sold, the retailer keeps f^*p and transfers $(1 - f)^*p$ to the manufacturer. The retailer salvages any unsold product for v. Depending on the value of f, two cases are possible:

- When $0 < f \leq 1$, the retailer shares $(1 - f)$ percent of her sales revenue with the manufacturer. This is interpreted as a *revenue sharing contract*. Note that the special case with $f = 1$ corresponds to a wholesale price contract.

- When $f > 1$, the manufacturer pays $(f - 1)p$ for each unit sold to the retailer. This is interpreted as a *rebate contract*.

With a revenue sharing (or a rebate) contract, the retailer's cost of underage is $c_u = fp - w$. Her cost of overage is $c_o = w - v$. Marginal cost–benefit analysis states that the retailer's optimal stocking quantity satisfies

$$Q^{rc} = F^{-1}\left(\frac{c_u}{c_u + c_o}\right) = F^{-1}\left(\frac{fp - w}{fp - v}\right).$$

The contract parameters (w, f) can be determined such that it is optimal for the retailer to order a quantity equal to the integrated firm's optimal quantity Q^I. Hence, the supply chain can be coordinated if w and f are set such that the retailer's critical ratio is equal to the integrated firm's critical ratio; that is, when $\frac{fp-w}{fp-v} = \frac{p-c}{p-v}$. Rearranging the terms, we obtain the following relationship between the parameters w and f^{rc} of a coordinating revenue sharing (or, rebate) contract

$$f^{rc} = \frac{w(p - v) - v(p - c)}{p(c - v)}. \tag{12}$$

Next we investigate the expected profits. For a given stocking quantity Q, the manufacturer's, the retailer's, and the total supply chain's expected profits are

$$\Pi_m^{rc}(Q) = (w - c)Q + (1 - f)pE[\min(Q, D)],$$

$$\Pi_r^{rc}(Q) = fpE[\min(Q, D)] + vE[Q - \min(Q, D)] - wQ$$

$$= (fp - v)E[\min(Q, D)] - (w - v)Q, \tag{13}$$

$$\Pi_{tot}^{rc}(Q) = (p - v)E[\min(Q, D)] - (c - v)Q.$$

The retailer's optimal stocking quantity Q^{rc} defined above is also the maximizer of (13). Hence, any (w, f) pair that satisfies (12) helps achieve channel coordination. Substituting f^{rc} into the retailer's expected profit in (13) yields

$$\Pi_r^{rc}(Q) = \left(\frac{w - v}{c - v}\right)\Pi_{tot}^{rc}(Q). \tag{14}$$

Because $\frac{w-v}{c-v}$ is a constant, the retailer's optimal stocking quantity coincides with the supply chain optimal stocking quantity Q^I. This observation offers another proof that the supply chain is coordinated for any (w, f^{rc}) pair that satisfies (12). Different (w, f^{rc}) pairs determine how the total supply chain profit and associated inventory risk will be shared between the two firms.

Let's first consider the *revenue sharing* contract, $f \leq 1$. Similar to the buy-back contract, the coordinating revenue sharing contract is not unique. A revenue sharing contract also allows arbitrary sharing of profits. At one extreme is the coordinating revenue sharing contract $(w = c, f^{rc} = 1)$, for which the retailer's share of the supply chain profit is $\frac{w-v}{c-v} = 1$. With this contract, the manufacturer's expected profit is zero because he sells at unit cost and his revenue share is $(1 - f) = 0$. All sales revenue, all supply chain profit, and all inventory risk is assigned to the retailer. Note that this revenue sharing contract is equivalent to a wholesale price contract with $w = c$. At the other extreme is the coordinating revenue sharing contract $(w = v, f^{rc} = v/p)$, for which the retailer's share of the supply chain profit is $\frac{w-v}{c-v} = 0$. Because the retailer's revenue share is v/p, the retailer's revenue per sale is only the salvage value v. The wholesale price is also equal to the salvage value. Hence, the retailer can recapture her payment to the manufacturer for any excess unit by salvaging. As a result, the retailer's expected profit is zero, and she is under zero excess inventory risk. This contract assigns $(1 - v/p)$ percent of the sales revenue, all supply chain profit, and all inventory risk to the manufacturer.

The continuum of coordinating revenue sharing contracts (w, f^{rc}) between these two extremes allows arbitrary profit and risk sharing between the firms. Note from (12) and (14) that a higher revenue share for the retailer f^{rc} is coupled with a higher wholesale price, and such a contract leads to a higher profit share and higher inventory risk for the retailer. Hence, the retailer or the manufacturer's expected profit increases as she or he is under higher inventory risk. This is similar to the result we obtained with buy-back contracts.

The coordinating revenue sharing contact is interesting from the pricing point of view. Coordination requires the manufacturer to charge a wholesale price less than or equal to his unit production cost. That is, $f^{rc} \leq 1$ implies $w \leq c$. By charging $w \leq c$, the manufacturer actually loses money for each unit that he sells to the retailer. The manufacturer's profit comes from his $(1 - f)$ percent share of the retailer's sales revenue. Because $w \leq c$, the retailer's cost of overage and underage are lower than the integrated firm's cost of overage and underage respectively. In other words, the revenue sharing contract reduces the retailer's excess inventory risk even below the integrated firm's inventory risk. Yet, the retailer's upside risk (potential loss from not carrying an extra unit) is also lower, which allows a coordinating solution.

Figure 29.5(a) illustrates the firms' payoffs as a function of demand realization d for a given stocking quantity Q decision of the retailer. The figure compares the payoffs between a wholesale price contract (the darker lines) and a coordinating revenue sharing contract (the lighter lines). We observe how the revenue sharing contract transfers part of the retailer's inventory risk to the manufacturer for demand realizations lower than the stocking quantity Q. Unlike the buy-back contract, the revenue sharing contract affects the payoffs for demand realizations higher than Q as well.

The best-known revenue sharing contract example is the one between video rental stores (such as Blockbuster) and the movie studios that produce films (see Mortimer 2002, and Cachon and Lariviere 2005 for details). Prior to 1998, a rental store would pay a wholesale price of around $65 per film copy to the studio. The high upfront payment discouraged rental stores from purchasing sufficient number of copies, leading to low product availability for consumers. In 1998, the leading rental store chain, Blockbuster, and the studios

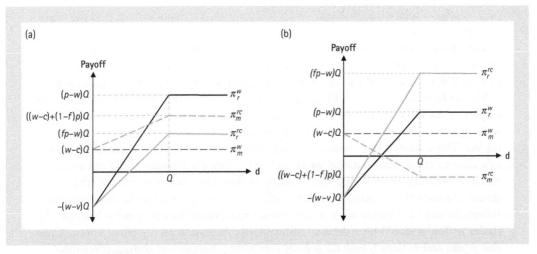

FIGURE 29.5 Payoffs as a function of demand realization; (a) with a revenue sharing contract; (b) with a rebate contract

signed a revenue sharing contract. The wholesale price of a copy was reduced to around $3–$8; in exchange, Blockbuster agreed to share around 45 percent of its rental revenue with the movie studios. Due to the decrease in the upfront price, Blockbuster ordered many more copies than before. Both Blockbuster and the movie studios benefited from the deal, and consumers enjoyed higher product availability levels. The interested reader is referred to Cachon and Lariviere (2005) for a comprehensive analysis and discussion of the revenue sharing contract.

Next let's consider the *rebate* contract, the case with $f > 1$. With the rebate contract (w, r), the manufacturer pays the retailer a rebate $r = (f - 1)p$ per unit sold. Note that a high wholesale price w increases the retailer's excess inventory risk, whereas a high f increases her inventory shortage risk. When $w > c$; that is, when the manufacturer receives a positive margin for each unit he sells to the retailer, we know from (12) that a coordinating contract requires $f^{rc} > 1$. In other words, the manufacturer in this case should share part of his earnings with the retailer through a rebate agreement to achieve channel coordination. Doing so would increase the retailer's cost of underage (or her upside risk) from $p - w$ to $p - w + r$. Her cost of overage $w - v$ is the same as the one with the wholesale price contract. Hence, the retailer would find it optimal to order and stock a larger quantity, increasing the chances of sales and profits. Note the difference between the pricing strategies of the rebate and buy-back contracts: The rebate contract offers an extra payment for the retailer's sold units; whereas the buy-back contract puts a price on unsold units. Consequently, the rebate contract increases the retailer's inventory shortage cost (the upside risk); whereas the buy-back contract reduces the retailer's excess inventory risk (the downside risk).

Figure 29.5(b) compares the payoffs between a wholesale price contract (the darker lines) and a coordinating rebate contract (the lighter lines). We observe the manufacturer's payoff to be negative for most demand realizations. This is because the rebate $r = f^{rc}p - p = \frac{(w-c)(p-v)}{(c-v)}$ that the manufacturer pays to the retailer for each unit sold is higher than the manufacturer's unit profit margin $(w - c)$. Hence, the manufacturer's expected profit in a coordinating rebate contract is negative. The *target rebate* contract

(w, t, r) offers a solution to this issue. With this contract, the manufacturer pays the rebate r to the retailer only for units sold beyond a threshold level t. Hence, the manufacturer makes a positive profit at each unit sold up to the threshold level. The rebate contract we studied is a special case of the target rebate contract with $t = 0$. One can determine w, t, and r values that achieve coordination and arbitrary profit sharing with a target rebate contract.

Microsoft, Hewlett Packard, Lotus, and Novell are among the firms that are known to employ rebates. Rebates known as *dealer incentives* are widespread in the auto industry as well. In some cases, the rebate is offered directly to the end-consumer, instead of the retailer. This is known as a *consumer rebate*; whereas the rebate form we studied is known as a *channel rebate*. In the model we considered, a consumer rebate would not affect the retailer's ordering decision and the resulting profits. However, a consumer rebate may stimulate demand by reducing the effective sales price of the product to the end-consumers. Hence, the story is different when demand D is a function of the sales price p. We refer the reader to Taylor (2002) for a detailed and complete discussion on the rebate contract. See also Aydin and Porteus (2009) for a study comparing channel and consumer rebates.

29.2.5 The quantity flexibility contract

The buy-back contract reduced the retailer's excess inventory risk by allowing her to return all unsold units for *partial credit* (i.e., $b < w$). Providing *full credit* (i.e., $b = w$) for all returns would be inefficient because this would transfer all inventory risk to the manufacturer. A possible alternative is to allow *partial returns* for full credit. This is how a *quantity flexibility contract* (w, d_a, u_a) operates. With this contract, the retailer first submits an initial order Q^{ini}. After observing demand realization d, the retailer is allowed to submit a *modified order* Q^m. The contract imposes limits to order modification, though. The retailer can cancel *at most* d_a% of her initial order at full credit (i.e., receive back the w per unit she paid), but she has to buy the rest of her initial order for w each. In other words, the retailer provides a minimum purchase guarantee of $(1 - d_a)Q^{ini}$ units to the manufacturer. The manufacturer, in return, guarantees to deliver *at most* u_a% above the retailer's initial order. Thus, the retailer's modified order needs to satisfy $Q^m \in [(1 - d_a)Q^{ini}, (1 + u_a)Q^{ini}]$. At the end of the season, both the manufacturer and the retailer salvage excess units at v per unit.

The manufacturer produces $Q = (1 + u_a)Q^{ini}$ units to honor his commitment.[11] The retailer is committed to purchase at least $(1 - d_a)Q^{ini} = \left(\frac{1-d_a}{1+u_a}\right)Q$ units of this production quantity Q. We define $R = (1 - d_a)/(1 + u_a)$ as the retailer's *responsibility parameter* which represents the fraction of supply chain inventory for which the retailer is responsible. Higher responsibility values correspond to lower *flexibility* for the retailer. In a sense, the quantity flexibility contract prices this flexibility to cancel a portion of the initial order after observing the demand realization.

With a quantity flexibility contract, the cost of underage for the retailer is $c_u = p - w$. The cost of overage, however, is not fixed. For a given initial order Q^{ini}, the marginal cost of having one excess unit depends on the total number of excess units ($Q^{ini} - d$). If the number of excess units is less than or equal to the quantity that the retailer can cancel for

---

[11] Alternatively, one might model a case in which the manufacturer decides how much to produce, and pays a penalty to the retailer if he cannot meet the guaranteed availability level.

full credit (i.e., if $Q^{ini} - d \le d_a Q^{ini}$), the retailer does not incur a cost due to not having ordered one less unit. Hence $c_o = 0$. Note that in this case the quantity flexibility contract operates like a buy-back contract with $b = w$. If the number of excess units is more than the quantity that the retailer can cancel for full credit (i.e., if $Q^{ini} - d > d_a Q^{ini}$), the retailer loses $c_o = w - v$ due to not having ordered one less unit. Because the cost of overage is not fixed, we cannot use the marginal cost–benefit analysis to determine the retailer's optimal initial order quantity. To this end, we investigate the retailer's expected profit function next. We carry out the analysis using the manufacturer's production quantity $Q = (1 + u_a)Q^{ini}$ that the retailer's initial order Q^{ini} implies. For a given production quantity Q, the manufacturer's, the retailer's, and the total supply chain's expected profits are

$$\Pi_m^{qf}(Q) = wE[Q^m] + vE[Q - Q^m] - cQ$$
$$= (w - v)E[Q^m] - (c - v)Q,$$
$$\Pi_r^{qf}(Q) = pE[\min(Q, D)] + vE[Q^m - \min(Q, D)] - wE[Q^m] \tag{15}$$
$$= (p - v)E[\min(Q, D)] - (w - v)E[Q^m],$$
$$\Pi_{tot}^{qf}(Q) = (p - v)E[\min(Q, D)] - (c - v)Q.$$

We calculate the expected value of the retailer's modified order quantity Q^m as

$$E[Q^m] = \int_0^{RQ} RQf(x)dx + \int_{RQ}^Q xf(x)dx + \int_Q^\infty Qf(x)dx = Q - \int_{RQ}^Q F(x)dx.$$

The second equality follows from integration by parts. We calculate the expected sales as $E[\min(Q, D)] = \int_0^Q xf(x)dx + \int_Q^\infty Qf(x)dx = Q - \int_0^Q F(x)dx$. The second equality, again, follows from integration by parts. Substituting $E[Q^m]$ and $E[\min(Q,D)]$, the retailer's expected profit function in (15) becomes

$$\Pi_r^{qf}(Q) = (p - w)Q - (p - v)\int_0^{RQ} F(x)dx - (p - w)\int_{RQ}^Q F(x)dx.$$

This function is concave in Q. The optimal production quantity Q^{qf} for the retailer satisfies the following first order condition

$$\left.\frac{\partial \Pi_r^{qf}(Q)}{\partial Q}\right|_{Q=Q^{qf}} = (p - w)(1 - F(Q^{qf})) - (w - v)R\, F(RQ^{qf}) = 0. \tag{16}$$

The quantity flexibility contract (w, d_a, u_a) achieves coordination if the retailer optimally orders $Q^I/(1 + u_a)$ units. In this case, the manufacturer produces $Q^{qf} = (1 + u_a)\frac{Q^I}{1+u_a} = Q^I$ units and hence, the total supply chain expected profit is maximized. Substituting $Q^{qf} = Q^I = F^{-1}\left(\frac{p-c}{p-v}\right)$ into (16) and re-arranging the terms, we obtain the following relationship between the parameters w and $R = \frac{1-d_a}{1+u_a}$ of a coordinating quantity flexibility contract

$$w^{qf} = v + \frac{c - v}{\frac{c-v}{p-v} + R\, F(RQ^I)}. \tag{17}$$

Note that the coordination relation depends only on the retailer's responsibility parameter $R = (1 - d_a)/(1 + u_a)$, not on the individual adjustment limit values d_a and u_a. Also note that the wholesale price w^{qf} in a coordinating quantity flexibility contract is decreasing in the responsibility parameter R, thus it is increasing in contract flexibility. This is how flexibility is priced in this contract: The retailer needs to pay more if she chooses a more flexible contract. Finally, we observe from (17) that the optimal parameters in a coordinating quantity flexibility contract depend on the demand distribution. This might lead to implementation issues. For instance, the manufacturer cannot use the same coordinating quantity flexibility contract in different markets that have different demand distributions.

Similar to the buy-back and revenue sharing (or, rebate) contracts, the coordinating quantity flexibility contract is not unique. Any (w^{qf}, R) pair that satisfies (17) coordinates the supply chain and achieves the maximum possible expected supply chain profit. Different (w^{qf}, R) pairs determine how this profit and associated inventory risk is shared between the two firms. At one extreme is the coordinating quantity flexibility contract $(w^{qf} = c, R = 1)$, for which $d_a = 0$ and $u_a = 0$. This contract does not offer any flexibility to the retailer at all. The retailer has to purchase all of her initial order Q^{ini} without any modification. The manufacturer's profit is zero because he sells to the retailer at his unit production cost. All supply chain profit and all inventory risk is assigned to the retailer. At the other extreme is the coordinating quantity flexibility contract $(w = p, R = 0)$, for which $d_a = 1$. This contract provides extreme flexibility to the retailer because she can cancel all of her initial order Q^{ini}. However, the retailer's expected profit is zero because the wholesale price is equal to the sales price. All supply chain profit and all inventory risk is assigned to the manufacturer.

The continuum of coordinating quantity flexibility contracts (w^{qf}, R) between these two extremes allows arbitrary profit and risk sharing between the firms. Because $\frac{\partial \Pi_r^{qf}(w^{qf}, R)}{\partial R} > 0$, the retailer's expected profit is higher with a coordinating quantity flexibility contract that has high responsibility R (i.e., low flexibility) and low w values. Hence, similar to buy-back and revenue sharing contracts, the coordinating quantity flexibility contract assigns the retailer (or the manufacturer) higher expected profit in exchange for accepting higher excess inventory risk. Note, however, that the retailer's expected profit is increasing in her responsibility parameter R because the corresponding wholesale price parameter w^{qf} in the contract decreases. Otherwise, for a given w value, the retailer would prefer a contract with less responsibility R, which offers higher flexibility (with high d_a and high u_a).

Figure 29.6 illustrates the firms' payoffs as a function of demand realization d. The figure compares the payoffs between a wholesale price contract (the darker lines) and a coordinating quantity flexibility contract (the lighter lines). With the wholesale price contract, the retailer places an order of Q units. With the quantity flexibility contract, she places an initial order of $Q^{ini} = Q/(1 + u_a)$ units, leading to a production quantity of Q units. Note that the payoff functions of the firms with the quantity flexibility contract change slope at the retailer's minimum purchase quantity RQ and at the manufacturer's production quantity Q. We observe how this contract allocates inventory risk between the two firms. For demand realizations lower than the retailer's minimum purchase commitment RQ, the retailer assumes all excess inventory risk and the manufacturer's payoff is fixed. For $d \in (RQ, Q)$, the firms share excess inventory risk. For demand realizations higher than the manufacturer's production quantity Q, there is no excess inventory risk to be shared. Hence, the quantity flexibility contract payoffs overlap with the respective wholesale price contract payoffs.

Tsay (1999), who provides an extensive discussion of the quantity flexibility contract, mentions that these contracts are being used by firms including Sun Microsystems, Solectron, Toyota, and IBM. Heskett and Signorelli (1984) discuss how Benetton uses a quantity

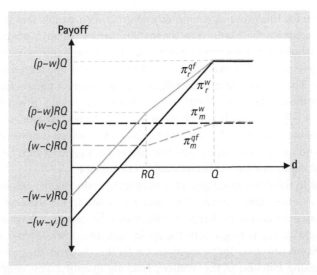

FIGURE 29.6 Payoffs as a function of demand realization with a quantity flexibility contract

flexibility contract with its suppliers. A similar contract called *backup agreement* is used in the fashion industry (see Eppen and Iyer 1997). Under a backup agreement, the retailer (a catalogue seller) first commits to a total quantity for the season. The manufacturer delivers some fraction of this quantity at the beginning of the season, and holds the rest as *backup*. After observing initial demand, the retailer may use as much as she wants from this backup, and pays a fee for the unused backup quantity. Note that this is different from a quantity flexibility contract in which the retailer does not pay for unused flexibility.

29.2.6 Other B2B contracts

We have discussed a variety of B2B contract forms that help a manufacturer and a retailer achieve channel coordination by reallocating the risk of inventory excess and shortage. These contracts, primarily through their pricing terms, align the retailer's (decision-maker's) objective with that of the integrated firm's (central decision-maker's). Most B2B contracts can be categorized under three groups. The contracts in the first group enable firms to effectively reduce the risk of excess inventory (downside risk). The contracts in the second group enable the firms to decrease the risk of shortage (upside risk). This can be achieved by increasing the cost of underage so that it becomes more costly to face an inventory shortage. The contracts in the third group provide flexibility to target both risks simultaneously. Below we categorize the contracts we discussed along this dimension and briefly mention a few more contract forms that are commonly used in practice or studied in the literature.

The first group includes the buy-back, revenue sharing, and quantity flexibility contracts. As we studied, these contracts target the downside risk of the retailer by reducing her cost of overage. They do not change the retailer's underage cost.

The rebate contract with parameters (w, r) is an example for the second group. The rebate increases the cost of underage for the retailer, thus increasing her upside risk.

Another example for this group is the *penalty contract* with parameters (w, z) (Lariviere 1999). With this contract, the retailer pays the manufacturer a penalty z per unit of lost sales in addition to a wholesale price w per unit ordered. The retailer's cost of underage increases from $p - w$ to $p - w + z$. The overage cost is the same as the one with a wholesale price contract, $w - v$. The supply chain is coordinated if the contract parameters w and z are chosen such that the retailer's critical ratio is equal to the integrated firm's critical ratio; that is, when $\frac{p-w+z}{p-v+z} = \frac{p-c}{p-v}$. This holds for $z^{pc} = (w - c)\frac{p-v}{c-v}$. Note, however, that the penalty contract requires the quantity of lost sales to be monitored, which is not easy. In addition, the retailer has no incentive to report any lost sale to the manufacturer. Such implementation issues are important for a contract's field performance.

The contracts in the third group generally operate by reducing the wholesale price that the retailer pays to the manufacturer. Note that a decrease in the wholesale price simultaneously increases the cost of underage and decreases the cost of overage for the retailer. By doing so, these contracts target both the upside risk and downside risk of the retailer. The *quantity discount contract* is one example. Under this contract, the per-unit wholesale price is a decreasing function of the retailer's stocking quantity. This contract, however, does not shift any inventory risk from the retailer to the manufacturer because the manufacturer's profit is deterministic once the retailer decides on her stocking quantity. We refer the reader to Jeuland and Shugan (1983) and Moorthy (1987) for a detailed discussion of the quantity discount contract.

Another example for the third group is the *two-part tariff* with parameters (w, F). Under this contract, the manufacturer charges the retailer an upfront lump-sum payment F in addition to a per-unit wholesale price w. The two-part tariff can achieve coordination and arbitrary profit sharing when the wholesale price is set equal to the unit production cost ($w = c$). The coordination problem is solved due to $w = c$, which eliminates double marginalization. Essentially, the two-part tariff makes the retailer's cost of underage and overage equal to that of the integrated firm's. Hence, it becomes optimal for the retailer to order and stock the integrated firm's optimal quantity. The lump-sum payment F allows arbitrary allocation of the supply chain profit between the two firms. The two-part tariff can be interpreted as a *franchising* agreement. The manufacturer's unit profit from sales to the retailer is zero because he sells at the production cost. His profit is from the lump-sum payment F. By paying the lump-sum payment, the retailer becomes the owner of the business and thus orders the supply chain optimal quantity. Note that the two-part tariff does not enable the firms to share excess inventory risk. It also requires an upfront side payment, which might not sound attractive to the retailer. We refer the reader to Moorthy (1987) and Tirole (1988) for more discussion of two-part tariffs and franchising. We summarize the retailer's (the decision-maker's) costs of underage and overage under various contract types in Table 29.1.

Next, we discuss the *options contract*, which provides a framework to replicate the payoffs of the other B2B contracts we discussed using three pricing terms. With an options contract, the retailer makes two decisions before observing demand realization: (1) She determines the number of *firm orders* to place at a *firm order price*. The retailer has to purchase these units upon observing demand realization. (2) She determines the number of *options* to purchase at an *options price*. Each option gives the retailer the opportunity to purchase a unit, if needed, after observing demand realization. The retailer needs to pay an additional *exercise price* for each option that she chooses to use after observing demand.

Table 29.1 The retailer's costs of underage and overage with different B2B contracts

Contract	Cost of underage	Cost of overage	Critical ratio
Integrated firm	$p - c$	$c - v$	$\frac{p-c}{p-v}$
Wholesale price	$p - w$	$w - v$	$\frac{p-w}{p-v}$
Buy-back	$p - w$	$w - b$	$\frac{p-w}{p-b}$
Revenue sharing	$fp - w$	$w - v$	$\frac{fp-w}{fp-v}$
Rebate[a]	$p - w + r$	$w - v$	$\frac{p-w+r}{p+r-v}$
Quantity flexibility	$p - w$	varying	varying
Penalty	$p - w + z$	$w - v$	$\frac{p-w+z}{p+z-v}$

[a] For units sold above the target level t.

Table 29.2 illustrates how the options contract framework can be used to replicate the payoffs with the different B2B contracts discussed. Note that the exercise price is positive with the contracts in the first group (i.e., those that target downside risk by reducing the retailer's cost of overage); whereas, it is negative for the contracts in the second group (those that target upside risk by increasing the retailer's cost of underage).

With a *buy-back* contract, for example, the retailer does not place any firm order. She purchases Q options at an option price of $w - b$ each. After observing demand realization d, she exercises $\min(Q, d)$ of these options by paying an exercise price of b each. With a *revenue sharing* contract too, the retailer does not place any firm order. She purchases Q options at an option price of w each. After observing demand realization d, she exercises $\min(Q, d)$ of these options by paying an exercise price of $(1 - f)p$ each. The *rebate* contract is similar to the revenue sharing contract, but the exercise price $-r$ is negative. With a *quantity flexibility* contract, the retailer places RQ firm orders by paying the firm order price w. She also purchases $(1 - R)Q$ options at an option price of zero. After observing demand realization d, the retailer exercises $\min(\max(d - RQ, 0), (1 - R)Q)$ options at an exercise price of w each. Finally, with a *penalty* contract, the retailer places no firm order and purchases Q options at a price of $w + z$. She exercises $min(Q, d)$ of these options at an

Table 29.2 B2B contracts in an options framework

Contract	Number of firm orders	Number of options	Options exercised	Firm order price	Option price	Exercise price
Buy-back	0	Q	$\min(Q, d)$	NA	$w - b$	b
Revenue sharing	0	Q	$\min(Q, d)$	NA	w	$(1 - f)p$
Rebate[a]	0	Q	$\min(Q, d)$	NA	w	$-r$
Quantity flexibility	RQ	$(1 - R)Q$	$\min(\max(d - RQ, 0),$ $(1 - R)Q)$	w	0	w
Penalty	0	Q	$\min(Q, d)$	NA	$w + z$	$-z$

Note: [a] For $t = 0$.

exercise price of $-z$, if needed. We refer the reader to Barnes-Schuster et al. (2002) for further discussion of the options contract.

A B2B contractual form that does not fall under any of the three groups is the *consignment contract*. With a consignment contract, the manufacturer keeps ownership of the inventory at the retailer until it is sold to consumers. The retailer pays the manufacturer only when the product is sold. The manufacturer essentially rents shelf space from the retailer. Note that such an arrangement does not allow risk sharing. It assigns all inventory risk to the manufacturer, leaving the retailer with zero risk. Consignment practice is popular in the US retail industry (Kandel 1996).

A related practice is Vendor Managed Inventory (VMI). Under VMI, the manufacturer keeps track of the retailer's inventory status and decides on the timing and size of the shipments. Various companies from consumer goods to high technology industries, including Procter & Gamble, Campbell Soup, Barilla SpA, General Electric, and Intel, employ VMI (Fry et al. 2001). In the grocery industry, similar practices are known as Continuous Replenishment Programs (CRP). A successful VMI program benefits the manufacturer by providing valuable demand information (hence, by reducing the bullwhip effect), and benefits the retailer through higher product availability levels. We refer the reader to Simchi-Levi et al. (2007) for further discussion of VMI programs.

29.3 INVENTORY RISK SHARING WITH A PRICE-SETTING RETAILER

So far, we have considered a manufacturer–retailer supply chain in which the sales price of the product in the consumer market is exogenously determined. In other words, the retailer (the newsvendor) decides on how much inventory to stock given a sales price to consumers. This scenario is possible, for example, when the retailer is selling a *commodity* (or, standard) product for which she does not have pricing power. For certain products, however, the retailer may be able to determine the sales price. This scenario is possible, for example, when the retailer sells a *custom product*. In this case, demand for the product is modeled as a decreasing function of the retailer's sales price, that is, as $D(p)$.

The manufacturer may want to fix the retailer's sales price to maximize his expected profit. In the USA, however, it is illegal to impose a sales price on the retailer (Tirole 1988). The manufacturer can only *suggest* a sales price. Nevertheless, the manufacturer can *influence* the retailer's sales price decision through the contract terms. The question is, whether the B2B contract terms between the firms will be able to induce the retailer to choose the integrated firm's optimal sales price and stocking quantity. Trying to align incentives along two decisions complicates the contract design problem because the incentives for one of these decisions might distort the incentives for the other. In this section of the chapter, we provide a brief introduction to some related issues and refer the reader to other papers for a detailed account.

Recall that to determine the conditions for coordination, one should first consider the integrated firm's problem. Consider a setting similar to the one in Section 29.2 but with two decisions: stocking quantity Q and sales price p. For simplicity we assume that the salvage value v is zero. The integrated firm determines the sales price p and the stocking quantity Q to maximize her expected profit

$$\Pi(p, Q) = pE[min(Q, D(p))] - cQ. \tag{18}$$

We can determine the optimal decision variables sequentially when $\Pi(p, Q)$ is jointly concave[12] in p and Q. To do so, we first determine the integrated firm's optimal quantity given a sales price p. This problem reduces to the standard newsvendor problem and, hence, the optimal stocking quantity satisfies $Q^I(p) = F^{-1}\left(\frac{p-c}{p}\right)$. Next we plug this quantity into (18) and formulate the integrated firm's problem as a function of only the sales price. The first order condition for the integrated firm's sales price decision is

$$\left.\frac{\partial\Pi(p, Q^I(p))}{\partial p}\right|_{p=p^I} = \left(E[min(Q^I(p), D(p))] + p\frac{\partial E[min(Q^I(p), D(p))]}{\partial p} - c\frac{\partial Q^I(p)}{\partial p}\right)\bigg|_{p=p^I} = 0. \tag{19}$$

The integrated firm chooses the sales price p^I that satisfies this condition and $Q^I(p^I) = F^{-1}\left(\frac{p^I-c}{p^I}\right)$ as her stocking quantity.

Next we consider a decentralized manufacturer–retailer supply chain. We check whether the buy-back and the revenue sharing contracts can motivate a price-setting retailer to choose p^I and Q^I; that is, whether these contracts can coordinate the supply chain.

With a buy-back contract (w, b), the retailer's expected profit function is $\Pi_r^b(p, Q) = (p - b)E[min(Q, D(p))] - (w - b)Q$. Coordination requires p^I to satisfy the following first order condition

$$\left.\frac{\partial\Pi_r^b(p, Q^I(p))}{\partial p}\right|_{p=p^I} = \left(E[min(Q^I(p), D(p))] + (p - b)\frac{\partial E[min(Q^I(p), D(p))]}{\partial p} - (w - b)\frac{\partial Q^I(p)}{\partial p}\right)\bigg|_{p=p^I} = 0.$$

Comparing this condition with the integrated firm's condition in (19) reveals that the condition holds only for $b = 0$. Thus, the buyback contract, with its two pricing terms, fails to coordinate the supply chain with a price-setting retailer.

With a revenue sharing contract (w, f), the retailer's expected profit function is $\Pi_r^{rc}(p, Q) = fpE[min(Q, D(p))] - wQ$. Coordination requires p^I to satisfy the following first order condition

$$\left.\frac{\partial\Pi_r^{rc}(p, Q^I(p))}{\partial p}\right|_{p=p^I} = \left(fE[min(Q^I(p), D(p))] + fp\frac{\partial E[min(Q^I(p), D(p))]}{\partial p} - w\frac{\partial Q^I(p)}{\partial p}\right)\bigg|_{p=p^I} = 0.$$

Comparison with the integrated firm's condition in (19) reveals that the condition holds for any (w, f) pair that satisfies $f = w/c$. Hence, the revenue sharing contract can coordinate the supply chain with a price-setting retailer.[13]

Although the buy-back contract does not achieve channel coordination, it may lead to higher channel efficiency compared to a given wholesale price contract. Bernstein and Federgruen (2005) show that coordination can be achieved with a modified buy-back contract $(w(p), b(p))$ in which the wholesale price and the buy-back price are functions

---

[12] $\Pi(p, Q)$ is jointly concave in p and Q if $\frac{\partial^2\Pi(p,Q)}{\partial p^2} < 0$ and $\frac{\partial^2\Pi(p,Q)}{\partial p^2}\frac{\partial^2\Pi(p,Q)}{\partial Q^2} - \left(\frac{\partial^2\Pi(p,Q)}{\partial p\partial Q}\right)^2 > 0$ are satisfied. We assume that the demand function $D(p)$ allows these conditions to be met.

[13] We remark that these results depend on the model characteristics. For example, the revenue sharing contract does not coordinate the supply chain with a price-setting retailer if the salvage value v is included in the model.

Table 29.3 Results for the specific demand function

Contract	Π_r or Π^I	p	Q
Integrated firm	$\Pi^I = (p-c)Q - \frac{pQ^2}{4(1-p)}$	$p^I = \frac{1+\sqrt{1+8c}}{4}$	$Q^I = \frac{\left(3-\sqrt{1+8c}\right)^2}{4}$
Wholesale price contract	$\Pi_r^w = (p-w)Q - \frac{pQ^2}{4(1-p)}$	$p^w = \frac{1+\sqrt{1+8w}}{4}$	$Q^w = \frac{\left(3-\sqrt{1+8w}\right)^2}{4}$
Buy-back contract	$\Pi_r^b = (p-w)Q - (p-b)\frac{Q^2}{4(1-p)}$	$p^b = \frac{3b+1+\sqrt{(1+8w-9b)(1-b)}}{4}$	$Q^b = \frac{2(1-p^b)(p^b-w)}{p^b-b}$

of the sales price. With this scheme, the retailer first commits to a sales price p. Then, the manufacturer determines the corresponding contract $(w(p), b(p))$. Finally, the retailer determines her stocking quantity. The coordinating wholesale price $w(p)$ is shown to be decreasing in the sales price p. The manufacturer encourages the retailer to decrease the sales price by *discounting* the wholesale price, hence by sharing the burden of the sales price reduction. The authors state that this scheme is similar to the bill-back schemes which are reported to be disliked by retailers. Song et al. (2008) characterize the properties of buy-back contracts for multiplicative demand models.

Cachon and Lariviere (2005) study the performance of other B2B contracts with a price-setting retailer. They show that the *quantity flexibility* and the *rebate* contracts cannot coordinate the supply chain unless the manufacturer earns zero profit. The *two-part tariff* and *quantity discount* contracts, on the other hand, are shown to coordinate the supply chain. Chen et al. (2007) study the effects of *consumer rebate* contracts on firms' profits with a price-setting retailer.

29.3.1 Numerical example with a specific demand function

To illustrate our discussion, we consider a specific price-dependent demand function $D(p) = (1-p)X$.[14] The term X is a random variable distributed uniformly on $[0,2]$.[15] The expected demand $(1-p)$ is decreasing in the retailer's sales price p and it is equal to zero for $p = 1$. The expected sales quantity is calculated as

$$E[\min(Q, D(p))] = \int_0^{\frac{Q}{1-p}} (1-p)xf(x)dx + \int_{\frac{Q}{1-p}}^2 Qf(x)dx = Q\left(1 - \frac{Q}{4(1-p)}\right), \quad (20)$$

where $f(x) = 0.5$ is the density function of the random variable X.

Table 29.3 summarizes the outcome for the integrated firm and for the decentralized supply chain under wholesale price and buy-back contracts. The table presents the retailer's

---

[14] This example follows from the model in Granot and Yin (2005), which is based on Emmons and Gilbert (1998).

[15] The demand form $D(p) = d(p)X$ is known as the multiplicative demand model first proposed by Karlin and Carr (1962). The other major alternative is the additive demand model $D(p) = d(p) + X$ (Mills 1959). The primary difference between the two alternatives is that the variance of demand is decreasing in the sales price in the multiplicative model, whereas it is independent of the sales price in the additive model. The choice between these two alternatives might lead to significantly different qualitative results (see Mills 1959; Emmons and Gilbert 1998; Petruzzi and Dada 1999).

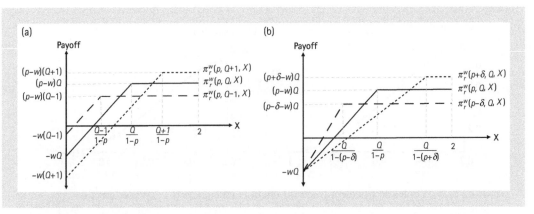

FIGURE 29.7 The retailer's Payoff with a wholesale price contract; (a) changing the stocking quantity; (b) changing the sales price

(or the integrated firm's) expected profit function, which is jointly concave in p and Q, as well as the sales price and quantity values that maximize this function.

Figure 29.7(a) illustrates how the retailer's payoff under the wholesale price contract changes when she changes the stocking quantity, assuming a given sales price p. We observe that the effect of increasing or decreasing the stocking quantity is similar to the effect in the fixed-price analysis of Section 29.2.1. Figure 29.7(b) illustrates how the retailer's payoff changes when she increases or decreases the sales price by $\delta > 0$, assuming a given stocking quantity Q. Note that an increase in the sales price increases the maximum possible profit for the retailer (due to the increase in the profit margin) but also decreases the probability of high demand realization. The retailer needs to consider this tradeoff when determining her stocking quantity and sales price.

Under the wholesale price contract, if demand were deterministic, the retailer would simply order $Q = D(p) = 1 - p$ units. In this case, she would set the sales price as $p^u = \frac{w+1}{2}$ to maximize her expected profit $(p - w)(1 - p)$. We have $p^w > p^u$ due to $c \leq w \leq p < 1$. Thus, inventory risk due to uncertain demand causes the retailer to set a higher sales price to consumers,[16] leading to a decrease in the expected consumer demand.

Under the buy-back contract, we observe that the retailer's optimal sales price is increasing in the wholesale price w, whereas it is decreasing in the buy-back price b. This is consistent with our earlier observation that the retailer's optimal sales price increases with excess inventory risk. A higher buy-back price b decreases the retailer's inventory risk, hence it leads her to choose a lower sales price. Note that our analysis with the wholesale price contract corresponds to a special case of the buy-back contract analysis with $b = 0$.

To further illustrate our discussion, we consider a numerical example with unit production cost $c = 0.2$.[17] In particular, we investigate channel efficiency under the wholesale price and buy-back contracts. Recall that channel efficiency is defined as the ratio of the expected

---

[16] This result holds for all multiplicative demand models under mild assumptions. See Karlin and Carr (1962), Emmons and Gilbert (1998), and Petruzzi and Dada (1999).

[17] Our observations would be valid for other production cost values $c \in [0,1]$ as well.

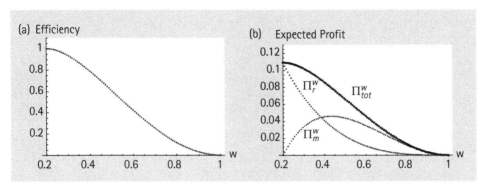

FIGURE 29.8 Wholesale price contract; (a) channel efficiency; (b) expected profits

total supply chain profit under a B2B contract to the integrated firm's optimal expected profit (i.e., $(\Pi_r + \Pi_m)/\Pi^I$). A contract with high efficiency provides higher total profits. By choosing specific contract parameters, the manufacturer and the retailer can negotiate to share the total profit based on their respective powers. For $c = 0.2$, the integrated firm's optimal price and quantity decisions are $p^I = 0.653$, $Q^I = 0.481$, leading to an expected profit level of $\Pi^I = 0.109$.

Figures 29.8 and 29.9 present the results as a function of the pricing term in the contract, the wholesale price w. Figure 29.8(a) illustrates the efficiency of the contract as a function of w. We note that the contract achieves coordination (i.e., 100 percent efficiency) only for $w = c$. Similar to the fixed-price analysis, efficiency decreases with w due to double marginalization. Figure 29.8(b) presents the expected profits of the manufacturer, the retailer and the total supply chain.

Figures 29.9(a) and (b) illustrate the retailer's sales price and stocking quantity decisions as a function of the wholesale price. As expected, the retailer chooses a higher sales price and a lower stocking quantity when the wholesale price increases.

Next, we consider a buy-back contract with parameters (w, b). Figures 29.10(a)–(b) and 29.11(a)–(b) present the results as a function of the buy-back price b when the manufacturer offers a wholesale price $w = 0.5$. When $w = 0.5$, the buy-back price that maximizes

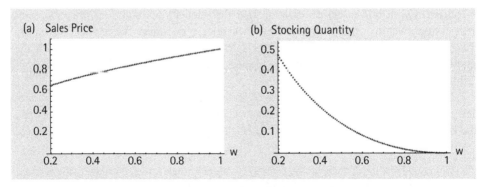

FIGURE 29.9 Wholesale price contract; (a) sales price; (b) stocking quantity

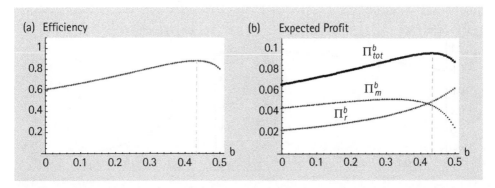

FIGURE 29.10 Buy-back contract with $w = 0.5$; (a) channel efficiency; (b) expected profits

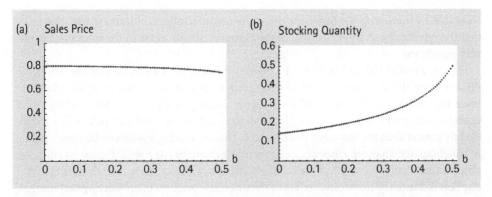

FIGURE 29.11 Buy-back contract with $w = 0.5$; (a) sales price; (b) stocking quantity

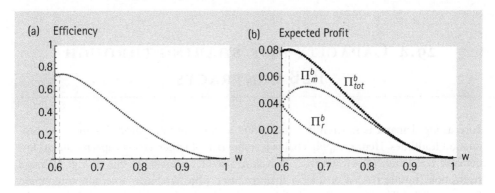

FIGURE 29.12 Buy-back contract with $b = 0.6$; (a) channel efficiency; (b) expected profits

the expected total supply chain profit is $b = 0.432$, leading to an expected total profit of $\Pi^b_{tot} = 0.096$. This profit level is below the integrated firm's optimal expected profit of $\Pi^I = 0.109$. This is because the buy-back contract fails to coordinate the supply chain with a price-setting retailer. We also observe that providing full credit for returns (i.e., $b = w = 0.5$) is not beneficial for the supply chain because it causes the retailer to order excessively.

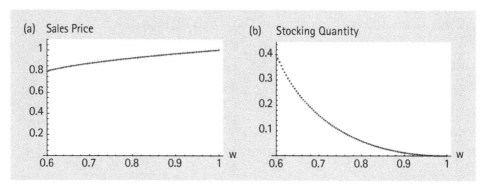

FIGURE 29.13 Buy-back contract with $b = 0.6$; (a) sales price; (b) stocking quantity

Note that by increasing the buy-back price, the manufacturer can decrease the sales price that the retailer charges to end-consumers. However, the decrease in the sales price is not very significant.

Figures 29.12(a)–(b) and 29.13(a)–(b) present the results as a function of the wholesale price w when the manufacturer offers a buy-back price $b = 0.6$. In this case, the wholesale price that maximizes the expected total supply chain profit is $w = 0.616$, leading to an expected total profit of $\Pi^b_{tot} = 0.081$. Note that the maximizing wholesale price value is only slightly greater than the buy-back price $b = 0.6$. Hence, offering a generous buy-back policy is beneficial for channel efficiency. Comparing Figure 29.13(a) with Figure 29.11(a), we observe that changes in w affect the retailer's sales price choice more than the changes in b do. This is due to the more direct effect of the wholesale price on the retailer's profit margin. The wholesale price w affects the retailer's profit margin on all units; whereas the buy-back price b affects only the margin with leftover units.

29.4 CAPACITY RISK SHARING THROUGH B2B CONTRACTS

Forecasting demand is inherently difficult due to short product lifecycles and long production leadtimes. Hence, supply chains face the risk of either excess capacity due to low demand realization (downside risk) or lack of product availability due to high demand realization (upside risk). Consider a manufacturer who purchases a certain component from a supplier. The manufacturer builds to order, that is, she produces after observing the realization of consumer demand. The supplier, on the other hand, needs to build his capacity to produce the component in advance of the manufacturer's order. If consumer demand turns out to be high, both the supplier and the manufacturer face upside capacity risk. However, if consumer demand turns out to be low, only the supplier faces downside capacity risk. The cost of capacity risk is exacerbated by a lack of proper risk sharing.

The severity of capacity risk for each firm depends on the contractual agreement. Under a wholesale price contract, for example, the manufacturer pays a wholesale price w to the supplier for each unit ordered. The supplier decides on the component capacity K to maximize his expected profit prior to observing demand. Let c_k be the unit cost of capacity. Next, demand D is realized and the manufacturer places an order. The supplier fills the order as much as possible at a unit cost c; that is, he delivers $\min(D, K)$ units. The manufacturer receives the order and sells at a fixed price $p > 0$. Unmet demand is lost without additional stockout penalty, and unsold inventory has zero salvage value without loss of generality.

Note that demand D is uncertain at the time when the supplier builds capacity. Suppose the demand forecast is such that $D = \mu + \varepsilon$, where μ is the mean, which is a positive constant, and ε is a zero-mean random variable with a cdf $G(\cdot)$ which represents the market or forecast uncertainty. Such information can be constructed by using information obtained from forecast error data or through a third-party market research firm (such as Dataquest services of the Gartner group). Under a wholesale price contract, for a given capacity K, the manufacturer's and the supplier's expected profits before demand is realized are

$$\Pi_m^w(K) = (p - w)E[\min(D, K)], \tag{21}$$

$$\Pi_s^w(K) = (w - c)E[\min(D, K)] - c_k K. \tag{22}$$

The supplier maximizes his expected profit in (22) by setting capacity to

$$K^w = \mu + G^{-1}\left(\frac{w - c - c_k}{w - c}\right). \tag{23}$$

Next, consider the vertically integrated supply chain in which a single firm owns both the manufacturer and the supplier. This integrated firm's expected profit and its optimal capacity would be

$$\Pi^I(K) = (p - c)E[\min(D, K)] - c_k K, \tag{24}$$

$$K^I = \mu + G^{-1}\left(\frac{p - c - c_k}{p - c}\right). \tag{25}$$

Note from (22) and (24) that the supplier's marginal profit is less than the integrated firm's marginal profit. This difference is due to double marginalization. The supplier, therefore, secures less capacity than the integrated firm's optimal capacity; that is, $K^w \leq K^I$. Note that $\Pi^I(K^I) \geq \Pi_m^w(K^w) + \Pi_s^w(K^w)$. Hence, the manufacturer and the supplier are leaving money on the table due to decentralized operations.

Because she builds to order, the manufacturer's payoff (realized profit) is always non-negative, whereas the supplier faces the risk of a negative payoff. The manufacturer may encourage the supplier to build more capacity by providing some protection against the downside risk; that is the risk of having excess capacity. Consider the *payback contract* (w, τ) (Özer and Wei 2006), under which the manufacturer pays the supplier w per unit she orders and τ per unit for unused capacity $(K - D)^+$. This would reduce the supplier's marginal cost to $(c - \tau)$ and induce the supplier to build a higher capacity. The manufacturer's and the supplier's expected profit functions under a payback contract are

$$\Pi_m^{pc}(K) = (p - w)E[\min(D, K)] - \tau E[(K - D)^+],$$

$$\Pi_s^{pc}(K) = (w - c)E[\min(D, K)] + \tau E[(K - D)^+] - c_k K.$$

The supplier solves $\max_{K \geq 0} \Pi_s^{pc}(K)$. His optimal capacity is $K^{pc} \equiv \mu + G^{-1}\left(\frac{w-c-c_k}{w-c-\tau}\right)$. To achieve channel coordination, we equate K^{pc} with K^I and solve for τ, resulting in

$$\tau^{pc} = \frac{(p-w)c_k}{p-c-c_k}. \tag{26}$$

Hence, the payback contract (w, τ^{pc}) can coordinate the supply chain using its two pricing terms. The supplier captures $\frac{w-c-c_k}{p-c-c_k} \times 100\%$ of the total expected supply chain profit (which is equal to $\Pi^I(K^I)$), and the manufacturer captures the rest. The coordinating payback contract is not unique. The firms can achieve arbitrary profit sharing by choosing different parameter combinations (w, τ^{pc}) that satisfy (26). Therefore, with the appropriate choice of parameters (w, τ^{pc}), the payback contract results in mutually beneficial terms; that is, the manufacturer's and the supplier's expected profits can be set at least as large as their profits under any wholesale price contract. Note that the payback contract is analogous to the buy-back contract that we study in Section 29.2.3.

The payback contract provides a reward mechanism that induces the supplier to secure more capacity. Another reward mechanism is the *quantity premium contract*. Under this contract, the manufacturer offers the supplier a wholesale price $w(Q)$ where $w(Q)$ is an *increasing* function of the order quantity. To motivate the supplier to invest in capacity, the manufacturer offers a *pricing menu* where higher order sizes correspond to higher wholesale prices. This is similar to the manufacturer contracting for expensive *surge capacity* that is to be used if demand turns out to be high. Tomlin (2003) shows that the quantity premium contract can achieve channel coordination. One can also induce the supplier to build more capacity with a *penalty contract* instead of a reward mechanism. Under this contract, the supplier is penalized for every unit of order that he is unable to satisfy due to capacity shortage.

Some B2B contract types can achieve channel coordination by passing the decision right to the party that has the same incentive as the integrated firm. A good example of this mechanism is the *capacity reservation contract*, under which the manufacturer pays K per unit of capacity to reserve product from the supplier. This contract transfers the capacity decision from the supplier to the manufacturer. It can be shown that the supplier would voluntarily reserve the optimal capacity decided by the manufacturer. That is, reserving the capacity that is optimal for the manufacturer becomes also optimal for the supplier; hence, their incentives are aligned. Özer and Wei (2006) show that the capacity reservation contract can coordinate the supply chain.[18] Note that the payment to the supplier does not have to be in monetary terms. Instead, the manufacturer can build the required capacity at the supplier's site, for example by purchasing the required equipment. A similar contract form is the *cost-sharing contract*. With this contract, the manufacturer reserves a capacity and pays a fraction of the associated cost. Depending on demand realization, the manufacturer either receives a refund or makes an additional payment to the supplier (Erkoc and Wu 2005). A disadvantage of the cost-sharing contract is that it requires the supplier to share his production cost with the manufacturer.

---

[18] The authors also show that this contract form can be used to screen private forecast information, as we discuss in Section 29.5.

29.5 Information sharing through B2B contracts

Another issue in the supply chain we considered in Section 29.4 could arise from sharing forecast information. To deliver on time, the supplier must secure capacity prior to receiving firm orders from the manufacturer who uses these components to build the end product. To do so, the supplier relies on a demand forecast. The manufacturer often has better forecast information than the supplier due to her proximity to consumers. However, the supplier does not consider the manufacturer's demand forecast to be credible because the manufacturer has an incentive to exaggerate her forecast to make the supplier build higher capacity. The supplier, therefore, relies on his own less accurate forecast, resulting in either insufficient or excessive component capacity. Lee et al. (1997) provide four reasons, such as order batching, for a downstream member in a supply chain to distort its demand forecast when sharing it with an upstream member. Özer and Wei (2006) show that another key reason for this phenomenon (which is known as the *bullwhip effect*) is the form of the contract between the firms.

Suppose that demand in the aforementioned supplier–manufacturer supply chain is modeled as $D = \mu + \varepsilon + \xi$ where ξ represents the manufacturer's *private forecast information* that she obtains before the supplier sets capacity. The manufacturer knows the value of ξ deterministically. If the supplier had access to ξ, he would set the capacity as

$$ K^w = \mu + \xi + G^{-1}\left(\frac{w - c - c_k}{w - c}\right) $$

to maximize his expected profit in (22). However, ξ is known *only* to the manufacturer. This concept is what is known as *asymmetric* forecast information. Can the manufacturer share this forecast information *credibly*? The answer is *no* because the manufacturer has an incentive to inflate her private forecast information ξ. This incentive arises because the manufacturer's expected profit in (21) is increasing in the supplier's capacity choice K, and the supplier's optimal capacity K^w is increasing in ξ. Hence, by sharing an inflated forecast, the manufacturer can increase her expected profit. The supplier, therefore, would never consider the forecast information provided by the manufacturer to be *credible* regardless of the manufacturer's sincere effort to share this information. Without credible forecast information sharing, the supplier cannot adjust the capacity to account for the manufacturer's private forecast. The consequences of this inefficiency could be severe for *both* firms. When the manufacturer's private forecast is high, both firms may lose sales, resulting in lower profits (as in the Boeing case mentioned in Cole 1997). When the manufacturer's private forecast information is low, the supplier may suffer from excess capacity (as in the Solectron case mentioned in Hibbard 2003). Consumers also suffer from high price tags and low product availability. The remedy for this inefficiency is to induce *credible* information sharing.

The supplier can hold the manufacturer accountable for her private forecast information by requiring a *monetary* commitment before securing component capacity (Özer and Wei 2006). To this end, he can *screen* the manufacturer's forecast information by designing a menu of prices for reserving capacity. Next we illustrate this approach in a setting where the manufacturer's private forecast information ξ can take only two possible values, leading to two possible *types* for the manufacturer: a *low-forecast* manufacturer who has information $\xi_L = -\mu$ (in which case demand satisfies $D = \varepsilon$), and a *high-forecast* manufacturer who has information $\xi_H = \mu$ (in which case $D = 2\mu + \varepsilon$). The supplier's belief is that the manufacturer has ξ_L with probability α and ξ_H with probability $(1 - \alpha)$.

The sequence of events is as follows. First, the supplier provides a *menu of two contracts* (K_L, P_L), (K_H, P_H). Given this menu, the manufacturer chooses the contract (K_i, P_i) that maximizes her expected profit, where $i \in \{L, H\}$. By doing so, she announces her forecast information to be ξ_i, which could differ from her true forecast information ξ. Depending on the chosen contract, the supplier receives the payment P_i from the manufacturer and builds capacity K_i at unit cost c_k. Next, the manufacturer observes demand D and places an order of size D. The supplier produces as much of the order as possible given the capacity constraint; that is, he delivers $\min(D, K_i)$. The manufacturer receives the ordered units and sells at unit price $p > 0$.

The supplier's challenge is to maximize his expected profit by choosing a menu of contracts (which elicit truthful information from the manufacturer), while ensuring the manufacturer's participation. To identify the optimal menu of contracts, the supplier solves

$$\max_{\{(K_L,P_L),(K_H,P_H)\}} \alpha((w-c)E[\min(\varepsilon,K_L)] + P_L - c_K K_L) + (1-\alpha)((w-c)E[\min(2\mu+\varepsilon,K_H)]$$
$$+ P_H - c_K K_H)$$

subject to

$$(p-w)E[\min(\varepsilon,K_L)] - P_L \geq (p-w)E[\min(\varepsilon,K_H)] - P_H \qquad \text{IC}_L$$
$$(p-w)E[\min(2\mu+\varepsilon,K_H)] - P_H \geq (p-w)E[\min(2\mu+\varepsilon,K_L)] - P_L \qquad \text{IC}_H$$
$$(p-w)E[\min(\varepsilon,K_L)] - P_L \geq \pi_m^{min} \qquad \text{PC}_L$$
$$(p-w)E[\min(2\mu+\varepsilon,K_H)] - P_H \geq \pi_m^{min} \qquad \text{PC}_H$$

The expectations in the supplier's objective are with respect to the demand uncertainty ε. The constraints labeled with IC are the incentive compatibility constraints. These constraints ensure that the manufacturer maximizes her profit only by truthfully revealing her forecast information type. Due to the IC constraints, a low-forecast manufacturer's expected profit is higher with the contract (K_L, P_L); whereas a high-forecast manufacturer's expected profit is higher with the contract (K_H, P_H). The constraints labeled with PC are the participation constraints. These constraints ensure the minimum profit level π_m^{min} for both manufacturer types. This minimum profit could represent the manufacturer's profit from her outside option, or her profit under other contracts.

We determine the supplier's optimal contract menu $\{(K_L^{cr}, P_L^{cr}), (K_H^{cr}, P_H^{cr})\}$ by solving this problem. Deferring the solution details to Appendix B, here we discuss the key characteristics of the optimal menu and the results. We use the superscript *cr* because we interpret this menu as a *capacity reservation* contract. Although the supplier does not know the forecast-type of the manufacturer he is facing, the incentive compatibility (IC) constraints mean that it is to the best interest of the manufacturer to choose the contract intended for her type. The Revelation Principle (Myerson 1979) assures that the incentive-compatible optimal menu of contracts that we identify provides the highest possible expected profit for the supplier under asymmetric forecast information.

When offered this menu, a high-forecast manufacturer chooses the contract $\left(K_H^{cr}, P_H^{cr}\right)$. In this case, supply chain efficiency does not suffer because the chosen capacity is at the supply chain optimal level (i.e., $K_H^{cr} = K_H^{I}$). However, this contract yields the manufacturer an expected profit larger than the minimum profit level π_m^{min}. The supplier leaves the high-forecast manufacturer this extra profit (known as a *rent*) so as to keep her from choosing the low-forecast manufacturer's contract in the menu. A low-forecast manufacturer, on the other hand, chooses the contract $\left(K_L^{cr}, P_L^{cr}\right)$. In this case, supply chain efficiency suffers because the chosen capacity level is below the supply chain optimal level (i.e., $K_L^{cr} < K_L^{I}$). The manufacturer's expected profit is only the minimum profit level; that is, she is not given a rent. The supplier does not lose profit due to rent; yet, his expected profit goes down due to the suboptimal capacity level. In summary, the contract menu approach achieves credible information sharing between the supplier and the manufacturer; however it can *only mitigate* the adverse effects of information asymmetry.

We observe how a supplier can use a deliberately designed menu of contracts, which price capacity reservation, to maximize his expected profit under asymmetric forecast information. While doing so, the supplier also learns the unknown forecast type of the manufacturer. However, this learning happens too late (i.e., when the manufacturer chooses one of the two contracts in the menu) to affect the outcome of the contracting process.[19]

Özer and Wei (2006) study a generalized version of this problem with a continuous type space for ξ instead of two types. They show that the optimal $P^{cr}(\xi)$ and $K^{cr}(\xi)$ values are monotone in ξ. Hence, one can construct a function $P(K)$ by setting $P(K) = P^{cr}(\xi)$, if $K = K^{cr}(\xi)$. This function can be interpreted as a capacity reservation contract under which the manufacturer pays $P(K)$ to reserve K units of capacity. Note that the optimal contract is independent of the manufacturer's forecast information. The supplier simply offers this contract as a menu of prices for the corresponding capacity that the manufacturer may reserve. Essentially the supplier delegates the capacity decision right to the manufacturer, who has superior forecast information. The distinctive feature of this pricing scheme is that the function $P(K)$ is nonlinear and concave. Concavity implies that the supplier charges less for each additional unit of capacity reserved. By doing so, the supplier provides more incentive for a high-forecast manufacturer to reserve more capacity and truthfully reveal her forecast information.

Another pricing-related method to acquire the manufacturer's private forecast information is to offer a reduced price for orders placed before the supplier builds capacity. This is how an *advance purchase* contract operates. The advance purchase can be costly to the manufacturer if the realized demand turns out to be lower than the advance purchase quantity. Intuitively, this commitment prevents a low-forecast manufacturer from communicating a high forecast. Özer and Wei (2006) show that the manufacturer can credibly *signal* her forecast information with an advance purchase contract.

---

[19] We assume that the firms will not re-negotiate after the manufacturer chooses a contract. If re-negotiation is allowed, one faces a totally different strategic interaction.

In summary, firms may be reluctant to collect, process, and share information because of conflicting incentives. The informed firm may have an incentive to distort or hide information to gain strategic advantage. In such cases, the uninformed firm can propose a contract to extract this information. This interaction is known as *adverse selection* or *screening* (e.g., the capacity reservation contract). Second, the informed firm may signal her information to gain cooperation. However, she needs to signal private information in a *credible* way. This interaction is known as a *signaling* game (e.g., the advance purchase contract). Another form of information asymmetry arises as *moral hazard* where one firm influences the supply chain profit through an action or choice not observable to the other. The non-acting firm designs a contract to maximize his own profit (Fudenberg and Tirole 1991; Salanie 1997). The supply chain literature that explicitly models asymmetric information can be classified into two groups. A group of researchers (including Corbett et al. 2005) focus on information asymmetry in production cost, and another group (including Porteus and Whang 1991; Cachon and Lariviere 2001; Özer and Wei 2006) focuses on information asymmetry in market demand and forecasts. Chen (2003) provides an excellent review of the use of these models in supply chain research.

29.6 CONTRACT IMPLEMENTATION ISSUES

Various B2B contract forms achieve channel coordination through pricing different attributes of the relation between the firms. Yet, these contracts require different sets of information and different levels of monitoring. Here we discuss some issues to be considered when choosing a contract type to implement. Contract choice depends on several factors of which the resulting expected profits and incentives are the most important. However, factors including complexities involved in administering contracts, transaction costs, legal considerations, and behavioral aspects might also play important roles. Considering such factors, a manager may prefer a non-coordinating but simple B2B contract that achieves sufficiently high channel efficiency over a coordinating but complex contract. Lariviere and Porteus (2001) argue that the efficiency of the wholesale price contract increases if demand does not exhibit sufficient variation. Given such a market condition, the wholesale price contract might be a good choice for the supply chain. In fact, commonly used contracts are observed to be simpler than theoretical predictions (Holmstrom and Milgrom 1987).

B2B contracts differ in their implementation cost and information requirements. Contracts that involve only price-related terms, such as the wholesale price contract, the two-part tariff, and the quantity discount contract are easier to implement than the contracts that have additional terms related to the realization of demand. For example, the additional term in the buy-back contract is related to the quantity of leftover units; whereas, the additional term in the revenue sharing and rebate contracts is related to the quantity of sales. Such contracts require the monitoring of sales, which is costly.

The *buyback* contract requires tracking unsold inventory at the retailer and reimbursing the retailer. In addition, the cost of physically returning the unsold units to the retailer can be significant. The *revenue sharing* contract requires monitoring the retailer's revenue, which might also be quite costly and difficult. In the Blockbuster case, for example, 10 percent of rental revenues go to Rentrak, an independent firm that monitors computer transactions to enforce the contract terms. The retailer does not have an incentive to report her sales, because she pays to the manufacturer for each sale. The *rebate* contract, on the other hand, poses less difficulty in this respect because the retailer has an incentive to report sales to take advantage of the rebate. Verification of sales is possible through accounting records. By contrast, verification of *lost sales* is notoriously difficult. This is what the *penalty* contract requires. In addition, the retailer has an incentive to hide lost sales to avoid penalty with a penalty contract. Thus, the penalty contract might be more suitable for inter-firm use rather than use as a B2B contract (Lariviere 1999).

Recall that some B2B contracts are designed to shift decision rights to another firm. Consider, for example, the *consignment* contract (or VMI). One major difficulty in implementing this contract is to convince the retailer to share her information and to delegate inventory decisions to the manufacturer. This requires a certain level of trust between the firms. In particular, the manufacturer should demonstrate that it will respect the confidentiality of the retailer's information and that it will be able to provide the agreed-upon product availability levels at the retailer's shelves. For example, Spartan Stores, a grocery chain, stopped the VMI program with one of its suppliers after one year of operation because it did not trust that supplier's forecasting skills and because the program failed to deliver acceptable inventory performance (Simchi-Levi et al. 2007). Implementing a VMI program also requires investments in information technology and significant changes in business processes. The program may cause resistance within the manufacturer's own organization because it shifts power from the sales department to the logistics department. For example, Hammond (1994) describes the resistance to Barilla's VMI program by its distributors and by its own sales department. However, the widespread adoption of VMI programs indicate that their benefits often outweigh their costs. In fact, empirical research has shown that VMI programs benefit both retailers (Clark and Hammond 1997) and manufacturers (Kulp et al. 2004).

The choice of attributes to contract on is also an important factor in implementing a contract. The level of an attribute might be *observed* by the firms who sign a contract. However, if a court of law cannot tell the level of the attribute, then this attribute is *non-verifiable*, in which case a B2B contract based on this attribute cannot be legally binding.[20] For example, the level of sales effort that a retailer provides for a manufacturer's product might be observed by both firms. However, it might not be possible to prove in a court that a certain level of effort is low. In this case, the firms cannot legally settle a dispute based on the level of sales effort. On the contrary, the number of salespeople that the retailer employs is an attribute on which the parties can write a legally binding contract because this number can be verified by a court audit.

The manager should also consider the legal ramifications when designing a B2B contract. For example, contracts that impose restraints on the retailer's actions, or that lead to anti-competitive price discrimination can be illegal in the USA. Such *vertical restraints*, including resale price maintenance (RPM), quantity fixing, and related practices are followed

---

[20] This distinction between observable and verifiable has been a focus of the *incomplete contract theory* in economics (Grossman and Hart 1986; Tirole 1999).

closely by competition authorities.[21] With RPM, the manufacturer determines a minimum sale price (i.e., a price floor) that the retailer can charge to the end-consumers.[22] Forcing retailers to hold a certain level of inventory (quantity fixing) is also illegal in the USA. This issue is important for a manager to consider when implementing a consignment contract. Another commonly encountered constraint is the Robinson–Patman Act[23] of 1936 that prevents a manufacturer from engaging in anti-competitive forms of price discrimination among retailers. The act requires the same terms to be available to all retailers in a given category. For example, when designing a *nonlinear pricing contract*, a manufacturer should be careful not to violate the Robinson–Patman Act in cases where she is selling to heterogeneous retailers. Another possibility for discrimination is with contracts that depend on demand parameters for coordination, such as the quantity flexibility contract. Such a contract may have legal ramifications when the manufacturer works with several retailers that face independent but nonidentical demand. In this case, the manufacturer needs to offer different contracts to coordinate each retailer.

The models we discussed (all models, in general) rest on certain assumptions regarding how the firms (or, the decision-makers) make decisions. For example, each firm's objective in the models is to maximize its expected profit. A firm that has relatively limited resources, however, would also be concerned about the variability in its profit level and act *risk-averse*. Rather than maximizing the expected profit level, a risk-averse firm maximizes its expected *utility* which is given by (*expected level of profit*)-*k*(*variance in profit*) where a high parameter k indicates higher aversion to risk.[24] When faced with two different contracts that provide the same expected profit, a risk-averse firm would choose the contract that offers a lower variance in profit. For example, a target rebate contract offers the retailer a chance to generate extra profits when demand is high and, hence, increases the variance in the retailer's profit. A buy-back contract, on the other hand, provides insurance to the retailer in low demand realizations and, hence, reduces the variance in the retailer's profit. Thus, a risk-averse retailer would choose a coordinating buy-back contract over a coordinating target rebate contract when the contracts offer the same expected profit level. We refer the reader to Eeckhoudt et al. (1995), van Mieghem (2007), and Özer et al. (2007) for further discussion of risk aversion in supply chains.

In addition to risk aversion, there are other *behavioral factors* that a manager could consider in designing B2B contracts. Since the seminal work of Kahneman and Tversky (1979), researchers have shown that decision-makers do not act rationally, and do not necessarily aim to maximize expected utility levels. Rather than optimizing, people use

---

[21] For example, in the USA, the Antitrust Division of the US Department of Justice is charged "to promote and protect the competitive process, and the US economy through the enforcement of the antitrust laws". This division provides guidance on legal business practices jointly with The Federal Trade Commission (http://www.usdoj.gov/atr/).

[22] Whether RPM should be allowed has been an issue of continuous debate among policy-makers. For example, RPM is shown to be beneficial in markets where destructive competition between retailers drive sales prices down (Deneckere et al. 1997). When the manufacturer imposes RPM, the retailers will order more, knowing that competitors will not be able to cut the sales price down. Krishnan and Winter (2007) discuss how price floors and price ceilings may help achieve supply chain coordination.

[23] The US Federal Trade Commission states: "A seller charging competing buyers different prices for the same commodity or discriminating in the provision of allowances (compensation for advertising and other services) may be violating the Robinson–Patman Act.... However, price discriminations generally are lawful, particularly if they reflect the different costs of dealing with different buyers or result from a sellers' attempts to meet a competitors prices or services." Source: http://www.ftc.gov/bc/compguide/discrim.htm.

[24] This is the mean–variance tradeoff approach to model risk aversion. See Luenberger (1998) for details.

heuristics when faced with complex problems. They exhibit certain biases that affect their objective functions. For example, they prefer avoiding losses to obtaining gains (loss aversion), and they are affected by the way the problem is described (framing effect). Rather than being selfish, decision-makers have social motives such as altruism and fairness that affect their decisions. *Controlled experiments with human subjects* can be used to identify such behavioral factors affecting decisions and contract choice. Experiments are particularly effective in capturing factors in *strategic interactions* between decision-makers that game-theoretic models might not capture. Managers often do not have enough time or knowledge to model optimization problems and/or characterize the best-response functions of other decision-makers (as is assumed in game theory) to design contracts. Mathematical modeling helps structure the human decision-making process. Controlled laboratory experiments help identify how humans act and react, and how, when, and why they deviate from theoretical predictions. Along this line, future research on B2B contract design could be to enhance optimization based on mathematical modeling approaches by incorporating decision biases that are not described by current modeling realms, such as the utility-based maximization. We refer the reader to Özer and Zheng (Chapter 20) for further information on this research.

29.7 CONCLUSIONS AND DISCUSSION

In this chapter, we discuss how pricing terms in B2B contracts can be used to achieve proper risk and information sharing in a supply chain. We begin with the study of inventory risk. We first outline the basic tradeoff between inventory excess and shortage considering a single firm's production/stocking decision. Next we study inventory risk in a decentralized manufacturer–retailer supply chain. We show that the wholesale price contract fails to align the incentive of the retailer with that of the supply chain, causing the retailer to order and stock less than the supply chain optimal quantity. Focusing on the costs of underage and overage, we illustrate the root cause of this inefficiency as improper inventory risk sharing between the manufacturer and the retailer. Next, we consider a series of B2B contracts that can coordinate the supply chain by aligning the incentive of the retailer with the supply chain's incentive. For each contract type, we determine the coordinating parameters and we discuss how the contract achieves arbitrary profit and risk sharing between the firms. Finally, we study the effects of B2B contracts when the retailer determines the sales price of the product in the consumer market in addition to her stocking quantity.

Next we study capacity risk in a supplier–manufacturer supply chain. We show that the supplier provides less than the supply chain optimal capacity level due to improper allocation of risk under a wholesale price contract. We illustrate how this supply chain can be coordinated through a payback contract. Considering the same supply chain, we also show how the manufacturer can use a B2B contract to credibly convey her private forecast information to the supplier. Finally, we discuss contract implementation issues including administrative costs, information requirements, and legal and behavioral issues. We confine our discussion to simple models to focus on the key issues and to achieve tractability. Next, we briefly discuss how these models might be extended in a number of ways.

We consider models with a single selling season. This scenario used to be typical of fashion and perishable goods industries. It now applies to many other industries such as high tech and toys because of shortening product lifecycles, increasing product variety, increasing manufacturing leadtimes (due to outsourcing and offshoring), and high demand uncertainty. A number of researchers study models that consider *multiple selling seasons*. For example, Lütze and Özer (2008) consider a multi-period relationship between a make-to-stock manufacturer and a procure-to-stock retailer. The manufacturer can produce any order in a given production leadtime. The manufacturer prefers the retailer to commit to purchase in advance, and wait for delivery. The retailer, on the other hand, prefers to delay commitment as much as possible, and prefers immediate delivery from the manufacturer. Lütze and Özer (2008) offer a *promised leadtime contract (t, K)* to align the incentives of the firms in this setting. Under this contract, the manufacturer guarantees delivery after t time periods in exchange for a per-period lump sum payment K. The promised leadtime contract reduces the inventory risk of the manufacturer by providing advance orders, and reduces the retailer's risk of product availability. Researchers that study general long-term (multi-period) contracting issues include Plambeck and Zenios (2000) and Zhang and Zenios (2008).

Another possible extension is to model *competition* at retailer, manufacturer, or supplier levels. Modeling competition at the retailer level requires specifying the interdependence of retailer demands. For example, total consumer demand may be allocated among retailers based on the price and/or stocking level decisions of all retailers. Unmet demand at one retailer may spill over to other retailers. Under such a scenario, in addition to the manufacturer's contract terms, a retailer also needs to consider the competing retailers' decisions when determining her stocking quantity. Consequently, a B2B contract that coordinates the channel with a single retailer might not do so with multiple retailers. Selling through multiple retailers changes the nature of the manufacturer's problem as well. For example, when the manufacturer's production capacity is limited, one needs to specify how inventory will be allocated between the retailers. In general, selling through multiple retailers would hedge the manufacturer against demand uncertainty from any single retailer. Similarly, sourcing from multiple suppliers would hedge the manufacturer against uncertainties in supply.

Lippman and McCardle (1997), van Ryzin and Mahajan (1999), and Bernstein and Federgruen (2005) are among the researchers who study supply chains with multiple competing retailers. Boyaci (2005) and Chen et al. (2008) study coordination and competition issues in *dual sales channels*, where an independent retailer channel competes with a manufacturer's totally owned direct channel. This setting offers an interesting strategic interaction because the manufacturer becomes both a supplier (in a vertical relation) and a competitor (in a horizontal relation) to his retailer. Bernstein and Federgruen (2004, 2007) study retailers competing in price and inventory in multiple selling seasons. Krishnan and Winter (2010) show that for highly perishable products, the pricing and inventory decisions of the retailers can be coordinated through either buy-backs or vertical price floors. For less perishable products, coordination is possible through inventory penalties or vertical price ceilings.

Modeling the effects of the retailer's *sales effort* offers another extension. The retailer might increase the demand in her store by undertaking costly activities such as investing in the store, training employees, or increasing advertising. The level of a retailer's sales effort generally cannot be stipulated by a contract, because it is not verifiable (see the discussion in Section 29.6). In this case, a contract that reduces the inventory risk of the retailer causes a decrease in the retailer's incentive to exert sales effort. For example, the revenue sharing contract reduces the retailer's incentive to provide sales effort because the retailer only realizes part of the sales benefit. Conversely, the rebate contract provides incentive to exert sales effort because the retailer is rewarded for sales. In fact, Taylor (2002) shows that a rebate coupled with a buy-back contract can coordinate a supply chain in which the retailer's sales effort affects demand.

A retailer might obtain a *forecast update* before the selling season starts. Under a wholesale price contract, such a retailer would prefer to wait and place her order after obtaining the forecast update. For example, retailers in the apparel industry usually place orders after a major trade show (Hammond and Raman 1996). This last minute ordering policy shortens the manufacturer's leadtime, leading to higher production costs. Hence, the manufacturer prefers the retailer to place at least part of the order before the forecast update. This arrangement also pushes part of the inventory and inventory risk to the retailer. To this end, Özer et al. (2007) study a *dual purchase contract*. This contract specifies two prices: a lower *advance purchase price* for retailer's orders placed before the forecast update, and a higher regular wholesale price for orders placed after the forecast update. The retailer faces a tradeoff between waiting for better information and taking advantage of the lower advance purchase price.

Risk and information sharing through pricing terms in B2B contracts is an active research area offering a number of avenues for additional research. Given the importance of the subject, several researchers and practitioners work on designing effective contracts. The following paragraphs present our final thoughts regarding some future research directions that might help bridge the gap between theory and practice in this field.

One important consideration is to develop models to take advantage of emerging business practices and technologies. For example, Internet sales allow a retailer to instantly change the sales price to end-consumers. What type of B2B contracts might improve the efficiency of the supply chain in this dynamic pricing environment? How would the inventory and capacity decisions of the supply chain members be affected? Another example is the increasing use of information technologies, such as RFID (Radio Frequency Identification) in supply chain management. RFID is a sensor technology that enables automatic tracking of products through the supply chain. The potential benefits of this technology include improved visibility, higher shelf availability, and reduced labor costs. Designing B2B contracts to realize the benefits and to share the costs of RFID implementation are important issues to investigate (see, for example, Gaukler et al. 2007; Heese 2007; Lee and Özer 2007).

Another opportunity lies in conducting behavioral experiments to understand how actual decision-makers act given certain contractual forms. To better understand the implications of using a contractual form, one can first build a theoretical model, and then test the predictions of this model with experiments involving human decision-makers. If experiments identify a significant behavioral factor affecting the decisions, the theoretical model can be extended to address this factor. Experiments can then be conducted again based on the extended model. Such a theory–experiment loop might lead to models that are more successful in capturing the dynamics of managerial decision making. Human experiments are particularly valuable in predicting the effects of potential policy changes and contractual arrangements between firms before such changes are implemented. Anticipating the potential, both academicians and industrial researchers have begun conducting behavioral experiments with human decision-makers. Hewlett Packard, for example, altered its policy regarding its retailers' MAP (Minimum Advertised Price policy) violations based on experimental results (Charness and Chen 2002).

Similar opportunities lie in conducting empirical and field studies. Empirical work regarding B2B contracts in supply chains is scarce. One reason for this scarcity is the firms' reluctance to share contractual data, in particular regarding their pricing decisions. Even when data are available, it might not be amenable to analysis because standards differ across firms and industries. The need for empirical work is even more pronounced for contracts that address capacity risk, such as the payback, capacity reservation, and advance purchase contracts. Controlled field experiments could be too risky and costly. Nevertheless, given recent technological advances, a tremendous amount of data is available from various industry segments such as retail and manufacturing. Mining these data may lead to information regarding the effectiveness of contracts. Such information can help identify when a certain B2B contract type is preferable over others and also help design better contracts.

Risk and information sharing through pricing terms in B2B contracts will constitute an important issue given today's fragmented supply chains. Although business practices, technology, and contractual forms may change over time, the fundamental issues discussed in this chapter and in the references will remain an important research area.

Appendix 29.A: Notation

Table 29.A1	
Inventory risk	
p : Sales price to end consumers	**Order and demand related**
c : Unit production cost at the manufacturer	Q : Production / Order / Stocking quantity
v : Salvage value	Q^{ini} : Retailer's initial order in a q.f. contract
Contract related	Q^m : Retailer's modified order in a q.f. contract
w : Wholesale price	D : Random consumer demand
b : Buy-back price	d : A particular realization
θ : Retailer's share of profit in a b.b contract	$f(x)$: Density
f : Retailer's share of revenue in a rev.sh. contract	$F(x)$: Cumulative dist. function
t: Threshold level in a rebate contract	$F^{-1}(x)$: Inverse cumulative dist. function
r : Rebate rate in a rebate contract	X : Random component of demand in §29.3
u_a : Upward adjustment limit in a q.f. contract	**Superscripts** (to denote the contract type)
d_a : Downward adjustment limit in a q.f. contract	I : Integrated firm
R : Retailer's responsibility prm. in a q.f. contract	w : Wholesale price contract
z : Penalty rate in a penalty contract	b : Buyback contract
F : Lump-sum payment in a two-part tariff	rc : Revenue sharing or rebate contract
Other	qf : Quantity flexibility contract
c_u : Cost of underage	**Subscripts** (to denote the firm)
c_o : Cost of overage	m : Manufacturer
π : Payoff	r : Retailer
Π : Expected profit	tot : Total supply chain

Capacity risk
p : Sales price to end-customers
c_k : Supplier's unit cost of capacity
c : Supplier's unit production cost

Contract related
w : Wholesale price
τ : Payback rate in a payback contract
$P(.)$: Payment to supplier
$K(.)$: Reserved capacity

Superscripts (to denote the contract type)
I : Integrated firm
w : Wholesale price contract
pc : Payback contract
cr : Capacity reservation contract

Other
Π : Expected profit

Capacity and demand related
K : Supplier's capacity decision
D : Random customer demand
μ : Mean demand
ε : General demand uncertainty
$\quad g(x)$: Density
$\quad G(x)$: Cumulative dist. function
$\quad G^{-1}(x)$: Inverse cumulative dist. function
ξ : Manufacturer's private forecast information
$\quad \xi_L$: Low private forecast $(= -\mu)$
$\quad \xi_H$: High private forecast $(= \mu)$

Subscripts (to denote the firm)
s : Supplier
m : Manufacturer

Appendix 29.B: Derivation of Section 29.5 results

To solve the supplier's problem, first we observe that the constraint PC_H must be redundant in the optimal solution. This is due to the constraints IC_H, PC_L and because $E[\min(2\mu + \varepsilon, K_L)] \geq E[\min(\varepsilon, K_L)]$. Second, we observe that PC_L must be binding (i.e., hold as an equality) in the optimal solution. Otherwise, increasing both P_L and P_H by the same quantity would improve the supplier's objective function value while preserving PC_L, and not affecting IC_H and IC_L. We also observe that IC_H must be binding in the optimal solution. Otherwise, increasing P_H by a small quantity would preserve IC_H, relax IC_L, not affect PC_L, and improve the objective function. Next, we determine the optimal payment values from the binding constraints PC_L and IC_H as

$$P_L^{cr} = (p - w)E[\min(\varepsilon, K_L)] - \pi_m^{min}, \tag{27}$$

$$P_H^{cr} = (p - w)(E[\min(2\mu + \varepsilon, K_H)] - E[\min(2\mu + \varepsilon, K_L)] \\ + E[\min(\varepsilon, K_L)]) - \pi_m^{min}. \tag{28}$$

Note that the low-forecast manufacturer's payment to the supplier leaves her with no expected profit beyond the minimum profit level π_m^{min}. The high-forecast manufacturer, on the other hand, obtains an *information rent* (extra profit) over the minimum profit level due to the presence of private forecast information. The magnitude of this rent is

$$(p - w)(E[\min(2\mu + \varepsilon, K_L)] - E[\min(\varepsilon, K_L)]). \tag{29}$$

Next, by substituting P_L^{cr} and P_H^{cr}, we observe that the constraint IC_L is redundant in the optimal solution. Hence, so far, we eliminated the constraints PC_H and IC_L and we showed that the constraints PC_L and IC_H must be binding in the optimal solution. Next we eliminate the two binding constraints by substituting P_L^{cr} and P_H^{cr} from (27) and (28) into the supplier's objective function. The objective function becomes

$$\max_{K_L, K_H} \; \alpha((p-c)E[\min(\varepsilon, K_L)] - \pi_m^{min} - c_K K_L) +$$

$$(1-\alpha)((p-c)E[\min(2\mu + \varepsilon, K_H)]) + (p-w)(E[\min(\varepsilon, K_L)]$$

$$- E[\min(2\mu + \varepsilon, K_L)]) - \pi_m^{min} - c_K K_H.$$

Note that the supplier's problem is converted into an *unconstrained* optimization problem over the capacity values K_L and K_H. Ignoring the constant π_m^{min}, we write the objective function as functions of K_L and K_H separately as

$$\text{Section L}: \max_{K_L} \; \alpha((p-c)E[\min(\varepsilon, K_L)] - c_K K_L) - (1-\alpha)(p-w)(E[\min(2\mu + \varepsilon, K_L)]$$

$$- E[\min(\varepsilon, K_L)]),$$

$$\text{Section H}: \max_{K_H} \; (1-\alpha)([(p-c)E[\min(2\mu + \varepsilon, K_H)] - c_K K_H).$$

We solve the two sections separately to determine the optimal K_L^{cr} and K_H^{cr} values. The expression in *Section L* is composed of two parts. The first part $\alpha((p-c)E[\min(\varepsilon, K_L)] - c_K K_L)$ is a constant α multiple of the integrated firm's objective in (24) with low forecast information. The rest of *Section L* denotes the loss of the supply chain due to information asymmetry. This expression includes the rent in (29) that a high-forecast manufacturer obtains from the supplier. The function in *Section L* is maximized at a capacity $K_L^{cr} < K_L^I = G^{-1}\left(\frac{p-c-c_k}{p-c}\right)$. Thus, when the manufacturer has low forecast information, information asymmetry causes the supplier to build a lower capacity than the supply chain optimal capacity. This decrease in capacity causes a reduction in the supplier's expected profit and in channel efficiency.

The expression in *Section H* is a constant $(1-\alpha)$ multiple of the integrated firm's objective in (22) with high-forecast information. We know from (23) that this function is maximized at $K_H^{cr} = K_H^I = 2\mu + G^{-1}\left(\frac{p-c-c_k}{p-c}\right)$. Thus, when the manufacturer has high-forecast information, information asymmetry does not cause inefficiency in the channel. However, the manufacturer captures the information rent given in (29) from the supplier.

One can determine the corresponding payment values P_L^{cr} and P_H^{cr} by substituting K_L^{cr} and K_H^{cr} into (27) and (28). One can then find the supplier's and the manufacturer's expected profits under asymmetric forecast information by using these parameters in the supplier's optimal menu of contracts $\left\{\left(K_L^{cr}, P_L^{cr}\right), \left(K_H^{cr}, P_H^{cr}\right)\right\}$.

References

Aydin, G. and Porteus, E. L. (2009) "Manufacturer-to-retailer versus manufacturer-to-consumer rebates in a supply chain", in N. Agrawal and S. Smith (eds), *Retail Supply Chain Management*. Norwell, MA: Kluwer Academic Publishers, ch. 10.

Barnes-Schuster, D., Bassok, Y., and Anupindi, R. (2002) "Coordination and flexibility in supply contracts with options", *Manufacturing & Service Operations Management* 4/3: 171–207.

Bernstein, F. and Federgruen, A. (2004) "A general equilibrium model for retail industries with price and service competition", *Operations Research* 52/6: 868–86.

—— and —— (2005) "Decentralized supply chains with competing retailers under demand uncertainty", *Management Science* 51/1: 18–29.

—— and —— (2007) "Coordination mechanisms for supply chains under price and service competition". *Manufacturing & Service Operations Management* 9/3: 242–62.

Boyaci, T. (2005) "Competitive stocking and coordination in a multiple-channel distribution system", *IIE Transactions* 37/5: 407–27.

Cachon, G. (2003) "Supply chain coordination with contracts", in A. G. de Kok and S. Graves (eds), *Handbooks in Operations Research and Management Science, Vol. 11*. Amsterdam: Elsevier, ch. 6.

—— and Lariviere, M. A. (2001) "Contracting to assure supply: How to share demand forecasts in a supply chain", *Management Science* 47/5: 629–46.

—— and —— (2005) "Supply chain coordination with revenue-sharing contracts: Strengths and limitations", *Management Science* 51/1: 31–44.

—— and Terwiesch, C. (2006) *Matching Supply with Demand*. Columbus, OH: McGraw-Hill.

Charness, G. and Chen, K. (2002) "Minimum advertised price policy rules and retailer behavior: An experiment", *Interfaces* 32/5: 62–73.

Chen, F. (2003) "Information sharing and supply chain coordination", in A. G. de Kok and S. Graves (eds), *Handbooks in Operations Research and Management Science, Vol. 11*. Amsterdam: Elsevier, ch. 7.

Chen K.-Y., Kaya, M., and Özer, Ö. (2008) "Dual sales channel management with service competition", *Manufacturing & Service Operations Management* 10/4: 654–75.

Chen, X., Li, C. L., Rhee, B. D., and Simchi-Levi, D. (2007) "The impact of manufacturer rebates on supply chain profits", *Naval Research Logistics* 54/6: 667–80.

Chopra, S. and Sodhi, M. S. (2004) "Managing risk to avoid supply chain breakdown", *MIT Sloan Management Review* 46/1: 53–61.

Clark, T. H. and Hammond, J. (1997) "Reengineering channel reordering processes to improve total supply chain performance", *Production and Operations Management* 6/3: 248–65.

Cole, J. (1997) "Boeing, pushing for record production, finds part shortages, delivery delays", *Wall Street Journal* June 26.

Corbett, C. J., DeCroix, G. A., and Ha, A. Y. (2005) "Optimal shared-savings contracts in supply chains: Linear contracts and double moral hazard", *European Journal of Operational Research* 163/3: 653–67.

Deneckere, R., Marvel, H., and Peck, J. (1997) "Demand uncertainty and price maintenance: Markdowns as destructive competition", *American Economic Review* 87/4: 619–41.

Eeckhoudt, L., Gollier, C., and Schlesinger, H. (1995) "The risk-averse (and prudent) news-boy", *Management Science* 41/5: 786–94.

Emmons, H. and Gilbert, S. M. (1998) "The role of return policies in pricing and inventory decisions for catalogue goods", *Management Science* 44/2: 276–83.

Eppen, G. and Iyer, A. (1997) "Backup agreements in fashion buying—the value of upstream flexibility", *Management Science* 43 11: 1469–84.

Erkoc, M. and Wu, D. (2005) "Managing high-tech capacity expansion via reservation contracts", *Production Operations Management* 14/2: 232–51.

Fudenberg, D. and Tirole, J. (1991) *Game Theory*. Cambridge, MA: MIT Press.

Fry, M. J., Kapuscinski, R., and Olsen, T. L. (2001) "Coordinating production and delivery under a (z, Z)-type vendor-managed inventory contract", *Manufacturing & Service Operations Management* 3/2: 151–73.

Gaukler, G., Seifert, R., and Hausman, W. (2007) "Item level RFID in the retail supply chain", *Production and Operations Management* 16/1: 65–76.

Granot, D. and Yin, S. (2005) "On the effectiveness of returns policies in the price-dependent newsvendor models", *Naval Research Logistics* 52/8: 765–79.

Grossman, S. J. and Hart, O. (1986) "The costs and benefits of ownership: A theory of vertical and lateral integration", *The Journal of Political Economy* 94/4: 691–719.

Hammond, J. H. (1994) "Barilla SpA (A)", *Harvard Business School Case* No 9-694-046, Boston, MA.

—— and Raman, A. (1996) "Sport Obermeyer Ltd.", *Harvard Business School Case* No 9-695-022, Boston, MA.

Heese, S. (2007) "Inventory record inaccuracy, double marginalization, and RFID adoption", *Production and Operations Management* 16/5: 542–53.

Heskett, J. L. and Signorelli, S. (1984) "Benetton (A)", *Harvard Business School Case* No 9-685-014, Boston, MA.

Hibbard, J. (2003) "The case of obsolete inventory", *Red Herring* 123: 34–8.

Holmstrom, B. and Milgrom, P. (1987) "Aggregation and linearity in the provision of intertemporal incentives", *Econometrica* 55/2: 303–28.

Jeuland, A. and Shugan, S. (1983) "Managing channel profits", *Marketing Science* 2/3: 239–72.

Kahneman D. and Tversky, A. (1979) "Prospect theory: An analysis of decision under risk", *Econometrica* 47/2: 263–92.

Kandel, E. (1996) "The right to return", *Journal of Law and Economics* 39/1: 329–56.

Karlin, S. and Carr, C. R. (1962) "Prices and optimal inventory policy", in K. J. Arrow, S. Karlin, and H. Scarf (eds), *Studies in Applied Probability and Management Science*. Palo Alto, CA: Stanford Press, 159–72.

Krishnan, H. and Winter, R. A. (2007) "Vertical control of price and inventory", *American Economic Review* 97/5: 1840–57.

—— and—— (2010) "Inventory dynamics and supply chain coordination", *Management Science* 56/1: 141–7.

Kulp, S. C., Lee, H., Ofek, E. (2004) "Manufacturer benefits from information integration with retail customers", *Management Science* 50/4: 431–44.

Lariviere, M. A. (1999) "Supply chain contracting and coordination with stochastic demand", in S. Tayur, M. Magazine, and R. Ganeshan (eds), *Quantitative Models for Supply Chain Management*. Norwell, MA: Kluwer Academic Publishers, ch. 8.

—— and Porteus, E. L. (2001) "Selling to the newsvendor: An analysis of price-only contracts", *Manufacturing & Service Operations Management* 3/4: 293–305.

Lee, H. and Özer, Ö. (2007) "Unlocking the value of RFID", *Production and Operations Management* 16/1: 40–64.

—— Padmanabhan, V., and Whang, S. (1997) "Information distortion in a supply chain: The bullwhip effect", *Management Science* 43/4: 547–58.

Lippman, S. and McCardle, K. (1997) "The competitive newsboy", *Operations Research* 45/1: 54–65.

Luenberger, D. G. (1998) *Investment Science*. New York: Oxford University Press.

Lütze, H. and Özer, Ö. (2008) "Promised lead-time contracts under asymmetric information", *Operations Research* 56/4: 898–915.

Mills, E. S. (1959) "Uncertainty and price theory", *Quarterly Journal of Economics* 73/1: 116–30.

Moorthy, K. S. (1987) "Managing channel profits: Comment", *Marketing Science* 6: 375–9.

Mortimer, J. H. (2002) "The effects of revenue-sharing contracts on welfare in vertically-separated markets: Evidence from the video rental industry". Working paper, Harvard University.

Myerson, R. (1979) "Incentive compatibility and the bargaining problem", *Econometrica* 47: 61–73.

Özer, Ö. (2006) "Inventory management: Information, coordination and rationality", in K. Kempf, P. Keskinocak, and R. Uzsoy (eds), *Handbook of Production Planning*. Norwell, MA: Kluwer Academic Publishers, ch. 14.

—— and Wei, W. (2006) "Strategic commitments for an optimal capacity decision under asymmetric forecast information", *Management Science* 52/8: 1238–57.

—— Uncu, O., and Wei, W. (2007) "Selling to the 'Newsvendor' with a forecast update: Analysis of a dual purchase contract", *European Journal of Operational Research* 182/3: 1150–76.

Padmanabhan, V. and Png, I. P. L. (1995) "Returns policies: Make money by making good", *Sloan Management Review* 37/1: 65–72.

—— and —— (1997) "Manufacturer's returns policies and retail competition", *Marketing Science* 16/1: 81–94.

Petruzzi, N. C. and Dada, M. (1999) "Pricing and the newsvendor problem: A review with extensions", *Operations Research* 47/2: 183–94.

Plambeck, E. L. and Zenios, S. A. (2000) "Performance-based incentives in a dynamic principal–agent model", *Manufacturing & Service Operations Management* 2/3: 240–63.

Porteus, E. and Whang, S. (1991) "On manufacturing/marketing incentives", *Management Science* 37/9: 1166–81.

Salanie, B. (1997) *The Economics of Contracts: A primer*. Cambridge, MA: MIT Press.

Simchi-Levi, D., Kaminsky, P., and Simchi-Levi., E. (2007) *Designing and managing the supply chain: Concepts, strategies and case studies*, 3rd edn. Columbus, OH: McGraw-Hill.

Singhal, V. R. and Hendricks, K. B. (2002) "How supply chain glitches torpedo shareholder value", *Supply Chain Management Review* July/August.

Song, Y., Ray, S., and Li, S. (2008) "Structural properties of buy-back contracts for price-setting newsvendors", *Manufacturing & Service Operations Management* 10/1: 1–18.

Spengler, J. (1950) "Vertical integration and antitrust policy", *Journal of Political Economics* 58/4: 347–52.

Taylor, T. (2002) "Supply chain coordination under channel rebates with sales effort effects", *Management Science* 48/8: 992–1007.

Tirole, J. (1988) *The Theory of Industrial Organization*. Cambridge, MA: MIT Press.

—— (1999) "Incomplete contracts: Where do we stand?" *Econometrica* 67/4: 741–81.

Tomlin, B. (2003) "Capacity investments in supply chains: Sharing the gain rather than sharing the pain", *Manufacturing & Service Operations Management* 5/4: 317–33.

Tsay, A. (1999) "The quantity flexibility contract and supplier-customer incentives", *Management Science* 45: 1339–58.

van Mieghem, J. A. (2007) "Risk mitigation in newsvendor networks: Resource diversification, flexibility, sharing, and hedging", *Management Science* 53/8: 1269–88.

van Ryzin, G. and Mahajan, S. (1999) "Supply chain coordination under horizontal competition". Working paper, Columbia University, New York.

Zhang, H. and Zenios, S. (2008) "A dynamic principal–agent model with hidden information: Sequential optimality through truthful state revelation", *Operations Research* 56/3: 681–96.

CHAPTER 30

PRICING AND
INVENTORY
MANAGEMENT

XIN CHEN AND DAVID SIMCHI-LEVI

30.1 INTRODUCTION

Recent years have witnessed phenomenal growth of successful deployments of innovative pricing strategies in a variety of industries. For instance, no company underscores the impact of the Internet on product pricing strategies more than Dell Computers. The price of a product is not fixed on Dell's website; it may change significantly over time. Of course, Dell is not alone in its use of sophisticated pricing strategies. Indeed, scores of retail and manufacturing companies have started exploring dynamic pricing to improve their operations and ultimately their bottom line.

Several factors contribute to the phenomenal growth of dynamic pricing. First, the development of sophisticated information technologies greatly facilitates the collection and communication of customer data. Secondly, costs associated with changing prices have been significantly reduced again due to the development of information technologies. Thirdly, active academic research provides analytical models and tools for price optimization. Fourthly, decision support systems for customer data analysis and price optimization have been developed and successfully implemented in a number of industries.

The purpose of this chapter is to survey academic research on price optimization models in which inventory replenishment plays a critical role. Our emphasis is on integrated production/inventory and pricing models that have the potential to be used for decision support at both the operational and the tactical levels. We also review strategic models on

The authors thank the editors of this handbook, Peng Hu, and Yuhan Zhang for helpful suggestions and comments. The first author is partly supported by NSF Grants CMMI-0653909, CMMI-0926845 ARRA, and CMMI-1030923. The second author is partly supported by ONR Contracts N00014-95-1-0232 and N00014-01-1-0146; NSF Contracts DMI-0085683 and DMI- 0245352; NASA interplanetary supply chain and logistics architectures project; and NSF Contract CMMI-0758069.

supply chain competition, coordination, and cooperation built upon these operational and tactical inventory and pricing models.

This chapter is not the first survey of this kind. In fact, several notable survey articles appeared since the publication of the seminal paper by Whitin (1955) who analyzes an EOQ model and a newsvendor model both with price dependent demand. Among them, Eliashberg and Steinberg (1991) review the literature up to year 1991 on the interface of operations and marketing with an emphasis on integrated inventory and pricing models. Three recent papers, Elmaghraby and Keskinocak (2003), Yano and Gilbert (2005), and Chan et al. (2004), survey the related literature up to 2004 from operations research and management science perspective. Elmaghraby and Keskinocak (2003) focus on a few key papers on dynamic pricing in the presence of inventory considerations. Chan et al. (2004) provide a comprehensive review of coordinated pricing and inventory models including markdown and clearance pricing. Our review is more aligned with Yano and Gilbert (2005) in which inventory replenishment is critical. However, we do not survey EOQ-type models and deterministic models emphasizing demand smoothing (as a result of convex production cost) which are comprehensively surveyed in Yano and Gilbert (2005). Neither are models involving initial inventory decisions in conjunction with markdown pricing decisions reviewed in Elmaghraby and Keskinocak (2003) and Chan et al. (2004). On the other hand, and more importantly, we cover many recent papers which appear after the publication of these three surveys. Our intention is not to provide a comprehensive review but rather to highlight key up-to-date developments and their historical roots.

The organization of this chapter is as follows. In the next section, we present commonly used demand models, which is followed by a survey of deterministic periodic review inventory and pricing models. We then present stochastic models distinguishing between single period models, multi-period models with convex ordering costs and multi-period models with concave ordering costs. Built upon the inventory and pricing models presented in the previous sections, we then review models on supply chain competition, coordination, and cooperation. Finally, we provide some concluding remarks and thoughts on future research.

30.2 DEMAND MODELS

To make optimal pricing decisions, it is critical to know the volume of a product that customers are willing to purchase at a specific price. The relationship between the volume and price gives rise to a demand model. Depending on the scenario, the demand for a product can depend on many variables other than price, such as quality, brand name, and competitor's prices. Here, however, we restrict our discussion to demand models in which price is the only variable.

Economic theory provides us with basic demand models derived from the classical rational theory of consumer choice (we refer to van Ryzin (Chapter 18) and Talluri and van Ryzin (2004: ch. 7) as well as the reference therein for more details). From this theory, it is typical to assume that the demand for a product is a decreasing function of its current price and revenue is concave as a function of price. Some commonly used deterministic demand functions include the linear demand $d(p) = b - ap$ for $p \in [0, b/a]$ ($a > 0$ and $b \geq 0$), the exponential demand $d(p) = e^{b-ap}$ ($a > 0$ and $b > 0$), the iso-price-elastic demand[1] $d(p) = ap^{-b}$ ($a > 0$ and $b > 1$), and the Logit demand $d(p) = N\frac{e^{-ap}}{1+e^{-ap}}$ which is the product of the market size N and the probability that a customer with a coefficient of price sensitivity a buys at price p.

We now present demand models for multiple products whose demands depend on prices of all products. Let $p = (p_1, p_2, \ldots, p_n)$ be the price vector of n products and d $(p) = (d_1(p), d_2(p), \ldots, d_n(p_n))$ be the associated demand vector. As is consistent with demand models for a single product, we often assume that $\frac{\partial d_i(p)}{\partial p_i} \leq 0$, which implies that the demand for product i is nonincreasing in its own price. The sign of $\frac{\partial d_i(p)}{\partial p_j}$ ($i \neq j$) depends on whether products i and j are complements or substitutes. In the former case, $\frac{\partial d_i(p)}{\partial p_j} \leq 0$ while in the latter case, $\frac{\partial d_i(p)}{\partial p_j} \geq 0$.

Some specific multi-product demand models can be derived by extending the demand functions of a single product. For instance, the linear demand model for multiple products, is given by $d(p) = b + Ap$, where $b = (b_1, b_2, \ldots, b_n)$ is the vector of coefficients and $A = [a_{ij}]$ is an $n \times n$ matrix of price sensitivity coefficients with $a_{ii} < 0$ and $a_{ij} \leq 0$ or $a_{ij} \geq 0$ ($i \neq j$) for complements or substitutes respectively. The exponential demand model is a composite of the exponential function and linear functions, given by $d_i(p) = e^{b_i + A_i^T p}$, $i = 1, 2, \ldots, n$. The iso-price-elastic demand model can be represented as $d_i(p) = b_i p_1^{-a_{i1}} p_2^{-a_{i2}} \cdots p_n^{-a_{in}}$, $i = 1, 2, \ldots, n$, where a_{ij} defines the cross price elasticity between products i and j. Finally, the logit demand is given by $d_i(p) = N\frac{e^{-a_i p_i}}{1+\sum_{j=1}^{n} e^{-a_j p_j}}$ which is the product of the market size N and the probability that a customer chooses product j as a function of the price vector p (the probability is derived from the commonly used multinomial logit model).

In stochastic settings, the demand of a product is often represented as a function of the price p and a random noise ε independent of p denoted by $d(p, \varepsilon)$. Sometimes it is important to specify the format that the random noise ε enters the demand function. If the demand is a deterministic function of price p, $d(p)$, plus the random noise ε (usually normalized to have zero mean), that is $d(p, \varepsilon) = d(p) + \varepsilon$, it is called an additive demand. If the demand is a deterministic function of price p, $d(p)$, multiplied by the random noise ε (assumed to be nonnegative and usually normalized to have unit mean), that is, $d(p, \varepsilon) = d(p)\varepsilon$, it is referred to as a multiplicative demand. More general demand functions of the following forms $d(p, \varepsilon) = d_1(p) \varepsilon + d_2(p)$ or $d(p, \varepsilon) = d_1(p)\varepsilon_1 + \varepsilon_2$ (where $\varepsilon_1 \geq 0$ and ε_2 are two random variables) are also used in the inventory and pricing literature. Stochastic multi-product demand models can be also defined correspondingly.

Observe that for additive demand, the demand variance is independent of price while the coefficient of variation (the ratio of standard deviation and mean) is dependent of price. In contrast, for multiplicative demand, the coefficient of variation does not depend on price while the variance does. In single product settings with decreasing expected demand $d(p)$, higher price leads to higher uncertainty for additive demand but lower uncertainty for multiplicative demand.

---

[1] The price elasticity of demand is the relative change in demand in response to a relative change in price. It is defined for a demand function $d(p)$ as $e(p) = -\frac{pd'(p)}{d(p)}$.

The above demand models derived from economic theory assume that the demand of a product only depends on its current price. This assumption, appropriate to models of impulsive purchasing, is unreasonable when consumers actively react to firms' dynamic pricing strategies, as demonstrated by plenty of empirical evidence. Modeling consumer behavior to explain and predict how individuals react to dynamic pricing strategies has been a very important research topic in the marketing literature (see Monroe 2003). It has also received considerable attention in the operations management community in recent years (see Aviv and Vulcano Chapter 23 for a review). Instead of providing a detailed review of the literature on consumer behavior models, we present in the next section one class of well-studied consumer behavioral pricing models in the marketing literature, the so-called reference price model, which has recently been incorporated into integrated inventory and pricing models.

30.3 PERIODIC REVIEW

DETERMINISTIC MODELS

In this section, we survey periodic review inventory and pricing models within deterministic settings. We first present a general modeling framework for a single product. Specifically, consider a firm that makes replenishment and pricing decisions of a single product over a finite planning horizon with T periods. At the beginning of period t $(t = 1, 2, \ldots, T)$, the firm decides on its order quantity x_t, which incurs a fixed ordering cost k_t (charged only if $x_t > 0$ and independent of the order quantity) and a variable ordering cost c_t per unit. In addition, an upper bound q_t may also be imposed on the order quantity x_t. At the same time, the firm also determines its selling price p_t. Demand of period t is assumed to be a deterministic function of the current period selling price p_t, denoted as $d_t(p_t)$. For simplicity, we assume that no backorder is allowed[2] and leftover inventory is carried over from period t to the next period incurring an inventory holding cost h_t per unit. The firm's objective is to find a sequence of order quantities x_t and prices p_t so as to maximize the total profit over the planning horizon.

Upon denoting a pricing plan $p = (p_1, p_2, \ldots, p_T)$ and its related demand sequence $d(p) = (d_1(p_1), d_2(p_2), \ldots, d_T(p_T))$, a mathematical model for the deterministic inventory and pricing problem is:

$$\max \sum_{t=1}^{T} p_t d_t(p_t) - C(d(p)) \tag{1}$$
$$\text{subject to } p_t \in [\underline{p}_t, \bar{p}_t], t = 1, 2, \ldots, T,$$

where a lower bound $\underline{p}_t$ and an upper bound $\bar{p}_t$ on the selling price p_t are imposed to prevent a low profit margin and an unreasonable high price respectively. In the objective function of the above problem, the first term is the total revenue, and the second term $C(d(p))$ is the minimum ordering and inventory holding cost over the planning horizon

---

[2] Models with backorders can be handled following a similar idea.

for a given pricing plan p, which can be obtained by solving the following classical capacitated economic lot sizing model: for $d = (d_1, d_2, \ldots, d_T)$,

$$C(d) = \text{Min} \sum_{t=1}^{T} k_t z_t + c_t x_t + h_t I_t$$
$$\text{subject to } I_t = I_{t-1} + x_t - d_t, t = 1, 2, \ldots, T$$
$$I_0 = 0$$
$$x_t \leq q_t z_t, t = 1, 2, \ldots, T \tag{2}$$
$$z_t \in \{0, 1\}, \ t = 1, 2, \ldots, T$$
$$I_t, x_t \geq 0, \ t = 1, 2, \ldots, T,$$

where the binary variable z_t indicates whether an order is placed or not at period t and the variable I_t is the inventory level at the end of period t. In addition, the first constraint is the inventory balance equation, the second one states that we start with zero inventory, the third one is the capacity constraint (in case of no capacity on order quantity one can simply replace q_t with an upper bound on the total demand from periods t to T), and finally $I_t \geq 0$ implies that no backorder is allowed.

The major focus of this literature is on designing efficient algorithms for finding optimal solutions to problem (1) and its extensions by exploiting their structures. To illustrate the basic ideas involved, we sketch algorithms to solve problem (1) under different assumptions.

We first focus on settings with no capacity constraint. The key is to observe that without capacity constraint, there is an optimal ordering plan for problem (2) which has the so-called zero-inventory-ordering (ZIO) property; that is, $x_t I_{t-1} = 0$ or equivalently no order is placed whenever the inventory level is positive. To see this, consider an ordering plan which specifies for a period, say t, with a positive initial inventory level I_{t-1}, an order x_t to be placed. Let i be the ordering period immediately before period t. We can either shift the entire order placed at period t to period i or shift an order quantity of I_{t-1} units from period i to period t. In the first option, no order is place at period t and the resulting cost change is $(c_{it} - c_t)x_t$, while in the second option, the initial inventory level at period t is zero and the resulting cost change $-(c_{it} - c_t)I_{t-1}$, where $c_{it} = c_i + \sum_{l=i}^{t-1} h_l$ is the marginal cost of satisfying period t's demand by an order placed at period i. Clearly one of the options leads to an ordering plan with a cost no more than that of the original plan. The same process is repeated on the plan with the lowest cost until we end up with a plan with the ZIO property in at most $T-1$ steps.

It is clear that for an ordering plan with the ZIO property, it suffices to specify the ordering periods. Specifically, if periods i and j ($i < j$) are two consecutive ordering periods in such an ordering plan, the ZIO property implies that the demand at period t ($i < t < j$) is filled by the order placed at period i only and thus the marginal cost of satisfying period t's demand is given by c_{it}. The associated optimal price for period t with $i \leq t < j$ can then be derived by finding the highest profit of period t:

$$\begin{aligned} v_{it} = \text{Max} \quad & p_t d_t(p_t) - c_{it} p_t \\ \text{subject to} \quad & p_t \in [\underline{p}_t, \bar{p}_t]. \end{aligned} \tag{3}$$

In the case with no fixed ordering costs, it is straightforward to identify all ordering periods t_l recursively by letting $t_1 = 1$ and $t_{l+1} = \min\{T + 1, \min\{t : t \in (t_l, T], c_t \le c_{t_l t}\}\}$ for $l \ge 1$. In the case with fixed ordering costs, it is not sufficient to compare the marginal costs. However, the ZIO property allows us to construct an equivalent longest path problem in an acyclic network $G = (V, E)$ with the node set $V = \{1, 2, \ldots, T + 1\}$ and the arc set $E = \{(i, j) : 1 \le i < j \le T + 1\}$. In the construction, an arc (i, j) means that the demands from periods i up to $j - 1$ are served by the order placed at period i. The length assigned to arc (i, j) is $\sum_{t=i}^{j-1} v_{it} - k_i$; that is, the total profit from periods i to $j - 1$ with the prices determined by solving problem (3) for $t = i, \ldots, j - 1$. One can show that a longest path from node 1 to node $T + 1$ in the network G gives an optimal ordering plan with the ZIO property whose ordering periods exactly correspond to the nodes on the longest path, and the associated optimal prices are derived through problem (3). The algorithm involves solving $T(T + 1)/2$ subproblems with the same structure as (3) and then finding a longest path in the acyclic network G.

One way to find a longest path in the acyclic network G is a forward-type algorithm which actually derives longest paths from node 1 to all nodes. Here is the sketch of the idea. For a given node t $(t = 1, 2, \ldots, T)$, once we have the longest paths from node 1 to nodes 1, 2, ..., $t - 1$, a longest path from node 1 to node t is the one with the longest length among $t - 1$ options: following the longest path from node 1 to node τ and then arc (τ, t), $\tau = 1$, 2, ..., $t - 1$. The computational complexity of the forward-type algorithm is $O(T^2)$; that is, there exists a constant $\rho > 0$ such that the algorithm solves the problem in no more than ρT^2 elementary operations (additions, multiplications, and comparisons).[3]

Wagner and Whitin (1958a) appear to be the first to incorporate the pricing decision into the now classical economic lot sizing model without capacity constraint (also commonly referred to as the Wagner–Whitin model; see Wagner and Whitin 1958b). They recognize the ZIO property and sketch a forward-type algorithm similar to the one described here. They also suggest using the planning horizon property (i.e., if for a problem with t periods an order is placed at period t, then all periods prior to t can be ignored in determining the optimal policy for future periods) to simplify the computation. These results are parallel to the ones in the Wagner–Whitin model (Wagner and Whitin 1958b).[4] Thomas (1970) analyzes a model similar to Wagner and Whitin (1958a) and illustrates explicitly that an optimal price at period t can be identified, independent of other periods' prices, by solving the single variable optimization problem (3) if demand of period t is satisfied by an order placed at period i. Geunes et al. (2006) consider several extensions by allowing for multiple price–demand curves and piecewise linear concave ordering costs and illustrate that these extensions can be handled easily by adapting the algorithm sketched here without substantially increasing the computational complexity. They also present an equivalent integer program formulation for problem (1) whose linear

---

[3] We refer to Ahuja et al. (1993) for more details on solving longest (shortest) path problems in acyclic networks.

[4] Interestingly, Wagner and Whitin (1958a) focusing on the economic lot sizing model with price-dependent demand precede Wagner and Whitin (1958b) which analyzes the economic lot sizing model *without* pricing decisions; see Wagner (2004) for a recollection of the background. In addition, surprisingly, Wagner and Whitin (1958a) do not refer to Whitin (1955), which, analyzing the newsvendor model with price-dependent demand, appears to be the first attempt to incorporate pricing decisions into inventory models.

programming relaxation does not have an integrality gap[5] under the assumption that the revenue at each period is a piecewise linear (with finite pieces) and concave function in terms of the satisfied demand.

We now focus on problem (1) with capacity constraints. We start with the case with no fixed ordering costs. Assume that the demand function $d_t(p_t)$ is strictly decreasing in the selling price p_t, which implies that there is a one-to-one correspondence between the demand and the selling price at period t. Thus, solving problem (1) is equivalent to determining a sequence of demands that gives the maximum profit, and in this case, problem (1) can be formulated as a min-cost network flow problem.[6] If, in addition, the revenue curves are assumed to be concave, it can be solved efficiently by standard algorithms for min-cost network flow problems with convex cost (see Ahuja et al. 1993). It can also be solved by an intuitive and interesting greedy algorithm. Assuming integer-valued inventory levels, order quantities, and demand, the greedy algorithm works as follows: starting with zero demand, at each iteration, identify a period and increase its demand by one unit if it respects capacity constraints and gives the highest profit increase among all possible periods; stop the process if no further improvement is possible. The greedy algorithm is proposed by Biller et al. (2005), who also present computational experiments suggesting that it is possible to achieve significant benefit with few price changes.

The capacitated inventory and pricing model with fixed ordering costs is not significantly different from the capacitated economic lot sizing (CELS) model (2) (see Geunes et al. (2006) for the model with piecewise linear concave revenue functions; Deng and Yano (2006) and Geunes et al. (2009) for the model with general concave revenue functions—all are with respect to the satisfied demand). Optimal ordering plans may not have the ZIO property any more for the capacitated models. Instead, it can be shown that there exists an optimal ordering plan consisting of a series of capacity constrained production sequences. That is, we can partition the planning horizon so that each member of the partition (called a production sequence) consists of a series of consecutive periods that starts and ends with zero inventory level, and holds positive inventory in between, and at each period of the production sequence, we either produce nothing or to the full capacity, except for at most one period (referred to as the fractional production period) at which one can produce a quantity strictly between zero and the full capacity. To prove this statement, observe that model (2) is a concave minimization problem with linear constraints and thus attains optimality at some extreme point, which exactly corresponds to an ordering plan consisting of a series of capacity constrained production sequences.

We can determine the optimal prices associated with any given production sequence independently of other production sequences. To simplify our presentation, assume that all inventory holding costs are zero (note that this can be assumed without loss of generality

---

[5] Similar integer program formulations for economic lot sizing models without pricing decisions are powerful in designing efficient algorithms for models with multiple products (see Pochet and Wolsey 2006).

[6] We first construct a directed network $G = (V, E)$, in which the node set $V = \{0, 1, \ldots, T, T + 1\}$ and the arc set $E = \{(t, t + 1) : t = 1, 2, \ldots, T-1\} \cup \{(0, t), (t, T + 1) : t = 1, 2, \ldots, T\} \cup \{(T + 1, 0)\}$. The flow on arc $(0, t)$ $(t = 1, 2, \ldots, T)$, denoted by x_t, belongs to $[0, q_t]$ and incurs a linear cost $c_t x_t$. The flow on arc $(t, t+1)$ $(t = 1, 2, \ldots, T-1)$, denoted by I_t, is nonnegative and incurs a linear cost $h_t I_t$. The flow on arc $(t, T + 1)$ $(t = 1, 2, \ldots, T)$, denoted by d_t, belongs to the interval $[d_t(\bar{p}_t), d_t(\underline{p}_t)]$ and incurs a cost $-d_t g_t(d_t)$, where $g_t(\cdot)$ is the inverse function of $d_t(\cdot)$. The flow on arc $(T + 1, 0)$ is nonnegative and does not incur any cost. With this construction, problem (1) is equivalent to finding a circulation in the network G with a minimum cost.

since we can reformulate problem (1) by replacing inventory variables I_t by $\sum_{l=1}^{t}(x_l - d_l)$ and rearranging terms). Under this assumption, the key observation is that at optimality the marginal revenue (with respect to the satisfied demand) at each period within a production sequence is essentially the same (we say "essentially" because exceptions happen when we take care of the boundary conditions on prices) and we can look at three different cases: (1) if the fractional production period is specified, the optimal price at each period can be easily determined by setting its marginal revenue equal to the variable production cost of the fractional production period; (2) if there is no fractional production period but there is a period, called a fractional demand period, in which the price does not attain the bound constraints, the marginal revenue at each period equals the marginal revenue at the fractional demand period, and if in addition we know the total production quantity of the production sequence, we can then determine the optimal prices; (3) if there is no fractional production period nor fractional demand period, we can determine whether the optimal prices are at their lower bounds or upper bounds by comparing the marginal revenues at these bounds. If we have equal capacities q_t at all periods, we can find the optimal production plans as we do for the CELS problem for all cases (1)–(3) and thus solve eq. (1) in polynomial time. Of course, in case (2), we first need to determine optimal price vector candidates. However, the number of price vector candidates is equal to the number of possible total production quantities which is no more than the number of periods of the production sequence. If the capacities q_t are time dependent, even the CELS problem is NP-hard (see Florian and Morton (1971); Florian et al. (1980) for the CELS model with equal and unequal capacities respectively).

The models analyzed above assume that prices can be freely changed from one period to the next. However, for certain products like catalog goods, firms may want to determine a price at the beginning of the selling season and maintain the same price throughout the whole planning horizon. We can use eqs (1)–(2) to model such a setting by simply adding constraints $p_1 = \ldots = p_T$ and end up with the so-called *joint inventory and static pricing model*. A heuristics for solving the model is the alternating coordinates minimization (ACM) type algorithm. That is, for a given price (and hence a given demand process) find an optimal ordering plan by solving an economic lot sizing problem; then for this ordering plan, find an associated optimal price using the approach we sketched earlier. The ACM algorithm alternates between these two steps until no further improvement is possible.

Kunreuther and Schrage (1973) were the first to propose and analyze the joint inventory and static pricing problem with no capacity constraint. They assume that the demand at period t takes the form $d_t(p) = b_t + a_t d(p)$ for some nonnegative coefficients a_t, b_t, in which the function $d(p)$ is a nonincreasing differentiable function. They propose to apply the ACM algorithm starting from a lower bound $\underline{p}$ and an upper bound $\bar{p}$ of price separately. Let p_l^* and p_u^* be the corresponding terminating prices after a finite number of steps. They prove that their approach does not skip any optimal solution in $[\underline{p}, p_l^*]$ and $[p_u^*, \bar{p}]$ (i.e., the profit of a newly generated price is always no less than the profit of any price between this newly generated price and the price generated in the previous step) and thus an optimal price lies in the interval $[p_l^*, p_u^*]$. Van den Heuvel and Wagelmans (2006) propose to restart the approach in Kunreuther and Schrage (1973) whenever there are unexplored intervals. They argue that the minimum total ordering and inventory holding cost is a piecewise linear concave function of the price effect $d(p)$ with at most $O(T^2)$ linear pieces and their algorithm involves solving $O(T^2)$ economic lot sizing problems each of which corresponds to a linear piece, which implies that the joint inventory and static pricing problem with no capacity constraint can be solved in polynomial time. The capacitated counterpart of Kunreuther and Shrage's model is analyzed in Geunes et al. (2009) (in addition to the capacitated inventory and pricing model with dynamic pricing).

Gilbert (1999) considers a special case of the model proposed by Kunreuther and Schrage (1973) with the assumption that the cost parameters c_t, h_t, and k_t are time independent and the demand takes the form $d_t(p) = a_t d(p)$. A key observation from these assumptions is that given the number of setups, say n, the minimum ordering and inventory holding cost (even though the number of setups is given, we still need to identify the ordering periods) is a linear function of the price effect $d(p)$, $nK + \gamma_n d(p)$, where the coefficient γ_n is independent of p and can be derived by solving a simple dynamic program in $O(T^2)$ time. Since there are T possible candidates for the number of setups, Gilbert (1999) shows that his model can be solved in $O(T^3)$ time under the additional assumption that the function $d(\cdot)$ has an inverse $p(d)$ and the revenue function $dp(d)$ is concave.

A predominant assumption made in the existing inventory and pricing literature is that price adjustment is costless. Yet, various empirical studies illustrate that price adjustment costs do exist and play a crucial role in shaping firms' pricing strategies. For instance, Levy et al. (1997) report that price adjustment may generate enormous costs for major retailer chains, and take up as much as 40 percent of the reported profits for some of these chains. A few papers that take into account price adjustment cost include Chen and Hu (2008) and Chen et al. (2008), which analyze a stochastic model and will be reviewed in the next section.

Chen and Hu (2008) assume that a cost of changing price tags, independent of the magnitude of the price change, is charged if the price at one period is different from its previous period. As both fixed ordering cost and price adjustment cost are taken into account, their model is much more complicated. Still, under the assumption of no capacity constraint, they develop exact algorithms for finding the optimal order quantities and selling prices. The idea is to partition the planning horizon such that each member of the partition consists of consecutive periods with a constant price. The total profit is then appropriately allocated to each member of the partition, and for each member they solve a joint inventory and static pricing problem to find a single constant price maximizing its allocated profit. Based on this result, Chen and Hu (2008) construct an acyclic network so that solving their inventory and pricing model with price adjustment cost is equivalent to finding a longest path in the acyclic network.

A few papers start to relax the assumption that demand at a period depends only on the current period's price. In the deterministic setting, Ahn et al. (2007) study an inventory and pricing model in which the ordering cost is linear and the demand at one period depends on the prices of the current period and previous periods. Specifically, they assume that at each period, new customers enter the market and a fraction of them may stay for certain fixed periods. The amount of new customers is a linear function of the current period's price. This model allows them to capture the size of the customer segment for a given valuation. If the price drops down to a level below the valuation of a customer in the market, the customer makes a purchase and leaves the market. The total demand at one period is then represented as a function of the prices of its current period as well as its previous periods. The authors develop effective heuristics for their optimization problem. When there is no capacity constraint and customers stay for at most one more period in addition to the period when they enter the market, they derive closed-form solutions for the case with stationary parameters and develop an efficient polynomial time algorithm for the case with non-stationary parameters.

Chen et al. (2009a) propose and analyze a deterministic finite horizon coordinated pricing and inventory model in which demand functions are specified by a class of reference price models. In such models, it is argued that consumers develop price expectations, referred to as reference prices, and use them to judge the purchase price of a product (see Mazumdar et al. (2005) for a review). Among many different reference price models, a memory-based model, in which the reference price is the weighted average of a product's own past prices, is commonly used and empirically validated on scanner panel data for a variety of products (see Greenleaf 1995). Specifically, in an exponential-smoothing memory-based model, the reference price at period t, r_t is determined as: $r_t = \alpha r_{t-1} + (1 - \alpha)p_{t-1}$, where p_{t-1} is the previous period price and $\alpha \in [0,1]$ is the smoothing factor.

The demand at period t, taking into account the effect of reference price, can be modeled as a kinked demand curve, namely $d_t(p_t, r_t) = b_t - a_t p_t + f(r_t - p_t)$ (see Fibich et al. 2003; Greenleaf 1995; Kopalle et al. 1996). Here a_t and b_t are some given positive constants while $f(u) = \delta u$ for $u > 0$ and $f(u) = \gamma u$ for $u < 0$ with $0 \le \delta \le \gamma$. The definition of f implies that the effect of $r_t - p_t$ on demand is asymmetric and consumers are loss-averse; that is, consumers are more sensitive to loss ($p_t > r_t$) than gain ($p_t < r_t$). Such a demand function is not only empirically validated but also supported by Kahneman and Tversky's (1979) prospect theory (see Mazumdar et al. (2005) for more discussion and Popescu and Wu (2007) and Nasiry and Popescu (2008) for extensions of the reference models).

The revenue function $p_t d_t(p_t, r_t)$ may not be jointly concave in p_t and r_t. Nevertheless, Chen et al. (2009a) develop strongly polynomial time algorithms for the cases with no fixed ordering costs under some technical conditions and propose a heuristic for the general case with an error bound estimation. Their numerical study illustrates that incorporating the reference price effect into integrated inventory and pricing models can have a significant impact on firms' profits. In addition, the more the reference price effect contributes to the demand, the larger the benefit of pricing and inventory integration.

All the above papers focus on a single product. Gilbert (2000) considers a multi-product inventory and pricing model in which there is a joint production capacity for all products and the fixed ordering cost is negligible. Assuming that the revenue of a product is concave in demand intensities, the author develops an algorithm to find the optimal solution by exploiting the special problem structure, which unfortunately may not run in polynomial time. Hall et al. (2003) develop an inventory and pricing model for products of a category with joint fixed ordering costs in which demand for a product depends on the prices of all products in the category. They develop a dynamic programming formulation to solve their model and demonstrate the benefits obtained via a category management approach.

30.4 STOCHASTIC MODELS

In this section, we focus on integrated inventory and pricing models with stochastic demand. We will first review single period models, which are appropriate for products with long production/order lead times but short selling seasons, and then move to multi-period models in which replenishment is possible in the planning horizon.

30.4.1 Single period models

A single period inventory and pricing model with stochastic demand is an extension of the classical newsvendor model and is thus often referred to as a newsvendor model with price-dependent demand. In this model, at the beginning of the period, an order with a quantity of x units is placed incurring a per-unit cost c. At the same time, a selling price p is decided. During the period, a stochastic price-dependent demand, denoted as $d(p, \varepsilon)$ with ε being a random perturbation, is realized. If the order quantity x is larger than the realized demand $d(p, \varepsilon)$, a per-unit holding cost h is charged for excess inventory (if $h < 0$, then it corresponds to the salvage value). On the other hand, if the realized demand $d(p, \varepsilon)$ is larger than the order quantity, excess demand is lost incurring a unit penalty cost b. The objective is to decide on the order quantity x and the selling price p so that the expected profit is maximized. Upon denoting $x^+ = \max(x, 0)$, the newsvendor model with price-dependent demand is formulated as follows:

$$\underset{x \geq 0, p \in [\underline{p}, \bar{p}]}{\text{Max}} \quad p\mathrm{E}[\min(d(p, \varepsilon), x)] - cx - \mathrm{E}[h(x - d(p, \varepsilon))^+ + b(d(p, \varepsilon) - x)^+], \quad (4)$$

where the first term is the expected revenue, the second term is the ordering cost, and the last term is the expected inventory holding cost and lost sales cost.

To simplify our presentation, we use $d(p, \varepsilon) = d_1(p)\varepsilon + d_2(p)$ (referred to as the mixture demand model), where $d_1(p)$ and $d_2(p)$ are two deterministic functions of price and ε is a nonnegative random variable. Note that when $d_1(p) = 1$, the mixture demand model is the additive demand model, and when $d_2(p) = 0$, it is the multiplicative demand model. Let $d(p) = d_1(p)\mathrm{E}[\varepsilon] + d_2(p)$ be the expected demand for a given p and $R(p) = (p - c)d(p)$, the profit function of the deterministic counterpart of the newsvendor model with price dependent demand. Define $z = \frac{x - d_2(p)}{d_1(p)}$, which can be interpreted as the stocking factor representing a surrogate for safety stock factor, the number of standard deviations that the stocking quantity deviates from expected demand (see Petruzzi and Dada 1999). Problem (4) is equivalently reformulated as

$$\underset{z, p}{\text{Max}} \quad \phi(z, p) = R(p) - (p - c)d_1(p)u(z) - d_1(p)v(z), \quad (5)$$

where $u(z) = \mathrm{E}[\varepsilon] - \mathrm{E}[\min(z, \varepsilon)]$ and $v(z) = (c + h)z + b\mathrm{E}[\varepsilon] - (c + b + h)\mathrm{E}[\min(z, \varepsilon)]$. It is clear that $u(z) \geq 0$ and $v(z) \geq 0$ for all z. Assume that the cumulative distribution function of ε, $F(\cdot)$, is continuous. Under this assumption, there is a unique solution z, denoted by $z*(p)$, maximizing $\phi(z, p)$ for a given p. In fact, $z^*(p) = F^{-1}\left(\frac{p + b - c}{p + b + h}\right)$ is the optimal solution for a corresponding newsvendor model. Let $\pi(p) = \phi(z*(p), p)$ be the induced expected profit function. The optimal price can then be solved by maximizing $\pi(p)$. Unfortunately, the profit function $\pi(p)$ may not be concave or quasi-concave.

Thus, one of the major focuses in the literature concerns structural results of the optimization problem (4), namely the existence and uniqueness of the optimal solutions and concavity or quasi-concavity of the expected profit functions, and comparative statics analysis. We first consider the deterministic counterpart. Note that a stationary point of $R(p)$ satisfies

$$p\left(1 - \frac{1}{e(p)}\right) = c.$$

Recall that $e(p) = -pd'(p)/d(p)$ is the price elasticity of the expected demand. If the expected demand $d(p)$ has an increasing price elasticity, which includes linear demand and concave demand, then $R(p)$ has a unique stationary point and thus is quasi-concave in $[c, \bar{p}]$. The newsvendor model with price-dependent demand can also be handled by analyzing the stationary point of the induced expected profit function $\pi(p)$. Since the derivation is rather tedious, we simply present the results (more details can be found in Yao et al. (2006). Essentially, if the expected demand has an increasing price elasticity and the random variable ε has an increasing generalized failure rate for the multiplicative demand case or an increasing failure rate for the additive demand case,[7] then $\pi(p)$ has a unique stationary point and therefore is quasi-concave in $[c, \bar{p}]$.

Another major focus of the literature concerns the relation between a stochastic model and its deterministic counterpart. Interestingly, the relation of the optimal price in a newsvendor model with price-dependent demand (referred to as optimal risky price) and the optimal price of its deterministic counterpart (a price maximizing $R(p)$ and referred to as the optimal riskless price) depends on how uncertainty is incorporated into the demand function. Specifically, if the demand is additive, that is, $d(p, \varepsilon) = d(p) + \varepsilon$, then the optimal risky price is no more than the optimal riskless price. On the other hand, if the demand is multiplicative, that is, $d(p, \varepsilon) = d(p)\varepsilon$, then the opposite is true, namely the optimal risky price is no less than the optimal riskless price.

We now sketch the analysis. Assume that $R(p)$ and $\pi(p)$ are quasi-concave and have unique stationary points in $[c, \bar{p}]$. The optimal riskless price p^0 and the optimal risky price $p*$ are given by $R'(p^0) = 0$ and $\pi'(p*) = 0$ respectively. From the envelope theorem,

$$\pi'(p) = \frac{\phi(z, p)}{p}\Big|_{z=z^*(p)}.$$

Let $z^* = z^*(p^*)$. We have that

$$0 = \pi'(p^*) = R'(p^*)(1 - u(z^*)w(p^*)) - R(p^*)u(z^*)w'(p^*) - d_1'(p^*)v(z^*),$$

where $w(p) = \frac{d_1(p)}{d_1(p)E[\varepsilon]+d_2(p)}$. Therefore,

$$R'(p^*)(1 - u(z^*)w(p^*)) = R(p^*)u(z^*)w'(p^*) + d_1'(p^*)v(z^*).$$

Note that $1 - u(z*)w(p*) > 0$.

If both $d_1(p)$ and $w(p)$ are decreasing, then $R'(p*) \leq 0$ and the quasi-concavity of $R(p)$ implies that $p* \geq p^0$. On the other hand, if both $d_1(p)$ and $w(p)$ are increasing, then $R'(p*) \geq 0$ and the quasi-concavity of $R(p)$ implies that $p* \leq p^0$. As a consequence, we have $p* \geq p^0$ for the additive demand model in which $d_1(p) = 1$ and $d_2(p)$ is decreasing and $p* \leq p^0$ for the multiplicative demand model in which $d_2(p) = 0$ and $d_1(p)$ is decreasing.

To provide some intuition to the interesting comparison between the additive demand and the multiplicative demand, observe that price provides an opportunity to reduce the risk of overstocking and understocking as a result of demand uncertainty. Thus, it seems reasonable to choose a price to reduce both measures of demand uncertainty if possible: the

---

[7] Let $f(\cdot)$ be the density of the cumulative demand distribution $F(\cdot)$. The distribution has an increasing (generalized) failure rate if its failure rate function $\frac{f(\xi)}{1-F(\xi)}$ (or correspondingly its generalized failure rate function $\frac{\xi f(\xi)}{1-F(\xi)}$) is increasing. This includes several commonly used distributions such as uniform, (truncated) Normal, exponential, Gamma distributions.

demand variance $d_1^2(p)\sigma^2$ and coefficient of variation $w(p)\sigma = \frac{d_1(p)\sigma}{d_1(p)E[\varepsilon]+d_2(p)}$, where σ is the standard deviation of ε. If both measures are decreasing in price, one can expect the optimal risky price to be no less than the optimal riskless price. On the other hand, if both measures are increasing in price, the opposite is true.

The newsvendor model with price-dependent demand was first proposed by Whitin (1955). He also sketches a sequential procedure to calculate the optimal price (first compute the optimal ordering quantity for a given price and then find the optimal solution of the induced expected profit function).

Papers that touch upon conditions for the existence and uniqueness of the optimal solution and concavity properties of the expected profit include Zabel (1970) (multiplicative demand), Young (1978) (mixture demand), Polatoglu (1991) (general demand), Petruzzi and Dada (1999) (both additive and multiplicative demand), Yao et al. (2006) (both additive and multiplicative demand), Chen et al. (2006) (additive demand), Song et al. (2009) (multiplicative demand), and Kocabiykoglu and Popescu (2009) (general demand). Among them, Yao et al. (2006) provide a nice summary of different conditions in many papers and also derive the conditions presented here. Chen et al. (2006) provide conditions for the quasi-concavity of the single period induced expected profit as a function of the order-up-to level for the additive demand case, while Song et al. (2009) derive conditions for the concavity of the single period induced expected profit as a function of the order-up-to level for the multiplicative demand case. These conditions, to be discussed in detail in the next subsection on multi-period stochastic models, involve assumptions on the expected demand and the failure rate function of the underlying random variable. Roughly speaking, they impose conditions that are slightly stronger than the concavity of the expected demand and assume that the underlying random variable satisfies properties closely related to the increasing failure rate requirement.

Recognizing that existing results and techniques depend heavily on how uncertainty is incorporated in the demand model, Kocabiykoglu and Popescu (2009) attempt to propose a unified framework for general demand by introducing a new concept called the elasticity of lost sales. Let $q(p, x)$ be the probability that the demand $d(p, \varepsilon)$ exceeds the inventory level x for a given p and x. The elasticity of lost sales is defined for a selling p and inventory level x as $-p\frac{q(p,x)}{\partial p}/q(p,x)$. Kocabiykoglu and Popescu (2009) illustrate that the concavity and submodularity of the expected profit and monotonicity of the optimal solutions are characterized by the monotonicity or bounds on the elasticity of lost sales, which are satisfied by most demand models analyzed in the literature.

A different demand model is proposed in Raz and Porteus (2006), in which the stochastic demand is specified by several fractiles. These fractiles are represented as piecewise linear functions of the selling price (with the same breakpoints for all fractiles). They argue that such demand models are tractable and allow them to capture certain settings in which additive or multiplicative demand is not appropriate, for instance, settings in which the lowest demand variability comes at either very high or very low prices or settings in which one has a good understanding of the market demand for a middle range of prices. They also illustrate that the optimal price may not be a monotone function of the ordering cost in contrast to most single period inventory and pricing models.

The relation between the optimal riskless price and the optimal risky price was first illustrated in Mills (1959) for the additive demand case. The multiplicative demand case was proven by Karlin and Carr (1962). They also extend their single period model to an infinite horizon setting, in which a single constant price is specified at the beginning of the planning horizon, and prove that the optimal price lies between the optimal riskless price and the optimal risky price (both for a single period) if demand is multiplicative with a uniformly distributed perturbation if demand is additive.

Hempenius (1970) studies a problem similar to the one in Mills (1959) with an additive demand and obtains the same result regarding the optimal risky and riskless prices. The author also investigates how ordering and pricing decisions depend on the variance of the additive random perturbation. In addition, models taking into account risk aversion (using a mean-variance utility) and additive price-dependent random perturbation are proposed (most results are derived for specific demand distributions and sometimes numerically).

The comparison of the optimal riskless and risky prices for the mixture demand model presented here is carried out in Young (1978). Young (1979) extends this demand model by introducing a new parameter b in the function $d_1(p)$, which the author argues represents competitiveness. The author performs comparative statics analysis of the optimal price, expected sales and average inventory and shortage costs with respect to the parameter b, and illustrates that uncertainty may lead to results that differ from its deterministic counterpart.

The intuition explaining the observation of the optimal riskless and risky prices under different demand models is offered in Zabel (1972) and Petruzzi and Dada (1999). The latter paper introduces a new price benchmark, referred to as the base price. For a given value of z, the base price is defined as the price maximizing the profit from expected sales; that is, the optimal solution of the problem

$$\text{Max}_p(p - c)(d_1(p)E[\min(z, \varepsilon)] + d_2(p)).$$

Petruzzi and Dada (1999) illustrate that the optimal risky price can be interpreted as the sum of the base price and a (nonnegative) premium for both the additive and multiplicative cases. Interestingly, in the additive demand case, the premium is zero since for a given z the expected understocking and overstocking are independent of the price p.

All the above papers assume that unsatisfied demand is lost. Simchi-Levi et al. (2005) analyze a single period inventory and pricing model in which unsatisfied demand is filled through an emergency order with a cost higher than the regular ordering cost c. In this case, the expected profit function is well-behaved and existence and uniqueness can be warranted under general assumptions. Simchi-Levi et al. (2005) prove that for the multiplicative demand case, the optimal risky price is no less than the optimal riskless price, which is consistent with the lost sales models. However, for the additive demand case, the optimal risky price equals the optimal riskless price.

Most papers assume that demand depends only on price but not a firm's inventory level. Dana and Petruzzi (2001) depart from this assumption by modeling customers' choice explicitly in view of product availability and their outside options, which leads to stochastic price and inventory-dependent demand. They illustrate that by internalizing the inventory effect on demand, the firm would order more, set a higher fill rate, and earn a higher expected profit.

Several papers incorporate risk aversion into single period inventory and pricing models. Among them, Leland (1972) develops a model of an expected utility-maximizing firm facing random demand whose relation with price is specified as an implicit function. Depending on whether the ordering and pricing decisions are made before or after the realization of the underlying uncertainty, Leland (1972) analyzes four models with different postponement strategies and compares risk-averse models with their risk-neutral counterparts.

Agrawal and Seshadri (2000) analyze a model similar to the one in Simchi-Levi et al. (2005). However, they assume that the decision-maker is risk-averse and use expected utility as the risk measure. They prove that for the multiplicative demand case, the risk-averse decision-maker sets a higher price and orders less compared with its risk-neutral counterpart, while for the additive demand case, the risk-averse decision-maker sets a lower price. A different risk-averse model is analyzed in Chen et al. (2009b), in which risk is measured by the conditional value-at-risk, a risk measure commonly used in finance literature. Focusing on the lost sales model, they derive results regarding optimal risky price and riskless price that are consistent with risk-neutral models. They also illustrate that the more risk-averse the decision-maker is, the smaller the optimal price will be (for both additive and multiplicative demand case), and the smaller the ordering quantity will be (for multiplicative demand case). A different and yet related model is proposed in Lau and Lau (1988) in which the objective is to maximize the probability of attaining a target profile.

Research on multi-product models is limited. This is not very surprising given the analytical complexity even for single product models. Aydin and Porteus (2008) further demonstrate the analytical complexity through a single period inventory and pricing problem with multiple products under price-based substitution and lost sales assumptions. They assume that a product's demand is a deterministic function of the prices with a multiplicative random perturbation, in which the deterministic functions are given by the attraction model from the marketing literature. Specifically, the demand for product i is given by $d_i(p) = \frac{v_i(p_i)}{v_o + \sum_{j=1}^{n} v_j(p_j)} \varepsilon_i$, where n is the number of products, v_o is a positive scalar and for $i = 1, 2, \ldots, N$, $v_i(p_i)$ are strictly decreasing in p_i and ε_i are identically and independently distributed nonnegative random variables with an increasing failure rate cumulative distribution function. Aydin and Porteus (2008) show that the objective function is not necessarily jointly quasi-concave in prices even for deterministic demand. Interestingly, under some technical conditions on the functions v_i, $i = 1, 2, \ldots, N$, they prove that their model admits a unique solution to the first order optimality condition and thus the solution is optimal.

Finally, we mention several papers that compare different postponement strategies in single period inventory and pricing models. Van Mieghem and Dada (1999) analyze two-stage decision models (under monopoly, duopoly, or oligopoly with perfect competition) involving capacity, inventory, and pricing decisions of a single product, Bish and Wang (2004) and Chod and Rudi (2005) study resource investment in settings with flexible resources and responsive price, and Tomlin and Wang (2008) focus on a co-production system with two products.

30.4.2 Multi-period models with convex ordering costs

In this and the next subsections, we review stochastic inventory and pricing models with multiple replenishment opportunities. The focus is on characterizing the structure of the optimal policies that provides important managerial insights and facilitates efficient computation. We first present a general model and then review relevant papers on models with convex ordering costs in this subsection and on models with concave ordering costs in the next subsection.

The sequence of events of the multi-period stochastic model is similar to its deterministic counterpart presented in the previous section. That is, at the beginning of period t ($t = 1$, 2, ..., T), the firm decides on its order quantity and selling price for period t. Demand in period t is assumed to be a stochastic function of the current period selling price p_t, denoted as $d_t(p_t, \varepsilon_t)$, and is realized after the ordering and pricing decision for period t is made. Let x_t be the inventory level at the beginning of period t, just before placing an order. Similarly, y_t is the inventory level at the beginning of period t after placing an order. For tractability, the order leadtime is assumed to be zero. Thus, the ordering cost is a function of the order quantity $y_t - x_t$ and is denoted as $C_t(y_t - x_t)$.

Since demand is stochastic, it is unlikely that all demands can be filled immediately from on-hand inventory. In this case, unsatisfied demand is assumed to be either backlogged or lost; both the backlogging model and the lost sales model are commonly used in the literature. In the backlogging model, the selling price for the backlogged demand is the price in the period at which the demand occurs. Let x be the inventory level carried over from period t to period $t + 1$. A cost $h_t(x)$ is incurred at the end of period t which represents inventory holding cost when $x > 0$ and backorder cost or lost sale penalty cost if $x < 0$ depending on whether unsatisfied demand is backlogged or lost. $h_t(x)$ is usually assumed to be convex.

The objective is to decide on ordering and pricing policies to maximize total expected profit over the entire planning horizon. That is, to choose y_t and p_t to maximize

$$E\left[\sum_{t=1}^{T} -C_t(y_t - x_t) - h_t(y_t - d_t(p_t, \varepsilon_t)) + p_t d_t(p_t, \varepsilon_t)\right], \tag{6}$$

where $x_{t+1} = \psi(y_t - d_t(p_t, \varepsilon_t))$. Here, $\psi(x) = x$ for the backlogging model and $\psi(x) = \text{Max}(x, 0)$ for the lost sales model.

We denote by $v_t(x)$ the maximum expected profit starting from the beginning of time period t with inventory level x to the end of the planning horizon ($v_t(x)$ is referred to as the profit-to-go function). We write a recursion of $v_t(x)$ as a dynamic program as follows. For $t = T, T-1, \ldots, 1$,

$$v_t(x) = \text{Max}_{y \geq x, \underline{p}_t \leq p \leq \bar{p}_t} -C_t(y - x) - E[h_t(y - d_t(p, \varepsilon_t))]$$
$$+ E[p(y - \psi(y - d_t(p, \varepsilon_t)))] + E[v_{t+1}(\psi(y - d_t(p, \varepsilon_t)))], \tag{7}$$

where the first three terms represent the ordering cost, the expected inventory holding and backlogging (or lost sales penalty) cost, and the expected revenue incurred at period t respectively, and the last term is the profit-to-go function. We assume for simplicity that $v_{T+1}(x) = 0$, that is, at the end of the planning horizon, no cost is incurred for lost sales and no salvage value is imposed on leftover inventory.

In this subsection, we assume that the ordering cost functions $C_t(\cdot)$ are convex, which implies that the marginal purchasing cost increases as one orders more. Under this assumption, the literature mainly focuses on developing conditions under which the so-called base-stock list-price type policy is optimal. In a base-stock list-price policy, at each period there is a base-stock level such that an order is placed to raise the inventory level to the base-stock level and a list price is charged if the initial inventory level is below the base-stock level, otherwise no order is placed and a discount is offered. In addition, the higher the initial inventory level, the deeper the discount. When the ordering cost functions are linear, a base-stock list-price policy is optimal under various technical conditions on demand functions and random perturbations.

When the ordering cost functions are general convex functions, such a simple policy is usually not optimal. However, an extended base-stock list-price policy is optimal under various technical conditions on demand functions and random perturbations. In such a policy, at each period there exists a critical point, say $x*$, such that no order is placed when the initial inventory level x at the beginning of this period is above $x*$, while for x below $x*$, the order-up-to level $y*(x)$ is increasing in x; the price $p*(y*(x))$ depends on x only through the order-up-to level $y*(x)$ and is decreasing in x. Here the critical point, the order quantity, and the order-up-to level are usually time dependent. The extended base-stock list-price policy can be refined when the ordering cost functions are convex and piecewise-linear.

A typical approach to prove the optimality of the base-stock list-price type policy is to argue that certain concavity properties on the value functions v_t can be preserved under dynamic programming recursions. To illustrate the idea, consider the case in which any unfilled demand is backlogged and the expected demands are linear in prices. In this case, single period expected profit functions are concave. If $v_{t+1}(\cdot)$ is concave, then problem (7) has a concave objective function with linear constraints and thus $v_t(x)$ remains concave. One can also show that the objective function is supermodular in $(x, y, -p)$ and the feasible set is a lattice. Thus, the optimal order-up-to level $y*(x)$ is increasing in x while the optimal price $p*(y*(x))$ is decreasing in x. That is, the optimal policy follows the extended base-stock list-price policy, which reduces to the base-stock list-price policy for linear ordering costs. The same structural policy remains optimal if the demand functions have the forms $d(p)\varepsilon_1 + \varepsilon_2$ with ε_1 and ε_2 being two random perturbations and at each period the expected revenue is a concave function of the expected demand. The idea is to reformulate problem (7) by replacing the price variable with a new variable representing the expected demand (for this purpose we assume that there is a one-to-one correspondence between price and its associated expected demand).

Problem (7) with linear ordering costs and backlogged demand is analyzed in Federgruen and Heching (1999). They use the mixture demand model $d_t(p, \varepsilon_t) = d_{1,t}(p)\varepsilon_t + d_{2,t}(p)$. They further assume that one period expected inventory holding and backlogging cost is jointly convex in inventory level and selling price and illustrate that this assumption is satisfied if $d_{1,t}(p)$ and $d_{2,t}(p)$ are linear in p. They prove that a base-stock list-price policy is optimal. Several extensions are discussed. In one extension, price is only allowed to markdown. In this case, again the optimal policy is given by a base-stock list-price policy with the base-stock level dependent on the price of the previous period. They consider another extension in which capacity constraints are imposed for ordering quantities and prove that a modified base-stock list-price policy is optimal. In such a policy, at each period, when the initial inventory level is below the base-stock level, an order would be made to raise the inventory level to the base-stock level if possible. Otherwise a full capacity would be ordered. Federgruen and Heching (1999) further prove that similar structural results can be extended to models with emergency orders (instead of backlogging) and to infinite horizon models under both the discounted profit and long-run average profit criteria. However, models with a nonzero leadtime for ordering impose a significant challenge, for which they propose heuristics.

Federgruen and Heching (1999) develop an efficient value iteration method to compute optimal policies. Based on data collected from a specialty retailer of high end women's apparel, they conduct an extensive numerical study to demonstrate the benefits of dynamic pricing strategies over static strategies and the impact of demand uncertainty and price elasticities on optimal policies and their corresponding profits and observe that dynamic pricing strategies may bring significant benefits even in a stationary environment.

Problem (7) with lost sales is more complicated. Indeed, strong technical conditions on both the expected demands and the distributions of the random perturbations are usually needed for the concavity of the single period expected profit. Mills (1962) recognizes the need and the difficulty of extending the single period model in Mills (1959) to multi-period settings and develops a single period approximation.

Miercort (1968) analyzes problem (7) with linear ordering costs. The expected demand is assumed to be decreasing, convex, and twice differentiable in price. Under some strong conditions on the demand density functions to ensure the concavity of the single period expected profit, Miercort (1968) proves that a base-stock list-price policy is optimal.

Ernst (1970) assumes that all costs are linear, demand is additive and linear in price in problem (7). In addition, the distribution of the underlying additive random variable belongs to the class of Pólya frequency functions of order 2 (PF2), which includes common distributions such as uniform, normal, and truncated normal as special cases. With additional assumptions on system parameters, the author proves that the optimal policy is unique and follows a base-stock list-price policy.[8] Ernst (1970) extends the results to infinite horizon models, conducts sensitivity analysis of the optimal parameters and compares the optimal policies of the model with uncertain demand and its deterministic counterpart.

Zabel (1972), motivated by observations made from a simulation study in Nevins (1966) on multi-period inventory and pricing models, analyzes a special case of the general model (6) with stationary problem parameters under the assumption that the ordering cost is convex, the inventory holding cost is linear, and unsatisfied demand is lost without incurring a penalty cost. The author demonstrates the difficulty of extending the uniqueness properties of optimal solutions from a single period model in Zabel (1970) to multi-period settings. Focusing on an additive demand model in which the expected demand is concave in the selling price and the underlying random variable is exponentially or uniformly distributed and imposing some additional technical conditions, Zabel (1972) argues that the profit-to-go function $v_t(x)$ is concave and proves that the extended base-stock list-price policy is optimal and in addition the optimal order quantity is decreasing in x. The author also makes an intra-period comparison of the optimal policy parameters and performs comparative statics analysis. For instance, Zabel (1972) proves that the critical point x_t^* is increasing over time and the optimal order-up-to level y_t^*, the optimal order quantity q_t^*, and the optimal price p_t^* are all decreasing in the unit holding cost for x below x_t^*.

---

[8] Ernst (1970) pays special attention to the possibility of having negative values derived from additive demand models and illustrates that a list-price policy may fail to be optimal if the additive demand model results in negative values at the optimal policy.

Focusing on additive demand, Thowsen (1975) proposes a model similar to Zabel (1972) with linear ordering cost. The author assumes that unsatisfied demand can be partially backlogged which makes the lost sales and full backlogging cases two extreme cases in a unified model, and a fraction of inventory may deteriorate from one period to the next. Some assumptions on cost and expected demand are also imposed, which essentially require that there is no motive to hold inventory, stockout and backlog demand, the inventory system is profitable, and the price constraint will not be binding (i.e., not attain its upper bound). Under these assumptions, Thowsen (1975) identifies conditions under which a base-stock list-price policy is optimal.

As acknowledged by Thowsen (1975), these conditions are hard to verify in general. However, they are satisfied in two settings. The first is the backlogging case with convex inventory holding and backlogging cost and concave expected demand (as a function of price). The second setting is the partial backlogging case as well as the lost sales case with convex inventory holding, linear stock out cost, linear expected demand, and a PF2 distribution for the additive random perturbation. In these two settings, the profit-to-go function $v_t(x)$ is shown to be concave. The author also allows revenue to be collected several periods after demand occurs or is satisfied (customers still pay the price of the period at which their demand occurs) and proves that the same structural results hold under similar conditions.

Chan et al. (2006) study a multi-period joint pricing and production model under a general, non-stationary stochastic demand function with a discrete menu of prices. In their model, the available production capacity is limited and unmet demand is lost. They also allow discretionary sales, that is, inventory may be set aside to satisfy future demand even if some present demand is lost. They analyze and compare delayed production strategies (in which pricing is determined upfront while production is determined at the beginning of each period) and delayed pricing strategies (in which production is determined upfront while pricing is determined at the beginning of each period). Chan et al. (2006) describe policies and effective heuristics for the strategies based on deterministic approximations. Their computational study illustrates that delayed production is usually better than delayed pricing except sometimes when capacity is tight.

Almost all papers in the inventory and pricing literature assume that the yield is certain. One exception is Li and Zheng (2006) who analyze a model similar to Federgruen and Heching (1999) but with additive demand and stochastic proportional yield (i.e., the received quantity equals the order quantity multiplied by a nonnegative random variable). Similar to inventory models with random yield but without pricing decisions (see, for instance, Zipkin 2000), they prove that the extended base-stock list-price policy is optimal and in addition the optimal order quantity is a decreasing function of the initial inventory level. They further study the operational effects of uncertain yield and prove that, in the single period case, the critical number is independent of the yield variability, while in the multi-period case, it is higher in a system with uncertain yield than in the one with certain yield. Moreover, the system with uncertain yield always charges a higher price.

Allon and Zeevi (2009) develop a model that integrates capacity investment (or disinvestment), production (inventory), and price decisions. In their model, at the beginning of each period, a capacity adjustment is first determined, which is then followed by the production and pricing decisions. Demand is additive with expectation linear in price, and unsatisfied demand is backlogged. Inventory holding and backlogging cost is assumed to be convex in leftover inventory level. All other costs, including ordering cost, and capacity investment cost and disinvestment cost, are linear. They prove that the capacity decision follows the so-called target interval policy. In such a policy, at each period, there exists two numbers L and U with $L \leq U$ such that the following action is taken: invest and raise capacity to L if the initial capacity level is lower than L; disinvest and decrease capacity to U if the initial capacity level is higher than U; otherwise keep the current capacity level. In their model, the two numbers L and U may depend on time and initial inventory level. The optimal production and pricing decision follows the modified base-stock list-price policy with the policy parameters dependent on capacity level. They also consider a different case in which inventory cannot be carried over from one period to the next and price can only be marked down. In this case, they prove that the optimal capacity decision takes the form of a price-dependent target inventory policy and the two target parameters are nonincreasing in price level of the previous period.

Qi (2010) analyzes an integrated inventory and pricing model with supply capacity uncertainty and linear ordering cost. She illustrates that the base-stock list-price policy is not optimal even under deterministic demand. Assuming additive demand, she proves that in the optimal policy, there exists a reorder point such that an order is placed when the inventory level is below the reorder point, and the optimal order and price are chosen to achieve a constant target safety stock.

Boyaci and Ozer (2009) consider pricing strategy in acquiring demand information to plan for capacity. They study the joint benefit of acquiring information for capacity planning through advance selling and revenue management of installed capacity through dynamic pricing.

Similar to Chen and Hu (2008), Chen et al. (2008) incorporate price adjustment costs into an integrated inventory and pricing model but with stochastic demand. Their model is similar to the one analyzed in Federgruen and Heching (1999), except that at each period, a price adjustment cost is incurred if the current period price is different from the price of the previous period, which may involve a fixed component independent of the magnitude of the price change and a variable component proportional to the magnitude of the price change. Acknowledging the complexity of the general model, Chen et al. (2008) analyze two special cases: a model without fixed ordering cost and fixed price adjustment cost and a model with fixed price adjustment cost and no inventory carryover. For each case, they characterize the structure of the optimal policy.

For the model without fixed ordering cost and fixed price adjustment cost, Chen et al. (2008) prove that the optimal inventory policy follows a base-stock-type policy, in which the base-stock level is a nonincreasing function of the price in the previous period, whereas the optimal price follows a target interval policy, in which the two target parameters are nonincreasing functions of the initial inventory level. For the model with fixed price-change costs and no inventory carryover, Chen et al. (2008) employ the concepts of k-concavity and symmetric k-concavity to provide a characterization of the structure of the optimal pricing policy for their model which allows for markdown, markup, or bi-directional price changes. For the general problem, they develop an intuitive heuristic policy to manage inventory and set selling prices. Compared with the optimal policy, which is likely to be very complicated, their heuristic policy is amenable to practical implementation. In addition, their numerical study demonstrates that it is quite effective.

A few works start to incorporate reference price effects into stochastic inventory and pricing models. In this case, the dynamic program (7) has to be augmented to include the reference price as a state variable in addition to the inventory level, which significantly complicates the analysis of the problem. Indeed, the single period expected profit is not a concave function in general. Focusing on additive demand, Gimpl-Heersink (2008) proves that a reference price-dependent base-stock list-price policy is optimal under general assumptions for a single period setting and under more restrictive assumptions for a two period setting. Their numerical study illustrates that with the presence of reference price effects, the integrated inventory and pricing model brings considerable benefits over a procedure that determines price decisions and ordering decisions sequentially. By introducing a transformation technique, Chen et al. (2011) prove that a reference price-dependent base-stock policy is optimal in multi-period settings with both additive and multiplicative demands. They also analyze the convergence of the price trajectory in the infinite horizon setting and characterize the limit. Guler et al. (2010) analyze a similar model where customers are loss-averse or loss-neutral with relative difference reference effects and provide conditions under which a state-dependent order-up-to policy is optimal.

Chen and Zhang (2010) introduce a stochastic term in reference price evolution dynamics to capture possible modeling errors. They derive an explicit solution for the optimal steady state price in a continuous time model and illustrate that the optimal steady state price in the setting with stochastic reference price dynamics is always higher than the corresponding price in the setting without stochasticity.

All the above models assume that inventory is managed at a single location. Federgruen and Heching (2002) extend their earlier work in Federgruen and Heching (1999) to a distribution system with a distribution center serving several retailer stores. At the beginning of each period, the distribution center, which does not hold any inventory, will place an order which will then be allocated to the retailer stores after an order leadtime and an allocation leadtime. At the same time, a single price across all retailer stores is determined. Federgruen and Heching (2002) present a tractable approximation of the stochastic model, which admits an optimal policy with a simple structure, and carry out an extensive computational study to illustrate the benefits of dynamic pricing strategies under a variety of different system parameters.

A few papers analyze multiple products in the stochastic setting. Zhu and Thonemann (2009) extend the model in Federgruen and Heching (1999) to the case with two substitutable products in which demand of each product depends linearly on the prices of both products. They prove that the optimal inventory policy behaves similarly to the base-stock policy for the one-product problem: when the starting inventory levels of both products are low, the optimal decision is to order both products; when the starting inventory levels of both products are high, the optimal decision is not to order; when one product has a high starting inventory level and the other has a low starting inventory level, the optimal decision is to order only the product with the low inventory level. In addition, the inventory policy of one period is given by a base-stock policy in which the base-stock level is nonincreasing in the initial inventory level of another product. They also provide a characterization of the optimal pricing and illustrate that in their model, the base-stock list-price policy, which is optimal for the single period model in Federgruen and Heching (1999), may fail to be optimal.

Ceryan et al. (2009) extend the model in Zhu and Thonemann (2009) by incorporating both dedicated and flexible production capacities for the two substitutable products. They characterize the structure of the optimal production and pricing decisions and explore the effects of various problem parameters on the optimal policy. Song and Xue (2007) analyze a model with multiple substitutable products with more general demand functions. They provide a characterization of the structure of the optimal policy and develop an algorithm to compute it. By developing a preservation result of submodularity property under an optimization operation in two dimensional space, Chen et al. (2010b) characterize the structure of the optimal production and pricing policy for models with either two complementary products or two substitutable products. In the case with two substitutable products, they provide a refined structural property and significantly simplify some of the proofs in Zhu and Thonemann (2009), Ceryan et al. (2009), and Song and Xue (2007).

30.4.3 Multi-period models with concave ordering costs

In the previous subsection we assume that the ordering cost is either convex or linear. However, in some practical settings, the ordering cost can be concave, as a result of economies of scale or incremental discounts provided by suppliers. Such cost structures impose a significant challenge for multi-period models because the value functions $v_t(x)$ are not concave anymore and base-stock list-price policies are not optimal either. The literature mainly focuses on developing conditions under which an (s, S, p) type policy is optimal when the ordering cost involves a fixed cost component representing economies of scale and a variable cost component. In an (s, S, p) policy, inventory is managed based on an (s, S) policy: if the inventory level at the beginning of period t is below the reorder point, s_t, an order is placed to raise the inventory level to the order-up-to level, S_t; otherwise, no order is placed. The selling price of the product depends (not necessarily monotonically) on the initial inventory level at the beginning of the period.

Interestingly, the structural results and the analysis depend heavily on how uncertainty is incorporated into demand models. Consider problem (7) in which the ordering cost includes both a fixed cost independent of the order quantity and a variable cost proportional to the quantity and unsatisfied demand is backlogged. Assume that for any period t, the demand function satisfies $d_t(p_t, \varepsilon_t) = \varepsilon_{1t} d_t(p_t) + \varepsilon_{2t}$, where the random perturbations, $\varepsilon_t = (\varepsilon_{1t}, \varepsilon_{2t})$, are independent across time satisfying $\varepsilon_{1t} \geq 0$, $E\{\varepsilon_{1t}\} = 1$ and $E\{\varepsilon_{2t}\} = 0$. Furthermore, the function $d_t(p)$ is continuous and strictly decreasing and the expected revenue $dp_t(d)$ is concave in the expected demand d at period t, where $p_t(d)$ is the inverse function of $d_t(p)$.[9]

When the demand process is additive, that is, $\varepsilon_{1t} = 1$, one can show that at an optimal policy, the higher the inventory level at the beginning of time period t, the higher the expected inventory level at the end of period t. Though the value function $v_t(x)$ is not concave, this result allows one to show by induction that $v_t(x)$ is a k-concave[10] function of x and the optimality of an (s, S, p) policy follows directly from k-concavity.

---

[9] Since $d = E\{d_t(p_t, \varepsilon_t)\} = d_t(p_t)$, the expected revenue can be represented as $dp_t(d)$.

[10] The concept of k-convexity is introduced by Scarf (1960) to analyze stochastic inventory models with fixed ordering cost. A definition of k-convexity, equivalent to the original one proposed by Scarf, is as follows: a real-valued function f is called k-convex for $k \geq 0$, if for any $x_0 \leq x_1$ and $\lambda \in [0, 1]$,

$$f((1 - \lambda)x_0 + \lambda x_1) \leq (1 - \lambda)f(x_0) + \lambda f(x_1) + \lambda k.$$

A function f is k-concave if $-f$ is k-convex.

Unfortunately, the (s, S, p) policy is not necessarily optimal for general demand models. To characterize the optimal policy in this case, a new concept, symmetric k-concavity[11] is needed. It can be shown that for general demand processes, even though $v_t(x)$ may fail to be k-concave, it is symmetric k-concave and consequently an (s, S, A, p) policy is optimal. In such a policy, the optimal inventory strategy at period t is characterized by two parameters (s_t, S_t) and a set $A_t \in [s_t, (s_t + S_t)/2]$, possibly empty depending on the problem instance. When the inventory level x_t at the beginning of period t is less than s_t or $x_t \in A_t$, an order of size $S_t - x_t$ is made. Otherwise, no order is placed. Price depends on the initial inventory level at the beginning of the period.

The above model was first analyzed by Thomas (1974). Although a counterexample is constructed to show that an (s, S, p) policy may fail to be optimal when prices are restricted to a discrete set, the author conjectures that an (s, S, p) policy is optimal under fairly general conditions if prices in an interval are under consideration.

Chen and Simchi-Levi (2004a) prove that the (s, S, p) policy postulated by Thomas (1974) is indeed optimal when the demand process is additive and construct an example which shows that the value function $v_t(x)$ may not be k-concave and an (s, S, p) policy may fail to be optimal when the demand process is multiplicative. The concept of symmetric k-concavity[12] and the (s, S, A, p) policy are introduced in Chen and Simchi-Levi (2004a) for the multiplicative demand case. Although an (s, S, A, p) policy may not be optimal in settings with general demand, surprisingly, Chen and Simchi-Levi (2004b) show by employing the concept of symmetric k-concavity that a stationary (s, S, p) policy is optimal for the infinite horizon model under either the discounted profit or the average profit criterion. This optimality result also holds under the average profit criterion if the single period maximum expected profit function, $Q(x) = \max_{p \in [\underline{p}, \bar{p}]} \pi(x, p)$, is quasi-concave, where $\pi(x, p)$ is the single period expected profit for a given inventory level x and price p. However, they demonstrate through one example that if prices are restricted to take values from a discrete set, a stationary (s, S, p) policy may not be optimal anymore.

Yin and Rajaram (2007) present a generalization of the model in Chen and Simchi-Levi (2004a) to allow for Markovian modulated demand. For Chen and Simchi-Levi's infinite horizon model with the average profit criterion, Feng and Chen (2004) prove that the structure of the optimal policy holds under slightly relaxed demand assumptions and develop an efficient algorithm to find the parameters of the optimal policies. On the other hand, Zhang and Fu (2005) derive sample path derivatives that can be used in a gradient-based algorithm for determining the optimal stationary (s, S, p) policy parameters in a simulation-based optimization procedure.

Focusing on additive demand, Chen et al. (2010c) analyze problem (7) with concave piecewise-linear ordering cost. Under the assumption that the additive random perturbation follows a positive Pólya or uniform distribution, they prove that the value functions

---

[11]   A real-valued function f is called symmetric k-convex for $k \geq 0$, if for any x_0, x_1 and $\lambda \in [0, 1]$,

$$f((1 - \lambda)x_0 + \lambda x_1) \leq (1 - \lambda)f(x_0) + \lambda f(x_1) + \max\{\lambda, 1 - \lambda\}k.$$

A function f is called symmetric k-concave if $-f$ is symmetric k-convex.

[12]   Building upon the concepts of k-convexity and symmetric k-convexity, Ye and Duenyas (2007) propose the so-called (k, q)-convexity, which finds application for capacity investment problems with two-sided-capacity adjustment costs and stochastic cash balance problems with fixed costs (Chen and Simchi-Levi 2009).

$v_t(x)$ belong to the class of quasi-k-concave functions[13] by establishing a new preservation property of quasi-k-concavity, which says that under mild technical conditions, $\max_d[\alpha(d) + \beta(y-d)]$ is quasi-K-concave if the one-dimensional functions $\alpha(\cdot)$ and $\beta(\cdot)$ are concave and quasi-K-concave respectively. Quasi-k-concavity of the value functions implies that a generalized (s, S, p) policy is optimal. In such a policy, inventory is managed based on a generalized (s, S) policy. That is, there is a sequence of reorder points s_i and order-up-to levels S_i (both are increasing in i) such that if the starting inventory level is lower than the reorder point s_i but higher than s_{i+1}, an order is placed to raise its inventory level to S_i. The optimal price is set according to the inventory level after replenishment. For the special case with two suppliers, one with only variable cost while the other has both fixed and variable costs, they prove that the (refined) generalized (s, S, p) policy is still optimal when the additive random component in the demand function has a strongly unimodal density.

Polatoglu and Sahin (2000) analyze problem (7) with lost sales. They show that an (s, S, p) policy is not optimal in general and provide some conditions for the optimality of an (s, S, p) policy, which unfortunately may be hard to verify.

In an attempt to attack lost sales models, Chen et al. (2006) make the following assumptions: first, demand is additive, and in the additive demand process $d(p) + \beta$, the expected demand $d(p)$ is decreasing and concave in p, and $3d'' + pd''' \leq 0$ for $p \in [c, \bar{p}]$, where c is the variable ordering cost and $\bar{p}$ is the upper bound imposed on p; second, the failure rate function of the underlying random variable β with probability density function f and cumulative distribution function F, $r(u) = f(u)/(1 - F(u))$, satisfies $r'(u) + [r(u)]^2 > 0$ for u in the support of β; third, all cost and demand parameters are stationary; fourth, both the inventory holding cost and the stockout cost are linear, and the salvage value at the end of the planning horizon is equal to the variable ordering cost. Under these assumptions, they prove that an (s, S, p) policy is optimal for their multi-period model. They also illustrate the difficulty of extending their approach to models with a salvage value different from the variable ordering cost and to models with multiplicative demand.

Huh and Janakiraman (2008) propose an alternate approach to prove the optimality of an (s, S, p) for problem (6) with stationary cost and demand parameters. In their model, the demand takes a more general form: $d(p, \varepsilon)$, where $d(p, \varepsilon)$ is monotone and concave in p for almost every value of the underlying uncertainty ε (their demand actually allows for other decisions that may influence demand). They impose two conditions on the single period expected profit function $\pi(x, p)$. Let $y*$ be the maximal point of the single period maximum expected profit $Q(x)$. Their first condition requires that $Q(x)$ is quasi-concave, and their second condition requires that for any $y* \leq y^1 < y^2$ and any given price p^2, there exists a price p^1 such that $\pi(y^1, p^1) \geq \pi(y^2, p^2)$ and $\psi(y^1 - d(p^1, \varepsilon)) \leq \max\{y*, \psi(y^2 - d(p^2, \varepsilon))\}$ for any realization of ε, where $\psi(x) = x$ for the backlogging case and $\psi(x) = \max(x, 0)$ for the lost sales case as defined earlier. Roughly speaking, their first condition implies that the closer the inventory level (after ordering) is to $y*$, the higher the profit the system can generate in a single period, and their second condition implies that if one starts with a better inventory position (i.e., an inventory position closer to $y*$), one can generate more

---

[13]   A one-dimensional function f is quasi-k-concave if for any $x_1 \leq x_2$ and $\lambda \in [0, 1], f((1 - \lambda)x_1 + \lambda x_2) \geq \min\{f(x_1), f(x_2) - k\}$. It was introduced by Porteus (1971) to analyze stochastic inventory models with concave ordering costs.

expected profit at the current period and end up at a better inventory position at the beginning of the following period (i.e., an inventory position closer to $y*$ or smaller than $y*$ so that the inventory level can be raised to $y*$ with one order) simultaneously.

Under the above two conditions, Huh and Janakiraman (2008) prove that a stationary (s, S, p) policy is optimal for the infinite horizon version of problem (6) under the discounted profit criterion (their approach does not work for the infinite horizon model under the average profit criterion). With a third condition, which requires that for any $y^2 < y^1 \leq y*$ and any given price p^2, there exists a price p^1 such that $\pi(y^1, p^1) \geq \pi(y^2, p^2)$ and $\psi(y^1 - d(p^1, \varepsilon)) \geq \psi(y^2 - d(p^2, \varepsilon))$ for any realization of ε, they prove that an (s, S, p) policy is optimal for the finite horizon problem (6) with stationary input data. For the backlogging model, they prove that the joint concavity of the single period expected profit $\pi(x, p)$ implies the first two conditions, and present an assumption that gives rise to the three conditions in the additive demand case. For the lost sales model, they prove that the assumptions made in Chen et al. (2006) are sufficient for the three conditions.

Building upon the approach in Huh and Janakiraman (2008), Song et al. (2009) analyze problem (7) with stationary input data and multiplicative demand $d(p)\varepsilon$. They assume that the expected demand $d(p)$ satisfies the following conditions: first, $d(p)$ is strictly decreasing and has an increasing elasticity $- pd'(p)d(p)$; second, $d(p)/d'(p)$ is monotone and concave; third, $p + d(p)/d'(p)$ is strictly increasing. In addition, the underlying random variable ε has an increasing failure rate. Under these assumptions, they prove that the first two conditions in Huh and Janakiraman (2008) hold and thus a stationary (s, S, p) policy is optimal for the infinite horizon model under the discounted profit criterion. With additional work, they prove that an (s, S, A, p) policy, optimal for the finite horizon model with backlogging in Chen and Simchi-Levi (2004a), is also optimal for their finite horizon model with lost sales and stationary input data.

All the above papers assume a risk-neutral decision-maker. Chen et al. (2007b) propose a general framework for incorporating risk aversion in multi-period inventory (and pricing) models, while Chen and Sun (2007) consider a corresponding infinite horizon model. They show that the structure of the optimal policy for a decision-maker with additive exponential utility functions is almost identical to the structure of the optimal risk-neutral inventory (and pricing) policies, and demonstrate computationally that the optimal policy is relatively insensitive to small changes in the decision-maker's level of risk aversion. Interestingly, since the additivity property of the expectation operator cannot be extended to a risk-averse setting (involving certainty equivalent operator), the proof approaches in Chen and Simchi-Levi (2004b) and Huh and Janakiraman (2008), built upon additivity of the expectation operator, may not be extended to analyze their infinite horizon risk-averse model and thus they take a different approach to prove the optimality of the stationary (s, S, p) policy.

Several papers analyze continuous review models with fixed ordering cost. Under the unit demand assumption (i.e., each arrival requests a single unit item), Feng and Chen (2002) prove that the optimal policy has a simple structure under the infinite horizon long-run average profit criterion. Chen and Simchi-Levi (2006) subsequently generalize their model and results to allow for more general demand functions and prove that an (s, S, p) policy and a stationary (s, S, p) are optimal respectively for the finite horizon case and the infinite horizon case under both the discounted profit and average profit criteria. In the infinite horizon case with average profit criterion, Chen and Simchi-Levi (2006) prove that the optimal price is a unimodal function of the inventory level. Finally, for the same model, Chao and Zhou (2006) develop efficient computational procedures to find the parameters of the optimal policy.

It is worthwhile to mention several other papers whose focus is not on characterizing the structure of optimal policies. Chen et al. (2010a) present an inventory and pricing model with demand modeled as a diffusion process and quantify the profit improvement of dynamic pricing over static pricing. Other related work includes Lodish (1980) who develops an integrated inventory and pricing model and Subrahmanyan and Shoemaker (1996) who develop an integrated inventory and pricing model with demand learning through Bayesian updating. Without focusing on the structure of the optimal policies, both papers propose to solve their models by brute force backward dynamic programming. Additional papers on demand learning include Petruzzi and Dada (2002), Aviv and Pazgal (2005), and Zhang and Chen (2006).

30.5 SUPPLY CHAIN COMPETITION, COORDINATION, AND COOPERATION

The research on decentralized supply chain systems received significant amounts of attention in the past decade and remains an active area. One stream of this research employs concepts and methodologies from non-cooperative game theory to analyze equilibrium behavior of the supply chain and supply chain coordination. As the literature on these topics is rapidly growing, we do not intend to provide a comprehensive review. Instead, our focus is mainly on decentralized supply chain models (mostly with demand uncertainty) that are either built upon or closely related to the integrated inventory and pricing models reviewed in the previous sections. For more comprehensive recent surveys on decentralized supply chain models, we refer to Cachon (2003) and several chapters in Tayur et al. (1998). We also refer to Kaya and Özer (Chapter 29) for a tutorial on supply chain contracts. Another, more recent and less extensive, stream of research employs concepts and methodologies from cooperative game theory to analyze the stability and formation of coalitions in supply chain settings. We review several papers on this stream in which inventory and pricing decisions play an important role.

Levitan and Shubik (1971) provide a duopoly model with two symmetrical firms competing on inventory and price. Even though a pure strategy Nash equilibrium may not exist in a deterministic model with capacity constraints, they illustrate through an example that it may be restored when demand is stochastic and inventory carrying cost is introduced. Since they model explicitly price-outs (i.e., a firm is driven out of the market) and customer switching in the case of stockouts, their demand model is very complicated, which prevents them from deriving conditions for the existence of a pure strategy Nash equilibrium.

Marvel and Peck (1995) consider a single period model consisting of a manufacturer and a retailer who orders from the manufacturer and makes a pricing decision. Demand is characterized by two independent random variables: the number of customers and customers' valuation of the product. A customer with a valuation no less than the retailer's price will purchase one unit. They illustrate that the attractiveness of a returns policy to the manufacturer depends crucially on the nature of the demand uncertainty. Specifically, return policies benefit the manufacturer if the only uncertainty is over the number of customers. On the other hand, it would induce retailer prices to go too high to be beneficial for the manufacturer if the only uncertainty is over customers' valuation.

Kandel (1996) studies the allocation of responsibility of unsold inventories in a setting with a manufacturer and a retailer. The author demonstrates that contract choice may depend on (among several other factors) whether the selling price is a decision variable and who is responsible for making the pricing decision. For instance, when the retailer decides the selling price, it is possible to show that in cases with sufficiently high price elasticity, the manufacturer prefers no returns policy, while the opposite is true when the price elasticity is not too high.

Emmons and Gilbert (1998) consider a similar setting but assume that the retailer faces a (stochastic) multiplicative price-dependent demand. They illustrate that under the assumption of a linear expected demand and uniformly distributed multiplicative random perturbation, there exists a return policy which leads to higher profits for both the manufacturer and the retailer.

Chen et al. (2007a) study a setting in which the manufacturer provides a rebate to end-customers of the retailer. Building upon the multiplicative demand model with an iso-price-elastic expected demand, they characterize the impact of a manufacturer rebate on the expected profits of both the manufacturer and the retailer. They show that unless all of the customers claim the rebate, the rebate always benefits the manufacturer, while an "instant rebate", where every customer redeems the rebate on the spot, does not necessarily benefit the manufacturer.

Granot and Yin (2005) analyze a model similar to the one in Emmons and Gilbert (1998). They show that for a zero salvage value and some expected demand functions, returns policies may not benefit the manufacturer. They also investigate the impact of returns policies on the supply chain. In a similar setting, Granot and Yin (2008) analyze the effect of price and order postponement on the equilibrium values of the contract parameters and profits, while Granot and Yin (2007) allow the manufacturer and the retailer to commit to contract parameters (wholesale price, retail price, buy-back price, and order quantity) sequentially and alternately, and investigate its effect on the equilibrium profits of the channel and its members.

Cachon and Lariviere (2005) discuss different contracts in single period supply chain settings involving a supplier and a single retailer or competing retailers facing price-dependent demand among many other things. In the case with a single price-setting retailer, they point out that many contracts that coordinate supply chains with a price-fixed retailer may fail to coordinate the supply chain. However, the revenue sharing contract (in which the supplier requires a percentage of realized revenue from the retailer) continues to coordinate the supply chain and is equivalent to the linear price-discount sharing scheme proposed by Bernstein and Federgruen (2005).

Li and Atkins (2002) study the coordination of production and marketing within a firm. Assuming linear additive demand, they make the following observations under linear transfer price: (1) if production commits to a service level[14] instead of an inventory level, both production and marketing are better off; (2) the same improvement can be achieved if marketing is at a dominant position (in the sense that it is leader in a Stackelberg game

---

[14] If demand is given by $d(p) + \varepsilon$ and the order quantity is y, Li and Atkins (2002) use $z = y - d(p)$ to measure service level. Also recall that z is referred to as the safety stock factor in Petruzzi and Dada (1999).

between production and marketing). In addition, they propose coordinating the firm through a quantity discount contract coupled with a buy-back policy.

Bernstein and Federgruen (2005) analyze a decentralized supply chain system with a single supplier serving multiple retailers in a single period setting. Each retailer faces a single period problem similar to the ones presented in the single period stochastic models subsection with lost sales and multiplicative demand. They consider both the noncompeting retailer case in which each retailer's demand depends only on its own price and the competing retailer case in which the retailers offer substitutable products and thus each retailer's demand depends on its own price and the prices of all other retailers. Since they assume linear production cost for the supplier, it is clear that in the first case, the noncompeting retailers are independent of each other and the qualitative results for a supply chain with a supplier and a retailer can be directly extended to the case with multiple noncompeting retailers. In their second case with competing retailers, Bernstein and Federgruen (2005) assume that the logarithm of a retailer's expected demand function has increasing differences in its own price and each of the prices of the other retailers. Under this assumption, the retailer game when wholesale prices and buy-back rates are constant belongs to a class of well-understood games, the log-supermodular game, and thus admits a pure strategy Nash equilibrium. In both cases, Bernstein and Federgruen (2005) propose contracts that coordinate the supply chain; that is, the expected profit of the decentralized system under the contract is the same as the maximum expected profit achievable in a centralized supply chain.

Ray et al. (2005) study centralized and decentralized supply chains in which a retailer, facing arriving customers with an additive price-dependent rate, makes replenishment from a distributor following a local base-stock policy, who in turn orders from an outside manufacturer again using a local base-stock policy. In their decentralized model, the distributor and the retailer play a Stackelberg game with the distributor as the leader setting its wholesale price and base-stock level. Ray et al. (2005) investigate the impact of price sensitivity, demand uncertainty, and delivery time variability on the decisions of the distributor and the retailer under both the centralized and decentralized settings.

Wang et al. (2004) analyze consignment contracts with revenue sharing in a single period setting in which the manufacturer and the retailer play a Stackelberg game but with the retailer as the leader in setting the percentage of realized revenues shared with the manufacturer. The manufacturer will then decide on the selling price and delivery quantity for the retailer and maintain ownership of the stock. Wang (2006) extends the model in Wang et al. (2004) to a setting with multiple manufacturers producing and selling perfectly complementary products (i.e., products that are always sold together) to the market through a common retailer under an identical consignment contract with revenue sharing.

Kirman and Sobel (1974) appear to be the first to analyze a periodic review infinite horizon model with competing firms facing stochastic demands. They assume that unsatisfied demand is backlogged and all costs (ordering, inventory holding, backlogging) are linear. Their principal result is to show that a pure strategy Nash equilibrium with a stationary base-stock level[15] for the infinite horizon game is specified by a pure strategy

---

[15] Kirman and Sobel (1974) do not articulate the pricing strategies of the firms, which presumably are mixed strategies. Bernstein and Federgruen (2004a) comment that Kirman and Sobel's characterization of the mixed strategy equilibrium requires a modification.

Nash equilibrium of a corresponding single stage game.[16] The existence of this equilibrium is guaranteed under certain technical conditions imposed on the expected single period expected profit (as a function of the order quantity and the selling price). Bernstein and Federgruen (2004a) consider a periodic review infinite horizon model with competing retailers similar to Kirman and Sobel (1974) with multiplicative demand. Under some technical conditions, they show that the corresponding single stage game is log-super-modular and thus a pure strategy Nash equilibrium exists, which in turn specifies a pure strategy Nash equilibrium of the infinite horizon game in which each retailer adopts a stationary base-stock policy together with a stationary price. They also perform comparative statics analysis regarding the impact of several system parameters on the equilibrium strategy and its associated expected profits.

Bernstein and Federgruen (2004b) develop a periodic review infinite horizon general equilibrium model with price and service competition in which the service level of a firm is measured by its fill rate—the fraction of demand filled from on-hand inventory. They assume that the demand of each firm is multiplicative and propose various forms of the expected demand as a function of firms' prices and service levels. Three different competition scenarios are analyzed: (1) price competition with exogenous service levels; (2) simultaneous price and service-level competition; (3) two-stage competition in which each firm first sets a service level and then chooses a dynamic pricing and inventory policy. The supply chain coordination under price and service competition is addressed in Bernstein and Federgruen (2007).

Competition models incorporating economies of scale in the operational costs and time dependent demand functions and cost parameters are limited and challenging. Federgruen and Meissner (2009) study a setting with multiple competing retailers each of which faces a joint inventory and static pricing problem similar to the one in Kunreuther and Schrage (1973). At each period, each retailer's demand is a function of the prices of all retailers set at the beginning of the planning horizon. They develop close approximations to the profit functions. In addition, they prove that under mild conditions the price competition game under these approximate profit functions has a pure strategy Nash equilibrium and, with slightly stronger conditions, it has a unique equilibrium, which is the limit of the *tatônnement* scheme starting from any initial price vector.

Several papers consider centralized and decentralized two-echelon distribution systems with a supplier serving a network of retailers, each of which faces an EOQ-type of setting with a constant price-dependent demand rate (i.e., each retailer places orders to satisfy a constant and continuous demand flow while balancing fixed ordering costs and inventory holding costs). Chen et al. (2001b) develop efficient algorithms to determine optimal pricing and replenishment strategies for different channel structures. Boyaci and Gallego (2002) study the problem of coordinating pricing and inventory replenishment policies in a supply chain consisting of one wholesaler and one or more non-competing retailers with deterministic price-sensitive demand and show that an optimal solution for the centralized system can be interpreted as consignment selling. Chen et al. (2001a) and Bernstein and Federgruen (2003) propose coordination mechanisms for the decentralized systems with

---

[16] Kirman and Sobel (1974) argue that all their results can be extended to the lost sales model by observing that a lost sales model can be equivalently converted to a backlogging model by granting a credit for each backlogged unit. This observation unfortunately is not true when prices are also decision variables.

non-competing retailers and competing retailers respectively. Bernstein et al. (2006) characterize supply chain settings in which perfect coordination can be achieved with simple wholesale pricing schemes and apply their results to decentralized distribution systems. For more EOQ-type supply chain models, see Yano and Gilbert (2003).

All the above papers employ the concepts and methodologies from non-cooperative game theory, which basically assume that no binding agreements can be enforced. However, there are numerous situations in which binding agreements, once reached, can be costlessly implemented. Another branch of game theory, cooperative game theory, provides concepts and tools to analyze these binding agreements and started to receive attention from the operations management community. We review two recent papers which apply concepts and methodologies from cooperative game theory to study supply chain models involving inventory and pricing decisions. For a comprehensive review of the applications of cooperative game theory to supply chain settings, we refer to Nagarajan and Sosic (2008).

Chen (2009) considers a distribution system consisting of a set of non-competing retailers, who sell a single product. The demand of each retailer depends on its own selling price and a common random variable representing the market condition, referred to as a market signal. To take advantage of economies of scale and risk pooling effects, the retailers may form a coalition by placing joint orders before the realization of the market signal and allocating inventory among themselves after the market signal is revealed. Given retailers' interest in inventory centralization, it is critical that they allocate the cost or share the benefit in such a way that no set of retailers gains more by deviating from the cooperation. Such cooperatively achieved allocations are called core allocations in cooperative game theory. The existence of core allocations implies that the grand coalition (i.e., the coalition with all retailers) is stable.[17] Chen (2009) shows that inventory centralization games with price-dependent demand have non-empty cores under very general assumptions regarding ordering costs. Specifically, under the assumption that the ordering cost follows a general quantity discount (which includes several commonly used discounts: incremental discounts, all-units discounts, and the less-than-truckload volume discount), he proves that an inventory centralization game in which all retailers share a single common warehouse has a non-empty core when (1) the retailers' pricing decisions are made after the revelation of the market signal, or (2) the retailers' have identical cost parameters and their pricing decisions are made before the revelation of the market signal.

The model in Chen (2009) assumes each retailer's demand is independent of other retailers' prices. When this assumption is relaxed, it becomes tricky to define core allocations as the value of a coalition depends on pricing decisions of retailers not in the coalition. In fact, in this case, the retailers may prefer to form different price-setting cartels. Nagarajan and Sosic (2007) study the dynamic alliance formation process for a system with multiple symmetric retailers competing on (price) substitutable products. In their model, the retailers, facing a deterministic (or stochastic additive) linear demand, make two-stage decisions. In the first stage, the retailers form coalitions. In the second stage, retailers in the same coalition agree on a single price to compete with the prices of other coalitions. In the

---

[17] Chen and Zhang (2007, 2009) study core allocations of distribution systems respectively in a similar single period stochastic setting and in a deterministic multi-period setting. Both papers assume concave ordering costs but do not consider pricing decisions.

case with demand uncertainty, retailers in the same coalition are assumed to make their own inventory decisions independently after the prices are set.

Nagarajan and Sosic (2007) apply two solution concepts from cooperative game theory, the largest consistent set and the equilibrium process of coalition formation, to study the stability of coalition structures in a farsighted sense. They identify conditions under which certain coalition structures are farsighted stable and investigate the impact of the market size, demand variability, cost parameters, and degree of substitutability on market structures.

30.6 CONCLUSIONS AND FUTURE RESEARCH

As can be seen from the above survey, many papers on integrated inventory and pricing models appeared in the past few years. Some notable progress includes: (1) the conditions for the optimality of an (s, S, p) policy for multi-period stochastic models with concave ordering costs have been relaxed; (2) researchers started to explore integrated inventory and pricing models incorporating customer behavior; (3) models that explicitly incorporate price adjustment costs started to receive attention; (4) research on decentralized supply chain models with price-dependent external demand grew rapidly; (5) models analyzing the stability and formation of coalitions from the perspective of cooperative game theory emerged.

Yet many important problems remain to be explored. First, our understanding of integrated inventory and pricing models incorporating customer behavior is still very limited. The reference price model presented earlier can be immediately integrated with existing inventory and pricing models, which unfortunately aggravates the difficulty of the already complicated models. However, given its strong empirical and theoretical support, it is definitely valuable to incorporate it into production/inventory models. Of course, the reference price model only provides one illustrative example. We believe that many more customer behavior models will be built and incorporated into operational models.

Secondly, it remains a significant challenge to incorporate leadtime into stochastic models. Indeed, the zero leadtime assumption is required for all the multi-period models reviewed here, which severely limits their use and our understanding of the interaction between inventory and pricing decisions in more general settings such as multi-echelon systems, assembly systems, and distribution systems. By contrast, for standard stochastic inventory control problems with backlogging, structural results of the optimal policy for models with zero leadtime can generally be extended to models with deterministic leadtime. The idea is to transfer a model with a positive leadtime to one with a similar structure, but zero leadtime (see Scarf 1960). Unfortunately, this technique is not valid for inventory and pricing models with a positive leadtime because in this case, the two decisions, the ordering decision and the pricing decision, will take effect at different times.

Thirdly, more research on multi-product models is needed. In inventory models without pricing, different products are linked together through joint fixed ordering costs and/or shared capacity and/or correlated demand. In integrated inventory and pricing models, they may also be linked together through cross-price elasticities. These linkages greatly enrich the applicability of models. On the other hand, they also impose enormous challenges in terms of collecting data as well as analyzing and solving multi-period models.

Fourthly, the structure of the optimal policy for the stochastic integrated inventory and pricing model with both fixed ordering cost and fixed price adjustment cost is still open. Indeed, in this case, unlike the model analyzed in Chen and Simchi-Levi (2004a), inventory level alone is not enough to specify the profit-to-go function and the previous period price has to be incorporated. As a result, we end up with a challenging dynamic program with two dimensional state-space for which the concept of symmetric k-convexity, important for integrated inventory and pricing models without price adjustment cost or without inventory carryover, is unlikely to be applicable. Yet, we believe that extensions of this concept (symmetric k-convexity) will prove powerful for two or higher dimensional dynamic programs. In fact, a deep understanding of this problem will not only allow the analysis of general integrated inventory and pricing models with costly price adjustment but also shed new light on another class of classical inventory models, namely the stochastic joint replenishment problems, given the similarities of their structures. It is worthwhile pointing out that the structure of the optimal policy of stochastic joint replenishment problems is essentially unknown despite several decades of intensive research on inventory models.

Fifthly, incorporating insights derived from decentralized supply chain models into decision making may provide tremendous value in improving how organizations interact. Unfortunately, limited research has been conducted on multi-period competition models. This is not surprising given the complexity of inventory and pricing models. But, the tremendous progress that has been achieved in the last few years will hopefully lead to new models that capture competition.

Finally, there are still significant gaps between academic research and industrial practice. Several vendors such as JDA, Oracle, and SAS provide both pricing optimization and inventory management modules. However, we are not aware of any decision support system that truly integrates production/inventory and pricing decisions despite their potential impacts. Several factors may contribute to this:

- The lack of efficient algorithms for general, multi-period, multiproduct models, slows the development of decision support systems. This is even true for single product models because of the distinctive features of these models: multi-period, uncertainty, and economies of scale. Indeed, even in deterministic settings, incorporating pricing decisions significantly increases the computational complexity relative to pure inventory models.

- The existence of organizational barriers. That is, inventory decisions are typically the responsibility of manufacturing, logistics, or supply chain executives whereas pricing is controlled by finance, sales, and marketing.

- The lack of empirical data to help companies identify the appropriate demand–price function. In some industries, such data can be collected through on-line experiments. In others, it is done through customer market surveys conducted before new products are released. Our experience is that retailers typically apply multiplicative demand models while the automotive industry applies linear, additive, demand models.

- Finally, the lack of experience in identifying when deterministic models are more appropriate than stochastic models and vice versa.

Thus, while significant progress has been made on the integration of pricing and inventory management, enormous challenges and opportunities remain.

REFERENCES

Agrawal, V. and Seshadri, S. (2000) "Impact of Uncertainty and Risk Aversion on Price and Order Quantity in the Newsvendor Problem", *Manufacturing and Service Operations Management* 2/4: 410–23.

Ahn, H., Gumus, M., and Kaminsky, P. (2007) "Pricing and Manufacturing Decisions When Demand Is a Function of Prices in Multiple Periods", *Operations Research* 55/6: 1039–57.

Ahuja, R., Magnanti, T. L., and Orlin, J. B. (1993) *Network Flows: Theory, Algorithms, and Applications.* Upper Saddle River, NJ: Prentice Hall.

Allon, G. and Zeevi, A. (2011) "A Note on the Relationship Among Capacity, Price and Inventory in a Make-to-Stock System", *Production and Operations Management*, 20/1: 143–51.

Aviv, Y. and Pazgal, A. (2005) "A Partially Observed Markov Decision Process for Dynamic Pricing", *Management Science* 51/9: 1400–16.

Aydin, G. and Porteus, E. (2008) "Joint Inventory and Pricing Decisions for an Assortment", *Operations Research* 56/5: 1247–55.

Bernstein, F. and Federgruen, A. (2003) "Pricing and Replenishment Strategies in a Distribution System with Competing Retailers", *Operations Research* 51/3: 409–26.

—— and —— (2004a) "Dynamic Inventory and Pricing Models for Competing Retailers", *Naval Research Logistics* 51/2: 258–74.

—— and —— (2004b) "A General Equilibrium Model for Industries with Price and Service Competition", *Operations Research* 52/6: 868–86.

—— and —— (2005) "Decentralized Supply Chains with Competing Retailers Under Demand Uncertainty", *Management Science* 51/1: 18–29.

—— and —— (2007) "Coordination Mechanisms for Supply Chains Under Price and Service Competition", *Manufacturing and Service Operations Management* 9/3: 242–62.

—— Chen, F., and Federgruen, A. (2006) "Coordinating Supply Chains with Simple Pricing Schemes: The Role of Vendor-Managed Inventories", *Management Science* 52/10: 1483–92.

Biller, S., Chan, L. M. A., Simchi-Levi, D., and Swann, J. (2005) "Dynamic Pricing and the Direct-to-Customer Model in the Automotive Industry", *Electronic Commerce Research* 5/2: 309–34.

Bish, E. and Wang, Q. (2004) "Optimal Investment Strategies for Flexible Resources, Considering Pricing and Correlated Demands", *Operations Research* 52/(6): 954–64.

Boyaci, T. and Gallego, G. (2002) "Coordinating Pricing and Inventory Replenishment Policies for one Wholesaler and one or more Geographically Dispersed Retailers", *International Journal of Production Economics* 77/(2): 95–111.

—— and Özer, Ö. (2009) "Information Acquisition for Capacity Planning via Pricing and Advance Selling; When to Stop and Act?" *Operations Research*: 1328–49.

Cachon, G. (2003) "Supply Chain Coordination with Contracts", *Handbooks in Operations Research and Management Science* 11: 229–340.

—— and Lariviere, M. (2005) "Supply Chain Coordination with Revenue-Sharing Contracts: Strengths and Limitations", *Management Science* 51/(1): 30–44.

Ceryan, O., Sahin, O., and Duenyas, I. (2009) "Managing Demand and Supply for Multiple Products Through Dynamic Pricing and Capacity Flexibility". Working paper.

Chan, L., Shen, Z. J. M., Simchi-Levi, D., and Swann, J. (2004) "Coordination of Pricing and Inventory Decisions: A Survey and Classification" in D. Simchi-Levi, D. Wu, and Z. Shen (eds), *Handbook of Quantitative Supply Chain Analysis: Modeling in the E-Business Era* 335–92.

—— Simchi-Levi, D., and Swann, J. (2006) "Pricing, Production, and Inventory Policies for Manufacturing with Stochastic Demand and Discretionary Sales", *Manufacturing and Service Operations Management* 8/(2): 149–68.

Chao, X. and Zhou, S. (2006) "Joint Inventory-and-pricing Strategy for a Stochastic Continuous-Review system", *IIE Transactions* 38/5: 401–8.

Chen, F., Federgruen, A., and Zheng, Y. S. (2001a) "Coordination Mechanisms for a Distribution System with One Supplier and Multiple Retailers", *Management Science* 47/5: 693–708.

—— —— and —— (2001b) "Near-Optimal Pricing and Replenishment Strategies for a Retail/Distribution System", *Operations Research* 49/6: 839–53.

Chen, H., Wu, O., and Yao, D. D. (2010a) "On the Benefit of Inventory-Based Dynamic Pricing Strategies", *Production and Operations Management* 19: 249–60.

Chen, X. (2009) "Inventory Centralization Games with Price-Dependent Demand and Quantity Discount", *Operations Research* 57/6: 1394–1406.

—— and Hu, P. (2008) "Coordinated Pricing and Inventory Management with Deterministic Demand and Costly Price Adjustment". Working paper.

—— and Simchi-Levi, D. (2004a) "Coordinating Inventory Control and Pricing Strategies with Random Demand and Fixed Ordering Cost: The Finite Horizon Case", *Operations Research* 52/6: 887–96.

—— and —— (2004b) "Coordinating Inventory Control and Pricing Strategies with Random Demand and Fixed Ordering Cost: The Infinite Horizon Case", *Mathematics of Operations Research* 29/3: 698–723.

—— and—— (2006) "Coordinating Inventory Control and Pricing Strategies: The continuous review model", *Operations Research Letters* 34/3: 323–32.

—— and —— (2009) "A New Approach for the Stochastic Cash Balance Problem with Fixed Costs", *Probability in the Engineering and Informational Sciences* 23: 545–62.

—— and Sun, P. (2007) "Optimal Structural Policies for Ambiguity and Risk Averse Inventory and Pricing Models". Working paper. *SIAM Journal on Control and Optimization*, forthcoming.

—— and Zhang, J. (2007) "Duality Approaches to Economic Lot-Sizing Games". Working paper.

—— and —— (2009) "A Stochastic Programming Duality Approach to Inventory Centralization Games", *Operations Research* 57/4: 840–51.

—— and Zhang, Y. (2010) "Dynamic Pricing under Stochastic Reference Price Effect". Working paper.

—— Li, C., Rhee, B., and Simchi-Levi, D. (2007a) "The Impact of Manufacturer Rebates on Supply Chain Profits", *Naval Research Logistics* 54: 667–80.

—— Sim, M., Simchi-Levi, D., and Sun, P. (2007b) "Risk Aversion in Inventory Management", *Operations Research* 55/5: 828–42.

Chen, X., Zhou, S., and Chen, Y. (2008) "Integration of Inventory and Pricing Decisions with costly Price Adjustments", *Operations Research* 59(6): 1144–58.

—— Hu, P., and He, S. (2009a) "Coordinated Pricing and Inventory Management with Reference Price Effect and Deterministic Demand". Working paper.

—— —— and —— (2010b) "Preservation of Submodularity under Infimal Convolution in Two Dimensional Space and its Applications". Working paper.

—— Zhang, Y., and Zhou, S. (2010c) "Preservation of Quasi-K-Concavity and Its Application to Joint Inventory-Pricing Models with Concave Ordering Costs", *Operations Research* 58/4: 1012–16.

—— Hu, P., Shum, S., and Zhang, Y. (2011) "Stochastic Inventory Models with Reference Price Effects". Working paper, University of Illinois.

Chen, Y., Ray, S., and Song, Y. (2006) "Optimal Pricing and Inventory Control Policy in Periodic-review Systems with Fixed Ordering Cost and Lost Sales", *Naval Research Logistics* 53/(2): 117–36.

—— Xu, M., and Zhang, Z. (2009b) "A Risk-Averse Newsvendor Model Under CVaR Decision Criterion", *Operations Research* 57/4: 1040–4.

Chod, J. and Rudi, N. (2005) "Resource Flexibility with Responsive Pricing", *Operations Research* 53/(3): 532–48.

Dana, J. and Petruzzi, N. (2001) "Note: The Newsvendor Model with Endogenous Demand", *Management Science* 47/(11): 1488–97.

Deng, S. and Yano, C. (2006) "Joint Production and Pricing Decisions with Setup Costs and Capacity Constraints", *Management Science* 52: 741–56.

Eliashberg, J. and Steinberg, R. (1991) "Marketing-production Joint Decision Making", in J. Eliashberg and G. L. Lilien (eds.), *Management Science in Marketing*, Volume 5 of Handbooks in Operations Research and Management Science, Amsterdam: Elsevier, 827–77.

Elmaghraby, W. and Keskinocak, P. (2003) "Dynamic Pricing in the Presence of Inventory Considerations: Research Overview, Current Practices, and Future Directions", *Management Science* 49: 1287–309.

Emmons, H. and Gilbert, S. M. (1998) "Note the Role of Returns Policies in Pricing and Inventory Decisions for Catalogue Goods", *Management Science* 44/2: 276–83.

Ernst, R. (1970) "A Linear Inventory Model with a Monopoly Firm". PhD thesis, University of California, Berkeley.

Federgruen, A. and Heching, A. (1999) "Combined Pricing and Inventory Control under Uncertainty", *Operations Research* 47: 454–75.

—— and —— (2002) "Multilocation Combined Pricing and Inventory Control", *Manufacturing and Service Operations Management* 4/4: 275–95.

—— and Meissner, J. (2009) "Competition under Time-varying Demands and Dynamic Lot Sizing Costs", *Naval Research Logistics* 56: 57–73.

Feng, Q. (2010) "Integrating Dynamic Pricing and Replenishment Decisions Under Supply Capacity Uncertainty", *Management Science* 56/12: 2154–72.

Feng, Y. and Chen, Y. (2002) "Joint Pricing and Inventory Control with Setup Costs and Demand Uncertainty". Working paper.

—— and Chen, Y. (2004) "Optimality and Optimization of a Joint Pricing and Inventory-control Policy for a Periodic-Review System". Working paper. *Operations Research*, forthcoming.

Fibich, G., Gavious, A., and Lowengart, O. (2003) "Explicit Solutions of Optimization Models and Differential Games with Nonsmooth (Asymmetric) Reference-Price Effects", *Operations Research* 51/5: 721–34.

Florian, M. and Morton, K. (1971) "Deterministic Production Planning with Concave Costs and Capacity Constraints", *Management Science* 18/1: 12–20.

—— Lenstra, J. K., and Rinnooy Kan, A. H. G. (1980) "Deterministic Production Planning: Algorithms and Complexity", *Management Science* 26/7: 669–79.

Geunes, J., Romeijn, E., and Taaffe, K. (2006) "Requirements Planning with Pricing and Order Selection Flexibility", *Operations Research* 54: 394–401.

—— Merzifonluŏglu, Y., and Romeijn, E. (2009) "Capacitated Procurement Planning with Price-Sensitive Demand and General Concave Revenue Functions", *European Journal of Operational Research* 194/2: 390–405.

Gilbert, S. M. (1999) "Coordination of pricing and multi-period production for constant priced goods", *European Journal of Operational Research* 114/2: 330–7.

—— (2000) "Coordination of Pricing and Multiple-Period Production across Multiple Constant Priced Goods", *Management Science* 46: 1602–16.

Gimpl-Heersink, D. (2008) "Joint Pricing and Inventory Control under Reference Price Effects". PhD thesis, University of Economics.

Granot, D. and Yin, S. (2005) "On the Effectiveness of Returns Policies in the Price-Dependent Newsvendor Model", *Naval Research Logistics* 52/8: 765–79.

—— and —— (2007) "On Sequential Commitment in the Price-Dependent Newsvendor Model", *European Journal of Operational Research* 177/2: 939–68.

—— and —— (2008) "Price and Order Postponement in a Decentralized Newsvendor Model with Multiplicative and Price-Dependent Demand", *Operations Research* 56/1: 121–39.

Greenleaf, E. (1995) "The Impact of Reference Price Effects on the Profitability of Price Promotions", *Marketing Science* 14: 82–104.

Guler, M., Bilgic, T., and Gullu, R. (2010) "Joint Inventory and Pricing Decisions with Reference Effects". Working paper.

Hall, J., Kopalle, P. K., and Krishna, A. (2003) "A Category Management Model of Retailer Dynamic Pricing and Ordering Decisions: Normative and Empirical Analysis". Working paper.

Hempenius, A. (1970) *Monopoly with Random Demand*. Rotterdam: Universitaire Pers.

Huh, W. T. and Janakiraman, G. (2008) "(s, S) Optimality in Joint Inventory-Pricing Control: An Alternate Approach", *Operations Research* 56: 783–90.

Kahneman, D. and Tversky, A. (1979) "Prospect Theory: An Analysis of Decision under Risk", *Econometrica* 47/2: 263–91.

Kandel, E. (1996) "Right to Return", *Journal of Law and Economics* 39: 329–56.

Karlin, S. and Carr, C. (1962) "Prices and Optimal Inventory Policy", *Studies in Applied Probability and Management Science* 159–72.

Kirman, A. and Sobel, M. (1974) "Dynamic Oligopoly with Inventories", *Econometrica* 42/2: 279–87.

Kocabiykoglu, A. and Popescu, I. (2011) "An Elasticity Perspective on the Newsvendor with Price Sensitive Demand", *Operations Research*, 59/2: 301–12.

Kopalle, P., Rao, A. G., and Assuncao, J. L. (1996) "Asymmetric Reference Price Effects and Dynamic Pricing Policies", *Marketing Science* 15: 60–85.

Kunreuther, H. and Schrage, L. (1973) "Joint Pricing and Inventory Decisions for Constant Priced Items", *Management Science* 19/7: 732–8.

Lau, A. H.-L. and Lau, H.-S. (1988) "The Newsboy Problem With Price-Dependent Demand Distribution", *I-IE Transactions* 20: 168–75.

Leland, H. E. (1972) "Theory of the Firm Facing Uncertain Demand", *American Economic Review* 62/3: 278–91.

Levitan, R. and Shubik, M. (1971) "Price Variation Duopoly with Differentiated Products and Random Demand", *Journal of Economic Theory* 3: 23–39.

Levy, D., Bergen, M., Dutta, S., and Venable, R. (1997) "The Magnitude of Menu Costs: Direct Evidence from Large U.S. Supermarket Chains", *Quarterly Journal of Economics* 112: 791–825.

Li, Q. and Atkins, D. (2002) "Coordinating Replenishment and Pricing in a Firm", *Manufacturing and Service Operations Management* 4/4: 241–57.

—— and Zheng, S. (2006) "Joint Inventory Replenishment and Pricing Control for Systems with Uncertain Yield and Demand", *Operations Research* 54/4: 696–705.

Lodish, L. M. (1980) "Applied Dynamic Pricing and Production Models with Specific Application to Broadcast Spot Pricing", *Journal of Marketing Research* 17/2: 203–11.

Marvel, H. and Peck, J. (1995) "Demand Uncertainty and Returns Policies", *International Economic Review* 36/3: 691–714.

Mazumdar, T., Raj, S. P., and Sinha, I. (2005) "Reference Price Research: Review and Propositions", *Journal of Marketing* 69/4: 84–102.

Miercort, F. (1968) "Some Effects of Advertising and Prices on Optimal Inventory Policy". Research Report.

Mills, E. S. (1959). "Uncertainty and Price Theory", *Quarterly Journal of Economics* 73/1: 116–30.

—— (1962) *Price, Output, and Inventory Policy: A Study in the Economics of the Firm and Industry*. New York: Wiley.

Monroe, K. (2003) *Pricing: Making Profitable Decisions*, 3rd edn. Columbus, OH: McGraw-HillIrwin.

Nagarajan, M. and Sosic, G. (2007) "Stable Farsighted Coalitions in Competitive Markets", *Management Science* 53/1: 29–45.

—— and —— (2008) "Game-theoretic Analysis of Cooperation among Supply Chain Agents: Review and Extensions", *European Journal of Operational Research* 187/3: 719–45.

Nasiry, J. and Popescu, I. (2008) "Dynamic Pricing with Loss Averse Consumers and Peak-End Anchoring". Working paper. *Operations Research*, forthcoming.

Nevins, A. J. (1966) "Some Effects of Uncertainty: Simulation of a Model of Price", *Quarterly Journal of Economics* 80/1: 73–87.

Petruzzi, N. and Dada, M. (1999) "Pricing and the Newsvendor Problem: A Review with Extensions", *Operations Research* 47: 183–94.

—— and —— (2002) "Dynamic Pricing and Inventory Control with Learning", *Naval Research Logistics* 49/3: 303–25.

Pochet, Y. and Wolsey, L. (2006) *Production Planning by Mixed Integer Programming*. Springer, New York.

Polatoglu, L. (1991) "Optimal Order Quantity and Pricing Decisions in Single-period Inventory Systems", *International Journal of Production Economics* 23/1–3: 175–85.

—— and Sahin, I. (2000) "Optimal Procurement Policies under Price-dependent Demand", *International Journal of Production Economics* 65: 141–71.

Popescu, I. and Wu, Y. (2007) "Dynamic Pricing Strategies with Reference Effects", *Operations Research* 55/3: 413–29.

Porteus, E. (1971) "On the Optimality of Generalized (s; S) Policies", *Management Science* 17/7: 411–26.

Ray, S., Song, Y., and Li, S. (2005) "Tailored Supply Chain Decision-Making Under Price-Sensitive Stochastic Demand and Delivery Uncertainty", *Management Science* 51/12: 1873–91.

Raz, G. and Porteus, E. L. (2006) "A Fractiles Perspective to the Joint Price/Quantity News-vendor Model", *Management Science* 52/11: 1764–77.

Scarf, H. (1960) "The Optimality of (s; S) Policies for the Dynamic Inventory Problem", in K. Arrow, S. Karlin, and P. Suppe (eds), *Mathematical methods in the social sciences, 1959: Proceedings of the 1st Stanford Symposium on Mathematical Methods in the Social Sciences.* Stanford, CA: Stanford University Press.

Simchi-Levi, D., Chen, X., and Bramel, J. (2005) *The Logic of Logistics: Theory, Algorithms, and Applications for Logistics Management*, 2nd edn. New York: Springer.

Song, J. and Xue, Z. (2007) "Demand Management and Inventory Control for Substitutable Products". Working paper.

Song, Y. et al. (2009) "Note: Optimal Dynamic Joint Inventory-Pricing Control for Multi-plicative Demand with Fixed Order Costs and Lost Sales", *Operations Research* 57/1: 245–50.

Subrahmanyan, S. and Shoemaker, R. (1996) "Developing Optimal Pricing and Inventory Policies for Retailers who Face Uncertain Demand", *Journal of Retailing* 72/1: 7–30.

Talluri, K. and van Ryzin, G. (2004) *The Theory and Practice of Revenue Management.* New York: Springer.

Tayur, S., Ganeshan, R., and Magazine, M. (1998) *Quantitative Models for Supply Chain Management.* Norwell, MA: Kluwer Academic Publishers.

Thomas, J. (1970) "Price-production Decisions with Deterministic Demand", *Management Science* 16: 747–50.

—— (1974) "Price and Production Decisions with Random Demand", *Operations Research* 22/3: 513–18.

Thowsen, G. T. (1975) "A Dynamic, Nonstationary Inventory Problem for a Price/Quantity Setting Firm", *Naval Research Logistics Quarterly* 22/3: 461–76.

Tomlin, B. and Wang, Y. (2008) "Pricing and Operational Recourse in Coproduction Systems", *Management Science* 54/3: 522–37.

van den Heuvel, W. and Wagelmans, A. P. (2006) "A Polynomial Time Algorithm for a Deterministic Joint Pricing and Inventory Model", *European Journal of Operational Research* 170/2: 463–80.

van Mieghem, J. A. and Dada, M. (1999) "Price Versus Production Postponement: Capacity and Competition", *Management Science* 45/12: 1631–49.

Wagner, H. (2004) "Comments on 'Dynamic Version of the Economic Lot Size Model'", *Management Science* 50/12: 1775–77.

—— and Whitin, T. (1958a) "Dynamic Problems in the Theory of the Firm", *Naval Research Logistics Quarterly* 5,1: 53–74.

—— and —— (1958b) "Dynamic Version of the Economic Lot Size Model", *Management Science* 5/1: 89–96.

Wang, Y. (2006) "Joint Pricing-Production Decisions in Supply Chains of Complementary Products with Uncertain Demand", *Operations Research* 54/6: 1110–27.

—— Jiang, L., and Shen, Z. (2004) "Channel Performance Under Consignment Contract with Revenue Sharing", *Management Science* 50/1: 34–47.

Whitin, T. (1955) "Inventory Control and Price Theory", *Management Science* 2/1: 61–8.

Yano, C. A. and Gilbert, S. M. (2005) "Coordinated Pricing and Production/Procurement Decisions: A Review", in J. Eliashberg and A. Chakravarty (eds), *Managing Business Inter-faces: Marketing, Engineering, and Manufacturing Perspectives.* Norwell, MA: Kluwer, 65–103.

Yao, L., Chen, Y., and Yan, H. (2006) "Analysis of a Supply Contract for Coordinating the Newsvendor with Price Dependent Demand". Working paper.

Ye, Q. and Duenyas, I. (2007) "Optimal Capacity Investment Decisions with Two-Sided Fixed-Capacity Adjustment Costs", *Operations Research* 55/2: 272–83.

Yin, R. and Rajaram, K. (2007) "Joint pricing and inventory control with a Markovian demand model", *European Journal of Operational Research* 182/1: 113–26.

Young, L. (1978) "Price, Inventory and the Structure of Uncertain Demand", *Journal of New Zealand Operations Research Society* 6: 157–77.

—— (1979) "Uncertainty, Market Structure, and Resource Allocation", *Oxford Economic Papers* 31/1: 47–59.

Zabel, E. (1970) "Monopoly and Uncertainty", *Review of Economic Studies* 37/2: 205–19.

—— (1972) "Multiperiod Monopoly under Uncertainty", *Journal of Economic Theory* 5/3: 524–36.

Zhang, H. and Fu, M. (2005) "Sample Path Derivatives for (s, S) Inventory Systems with Price Determination", in B. Golden, S. Raghavan, and E. Wasil (eds), *The Next Wave in Computing, Optimization, and Decision Technologies*, New York: Springer Science + Business Media, 229–46.

Zhang, J. and Chen, J. (2006) "Bayesian Solution to Pricing and Inventory Control under Unknown Demand Distribution", *Operations Research Letters* 34/5: 517–24.

Zhu, K. and Thonemann, U. (2009) "Coordination of Pricing and Inventory Control across Products", *Naval Research Logistics* 56/2: 175–90.

Zipkin, P. (2000) *Foundations of Inventory Management*. New York: McGraw-Hill.

PART V

ORGANIZATION AND PROCESSES

CHAPTER 31

STRUCTURING AND MANAGING AN EFFECTIVE PRICING ORGANIZATION

MIKE SIMONETTO, LARRY MONTAN,
JULIE MEEHAN, AND JUNKO KAJI

31.1 THE NEED FOR A PRICING ORGANIZATION

Pricing is a pressing marketplace challenge and a vital business discipline. Today's marketplace forces—including shorter product lifecycles, rising raw material costs, increasing price sensitivity from both business and retail buyers, and a greater Wall Street focus on pricing and margin growth—are driving companies to pay closer attention to pricing as a key driver of performance. Along with these challenges have come new approaches, tools, and methodologies for addressing them. The advent of electronic data storage and the rise of e-commerce allow companies to collect vast amounts of data on transactions, customers, and products. New pricing technologies and mathematical tools now enable companies to analyze data in ways never before possible. Price waterfalls, price optimization algorithms, price demand/elasticity analyses—these techniques and more have taken pricing from an art to a science and have opened the door for companies to use pricing as a significant driver of profitability.

The growing recognition of pricing's business impact has placed pricing on the same trajectory that areas such as procurement, information technology (IT), risk management, and quality followed in the past: from an informally managed, fragmented activity to a rigorous business discipline with an acknowledged need for an organizational infrastructure to manage it effectively. As more companies appreciate pricing's strategic importance, the pricing organization is becoming as common a feature of the corporate landscape as supply chain, customer service, and quality organizations.

This chapter presents the authors' views on why companies should consider establishing a dedicated pricing organization, and proposes an approach for structuring such an organization. The chapter also discusses how to effectively manage a pricing organization, and concludes with a four-step process for creating or reorganizing a pricing organization.

31.1.1 The pricing organization's purpose

The purpose of a pricing organization is to *efficiently and effectively set, execute, and monitor the performance of prices that support the company's strategic goals.* Specifically, a company's pricing organization should, at a supportable cost and in a manner that furthers corporate objectives, perform the following three activities:

- *Price-setting:* Price-setting refers to the derivation of the optimal price to offer for a product, service, or product/service bundle, at a given volume, through a given channel, in a specific competitive landscape, at a specific time in the product lifecycle, for a specific period of time, while supporting branding and product positioning objectives. The goals of price-setting could be profitability, market share, competitive positioning/disruption, brand management, product lifecycle management, or other factors.

- *Price execution:* Once an optimal price offering has been determined, price execution focuses on delivering prices to the marketplace in a way that induces customers to pay the prices required to drive expected revenues and margins. Price execution activities can range from tagging products at retail stores to complex one-on-one sales negotiations. They also include order fulfillment activities that impact the economic or "pocket" margin produced as a result of a specific transaction.

- *Price performance monitoring:* This activity includes processes for monitoring, evaluating, and managing price to achieve the stated tactical and strategic goals. Such monitoring goes beyond simply determining if the expected margins have been achieved. Effective monitoring should also evaluate and support improvements to product service/differentiation, salesforce effectiveness, and the ability to sell on attributes other than price, in addition to monitoring pricing process adherence.

An effective pricing organization must include both pricing resources and a variety of people from other corporate functions, including sales, marketing, finance, operations, and technology. In this chapter, the term "pricing organization" is used to refer to all individuals at a company whose activities affect price-setting, execution, and monitoring. The term "pricing department" is used to refer to the group of people who focus on pricing as their primary or sole responsibility—usually a far smaller group than the extended pricing organization.

31.1.2 Real-life pricing organizations: some common issues

Much of modern pricing strategy draws heavily on newly developed methodologies and technologies (i.e., pricing software applications). Hence, pricing has only recently begun to evolve into a sophisticated management discipline. In fact, many companies are still in the process of establishing effective pricing organizations.

At a typical company, pricing activities are often fragmented, poorly managed, and lack overall strategic direction. The fragmentation often manifests itself in the multiplicity of departments in the organization with some degree of pricing responsibility. For example, product marketing may set prices, sales may propose prices to customers (often different prices from what product marketing has set), and finance may analyze deals for profitability based on considerations such as warranty or promotion costs that neither sales nor marketing factor into their pricing decisions.

Organizational issues common among companies with less well-developed pricing capabilities include:

- *Uncoordinated pricing groups.* Instead of managing pricing through a single enterprise-wide organization, many companies maintain independently run pricing groups in each business unit, division, or location. In functionally decentralized organizations, these groups typically do not coordinate their efforts, and they often implement conflicting pricing practices and initiatives. Lack of coordination makes it difficult to set and enforce a company-wide pricing strategy, implement effective practices across all pricing groups, and establish consistent metrics to track pricing performance.

- *Low organizational status.* Often, responsibility for pricing rests with middle management rather than with a top-level executive. In a 2008 AMR Research survey, only 37 percent of the 219 companies surveyed had a director-level or higher pricing position within the organization. "This indicates," the report observes, "that the majority of companies have yet to make the necessary organizational alignments to improving pricing practices" (Tohamy and Keltz 2008).

  Due to this low organizational status, pricing decisions can easily be swayed by more powerful (or simply more vocal) constituents whose agendas may not necessarily align with each other or with the company's overall goals. The sales function may want to lower prices to increase volume, marketing may want to increase prices to support a premium brand image, operations may want to widen price bands to reduce the frequency of exceptions and thereby streamline the sales process, and so on.

- *Misplaced decision-making authority.* Pricing decisions should be made by people who have the appropriate data, who are in a position to take or enable timely action, and whose goals are consistent with those of the company. Accountability and authority must be aligned in order to realize the value pricing can drive for a typical business, and that alignment must focus on corporate performance and not the performance of a single function or group.

- *Limited responsibilities.* Pricing professionals' responsibilities at some companies tend to be limited and reactive: performing historical research, managing price books, and tracking prices in the field. Missing from this set of responsibilities is the entire realm of pricing analytics and optimization. In addition, many organizations today have primarily manual pricing processes, which can result in increased costs, understaffing,

Box 31.1 Top 10 signs of an ineffective pricing organization

1. Customers have difficulty obtaining price information on a timely basis.
2. Inconsistent or untimely internal and external pricing communications.
3. CxOs cannot obtain information about the impact of price on company performance except at the gross margin level.
4. Little or no transactional insight as to customer, product, segment, channel, salesperson, or geographic profitability except at the gross margin level.
5. Inconsistent or conflicting pricing by channel.
6. Inappropriate or excessive discounting.
7. Frequent turnover in pricing resources.
8. Significant volume of pricing errors.
9. Inability to identify and deal with negative-margin customers or deals.
10. Significant time spent researching and resolving pricing requests and errors.

a high error rate, and a focus on getting it done now over getting it done right. The results are predictable: lost sales, frustrated salespeople, unhappy customers, and poor margin performance.

- *Misaligned reward and compensation structures.* A major barrier to effective pricing is a reward and compensation structure that works against setting and executing prices that support corporate goals. Respondents to the 2008 AMR Research survey identified "changing the compensation to align with project goals" as one of pricing's top three organizational challenges (Tohamy and Keltz 2008).

One common example of misaligned compensation is the practice of compensating the salesforce solely on volume. In this situation, the salesforce no longer works in the best interest of corporate objectives, but typically becomes a customer advocacy group that consistently gives away margin in order to meet their personal sales objectives. Even if they cannot directly lower prices, salespeople compensated purely on volume often find ways to make concessions on terms, service levels, or other factors that amount to an additional discount on price.

31.2 DESIGNING THE PRICING ORGANIZATION

The pricing organization should be based on a careful understanding of a company's specific pricing requirements. It needs to be organized in a way that drives the achievement of corporate objectives, not functional or political considerations.

There are two primary dimensions to assess in developing a pricing organization (Figure 31.1). First, what is the degree of influence the pricing organization should have? Should it provide general guidance to the organization, or should it be given "teeth" to define policy and procedures and to make decisions? Secondly, what should be the pricing organization's scope and focus? Should it focus only on analytics and reporting, or does it need to have a broader scope that includes pricing strategy and execution as well as

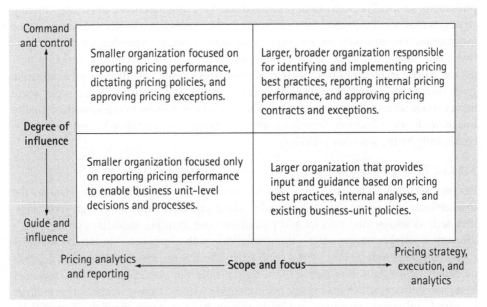

FIGURE 31.1 Two dimensions to consider in developing a pricing organization

analytics? These dimensions can be further explored in light of the company's pricing capabilities, environment, and culture.

The basic process for designing a pricing organization can be summarized as: (1) identify core capabilities and environmental factors; (2) define and design pricing processes; and (3) define pricing roles and map these roles to job positions.

31.2.1 Step one: Identifying core capabilities and environmental factors

A critical first step in designing a pricing organization is to understand what core capabilities are needed to set and execute effective prices. Understanding the impact of environmental factors—both in the external marketplace and in the company's own corporate culture—is also essential. These environmental factors can influence the importance of core capabilities in addressing the company's pricing needs.

31.2.1.1 Core pricing capabilities

Effective pricing depends on coordinated efforts among six core capabilities: pricing strategy, price execution, price analytics and optimization, pricing technology, tax and regulatory considerations, and organizational management and governance.

31.2.1.1.1 Pricing strategy

Pricing strategies define and articulate the guiding principles behind a company's efforts to price its goods and services. At the highest level, for example, a company might adopt a philosophy such as "We will not be undersold" or "Our products never go on sale." Pricing strategies may also be defined for specific products, channels, customer segments, and/or geographies. The goal may not always be to maximize margin: Depending on the competitive environment, the stage of the product lifecycle, and other factors, a company may decide to price its offerings in a way that suboptimizes margin but advances other strategic goals such as increasing market share or undercutting a competitor. For example, some luxury goods sellers will not discount below a certain level in order to maintain their quality image, while some discount chains will sell some items at cost or close to cost in order to consistently be the low–cost provider.

31.2.1.1.2 *Pricing execution*

Pricing execution includes all processes by which a company delivers its prices to the marketplace, both internally and externally. These processes range from high-level activities such as setting sales policies and procedures—for example, guidelines on how big a discount a salesperson can offer without checking with a manager—to tactical activities such as tagging products for sale at a retail store. Effective pricing execution often depends on delivering the right information to the right people. For example, one global consumer beverage company, which made large investments in fixtures, storage, and displays in order to attract and retain customers, needed to inform its salespeople about the cost of these investments and educate them to take those costs into account when negotiating deals.

31.2.1.1.3 *Analytics and optimization*

A state-of-the-art pricing organization should arm its decision-makers with fact-based analytic insights and projections that both guide and show the probable results of pricing decisions. Two of the most important types of analyses are pricing analytics and price optimization.

- *Pricing analytics*: This activity involves looking at past customer transactions in order to better understand profitability. A pricing analysis collects and studies historical data on product cost, prices paid, and cost to serve. Using this information, companies can develop profit-boosting strategies such as discontinuing unprofitable products or customers, changing pricing policies, or adjusting prices upward or downward. Pricing analytics can also help a company develop a deep understanding of what aspects of a product their customers truly value. For example, to what extent does the customer value on-site technical support, consigned inventory, or special terms or conditions? This information can help position the company's products or services on the value delivered rather than the company's own cost of acquisition.

- *Price optimization*: This discipline uses mathematical models to determine the price that maximizes an outcome (such as profit, revenue, or market share) based on historical customer, marketplace, and competitor information. A price optimization model can help management select an appropriate price, and it can also determine the probable outcome of any pricing changes. For example, a company may use such a model to determine how a new product launch at a certain set of price points may or may not cannibalize other sales of similar products. The chapters in this handbook provide several examples of pricing analytics and optimization (for example, see Chapter 26 by Talluri on Revenue Management and Chapter 25 by Ramakrishnan on Markdown Management).

31.2.1.1.4 Pricing technology

The sophisticated pricing software applications available today can uncover customer, channel, and product profitability patterns across millions of transaction records. They can also give salespeople real-time access to customer and profitability information during sales negotiations. Such information can allow them to calculate a deal's profitability under a variety of price and product combinations before closing a sale.

31.2.1.1.5 Tax and regulatory considerations

Identifying and dealing with tax considerations can significantly improve after-tax margins. For example, evaluating the impact that recognizing profits in different countries would have on the company's global effective tax rate can be an important input into pricing decisions. Where and how certain pricing decisions are made can also influence the tax jurisdiction where the revenue should ultimately be recognized. For today's multinational or global companies, transfer pricing is another key tax issue. The Robinson–Patman Act of 1936 restricts the ability of companies to sell the same product to competing customers at different prices. The Sarbanes–Oxley Act requires that companies assess the adequacy of internal controls over financial reporting, which can have significant implications for a company's pricing-related controls and documentation.

31.2.1.1.6 Organizational management and governance

This refers to the establishment and management of a pricing organization that will enable the aforementioned capabilities. In addition to putting the right people in the right roles and giving them the right information at the right time, an effective pricing organization must be able to manage all the behavioral and cultural factors that affect pricing outcomes. These factors could be both internal and external to the company (see Özer and Zheng Chapter 20). An effectively managed and governed pricing organization will have processes and procedures for activities such as enforcing price policies and procedures, training field personnel to interpret and use analytical data, and evaluating and approving price exceptions.

31.2.1.2 Key external environmental influences

The specific pressures on a pricing organization, and therefore the pricing capabilities it needs to emphasize, depend largely on external factors such as the degree of product commoditization, the attributes of the company's target customers, and the company's corporate culture. External influences also include factors unique to an industry, product set, or geographic market, such as the competitive landscape and supply constraints or surpluses.

31.2.1.2.1 Product commoditization

Pricing for highly commoditized products—products that are widely available and essentially interchangeable with competitors' products—generally focuses on undercutting the competition to become the lowest-cost provider in a given market. To execute this strategy, a pricing organization must have excellent competitive research and analysis capabilities as well as detailed cost accounting. Pricing execution, too, must be top-notch in order to gain a competitive advantage. On the other hand, the range of acceptable prices is highly constrained by the marketplace. Because of this, advanced pricing analytics and optimization techniques—although they are certainly used—are less important in commodity pricing than for products for which the marketplace allows greater latitude on price.

With highly differentiated products, where price is only one of many factors that influence purchase decisions, there is much more latitude in price. In this situation, effective price-setting requires strong analytic capabilities to untangle the complex relationships between price and buying behavior. Effective price execution, in turn, requires value-based selling skills to enhance customers' perceptions of product value. If prices are open to negotiation, the pricing organization also needs policies, procedures, and technological tools to help salespeople and other market-facing personnel identify pricing adjustments that strike an appropriate balance between the customer's satisfaction and the company's own interests.

31.2.1.2.2 *Customer attributes*

Customer attributes that significantly influence a company's pricing decisions include buying style, the customer's view of the total cost of ownership, channel choice, and intended use.

In our experience, customers tend to fall along a continuum from "transactional" to "relationship-based" buyers. Transactional buyers are those who place a higher value on price, terms, and conditions than on the relationship with the seller. To these buyers, the product's price and availability matters more than who sells the product. Because of their high price sensitivity, transactional buyers often require pricing that allows the seller to match or beat the competition.

On the other end of the scale, relationship buyers view their relationship with the seller as part of the value they obtain from the transaction. They tend to value high-touch, personal attention and, given a high-quality relationship, are apt to be less price sensitive than transactional buyers. Extracting value from relationship buyers depends greatly on value-based pricing capabilities such as analytics and optimization, coupled with relationship-building sales techniques and solid pricing execution.

Another attribute that influences pricing decisions is the customer's sophistication about the *total cost of ownership* (TCO). TCO evaluates the cost of a product or service based not only on its purchase price, but also on the total cost and benefits associated with the purchase, from acquisition through use and potentially on to disposal. In general, the more sophisticated a buyer's understanding and use of TCO principles, the easier it is for a seller to differentiate its products and/or services and compete on factors other than price. Customers who employ TCO techniques are usually more open to negotiation on non-price-related matters, and they are typically willing to engage in discussions about the price/profitability waterfall.

Customers' channel choice also affects pricing decisions. The demand faced in each channel depends on the service levels of each channel as well as the consumers' valuation of the product and shopping experience (Chen et al. 2008). To incorporate such complexity and make effective pricing decisions, a company requires advanced analytics to understand the role of price in customers' buying decisions. A medical supply company, for instance, may sell its products through several different *group pricing organizations* (GPOs), each with its own pricing structure, and each of which imposes different terms (such as minimum purchase requirements) on its members. A hospital that belongs to more than one GPO makes purchasing decisions based not only on price and product, but also on the need to allocate its purchases among GPOs in a way that satisfies all membership terms. This can add significant complexity to any attempt to build an analytical pricing model.

Selling to a distributor or manufacturer often requires different pricing approaches than selling to end-consumers. Unlike end-consumers, distributors and manufacturers can be influenced by tactics that help them offset higher purchase prices by passing along the added cost to their own customers (such as rebates and buy-back contracts). Executing such tactics requires the seller to understand the customer's business, the seller's own costs and business drivers, and the impact of price and value on buying behavior at a much deeper level than typically required for consumer-focused price execution. Chapter 29 by Kaya and Özer provides a discussion on pricing contracts among firms.

31.2.1.3 Internal environmental influences: corporate culture

A company's basic cultural orientation can have profound implications for effective pricing management. Is the company sales-driven, where closing the deal is the ultimate measure of success? Does it have a research and development (R&D)-driven culture, where developing leading-edge products or services is the path to a C-level position? Is the corporate culture finance-driven, where meeting the numbers determines personal success or failure, or is it an operations-driven culture, where efficient manufacturing and supply chain performance are the top priorities?

Understanding the company's basic cultural ethos, and structuring the pricing organization in a way that helps it be effective within that context, is critical to any pricing organization's success. Table 31.1, lists nine cultural drivers (following the classification of Tregoe et al. (1989)) of corporate culture and the implications for pricing.

- *Decision-making style.* A company's decision-making style—participative, authoritarian, or somewhere in between—can have a major impact on the pricing organization's decision-making processes and approach.

- *Capabilities and attitudes around information.* Because much of pricing's power comes from gathering, analyzing, and distributing information, companies that value and enable effective information-sharing will find it easier to establish an effective pricing capability than companies where information is not as well managed or shared.

- *Leadership attitude toward pricing.* The degree to which top executives view pricing as a strategic priority as opposed to a tactical, mid-management concern has a major impact on a pricing organization's effectiveness. One way to raise pricing's visibility among corporate leaders is to require C-level ownership of the pricing organization and its performance.

- *Existing pricing skills and competencies.* A crucial step in designing a pricing organization is to evaluate the pricing skills and competencies the company currently has in place. This evaluation can help guide the structure of the pricing organization. It also sheds light on the talent management issues the pricing organization may face in both the short and the long term.

- *Functional influence.* If a particular functional area in the company tends to drive key decisions, then this function's political power must be taken into consideration. For

Table 31.1 Cultural drivers and pricing implications

Cultural driver	Description	Likely pricing implications
Products or services offered	The company is committed primarily to a product or service and limits its strategy to increasing the quantity and quality of that product or service.	• Pricing typically owned by product managers • Price optimization is important to help maximize share • Pricing goals typically focus on product profitability and market share • Pressure to get it right the first time (with new product launch) • Pricing can be relatively tactical around the products
Market needs	The company continually surveys potential customers to discover unfilled needs for goods and services, focusing on specific markets (industries).	• Relatively strategic pricing approach • Offers a relatively wide range of options for price-setting and execution • Pricing goals typically focus on account profitability; marketplace objectives may supersede product profitability at times • Pricing is relatively complex
Technology	The company continually tries to develop products and services that are based on the latest scientific breakthroughs.	• Pricing processes reflect long R&D and product development cycles • Pricing aligns closely with the product lifecycle: value-driven for newer, more highly differentiated products, cost- or market-driven for older, more commoditized products • Execution less important in the beginning of the lifecycle • Cost-to-serve elements less important in setting prices
Production capability	The company has a primary commitment to keeping its existing production capacity utilized (e.g., to have hospital beds filled or to keep the continuous-process plant from shutting down).	• Execution is critical in order to effectively capture price waterfall elements • Optimization critical to keeping plants running 24/7 • Effective price-setting and minimizing revenue leakage are major concerns
Method of sale	The company's strategy is directed by the method of sale (e.g., door-to-door selling, direct mail, premiums, and bonus programs).	• Process and policy side of pricing is critical; price guidelines must be robust and effectively enforced
Method of distribution	The company is driven by its current method of distribution (e.g., regional warehouses,	• Pricing is pushed down to the distributors who are responsible for their margins, price-setting, and price execution • Pricing typically focuses on competitive

	manufacturer's representatives, pipelines)	price-setting; the distribution channel owns price execution • Pricing is highly customized to the distribution channel's competitive situation, market, and customer
Natural resources	The company is strategically driven by a dependency on natural resources (e.g., coal, timber, petroleum, land, metals)	• Pricing is highly commoditized with a high degree of price fluctuations • Pricing organization focuses on constantly monitoring market price, demand, elasticities, and optimization • Highly quantitative approach to pricing
Size and growth	The company is driven by set goals regarding size and growth. It constantly strives for continuing, significant growth above current performance.	• Pricing goals typically focus on volume or market share • Pricing organization must understand the impact of pricing waterfall elements on volume • Heavy use of forecasting and advanced analytics to predict the impact of price and waterfall elements on demand and volumes • Pricing tends to rely on broad price bands with relatively few controls or reviews
Profit/return on investment	The company sets a high priority on profit margins or return on investments and makes strategic decisions in order to achieve these goals.	• Pricing viewed as a powerful profit driver • Sophisticated pricing capabilities and competencies • High level of pricing controls and monitoring • Heavy use of analysis to understand cost to serve and price waterfall elements

example, if a company's last three CEOs came from the sales organization, then sales is likely to have disproportionate influence over how prices are set and executed. The pricing organization should be designed in a way that reduces or eliminates undue functional influences.

• *Communication and change management capabilities.* Establishing an effective pricing organization often involves communication and change issues that are unique to the pricing discipline. First, the newness of the pricing discipline, and the resulting lack of familiarity with pricing's importance and capabilities, can make it difficult for people to understand and accept their new pricing-related roles. Secondly, the adoption of advanced analytics may meet resistance from people—especially salespeople—who are unaccustomed to using a data-driven pricing approach. Thirdly, the need for cross-functional collaboration in pricing is greater than in many other business areas. For all these reasons, a company that focuses on effectively communicating and managing change has a better chance of establishing effective pricing organization roles than companies that invest little in formal change management capabilities.

31.2.2 Step two: Designing pricing processes

A thorough understanding of the company's pricing needs will provide the foundation for defining and designing specific pricing processes. These processes fall into the nine major areas illustrated in Figure 31.2.

Most companies need processes in all nine areas; however, some may find that their pricing activities may not require one or more of the areas. For example, a company that never has a price exception or never runs sales programs and promotions does not need processes relating to these activities.

Pricing processes should be designed so that the majority of a company's prices are determined without having to undergo an exception. If the company's pricing strategy and price-setting are accurate and reflect both market realities and company objectives, there should be few price deviations and requests for exceptions. A high number of exceptions suggests the company needs to rethink its pricing strategy and price-setting process. One medical device company, for example, found that more than 70 percent of pricing decisions required extra levels of approval, costing it an extra 7 to 10 days in getting a price to a customer. This was a clear signal that the pricing process needed improvement.

By describing each process in detail, a company can ultimately arrive at a list of specific activities that describes all the tasks needed to execute each process. A process map—a flowchart that depicts the steps of a process—can be helpful in identifying and articulating the required activities and who is responsible for each one. The goal is to define all process activities in sufficient detail such that these activities can be grouped into roles.

31.2.3 Step three: Establishing roles and responsibilities

A pricing organization's roles and responsibilities can be established through two steps. The first step is to define and develop roles by grouping pricing activities into logically related sets of tasks. The second step is to map roles to job positions. This involves assigning pricing roles to specific job positions that are responsible for executing those responsibilities.

31.2.3.1 Defining and developing roles

A *role* is a focused series of tasks that can be logically grouped as part of a process (Figure 31.3). As an example, the set of activities required to approve a price that will be offered to a customer can be grouped into a role called "price approver." This role can then

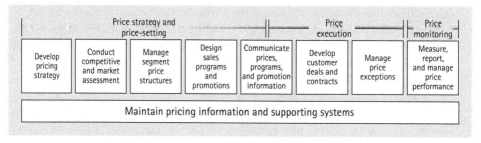

FIGURE 31.2 Nine major pricing process areas

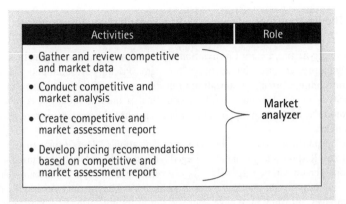

FIGURE 31.3 A role is a focused series of tasks that can be logically grouped as part of a process

Table 31.2 Sample pricing roles associated with pricing processes

Process	Sample roles
Develop pricing strategy	• Pricing strategy developer • Market analyzer • Marketing manager • Executive leadership team • Field sales leader
Conduct competitive and market assessment	• Customer relationship manager • Market analyzer • Analyzer supervisor
Manage segment price structures	• Base price approver • Base price determination coordinator • Discount/premium coordinator • Pricing data entry coordinator
Design sales programs and promotions	• Customer segmentation owner • Programs and promotions developer • Programs and promotions approver • Promotional materials developer
Communicate prices, program, and promotion information	• Communication strategy developer • Contingency plan approver • Customer relationship owner • Pricing/program/promotion information communicator
Develop customer deals and contracts	• Business approver • Legal approver • Quote/contract developer
Manage price exceptions	• Price exception negotiator • Price exception approver
Measure and report price performance	• Pricing strategy developer • Product strategy developer • Sales strategy developer • Supply-facing strategy developer
Maintain pricing information and supporting systems	• Pricing system administrator

---

Box 31.2 The Responsibility-Accountability-Consultation-Inform matrix

The *Responsibility-Accountability-Consultation-Inform (RACI) matrix*, originally developed for use in Six Sigma projects (see Chapter 33 on "Six Sigma Pricing" by Sodhi and Sodhi), can be a useful tool for refining a pricing organization's role descriptions. In a RACI matrix, the ownership of each activity is allocated among roles based on whether the role should be *responsible* for the activity, *accountable* for the activity, provide *advice* regarding the activity, or receive *information* about the activity.

People in "responsible" roles are the pricing organization's "doers"; they answer to the "accountable" roles. Responsible people are charged, at a tactical level, with executing a given task. More than one person can be responsible for a given activity. People in "accountable" roles are those ultimately responsible for the results of an activity. They do not necessarily execute the activity themselves, but they may have approval authority and provide guidance and strategic direction. For example, the person(s) responsible for issuing a new price back to dealers are in an accountable role regardless of who actually communicates the price to the dealer. People in "advisory" roles have information or skills that are important to completing an activity. They should have the opportunity to provide input on decisions that affect their areas, but they do not make the final decision or grant approval. For example, a product manager may consult with field sales on updating a new price list or a promotion campaign. People in "informatory" roles are those who are affected by activities or decisions and therefore need to be kept informed. They do not participate in the effort, and they are usually informed after decisions are made but before action has been taken.

---

be assigned to one or more jobs as appropriate, such as Product Manager, Regional Sales Manager, and/or Division Controller.

Table 31.2 lists typical pricing roles associated with each of the nine high-level processes. This list is for illustrative purposes only. The specific list for a given company depends on a company's business drivers, specific pricing needs, the overall corporate structure, as well as the responsibilities of any pricing roles that the company may already have in place.

31.2.3.2 *Mapping roles to job positions*

With pricing roles clearly defined, the next step is to map each role to a specific job position within the company. As illustrated in Figure 31.4, a job position may include one or more

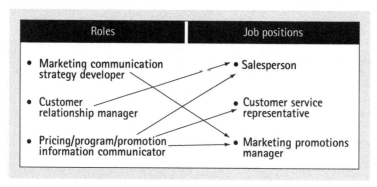

FIGURE 31.4 Roles map to specific job positions

roles, and a role may map to one or more jobs (e.g., both salespeople and customer service representatives may fill the role of Pricing/Program/Promotion Information Communicator). New job positions may need to be created to assume certain roles, while other job positions' responsibilities may need to be expanded, diminished, or eliminated in order to align them with the appropriate roles.

In addition to involvement from stakeholders throughout the functions and business units, an effective pricing organization will likely need a dedicated "pricing department" to house specialized pricing capabilities. Table 31.3 gives a sampling of common pricing department job titles and their associated responsibilities.

Roles within the pricing department often require a variety of specialized competencies such as familiarity with pricing software, sophisticated analytics, and capabilities around competitive market research and analysis, as well as project management skills. Table 31.4 lists some of the important competencies typically found among pricing professionals.

Finally, one of the most critical decisions about roles in the pricing organization is the question of who should lead the organization. A strong argument can be made that the pricing organization should report to a C-level executive, or at least an executive immediately below the C-level. Having the pricing organization report to such a highly placed executive can give pricing the presence in the executive suite needed to align pricing strategy with corporate strategy. It can also give the pricing organization the visibility and influence it needs to set and enforce pricing policies and procedures, and can institutionalize pricing as a core competitive competency within the organization. Finally, having a C-level executive in charge of pricing can give the executive team a single, highly visible point of contact for pricing questions and issues.

Which C-executive is the most appropriate leader for the pricing organization at any company depends largely on the extent to which pricing is aligned with each executive's functional role. This choice, in turn, depends on each company's unique priorities, strategy, and pricing needs. Table 31.5 summarizes some of the possible pros and cons of having the pricing organization report to various C-level titles.

31.3 MANAGING THE PRICING ORGANIZATION

Effective management brings a pricing organization to life, providing the rules, policies, and activities that help personnel understand, accept, and effectively carry out their responsibilities. Important aspects of pricing organization management include governance, multifunctional involvement, organizational tensions, talent management, and change management.

31.3.1 Pricing organization governance

The term "governance" refers to the rules that define and regulate an organization's decision-making authority, reporting relationships, and the involvement of stakeholders from multiple functions and other areas of the business. Pricing decisions should be made by individuals who have the relevant information required for informed decision making;

Table 31.3 Sample pricing department roles

Common job title	Common responsibilities
Pricing operations manager	• Develop and implement product pricing • Manage the financial analyses that support the development of pricing strategies (cost plus, competition oriented, value-based, or hybrid), price execution policies, and overall optimization of price management. • Oversee the end-to-end price book publishing process • Provide centralized pricing support to the organization with ongoing pricing analytics that delivers timely and accurate information to support overall market, product, and customer objectives
Pricing analyst	• Conduct and document financial analyses that support the development of pricing strategies, price execution policies, and overall optimization of price management • Provide product managers with ongoing pricing analytics that delivers timely, accurate information to support overall market, product, and customer objectives
Pricing support specialist	• Provide detailed support for price book production • Research and resolve pricing discrepancies • Investigate and recommend resolutions for standard/day-to-day pricing issues originating from departmental management, field sales personnel, regional management, and/or senior management
Product segment manager	• Provide marketing support to the company's product lines, including support related to company product offerings, pricing, distribution, service, and promotional strategies • Conduct and analyze market and product performance research studies to determine market potential, profitability, positioning, and strategies • Develop and test market and product hypotheses around product lifecycle, extensions, new products, suppliers, pricing, segments, competition, value analyses, and distribution/inventory
Revenue controller	• Establish, report, and maintain appropriate measures and processes to track and govern contractual sales obligations, concessions, and purchasing deals • Review contractual obligations and ensure they are documented and reported in compliance with sales and accounting policies and guidelines • Design and maintain internal controls for the company's business units to support accurate, timely, and regulation-compliant financial reporting
Business system analyst	• Provide leadership and guidance in gathering, clarifying, and documenting requirements for pricing application projects, service, and support requests • Work to implement solutions to meet company business requirements related to purchased software packages • Facilitate work throughout the entire IT lifecycle, including working with IT architects to identify a technical solution, facilitating IT estimates and staffing needs, providing work oversight and customer status, and facilitating Quality Assurance testing
Pricing organization leader	• Executive leadership and direction for pricing activities • Typically is or reports to a C-level executive

Table 31.4 Sample pricing competencies

Competency name	Description
Pricing strategy	• Ability to set and evaluate pricing objectives and determine appropriate approaches to product pricing, including cost, value, competitive, and hybrid approaches • Ability to establish pricing strategies that are aligned with corporate strategy and pricing objectives
Price analytics	• Knowledge of pricing analytics and ability to apply analytics to determine product profitability and margin performance • Ability to develop and implement recommendations for margin improvement
Price execution	• Understanding of corporate pricing goals • Ability to make pricing decisions that are aligned with corporate pricing goals and communicate them accurately and rapidly to the field • Knowledge of technology required to capture pricing requests and to identify and report high-visibility activity requiring formal action by senior management • Ability to measure and report pricing performance
Pricing technology	• Experience in maintaining pricing information, applications, and supporting systems, including maintenance of price structures, process policies, performance metrics data, programs and promotions information, and data integrity. • Ability to manage the design and development of new pricing systems, processes, and reports, including researching new pricing systems or upgrades
Competitive pricing analysis	• Ability to analyze competitors' pricing and value propositions and apply the findings to help develop the company's own pricing and value propositions

who are in a position to make or enable timely decisions; and who are pursuing goals aligned with corporate goals.

To determine what constitutes "relevant" information and "timely" action, a company needs to examine its corporate and pricing strategy, its pricing-related business needs, the circumstances under which each decision is likely to be made, and the level of risk and opportunity associated with the decision. These considerations should be taken into account when allocating decision-making authority to specific roles and job positions. For example, at one consumer foods company, promotional programs are developed by marketing, but sales has the final decision on which promotions to offer to which customers. This reduces the risk that promotions will be given to customers who, in the judgment of the sales team, are unlikely to respond in the desired manner.

Risk management is another important component of pricing governance. Because pricing can have such a large impact on business performance, many pricing decisions are risky, making it important for the pricing process to include the appropriate people to evaluate and manage that risk. The riskier a decision, generally speaking, the more senior the individual or group making that decision should be.

Table 31.5 Pros and cons of having pricing report to various functions

Function (executive)	Pros	Cons
Finance (CFO)	• Ready access to financial data used in pricing analytics • Financial analytic capabilities can support effective pricing analytics	• Not close to the marketplace; less insight into customers, products, and market strategy than functions such as sales or marketing • Accounting method of calculating sales, general, and administrative expenses may impede accurate calculation of economic cost to serve
Marketing (Chief Marketing Officer)	• Traditional home of pricing as one of the "four Ps of marketing" (product, price, place, promotion) • Takes a holistic view of the pricing process, from price-setting to execution • Typically oversees the entire product lifecycle • Ability to tie in market, customer, product, and sales strategies • Ready access to value and competitive information	• Tends to focus more on price-setting than on price execution • May lack visibility into or understanding of price waterfall and detailed cost to serve
Sales (VP of Sales or equivalent)	• Closeness to the marketplace can facilitate information-gathering and improve responsiveness • May make it easier to implement/enforce new sales compensation programs, pricing policies, and other initiatives among the field salesforce	• Short-term, reactive view of pricing may hinder the development and execution of a strategic pricing approach • Sales often characterized by discounting behaviors that may diminish the effectiveness of price-setting and execution strategies • Potential for misaligned sales compensation structures that drive success for the sales organization but sub optimize corporate performance
Operations (COO)	• Ready access to information about accounts, fulfillment, order-to-cash activities, and other operational information	• Unlikely to have appropriate pricing skills • Operations typically not involved in setting market, product, customer, and sales strategies
IT (CIO)	• High degree of ownership of the data, analytics, and technology that enable pricing	• Removed from the market and customers

		• No ownership over customer-facing functions (i.e., sales, customer service and support)
		• No responsibility for demand generation strategies and activities
		• May limit pricing to analytics and transaction management
Pricing reports directly to CEO	• High-level visibility • Can give pricing greater scope and authority • Can improve access to resources • Reinforces the importance of pricing to the company	• Potential confusion or conflict around the CEO's responsibilities and authority versus other functional executives (e.g., CFO or COO)

In addition, proper controls and processes for the recording of price and revenue are required for meeting the present standards concerning financial reporting.

31.3.2 Multifunctional involvement

Without a structured effort to maintain cross-functional collaboration, supported by a realignment of functional goals to support corporate pricing objectives, it is very unlikely that a company will set prices effectively. Companies seeking to foster productive collaboration should formally structure discussions about the tradeoffs between functions, develop functional performance metrics that reward cross-functional collaboration, and develop cross-functional action plans for dealing with the more difficult integration points.

Senior executives play an important role in managing the push and pull among different functions in the pricing organization. It is essential for senior leaders to set the pricing organization's strategic direction and provide all functional stakeholders with the guidance they need to align their pricing activities with corporate objectives. Absent such guidance, each function will naturally behave in a way that supports its own functional metrics, which can potentially interfere with the achievement of the company's larger pricing goals. That said, the goal is not to achieve unanimous agreement among functions, but to consider all appropriate perspectives when making pricing decisions. In fact, disagreements among functions can point to areas of legitimate concern, alerting a company to the possibility that a pricing decision may need to be reconsidered.

Operational processes and policies must be defined for pricing activities that require coordination across functions. For example, the pricing organization must agree on how it will manage price exceptions. To do this, it should first define guardrails (suggested minimum and maximum prices) based on the type of deal and customer under consideration. For example, deals involving low-margin products or long-standing customers would have different guardrails than deals involving high-margin products or new customers. Once these guardrails are established, it is desirable to limit the number of deals for which the salesforce requests exceptions. When an exception request is made, it should be examined by a cross-functional team that includes representatives from sales, marketing, and finance to determine if the exception should be approved. In this way, the pricing organization's operating model becomes a lens to focus individuals on the right actions, and does not leave important decisions that affect overall profitability in the hands of a single function.

The following general observations about the role of each function in pricing apply to most companies:

- *Sales.* Salespeople should use analytics to guide sales negotiations and stay within the organization's pricing guidelines. In addition, they should gather information about how customers make buying decisions and provide this information to the pricing function.

- *Marketing.* Marketing can support price execution by adopting a data-driven approach to promotions and programs that considers the impact of discounts and incentives on pocket price. One digital media company, for example, establishes and monitors the return on investment from all demand generation programs down to the product, service, and account levels.

- *Research and development.* Price should be considered very early in the product development process. R&D personnel can offer insights on, for example, how much a new product might cost to produce, the product's target customers, and the new product's point of competitive differentiation. Pricing considerations can also direct some aspects of the new product development process. For example, product designers should know what a product would need to cost in order to compete effectively with competing products. This can affect decisions around what features to include in a product or the materials from which the product should be built.

- *Manufacturing and operations.* Manufacturing, operations, and logistics should monitor the costs to manufacture or source, warehouse, package, and ship products and report changes to the pricing organization. Leaders from these functions may also be involved in setting pricing strategy, contributing their knowledge of operational considerations (such as the desirability of maintaining a certain asset utilization level).

  In industries that are more commoditized and/or use a cost-plus approach to pricing, the involvement of manufacturing and/or operations is especially critical. Consider, for example, advance selling. Some customers can be induced to place their orders in advance through providing discounts. The value of advance selling is that it helps the company to better plan/forecast and reduce production, logistics, and inventory costs. If the firm does not accurately calculate cost reduction, however, then it runs the risk of offering discounts that cost more than the benefits.

- *Customer support and logistics.* Customer support and logistics should be closely evaluated in the price-setting process. In both areas, aligning service levels with the value of the service to the customer is critical in managing transactional profitability. For example, companies with sophisticated products usually offer technical support. Often, support is intended for high-volume customers. But these customers, in many cases, have their own technical support groups. As a result, smaller customers who lack internal support capabilities consume the majority of technical support services—but in many cases, the prices charged to these customers do not reflect the higher service costs.

- *Finance.* The finance function may control much of the transactional data used in pricing analytics and optimization. Hence, it usually has both data and analytic capabilities that are important inputs to the pricing organization. Finance often also determines revenue and margin targets, which become key drivers of profitability targets.

- *Legal, regulatory, and tax.* The pricing organization should involve the appropriate legal, regulatory, and/or tax professionals in making pricing decisions for industries where these factors are important. For instance, a company's legal counsel may provide useful assistance in evaluating compliance with the Robinson–Patman Act. In heavily regulated industries such as pharmaceuticals or medical devices, a company's regulatory professionals can help determine the impact of regulatory approval costs.

- IT. The IT function needs to effectively manage both the data and the applications required by the pricing organization.

31.3.3 Organizational tensions

Tensions between stakeholders (such as departments) with different opinions or goals often exist within a pricing organization. Pricing leaders should carefully monitor such tensions, both to consider opinions of all parties when setting pricing strategy and to take steps to defuse potential conflicts when they threaten to paralyze the organization.

A frequent source of tension is that each of the multiple corporate groups involved in pricing—functions, geographies, and business units—may have different performance metrics, compensation structures, and goals. An effective pricing organization must transcend the possible conflicts of interest that may arise among these groups. Clearly defined pricing processes and roles, common goals and objectives, and the use of performance metrics for pricing roles that evaluate each individual's fulfillment of any collaborative responsibilities can help drive collaboration.

One approach that many companies find effective is to establish a multidisciplinary pricing council as a venue for offering input, discussing issues, and setting policies. Such a council, typically headed by the executive leading the pricing organization, may include representatives from different functions, geographies, business units, product lines, or any other stakeholder group that plays a significant role in pricing. In addition, companies may wish to institute a "fast track" process for resolving issues that cannot wait for a council meeting.

Another common source of tension relates to the extent of control over pricing decisions exerted by different levels of the corporate hierarchy. In general, people in lower-level roles, who execute day-to-day tactical activities and often interact more directly with customers, usually take a more tactical view of pricing than people at higher levels, who are more concerned with overall pricing strategy and performance. Placing certain tactical decisions at too high a level—for example, requiring management approval for very small price adjustments in the field or for making a one-time investment in a new account—can impede responsiveness, reduce flexibility, lower efficiency, and fail to take critical contextual information into account. Placing certain strategic decisions at too low a level may create the risk of subordinating strategic objectives to the pursuit of tactical gains.

The classic example of a hierarchical tension is the one that nearly always exists between the field salesforce and the "home office"—a general term describing the pricing organization that sets the rules and regulations that guide pricing decisions. A pricing organization in which the home office controls most of these decisions can be described as "centralized," while a pricing organization where the field salesforce has considerable autonomy in making pricing decisions can be described as "decentralized." Generally speaking, decentralized organizations offer greater speed, flexibility, and responsiveness, while centralized organizations offer greater consistency, standardization, and control. Companies whose pricing and marketplace strategies require the former may do well to place greater authority in the hands of the salesforce; companies whose pricing and marketplace strategies require the latter may want to give the home office more control.

31.3.4 Talent management in pricing

Pricing poses a number of unique talent management challenges. One common issue is the relative scarcity of professionals with the right combination of skills to work effectively in a pricing department. Many pricing roles require not only strong analytic and mathematical skills, but also strong communication skills and interpersonal savvy to present and explain analytical results to non-specialist stakeholders. Companies may need to take a combined "buy and build" approach to filling these roles, training its existing pricing resources on needed skills to supplement the resources it may be able to hire from outside the company. The positive side to this is that a broad range of skill sets and backgrounds are relevant to building a strong pricing organization. According to a 2009 survey of more than 300 pricing professionals, the pricing profession (and organization) draws upon many functional skill sets, with financial and marketing backgrounds reported as most prevalent (Figure 31.5) (Deloitte Development LLC 2009).

Another significant challenge is that pricing rarely has the political clout or the career path opportunities that would attract talented, qualified professionals. Companies who

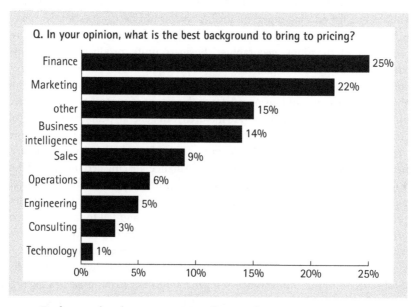

FIGURE 31.5 Backgrounds relevant to pricing ($N = 317$)

want to establish pricing as a sustainable competitive capability must position pricing as a critical function that can lead to senior-level career opportunities.

Further, few companies have implemented clearly defined career paths and advancement opportunities for individuals in specialized pricing roles. The reality is that pricing roles can and often do offer advancement opportunities equal to those available in other, more established functions. Often, pricing specialists rise to become product managers, marketing managers, or general managers—all positions that leverage a former pricing specialist's knowledge and experience. But because these higher-level positions usually lie outside the pricing department, pricing's role as a stepping-stone to advancement is rarely obvious.

A talent management strategy for pricing professionals should focus not only on developing pricing professionals' skills, but also on highlighting the relevance of pricing experience to high-level positions in other areas of the business. Steps to make pricing an attractive job choice might include formalizing career paths for pricing specialists, clearly communicating the value of a pricing background to various roles in the business, and encouraging leaders to look for pricing experience when evaluating job candidates.

Another opportunity for attracting the right talent into pricing is the establishment of pricing as a key rotation in any management development program. Requiring senior-level managers to spend time in pricing can improve the perception of pricing as a critical function within the organization, provide a steady stream of talented, motivated individuals to the pricing organization, and help build a network of pricing professionals within the ranks of corporate leadership. In addition, a pricing rotation program can help strengthen the company's support of pricing by giving its future leaders personal insight into the pricing challenges that face the company.

31.3.5 Change management challenges in pricing

Companies often encounter several pricing-specific change management issues in their efforts to improve their pricing organizations. Because pricing is a relatively new field, and pricing typically lacks a great deal of visibility or organizational status, companies often encounter resistance to the changes needed to establish an effective pricing organization. To gain both leadership and rank-and-file buy-in, it may be necessary to educate stakeholders about the value of pricing as well as the utility and validity of advanced pricing techniques such as analytics and optimization. A company may also need to offer training on pricing skills to individuals who are not familiar enough with pricing concepts and techniques to effectively carry out their new pricing roles.

Gaining salesperson buy-in to the use of quantitative pricing techniques can be a particular challenge. Data-driven pricing techniques can enable marketing and sales professionals to model multiple deal configurations in real time and understand the impacts of different concession levels. Frequently, however, salespeople resist the use of such tools and techniques on the grounds that a computer can have nothing to add to their knowledge of customer needs and their relationships with buyers. In addition, the insights driven by data analysis can deliver recommendations that are counter to the conventional wisdom among the salesforce. If a company does not recognize and deal with these resistance points, building advanced analytic capabilities can be a waste of time.

One helpful tactic for gaining salesperson buy-in is to involve them and other end-users in developing the technology itself. Seeking the salesforce's input in the data requirements stage of application design—asking them what information would be most useful to them and how they would like it to be organized, for instance—not only can help software developers better tailor the software to user needs, but can also foster a sense of ownership of and confidence in the technology among the salesforce, making them more likely to use it. Once buy-in is obtained, effective training is a must. In the 2008 AMR Research survey, "Training the sales force on fact-based pricing" was named as one of pricing's top organizational challenges (Tohamy and Keltz 2008).

31.4 STEPS TO DESIGNING AN EFFECTIVE PRICING ORGANIZATION

Pricing leaders seeking to design or redesign an effective pricing organization should consider approaching the effort in four phases: Define strategic objectives and assess organization; define core capabilities and operating model; design organization; and implement and adjust organization.

31.4.1 Define strategic objectives and assess organization

Pricing leaders need to examine the company's strategic goals and drivers, determine how pricing can help advance those goals, and document the pricing organization's mission, vision, and strategic objectives. Next, pricing leaders need to define and identify improvement opportunities and develop a business case. They should evaluate the state of pricing as it exists at the company today and compare it to what they have defined as the required future state. A major milestone in this step is the development of a compelling business case that can persuade corporate leaders to invest the time and money needed. Finally, pricing leaders need to develop design requirements that articulate what the pricing organization needs to accomplish.

31.4.2 Define core capabilities, performance metrics, and operating model

This phase lays out the broad brushstrokes for the future pricing organization. Pricing leaders should first examine the strategic drivers, improvement opportunities, and organization design requirements identified in the previous phase to clarify the core capabilities needed by the new pricing organization. Next, pricing leaders should define the metrics on which the pricing organization's performance will be evaluated. These should include metrics for measuring the pricing organization's advancement of the company's goals (such as revenue, margin, and/or volume targets) as well as metrics to measure the pricing organization's operational efficiency (such as decision turnaround time or the time to complete pricing-related support tasks such as price book production).

Pricing leaders can then develop the new pricing organization's operating model—a high-level description of how the pricing function interacts and aligns with other functional areas such as marketing, sales, operations, supply chain, finance, and IT. High-level strategies, decisions, and price execution responsibilities should be articulated here. Overall financial contribution expectations (performance metrics) should also be defined and aligned to the creation of shareholder value.

31.4.3 Design organization

This phase develops the details of the new pricing organization: processes, roles, responsibilities, job positions, governance, and reporting. First, a high-level organizational design should be created based on the operating model developed in the previous step, and processes designed to allow the pricing organization to effectively and efficiently carry out its goals. Then, the pricing organization's governance and decision rights must be determined, a high-level rewards strategy developed, and the pricing organization's specific roles, responsibilities, and reporting relationships defined. Finally, leaders must decide what job positions are needed to cover the pricing organization's roles.

31.4.4 Implement and adjust the organization

This step involves planning and executing the transition from the old pricing organization to the new. First, pricing leaders should work with executive stakeholders across the enterprise to plan the implementation of the new pricing organization, identify change

---

Box 31.3 Steps to a more effective pricing organization

1. Define strategic objectives and assess organization
   - articulate strategic drivers;
   - define improvement opportunities and business case;
   - develop organization design requirements.
2. Define core capabilities and operating model
   - define core capabilities;
   - define performance metrics;
   - develop operating model.
3. Design organization
   - develop high-level organization design;
   - define pricing processes;
   - determine governance/decision rights;
   - define rewards strategy;
   - develop detailed organization design;
   - develop job profiles.
4. Implement and adjust organization
   - design organization transition strategy;
   - develop detailed workforce transition plan;
   - transition workforce and execute training plans;
   - adjust organization.

management issues, and develop strategies to address them. Pricing leaders should then work with human resources to create a detailed transition plan for any current employees affected by the shift to the new pricing organization. Issues to consider include employee selection, compensation/rewards, severance, outplacement, on-boarding, training, workforce continuity, and communications. The pricing organization employees must then be redeployed, on-boarded, outplaced, and trained as needed.

Finally, the company should continually monitor and adjust the performance of the new pricing organization, identify and execute opportunities for improvement, and continuously evaluate the need for changes to keep the pricing organization aligned with the company's business strategy.

31.5 Future trends and conclusion

While many of the core concepts of pricing have been in existence for decades, the application of these concepts across both geographies and industries continues to evolve. We see three major trends in pricing organization.

31.5.1 Pricing will become more centralized

As the importance of pricing as a discipline continues to increase, and as sophisticated pricing tools become more generally adopted, we expect more companies to move toward greater centralization in their pricing organizations. In many industries, conventional wisdom has dictated that pricing decisions be made as close to the customer as possible. This has often meant that the salesforce had the final say in what price and what terms, conditions, and discounts were offered. In addition, the sales team has traditionally been regarded as the part of the organization that best knows customer needs, the attributes on which customers base buying decisions, and, ultimately, what price a customer would accept. In many industries, this resulted in a very decentralized approach to decision making, often with the salesforce possessing "total flexibility" on price.

In addition, the level of detailed analysis to support pricing decisions has historically been marginal at best. This led to an over-reliance on the salesforce to identify the product or service attributes driving the buying decision. Often, the need for a quick response to pricing inquiries precluded going back to a central organization for a decision, since checking with the central organization would take too long for the short response times expected or demanded by the customer. All too often, the result of these decentralized pricing decisions has been a total lack of consistency and control of both price and profitability.

As pricing continues to mature, this decentralized approach has increasingly been called into question, to the point where we believe that it will be replaced with a more centralized model at many companies. Analytic tools and additional information sources have demonstrated that the salesforce does not know the customer as well as once thought. Salespeople are apt to misunderstand, misprioritize, or misjudge the product or service attributes that drive buying behavior. In addition, executives are coming to appreciate the extent to which volume-driven compensation models incent the salesforce to close the deal at any cost. Finally, the widespread adoption of tools that allow near-instantaneous communication with the salesforce have radically altered what information is available to the individual making the pricing decision.

There is also the fundamental question of how the salesforce should be spending their time. Do leaders want them running detailed analyses, or do they want the salespeople in front of the client, selling? How much autonomy should salespeople have, and what is the appropriate level of corporate guidance and control that leads to the optimal mix of revenue, volume, and profit?

31.5.2 Integration of salesforce automation tools and pricing tools will drive greater cross-functional integration

We anticipate that the integration of salesforce automation (SFA) and pricing software will accelerate. There are already examples of ad hoc alliances between pricing software vendors and SFA vendors. We expect formal alliances, acquisitions, and other market activities to drive this integration even further and faster in the future.

What does this mean for the pricing organization? Further, deeper, and faster integration with other functions. While sales, marketing, and finance are obvious collaborators with pricing, operations will also be a key part of the integrated pricing organization. Managing customer relationships at the transaction level will require significant integration among operations, customer service, supply chain, finance, engineering, sales, and marketing.

This degree of integration will require governance models that gather and include the perspectives of many disparate and often competitive corporate functions. Today, few sales organizations have the required information to have those conversations, and even fewer are trained to target the right tradeoffs in terms of price, volume, and cost to serve. Old boundaries will no longer apply. For example, it will become standard for the salesforce to include "cost to serve" as a critical consideration when setting a price.

The right governance model will be tailored to a specific organization's needs. It will enable fast and accurate decision making, terms that are not really compatible with decision by committee. Rotational leadership models, rotation of decision-makers and support staff through the various functions, and the use of the pricing organization as a management trainee stop over are all beginning to occur now. As information availability continues to improve, we look for these trends to accelerate.

31.5.3 Pricing as a profession will continue to emerge and grow

As the strategic imperative for pricing continues to grow, we believe that more people will be making a career in pricing. Pricing professionals come from a broad range of backgrounds, and it is this diversity that helps set pricing apart from other professions. As the pricing profession has matured, more professional organizations dedicated to its growth, such as the Professional Pricing Society, have emerged. The results of a 2009 survey found that over 85 percent of survey participants believed pricing to be a strong career enhancer and that 40 percent planned on staying in the pricing field (Figures 31.6 and 31.7) (Deloitte Development LLC 2009).

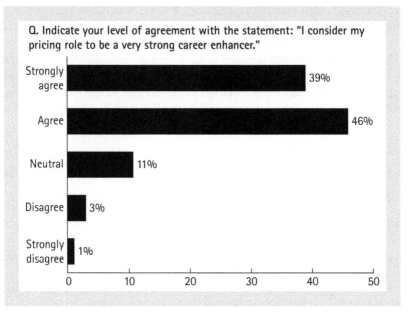

FIGURE 31.6 Pricing professionals' views of their pricing roles ($N = 317$)

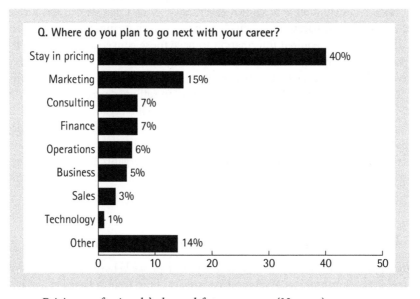

FIGURE 31.7 Pricing professionals' planned future careers ($N = 317$)

The business imperative is clear. Pricing's potential for driving business results is too great to be left to informal processes or managed in disconnected pockets of the enterprise. Companies that organize around pricing in the same way that they have organized around supply chain, quality, and other strategically important activities will be much better positioned to use pricing as a powerful tool for pursuing business strategies—and for achieving competitive advantage in the marketplace.

References

Chen, K., Kaya, M., and Özer, Ö. (2008) "Dual Sales Channel Management with Service Competition," *Manufacturing and Service Operations Management* 10/4: 654–75.

Deloitte Development LLP (2009) "Is there a career in pricing? An insider's view of the pricing profession." Survey of 250 pricing professionals conducted by Deloitte Development LLP.

Tohamy, N. and Keltz, H. (2008) *Building a Bulletproof Business Case for Pricing Improvement Initiatives*. Boston, MA: AMR Research, Inc.

Tregoe, B. B., Zimmerman, J. W., Smith, R. A., and Tobia, P. M. (1989) *Vision in Action: Putting a Winning Strategy to Work*. New York: Simon & Schuster.

CHAPTER 32

....

GLOBAL PRICING
STRATEGY

....

GREG CUDAHY, THOMAS G. JACOBSON,
TIAGO SALVADOR, AND JULIAN SHORT

Pricing has long involved international implications, as trade routes over oceans and deserts connected local merchants with far-flung customers. A thousand years ago, for instance, a Venetian artisan priced his elegant glassware based not only on the costs of material and apprentice labor, but also according to the particular customer's values and the latest intelligence on rivals' wares along those trade routes.

Today, the globalized nature of pricing has become hyper-fast and significantly more complex. Information about prices moves at the speed of light, not the speed of a camel or caravel. Advances in technology—particularly the greater price transparency afforded by the Internet—combined with the rise of the procurement function's role and skill in price negotiation have increased the need to balance local and global differences when setting prices for products and services. Globalization poses a big problem for businesses that are marketing and selling the same product (or with minor variations) in many different markets. For many multinationals, the rapid evolution of the "multi-polar world"—where regional centers of commerce such as Dubai, Mumbai, Shanghai, and Sao Paolo begin to challenge the long-time dominance of the economic triad of the USA, Europe, and Japan.

Marketing and selling no longer take place at only a local or only a global level, but at several levels to different customer segments—customers who can access a wealth of price information quite quickly. A luxury goods maker may operate physical stores from Boston to Tokyo, each of which may require different price points for the same handbag in order to reflect the different values of local buyers and the dynamics of local competition. But the company may also sell through its own website and even through other web retailers, so the same shopper may find three or four different prices for the same product through these various channels.

Effective global pricing thus entails what might be termed a "pan local" approach, with potentially different tactics for each local market, yet all adding up to a coherent overall strategy. Ad hoc pricing decisions can damage the brand and wreak havoc on revenues and profitability. All the components of the business model, from the supply chain to channel partners, have to be considered and harmonized in order to build a successful global pricing strategy.

Consider the matter of seasonality from the standpoint of a clothing retailer that is based in the United States but selling globally through its website. It may be summer in July at home, when the retailer wants to get rid of sweater inventory through closeout prices; but it's winter in Australia and Argentina, when sweater demand is highest. The retailer will want to choreograph seasonal prices appropriately through such methods as shipping or handling costs.

To be a true high-performance business today—an organization that, over successive economic cycles, outperforms its peers in terms of returns to shareholders, revenue growth, profitability, consistency, and positioning for the future—it is essential to have a well-crafted and well-articulated pricing capability and to develop and embed all of the necessary components to sustain it. A company that aims to be a lowest-price competitor in many regional markets, for instance, will need the low-cost suppliers and shippers to execute that strategy.

It is no secret that even small pricing increments can produce large bottom-line improvements, giving changes in pricing more impact than just about any other profit-generating initiative. Our case experience and research has shown that for most businesses selling tangible products, a 1 percent increase in average prices lifts operating profits by anywhere from 7 percent to 15 percent. But for there to be a lasting impact, those changes must be based on more than feelings about "what the market can stand today". While it's true that many an exploratory hike in prices can buoy up a financial quarter or blunt the edge of temporary increases in raw materials costs, prices must be managed strategically— managed for the long term, integrated with other business processes, and recognized as a key driver of profitability.

An effective global pricing capability will encompass:

- A *pricing strategy* that harmonizes local and global markets. The goal is not a common price across all markets, but rather harmony and reconciliation among the different markets. Discounts, for instance are culturally acceptable in some regions but not others, so a company will have to rely on rebates for certain regions. Strategy needs to take such variations into account.

- *Pricing analytics* that tease out nuances within and between customer segments, regions, or populations that appear to be homogeneous at first blush or have been historically served with a "one-size fits all" approach. For example, a company's pricing strategy may require data to be aggregated differently than how it has previously been aggregated for the company's financial reporting. Understanding how business units in Europe contribute to the overall business performance is one thing; being able to understand how prices in Italy are affecting the local business *and* influencing prices in Paris is quite another. Similarly, analytics allow a firm to set local prices informed by the impacts of currency, warranties, terms and conditions, taxes, negotiating styles, and other local variables.

- *Price and rule setting* with adequate precision to generate value in a host of different micro-markets (whether country, industry, product, or customer segments) served by the business. Multiple prices are more effective than one global price adjusted for currency differences, which ignores local market conditions. Being able to isolate feedback from prices at the micro-segment level is critical to achieving such precision.

- *Price execution* with sufficient speed and accuracy to reach the far corners of customer markets and the supply chain in a timely manner.
- Support from the appropriate *governance* that balances the interests of central headquarters with the regional locations, where both brand strength and cost structure might vary to a large degree.
- Support from *data infrastructure* to achieve a closed-loop approach. Most multinationals have a legacy of different IT systems from mergers, acquisitions, and country-specific IT initiatives. Definitions and semantics around pricing can differ from system to system. Technology greatly facilitates the process of scaling up to reach more markets, so success in global pricing hinges on having a common pricing language, common accounting systems, and a common IT backbone.

It is critical to align the pricing strategy in a local market with the business strategy for that market. For example, when a UK-based maker of household cleaning products or a US maker of smartphones enters rural China, the primary objective will be to build brand awareness; pricing should be tuned to meet that objective. At the global level, pricing strategy should support the target profitability overall, but pricing strategy also consists of a roll-up of differentiated local strategies. The strategy provides the platform for how pricing decisions are made and implemented in practice by salespeople and contract administrators who can be distant, culturally as well as geographically, from the nexus where strategy decisions are made. Importantly, the strategy gives the organization a common ground for discussion among the expanding roster of those involved in pricing decisions these days.

In many companies, however, pricing is a much more scattershot affair, and getting to a true global pricing approach will call for a transformation of current processes. To embed pricing decisions into operations, a company should give explicit decision-making authority to one senior executive (or, at most, a very small set of executives), guard against assuming that a trend in one region will apply elsewhere, and ensure that the right incentives are in place for local business leaders. It can be quite challenging to develop a compelling vision of a pricing capability, let alone communicate it effectively or execute against it. To start, there are plenty of "cooks in the kitchen", ranging from sales teams to product engineers to marketers to pricing coordinators, yet few head chefs. According to market researcher AMR Research, in 2008, only 37 percent of companies had a dedicated pricing position at director level or above—a position that spans functional areas and business units (Tohamy and Keltz 2008).

It is harder still to make a pricing transformation cohesive and effective worldwide; too many companies rely on pricing that is developed centrally and then rolled out locally. The emotional and political factors regularly interfere. And as a constant, the commercial world is in flux more than ever. Businesses are stretched to compete worldwide, in new markets and against emerging-market contenders that were not in the picture a decade ago or even five years ago. Ideas travel faster, and innovation breakthroughs and brands are perishable. In addition, the demands of customers and investors continue to grow in scope and complexity, for example, customers caring about "green" products.

The good news is that pricing issues have risen on the agenda of senior executives. At industrial parts maker Parker Hannifin, new CEO Donald Washkewicz was the driver for a company-wide shift in pricing, moving away from a cost-plus approach to setting prices by what customers are willing to pay. His pricing initiative is widely credited with boosting operating income and return on invested capital (Aeppel 2007).

Moreover, there is a growing realization among senior managers that pricing is not just a seasonal initiative or a tactic to deal with economic downturn, but rather a *capability*—a set of strategies, business processes, and organization models—that needs to be built into the fabric of the organization. The IT function will have to reconcile differing legacy systems across the various business units of a global organization, so that local feedback can be analyzed and rolled up to inform the different pricing decisions that need to be made. Fortunately, there are now more software tools and proven methodologies available with which to make fact-based pricing decisions and to coordinate responses to pricing lifecycles and pricing patterns.

This chapter establishes the case for a strategic approach to pricing. In addition it discusses what is required to move from a vision of robust pricing to the actual capability, to affirm that pricing strategy is an inextricable element of pricing capability, and to show what is needed to make that capability truly effective worldwide. We acknowledge the many challenges that stand in the way of making that capability sustainable—the factors that must be addressed before pricing can become a consistent way of doing business rather than a one-off project. Finally, we explore the growing role of information technology and the critical interdependence between pricing strategy and technology. Of course, this chapter cannot lay out a definitive blueprint for any one company's pricing transformation. However, we believe that the best-practice experiences shared and the obstacles to success identified contain enough general guidance to help most companies consider how to develop the global pricing capabilities that will work for them.

32.1 LAYING THE FOUNDATIONS WITH THE RIGHT PRICING STRATEGY

A company's pricing strategy should be tightly linked with its capabilities in supply chain, IT, and other operational areas. Constraints in those capabilities will undermine the pricing strategy and leave value on the table, as shown conceptually in Figure 32.1.

A simple example: The strategy may determine that there is a segment of customers who want to pay more for overnight delivery. But unless the provider has an overnight delivery capability or a channel partner with that capability, the strategy will never get off the ground. Similarly, a company that segments its markets in simplistic ways risks limiting itself to a "one price fits all" choice. A competitor that segments more thoughtfully, leveraging detailed customer behavioral data, will have far more opportunities to optimize prices, react more easily as markets shift and capture more profit potential.

So the half-life of pricing strategy will be very short if it is not institutionalized in supporting processes, organizational structure, and technology. On the flip side, using

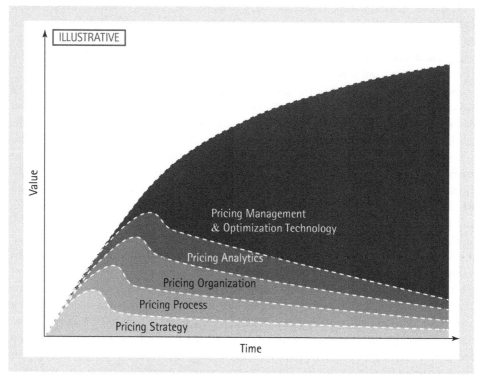

FIGURE 32.1 Unlocking the value of price strategy transformation

advanced pricing technology in the absence of a well-developed pricing strategy is like putting a Stradivarius violin in the hands of a novice.

The basis of any pricing capability is an appropriate strategy for pricing. Only when the strategy is designed in parallel with other components of pricing capability can there be meaningful discussion of the processes needed for proper management of pricing activities, the organizational structure needed to support the processes, or the analytics and technology solutions available to optimize pricing decisions. Without parallel development of a strategy for pricing, it is all too easy for a "one price fits all" philosophy to take hold.

Note that most companies *do* have pricing strategies, even if they are not explicit across the organization or if they lack adequate processes and organizational structures to make them actionable. *Cost-plus pricing* is the de facto standard in many businesses, where managers calculate how much it costs to make and deliver each product and then add a flat percentage on top, say 35 percent. Many managers like this method because it is straightforward, gives them broad authority to negotiate deals, and is useful when sales volumes can be predicted fairly accurately. From a global perspective, cost-plus pricing should consider the following factors: the company's supply chain capability to optimize sourcing decisions, the asset and yield management economics of the business model (such as owning versus leasing), transportation costs, and raw material costs. Changes in cost for raw materials, for instance, may dictate going abroad for sourcing the materials, so the company will want to be sure that its supply chain is up to the task.

Cost-plus pricing has several major drawbacks. No matter how much a product improves, the company ends up charging the same premium it would for a more standard item. If the firm finds a way to make a product more efficiently, it cuts the price as well. If input costs jump higher, the automatic price hike will surely discourage customers. Worse, cost-plus takes no account of how the customer might value the product. As a result, cost-plus pricing leaves money on the table and leads to a low return on invested capital.

Competitive pricing, where managers peg prices to what's charged by certain competitors, can be a valid strategy where a company is striving to be seen as providing the best value at a given price. On a global scale, competitive pricing takes on a whole new definition. In each local market, one has to understand the new competitors, their cost structures, and their product mix. However, competitive pricing also has several drawbacks. It encourages the perception that the company's offerings are commodities (as with gas stations); the competitor's pricing system itself may be irrational; the product's value may not justify the price; and the strategy cedes leadership in the market to competitors.

Value-based pricing opens up the largest spread of pricing possibilities; it is the strategy that best matches what different customers will pay and is ideal for offerings for which customers have fewer alternatives. Airlines can charge more for Cleveland-to-Tampa flights in January than in August. Smartphone manufacturers charge more for version 1.0 because early adopters will pay more for the latest cool gadget. A successful value-based strategy, though, hinges on having a deep understanding of what customers want and are willing to pay for, and how to anticipate and respond to fast-moving market transitions—as when streaming Internet videos start to displace DVDs, or an Mp3 player gets displaced by the new iPhone.

These considerations can be complex to manage when a company serves global markets, as behavior and demographics will vary greatly at the local level. On a global basis, consider the simple examples of beer imports. On a relative basis, some consumers in the USA may be willing to pay more (beyond the additional cost of distribution) for a can of Foster's, because of its import cachet, while elsewhere, the brand and price may lack that same premium.

Indeed, none of the three traditional pricing strategies is totally sufficient for the complexities of a global marketplace. It is not unusual for companies with declared pricing strategies to believe that they need only execute properly against that strategy. Consider the hypothetical case of a retailer whose pricing strategy is to match competitors' price moves. Even if the retailer does everything right in terms of pricing execution and quickly responds to competitors' changes, it still may miss out on profit opportunities. If products that could garner higher prices are not broken out, the company has no way of determining what profit opportunities it is missing. In effect it may be "overmuscled" in one area, but a weakling in others such that competitive pricing is inadequate.

No single pricing strategy can serve the broad portfolio of products now offered by most multinationals. What is more effective is to pick the right pricing strategy for the right segment, geography, or product offering—one strategy for high-value customized offerings and another for "catalog" products. An investment brokerage may have a set price for its standard trading transactions but may also vary price points for advisory services tailored to high-net-worth individuals. Managers must have a holistic view of the product/service

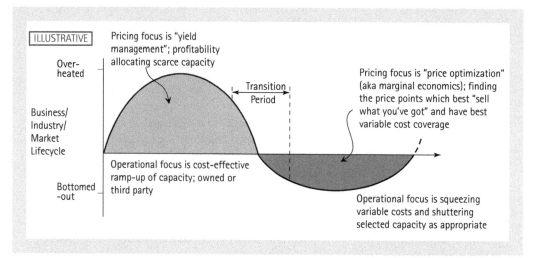

FIGURE 32.2 Business/industry/market lifecycle

portfolio and its various contributions to overall strategic and business objectives in order to maximize profitability.

The three basic pricing strategies neither automatically account for market flux nor for the fact that pricing has a lifecycle of its own as shown in Figure 32.2.

To sustain effective pricing practices over time, organizations need to ensure that business cycle fluctuations are reflected in pricing approaches and embedded in operational decision making. The basic approach is to leverage "yield management" tactics in times of excess demand—like those used by the airlines to price seats—then to shift to "marginal economics" during periods of excess capacity while working with the supply side to cut costs or adjust capacity.

The fact that the timing and intensity of these market fluctuations can vary across regions and industries further adds to the complexity of operational decision making. High performers excel at knowing when to manage the transitions between business cycles as the balance between supply and demand changes, reacting to the environment long before their competitors do.

Furthermore, the three strategies do not address the changes in perceived value during a product's lifecycle. It is no mystery that new and innovative products can command price premiums. However, when more competitors enter and the market starts to mature, pricing gets more difficult to manage, because high quality products become widely available. High performers' pricing strategies acknowledge and accommodate such transition points—as, for instance, Apple deliberately rolled out more and more versions of the iPod, each at different price points.

So how does an organization begin to craft a pricing strategy appropriate to the dynamics and complexities of its product mix and its market conditions? Three steps are useful here—and each involves discussion at the most senior levels of the organization.

32.1.1 Assess pricing performance in the context of the current business environment

This first step calls for senior managers to analyze the company's profit model or models from both the revenue and margin points of view against the backdrop of world markets, where globalization, electronic commerce and the shifting sands of geopolitical and industrial actions have created an environment of "permanent volatility."

For example, a retailer's "me too" pricing strategy resulted in lost opportunities and impeded the company's push for the larger profits needed to consolidate its market-leading position. A large portion of its product prices hadn't been changed in years, since they were modified only when the competition made a price move. Essentially, the retailer did not display the confidence it could have shown as a market leader, nor the responsiveness required in an increasingly volatile market.

At the same time, the retailer had the ability to price at the area and store level—a powerful tool, but one that risked creating disgruntled customers who might feel cheated when seeing a lower price elsewhere compared to what they had paid. Harmonizing prices across geographical areas could eliminate these inconsistencies.

Structured analysis showed the company's leaders that their corporate brand, product assortment, operations, and corporate pledge were all centered around *customers*—yet their price strategy was centered on *competitors*. By breaking down the retailer's profit model by product line—digging deeply enough into the sales and operations data to determine the cost to serve customers of each product offering and to identify the profits available at different price points over the lifecycle of the offering—it was possible not only to determine the appropriate prices and to quickly test customers' responses, but also to decide how often and how quickly to change prices. We found, in this case, that 20 percent of the product portfolio could be priced at a premium, in many cases at a premium of 8–10 percent more than competitors' like products (the premium was driven by highly-perceived in-store customer service levels). Of course, when tackling product pricing issues globally, decisions have to be made in light of whether a firm has global procurement capabilities, and also in light of local regulations and local selling considerations, which call for customization wherever possible.

32.1.2 Segment products/customers and align pricing strategies and positioning

Next, it is necessary to understand the various segments of customers a company serves and align strategies and price positioning, leveraging visibility to price elasticity and offering preferences in each of those segments. At the retailer mentioned earlier, the leadership team gained further insights after completion of a detailed study of the company's various customer segments (e.g., loyal customers versus transactional shoppers) and store segments (e.g., low-density population versus high-density population or close proximity to competition). Then the retailer was able to compare its business strategy to market conditions to determine how to set pricing in each segment (i.e., keeping the price high but using either loyalty points or promotions for particular customer segments). The market study confirmed the boundaries of the market segments and gauged the size of each; it also mapped out the evolving needs of customers in each segment, the positions of the retailers' suppliers and the strengths and weaknesses of its competitors in each market.

These insights provided the essential context for overhauling the company's pricing strategy. The core customers were becoming more conservative as the economy turned downward; they were driving fewer miles to retail locations. Meanwhile, suppliers hurt by rapid rises in commodity prices were getting tougher in negotiating with the retailer on both the size and timing of their price increases. And the quality of their products was increasing, lifting base prices. At the same time, several prominent competitive chains were becoming more aggressive with competing volume products. And mainstream rivals were hiring new management, exploring pricing optimization software and gaining strength through acquisition.

For this retailer, as with many companies, such comprehensive marketplace analysis can show how to segment the business and determine the market-relevant prices that balance customer needs, competitor response, and underlying cost position of the product/ segment (Figure 32.3).

Returning to the Parker Hannifin case, the company abandoned its long-time cost-plus strategy in favor of strategic pricing that capitalized on the niche characteristics of many of its products. The unit that makes industrial fittings spent half a year gathering data on 2,000 different products—mostly metal components for oil rigs and power plants. Discovering that more than a quarter of the parts were priced too low relative to demand, the unit's management team deployed a full-blown pricing program, raising prices an

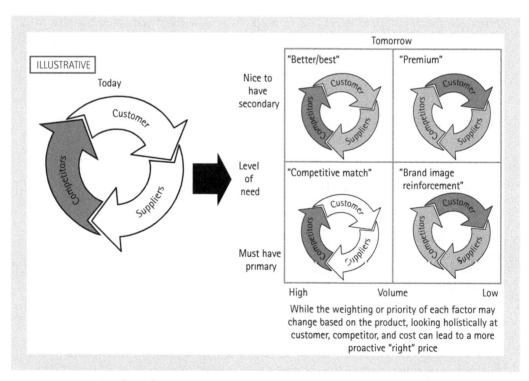

FIGURE 32.3 Market-relevant pricing

average of 5 percent and in some cases by as much as 60 percent to reflect market opportunities (Aeppel 2007).

There are a myriad of global and local factors that go into effective alignment of pricing strategies and positioning, not least of which include geographic and cultural differences. Competitor sets, customer preferences and regulatory constraints will be quite different for, say, a European retailer doing business in China or a US manufacturer selling in Latin America.

The relationships between global brands and regional sub-brands also have a strong influence on what pricing strategies to deploy. Additionally, relationships with channel partners, local market capacities, and product/industry lifecycles will vary by geography. A truly global pricing strategy will optimize the differences of these inputs across the globe to formulate sub-strategies that effectively get the best possible profit potential from each regional microsegment.

32.1.3 Incorporate the appropriate pricing structures and presentation into price-setting considerations

Price structures that may have worked for earlier products may not automatically translate for new products. When there are inadequate data with which to make concrete decisions, it is tempting to default to reference products. But that tactic can have its pitfalls.

Launching a new product requires more considerations than simply the price of the reference product being replaced or augmented. Research on customer tradeoffs might indicate that a substantial cut in price will greatly increase the size of the market, regardless of the reference product price. The same logic might apply to the launch of a new website that offers the existing product line. Returning to the experience of Apple, when it launched the 3G iPhone it could have used reference products to price the new phone at a very large premium. Instead, it offered one version at a relatively low price in order to expand the market, and reserved the premium price for a version with more memory (which likely was not costly to add).

Once a company determines the pricing structure, an important decision is how to present it to customers, competitors, even to employees. On the customer front, complete transparency can cause trouble. Consider the white-goods appliance market. Customers for a high-end dishwasher would probably accept a flat house-call service charge of $200 plus parts. Customers at the low end of the market would balk; a more palatable presentation for them might be $29.99 upfront charge plus parts and labor. Even though the economics wind up being the same on average for both approaches, the presentation should be tailored to the appropriate segment.

Serving customers globally further complicates price setting, as there are more segments to consider and potentially more providers they can choose from. Consider the many students who live abroad but attend college in Boston. They travel frequently, search via the Internet, and thus potentially see several price points for the same product. Any company serving them will have to think through the implications of its pricing structure and presentation.

Pricing structures also play critical roles in business-to-business sectors. The price of a product or service or bundle, and the negotiations that follow, incorporates a number of elements such as product grade and specifications, distribution priority, and terms and conditions such as early-pay discounts. Managing these elements of price and aligning them to the various customer segments is critical to achieving profit growth objectives. These pricing structures also affect firms' incentives regarding whether to share information and coordinate decisions. (See Chapter 29 by Kaya and Özer.)

Secondly, it is crucial to get each product's "introductory" price right. Every price point that follows during the product's lifecycle is essentially a subject for negotiation. Apple's iPhone is a fine example of how to do this well: In the initial market cycle, the price was geared higher to appeal to early adopters. In the second sweep through, the phone was priced to capture premium payers, then, in a third sweep, it was pitched at a lower price point to pick up the larger mass of more price-sensitive customers. Important decisions here are how high or low to set the initial price, when to move to a lower price, and how to quantify the impact of these decisions. (See Chapter 23 by Aviv and Vulcano; Chen and Simchi-Levi Chapter 30.)

One concept that high-performing companies are adopting is *design to price*, an approach that can be very effective for new product introductions. Rather than using a cost-plus approach, leading pricers start with the market opportunity to be addressed and test market sizes at different price points. Then they work backward to design a product at a cost that can be delivered at the desired price while still meeting margin expectations and overall business objectives.

Starting with a well-grounded understanding of the price the market will bear and then designing to meet that price is a great forcing function for cost-driven innovation. Tata Motors Chairman Ratan Tata got the idea for the Nano car from watching families traveling on motorcycles and scooters in rural India. The company pegged the car's price at about $2,500 to attract lower-income families that could afford motorcycles but not cars as traditionally priced (Kurczewski 2010).

Designing to low price can help companies open up new markets and new revenue streams, particularly in the emerging economies where more people are climbing out of poverty into low-wage households and aspiring to consume a broader range of goods and services—if they are priced within reach. This strategy can also address the increased frugality in developed markets, where cost-conscious consumers are demanding more value at lower prices.

Of course, designing to price must be supported by an appropriate cost structure. JetBlue has succeeded as a low-cost carrier in part because it matched its cost structure to its pricing. By contrast, several major airlines that tried to launch low-cost versions were not able to reduce their costs to the point where they could make sufficient profit at the low prices.

Another factor is how prices are perceived by customers. When it comes to setting the appropriate price, perception really can be everything. Pricing optics—the perception and emotional impact of a price—lie behind the preference to buy at $19.99 but not $20.25. It also means paying close attention to how prices are packaged in more nuanced ways. For example, a monthly lease fee of $599 with $7,500 down for a 2008 BMW M5 sedan looks a lot more appealing than the manufacturer's suggested retail purchase price of $88,495 (BMW 2008). Other cases where perception of value is important are the "triple play" bundles from phone and cable companies and service warranties for home appliances. (See Özer and Zheng Chapter 20.)

Other factors will make a price look more or less attractive—factors that include the customer's experience. In retailing, the sales channel is especially influential in shaping the shopper's perception of value. Costco sells high-end watches, but the discount club is not where most customers of expensive watches will go. So the upmarket watch purveyor has permission to sell the same watch for substantially more than the mid-market or discount channels can. And to a large extent in the business-to-business world, terms and conditions will shape the price, requiring a sub-strategy that becomes part of the overall pricing capability. The terms may govern everything from payment period to warranty details to seller financing.

Price setting and optics have different implications in the multi-polar world; setting prices higher with the expectation of negotiating down in one region of the world will not work in other regions or situations where price is seen as non-negotiable. (See Phillips Chapter 2.) Similarly, regulatory, legal, and tax constraints can impact the ability to offer the same pricing structures across regions or even within regions. Tax law across the various US states provides a simple example: Some states offer benefits for leasing a car, but when that tax break changes, leasing loses its luster relative to buying.

32.2 Pricing as a "closed-loop" process

Setting the appropriate pricing strategies and the prices themselves are the first steps—but they are by no means all that is needed to create a sustainable pricing capability. It is essential to execute those strategies consistently, and to constantly test and refine the pricing tactics using a closed-loop approach. On a global scale, the loop often starts with an accretion of mini-loops, as each locality works to tune its own feedback loop of local pricing decisions. The global overlay is the set of capabilities discussed earlier (strategy, governance, analytics, and so on) that continue to determine what "local" means. The definition of "local" tends to fluctuate as the regions themselves change: At first, "rural China" may be good enough as a meaningful market, while in the following year it may be important to distinguish among individual provinces, which have sharply different dialects, customs, patterns of buying behavior, and industry profiles.

The closed-loop process serves another purpose at the global level, namely to take an enterprise-wide view of how pricing affects the business. A business and pricing strategy may be highly successful in one local market, but if the company looks at the global investment involved in serving all local markets, it may become apparent that the best decision is to exit that particular business.

For consumer-facing businesses, where point-of-sale data are increasingly available, pricing teams need to be able to sift through data to draw the right conclusions for updating pricing tactics. They also should understand what affects the customer's preferences and why those preferences change—a tricky challenge. Add to that the need to balance promotion activities with price increases and the need for a closed-loop, sense-and-respond model, becomes evident. (See Chapter 24 by Blattberg and Briesch.)

By adopting a closed-loop process, an automotive goods retailer was able to align its business strategy with its pricing strategy. For several decades, the retailer invested in differentiating on service, support, and availability of hard-to-find parts. Under price pressure from competitors, the firm decided at one point that it would try to match low prices on all its goods. But that decision did not mesh with its strategy, which involved extensive call centers and competitive shop capabilities. A more nuanced pricing approach was called for, and the company responded by offering value choices to customers at different price points. The company was able to drive increased profitability by increasing volume on items for which pricing was competitive, holding ground with mass merchandisers on other items for which service was superior, and commanding premiums on items that were differentiated—all with a more efficient approach to price promotions.

Business-to-business companies face similar challenges but with different emphases. For instance, because they typically have fewer customers and transactions than consumer-facing businesses, there is usually more detail around each customer and transaction to analyze but smaller volumes of data available. At the same time, there is generally a better understanding of customers' shifting needs because the supplier–customer relationship is much more personal and rich, with deeper interactions. The key challenge comes in executing against pricing strategies and in managing the approval processes needed to enforce them.

Ongoing face-to-face negotiation adds uncertainty, underscoring the case for a measured sense-and-respond model that provides flexibility while bringing together data analysis and negotiating skills to win deals at the desired price and profitability—and managing discounting appropriately. (See Jacobson et al. Chapter 34 and Phillips Chapter 21.)

A closed-loop pricing process can enable further analysis of customer purchasing data, allowing marketers to refine and tailor sales and marketing messages and materials for future customer interactions. This approach provided a pharmaceutical company's marketers with a direct feedback mechanism between the field sales and brand teams, enabling the brand group to collect quantitative data on its programs and use it to effectively segment target markets of physicians.

Managing the overall portfolio of prices is a critical part of the closed-loop process for all businesses. It enables an organization to understand the impact of pricing decisions on corporate performance, helping to determine how pricing decisions tie to profit and growth objectives and align with overall business strategy. It is vital to become familiar with the interdependencies of pricing decisions across the product portfolio, and to be able to manage product/channel conflict and cross-border issues. (In some cases, "channel" can be a single large customer such as a mass retailer.) However, with the right toolset in place, portfolio management allows organizations to conduct what-if scenarios, making more informed decisions on promotion and discounting decisions and testing the impact of potential pricing increases or the likelihood of lower profitability.

By taking a product portfolio management approach to pricing, a global retailer was able to determine which items truly required low prices in order for the business to retain its image as the low-price leader; the retailer then priced those items accordingly. At the same time, the company was able to apply more moderate value pricing to less price-sensitive items. The overall result: increases in gross margins in key product categories and a simultaneous boost to customers' perceptions of the retailer as a price leader.

The closed-loop approach also requires the right metrics and incentives to be in place to support the sales behaviors that will support the new pricing capabilities right through to the point at which the contract is signed, as well as to help with monitoring and measuring sales performance.

In short, the closed-loop model aligns a business's pricing strategies with a powerful ability to sense and respond to market feedback and competitors' actions, and with the ability to analyze data to continually improve its micro-segmented strategies across the globe.

32.3 RETHINKING THE PRICING ORGANIZATION

The next questions concern who will drive the strategy and the pricing processes once they have been agreed upon. Typically, responsibility for pricing at most companies is spread among sales teams, marketing managers, product managers, pricing analysts, pricing coordinators, campaign managers, and contract negotiators. Pricing teams can comprise a mix of any of these roles—and can be led by individuals from any of them.

Some companies are recognizing that, because of its importance to profitability, pricing requires a higher level of management attention. As a result, we are now seeing the rise of the chief pricing officer (CPO) or a recognized senior pricing executive with a similar title such as chief revenue officer or chief value officer. Whatever the actual title, it is typically a C-suite role or direct report in high-performance businesses charged with profit optimization and portfolio management in addition to pricing. The role may report to the chief operating officer (COO) or may be a profit-and-loss-level report, whether divisional or corporate. CPOs have become prominent in insurance, for instance, with insurers such as ACE, Swiss Re, and TransAmerica being notable examples.

In some cases, partnerships between the CPO and chief strategy officer (CSO) manage the balance between supply and demand, with the CPO taking on short-term responses and analytics tasks and the CSO driving mid- to long-term planning. The CPO's goal is to shift from revenue maximization to profit optimization—that is, profitable growth—so the supply/demand balance is key. As such, in practice CPOs rarely report to the chief sales officers due to the latter's focus on growing sales volume (often at any price).

The organizational issues grow more complex in highly international or decentralized organizations. In such cases, there can be unproductive tension between corporate pricing decision-makers and those in far-away offices. Central initiatives may be viewed with suspicion—done "to me" rather than "with me"—which makes the selling of any pricing transformation that much trickier.

Companies with leading pricing practices are also aware of the need to support their pricing decisions right through to the negotiation with the customer. (In many cases, that support must be extended further, to the contract administration staff who can ensure that the pricing terms in the contract are upheld. See Jacobson et al. Chapter 34.) Not only do companies with leading pricing practices train their sales staff to better understand the rationale behind their pricing decisions, they also give more attention to the metrics and incentives that largely determine the behavior of the salesforce. For instance, in many manufacturing businesses with large direct salesforces, traditional sales incentive plans that were based solely on sales volume are shifting to focus more on profitability.

32.4 A VITAL ROLE FOR INFORMATION TECHNOLOGY

It is difficult to master all the complexities and dynamics of a pricing capability without the benefit of information technology. Indeed, pricing and profit optimization (PPO) tools now significantly expand the number of viable pricing strategies that a company can have. The software quickly allows pricing analysts to drill down to the transaction level, to develop a wide range of "what if" analyses and to roll up high-level reports for managers. Importantly, the tools can give rapid feedback about which pricing maneuvers work best.

In the past decade, a host of providers have created software solutions that help to analyze pricing data, determine which prices on which products will optimize profits, automate decisions such as post-sale markdowns, and more. Demand for those offerings has been healthy—a clear signal that senior managers are interested in improving their pricing capabilities.

However, there are no silver bullets. Software solutions are only as accurate and as timely as the data that they can access. As point solutions, they almost always require levels of integration not only with other comparably focused solutions, but also with ERP software suites. Nor can the PPO tools be relied upon to solve more than they are capable of. "Implementing a pricing technology without a minimum amount of process redesign is almost always the wrong approach," notes a 2008 AMR Research report (Tohamy and Keltz 2008). The researcher's survey indicates that only 5 percent of companies say they are implementing or planning to implement the technology prior to changing processes.

Indeed, pricing software can be a double-edged sword. While it enables strategy to be implemented quickly and efficiently, it also allows strategic mistakes to occur instantly. In one case, a healthcare provider piloted pricing software in a key part of its business, and the software brought to light major flaws in a pricing strategy that had been implemented prior to the software pilot.

Leading companies recognize that effective pricing capability needs top pricing talent as much as it needs software tools and infrastructure, so they push to use both sets of resources better than their competitors do. That means that they use the software to automate the routine decisions (a retailer's post-holiday sales markdowns, for example), while leaving the more volatile and higher-impact decisions to the scarcer resources: their talented pricing analysts. Technology should focus on the routine, repeatable tasks, and should point out outliers and exceptions that require attention; people should concentrate on business decisions such as where to intervene and how to deal with exceptions. This runs counter to the natural tendency for staff to gravitate toward the more familiar, comfortable work, regardless of its value or impact.

32.5 BARRIERS TO SUCCESSFUL PRICING TRANSFORMATION

Many organizations are equipped to deal with the analytical factors that involve data availability and accuracy and the pricing rules and algorithms used to make pricing decisions. But the workplace is rarely an analytical place alone. In practice, business leaders must confront two other critical factors if they are to successfully transform their pricing capabilities.

Psychological factors masquerade as analytical obstacles all the time. In one case, an electronics manufacturer, with no shortage of talented pricing analysts, failed to get its analysts to use its new pricing software. The tool was complicated, and while it yielded accurate and predictive results, its findings were second-guessed and eventually viewed as irrelevant. In reality, the salesforce did not like the tool because it challenged their credibility. In implementing the new tool, the manufacturer had failed to address the salesforce's incentives and resistance to change.

Psychological responses intersect with analytical behavior when it comes to ensuring that the sales force follows through on pricing decisions made. (See Jacobson et al. Chapter 34.) Since sales professionals are so geared to the rewards of successful transactions, companies that put in place the right metrics and the incentives programs that support new pricing capabilities will be best placed to capture the full value of their pricing moves.

Managing the cycle of psychological change is critical to successful implementations and sustainable results. Essentially, there must be recognition that for those involved, change involves both anxiety and excitement, and that large-scale change initiatives often move from uninformed optimism to informed pessimism before entering a period of hopeful realism—followed by the informed optimism that underpins real commitment.

On the organizational side, it is easy to forget the power associated with a change in control of pricing decision making. Regardless of their past successes, those who have historically owned pricing decision making are often on the look-out for challenges to their position and authority. Perceived power shifts away from their control, even if small, may cause them to covertly undermine initiatives designed to align pricing with performance.

These complexities are exacerbated by the varying cultures across the globe, and the challenges of dealing with the array of psychological and organizational factors that can affect a global pricing transformation become all too apparent. Different regions' interpretations of pricing terminology are only the start of it; cultural variations are regularly held up as "the way we do things here", and varying approaches to conflict resolution need to be anticipated and addressed when the need arises.

At the same time, local dynamics that affect pricing and promotions require careful consideration. Currency issues come into play, and with them, prevailing and projected exchange rates. It is usually a mistake for corporate headquarters to set one price that then gets adjusted by currency differences for each country. That approach ignores local market differences. For example, a US-set price may assume there will be some level of discounting or negotiating. But that won't translate well to a region where negotiation rarely occurs, where there are supply/demand imbalances, or where the brand is weak or young. A more effective approach is to engage in currency hedging, which can reduce volatility without affecting profitability.

32.6 BREAKING DOWN THE BARRIERS

Companies pursuing large-scale pricing transformation initiatives should consider several techniques to overcome resistance to change. To begin with, all key stakeholders have to be identified and their expectations established at the start of any program. Communications are equally important and must be aligned with the stakeholder analysis and planned with the rest of the program. Stakeholders must then be managed proactively throughout the program to avoid a dip in commitment. And communication has to be executed throughout the program with the same rigor as the rest of the delivery. It is also essential to build a powerful network of sponsors—not only senior executives but also key managers. (See Box 32.1 "Making change stick" for a glimpse of these techniques in action at a leading chemicals company.)

In the global context, readying the organization for change also means balancing pricing standardization with local customization. As mentioned earlier, it is all too easy for local managers to feel that a new pricing capability is being imposed by the corporate center. However, that is not to say that local requirements must be met at all costs. The increased business benefits of meeting them must be viewed in light of any increase in overall total cost of ownership. A pricing design can often be standardized at a high level and then allowed to differ at a more granular level, but at little incremental cost.

Significant business benefits were achieved by a global energy company that took a staged approach to implementing a worldwide pricing model. When the company piloted the global pricing model, a model that provided insight into deal profitability, the salesforce initially resisted because they didn't believe that it would benefit their careers or compensation to walk away from low-profit deals. As a result, senior leadership restructured sales incentives (i.e., changing from volume-based compensation to a combination of volume-and-profit level compensation to make it more palatable) and raised the criticality that profit plays not only in the organization's success but in that of its leaders and its salesforce. Achieving early success in Europe, the company rolled out its global pricing model localizing it for each market by incorporating variables such as market risk, credit risk, and lag factors. Gross margins improved as the company shared best pricing practices among local implementations while applying a core set of uniform predictive pricing assets and aligning pricing capabilities with value chain capabilities.

32.7 SUSTAINING A GLOBAL PRICING CAPABILITY

Just because a company has crafted a cohesive global pricing capability does not mean it will be able to sustain the effort. Sustainability is far from inherent: The capability and its benefits can quite quickly degrade as the operating model ages and the old rules no longer apply.

The closed-loop process referred to earlier can help ensure that the chosen pricing strategy stays in sync with the other components of the business model. Properly designed and utilized, a closed-loop model will flag the inevitable imbalances that occur over time and allow managers to correct them. For instance, if there is a change in organizational structure, the model will quickly allow a manager to understand the unintended consequences of that change on the rest of the company's pricing capability. Or if the manager overreaches a strategy that cannot be implemented because of not having the necessary capabilities in place, then the model shows that the intended business benefits cannot be achieved.

Box 32.1 Making change stick: a case study

Pricing transformation needs to take a root with a systematic approach to managing change. For example, at a large chemicals manufacturer, in the earliest conversations about the initiative, the company's top management team was explicitly advised on what the transformation initiative would entail, including a rough idea of the time it would take and the issues it would raise. The goal of those conversations was to seek and obtain commitment at the highest levels to the plan. Follow-on conversations identified and designated one senior manager as the lead change agent—a professional who held a global role in the company's commercial operations—essentially its sales, marketing, and business development activities.

Then one-on-one sessions were held with the company's new change leader to ensure that he properly and fully grasped the necessary approach. The next move was his: to pick a team of about ten professionals from within the commercial operations, with an emphasis on customer-service excellence. The selection process took a solid two months; the change leader had to present a high-level value case for the change effort and then ask for the candidates' commitment to participate, while carrying out their regular work. One factor was critical: Prospective team members had to be receptive to dealing with new technology.

During the first meeting with the full change team, the group identified the size of the opportunity to transform the pricing function, the gaps that needed to be filled, the expected changes to work processes, the pricing and analytics software that would create value, and more. Successive meetings started digging into more specific questions about timing and about the detail of the transformation rollout plan.

One key theme ran throughout: the need to signal clearly to the whole organization that new pricing structures were coming. So the change team was tasked with figuring out the best ways to communicate the imminent changes. The team engaged key people from a variety of different geographies and businesses to get input. At the same time, the change teams set up a small group whose job was to consistently and clearly communicate progress to the company's senior marketing and sales executives.

Separately, the change team launched another more tactical group: the business steering team whose members were drawn from a range of functions that would be affected by the pricing transformation. The objective was to have experienced and insightful business leaders review the transformation plans—providing crucial checks and balances and regular "sanity checks"—as well as to use them as another communications point back to the business. For instance, the sales executives on the steering team were tasked with taking the plan back to the other sales leaders, a role that took quite a bit of time. It was crucial to have them act as familiar faces to represent the initiative.

The change team also made certain that they used entertainment as a mechanism to encourage buy-in and retention of the ideas. So the change initiatives were wrapped around a theme named "Let's get in the game". The development of a key phase of the change plan was timed to coincide with a national sales conference to provide the best possible platform for buy-in across the organization. As part of this theme, the change leaders organized a citywide event modeled on the "Amazing Race" TV show. Lasting 90 minutes, the evening event involved activities that were peppered with fun trivia about the project.

Concurrently, the team reinforced the transformation messages with hands-on classroom training where the presentation slides used a game-show theme, rewarding top players with prizes. Other training exercises used similarly creative devices to make the messages stick.

Essentially, the guiding discipline for the change management process was the need to pay attention to the culture of the organization. "We knew we had to have a relationship kind of approach for the sales organization," said one senior participant. "Most of the message was carried by the commercial vice president. We made sure he was very visible and verbal; if he said it, people believed it."

The "observer effect" also plays a part: That is, individuals tend to return to previous familiar habits when not being monitored, so if a company's leadership is not monitoring employees' behavior, the leadership may be perceived as not being committed to driving the new focus. The capability loses its effectiveness when the company's ability to make speedy pricing decisions and putting prices into play lags that of its rivals or customers. Over time, other organizational decisions outside the core pricing function begin to blur the lines of pricing accountability and authority. In addition, there can be over-reliance on regular periodic reviews rather than responsiveness to trigger points such as sudden shifts in demand or rapidly changing competitive dynamics.

The objective should be to look beyond an immediate price lift to a pricing *system* that enables better-targeted, more market-relevant, and consistently applied pricing strategies, policies and rules. (See Box 32.2 for the kinds of points that the management team must discuss.) The ideal system will be much more adaptable to increasingly volatile supply/demand markets. Such a system can significantly improve the customer experience because it will shorten pricing cycle times, cut errors and rework, and better match value to price. The system can also enable the company to manage its product portfolios effectively, anticipate or at least respond promptly to competitors' moves, and give the company's pricing professionals more time to focus on the pricing decisions that matter most.

Box 32.2 Checklist questions

PRICING STRATEGY

- Do you have a clearly articulated pricing strategy?
- Does your pricing strategy account for the complexities of the various dimensions of your business, including product, channel, and geography?
- Do you fully understand the potential "unintended consequences" of your strategy: on competition, workforce, suppliers, and customers?
- Do you have a system of checks and balances to adjust your strategy as needed?
- Are some local markets overly favored by headquarters in pricing strategies?
- Do price strategies adequately reflect differences between emerging and mature markets?

PRICING ANALYTICS

- Are your analytical capabilities automated and standardized or do they require significant manual effort from your pricing experts?
- Are your reporting capabilities customizable to see the key metrics for your particular organization in your local market?
- Are your analytics and reports set up to focus on areas with the greatest opportunity to grow the bottom line?
- Is there a standard procedure to reassess the relevancy and effectiveness of your analytics?

Price-setting/negotiation

- Are your pricing rules properly documented, systematic, process-driven, and dynamic?
- Can you adjust pricing in accordance with internal supply levels in the same fashion as with external demand, market factors?
- Have you built the appropriate algorithms to support pricing optimization?
- Do you have distinct responsibilities identified during the negotiation process that will balance profitability with buyer satisfaction?
- Do they reflect cultural differences in the markets you serve, such as the propensity to bargain?
- Is the salesforce properly trained in negotiation techniques?

Pricing execution/management

- Is your transactional pricing as dynamic as your competition?
- Is your compliance capability robust enough to track the lifecycle of a transaction?
- Is your organization aware of where to focus most effectively to reduce pricing "leakage"?
- Do you spend more time with the buyer or are you too entrenched in the internal deal approval process?
- Is the supply chain robust enough to profitably source products in local markets?
- Do your local market leaders structure prices to take into account currency impacts, warranties, and terms and conditions?

Governance/infrastructure

- Are there distinct responsibilities around strategic, tactical, and transactional pricing decisions—at both the local and global levels?
- Is there an appropriate balance between growth and profitability in your organization? Are metrics and incentives aligned to this?
- Does your process allow for systematic analysis and refresh for a true "closed-loop" pricing capability?
- Are you prepared to continue to grow your pricing capability over time with increased data detail and rigor?

32.8 Summary

Multiple factors are converging to make it crucial for business leaders to develop and implement effective global pricing capabilities now. The global economy is more tightly coupled than ever before—and significantly more volatile. Well-capitalized and highly capable contenders from developing markets are emerging to add to the competitive ferment. Customers are less wedded to brands, more knowledgeable and more assertive about what they want, and much more willing to jump ship if they don't get what they want. And managers can no longer rely on even the most efficient supply chains to respond to supply/demand balances without taking advantage of pricing and promotion tactics.

Business leaders who have proceeded under the assumption that pricing is something of a dark art must now reframe it as a bright science. They have to think much more in terms of the capability as distinct from strategy—with an emphasis not only on the foundational frameworks that link pricing to the business strategy but also on the processes, organizational dynamics and tools that can bring the results of informed pricing decisions directly to the bottom line quarter after quarter, year after year. In short, they must add pricing to the line-up of business disciplines that merit a regular place on top management's agenda.

As we have described, there is no easy path for the transformation to a sustainable, world-class pricing capability. Yet many world-class businesses are already well down that path. In most industries, it will soon be impossible to be a high-performing business without having a substantially superior pricing capability. The long-term benefits are too great not to make that transformation now.

REFERENCES

Aeppel, T. (2007) "Seeking Perfect Prices, CEO Tears Up the Rules," *Wall Street Journal* March 27.

BMW (2008) Actual BMW dealer listing, November: http://lease.bmwpeabody.com/cars/2008/2008-bmw-M5-space-grey-boston-mass-699.html.

Kurczewski, N. (2010) "Another Low-Cost Car Coming to Indian Market", *New York Times* March 10.

Tohamy, N. and Keltz, H. (2008) "Building a Bulletproof Business Case for Pricing Improvement Initiatives", AMR Research, August 15.

CHAPTER 33

....

USING LEAN SIX SIGMA TO IMPROVE PRICING EXECUTION

....

MANMOHAN S. SODHI AND NAVDEEP S. SODHI

33.1 INTRODUCTION

....

To implement their pricing strategies, companies develop pricing guidelines for different market segments and geographical regions. In practice, realized prices occasionally breach the floors of these guidelines. As a result, prices, margins and even revenues are lower than they could be. These price breaches reflect loose processes that additionally have other problems such as excessive turnaround times for price approvals.

In manufacturing and services (Snee and Hoerl 2005), Six Sigma, Lean, and similar approaches have been used to reduce or even eliminate defects and to remove waste such as excessive inventory or excessively long cycle times. We adapt Six Sigma and Lean methodologies to improve pricing processes through *Lean Six Sigma Pricing*. In this article we discuss how and where Lean Six Sigma Pricing can be applied, and present a case study.

We note that just as continuous improvement cannot solve all the problems of a manufacturing company, Lean Six Sigma Pricing cannot solve all the pricing-related challenges. Pricing is a challenging area requiring solutions at different levels: industry price level; product or market strategy level; or transaction level (Marn and Rosiello 1992). Improvements to pricing through changing strategy, through changes in incentive structures, through incorporating pricing in new product development, and through creating the "right" pricing roles and organization for a company's setting—see for instance, Nagle and Holden (2003); Stein et al. (2006); Simon et al. (2006); and Baker et al. (2010)—cannot come from improving pricing processes at the transaction level or contract level. As such, these are not the subject matter for Lean Six Sigma Pricing. On the other hand, transactions and transaction-level processes are where the rubber of pricing strategy meets the road, often making the difference between a company being profitable or not. Lean Six Sigma Pricing can improve these processes and consequently the realized price, directly impacting profitability.

33.2 SIX SIGMA AND LEAN IN MANUFACTURING AND SERVICES

Six Sigma and Lean are two approaches to continuous improvement and they target repeated processes. The fundamental objective of the Six Sigma methodology is the implementation of evidence-based process improvement by reducing process variation. The objective of Lean efforts is to reduce waste, where waste could be inventory, customer waiting time, or scrap. Lean also targets the "over-burden" of resources and "unevenness" of workload over time in the process. One way to distinguish Six Sigma and Lean at a high level is to characterize Six Sigma as directly targeting *variation* of process-related characteristics and Lean as directly targeting the *average* level of, say, time or resources consumed.

33.2.1 Six Sigma

Six Sigma is associated with Motorola, where Bill Smith first formulated the specifics of the methodology in 1986 (cf. Larson 2003: ch. 1). However the roots of Six Sigma go back to at least the 1920s as the methodology follows quality control, TQM, and similar approaches advocated by Walter Shewhart, Edward Deming, Joseph Juran, Kaoru Ishikawa, Genichi Taguchi, and others in order of historical appearance.

Like Quality Control and similar approaches, Six Sigma seeks to reduce the variation in process inputs at any step that results in variation and hence defects in the process output. It does so by focusing on process-related facts and data that relate the variation of inputs to variations in the output. However, Six Sigma differs from preceding methodologies in an important way: it focuses on achieving measurable and quantifiable financial returns and each project seeks to identify the bottom-line impact. Top management support is actively sought to ensure that Six Sigma projects are aligned with the organization's overall objectives rather than being purely "bottom-up" initiatives. In addition, Six Sigma creates a lasting infrastructure by way of creating "champions", "master black belts", "black belts", and "green belts"; however, this infrastructure can become a rigid bureaucracy.

33.2.2 Lean

Lean manufacturing is typically associated with Toyota and its famed Toyota Production System. Its roots as an approach seeking efficiency (thus reducing waste) go back even further than Six Sigma, to the end of the nineteenth century, in particular to Charles Babbage (who also designed the first computer and the penny post in addition to his study of industrial manufacturing and the division of labor), Frederick Taylor (and the time-and-motion studies), and Henry Ford (and the assembly line) in order of historical appearance. The Toyota Production System was developed by Taiichi Ohno and Shigeo Shingo (Liker 2004: ch. 2).

Lean seeks to reduce waste due to overproduction such as unnecessary transportation of the produced item, inventory, motion of the worker or equipment, product defects, over-processing, and excessive wait times (Womack and Jones 2003: ch. 1). Mapping a process in detail to identify which steps are value-adding and which ones are not is an important part of any Lean project. The modification or elimination of non-value-adding steps is a way to reduce waste.

Although Lean focuses on reducing waste, proponents may target unevenness of work-loads, overburden of resources, and other sources of variation that also lead to waste. *Unevenness* results from the reality of irregular production schedules and fluctuating production volume. *Overburden* occurs when people or machines are pushed beyond their natural limits, which can cause machine breakdowns, defects, low morale, and absenteeism.

33.2.3 Lean Six Sigma

With Six Sigma and Lean both being approaches to improve repetitive processes incrementally as part of continuous improvement, it is natural to compare the two and determine if we could use a "best of both worlds" approach.

Both approaches come with sets of sophisticated tools although Six Sigma's toolbox is arguably more prominent (cf. Breyfogle 2003 or Pyzdek and Keller 2009). Depending on the organization, Lean and its simpler toolset, in particular Lean's view of processes as a "value-stream" (Womack and Jones 2003: ch. 2), could provide an easier start than with Six Sigma in terms of requiring less training to get started. However, Six Sigma arguably provides a better structure and prepares the team for larger projects that are better aligned with top management goals. This suggests the two approaches can be combined using Lean's tools in Six Sigma's structure, which also helps loosen up the rigidity that one observes in practice for Six Sigma projects.

In an area like pricing with multiple stakeholders who may not even recognize there is a process or there are roles other than their own, the attraction of combining Lean and Six Sigma is greater than in areas like manufacturing or services. Lean's approach can help identify processes and increase a team's confidence by identifying easily achievable improvements while leaving the challenges of price variation and guideline breaches to the rigors of Six Sigma. Rather than training people in two different approaches, we could stick with one hybrid approach with a carefully selected initial set of tools that could be extended over subsequent projects.

33.3 Lean Six Sigma Pricing

Given our focus on the pricing execution, effectively the process for a single transaction, the "defect" could be an excessive discount relative to the guidelines sales personnel, customer service representatives, and pricing analysts and managers are supposed to follow. Or, the "defect" could be an excessive turnaround time for price approvals. There are also other pricing contexts such as revenue management or markdown management (see the chapters in this volume on the tactics of pricing and the book by Phillips 2005). Such pricing contexts can have "defects" when it comes to execution. We can apply Lean Six Sigma to improve pricing execution, we call this adaptation *Lean Six Sigma Pricing*.

Lean Six Sigma Pricing borrows from Six Sigma and Lean but is additionally cognizant of the complexity of cutting across multiple functions and groups with different objectives (Sodhi and Sodhi 2005, 2008). Pricing projects include various internal stakeholders including functional groups such as Finance, Marketing, Sales, and IT as well as top management. As internal "customers" of any Lean Six Sigma Pricing project, these stakeholders have diverse requirements that affect the scope of any project because, unlike manufacturing projects, a Lean Six Sigma Pricing project would require approval or buy-in from this diverse group of stakeholders. Therefore, the makeup of the project team and of the Steering Committee is crucial in ensuring agreement from all stakeholders to proceed.

We emphasize that Lean Six Sigma Pricing—or indeed any approach based on continuous improvement—is not intended to *create* or *improve* pricing strategy but to improve repetitive operations pertaining to pricing processes and thus improve both adherence to strategy and execution in general. It applies to pricing operations and repeated processes, for example to control discount levels off list prices in contracts or in individual transactions and not to position the company's prices relative to the competition.

A company usually centralizes its strategy setting, which would also not be repetitive. However, the execution of any resulting strategy at the level of each of the tens of thousands of individual transactions or more a year is typically decentralized. Even in a business-to-business (B2B) company with a relatively small number of large customers, where one could expect centralization in pricing execution, there may be a number of different locations for the same customer, each requiring adjustment based on local needs. Such an environment is prone to pricing-related defects. Pricing execution can often benefit from the improved controls and discipline that Lean Six Sigma Pricing can bring.

Benefits from Lean Six Sigma Pricing can go beyond individual transactions if there are other processes that are repeated a few times a year or even once a year across many product families and individual products. An annual list-price-setting or a quarterly list-price-adjustment may be repeated across thousands of products and Lean Six Sigma Pricing can help bring rigor and improvement to both.

Below are the five DMAIC steps taken from Six Sigma, adapted for dealing with the transaction pricing process and using tools from Lean:

I. *Define*: The Define phase includes identifying a pricing-related process for improvement and making a sales pitch to senior management for project approval. The output of this step is the scope, a time line, and expected improvement to the bottom line in quantitative terms—sometimes only a guess—and expected benefits other than bottom-line ones. The defect has to be described; for instance, that the price in some transactions is too low relative to the company guidelines. The goal may state reducing the level of defects by a target that is both meaningful and achievable, for example reducing pricing defects by 50 percent. Scope has to be chosen carefully because the scale and size of the project can be a pitfall. If the scope of a Lean Six Sigma Pricing project is too large, we are setting up the project team to fail and if the scope is too small it just may not get the attention from stakeholders needed to succeed.

II. *Measure*: In the second step, the team maps the targeted process in detail as it is executed currently in reality rather than in any idealization on paper; gathers data and other relevant information; verifies the quality and reliability of the gathered data; and prepares these data and other information for analysis. Mapping the "as is" process using tools such as SIPOC (Supplier-Input-Process-Output-Customer) from Six Sigma or Value Stream mapping from Lean helps identify many problems and sources of friction between Sales and Pricing that could be fixed as the project progresses. Before collecting data, the project team decides what to measure; how to sample the data and test its reliability; and how to define operational terms across the team and the steering committee. Testing the quality and reliability of the data is part of the so-called measurement systems analysis (MSA), which is essential because pricing analysis is quite vulnerable to inaccuracies from personnel manually entering erroneous numbers as well as data input for key variables that is missing. Data collection acquires even more importance when multiple stakeholders have differing interests, as is the case with pricing. While it may be politically incorrect to openly discuss the different and potentially conflicting incentives as motivating the actions of different stakeholders, the team can and should collect data to show evidence for the extent of variation in realized prices by customer sales volume, region, product line, etc., letting the facts speak for themselves.

III. *Analyze*: Analysis is the heart of Lean Six Sigma Pricing projects to identify and understand the reasons for variation. There are three types of analysis: (1) *process analysis* including that following Value Stream or SIPOC mapping to understand process failures that lead to defective prices (or other output); (2) *root-cause analysis* to hypothesize reasons for defects and validate a plausible subset; and (3) *data analysis* to understand the source and extent of price variation in terms of process inputs or steps. While data analysis is primarily statistical, we do not necessarily require statisticians for pricing analysis. For some projects, analysis may comprise only process analysis (using, for instance, a cause-and-effect matrix) or root-cause analysis (using a tool like a fishbone diagram) so it is possible, in some cases, to do an entire Lean Six Sigma Pricing project without any statistical analysis.

IV. *Improve*: The purpose of this phase is to list and prioritize solutions for presentation to the Steering Committee. To prioritize proposed solutions, the team can use different tools such as the prioritization matrix or a cause-and-effect matrix to build a shared understanding among the team members from the different functions. To identify and communicate the risks associated with implementation, the project team may use Failure Mode and Exceptions Analysis (FMEA), a tool to help identify and prioritize potential failures based on how serious their consequences might be, how frequently they could occur and how easily they could be detected (cf. Breyfogle 2003: ch. 14). Such analysis, whether done formally with FMEA or informally, helps set the stage for the next and the last step.

V. *Control*: In the final stage, the team recommends controls on an ongoing basis to prevent failures and to sustain the improvements. In Lean methodology, the emphasis is on error-proofing at the outset without ongoing controls. These recommendations entail the development, documentation, and implementation of an ongoing monitoring plan to check (1) if the approved recommendations are actually being carried out, and (2) if the results being sought in terms of process improvement are actually being achieved. A control plan is thus part of the modified process to ensure that it is standardized, i.e., the process takes place as expected and as agreed and therefore it produces far fewer pricing defects.

Implementing pricing solutions may remain tricky despite support from top management and approval from the steering committee. Therefore controls on implementation, even if these are simple progress reports, can be quite useful. However, the project team should

Table 33.1 A summary of the steps and some of the related tools for Lean Six Sigma Pricing

Step	Key actions	Tools
Define	Develop project scope around defects that are specific, measurable and affect pricing performance.	Baseline ("as is" situation in quantified terms, for later comparison)
	Identify project leader, project team, project sponsor, project champion, and steering committee.	Project Charter
	Set up goals and a financial target to be achieved by eliminating defects.	
Measure	Develop a detailed map of the existing process.	Supplier-Input-Process-Output-Customer (SIPOC) from Six Sigma or Value Steam Map (VSM) from Lean
	Identify key requirements from senior management regarding pricing and use these to prioritize which process steps to focus on.	Cause-and-Effect Matrix (C & E)
	Check whether the data about the process output and process inputs for the identified steps exists and is reliable.	Measurement System Analysis (MSA)
Analysis	Carry out a process analysis: why do problems occur?	Value stream analysis; SIPOC
	Carry out a root-cause analysis.	Fishbone diagram/why–why analysis
	In terms of data, analyze the variation of the Ys in terms of the input variables (Xs).	Multivariate analysis: regression, ANOVA, etc.
Improve	Make recommendations for improvement by way of process modifications; prioritize these and document the effort needed (expected).	
	Document the risks associated with making the process change(s).	Failure Modes and Effects Analysis (FMEA) updated
	Develop plan to hand-off responsibility to the process owner(s).	Transfer Plan with what-who-when
Control	Document and implement actions to prevent defects creeping back.	Control plan, FMEA
	Validate gains from the project and track improvement relative to baseline (see Define).	Dashboard metrics

strive to ensure that the proposed controls are not onerous otherwise the solutions will become unpopular and vulnerable to backlash. On the other hand, the project team must seek an understanding that the controls would not be removed over time, something that is quite possible in pricing-related projects.

Table 33.1 summarizes these steps and possible tools to be used at each step (Breyfogle 2003).

33.4 CASE STUDY

We now describe how a US-based global manufacturer of industrial equipment, which we will call "Acme", applied Lean Six Sigma to its price-setting process for one product line.

A change in market conditions had put Acme under considerable pricing pressure. The price of two key raw materials—steel and petroleum—had risen quickly and sharply, with Acme's steel suppliers refusing to honor existing contracts. As a result, raw material costs for Acme increased twofold within the space of a few months. The company had no choice but to raise list prices. The question of "how much?" was a difficult one. In addition, there was an operational challenge: Acme could not be sure whether a nominal increase in list prices would even hit the bottom line because sales representatives could also provide additional discounts to customers!

Sales and Pricing did not typically see eye-to-eye on transactions. Acme's sales representatives saw their mission as building market share, which was senior management's stated aim. Being close to the customers, sales representatives felt they knew the best price. They saw the pricing managers and analysts as obstructions, out of touch, and too slow to respond to changing conditions on the ground. They would therefore circumvent the necessary checks and controls on invoiced prices, but this potentially eroded the company's profit margins. On the other side of the fence, pricing analysts saw themselves as guardians of profitability, providing essential pricing analysis and, in their opinion, a quick turn-around on approvals.

Each transaction had its own discount and hence its own invoiced price. Pricing guidelines about discount levels were set by the Pricing team. At Acme, Sales had market-specific blanket ceilings for percentage discounts on all products, and sales representatives had to obtain authorization from Pricing to offer deeper discounts. A Pricing analyst or manager either approved the request or recommended a slightly lower discount. The sales representative would then complete the transaction and invoice the customer with a final price, which was (in principle) the same as or possibly slightly higher than the approved price.

But top management did not like losing market share and the absence of any effective controls encouraged some salespeople to short-circuit the price-approval process. A sales representative would ask Pricing for discounts that were much deeper than the guidelines allowed for, and even if Pricing complied, the representative might offer a further, unapproved discount to close a deal. For instance, one order approved by Pricing at $81,000 was actually invoiced at $75,000, and another was approved at $31,000 but invoiced at $28,000. With tens of thousands of sales transactions per year, the task of making sure each invoice complied with the guidelines or even with the approved prices was a challenge.

This was all well known within the company but now there was the urgency of increased costs that would hit the bottom line if they could not be passed on to the customer. This motivated senior managers to look "outside the box". They knew that Acme had enjoyed considerable success in reducing manufacturing variability by applying Six Sigma discipline (indeed, Acme was one of the early adopters). It seemed that pricing a transaction closely resembled a manufacturing process and the invoiced price could be considered the result of a "manufacturing" process encompassing several stages. The management therefore decided to pilot a Lean Six Sigma Pricing project in one of the company's North American subsidiaries. If the project led to better control of final prices, they could roll out the approach throughout the company's entire global operations.

A manager from Pricing was appointed as project manager and was given the help of a Six Sigma expert, or "Master Black Belt", recruited from the manufacturing side. The project sponsor was the senior executive responsible for Pricing. To ensure everyone's buy-in for any subsequent implementation, the project manager enlisted people from the pricing, finance, marketing, IT, and sales divisions to be part of the Six Sigma team. The various members of the team were chosen for their functional and analytical expertise. The finance person, for example, was chosen because she was familiar with the many pricing-related reports Acme was currently generating and was also familiar with many of the company's data sources.

In addition, to endow the project with institutional backing and ensure that team members had good access to data, the project manager asked people in positions of influence at Acme to serve on a steering committee for the project. The chair of the committee was the project sponsor. Other members included the director of sales, the vice-president of IT, the vice-president of finance, and the vice-president of marketing. They agreed that the project manager would meet with the team and the steering committee as needed to keep them apprised of the project's progress.

The project manager and the rest of the team then carried out the five steps of Six Sigma, employing some Lean tools as well.

33.4.1 Define

33.4.1.1 Defect

The project manager proposed a narrow but meaningful definition of a defect: a transaction invoiced at a price lower than the one Pricing had approved (or lower than the current blanket guidelines, when approval had not been sought). Once the definition of a defect was set, the project manager, with the help of the sponsor as well as the rest of the Steering Committee, recommended an appropriate scope for the project, limiting it to only one particular product line in one geographical region only, in this case, North America.

33.4.1.2 Goal as bottom-line benefit

The first duty of the team was to confirm the proposed problem definition and project charter and to set a financial goal for the project. Nonetheless, the team set a goal of increasing the selected product line's revenues (and profits) in North America by

0.5 percent or $500,000 in the first year following implementation. This additional revenue was to come entirely from a higher realized price, that is from actions that did not incur any losses in market share or unit sales volumes. Interestingly, the targeted increase in bottom line benefits, although small as a percentage increase, was in absolute terms a far more ambitious number than Acme had ever set for comparably sized manufacturing or service Six Sigma projects that typically delivered average annual bottom-line benefits of less than $100,000.

33.4.2 Measure

33.4.2.1 "As is" process map

The project manager began by mapping the price agreement process, with team members helping to fill in process details. To generate and verify the information he needed, the project manager formally interviewed eight colleagues from five functions: Sales, Marketing, Finance, Pricing, and IT. He also sought informal feedback from other people in these functions.

The team then was able to draw a high-level process map with six steps including the function (Sales or Pricing) mainly responsible for that step. Although straightforward in principle, the pricing process did not work smoothly in practice. It was replete with exceptions and shortcuts and the quality of inputs available to Sales or Pricing personnel in any step could be quite poor. The six steps in the process can be depicted as a SIPOC, that is Supplier-Input-Process-Output-Customer, table (Table 33.2).

The six-step process map was supported by documentation detailing the inputs (called Xs in Six Sigma parlance) and outputs (Ys) associated with each step, showing all the people and IT systems involved, and specifying whether the decision-making inputs could be controlled by Pricing or Sales. The eventual output variable for the entire process is the final transaction price, but intermediate steps have their own intermediate outputs as reflected in Table 33.2.

33.4.2.2 Value Stream map

Then, with the help of a larger group that included sales representatives as well as pricing analysts, Acme proceeded to do a more detailed Value Stream map—a key Lean tool—of this process capturing various discount mechanisms, communication media, and workflows used by different functions. Doing so brought out a number of process-related issues:

- a lot of handoffs in the process;
- too much time taken by Pricing compiling and analyzing information and data;
- too many decision-makers—multiple owners in process;
- too many silos, not enough delegation;
- a lot of time passing in sales;
- no clear process owner;

Table 33.2 A high-level map of Acme's existing pricing process

Step	Supplier	Input	Process	Output	Customer	Issues/work-arounds/shortcuts
1	Sales representative	List price (MSRP), discount guidelines	Initial price assessment with customer; customer seeks price exception	Tentative price based on discount off of List; needs approval from Pricing	Customer	Sometimes Sales rep offered a final price to the customer, skipping the remaining steps.
2	Sales representative	Tentative price, product details, and customer information	Request approval to price exception	Information about the proposed transaction and about the customer along with justification	Pricing	The sales rep did not sometimes provide adequate information for the quotation.
3	Pricing	Information about the customer, the specific transaction proposed, justification for discount, and discount guidelines	Compile information into a formal quotation	Completed quotation, with some historical information	Pricing	The absence of adequate information resulted in the Pricing analyst having to chase for the required information, thus wasting time.
4	Pricing	Completed quotation, history of similar transactions with same or other customers	Review and analyze quote	Tentative approved price ready for communication	Pricing	Guidelines available to the pricing analyst could be quite poor. Or a quick turnaround could leave little time for this step.
5	Pricing	Tentative approved price	Communicate price approval to Sales office	Approved Price	Sales rep, senior and marketing managers, etc.	This could go back-and-forth between Sales and Pricing. The final approved price could end up quite a bit lower because of pressure from a senior sales or marketing manager.
6	Sales representative	Approved price	Submit price to customer	Approved price for invoicing subject to customer agreement	Customer	The price Sales rep offered to customer could be quite a bit lower than the approved price if the sale went through.

- concession process may vary by product;
- inconsistent application on margin-based pricing rules;
- process for accessing price/cost info is too long;
- multiple media for communication—phone calls, e-mails, faxes—are a source of confusion;
- sales reps do not fill out discount request forms with required information when seeking price approvals;
- Pricing provides weak competitive analysis;
- no clear rationale—why we give (by way of discounts) what we give;
- there are no metrics for pricing.

These issues became the basis for future analysis; some as part of this project, others being postponed to subsequent projects in the spirit of continuous improvement.

33.4.2.3 *Measurement systems analysis*

Finally, the team assessed the quality of the input data that supported the pricing process—this is MSA or measurement systems analysis. The team needed to have faith in the numbers on which it was going to base its findings and recommendations. They also had to check if the current steps were systematically producing faulty data. By examining representative samples of data in detail, the team was able to confirm that the actual sales transaction data were by and large stable and reliable, even though different reports presented and summarized the information in different ways.

33.4.3 Analyze

33.4.3.1 *Root-cause analysis*

The team members started by meeting to identify the ways in which people fail to act as needed or fail to assert effective control at each stage. At first, it was natural to take the results of the Value Stream exercise and do a why–why (or fishbone) analysis especially in regard to the sales representatives complaint that pricing approvals took too much time, thus causing "waste" in Lean parlance. As a result, it was clear that "overburden" and "unevenness"—key ideas along with waste in Lean—resulted from pricing analysts getting lots of pricing approval requests on transactions that ranged from $100 to more than $100,000. As a result, the team was able to suggest recommendations that were implemented right away.

33.4.3.2 *Prioritization*

To narrow the focus on specific steps within the transaction pricing process, the Acme team used a Six Sigma tool called the cause-and-effect (C&E) Matrix to guide discussion. With the help of the Master Black Belt, the project manager held a workshop using the tool to identify problems and put them in order of priority. The rows on the C&E matrix

Table 33.3 Cause-and-effect (C & E) matrix for prioritizing which process steps to focus on, with scores *a–f* reflecting the importance of a step in terms of customer requirements

	Process	Customer requirement, weight w_1	Customer requirement, weight w_2	Total weighted score for step
Step 1	Initial price assessment with customer; customer seeks price exception	a_1	a_2	$a_1 w_1 + a_2 w_2$
Step 2	Request approval to price exception	b_1	b_2	$b_1 w_1 + b_2 w_2$
Step 3	Compile information into a formal quotation	c_1	c_2	$c_1 w_1 + c_2 w_2$
Step 4	Review and analyze quote	d_1	d_2	$d_1 w_1 + d_2 w_2$
Step 5	Communicate price approval to Sales office	e_1	e_2	$e_1 w_1 + e_2 w_2$
Step 6	Submit price to customer	f_1	f_2	$f_1 w_1 + f_2 w_2$

correspond to the six steps in the current process, and the columns list all of the requirements of the customers of each step, each requirement weighted according to how important it is to the customer. For the Acme team, "customers" were senior executives who wanted better controls in, and eventually better price performance from, the pricing process. The impact of each step on the customer requirements is a score that is a table entry, with a total score weighted by the importance of the customer requirement in the last column indicating the priority of the step (Table 33.3).

33.4.3.3 *Process analysis*

The project team did not actually assign number scores to the C&E matrix to prioritize steps. Instead, the team members used the structure of the matrix to focus on possible causes for lack of control at each step. The process diagram was projected as a slide, and team members used a whiteboard to discuss each step in turn. The main findings from this exercise suggested that the defects arose largely from problems in steps 1, 4, and 6, and from failures in reporting.

Step 1: The team found that the ability of the sales representatives to help customers select the right products, and the right features for those products, was critical to managing customers' price expectations. Unfortunately, sales representatives' failure in assessing customer requirements could not be easily detected and controlled.

Step 4: The key constraint here was time; sales representatives sometimes wanted discount approval within hours of forwarding a request, which made it difficult for pricing analysts to work out whether or not the discount was reasonable. Giving Pricing more time for analysis would make it easier to reduce the incidence of defective prices.

Step 6: Sales representatives sometimes offered final prices to customers without prior approval, leaving Pricing with little choice but to approve the price after the fact. The team agreed that such situations should be tracked.

Reporting: Information about transactions was not gathered or presented in a consistent manner. The unit's various functions generated more than a hundred different transaction reports that summarized sales data by product line, market, and other ways at weekly, monthly, or quarterly intervals. Discrepancies and redundancies in those reports led to variability in prices. This meant that managers could neither track pricing defects easily nor obtain the data they needed in time to do adequate due diligence on price quotes (Step 4).

33.4.3.4 Statistical analysis

The project manager did a standard statistical analysis of transaction-level data for all of the individual transactions that occurred in the two years before the project started. He discovered that actual transaction prices were distributed along a bell-shaped curve around the average transaction price, demonstrating the classic problem that Six Sigma targets— that the high rates of defects (in this instance lower-than-approved prices) stem from high variability. Moreover, the price ranges for transactions of different sizes overlapped significantly, suggesting that pricing guidelines were not differentiated enough for different-sized transactions. If the Six Sigma team could reduce the variability of transaction prices, it would address both problems.

In addition, the analysis revealed that salespeople serving certain territories within the same market had a greater tendency than their colleagues in other territories to invoice at prices either significantly higher or lower than approved. The team concluded from this analysis that different pricing guidelines needed to be set not only for different transaction sizes but also for different territories within the same market and possibly even for customer groups. Pricing guidelines had always been market-specific but were not differentiated by transaction sizes, territories, or, for the most part, by customer group.

33.4.4 Improve and control

Recall that the main aim of the project was to recommend modifications to the existing process to decrease the number of unapproved prices but also without creating an onerous approval process. Response speed was critical for salespeople, so they could continue to act quickly and close deals. What the pricing analysts needed, the team concluded, was clear guidelines to help them decide when they should or should not approve any deeper-than-usual discounts that Sales had requested or promised to customers.

Following the Lean analysis in the previous stage, the team recommended that to reduce the "overburden" of the pricing analysts in the number of requests they had to deal with and remove the "unevenness" of the different requests in terms of highly varying transaction size, discount thresholds by transaction size should be established below which the sales representatives would not have to seek pricing approvals. Pricing would get involved only in the larger transactions. These recommendations were immediately implemented as both Pricing and Sales were in agreement. No controls were needed or sought on this improvement. As the number of such small transactions exceeded the number of larger transactions, the workload involved in approving discounts for pricing analysts and sales representatives decreased and the transaction sizes for pricing approval requests became more "even".

33.4.4.1 *Pricing guideline structure*

To simplify and centralize the guideline structure, the team proposed giving product-specific, region-specific, and transaction-size-specific graduated discount approval authority to individuals at three levels: sales representatives or managers, pricing analysts, and the pricing manager. Finally, top executives could continue to approve discounts without any limit. For example, in one particular market, say the south-west region within North America, a sales representative could offer any discount up to 30 percent at his discretion for a transaction size between $100,000 and $150,000. To offer an even lower price to a customer, the sales representative would have to contact a pricing analyst for approval. The pricing analyst would first check against the guideline price for that region, type of product, transaction size, and perhaps other criteria, and use this to negotiate with the sales representative for any further discount, up to a limit of 35 percent. If the sales representative felt that the situation demanded an even lower price than the analyst could authorize, the request would be elevated to the pricing manager, who could approve a discount of up to 40 percent. If the sales representative was going for an even lower price, the request was passed up to a specified group at the top leadership level, which alone could approve a higher discount.

The new distribution of pricing responsibilities required a process for developing, and, from time to time, re-evaluating all discount guidelines and the different floors as per the revised process. To ensure regular updating of these guidelines, the team created a spreadsheet tool that let Pricing work off recent transaction history.

Making both the guidelines and the escalation process clear speeded up the process by making it more efficient. In addition, the pricing organization would now have 24 hours to perform due diligence before approving a price request.

33.4.4.2 *Tracking exceptions*

The graduated discount guideline structure described is not unusual and a similar process already existed at Acme. To control variations better, the project team created exception codes that enabled Acme to track variations in prices relative to guidelines and the stated reasons for the variation. The codes made it clear who had been involved in the decision to deviate from guidelines. For instance, if someone from the leadership had approved a deep discount, the eventual transaction was tagged with a "Leadership Approval" code. If Acme needed to match a competitor's aggressive price, the pricing manager could approve a low price that was tagged with a Competitive Match code. If a sales representative had already promised a price to a customer before getting approval, the transaction would have to be tagged with a Sales Error code. The team also recommended tracking which sales representatives consistently asked for turnarounds that were faster than the now required 24-hour period.

While the new process allowed flexibility to sales representatives in occasionally submitting final prices to customers in the first step, any such deviations would now be tracked. In cases where sales representatives had already offered a customer a price and needed post hoc authorization, the new process required that the rep involve his boss, who would have to e-mail or call Pricing for approval. The price already offered would still be honored, but now representatives could be held more accountable for making unauthorized commitments.

33.4.4.3 *Tracking progress*

Acme set up a monthly "price review" meeting at which executives—mainly the vice-presidents of marketing, sales, and finance, along with their direct reports—looked not only at the company's overall performance and at particular geographic markets and transaction sizes but also at the exception codes to see if the new process is indeed resulting in higher average transaction prices and fewer exceptions without loss of market share. If the company were losing market share, it might be a sign that Acme needs to review pricing guidelines or take a look at how sales representatives are managing their territories.

If the price-review group were to notice that a particular sales representative was frequently making Sales Error transactions, the rep's boss would take a closer look at how the rep was negotiating. And if the review group were to see that transactions of a particular size regularly require the pricing manager's approval, the group could instigate a re-examination of the pricing guidelines for that transaction size.

33.4.5 Results

The initial goal of generating $500,000 in incremental revenues in the first year was handily exceeded in only three months. More important, following a subsequent across-the-board list price increase, the average transaction price for the pilot product went up by slightly more than the list prices; in other words, the increase was fully reflected in the top line. But other product lines realized less than half the increase. That list price increase, together with the tighter controls the Six Sigma team developed and implemented, resulted in $5.8 million in incremental revenues in just the first six months following implementation, all going straight to the bottom line.

From an organizational perspective, the exercise of systematically collecting and analyzing price transaction data has given pricing analysts hard evidence to counter the claims sales staff had typically advanced in negotiating discounts. A frequent claim, for instance, was that "My customers want just as high a percentage discount for a $3,000 transaction as they would get for a $300,000 one." Now that Pricing knows for certain that Acme's customers tend to accept lower discounts on smaller transactions and that some customers are willing to pay higher prices than others, analysts can more easily push back when negotiating price approvals with sales staff. They can respond confidently and authoritatively when sales representatives ask questions like "Why is my authorized price higher than those in another market?" or "How come we don't authorize the same price for all customers?"

Sales representatives at Acme can use the same data to press their own points. It became clear, for example, that some sales offices that had previously been under scrutiny for aggressive pricing practices had in fact been acting reasonably given their local market conditions.

33.5 LIMITATIONS OF LEAN SIX SIGMA PRICING

Six Sigma and Lean can be misrepresented as a cure-all for all management problems just like any other business improvement approach. Goh (2002) has taken a critical look at Six Sigma and highlighted its limitations. Likewise, Lean Six Sigma Pricing needs to be viewed carefully in terms of what it can do and what it cannot do rather than as a panacea for all pricing woes.

First and foremost, Lean Six Sigma Pricing needs top management support to implement and to sustain the changes implemented. Pricing involves multiple functions and top-level direction is needed. However, top managers have changing priorities: once good results have been obtained in even one area of pricing, attention may move on to other pressing matters in the organization and Lean Six Sigma Pricing or other initiatives may suffer.

Lean Six Sigma Pricing aims to improve pricing execution through incremental changes and controls rather than devising completely new processes even when they are warranted. The focus is on step-by-step rigor rather than creativity. If there are many different types of defects, continuous-improvement rigor demands that the changes made initially target only a small subset of these defects so that before-and-after changes can be compared for impact. However, unbridled "creativity" can and does lead to unmitigated disaster in pricing, and the step-by-step approach can be better in general.

Lean Six Sigma Pricing is defensive in that it seeks to decrease pricing defects and thus improve margins rather than seek new opportunities for revenue growth, the aim of senior managers. Still, it is possible that the discipline of carrying out the initial steps of Define, Measure, and Analyze may trigger ideas of brand new business processes to support a new business, or at least bring some discipline to the pricing of new products in existing markets or of existing products in new markets.

Both Six Sigma and Lean rely heavily on customer input to identify problems. However, for improving pricing with Lean Six Sigma Pricing, the "customer" is not the company's customer. Instead, the "customer" here is the company's senior management who are seeking to improve pricing execution and margins. And, senior managers may have different and possibly inconsistent goals unlike an external customer.

Lean and Six Sigma establish quantitative goals at the start of a project, although Six Sigma carries this further by estimating bottom-line benefits in the Define phase. However, when using Lean Six Sigma Pricing, quantitative goals such as an improvement of prices by 0.50 percent points, are hard to devise at the outset. Of course, this may simply be a matter of experience: with multiple projects, concrete goals should become easier to devise.

The focus in Lean Six Sigma Pricing is on the aspects that can be measured rather than on nebulous but troubling areas like inter-department friction. Such friction, or more broadly, clarification of management goals and having incentives that are consistent with these goals, is not the subject matter of continuous improvement through Lean or Six Sigma. Still, a fact-and-measurement-based approach like Lean Six Sigma Pricing can take the attention away from personality conflicts to specific process shortcomings with concrete data and other facts.

More broadly, Lean Six Sigma Pricing does not provide guidance on whether the pricing strategy is misguided or on whether pricing guidelines are too unrealistic—its focus is improving pricing execution. Even Toyota, famed for its Lean Manufacturing or Toyota Production System way, has discovered through its 2009–10 recall that there are problems that cannot be handled with continuous improvement. In pricing, problems are especially challenging because Sales and Marketing may not see eye-to-eye on pricing strategy or on guidelines: disagreements that appear as guideline violations may actually be problems of changing incentives that are not a subject for Lean Six Sigma Pricing.

33.6 SUMMARY AND CONCLUSION

We have described how continuous improvement methodologies that have helped manu-facturing or services can be brought to bear on the improvement of pricing execution by way of Six Sigma and Lean. These two approaches are different due to their different underlying philosophies. The fact that the concepts underlying these approaches span nearly a century underscores their power. Our goal was to show that these approaches can be used for improving pricing execution and we called our adaptation—use of Lean tools but within the Six Sigma framework—Lean Six Sigma Pricing.

We also presented a case study. Companies may benefit from the outcome of this case study as they look for ways to exercise price control without alienating customers. Many companies stay committed to legacy pricing systems, processes, and organizational struc-tures by exercising sporadic control. The benefits, if any, are short-lived often leaving the organization with new problems. These companies can transform the relationship between their Pricing and Sales staffs from adversity to relative harmony by giving them a process for making joint decisions that are aligned with company objectives and based on solid data and analysis.

While Lean Six Sigma Pricing targets pricing execution, we should note that not all pricing challenges pertain to execution: there are also strategic and organizational problems that are best handled at a strategic level rather than an operational one. Indeed, improve-ments in execution by way of Lean Six Sigma Pricing may actually postpone taking the pricing strategy and organization bull by the horns. Still, continuous improvement is what made the Japanese carmakers competitive against their US counterparts in the 1970s and made Motorola successful in the late 1980s. It could be argued that Lean Six Sigma Pricing improves the capability of an organization (Dutta et al. 2003) and is therefore of enough strategic value to be part of its pricing infrastructure (Baker et al. 2010). As such, Lean Six Sigma Pricing as a continuous improvement methodology has a valuable role to play in the complex domain of pricing.

REFERENCES

Baker, W. L., Marn, M. V., and Zawada, C. C. (2010) "Building a Better Pricing Infrastruc-ture", *McKinsey Quarterly* August.

Breyfogle, F. W. III (2003) *Implementing Six Sigma: Smarter solutions using statistical analysis*, 2nd edn. New York: Wiley.

Dutta, S., Zbaracki, M. J., and Bergen, M. (2003) "Pricing Process as a Capability: A resource-based perspective", *Strategic Management Journal* 24: 615–30.

Goh, T. N. (2002) "A Strategic Assessment of Six Sigma", *Quality and Reliability Engineering International* 18: 403–10.

Larson, A. (2003) *Demystifying Six Sigma*, New York: Amacom.

Liker, J. (2004) *The Toyota Way: 14 management principles from the world's greatest manu-facturer*. New York: McGraw-Hill.

Marn, M. V. and Rosiello R. L. (1992) "Managing Price, Gaining profit", *Harvard Business Review* (September–October): 84–93.

Nagle, T. T. and Holden, R. K. (2003) *The Strategy and Tactics of Pricing: A guide to profitable decision-making*, 3rd edn. Englewood Cliffs, NJ: Prentice Hall.

Phillips, R. (2005) *Revenue Management*. Stanford, CA: Stanford University Press.

Pyzdek, T. and Keller, P. (2009) *The Six Sigma Handbook: A complete guide for green belts, black belts, and managers at all levels*, 3rd edn. New York: McGraw Hill.

Simon, H., Bilstein F. B., and Luby, F. (2006) *Manage for Profit not for Market Share: A guide to greater profits in highly contested markets*. Boston, MA: Harvard Business School Press.

Snee, R. D. and Hoerl, R. W. (2005) *Six Sigma Beyond the Factory Floor: Deployment strategies for financial services, health care, and the rest of the real economy*. Upper Saddle River, NJ: Pearson Prentice Hall.

Sodhi, M. and Sodhi, N. (2005) "Six Sigma Pricing", *Harvard Business Review* (May): 135–42.

—— and —— (2008) *Six Sigma Pricing: Improving Pricing Operations to Increase Profits*. London: FT Press.

Stein, A. D., Lancioni, R. A., and Smith, M. F. (2006) "Inter Departmental Price-Setting in Industrial Markets: Organizational Perspectives and Recommendations", *Journal of Professional Pricing*, 131.

Womack, J. P. and Jones, D. T. (2003) *Lean Thinking: Banish waste and create wealth in your corporation*, rev edn. London: Simon and Schuster.

CHAPTER 34

MASTERING YOUR PROFIT DESTINY IN BUSINESS-TO-BUSINESS SETTINGS

THOMAS G. JACOBSON, TIFFANY GILBERT,
MICHELLE MAHONEY, AND TIAGO SALVADOR

He's a man way out there in the blue, riding on a smile and a shoeshine.
Death of a Salesman *by Arthur Miller*

When is the price really the price? Short answer: Almost never.

In business-to-business transactions, pricing decision making continues to be one of the least-understood levers influencing a company's ability to achieve high performance. Regardless of how well the pricing strategy has been crafted and how carefully it has been rolled out to the sales territories, the price comes down to what customers actually agree to pay—that is, what salespeople *allow* their customers to pay.

The challenge is that many sales professionals instinctively resort to price-cutting, discounting, or conceding on terms and conditions when they hear "you are too expensive" or "your competitor will provide this for less", even if the buyer shows no evidence for such claims. The primary motivation of the salesforce is almost always to make the sale—not to sell more profitably. The secondary motivation is usually to develop a good relationship, under the belief that the relationship aspects of the negotiation can be "win–win". Even though intensive training on negotiating tactics has been available for many decades, too few salespeople have the right focus, orientation, or motivation to be able to effectively counter this game of inches.

Improvements in sales compensation, where used, have made some difference, but not enough. Although more compensation plans now include incentives for deal profitability, it is not uncommon for salespeople to justify their actions by saying, "no one ever lost a job for giving a bigger discount...but if we lose the deal, it's a whole other story."

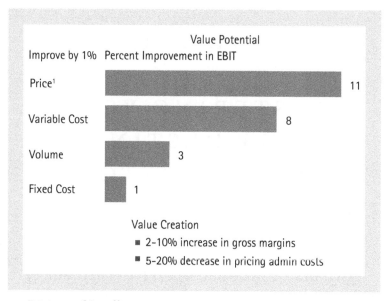

FIGURE 34.1 Pricing and its effect on margins

Note: 1 Represents a 1% increase in price and assumes no loss in volume.

Source: Accenture analysis

The consequences are worrisome. Price is far and away a company's single-biggest driver of profitability; for many businesses, a 1 percent increase in average prices lifts operating profits by anywhere from 7 percent to 15 percent, as shown in Figure 34.1. Yet salespeople may relinquish as much as 15 percent on price if management fails to set tight boundaries. Even when management *does* set strict pricing guidelines, some sales professionals will concede more. The erosion can be evident in what are often thought of as innocuous selling traditions, such as rounding down on price on the customer quote or even on the price sheet.

Furthermore, failure to adhere to the pricing strategy and structured negotiating framework means an outright waste of investments in sales training and development and support of the product's brand, if not of the corporate brand. It squanders investments in service quality in retail outlets. And it undercuts development of the price strategy and pricing processes in the first place.

Given these potentially debilitating impacts, it is important to re-energize the discussion of negotiation and sales effectiveness. The point at which the seller sits down with the buyer is the moment of truth when many of the pricing factors discussed in this book come together. The most sophisticated price optimization models mean little if they are not manifested in the decisions made by salespeople every day. Furthermore, no literature about negotiation can be conclusive if it does not address the concept of pricing *with confidence*.

Although the past few decades have seen a tremendous body of work on negotiation—from sources such as the Harvard Negotiation Project and Oxford University's Programme on Negotiation—the emphasis has been on creating an environment that aligns value and price. Such sources have coached professionals to remain unconditionally constructive—to consider the participants as amicable problem solvers rather than adversaries (see, e.g., Fisher and Ury 1991).

However, sellers have had only limited visibility into how procurement teams are gaining strength at the negotiating table. Procurement professionals have been steadily amassing a rich repertoire of capabilities that help them understand what motivates sales teams and that allow them to deploy psychological, organizational, and even theatrical negotiating tactics. In pricing negotiation, the balance has increasingly shifted in favor of procurement. It has thus become essential for sellers to add new negotiating skills.

In fact, procurement teams have been schooled not only to understand a seller's unconditionally constructive stance, but also to hold firm with what some term a "professionally adversarial" approach. The mismatch regularly works in the buyer's favor. Indeed, we regularly hear from procurement teams that buyers persist with an adversarial approach because it works so well with sales negotiators who want to "close at all costs".

We seek to restore the balance of power. A constructive stance should include the possibility—indeed, the likelihood—of conflict. Only when conflict is openly acknowledged can the opposing parties deal with the underlying issues and come to agreement more quickly.

This chapter explores what undermines sellers' confidence, with an emphasis on procurement's power, and on the common problems with seller–buyer relationships. We review what is needed to restore confidence to the point where the seller not only closes the sale but is able to capture the extra couple of points of revenue that generate large profit improvements. Specifically, we highlight three areas that can help create an environment that encourages sales professionals to work through conflict without unnecessarily giving in to all of procurement's demands. The focus throughout is on large, complex business-to-business sales—whether products, services, or a mix—rather than simpler or routine transactions such as those involving parts replenishment or retail restocking. There is no "silver bullet" to getting fair compensation for value delivered, but there are clear payoffs to raising awareness about confident pricing.

Confident pricing starts with foundational negotiation skills, including those taught in university and commercial courses. It also includes an understanding of negotiating differences among various customer segments, so that sellers can anticipate the most likely responses and how customers will make tradeoffs—all of which affects pricing elasticity.

From there, confident pricing is built by addressing the fact that sellers' negotiation weaknesses are largely systemic; there is little in the typical company's organizational infrastructure to hold salespeople accountable for capturing the last percentage point on price. An analogy in the real estate sector: Sellers often find their broker will settle for a lower price than they might find desirable because the realtor's share of the *increment* in selling price is outweighed by the real costs of further marketing of the property as well as the opportunity cost of moving quickly to another sale.

Confident pricing is also a function of other factors, where the company is in the economic cycle and within its geographic markets; and where along the product lifecycle, as new products will have different value propositions than those being phased out. Negotiating styles that work when markets are buoyant and demand is robust are unlikely to be effective during a recession. If the sellers cannot identify their company's place in the economic cycle, they will lose leverage, because they are unlikely to be able to say with certainty what overall demand patterns look like or what is their company's current and planned capacity.

The necessary responses also include a clear-eyed, dispassionate perspective of the psychological and organizational aspects of negotiating. While there is, of course, a rational aspect to negotiating price—it is reasonable to use price to stimulate or shape demand—a host of other factors come into play. In hard economic times, for instance, sellers may feel under great pressure to close deals or lose their jobs. Rebuilding real confidence in pricing is not a simple matter. So let's begin to give meaning to that task by describing procurement's growing strength.

34.1 PROCUREMENT'S NEW MUSCLE

In the battle between suppliers' sales teams and customers' procurement professionals, the latter have been steadily gaining skills and influence over the last few decades. In fact, procurement departments are often better trained to disrupt sellers' pricing strategies than sellers are prepared to exert those strategies.

Procurement has moved beyond a largely clerical task to a more important, often strategic, role in many companies. Buyers don't simply procure materials and components for goods sold; today, they have wide spans of control over indirect spending on everything from office equipment and electricity use to travel and outsourcing services. A report by executive recruiting company, Spencer Stuart, notes that the role of the chief procurement officer (CPO)—relatively recent in itself—has become completely strategic, controlling the majority of the total cost of sales and deeply involved in long-term planning of new business models, with a strong emphasis on the demand side of the supply chain (Spencer Stuart 2009).

This change coincides with marketplace recognition that supply chain performance is directly tied to a company's overall success; for example, Accenture's High Performance Business Research demonstrates the business impact of procurement and supply chain excellence. Given ongoing market complexities and companies' need to be agile, chief procurement officers will likely continue to gain influence.

Shelley Stewart, Jr. exemplifies the leverage of the new breed of chief procurement officer. As chief procurement officer of Tyco International, Ltd., he reportedly manages $13 billion in procurement spend. But he is also the conglomerate's senior vice-president of operational excellence, leading the cross-divisional teams whose job is to reduce costs and boost efficiency company-wide and heading the company's Six Sigma, lean manufacturing, information technology, working capital, real estate, and supply chain initiatives. Stewart is also responsible for some $600 million in IT spending.[1]

Increasingly, chief procurement officers are reporting directly to CEOs—and more boards are appointing directors with strong supply chain backgrounds. Chiquita Brands

---

[1] http://www.ism.ws/about/MediaRoom/newsreleasedetail.cfm?ItemNumber=21593 and http://www.mbnusa.biz/articles.php?aid=084af6d072-20091109172854&CatID=12&SubCatD=2.

International, Inc., for instance, named Bill Camp as a director, a 30-year veteran of the agricultural processing value chain. Many new supply chain leaders have had comprehensive profit-and-loss experience, running their own business units or product lines. Indeed, there is empirical evidence to show that many new Masters of Business Administration (MBAs) are targeting supply chain and procurement roles in industrial companies.

In tandem with procurement's growing strength, professional associations such as the Institute for Supply Management (ISM) and the Council of Supply Chain Management Professionals (CSCMP) now offer many more negotiation courses, workshops, and levels of professional certification. Partner organizations such as ADR North America advise on tactical negotiations, focusing on specific skills such as "questioning for control" and mastering the use of "agreement staircases".

Excellence in negotiation has long been a staple of the purchasing skills portfolio. For many years, negotiation experts wrote a lively column in the *Journal of Purchasing*; today, the journal runs a column titled "Black Belt Negotiators" that celebrates a negotiating "win" by a procurement team. The editors regularly invite readers to submit examples of excellence in negotiations. A good procurement group uses multiple approaches at different times for different product types and business needs—everything from hardball price-focused tactics that concentrate on price or emphasize urgency to total-value approaches and amicable tactics based on long-term collaboration. There is no shortage of approaches, but five in particular are in wide use:

- *The hard case.* Buyers who favor this approach are trying to dominate the discussion—to dictate "take it or leave it" rather than negotiate. They are strict price list advocates whose default is to reject any price or cost factors advanced by the seller. They can come across as aloof at best and hostile at worst.

- *The total value case.* These buyers express concern about the overall value presented. Their total-cost approach digs for as much detail as possible—for example, on how value will be measured—to gain an advantage for negotiation. Generally professionally trained in negotiation, these buyers are relatively open to different ideas and approaches. They want abundant detail about, for example, what is behind the cost, what the seller's profit margins are, and sources of markups. Such buyers want to have a start-to-finish understanding about the business so that they can gain a position of strength.

- *The friendly case.* Friendly buyers generally want to (or profess to want to) know about you personally and appear eager to build a positive and lasting relationship. They lead conversations along different tangents and will press for details. They want to know what can be done for them personally—anything that can "help them out."

- *The cost case.* The unwavering focus of these buyers is the cost to the business. New ideas and potential future opportunities to save money are of no interest to them. They regularly argue that the seller's prices are too high.

- *The urgent case.* The ploy in this case is the request for "something" right now. This approach, where everything is deemed to be urgent, is used to keep the seller off balance. A favorite device is to request a number while insisting "the buyer won't hold you to it".

Procurement professionals routinely use these tactics because they tend to be effective, regardless of the true competitive reality or the likelihood that buyers are willing to pay more.

Importantly, much of the edge of today's professional procurement specialists comes not only from their higher education and levels of certification, but from their broader access to information on costs and stronger analytical abilities. It is increasingly common for procurement professionals to interact closely with their peers in the finance department to develop more complete cost pictures, to more closely control costs, and to project future savings. "To maximize the business benefits that can be achieved with procurement and supply management...your supply-management organization cannot work alone," Robert Rudzki, former CPO of Bayer Corp., told *CFO* magazine. "Finance is often the most important internal 'partner' with the procurement or supply-management organization" (Rudzki 2009).

Procurement professionals benefit from an arsenal of software tools that are designed to help them improve their effectiveness. Sales and operations-planning tools have been particularly useful for arriving at the negotiating table with a wealth of data about demand and production scheduling and with a range of options already sketched out. Widely available global trade-management tools allow purchasers to squeeze new efficiencies out of what has been referred to as the "financial supply chain"—the trail of everything from requests for proposal and letters of credit to purchase orders and bank confirmation records.

Procurement spend analysis is also emerging as a valuable solution for reining in maverick spending. Companies that apply spend analysis can save up to 40 percent more than those that do not, according to a report from Aberdeen Group. Aberdeen encourages companies to directly apply spend analysis results in strategic-sourcing initiatives, to tightly link spend analysis systems with contract lifecycle management and e-procurement systems, and to use web-based reporting and dashboards to track key spending and savings metrics (Aberdeen Group 2008).

Third-party procurement advisors add further complexity to any sales negotiation. In larger sales, and in particular in situations in which the product may be a complicated mix of, say, equipment, aftermarket parts and a range of services, it is increasingly common to see independent consultants brought in for their experience in negotiation or their familiarity with the types of offerings available.

Procurement professionals create additional headaches for sellers when they use auctions. E-auctions have become another weapon in the buyer's arsenal, adding complexity, driving unhealthy levels of internal negotiations at the seller, and forcing uncomfortable decisions about whether or not to participate in the e-auction.

34.2 THE PROBLEM WITH RELATIONSHIPS

Part of the problem for sellers on the front lines of negotiation is that they can become confused about the role of "the relationship"—a charged term if ever there was one. Macro factors such as globalization exacerbate the challenge; that is, sellers have an emotional disadvantage when coming to negotiations expecting a relationship, but the procurement team is only interested in a transaction.

In the midst of difficult negotiations, and under pressure to close the sale, many salespeople misconstrue the role of being customer-focused and allow the relationship to become a lever that the buyer can use to extract an unjustified concession: "Come on, it's only $22,000. Can't you do it for free, *for the good of the relationship*?" Such a request signals something is wrong: Two starkly different perceptions of a "good" relationship are at play. Conceding without a reciprocal commitment—effectively trying to buy one's way into a relationship—puts the seller's interests at risk and signals the buyer's true perspective. Such strategies simply establish bad precedents that may escalate into requests for larger favors in the future.

So can there ever be a good relationship with a customer—one in which there is openness and honesty about the value of the relationship to each side? And, does a good relationship really matter anyway? The answers are "yes" and "yes". It matters because, by definition, a good relationship means efficient interactions and consistent, repeated wins for both sides. When transactions were the order of the day and total costs were not well understood, relationships mattered less. But today, three factors make relationships more important:

- More customers have been anxious to pare their supplier rosters in order to reduce their operating costs. Many have calculated the actual total costs of running supplier evaluations, issuing and responding to requests for proposals, managing purchase order variables, and dealing with different business processes—all of the moving parts for which cumulative costs can soon outweigh the advantages of having a diverse supplier base. As the focus has shifted to working with fewer suppliers, it has become more important to forge long-lasting relationships with them—in effect, to treat more suppliers as preferred suppliers.

- The trend to outsource business processes deemed to be non-core—third-party logistics or payroll processing, for instance—has required deeper relationships. Many companies now characterize and even define some of those relationships as "partnerships".

- More businesses that have long made tangible products now sell services as well. A classic example is jet engine maker Rolls Royce, which now derives a substantial portion of its revenues and much of its growth from servicing those engines. Selling services, of course, is much less transaction-oriented than selling products.

In fact, there are now more and more situations in which the ability to build and maintain relationships can be a winning element in a competitive bid. Where procurement professionals wield the relationship as a bargaining chip—perhaps encouraging the seller to compensate for alleged past difficulties by agreeing to its proposed terms for the sake of the relationship—skilled sales negotiators work to separate the substance from the relationship, and they deal with each on its merits. Every negotiator must juggle two balls at once: the substance of good deal terms and the relationship, which involves addressing differences. The challenge is to devise a strategy where you get both a good deal and a good working relationship (see Figure 34.2).

To build the kind of relationship the seller wants, one must first understand the kind of relationship that exists. An honest assessment is essential. If the seller feels that the buyer is—intentionally or unintentionally—confusing substance with relationship, it is time to evaluate how the parties communicate and deal with their differences. You can have a strong transactional relationship, but it's important to understand that it *is* mainly transactional. It's also possible to have a long-term relationship that has a detrimental effect on your ability to negotiate pricing.

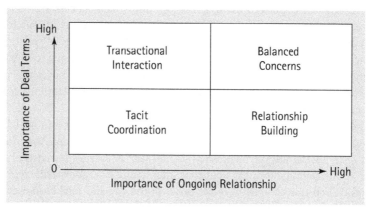

FIGURE 34.2 A framework for picking a negotiation strategy

Once a relationship has been evaluated, it's useful to determine the nature of the relationship—whether it leans toward a true partnership or toward a "master/servant" link in which the customer acts as the dominant partner, with the supplier expected to comply. The primary questions to ask are these: What is the history between the parties? Has either side acted in ways that could be construed as being difficult to do business with? How committed is the other party? Does he or she have the appropriate budget or resources allocated for the proposed work? Does the other party show a willingness to work with you?

If the customer has proven it is committed to the current relationship, the relationship will probably continue to prosper. However, if the customer has already shown untrustworthy behavior coupled with empty promises, why would its behavior change in the future? Likewise, why would the customer alter behavior if the sellers have shown that they will accept it? If the results of these efforts reveal that the buyer really is not particularly interested in mutuality and does not view the seller as a potential business partner, the seller can take steps to try to salvage a relationship.

In business-to-business environments, the seller–buyer relationship is not limited to one individual from each side; the buyer's team may include evaluators, technical buyers, procurement professionals, key influencers, business customers, and others. It is important to identify and build a special relationship with the "value champion" on the buying team—the person who has some ownership of the outcome, who understands the business needs and understands the value that the seller's offer can add to the company.

Because the value champion supports the project in principle and is well placed to get others to agree to the value that the project will deliver, it is crucial to find and engage that person and to deeply understand his or her perspective. If the supplier does not do this before sitting down with the customer's procurement team, a struggle over pricing is almost guaranteed regardless of quality and differentiation.

The seller must confirm, early on, that the value champion is in fact an influencer and ideally a powerful one for the deal at hand—just because that person was the value champion for other work does not mean that person is right for all subsequent work. It is easy to become friendly with a particular value champion, which means it is easy to make the wrong choice about the right person later on.

Finally, once the right champion has been identified, it is necessary to figure out the best way to work with him or her. Value champions may fall into one of several categories, which we've characterized for illustrative purposes here. Each category has its strengths and weaknesses: the assertive but potentially less-experienced person who wants to ignore the details and get started right away; the fearful person who contends that the new proposition won't work but who can be very useful once he or she is persuaded of the proposition's value; and the skeptical person who argues that the proposition didn't "fly" before, so it won't work now. Paradoxically, this last category of skeptics can yield some of the best value champions because they weigh the risks, take the time to research, analyze and understand, which can lead to their fully supporting the work at hand.

34.3 THE RELEVANCE OF TRADITIONAL NEGOTIATING APPROACHES

Regardless of the duration or type of the relationship, the basics of sound negotiating always apply. Five negotiating practices should be considered prerequisites for continually pricing with confidence.

1. *Remain unconditionally constructive.* There are two goals to any negotiation—a good agreement in the current negotiation and improved relations to facilitate the current discussions and potential future negotiations. A joint problem-solving negotiation process that improves the relationship is more likely to resolve disagreements quickly and amicably than one that creates tension and suspicion.

   The key is to remain unconditionally constructive. Admittedly, this can be difficult to master in the face of hostility. It calls for actively promoting understanding; the salesperson's willingness to hear the buyer's input underscores his commitment to a mutually beneficial relationship. The seller also has to accept the buyer's concerns as worthy of his consideration, even when he and his concerns are dismissed or devalued by the buyer. It is essential to remain rational even if the buyer acts emotionally or steps over the line. At the same time, the seller must be consistently reliable and trustworthy regardless of the trustworthiness demonstrated by the other side. And the seller must never use coercive behavior, even if the buyer uses it regularly.

2. *Focus on strategic interests.* The second fundamental of negotiating is to stay focused on strategic interests. The goal of every negotiation is to create value for the customer and for the supplier by crafting a deal that satisfies both sides' core interests. Understanding a customer's interests can challenge even the best negotiators. The customer can be reluctant to share information for fear of giving up leverage, or their negotiator may simply not have the information. Typically, buyers will obscure their core interests by emphasizing their positions—their statements of what they say they will or will not do.

   Positions can appear irreconcilable; they certainly can obstruct understanding. Consider the case of a buyer who expresses concern that a supplier's solution may not work properly. He may take the position that the supplier accepts "unlimited liability". They want a sufficient remedy, and they want to ensure that the supplier is properly motivated. Although that is the position, the underlying interest is to make sure the solution works before it goes into production. A skilled negotiator would base the compromise on that interest and focus on the solution working, not on what happens if it fails. The negotiator might suggest detailed acceptance testing and a warranty, which would enhance the probability of success, instead of increasing the limitation of liability, which rarely improves that probability.

3. *Maximize legitimacy*. Each side must be able to measure a deal's success. Both need standards of fairness—or legitimacy—as a foundation for agreement. Legitimacy matters because negotiations can end with one party feeling exploited and reluctant to negotiate with the other party again.

   Simply put, the seller must explain why a proposed agreement is fair, appropriate, or justifiable. Instead of making each negotiation a contest of wills, the seller must reference its principles as legitimate criteria or benchmarks that a disinterested third party could endorse. Rather than haggle over somewhat arbitrary positions, both parties can discuss which objective standards apply best to a particular negotiation and how they should be applied. Because neither party has backed down to the will of the other, negotiators find it easier to accept and justify to others terms based on such discussions.

4. *Create value by being firm but flexible*. In any negotiation, both sides can almost always find a range of potentially acceptable solutions. Skilled negotiators recognize the value of designing a solution that costs one side as little as possible while benefiting the other side as much as possible. It is important to understand how best to work within a "zone of possible agreement". Some sales negotiators, pressed by time constraints and worried about losing the deal, may be tempted to agree to the first proposal that falls within an agreed-upon zone. In the spirit of being flexible and cooperative—in the bid to build a good relationship—they may try to accommodate each of the customer's concerns. However, the best approach is to avoid agreeing to the first minimally acceptable proposal. Negotiators should firmly seek and create options that will be more satisfying to one party's interests without decreasing the other's satisfaction.

5. *Create a clear choice—"commercially viable" or "willing to walk"*. Sales negotiators have to evaluate whether the proposed deal structure meets their company's interests or whether the company would be better off walking away. However, they must also be able to rely on their company's management team to support good decisions to walk away from bad deals.

   The concept of the "best alternative to negotiated agreement" (BATNA)—developed by the Harvard Negotiation Project—is helpful here. Having carefully thought through the BATNA—what one party would do if it walked away from the negotiation with no agreement—ensures that rigorous qualification and decision making is applied to every deal. Skilled sales negotiators know that any deal reached must be better than their best alternative. BATNA applies to consumer markets as well. A buyer whose heart is set on a high-end, electric-drive sports car has few alternatives to a Tesla Roadster, whereas the same buyer looking for a standard sedan for his daughter has a wealth of choices.

34.4 Toward mastering your profit destiny

The five fundamentals discussed above stand as prerequisite skills for any significant business-to-business negotiation. However, collectively as well as individually, they do not prevent the price leakage that stems from a lack of confidence on the part of the seller. The tools of procurement's trade are powerful in their simplicity, but devastating to the sales professional—demands for a 15 percent volume discount, say, or a declaration that the seller is 30 percent more expensive than a key competitor.

The ability to hold firm on a seller's price calls for an understanding of the value of the offering at any point in an economic cycle and for an ability to think in terms of narrowing the customer focus and fine-tuning the product mix. How does a company create an environment that promotes confident price negotiation and alleviates negotiating pressure? Improving capabilities in the following areas will allow sellers to work through conflict instead of routinely accommodating buyers' demands.

34.4.1 Understanding and embracing the 1 percent principle

Even a 1 percent increase in price can have a significant impact on the bottom line, and typically, 1 percent does not impact the win/loss ratio. This concept works both ways, so a 1 percent decrease in price can be detrimental. Educating a salesforce about the collective impact of its actions is just one of many actions that can help alleviate price-diminishing behaviors.

One large industrial services company used a pricing model to determine prices for its offerings. But its sales teams had a practice—unstated, of course—of rounding their quotes down to the nearest whole amount. This rounding-down process had nearly a 7 percent impact on pre-tax income—before the salespeople began actively negotiating with the customer. By educating its sales teams about the bottom-line impact of rounding down, the company was able to modify the teams' behavior and improve its profitability.

Lack of awareness of the 1 percent principle surfaces in other ways—for example, in the tendency of many salespeople to "split the difference" to come to terms with a customer. The deal may close, but at what price? Another example is the "giveaway"—a complimentary product or an add-on service that is provided *gratis*, which typically has a negative impact on the bottom line.

Sales teams that understand the 1 percent principle are far more likely to embody the confidence necessary for difficult and protracted negotiations and to seek out the easy wins for their company rather than easy ways out of a challenging discussion with procurement. Going into negotiations, every salesperson should be looking for the flat spot on the pricing curve—the 1 percent to 2 percent that they can work on without affecting their ability to close the sale (see Figure 34.3).

The linkage between price and volume needs to be made clear. Based on the history and understanding of customers, sellers should be able to identify the points at which they can increase price without it affecting their ability to close the sale.

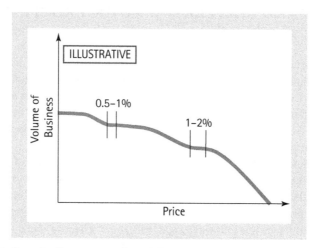

FIGURE 34.3 Finding the flat spot on the pricing curve

Note: Assumes a distinct relationship between price and volume exists.

34.4.2 Maximizing pricing levers

Negotiation concessions such as splitting the difference and rounding down may not be noticed at the level of the individual deal, but when magnified across hundreds of deals, the cumulative negative financial impact can be substantial.

Terms and conditions are another area where little concessions accumulate to become big givebacks. Consider the case of the industrial services company that had engineered its early-pay discounts so effectively that every customer took that option. Instead of the normal 30-day payment terms, the company offered discounts if customers paid in 14 or 15 days. Although the industrial firm certainly saw some benefits from the cash-flow perspective, the early-pay plan's impact resulted in a 33 percent operating loss.

Be leery of volume discounts, a negotiation ploy that can be challenging since little is done to ensure that purchasing promises are kept. Making discount concessions on the basis of potential volume purchases can be seemingly harmless, but if not coupled with assurances of predictable volume, the results can be crippling. True savings can only be passed on to the buyer in situations where the buyer is purchasing predictable and profitable volume.

The key is for sales teams to understand the context of the buyer's request in order to separate theatrics and idle threats from realistic, meaningful requests. When preparing for a negotiation, the seller is trying to preserve volume and improve or at least to preserve profit. The seller should use the negotiation as an opportunity to change the customer's buying behavior by addressing the components that have been eroding margin and ensuring that the resulting agreement allows the seller to measure and see when the situation changes.

Consider a price discount request. The ultimate goal in the negotiation process is to change the momentum of the discussion away from a pure pricing exercise. Sellers should follow a simple step-by-step process to achieve this goal.

The first step is to resist the immediate reflex to react to the price discount request. Instead, listen to the buyers' request and make sure buyers are well informed about why they are making the request in the first place. Essentially, the seller should want to commit to a partnership with the buyers—not simply a "we'll give you everything you ask for" relationship.

The next step is to seek to understand and subsequently respond to the request. It is crucial to find out what is driving the request: Is it driven by the budget or mandated by corporate management? Does the request apply to all departments, projects, and vendors? The seller should try to determine the various potential outcomes if the seller were to agree to the buyer's request. If the customer put a halt to the project, how would it impact its operations? Will the customer share the imposed project burdens? What is the BATNA?

With an understanding of where the request is coming from, the seller can then preempt the customer's requests by building a top-down view. For example, it is good practice to identify a value champion for the deal and to refresh the business case to remind the buyer of the value of the project. A contingency plan is very useful to prepare for situations where, say, the customer requests an additional discount or where it is critical to have a clear picture of the customer's current financial situation. A good contingency plan will tease out answers to all the right questions: What is the seller's profitability on the deal? What will a discount mean to the seller's profitability and to future negotiations, since the discount is setting a precedent?

At this point, it is appropriate to explore potential pricing levers to pull when responding to the buyer's request. Consider factors such as the resource intensity on the project, modified payment structures or schedules and the terms and conditions required to meet mutual objectives. Price is tightly linked with terms and conditions, of course; in most cases, a price assumes certain terms such as a standard delivery window or the use of particular resources.

Finally, sellers must work on structuring their responses to the buyers so they can arrive at mutually beneficial decisions. How will they develop an ongoing "give–get" relationship? How will they change the discussion from a one-sided price mandate to a shared effort? How can there be any certainty that decisions made now will not hurt future profitability? The objective of structuring responses to such questions is to get the customer to under-stand—and agree—to an outcome that is much closer to the seller's stance while main-taining mutual benefit.

These levers will change according to the nature of the company's industry and the products and/or services provided. By encouraging deal teams to be less reactive, to plan for each scenario, to lay out contingency plans and to educate salespeople on the implications of these negotiating considerations, companies can modify not only selling behavior, but also improve profitability.

34.4.3 Controlling the behaviors that destroy confidence

Experienced salespeople are familiar with buyers' standard ploys—everything from threats that "if you don't do it our way, we will exclude you from the bid" to demands for volume discounts and extensions of payment terms and favored treatment "since we're a big

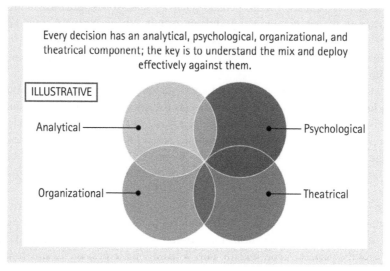

Every decision has an analytical, psychological, organizational, and theatrical component; the key is to understand the mix and deploy effectively against them.

ILLUSTRATIVE

Analytical

Psychological

Organizational

Theatrical

FIGURE 34.4 Pricing spheres of influence

customer". However, not all salespeople respond in the same ways to those tactics. Some will be spooked into early concessions.

Expert sales negotiators hold firm not just because they exhibit the confidence born of deep preparation, practiced use of the five fundamentals and their innate drive, but also because they grasp the differences between the analytic, psychological, organizational, and theatrical aspects of negotiating (see Figure 34.4).

Few human interactions are wholly analytic, yet sellers spend the vast majority of their efforts on the rational aspects of their value propositions. Most skilled procurement teams excel at using seemingly rational stances to disguise psychological or organizational tactics. They may deliberately choreograph the outcomes they want, planning and rehearsing theatrical responses to induce angst in the seller. In one case, a procurement group changed the room assigned for the negotiation at the last moment. When the supplier's team found the new room, they were asked why they were late. In other situations, buyers impose conditions that elicit emotional and often overhasty responses—for example, by insisting that payment terms are stretched from 30 days to 60 or even 120 as a precondition of being included in the bid. Other buyers enforce reverse auctions, knowing that the subsequent long pre-bid negotiating cycles will bring early concessions from sellers.

It is important for the supplier's sales leadership to examine their company's behavioral landscape as well as that of the customer. Does the seller's company have a reputation for being collaborative? Is it usually the first party to mention pricing? How willing are our salespeople to say "no"? Do we have a negative reputation for a "no–no–yes" pattern of negotiation? Do our sellers radiate calm and reason, or do we have hotheads who rise to the emotional bait offered by buyers?

At the same time, sales leaders must equip their sales teams with the means to assess the behavioral landscapes of their customers and prospects. Behavioral elements, such as anticipating a response to good cop/bad cop tactics, should be as much a part of the preparation as discovery of the customer's financial status and supplier options.

A seller's recognition and rewards plans need to align to the pricing strategy and not send conflicting messages to the field. If, for example, there is acceptance of "win at any cost" deals, then confidence at the negotiation table is compromised. If the selection criteria for who wins the Mediterranean cruise are based on volume alone, without looking at profitability, salespeople are less likely to have confidence in negotiating price and more likely to be driven by simply closing the deal.

Clearly, compensation incentives must align with firmly established pricing targets, roles, and alternatives while recognizing precedent-setting behaviors. If the right metrics are in place to measure price and profitability, salesforce behavior will shift to a focus on incremental price positions and relentlessly qualify their prospects based on price, not just on the likelihood of winning the deal.

Sales *reporting* also needs an upgrade, since people deliver on what they're measured against. The vast majority of final reporting today highlights factors such as cost but not price performance. One can change sales compensation structures, beef up training and so on, but if a firm does not also enhance the visibility of price performance in reporting and give it the same visibility as cost issues or market share factors, price performance will be hard to enforce.

34.4.4 Improving the balance of resources and skills

Restoring confidence also involves ensuring a more even match between buyer and seller. As discussed earlier, procurement teams have made great progress in recent decades, acquiring skills and leverage that eclipse those of many suppliers' teams. To redress this imbalance, it is necessary not only to augment suppliers' skills in negotiation and solution selling, but also to ensure that the right teams are fielded for the negotiation situations encountered. Further, the sales organization must have all of the appropriate pricing capabilities, including the metrics and incentives that support the right skills.

What are the right skills? At a minimum, sales leaders must ensure that their teams understand the pricing strategy of the company or business unit, that they are deeply knowledgeable about the product and its market environment, and that they have mastered the five negotiation fundamentals. Beyond that, sales executives must acknowledge the variations in negotiating circumstances and in the skill levels required for each.

Clearly, not all negotiations are marked by fierce confrontation. By the same token, no two salespeople have identical performance characteristics. Individuals who sell exactly the same product can produce drastically different pricing results despite being compensated in the same manner and having equal access to the same selling tools. Some sellers have the fire in the belly, an innate ease with conflict situations—in fact, they have fun when the pressure is on. Those who don't will never have the confidence necessary to deal with the most contentious negotiations, regardless of how well they understand the five fundamentals or how well they grasp the 1 percent principle.

Raising the overall skills of a salesforce in handling complicated pricing negotiations should be a high priority. World-class price negotiators probably make up no more than 15 percent of a typical team; these standouts should be identified, coached, and deployed as a specialized team that is fully equipped to handle some of the biggest and potentially most challenging pricing opportunities.

Thus, sales leaders must take stock of the core skills of all those who are most likely to have to negotiate directly, using metrics and formal assessment techniques to monitor and track skill levels over time and across different negotiation circumstances. How well does the selling team grasp the overall pricing strategy? How does it score against the company's benchmarks on the five negotiation fundamentals? How clear is it about the company's BATNA? How do the team members demonstrate that they understand and regularly apply the 1 percent principle? How suited are they to team selling situations? Where the assessment reveals that skills fall short of what is needed to fulfill the pricing strategy—skills that will vary according to the intensity of the negotiating situation—sales leadership must invest in appropriate training—from self-paced instruction to role-playing sessions.

All of the mechanisms that make for a premier learning environment—from easy reuse and sharing of learning content, to integration of training with a skills database, to the use of workflows to automate the administration of training tasks—must be deployed in the sales training program. Sales leaders must also rethink performance evaluation systems and sales compensation structures to achieve the proper tradeoffs between volume and profitability. And they should ensure that their regional and other mid-level managers are held accountable for recruiting, training, managing, and retaining salespeople who embody the principles of pricing with confidence.

Redressing the imbalance of negotiating capabilities also calls for better market tracking and analysis of supply–demand patterns. Currently, market-tracking efforts at many organizations suffer from limited resources, flawed processes, and substandard or non-existent technology solutions that can facilitate price tracking, monitoring, and prediction.

At the same time, adjustments to list price can be highly complex, requiring multiple checkpoints and approvals. Sales teams often lack the capabilities to grasp the subtleties of balancing supply and demand—crucial information for confident negotiating. With only limited knowledge of industry supply and demand constraints, they cannot predict price fluctuations. They don't have sufficient data or resources to analyze industry cost curves and assess marginal economics.

Redressing the imbalance of negotiating capabilities becomes all the more important in a multi-polar world, where old assumptions about the developing world no longer apply. Increasingly, globalization puts sellers in front of buyers from cultures quite unlike their own. In Japan, there is no "no", while the word "yes" translates to "I heard you" or "I understand you", rather than inferring agreement. In China, a common response is to indicate "no problem", leaving in question whether the speaker agrees or disagrees.

A buyer from another culture is quite often the product of the style of behavior accepted as the norm in his or her culture. National stereotypes often do bear out: The British may appear quite formal. French negotiators tend to be process oriented. Italians may consider themselves the best bargain hunters. Importantly, while many will adapt their culturally shaped negotiating styles in specific one-to-one situations, few will veer from their cultural norms in front of colleagues of the same nationality.

Less well understood is the degree to which aggressive buyers from other nations will use cultural disparities as part of their negotiating tactics. In some places, it is not unheard of for procurement teams that are conversant in the seller's language to minimize their proficiency—and then express frustration that the seller did not bring a translator. Buyers may also use foreigners' desire to negotiate in their culture as a form of theater—essentially exploiting the urge to build good relationships.

34.5 Summary

The hard truth is that most companies fail to generate the levels of revenue and the profitability that their pricing strategies and pricing processes ought to deliver. Because price is indisputably a company's biggest driver of profitability, it is incumbent on business leaders to ensure not only that their sales teams and sales management structures are armed with conventional best practices in negotiation, but also that they are truly able to price with confidence.

Carefully crafted pricing strategies and diligently managed pricing processes will take financial performance only so far. At the end of the quarter and the end of the year, the top and bottom lines are still dependent, to a large degree, on what the sales teams allow their customers to pay.

This chapter has laid out reasons why so many capable salespeople today fall short of their potential to deliver more value for their organizations. It has described current best practices in negotiating strategy and tactics, and then extended those practices to focus specifically on the issue of confident pricing, offering guidelines that can help sales professionals work through conflict without yielding to procurement's demands.

Sellers should also take advantage of advances in technology, particularly information search and data analytics, to prepare for negotiations. Web-based research, for instance, can give sellers greater visibility into tradeoffs, terms and conditions, and the buyer's priorities. In addition, technology allows a company to gather more data about a buyer's spending history with the firm, across geographies or business units. To the extent that better data and analytics go beyond guesswork, technology can be a force for raising one's level of confidence.

Technology is changing sales negotiations in ways that are not fully understood, especially through on-line auctions. We urge researchers to explore the role of e-auctions, specifically by examining: How pervasive are they? Where are they most prevalent—by industry and by types of good and service? How do they benefit both buyers and sellers, and what are the drawbacks?

Technological change, however, does not undercut the best practices and principles described here. By adhering to these principles and focusing squarely on behavioral change, sales teams can produce substantial improvements in profits and help their organizations in the quest for high performance.

References

Aberdeen Group (2008) "With tough times ahead, procurement leaders go 'back to basics' and save more by performing spend analysis", press release, November 12.

Berg, M. B. and Billington, C. (May 1, 2008) "Supply chain attracting—and rewarding—MBAs," *Supply Chain Management Review*, http://www.highbeam.com/doc/1G1-179568968.html.

Fisher, R. and Ury, W. (1991) *Getting to Yes—Negotiating Agreement Without Giving In*, Harvard Program on Negotiation (PON). New York: Penguin Books.

Rudzki, R. (2006) "Adding value where it matters", *CFO* magazine January.

Spencer Stuart (2009) "The rise of the global supply chain leader," http:www.spencerstuart.com/supply/1380/.

PART VI

CURRENT
CHALLENGES
AND FUTURE
PROSPECTS

CHAPTER 35

....

CURRENT CHALLENGES AND FUTURE PROSPECTS FOR PRICING MANAGEMENT

....

ÖZALP ÖZER AND ROBERT PHILLIPS

As many of the chapters in this book make clear, the field of pricing contains many opportunities for research. Many of the chapters identify important research topics. Furthermore, none of the major areas of pricing are "closed" and no industry has "solved the pricing problem"—there are great opportunities to extend the current state-of-the-art in pricing almost everywhere. But, "pricing" is a scattered field. Researchers from different disciplines have studied pricing using the approaches and tools specific to their disciplines. Pricing managers and analysts have developed tools and methodologies that address problems specific to their industry without worrying if the same tools and methodologies might apply elsewhere. As a result, research into pricing has not progressed uniformly across all fronts. Some areas of great practical importance such as customized pricing have seen little research, while some of the most widely studied topics in pricing, such as auction theory, do not play a major role in day-to-day commerce. Pricing in some industries—notably the passenger airlines—has been the subject of tremendous amounts of research and development while pricing in industries with similar levels of complexity—for example, television advertising—has been very little studied. There are, of course, good reasons for the discrepancies between research focus and commercial importance: research is usually driven by what a researcher perceives as interesting or deep instead of what is commonplace. And, of course, pricing analysts and purveyors of pricing software seek to solve the pricing problems of the companies who are willing to pay for them—which may not correspond to the ones with the hardest or most interesting problems.

We gratefully acknowledge the very helpful comments of Michael Harrison on an early draft of this article.

One implication of the scattered nature of pricing research is that there are many research topics that cut across industries and disciplines. In this chapter, we discuss two such areas:

- empirical studies of pricing;
- pricing with unknown response.

In each case, we briefly describe the issues and the associated areas of research.

35.1 EMPIRICAL STUDIES OF PRICING

As noted in a number of chapters in this book, pricing is often a messy, difficult, and uncertain process. Organizations within the same industry vary widely in how they organize, execute, and evaluate pricing decisions. There are consultants who will provide guidance on how a pricing department should be run and how prices should be set in different environments—see the chapters by Simonetto et al., Jacobson et al., and Sodhi and Sodhi in this volume. Some companies have implemented "pricing optimization" or "pricing analysis" software systems. However, very little is known with certainty about "what works best" in pricing processes and organizations. While there are plenty of anecdotes and experience, there have been almost no systematic studies comparing how different approaches influence profitability or shareholder value. There are three major areas of interest.

- *How prices are determined.* There has been very little empirical research studying how prices are actually set within different companies. Very few researchers have spent time with pricing groups, pricing analysts, or pricing managers to observe how they make decisions, process information, interact with other groups within an organization, etc. One exception is Zbaracki and Bergen (2010) who studied the price-adjustment process at a Midwestern manufacturing firm as an example of a "truce" between the sales and marketing groups. Their ethnographic approach is useful in understanding how prices were set within one organization. However, much more is needed. Without a better sense of who exactly is setting prices with companies, how they are setting them, and what the company is trying to achieve, it is difficult to say very much about the nature of current prices nor how pricing could be improved.
- *Effectiveness of different pricing organizations and processes.* There is a strong need for research to determine what pricing approaches work best in which situations. Do retail chains or hotel chains that decentralize pricing perform better or worse than those that centralize the function? Do manufacturers who adopt an independent pricing function perform better than those that have pricing embedded within the sales, finance, or marketing organization? How does the distribution of pricing authority within a company affect relative performance within an industry? The appropriate distribution of pricing authority between centralized and decentralized functions is a particularly intriguing area for research. As noted by Simonetto et al. (Chapter 31) there is often considerable tension between local pricing functions—who have better knowledge of local conditions and competition—and centralized

functions who have a better understanding of the overall corporate situation. How to create incentives and information flows that best align centralized and decentralized pricing as well as determining which approaches work best in which situations is an open topic for research.

- *Effectiveness of automated systems.* Over the past twenty years, companies in many different industries have invested in automated systems to support complex pricing decisions. As one example, airlines have invested many millions of dollars in revenue management systems (see Barnes and Talluri, Chapters 3 and 26 respectively) as have rental car companies, hotels, and cruise lines (see Lieberman, Chapter 12). Many retailers selling fashion goods have invested in automated markdown management systems (see Ramakrishnan, Chapter 25). Companies in other industries have invested in automated dynamic pricing and customized pricing systems. Published reports of these systems often claim substantial benefits for individual implementations. For example, Barry Smith and his collaborators at American Airlines claimed, "We estimate that Yield Management has generated $1.4 billion in incremental revenue in the last three years alone. We expect Yield Management to generate at least $500 million annually for the foreseeable future". (Smith et al. 1992). Unfortunately, despite such claims, it is extremely difficult to ascertain the benefits that have been derived from implementing automated systems for three reasons.

1. There is no commonly accepted benchmark for estimating benefits. The "gold standard" for comparing two alternative treatments is the randomized trial—however, it is often difficult or impossible to perform a randomized trial of pricing approaches in the real world. For this reason, benefit estimates of pricing systems are often based either on non-randomized trials, historical comparisons (before and after), or simulations. Each of these approaches has difficulties—see Talluri et al. (2010) for a discussion. Furthermore, benefits estimates are often presented without a clear explanation of how they were calculated. In the vast majority of cases, the data used to calculate the benefits is proprietary and therefore not available to others. As a result, most (if not all) of the benefit estimates of pricing improvements published literature are non-verifiable and not capable of replication in any meaningful sense.

2. The people calculating and reporting benefits often have a stake in the magnitude of the benefits. Both the sponsors and the developers of an automated pricing optimization system have a personal stake in the perceived success of the system. Given that they are usually the parties estimating the benefits, the possibility of bias (conscious or unconscious) is often present. Benefits are rarely (if ever) calculated by disinterested third parties as they would need to be to eliminate these biases.

3. Finally, systems that fail to produce a certain level of benefits (or simply fail) are generally not reported. For this reason alone, any meta-research that relied on published or reported benefits would almost certainly be biased upward.

Empirical research into how companies really price, what types of pricing processes and organizations work best in what situations, and the extent to which automated support systems can actually improve pricing are badly needed.

35.2 PRICING WITH UNKNOWN RESPONSE

Most of the time, companies set prices without a clear knowledge of how customers will respond. It is unlikely that any company, in any industry, knows the price-elasticity of their customer segments with certainty. The only way that most companies can learn about how customers will respond to different price is "by doing"—that is, by changing prices and observing how demand changes. However, explicit price-testing is potentially costly and may be difficult or impossible in some markets. This means that many companies follow a four-step, dynamic pricing and updating approach:

1. The firm begins with an initial model (possibly very inaccurate) of market response for its products.

2. The firm sets prices to maximize profit given its model of market response and observes demand at those prices.

3. Based on its observation, the firm updates its market response model.

4. Based on the updated model, the firm sets new optimal prices and the process continues.

This view of pricing behavior is quite plausible. In fact, it is equivalent to the "closed loop process" of pricing recommended by some authors (Phillips 2005). However, there are a number of questions that can be asked about this process. Under what conditions will it converge? If it converges, does it converge to the right price? What happens if there is a number of competitors, each using a similar process? Is there a better process—in particular, would the firm be better off doing some explicit price testing to estimate the underlying model more accurately before optimizing prices? What happens if market response is changing?

The question of convergence was addressed by Rothschild (1974) who considered a seller who has a finite number of prices at which he can sell his product but he is uncertain about the demand for his product at different prices. Rothschild considered the case in which demand at each price consists of a mean with a normally distributed noise term. In each period, the seller chose which price to charge and would then observe the resulting demands and realize the resulting profits. The firm would then update his prior probability on the mean and standard deviation at that price by applying Bayes' rule. Rothschild showed that a seller who updates his estimate of demand after every customer interaction and then chooses the optimal price will, almost surely, ultimately converge to charging a single price in perpetuity. However, there is a non-zero probability that the price chosen will not be the optimal one. An implication of this finding is that if there are a number of companies in the market, some of them may converge to the "right" price but others may converge to various "wrong" prices. He views this as a potential explanation for price-variation in many markets: "Since price variability is such a pervasive phenomenon, it seems unsatisfactory to regard it as simply an artifact of disequilibrium" (Rothschild 1974: 187). McLennan (1984) obtained a similar result when the seller's prior belief was over a family of continuous demand response curves and the seller could choose any price within a continuum. Harrison et al. (2011) consider the case of a seller facing one of two possible demand models. The seller has prior probabilities p_1 and p_2 of which demand model represents the true state of nature with $p_1 + p_2 = 1$. They consider a seller who sets the optimal (profit-maximizing) price based on his current values of p_1 and p_2, observes the demand and uses Bayes' rule to update p_1 and p_2, continuing the process indefinitely. They show that this so-called *myopic Bayesian policy* can converge to a sub-optimal price with non-zero probability in many cases. Their key insight is that there can exist a non-informative price r such that (1) r is the optimal price given p_1 and p_2, (2) for the real state of nature—which might be either demand model 1 or demand model 2—the sequence of demands generated by the demand model is consistent with posteriors of p_1 and p_2, and (3) r is not optimal for the real underlying demand model. In this case, there can exist an attraction basin of initial prices such that the sequence of prices will converge almost surely to r. Lobo and Boyd (2003) achieve a similar result for the case of a seller facing a linear demand model with unknown slope and intercept.

This stream of research implies that the seemingly rational approach of updating the demand with the latest demand information and then charging the optimal price based on the updated model can lead to bad prices. The solution to this situation is far from clear. Lobo and Boyd (2003) find that adding a random component to the calculated optimal price—an approach that they call "dithering"—can improve overall performance. However, finding the right amount to "dither" is a challenge: adding a random variable with too much dispersion can lead to substantial losses from bad pricing, adding one with too little dispersion can lead to very slow learning. Harrison et al. note that bounding the actual price away from the recommended price can reduce "regret" defined as the difference between achieved profits and optimal profits. Unfortunately, pricing managers are likely to find both of these policies unappealing. Both policies say that "based on our best understanding of the market, we have determined the price that would maximize your expected profit, but we want you to charge something else." The two approaches also might be difficult to implement in practice. A more realistic approach might be for the seller to periodically indulge in some price-testing to test its current understanding of the market. What prices to test and how often to test are unknown and are potentially fruitful areas for research.

The work mentioned previously has considered the case of a seller who does not observe competitive prices but reacts only to demand. The case in which there are two competitors observing each other's prices and trying to determine the underlying consumer demand model has also been addressed. Kirman (1975) investigates the case of two sellers facing deterministic linear demand and shows that, if each seller knows the "true slope" of his demand but uses the sequence of observed price/demand pairs to estimate the intercept; the sequence of prices will converge to the Nash equilibrium of the game in which both sellers know the full true model. Brousseau and Kirman (1992) consider the case of two symmetric sellers in which both the "true slope" and "true intercept" of a linear demand model are *ex ante* unknown to both sellers. The sellers proceed in stages by using least squares to estimate the slope and intercept in each stage based on previously observed demand. They show that prices will not necessarily converge under this process given arbitrary starting points. These results and some related work are summarized in Kirman (1995). Cooper et al. (2009) extend these results to confirm that (1) when the slopes are known and the sellers estimate the intercepts, the prices converge to the competitive solution; (2) when intercepts are known and sellers estimate the slopes, the prices converge to the cooperative solution, even in the absence of explicit collusion; (3) when sellers estimate both the slope and the intercept, prices can converge to different limits from different starting points.

We believe that this type of research is quite interesting from a number of points of view. As noted above, the finding that a seemingly optimal updating policy can lead a seller to get trapped at a sub-optimal price leads to the question of what practical approaches should be taken to keep this from happening. A key implication of much of this research is that sellers that are identical in terms of product and cost structure might charge different prices in the same market if they start from different points. It would be interesting to know the extent to which this finding explains some of the price-dispersion that characterizes real-world consumer markets. Finally, a key insight of these models is that *price dispersion in a market is not necessarily a disequilibrium phenomenon*. To the extent that this is the case, standard general equilibrium models might need to be modified to allow for the case of identical firms selling the same product at different prices in the same market at equilibrium.

35.3 CONCLUSION

While pricing and the nature of prices have been studied at least since the time of Adam Smith, "pricing science" remains a work in progress. On the more theoretical side there is still a gap between the relatively simplistic view of pricing prevalent in classical economics and the messy, uncertain, and stressful activity of pricing in many businesses. On the practical side, ever increasing amounts of information and the decreasing cost of computation has resulted in ongoing interest in automated decision support systems of increasing complexity to support the pricing process. The rise of Internet commerce has given rise to entirely new markets and pricing opportunities as exemplified by eBay (on-line consumer auctions), Priceline ("name your own price" for airline tickets), and Groupon (on-line demand aggregation for discounts). We believe that there will be great opportunities for research and development in these areas for many years to come. We hope that the chapters in this book will inspire and guide some of this research.

REFERENCES

Brousseau, V. and Kirman, A. (1992) "Apparent Convergence of Learning Processes in Mis-specified Games", in B. Dutta, D. Mookherjee, T. Partasarathy, T. E. S. Raghavan, D. Ray, and S. Tijs (eds), *Game Theory and Economic Applications*. Berlin: Springer-Verlag.

Cooper, W. L., Homem-de-Mello, T., and Kleywegt, A. J. (2009) "Learning and Pricing with Models that Do Not Explicitly Incorporate Competition". Working Paper. University of Minnesota. Minneapolis, MN.

Harrison, J. M., Keskin, N. B., and Zeevi, A. (2011) "Bayesian Dynamic Pricing Policies: Learning and Earning Under a Binary Prior Distribution", *Management Science* forthcoming, available at < http://faculty-gsb.stanford.edu/harison/Documents/hk2-1.pdf>.

Kirman, A. (1975) "Learning by Firms About Demand Conditions", in R. H. Day and T. Graves (eds), *Adaptive Economic Models*. New York: Academic Press.

—— (1995) "Learning in Oligopoly: Theory, Simulation, and Experimental Evidence", in A. Kirman and M. Salmon (eds), *Learning and Rationality in Economics*. Cambridge, MA: Blackwell Publishers.

Lobo, M. S. and Boyd, S. (2003) "Pricing and Learning with Uncertain Demand". Working Paper. Stanford University. Stanford, CA.

McLennan, A. (1984) "Price Dispersion and Incomplete Learning in the Long Run", *Journal of Economic Dynamics and Control* 7/3: 331–47.

Phillips, R. (2005) *Pricing and Revenue Optimization*. Stanford, CA: Stanford University Press.

Rothschild, M. (1974) "A Two-Armed Bandit Theory of Market Pricing", *Journal of Economic Theory* 9: 185–202.

Smith, B., Leimkuhler, J., and Darrow, R. (1992) "Yield Management at American Airlines", *Interfaces* 22/1: 8–31.

Talluri, K., Castejon, F., Codina, B., and Magaz, J. (2010) "Proving the Performance of a New Revenue Management System", *Journal of Pricing and Revenue Management* 9/3: 300–12.

Zbaracki, M. J. and Bergen, M. (2010) "When Truces Collapse: A Longitudinal Study of Price-Adjustment Routines", *Organization Science* 21/5: 955–72.

INDEX

Cabral, L. M. B. 313
Cachon, G. P. 382, 444, 446, 563–5, 567, 676, 739–40, 750, 752–3, 762, 772, 809–10
Caldentey, R. 549, 581
call options 554
callable services 715–16, 731
Camerer, C. F. 17, 329, 397–8, 411, 425, 518
Camp, B. 897
Campbell, M. 440
Campbell, W. M. 682
Canadian Broadcasting Corporation (CBC) 193–4
cancelations 657, 658, 676
cannibalization 165–6
Cannon, J. 427
Cantillon, E. 701
capacitated economic lot sizing (CELS) 790
capacity:
  adjustment 802–3
  commitment 566–7
  constraints 790
  rationing 554, 561–3
  risk 775
Capen, E. C. 682, 695
Caplice, C. 701
Carare, O. 688
Cargill 230
Caribbean islands 201–2
Carmin, J. 116
Carnival Cruise Lines 200, 203–4, 210
Carr, C. R. 531, 762–3, 796
Carter, J. 51
Carvalho, R. 550
cash flow, expected 168
Cass, D. 299
Cassady, R. 519, 680, 684, 686
Casson, L. 29, 107
Castleman, H. 24
Castro, J. 64, 69
category expansion 596
cattle 231–4
Caufield, S. 469
cause-and-effect (C&E) matrix 885–6
CBS 183, 195
Celebrity Cruises 200
central planning 308
Ceryan, O. 804–5

Chakravarti, D. 728
Champ, P. A. 308
Chan, L. 531, 785, 802
Chandon, P. 587
Chandukala, S. R. 608
Chang, K. 435
change:
  management 847–8
  resistance to 869–70
channel inefficiency 745
Chao, H. P. 515, 517, 519
Chao, X. 809
Charlton, M. 684
Charness, G. 424, 453, 778
Chehrazi, N. 331
Chen, F. 715, 812
Chen, H. 809
Chen, J. 804, 813
Chen, K. 444, 452–3, 832
Chen, X. 8, 531, 793, 798, 803, 805–6, 808, 810, 813, 815, 864
Chen, Y. 796, 798, 803, 806–8
Chernev, A. 593
Chevalier, J. A. 612
Chicago Mercantile Exchange (CME) 233
chicken 231, 235
chief pricing officer (CPO) 867
Chile 530
Chintagunta, P. K. 378, 402–3
Chipman, J. 290
Chiquita Brands 896
Cho, I.-K. 320
Chod, J. 798
Choi, S. C. 403
choice 341
  consumers' 574–6
  set 346
  theory 417–23, 430–7
  see also preference
choice-based deterministic linear programming (CDLP) 574, 673–4
Chone, P. 727
Chopra, S. 740
Christie's 684
churn 159, 162, 164, 168
Cingular Wireless 165
Ciso 739

labor 174, 176
  costs 49–52, 73, 104, 173, 265, 271, 276, 368
  in exchange value 282
Laffont, J.-J. 320, 519
Lagrangian methods 671–2
Lai, G. 440, 570–1
Laibson, D. 423
Lal, R. 396–7, 400, 406, 409, 519, 599–600, 613
lamb 231, 236
Lambert, Z. 436
Lambrecht, A. 724
Lambropoulos, S. 689
Lancaster, K. J. 317
Land, A. 704
Land's End 560
Landsberger, M. 556
Lariviere, M. A. 117, 444, 446, 740, 752–3,
    762, 772–3, 810
Larson, A. 876
latent segments 349
Lattin, J. 435
Lau, A. H.-L. 798
Lau, H.-S. 798
Lawdog 222
Lazear, E. P. 16, 525, 545–6, 612, 688
Lean 8, 876–7, 890, 896
Lean Six Sigma:
  analyze 879, 885–7
  case study 881–9
  control 879–80
  define 878
  improve 879, 887–9
  limitations 889–90
  measure 878–9, 883–5, 885
  pricing 877–81
Learmont, B. 680, 687
learning 525, 560
  demand 646
  with dynamic list pricing (DLP) 545–54
  with intertemporal valuations 552–4
  passive 548
  and pricing 550–1
Lee, E. 403
Lee, H. 173, 740, 769, 777
Lee, H. L. 381
Lee, K. 378
Lee, T. 541–2

Leeflang, P. S. H. 406, 408, 630
Lehmann, D. 701
Leland, H. E. 303, 797–8
length-of-stay control 668
Lerman, S. 347, 349, 378, 675
less-than-truckload (LTL) industry 217–29, 479
  bid review 225
  bid submission 223, 225
  common carrier agreement 223–4
  contracts 223–4
  described 218–20
  Freight All Kinds (FAK) 224
  general rate increase (GRI) 226–7
  Household Goods Mileage Guide 223–4
  legislation 220–2
  pricing decision support 224–6
  pricing process 222–7
  profitability analysis 227–8
  revenue management 226
Leszczyc, P. 686
level-k thinking 428–9
Levin, D. 680
Levin, Y. 552
Levitan, R. 809
Levy, D. 792
Lewicki, R. 427
Lewis, R. C. 110
Li, Q. 802, 810
Lichtenstein 593
Lieberman, W. H. 203, 215, 392, 732, 915
lifeboats 214–15
Liker, J. 876
Lilien, G. L. 197, 378
Lim, N. 451
Lindahl, E. 307
Lindahl equilibrium 307
Lindqvist, T. 306
Lindsay, D. 436
Lindsey, J. K. 477
linear programming (LP) 641
linear regression 635–6
linear-in-parameters 346
Lippman, S. 776
Lissner, W. 697
List, J. 426
list pricing 6, 38–40, 127
Little, J. D. C. 349, 399, 605–6